KEEWAYS    MEDITATION ONENESS  written by Roy l

*Wishing you all the very best in your development in the Divine Light and within the
the highest realms, I will be thinking of you helping others. Love, light, and loving h*
*Roy x x x*
*xx*

This full edition incorporating Part One and Two was more or less completed in the Nov 2006 at home, then it will be tweaked about a bit, probably finish early February 2007 and published.

Please write to me if you think something is wrong or needs adding to help others.
I have been putting this book together since late 1970's and I am still continuing to add information for the benefit of all mankind of every culture, affiliation, opinion, no matter what religion or belief. This is so all on this earth plane can know the truth by experience, not by hearsay or blind faith.

© No part of this book is to be reproduced or utilized in any form or by any means electronic or mechanical or stored in any database or retrieval system without prior written permission from Keegan family Quayle family and Carolan family who all had an input from first in 1970-2007.

**Published by D R T Keeghan 34, WA2 0BS U.K.**
Post any comments :- Email  keeways@hotmail.com

ISBN No 978-0-9554590-0-9
978-0-9554590-0-9

Please remember
This book is for the **PROFESSIONAL**
as well as the absolute **COMPLETE NOVICE**
who knows nothing, and learns slowly.

I dedicate this book to those I love with their beautiful sunshine eyes.

A saying given to me which sums me up beautifully is :-

"I AM NOT ALL THAT YOU SEE"

I send you all Love, Light and wishing you Loving Spiritual Harmony in your progression within your searching for truth and proof of the continuance of life after our so called "death" or as I like to call it "life across the veil [until you see **the veil** you will not understand **it**] please learn within the Light of the Divine Spirit, who many call God".

Firstly I must apologise, for the simple reason I have tried to cram into the space available as much information as possible, and tried to keep it all together in this now one volume. I hope it will not be too much of a struggle reading it in the format I have put it in. It is only me in my none professional status, my dyslectic writing and in my honesty informing you, please enjoy. All the thoughts written in this book are personal to me, Derek, Roy, Tom, Keeghan.

All the writings are **mainly** from my **own experiences**. Myself doing a **great many years of "practical" research** and at the same time developing my own gifts from the late 1970's until the present day 2005, but also adding where needed with the help of others far more experienced than me, their experiences. **I am continually learning and adding to the information** on paper each and every day for the benefit of others, to help them with the knowledge of how to start linking with those within the higher vibrational realms of the World of Spirit where we all will end up in when our life on this earth plane has finished. One thing is certain in this life, we will all leave our earthly body. Yes, we all will what we call, die. Take comfort in knowing and proving to yourself and others, life continues when you cross the veil.

This book is for the **ordinary individual** helping them in different ways **how to develop, and within its pages, explains how with sincere dedication become a TRUE Medium,** whether "**Mental**", "**Trance**", "**Physical**", or a "**Healer**". This is so the reader can prove to others there is life after our so-called death. I have put into this book all the things I think are relevant at this time of writing. I have also included ways I have found that were not suitable for me in my development. These are included because everyone is different. **There is no quick fix.** What suits me might not suit another person. **BUT it should be realised there has to be a constant, which will be seen throughout the book, those constants are :-**

**When linking, constantly talking to Spirit through SINCERE thought to bring those Helpers in the Spirit World close to you; SINCERITY when talking to Spirit; Very regular Meditation; When Spirit is close, slowing as much as possible the thoughts going through the mind to let Spirit do the things necessary for your development** [ways for this to happen will be shown later in the book]; **and Negativity slows, and many times stops development and links. LIES are negativity. DO NOT LIE to yourself, to Spirit, or others, otherwise your development will suffer.**

You might see my points of view change in places, I have left them in so all who read this book can see how I have developed and blossomed in the ways of linking with those angelic helpers in the Spirit World. So on saying this, it is best to read the entire book if you do not agree with my words written on one single page of the book. After reading this book it is so important that people decide for themselves and not be coerced.

**REMEMBER.** What people do not understand they always ridicule. Are you going to be that sort of a person? Or **are you going to have an open mind?** Please read it **ALL**, then try, experiment, **THEN** criticise.

## There are none so blind as those who do not want to see.
## There are none so deaf as those who do not want to hear or do not want to listen.
## There are none so insensitive as those who do not want to be aware or to feel.

There are many people on this earth within the manmade religions who would rather this book not be put into print to teach the ordinary person how to link with the higher realms and prove to themselves and others that LIFE **IS** AFTER LIFE, IT CONTINUES FOR EVERYONE, **NO MATTER WHO THEY ARE**.

This is a book of **how to do all the things relevant to linking** with the angelic Spirit Helpers, so the reader can help others understand that life continues when the shell used on this earth plane is finished. I have set this book out in a format **for teaching as well as for the personal development of the reader. Please use it to help others understand, NOT FOR your own EGO, BUT on saying that be PROUD of what gifts you have been given and allowed to use by Spirit from across the other side of the veil to help others.**

I have been told by so many older experienced Mediums who teach the subject of Mediumship, who after reading my first book, [190 pages] said that they had forgotten a lot of the basic steps that they went through in their years of development. It is all now here in my expanded book [481] just for you.

The **most important thing** I would like to say here is; no matter what you read about and see in this world, you have to **experience it,** most importantly I will say it again, **experience "it"** and **be able do "it" yourself** before **you** as an individual have any knowledge of **"it"**. No matter what **"IT"** is.

**If you cannot do "it", you do not know "it".**
**This book is written for all peoples of the world,**
**no matter which country they live in, what language they speak, what belief they hold or religion they belong to.**
**This book is for YOU !!**
**This book after reading it is to be used to prove to yourself and others that life after our so-called death continues, and to enable you through that knowledge to help and comfort others in their time of need.**

I was in conversation with some people when my first book was mentioned. One person said, "it is written how Roy speaks". I hope you can understand my meanings and what I have intended to say in that special edition of 190 pages and now in its 470 plus pages. I was writing this for ages and went on right through the night many times to get it completed for all who bought it. It was as though I was on a mission for Spirit to help others learn the true ways of how to link with the Spirit World and it did not stop there. I have written truly and sincerely from my heart to help others learn and it has been a long journey and is still continuing. I have now hopefully finished writing this book after the start in the 1970's; it was half way through in June 2003, now near completion in 2007. Each time I thought it was finished I found something else to put in. I hope you enjoy every part of the book in both sections. In the first section "One" is mainly about Mental Mediumship, and in section "Two" about advanced Mediumship of Trance, Transfiguration and Physical Mediumship. I feel now the time has come to close this book and concentrate on my own personal development, and put it all in one volume. Love and Light, may your God go with you.

## FOREWORD

I firstly dedicate "Meditation Oneness" to all my friends in the World of Spirit for helping me to understand.

I also dedicate this book to the memory of my Dad, "Thomas"(Tommy/Tom), born 10$^{th}$ October 1910; died 12$^{th}$ June 1965. A person who I would have liked to have known better. He has now gone to a better place after suffering for 14 years after being diagnosed with a tumour on the brain. Collapsing in fits because of it from the very start a few years before the diagnosis. The last two years of his life bedridden in my family home in our sitting room downstairs, his earthly body was like a wasted, 4 stone, thin shell of his former self when he finally crossed over the veil.

To my mother, maiden name Gladys Malvina Taylor, born 14$^{th}$ July 1914, now 90, and still dancing, who with her love unselfishly looked after my Dad in his suffering.

To the memory of James (Jim) Senior born 10$^{th}$ October 1904, died 27$^{th}$ July 1977, my stepfather who always said I was the son he never had, my stepsister Grace now gone, who lovingly and caringly called me "bruv".

To the love of my caring sister Joan, and her husband Mike Corrigan, the really good caring people who stood by me through good times and especially the bad ones.

Last, but not in any shape or form least, this book is written and dedicated to the loves of my life, my four lovely children with their beautiful sunshine eyes; Julie born 1$^{st}$ January 1965, and Tom born April 1970, who I had living with me as my support after my divorce from the ages of 13 and 8, Julie bringing Tom and myself up worse ["better"], yes, better than any wife from that time, making sure we were kept in line as "good ladies" do and still makes sure I am OK to this day and I do not get too far out of line;

she is a treasure and always has been; and Pauline born 13th January 1966 and Derek born 19th May 1968, who chose to live with their mother. All without whom I would have given up and crossed the veil years ago. They all make and have made my life what it is now, I thank you all for the help, support and the making my life what it is today.

Also to the memory of a good friend I had, who was with me from her small bottle fed three weeks old and beside me nearly 24 hours of every day for 14 years; a truly loyal four legged friend I still very much miss, "KITTY" my wonderful faithful Alsatian dog. An animal I still hear around me; shaking her head just as she did when alive on this earth plain rattling the metal tags attached to her collar; this lifts me up when I am sometimes down in the mouth whilst on my own. Lately I seem to be more and more on my own with Spirit.

---

I feel very privileged to have been asked by Mr Roy Keeghan to comment on his new book. As a Teaching Medium, I am constantly being asked for details of a book to which my students may refer. They want a no nonsense information book which explains fundamental issues in Spiritualism and the mechanics behind Psychism and Mediumship. Well, here it is.

This is a book in which you can find details about things as diverse as "Brain Wave Patterns", "How to Follow a Guided Meditation". The highs, lows and "Development of the Trance State", the fascinating explanation of "Ectoplasm" and the whys and wherefores when sitting in a "Physical Phenomena Circle". I have used information in Roy's book on numerous occasions as a guide to teaching and helping others to understand. I like his personal anecdotes and the way he puts in his own opinions. It's great to read about other people's experiences in their Mediumship.

We need to share our education and help the next generation of Mediums to be better than we are. We will not achieve that unless we talk to each other in a manner that is clear and uncluttered. I am sure Roy is happy to hear about your experiences too as he is very involved in the study of Mediumship. He is travelling about all over the place, armed with his drums for Shamanic Trance workshops. With his portable cabinet to sit in going around to learning centres and home Circles, capturing phenomena in daylight, red light, and in complete darkness with his infrared cameras, video recorders and other experimental equipment.

I would like to wish Roy continued success with this, his now completed book, knowing that he is very much guided by the Spirit World.

Love, Light and Peace to you all.

**Melanie Polley.**     From Nr. Rugby U.K.     **S.N.U. Tutor; Mental, Deep Trance, and Physical Medium,**
(Who is a truly nice, genuine, deeply sensitive person. I first met at Ayr University complex in 2001 whilst I was attending a course, and all Mediums were being tested by a doctor whilst in an altered state. Roy the author).

---

Roy has been a very good friend of mine for over twenty years. I now realise he is correct in the ways he was talking to me about the progression of myself and my development as I went through life and now looking forward in a few months time, my life after death. Roy hardly ever talked about what he did within the religion he followed. I would not allow him to place his hands on me for healing; that I now regret. I did not know for many years he had been looking into and developing his awareness into the aspects of what happens when we part from this life. I am now in the last few months of my life through the ways I have led my life and smoking. I am sorry now I did not understand at times what I dismissed as rubbish the words of Roy. This very thick book now up to 280 pages of A4 he gave me to read. I hope it can help people to understand, and help others to realise what we have been brought up in our own lives to believe in, within our own religions and our own home doctrines is not always true. I now know it is up to you as an individual to put your own brain in gear and think, then deliver what you want in this life. It is up to you; what you sow, then you WILL reap. I now have realised that too late. I hope this book can help others to understand the complexities of life; it's many facets, and the knowledge of life continuing after life. Please think of me when I'm gone so I am not forgotten. Then put a little time aside to think of your friends and loved ones who are not now with you, but are still alive in another dimension. Send your thoughts out to them, tell them you now know and you still care.

Yours sincerely

**Peter Whitaker**.
From Warrington Cheshire U.K. **Died October 2001 through the ravages cancer at the age of 56.**
(A very good friend, who was confused and lonely through his anger in his mind, which then through drink and the suffering he kept to himself, the anger was often transferred through his mouth to others around him in his life, gone but not forgotten. Roy the author)

---

I would like to personally thank from the bottom of my heart, "The Harry Edwards Spiritual Healing Sanctuary", and Ramus Branch, Joan Branch, and Vincent Hill, for the kind permission for me to put in my book, photographs from **Harry Edwards'** book **"The Mediumship of Arnold Clare" and the book itself,** which unfortunately is out of print. I have included from it most of the relevant information here, which I think is so necessary for people who are trying to understand and develop Physical Mediumship, as I feel this wonderful information should not be left to die forgotten in an old book, and decaying on book shelves even if the healing trust did not. I have included at the end of my book, a list of the wonderful books still available, which should be read by everyone. They were written by the world-renowned healer Harry Edwards and are still on sale at the Harry Edwards Spiritual Healing Sanctuary, Arthur Findlay College, in the Stansted Hall bookshop and other good bookshops. People use to travel to Harry Edwards from all over the world to attend his spiritual healing clinics; this work of healing the sick and infirmed taught by Harry Edwards, is still being carried on by the dedicated healers in that sanctuary. His books are well worth a read. They are still relevant to today's ways of teaching and linking with Spirit World. Roy (author)

# MEDITATION ONENESS
## or
# LINKING WITH ANGELS

In this book I will, with your permission, show you a wonderful world starting within yourself. That then will open your eyes to the many wonders of this physical world of ours. Then progressing further onwards if you like; with the help of the kindly Angels in the world of love and harmony in Spirit, you can help others and yourself within :-

## "Oneness"

**Oneness is defined in dictionaries as:-** in harmony with, harmony, bonding, synchronization, entirety, totality, togetherness, as a whole, solidarity, as one, singleness, singularity, agreement, contract, sameness, balance, uniqueness, mixture, union, unity, unified, wholeness, merged, combined, united, mutual, bonding, connected, linked, in tune with, symmetry, fused, combination of, coming together, blending, amalgamated, coupled, attached, joined, complete, whole, completeness, fullness, inclusive, all-encompassing.

**When you are in meditation and truly link with God, the Divine Spirit, in the Divine Light, you are all of these when in "ONENESS".**

### "Angel" comes from the Greek word for "messenger".

In English dictionaries "ANGELS" are "Messengers of God", "Heavenly Messengers", "Divine Messengers", "Spirits who conveys God's will to man", A kind and lovely person", "Emissaries from God to man".

# This is a book to teach you how to develop through meditation

# Stress Relief

# Spiritual Healing

# Spiritual Development

# Spiritual Mediumship

# Spiritual Trance Mediumship

# And

# Spiritual Physical Phenomena

### This book helps you prove to yourself and to others there is life after our so-called death

The book is one of no religion and should be seen as such. I have of course put my own opinions in it, but in the main it is an all-encompassing humanistic book. A way of life that can be enlightening, a way of bonding your own inner higher self with the higher side of life amongst the highly developed Angels who are in the world we will all end up in across the veil, in the world of higher vibrations of those we call Spirit.

All in this book has been achieved, and also can be achieved by you. If you have the **positive sincere attitude of mind needed**, and knowing it will happen, it can. If you have the <u>**sincerity**</u> to help others here on the earth and those gone before, it can and will happen. If you have **dedication**, the belief in yourself and are willing to link **within the peaceful loving harmony** with all in the higher side of life, starting within the most powerful of vibrations, which are **Love and the Divine Light,** it truly happens.

### I MAKE NO APOLOGY FOR REPEATING THIS SAYING THROUGHOUT THIS BOOK, AS I KNOW IT IS <u>SO</u> NECESSARY.

**It is all here for you when asking the Spirit World within your own mind through "SINCERE" thought :-"Please come with only goodness, kindness, happiness, love, and truth, and to blend in peaceful, loving harmony within the Divine Light of Spirit, come to me with all the help that can be given from the Angels in Spirit from within the loving harmony of highest realms of Spirit".**
**If you are genuine in ask for it, over time <u>it does happen</u> !**

As you go through this book you will find it is the simplest thing in the world to link with your higher self and the Divine Light, which can lead you on into the linking of the realms of Light of Angels and onto the truth and understanding of, and learning within the Divine Light of God. This is something that the leading religions of the world have been trying to keep from the common man, trying to keep it to themselves within the circle of the high up in the churches. Keeping the ordinary person in ignorance of the true meanings of the old teachers in the main religions.

**Every religion in the world; bar none;** started by their pioneers talking to Spirit, [a messenger of God, some say God him/herself], talking and communicating with those who had passed on into the higher realms, in other words, those pioneers being Mediumistic people. **All Religions** are man made; there are no religions in the Spirit World.
READ THE SECTION OF THE BOOK YOU WISH TO LEARN ABOUT BUT KEEP ON GOING BEYOND THAT SECTION TO STRETCH YOUR MIND.

All it is the finding of yourself within, then the expanding of your higher self to blend with the Angels in peaceful loving harmony within the Divine Loving Light of God, the Divine Spirit.
Please do not think all your contacts with the Angels are going to be there all of the time, and it is going to happen immediately. It takes **a lot of dedication, self-discipline and that precious commodity for most people, "TIME". Yes, <u>time</u> put aside to meditate and blend with those teachers in Spirit** to have a good firm link with the higher realm. Yes, those who look after you will come to you in the hours of need, but please remember those Angels have other work to do in the higher realm in the higher vibrational level, learning themselves in their own environment and helping others in their needs. Make your appointment with those helpers in Spirit and try to stick to that time on a regular basis.
Please do not be selfish in your asking, have humility and compassion for others when linking, developing and when teaching. Always be **truthful** and **sincere** to yourself and to those in the World of Spirit.
What every person should be doing when linking with the Angels, is to think not of themselves, but of the others that they are going to help, not being selfish and thinking of their own personal gain, ego, what do people think of me attitude. Their personal angelic friends in the World of Spirit, will think far more of their helper, the open vessel, the budding Medium; if they would only put themselves aside for a moment. Then they, who are in the higher plane across the veil could come in and help all they can in that person's endeavours, which are hopefully, helping others in need.

When working with our friends in Spirit it must also be remembered all in the Spirit World are not all Angels. As we progress along in our learning of the World of Spirit, most find they will perhaps at sometime; have to contend with the unwanted links. A kind of person now in the Spirit World, who whilst on the earth plane, would have been a problem of one sort or another. Sadly a lot of them are there in Spirit and do not want to progress onward towards the true Light of God. If this happens, ask them to go and they will if you are **sincere in your asking**. Do not ever be intimidated by those lower forms in the World of Spirit, they will never harm you, **goodness, kindness, love and truth** will always beat badness. Neither will the higher levels in the true Spirit Light do any harm to you if they are going to work with you. Always ask for the highest and best links that are in the true Light of the Divine Spirit.
Never let the lower elemental level from Spirit come to you, never allow their presence around you without the help of your personal Divine Helpers [as you read more of this book in the Physical sections, you will see that the lower elementals (Nature Spirits) are sometimes needed in your development]. Get to know those Divine Helpers [some call them Angels], the ones that will be looking after your welfare **it is NOT** necessary to know their names just know them, fell them near close to you and they will get to know you as you are, it will then be a blend of harmony, one of togetherness within the Divine Light of Spirit. "Oneness".
Always remember **you** are the one in control in every circumstance.
**It is <u>not</u> the ones in Spirit that do you any deliberate harm if they want to work with you; it is the people on this earth you should worry about.**
<u>**It is the not so nice people on this earth plane that do us harm**</u>.
Your Guardian Angels will look after you, **if you sincerely ask** within your mind and **give permission** by your sincere thoughts to be used by Spirit. It is always the asking through sincere thought that the contact is made when linking with your friends in the World of Spirit. Do not think it is different talking to your friends in the World of Spirit than it is talking to your friends on the earth plane. Just because you

cannot see them in the Spirit World, it does not mean they do not exist. I hope in this book you will find ways that you can use with the help of your kind angelic helpers, ways to help and benefit others also show them there is a way of life that continues after this earthly body has been worn out and discarded. (In other words, prove you and everyone continue to live after you and they "die").

Angels and helpers in the Spirit World mainly show themselves and link with the people in the earth plane in the hours of need, and a lot of people are in need. This is why there is a need of more people to help the kind people in Spirit, those Angels in Spirit to help others here on our earth plane. There is a constant need of selfless people who do not think of themselves first. Any person can with the help of those kind, caring, selfless, angelic people in Spirit, learn and progress to be a better person, a kinder, caring person to their fellow man and woman. One who thinks of their surroundings and what it is going to be like in later years. A person who thinks of their neighbours, and friends and how they can be helped with the help of a higher force, a force that every person has the ability to link into if shown how. Each caring person has his or her own special roll to play, in the great universal plan of the Divine Spirit, GOD.

Never be negative, as negativity halts any links with the World of Spirit or development of any forms of mediumship. This applies to the person themselves or persons around the developing Medium or in any Circle that has been set up for the purpose of bringing the Spirit World forward into that Circle of friends. Always be positive in your attitude and positive in your linking with Spirit. Bring forward Spirit in an atmosphere of happiness and make sure it is the truth not something you would like it to be. It is the lies that stop and halt any development in a Circle and the person.

[Never impose onto others your opinions of your beliefs, let the people find God and the higher life in their own way. You cannot impose Spirit on others, you cannot bring the Spirit World to another person, they have to find it all within themselves. Yes, you can show exercises and demonstrate your gifts BUT if it is not being accepted, the truth will fall on infertile, closed minds because of their possible subtle indoctrination from childhood. It is only the individual that can bring the Spirit World link to themselves, they have to be subservient to the love of the higher realms]

As Battling Bertha [Harris] said "Mediums get up on the platform before they are ready. They need training, and time to prefect their Mediumship. The budding Mediums have not learned the difference between imagination and Spirit intervention. A budding Medium should not be allowed on a platform until he/she has disciplined his/her Mediumship. Some would be Mediums do not have the faculty, so, if things are not going well they imagine or fabricate a few pieces of evidence. I get more help from Spirit by admitting my limitations, then they help me sort things out. With regard to deception I know there are many distinguished names who pad out their demonstrations with facts gleaned anything but spiritually. I am an old woman now, but I swear on my oath I have never cheated. Once you do that Spirit will drop you. They can't be bothered wasting their time on frauds".

Here we come back to the basic thing in Mediumship development **get your link with the Spirit World STRONG FIRST before all else**. This all applies to the present day as it did in Bertha's days.

## WHAT IS MEDITATION?

**It is only "Focused attention"**
**That is all this book is about.**

## "FOCUSED ATTENTION"

**"If it is the will of the Divine Spirit and you give your permission".**

**You will be able to go forward**

## and link with the higher vibrational "Angel Force" within the realms of Spirit.
# The only thing that is here now to stop you, is yourself.

A most important point that I should be put in here is an explanation of **BEING SINCERE** as it is a basis of linking with the Spirit World:- "If you want to go through all of your development stages in linking with the Spirit World, everything should be done with **sincerity,** everyone has to be **sincere** in their talking to Spirit, when talking within their thoughts and asking of the Spirit World when in any development class or development situation. This book starts at the basics as it is for the people who are coming in from the very beginning of any learning, I will continue through to the very pinnacle of Mediumship development.

I will explain what being **Sincere** and **Sincerity** is. Starting with the dictionary meanings.

**Sincere** :- free from charade, fakery, trickery, pretence or deceit; not assumed or put on; not a sham; not make-believe; being genuine, honest, frank, truthful, candid, straightforward; not assumed or merely professed. **Sincerity, Sincerely, Sincereness** :- State or quality of being sincere; honesty of mind or intention; integrity, genuineness, truthfulness, openness, reliability, faithfulness, dependability, trustworthiness.

**Being sincere** with your links with the Spirit World and the asking of it. It is the really, really, really wanting of your development, you want that link, it is the one thing in the world you want. Everything else in this world is insignificant in relation to your link. You honestly want what you are asking the Spirit World for. You do not want your gifts to build up your own ego. The gifts are for the others you wish to help along your pathways in life and to show them and prove to them there is life after our so-called death. You have to be true when going through all stages of your development. That is being true to yourself, to those you show your gifts to and most importantly true to those in the Spirit World you link with and are there to help and guide you in everything, **IF** you let them. You must not make anything up, being true all the time as it must be realised this is a very big responsibility you are taking on. You have got to try to be there when Spirit needs you for others. They will show you where and when in their own particular ways. Yes, you have to have a life of your own, as in everything in life it is a balancing act. Keep your feet on the ground. Once after I had come out of a trance state, after doing a demonstration of Transfiguration I was feeling very groggy and I was told to go and hug a tree. What are people being taught by some tutors? I went and lay down asking the Spirit World to take the conditions away as I know it generally takes a little while but I have learned to deal with it and I let the Spirit World who put me into that state bring me back to my everyday life bodily functioning.

A few words that I feel should be placed here so people can really understand them, as they are necessary and are vitally important in the linking with the Spirit World.

**LOVE,** a person held in high esteem, attachment, strong liking, more than fondness, placed above all else, affectionate devotion, personified influence, or a God, beloved one, goodwill, devoted attachment to, passion, desire, object of affection, the personification of love, delighting in, deep admiration.

**HONESTY,** fair in speech or act, upright conduct or disposition, not lying, cheating or stealing, dealing fairly, just, faithful, unadulterated, sincere, good, earned by fair means, worthy, truthfulness.

**TRUTH,** reality, fact, quality, genuineness, honesty, accuracy, integrity, loyalty, state, of being true.

**TRUST,** have faith or confidence in, unconditional giving of self to another, implicit faith in, to entrust, to believe, reliance on, moral responsibility, hope, obligation of one in whom confidence is placed or authority vested, committed to one's care, rely or depend on, rely on truthfulness, commit to care or safety of, without fear of consequences.

Use all of these words and the actions as you go through your life as a mediumistic person and you will not go far wrong.

# MEDITATION

**First of all there has to be basics to gain a link!**

When you meditate, you get in touch with your own feelings and are able to work out problems far more easily than normal. It is as though you are able to see things more clearly within. It is only your own higher self that is coming into a better state of awareness. The deeper you go into that meditative state the more aware you become.

Some people call this meditation but really it is contemplation, it is the same with so called guided meditation' this is also contemplation. You have to go through this process of contemplation, as most people cannot stop their thoughts going through their mind. This slowing down of thoughts and ultimately stopping the thought process will continue until you achieve "Oneness" in the Divine Light of Spirit.

All the religions of the world meditate (or contemplate, using their thoughts) to some degree or other no matter which one.

You as a Christian, Muslim, Hindu, Jew, Buddhist, Hindu, Sikh, Sufi, Aborigine, Voodoo, etc., or a person in any other religion might dispute that. BUT look how you sometimes pray, **if you mean it**. Probably you will go into the silence and think one thought. Focus your attention on that one thought while in the house of your God. Blending within that power of your God. Yes! That is all meditation is "focused attention". **BUT true meditation** is focusing on one **single** point, the light within the third eye point, the void, the **single** colour, the **single** sound, etc.

This is a book I have been writing since the late 1970's. I have been collecting as much **personal experience** as possible for the benefit of the Angels in Spirit. Also for others on this earth plane to learn the art of linking with those Angels, perhaps I might eventually complete this particular book. I have never stopped learning about the higher life even when I was very, very young, even though I did not know it at the time. I started, then stopped, then started again when the times were right for me, but I never stopped believing in the Divine Power. I always said my prayers in my head each and every day mainly at night right from the time when I was very, very small, and I am not very big now. (Only 5ft.6in and shrinking with old age now I am 23 and a bit. Born in 1942, I won't say that too loud)

I have placed in the book different methods of development so experiment, because what is suitable for me might not be suitable for others, BUT remember there has to be a constant. I only hope it is useful to the many people that will be learning from this book. I can only say now on "proof reading" this book through [before it was published], I wished that I had, had the benefit of a book like this a great many years ago when I was first starting my way of an upward curve of learning. I was fumbling in the dark for a great many, many, many years. I now can say the developing of my link with the Angels in Spirit would have been much different and easier, BUT it must have been for a purpose, perhaps the writing of this book by me was needed. I look back now over the many years and I can see that I was sitting in Circles mainly for others to develop their link with the Angels **BUT** over the past many years gaining my experiences and development at the right time as well.

I only wished that I had attended courses at "The Arthur Findlay College" at Stansted Hall Stansted, Essex, U.K. earlier than I had. I have learned something different each time I have been there, even when attending the same courses with the same tutors over the years. I have tried to sit in different tutor's lectures, in different tutor's development Circles and go on different weeks to Stansted when different things take place. This was to gain the experiences, some being better than others if I can put it that way kindly. With spiritual development, as with most things in this life you have to experience it to have the first hand knowledge of it. Then and only then can it be classed as reality for you.

**Remember** you are an individual and what works for you, might not work for another person, so please do not think one method explained is better than another; "**You** and only **You**" will know which method is best for yourself, so you have to experiment, no one gives you anything on a plate. Most people have to work for their development, so be patient. Also **please give one method a chance to work with you** over a period of at least a great many months, never give up after a few weeks, certainly not after a few days. You will learn for yourself while being **sincere, patient, disciplined**, and most of all **in harmony** with those around you. You will then have learned to be **in harmony with the high vibrational level of Spirit** across the veil, when that happens, from that moment on you will progress. After talking to and asking those in Spirit, within your mind, for your progress in the field of learning you have in mind, you then have to learn to be passive whilst meditating so Spirit can do their work unhindered. This is the only way I know of how to become mediumistic. Yes this is the constant that is needed, MEDITATION after constantly sincerely talking to the World of Spirit through your thoughts.

If only every person in the world would learn to discipline themselves.

I truly believe every person in this world of ours at a very early age should be made to learn to meditate regularly each day. If disciplined meditation was done by all, taught in schools at an early age, we could all learn to get rid of all the stress, anger, evil, and hurt from this earth plane of ours.

When you are angry, fight, or deliberately hurt someone, the only person you really do any lasting damage to, the main person you hurt **is yourself.** It always lasts in yourself a lot longer than in the person you have done the wrong to. That hurt and anger stays with you for a great many days [in some instances months, it can even last for years within some people], festering like a sore in your mind bringing stress to you yourself each and every day, how ever long it goes on for. Life must go on, let life for you go on in a nice, smooth anger free, stress less way. Quite often the hurt done to others can fester in your own mind so much, it can rebound back on you as a medical problem, so making you ill. As a lot on this earth have found out to their cost.

Do you know what, it really is nice to be nice.

**Here ask yourself a few questions!**

Are you not always calm and kind to others?
Are you sharp and aggressive?
If you are upset, do you lash out or fight?
Do you look for trouble at the first sign of people having a different opinion than yourself?
Do you not let others have a way of life that is different to your own?
Do you not like people who are different to you?
Do you have to control the way things turn out in your family situation?
Do you look for problems before they arise?
Is everyone causing problems for you? **OR is it you, yourself?**
Do you get angry at the little things that the neighbours do contrary to what you think should be done?
Do you think others are always against you? **OR is it you, yourself?**
Are the neighbours not nice, **OR is it you, yourself?**
Do you have anger in you mind when something goes wrong at work?
Are you blaming everyone else for the problems around you? **OR is it you, yourself?**
Is work getting too much?
Is it all getting you down?
Are you getting angry with your family and friends?
Does all that you do in your life seem to be getting too much?
Are the children or your partner annoying you all the time? **OR is it you, yourself?**
Do the little annoying things turn out bigger in your mind than they should in reality?
Do you want a calmer way of life?
Do you want a better way of living?
Do you want to link with the Angels, with those in the Spirit realms?
Do you want to help others?
Do you want to progress towards inner peace?
Do you want to prove to others with the help of Angels in Spirit, there is life after our so-called death?
Do you want to be a Medium?
Do you want to enhance your psychic abilities?
Do you want know how to heal others?
If any one of these statements and many more I could put in here apply to you, **then this book is definitely for you**, and **meditation is a must for you**.

Think of an athlete or sports person who has to train his/her self each day to achieve their goal for their one day performance in an arena, or in a track or field event, to bring themselves up to their very best standard, the best for that certain individual person in their field. They are always training building up their muscles, eating correctly, having the right frame of mind, thinking positively, and doing things correctly. Sleeping and resting as and when necessary when their trainer says so. They are honing and fine tuning their body and mind for their goal in life. Even when fully fit at the height of their profession, they do not go away to relax each day, forgetting what they have learned. They do not let it all go by the wayside, then at intervals come back and expect it all to be the same. They keep up the regular training, perhaps not as much, but they still keep doing their training to keep their muscles toned, and their mind focused. So should you do so when you are developing and when developed. **You should** keep up the regular meditation and practice. Meditate, meditate, meditate, practice, practice, practice at the beginning of your Mediumship and throughout your life as a medium.

So it is with linking with the Angels in Spirit and with Mediumship. If you do things correctly you will succeed. You also have to exercise to keep your body healthy, eating and drinking the correct things, having a **good mixed diet**, doing all things in moderation, being happy, and having the right frame of mind for life around you. To be open, ready, and willing to receive each time you sit for the Angels in Spirit, so they can be fine tuning your mind for you ready for the task in hand. To be positive in your outlook, having a good and restful sleep each and every night. Being truthful, positive, and sincere to all around you, **at all times**. Most of all being truthful to yourself. Do not ever forget to **meditate regularly and punctual** to keep your link with the Angels in Spirit strong, it is called respect.

Most importantly **PUT TIME ASIDE FOR YOURSELF** so you do not burn out.

Meditation is the most important way to develop your link with the Angels in Spirit and to make it stronger for yourself. **Regular**, **punctual**, meditating builds up the development and the strengthening of your psychic abilities and your mediumistic skills, which might be needed to help others in the future.

**A most important point that "cannot be over stressed" is :-**

**"People in meditation are not to be touched at any time"**

People who are in meditation are in a state of altered awareness. **You** or **any other person "cannot know"** and I repeat, **"cannot know:"** how deep the other person is in that altered state of awareness with their meditation; **so do not touch**. The person in meditation; if you are with them; should be softly talked back using their name, which should bring them back to their normal state of awareness. This is the only time to ever use their name to them while they are in meditation. By saying their name, it acts as a trigger within their brain to bring the person back to reality, back to their normal, everyday, earthly state. Please think on about the law of the land in Great Britain, it says if you just touch a person, you are committing an offence of "assault". If, as could happen, you touch someone and they have a shock (if they are in an altered state of awareness, meditation), You could be accused of "an assault causing actual bodily harm". If a person has a heart problem and they get a shock off some foolish person, think of the unthinkable.

# YES; danger in whatever form. BE SENSIBLE.

**Meditation** is mainly done with the eyes closed to avoid distraction and focusing your attention in the third eye area on **"a"** fixed point, be it light [the divine light of Spirit] within the mind's eye, or **"a"** colour, or **"an"** object, or **"a"** black bean on a white background etc. notice the singular. A single phrase, about three words, can also be used, if it is too long, you have to think and that in not meditation, it is contemplation. For advanced linking with the World of Spirit this is the main method of linking and quietening the mind that is so necessary for the Spirit World to develop the budding Medium. After asking for whatever development you require you have to become part of that light and belong there in your mind's eye within that colour, the void, or the divine light of Spirit as your development is enhanced by the unseen power.

**Contemplation** is with outer influences;{which people can confuse with meditation} it can be words, anything verbal, pictures within the mind like a "guided meditation"(which it is not), in music being the notes. Listening to the music instead of trying to still or quietening the mind. Thinking thoughts, thinking about a piece of music you are supposed to be meditating to, thinking about your sitting position as you sit there with your eyes closed, thinking about the things you have to do later on, thinking about your troubles, thinking about if you are doing things correctly. Look into the light within your third eye region and your mind automatically goes quieter. It is holding that light that is the hard part, it needs practice, dedication, time, and patience.

Guided contemplation (in many instances it will be called meditation) in this book is needed in your development to put into your mind **pictures, from words, from others** who read out to you the exercises from this book, or the pictures being put into your mind from the words off a tape recording. From that simple start over time if done in the quiet of your own space, whether it is on your own or in a group setting, Spirit will come closer to you as and when you **give them permission** to develop you in what you want through your thoughts. But firstly you have to **invite** through, your thoughts, those in the Spirit World to come closer to you. First going over and over and over and over again and again, the bringing to yourself the World of Spirit, repeatedly encouraging Spirit to come closer to you.
**Then at a separate time**, with practice, as you focus your attention (meditation) to still your mind as much as possible on the colours, light or a fixed point within your third eye, Spirit will be able to put **their words** through the stillness of your mind into your thought pattern along with **their pictures/images.**

There are different levels of linking for different disciplines. Starting off from awareness of Spirit, going on to Mental Mediumship, Healing others, then through to Physical Mediumship.

Do not think one method of meditation is better than another BUT remember **there has to be a constant,** a set format that works for most people for most of the time. I am not going to put any one person onto any one set format because we are all individuals, having different requirements, and can need different things to help us to react together with our own individual personality, our own free Spirit, then link with those in the World of Spirit. That set formula is MEDITATION and stillness of the mind within that meditation. Negativity **STOPS** development and **STOPS** spiritual phenomena.
Our own individual Spirit within each and every one of us [because each of us is an individual physical body and an individual Spirit/soul] has to learn to blend with the Angels in Spirit, and the Divine Spirit and become as one, within **oneness ("stillness within the mind when in meditation")**. For that we individually need individual things, also each person needs to be completely relaxed to achieve this, especially in the deeper forms of meditation.

If you have ever wondered what happens when we join up or link with the higher vibration level of those in Spirit, or when we depart the earth plane or how we are part of the higher levels of the Spirit World. I will try to put it in context.
Think of your Spirit within you, as if you are an atom of water vapour, that forms a cloud, which then forms an individual droplet of water, that falls to the ground in the form of a shower of rain, that forms a stream, that forms a river, that forms the sea; you are then part of the whole. You are still an atom of water, yet you are part of the whole. That is what happens when you develop and progress through the seven vibrational levels of consciousness (but are there seven of seven of seven, of seven of seven???), become as one, oneness with the Divine Spirit, part of the whole, pure thought, as you progress, pure light. This is also what has been told to us what happens when we pass over to the other side of the veil into pure thought. Sorry it should be only the Divine (light of) Spirit is **true** pure thought. Anyway to continue.

**REMEMBER**
**You are what you are in your own head; let it always be good, beautiful, positive, true, and full of happiness and love. Being sincere in everything you think and do.**

To get things into prospective for you simply put, all that it is.

## "Meditation is focused attention".

A very important thing that must be said here is
For you to remember **always**;

## " THOUGHTS ARE A LIVING ENERGY "

Be careful how you use them. Prove it to others it being so, look in the dowsing section.
Remember the pendulum of life.
What you give out comes back to you ten fold.
**Once you have sent your thoughts out you cannot retrieve
or change any of those thoughts.**

Let your thoughts always be **"GOOD"** for your own sake and for the sake of others.

## " PLEASE USE YOUR THOUGHTS WISELY "

There are healing thoughts as well, please use them for others less fortunate than yourself.
Importantly **"do not forget yourself."**

# STRESS REDUCTION

Meditation has been used by countless generations of humans on all continents, Shaman of the British Isles and Europe, Aborigines of Australia, North American Indian Medicine Men or Holy Men, Asian Holy people and many other groups on different continents of the world since time began. It is now known, or should I say has been accepted by the "all knowledgeable [are not]!" western medical profession [**sadly,** a lot of them now seem to be legalised drug pushers who bury their mistakes and are in some/many ways owned by the all powerful money making drug companies], which has been going for only about a few hundred years or so. The modern medical profession after dismissing it as a crank's or weirdo's form of doing their own thing, are now saying meditation is definitely a good form of relaxation, stress management, and a help to gain stability in every day life, which is beneficial for everyone to use.

If a person has never done meditation before, it might seem a strange way of sitting upright in a comfortable position, and not crossing the legs as the people of some religions of Asia go about it. Sitting with legs crossed for the westerner in a cramped cross-legged position is not always necessary, please think logically. If a person is not use to sitting in a crossed legged position then their blood can be restricted in the legs so leading to cramp. Look at the pages ahead and see what can happen to a person when they meditate. Their blood flow alters; this is not the person themselves doing it consciously. It is the person relaxing and their Spirit being joined with the higher force of Spirit in the higher realms. They are then linked and being developed, being attuned, being made as one, blending with Spirit. Spirit has a need in some circumstances to alter the blood flow of the human body. This is not a fantasy, it is fact. Look at the figures that are printed later on in the book. They are of Mediums that have been tested by a doctor just recently and this is an on going thing.

I want to try and help you have a go for yourself in the privacy of your own abode to grow to learn how to link within with your own higher self. This will not only help you in your every day life, if you use meditation regularly for help with your development of your link, **if asked for sincerely** within your thoughts, you will be blending with the Angels in Spirit and enhancing your psychic ability. **If asked for sincerely** this will also help in a business life or you in your life, helping you to grow calmly in stature in the everyday things more than you can imagine. In fact this can be used in any part of business life whether you own it or not. Try meditating each day for ten to fifteen minutes, more if possible if only to relieve your everyday stress, it can build up your own inner strength to face the growing pressure of life in this fast world around you.

When you meditate you feel a lot calmer, better able to handle whatever this life throws into your pathway as you carry on along that bumpy pathway, whether it is within your work place or in your home life.

When starting to meditate, make sure you are in a quiet, comfortable place, where you are not likely to be interrupted, by that I mean not being disturbed, surprised, no telephones or door bells likely to startle you, or touched by others, especially if you do go into deep meditation, bad psychic shock can occur if you are suddenly disturbed, BUT it depends on the individual. If meditating with others never touch them as you do not know what level of meditation (which is altered/heightened sense of awareness) they are at, keep a space in between you and them.

Meditation is the easiest thing in the world to do. All you have to do is to close your eyes and concentrate on the colour you see. If you do not have a colour in your mind open your eyes, look at an object and its colour then hold it in your mind, if the object/colour stays in your mind hold that. Probably your mind will have all different thoughts going in and out all the time don't worry about it, try to abandon any thought, don't force it, for this there are many exercises on how to do this later on in the book. What you are doing is focusing your attention. With practice you will hold either the colour or the object for a longer period each time in your mind. You will find as I did, your thoughts have a way of finding out any problems you have in your life and sorting them out. Life becomes a lot more bearable for you and the people you come in contact with, because you become a better person within yourself, you will know it, and feel it yourself. A lot more people are meditating, and happily they are finding it helps in many different ways, because it calms you down, it can help with your business, your home life, your relationships, your place of work, it can help to reduce stress, all these things are known and proven facts. I only wish meditation was practised in schools and institutions (especially mental institutes), where people have had problems and have been shut away from society. I think it should be compulsory for **all** in there, staff and the others. Perhaps one day it might happen! It would make people go within themselves and think about the things they have done to others and how they could have avoided it. How they could help themselves, why they are in that position, where have they come from, when did it start, who is there to help, what are they going to do about the situation, how are they going to resolve the situation. Also the patients in those institutions would I think be helped greatly, and not put on so many drugs.

To help with any of your problems, go into the meditative state, then go through your problem by using the five "W's and the "H". They are "why, where, when, what, who, how". Close your eyes and go through the words thinking of how you can solve the problem by the key word it will surprise you. If you forget them write them down so you can remember them. Concentrate on one word at a time as you contemplate your problem. By using the key words and going through all the scenarios, most problems will be sorted out, perhaps not immediately, but over time they definitely will.

I have written down many exercises that can be done alone or in a group situation later on in the book. With any of these exercises they can be used for your own personal use, using your own voice on a tape recorder. (The reason I say your own voice is, you are use to hearing your own voice and your subconscious will react easier and quicker to your own voice as your subconscious knows and trusts it) Record each exercise on a tape recorder and you should find each exercise far easier to deal with and go along with. If you do not have the confidence to do any of the exercises I will try and record some of them and have them here for you (address on the front cover) or at Stansted Hall's shop.

One exercise that I have used to clear my mind a little better, or what I should correctly say is, slowed down the thoughts going through it. I do not know many Mediums (**a Medium** is a person who is a link between the people on the earth plane and those Angels in the Spirit World) that can completely clear their minds with the exception of a handful of Deep Trance and Physical Mediums, and even then most of them if they are truthful will admit they are still aware of the outside happenings and they have only been out of touch fully, only on a handful of occasions. I seem to be able to look into the light within my mind for a lot longer without any thoughts coming into my mind now after a great many years of practice. The trouble is if you leave alone the exercise of stilling the mind or not meditating so maintaining your spiritual link for a few months, it is harder to bring yourself back to the stage where you were at. Most of these exercises can be used to improve your link with the Spirit World. It helps by putting images into your subconscious so allowing Spirit to see how they can then put images into it for you to use, BUT always remember first you have to **ask and allow** Spirit to work with you with your permission. They cannot use you until you give permission, it is the divine law. Spirit cannot come to you unless you allow them to so, so do not worry, **you are the one who is <u>always</u> in charge remember that**.

Anyway back to the exercise for a leader of the group to read out in development classes (this is also a good one for yourself to record, so substitute, "I" for "you"): -
Firstly **ask <u>sincerely</u>** in your mind for goodness, kindness, truth, happiness, love, light, and to blend in peaceful Divine Light within the loving harmony of the highest realms of those Angels in Spirit. After the prayer keep on encouraging Spirit to come closer and help you for a good few minutes [ten at least, as with all the exercises]. This is a beginner's exercise.

Sitting comfortable in a chair feel your feet firmly on the ground.

You **see** and **feel** in your mind the power of the mother earth being drawn up into your legs, see it as a light. (if at first you do not see it, **<u>sincerely sense it</u>** as you go through the exercises).
You **see the power** in your mind as such, visibly as a colour. [I see it most times as a clear white light, with me it can change, but any colour of light will do].
**Pause,**        **See and Feel it.**
As it does the light goes upwards, it goes into your lower body, filling it up with power.
You **see the power** in your mind as such, visibly as a colour.
**Pause,**        **See and Feel it.**
The light keeps coming slowly into your upper body, building and filling upwards.
You **see the power** in your mind as such, visibly as a colour.
**Pause,**        **See and Feel it.**
The light is coming upwards, flowing ever upwards, filling your arms from the hands upwards to the shoulders.
You **see the power** in your mind as such, visibly as a colour.
**Pause,**        **See and Feel it.**
The light is flowing upwards through the neck to the head, filling it up and flowing over your body on the outside it is keeping your body warm and comfortable.
You **see the power** in your mind as such, visibly as a colour.
**Pause,**        **See and Feel it.**
Now you **see it** in your mind flowing over your body and it is going upwards in a cone of light towards the Divine Light, the power of the Divine Spirit.
**See it** there joining up with that power. You **see the power** in your mind as such, visibly as a colour.
**Pause,**        **See and Feel it.**
**See it** as it is filled with the Divine Light of the Divine Spirit, flowing back downwards to your head, filling your head with the power of light.
**Pause,**        **See and Feel it.**
**See it** filling and flowing through your head and neck into your shoulders and arms and back up to the neck until it over flows all over you inside going downwards.
**Pause,**        **See and Feel it.**
**See it** going all over into your body, downwards through the upper half of your body into the lower half, filling it up with the most powerful of light, the Divine Light of Spirit.
**Pause,**        **See and Feel it.**
See the all-powerful Divine Light going downwards, into your legs flowing into the ground.
**Pause,**        **See and Feel it.**
**See it** flowing and going all over arms, your whole body, down over your legs then to the floor.
**Pause,**        **See and Feel it.**
**See the <u>Divine Light of Spirit</u>** there, where it is drawn up **again** into your body, where it now has a **<u>double strength</u>** to it, more powerful.

Each time you **see in your mind** the light going up to meet the Divine Light of Spirit, then recharging.
You **see it** in your mind coming down all over you, down to your feet where it is again drawn up, more

powerful each time, **see it** happening, **feel it** happening.
Repeat the exercise in your mind, up and down for about five or seven times on your tape recording. More of course if you want to dwell in it. It can be a wonderful experience.
Then you concentrate on that light becoming part of it, the more you become part of it, the more you want to do so. So loose yourself in it, become as one with the light. That way you let your own Spirit help the Angels in Spirit to help you in your development or the clearing the mind of your worries. Give permission to the higher life force if you would like this development. **If you do not ask, you do not get.** Ask for the development you would like (that is if you would like to e.g. clairvoyance, clairaudience, clairsentience, Clairknowing, physical Mediumship, becoming a Healer, etc)

Keep this up for as long as you can, at first it might be only for a few minutes; as you get more confident with this practice, try to extend the length of time each time you meditate. There are many exercises in this book try them all. One will suit you. You should enjoy them all. That is I hope you do.

When you come back into the normality of your surroundings, you will feel better able to handle the problems of your life, also it has been found when people meditate that people's heart rate have been slowed and also their blood pressure lowered, making the ageing process go slower. Look at the Swamis or Holy people that have been meditating for years, they never look old. Even though they might be in their 70's they look no more than 40-50. Try it and take the pressures of life off your shoulders, and you will stay younger looking and a lot more healthy. You are what you are in your head!!!

Another small exercise is to try to take into your mind a place of safety for yourself, anywhere at all. Like walking down a path, through a gate then into a lovely garden where the sun is shining and in the garden there are lots of beautiful flowers. There is a seat in this garden where there is someone sitting on it. If you want to find an answer to a problem, you go to that person to talk to them in your mind, it is one of your Guardian Angels. You discuss the problem with them, asking in your mind for some help with this problem. Ninety nine times out of hundred the problem gets resolved between the two of you in your own mind. It is best for a person to talk you through this exercise or make a tape recording for yourself of the following pages.

Before starting any meditation, I always pray **sincerely asking in my mind** for goodness, kindness, happiness, love, truth and to blend in peaceful Divine Light of Spirit within the loving harmony of the highest vibrational force of those Angels in the highest realms of Spirit.

I will expand on this exercise for you so you can record it for yourself **for your own personal use only**:-

Close your eyes. (Have a soft gentle music playing in the background, **if you want to**).
Each time pause, **see it, feel it, sense it** in your whole being, you **are** there within this scene. (even if you cannot see within your mind at first, be aware of the situation if only sensing the picture painted by the words. This is practice for putting images into your mind ready for Spirit to generate them when you are ready).
You are facing a garden gate, looking into the nicest, the most beautiful garden you have ever seen.
Pause, **see it, feel it, sense it** in your whole being, you **are** there.
You open the gate and walk in, as you go in; you look up at the welcome sign above the gate, read it; what does it say for you, it is a personal welcoming message (you might not see anything do not worry just carry on).
Pause, **see it, feel it, sense it** in your whole being, you **are** there.
You turn and close the gate behind you closing out all the problems you have had in your life, and all the ones you are having now.
Pause, **see it, feel it, sense it** in your whole being, you **are** there.
You are feeling safe and comfortable here in this garden, there is a sense of warm welcome that surrounds you.
Pause, **see it, feel it, sense it** in your whole being, you **are** there.
Here you can see the humming bees around the flowers, you can hear the singing birds in the trees and bushes and you marvel at the multi coloured butterflies all gently going about their business.
Pause, **see it, feel it, sense it** in your whole being.

You can smell the perfume from the many coloured flower blossoms that is getting wafted gently towards you by the multi coloured butterfly wings as they fly past you in the gentle, warm soft summer breeze.

Pause, **see it, feel it, sense it** in your whole being.

The clear, blue, sky is letting the warm gentle sun come onto you, it is warming the whole of your body in the nicest of ways, there is no risks here, nothing at all to be afraid of as you walk slowly along the crunchy, gravel, path.

Pause, **see it, feel it, sense it** in your whole being.

You are passing the most beautiful, sweetest smelling, flowering, white, shrub you have ever seen or smelt. Here you pause and take in all that is around you in the garden. You see the many butterflies feeding on the nectar out of the yellow centre of the flowers they are both spectacularly beautiful. Their colours are so varied and vibrant, there are plain coloured ones and many with a multitude of colours on their wings, it is making you feel good within yourself.

Pause, **see it, feel it, sense it** in your whole being.

You can see the borders full of flowers of different shades of pastel colours, and others which truly take your breath away, beds of small soft coloured flowers, beds of tall brightly coloured flowers and in the background you can see there are spaces along special paths. Here you pause and take in all that is around you in the garden. You are drinking in the colours from the surrounding area, it is making you feel better than at any time in your life.

Pause, **see it, feel it, sense it**.

Your eyes can see along these special paths it is as though you are drawn into one of these spaces, this is where there is someone who is waiting especially for you, they have made this special journey to come to be with you there on your special journey of enlightenment.

Pause, **see it, feel it, sense it**.

As you walk towards this person along this special path that has been put there, just made for you. You look towards them, this person looks so kind and caring.

Pause, **see it, feel it, sense it**.

Going closer you see this person is beckoning to you to come over to them; it is that special angelic person who is going to help you. (They do not have wings; they look normal to you). This person has a caring, kind, wonderful presence about them.

Pause, **see it, feel it, sense it** in your whole being.

They are patting the wooden seat for you to come over and sit beside them.

Pause, **see it, feel it, sense it**.

You sit beside them in the warmth and comfort that is surrounding this place, you cannot hear any voice, but you know what they are saying to you and you listen with your thoughts. Your thoughts are mixing with their thoughts, you are communicating like this, and it is the most natural feeling in the world for you in this new way of communicating.

Pause, **see it, feel it, sense it**. (here you **pause a lot longer** in their presence)

As you are talking with your thoughts you hear the pleasant bird songs from the warm brown mottled and some brightly coloured birds singing in the background.

Pause, **see it, feel it, sense it**. (here you **pause lot longer** in their presence)

After a while you have to come back, so you bid this kind, caring, wonderful, angelic person farewell for now, you say (if you want to) you would like to come back, and see them the next time you are in this garden, and you make arrangements with them, which **you know** you will keep (at that certain time, on that particular day arranged. This is the time you will normally regularly do your group meditating).

Pause, **see it, feel it, sense it**.

You get up, give them a hug, wave goodbye, and you slowly go down the crunchy, gravel path.

Pause, **see it, feel it, sense it**.

You get the smell of the whole garden as you go passed the flower beds and the beautiful, sweet smelling, white bush.

Pause, **see it, feel it, sense it**.

You see the butterflies and the bees in the flowerbeds going about their daily lives drinking and collecting the pollen, the birds are singing to you as you walk along the path towards the gate; it is fantastic to be alive.

Pause, **see it, feel it, sense it**.

You reach the gate all renewed in yourself, you turn around to wave goodbye but the person is out of sight around the bend, so you make a conscious decision in your own mind to return when you can, the next time you meditate, remembering the time and date arranged.

Pause, **see it**, **feel it**, **sense it** in your whole being, you **are** there.

You open the gate and step out into the real world and close the gate behind you. You are a different person now within yourself for taking this journey. It has filled you up with a renewed vigour, which you have not experienced before, it truly feels fantastic. This feeling will last in you for as long as you wish it to, you can go back at any time to be re-invigorated.

For the last time. Pause, **see it, feel it, sense it**.

Come back out of meditation when you are ready.

Do not worry if the image does not come into your mind at first, it will with practice. Rome was not built in a day.

I must say here, before you start reading this book do not try to put yourselves into any helping or mediumistic category. The reason is I feel if you do, you will find others will start to try and categorise one Medium to the next, remember, we all should be trying to help others come to terms with death of loved ones and proving to people that we do not die, but continue after the body ceases to function, and then with the help of the Angels in Spirit to help the other people around you, **nothing else, no ego trips**. Also as you progress with your gifts if you label yourself you will be stuck with that category by others. Let people see you as you are and go by what you can do for them, so let it always be the truth and sincerity. Be especially true to yourself, and then everything else will follow true. Forget about labels.

Another thing that should be said here is this thing about Guides, Helpers, and Angels in Spirit. I hear people say I have a "China Man" here with you, an "American Red Indian", an Indian with an elephant, etc. this is your guide, helper, Angel in Spirit. Steer away from this as it has been said time and time again from the higher side of life, it takes about upwards to 60 people plus (Angels in Spirit) [depending on the circumstances], a group soul, the group thought, the thought of people (Angels in Spirit) who have passed into the higher realm, those who are specialists in their own field on the other side of the veil, just to help a single person come through to the lower plane on earth to make and keep regular contact through a Medium or the earth bound helper. The same thing applies with healing, it also takes about 10-60 people plus [depending on the circumstances] a group soul, the group thought of the angelic helpers in the realms of Spirit to help adjust the chemicals in the body of the patient and the Medium (earth bound helper) to help the patient become a person who is feeling better, hopefully well and fully recovered. So you can see, you are placing only one angelic person on a pedestal. Don't do it, they are one of many angelic helpers. You are doing an injustice to all the other angelic helpers in Spirit, within the group that is helping you.

I feel it so, so, very, very much important that people in every society should teach the young to meditate from the start of their academic learning process. The simple reason is:- if before the half hour to and hour of meditation they are told by a truly sympathetic tutor of the practical reasons for the things and the reactions of the things they do wrong to others and **most importantly** do right to others [**dwelling on the good**] and how it reacts for and against everyone and very much the consequences of anything, no matter what they do, the young will begin to think and then begin to understand and hopefully change the society they live in for the good, **BUT IT MUST BE STRESSED** the trouble is if you get a person in these circumstances who wishes to control others in their way of thinking, they will be able to turn the young against the whole of society. This is a reason for people in control of the young [can I say sadly after a lot of thought] to be monitored. BUT IT THEN leaves the society they live in no matter where, in the hands of **what could be** the controlling manipulating people, GOVERNMENTS, COUNCILS, religious cults, etc. of all kinds throughout the world. We are then under the control of the few controlling the many, coming back in a full circle to religion and their control of the people and what they did and now do. Every young person in this world has to be taught to be thinking independently and the consequences of every action they do and that should start from an early age. By going into meditation [really contemplation] every day each individual will think of the action they are dealing with in their every day life and that surely must be better for all.

# SHAMANIC TRANCE

The Shaman of every nation used, (and many still use) different methods of inducing a Trance state so they can/could link up with the worlds of the so-called dead. I have come to the same conclusion time and time again, it is repeating something simple over and over again [self hypnosis] that puts a person into the right frame of mind to link with the World of Spirit. The people who lived many centuries ago knew this. It is only people in this day and age who are making it look complicated to make themselves look good.

Remember the saying, "**It is a clever/wise man that makes things** (look) **simple, it is** (a fool) **an ignorant man that makes things complicated to try to make himself look clever**".

I have been looking into the ways of the people in the different parts of the world who practice the art of Trance to contact Spirit.

People think that music when meditating has to be nice and serene, calm and low in volume. I have tried one method that is used by the North American Indians. This method was using their drums to go on a journey while meditating. It is one of their ways of journeying in the mind, discovering your inner self, so dismiss out of your mind that you have to be only quiet and calm whilst meditating. If you can, try this drum method out, because if you can meditate in the noise of the drums you can meditate anywhere. It is a different method of trying to have focused awareness, focused attention. There are many peoples of the world using noise for altered awareness.

The first time I tried this form of meditation with the drums, was when I attended a workshop run by Barbara Meiklejohn-Free at "The Arthur Findlay College" at Stansted, Essex. I was surprised at the depth of the meditation state I achieved whilst the drums were beating out their rhythm, also what surprised me was the amount of different things that I received in my mind from Spirit when I went on that journey of discovery within my mind, all while the noise of the drums and rattles was going on all around me.

The workshop was about the ways the North American Native Indians use the drums, and their rhythms to help the North American Native Indian Holy Men to bring in the Spirits around them, to heal the Native Indians, to guide them in times of uncertainty, and of course to dance to in times of happiness, sadness, and in times when help was needed for the tribe. Bringing on the rain and such.

The time that stands out for me, was when most of the people who were on the course, all attended the workshop in the large hall at Stansted. There were 30 people using handheld Native North American Indian drums, and Celtic drums, with others on corn rattles, and at the side a very large [3-4 foot across] POW-WOW drum with four people on it, all playing at once while there was a circle of twelve people meditating in the middle, all going on a journey of discovery. We all had a turn of sitting in the Circle, **what an experience!**

A tape recorder has been used many times when the drums have been played in this situation and there have been recorded on the tape, Spirit voices. Whilst you are playing the drums in this event, it is as though the drums are talking or singing to you as you play, it is truly amazing. (You can sometimes hear within the beat of the drum you are holding, a vibration that brings with it voices and singing).

Barbara has a close working relationship with the teachers from the various Native American tribes, and spends a part of each year working on different reservations. In 1999, she was working on the Crow reservation in Montana also at Pine Ridge in South Dakota, striving to learn from their wisdom. Barbara was also taught by Red Bird from the Cochiti Pueblo people.

Another workshop I attended, I had the good fortune to meet two Sioux Indians who came over to lecture at the college. I found them very informative and entertaining. As Barbara says; the drum is a very ancient instrument, which has been used, by Shaman, Healers, and Medicine people in virtually every culture for hundreds of thousands of years. It has proven equally effective in the present day, as it was in days gone by, for Healing, Mediumship, and Trance work. Here we are again with the vibration of the airwaves to attract Spirit. (as singing is in our Physical Circles)

I also go around to different centres with my dozen drums, shakers, and sticks, to help people with their knowledge of Shamanic Trance. It can be a wonderful experience.

The native Asian cultures also have their own method of bringing people into the trance situation. They use the natural materials available in their surroundings as all cultures of the world do.
The peoples of the Malaysian continent use the forest to pick from and use the materials for house building, so what could be more natural than using the building material for producing a rhythmical beat noise so inducing a Trance state. BUT a lot of tribes actually use the forest herbs to produce hallucinogenic effects as well NOT TO BE RECOMMENDED.

**What ever altered states that can be produced by drugs can be produced by you as a Human Spirit by meditation if done properly. PLEASE DO NOT USE DRUGS.**

The material mainly used by the Asian and Malaysian natives is bamboo, which grows in abundance in that part of the world. The natives did not often make many bamboo instruments for trance work, but they have special huts for their trance work and they hit the bamboo floor in a rhythmic beat, often while drinking the local home brew.

The Native aborigines of Australia use bones of animals, hard sticks, and stones. They then can create a constant beat by striking them together. Mainly they go into the outback to special dreamtime places and go into what they call dreamland, we of course call it meditation.

Then there are the native African people who have large forest areas and hollow out logs to make drums of many types and styles, some covered with animal skins some are not. There are many instances of medicine men having special dark huts to meditate in. (The North American Native Indians have darkened [blacked out] sweat lodges they use).

There have been instances written about were people have travelled along a track miles from no where, only to be greeted by a medicine man coming out of the scrub, taken to a hut miles from the nearest white settlement and a séance has taken place. There the person's relation who had passed years ago, has appeared out of the air/ether before them. I will have to dig out the old book where full explanations are written. I cannot remember the name.

There are many tribes who meditate in the open while they are on foraging trips.
The peoples of the forest in the South Americas use the trees and their exposed roots that resonate when beaten. There are many trees/woods that give different sounds out when hit so each tribe has their own favourite ones.

If you would like to have a go at Shamanic Trance inducement, all that is needed is a friend with drum and stick, or a piece of wood and stick, or died bone and stick, or a bundle of bamboo and a stick, one or a set of shakers (type of rattle) perhaps a dried gourd with the seeds still in it. Some of the North American Native Indians use the dried rattles of the Rattle Snake. The African Natives use dried gourds and large long dried tree/bush seedpods with their seeds rattling inside, as do the South Americans. It is best to have more than one friend with you playing the beat, BUT this can be done with only two people. IF you cannot get hold of a friend then all that is needed is a tape recorder to record your own beat on whatever instrument you have. Remembering we are all different with different needs where rhythm and noise is concerned.

Sit in a comfortable position on a chair or the floor. Relax and close your eyes. Concentrate on the breath, breath gently and slowly through the nose and be aware of yourself gently drawing in the etheric part of the air to the root of the nose and put your own character onto it, implant your good thoughts in it by saying a few words in your mind through your thoughts to those you would like to draw close to you. Ask them to help you in your quest for knowledge and wisdom. Ask as I do for them to come closer but only ever come with goodness, kindness, love and truth, to come within the Divine Light of Spirit from within the loving harmony of Spirit of the highest realms. Whilst looking into the light (colour) in your third eye, let the rhythm go over you, get involved with it, do not listen to the beat but be part of it by looking into your third eye area, ask those in Spirit for knowledge and guidance in your thoughts, to be shown pictures, I assure you, you will be given some by them, by Spirit. It might be mixtures of coloured light, a scene, a face, a landscape, something you might have been thinking about previously; in fact anything; this can be your own awareness coming to the fore. Write down what ever comes into your third eye so you can go back to it at a later time to see if it is of any relevance to you now.

If doing the Shamanic Trance inducement in a group situation. Divide the group into two, place one group of people around in a circle formation, asking the people who are meditating to ask Spirit within their thoughts, to keep encouraging Spirit to come closer and help them in their development, then after a time let go of their thoughts, still the mind by looking into the light and become part of the rhythm. The others are to be given the instruments to be used in the beat/rhythm. Arrange to have a rhythm/beater leader who takes the lead, a person who has the knowledge of a rhythm, because the rhythm should change at different times throughout the session. So you can see it is necessary for a person with some knowledge of rhythm has to be the leader.

Suggested rhythms are as follows :- (each number is a beat) on the capital wording the beat is stronger. **ONE** two three (space), **ONE** two three (space), **ONE** two three (space), **ONE** two three (space), **BOOM** boom boom (space) **BOOM** boom boom (space), **BOOM** boom boom (space), and so on for about five minutes or so.
Then change to, one two three **FOUR** (with a slightly heavier beat on the four) one two three **FOUR**, one two three **FOUR**, one two three **FOUR**, boom boom boom **BOOM**, boom boom boom **BOOM**, boom boom boom **BOOM**, boom boom boom **BOOM**, and so on for another five minutes or so.
Then go back to the:- **ONE** two three (space), **ONE** two three (space), **ONE** two three (space), **ONE** two three (space), **BOOM** boom boom (space), **BOOM** boom boom (space), **BOOM** boom boom (space).
Then go to a same beat throughout with no heavy strike for another five minutes or so. One two three four five six seven eight nine ten :- etc. boom boom boom boom boom boom boom boom boom boom boom boom boom. Then do the sequence over again.

When beating, the people with the instruments should walk around **"slowly"** behind the meditating group as they beat out the rhythm on the instruments, **DO NOT TOUCH THE PEOPLE WHO ARE MEDITATING.** Lots of people make up their own simple rhythms, but really there are only four types of beat the other one being :- one two (space), one two (space), one two (space), one two (space), boom boom (space), boom boom (space), boom boom (space) etc, etc this could also be included.
After about a half an hour or so, the leader has to stop the beat and talk to the people meditating in the Circle. Ask them to let the conditions go and come back to the normality of their normal self. Any person not coming back, staying in meditation, should be talked to gently saying their name and ask them to let the conditions go and come back. **"AT NO TIME MUST THEY (the meditating people) BE TOUCHED OR SHAKEN."** Allow each individual to come back in their own time
When all are back to normality the leader of the groups should go around the Circle and ask each person in turn to relate to the group as a whole what experiences they had if any. There must be no stigma attached to any one who does not experience anything, we are all made different. Remember to praise the people for what they have achieved.
The groups then swap over. The rhythm section meditating, the people meditating playing the instruments.

I have found that the Bodhran type drums are the best as an all round instrument, as they are reasonably priced, coming in a large range of sizes and they can be painted how ever you like by using acrylic paints. And they can be played in so many different ways. The American Native Indian drum is higher priced and has a deeper, heavier beat. This could be used as the lead drum for the beat from the rhythm/beater leader if only one is bought. There are many dried gourds on sale now in farm shops where they grow them and in craft shops. So you can paint on your own designs. Why not try to make your own by buying one, drying it out in an airing cupboard and then painting it in your own design. Remember, also, no one need go out with a headache, the constant monotonous rhythm is the main thing, **NOT** the loudness of the beat.

# ANOTHER METHOD OF MEDITATION

Here is another very good way for learners to start to meditate, for relaxation, for stress reduction, for healing of many kinds and also for linking with the Angels in Spirit or the inner self [your own Spirit]. I have made a tape of this if you would like to buy it from Stansted Hall to use on your own. But for now, try it this way. Have the leader of your group read it to you all.

Each person has to talk to Spirit within their own mind encouraging them to come closer each time they sit for a link. This should **always** be done and it should be done **with sincerity**. Asking for Spirit to come with only goodness, kindness, love and truth, to come within the Divine Light of Spirit, from the loving harmony of Spirit of the highest realms. This should be done at every time of sitting for a link with those in Spirit. If you sit in any Circle, then each person should have been talking to Spirit within their minds, constantly asking Spirit to come closer and help them, this should be done as a matter of course hours before the sitting, getting ready for the linking, and/or development. You or any other person cannot expect those in Spirit to come to you immediately when you sit down to meditate. Yes Spirit can be around you at any time. But I have found out over my time experiencing Spirit within my own development, if you wish to have a strong link with Spirit you have to sit and talk to them within your own mind.

The person/persons just have to close their eyes, ask them to concentrate on the breath, breath with intention, see and feel it going in and out of the nose in a steady stream, put good thoughts on the air as it goes into the lungs feeding the body, see it for a few minutes then let it go. Imagine they are going on this journey. Let them see it in their minds eye, in their imagination. This is a practice sequence to help you form pictures in the mind. Many call this meditation but it is really contemplation. You are using thought. Not stilling the mind BUT it is all practice for later on. I believe helping Spirit by placing yourself in a situation where they can know you are willing to link and then helping them to see how your linkage in the brain functions when you link and how you are shown the images within the third eye. Spirit then can place images into your mind as your link becomes stronger and you develop together with the Spirit World.
It is in the early stages (a little later on than this) you have to take notice of the positions of the images given by Spirit and what they mean. I am shown images in my third eye area when using clairvoyance, for the past the images and the words are on the left, for the present at the front, and the future on the right. Below front, is the position set by Spirit for me to be shown things given in the past and the person still has it at this present time. Work out with your friends in the World of Spirit what rules you would like them to work by and then stick to them so you can have a good strong solid link. I would advise you to write the rules down before you send out any thoughts to Spirit and go over them a few times to make sure they are correct for you and Spirit when are both linking together.

Now to the Meditation sequence.
In the background is a low meditation tape playing. Have your group, or your partner close their eyes, ask them to concentrate on their breathing for a few minutes and within the mind, to place some good thoughts and what you wish to get out of this meditation, place those thoughts onto the breath to impress them on the ether that is being held at the root of the nose, after about a minute ask the person/people to look into the third eye into the light /colour and let the thoughts go, still the mind by just looking into the light. If any thoughts come into the mind just let them drift through, do not think of them, go back to the light and look into it, (keep on doing this, if you break from the light (or a colour) go back and start again all that is needed is practice).
Then have someone very softly and gently, and very slowly read out all of this, hesitating, for a while where the commas are, stopping, where the full stops are for a few moments longer, longer where there are many full stops. Very slightly emphasis the words in bold:-

All close your eyes. As always say a prayer to the World of Spirit.
**Ask with sincerity** for goodness, kindness, love and truth, and to blend in peaceful Divine Light of Spirit within the loving harmony of the highest vibrational force of those Angels in highest realms of Spirit.
Now see yourself in a beautiful flowery meadow with many different vibrantly coloured butterflies flying

## KEEWAYS   MEDITATION ONENESS   written by Roy Keeghan

all around the flowers, you have no shoes on your feet, in part of the meadow the grass has been cut, you can smell the new mown grass... All the grass is still damp, it has dew on it from the night before; you can feel the coolness of the wet dew on your bare feet...The warm sun is out in the bright beautiful blue sky, you can hear the birds singing melodiously in the differently shaded coloured leafed trees....There are more birds singing in the mixed sweet smelling blossom of the bushy hedgerows, you stop for a while listening and absorbing the wonder of nature and it's beauty.......

As you walk along through the meadow you start looking up into that bright blue sky, there are very light fluffy white clouds like flimsy cotton wool floating about, you see and hear the skylarks singing at the top of their lungs as they fly so high above you and the flowers in the meadow.....

As you walk along deeper into the meadow away from the hedgerow, the sun in the bright blue sky is starting to feel lovely and warm on you; there are a few more skylarks competing for their song to be personal to your ears...

It is good to be out here in the meadow with the smell of the new mown grass, and the feel of the wet dew on your feet, and the life giving sun in the beautiful blue sky is feeling warm and comfortable on you...

As you walk through the wet dew laden green grass you can feel the moisture on your feet, the dew is feeling nice and cool on your feet and toes...

The warmth of the sun is feeling good on your body as you go through the meadow grass, it is as though the birds are singing just for you to brighten up your day...

You can smell the new mown grass as the steam is rising from it; the warm sun is doing its work of drying it ready for harvesting...

As you walk along in the meadow you can hear in the distance the occasional sea bird calling, you look towards the sounds and now can see the blue green sea in the far distance with a crop of rocks leading down to the seashore...

What a wonderful smell you are getting from the newly mown grass as you walk through it...

The smell of the blue green sea and the new mown green grass are now mixing, what a wonderful livening aroma it is bringing you...

The sounds of the sea, the sea on the shore and the seabirds are getting louder....

Through the meadow you are walking towards the crop of rocks, you can clearly hear the sounds of the sea on the foreshore, you see the rocks glistening in the sun with the water still on them, it was left there from the receding sea making the warm sun reflect on them. The refection is joining together now as you walk towards the rocks; they all look like one sheet of glass glistening together in the distance....

Walking onward the mixed smell of the new mown grass in the meadow and the smell of the sea is making you feel good about yourself...

The warmth of the sun on you is making you feel happy with yourself and with life itself.

By the rocks in the distance there is what looks like a bent fallen tree...

As you get closer you can see it is a tree.

This tree looks as if it has been blown over by the storms many years ago...

The tree is still alive with branches sprouting up from it's trunk, the branches of the tree has formed an unusual shape at ground level, that shape to you looks like a nice comfortable seat....

On going across the cool wet flat sea-smoothed rocks towards the tree you see the storm damage **has** formed a seat **it is there**....

You can feel the nice, wet, coolness of the water worn, smooth rocks on your feet...

You go across to the bent fallen tree and sit in the tree seat with your feet resting on the cool, smooth, wet, flat, seashore rocks...

You are now in the warmth of the sun and the comfort of the tree seat, your feet are on the cool, sea worn, smooth rocks...

Your whole body is nice and relaxed in the healing, life giving, warmth of the sun, there is a very light gentle sea breeze bringing into your nostrils the clean healing smell of the sea, you can feel the life of the tree as you relax in it's branches, it is sharing it's life force with you, the tree is sharing it's strength and giving you comfort as you relax into the soft subtle supporting branches and all is well with you....

Take a few minutes to absorb the feeling as you relax in the tree seat looking out to sea and the wonderful view around you.......

As you are sitting there relaxed you can see a fantastic pure coloured bright white light coming from that beautiful blue sky, surround yourself in that fantastic, pure coloured, bright white light.....

This pure coloured white light is going all over your head, it is tumbling down covering your shoulders and all over your body, this fantastic pure coloured white light is now all around you and you feel the safest you have ever felt anywhere in your life…..

This light is giving you all the strength that can be given to anyone; it is being given to you for good health, happiness, relaxation, protection, and the development of your inner yourself.

Within this light you can feel there is someone there protecting you, you turn round and see this angelic, kind, warm, comforting person standing there. (you might see this person with you, do not worry if you don't, they **are** there with you in the light, sense them with you).

Take a few minutes to absorb the feeling….

Now is the time to ask the question that you have wanted to be answered…..

This question is not always answered right away, or at this time or on this day.

You ask that question in your mind and wait…..

Take a few minutes to absorb the feeling, and to see if your question is answered…**(wait a longer period of time here)**……

Your attention is now drawn to the ground around you, you had not noticed before all the splendour between the smooth rocks around you. Was it the bright Divine Light that made it happen? Was it the person who was there with you who brought all the splendour for you? What ever it was, it has heightened your awareness.

There are rock pools with brightly coloured life in them…..

You take a few moments of your time to look at the brightly coloured life in the rock pools and drink in their splendour……

You look around and see there is now springing up bright beautifully coloured flowers all around you as well as under the tree seat you are sitting on…..

You bend down to pick up the most beautiful flower you have ever seen and hold it up to your nose.

As it comes to your nose you become aware of, and see the beautiful coloured perfume coming from the most beautiful flower you have ever seen; the one you are holding in your hand, and all the others around you…..

You breath in deeply that beautifully coloured perfume and it is clearing all the hurt that you have in your mind…..

The beautifully coloured perfume is taking away all the aches and pains you have in your body……

The beautifully coloured perfume is healing all your ills that you have in you, and it will go on healing you each time you bring that beautifully coloured perfume from that bright beautifully coloured flower back into your mind no matter where you are…..

Take a few moments to deeply breath in the fragrance that is surrounding you…….

You slowly get up and start to walk towards a stile over which there is a field full of brown ripening grain growing, mixed in with the brown grain the field is also full of brightly coloured red poppies they are all together moving with a life of it's own in the very gentle sea breeze…

There you pause for a while at the stile and start leaning on it in the warmth of the life giving sun……….

As you look into the field full of grain and brightly coloured red poppies swaying very gently in the light sea breeze, you become aware of the person beside you, you turn round and see it is the angelic, kind, warm, comforting, person who you asked the question of. This person is there just to let you know they will be there beside you whenever you need them. (It might be just one person or a few)…..

If they have the answer to your question they will give you the answer and then leave when they are ready, they might at this time want to leave the answer for another time…..

You now have time to reflect on that answer if you were given one, you can also reflect on the person who is going to be there to help you in different difficult situations you might have in your life and help you with the questions you might ask in the future…….

As you look back into the field of ripening brown grain with the brightly coloured red poppies swaying gently all mixed together, you can now take a few moments to go over and absorb all that has been given in this time of meditation……...

You turn and now start to walk back away from field of grain that is full of poppies and the stile, going towards the comfortable soft subtle supporting tree seat….

You can still smell that light clean healing sea breeze that did you so much good...

You cross back over the nice cool smooth rocks in your bare feet as you breath in the smells, the rocks now are drying in the warmth of the sun, they feel slightly different on your feet now….

On passing the strong fallen bending tree, you see all the beautiful brightly coloured flowers with their beautifully coloured perfume that healed all your problems, you give some words of thanks within your mind to the high realms of Spirit for all you have seen, smelt and felt….

You take a long lasting, deep breath to keep you going, so it can forever go on healing your inner self.

You start to cross back over the warm drying dew grass in the green meadow hearing the birds singing in the warmth of the sun, they are singing especially to you from the hedgerows, bushes, trees, and sky making you the happiest person alive..

You **are** lucky having all this around you, you feel you are as one with nature…

Take a few moments to absorb the feeling……..

You are walking slowly back over the rest of the meadow, going through the meadow flowers with the butterflies flying round them, past the blossoming hedgerows with the birds singing in them, at the gate you open it, turn around and look across the meadow,,,,, then go through the gate, closing the gate behind you at the same time thanking the higher force for all that is good in the world, and asking for only goodness, and kindness in every form to continue ….

Come back out of meditation gently and slowly at your own pace, do not rush it………..

The leader of the group should talk the group back now slowly and gently. If any one person/persons are staying in the meditative state then the leader should continue to talk to them using their name to bring them back, the use of their name acts as a trigger in the subconscious. Tell all there it is discipline that is needed when you are in a situation that is wonderful and you do not wish to come out of it.

Whenever you want to go back into that beautiful atmosphere, you can do so at any time for healing, answers, or relaxation. If you want to heal yourself, remember the smells you have conjured up in your mind and bring them back as they were seen for you in your meditation.

You will all be amazed how much good that little passage will do for you when read out with care by another. If you cannot get anyone to read this out for you please for your own sake try to get the tape of this meditation. Better still read it out for yourself and record it. Your own voice is the best thing to listen to.

Before any person goes into a relaxed state ready for meditation. The leader or the person talking should ask for the person/persons to say a **sincere prayer** within their mind, then to concentrate on the breath. Breath with intention. See the breath going into the nose, as it goes into the nose, the air is taking the ether into the nose where it is held at the root of the nose, the rest of the air is going into the lungs and feeding the body making it relaxed. Let the thoughts be good and send those good thoughts into the breath going into the nose, impress on the ether what development you would like Spirit to help you with. On an outward breath send out through the nose any badness from your mind and body. Do this for a good few minutes.

With this sort of contemplation (meditation) many people start to see images, feel the air, the breeze, the smells, the sounds, this can be in stages over a period of time, it is your awareness coming to the fore. It gives Spirit a chance to impress on you the sensations, it is the start of your development.

## ANOTHER METHOD OF MEDITATION

One method of inducing another relaxed form of meditation is for someone to count while sitting or standing in front of another person. A lot of people prefer to have the person on the chair for meditation and the other person on the floor sitting, or a lower seat. This saves the point of talking down to the person in the chair making them feel inferior. This following method is a form of mild hypnosis. It is one method you can use yourself for self-hypnosis.

This method can also be done one to one, or in a group with just one person counting and all the rest meditating. As the one person counts slowly the other person/persons who is/are going to meditate, start with their eyes open. When the number one is spoken "one"; then they close their eyes as the number two is spoken "two"; on the number three they open their eyes; on the number four they close their eyes; and so on until they raise a finger on their hand when they are relaxed. So it is:- 1 eyes open, 2 eyes closed, 3 eyes open, 4 eyes closed, 5 eyes open, 6 eyes closed, 7 eyes open, 8 eyes closed, 9 eyes open, 10 eyes closed, 11 eyes open, 12 eyes closed, 13 eyes open, 14 eyes closed and so on until all there have relaxed and raised a finger on their hand **slightly** or their hand slightly. The hands of the person previously having been resting comfortably on their knees. Each person goes into a relaxed state at different stages, some at ten, others at one hundred and ten, there is no set time, but the people must be relaxed and not fight the sensations. Each person can come out of the meditation whenever they want to.

Each person **first** should always remember the saying of the **sincere prayer** and then the talking, asking, the encouraging of Spirit to help and develop you in what ever you would like. (this is done within their own mind through **sincere** thought)
Ask for Spirit to come only with goodness, kindness, love and truth, to come within the Divine Light of Spirit, to come only from within the loving harmony of Spirit of the highest realms.

If a person is not feeling relaxed for meditation, another way of dealing with this can be to comb their aura. It might look strange to the outsider but it does work. The person ready to meditate sits in a comfortable chair with their eyes closed. The worker stands in front of them bending over the "meditator" not speaking. The "worker" now starts to do a stroking downward action over the person, their both hands being about an inch to three inches away from the head or body of the "meditator", **never touching**. The worker starts with both hands at the top of the head going down in a **very slow** action, over each side at the same time, the side of the head down to the shoulders and down along the arms and then sweeping both hands at the same time, palms outwards to the side away from the person and the "worker" then starts again at the top of the head with each hand going down at the same time in a **very slow** action, over the side of the head down to the shoulders and down along the arms and then sweeping palms outwards to the side away from the "meditator" and then "worker" starts again, again, and again, until the person is totally relaxed. This method of combing the aura can be used for the healing of headaches and migraine. The older mediums of the last century used this method to be mesmerised for half an hour plus, before going onto the platform to demonstrate.

## CLAIR-VOYANCE    CLAIR-SENTIENCE CLAIR-AUDIENCE
Here I have put categories that should also be used within Mediumship and they are
## "CLAIR-KNOWING and others

I have put these together because a lot of people who have clairvoyance also have or I should say **can** have, clairaudience and most of the developed Mediums have clairsentience, and other clairs, they all are developed in a similar way, i.e. Closing the eyes concentrating on the breath as it slowly goes in and out of the nose, expel all the breath each time but do not breath in deep, then after the first six breaths go steady with the breathing, stilling the body. Then asking Spirit through thought, to place on the breath that is going into the nose through the filters of the nose, to the root of the nose where the ether part of the air is collected. Place those good thoughts on that ether (you are to impress your character on the ether), **asking Spirit sincerely** for the development you wish to develop. It is necessary to impress on the ether the thought intention (what development you wish to be helped with). Do this whilst sitting in meditation at home alone, in a Circle, or in a group awareness Circle, or in a development Circle. Quite often the three gifts develop together. BUT not always! One of the top Mediums I know who travels the world, and I have sat in his development Circles, is only clairsentient. Remember to ask by thought [the living energy] for the gifts that you wish to receive from those Angels in Spirit, they will be given "if it is the will of the Divine Spirit" and that is important here **IF IT IS THE WILL OF THE DIVINE SPIRIT.** You should ask being **true, positive, sincere,** sending out **love** and wishing/wanting/asking to blend in peaceful **loving harmony**, and with the understanding that the Angels in Spirit have the knowledge of which gift is best for you to use. You should be saying you are going to put the gifts to good use for the benefit of others to understand there is life after our so-called death **and mean it.** Then you will be able to bring help to your fellow man/woman giving them comfort in their hour of need.

I repeat the one very important thing. It is up to the Angels in Spirit in your development and what gift they want to bless you with. If it is their will, you can and possibly will receive that gift. The Angels in Spirit know what you are, what your potential is, and what you are capable of doing. Have the knowledge to let the Angels in Spirit decide for you, also by trying everything in the psychic field, all that is within this book, that gift; which is ready to be given to you by Spirit will slot into place at the correct time, so experiment.

**"BEFORE" EVERY CIRCLE AND EVERY TIME A PERSON SITS FOR A SPIRIT LINK. THEY SHOULD IN THEIR MIND, BE SINCERELY ASKING AND ENCOURAGING SPIRIT TO COME CLOSER TO THEM AND HELP AT ALLOTTED TIME FOR THE SITTING FOR DEVELOPMENT OR DEMONSTRATION, ENCOURAGING OVER AND OVER AND OVER. AT LEAST AN HOUR OR TWO "BEFORE" THE ALLOTTED TIME. YOU CANNOT EXPECT YOUR LINK TO COME AUTOMATICALLY AS SOON AS YOU SIT DOWN IN A CIRCLE OR DEMONSTRATE YOUR SKILL OF A LINK WITH SPIRIT TO PROVE TO OTHER THERE IS LIFE AFTER OUR SO CALLED DEATH. You have to cultivate your gifts together with those helpers in Spirit and then keep it nourished by talking to Spirit within meditation.**

It would seem that sitting for Trance, [I go fully into telling about trance in the later parts of the book] brings in most of the gifts to people sooner for some reason. I think personally it is because the developing Medium or earth bound helper, blanks out, quietens, stills, or makes his/her mind more tranquil, and lets the Angels in Spirit get on with the task in hand, [that being altering/setting up the connections in the brain needed by Spirit to act as a receiver {a link, a medium}], and when the Medium is in the Trance State, they then have no interference to contend with, that being the interference of the activity of the mind of the Medium.
It is the easiest thing in the world to close your eyes and think, to have thoughts run through your mind; it is the hardest thing in the world to slow down and eventually stop any thoughts running through your mind. BUT that should be the aim of us all. It is only by having a quite mind (a quietened mind) and looking into the Divine Light within the third eye area of the mind that this will be achieved. This is the way I do it anyway. So I know it works.

Often a Medium (the earth bound linking person) can have a mental block, a point in their life when all their gifts are taken away, and nothing at all seems to happen when trying to link with those in Spirit. This is sometimes due to the fact the Medium takes everything for granted from the Angels in Spirit, so the link is lost for a while (I believe it can be and **is taken away** for any number of reasons). Sometimes it is when the Medium does not meditate alongside their work; only working, forgetting about time they should put aside for the development link with the Angels in Spirit, it should be pointed out here none of us are ever fully developed we keep on developing until we pass across the veil and join with those in Spirit, even then we have to keep on developing whilst we are there in Spirit. Sometimes it can be because their lives are in turmoil and the person cannot get the thoughts out of the mind or cannot stop them from coming into the mind all the time while meditating. It can be because of negativity, or badness within the Medium or to many distractions in the Medium's life. If left too long, quite often the Medium has to start from nearly scratch again to build up their link with those in Spirit. If you receive the gift from Spirit treasure it, and remember to link with the Angels in Spirit at the very, very least once a week for an hour, better once a day even if it is only for fifteen/sixty minutes in those quiet moments of meditation on your own with Spirit.

I now go to the technical points of seeing, hearing, and the things I was taught about at school in physics. To see colours, you have to pick up the wavelength of each individual colour that is reflected off the object. So to see a person you have to see/pickup all the colours being reflected off their clothing, skin, hair, eyes and anything else they have on, and/or off the person you are looking at, at the time. You see, now it is for you a solid body, which is sending off slow vibrations, which you can now pick up because you have learned it from experience from birth. It is also known if a person has not seen from birth, being blind and they get their sight back in later life. They also have to learn to see/pickup the vibrations, learn to read/see/pickup the vibrations over periods of time possibly up to twelve months. This is so the brain can grow connection to interpret those signals and go on learning so the person who was blind can see as a normal sighted person.

Please think logically about seeing anything; I remember seeing this middle aged person who was blind from birth, he lived in America. This man was on a programme on television about his progress and how he had to learn to see and what he went through. He had not seen anything through his eyes before the doctors found after an operation to repair a section of nerve there was nothing to stop him seeing, so from being blind from birth he then had to learn to see at the age of thirty-forty. This man had to teach his eyes and the rods behind the eyes to transmit signals to form images that his brain could learn to interpret as sight that most of us have. He then had the use of his eyes every day in our normal way, YET IT TOOK HIM in his developing of seeing properly with his newly found sight, using his eyes **twelve to fourteen hours a day,** may be more, this was from the time he awoke until he went to bed over this period of time; I think it was over a period of twelve months this man had to educate his eyes, the rods behind the eyes, and his brain to see as most of us do. Work it out 12 x 365 = 4380 hours that man had to practice and educate his natural ability that most of us have, just for him to learn to see. So it is with you as a Medium. You have to learn, **over a great many hours,** to learn how to pickup/see (Spirit World has to alter [if seeing Spirit objectively clairvoyantly, altering and adjusting the lenses of the eye and then in turn the rods behind the eyes which send information to the brain] and increase the brain's connections as well for the Medium to develop things within the body for Spirit's purpose) the vibrations of the higher frequency to see clairvoyantly the forms or images of the things given by the Angels of the Spirit sphere and to see those In the Spirit World who come to show themselves. You have to learn, whilst in meditation with the help of those in the higher realms, to expand your frequency range, of seeing/picking up the vibrations of the airwaves. You the budding Medium being as passive as possible in meditation.
This should be seen just as a natural process, which the Mediums are using to help others come to terms with our term "death," **yes! This is open to all NOT JUST THE CHOSEN FEW, it takes <u>dedication</u> that is all. Ask with <u>sincerity</u>** from the World of Spirit for what you want as you meditate, talk to those helpers in Spirit they are there for you to get to know and they WILL become your friends. After asking and talking (within the mind) to those Spirit friends in the realms of Spirit, the Medium does nothing but meditate, trying to still or quieten their mind and that then allows those in Spirit to do what they need to do. I assure you, it will not hurt or injure you. So it is with the hearing of the Angels in Spirit, a Medium within meditation puts their time and mind aside to tune into vibrations that others without **love, harmony, dedication** and <u>**sincerity**</u> cannot normally attune to. The passive developing Medium is allowing the Spirit World the setting up, a re-tuned or expanding the frequency range tuner within the Medium's head (within the brain/mind with newly formed connections) with the help of the Angels in Spirit. A frequency that they can use and listen to, one that is higher than the ordinary person in the street can hear.

I believe some deaf people could also hear the voices/vibrations from the Angels in Spirit if they trained as a clairaudient, just as hearing persons can. It is just as I believe a blind person can see clairvoyantly as has been proved at our Liverpool, Daulby Street church many times by the blind Mediums Mavis Michel, also the blind husband and wife Medium team of Joe and Wendy Hunter. They would be tuning into the vibrations that are invisible to the ordinary person's eye frequency. The eye not being able to pickup/see the vibrations because they are of a higher/different frequency range. So it is with the voices/vibrations of the Angels in Spirit that are turned into voices in Mediums' heads. Now with training and tuning the brain by Spirit and meditation time put aside by the person, **allowing it to happen**, more importantly <u>**giving permission**</u>, the budding Medium can pickup/interpret higher than normal vibrations such as voices/images of people, helpers, and Spirit Angels messages from the higher vibrational level, because they, the Mediums have had the intelligence to put some time aside in meditation and to quieten their brain activity to link into the Angels in Spirit for their help. Please remember this is different to physical seeing and hearing this applies to any of the other Clairs.

I was watching a programme on TV about the body and the development of the brain in newborn child. This I feel was put on for the explanation not just for the curious but also for people who want to understand how Spirit uses the channels in our brain whist linking. I will add more in the Physical Mediumship part, but I will say here this programme clarified for me that I was correct in my findings. In as much as if you do not use your brain regularly for the purposes you use it for, whether for everyday life or meditating for the purpose of linking with Spirit, the connections made within the brain, die. More so as we grow older because the regeneration of new tissue does not become as easy for our human form in old age, it is best to start when young, the younger the better. But the linking mechanism of the Medium is slightly different, as it is done not entirely in the brain itself. Spirit uses every part of the person including the etheric part as well. So the mechanism for linking with Spirit is not entirely lost if for one earthly reason or another a lapse of time is not too great in between the regular meditating starting again. Please to not chance it too often though as continuity is the vital key here. If you want to become a Mediumistic person, you must develop **with** the World of Spirit on a **regular basis**. You talking to them through thought and them talking to you it goes both ways NOT just one way.

## How the system of communication with Spirit works

The group thought in Spirit of unknown size ⇄ From one spokesperson of the group Information goes to ⇄ Medium's Spirit then to Medium's Subconscious Medium's Conscious then ⇒ Out of the Medium's mouth to the recipient

**Please remember this is a <u>two-way</u> communication that has to be in "HARMONY"** also I have put in the diagram "from one spokesperson of the group". In the realms of Spirit it should technically be "from one thought person", or "from one person through thought".

**Clairvoyance or Clear Seeing** is the gift of seeing objects, animals or people in the mind's eye, in fact anything that others cannot see. For some, this is at times, mixed up with their normal vision state, others have to adjust their mind with training in meditation alongside Spirit helpers to pick it up.

Some Mediums [the Clairvoyant] see a Spirit form in the flesh so to speak, as though the person is real, seeing the vibration of the bodily form here on the earth plane beside others perhaps beside themselves, this is classed as seeing "objectively" (the object, as an object), It should be pointed out here that the Spirit form is being seen through the clairvoyant mechanism of the brain/mind of the mediumistic person seeing the Spirit form, otherwise it would be physical phenomena where by everyone there could see the Spirit form, this applies to all the Clairs. The Spirit World have to alter the vibrations of the Medium [heightening them], this is done naturally during meditation if asked for, and the Spirit World have to lower their vibrations to match [or as is said "to link with the Medium"].

Some Mediums see the Spirit form in their head [minds eye], also they can see things as a movie or a television programme in their third eye, some just get a still form like a photograph in their mind, this is classed as seeing "subjectively".

Quite often as Mediums develop they get them all, **BUT not always**. To progress with this gift it is best to put at the very, very least two hours a week [an hour daily is best, you will progress quicker] aside at a set time to meditate to get a better/stronger link with those in Spirit while sitting within the power of the Angels in Spirit. **Remember to ask with a thought** to your Guardian Angels for the gift you would like to develop at the start of the meditation, if you like, during as well. I personally talk to Spirit in my mind encouraging them to come closer to help me develop or help me link with them to help others when giving messages in any of the Claire------s. I get a mixture of words and pictures and I have a more heighten sense of awareness because I meditate very regularly, by that I mean meditate each day, many times twice a day, and sometimes more.

I am shown images in my third eye area when using clairvoyance, for something **in the past** they placed by Spirit are **on the left** in my mind's eye, **for the present at the front**, and **the future on the right**. Below front, is the position set by Spirit for me, to show things given to the recipient in the past and the person still has it (in this present day). Work out with your friends in the World of Spirit what rules you would like them to work by and then stick to them so you can have a good strong solid link. I would advise you to write them down before you send out any thoughts to Spirit and go over them a few times to make sure they are correct for you and Spirit when are linking together. Then meditate on that set of rules quite a few times to make sure Spirit can carry on your development whilst using those rules, of course they might change over time only you and your Spirit Helpers/links will know in which way it does through practicing together in that all important harmony with each other.

People often ask how do you start seeing a house number, the name of a street and full names. It is no great secret, just ask Spirit for them to be given to you. Keep on asking over and over again they will come when they are ready to be given. Nothing is ever given without being worked for in some way. So start meditating regularly to bring that harmony with the higher vibrational force and self, be sincere in your asking and what you are asking for and especially sincere in what you are going to be using it for; **that,** I believe strongly, **your gift should be to help others.**

There are a few exercises that can be done to help though. Spirit has to get to know how you are seeing clairvoyantly as you start to develop, yes they learn just as you do, you progress alongside each other. The most important single thing is to have a GOOD STRONG LINK WITH SPIRIT. The only way to get that is to talk to them in all sincerity, and encourage them to come near to you, to be part of you as one. You blend in **LOVING HARMONY** with the Spirit World bringing in helpers from the World of Spirit to become part of your harmonious group while working as a Medium. They also have to allow you to be part of the working group, yes, with their permission you develop while regularly meditating.

Now to the exercises for numbers. Have the numbers from one to ten, and a nought, each one individually **CLEARLY** written [in a solid black font (type setting) that is easily read] in the centre on its own single piece of white A4 paper. Going through each number in sequence. First look at the number "one" on the paper; have it right in front of your eyes but in focus; look at it for a few minutes then close your eyes, you will see that number in front of you in your mind's eye with your eyes closed. When it fades or goes away repeat the exercise again. Do this about five times then go onto the next number "two" on it's paper, going all the way through the numbers. Then place the numbers at random together and put them on a piece of paper in the centre of a piece of A4 in pairs and then later on in groups of numbers. As you are doing this exercise keep on talking to your Spirit helpers, asking sincerely for them to help you in your task and for you to use it in the helping of others so you can prove to them there is life after our so called death. Talk to the Spirit World as though they are your friends and are beside you and within your mind, because that is what they are and if done honestly and sincerely they will become your best friends. Do this for a few weeks while on your own in a quiet place and before the start of a meditation.

It is the same for street names, [or road names and the names of towns, cities and countries. Even the names of people and animals]. Look through a telephone directory for the names of streets and roads; it does not have to be your own local directory. This exercise is only to get yourself and the World of Spirit get used to seeing the names in your clairvoyant vision and how it is achieve. This is so the World of Spirit can place them in your clairvoyant vision in your later development. Have the name of an individual street or road **CLEARLY** written in the centre, on a single piece of A4 paper, going through each individual name in sequence. First look at the name on the paper; have it right in front of your eyes but in focus; look at it for a few minutes then close your eyes. If done properly you will see that name in front of you in your mind's eye with your eyes closed. When it fades or goes away repeat the exercise again. Do this about five times, then go onto the next name of a street or road on its paper. **MOST OF ALL** remembering to be talking to the World of Spirit whilst doing this exercise. The asking and talking to the World of Spirit **in all sincerity** is the most important part of the exercise and the bringing in the link with Spirit helpers. Please remember these exercises have to be done regularly on a daily basis, each person is different in the length of time these exercises must be done for.

Talk to the Spirit World as though they are your friends here on this earth plane and are beside you and talk to them within your mind, because that is what they are **they are your friends** and will become more so as you progress along side them, and if done honestly and sincerely they will really become your **best friends**. Do these exercises for a few weeks while on your own in a quiet place and before the start of a meditation.

After you have done these exercises there is a contemplation; or as most people call it guided meditation; that can be used for the enhancement of your clairvoyance. See the section on running a course for enhancing within in the third eye area with the help of Spirit; the giving of names, places, numbers of houses, and street names, areas, cities, and countries.

## Clairaudience or Clear Hearing

is the gift of hearing Spirit voices from the Spirit World, which are not audible to other people who are even next to the Medium [the Clairaudient] who is hearing the Spirit World. Some Mediums hear as though they are listening to a person talking to them on the outside of their head, it is as though the Spirit is next to or near to the Medium, this is said to be hearing "objectively" (the object is next to/near them, just as you and I would be in our earthly body), and other

Mediums hear the voices within their head/mind as a thought verbalisation of a thought, this is said to be hearing "subjectively". Some Mediums develop both ways of hearing messages from Spirit. To progress with this gift it is best to put at the very, very least two hours a week [daily is best, you will progress quicker] aside at a set time to meditate to get a better/stronger link with those in the Spirit World while sitting within the power of those Angels in Spirit. **Remember to ask** constantly with **sincere** thought within your head, keep asking the Guardian Angels for the gift you would like to develop at the start of the meditation, if you like, during as well. If the link is not strong, keep on encouraging Spirit through that **sincere** thought to come closer to help you. Talk to them through thought, just as you would talk to a friend, because that is what they are and will become to you. There are many exercises that can be done for this. Go along the Buddhist way of exercising, mindfully listen to people talking, purposely listen to they way they talk, the way their voice comes to you, the way music comes into your ears, truly listen while talking to the Spirit World asking them for this gift of clear hearing.

**Clairsentience or Clear Sensing** is the gift of extra feeling, or having an impression of what is being given by the Angels in Spirit, it is received by the Medium [the Clairsentient] from the higher vibrational plane of Spirit. Quite a lot of people throughout the world have this gift but we do not call them Mediums, nor do they wish to become Mediums, they are generally just called Sensitives or extra sensitive people. But this section of Mediumship can be mixed up with subjective clairvoyance when a person within their head can nearly see the Spirit images but it is in a haze NOT CLEARLY seeing not fully shown yet they clearly feel the images that Spirit would like impressed on the person. That is the difference.

A lot of people that have the gift of being a Medium, a Sensitive, their sensitivity is such they often have a feeling of [the person in Spirit], their looks, their build, their age, their character, what they did when on earth, and what they died of before they, the person crossed over into the World of Spirit. To progress with this gift it is best to put at the very, very least two hours a week [daily is best you will progress quicker] aside at a set time to meditate to get a better/stronger link with the Angels in Spirit while sitting within the power of those in Spirit. **Remember to ask**, through **sincere** thought within your head, from the Angels/helpers in Spirit for the gift you would like to develop at the start of the meditation, if you like, during as well. Keep talking over and over and over again to Spirit in your mind. Ask, ask, and ask with sincerity. As always starting and finishing with a **sincere** prayer.

**Clairsensatience or Clear Feeling,** this is a gift where the Medium [the Clairsensatient] giving proof of the existence of life continuing, can take on the ailments of the person who is now in the World of Spirit, feeling the same problem of that person they had whilst they were here on the earth plane. If they had pains in their joints when this person was on this side of the veil the Medium will feel it. As they will if the link in Spirit suffered with heart problems, cancer, stomach problems, loss of a limb, tumour on the brain, etc. It will go when the link goes, and/or when the Medium goes onto another link or when the Medium asks for the symptoms of that particular link to go even if carrying on with that same link. Remember you are always the one in charge. This is feeling objectively.

The Medium can feel it as though the person who is in the World of Spirit is near them but only sensing them, this is being "subjective" in your feeling. But when the person in Spirit tugs and pulls at your clothing, feeling the pains those in the World of Spirit had when on the earth plane this is feeling "objectively".

When the Medium is feeling Spirit subjectively they only have a sense of it, and so it crosses over into the realms of Clairsentience or Clear Sensing.

**Clairsentirience or Clear Smelling**, this Clair should also be put into this book as it is part of Mediumship. A lot of sensitive people can smell the odour of the person who is not on the earth plane. They can sometimes smell their pipe tobacco, cigarette tobacco, food smells, different spices as though they are coming from a kitchen. Some Mediums [the Clairsentirient] can smell the places where the deceased person worked like a chemical factory, the docks, the places to be reminded of for the recipient of a message off the platform in the church or meeting place or in a development Circle.

Some Mediums smell the actual smell of the odour [objectively], others the smell is planted by Spirit within the mind. [Subjectively] being aware of the smell through thought.

**Clairgouterience or Clear Tasting,** this is where the Medium [the Clairgouterient] can taste the foods, liquid and anything that goes into the mouth of the deceased person, it is tasted by the Medium. This is given by those in Spirit to confirm it is the correct person being contacted. This has to be interpreted by the Medium through their link with Spirit to say whether it is liked or disliked. This is where one of the other Clairs come in. It not very often any of the Clairs come on their own. They are mainly given in two plus, then increased as the Budding Medium meditates more and links better with those in the World of Spirit, becoming more aware of the different messages and signals given by the World of Spirit through the developing mediumship of the Medium. The actual taste within the mouth can at times be strong as though the medium/sensitive has taken it in their mouth this is "objective" clear tasting. "Subjectively" is when it is put as a thought in the mind.

**Clairsavoirience or Clear Knowing,** is the gift of knowing a message is correct or something about a person or situation is correct without getting a clairvoyant, clairaudient, or clairsentient message from Spirit, it is when you just know. It is more than a clairsentient feeling. A feeling of clear certainty. **BUT** this generally has to be built up within your link with Spirit over your period of time whilst developing a very good trusted link with those who you learn to trust across the veil, in the World of Spirit. The budding Medium [The Clairsavoirient] learns to know that a message from the Spirit World being given for a person, **is** for that person even though they are being rejected by the recipient by the no's; "It is not me", "I do not know that person", I do not know that name", "I do not know that place you are talking about". Or "I have no knowledge of a relation of that name living there in that place", ETC. That Clair-Knowing only comes with experience and when you trust your link in the Spirit world.

The Medium learns to differentiate between their own thoughts and the information given by the person/persons/group who is guiding them from World of Spirit. That comes back to **TRUST**, because you, the Medium, have over the period of time learned that trust of the things given by Spirit in a **slightly different way, a subtle way** within your mind. You have within the partnership of yourself and the Spirit World learned that subtle difference which is the knowing of that special informational link rather than take and mix it up with the normal everyday thoughts that keep on going through your mind. Some people say it is a GUT FEELING (these words are from every day life which every day people use, it is the area of the solar plexus coming into play) but Clairknowing is more than that. It is the **certainty of knowing** you are correct in what you are giving out to the person. Clairknowing comes into Mediumship also when information and messages are given through the means of clairvoyance, clairaudience, and clairsentience, etc. to a lesser degree when learning and very much so when the Medium is at a higher stage in their development, knowing and fully trusting in their own Spiritual Link.

I personally when linking with Spirit, then with the person/recipient, linking into the both vibrations for a message to be given to the recipient, if the person I am talking to is the correct one for the message I find I get a tingling feeling down my spine. I then know I am on the correct vibrational link to give the message to the person that responds. This also applies to when I have my eyes close when I am in trance, also when doing transfiguration, this is when I am slightly aware of what is happening but not altogether there, if you know what I mean. You will understand the latter when it happens to you.

IT IS MOST IMPORTANT for the budding Medium to realise that only the things given by those in the Spirit should be given to the recipient and **"NOT" to make things up** and NOT put in words and things that they have not been given, as the subtle little messages from those loved ones in the World of Spirit will be missed. The truth must be said as it is important BUT again it is the responsibility of the Medium not to bring hurt into the life of another. It is very rare for those in Spirit to bring ills onto those here on this earth plane of ours. It is mainly the Medium themselves bringing out what they within their own mind **"think"** is the message. The Medium even then should take that the responsibility of their actions and possibly not give the bad message if it means hurt. Or censor it slightly. It is not the Mediums job to make up stories for entertainment, it is the Medium's job to tell the truth and give what is given to them from their link in the World of Spirit, even if it is a short sentence or one word or a single picture. I know one egotistical Medium who travels all over the world and used to embellishes the things he got from Spirit, he could make up stories. He is/was always saying "I am the most famous, well known Medium in the world, so what". BUT he loves saying it and the trouble is HE BELIEVES HE IS. A self-imposed status of "Pima Donna". He is changing the way he works now thank goodness at long last after sitting since the 1970's under the famous Physical Medium, Gordon Higginson. He is taking notice of others and Spirit. Seeing the foolish practices that some Mediums put out to the general public often makes me smile to myself.

**Clairdelusion.** Here is one of the most commonly used Clairs, it is when a so called Medium uses the figments of their imagination, they fantasise, they create their own thoughts into the words that they think the recipient wants to hear. This person is a charlatan, one that fantasies, hallucinates, invents and creates stories within their own mind for others to hear. They have a false opinion, a false belief of their gifts. These **Delusionists deceive themselves** and raise the hopes of others vainly fooling them, as it all becomes one great big lie, which they become to believe them selves. Many is the time these people do not realise they are doing it; they are so into their own way of doing things. These people very rarely putting time aside to link with the Spirit World. They think, they are a natural Medium linking with the Spirit World when it is NO MORE than the thoughts going through the mind of this so called Medium. The only way to keep your link strong with the Spirit World is to sit in the peace of meditation and talk to them through **sincere** thought, asking Spirit for what ever you want developed. Then after a time of say quarter to half an hour allow them in the higher realms develop you in the peace and stillness of meditation whilst looking into the third eye into the colour, the void, or the white light of Spirit so you can slow down the thoughts going through the mind. The Spirit World can only develop you when you have a quiet mind. Please remember you have to get your link with the Spirit World developed before any strong and true messages come into your Spirit linking mind. When that happens, then and only then, saying the first thing that comes into your mind and say only that which is given, not adding onto the thought link from Spirit otherwise your mind comes into the equation. It is only done through putting time aside for Spirit. Practice, practice, practice.

I would like here to put in some exercises for the budding Medium who cannot see, hear, feel or sense anything from Spirit. These are some of many in the book.

**For development of the gifts for linking with the Spirit World**

**All the exercises in this book must be done along side meditation, "not instead of".**

**This includes every exercise in this book.**

# MEDITATE, MEDITATE, MEDITATE, if possible each and every day.

This is called visualisation exercising, which is an exercise that is a must for those who cannot see or hear within their third eye, and within their minds.

**First** you have to say a **sincere** prayer, **truly meaning it**, talking to those helpers in the World of Spirit asking them to come near, to come closer to you and link to help you develop so you can be used as an open vessel to help others understand there is life after our so called death. ( I always ask Spirit to come only with goodness, kindness, love, and truth, to come within the Divine Light of Spirit from loving harmony of Spirit of the highest realms). After that prayer and after a good few minutes [up to half an hour] of asking and encouraging Spirit to come near and help (over and over and over again), you will begin to feel their presence, start to meditate for five minutes, then start to talk again (within your mind) to your helpers, **being sincere** about your task ahead asking them to come near and help you develop your clear seeing, (or what ever development you wish to expand; I ask for the mental mediumship) knowing your helpers will be able to see the way your brain linkage is used for imaging and your etheric body can be used by Spirit so that you can pick up their images and words sent. They will be able to fine-tune it into a receiver for you. You are only educating your brain back to your natural ways that were there when you were little and younger, a natural way of linking with those in Spirit, a way you have let lapse and so decay. It is using your own natural thought pattern, educating it once again in conjunction with your Spirit friends, trusting those in Spirit to know what is best for you. A way that you will begin to bring that natural pattern back for your use.

Try this exercise for your self.
Have a piece of plain white paper with coloured pictures on. You can cut your own pictures out of books and stick them on a piece of plain white paper, could be any **single object**, an animal or a human form, start with a **single object** at a time, you could use the image of a star, triangle, square, wavy line, circle, sun with rays going out from it, a crescent moon, a ship, a simple car, make up your own list.

Place the picture in front of your eyes, looking at the picture for about a minute looking at every detail, saying within your mind each detail quietly to yourself. Then close your eyes and look into your third eye region, seeing that picture. Going over each and every detail, seeing each detail within your mind. If the image fails go back to the picture again and look at it with your eyes open for another minute, close your eyes again and see it in your third eye region. Keep on going back to the picture over and over again until the image is fixed in your mind for a period of time that you can hold on to it; about a half a minute to a minute is well long enough. When you can do that, go to the next picture and go through the process again. Often the picture is not in picture form like you can see with your eyes, the image is in a thought form that can be remembered and brought out though memory and described. So do not be too disappointed if you cannot see the image in true picture form within your mind. It is only you yourself that can say what is suitable for yourself. Know that everyone is different. Think of looking into a light bulb, which is lit, and remember how it is impressed in your vision so when you close your eyes it is still seen.

Then after this exercise has been done about twenty or thirty times successfully, increase on the continents of the single coloured image picture. I say coloured because I like colour but can be in black and white. REMEMBER if you go too quick and miss steps out it is only yourself you are cheating. I would practice this exercise for about an hour a day, for a few months. But it is up to the individual.

Look at the multi-imaged picture for a while say about a minute, then with your eyes closed try to hold it in your mind at your third eye point. If you cannot hold it, go back to looking at the same multi imaged picture and try again. You will naturally miss something out you have not seen the first few times if the images are not simple but do not worry this is a learning process, use it as a fun thing perhaps with like minded friends.

The keeping hold of the image within your third eye does not have to be for many minutes BUT it has to be for at least half a minute to start with. The reason for this is to let those in Spirit connect the correct points and to help them know what is where, and what does what in the individual. REMEMBERING we are all slightly different in our own individual make up, so it is with our brains and our etheric body and the connections therein. At the end of the exercises see if any images start to come while you are looking into your third eye while you are just meditating.

Please remember the images given by those in the World of Spirit can come very, very quick so be prepared for it. (as can the words). Also the pictures given to you within your mind from Spirit can be in many forms, single images, multi images, going up to a rolling film like on a video screen. This is why it is important for you to gain as much knowledge of how to educate your own recognition skills and this is not just visual recognition. And then the budding Medium has to learn how to give off the things recognised from Spirit to others as a true reflection of the person who is in Spirit.

To start seeing the images moving within your mind, you can use a video player as a short repeating sequence, or, if you have not got a video recorder use the images on the TV screen.
Sit quietly talking within your mind, say a prayer to those helpers in Spirit asking them to only come and help from the highest realms and to come within the loving harmony within the Divine Light of Spirit bringing only goodness kindness love and truth. Give Spirit permission to use you as an open vessel for the use of helping others. Look at the screen at the required sequence of images then close your eyes and try to bring the image back into your mind. Keep on practicing this over a set period of time the longer the better, one that suits you. This is why a set sequence is really needed and gone over and over as a lot of the imagery can be missed. The sequence only has to be about five to ten seconds [you will find at first ten seconds is a very long time because a lot of information can be put into the mind] or half a minute to a minute or so. Remembering to always keep on meditating along side the linking with the World of

Spirit as you are doing any of these imagery exercises. The video recorder can be very good for practicing recognising the images of sight and bringing in the sound into the mind ready for the World of Spirit to recognise how the individuals mind linkages work in the individual they then can implant their own superimposed images sounds, feelings etc. Yes there has to be a constant in all, but the subtle differences in the individual and in the individual's development make for the difference in the ordinary person, the Medium, the good Medium and the excellent Medium. Which one are you going to aim to be?????????? The latter I hope.

With the sounds this can be slightly different but bringing in more expansion of your imagery. Remember the sight is taken into our mind through waves of light, just as is sound going through the air along waves of vibration through to the ears. Both are then changed into electrical signals for the brain. This is the way Spirit actually put their thoughts into our brain system. So now it should be obvious to you the reasoning for the practice **while linking with Spirit** this is so they can see what connections go where and what does what. If things get wrongly connect all sort of strange things can happen see in the trance section in the other half of this book [volume two trance section]

**ALWAYS, First** you have to link, you have to say a **sincere** prayer, **truly meaning it**, talking to those helpers in Spirit asking them to come near to come closer to you and link to help you develop so you can be used as an open vessel to help others understand there is life after our so called death. Record many different simple sounds e.g. a single word, perhaps your own name. A single door bell ring. A single hand held bell ring. A single bang of a gong. A single church bell toll. A single door knock. Any single sound at first. Hold that in your mind trying to hold it as long as possible. Keep going back to the same sound until you can hold it in your mind and recall it in a thought form sound. After, have a sequence recorded where you have the word of the sound spoken and you have to test yourself to see if you can recall within your mind the noise of the word spoken. Then increase the number of sounds e.g. A street noise sequence. A school playground noise. A railway station with a train passing through. Record some sounds from a riverbank, perhaps a dockland noise with ships hooting in the background. An entertainment complex, a shopping mall. A busy street with traffic going along it. A full happy peel of bells. A dog barking. Then again have the words spoken about the happenings, scenes, and sounds.

All these noises **should** conjure up images for you as well as you practicing holding the sound within your mind as the images are there when you as the budding Medium have your eyes closed.

Go to a swimming baths record different activities there. Someone diving, someone playing and splashing, another swimming. Have **someone** saw a plant of wood, someone doing a tap dance on a wooden floor. A drummer playing the drums. Get a friend to run past you as you are recording, then next to walk past you and hear the difference. When you have finished your exercises, ask Spirit to help you progress by saying your **sincere** prayers talking to Spirit, go into meditation, trying to still your mind, just looking into the light within your third eye **(see the next sequence on how to meditate).**

These next exercises are for stimulating your **"clear-feeling"** whether it is through your taste buds, through your **"clear-touching"**, your tactile senses or through your **"clear-smelling"** they are all for part of your enhanced development. To give your awareness a boost. So the subtleties of different things given by Spirit are stimulated and slot into place at the correct times whilst giving a message from Spirit to a recipient.

**Always, First** you have to say a **sincere** prayer, **truly meaning it**, talking to those helpers in Spirit asking them to come near to come closer to you and link to help you develop so you can be used as an open vessel to help others understand there is life after our so called death. As you go through this book you will see that the prayer I say is a set one, one that is for me my guiding rod. My all-encompassing embrace with the link with my Spirit helpers. A prayer for me that works is:- Please help me prove there is life after our so-called death to others. Come only with goodness, kindness, love and truth; come within the divine light of Spirit within the loving harmony of Spirit from the highest realms. You can use this one or make your own up, BUT the most important thing to emphasise here is that your prayer should come from your heart and **with all your sincerity**, really meaning it.

Have a tape recording of a person guiding you through experiences like the ones in this book, a guided meditation (which it is not, it is guided contemplation). Also have the tape made for your own sequences.

This is best done with a friend, first one meditating then having turns about, that way you both can progress together. Or it can be done in a group situation. If on your own; simulate having someone there with you.

In this case make ready a list similar to the one here:-
Have things placed ready like sawdust, newly mown grass, fresh bread, (or put some sliced bread in the oven ready), nail varnish, sulphur, cinnamon, thyme, sage and onion mixture (or separate), curry powder, a scented flower (e.g. rose), perfume, drinking spirits of different kinds. A beer and/or cider (only need be a thimble full), a citrus fruit (orange, lemon, grapefruit), salt, flavoured ice or ice cream, freshly sawn piece wood, fresh cream, yoghurt, cream cheese. And many more you can think of.

By having the things ready and smelling, tasting and/or touching them all, the awareness is more intense when doing the second stage without smelling, tasting or touching the actual substance and recalling it within the mind, how it has smelt, how it has tasted and how it has felt.

The person (student) who is practicing the technique closes their eyes, after saying their own personal **sincere** prayer, bringing Spirit near to them in the task ahead, asks Spirit to help them in their task. This is to help both the student and Spirit helpers work together, and get to know how each other works, remembering it is always a two way learning process.

The helper says the name [by saying the name of the substance and or object this will conjure up an image within the mind] of the substance that is being brought to the nose of the closed eyed student, allows the student to smell (or guides the student to dip their finger into liquid rub it in between the fingers and taste, or guide their hand to hold the fruit and dip their finger, of the other hand, over the surface to taste while holding it and feeling it, they can smell each one as well), remembering to use all the senses, that is touch, smell and taste. After each time the student should after a little time of playing over in their mind the taste, smell and/or feeling of the substance, they should open their eyes and go through the procedure again and again until that substance is fixed in their mind, and they are able to recall it when ever it is spoken of. To practice this, the helper says to the student in a random order the names of the substances on the list this is done slowly and with an interval to let the student's mind focus on the substance's smell, feel, and taste, also to bring an image into the mind of the Sensitive/Medium of what is being practiced with. The student with the eyes firstly closed slowly goes through the remembering of the sight of, smell, taste, or feeling of the individual substances. Then with their eyes open goes through the list in a different sequence. Each time giving the student time to recall the substance in their mind's memory bank. Bringing back the sight, taste, feeling and smell to the fore.

When giving a reading, you always first have to make the contact [bring in a link with Spirit] with those who have passed into the next life across the veil, give off what you receive from those in Spirit, **most importantly,** at the end of a reading/message to a person make sure you give the recipient some personal evidence, anyone can give general names and numbers at random. It is the last piece of evidence, which no one else knows about which is personal to the recipient that makes a reading of truth from those in the World of Spirit. It is that last piece of **EVIDENCE** from the World of Spirit that will stick in that person's mind for the rest of their life, make sure it comes with the truth of your link.

As well as meditating on your own, all of these gifts can also be developed earlier by sitting in an awareness Circle or development Circle. **BUT MAKE SURE THE CIRCLE YOU SIT IN IS "HARMONOUS"**. With all of these gifts you always have to put a thought out to the loved ones in the higher vibrational level who look after you. Yes, they will and do look after you. Ask them to come near to you to help within the Divine Light of Spirit, bringing goodness, kindness, love and truth from the highest realms of Spirit.

A lot of Mediums who teach at the awareness classes, place the Mediums who see subjectively or hear subjectively as seeing and hearing "clairsentiently", because it is not for them, that individual, seeing clearly clairvoyantly, and not hearing clearly clairaudiently, outside the head. BUT I must say to them again and others, I see and hear clearly inside my head, yes I sometimes see and hear differently outside my head and sometimes it is as though I sense it. So please believe the person who is doing the seeing, hearing, and feeling. And **NOT WHAT YOU EXPERIENCE.** Everyone is an individual. Anyway why be so dogmatic and pigeonhole people, what is in a word?

If you think this gift of Mediumship is easy, think again. It means a lot of hard work, being disciplined, being positive, being sincere, truthful, having regular, special times put aside for Angelic Spirit Link in meditation and dedication to achieve any of these gifts if you have not retained them from birth. Yes, I say that because we all have that gift at birth when we are young in some stronger than others. Some retain the gift, others forget perhaps wanting to forget, others let it lapse. Trust in the World of Spirit but remember you are the one in charge of what happens not the Spirit World so do not blame them for something when it is your fault. Spirit cannot interfere with you or link with you unless you allow them to do so, it is Divine Law. Spirit is always there ready and waiting for us to ask for the help that we need. We have to be willing and subservient and allow Spirit to come to us with our own, personally given permission.

Lots of us have had some experience and remember snippets of that gift from God, the Divine Spirit, the memory of the link with other side that has been with the Spirit, our own Spirit from the day when we were born into this earthly plane, seeing things others did not, feeling things others around us could not believe, having things happen to us when we were young and we had to suppress because others made fun of us, just because we were more sensitive than our other friends.

A lot of mediumistic people start their voyage of discovery after a traumatic experience, after an accident, after a near death experience. It is though that shock or jolt in their life brings to the person a sense that they are doing things wrong, going along the wrong path to enlightenment. They become to have a need to help others more, to become more sensitive to life in general, caring about what goes on around them and their surroundings, wanting to find out more about what happens if they go along another route of development, want to develop within themselves a knowledge that can help their fellow man. There becomes an extra need. Strange but true. Look at your own start, and those of others.

When starting with the exercises for your awareness or guided meditation (it should be called guided contemplation) where the mind is used (and you are thinking about the story) to put images into it away from the outside, doing unseeing imagery (eyes closed), placing them into the third eye region of the brain. These images are at the start of your development mainly you, the developing Medium, you yourself producing the images from your own brain out of your imagination, the equation being, 90% plus, and 10% coming from the linking with Spirit. This is why it is vital, so imperative, at separate times put aside, to try and look into the light within the mind after asking Spirit to come near and help. As the link gets stronger the Medium learns to slow down the thoughts going in and out of the brain, the link becomes better, 40% self and 60% from Spirit help. As you progress the link gets a great deal stronger, **IF, the discipline of focused attention (meditation) has been applied**. The aim is for most 10% or lower of self, and 90% plus information from the Spirit World. It should be the aim is for, 100% information from the Spirit World. You the Medium being passive to the thoughts going through the mind.

# MINDFULNESS

The ways of most meditation that the Buddhist do, **are not** generally for the development of a link with the Spirit World and for Mediumship but can be adapted while talking to Spirit through thought. The exercises are very good for the enlightenment of self, ways of going within and thinking about what you are doing in everyday life and not taking everything you do in your everyday life for granted. Mindfulness helps a person to live life to the full and gain an insight of what is happening around you when interacting with everything. Use these exercising methods for yourself for practice while linking into the World of Spirit, talk to Spirit ask for help for the development of your gifts.

There are many exercises that can be adapted to this form of "mindfulness" to make yourself aware of what is happening when you do all things in your life, this is so nothing is taken for granted also they can be used to help with your link with the World of Spirit I will give a few here.

I feel sorry for the way modern Buddhism has gone. The Buddha started off by renouncing all worldly goods and lead a life of chastity and none materialism. The Buddha did not write anything down, neither did any of the people who are at the start of most of the of the world religions, this includes Jesus, and Mohamed. The religions they were said to have founded are man made e.g. Christianity, Judaism, Muslims, Hinduism and Sikhism, etc. Their leaders who started off their particular religion said not to be materialistic, do not worship idols, not to kill, live a life of peace, help others along life's pathway. Mostly giving a good guidance to their followers. Each religion has fallen under the spell of the manipulative people who controlled/control from within. The modern day leaders try in many ways to suppress the true teachings of the founder to keep their comfortable place in that religion. Look at all the gold and finery that each religious place of worship has within its walls. Anyway I will get off my soapbox for now.

**Back to the exercises of mindfulness**.
If you are washing the dishes do not do it as a chore doing it on automatic pilot, not thinking what you are doing, know you are washing the dishes, be thankful for it. Wash the dishes and know you are washing the dishes. Wash the dishes to wash the dishes.
As with most things in this life of ours we take too many things for granted we do not think about the gifts we have been blessed with. Do the same with walking, walk and know you are walking. As you walk along the road think about the action and what is happening within your body how it is interacting with the floor, then go to your feet. Think how they are interacting within the enclosure of skin that you have on your feet how does it feel for you. From there go to your ankles feel and see them within your mind how they are acting, think about them for a little while as you go along your pathway. Be thankful that you have the use of your feet and ankles, thank your higher source of power the Divine Spirit. Go along the whole of your body as you walk Do every day chores in the same spirit, this will help in your development of sensing, clairsentience. But you have to be talking and asking Spirit at the same time.
Ways of mindfulness can be adapted to your Mediumship by thinking of what is happening around you. The difference with doing the exercises of Mindfulness for your own inner self and gaining the gifts of Mediumship, is at the same time to be asking the World of Spirit within your mind to help you in your quest to have the gifts of Mediumship. I will give another instance on hearing, clairaudience and the development of seeing, clairvoyance. Whilst listening to your favourite records close your eyes say a **sincere** prayer or **sincere** affirmation to the World of Spirit. Then see the group, band, orchestra within your third eye playing their instruments, look at each individual player as they play each note, go to them in your mind, be along side them as a whole group of people, then as you progress listening intently, go to just one persons playing one instrument from amongst the whole musical harmony, be with that individual. Try to feel what they are feeling as you see them playing, hear what they are hearing as they play, you are part of that harmonious musical extravaganza. Always remembering your **sincere** talking through thought and the **sincere** asking through thought within your mind of the World of Spirit for what you require of them.
When you are planting in the garden or pruning the trees and bushes do it deliberately, know what you are doing. Talk within your mind to the plants, tell them what you are doing and why. It will change your prospective of life and the things around you, if you go about mindfulness in the correct manner. Let it start today for you as a mindful person. Think about what you do for living things around you and this means not only the plants but also the animal, human species. It is the intent that counts.

# HOW DO I MEDITATE

Lots of people have said to me "I cannot meditate", "I cannot see through my third eye", "I cannot clear my mind", I cannot get every day thoughts out of my mind". To those people who have tried every method and still have trouble I say to them, "**AT FIRST** until you learn, use an aid/crutch". "Have something tangible to look at as though it is inside your head". Use the **KEEWAYS'** method that I teach. "Make yourself a pendant of any sort, for example a piece of wood tied with a piece of string, a piece of jewellery, a gem/birth stone on a chain, an Angel pendant, a ring, anything". "Make the length of string/chain long enough to go around your head and position the pendant to rest on the centre of your forehead just above the join of the eye brows, outside the third eye position". When you start to mediate with your eyes closed you now have something tangible to concentrate on. Looking at it with your **eyes closed** through your third eye, it now becomes real, something to focus on. Use this aid for the length of time you think it is a help to you. When you have finished with that aid/crutch put it aside. Let your thoughts go in and out of your mind as you are doing it, keep going back from the thoughts to concentrate on the pendant, a colour, or light. I have not met any Medium yet that has said to me I stop my mind from working completely **all the time** when going into meditation. Some see a light or colours at first, I personally didn't, for me it took a long time, sitting once a week.

When I started meditating I saw nothing only darkness, then after a few months of sitting in a Circle I started seeing a small light the size of a pinhead at the end of a passage/tunnel/through a darkness, that light was as though it was a hundred yards away at least. Gradually as I sat longer the light became brighter, now I can close my eyes, ask the Angels in Spirit within my mind for help and it comes practically straight away {BUT not always and sometimes not easily, because of thoughts I cannot stop that might be going through my mind after a traumatic time that day} remember you have to ask those Angels in the Spirit World for the help that you need in development. The Angels in Spirit do not know what you want until you ask in your head, they are only a thought away. **Thought** is the most powerful thing in the universe, **use it wisely**. Once you send out a thought it cannot be retrieved. Make sure they are good.

I have tried all sorts of different methods to develop. Sitting on my own, sitting in different Circles and with different friends, some ways I found better than others. Some Circles are better than others because of the makeup of the people sitting in them, all Circles are different, they all vary, find the one that suits you, otherwise it is best sit on your own. You have to find the method, which is comfortable for you to use and develop it, because everyone is different. What works for one person might not work for another. Please experiment.

Remember to always ask the Angels/Spirit to come near to you to help, coming with happiness, goodness, kindness, love and truth, to blend in the peaceful Divine Light within the loving harmony of those in the highest realms of the Spirit world. (Some call Angels the messengers of God, as I believe they are just another name for Spirit).

Another way to try meditating and bringing a point to focus on at your third eye is by pressing your finger on the third eye point, (which is inside your head, behind the centre of your forehead [between the two eye brows] about an inch above the eyes) and then close your eyes and concentrate on that point you pressed.

If you want to get a light within the third eye to concentrate on while meditating, try getting a sheet of coloured A4 or A5 paper. A colour you think would be suitable for you personally. Yellow, pink, blue, purple, green, white, any colour you like, perhaps one of each to practice with at different times. Hold the piece of paper in front of your eyes about a foot away from you. Look at the colour of the sheet of paper for a length of time [about half a minute, maybe a little less] absorb the colour, so you can hold the colour in your mind's eye. Close your eyes and you will see the colour. If you lose the colour in your mind's eye, open your eyes and start again. You will with practice soon get the colour staying in your mind longer and longer. This is a way of getting absorbed by the light when going deeper into meditation. Remember light is colour. You will find the colour changes within your mind's eye, so do not worry, if it does or does not.

A place I would whole-heartedly recommend for the power it has in the building and it's grounds, is the Arthur Findlay College. If you go to the Arthur Findlay College, Stansted Hall, Stansted, Essex. U.K. go different weeks to try different tutors for they have differing methods of training, the one to suit you will be found when you are ready to link with those Guardian Angels in Spirit, only those in Spirit know when that is.

Go to different open Circles in the Spiritualist Churches. Start a Circle of your own in your house or a local centre with a few others of like minds. Learn as much as you can from Mediums there, BUT do not take everything they tell you as law or gospel. They might think it is true in their own minds, but it is only their opinion. Check, check, and double check. I have heard some very strange opinions from some "**respected Mediums**". Try to look at things logically. I am trying in this book to give you as many options that I have come across so you have a choice. Look at all the professors in the colleges and all the learned people who run our country they had to go and learn as they progressed in their specialist subjects, do yourself a favour from the start, learn from the different tutors and different subjects in the Spiritual Mediumship field at a psychic college especially "Stansted Hall". Remember every person in the teaching field has something different to offer, and please remember they do not know it all. Neither do I.

**ONE THING THAT SHOULD BE PUT TO YOU ALL IS :- DO NOT TRY TO FOOL YOURSELF OR LIE TO OTHERS ABOUT YOUR GIFT/GIFTS OR WHAT YOU GET. IF YOU**

**DO LIE, IT ALWAYS COMES BACK ON YOU. THIS IS NEGATIVITY. NEGATIVITY STOPS DEVELOPMENT IN SPIRITUALALITY.**
**NEVER MAKE THINGS UP ABOUT WHAT IS GIVEN TO YOU FROM THE REALMS OF THOSE IN THE WORLD OF SPIRIT.**
**TELL THE TRUTH TO THE OTHER PERSON HOW YOU SEE IT, FEEL IT, OR THINK IT. THIS IS ABOUT A SITUATION YOU MIGHT BE DESCRIBING FROM THOSE ANGELS IN SPIRIT.**
**BE TRUE TO THOSE IN THE SPIRIT REALMS AND TO YOURSELF.**
**BUT BE AWARE OF YOUR IMAGINATION. TEST, TEST, AND TEST AGAIN YOUR LINK IN THE SPIRIT WORLD BY CONTINUALLY ASKING OF THEM one question at a time**, each time waiting for the answer.
Remember **WHO**, **WHAT**, **WHERE**, **WHEN**, **WHY**, **HOW**, FROM THE LINK YOU GET.
If you are giving a message to a person and get stuck, use these five "W's" and the "H" to expand your message from Spirit, keep on going back to your link in Spirit and ask the next one of the "W's" & "H" of them.
Never try to deliberately hurt other people. Remember cause and affect "The pendulum of life". What goes out comes back to you ten fold, what goes around comes around even more so when in the spiritual field, with beneficial or devastating consequences. Make sure it is for you beneficial, from the goodness you have given out to others, and it comes from your heart as it goes out to others.

# MEDIUMS
# MEDIUMSHIP

If you think you are going to get the type of Mediumship you are looking for, think about it very carefully. I say that because we do not know what we are capable of, **BUT THOSE IN SPIRIT DO**. So do not be surprised if over the years of development you are guided towards a different direction than the one you had mapped out for yourself, it does not matter if you wanted to be a Physical Medium, and you turn out to be a Healer (which is Physical anyway). It might have been mapped out for you from the start by the Angelic Helpers. All that should be in your mind is that you are helping others for their benefit and that of those in Spirit, and so it will come back to you ten fold in benefits of your own. What you give out always comes back to you many, many times over; make sure it is from the goodness of your heart.

A Medium should make sure a person is uplifted after their reading/sitting **DEFINITELY** not down or a low ebb in their mind. A Medium should **NEVER** tell any person or the enquirer when or how they are going to "die/pass". A Healing Medium should **NEVER** take on the responsibility of an earthly doctor; the medium must remember they are only a channel for doing the work of those kindly people in the Spirit World, those helpers in the higher realms who tirelessly put time aside to come and help us here on the earth plane. It is your own personal responsibility to have the best ethics possible.

If people are termed as being a Medium, it is because they are the person in the middle of Spirit, [the link, the person who has passed over to the higher vibrational level], and another who would like information, so the Medium is a catalyst in the middle of Spirit and the enquirer. They are contacting Spirit in the higher realm, by using their own Spirit, then passing on the information through to the Spirit of the person who is getting the message. Using the link of all three. The person [the Spirit], who they are in contact with could be a person in the close family, a relative, a friend, an intermediary often classed by some as a guide, helper, helping Angel of the Medium. Here it must be said again, it takes more than one person to form a link [between about 10-60 plus depending on the circumstances] so keep away from naming this link, you will be doing a disservice to all the other people in the Spirit Group who are helping. The Spirit helper, guide, angel are only at the forefront of the action. Do not put your Spirit friends on a pedestal.

A Medium's main aim should be one of comforting the bereaved, showing and proving to all, there is life after our so-called "death". Proving life in Spirit continues in an area of vibration, which we know about but do not fully understand as yet. [we are all still learning and will continue to learn]. Giving information to enquirers, from their loved ones, family and friends, even love and memories off people they have only met slightly while they were here on this earth plane. Another aim should be to try and remove the fear of death that some people have, showing others that life goes on only in a different form in a higher vibrational level, if you want it, without all the badness that the earth plane has and you develop in yourself spiritually and hopefully try to rise above.

Other Mediums as they develop will hopefully help people who have fallen into a trap of their or another person's making, having a distressed Spirit around them, which is often nerve wracking for the earth bound person, a Spirit who is trapped here in limbo, enclosed in their blinkered mind. The Medium helping to release the poor Spirit, by getting that Spirit to send out their own thoughts to the "White Brotherhood" for their help, their guidance and go forward into the light and so solve a problem for the earth bound person/Spirit. It will be seen in the chapter "R'Help Circles" a person has to ask for help it is the divine law, that those higher up in the Spirit world cannot help until asked, they will be there beside the person but have to wait for that asking thought of help. The people in Spirit are always there ready to help anyone in the Spirit World to progress.

Try to read as many books as possible of the lives of the Mediums of the past. The Rev Stainton Moses [Trance, Automatic Writing, Physical Phenomena and more], Ena Twigg [Clairvoyant, Clairsentience, Trance], Gordon Higginson [Physical Phenomena, Independent Direct Voice, Trance, Clairvoyance and very much more], Jack Webber [Trance, Physical Phenomena and more]; Arnold Clare, (Deep Trance, Physical Phenomena); Helen Duncan [Trance, Physical Phenomena, Clairvoyance, Clairaudience and more], Helen was the last person to be prosecuted in 1944 in England under the Witchcraft Act of 1735. Harry Edwards and John Cain, who were two extraordinary Spiritual Healing Mediums and good all rounders, Betty Shine, Harry Boddington, Andrew Jackson Davis and many, many other mediumistic people .

It is a pity a real true book of the life of Gordon Higginson has not been written by someone responsible. I would have liked to have done so but was stopped by the people who sat with him in his Circle for most of his lifetime. After they read the book on the bookshelf about him, they said they did not recognise him from the things given in the book. "That was not their Gordon," they said when asked. This was from people who knew him for over sixty years, and from the people in his church at Longton, Stoke on Trent. They had given a lot of information to the author and said they would never give any more information because of the way it was put down in the book, it was nothing like Gordon. Gordon's friends refused point blank to give me or anyone else any information. It was only his sister Hazel that allowed me to talk about the things that went on with Gordon BUT unfortunately the lady (now in her 80's) is very, very deaf, and did not know half of what I knew as true.

To become a good Medium you have to explain fully what you get in your mind from your Angel Spirit Link. You have to be clear to yourself and most of all to the person you are giving a reading for [the enquirer]. You have to learn how, what, and why information is being given. (Each time not forgetting to use every time **Where, When, Why, What, Who, and How**. Remember to only ask one question at a time and wait for the answer from Spirit) You don't have to understand what is given at all and quite often you don't, that is for the enquirer, for them to understand. Trust in those Angels in Spirit **BUT** get to know who you are dealing with, then and only then trust fully. But what is important for the Medium is for them to get to know how Spirit is giving the messages. Is it a prompt? Is it an exact scene? You have to learn as you progress along with your link, your Spirit communicator/guide/helper/angel, yes, they also have to learn along side you. For they are only people who have passed into the higher vibrational level our so called "death state"; YES it is a two way learning process. You must aim for the highest links who are developed in the Divine Light and stick to that; always ask for the best. There is an old saying aim for the stars and you might reach the sun; aim for the sun and you might reach the moon; aim for the moon and you might reach the mountain. Aim for the mountain and you might get over the hill. Aim for the hill and you might get up the road. Where do you want to be? Just up the road or on the moon or sun? Aim for the highest.

When telling others about your linking, whether it is in clairsentience, clairaudience, clairvoyance or Clairknowing, etc. Explain to your enquirer, the person who you are in contact with or being shown or hear or feel, explain their personality; happy, sad, angry, etc.; describe the face, round, long, chubby, thin, etc.; the hair, long short, fine, thick, grey, white, blond, black, brown, red etc; their build, if the person is fat, well rounded, thin, kept themselves well; well built, slim, tall, short etc. "**What** age group; old, young, middle age, toddler"? "**What** sort of clothes they are wearing"? If they are untidy, well dressed, tidy, are they wearing work clothes, old fashioned, modern day; that will tell you about their job of work, the approximate dates they were alive on earth. **Ask your helper, guide, Angel communicator in Spirit** "**What** the person is there for?" "**What** to they wish to be said to the enquirer?" "**Who** they have come to present themselves to"? "**Who** do you want to go to talk to"? [if you are in a group situation] **Who** are they? Mum, dad, brother, sister, auntie, uncle, friend, relation, etc. If you get a wrong response off the enquirer, a "No" with their recognition, go back to the Angel communicator in Spirit and ask in your own mind a question you would like answered. **Why** has the person come? **Where** did the person live? **Where** did they work? **When** did they pass into the Spirit world? **When** were they born ? **How** old are they? **How** did they pass into the Spirit World? Tell the enquirer what sort of scene you are looking at, **Where** the person is in/on the scene. Learn to expand the scene verbally. Remember you are the one who is looking at the scene if you are clairvoyant; if you are clairsentient describe the scene you can sense. You should be explaining to the person as though they are blind, which of course they are to the scene in your head. You as the Medium should be asking Spirit in your own head the next question as you are giving out information to the recipient, ready to give a continuous message without any pauses. This is the perfect way but of course we are not all perfect, and the conditions are not always perfect in most links.

A good way of practicing is to look at and practice by explaining a picture, a drawing, a photograph, a scene out of a magazine etc. and then after looking at it for a minute or less, start describing to a friend or an audience, what was in the picture you were looking at. If there are no people who you can practice on, you can even explain to yourself onto a tape recorder. Then if you can get a picture from the explanation of the playback you might be going in the right direction, **BUT** if you do the explaining of a picture using this method do not kid yourself and pretend you are doing it right when you are not. Be very self critical, it is the only way you will go forward.

Sometimes the Angel Spirit Links can be very quick in their showing of pictures within your mind so learn to pick up as much of a picture scene you [the picture you will be holding in your mind at the time] can in the shortest time possible when you practice. At first take your time looking at all the details, then as you go along with your practice make the time you look at a picture shorter each time for yourself. Go to art galleries and look at a certain single picture for only a moment, look away and then try to remember as much of the picture you can, go away from it and write it down, or record the things you have seen in the picture, then come back and check it out for yourself to see how much detail you have taken into your brain's memory pattern.

If when you are doing a reading and the response of your enquirer is negative, keep on going back to the helping Angel communicator in Spirit for your answers, keep asking questions again and again in your mind. Learn **how** your Angel communicator in Spirit is giving you your messages. Are they in picture form? Are they in exact movie form explaining and showing everything to you that was true for the enquirer? Are they in cryptic form? Are those in Spirit only showing you symbols and hints that have to be worked out by practice. Remember your Angel Spirit Link is learning as well to work with you, as you will be learning to work with them. At the end **ask** for evidence of the communication for the questioner so the enquirer can be certain of the link. **Ask, ask, ask, ask** in your mind by the way of thought. Keep on going back to your Angel communicator in Spirit. It is the only way you will learn to have two-way trust and build up a stronger link as you go along developing together with your Angels in Spirit. **Practice, practice, practice,** in your **"harmonious"(A MUST)** Circles, and then **practice, practice, practice,** on friends and relations some more, giving everyone and anyone free readings. As you go along you should always put aside some time to be sitting in meditation for the power of Spirit to strengthen your link, and to keep on doing meditation no matter how long you have been linking into the angelic people in Spirit.

When you do start giving a reading for a person, or give messages to people, go to them afterwards and explain to them how you received the message, in what form, how it was given. I tell them as I am giving the reading. If it was Clairvoyance, or Clairaudience. Was it from the left? Was it from the right? Was it straight ahead? If it was clairsentiently did you feel it was from the left? Did you feel it was from the right? Did you feel it was straight ahead? These little details are the start of your learning; you have to learn how your "angelic help link" in the Spirit World is giving you these messages. I personally receive the past on the left hand side of my mind; I receive the future on the right hand side of my mind, and the present straight ahead. BUT and a **BIG "BUT"** it is **you** and **your link** in the World of Spirit that have to learn together, not me putting my interpretation on to your given links. Another Medium I was talking to said her helpers in Spirit and herself have worked out together; if the Spirit to be brought forward to the enquirer is a father/father figure or on the father's side of the family she is aware of or sees the Spirit on the right hand side of the enquirer; if Spirit is seen or the Medium is aware of Spirit on the left hand side of the enquirer then the communicator is from the enquirer's mother/mother figure or from the mother's side of the family. If the communicator stands in front of the enquirer then she knew that the communication was of a child. If the communicator in Spirit stands behind the enquirer then it is a grandparent, to the left at the back it is from the mother's side or it is the grandmother and to the right but at the back of the enquirer it is from the father's side or the grandfather.

Please remember you never stop learning or developing, and so it is logical that you should never stop meditating, this is so you are able to still develop/strengthen your link with the Spirit side of life. Put a set day aside, at a set time to develop those gifts you would like to be given. If it is the will of those angelic helpers in Spirit you will be given them. Put say a Monday, Wednesday, and Friday at 7.00pm aside for Mental Mediumship, which is Clairvoyance, Clairaudience, Clairsentience, all the Clairs----; Tuesday, Thursday, and Saturday at 7.00pm for Physical Phenomena. And perhaps 10.00pm each evening put that aside for Automatic Writing. Of course this would be a strict timetable, so adjust it to suit yourself. An hour every other day might suit you, or two nights a week might be better. Even one night a week might be the only time to put aside because of your life style. Please do not kid yourself though, time can always be found if you are serious about your own development.

I will always remember a busy housewife saying to me "I could never find time to meditate until I had the idea from my husband who found his own private space to read his paper without any interference from myself and the children. He would vanish into the bathroom with a cushion and sit on the toilet for up to an hour with everyone in the household thinking he was doing his ablutions". I then had the idea, which now works for me, I started to take the cushion in and meditate in the smallest room in the house as well. I had found a bit of time and space for myself." Not the best of places you might say BUT it shows what can be done if you really want to do anything, nothing will stop you if you want it badly enough, a way will always be found. Another person I know, Maureen for the North East, meditates in her bath with scented candles lit around the bathroom. Another lady, Denise from Leigh, Lancashire, meditates as soon as she is in her bed at night time, as well as Saturday and Sunday mornings, and this lady is becoming one of the best mediums I have seen of late.

**Please remember you have to put in the time and effort to develop anything to the full**.

Also you must remember to ask your Angels in Spirit for the things you want. One last thing that all budding Mediums must be told. "It is not you that decides what gift you are going to be working with, it is the decision of the Angels in Spirit, **IF IT IS THEIR WILL.**"

You have to be truthful, dedicated, sincere, and positive, as you progress towards a certain development link. **BUT REMEMBER to ASK!** Then you might receive your gift of linking with those in Spirit, if you send out goodness, kindness, happiness, light, love and are dedicated to link in peaceful loving harmony, of Spirit of the highest realms, look into the light, most gifts **are** given by those helpers in Spirit.

Time put aside for meditation and time given to those in the angelic World of Spirit is the factor that makes the difference between a very good Medium with an excellent link, good Medium with a good link, a poor Medium and a bad link, a Medium that kids their own-self they have a link, and the ordinary person.

## **Time put aside for those in Spirit is never wasted**.

What you should always think of is yourself and put some time aside for yourself. Never neglect your own health and well being, if you are not well, or you are tired you will not be any use to your Spirit Angel helpers and your link will suffer. When you are not tired and you feel "bright eyed and bushy tailed" [as they say here], a sparkle in you that everyone you come across will see, you will feel better able to put in more effort and so the Angels in Spirit will be able to link with a strong, healthy and vibrant body and mind, using you as a good catalyst here on the earth plane. Some Mediums lose their gifts for a time, for whatever reason. What has to be done is for the Medium to go back to square one, back to basics, meditate, meditate, meditate. Perhaps they have lost sight of their true path and need to find it again. Do not ever think of trying to fool the public, it will rebound in your face if you do, and you are only fooling yourself if you do.

## Always be "honest and true" to those in Spirit, others, and especially yourself.

Mediums should meditate asking those in Spirit to strengthen their link and to ask the Divine Spirit to bring their Angel Spirit helpers closer to them always before giving a service, a reading, a sitting for the general public. Then after their work with Spirit, the Medium should be thanking them for their time and help, also making arrangements with their Angel Spirits within their own thoughts for the next time they are going to link.

The best Mental Medium I have ever seen work on the platform bar none was an English man called Gerard Smith. I had the privilege of seeing him at the Burslem Spiritualist Church in Stoke June 1999, and I have seen Gordon Higginson and many of the older Mediums working on the platform in the late 1970's -1980's. Gerard was taught by Gordon Higginson. Gerard gave as evidence from the Spirit realm; Polish names and surnames, place names, numbers of houses, the street names where people had lived, first names of the people who had passed over, and the descriptions of them.

Gerard also linked two unconnected people who were sitting about 10 seats apart. Both denied the link to each other. He at first thought they were related but the link was one of the lady's brother in Spirit who had visited the other lady's house, giving the number house of 146 and the name of the road. Gerard had given these out to this person previously and the name of the occupier who was the other person's husband in Spirit. The husband and the ladies brother was the link to the two of them.

After the service I went over to ask him how he received the information. He was seeing them subjectively and objectively from those in Spirit and he was always going back to his Spirit helpers in his head/mind and constantly asking for the information. He received his information clairvoyantly, clairaudiently, and clairsentiently, while asking, asking, asking, and asking Spirit again and again while working. His mind was never still. BUT he only gave what he received from Spirit, and did not add anything at all even if he thought it was what Spirit wanted to be said never letting his imagination interfere.

Another very good Medium is Ron Jordan. I was speaking to him while we were having a pint of beer in the thatched roofed pub "The Ash" in the village of Burton End ½ mile away from the Arthur Findlay College at Stansted Hall, Essex UK on the Saturday before the courses started and he said his trainer was a very strict person when he first started off with his craft. [Ron is also a very good trainer himself]

The trainer stood in front of him, he had Ron link with Spirit, and then without any time to think Ron had to say, "I see a person".

Trainer very quickly asked, "Is it a man or woman?

Ron "it is a man", [or woman which ever came into the mind first without thinking; in other words not letting his mind interfere].

Trainer very quickly said, "What do they look like?"

Ron then described the person. When he said it, it became reality in his mind because of the link with Spirit there. There was no time for his **own mind** to come into the equation.

There was always **no time to think**. Each time the trainer had a quick question for Ron, which any fully trained Medium would normally (or "should be" saying quickly to Spirit as they are giving their messages to the recipients) have been putting quickly to Spirit in his own mind anyway, just to keep the

link flowing. Ron now always works that way with Spirit helpers and he is very accurate with his messages. I have heard Ron give a very good session on the platform of a church a few times he is excellent. Picking up one time in the Stansted Hall Sanctuary (church) from a very well known Medium that had failed in their presentation. Yes a lot of the good working Mediums can have off days.
The questions to keep asking are who? what? why? where? when? how? The 5 W's and the H.

A very good method of getting your mediumship honed is to have your eyes blindfolded (so you cannot see anything), and your ears blanked off (an ear muff on them to stop any noise, or outside interference). Be in the room with others or even just one friend. Then link with Spirit and give off all you see, and hear from Spirit. Record the session so you can hear the two way conversation. The person giving a thumbs up or thumbs down for correct or wrong information. As the link becomes stronger, with the going back to your link in Spirit, **asking for the information** in your mind, and **keep on going back to your link in Spirit asking, asking, asking** for that information. (Remember the who, what, where, why, when, and how, the asking of Spirit rule). You will be able to give off house numbers, street names, and the full names of those in the Spirit World who wish to be remembered. All it needs is dedication, sincerity, and practice, most of all that harmony with Spirit. This is what all the good Mediums of the past used to do. The reason for the earmuff and blindfold was for the Medium not to be influenced by any reaction of the person the message is for. The messages you receive from your Spirit helpers you know then can be relied on to be unadulterated.

One way I was shown how to practice my work with my Spirit helpers on the platform, was by Eileen Mitchamson, a very good Trance and Platform Medium, this was at a course in the Arthur Findlay College, at Stansted Hall.
This young lady of 23 and a bit, Eileen had us up on the platform one by one, facing **away** from the audience. We had to Link with Spirit, and then say what came into our minds each time we gave any information to the audience. Then when the single person (remember there could be a few people at first accepting the message they have to be whittled down to one as more information comes from Spirit) in the audience who took the information as their own loved one coming through, Eileen was the one who said whether the information was correct or not, she was the only one talking. The audience at first putting their hands up to accept the message was for them, then afterwards just nodding yes or no. The budding Medium was not influenced in any way by reactions. Whenever we got a pause Eileen was telling us, reminding us, cajoling us, to go back to our Link in Spirit, as she was saying if we were correct or not and to ask the helper in Spirit for some more different information to clarify the person's identity as each piece was given to the person who had taken the link. We were constantly reminded by her, one at a time, when relevant; of the who, what, where, why, when, how? The five "W"s and an "H" during the message giving.

It is paramount that you keep on talking to your Link in the Spirit World **within your mind**, through thought, as though you are in conversation with someone here on the earth plane.

At the end of the message we had to give out extra solid proof, Eileen asked us to go back to our Link in Spirit, and ask for some extra evidence to give to the person before we left them to go to another person in the audience. This is something that is forgotten about by many platform Mediums and should always be done at the end of any message.

## ONE METHOD

To start off meditating you have to find yourself a comfortable chair to sit in, [you can make yourself comfortable in a laying down position as well if you want to]. Relax, rest your arms on your lap, or [if laying down, place your arms comfortably by your side], the palms of your hands open and facing upwards {I do it this way, but at other times I have my palms resting on each leg}, some people place their thumb and one finger together, generally the index finger. I personally don't as this also can have your muscles and tendons tensed up, so leading to cramp, just do things naturally that is all that is needed. **Close your eyes,** have a few words to the person in Spirit who you believe in, The Divine Spirit, the one who helps you in your time of need while you are on this earth, (your personal gatekeeper, your Guardian Angel) perhaps your God, a relative who has past on before, or a close friend who you can still feel is around you even though for you they are not still here on this earth, ask them for their help and protection, ask them to link with you bringing goodness, kindness, happiness, love, truth, and pure Divine Light of Spirit and to blend within the loving harmony of those in Spirit from the highest realms. Look into your forehead or third eye for fifteen minutes; a half hour, an hour [or two], remembering **eyes still closed**, whichever time length is best for you, there is no set time limit.

Remember the breath. Breath with intention. Before any person goes into a relaxed state ready for meditation, the person should be saying a prayer within their mind, then to concentrate on the breath.

See the breath going into the nose, as it goes into the nose, the air is taking the ether as well into the nose where that ether is held at the root of the nose, the rest of the air is going into the lungs and feeding the body making it relaxed. Let the thoughts in the mind be good and send those good thoughts into the breath going into the nose, impress on the ether through thought what development you would like Spirit to help you with. On an outward breath send out through the nose any badness from your mind. Do this for a good few minutes.

If you start to do readings for people, remember to use this method of meditating and asking Spirit for help and guidance five minutes "at the very least" **before each reading**, it will help you compose yourself and you will get inspiration as well as a rejuvenational rest. Have a drink of water beside you, have a drink as and when needed; you will find you quite often get thirsty, and then start meditating again.

When you have finished, always thank the people above for helping you, ask for the condition to be taken away, close the power points, if you have opened them [rub your hands {an option}], and relax, you will feel better. The longer and more often you do this the quicker/earlier you will develop your psychic abilities to the full. BUT remember no person is ever truly fully developed so keep it up always.

Some people open their power points when meditating; it is entirely up to the individual. I will explain these later on in the book. To clean your power points (chakras) ask for power of the cleaning light to bath your body going from the top to base, then from the base to the top. Or think of yourself under a shower, instead of using water it is light, and it is not only going over the outside of your body it is cleaning all of the inside as well.

**Do not worry,** deep meditation and mediumship is **not harmful**.

Just remember         Ask for **goodness, kindness, happiness, love, light, truth, and to blend in peaceful harmony with those in the Divine Light of Spirit within the loving harmony from those in the highest realms in Spirit.**

# Good attracts Good:     Evil attracts Evil :

# YOU can make your own EVIL environment.

### So control what you are and what surrounds you by "good" thoughts and "good" deeds.

### This you will find is a new, good way of life you are embarking on.

Your mind is only the receiver, the instrument, and you are the speaker, accept your mind and self as such, and don't get big headed if you do develop into a good Medium, as I hope many of you will. Never be jealous or envious of other people's abilities, it can bring you down, inhibiting your own true development. Accept people as they are. Helping the ones who need or ask for your help. Never lie about your abilities as lies are negative, and as should be pointed out negativity can halt development and linking with the highest of the Spirit realms. It is the highest realms I always want to link with, NOT the lower elementals, as I hope you do.

Budding Mediums over periods of time ranging from days to months, for a great many hours when going into deeper meditation, people try to see things within their third eye, but a lot of them cannot see anything at all through their third eye, some never do, only giving their power to the others when in a Home Circle or set Circle with friends, then suddenly as they progress, they start to see different colours in their third eye at different sitting times. Some people do not remember to ask for whatever development they want in their mediumship, thought is the way to talk to the higher realm, so they do not progress. As some people get further along into deeper meditation, they can actually start to see a tunnel/tube with a small light at the end, then a few more hours along in their meditation the light starts to get brighter and then they start to see different things, this is the opening up of their own spiritual, psychic awareness. Do not force any results, they will come naturally as you progress within your meditation.

When on your own always **ask** for that what you want first out loud and then keep repeating your request quietly in your head [this is always your link to Spirit, your request in thought] as and when you feel it is necessary, (some people find it is better to repeat their requests all the time out loud), **ask** also for your angelic Spirit Helpers to come closer. Do not worry it will not harm you, just keep good thoughts in your head at all times, even when you are doing normal things in your life. It also helps you lead a better life if the thoughts are always good. If you ever get anything that you consider an adverse effect at any time, remember you are the one who is in control no one else. If anything you do not like happens, all you have to do is to close your eyes and ask your angelic helper who you believe in to take away any bad condition you do not want, bring in Divine Light to your power points/chakra into your whole inner body to clean away any badness and evil and "**it will go**", remember that shower of Divine Light. Always remember to **ask** for help and protection of the Divine Light of Spirit at the start of deep meditation, and at the end thank the ones helping you and protecting you, **asking** for the condition to go away. If any power left is felt, **ask** for it to go out to others who need it in the way of healing, try to do this automatically. Always think of others and try to help them to be good, healthy, and happy. Remember whatever you give out in this life comes back to you ten fold. Let it always be true, full of love, goodness and kindness, and for you to mean it from the bottom of your heart (sincerely). **Ask** from above for what you want to happen. Always remember to close down your power points (your chakra **if you open them**) and to **ask** for your taken in conditions to go. It is the power of your good, positive thoughts and the help of a guide in later development that you will find amazing. Please remember Spirit friends will never bring to you any harm, evil or badness if they are going to work with you, it must be trust both ways. Have absolute total trust in the higher realm of Spirit as you get to know them. I certainly do.

Before I go into the ways people do this form of bringing in the power. It has to be said that if you sit in meditation and bring into your being the Divine Light, the power of Spirit, you are doing the same as is going to be told to you in the chakra sequences. This way of opening the chakra I feel is only a way of heightening the parts of your body so you are aware of them and then you can put them out of your mind to let Spirit blend with your mind. Perhaps making yourself more aware of the points in your body more than you would normally do if you just use the drawing in of the Light and let it over flow your being. Please remember the people in the old days did not have any knowledge of any of their chakras and they were the "best" documented Mediums the world has ever known. I say, "documented" the reason being they were written about when they were still working as Mediums and being seen to do their work. I could class the people in the religious books but as we all now know, those books were written many hundreds of years after the deaths of the Holy Men. So how can any sane person with a little bit of common sense believe totally in every word written down that they allegedly said is for me beyond belief. Those Holy Books should be looked at those books as history books only, and not very accurate ones at that, and as a **possibility** of some things happening in them, most should be classed and read as legends.

People say about those looking into their own spirituality trying to link into the higher life of Spirit Angels is all a con, BUT look at all the religions around you; NOT ONE other religion in this world proves there is life after death day after day, except those people who do follow Spirit and yet in the other religions they have thousands of followers going along in **blind faith** being indoctrinated from birth, brain washed. Remember all of the other religions used to have Holy Men to bring forth the Spirit people, see the Spirits clairvoyantly or talk to the Spirit World clairaudiently, those who had passed BUT when the Holy Men of those religions saw the ordinary man was doing it as well, they started calling them witches and wizards and condemned them to death because the Holy Men were losing their power over their flock. They started losing the finance from the money spinning religion, which was making them a comfortable life style that was for them being lost. Through this, a great many innocent people throughout the world were put to death because of it and are "still being slaughtered today" in the name of religion.

## RELIGION IS ONLY ABOUT MONEY AND POWER OVER PEOPLE.

## IN OTHER WORDS, CONTROL!
### Think about it!

With following Spirit I have found and so have many. You look at the religion/movement of those in Spirit and if you are not ready for it, you go away for a period of time. Then you come back to find out more. It is as though you need a little bit more knowledge at each time you enquire and go to the stage you want, then go to your own spiritual point in your own personal development but those Angels in Spirit never leave you. The reason I say that, it is from my own experience and that of others I have spoken to.

When most people have had some loved one pass into the higher sphere of Spirit, the curiosity comes in. Then the person begins to wonder where do I go, or where has their loved one gone to. Most other religions do not give the full answers to their congregations, which is sad for the people and their need to know. Most religious leaders can agree with the ideas of those people who die going to the World of Spirit and talking to those in Spirit, in an each way conversation, BUT when they go back to their flock they deny it because to accept it would be putting them out of a job, anyway that is what I have found. And to continue, I will get off my soapbox for a while.
Even the Pope in Rome is now saying it is not a sin to talk to the dead, at last they are waking up.

# MUSIC, SOUNDS, and BRAINWAVES

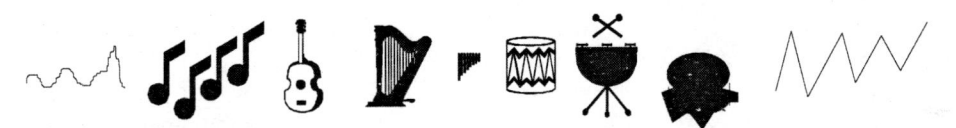

Music, notes, rhythm, and singing are said by many, "to be the life of the soul"

There are different levels of brainwaves that we all have, even in a Medium's and your own, that are different. These brainwaves come into operation when you start working at different levels of Mediumship and looking into the way Mediums work.

The brainwaves have now been measured in hertz by scientists on an electroencephalograph in cycles per second or CPC.
Here in a list are the levels of brain waves in hertz and their true range. I say true range, as a lot of writers place the wave forms in a very general list which are not fully accurate, but I have written them as well as such, I have also placed the true list for the sake of the technically minded.

| | |
|---|---|
| High Beta | 30 plus - 23 Hz |
| Beta | 22.99 – 16 Hz |
| Low Beta | 15.99 – 14.50 Hz |
| Beta/Alpha | 14.49 - 13.50 Hz |
| High Alpha | 13.49 – 12.40 Hz |
| Alpha | 12.39 – 9.90 Hz |
| Low Alpha | 9.89 – 8.20 Hz |
| Alpha/Theta | 7.19 – 7.70 Hz |
| High Theta | 7.69 – 7.10 Hz |
| Theta | 7.00 – 4.90 Hz |
| Low Theta | 4.89 – 4.30 Hz |
| Theta/Delta | 4.29 – 3.90 Hz |

| | |
|---|---|
| High Delta | 3.89 – 3.00 Hz |
| Delta | 2.99 – 1.50 Hz |
| Low delta | 1.49 - 0.50 Hz |
| Panning | 0.49 – 0.01 Hz |

The reason I have not put the following meanings in a chronological list is, all people are individuals so the "Hz" level measured for one person and their response to it or within that measurement is not necessarily the same for the next person. These are in a very general list.

At the levels of **beta,** people have a brainwave range of **30 Hz and above –down to 14 Hz**
Starting at the top of this level you are from a state of panic/stress, hyperactivity, at the top of the Hz range going downwards in the Hz range through to your normal self, down to a quietness in your self. This is the general state that most of us mortals go around our normal life in.

At the levels of **alpha,** people have a brainwave range of **14-8 Hz.**
At this level you are from the start of the meditation, settling down, going downwards through to the your inner awareness, starting of altered awareness, working things out in your mind, being inspired, telepathy, down to where you start experiencing clairvoyance, clairsentience, clairaudience. Still further down to the Light Trance, and a lot of people get a deeper inspiration starting inspirational speaking here at this low level range. Very sensitive awareness. Down to a deeper altered state of awareness (deeper state of trance), linking with Spirit from a light link to a stronger link.

At the levels of **theta,** people have a brainwave range of **8-4 Hz.**
Stronger Trance State. At this level you can have the start of loss of awareness, you are at the deep yoga state. Passive, still mind, where Spirit helpers can have control. Start of out of body (and quite often full out of body when the mind is still in a functioning roll), Start of physical phenomena, much stronger Trance State. Ultra sensitive awareness. In some, a comatose state. The body and mind is in a passive state ready to be used by Spirit for Physical Phenomena. Full experience of out of body (when fully trained). Start of comatose state.

At the levels of **delta,** people have a brainwave range of **4-0 Hz**.
There are not many people, if any, can be shown to be in this lower state of brain pattern (or is it none have been tested to be shown that it is achievable). Here you let those Spirit helpers have the full control. Your whole body and mind is totally passive for spirit control. Full strength trance situation. Loss of awareness. Physical Phenomena of different sorts. Into the realms of a comatose state

Scientists have found out now that the use of certain vibrational notes or certain vibrational noises can help to train a person to take themselves into any of the altered states of the mind/brain. Altering their states (Depth) of altered awareness. Whether it is beta, alpha, theta, or delta. Many people have used music on tapes to educate the right hemisphere of the brain to better receive and to bring incoming vibration levels to a more equal state. The right hemisphere of the brain is used by people more in the development of a person's psychic functions, their awareness, their sensitivity, and possibly enhance their Mediumship.

By using certain musical notes any person can enhance their abilities to a greater degree earlier than others can achieve through a great many hours of meditation to control their mind. "BUT" Please do not run away with the idea that you can get away with not meditating, you can't, the musical notes on tapes are only another tool, a help towards earlier linking. But it must be said that a lot of people, older ones who have had traditional training, pooh, pooh the idea. I say sorry to them because **this method has been shown to work in a great many cases.** Especially by the military of many countries, Especially the U.S.A. Russia, Israel, U.K. Germany, and France, and I should imagine a great many more. It should be pointed out here there has to be alterations in a Medium's brain linkage (the connections) by Spirit to produce whatever form of Mediumship they are going to work with within the Medium. **BUT** it is the individual's body that has to alter to the makeup of the things necessary for the link with Spirit. i.e. the brain linkage/connections, the blood flow, so the vascular system, and many other parts of the human body. (see in more detail later).

It should be noted that many ladies are more right brained than most men in general, in other words they are more sensitive to the Spirit vibrations than most men BUT it seems men when trained and link strongly with the World of Spirit have a stronger link than women SOMETIMES. Even so women too have to learn to get a better link with Spirit by lowering their brainwaves, to link into the different wavelengths of energy vibration from Spirit. Which is at a higher vibrational level than the ordinary person on this earth plane of ours. Spirit lowers their vibrations; we on this earth plane have to learn to heighten ours by meditation by asking Spirit and giving them permission for it to happen. The person has to be passive in their link with Spirit no matter what form of mediumship is required.

I am going to produce some tapes for people so they can train themselves to lower their brainwaves to go into the different states of altered awareness. From 24hz to below 2hz, which ever they want (any lower than this you will be comatose and classified by doctors as possibly brain dead). This can save a lot of time for the person in meditation at the beginning of the linking with their angelic Spirit friends. Also I will produce some tapes for men and the less sensitive ladies to educate their right brain to become a more receptive implement. **(If I have time).** Both sexes will be able to use them. Please remember here that there is no known way to bypass meditation as your main development way of linking with the World of Spirit.

There are many ways to use music to help with the calm meditation within your own safe environment each one being personal to the individual. A lot of people like the mantras of the eastern religions. Mantra means :- "That which protects the mind." A great many like the hub bub noise of the mixed up chanting of a different sect of religion. A lot more like the oomm chant of the Tibetan monks. Different again are the chanting of the English monks. Then there is the chants or singing of the Indians from North America, the Indian holy men from India. Whales calling to each other under water, birds singing. Orchestras playing different music, pipes of pan being played, the harp, the guitar. The constant, monotonous drum beat, and so it goes on, and on and on, there are many noises and there are many more to be found. Why not make your own, that way you know what suits yourself. I have made some calming tapes.

One person might use the music for background music. Allowing the music to flow around in the air like a cloud, not getting involved with it.

Another person might start to meditate with a different piece of music, or even the same but will have a different approach. One person will start to concentrate on one single note and focus on it each time it comes up in the musical piece. The best way is to do this is with a single note or two of the musical scale on a tape, this is if the person meditating is just being peaceful in their meditation.

If the person would like to become deeper in their meditation, a scale of notes is best. Each time the notes are finished the person can see themselves at a certain point in the meditation. Then as the scale of notes start again, the level of the meditation alters going more into the altered state of meditation, and so it continues going more into the altered state. Like descending down the scale ladder of notes.

Another way is to use the music as an air vibration enhancer. This is mainly to bring the airwaves to a point of attraction where those in Spirit can communicate through a Medium in a Physical Circle. The whole of the Circle is generally involved in this with their singing along to pieces of music chosen for their happiness and liveliness. Spirit is brought quicker into any Circle when the airwaves are vibrating well, so it seems. Many Circles do not conform to the one set of songs, BUT it has been found that some songs work better than others to attract those in Spirit to a Circle.

Some people prefer the sound of the monks chanting, or singing their mantra to meditate to; this also can bring good results for the individual and Circles. Never rule anything out. As I have mentioned I had a wonderful experience in a Circle when the very loud noise of the North American Indian drums were hammering out. Remember it is the vibration of the airwaves from the banging of the drum skin that was altering the airwaves. You could feel the vibration echoing in the hollow parts of your body as you became more sensitive to the beat, especially around the hollow chest and solar plexus area.

It is what is comfortable for you that matters BUT please for your own sake don't stop just on one type or piece of music, experience them all if you can.

After looking at the mantras, and affirmations, the medical profession found that anything said over and over, more than seven times in succession goes into the subconscious and is there for the rest of the day controlling/helping the person to be so. E.g. if you say you are going to be happy all day and you start the day off by saying the affirmation:- I am going to be happy all day, I am going to be happy all day, I am going to be happy all day, I am going to be happy all day, I am going to be happy all day, I am going to be happy all day, I am going to be happy all day,

By putting that thought into your mind it now has a profound effect on your outlook for the rest of the day. Don't believe me? Try it!!!! You could use any sentence you wish to make up for that particular day so wish to put to better use. It could be:- "I am going to meditate twice today and progress in my development". "I am going to a better person today and help where I can." "I am progressing in my development with Spirit when I sit." These form of words (or any you say) to yourself over and over and over again reinforce to your subconscious mind that those things you really want to do, and so it gets done. This has been known about by the sales people of the world for years and especially so the monks of the Eastern Countries over the centuries.

Mantras can be repeated over and over to help still the thoughts that go through the mind. **But remember,** it is still having your mind working to be saying the words of any mantra.

Look at the experiments that were done in the 1900's by George Jobson with vibrations, to try and have earlier and stronger contact with those in Spirit. He actually invented, with the help of those in the World of Spirit, a clockwork activated tuning fork, which was used first of all inside of his re-designed "Reflectograph," which he called the "Communigraph." This separate clockwork vibrating mechanism was then advertised for people sitting in Home Circles, for use to help them with their power build up in those newly formed Home Circles. The clockwork vibrating tuning fork was advertised for enhancing the power of Spirit in the Circle to help with Direct Voice, Physical Phenomena, trumpet movement, table rapping and levitation, and every kind of séance held.

The noise of the vibration when set was said to be a whirring noise then when properly adjusted it became a humming sound.

Jobson also found out through his experiments and through Spirit advice from a Deep Trance Medium Mrs Singleton, that the frequency of the lower "A" tuning fork, which vibrates at 220 cycles per second, "gave the note most pleasing to Spirit contact". That tuning fork note was found to be the best, **except** for the lower "A" double-diapason note of a large pipe organ, which of course was not practical for the Home Circles, perhaps that particular note could be recorded by the ordinary person, by going to a large cathedral and asking the organist to play the notes required.

Mr Jobson also states that that some notes of vibration, notably music can cause a disagreeable reaction with those in Spirit, even though it might be harmonious to us here on the earth plane. Only certain parts of the harmonics are said to be potent.

A long sustained note is much more potent, a discovery that probably accounts for the low, monotonous chanting of the Holy Men in the Eastern religious temples.

It has been found sounds made in the human throat area, by the human can be used to help with different healing techniques for the head area as sound vibrates within the round-ish bony structure, helping within it. Also sound can help with the air passages from the lungs upward. Sounds from the vocal cords vibrate throughout the body through the liquid/fluid of the human body. I have placed some exercises with sounds made by the individual in the healing section of this book.

# POWER POINTS
## Chakra (the Sanskrit word for "wheel") or Energy Centres.

Some people when going into deeper meditation, will later on actually say they open at first with what they call their chakras opening up or activating their main chakra, when going into a development of themselves for Clairvoyance, Clairaudience, Clairsentience, Clairknowing, psychometry, aura reading, healing, physical phenomena and others, what is known as Mediumship.

The chakras are said to be in the body at differing power points or energy centres that we all possess, I am only giving you the main ones, because there are a lot more of course. To enhance the main power points/chakra some draw in colours at each breath as they think of each power point. Please think on about your own personal colour range, it might not be the same as another person's colour. There must be hundreds of different shades of reds, greens, yellows, browns, blues, purples, etc. so chose your own. There are said to be 88,000 chakra or power centres of different degrees in and around the human body. Some sitters can get their main chakra spinning and feel it, others just image it.

Please remember, if as the books or teachers say "close your chakra" this is only a figure of speech. What they mean is to take the extra energy or power created from them by means of your thoughts.

## The only time your chakra or power points are closed is when you are dead.

The main chakra points are situated at :- I will only number the ones known by most.

**0:- feet of the person;** Here is a chakra that is forgotten by most people it is a position of balance and stability and is linked to mother earth; the colour of this chakra is **brown**.

**1:- spine base centre;** (mooladhara) [is always open but should be activated at the start of your need and cleanse when finished]; colour associated with this power point is **red**.

**2:- sacral centre;** (swdisthan) Just below the belly button. Colour associated with this power point is **orange**.

**3:- solar plexus centre;** (nabhi) Just above the belly button. Colour associated with this power point is **yellow**.

**4:- heart centre;** (anhata) colour associated with this power point is **green**, [please remember the thymus gland is a half chakra being developed in the human body by the higher side of life, this is in-between the throat and the heart, open and develop this as well].

**5:- throat centre;** (vishuddhi) colour associated with this power point is **blue.**

**6:- brow centre;** (ajna) between the eyes centre [third eye]; colour associated with this power point is **indigo**.

**7:- crown centre;** (sahasrara) top of the head centre; is always open, but should be activated [or should I say in this instance and in spine base, stimulated more] at the start of your need, and cleanse when finished. Colour associated with this power point is **Lilac**. [some say **purple or violet**].

The main chakra when they are used correctly; opening them individually is said to help with the development in each chakra of as follows in :-

**0:- Feet :- Balance and stability.**
**1:- Spine :- stability and the start of development.**
**2:- Sacral :- feeling.**
**3:- Solar plexus :- travelling.**
**4:- Heart :- understanding.**
**5:- Throat :- clairaudience.**
**6:- Brow :- clairvoyance.**
**7:- Crown :- continuity of consciousness.**

After you reach a higher level of learning of your craft, you will be informed that some of the centres/chakras or power points within your body interact with each other; this is so the vibration level necessary for a particular Mediumship gift that is being given to you and developed by the World of Spirit can be more fully developed. **Here I must say you can fill yourself with the Divine Light of God and have the same effect.** I am giving you as much information I have at my disposal for your development so you can use whichever method you choose to do so.

The Kundalini method of opening the chakras is very similar but there are said to be a few more power points. The books of the Kundalini methods go into far more detail than I can give here. The famous Healer Mr John Cain from Birkenhead Merseyside used to use this method to open his chakras. By the way do not dismiss these points of the chakras that you have. The energy that is put out by the chakra can be measured by electronic/mechanical instruments. **But importantly** what should be remembered, the Fox sisters did not have any knowledge of the chakras when they heard the intelligent rapping's in their little American home, and that sparked off people experimenting with all that encompasses modern Spiritualism. None of the early pioneers who linked with the Angels knew about any of the chakras. It has only now recently crept in from the eastern religions. Also what should be taken into consideration, the early pioneers who put more time aside for their own development, were in the main better Links/Mediums than the people today and there were a lot more good and more powerful Mediums/Sensitives in the past and they had no knowledge of chakras. All this was because of their dedication to link with "Angelic Spirit Helpers", and putting their own special time aside to become as one with the Angels in Spirit. Sitting in a passive state and being in the Divine Light within the "Oneness" with God.

There are many other methods to use when sitting for development.

This one is done by at first asking for the higher life's help, closing the eyes, when sitting or laying in a comfortable position, Asking for goodness, kindness, love, truth, and to blend in peaceful Divine Light of Spirit within the loving harmony of the Angels/Spirit of the highest realms of Spirit. Then imagining each chakra in the sequence laid out 0,1-7, start the power points/centres/chakras spinning as they build up the power as you open them up with eyes closed **see them** spinning upwards in bright light blending upwards into each other, while looking into your third eye.

Or some people when starting at the spine base centre, imagine each power point/centre/chakra as a bud [or ball when it is full of light it explodes upwards] opening up into a flower which then goes into a seed pod then explodes upwards in a bright light into the next chakra. When doing this method, go through each chakra in sequence **"slowly"**, then when the light reaches the top of the head the seed head explodes in light into the higher side of life and joins up with the Divine Light from above to you, so connecting you consciously to the Divine Light. The light flows also over yourself and where you are sitting going back around into yourself at your feet so building up more power, (do this as many times as you feel is necessary), so every time it goes to your feet it is stronger, each time it comes out of your head it goes upwards so making a stronger connection up above to the Divine Light.

At the end of your session, to close; imagine each chakra going back into a bud formation and closing up tightly in a ball of light, so cleansing each chakra, then thanking those who helped you. As you open so you close using the Divine Spirit's Light. Or use the method of letting the Divine Light of Spirit wash you as though you are under a shower. But not only is the light going all over you, it is washing all your inside as well.

Remember people all over the world have been developing their psychic abilities without using these methods, but this is now a very well documented and recognised as **"one"** way of developing. It is up to you alone which method you use.

As you progress along in your own correct way of opening and closing in meditation, it will be found when you start to meditate deeply asking for the higher life's help it will come to you easily, only you will know when that is. As you progress it will be found when you start to meditate deeply asking for the higher side of life's help from those Angels in Spirit, the power will automatically come to you as you **ask** for it; but at this point I should say that your mind has become attuned to the opening of the chakras without the need of thinking of opening the chakra when starting meditating. **BUT ALWAYS CLOSE AS YOU OPEN** whatever method use. Always remember to close down your power points (main chakras) if you open them and to ask those in the higher life side for your conditions to go, then; always, cleanse yourself inside with the light from the top of your head as though you are in a shower of light and **see it** going downwards through your body expelling it out of your eyes, ears, nose, mouth, along your arms to your fingers tips and out, through your body, legs, feet, and out of your toes. A full flow that will cleanse your body with light, taking away any darkness that is there, this can be done anywhere and at anytime, filling you with the Divine Spirit's Light and spiritual energy. The **MOST IMPORTANT** thing to remember is to **ask** and it **WILL** be given and so received, **BUT** not always right away. If people across the veil or the higher side of life do not know what you want, how can you receive it. Even if it is only development of yourself, and letting the higher realm decide as you progress. That is what I am doing, **I ask**, but also saying I am an open vessel here to be used and developed in what ever way the Angels in Spirit wish, giving permission to develop a stronger link with the Angels in Spirit and letting them decide. Those in Spirit know better than us mere mortals what they can work with, and mould into their catalyst, for whatever mediumship works best with an individual person.

In your life have a laugh, be happy, and do not be too serious about your life when working with those in Spirit, but do not be flippant whilst meditating or linking. Always remember you are always in control. If you do not want to work at a particular time and the messages keep on coming into your head just ask positively, sincerely, and nicely for them to go, thanking the link in Spirit for coming, then arranging when it will be best for them to work with you, so being more convenient for both parties.

Another method used for enhancing the main chakra is for you to sit in a comfortable position. Ask for Spirit to come to you at this time and help you develop in you ????? ("what ever" Mediumship in you). To bring only goodness, kindness, love, and truth, from within the Divine Light of Spirit, within the loving harmony of Spirit of the highest realms. You then think of the each of the main chakra being coloured or moulded into a ball of colour, their own particular colour. One at a time, starting at the balls of your feet at the ground. You can feel you feet resting on the ground, there you see a ball of warm brown growing around you and inside your feet and legs, it is expanding upwards. As that warm brown expands, you feel the warmth as it goes up into the chakra at the base of the spine, the colour starts to change into a red, it is starting to glow red and fill you with the power of the colour, you can still feel the warm brown it is still part of you, as the red swells, growing bigger, as it grows bigger it expands going into the sacral chakra, as it does, the power of it changes forming an expanding ball that starts to turn orange. But the power of the brown and red are still there in your body, you can feel it, you are aware of what is happening in your body. The orange ball starts to expand growing bigger and as it expands it flows upwards into the solar plexus chakra where it starts to turns yellow. The power of the orange stays in your body at that place, you can feel it, you are aware of what is happening in your body you have the colours of brown, red and orange in you. The yellow of the solar plexus starts to expand and it grows ever bigger, expanding, swelling into the heart and there it starts to turn green, a good green ball is forming and expanding. The power of the yellow stays in your body at that place, you can feel it, you are aware of what is happening in your body, you now have the colours of brown, red, orange, and yellow in you. That green starts to swell, expand, it starts flowing upwards to the throat area where it starts turning into blue colour it feels wonderful to have all the colours flowing in your body like this. The power of the green stays in your body at that place, you can feel it, you are aware of what is happening in your body, you now have the colours of brown, red, orange, yellow and green in you. As the blue at the throat starts to grow and become part of you, it is as though you are becoming more aware of the things happening in your body. It is a good feeling for you. The blue starts to grow, flow, and expand into the brow chakra where it starts to become a wonderful indigo colour The power of the blue stays in your body at that place, you can feel it, you are aware of what is happening in your body, you now have the colours of brown, red, orange, yellow, green, and blue in you. You are getting more conscious of the feeling of the colours and what they are doing within your body. The indigo in the brow as it expands is starting to make you become more relaxed because of the anticipation of what is about to happen. The colour is starting to expand into the top of your head at the crown chakra, it is now turning purple, the most beautiful purple you can imagine it is making you feel good to be alive. The power of the indigo stays in your body at that place, you can feel it, you are aware of what is happening in your body, you now have the colours of brown, red, orange, yellow, green, blue and indigo in you. You are getting more conscious of the feeling of the colours and what they are doing within your body it is a glowing feeling. You now can see and feel the colours in layers in your body see it in your minds eye, it feels strange but exciting to be part of this development inside yourself, the purple is getting stronger it is expanding at a fast rate and the purple is starting to go upwards to the higher side of life and it starts to become a bright white divine light as it mixes with it. The light is starting to come back down over you, going inside you, changing all the colours in turn to the white Divine Light of God, the Power Supreme. You see them changing. They change the feeling in your body to that of one of oneness with the Light, it is where you now belong, you belong in that Light. You now can sit and develop within that Light asking for the development you require. After asking sincerely, you now can sit and let Spirit do their quiet work unhindered for whatever length of time you wish.
I was at a teaching centre and the tutor who had experience of more years than me was using a method of opening the solar plexus for healing and was jumping from the third eye to the solar plexus, I was very surprised at what method he was using. He was saying to the Healing Circle open your solar plexus

chakra, concentrate on it, then look into your third eye as you are doing it, keep on concentrating on your solar plexus. Build up the power as you are doing it, look into your third eye. Keep on building up the power in the solar plexus and when I say push, I want you to push the energy to the person you are sending healing to into the top of the head and see it flowing into the person. One, two, three, push. That for me it you and not Spirit using the energy of your own body, that can very much deplete you.

I was very, very surprised, for me, it was us doing the healing NOT the Spirit World healing. At no time were we asked to link with the Spirit World. I could not get my head around the method of swapping from the third eye area to the solar plexus and back again. My mind was so active, the others and I were not giving the Spirit World the still mind for them to do their job, while we sat as a passive instrument of their work, it is not our job to do anything when healing. Not very much happened, so I did my own method after the first session, and things happened and were very much felt by the person opposite me, my fellow student. I always try to go to other peoples tutorials, the reason being, I can see their methods and if I get just one extra piece of information from a full week of tutorials might help me in my development I am over the moon and I meet others of mixed levels of experience and learn from them and help them on their way, but most times I see the things I teach about Spirit are the correct ways to go about linking and developing.

In my tutorials no matter what sort of development tutorial I take, I always insist that my students talk to the World of Spirit within their minds asking for what they want for at least 10 to 15 minutes in the Circle to gain a link BEFORE WE START.

## SUGGESTIONS FOR A SAFE CIRCLE

**WHAT IS A CIRCLE in the meditating, spiritual sense?** All that a Circle is, it is a group of people all sitting comfortably, reasonably close but not bodies touching, (sometimes it can be necessary to hold hands, or hand to wrist so there can be no messing around, or if a table is in the centre, their little fingers touching the person next to you, with hands flat down on the table) facing each other inwards towards a centre, generally in a room put aside for that moment, all in unison, all bringing in the love of all on this earth. Quite often the Circle is with friends of like minds sitting just for development. It can be just to join together with the Angels in Spirit for a few moments in time for relaxation or healing the stress of this world around us, also for development of one person, or all there sitting the Circle. Then it could be to have contact with the Angels in Spirit through a Medium who is clairvoyant, clairsentient, clairaudient, clairknowing, or the Circle can be to produce with the help of those Angels in Spirit, Physical Phenomena. A Circle can consist of two people to many.

**BEFORE EVERY CIRCLE AND EVERY TIME A PERSON SITS FOR A SPIRIT LINK. AT FIRST CONCENTRATE ON THE BREATH, THEY SHOULD IN THEIR MIND, BE ASKING AND ENCOURAGING SPIRIT TO COME CLOSER TO THEM AND HELP AT ALLOTTED TIME FOR THE SITTING FOR DEVELOPMENT OR DEMONSTRATION, OVER AND OVER AND OVER. AT LEAST AN HOUR OR TWO BEFORE THE ALLOTTED TIME. YOU CANNOT EXPECT YOUR LINK TO COME AUTOMATICALLY AS SOON AS YOU SIT DOWN IN A CIRCLE OR DEMONSTRATE YOUR SKILL OF A LINK WITH SPIRIT TO PROVE TO OTHER THERE IS LIFE AFTER OUR SO CALLED DEATH.**

**GENERALLY NO TWO CIRCLES HAVE THE SAME REACTIONS**

BUT ! Here are some constants that work for most.

Pick a leader to run the group from the start.
All rules should be set at the start of the Circle sitting, and all there told of them by the leader.
Have a comfortable room to sit in. [Some people do not alter their Circle room in any shape or form, some have **no** heating as well, allowing the room to find its own temperature].
A separate room preferably put aside just for purpose of sitting for any development [but is not essential].
A few bowls of water placed in the room each time for the sitting. This helps to prevent the Medium and the sitters getting too dehydrated. [a large mixing bowl or fruit bowl is ideal. I now have three large ones in my séance room (10ft x 9ft), and a drink of water for myself]

Have a glass of water for each sitter, always drink plenty of water while developing it can save some people getting headaches, remember you are developing/using parts of your brain that has had very little use, probably it has been dormant for many years. Think of the times you have not used a muscle for a length of time, then if you use that muscle more than normal, the next day it hurts, it can be the same when developing, also your linking parts of your brain has to make new connections for Spirit's use.

An exercise that might seem strange but it can be used to bring harmony to the Circle.

## YES it does work!!!

Look at each person individually in the group and smile at them, it does not matter if you feel uncomfortable and laugh, that will raise the vibrations. When that is done ask everyone to close their eyes, and smile inwardly to those in Spirit you are going to meet. Feel happy about meeting them as they draw near to the Circle welcome them, feel the happy anticipation, the warmth of the feeling, be sincere about the love you are giving out to them and the Circle.

To start or open a Circle, a sincere prayer or a few sincere words should be said to Spirit for what is required by the sitters. Just talk to Spirit as though you were talking to a friend, as you of course are, they certainly will be your friends. Friends of the best kind you will ever get.

All in any Circle should meditate in happiness, after the prayers or an affirmation at the start for at least ¼ to ½ an hour in the room to build up the power within the room and build up the link with the Angels in Spirit with all of the sitters individually within themselves, bringing each person into happy, warm, loving harmony with all that are gathered there. Each person through thought while meditating should be sincerely asking and encouraging Spirit to come near and help with whatever development or phenomena is required. If one person is developing or is the Medium being used for Physical Phenomena each person should be asking Spirit Helpers to send the power collected from themselves to go to the single person. (the more you sincerely give out unconditionally to others, the more you will receive from Spirit yourself).

A Circle develops quicker if it is of the same people each time. [better, early results work when sitters are placed man, woman, man, woman, etc. or masculine, feminine, masculine, feminine etc. or positive, negative, positive, negative etc.]. Some Circles prefer odd numbers, some don't.

When sitting for Spirit in any regular Circle, it is so important that people use the same seats, and are in the same sitting positions in the room. The Circle that sits this way brings earlier results. (If the use of a table for tilting is used for guidance, then the Angels in Spirit can advise where each person should sit for the best results, this was the way of doing things in the 1800's. They used the table for any advise of improving the Circle's development)

**Do not move around in the Circle by getting out of your seat and wandering around, have everything prepared first at the start of the Circle.**

Cleanliness of all sitters in mind, body and clothing (best if the same clothes are worn for each sitting, BUT don't forget to wash them).

Individual adjustable lighting of separate red and white lights. If only one can be dimmed, use a dimmer on red light which should be used throughout the sitting of the Circle (except for Physical Phenomena Circles which are generally in complete darkness, or the lowest point on the red dimmed light and then it is often covered) at the lowest point for all to just about see after the light has been on for five minutes. The eyes will be adjusted to the light by then. [Careful about switching the light on after the Circle, warn everyone to expect it, the immediate, sudden, bright light hurts the eyes].

Some Circles have no external daylight at all, just using the illumination from a bulb being either red, green, or blue, and have that on for all the time of the sitting of the Circle, so experiment. Most use a very low red light when going in for the deeper Trance Mediumship.

A lot of Circles are using ordinary white light on a dimmer as well so the Angels in Spirit can adjust the light if it is necessary. So there are two lights that are dim, the red one to see with and the white one dimmed down but not brightly shining out. A lot of Circles sit in full white light to develop. So you have many options.

All sitters having sincerity, dedication, peaceful loving harmony with each other.

Incompatible people will stop or hinder development, get rid of them.

No negativity allowed at all in the building or room. No bad or evil thoughts or deeds. No bitchiness, or gossip. No criticism of others at all within the room or Circle, even the building it is held in.

NO LIES in any person's development. This is negativity, and it should be pointed out here that negativity can stop any spiritual development.

No person is to have any preconceived ideas about what might happen within the Circle, with other sitters' development, or with their own development.

Total trust by all sitters in their personal higher self, total trust in the Angels/Spirit, and total trust of the higher life of Spirit.

Comfortable seats for all should be wooden, as the wood collects and stores the energy from the Spirit World and acts as a battery. Perhaps cushions to support the backs of sitters, not too mush soft furnishing in the room. All sitting upright, hands resting comfortably on the laps.

Legs not crossed, feet on the floor a comfortable distance apart. [crossed legs can restrict blood flow so causing cramp, it is also said to block some power points].

Body and brain completely relaxed, minimal thoughts so those angelic people in Spirit have full access to the inner workings of the brain and so to link better with the higher self [this is each individual trying to slow the thoughts and nerve impulses from the brain or electrical activity to the muscles, which tenses them. I just look into the light within my third eye position]

Nothing moved if possible. [meaning changed around].

Nothing being taken out or brought in.

New things brought into the special room or Circle gradually over a period of time.

Punctual starting times.

Do not start letting people in or out of the room after the starting of the Circle.

Stipulate a prompt time of starting. After that no entrance by any person **what so ever**.

Any person who is continually late, or a spasmodic sitter, only coming occasionally to the Circle. The best thing is to ask them not to attend again. It is not fair to the other sitters, neither is it fair to the Angelic link of the Spirit realm to think they all can put every bit of their effort into the Circle and not have a constant setting to help to make things happen for the benefit of all there.

Sitting at the same time, on the same day/days of the week is a must.

Any late starting of a Circle can put back the progression of that Circle, sit in the room at least five to ten minutes before the start of the Circle talking and laughing about things in general, But no nasty talk or negativity.

Do not wear anything restricting, undo belts, scarves, collars etc. Be comfortable in yourself.

Go to the toilet before sitting in any Circle so there is no interruption later when the Circle is in progress.

**Prayers to start and finish** the sitting of the Circle, with the asking for what you want from the Circle at the beginning. Also asking **sincerely and positively** for the Angels in Spirit to bring truth, goodness, love, light, happiness, kindness, peaceful loving harmony and protection of all there within the Divine Light of Spirit and to blend in loving harmony of Spirit in the highest realms.

No person to move out of their seats during the Circle sitting without permission of the leader of the Circle or the Angels in Spirit.

At the end just before the close, everyone is asked to send any power left to those in need of healing, within a quiet moment of at least two minutes. Then close down the conditions of the Circle in the form of a prayer thanking the Angels in Spirit, asking those Angel Links in Spirit to take conditions away returning everyone there to their normal self, telling those up stairs [in Spirit] you will be back and when, it is a commitment from all there to the angelic realm in Spirit.

Have a space between sitters, enough room so no sudden movement can interfere with another sitter. If any person does move suddenly, they cannot touch the person next to them and give them a nasty psychic shock, especially if that person is in deep meditation, very much in an altered state of awareness.

At the start, all there present being told if anything happens, not to touch any other person as they could be in deep meditation, a state of altered awareness. If the person is touched there is a possibility of a bad psychic shock occurring. In the extreme cases a psychic burn can occur, or internal bleeding, but this is mainly with the Physical Medium in the Physical Circle.

Bring back any person in deep meditation, by talking to the person in a low, gentle voice, **saying their name**, repeatedly asking them to let the conditions to go, and to come back to normality.

Only eat a very light meal before any Circle sitting and no nuts, especially peanuts, as they are hard for those in Spirit to deal with, so it has been told to us by the angelic helpers in Spirit. Those helpers in Spirit have to adjust the chemicals in the sitters' bodies in some Circles, to help them with the correct vibrations necessary.

Some Circles [mostly done in low wattage, dimmed, covered red light Circles, including development Circles] have on the floor or on a table [some have a table, some don't] in the middle of the Circle, a small bell, a little tambourine, concertina, a rattle for the Angels in Spirit to use as a form of communication, some have very light, wind chimes hung up, to see if there is any psychic breeze happening in the room and some a trumpet (shaped like a megaphone, or a dunces hat. I have known of four being used at once in established Circles), in the middle of the Circle for those Angels in Spirit to build a voice box in.

When any lights are switched on (or off), all there should be warned, including the helpers in Spirit, this is so those helpers in Spirit can withdraw any power or ectoplasm that might have been produced back into any Developing Mediums, and then the lights should only be turned up gradually to protect peoples eyes.

Have a sweet drink and/or sweet cakes/biscuits after sitting in any Circle to revitalise the sitters.

Each person should individually meditate in their own homes each day at the same time for ten to sixty minutes a day; longer if possible even if you do not want to sit in a Circle, the benefits to yourself will become self evident. Rome was not built in a day.

Some people try holding hands while sitting as in a joined Circle, [this can become uncomfortable sometimes, **BUT** this is how they used to sit in Circles in the early days], so their power developing is said, came stronger. Others just touch the fingertips of the person next to them in the Circle for five minutes to raise the power in the Circle (finger tip to finger tip, generally on a table top). This I feel would better as no squeezing of hands, or any playing around could occur.

Others in Circles placed their hands downwards on a table that they have placed in the middle of the group with their fingers touching, the sitters' little fingers touching the next person's. Some have their feet touching as well. Holding hands and but more so feet touching I think was a way of making sure the people in Physical Circles could not cheat in the dark, but on that point I am not certain. Some Circles say holding/ touching of the hands in the Circle, makes the Circles power more powerful quicker, of that I cannot make a judgement, but in the older books they did it as a matter of course.

Lots of the Circles in the 1800's-1900's used to go to the "truthful, very deep, Trance" Mediums [or have one in their Circle] so as they progressed they used to ask what they should do to help improve the development of people there in their Circle. I personally would be very careful of the people I would go to for advice. From what I have seen of the work of some Mediums, they are kidding themselves about their Trance depth and their link with a higher force. Go to see them work and then decide. As said before the tilting table and raps were used as advice in the early days.

Some Circles have their music playing in the Circle room throughout the day [or an hour or two before] of the Circle sitting, this is to build up the vibration levels and the atmosphere in the room before everyone comes to sit in the Circle.

The leaders in some groups keep asking for their requests for what they would like to happen out loud at intervals throughout the Circle. Remember it is the power of thought that is mainly used for contact with those in Spirit. If you feel that talking is best, try it, remembering it is the vibrations of the air through the human voice and music that the Spirit World seem to need for help come closer and have a more powerful link so always experiment. Remember the jokes that you hear about the Spiritualists in the Circles "is there anybody there". Yes, it is still used to bring in those in the Spirit World closer by some. But always remember to attract the good in the Spirit World, the angelic, the higher vibration level people by sincerely, and positively, **asking** always for goodness, kindness, happiness, truth, light, love, and to blend in peaceful Divine Light within the loving harmony of Spirit in the highest realms.

Each person should be sincerely **asking** in their minds throughout the Circle sitting, for the Angels in Spirit to come closer into their auric field and help in the task for what the Circle is sitting for. Whether it is one person where the power is directed to, or each individual developing in the group Circle as part of a whole.

A Circle does not have to be confined to just once a week but the people should keep to the same time, on the same days. A lot of Circles I have heard about lately meet Mondays and Fridays; or Mondays, Wednesdays and Fridays. Most seem to start at 7.30 or 8.00 [when people have finished work and are able to get there] to until whenever o'clock. The Circle is finished when the sitters start to get restless or the power is felt to wane. Some stick to set finishing times. It is best to let the conditions and those in Spirit decide.

A lot of Circles I have read about in the olden days at the start of Spiritualism, and ones I have heard of lately for sitting for the link with the Angels/Spirit met/meet in the daytime, when house persons are free, and they have very successful meeting. The daytime Circles at Stansted and the other colleges are also very good. Most of them are in the day and quite a lot in full daylight, except Physical Circles. These I think should be attempted in the light as well. But that is up to Spirit. Not us who are sitting.

Remember you are the one who is always in control. If those in Spirit you are working with want to work when you do not, mentally tell them you do not want to work and to go away until you ask for them to come. Saying " Thank you friend for coming to me at this time but I do not want to work, please come only when I invite you to come and work with me" "I do not want to work now but thank you for the link"
Try differing methods, I would be interested to find out which ones work best for you. Try to read as much material as you can on the subject of development of the psyche especially from the old out of print books that they have in libraries, those of the 1800's-1940's. I now have a collection of over 700 books.

Most of all try to attend some courses at the world-renowned Arthur Findlay College in Stansted Hall; it is like a large hotel with many lecture rooms. This is a college for psychic development; I use my weeks as a learning holiday. The power and atmosphere you will pick up is unbelievable when you stay there, so make sure you drink plenty of water while you are there for your first time. The power is different than a home Circle; it is like putting yourself under a high-powered battery charger. The power there actually gives you a boost if you ever feel you are not moving ahead or stagnating. They have a very well stocked bookshop. You will meet people from all over the world who go there to attend the lectures. You join in the development exercises, the Circles of development, sit in the experimental Physical Circles and are shown different methods of development of Mediumship. Probably you will have a drink and conversations with the friends from all over the world in Dining Hall and at night in the college bar. I have met people from Iceland, Australia, New Zealand, U.S.A., Germany, Sweden, Holland, Egypt, Canada, Ireland, Scotland, Wales, and Switzerland in just one week when I stayed there for a trance\physical week in 1998. You could even camp out in local farmers fields, or book into local hotels, just paying for and attend the courses on any of the 60+ courses that are held there throughout the year not one week is missed, **BUT** be careful though, remember you might well pay London prices, as Stansted Hall is close to the Stansted Airport, Essex. It is far better [and cheaper] to stay at the college though, you get mixing better while you are eating, talking and drinking with the new friends in the college restaurant, then you also can mix with others in the evening in the college bar, or in one of the lounges, perhaps the blue room where Arthur Findlay and his good lady used to sit for their development. The time while you are there at Stansted Hall goes far too quickly, it all makes you want to return again and again for other weeks on the different courses. Each time is different and you always pick up something new. The very least you should do if you do not go to Stansted, is to read some of the Arthur Findlay books and those of the older pioneer authors who have written about spiritual matters, the college does mail order. They also have open days. Please remember it can be a hectic learning week on some courses, others are completely relaxing. Choose the ones that suit you for your development purpose. The college has a yearly booklet with the entire weekly and weekend courses in it. Their phone No. 01279 813636. England.
While you are there if you want to have a break from the routine one day, try to go down to the little thatched roof village pub "The Ash" in Burton End, just come out of the college turn left over the motorway bridge then left into Burton End Village, the pub is about one/two hundred yards on the other side of the village, on the right hand side. It sells nice meals and a good pint of beer.

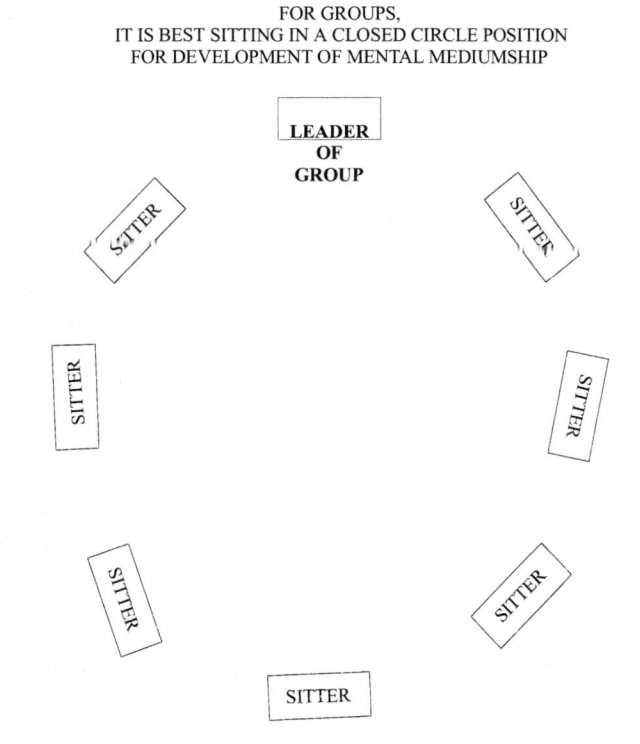

FOR GROUPS,
IT IS BEST SITTING IN A CLOSED CIRCLE POSITION
FOR DEVELOPMENT OF MENTAL MEDIUMSHIP

```
                    LEADER
                      OF
                     GROUP

      SITTER                        SITTER


   SITTER                              SITTER



      SITTER                        SITTER

                    SITTER
```

A circle can be from two to many.
A SPACE TO BE LEFT IN BETWEEN EACH PERSON,
**ESPECIALLY IN A DEVELOPMENT CIRCLE**
where everyone is going into meditation development at once.
That way no one can knock another sitter accidently if they bend down
to pick up their water at the side of them on the floor to have a sip.
The leader should always keep watch throughout the sitting of the Circle.
The leader may meditate at the start of the Circle to build up the power.

# DEVELOPMENT CIRCLE

**BEFORE EVERY CIRCLE AND EVERY TIME A PERSON SITS FOR A SPIRIT LINK. AT FIRST CONCENTRATE ON THE BREATH, THEY SHOULD IN THEIR MIND, BE ASKING AND ENCOURAGING SPIRIT TO COME CLOSER TO THEM AND HELP AT ALLOTTED TIME FOR THE SITTING FOR OF THE DEVELOPMENT THEY WANT TO HAVE OR HELP IN THE DEMONSTRATION THEY ARE ABOUT TO DO, OVER AND OVER AND OVER. <u>AT LEAST AN HOUR</u> OR TWO BEFORE THE ALLOTTED TIME. YOU CANNOT EXPECT YOUR LINK TO COME AUTOMATICALLY AS SOON AS YOU SIT DOWN IN A CIRCLE OR DEMONSTRATE YOUR SKILL OF A LINK WITH SPIRIT.**

**Each person should be looking forward to the Circle and linking in with Spirit in all sincerity with excited anticipation, especially in Trance and Physical Circles.**

From the start it should be stressed that every Circle is different, no two Circles in general are the same, they cannot be because of the different individuals sitting for their own personal individual development.

The better and quicker way of developing is to get a few like minded friends in loving harmony from two [Arthur Findlay used to sit just with his wife at home in the blue room of the college] up to about twelve-ish, [much more than this can bring in too many problems of incompatibility to the Circle.
The best loving harmony in Circles that last, seem to work with 4 to 8 people] in a quiet, comfortable room with comfortable seating, any more can bring different problems BUT they (Spirit) always sort out

the ones who cause them, and some how or other they leave or drift away from the Circle.

Pick a leader, then together in the same place/room/house once, twice or three times each week it is up to you. At the same time say "7.30pm start on say Monday and Thursday, finishing at say about 9.00 – 10.00pm". All sit comfortably around in a Circle [not exactly but figuratively speaking; a group with a centre] in a very, very low covered red light, reducing the intensity as the eyes get use to the subdued light, no outside light coming into the room, it might seem dark at first but the eyes soon get used to it very quickly. [Some Circles sit in complete darkness, in red light of varying brightness, less it seems is best, but some sit in full light for development. Experiment, with your group, the better results seem to be in subdued red light, it is nice and relaxing, try one method for six months or longer (or on different nights) then another way for six months, but give one method a chance to work and stick to the same times and nights of the week. What works for one group might not work for another] Please remember it needs **a constant** to develop your personal gifts, **regular attendance** and **dedication** by **all the sitters**. **All the sitters** should have sincere and positive thoughts and be in peaceful loving harmony with each other to build up any form of mediumship in any person in a group situation, so they then can be in peaceful loving harmony with the higher side of life across the veil, if a person is not comfortable with the others, nicely ask them to leave, have no negativity in the Circle in the way of thoughts, deeds, no bad talking, no bitching, leave all badness or bitterness no matter trivial or how small, outside of the building where you are going to sit.

Importantly, prepare yourself for the sitting in the power [in meditation] by washing yourself, [what you are doing is preparing your mind] not putting any scented things on yourself, [this is just in case any smells come through to the Circle as a contact while sitting].
Having a glass of water beside each person for them to drink as and when necessary.
Have each person arrive early to the house/building (about a quarter of an hour before) to settle in.
Make sure everything is ready and not left to the last minute.
Start the sitting with a good atmosphere, laughing and joking with each other bringing happiness within the Circle. This is to raise the vibrations.
Compose yourselves about five minutes before the red light is turned very dim or is turned off by one of the sitters [have a dimmer switch attached to the red light; but experiment with ordinary white, red, green and blue lights].
Start with some sincere prayers, always asking for goodness, kindness, happiness, love and truth to come to all in the Circle everyone there to sit in harmony, ask Spirit to bring in the Divine Light of Spirit and the helpers to come from the loving harmony from those in the highest realms. Possibly singing of a hymn, or any song, one that all know, you could have it on a tape and play it as you sing, then asking from the Angels in the Spirit World for the protection of the Circle, inside and around the outside of the Circle, also around the room you are all in, the place you are in, the surrounding area, ask from those above in the higher life from the highest developed possible [those upstairs as I say].
The leader should talk all there in the Circle through the sequence of events they are going to use.

One way is :-
Ask everyone to close their eyes. Say to the Circle :- "See that protection as a pure white light going clockwise all around the outside of the Circle". Repeat this a few times each time waiting a few moments then after the last repeat and after waiting a few minutes, then say, "See the pure white light also going around clockwise the inside of the Circle". Repeat this a few times each time waiting a few moments then after the last repeat and after waiting a few minutes, then say :- "The pure white light on the inside and the outside of the Circle is starting to build up and join up above everyone there, covering them, and then forming a cone of light from the middle of the Circle to join up to the Angels, and their purest highest love light of the Divine Spirit". {At this stage some Circles put on some very, very soft classical music or some very, very soft meditation music/chanting/drum beats/sounds, I personally found it distracting at first, but in other groups I have sat in I found the sounds actually enhanced the vibration levels within a Circle, this is why you should experiment with the sounds, try with, try without, try at the start, then try just in the middle of the sitting, then towards the end, and also try a meditation session just with different types of sound ten minutes of each on the one tape, [your group will find the sound best suited to it]} the leader Repeats this a few times each time waiting a few moments then after the last repeat and after waiting a few minutes, the leader lets the group of the Circle absorb the atmosphere and

talks to Spirit asking for the development of everyone in their own individual way to gain a stronger link with the World of Spirit.

The leader then asks the group after a few minutes to individually ask within their own minds for the development of whatever gift of a link they wish to gain from Spirit

Each person in their own mind, should be asking the Angels, the Helpers in Spirit for the sort of development they wish to have, also giving permission for Spirit to develop them in the field of work they would want them to do and keep on encouraging those good Angels of Spirit to come near, into their own individual auric field, and help with that development. Each person should then be trying to still the mind as much as possible to give Spirit all the help they can. Look into the light within their mind, the third eye. This is as they go into a meditation state, which will put them into an altered state of awareness ready for Spirit to do their work of developing the Budding Medium.

So it is; talk to Spirit, then still the mind by looking into the light within the mind [the third eye area].

Lots of different methods can be used. So read first, then plan, and then try.

The leader of the Circle should start by saying to all there, what they should do. Set the rules at the start; have them written down so you do not forget some of them. Especially if it is a new Circle or you have new sitters, if that is the case pick up your note and remind everyone of the rules and that way you do not forget anything.

In the very early stages of a Circle, at its start try this method, especially if it is a new Circle or the people are new to any Circle and cannot relax. This first part is to make each person aware of the different parts of the body then forget about them.

In a calm soft voice, the leader tells everyone to close their eyes, and very slowly goes through all the stages of relaxing all of their body, starting at the head going down to the feet.

Each person does this sequence at the start of a meditation if they cannot get relaxed.

The leader says this very, very, very, slowly so every person can feel each sequence of the relaxation. (This method can be used just for a stress management meditation and not just for development of Mediumship if needed)

"Relax your head, all the parts of your head." (Pause for a few moments.)
"Relax your scalp, feel your scalp being relaxed." (Pause for a few moments.)
"Relax all your muscles in your face, feel them all being relaxed." (Pause for a few moments.)
"Relax your jaw, feel your jaw being relaxed." (Pause for a few moments.)
"Relax your tongue, feel your tongue being relaxed." (Pause for a few moments.)
"Relax your mouth, feel all the parts in it being relaxed." (Pause for a few moments.)
"Go back and relax the parts you think might not be fully relaxed." (Pause for a few moments.)
"Relax your neck, feel your neck being relaxed." (Pause for a few moments.)
"Relax your neck, feel your neck being relaxed." (Pause for a few moments.)
"Relax your hands, feel your hands being relaxed." (Pause for a few moments.)
"Relax your shoulders, feel your shoulders being relaxed." (Pause for a few moments.)
"Relax your chest, feel your chest being relaxed." (Pause for a few moments.)
"Relax your stomach, feel your stomach being relaxed." (Pause for a few moments.)
"Relax your lower body, feel your lower body being relaxed." (Pause for a few moments.)
"Relax the skin of your body, feel all the skin of your body being relaxed." (Pause for a few moments.)
"Relax the top half of your legs, feel the top half of your legs being relaxed." (Pause for a few moments.)
"Relax the lower half of your legs, feel the lower half of your legs being relaxed." (Pause for a few moments.)
"Relax your feet, feel your feet being relaxed." (Pause for a few moments.)
"Rest in that peace and tranquillity for a moment." (Pause for a few moments.)

The leader then starts the power build up of the body, and then links it with those in higher realm.

The leader asks the group to imagine the power coming up from the ground in a beautiful, warm, light, brown, solid power in the form of light; it is the power of mother earth.

It is coming up through the feet, then slowly the leader in a soft voice goes through the chakras [that is if you use the chakra method, if not, just use pure white light through the sequences] telling people the sequence they want, so they can open up the chakras.

The power is coming up from the feet out of the warm brown of mother earth, the brown starts to fill the legs in the colour it is a wonderful warm brown, the brown goes up until it joins with the spine, it now becomes a red, it is a beautiful red, the likes of which you have not seen before, it is filling the **spine base centre with** red, see and feel it, it is a powerful light, it is making you feel so good about being given this power in this way, it is now, as you can see, and feel at the **spine chakra**, it is full of red light and over flowing up.

The red power is coming upwards and is going to the **navel centre,** it is now changing into such a beautiful orange light, as this orange power fills the navel centre this power is making you feel so good in yourself, you can feel it filling up, it is a beautiful feeling, it has now filled the **navel chakra** with the orange light, it is over flowing.

The orange power of light is going upwards towards the **spleen centre.**

The colour of the power has now slowly changed as it comes towards the **spleen centre**, it has now changed into a yellow, and is now filling up the **spleen chakra**, it is a colour of a powerful brightness, you can feel the brightness in the way of a subtle glow, it is making your body now feel different about being half full of this powerful sense of light. As your **spleen chakra** is filled up with yellow, no one could have told you about this feeling. You can feel it filling up and see it is now flowing over, and ever upwards to the **heart centre** where it is changing to a green.

You have seen greens in the fields as grass, the green leaves on the trees, and in plants. This green is not like that, it has a serenity about it, something you cannot describe, the beautiful green is filling the **heart chakra**, you hold that green colour in your mind, as you see the green filling your **heart chakra** up to the brim. This green in the heart chakra adds a different feeling to your body as it is filled and starts to over flow upwards to the **throat centre.**

You can see the magical, mystical change of the power into blue, it is not the blue of the sky or of the sea, it is the power of love as are all the other colours, you are feeling the loving power being drawn up into the **throat chakra** and slowly filling it up ready to be used when linking with the power of those in spirit, you can feel the power of this special blue overflowing upwards into the **brow centre** [third eye].

The special blue power is now turning into an indigo colour in the **third eye chakra;** it is not how you imagined. The blue is another very special powerful colour, from the power of those who look after you. By this colour, you know you are getting closer to those in the higher vibrational level who you love, and want to help. You can see and feel the very special indigo power filling up the third eye chakra, and overflowing upwards to the **crown centre,** where the power turns into a lilac or purple colour.

As the **crown chakra** is filling up, you now know you are close to the link with those in Spirit, it won't be long now, you can feel the wonderful vibrant purple going into **crown chakra** filling up and over flowing all over your body, the power that has built up is now changing into the power of bright light that is a constant flow ever upwards to meet the power above from those in the World of Spirit, it is changing once more into the pure bright white light of those in Spirit and Spirit have the light now to flow all around each person and in each person and it is flowing into the Circle. See it happening, feel it happening.

Every person there should be building up the power in the Circle, to see it, and feel it filling up the Circle with the light, it is coming from those Helpers in Spirit, asking all there in the Circle to expand the power [imagine the strength of the power or see it in your mind as a colour, or a strong white light] going outwards around the inside and the outside of the Circle, expanding the power outwards, every one should be expanding their aura [an aura is a person's power that surrounds everyone, some people when developed can see it's colours so telling what sort of health condition the person is in. This is done by thought] so it joins the person next to them [some people hold hands to join the power of the Circle in certain Circles this happened in the 1800's & 1900's Circles they got better results]. Experiment.

The leader asks gently, out loud for all to <u>**see**</u> through their third eye, (eyes closed of course,) and feel it all happening. (after a few minute of building up the power let go of the hands) Then each individual meditates, letting Spirit take each person individually along their own chosen pathway of development. This Circle should be practicing for about an hour at first, more later if required. When people come back out of meditation, they each in turn should say what occurred while they were in the altered state. What they were aware of, what they saw, felt, or heard, etc. each one should be told it is not a crime not to have anything, it will come when ready. When I started, I did not have anything for a great many months. The main thing is to be truthful.

Here are a few different sequences that you might like to use. There are many, make up your own. Go along with the story and then come back along the same route, this is to bring the people back to reality, out of meditation. They all should be said slowly, and pausing at the appropriate times so people can visualise the scene and get involved with it. All the sequences are done with the eyes closed, and only the leader talking, taking every person through the journeys of the mind, in the meditation (contemplation).

**REMEMBERING most importantly**, every time you sit for a link with the World of Spirit there must be **SINCERE prayers or SINCERE words** in the asking for what is require in the development of the individual or the group, this should be done over and over for many minutes to gain a link with the Spirit.

(1) See yourself crossing over a wooden stile, there is a path in front of you, it is an inviting sort of a path which you go along towards the noise of running water as you go along the long bending path. This path is leading you to the water you hear running along gurgling splashing in a gentle sort of way. The path is now at the side of a deep slow moving stream, you can see the fish swimming in the clear waters, they are gently flicking their tails as they swim against the flow of the stream as it flows past you. As you walk along the path you can feel the nice cool air under the overhanging trees where the dapple rays of sunlight are coming through the leaves. The water is starting to make a noise as you come up to a waterfall cascading the water off the mountainside. When you reach the waterfall there, you go into the back of the waterfall into a cave that is there, you look into the cave, and you can see through into the back of the cave, where there is an opening there, you look to see what you can in that opening. There is a an angelic person there waiting for you. This person is there ready to be asked questions of, and ready to give you answers in the way of help, you stay there, talking and listening to the wonderful person you have just met. Perhaps they want to take you on a journey of discovery. They might help you come to terms with something that has been troubling you. They might be helping you develop some gifts you have asked for. You are now in such a wonderful comfortable place everything else does not matter at this time. You know you are being well looked after by this person and always will be.

(2) To come back from meditation. The leader after a certain length of time; perhaps a half an hour to an hour; then starts to talk to the group and goes through the little story in reverse.

(3) It is time to come back now, in your mind you thank the person for being there and helping you in the things you needed, you bid them goodbye making arrangements to see them again, so you turn away from the opening in the cave, and walk towards the entrance under the waterfall. You come out of the cave from the back of the waterfall, and start walking down the gravel path beside the stream which seems to be flowing along with you in the sprinkling of sunlight that is coming through the trees above, the leaves, which are shading more of the sunlight seem to make the air cooler now it is definitely time to come back as you walk alongside the slow moving stream, it is as though the fish are looking up at you bidding you farewell as they swim alongside you, you see the stile in the distance away from the stream, you are walking towards it, when you reach the stile you turn and look back at the falling shadows knowing you will return at a later date after you come back to reality, you cross over the stile and come back to normality.

(4) The leader then gets every person to come out of meditation by saying their name, making sure at the end; each individual is back to their normal state of awareness.

(5) **OR** in your mind/third eye **see** yourself going along a winding pathway towards a house, as you go along the pathway you pass the rose beds along the way, here you stop for a short while to smell the roses. As you go through the garden along the path towards the house you hear a bird singing all alone in an apple tree. This bird is making you feel good to be alive it is singing to make you happy, you stop to look and listen to him, he is singing you a welcoming song. As you go further along the path, you reach the door of the house, which is open. You push the door open wide and walk into the hall, you go through another door into a room, in that room is a picture frame with just glass in it, it is a magical picture frame, it is going to show you things you want to know. You then walk across the room and go to the beautiful picture frame on the wall, and look into that magical picture frame seeing what is there within the picture.

(6) (It can be said here that there is an angelic person there waiting for them. This person is ready to be

asked questions of, and answers to be given in the way of help)
(7) To come back from meditation, the leader after a certain length of time; perhaps a half an hour to an hour; then starts to talk to the group and goes through the little story in reverse. The time is getting on now, you hear a clock chime, so you have to come back to the gate, so you turn away from the beautiful magical picture frame and walk across the room towards the door. You go through the door into the hall towards the front door of the house that has been so welcoming to you. You turn and close the front door after you so the house will be safe for you to return to at a later time. You are now in the garden walking towards the tree with the bird still singing in it the song that is all his own, his singing has changed, it is singing farewell to you, farewell until you come back again. You walk past the rose bed and take one last smell of the roses, pause and look back at the house knowing you will return again. You walk further down the path to the gate, as you come to the gate, you turn one last time and look back before walking through the gate back to reality. You go through the gate and close it behind you as you are now back to normality.
(8) The leader then gets every person to come out of meditation by saying their name, making sure at the end; each individual is back to their normal state of awareness.
(9) **OR** In your third eye **see** yourself going through an open space in a fence where there must have been a gate at one time. You walk through this gap in the fence over towards some sand-hills, the dry sand on your bare feet is hot in the sun, so you walk down towards the sea, you look to the sea and notice the tide is slowly going out. There you walk along the shoreline, the sand is wet and cool on your bare feet. As you walk further along you are watching the gentle wave action on the sand, there are many small fish in the rock pools and puddles that have been left by the receding sea, you notice the crab there scurrying along to a pool for safety. You look up into the distance there you can see a beach hut off away from the shore line it looks inviting to you, so you start to walk along the beach towards it. You cross over the rocks, which have been washed smooth by the action of the waves in winter. When you come to the hut, you see there the door has no lock on it, so you go into the hut where on the other side of the hut is an open window through that window is a remarkable view it is not a view of the sea or anywhere you could have imagined it, it is as though it is magic. You can see what ever you want to see through this window, with this in your mind; you look and start **seeing** what you can see through the window. (It can be said here that there is a person there waiting for them. This person is ready to be asked questions of, and answers to be given in the way of help).

To come back from meditation, the leader after a certain length of time; perhaps a half an hour to an hour; the leader then starts to talk to the group and goes through the little story in reverse.
The sun is starting to cool down, now it is time to go. So you turn away from the window and what you have been looking at, and bid it all farewell, thanking all who you have met. You turn towards the door and go through it. You can see there is a wateriness, a dullness in the sun; it is time to come back. You start to walk out across the smooth rocks towards the sea which is now coming back in towards the shore very slowly covering up the sand in a gentle sort of a way, you notice most of the rock pools are not there now they have been covered up by the incoming sea. It is time to hurry before you get cut off by the incoming tide. The sand on your feet is starting to feel cool, not how it was when you first started your journey. You start to go up over the sand hills, the sand on your feet is cool on your feet now, you turn and look back towards where you have been, knowing you will return at a later time. You walk back towards the gap in the fence and come through back to reality.
Then the leader gets every person to come out of meditation by saying their name, making sure at the end; each individual is back to their normal state of awareness.

In each instance after the meditation (contemplation) has been finished, each person in the group is asked individually about what they saw, while they were on the journey, they relate what images they saw. What they looked at? Who/what was there? What/how they felt about being there? What they were told, if anything? Did they meet anyone?
Throughout the time at intervals in the Circle from the start each person should have been asking within their minds help for development from their unseen angelic helpers, asking positively and sincerely.
Some people will at first keep going into and out of meditation. Do not worry, let them have a quiet drink so as not to disturb the others, if anyone coughs let them, and for that person to have a drink, do not try to

suppress the coughing **BUT** they should put their hand over their mouth or cough into a handkerchief, suppressing the cough can make it worse, then the person should go back into their meditation, as time goes by all there will achieve their goal. [Many a coughing session can be prevented by not having a cigarette, dairy products, any milky drinks, or chocolate things that make your throat cloggy for a few hours before the sitting in the Circle, drink only water if possible perhaps a banana to help with the sugar content for your body].

Then after an hour or longer, the leader will ask in a calm, soft, gentle voice, importantly not making any sharp noises, not touching or getting hold of anyone, the leader should say each person's name repeatedly and asking the others who are not back out of their altered state of awareness to let the conditions slowly go, for everyone in the group to come back into the room to everyone there, [only figuratively speaking, as no one there has left,] back to reality in the mind, some people come back into reality quicker than others so be patient, some will even want to stay in their new found serenity, you or the leader has to be in control. If a person stays in their meditating condition, repeat their name, keep on asking them gently to let the conditions go **DO NOT TOUCH THEM. Tell them letting go of the conditions is a discipline that has to be adhered to.**

When everyone has come back to reality, out of the meditation, the leader will ask the others in turn to relate to the group what they have seen, it is amazing what comes out, try writing it down each week, or record it. Do not try to make things up just to boost yourself, you are only kidding yourself no one else. If you do not see anything say so. **Be truthful** to Spirit, yourself and to the others there with you. Lies are negativity and negativity halts any progress/development.

If one person in the group is not getting anything for a number of weeks, try sending that individual off into meditation on their own, and the rest of the group to meditate for a few minutes to take in the power of those in the Spirit realm each individual asking Spirit to fill them up with the Power of Spirit and for them to come closer, (keep on asking over and over again within the mind), all there asking the higher realm for help and each individual then after those few minutes all open their eyes (except the single individual you are all helping to develop, the leader telling them when to come back), asking in the mind for the higher realm to send all the power they have individually just collected to that one person who is in need of help. Keep that up for about twenty minutes, let the leader bring the person back, then see what the person gets from those in Spirit. If at first you do not succeed; try, try and try again each week, for that one person.

After the group has gone around to each person in turn and finished what they want to say about what they felt and what they saw. Discuss it and say how you the leader felt while all there were in meditation.

**IMPORTANTLY** AFTER EACH SESSION, have every person close their eyes and the leader to say some **sincere words of thanks** to the Spirit World and ask for the power that has been built up in the room to be sent in the way of healing to the people who need it.

Try other exercises when you get together on different weeks. Go along a path to meet your guiding angel, perhaps at the waterfall, the beach, the picture, in a room, by a lake, by boat to an island, or somewhere nice. Sometimes ask the person you go to meet, perhaps it is your guide, an angel helper, for them to take each person individually to the halls of learning then afterwards each person individually relates what they saw and what they were told, write it down for future reference.

**Here is another exercise to do at different times.**

After the ¼ of an hour to an hour of a break, go back into meditation, letting the conditions return, [if you use the chakras, open up the chakras again], the leader will ask the group to look at the person next to them on their right hand side then close their eyes again and ask the higher life force, or the angels each person has now helping them. Each person has to **SINCERELY ask** in their mind for a message for that person next to them, and keep on **SINCERELY** asking over and over and over again, then later see what each person gets [at first after about ten minutes to ½ hour] when they feel they are ready [the time can be gradually reduced until the time becomes only a minute or two, as people become more attuned], coming back slowly, letting the conditions go when the leader says so in a quiet, soft voice. The leader then asks each and every person to relate what they got, even if they only imagine it, quite often people get nothing, but do not despair it comes with time with some people being quicker developers than others. Each person as they do this exercise should be asking the higher force of Spirit or the Angels in Spirit for help in the exercise. They should be talking to those in Spirit in their own mind as though they are talking to their friend, because that is what those in Spirit are going to become, their special friend. They should be **sincerely** asking them to come closer and help. Encouraging Spirit all the time to come closer.

**Another exercise.**
After the SINCERE prayers or affirmation. Remember the breath. Before any person goes into a relaxed state ready for meditation. The person should be saying a sincere prayer within their mind, then to concentrate on the breath. See the breath going into the nose, as it goes into the nose, the air is taking the ether as well into the nose where it is held at the root of the nose, the rest of the air is going into the lungs and feeding the body making it relaxed. Let the thoughts in the mind be good and send those good thoughts into the breath going into the nose, impress on the ether through thought what development you would like Spirit to help you with. On an outward breath send out through the nose any badness from your mind. Do this for a good few minutes. (At this stage if the leader feels the group needs to go deeper into an altered state of awareness for some trance development, the group then is asked to look into the Light within their own minds and become part of it).

The leader then asks the group to meditate to get close to those in Spirit [take the conditions back by asking Spirit to come closer and help in the task ahead, keep on encouraging Spirit to come closer, say it through **sincere thought** over and over and over again and again and again in your mind], then each person should open their eyes to look at the face of another person, any person in the group **not** the person next to them. They then close their eyes and ask the people in the higher realm through a thought in their head, ask for a message for that person, when the message is given the person should then ask, (again within their head) the higher realm of Spirit for the evidence of that message after a certain length of time say allow 5-10 minutes to start with, a shorter time span as people get better. Each person in turn gives the message to their own person they picked, and then at the end of the message the person should go back to Spirit and ask and give them a special piece of evidence that was given for that message. [E.g. perhaps your angelic Spirit Link/Helper might show or ask you to tell the person you are asking for, tell them about a lady (shown or told about) about 5ft 6in tall, grey hair, round face with a ruddy outdoor complexion, she looks about 56-ish. She was working at a sewing machine in a factory. Her name was Jane. The special piece of evidence at the end was given by Spirit in word form. This person still had a broach that the person in Spirit had left them].

In each message after seeing and/or hearing all this from Spirit, the person should always ask within their head for some special evidence for the recipient at the end of any message. Perhaps they will be given a picture in their mind of a watch or a broach (these were probably given to this person before they died, **but** do not add anything that you do not get from your Spirit Helpers) only just these details are then given to the person nothing else.

After practising for a while over a number of weeks, the group then does the same thing, but this time as each person gets the message and the special evidence at the end. They say the message and then give out what the special evidence was to the group as things come into the mind. [**REMEMBER** you always should ask in your own mind for the things you want and say whatever comes into your mind immediately without your own mind interfering] Later on write down what comes out, this is for the group's future reference. Some can see into the future, others the past of others, the fully developed both. Remember ask, but <u>**do not ever add** anything</u> that you do not get from your Spirit angelic helpers.

My helpers fix the thoughts and images in my mind on the left when it is the past. The front and the top of my head when it is the present, and the right hand side of my head placement of my thoughts and images within my head is the future. From the start, try to set your rules, which you are going to use during your partnership with your Spirit helpers.

**Another exercise**
Remember the breath. Before any person goes into a relaxed state ready for meditation. The person should be saying a **sincere prayer** within their mind, then to concentrate on the breath. See the breath going into the nose, as it goes into the nose, the air is taking the ether in as well into the nose where it is held at the root of the nose, the rest of the air is going into the lungs and feeding the body making it relaxed. Let the thoughts in the mind be good and send those good thoughts into the breath going into the nose, impress on the ether through thought what development you would like Spirit to help you with. On

an outward breath send out through the nose any badness from your mind. Do this for a good few minutes.

Each person has to close their eyes and say a few **sincere** words to Spirit asking for help within the task in hand. Everyone has to first pick out a single individual in the group and then for each person in the group in turn, to give that single individual what ever comes into their mind. This can be done with every person. It is another form of practice giving a message to the one person. Each person in the group, should be linking into the same message to the individual and expanding it in turn when the previous person has got stuck for words, always do it with the help of those in helpers in Spirit. If a person does not receive anything they can try next time. Never force anyone, BUT quite often when a person says they have not received anything they quite often do, so ask questions of them. A person who got nothing or so they think, might get a **feeling of something, a smell, an image, an object, a name, a place, a picture**, in their mind while another is talking giving the person their message, so encourage the person with nothing in their mind to open their thoughts. Then praise them for even the one single given event, name, or picture, because that way they will know they are developing and not being left out. Put a time limit on the message as some people can hog the exercise and make it their own. It is important to let everyone have a turn of giving and receiving a message.

When the Circle is finished, each person in their own mind thanks sincerely their angelic helpers then, one person [each person there should have a time when they do the opening and closing of a Circle as it binds the Circle as a matter of course] adds their own personal thanks out loud for the Circle and asks the people from the higher life to take away the conditions, and any power left to be sent out to those in need of it in the way of healing. Perhaps pick out and name individuals you know, who are in need of healing powers to be sent to, then give a few minutes for the power to be sent, then close completely. Each person there in the Circle, in their own mind, should be doing this as a matter of course. Ask for the Circle to be closed down and every person there present to be helped and protected from the evil out in the world at large.

**REMEMBER** conditions have to be built up over a great many weeks at the same time on the same day or days of the week. If a Circle can meet more than one day a week do so, remember more is best for the early expansion of development. If you can, try to meditate each day even if it is only five to ten minutes. Go somewhere quiet, I am sure every person in the land can always close themselves away somewhere in the house, even if they have a family, as I said before try say in the bathroom, take a cushion and sit for ten minutes at some stage in the day.

Please Remember; do not believe any person who says you are only allowed to sit in one circle at a time. Or you should not sit and meditate on your own. I have found, these messages are being given out generally because people are only trying to keep you from going to another Circle just in case you like it better and they lose you from their Circle, or to keep control of you. There can be a lot of jealousy in the development of some people, do not let yourself become one of these people. Stand beside the people who help you and those who are kind and generous with their affection and especially their time, and ask no reward. There was an 82 year old lady Gladys Owen, who started in Spiritualism at the age of 2 by giving out hymn books at the church, she was the president of the Liverpool church I attended for many years, she told me that she belonged to three Circles at the one time and was a very, very good kindly, strict, Medium with a great many strengths. Her father whilst in their Home Circle used to levitate whilst sitting in the chair and four people, with permission of their Helpers in Spirit, used to hang onto the four corners of the chair to try and bring him down from the ceiling. The longer and more frequently you sit for the development of the gift of linking with the Spirit Power the more competent you become. Also the people I have spoken to at Stansted sit in different Circles. So watch out for people who want to control. **Do things that you feel comfortable with. Experiment yourself.**

No matter what stage you are at in your development, remember you never stop developing, so never stop sitting in meditation.

# MEDIUMISTIC INSPIRATION

Perhaps this subject should not be called mediumistic because a lot of people can have inspiration without being what is termed mediumistic. But I would only counter that claim by saying the people who are inspired are more sensitive than most, being more sensitive to their own higher self, their own Spirit. Then if that is correct what are Sensitives called? They are called Mediums. What does an artist, an inventor, a writer, a sculptor, a poet, an orator, do? They most times before starting their work, meditate to gain inspiration. A lot of them would say, "I don't". But take a look at what they do, do. Most times before a project they will sit down, somewhere quiet, some close their eyes and think of one single thought. HOW? What is meditation? It is focused attention. That is exactly what they are doing, the start of mediumistic development. The artist, sculptor, inventor, writer, orator, poet, focuses their attention on the project in hand. They might be still, be in the quiet of their own little world to try and build up in their own mind, ideas, not knowing what is going on. Let us look at what is going on.

To my mind what they are doing is linking into their higher inner self, which is Spirit. Most will put out a thought of "I wonder how I can go about ***** ?" What is it said about thought? "It is the way to communicate with those in Spirit". Whether it is your own Spirit you are being in touch with or the higher life Spirit, remembering that we are one, part of the whole. Remember the atom or droplet of water going to the sea becoming part of the whole! So in effect the artist is linking with those in Spirit for their inspiration without really knowing it, asking in their own small way. Imagine what inspiration the artists would gain if they truly, fully linked in with the Spirit Helpers of the higher realm.

The linking in with those in Spirit for the artist's benefit should be done, by the tried and test way of meditation. Close the eyes, **ask** the higher life, the good angelic helpers in Spirit, to come close and **ask** for their help in the task ahead. Keep your eyes closed and try to let your mind go blank allowing Spirit to do their little bit to help. Then trust in them for their help. Quite often the artist will get ideas [messages] in their mind of how to do their task better. Often inventors solve their problems like this, by going into the quiet and mulling things over in their mind.

Have you ever gone to bed with a problem you wanted working out for the next day, and then started thinking of it for what seems like all of the night? What happens generally is you wake up with that problem solved? You have been inspired. You have expanded your normal thoughts to a higher level than normal becoming part of the whole, being in oneness with the higher vibrational force. Generally it is when you are in altered state of awareness, in a dream like state, half asleep. Yes you have done it yourself by looking into your own inner self, and let the higher self and a link, blend on a softer level, a quieter level, perhaps not a fully developed level. Imagine what you an artist, inventor or an ordinary person could achieve if your link was stronger, and was fully developed.

**An exercise** to try is. Each person is to have an A4 piece of paper (or A5) marked out into six sections. A selection of coloured pencils, or wax crayons, or chalks and boards to rest on. Perhaps sections of hardboard of A4 size for each person to rest the paper on.

In each section of six sections of the paper, draw some lines, any that that is take takes your fancy, any six different shapes. Could be a square, a circle, a diamond, a couple of snake type of squiggles mixed in with a couple of boxes, two triangles and squiggles, a couple of interlocking tent like structures, bottle shape, totem shape, anything abstract in fact. Duplicate them if you want to, [far easier] or make your own individual ones to give the entire group each time, then perhaps photo copy them for the next time.

These pieces of paper are given out to the group.

Place a mixture of coloured crayons, pens pencils or chalks in the middle of the group. If the group is too big place them into smaller groups.

All in the group have to colour the drawings in any way they wish at random in no set order, (see the drawing example on the coloured plates) the more they fill the picture in, the better the reading each individual will receive later.

As they are putting colour onto each individual randomly drawn markings within the squares, each person has to put on the paper a number **one to six** in each of the sections, in what order they coloured them in.

After the six sections with the randomly drawn markings in them have been coloured by each individual. Each individual puts a number or a letter on the back of the paper, which they will be able to recognise later on; importantly **NOT** their initials. The reason for this is the person's drawing might get recognised as being theirs and a knowledgeable reading from the person known could be given.

The papers are then collected by the leader of the group, and mixed up.

The papers are then to be given out to another person in the group. No person has to have their own paper that they coloured. If anyone receives their own back, it is to be swapped.

Each person then is told to start at the left hand corner square and write on the paper in each section, in the order given by the leader, (the leader has to keep to the same names for the same squares each time, going from left to right along the top first, then along the bottom, do not mix them up or cheat on this}. As follows:- in the top left square write **Self**; in the middle top square write **Family/home**; in the right top square write **Spirituality**; in the bottom left square write **Past/Background**; in the middle bottom square write **Present/Current**; in bottom right square write **Future/Pathway.**

Each person then has to give a blind reading to their best ability from the paper using the colours drawn, and the numbers they placed in each square and to the importance of each in the life of "the artist/drawer", the person who put the things on the paper, then sit down. No comments should be made until all there have done their readings. The paper is shown to the group, but they must not comment on it as yet or who's it is.

All there in the group, in turn has an opportunity to say if the reading was true or not so true for the person whose paper it was. Pointing out any truths or mistakes they would like to comment on. Each person in the group can help (if required) the person doing the reading if they get stuck, as this is a learning/practice exercise.

# SYMBOLISM

Spirit contacts can sometimes give you their thought messages in symbolic form. They can be black and white or in colour. Symbols come through from Spirit mainly in clairvoyance, but also sometimes through clairsentience. These you will have to learn to interpret for yourself. (If you go along this road) As you progress and learn alongside your angelic Spirit Contact, write the symbols down for next time or record the message and explanation as you give it so they can be gone over at a later date alongside their meanings to you and those in Spirit. Spirit has to know what symbols you can recognise and are able to pick out their meanings from their quickly given thought code, remember it is always a two way link of learning, Your angelic Spirit Helper is also learning alongside yourself learning what you can recognise and interpret in the correct way for them to get the message across to the people who need it. There have been many books on symbols written by many different authors, **all of them I have found to be different in their interpretation of the symbols.** If you use symbols, I think you or any person are going more along the PSYCHIC route NOT THE SPIRITUAL route. The book that you might choose might not suit me, and the book that I might choose might not suit you, AND MOST IMPORTANTLY the book you choose might not be the correct one for yourself and those in Spirit. So please pick your own carefully, but remembering the book that you choose is only a **ROUGH** guide of the meanings from Spirit, and **only COULD** be the meanings of the symbols being given by those helping you in Spirit. Each angelic Spirit thought contact is individual to each one of us, just as we ourselves are individual in our link with the Angels in Spirit. A Spirit contact is as individual as we are here on the earth plane. As you read the symbol interpretations look beyond the meanings and see how the author arrived at their meaning, use logic alongside your interpretation, then you will not go far wrong. You also will learn quicker that way, because that is what I feel those in Spirit are doing when they give symbols. They too use their logical way of thinking, knowing, you will [should] do the same, so help them out as well as yourself. But get to know "all" the meanings of the single words as soon as you can if you are going to work with symbols. Look at for instance at the word "horse". Every person generally knows what a horse looks like, but have you thought about the single word of horse? It conjures up more than you think of at first. One sort of horse is a Welsh wild horse (they used to be used in the pits, a pit pony), one a very large shire/cart horse pulling heavy wagons **there are many different types of these** as well, they were all used for many jobs in different industries, and for use in different types of jobs on different types of farms. Another one is a very small Shetland pony for children to ride, a pony for the teenager, a larger horse for the adult, a large horse for the cavalry. There are horses that do racing, one type for over jumps, another breed for racing on the flat, one a white horse from southern Spain that does dancing and is shown off in a ring doing displays, as do the circus horses. There are wild American Indian horses, also many types of ponies and mules, and then there are the Asses and donkeys in their many different breeds, which carry loads for their masters. This is just a very small list of the horses that there are in the world and the things they are used for. Look at the word "bird" and all the different birds there are, ones that are beautiful, richly adorned with bright colourful feathers, ones that are drab, in plain feathers. There are ones that hunt fish, ones that hunt others birds, ones that swim, ones that cannot fly, ones that live in the jungles, ones that live in the desert, ones that live in the tropics, ones that live in the polar regions, As you can see symbolism can be a complicated subject. I think it is far better to use the simple, easy things direct from Spirit rather than make it too complicated, BUT on saying that a lot of the top Mediums are now using this method. **ARE THEY ONLY USING THEIR PSYCHIC ABILITIES and NOT USING THEIR SPIRITUAL LINK FULLY?**

Are those Mediums being lazy by not getting themselves to work with Spirit that little bit better? Are they NOT meditating that little bit longer to get the link with their Spirit helpers stronger?

Do those Mediums who use symbols let their own mind, their own thoughts, come into the equation? Of course they do. Every person should only give out what they get from Spirit not make up stories.

Go to see how all Mediums work and analyse their ways. Look and listen closely and you will be able to see how they work. AND BE SURPRISED how many Mediums (so called; only give evidence Psychically).

Read as much about the everyday things and what people have done with their lives, go to the history books to see what information you can get out of them. Your Spirit Helper will generally use the information you have in your brain storage system to show you what they mean, so expand on the information what you have in your brain so you can have a better, more varied information store. The more you practice and read up on all the subjects you know about, the easier it becomes, then it will be like second nature for you to interpret. You have to practice, practice, practice. Have a reading book beside your bed to read for about ten to fifteen minutes before you drop off to sleep. Each night before you go to sleep give permission to your angelic link in Spirit to use you as an open vessel, as I do each night, ask the Spirit helper to help you progress in your development as you sleep bringing only goodness, kindness, happiness, love, and truth, and to blend in peaceful Divine Light within the loving harmony of those in Spirit from the highest realms and for you to have a good restful sleep waking up fully refreshed.

When you get the symbols given by Spirit look how they are all given. I have had the symbols [I say symbols, these were factual pieces of evidence from Spirit and I gave them as such with no extra embellishment to the recipient, so they were not symbols as such] given subjectively at the same height as my eyes, then at other times as though they have been given at my knee level. Then the next time during the sitting they have been given above, so make sure you clock and register in your mind for a later date, how they come as well as what they are, and what they have meant. They might come from left to right, or right to left. Stay at the right, or stay at the left. Some are given as a single symbol others are given within a group picture. Watch for these subtleties. If you are not too sure ask the enquirer they are only too willing to help, they generally think it is all part of their reading. Also remember to always ask your Spirit Helper for clarification. Keep going back to your Spirit Link in your mind SINCERELY ask, ask, ask, ask. Keep talking to them in your mind.

I will finish off by telling you about what the older Mediums have been telling me about using the symbolic methods of working with Spirit [most say it is a very low level of linking]. A psychic reading not a spiritual.

""It can become a minefield way of getting messages and working with those in Spirit because it can be a double edged sword. Easy to start yet hard to truly master with a true Spirit Link without the Medium's mind, their own thought coming into the equation, and then even harder still to get out of the habit of using the method of symbolism with messages. A lot of "Mediums"(I use that word loosely as most of them are not in my opinion), get what they think is a message from Spirit in the form of a symbol yet it is only their imagination. Making up a story from that single symbol so missing the true message from Spirit.""

One person who does readings said she gets symbols for her numbers. But at times it can become confusing, as sometimes she does not know whether it is the symbol itself or the number or the colour she should be giving. So she ends up giving the lot to the recipient of the message in a story she thinks the World of Spirit wants her to give. This person at least was honest when she was speaking to me about her link. I advised her to go back to basics and start meditating again SINCERELY talking to the World of Spirit about the gift she wanted to be helped with.

The numbers for her were given in colours and symbols, the numbers one to ten and the number 0. 0 was given as a round coloured orange. BUT it could be the fruit orange or the colour orange to be given to the person or the vitamins from eating the orange. The same as the number six which was given as yellow the same yellow as a banana, and/or at times as a banana. Again as a confused message. Was this her imagination or was her link so weak that all she could get from Spirit was symbols. This is why it is most important to gain a good link with Spirit from the start then you will get GOOD information from that GOOD Spirit link.

One way it can work and **can possibly** make the single image far more interesting to the enquirer and to the audience which might be good story made up at the time, **But** the Medium might have missed the point that Spirit was trying to make for the recipient, as the Medium can spin a reading out a lot more, not relying on Spirit for as much information as those in the higher plane could give. BUT is it coming from the Mediums mind alone and NOT from Spirit? Think about that and DON'T KID YOURSELF. A lot of people who think they work with those kind helpers in Spirit, do not have a link with Spirit at all, they only work psychically.

Working with symbols also has the disadvantage of making a Medium lazy in their working with a possible GOOD LINK if worked on over time with those angelic helpers in the Spirit World, those Spirit Helpers want to help and do good for us here on the earth plane. Yes it might take longer BUT IT IS WORTH IT IN THE LONG RUN.

It also gets the Spirit who links with the Medium to only get used to giving the Medium symbols, and so restricting the Medium's development, and they are ending up not asking for far more than they are getting at the present. Each Medium should be striving to improve their own link each day and every day in each personal reading, and each platform reading. Make yourself work, BUT, also make your helper who is the Spirit link work up to a far better standard, raise your standards to the highest levels. Yes you have the right to ask for that. It might take a bit longer but it will be well worth it.

Symbolism also has the disadvantage of possibly bringing into play the Medium's own mind into the reading more than any other form of linking with Spirit, so **colouring the message from Spirit** to a message of the Medium's thoughts, **their imagination comes into play** and so the message is **not the full true meaning from Spirit**, they only think it is"". SO PLEASE BE CAREFUL if you use this method. PLEASE **BE TRUE** TO **YOURSELF AND SPIRIT**. A Medium can be conning themselves and the public.

**ARE YOU GOING TO BE ONE LIKE THAT?**

In the long run it has to be said, it is best not to go down this route of getting interpretations of symbols from books in the first place, it is only **another person's personal opinion** of a meaning, and it is up to you and Spirit to work out your own interpretations.

**Learn alongside/with your own Spirit Link. Trust in them always when you have a good link.**

**REMEMBER** it should only be a two-way thought conversation between the Medium and the Spirit Contact **without** the thoughts of the Medium coming into the equation. The Medium should only be giving what Spirit gives to the Medium for the enquirer. **Not** anything they the Medium **"think"** their Spirit link means. I think by buying this book you are now reading you do not want to be a fortune teller, but be a person who proves there is life after our so called death through Spirit Helper link contact. Please go about it correctly.

# OVERSHADOWING

This is when a person has a Spirit Form which is often seen clairvoyantly by others in the group being replaced or shadowed over the body, and/or face of the Medium, (but that is possibly more of transfiguration), but over shadowing is more like a Spirit form coming into the auric field of the Medium. It can quite often be felt by the Medium in question. This can be Spirit being seen only clairvoyantly, this is when every person in the group does not always see the Spirit Form. This quite often can be seen in the early stages when a person is in the cabinet within a Circle, the lights on, (or in red light), the curtains open and power is being sent mentally by others of the Circle to the person sitting in the cabinet. As a person/Medium progresses, the overshadowing can be seen by many when the Medium is on the platform in church or in a Circle when the Medium is working, this could be their Helper, Guide, or Guardian Angel being shown to the clairvoyant, or could be the person who is linking with the Medium for someone in the congregation. Remembering those seen can also be a few not just one Helper, Guide, Angel coming through, then as more people come through, the face/body overshadowing changes for the clairvoyantly gifted Mediums to see.

Some Mediums take on the feeling of the person coming through from the other side. They feel the Spirit and their complaint [more in the realms of clairsentience] they also can be overshadowed to such an extent that they feel they are the person in the Spirit World; this is generally when they themselves are not in full control of their own link in Spirit. This it should be said here, any Medium when doing a reading for any person and/or they have finished working, and their helper wants again to comes into their auric field wanting to work, that person must have the strength of character to say "I am the one here on earth working, take this strong feeling away it is not very nice for me, but thank you for showing it to me, please do not give me the message like this so strong next time." Spirit when they come close to the Medium can bring to them all sorts of symptoms of the person who has passed into the higher realms. It is the way some links in Spirit work with their Mediums.

## PRECOGNITION

Precognition is classed as "previous knowledge" in the dictionary. In the psychic field, it is when a person has the foresight of events that will happen in the future, forthcoming events, good, bad, or any sort of ordinary everyday events. It would seem the most publicised events that are foreseen by people are of ones that stand out in the media. They make good publicity for the media itself. Don't think that this is always the case of someone having foresight. A lot of ordinary people have what I would call daydreams, an altered state of consciousness. In this state they can be having a clairvoyant type of experience that shows them the event/events that are about to happen in the future. How many times have you walked into a place, somewhere you have never been before and thought this looks familiar, I have been here before, or you have been doing something, and you have thought I have done this before. This **could** be your "precognition" coming into play; something you have foreseen in your mind but it has not been registered properly in your brain as a memory. It has only been brought to the fore because you have re-run it. If at the time you had written the daydream down you could have referred to the incident.

What I suggest is, if you ever have these things happen to you. When you have these incidents/events put into your mind, immediately after, it is most important for you to write your daydreams down **twice**, place one copy in a sealed envelope post it to yourself so that there is a date stamp on one. Mark the both envelopes the same to distinguish them from any others. Keep the other copy for yourself to look at as a reference to the incident/event that might happen in the future. Mark the both envelopes the same to distinguish them from any others. I have called the happenings daydreams yet there are people who have the event/incidents foretold in their mind at night. It would seem to be the case of these things happening when the mind is still.

We now come back to the way most Mediums work with their mediumship. It is through a "still mind" or "a less than fully active mind", lets call it "a quieter than normal mind". When this quietening of the mind occurs, those helpers in Spirit can then do their work of communication with their human Medium link on the earth plane. If this was controlled, the Medium should **in theory** be able to with practice, to link with Spirit and ask for the forthcoming events to be shown to them. If it is the will of Spirit those events/incidents should be able to be put into the Medium's mind to forewarn the people of happenings in the future.

Some Mediums actually do this already on the platform even if it is frowned upon by the churches. Yes they give out messages for the future. Will you watch out for this? Will you hold what I have said and when it happens come back and tell me, because this is what I am being told? How many times have we heard those statements? So ask and perhaps you will receive.

# SEERS

These people are classed in the dictionaries as prophets, divinely inspired persons, gifted ones who look into the future, foretelling of people's destiny.

Throughout the centuries there have been many seers as it is put, we now call them Mediums in our modern language. You only have to look in the Christian bible and the Old Testament [which is mainly the teachings of the Jewish religion] for evidence of happenings foretold by the seers of the time. Many spoke to God and Angels [Spirits] in their own way and gave out to the people the messages they received. Those people/Mediums were not condemned by the church at the time, neither are they today by the church, they are revered. Yet Mediums of our time are condemned by the Christian church. What is a "Medium"? A Medium is classed as a link that is in the middle of the ordinary person and God or the people who have gone before, and the people they give off information to. Christ materialised three days after his death this was through the Medium there at the time and this is held in high regard by the Christian church. Yet when Mediums now bring forth a materialised form they are condemned being told it is evil because the high up in the churches want to control the masses. These instances are the ones that stand out. LOOK and you will find a great many more, there also books written on this subject. Remember also the forecast of the plagues, famines, etc. The healing powers of the Mediums, the inspired speaking, speaking in different languages that the person did not know or understand whilst in an ordinary earthly state.

There were many seers in ancient Egypt as the historians through deciphering the hieroglyphics are showing it.

The modern seers, I say modern only because they are documented from the 14th century at the very time the people lived. Not written 345 years later as the happenings in the New Testament were. The Christians in the city of Alexandria destroyed most of the important information that was contained in the history books of the time. That city had the most important history library of the time bigger than anything we have in modern times. It was destroyed because of the Christian church wanting to put out only the information that they wished to pass on to their followers a blinkered belief, one of no other path to follow if you so desired.

A lot of the people in high places in England of the time went to seers for advice. Quite often they mixed astrology with their craft. You as an astrologer might dispute this but I will put it to you there are new planets now in your charts that have been added by man again in his advancement in his craft and so it will be in any forecasting of the future if used in this way. The only true way is through those in the Spirit World, yes you can use props, and prompts if that is the way you work, but the information has to come from somewhere and that somewhere is from within the Spirit of you, which is part of the whole, a part of Spirit. So it comes from the link with Spirit unseen, please learn to connect properly in your search for the truth.

The seer Mother Shipton, [Ursula Southeil] born in 1488, an unfortunate deformed lady, who was classed by many in different ways, by many in the past as a gypsy, an old hag, a sorceress, a prophetess, a sibyl, a fortune-teller, **but** she was held in high regard by all who met her.

Mother Shipton was a kindly lady who had inherited her gifts from her mother, so the locals in Yorkshire, England said at the time. She lived in Knaresborough, which is on the river Nidd, Yorkshire England. The poor lady was orphaned early in her life as her mother died soon after giving her life, and she was brought up in the early days by the convent her mother died in. When she left the orphanage she had to resort to begging to survive. Her clairvoyance was given to her in symbolic form, predicting many things throughout her life. Mother Shipton was brought to trial on numerous occasions but was always acquitted. Amongst the many things she forecast to happen were falling apart of the monasteries, and the building of iron bridges over the rivers, the tunnels under them, and iron ships floating, never believed of in her time. She died in 1561 when she was seventy-three. She had even predicted her death to the very hour and day a great many years before. She was so well thought of and remembered with affection, that the people of Yorkshire have placed a stone in her memory at Clifton, near the City of York. There are the Mother Shipton caves that turn things to stone, which are still an attraction to this day. There are different things hanging up from the cave walls covered in stone, things like old hats, shoes, etc.

I suppose the most famous of the seers that people know was Nostradamus. He was a Frenchman who was born on the 14th of December in 1503 into a converted Christian catholic family. The boy "Michel de Nostredame" at an early age was educated by his Jewish grandparents, mainly taught by both of his Jewish grandfathers. They taught him their own language of Hebrew alongside astrology. At school he learned philosophy, then progressed into medicine at University of Montpellier. He helped at the start of the plague in France, and was more successful than most in the curing of the sick because of him not purging the sick [bleeding the sick], as was the custom. Nostradamus was an avid reader seeking the truth about the occult of the time, magic, herbalism, and he was always experimenting with the chemical makeup of mixtures and of remedies, which was called alchemy. He was appointed as the physician to Charles 1V in 1560.

Nostradamus had his first prediction pamphlet published in 1555 called "Centuries" it was last published 1558. The almanac was written in verse called rhyming quatrains [four lined verses], this was to protect him from being hounded by the church run establishment, and to stop him being classed as a witch. From that date onwards he had them produced each year for the following years. They sold like hot cakes as people found out that his predictions were coming true, later he started to write down predictions for the far distant future, in fact up until the year 7000 so he had his prophesies published in ten booklets each one containing a hundred prophesies. All his books are written in verses of four lines with no dates for the predictions. So now it has been left to scholars to try and work them out. With some of the quatrains there have been a mixed meaning from the scholars, each scholar interpreting them differently because they can be obscure and open to many interpretations, but in the main they agree on the vast majority of them [so they say]. You would all like to know that not all the predictions have come true. But uncannily most have been true and accurate to the extent he allegedly gave names and dates. It is said he forecast the plague in Europe, the great fire of London, and the Second World War with Hitler's name given but one letter different he said "Hister". He actually forecast his own death in 1566. He instructed an engraver to place in his coffin a plaque unknown to others with a date on it. The coffin of Nostradamus was moved 134 years later and the people who moved it looked inside to see if there was a body still there and they found the plaque that was placed on his body with the date of 1700 on it. I could go on with the things he has predicted but I would need another few books. I also would advise anyone looking for his predictions to go and read the **original text** to find things out, as there are so many unanswered questions about the true meaning of his verses. The meanings have been distorted over the centuries by people **who have not** the knowledge of **THE "OLD FRENCH" language**. The meaning of the true text about Hitler is originally said to mean the now River Rhine as being the old meaning of the word Hister, the original "**Old French**" name of the river Rhine. **NOT Hitler**. I would ask you to read up on him from the start if you are interested. Go for instance to the Internet and see how many different meanings of one verse you can find, it might put you off his predictions forever. This is always the trouble with symbolism reading, coded verses and their interpretations and trying to make some sense of them after the person is on the other vibrational level, our so called death across the veil. Yes he was a seer in his own time, of that many are convinced through his "CENTURY ALMANACS" BUT what should be taken into consideration the man was talking in riddles for the sake of fooling the authorities; if he fooled them when he was alive, he can fool the general public now. Find out for yourself and read up, as I would ask you to read up on the other seers.

John Dee can also be checked up on in the history books of the 16th century at the time of Queen Elizabeth 1st. He was a man who eventually, after being put under house arrest and a session in prison, was the Queen's confidant, and personal astrologer and yet a person who was said to go into a Trance like state and talk to the Angels. But because of his favouritism the Queen allowed him to continue with his practice. He was thought by many foreigners and those on the British shores to be not all there in his head; and so because of this, his intelligence and knowledge of diplomatic matters, he mixed in the diplomatic circles as a spy of the time all around Europe. He was so intelligent he was an undergraduate at Cambridge when only fifteen. At nineteen he was a fellow at Trinity College where he was said to be experimenting with the occult. He was widely travelled through his studies lecturing on mathematics and astrology. An Abbot Trithemius introduce John Dee to "Angelic Magic" as it was called then, though in the manuscripts it was called "Seganographia". Yes a Christian churchman wrote about it even then. During his time around Europe he met and worked with different Mediums. John predicted the Spanish Armada, and the execution of the Mary Queen of Scots. He died in 1608.

**Sadly the people in the media (on TV) as usual, have made a not so FULL factual story of his life only dwelling on his quest to make gold in Russia through the old form of chemistry, alchemy.**

# EXTRASENSORY PERCEPTION
# ESP

This is a subject that has been used by the establishment and the people in the many moneymaking religions of the world, to get away from the words like Mediumship and all it entails. ESP is put down as the acquiring of information that is not normally accessed by normal means. E.g. spoken, written, media, etc. The Dictionaries class it as only as meaning clairvoyance, telepathy, and precognition. Mind reading. Receiving information over a distance through thought. But to my mind it should be looked at as being an all encompassing word to cover the many forms of mediumship as a whole and include clairvoyance, clairaudience, clairsentience, clairknowing, psychometry, crystal ball reading, the reading of hands, feet, head, colours, auras, cards, tealeaves, coffee grounds, beer froth, sand, flames, clouds, objects, etc. and many more

The opening up of a person and the development/practice of ESP and telepathy can be done by the methods of using cards.

**Exercise.**
This can be done with a full pack of ordinary playing cards, when a person ["A"] holds the card up in their hand with the back of the card facing towards the other person ["B"]. "B" then concentrates on the thoughts "A" is sending out. "B" then has to put down the card's colour, at first, but later on as they advance. "B" can also put down the suit, and/or picture of the card in question, but start simple, and then progress further.
Or person "A" draws a picture, then "B" has to try and draw the same picture. With these methods it is best to again start simple then progress to harder things. Perhaps start with four or five simple pictures. A square, a circle, cross, wavy lines, and triangle.
Or perhaps just try to guess the colours of any simple pack of cards. Black or red. Many people can get remarkable results with practice; we all have this ability to a greater or lesser degree. Remember to write down your score so you can see how you progress.
There are many ways you can improve. First ask for Spirits' help. When the phone rings you can try to guess who is on the other end of the phone before picking it up. Try to also think of the next person to come through a door of your choice, start simple say adult or child, male or female, perhaps a man or woman. Or what make of car is going to come around the corner next; this can be done easily as you wait for the bus. How long is the bus going to be? What time is it going to arrive? Etc. Use simple everyday things to enhance your psyche.

A way of practicing and improving a person's sensitivity is to have a group of people working with a range of coloured cloth; these can be plain or mixed [best with mostly plain, can be done with coloured "felt squares" also].
Have a group of people [say three or four] sit in chairs facing away from the box of coloured off cuts of cloth. Have the sitters close their eyes, or blind fold them, if they look they are only cheating themselves, at the same time the sitters should be asking for the help of Spirit in this exercise bringing them near by talking to Spirit in their thoughts.
Pick one person to choose one length of cloth and quietly place it on the shoulder or around the shoulders of each person sitting facing away from the box, the sitter still not opening their eyes. The colour of the cloth can be the same for each or different [best is a good mix].
The sitters are asked to bring Spirit near to them and to ask within their minds through thought for help in distinguishing the colour [they can be shown by Spirit the colour in their mind]. Allow a little bit of time, a minute or so. The sitters in turn have to say how they feel about the cloth that has been placed on/around their shoulder and the colour they think it is.
When everyone has finished, each person is asked if they wish to change their minds about the colour or if they have a different feeling about the cloth now they have had a bit more time. They are then asked to

open their eyes or remove the blindfold to see the colour of the cloth. There are no points for correct answers; it is purely an exercise for sensitivity and linking with Spirit. It will be found that with practice correct results will come when the link with Spirit gets stronger.

# TELEPATHY

Here is a word that encompasses a lot yet it is misunderstood. It is said by some dictionaries to include meanings that are similar those of ESP. Telepathy is the linking, or communication of minds. The sending of thoughts, maybe ideas from one person to another/others. I say others because it does not need to be one to one. It can be one to the many minds of many people. This is done without the use of the other senses that us humans are only normally supposed to have. But it should be looked at further, because it is or should be classed as a two way street, receiving and sending out thoughts to/from another source/person. I say source because it could be said that the two way contact of Mediums could be classed as using telepathy. The Medium's mind [and for that matter the person using telepathy] is attuned to the signals/vibrations given out by the thought link be it a human or Spirit. What must be remembered all of us humans are Spirit, all life is Spirit, all part of the whole of Spirit. Mental telepathy is thought-transference between people [whether they are on the earth plane or in Spirit]. Or when using links on earth, could it be the link is a three-way link? The person sending the thoughts out, those thoughts being picked up and sent out by Spirit, then the thoughts being received by the subject from Spirit. Remembering that we are all as one Spirit, part of the whole. That is something to think about isn't it?
There are many exercises that can be done with this subject make up your own, perhaps the sending of messages of a single words, a sentence, a story, a drawn object, or letter after writing it down so it cannot be changed by the sender. Have the things placed inside an enclosed envelop or box of some kind.

# PSYCHOMETRY

Psychometry is a where a Medium/sensitive can pick up the radiated vibrations or sense the surroundings of an object they hold. Saying what has happened to it and all about the person who owned it, who it belonged to and the happenings that it might have been involved with throughout its life of existence. Or it could be the vibrations of a building when they walk into it, saying what has gone on within the walls of the place, or, correctly work out, sense or be acutely aware of a person's character on the first meeting. But it is mainly "an inanimate object" that is read.
Some Mediums have the ability to turn on, switch on, or tune into the radiated vibrations that are given out by another person's personal gifts whether they have the ability to see clairvoyantly, or sense clairsentiently. There have been a number of theories of how this is done but I will keep out of the how and just say it is a fascinating way of practising your skills. I believe it is in the main the vibrations that are picked up from the "objects".

To build up or to practice this skill, **as with all the Mediumship skills**, you should first say a few words to Spirit in your own mind asking for their help bringing in a harmonious link with them in your task ahead, being positive, and sincere. Meditate to bring up the link stronger between yourself and Spirit, ask in your mind for only goodness, kindness, happiness, love, truth, to bring it in from within the Divine Light and within the peaceful loving harmony from the highest realms of Spirit.
There are a number of ways to explore this form of mediumship.
To exercise your mind and to improve your awareness, it is necessary to have at least one friend with you. For the person with you to have an object that you have no knowledge of. It is best to have an object that they or some other person has handled/worn daily. In the early days of this exercise do not let any other person handle the object at all. Then you as the Trainee Medium should proceed to tell your friend all about the object and what you can feel about the vibrations that trigger thoughts in your head, as you can see. The friend should know all about the object and all about the person who owns it. You will find the more you do this form of mediumship the more accurate you become about the information given. As you progress you should be able to give all the information that surrounds the object and those of the owner. The important happenings that have happened around the object and the events that the owner has been involved with in their life, what has gone on whilst they owned the object.
If your friend collects the object have the owner place the object in a bag so the carrier friend does not

handle the object at all. You then can take the object straight from the bag, or your carrier friend can pour the object out of the bag onto a tray, not handling it at all.

Remember to ask those helpers in Spirit for their help before starting the task in hand (any task at all). Also try and feel for yourself the vibrational link from the object. The more you practice the easier it will become, close your eyes, ask for help in linking, and then start letting the thoughts flow into your mind, giving them off to your friend what thoughts come into it, do not analyse any thoughts. The more relaxed you are, the easier the thoughts come into your mind. By the way most people do not physically feel the vibrations only picking up information in their mind to give out to the recipient.

# PSYCHIC AWARENESS

Where does psychic and spiritual awareness start and begin. Where does working alone with your own Spirit (your own heightened awareness within self) and working with the link with Spirit across the veil start and begin. No one knows. Yes we all have our own ideas about it but who can say where and when one starts or the other begins. This is the reason I am giving you as much information in the book to develop AN AWARENESS OF **"SPIRIT"**, whether it is your own, or being aware of those in Spirit across the veil. Please remember we are all Spirit, all part of Spirit, all part of the whole.

Exercises to help you become more psychically aware can be done in the comfort of your home, but it is best within a group situation so each person can help the others in things missed. The idea is for you to become more aware of your own surroundings and the ordinary things that you deal with in your own life, for you to take more notice, to care more, to have more sensitivity, to become closer to the pure light of your own Spirit, which is part of the whole of Spirit in the highest angelic realm and all that it has to offer.

If you heighten your senses, you become more aware of them, as a natural progression within yourself. This is the beginning of the opening up and the seeing of the true self within. Your true sensitive Spirit. Becoming closer to your Spirit of God, The Divine Spirit, knowing you are part of God, part of the whole.

First you must heighten ALL the senses that you have. If some are missing because of your disability, do not worry just use the ones you naturally have now. Explore them in any order. But each time something is pointed out pause a moment and look at it, listen to it, smell it, taste it, feel it, and be aware of it.

The more things you practice with, the better you will become.

You carefully and minutely look at things. You are to hear with sensitivity trying both ears not just one. To taste in your mouth, keeping what ever it is in your mouth very much longer than you would normally, also taste the different, subtle smells, that are coming into your nostrils, to smell the delicate odours, smell the powerful ones, notice the differences how they effect you inside your nostrils and possibly the taste in your mouth from that smell. Feel every object, everything you touch, slowly touching them with every fibre of your fingers, feel all the cracks, all the bumps and dips, are they smooth or harsh etc. Touch all different things with your bare feet and to be aware of the differences in all them, put them all in your special lists within your mind. Please try and keep these small exercises going within your life each and every day and do not take things for granted, I am sure you will find life a lot more fulfilling for yourself. You will in this way become more aware and a lot more sensitive within yourself and in your surroundings. It will help you care and be more concerned about the whole world at large and everything in it. **You will surprise yourself. This is and exercise that can be done in a group situation for fine-tuning the senses.**

### Seeing :-

Do all the exercises eyes **open first**, [seeing objectively] look at an object/subject; then eyes close to see the object/subject being looked at with closed eyes within your third eye [seeing subjectively]. Each time noticing the subtle difference, doing the exercise slowly and deliberately.

Look at the things around you. Pick one thing out and study it carefully pointing out to yourself or another person there with you, the different little things you would not ordinarily notice as you pass it by each day. See and be aware of the shape and form. How tall it is against the other things that are near. Look and see the material and how it is made to function, how it is now. How is it different from the other things around you? Look and see the colour. Compare it to the other colours near, does it blend does it clash, does it soften, does it stand out, or does it go into the background. Look for any imperfections. Look for the good points; notice the perfect points that you can see. Look for any unusual markings. Look for any mixing of the colours, see if any blend, look at the colours that are not blending and point them out to the others to help them be more aware, help each other in these exercises be part of the group. Remember to be part of the whole for the benefit of the group in every situation; it will help you for later times. Try these exercises with pottery, plants, food, manmade things of every description, pictures in glossy magazines, living animals, insects, pets, etc. etc. etc.

E.G. Each person in the group in turn holds a piece of pottery, they should say one point about the piece of pottery in turn to enlighten the others how they feel about their experience with that piece of pottery. How they see it, how they feel about it, what use it could be put, what good points about it, what is standing out about it, what imperfections there are with it, etc. And keep on going around until the group runs out of pointers. This is the bringing together of the group, the sharing their experiences together. It is to bring each other closer, to share feelings, to share what each other sees in other things; of how each person picks out the wonderful individuality of the things that are around each person in their every day lives.

### Hearing :-

Start **first with eyes open** then eyes closed. Each time noticing the subtle difference.

Listen to all the sounds that are around you, some are near some are further away. Concentrate on the sounds nearest that you can hear. Can you hear the heart beat of yourself concentrate on that for a while think how it is pumping the blood around your body feeding the muscles, cleaning the rubbish away into the liver and the kidneys, how the blood is being protective for you killing all the bacteria and viruses from all the illnesses you could be stuck down with. Listen to your breathing concentrate on your breath and how that is going into your lungs feeding your blood with oxygen, to the heart then out into your body. Listen to the people around you breathing, listen intently. Then try with the person next to you listen to their heart. Get a tube, or a rolled up piece of paper made into a tube, to listen with that. Concentrate on it and think what it is doing within that body. Listen to the noise which is furthest away from you, point it out to the others so they can be listening for it, see if they can hear something that is more of a distance away, see who can find the one at the furthest point. It could be an aeroplane, a train, the breeze in the air, the waves in the sea, a distant clap of thunder. Then come back to the second nearest sound, perhaps the person near breathing, then go to the next to furthest noise you can hear. Then come back to the next to nearest after the breathing, if there is none have someone make one, use your imagination. Perhaps someone tapping out a tune on their seat. Dwell on that sound think of how it is made, how it is sounding different to the other noises. Each time go far away then come back near, going from one sound to the other, each one being different in its resonance. Hear the differences and make a mental note of them to make yourself aware of the whole of that individual difference. Do not go to the same sound twice. Each person in the group should say one point in turn to enlighten the others how they feel about their experience. And keep on going around until the group runs out of pointers.

### Smell :-

With this exercise **start with the eyes closed** then repeat with the eyes open.

Here you can do this exercise in many imaginative ways. These exercises should really be done at the backs of the people taking part, so they cannot see what is going on. I would recommend having an adjustable speed fan so any scent of a smell left in the air can be blown away, but you can use the mixtures to your advantage if a fan is not used. Strike a sulphur match and carefully waft the scent over to the persons with you. Neither the leader of the group nor does the group say anything until the leader sees that all there have picked up and registered the smell in their mind. Light a candle; waft the smell towards every one. They are then in turn asked to describe the smell. The group then opens their eyes and the exercise is repeated and the differences noted out loud each person pointing out the differences to the others. The same is done with a joss stick, a bottle of perfume, gents' after-shave, a bar of soap under the noses of the group. But are not held by anyone only the one person going around with the smell producer. An apple, fruit of any sort. Onion, celery, garlic, etc. A lot of things out of your cupboard can be used. Scented things out of the garden. Anything at all that smells, from the subtle to the strong scented. **After** everyone has had a smell. Each person in the group should say one point in turn to enlighten the others how they feel about their experience. And keep on going around until the group runs out of pointers.

The exercise is repeated with the eyes open. Each time noticing the subtle difference.

### Taste :-
**Start** this exercise with your **eyes closed**, then open. Each time noticing the subtle difference.

Make up some jars of different tastes about a dozen or so and many in slices to run the teaspoon over wash the spoon after each tasting, use things like orange juice, lemon juice, weak vinegar, mild mustard, milk, lime juice, sliced onion, salt, pepper, garlic, sugar, syrup. And many more you can think of. The Idea is to have the jars and the slices out of the vision of the group so they cannot see what is coming next. The mixture should be sweet, sour, sharp, and subtle. Do not give the group anything you would not have yourself and ask beforehand if anyone there does not like anything. A lot of people have herbs in their cupboard use them. Do not use chilli or any very strong herb or spice. Always test them on yourself beforehand. **After** everyone has had a taste, each person in the group should say one point in turn to enlighten the others how they feel about their experience. With the teaspoon, just dip it into the liquid then pour it back, there should be enough of a taste on the metal for this exercise. DO NOT give teaspoons full of the liquids. And keep on going around until the group runs out of pointers.
The exercise is repeated with the eyes open. Each time noticing the subtle difference.

### Feeling, touch :-
This exercise should be done **first** with the **eyes closed** then with them open.
Have a variety of objects, pottery, materials, plants, fruits, foods, branches, leaves, papers of every description, if fact anything at all. Everyone there should in turn to hold, feel, touch the object in question without saying anything at all until the last person in the group has held and explored the object. If you can, have a number of objects the same so all can participate together. When all there have experienced the object, the leader will instruct each person in turn to say how they felt about the object whilst feeling it, holding it, touching it. The exercise is repeated with the eyes open. Each time noticing the subtle difference. You can try with your feet this is another exercise that can be fun and very much enlightening, especially to the senses.

### Sensing, and stronger awareness :-
This exercise is best done with a person having their eyes closed and a blindfold on or with the people standing with their front facing the wall and their eyes closed but even then with a blindfold on. Better still if you can use an earmuff to blank out the noise.
If the blindfold is used, then do one exercise facing the wall and then the next with the back to the wall and then note the subtle difference of each experience. Do these exercises alternately front to the wall then back to the wall.

This is one exercise that should be practised often within the awareness groups.
One person **A** is facing the wall, the group is spread out after the person **A** has been placed. The group are all in the area at the back of **A**, larger the gap the better it is. The leader picks a person from the group after **A** has been blind folded, then gives a hand signal to the individual from the group to slowly creep forward towards the person's, **A's** back to try and get as close as possible to them. This is without the person standing facing the wall **A** detecting them moving in towards them. If the person **A** can detect a person coming towards them, they say and from what direction. The truth has to be maintained, so the person standing facing the wall **A** can learn from each experience. Sometimes the group will not move at all. The group never talks throughout this exercise only the leader is to say if **A** has got their awareness of the person creeping up to them correct. This exercise should be tried with each person for about ten to fifteen minutes, longer if the group enjoys it. But give everyone there a chance to experience it. It is best done without shoes on or on a carpeted surface. Remember it does no harm what so ever to ask for help from your helpers in the other side of life in Spirit, you should always be learning alongside them, every time you link your awareness gets heightened by the World of Spirit. That means in any exercise in this book that you do.

If any person cheats in any of these exercises they are only cheating themselves so do not worry about that person not fully participating, just ignore them, they will be the loser, not the group. It is always best to have a blindfold for the eyes closed part of the exercise; it helps stops temptation, as people are naturally curious.

**Exercise**
While in ordinary light in the Circle, within or even out of the Circle, even at home with just another person is to put things [a ring, a drawing, a picture, a piece of cloth, a button, a medal etc.] singly into a sealed container or envelope so others cannot see what is there, then ask the group [or just yourselves, even if it is just you and a partner] First you should meditate; ask for help, bringing back the conditions of blending with Spirit, asking the higher life for help [closing the eyes, always asking sincerely and positively in your mind asking for only goodness, kindness, love, and truth to develop in the Divine Light and bring help from within the harmony of Spirit of the highest realms; opening the chakras if you want to] and to see if the other person can get any messages of what is inside the envelope, who is it off, where did it come from, what colour, what shape, any shapes, what is it made of. In fact anything at all relevant, what it is surrounded by, etc. The objects should NOT be handle to determine what they are, OR, they should be wrapped up in such a way that the person doing the reading cannot feel the object inside the wrapping. With practice you will be surprised at what comes about over the weeks as people develop, and how accurate they can become. By the way the number of people does not matter, can be from yourself and another, upwards to many. Another exercise is to have people bring in possessions or an ornament, the history of which the group does not know and let the group take in the conditions again, and try to give the owner as much information about it, who's it is, where it was bought, where it is kept, who owned it before, anything at all about the owner, etc. Some find it better to hold the possession piece in this type of exercise, but the idea is to ask for Spirits to help in your quest not to use psychometry.

**Another exercise** is to write down something on paper or to draw a sign, a house, boat, a picture on paper, have a photograph, anything. Place it inside an envelope and for the person or person's to try and mentally send the details of the contents to another person or persons and get them to draw it. But all should be first linking into Spirit each exercise.

In groups of two, some have an exercise where they draw five separate pieces of art in the form of :- 1, a square; 2, a circle; 3, a wave/waves or squiggle/squiggles; 4, a cross; 5, a triangle. The person who is trying to receive the thought of the sender has to draw each one, **singularly sent** to them by the way of thought in the correct order.

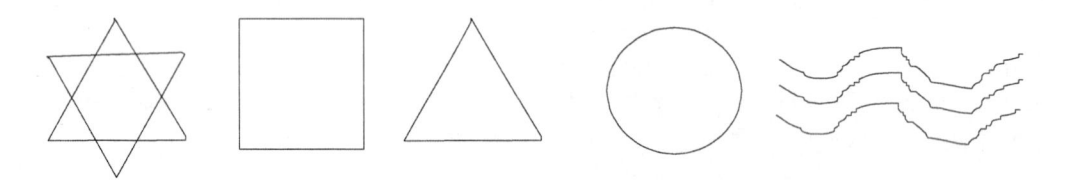

If one person is finding it hard or difficult to get any information out of another person's mind Send them out of the room, arrange what word or object is going to be sent to the mind of the one person who is outside of the room, then allow them back into the room, let the group of people there send out **one message/word** at a time to the individual. All the people there concentrating on the one thought at once. [This concentrates the power] E.g. all think of a circle and send that thought of a circle to the single person with every person in the group being sincere and positive with their thoughts and each person asking the unseen helpers from upstairs for their help. This is a very good exercise that can be used at first, for all, or singly one at a time. Remember all these skills do not come suddenly they have to be worked at over a length time with the help of your unseen helpers to develop together, always remembering it is a two way street of learning. Ask, ask, ask and keep on asking for the help from Spirit. The better results come when all there are happy and enjoying themselves.

Yet **another exercise** is to again have a friend help you with this. After asking sincerely and positively for help from Spirit from within your mind, build up the power as suggested. Have an ordinary set of playing cards or the set with the Keeways Tarot business pack and book. Have your friend place two pieces of paper in front of you, one with "red / R" on it, the other "black / B". Get your friend to shuffle the cards with only the suits in it [spades, hearts, clubs, and diamonds]. Have the cards facing towards your friend, the backs to you. Have your friend look at the card and get them to fix its colour image in their mind [red or black] and you to try and pick the colour up from their mind. You say whether it is either red or black pointing to the pile you want it to be placed on. You do not look to see if you are correct, the friend places the card face down on the pile you have indicated R or B [they do not correct any mistakes you make], do not try to go slowly, go at about one card a second or two, to two cards every four or five seconds, count your result at the finish. See if over a period of time you get a better correct score. Then as you go along, try to the same exercise with suits (red and black) and picture cards. So then there will be three piles R, B, P. With the set that comes with the sister book of the Keeways Tarot you will be able to go a little bit further having six piles [or more if you split them up into their face cards] R [red], Bla [black], G [green], Br [brown], Blu [blue], and T [tarot], as with other things go simply and then add as you improve.

Try using the planchette [an arrow or heart shaped piece of wood on casters, some planchettes I have heard about have been used on a shiny surface with felt pads on them instead of casters.] for Spirit writing or drawing by placing your fingers very lightly on the planchette. Some people have wonderful results with this method Always ask sincerely and positively from those above for the things you want them to help you with. When you finish always remember to close down your power points (chakras) if you have opened them of course, and to ask positively for your conditions to go, then clean your power points with pure light within your mind. Always after each session write down what happened, what was foretold, in what environment, and how it was achieved. Even if you were meditating alone. As you begin so you end.

**Another exercise** is to use a dowsing implement, a pendulum. At the start meditate to gain a link with your Spirit helpers, asking for their help. Also make the rules for the pendulum at the start anti-clockwise for NO, clockwise for YES. But test it first. I ask which way is yes? Then, Which way is no? Have a person put on a piece of paper a number then place it into an envelope. Then the other person has to use the dowsing pendulum to find out what number is written on the paper in the envelope. By asking questions while holding the pendulum about what number is it. Is it number one? Is it number two? Is it number three? Going through one to ten and seeing which way the pendulum swings. With practice it will be found out that an accurate score of the number will be found. Then progress trying two, 24; then three, 756; then four, 936; until a series of numbers are tried, and to be found out, say up to about four or five. E.g. 12648.

I personally do not have a heavy meal when I am sitting for a Circle or doing any psychic work. As the human body was designed for little and often that is what I mostly do. I just eat sensibly, having cereals mainly porridge now in the mornings, as this warms me up for the day and the sitting in the physical circle when it gets cold. I eat meat; fish twice a week if possible, plenty of vegetables, milk, cheese, eggs free range if possible, mixed herbs and plenty of fresh or frozen vegetables in home made soups with herbs and spices mixed in once or twice a month, and wholemeal bread. I grill most of my food and try to eat my vegetables fresh or frozen cooked with all my meals if possible without any preservatives in them. I try not to eat too much tinned foods as they all have preservatives in them. You see I vary my diet so inputting many different trace elements, minerals and vitamins. I am writing them down so you have a choice. PLEASE Remember you have to have a reasonable input of food to keep your body and bowels in good working order. But in a Physical Circle it is best to have only a small amount of food on that day at an early time before the sitting, that way Spirit, who will be working with you on that day will be able to work with your internal bodily chemicals easier, especially if you have the same food [this will be personal but logical] each time on that particular day until you are developed. Probably sticking to your own personal diet on that day after you do develop.

Some people/Mediums (especially the developed ones) wear the same clothes for each weekly Circle because it is said the vibrations or psychic power somehow builds up in them, but do make sure you keep them clean and washed. This is why a room put aside to be only used for Spirit communication is used and generally it achieves the quicker and stronger results. Some do not eat on the day of the Circle. Others eat very little. Some go vegetarian on the day. Some eat only vegetables on the day of the Circle. [Before you go completely vegetarian. Get the Medium Matthew Manning tapes and listen to the experiments done with himself and scientists, because it was found out that plants have feelings as well] Others eat only fish on the day of the Circle sitting. Most I have spoken to, eat their last meal about three/four hours before any Circle, a lot longer if sitting for Physical [not eating that day]. Some do not wear shoes for the Circle; as you can imagine the smell can be something else if people do not look after their personal hygiene, best to use your own personal slippers if you feel that way. That is another point to remember, your personal hygiene. Cleanliness is next to Godliness. It is a good idea to have a bath, a shower or body wash before any Circle to prepare yourself for it. Use a none scented soap as you might not pick up any other smells that are brought into the Circle by those who have gone before [who are in Spirit] as evidence showing that they are present as well as the sitters. Remember you are sitting to meet friends from Spirit, prepare yourself and your mind in anticipation, as though you are going out to meet friends on a social occasion.

People start to meditate in a wide variety of wonderful ways. Always remember that it is the many ways people of many continents have been doing it on their own and with others in a group for hundreds of thousands of years, "focusing their attention" in other words meditating, all get results in their own personal ways.

Some visualise a colour and concentrate on it. Others concentrate on a sound while meditating. They do not listen as such to the noise but get involved in it, becoming part of it, part of the vibration. Most people have seen some religions of the world who while meditating with their eyes closed, humming or repeating "aaaaaaahhhoooommm" or chanting a word over and over again, or saying a group of words over and over [a mantra]; this is another way. Other circles have the sounds of meditation music, this can consist of the buzzing of bees, the gentle patter of rain on a roof, waves on the shore, tinkle of bells, gentle beat of a drum [American Indians, African, South American, East Asian tribes people], slow easy strumming of the guitar or harp, the mellow sounds of the flute, the sounds of the deep ocean, whale sounds, the pumping of blood around the body, etc. This is a very personal feeling in each individual for the correct vibrational sound to bring about personal reactions. Remembering we are all individuals with our own feelings.

Some find it better to concentrate on their own breathing while going deeper into meditation. Some feel each deep breath in and each slow breath out. [The breathing goes shallower when you go deeper into meditation, some who have been doing it for years can get their breathing rate down to 8 breaths a minute and less].

Some with each breath, draw in the power of light from above seeing it being sent to the mind to build up their own inner strength, their own healing power to help their own well being, some use this method to increase their own antibodies to fight what ever diseases they have in their body. Yes it can be done, try it using your positive mind and be sincere about it when asking from above.

Some take a breath through the nose seeing it going into their lungs as the Divine Light filling the whole body up at each intake of breath, then they breath out through the nose seeing each breath take all the badness out of their body. They generally go through the sequence to relax but others can use this method until they are deep in Trance, if at any time the mind wanders the person goes back to the breath again, if any thought comes into the mind again, go back to see the breath again going into your nose, into your body, filling it up. If any thoughts come into your mind again go back to the breath see it going through the nose, into your body filling up the lungs and again keep on going back, and back, and back to the breath until the mind stills it's self of any thought, it is very hard at first but it gets easier. Practice, practice, practice, and more practice, there is no easy way I am sorry. [This method for me is still thinking using your own mind; I still prefer to look into the light within the mind after this exercise to help me go into a more altered awareness state].

Some try self hypnosis, which is a method of concentrating on a fixed point with the eyes open, not blinking until the eyes get tired and start to close, keep on looking at the fixed point until the eyes are shut with the wariness of concentration and staring, then the **start** of your meditation then deep meditation begins. This is a good way for people to go to sleep if they have problems when they go to bed, no need for tablets then. BUT remember the constant. That is to keep on encouraging Spirit to come closer and help in your development as you are looking at the fixed point.

One way I saw a group meditating [I asked them later what they were doing] was for them to close their eyes and then while they physically went through the actions, they imagined themselves opening a pair of curtains of a window for them to look through within their third eye, they acted it out. When they finished their meditation they then physically acted out the closing of the curtains, as they imagined the closing of the curtains. You could use this method with or without the actions. Try it and ask your helpers, guides, Angels to be there and to take you along on a journey. When you are ready, after using one of the methods of development, your own personal guide, helper, angel will appear to help you along your journey of development. They are seen within the third eye. You have a gatekeeper (or a Guardian Angel who is in the forefront of the others who are helping) who will be there with you all the time to help with the regulating of the power flow [or vibration levels] you need for the differing needs of development. This "person" generally stays the same until you need a person with more skills. You will through the course of time have different guides or more developed angels from a more knowledgeable group to help you as you develop.

If you find a method that suits you and you feel comfortable with it, use that method over and over again, only you will know, because you are an individual not like others.

By the way get away from the idea of one special guide or angel being with you. We have been told by the higher side of life that when a person is doing clairvoyance on the platform in a church they can have up to fifty/sixty helpers of that group (of thought) with them, of course some might be more prominent than others.

The best harmonious development Circle I have sat in was in the 1970's/1980's in a room above a shop, which was only used for us sitting in each week and nothing else. The best results happen earlier if you can find a room that is put aside for only sitting in for the development of communication with Spirit. We started the Circle in this room with a prayer and a hymn. Asking for goodness, kindness, love, truth, and asking to blend within the peaceful Divine Light, within the loving harmony of our Spirit friends in the highest realms of the Spirit World. The leader then started us with our meditation by us all relaxing all of our body first. This sequence can be gone through with a quiet, very low volume tape being played; in fact any taped meditation music. A way to start the session off is to play any music that can raise the vibration levels before any meditation music is played, try "Great Spirit" with American Indian drum accompaniment, or a chant of the Tibetan Monks, or similar to raise the vibration levels any music in fact, this is an option of the leader and of how the group feel.

We started the relaxation from the guidance of the leader of the Circle gently talking the group through all the sequences.

Start by first relaxing the head, then down to the neck, starting on the left side relaxing the fingers, going along to the hands, relaxing along up the arm, to the shoulders [first the left side then the right side], slowly relaxing at the top of the body then down to the lower parts of the body, at the top of the left leg relax, slowly going down to the knee, relaxing the calf then the feet and then the toes [one leg at a time], working downwards, when the all body is fully relaxed, each person is guided by the leader's gentle voice bringing in the power into the body through the feet, drawing it upwards. [[[The reason is that the power "which incidentally can be felt as you progress" is built up in the centre of the Circle and can sometimes be felt as a very cold air. As it comes in, try thinking of it as a cold blanket or a ball [the height of which can at many times be felt by the palm of the hand, pointing it to the floor], the group can be asked to feel the air, it can be felt usually by the group at a similar level but it can be felt to shift as though it is a wave action. This is a change of the vibration level of the air; [Try having maximum/minimum thermometers in the room at different heights]]] and being guided upwards through the power points/chakras. Drawing the power up from the floor up through the feet and legs to the base chakra, when that is filled up with light, let it overflow upwards into the solar plexus chakra filling that up with the light power and overflowing up to the sacral chakra, which is filling up with that bright light and flowing upwards to the spleen chakra filling that up with the bright light, when that is overflowing let it flow upwards to the heart chakra filling that up with light letting it overflow upwards to the thymus half chakra filling it up until it overflows upwards to the throat chakra filling it up to overflowing with light spilling over upwards to the brow chakra filling that up and overflowing upwards to the crown chakra filling that up until that light which has filled the whole body overflows the body but as it is filling up and overflowing, it is gaining in power going outwards around the Circle, and in the Circle, and now it is rising upwards to meet the light of above to the divine light it is now joining all in the circle as one to those in the higher life above, then expanding it out into the individual aura's, and going out to join up with the person next to them in the Circle, so binding and protecting with the Divine Light all of the inside and outside of the Circle as a whole. Each person asking in their mind, being positive and sincere about the asking of the power and guidance as it is being taken in by all. Each person then continues to look into their third eye, asking silently for the development they want to be helped with.

The leader of the Circle went in front of each person, each individual in turn, bringing more power to them by softly asking the unseen helpers in a low, soft, gentle voice, encouraging the power through the power points in the person's body, upwards from the feet to the crown chakra with a gentle upwards movement of the cupped hands in front of the person as though scooping water in front of the person and gently encouraging it ever upwards, **IMPORTANT NOT TOUCHING AT ANY TIME.** [The music or vibration sounds can be slowly/gently turned down at this point and then off] this is a time when each person should be asking in their own mind sincerely and positively for whatever they want. Development does not come overnight, it can take months sometimes years so be prepared BUT most of all be happy with your friends there and enjoy it, be happy with their development even if you do not get much yourself.

Most of the best development comes when a Circle is happy, lively and there is a togetherness, a peaceful loving harmony with all [any bad feelings, nastiness or jealousy should be nipped in the bud and the offenders asked to leave, if this happens when a Circle is in progress it should be terminated immediately and not started again for the rest of that day]. Within that Circle above the shop most people gained a lot of psychic development over the period of time I was there with them, a lot doing healing, some helping others with their new found clairvoyance, clairsentience, others amazing us all in the Circle when they developed their own individual gifts, one lady talking with a totally different voice to her own, a mans voice, that was a great surprise to me at the time, as I had not known anything like that at all.

At the end of the Circle when a few times a person was in really deep meditation, enjoying it too much, staying there, they did not want to let go of the conditions, the leader went in front of the person (**NOT TOUCHING THEM**) and talked to them in a soft and gentle voice saying "let the conditions go come back to us [saying the person's name]" as the leader used his hands in a downwards movement as though he was scooping the power [water] downwards to the ground and into the centre of the Circle and in every case the person was helped with their conditions and brought back to normality each time gently and calmly. (This by the way I have not seen done before or since in any other Circle).

**Another meditation technique** is to plant your feet firmly on the ground. **See and think** of the power of the earth being drawn up inside through the feet upwards through your body. **See and think** of it as power, white light or a colour being draw into yourself going ever upwards filling your body with it. <u>Feel and see</u> the power/colour/light as it fills you up until it reaches your head where it flows over your head and your body outside until it flows down to your feet. It is then **seen** [in your mind] starting to spill outwards to others in the Circle flowing every where; it starts to flow gently around the Circle going clockwise, when it comes back to you it starts another journey into your body through your feet going again upwards in the same fashion, flowing up and out and over, but now it is stronger because of all the benefit it has gained from the others in your group. It starts to form a cone in the middle of the Circle which is going higher in the middle, it is drawing the blended harmonious power from each person there, going ever upwards to the Divine Light which is flowing back and forth up and down to the Circle building up the power for each person.

If you do this on your own it is the same but each time it goes out of your head and flows over your body it gains strength from the air that surrounds you, you then feel it spreading outwards, pushing your aura, your power out to as far as it can go. You see it going upwards to the Divine light where its strength is increased and it come back to you as help and strength of power in your development.

Then you can start working, each person giving messages [or if on your own to a tape recorder] as you receive them but do not forget to ask for information each time, the type you require, if you do not ask, you do not get.

If the development Circle method is used and the leader wants to develop more themselves. Have a break after say ¼ -¾ of an hour, have some tea; talk about what went on. Then after the break, all the sitters there could sit for the leader for half an hour, or an hour or so. I suggest this for the simple reason leader, your sitters are there, they do not have to come back another time and the power has already been built up in the room from the development Circle. When doing this for the leader each person takes in the power and then asks the higher side of life [within their own mind] to give the power to the leader and keep asking for the power to go to the leader [or the person placed in the cabinet or the person placed at the end of the Circle, or in the middle of the Circle or at the opening of a horse shoe shaped Circle]. This method can also be used to empower a person who is finding it a little bit of a struggle to see anything in their third eye with or without a cabinet. For any Circle try building a cabinet for the leader to sit in as the older Mediums did, it concentrates/confines the power as it builds up. BUT it is not always necessary. A normal cabinet is an open fronted wooden box like structure, like a single wardrobe with a curtain across the front from the top to the ground, about three feet square and 6-6 high with a top piece or could be a frame with material placed over it. Room enough for the person to sit in and then stand up safely when leaving. A covered/shaded, able to be dimmed red light at the top front. Just a curtain across a corner of a room has been used in the past. Some people are experimenting using a double cabinet where two Mediums sit in it.

When in a Circle it is best to let your hidden helpers guide you and not to ask for the impossible. I just ask for help with my development to let me see, hear, and feel Spirit so I can help others to understand there is life after death and let those who know decide. Some people want clairvoyance, others would like different gifts of Mediumship, remember to ask. If when you are sitting for development you feel as if you have a spider's web feeling or an itch on your face or elsewhere on your body, don't scratch it. Or your feet and legs go cold or the room goes cold, it is only the change in vibration around you that you are picking up, it means you are becoming more aware of your surroundings and your development. Feeling the Power of Spirit. Experiment with different sounds when meditating. You will soon get the right music, use chants, drums, Tibetan begging bowls/singing bowls, Tibetan prayer bells, or any of the many sounds you can get now recorded to heighten your sensitivity and feelings of vibration. [I say again, try most of all to attend the Arthur Findlay College for a week and experience the atmosphere there, it is amazing. I assure you, going there once will not be enough]. With different sounds, you will feel the vibrating airwaves right through your body like a tingling, a wave, a shiver, your hair standing up, goose bumps, or a sparkle running down your spine. This is you being more aware of the changing vibrations and becoming more sensitive. When you feel it; it is amazing. One piece of music to start a Circle with could be "O Great Spirit" with the American Indian drums as a backing. It is a good vibration build up, get the recording and write out the words and learn them. By the way do not always be reverend, it is OK at the right time, but remember the higher life are not all stuffy, imagine this life without laughter and happiness, so it is over there. Most of all, DO NOT be flippant. Be positive and sincere bringing in happiness, goodness, kindness, love, truth and peaceful Divine Light within the loving harmony from the highest realms of Spirit, do this at all times in any Circle.

Something I found difficult while I was developing, when looking into a cabinet at the developing Medium in trance, was trying to see if there was any Spirit person that was building up with the person/Medium sitting in the cabinet. I found it easier when I slightly close my eyes until I was slightly squinting them and defocused and staring. [Let me explain what is happening. What you are doing you are allowing your muscles in your eyes to adjust the lens of the eye; as you do if you wear glasses and forget to put them on; the lens of the eye focuses the light going into the eye and onto the rods at the back of the eye, those rods then convert the wavelengths of light into an electrical signal, those rods at the back of the eye then put out the signal through to the brain in the way of that electrical impulse to get interpreted within the brain as a signal of sight. What you are looking at, by slightly squinting, you alter the focus of the lens of the eye allowing SOME people SOMETIMES to see the higher vibrational level of Spirit, who have themselves lowered their vibrational level to show themselves.], I gradually saw people building up from nothing [some do not look directly at the subject only looking to the side of the Medium]. This sometimes worked for me when I used the crystal ball, another way is to just stare into the crystal ball not blinking and the images came. For me to the left is the past and to the right is the future in the crystal ball. Try mirror scrying as well, this is similar to the crystal ball, only you look into the mirror at an angle to see things, (see colour plates) it is all exercise for you to start opening your psychic ability to see other things in life and to open up your own brain which is totally under used within every person. If you ever get a headache while developing drink plenty of water, it is only you using the under used parts of your brain. The main thing is to meditate and gain a closer link with the higher life and for them to develop with you. They will help you if you ask. "Ask and you shall receive" (but do not stop at one mediumistic discipline as it might not be best for you were Spirit is concerned). A lady I was talking to at Stansted said she started seeing people's auras from the time she was looking at a hawk in the sky through a pair of binoculars [the lens must have been out of focus] then there was all these bright colours around the hawk. From that day up until the present day she could see people's coloured aura. She said it was best if she did not look at the person in question directly, but looked at them slightly to the side of them and the colours were much clearer. So try it yourself. When working with those friends in Spirit I always close myself by a pray of thanks in my own words within my mind for the occasion.

The other way is when you have finished completely, is to always clean your power points (chakra), ask sincerely and positively in your mind for power of the cleaning light to bathe your body going from the top to base, then from the base to the top, then back down from the top to the base, and **see** in your mind's eye the light doing the job of work going from one chakra to the other within your body as it goes about its work of clearing the darkness out of your body bringing in the all powerful healing, cleaning, light.

Some imagine at the end of all the cleaning on the inside, they think of themselves under a shower, instead of water coming out of the shower, it is light they are being washed with on the outside. It runs all over their body both inside and out. What you are doing is to bring in the bright, higher force light of "The Divine Spirit", "The Great Spirit", "God" into your whole being, and accepting it, as you should to help you, then thank the higher realm in your own words within your mind.

**MOST OF ALL trust in the higher side of life**, BUT question all things yourself and do not believe everyone as you go through this wonderful new way of living, and do not believe everything that people have seen and done, I certainly don't. I want to see and do things that others say they have experienced THEN only that way will I truly believe. Also do not believe all that comes from the Spirit side of life, as over the other side of the veil, they are only ordinary people who have gone to another level, and they might not have developed as much as they should have and want to still cause mischief on the earth plane. As you progress you will find there are a great many different ideas, and points of view from the Spirit Realm so please question, question, question, and question again the spokesperson for the group in Spirit, the Spirit control of the Medium, the Spirit you will be talking to at any time whether it is when a person/Medium is in Trance, using the table, the planchette, within your own mind, or any other time. That one person is only the mouthpiece for that one group of Spirit people that comes through, like a chairperson of a committee. If you go to another Trance Medium and speak to their control, you will find sometimes that they have a different point of view of any situation. This is why you should NOT TAKE EVERY WORD FROM SPIRIT AT ITS FACE VALUE. Please think on about the way Spirit progress; they too have to develop in the higher realm. The person who first comes through might not be as highly educated/developed as the other person who comes through the next time. A Spirit might have been over the other side of the veil for eight hundred years and learned nothing. Another person in Spirit might have been in Spirit for a hundred years and progressed much further, learning something new each moment they had crossed the threshold into the light. So it is here people learn at different rates in all levels learning.

A Spirit who is higher developed than the ordinary person in the higher realm that comes through a Trance Medium, if they do not know an answer to a question. They will sometimes go to someone up there in the higher vibrational level who has better knowledge or go to the halls of learning and will try to give you the answer the next time you sit with the same Trance Medium and they come through. (Or the table or planchette, etc)

Before I finish on this subject, the best way to practice clairvoyance is to get a few friends together and give each other a reading, better still someone you do not know very well. Perhaps practice in a church Open Circle. First bring the power into yourself for a few minutes by meditating for a while, to get your link with Spirit in your own way. (Remember the asking for the goodness, kindness, love, truth, and to blend in peaceful Divine Light within the loving harmony from Spirit of the highest realms). Then close your eyes and see what you get in the way of pictures, voices, and what you feel about the person you start to give a reading for.

Try to keep opening your eyes open when you are doing the reading, even if it is only for a short while at first, people will think you are falling asleep if you don't. Most Mediums have to close their eyes at sometime while working; so do not worry about it. Start by asking by a thought (some Mediums ask Spirit out loud, it is up to you) to the higher life for some help to give the person a reading, asking if there is any message for them. Quite often you will get a person or a scene. Describe to the person what you see and see if they accept it. If they do, ask Spirit in your own mind for some more information, and try to keep on going with the message. If the message starts going wrong and the person cannot accept it, bring the person in Spirit back into your head, the one who you first started with in your head by asking them to return, then asking your contact in Spirit by thought, what it is you require. It might be your own thoughts picking up something instead of sticking with Spirit and trusting them with what is given in your head. Practice, practice, practice, practice, practice, it is the only way you will find out what way the Spirits that are guiding you are going to work with you and you with them. I will give you a few ideas as to the questions to go back with and **ask by thought** to the higher life.

Please Divine Spirit help me with the reading for this person, John. [At the start]
What is it I should tell John? Or
Is there a certain person who wants to contact John?
Who are they? Please show or tell me.
What do they want to tell John?
What sex are they? How old are they? [If you have not been shown]
Do they have any children? What children do they have? Who are they?
Is this a relation? (What relationship? is it a grandfather/mother link? Is an uncle/aunt link? A father/mother link? Etc.)
Is it a friend?
Where did they live?
Is there any other information for John?
At the end; "Have you any evidence I can give them?" Etc. [you might be given a watch, a car, a house, a book, a medal perhaps that was left for them when this person died. This is why it is a very good question to use and a way of finishing your link from Spirit and the presentation of clairvoyance for a person].
The five "W"'s and an "H" to ask of your Spirit link are; **Who, What, Where, Why, When**, also use **How**.
Please remember that a voice is produced by your vocal cords vibrating the air and it sends a wave of vibration from one point to another. When a Medium is working linked into Spirit whether it is clairvoyantly, clairsentiently or clairaudiently with one person, if another person interrupts with their voice, a cross vibrational link can be brought into the situation so SOME Mediums quite often cannot work accurately in that situation. So it is said, BUT it can be an ordinary interruption, which cuts off the flow of the quiet mind link through the Medium thinking of the person who has interrupted. BUT here it must be said that the thoughts that the Medium gives out to the Spirit World are also vibrations of a finer type and they should not get interrupted by others talking they can un-still the still link with the Spirit World **IF** the Medium is not attuned properly, it is a distraction only or should be only a short distraction. DO NOT TALK when Mediums are working, as most Mediums, it is said, work on a voice vibrational link. **It should not be so** but that is what they seem to put out to the public.
This goes for the clairvoyance, clairsentience, and clairaudience forms of mediumship link with Spirit.

**Another exercise for a group situation.**
In a group gathering, one exercise that can be useful for bringing awareness to the fore is to pick a leader. The group is placed in pairs sitting opposite each other, it best if each person does not know the other very well. (have some paper and a mixture coloured crayons or pencils ready). Everyone goes into meditation for a while (ten to fifteen minutes) asking within their minds from those in the higher realms (a prayer to Spirit) for help with the coming task. When in meditation the leader talks the group through the meditation while a low, calm, piece of music is playing. The leader saying " you see yourself in a garden, you are there with your friend opposite, within the garden and in the borders are flowers, your friend opposite is picking flowers for themselves, look at the flowers they are gathering, note what they are and how they look, note their colour. Coming out of meditation each person is given a piece of paper and a choice of coloured pencils to pick from. Each person then has to draw the flowers and how they all appeared to them in the meditation. It can be an interpretation of the flowers or just the colours as they

were seen. Each person in their own little group in turn has to give a reading for the person opposite. Then each person has to get up in front of the group and explain the scene they saw in their meditation and give their own interpretation of the scene, colours and the flowers and what it means to them, in a reading for the person who is sitting opposite them. Showing the group the picture, as the reading is taking place, everyone in the group at random has to say what they think and feel about each thing that is pointed out, as well as the colours and the flowers means in their opinion psychically spiritually and clairsentiently. This way all in the group learn and expand their own knowledge and the ways of interpreting the scenes, flowers and colours. This is NOT an artist's forum where the drawings are put under any scrutiny, it is the colours that are of importance and the feeling each person gets about the drawings and the person they are giving the reading for.
Always start and finish with a prayer to Spirit.

**Another similar group exercise is:-**
The leader has the group placed in pairs, the two people opposite each other. It best if each person does not know the other very well. (Have the paper and coloured crayons or pencils ready also a large plain wipe board or a large piece of paper [like the back of wallpaper] would be of benefit). Everyone in the group meditates for a while (ten to fifteen minutes), asking Spirit to come closer for the task ahead in interpreting colours for the person opposite, ask for some colours to be shown to them within their mind. This can be done with music or without. When coming out of meditation, each person looks at the other sitting opposite to them looking slightly to the side of them or through squinted eyes. To try and see any colours that might come in to their mind. It does not matter if the colours are not seen, they can be felt clairsentiently. On the paper each person draws a person in a standing position, putting the colours in the appropriate positions around and on the body that represents the person opposite. A reading is the given to each individual in the pair group about what it means to them.
Then each pair has to get up at the front of the group, one at each side of the board or holding their drawing up for all to see. There is a drawing of a person in a standing up position on the board or paper. Everyone in the group is asked to close their eyes and ask for help in seeing colours around the person who the reading is for, Perhaps the person on the left of the board. They can squint, see clairvoyantly, see the auras, or any other way; each person can even feel as though there are colours around a certain points of the person clairsentiently. One person at a time has to tell the group what colour/colours they see around the person who is standing at the front next to the drawing and where they saw it, this is then drawn on the paper drawing of the person. It might be a ball, a line, a circle or a ray of colour at a certain point. Everyone in the group has an input to the drawing. When the entire group have said what they saw and it has been placed on the drawing, the person who was sitting opposite this person now says what they saw and where they saw the colour on their partner. This is now placed on the drawing (there are two ways this can be done, this person's input can drawn first before the group, or at the end). The group's and the person's colour on the drawing is talked about and compared. A reading by everyone's input is then done on the drawing for the person. Everyone in the group at random has to say what they think and feel about each colour in their opinion, and what it means in this situation for the person psychically spiritually and clairsentiently. This way all in the group learn and expand their own knowledge and the ways of interpreting the colours that surround a person. This is done for each person in the group
Please remember there is no set way of interpreting the colours DO NOT think your way is any better than the next person. It is what comes into your mind that matters in any reading not what others see in theirs.
In every group development, it is a learning situation of what can be said, so may be you can use another person's interpretation in one of your readings later on. That little particular part might well be brought to mind as and when necessary. So take note of finer details.

Another method of teaching awareness, is to have a large board to draw on, on which is first drawn an outline of a person on the board. Have the whole class meditate to bring their link with Spirit closer link for about a quarter of an hour, then one person is brought forward to stand at the front. Have your pupils look at that person to try and see or feel if there are any colours around that person at the front. Each person as they see the colours should say where they are on that person. The tutor draws onto the outline of the person in the colours, the position and style it is seen as said by the participants. When everyone there has had an input, the tutor asks everyone in turn what they think the colours represent. A few examples are :- (1) There is a yellow glow above the head with a black or grey covering. (2) There is red over the elbows of the person. (3) There is blue under the chin. (4) There is orange in the stomach region. (5) There is a wavy colour of green with a shimmering coming from the chest area it has a funny grey green colour around it as well.

Of course these are only my interpretations of this, yours could be totally different. I hope you get the idea though. It can be fun to see how others interpret the picture. Everyone there should be encouraged to have their own individual input so the rest of the pupils can pick up the little subtle interpretations from the more experienced readers.

Here goes, this could be a reading from this picture. (1) This person is bright in their outlook but has had problems in the past, there is still a cloud hanging over them. The brightness will come through if they clear the cloud from their lives and live it to the full, they can have everything going for them. (2) This person has problems with the soreness around the joints of the arms mainly around the elbows, suffers from a joint disorder. Should go to the doctors to have it checked out, possible rheumatism or arthritis sufferer. (3) Here we can see this person is good at communication, they will if they sit for it on a regular basis, talk in trance. (4) I feel here this person is in need of vitamin "C" it seems to be lacking in their dietary needs, should be encouraged to eat more fruit and vegetables. (5) This person in suffering inwardly, they are taking things to heart at present, the wavy lines are an unstable outer influence, and it is casting shadows over their normal life. There is a possibility of a heart problem, which they could be worried about. Again go to the doctors to have a MOT of the body.

# HEALING

This is a part of Spiritual/Mediumship development every person in this world of ours, and especially those who are training to be a mediumistic person should take training for. If you have a link with the Spirit World you should put it to good use. This is the putting aside a little of your time for the help of another person, animal or any living thing on this earth plane. You have to be positive, sincere, truthful, and in peaceful loving harmony with the power of Spirit and caring with inner love of **all here** on the earth plane (Human, animal, insect, vegetable, and mineral) and those in Spirit.

It does not matter or should I say, "it should not matter if the Spirit you are linked with or the Spirit of the person in need of healing is used as long as the person gets better". You do not need to know the Spirit helper either.

To become a **GOOD HEALER,** and I hope you all want to become one. The most important thing is firstly to have a good link with those in the World of Spirit. Talk to Spirit over and over through thought to bring them near to you when needed.

To bring in a stronger link with those in the World of Spirit you have to be **PASSIVE**. Allowing Spirit to do their job without any interference form the Healing Medium. It is not the Healing Medium that is doing the healing; it is those in the Spirit World. The link should be the Medium and the World of Spirit NOT the Healing Medium and the patient. The Medium acts as a sort of catalyst not being changed but needed there for the process of the healing. The stronger the Medium's link with Spirit the better the results. This is why it is so necessary for the Healing Medium to meditate as much as possible, and to get closer to those in Spirit to let them do their work while the Healing Medium's mind is as still/quiet as possible. Remember the breath and the impression of thoughts on the ether at the root of the nose.

People can dismiss this form of Mediumship as being false because it cannot be proven by another who has not had the pain, suffering, or the burden of a disabling illness. The misinformed, not fully educated scientific and medical professions quite often put it down as "Hocus Pocus". I put it that way kindly as some of them are now coming around to the way of thinking it does actually work. (The hospital in Liverpool, Walton hospital is using Healing Mediums and good for them I say). They, the medical profession knock down healers by saying you cannot prove it because they [the Healers Mediums] have not used the placebo tests/effect, how sad. BUT they do not say anything about experiments done with microbes in test tubes and how they are altered for the good. Like the experiments done in laboratories by the Healing and Mental Medium Matthew Manning, scientists tested him many times. Spiritual healing can help where those in the medical profession sometimes cannot. There are many in the medical profession who will not allow themselves to even look at the way natural spiritual healing is helping others nor the way healing is done because of their religious upbringing.

It must be remembered when a person is healing it is the most simple of acts. Some Healer Mediums try to be doctors and **they are not**. Please do not allow yourself to go along that route. All that should be done is to link with Spirit asking for their help and for them to come closer to you as you become a channel for their work, try and still your mind and become as one with Spirit in the bright Divine Light within your mind, then place your hands about 1-2 inches over the patient and your work for Spirit begins, some touch the patient on the shoulders (BUT ask permission first). You are only the channel; please keep that in your head nothing more, nothing less.

The outstanding powerful Healing Mediums who I remember are Harry Edwards, who used to practice in Guildford, Surrey, England, and John Cain who was a working blacksmith, he left that line of work, then started to practice healing full time in Birkenhead, Merseyside, England. Both men had people coming from all over the world to be healed. I know John Cain used to have the good healing effect on people just by them being in his presence, also I know a lot were helped by just having his photograph there and the effect happened when they closed their eyes to be healed. People have been known to come into the Birkenhead healing centre by the coach load for healing that was what sort of a reputation he had. The man had the power/ability through his helpers in Spirit, to put people into a dreamy trance like state for their healing. He also went into Trance himself sometimes to heal. There are many documented incidences of people with "incurable", if that is a word that Spirit knows, being cured; I certainly don't think it is a word Spirit knows if the conditions are made right for them. There have been a quite a few books written by and about the two healers. They are worth reading about. Neither ever said they could cure anybody; please keep that in your mind if you do become a healer. Humility! It was not them that healed, it was Spirit. They were only the open vessel that Spirit used. The link should be the Healing Medium to those in the World of Spirit, **NOT** the Healing Medium to the patient. The Healing Medium should be passive and let those in Spirit get on with the job in hand and not interfere with their own thoughts of what should happen.

But here it must be said there are a great many alleged healers doing the work of healing who have not the training/guidance from fully experienced Healing Medium teachers, sadly there seems to be only a few really very good outstanding Healing Mediums now compared to the amount of healers there are in the world today that can stand up fully to the scrutiny of the enquiring media circus. Perhaps the mediocre healers are forgetting to put some time aside to link each day with Spirit to help themselves and Spirit to develop a good harmonious link. Perhaps they are taking their gift for granted. I feel this could be perhaps the healer wanting all the glory and the adulation from others, many of them being on an ego trip, instead of just accepting the gift from Spirit as being natural for all if worked with and built upon to keep the healing gift from Spirit. They should keep on linking each day to strengthen their beautiful God given gift. That way they would become a better blending healer. Remember folks the media loves nothing better than to find the charlatans and expose the fakes, so for your own sake do not even try to go along that pathway, you will be found out in what ever branch of Mediumship you choose, if you fake.

**BUT** here I must add, and I must also say there are a great many more unsung Healing Mediums who are doing a great job of work for the sick, putting their time in for their patients and not asking for any reward only expenses, most not even taking that. These are the dedicated people who ask for no recognition and little reward, only receiving the satisfaction of a happier person and a smiling face at the end of the session. Quite often they lay their hands on others for hours at a time even though it can make them so tired. Many can do too much and put their own health in danger of collapse. If you become a Healer leave time for yourself, because if you don't, you will not be any use to any ill person, never mind yourself, if you make yourself too tired to work efficiently. If you put time aside then you will become a good passive channel for Spirit.

You will find a lot of your patients will want the time to talk to you, so let them. This is where a counsellor course would be of use to some healers. I took one while I was working as an industry trainer so I can see from my own experience it can be helpful in some circumstances. BUT I must say here, I found when I was taking the counsellor course, that I already had the where with all through life's experiences and the bringing up my two children on my own. Helping with the children only holidays as a courier so my children could get a holiday. I had been doing counselling all the time. Listening, supporting, empathising, and sympathising with people and their problems. So do not think a course is necessarily going to make you a better person to deal with life's ups and downs.

I also found there were a few not so nice allegedly caring people who were taking the course for their portfolio and they were there only for how it would look good for them in their place of work, and not taking the course for the sake of helping the unfortunate. They were also talking about different people's problems in the bar afterwards that were brought out in the individual **private** practice sessions, all of which were supposed to be highly confidential.

If you do decide to take up healing, here are a few things that I feel should be kept up to help yourself to help others. Perhaps when doing healing in a place where there will be a special link with Spirit, a Healing Sanctuary.

## A few ideas for when you do healing.

**Have comfortable places to work in :-** Have a place where you and perhaps others can perform their task of healing in a happy, comfortable, tranquil atmosphere that has comfortable seats for you, other healers and the patients. Please think of the healers when getting chairs. Some healers will have to bend down if they do healing on the legs of a patient so it follows the best chair in that circumstance would be a very small one like a stool in those circumstances. Perhaps have soft meditation music in the background.

**Always respect the wishes of your patients** and never give out their names or addresses to any person without their prior permission. Keep personal details to yourself, never discuss a person's illness unless they themselves start to, even then I would not, just empathise with them, remember you are not a doctor.

**Keep records :-** It is always best to keep records of each healing session of each individual patient for your own benefit and for the evidence that might at sometime be needed by some authority.

**Washing your hands :-** Some Healer Mediums for the sake of cleanliness and to reassure the patient, generally wash their hands after each healing. I believe this should be done as a matter of course. Sometimes the Healing Medium can get sweaty hands when healing, so it makes sense to make washing your hands a normal practice. Have fresh soap, water, and clean towels as well as clean bowls ready at the start of each session.

**Uniform :-** Some Healer Mediums have started wearing white coats to reassure their patients they are a healer in the place where they are working. Please do not think a white coat turns you into a Healing Medium. Think of the situation, if a white coat is dirty, it can put people off. Always be clean and tidy in your dress code no matter what you wear.

**Be clean in yourself :-** Make sure you are clean in yourself and do not smell. Have a bath or shower each day before the healing session. There is nothing worse than a none smoking patient having to be healed for a quarter/half of an hour by a Healing Medium who smells like a stale smelly ashtray. Neither is it pleasant having to stand next to someone who smells of body sweat, or their clothes smell. Make sure your breath does not smell either. Clean your teeth before healing, perhaps have a mouthwash handy.

**Advertising your healing :-** When advertising never promise results. It should be enough for a Healing Medium to get known to others through the word of mouth through recommendation and this will come when they have gained enough strength in their link with Spirit. The public will be guided to the place of healing as and when necessary. The best recommendations are always former satisfied patients. A simple notice "Spiritual Healing", "Healing Centre" or just "Healing" and the times when it is taking place should be enough. Please, if you do advertise the Spirit Communicator who is helping you as you do your work as a healing Medium. Remember this, the Spirit Communicator is only a person who is in the forefront of a group of knowledgeable people in Spirit who are helping the Healing Medium.

**Selling of Medication :-** Please be very careful on medication. There is not a Healing centre in this country, the U.K., where Healing Mediums sell medication to their patients. **DON'T** do it. There are very stiff penalties for people who sell medication of any sort and are not qualified. Even be careful of selling the natural remedies. So look into your country's laws on this one. Never recommend any medicines nor should any Healing Medium go against the medical doctors in their advice of medicine or surgery. If you think a doctor has given the wrong diagnosis or wrong medicine, ask the patient to go back to their own doctor or another doctor of THEIR own choosing for a second opinion. The only thing you can say in those circumstances are "if it was me I know what I would do". It is then up to the patient. Never give medical advice it can lead to lawsuits.

You can get specimen cards from the Spiritualist National Union Healers, The Sanctuary, Stansted Hall. Stansted, Essex, England. And from the National Federation of Spiritual Healers, Shortacres, Church Hill, Loughton, Essex. England. It would be best to belong to one or the other of the healing organisations as a lot of advice and support can be had from them. Both organisations have courses that lead to world wide recognised diplomas.

To progress along the path of healing, a person should I feel, always say a sincere prayer to those in Spirit who you believe in [or to your God] the Divine Power of the highest realms.
Always after sitting in meditation, I sincerely ask the higher life to send out any power that I have built up around me and whatever is left in me to go out in the way of healing to others who need it, or to a special sick/ill patient, remembering every person is special. I see [in my mind; remember thought and it's power, it is a living energy] the healing going out to the people who need it in the way of the Divine Light. I first name people and then include all persons, animals and beings inhabiting the earthly plane that need healing, pause for five minutes or so, then say a sincere closing prayer. I always include the sending out of the power in the way of healing just before I close a Circle when the power is still there, then I close any Circle sincerely thanking all that have come to help within the Circle from the other side of life. Please try to do this each time as it can mean a lot to a great many people.

When doing healing I first meditate sincerely asking my helpers to come closer to me saying a sincere prayer asking for the higher side of life to help. I sincerely ask Spirit through thought to let me be used for the benefit of my fellow man, to be an instrument of healing, to be used as an open vessel. I see [in my mind] myself being filled with the Divine Power of Light of the Divine Spirit and encourage Spirit to come close over and over, over and over, over and over, over and over again until I feel them near and for the Spirit World to help me in my task ahead.
When I first started I went though this sequence. I give Spirit permission to use me as an instrument of healing. I meditate first bringing the Power of Spirit into myself, see it filling me up as an open vessel. When I have finished meditating bringing in the power of Spirit to myself, I go to the person in need of help, who is generally seated. I place my hands about 1-2 inches above the head of the patient or lightly on their head or on their shoulders after asking for permission of the person. I then see myself again being filled up with the healing light of the Divine Power; seeing it fill the whole of my body flowing over the patient, and myself I also see and feel it going out through my hands to the person in need of the healing. I then see the light, the power of Spirit being fed into the person and destroying the darkness of them inside, I see it filling them up and see it spilling over them in every direction as though it is washing away the dirt, muck, disease, hurt, pain, mental turmoil from the inside the patient into the ground. Most times now I see myself immersed in the Divine Light as well as the patient, both of us becoming as one in the Divine Light, being fully part of the Divine Light, it does feel good. I then let the Spirit World get on with the job in hand without my mind interfering. When I first started to get the healing power flowing in my body, also sometimes now, I got a strong pain in the muscles of my forearm when the power flows strongly I do not know why, but I accept it. Depending on the patient, I also can get very hot in myself in my body. Sometimes [well most times] a tingling in the palms of my hands, I know by this when the healing for the patient has finished. Sometimes the tingling can be only one hand for some reason. Sometimes hot sweaty hands. Sometimes cold hands. Sometimes I feel very cold all over. Sometimes I can have one hand hot and the other cold. Sometimes if the power is too great I have to bring my hands further away from the patient as the power can make my hands jerk and shake. Sometimes I can tell where the problems are in the patient. Sometimes I am directed towards the area in need of healing. Each person is different. Incidentally **I "sometimes" <u>do not touch a patient</u>**, (unless the permission has been granted), the reason being it is not necessary for one, and it can be sometimes an invasion of their space reason two, and reason three touching can be misconstrued sometimes by the opposite sex (always ask permission). I, at times **try** to keep about and inch or two away from the skin area within the auric field of a person. Also I try to have another person there with me when healing, especially when healing the opposite sex. If I ever feel a need to touch a person I always ask permission first. Remember the law in our country (U.K.) do not touch a person without their permission; you can be accused of an "assault".

Think about Trance Healing and the way it works; then try to get as close as possible to the Trance Healing Medium's way of doing things without going into a Trance state. (But what is Trance? It is altered awareness. A lot of healers are now calling it **"channelling"** because it seems Trance Healing is frowned on by the British and European establishments). The reason for being in a Trance **(channelling)** state is the Healing Medium will have the better stronger link with Spirit World. The Trance **(channelling)** Healer has a **still mind**. So should the healer, they should be trying to look into the light within their mind's eye, **to still the mind** after they have asked through a sincere prayer for the help from the Spirit World/ the God Force. This is for me is the aim; to allow Spirit to use the Healing Medium's mind/body as a catalyst while the healing takes place. This for me should be done without any outside interference from the healer's mind it is not the healer that is doing the healing it is the people who are allowed to be within the presence of the Mediumistic Healer. You look at things from a logical point of view this is the way of all the very well developed forms of Mediumship; <u>a still mind</u>. Well as still as possible, as Spirit gets on with their work unhindered. YES I say allowed!!! There is a natural law that says the Spirit World must not interfere unless given permission by the person of the earth plane, in this case the Mediumistic Healer.

This is the method I use now. I sincerely give permission to Spirit for me to be used as an open vessel for Spirit healing to heal the person there with me, then try to have a still mind for those in Spirit to work easier with me as I look into the light within my third eye and become part of it. I am up to the stage of trance healing where the Spirit helper showing self on my face and my body is made to look smaller and bent.

When healing **"NEVER"** ASK FOR THE ILLNESS OF THE PATIENT TO BE TAKEN INTO YOURSELF IT MIGHT STAY THERE. It is a very powerful thing this what we call "THOUGHT"; it is a living thing, a living energy. Be sensible about it. I have known Healers get the mild symptoms of their patient and those symptoms have stayed with them for a long time; about a day or so; this has made the Healing Medium ill, admitted it has only been a short while, but imagine if the illness stayed with the Healing Medium for a longer time and the symptoms had become stronger. The Healing Medium would become really physically ill themselves. The Healing Medium then would not be of any use to their patients or to themselves.

## How the system of communication with Spirit works if done correctly when linking with a Healing Medium

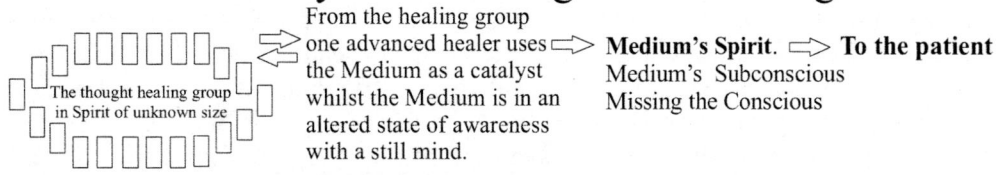

The thought healing group in Spirit of unknown size ⇌ From the healing group one advanced healer uses the Medium as a catalyst whilst the Medium is in an altered state of awareness with a still mind. ⇨ **Medium's Spirit.** ⇨ **To the patient**
Medium's Subconscious
Missing the Conscious

# ABSENT HEALING

Remember healing power does not need a person near to reap the benefit of it. This is classed as **Absent Healing.**

To help others away from you, meditate for a period of time. With sincerity see yourself filling up with the Divine Light, I try to make it about 15-30 minutes to link and build up the power. (shorter when you get experienced but do not cut it short because you are in a hurry, only finish when you feel it has been enough. It is not up to you to say what is enough, it is the World of Spirit who is in control, you should feel it through your hands when the healing power diminishes,). With your eyes closed think of the person who needs the help as being there near you, see them there, see yourself having your hands on the problem spot (near or on the shoulders if you do not know where the area is), asking your helpers in the World of Spirit to bring you the healing power over to you so you can link with the help of Spirit with the person in need of the healing as you are being used as a channel for their healing, ask Spirit to use you as an open vessel. Keep on looking into the Divine Light within your mind as you are healing. It stills the mind for Spirit to do their work, the Medium does nothing but allow the Spirit World to do their job. Do this over the period of time you think is suitable to help the recipient; about half an hour to an hour [longer the better]; when you have finished ask your helper to take away the conditions, (close down your chakra if that is what you open), thank your unseen helpers [and rub your hands {option}] and ask Spirit to let the contact go, to break the conditions and then clean your chakra [as some will want to do this [I personally don't], see yourself being under a shower in which the water is replaced with the Divine Light of Spirit and it is flowing over and into yourself for what ever length of time suits you the individual]. Different amounts of healing are sent out for different complaints, about thirty to sixty minutes is about right for most. For the most serious illnesses have a lot of healers gathered together in a Circle at the same time and perhaps send out the healing for a lot longer.

What a lot of churches and groups do is to have a healing book in which the names of the people who are on a sick list are put. This book is included in the sincere prayers at the start of the session of absent healing for all the people included in the book. This I would advise for all who do absent healing as all who are put forward for healing within the pages of the book will be included for absent healing as a group. A lot of healing groups and churches have the healing book placed in the middle of the Circle or at the front of the healing group or on the lap of the individual healing Medium or on the floor in front of them.

What should also be taken into consideration is when a person has anything wrong with them; it can be self inflicted or should I say; a person might be getting healed and they will go back into the situation that has been causing it in the first place, and so they do not get any better, they blame the healing Medium or healing they have been given not working.

Remember do not get big headed because you can heal others, you are only a channel for your unseen helpers, as you are when doing any work in any branch of Mediumship. Clean your chakras [if you opened them] or as some people do, shower yourself with the Divine Light of Spirit after doing healing so you do not retain any of the sick person's symptoms, and/or close with a sincere prayer thanking those up stairs in the higher life, all that is needed is to simply sincerely ask for the conditions you have received to go.

Some Healing Mediums doing absent healing go into a deep Trance State and let their Spirit helpers take over completely to do the work. Importantly most Healing Mediums should be passive, try to have as still a mind as you can to help Spirit do their work unhindered, to be used as an open vessel so to speak.

Please try to help others of this world of ours and the next by sending out sincere healing thoughts within the healing minute at the set time of 10 pm Greenwich Mean Time. I try to make it that I send out healing thoughts over a ten minutes period, five minutes each side. This should be done for all the living things on our planet and for peace in our world and to heal the world itself.

Every time a person sits for meditation and the linking with the World of Spirit [God], energy is built up. At the end of the meditation I always sincerely ask for Spirit to send out the energy that has been built up, for it to go out to others in the way of healing, I allow about a minute of silence and thought to direct it. Please every caring person, always do this exercise yourselves.

Please remember you are giving to others something from yourself and Spirit. This should be done whether on your own or in a group situation, or a Circle whether development or in a séance situation.

I think I should put here a method that I use to still my mind as much as possible. What I do is to close my eyes then start speaking to the World of Spirit within my mind through my thoughts. I say it over and over and over, again and again and again at first to bring Spirit closer, then when I know Spirit are there, I sincerely ask Spirit for what is needed. Being truthful to myself and Spirit and most of all being sincere in what I say. I then start concentrating on the light or colour that is within the area of the third eye. Trying to become part of it, dwelling in it. This cuts down on the thoughts going through my mind. You will surprise yourself. Yes it will be a struggle at first but it will come with practice.

# HEALING CIRCLE

This is not the only method by the way.

I had the privilege to be part of this particular Healing Circle with Janet Parker, taking it in the blue room at Stansted Hall, this was one of many I have attended and it was amazing. Chairs placed around in a Circle, a horseshoe shape type, the person in need of healing was placed sitting at the open end of horseshoe.

The Circle was started by the person in need of being healed being placed in one of the chairs in the

Circle [in a round/rectangle/oval shape] at the open end of the horseshoe shape, all the others also sat around in the Circle, every person present being asked to hold hands, the two people next to the person being healed placed their hands on the head [or use shoulders] of the person in need of healing. (Janet talked us through the sequence of events.) Then all close their eyes [imagining, trying to **see it** in your third eye] bringing in the Divine Healing Light to the Circle, We were asked to see the Healing Light going around us all, to surround the Circle with the Healing Light, have the Healing Light lapping gently over us into the middle as though it was the waves of the sea water being turned into Light.

We were asked to **see** [in our mind's eye] the power/light, "The Divine Healing Light" coming down from above and then **see it** building up as a shaft of Healing Light in the middle of the Circle, all the Healing Light started filling up the Circle, mingling all around each person, **see it** filling the Circle then spilling over to the outside of the Circle of Healing Light, building up around us and all asked to **see it** [in our mind's eye]. See the Healing Light starting to build up again in the middle of the Circle going ever upwards in the form of a pillar of Healing Light which formed a cone from us all in the Circle to the centre so joining both worlds for the help needed, as we saw the Healing Light in our mind, we were asked to start the power moving around Circle, to start it spinning from left to right, starting it at the bottom of our feet and getting it going faster and faster, **see it**, feel it spinning, as it rises upwards letting it take the badness away from the person in need of healing. I could feel the power shoot through my body at the tummy area [solar plexus] going sideways [this is something I have never felt before] as it spun around, (the power of the Healing Light) we were asked to see it going higher and higher into the more powerful, stronger Healing Light, it was amazing after the session of about ten minutes/quarter of an hour even I felt rejuvenated as everyone in the Circle did.

We were gently, softly, gradually talked through the steps as and when it was needed by the leader (Janet Parker) of the Healing Circle. We then were asked to see in our mind the Healing Light/Power as we all aimed the power towards the person who was ill, helping the power of Divine Healing Light to take away the illness upwards in the cone of Healing Light for about ten minutes to a quarter of an hour. Then the leader (Janet) talked us back down, asking us to let the conditions gently go. At the end we were all asked to send the healing energy out to people we knew who were sick/ill.

In another Healing Circle, we started with a full Circle and went through the same procedure but this time we were each asked to name a person out loud **or two only** that we knew, for the Healing Power to be sent to them aiming the cone of Healing Light to them; at the end of the session we were asked to send any Healing Power left in the Circle to those person who were in need of it around the world or in hospital. This method can be used for any person who is not there within the Circle. Start the spinning and then ask the group to aim the healing light out to those who have been mentioned. Always seeing it in your mind's eye. The reason only one or two people are mentioned, the time factor comes into the equation. It also gives a better response.

## SELF HEALING

Self Healing can be used by any person who is able to put their own mind to good use, and remember we all can if the conviction is there. We all have the strength, the ability within us to change most things in our life that go wrong with us as an individual, just as we have the ability to change things for others; make sure it is always good and for the best.

Here is a self healing method of rejuvenation, a very good way of getting yourself back on par. It is very easy to use. By making yourself a recorded tape to play, you now will have the means to relax and have healing at the same time. (If you like it, have a smell in the room that is nice for you and when you smell it each and every time after this healing session, that will trigger the healing effect for you unconsciously).

Find a place where you are going to be comfortable and not be disturbed, take the phone off the hook and put a notice across the door of the room where you are going to rest/meditate in.
First you can have a nice relaxing tape playing to yourself for a few minutes say about quarter of an hour before you play the healing tape.
Go through one of the relaxing of the body techniques in the book, so you now can concentrate on the clearing of the mind. This is to let good relaxing conscious and unconscious thoughts have the best

chance of success.

After this sequence has been recorded, play the following recorded sequence for yourself.

**This tape can be used for group healing as well.**

**I can see myself walking into a wonderful place that is filled (with all the things you feel comfortable in) with flowers, pictures, nice ornaments, and a wonderful smell that I always like. There is a wonderful plush healing couch on one side of the room. There is a wonderful smell filling the room.**

(you could say a garden, [and you could lay on a bed of saxifrage, camomile, thyme or anything you like], a room, a hall where ever you would like to be. The directed Divine Light could come through a special cloud overhead).

**Going over to the special couch, I breath in the smell the couch has, it is very special, it has a wonderful healing smell. I breathe in deeply taking in the healing from it, I touch the material I am going to lay down on, I feel it is also special. It is so soft, warm and deep in comfort.**

**As I sit on the healing couch I put my legs and body over into the middle of the material, I sink into the warm luxury of the healing couch. It has a feeling of goodness that is holding me snug in the warm special healing material as it closes around me, it is giving me comfort. I know healing has started already, as it is a very special healing couch. As I relax in the snug warm wonderful smelling material, I notice the light is fading. It is the slow shutting of the windows that is doing it. One special window above me starts to open and through it comes the warm, bright, Divine Healing Light that is directed onto the healing couch where I am laying. I feel the healing from the couch, I breath in the healing smell at each breath, I see the Divine Light healing me, I feel it around me and going into my body, I know it is all doing me good.**

(here have a pause for you to have time to absorb the Divine Light and warmth of the Spirit World. Each time you should in all sincerity within your mind, see it, feel it, know it is doing you good).

**The warmth and the Divine Healing Light are now getting stronger as the window very slowly opens. I breathe in the wonderful healing smell off the couch I feel it going deep into my body each time I breath in. I feel the healing coming from the special material that is around me it is the reflection of the Divine Healing Light from Spirit that is doing it, the material has absorbed the Divine Healing Light over time, the material is now giving it all to me, I see the Divine Healing Light coming all over me, I feel the power of the Divine Healing Light on me and going into my body, I know it is doing me good.**

(here have a pause for you to have time to absorb the Divine Light and warmth of the Spirit World. Each time you should in all sincerity within your mind, see it, feel it, know it is doing you good).

**I can feel the Divine Healing Light and warmth penetrating my body. It is filling me up with goodness, making me feel better than I was before. Each time I breath in the smell of the healing couch this healing me also, I see the Divine Healing Light coming from above and falling all over me it is penetrating my whole being, killing all the badness and the sickness that I have in me, I feel it. I feel the healing material that surrounds me reflecting the Divine Healing Light into me from underneath, I know it is doing me good.**

(here have a pause for you to have time to absorb the Divine Light and warmth of the Spirit World. Each time you should in all sincerity within your mind, see it, feel it, know it is doing you good).

**As I lay here in the Divine Healing Light, the warmth is getting stronger and it is flowing all around my body. The Light is being reflected from the healing couch into my body. Each breath I breath in I can feel the special healing smell permeating my lungs, which is sending the healing all around my body bringing in and doubling the healing within the Divine Healing Light. I can feel the benefit it is bringing into me. <u>I smell</u> the healing smell, <u>I see</u> the Divine Healing Light all around and inside me, <u>I feel</u> the warm Divine Healing Light around me and <u>I feel</u> the healing warmth penetrating my whole being from the reflection from underneath me it is coming off the healing couch and from the Divine Healing Light which is coming through the window all over and inside me. I know it is doing me good.**

(here have a pause for you to have time to absorb the Divine Light and warmth of the Spirit World. Each time you should in all sincerity within your mind, see it, feel it, know it is doing you good).

**I breathe in the wonderful healing smell at each breath, it is going into my lungs and into my body being pumped around by my heart through my blood system. I see the stream of the Divine Healing Light; I feel the warmth and the Divine Healing Light getting deeper into my body. It is**

now filling me slowly with that wonderful thing called the power of the healing love light from God. It is coming into me as warm healing light from all who send it out each time they link with Spirit in their thoughts for the benefit of others. Each good healing thought sent out, is joining up and going into my body to help make me whole again. I smell the healing smell, I see the Divine Healing Light over and inside me doing it's good work, I feel the Divine Healing Light penetrating my whole being making me well again, I know it is doing me good.

(here have a pause for you to have time to absorb the Divine Light and warmth of the Spirit World. Each time you should in all sincerity within your mind, see it, feel it, know it is doing you good).

**The healing of the wonderful smell from the special healing couch, the healing power from the special material on the couch that is wrapped around me, the healing thoughts of others sent out to me, and the warm Divine Healing Light that is going over me, around me, and inside my whole being, they are all penetrating the deepest parts of my body and are making the healing power, more and more powerful. The healing combination is being made ten fold now as they are all joined together, it is all being sent into my body and the healing is taking place with the direction of the Spirit World. Those in Spirit know where it is most needed. They are now taking the healing power and placing it into position where it will do most good for my body. <u>I can smell</u> the healing smell as it fills up my lungs ready to be taken around my body, <u>I can see</u> the healing power as it flows all around my body, <u>I see</u> the Divine Healing Light as it goes inside me through my skin, <u>I can feel</u> the Divine Healing Power from Spirit as it is healing me on the outside and the inside, <u>I know</u> it is doing me good.**

(here have a pause for you to have time to absorb Divine Light and warmth of the Spirit World. Each time you should in all sincerity within your mind, <u>see it, feel it, smell it, know it is doing you good</u>).

**As those healing thoughts, healing smell, and warm Healing Divine Light are blending as they go healing deeper into my body, I am fully aware of the benefit it is giving me. <u>I smell it</u>, <u>I see it</u>, <u>I feel it</u>, <u>I know it</u> is doing me good.**

(here have a pause for you to have time to absorb Divine light and warmth of the Spirit World. Each time you should in all sincerity within your mind, <u>see it, feel it, smell it, know it is doing you good</u>).

**I am going to lay here now and relax in the healing warmth and the healing smell of the special material letting the Divine Healing Light of Spirit do it's healing work. <u>I smell it</u>, <u>I see it</u>, <u>I feel it</u>, <u>I know it</u> is doing me good.**

(Lay there for however long you wish being comfortable and relaxed knowing you are in a secure warm place and getting the healing benefit within the Divine Light and warmth of the Spirit World).

(here you are having a pause for a time to absorb the light and warmth. Each time you should in all sincerity within your mind, <u>see it, feel it, smell it, know it is doing you good</u>).

**You can come back from that couch whenever you feel you want to.**

If you would like to make a long tape of this which would be better for a sustained attack on any illness, put in every two or three minutes as a trigger point for your subconscious, as follows.

**At each breath I smell the wonderful healing smell in the air as it goes into my body healing as it does, at each breath I feel the wonderful healing feeling in the air as it goes into my body healing as it does, at each breath I hear the wonderful healing noise in the air as it goes into my body healing as it does, I can feel the healing warmth and the healing comfort of the healing couch under me, I can feel and see the warm Divine Healing Light penetrating my body to the points where it is needed for healing making my body whole again. The healing power is getting stronger each time now it is all combined. I can see the Healing Divine Light coming all over me and going inside me, healing as it does so. I feel the Divine Healing Light falling all over me; it is washing away all the badness into the earth healing as it goes. As the Divine Healing Light goes inside me, it is dissolving all the illness that is inside me, it is being made into water and my waste product and it will come out as waste when I go to the toilet. The Divine Healing Light is healing the bad parts and making the bad whole again as it goes into my body, I know it is doing me good.**

Then at the end of the tape put in something like this.
**The window where the Divine Healing Light is coming through is closing and the other windows showing the daylight are opening. The light has changed now for the time being. The healing will be continuing all the time whether I think of the healing or not. The Divine Healing Light will be**

**here all the time when needed within me and around me, always making me feel better in myself, when I come out of this meditation the healing effects will continue all my days and nights. The next time I listen to this tape it will be stronger in the healing it does for me.**
Be sincere in the thoughts that are in your head, so the Divine Healing Light will continue doing it's work within you. Pause again slightly then continue and end with these words.
**I sincerely thank the people in the Spirit World for their time and effort in doing their work of getting me better. I am getting up from the couch and going to the door of the room I was having healing in. I open the door and step into the daylight, which has woken me up.**

Another way to help yourself whenever any health problem raises its ugly head, try to meditate each day. Do not make an excuse that you do not have any time during the day. We all can make time even if it is only a quarter of an hour. Meditation is to get yourself closer to the higher self that is within us all, to also join up with the higher force who ever you personally believe in. Sincerely ask for the help from the God force, the Spirit World while you go through these exercises.

What you do in this sequence is [there are many ways] sit or lay down comfortably, somewhere you won't get disturbed, close your eyes sincerely ask for help from the higher planes, those in Spirit. **Imagine, see** your complaint as being a dirty colour [or a bad image; a bad, an awful looking black/brown/red/yellow mixed coloured bug type thing, as in a cancer], a soreness of the bones could be **imagined/seen** as redness [as in arthritis or rheumatism]. With your eyes still closed, **imagine/see** yourself looking at your painful part of your bone (or anything in your body that is a problem) and **seeing it** as being a painful red (or the awful looking black/brown/red/yellow mixed coloured bug). Bring into your mind's eye the bright cleaning white light, the power of the inner self, joined up with the power of the higher force. You should **see** within your mind the power being aimed through that all powerful of things "thought"; **see** the true Divine Healing Light going to and surrounding the painful area. Surround it with the Divine Healing Light, **see** the area of redness changing to the true, natural, none painful whiteness of the bone in it's natural state as the light surrounds it. Each time you do this, concentrate and **make it so** and **believe it, it does happen**, the pain goes, perhaps not immediately but it will I assure you it will if this is done with the asking of the help of Spirit and if it is done sincerely.

As I mentioned before about cancer, I will tell you about this terrible illness and a way it can be killed. Try looking at the cancer in the body as a lot of evil looking bugs/reptiles type things (the most awful looking black/brown/red/yellow mixed coloured bugs you can imagine), after all; that is all that cancer is. Cancer is a part of your body that multiplies quicker than your anti-bodies can kill them, so with your own help and the sincere asking of the Spirit World, this disabling process can be reversed. Close your eyes; imagine the cancer as terrible as you want to see it, **but see it in your mind,** bring in the power of the pure, white, Divine Healing Light, the God Force from Spirit. **See this light surrounding** the cancer images individually with the pure Divine Healing Light the God Force from Spirit, **see the light trapping them** so they cannot multiply, "**see them being consumed**" "**being shrunk**" by the Divine Healing Light, "**see them being killed**" by the Light, [perhaps eaten by the Light] **see them made into waste** and **see them flowing away** in a flow of Light and **see them going down a drain** [or to your bladder or to your bowels see them being expelled out in your waste each time you go to the toilet. Have a very, very good drink of water before you start this sequence is something some do; that way the person will go to the toilet and the person can then physically **see the waste going down the toilet** when the person finishes the meditation]. As it is happening sincerely say to yourself inwardly "bring in the highest form of Divine Light to me and surround the cancer with the Divine Healing Light, killing it off with love, light and goodness, take it away into the waste and let be consumed by the Light making my system good again". Remember; **see it** happening, **feel it** happening, **know it is happening**, do this within your mind and most of all sincerely **believe it**. Have trust in your own Spirit and the power it has when it is being helped by being part of the whole of the higher developed vibrational level of the Divine Healing Spirit. Then look into the Light (or colour) within your third eye and let those in Spirit do their work with you being passive.

Use this method with any illness being in the state of meditation for 15 to 30 minutes or longer. I do not put a time limit for you as I do not have your illness, also I do not know how badly you want to get better. Do it as many times a day as you like. At the end of each method you use, I would recommend that you try and still your mind and just look into the God force the Divine Light after you have gone through sequence of killing the bugs and let the Divine Healing Light do it's work for at least a quarter of an hour after.

If you do go to a healer, help him/her to help you, while they are doing their healing on you. Get in touch with your higher self and link with the higher vibration level of Spirit by saying a sincere prayer. You then should try and **see** the Divine Healing Light entering the body and going to the problem area. See it working away; see it clearing the badness out of your body.

Keep on saying to yourself; **it is** getting better, **it is** getting better. **I can see it** getting better. [YOU MUST **SEE IT** GETTING BETTER.] **I can feel it** getting better. [YOU MUST **FEEL IT** GETTING BETTER]. **I KNOW IT IS GETTING BETTER.** [YOU MUST SINCERELY BELIEVE IN THE POWER OF THE SPIRIT WORLD DOING Its JOB OF HEALING].

It might be classed as positive thought, but to that I say it is your own positive higher self that is doing the healing with the help of the positive Divine Healing Light of Spirit by your thought reaching out to them. We come again to that **living energy "THOUGHT"**. If you do this regularly, it certainly works. It has also been done on people with broken bones, which have healed very much quicker than normal. The person has to see within their own mind, the bone knitting in the Divine Healing Light, and the person can quite often feel the effects of their own treatment. If you have brittle bone problems, try **seeing** the bones as being fixed by the Divine Healing Light, **see them being made whole again** being back to normal. Try to still your mind as much as possible and look into the Divine Healing Light after saying a few words up stairs [as I say] to those people in the Spirit World or within the God Force you believe in, while the healing is going on.

Some might heal using the method of seeing a shaft of Light being aimed at the spot on the body where the sickness or the diagnosed problem is. This can be in the form of a laser type of beam of the Divine Light of Spirit, a specially aimed beam of that most wonderful of gifts given to us by Spirit. Many healers can see the beam being used in this way and use it to the advantage of the patient. Use it on yourself for the benefits it can bring from God, the Divine Spirit.

## HEALING EXERCISES WITH SOUND

It has been found sounds made in the human, and also by the human can be used to help with different healing techniques for the head area as sound vibrates within the round-ish bony structure helping within it. Also sound can help with the air passages from the lungs upwards. The sounds vibrate through the body through the liquid/fluid of the human body [or any **anima**l body structure] also in the air cavities.

The ways to help yourself in this method are to make the sounds whilst breathing out after a deep breath repeating the sounds for a period of at least five minutes each day, morning and at night.

Make the sounds by producing the following English lettering and made up words.

These exercises can be used with groups of friends; they become very effective this way.

A E I O U          Pronounce these letters in sequence whilst breathing out your deep breath and opening your mouth wide and form the letters **deliberately and holding each letter**, drawing it out longer as a note, as you say them. These help with the whole of the body bring it into balance.

HUM HUM HUM          Pronounce these words over and over whist breathing out, it will help the airways from the lungs (as all these sounds do) going up to the bronchial tubes, the sinuses, and you will be able to feel the vibration in the skull.

N N N N N          These letters if pronounced correctly will help with the functioning of the passages in the ears. Remember to be breathing out that deep breath as you are doing these exercises.

MA MA MA MA MA          Helps with problems caused by the sinuses and the passages of the nose and the back of the throat area (nasal passages). Say them quickly and sharply with a quick out pouring of breath. Then try saying them slowly and slowly push the breath out as you say it.

YA  YOU  YAI   These words should be formed by exaggerating them with the mouth as they are exercises for the jaw muscles, and said to help with inner tension and migraine headaches.

HUH  HUH  HUH  HUH   These words should be said with an action of forcing the breath outwards **quickly** from the stomach area. They clear the mucus from the airways; help strengthen the stomach, so helping in turn the digestive system, and with appetite.

Try different sounds for yourself and add to this list.

Please think about the different frames of mind you can have when a noisy heavy rock band is playing, or a calm piece of music being played by a violin. Look also at the music you can now buy for meditating with, they calm the spirit within yet others can jar the senses. Sound is a very personal thing, what one person likes, another will find uncomfortable to sit and listen to. It has been told through mediums of old, coming from their messages off Spirit that the lower A double diapason is the best for attracting Spirit so try and get hold of some music in this key I personally do not know any. The large organs of the cathedrals are about that key in some pieces.

In 2001 at a Trance course in Stansted hall, a student trance medium was asked to demonstrate her skill whilst linking in with Spirit in a Trance state. It was a very unusual gift she had; I had heard her before a few years previous. The lady I think came from Denmark. She went into her Trance state linking into Spirit, then started to sing in what I can only describe as a mixture of different foreign songs and different notes, many of the songs and notes hit a vibration level that sent shivers through you, doing something inside of you, affecting the workings of the body and other notes uplifting your Spirit inside while listening. It was truly amazing. Emma Hardinge Britten describes singing healing Mediums in her books of the 1800s. So you can see what can be done with notes of vibrations, music and song.

## TRANCE HEALING

The word Trance in healing is being frowned on by those in the EEC of which we are now a part. So it has been decided by most healers to call it **"Channelling"** the American way of saying Trance healing. The word Trance for those allegedly intelligent people who run the EEC; is a person who is not under their own normal control, I personally believe the people in that organisation do not know what they are doing. Every time each person in the EEC parliament closes their eyes they are in a light Trance state, an altered state of awareness. So those "guardians" of our European Parliament have decided that for them to root out the people of not (as they think of them) so high a moral ground they are trying to pass a law to ban Trance Healing. I think the medical profession and the Christian churches might have had something to say in this matter, yes them having words in the ears of the EEC politicians so to speak, so getting it pushed through the EEC Parliament as law. But who can prove that a person who is doing healing is in Trance and another is not? Who is to say when are we not in Trance or when we are when doing healing? When we close our eyes we are in an altered state. What is Trance? It is being in an altered state of awareness and that altered state starts from the time our eyes shut.

Deep Trance **(channelling)** Healing is a very advanced form of healing where the "Healing Medium" is under the control of the Healing Spirits, who are generally doctors or specialists who had practised their medical skills while they were on the earth plane. But not always, those in Spirit could have learned their skills while across the other side of the veil.

The Deep Trance **(channelling)** Healing Medium is being used as an instrument, a vessel for the goodness, kindness, love and truth to be given to their fellow man. When a Deep Trance Healing Medium stills their mind to allow Spirit to take control of their body. They trust and know Spirit's judgement is far greater than their own in what is about to take place for the patient. All the Deep Trance Healing Medium should do is to be passive and let the Spirit World do their work. The link should be Medium to Spirit and the passive part on behalf of the Deep Trance Healing Medium then begins. The Healing Medium should not direct anything to the patient, that is Spirit's job.

I often see Trance **(channelling)** Healers advertising their services, putting their own, specialist/doctor in Spirit forward as though there is only one person who is there helping them. This is for me is doing a disservice to all the many Spirit helpers who are in the group of Spirit helpers that are necessary to perform such fantastic forms of help in this type of Mediumship [healing]. The mending of bones, healing terminal diseases, healing the mentally ill, and doing extraordinary operations. There can be upwards to approximately sixty in the medical team in the Spirit World helping the Spirit in the forefront of the healing situation all having their own specialist part to play. THIS IS WHY THE **PASSSIVE STANCE** OF THE TRANCE HEALING MEDIUM IS SO NECESSARY. None of these people in/of Spirit who are in the team of Spirit helpers, do not seem to get any recognition at all by the Healing Mediums who advertise their services. I realise the Trance **(channelling)** Healing Medium has to attract the public's eye, but, every person should recognise the fact of more than one Spirit helper being used with each helpful medical happening.

Some might dismiss the fact that miracles happen on a daily basis, especially the orthodox churches, which now seem to thrive on the so called miracles of the past and earn lots of money from them. Those churches thinking miracles can only happen in the books of their religions, only happening many years ago, and they think established churches alone have the monopoly on miracles. Forget about that, it still goes on today. Look and you will find a person of integrity who is each day quietly doing the work of Spirit healers for sick, handicapped, and infirm people, tirelessly working away not being publicised by the media because it might upset the money making established churches we have around us. The taking away of the peoples blinkers unlocking their fixed minds and making them open to other thoughts would take away the people from their congregations and so their comfortable monetary monopoly within their churches.

Simple ordinary people have been used as an instrument of Spirit doing Trance healing work for many years to help others, the healers still work tirelessly today. In Brazil there was an ordinary peasant farmer who did Trance healing for many there. Even Presidents were said to have gone to him for healing, they had to stand in the queue like all who were there. There are many still working today throughout the world.

The people who try to put all the Trance **(channelling)** Healing Mediums in the category of conjurers fall flat on their face when they go around investigating more than three Trance Healing Mediums because they then find there is no rational explanation that they can see for what is happening. BUT they, the investigator get the publicity because they have been courting it all their working lives and know how to manipulate publicity, the hard working Healing Medium gets very little, perhaps none; and lots of times adverse publicity. The conjurers are the only people the public listened to, it also makes a good story for the media, who in my opinion do not like the truth. What is it said by them? "Why let the truth get in the way of a good story". Those who believe do not need any evidence, those who do not believe none will suffice.

Please for your own sake do not go into a Trance **(channelling as some people call it)** state unless there are people who you trust there with you. You are likely to get into trouble if they are not.

When a Trance **(channelling)** Healing Medium sees a patient they do not need to know the ailments of the patient. At first they are generally in conversation with the person in need of healing, then as the Medium has the Power of Spirit come closer into them they start to go into a dreamy state. The conversation then stops. Spirit then takes over. The Medium must have total trust in the Spirit realm. As they get deeper into the Trance state, Spirit takes over the bodily actions of the entranced Healing Medium. This is why it is a must to have a trusted person/persons [<u>**never touching** the entranced healing Medium, unless they allow it</u>, everyone is different] by the entranced Medium's side at all times when they are in that Trance **(channelling)** state. This is a safeguard for the Trance Healing Medium and the patient, so there will be no misunderstanding at all in the Deep Trance Healing Medium's actions. The less the entranced Mediums knows about what is going on when they work in this state the better Spirit Healers can work. The mind of the entranced Medium must be detached from what they are doing otherwise they will block the link with Spirit, the mind of the Medium if used in thought by the Medium will interfere with the actions of Spirit Healers. A Deep Trance Healing Medium must be able to disassociate themselves totally from what they are doing otherwise they will block any link with the higher vibrational level. A very well known Trance **(channelling)** Healing Medium, and tutor, once told me "When I was first starting healing, I thought anything that a Healer could do in a Trance state to heal anyone, they could do in a normal state. This I found out later in my development was not true". "Spirit needs the Trance **(channelling)** State Medium to gain that greater link to the patient's own

Spirit". Remember, it is the saying of the Medium's name that brings the person back to reality; so do not use it while they are healing in Trance, but of course, this does not apply to all.

Sometimes a patient will have their eyes closed and they will get strange feelings when the healing is taking place. Some feel as though they are turning over, even though they are still remaining motionless on their back or sitting. Some feel as though they are having their stomach turned over or it being turned inside out. Some feel things happening in the area of the problem, others find that the healing gets done away from the supposed problem area. All healing varies. Some healers just stand still with their hands on the shoulders of their patient. Yet others when doing their work, the Trance Healing Medium seems to be manipulating the air around the patient. The purpose of healing is to make the patients Spirit and the earthly body whole again. Remember you are a "Healing Medium", not just a healer. You are the link in between the Spirit World and the patient; you are the catalyst, the "MEDIUM" by which things happen. Practice, practice, practice trying to still your mind the best you can for any healing work. Keep looking into the void, colour, or the divine light of Spirit in your mind's eye area [the third eye] become part of it. That is the best way I have found as yet BUT never forget you are only the instrument. Practice the passive state that the Trance Healing Medium is trying to achieve.

When going into a healing trance state, for three years I had a problem with letting Spirit influence me with their energy into letting them manipulate me into a stance that I at first found strange in so much as Spirit changing my face and my body which was bent over into a very elderly person's stance. I let my mind think it was not what I wanted others to see me in this, for me, was an abnormal state. When I relaxed into this state the naturalness of the flow of healing became a lot better and my patients felt a lot more in their healing even though I did not, I was still in what I thought was being passive for the Spirit World to use me. The strange thing was even after over half an hour sometimes more, I did not feel stiff or uncomfortable when I had finished healing in that bent over state.

## Always work in __truth__ and __sincerity__.

Trance **(channelling)** Healers are the better sitters for Physical Circles; also they can become very good Physical Mediums in their own right. The reason is the vibration level link Trance Healers work with the Spirit World are similar to the vibrational level linking the Physical Mediums work within with the Spirit World. So if you are going to sit for Physical, try to become a Trance **(channelling)** Healing Medium. Go to the courses that are run in the Arthur Findlay College, Stansted Hall, Stansted, Essex CM24 8UD. UK, Telephone 01279 813636 Email afc@snu.org.uk . website www.snu.org.uk **or at** Hafan y Coed, Heol Tawe, Abercraf, Swansea SA9 1TJ Telephone 01639 730 985 Fax 01639 730 704 E Mail hyc@btconnect.com website www.hafanycoed.com, on the ways of how to do Trance healing so you have good grounding of your subject.

I was in a Trance Healing experimental workshop class with a Healing Medium, during the Judith Seaman Trance week at Stansted Hall in April 2002 in the library. Where I had a wonderful experience. (It was the best group I had sat with there BAR NONE the loving unselfish harmony in Eileen Michamson's [she was the tutor of the group I was in that week such a wonderful genuine person] group was fantastic that week). The Healing tutor in his workshop with our group on the Thursday, had split us up into three sets of three. During my turn for healing I was healing a Canadian man called Andy whilst in Trance but still aware, under my left hand I could feel the skin on his left shoulder, moving like an undulating wave, a rippling effect. It was fantastic to feel Spirit move it. The Canadian male patient did not feel a thing only strong heat from my hands. He said he thought I would have gone to his back problem as he had mentioned it while in the group. I told him I always did healing with a passive mind; I link with Spirit and let them get on with the work necessary. He said he had had a problem with some disease of the skin from when he was young and did not talk about it. See Spirit knows best, there is no reason to apply your own mind or to know what disease the patient has. Just place your hands on the head, shoulders, or within the auric field of the patient then be passive.

During our turn to observe the tutor asked each three of us (there was nine in the group) to feel with our hands, the power of the energy produced around the placement of the set of six chairs; placed three sets of two. One each for the Healing Medium and one for each patient. The power formed an oblong and was domed over the group. This was felt by a tingling in the fingers, and sometimes full on the hands as we walked closer to the healing group from the furthest points of the room. I had previously done this exercise in Havan-y-Coed two years before but the power in this group at Stansted Hall was far, far, far stronger because of the loving unselfish harmony we all had built up during the week within our group. The Spirit World calls this surrounding force that we felt over and around the healer and the patient the "bowsing" effect.

# PSYCHIC SURGERY

I think a little of this miraculous of gifts should be placed in this book as there are still people who are dedicated enough to perform this skill with the help of those unseen in the World of Spirit. People who have the expertise to go into a **TRUE full deep passive Trance state** and let themselves be an instrument of highly developed surgeons and their team of helpers in the World of Spirit. It needs the team effort to accomplish this invasive event, as skilled Spirit doctors/surgeons have to be there ready to perform the operations. Other parts of the Spirit Team across the veil have to be there to manipulate the Trance Healing Medium in his/her actions through the nervous system, through the **still and passive mind** of the Healing Medium. Most of the Healing Mediums who are Physical Spiritual surgeons go into the Trance state and are in world of their own, they are not fully with us, as happens when a Medium practices **"Physical Phenomena"**. For most this is the natural state of a Medium in a **TRUE** Trance state. The Medium who practices this craft as a invasive Spiritual Surgeon, some mistakenly call it Psychic Surgeon, will be seen to cut open the body of the patient with unseen psychic tools of the doctor in Spirit (some use tools that can be seen), then proceed to delve into the body, which can be seen bleeding and draw out some sort of tissue or lump of the internal problem to the patient. The Medium will then draw his/her hands over the patient where there is a gaping wound and the wound will close instantly or in a very short time, most times leaving no scar or maybe a small one as well as little or no after effects for the patient.

One such man was living in Brazil called Jose Arigo; he is now in the Spirit World and helping in the Spirit Team who support Steven Turoff.

Others in the London area around the 1920's performed Physical Spiritual surgery. One such person, a white man then called the "Medicine Man" no name give but his practice was in Marylebone House. He used to place his hands inside the patients body and produce the tumours out of the open wounds place them into bottles they would then miraculously disappear, as would the great amount of blood that was accompanied with the open wounds. Another person in that area at about the same time who did the same was Evan Powell. His helper/guide was "Black Hawk".

A Philippine's Medium, Tony Agpaoa, is a very dedicated person and works relentlessly healing the sick and infirmed. BUT there are a lot of fakes in that part of the world many a conjurer there claiming to be a Physical Spiritual surgeon.

A Physical Spiritual Surgeon who works in England is Steven Turoff, a very hard working gent. He works with Dr Joseph Abraham Kahn who died in 1950's, a nurse Grace and a Mr R James. Steven is said to have a team of seventeen behind him and his hands, helping from across the veil. There is a very good book out about him called Steven Turoff Psychic Surgeon by Grant Solomon ISBN 0-7225-3890-1. His work is world renown, he has even demonstrated his skill at the Arthur Findlay College in Stansted, where people were asked to come up on the platform to watch the operation and the wound heal up on the person and close after a Physical Spiritual operation.

I have just recently found out about another Brazilian Healer, Joao Teixeria de Faria, who does spiritual healing and psychic surgery and is still performing operations today in 2004. He is affectionately known as Joao de Deus [John of God]. Joao started as a boy and he has dedicated his life to the healing of the sick in every way; each person's Mind, Body, and Spirit. It is said by the people who go to him, "he allows the team of over thirty "entities" [as it is put] to take control of him while operating on the seriously ill". These "entities", or as we say "those in Spirit in a higher vibrational plane", were while on this earth plane of ours [when alive] gifted doctors, surgeons and prominent people in their specialist field of healing. When Joao is in the trance state and the "entities" are there with him, he performs operations of different kinds some are visible others are invisible. There is no pain or blood or very little blood when the visible operations are performed on the patients. The patients are asked if they would like a visible or invisible operation before the start of the proceedings. I am told most of the operations are done invisibly. All of the operations are done without anaesthetic. There are literally thousands that have been through its doors, few, it is said have come out disappointed. The Sanctuary is like a small hospital set out in its own grounds where a lot of people go to sit within its gardens to meditate and contemplate.

The sanctuary is placed in the quiet of the surrounding hills in the village of Abadiania, which is built on a natural bed of quartz crystal.

A lady, Lynn Debenham, who had a miraculous operation by Joao de Deus and his helpers in Spirit to remove a lump off her spine, now runs trips across to Central Brazil to the Casa de Dom Inacio Healing Sanctuary. She can be contacted at :-  Edw Cottage, Llwyn Farm, Aberedw, Builth Wells, Powys, LD2 3YD. United Kingdom. Tel/fax  01982 570 449

"**Please**", if you go into this field of Mediumship **DO NOT FOOL YOURSELF WITH LIES!!!! Don't say to the public you are doing things with Spirit, when you are not.!!!!! You could hurt so many people and eventually yourself!!!!! <u>Please be truthful and sincere just as you should be in "any" Mediumship you do!!!!!</u>**
<u>**It is the Spirit World that decide if you are suitable NOT YOU**</u>**. They in their wisdom will guide you.**

Some **"Psychic Surgeons"** only do what can be described as passes over the body as though the Healing Medium is performing actions a doctor would if doing a surgical operation. It leaves some people to wonder if anything is happening when the Healing Medium goes into Trance BUT only the Healing Medium, Spirit and the patient can know this truth. This sort of action can leave people (a Healing Medium) open to abuse and be called a charlatan as have many have found to their own cost, even if they have the best of motives, that of helping others for no payment at all. Many have good results through the Power of Spirit BUT only when they are **truthful and sincere** with everything they do.

The Healing Medium still has to meditate and link into the Divine Light **regularly** to keep the link strong with those helpers in the World of Spirit. So please do not forget to do so, if you want to progress.

I would like to point out there are many instances where the Healing Medium themselves have set up the link with Spirit, the Healing Medium acting as an open vessel being there with the patient, then the Spirit Team takes over, while the Healing Medium's Spirit, and their physical body stands aside for the moment BUT staying near the patient as Spirit Team gets on with the work needed. Many is the time the manipulation can be felt in this instance by the patient, and people who have been within the healing room environment have seen the body in front of them being manipulated by an unseen force. Instances of this can be read about in the books of the healer Betty Shine, who sadly just recently has gone to the higher life in April 2002.

As all these instances should show you, it is the link through the Healing Medium while they are in a PASSIVE altered state, that is they are an activated passive catalyst (the entranced, passive Healing Medium) for the job in hand, which is needed most times for the healing of another living thing.

I asked Spirit once, "Why don't you heal all that ask for the healing to be done to others". The reply I got was :- "Not all people, many of whom class themselves as Mediums, who ask for others to be healed are **sincere** and **really mean it**, not taking the time needed, some stopping in mid-stream as though **they** have decided when enough is enough. Quite often many are flippant about it. It takes **much time and sincere effort** on the person's part to send out the **sincere healing linking thoughts** needed and **a lot more effort** on our side of the veil, on our healing group's part as well to link and act in a meaningful, constructive way. Some people can waste the gifts given to them because of self glorification. Many are those patients who go for healing, when they have had healing done, immediately return to the situation, which brought about the problem in the first place, and then blame the Medium and those in Spirit for healing not working. To gain a strong link with us here in the Spirit World, we need a <u>**sincere, passive, truthful**</u> subject for our work to be done unhindered ".

# Miracles <u>CAN</u>, <u>DO</u>, and <u>WILL</u> happen if healing is done in <u>TRUTH</u> and with the <u>SINCERITY</u> of the person when asking of the help needed from the other vibrational level, the Spirit World within which is the God force.

# MIRROR SCRYING
## Psychomantium

In the last century people used a mirror to try to see people who had passed into the higher sphere, their loved ones, in a mirror. Remember the fairy tale where the line says? :- "Mirror, mirror on the wall who is the fairest of them all," Is this part of the looking into the mirror being told of another person being shown to the seer in that fairy tale of many years ago? Was that person in the looking glass and being shown psychically a face of another?

This form of scrying is something that could be tried by anyone. When set up, the device is called a psychomantium.

You use a mirror that should be placed at an angle, where, when you look into it you cannot see your reflection in it. Or two mirrors which are in line with each other so you cannot see your reflection nor the reflection of the other mirror in the other, that should be tilted slightly at an angle, sit yourself in a comfortable seat, in a comfortable position, have the light [or candle] very, very dim/low at the back of the mirror, or to the side, so you cannot see the light or the reflection of it. A very low shaded/covered red light is said to be best, lots of people in the days far gone, have used a candle for lighting when scrying, some people use no light at all, sitting in the dark. The dark can have some wonderful effects in the mirror. A lot of sitters find this is the best way for them but try every form of lighting as well. The mirrors are set so you cannot see your own reflection in the mirrors.

Always start the sitting by saying some sort of a prayer, to your Divine Spirit, your God. I would always include in any sincere prayer the asking for only goodness, kindness, love and truth from within the Divine Light of Spirit and help to come from those in the loving harmony of the highest realms. Always you should ask and want complete peaceful loving harmony and ask for the help of the highest dimension, and asking sincerely to see the loved ones who you know, the people of the other vibration level who have gone before. [Ask for what you want answered also] Look into the mirror at an angle [try at different angles for yourself] and stare into it steadily for about 10-15 minutes, try to cut down on your blinking [by the way it does not always come at the first few times of sitting. You have to be patient, as you have to be with all the psychic developments]. Some people try defocusing their eyes or do not look directly at the point of vision, look beyond it. A lot of ancient people used a bowl of water in candlelight, or looked into a pool at dawn or dusk. As their psychic development progressed they could do it in the daylight. This might have been clairvoyance being used. De-focusing [as happens naturally when staring without blinking] their eyes as you do in crystal gazing.

Another method to try is:- Have a special room put aside for Spirit [best, but not always necessary].

The best way is to try to see into the mirror is for you to sit in front of the mirror in a dark room; no light at all is to come into it. Must be completely dark. Sit in front of the mirror in the light to set it up. The mirror is set at an angle so you **cannot** see your refection in it when you are in the light.

In the dark, as you look into the mirror, say a sincere prayer to your Divine Spirit, your God. I would always include in it the asking for only goodness, kindness, love, and truth of the highest Divine Light to come around you, wanting complete peaceful loving harmony with the highest vibrational level to come into the room and around you. In the dark sit comfortably and look into the mirror while you send out love to your loved ones. As you sit you will see faces being shown to you. If you are lucky you will be shown different scenes. Most people sit for about half to one hour. Some do not want to come out of the room, as they get engrossed in the scenes. You must discipline yourself and have a restriction on the time so as to not get hooked on it. I would recommend an hour at the most. You can then leave it for another day.

Try doing this method in the light as well. Experiment in the candlelight, diffused red light, diffused blue or green light. Place the lights so you cannot see yourself, the lights, nor can you see the reflections of the light in the mirrors. Experiment, experiment, experiment. Best results it seems take place when the mediumistic person is in the dark or very, very subdued light.

One person I was talking to at Stansted Hall, said he was looking into a mirror full on, straight on, he could see his own face, and the face turned and went off the mirror to the left, so experiment with every angle BUT give one angle of the mirror a chance to work, say about a month of doing it every day.

# CRYSTAL BALL GAZING
## Crystallomancy

A crystal ball is a slightly different form of looking into a person's past and their destiny in as much as the person who owns the ball has to be the only person who cleans it with warm soapy water and handles it, with the exception of when a person needs to know of their destiny, the person who you are going to scry for [scry is to look into the crystal ball and give information to others of what you see within it], BUT on saying that I have heard of a lady who was local to me, Mrs Yates from Leigh, Lancashire in England who used to use a "**crystal**" ball [her crystal ball was a large glass one] slightly differently, because when she brought the images through into the crystal ball, she used to give it to the sitters [who she was giving the reading to], and show the "**crystal**" ball to all the sitters who were there so they could also see the visions in it as well, and they did. There are always exceptions in all things psychic as I keep saying we are all individual in our links. A scrying ball that was generally always in the past, was made of clear quartz crystal, but as crystal is now being so dear to buy, people are using a clear glass ball, or the modern ones of clear plastic or clear resin. To start it is best for you to link into Spirit, ask sincerely within your thoughts for help from your friends, and the people above to help you. Look into the ball of your choice steadily for about ten/fifteen minutes to start with, not much more otherwise your eyes get tired and possibly blood shot. When you start always ask for help from Spirit in your thoughts (or out loud). Always thank your higher force and close the conditions with your thoughts. If you do not see anything, say so. You will be much better thought of in the long run.

For me, the information in the ball to the left is the past, the centre is the present, and to the right is the future. When you start looking into the ball always stipulate this to your helpers then they can work closely with you, it soon becomes second nature to both you and your helpers in the Spirit World. Set your own rules **first** to your way of looking into the crystal ball from the start.

Try to get some dark cloth to place the ball on, it can be placed on your lap, on a plinth, or cupped in your hands when reading. Try them all and find the way that suits you. I find reading in a subdued light is best; this comes from the back of me, not direct light as the reflection of the light can distract. Many find that candlelight is best. It is best to meditate before any reading, **sincerely asking** for help from above bringing goodness, kindness, love, and truth to come within the light of the Divine Spirit from the highest realms, and to blend in peaceful, loving harmony, bringing what ever you want to ask for. When reading, it is best not to be interrupted. Some say they see a clouding over of the inside of the ball. Others have different ways; this is because each person is an individual. Some only see writing, some pictures, some people, others see everything. Best to have the person who you are reading for across the other side of the table, within an arms length of the crystal ball, never have too many people there with this person as the messages can become mixed up. Best is always one to one. If that cannot be managed try to have the other people you are not giving the reading for at least about a metre, to a metre and a half away.

People use their crystal ball in different ways, the reason being we are all individuals having different strengths. Some have the ability with the help of above to charge their personal ball with an energy that always works for them as though there is a screen switched on inside the ball for them as and when necessary as they work. Others seem to use the ball as their focal point then draw on their own ability as a clairvoyant, some using the crystal ball as a hypnotic aid going into a light Trance. Yet others seem to have their crystal ball as a direct link to a higher level. Use whatever way is suitable for you. Some see their visions symbolically, others as though they are seeing actual happenings, you will have to practice and see which one comes for you. This is what happens with different platform Mediums so do not worry. Always talk to the Spirit World and say what you would like to happen then let it over a period of time.

I go into meditation first asking for a link for the person I am going to give the reading for. The crystal ball for me goes cloudy then clears, and then I can see the scenes or message for the person it become like a small TV.

In the 1900's there weere experiments done with globes of glass that were filled with pure, distilled, water. These were placed on a special stand, which underneath it had an enclosed, red light, shining up into the base of the water filled glass dome. A low wattage bulb which was battery operated was used by some under a cloth; the defused rays of soft, red, light was said to be suitable for illuminating ectoplasm which was said to be produced in some circumstances by the reader of the images in the ball. Some

Scryers are said to produce the ectoplasm in the crystal ball itself and this is what is showing/forming the images in the ball. How true that is I do not honestly know. **I would not** say my fog/misting/cloudiness was ectoplasm I think it was a focus for my Clairvoyance, BUT I might be wrong.

Some Scryers used to use shiny thick black oil or a strong black dye in water in vessels like a bowl to receive messages for others. Some use ordinary cooking oil floating on the water to interpret the reading for a person. Or a spot of motor oil, which turns into a myriad of colours on top of the water, it is like a shimmering rainbow of colours. Another way to use a dye for scrying is to use a round bottomed flask as you used to use in the chemistry experiments at school, then use the flask for looking into the blackness, another way is to swill a some black gloss paint around in a round globe like glass container (try an upturned goldfish bowl) and then let it dry, this will give a shiny round glass container to look into like a black glass crystal ball. A lot of the older books describe using black mirrors for scrying. There is nothing sinister in using the black globe or a black mirror. You can use any strong dark colour if you wish if you do not like the thought of black. Like everything in the linking with the Spirit World please EXPERIMENT.

# AWARENESS
# Sensitivity

When going into deep altered awareness in meditation, some feel their heart start to pound while in that meditation, this is I feel Spirit and your body adjusting to the levels needed for the higher realm to work, often the feelings go very quickly at other times it seems to stay a little longer but do not worry most deep meditators get this feeling at one time or another. It also means you are also becoming more aware of yourself and of your link with Spirit. Quite often people feel/hear a clock noise, the tick-tock, more so, a watch ticking can be heard louder, whereas before the meditation all was silent to the ear. For many when in this altered awareness, a normally quiet noise if given suddenly can shock, or make you jump when you are in this sensitive state, try to go deeper into your meditation and all noise will go. When in this sensitive state after meditation try the sounds of the beating of a drum, or ringing of the singing bowls, perhaps the Shaman's drum chant, the Tibetan gong, the mantra of the Monks, or Native American Indian's chants. These and many more sounds have a profound effect on your system when it is in this sensitive state. It shows you that you are progressing into a more sensitive person as a whole, feeling things that others do not. Music will start to sound different to your ears; you will also feel the music through your body as well. Some music in this state can be invasive to your system and can have a profound effect on the senses, experiment to see what suits you and what does not; it **will surprise you**.

As you progress you will find, I hope, that you will become more sensitive to other people's feelings. You will become far more sensitive in yourself and in your outlook throughout life, becoming a better person and more emotional, sympathising and empathising with other people more. Progressing still further with your feelings, you might find that you will be able to pick out people in a crowd who are good, sort of alright, passable, not so nice, bad, evil. But do not try too hard with this because there is many an occasion that first impressions can be wrong. Just look, listen and learn in whatever situation you are in, you will find you will learn a lot more than the other person who goes into a given situation with their mouth open first. [The owl is a wise old bird who sat in an oak, the more he heard the less he spoke, the less he spoke the more he heard, I wish I was that wise old bird], I hope later on you will be able to look for the good in everyone and put their faults aside and say; "there but for the grace of God go I". In other words it could have been be me in that situation if I would have been born into that family. I am lucky in what I have around me. It might not be perfect but I will make the best of what I have from God and improve on it. There are people in much worse situations than yourself, look around you.

Please be sensitive to the person who is always angry and hurting others, they have to put up with themselves all day and night long; **"YOU"** can walk away from them.

Remember the word "sensitive" was often and is still used for a describing Medium.

There are many exercises you can do to enhance your awareness. Try some of the ones used in the "Out of Body" experiments, and the others in this book, they will help a lot.

Most of all sit and talk within your thoughts [best silently for your own sake as people in our western society who talk to themselves can be classed as insane] or if you like out aloud to the Spirit World just as you would a friend. You have to talk over, and over, and over, and over again, and again, and again, many, many, many times for about fifteen to sixty minute and more at the start of your development please continue even if you do not think anything is happening because every person in this world on the earth plane can become sensitive to the linking with Spirit and become a Medium. No matter what others say, it is the depth of a link with the Spirit World that counts. It is the **truth** and **sincerity** you do things for Spirit and others that counts the most.

# IMAGERY CLAIRVOYANCE

I am putting this down in a separate listing as a lot of tutors are now it seems getting their pupils to ask Spirit to have them visualise different things in their minds rather than ask Spirit to give them pictures of people, names, numbers, streets, and events to give the enquirers, this they are saying is an exercise for the mind. That it may be, BUT the path they are taking their pupils along could be a one way movement and no way back if not taught properly, this could also be a crutch for some, (a support) thinking they have the gift of clairvoyance and stick to that one and only clairvoyant way of linking and possibly using just symbolism [then guessing what the Spirit World want to say to the recipient of the message]. Also the link that you get, you might become used to that way of working with the imagery you are given and then Spirit might only give you the imagery all the time to work with. You as the pupil might also become used to working with Spirit in imagery and will become satisfied with it as your link, then perhaps not asking for a stronger link and not progressing properly to the clear seeing of people and events, being given names of the persons who have passed into the World of Spirit, all that have surrounded the person throughout their lives. You might not get the clearer picture from Spirit to use when you are giving a reading. Each budding Medium should be asking for more each time they link with Spirit, trying to bring the link in stronger by meditating and talking within their mind to those in Spirit who help them. Treat them as friends because that is what they are, your friends to work with you for the rest of your life.

I am going to put this method down anyway because some might like to use it as an exercise then hopefully move on. I must admit I have used it on occasions as an exercise in awareness classes. I class it as "imagery psychometry". If there is such a thing.

I think this method is expanding your psychic ability. Use this method then progress along with other methods of your development.

Have a person who you do not know very well to sit with you, best opposite you. First go into the stillness of meditation. Ask Spirit, **in your thoughts,** to give you a flower for this person [seen within your mind's eye], a flower from which you can give off a message for the person from it. Ask for it to be shown being grown from seed, a bulb, or a root. Ask for them to show you the whole of the plant, the growing of the plant, the leaves, then the flower, and ask to be told what it is going to mean to you in the way of a reading for that person. You then give a reading for the person from what you have been given in your mind.

The last time I can remember doing this exercise I received in my head/mind [in my mind's eye] the ground, earth, and in that earth, the growing area, there was a root that grew stems, then leaves that were bright green, then from those stems and leaves there came a flower, a flower that looked like a very large daisy. It had a large bright, yellow centre with straight white petals all around it. As I looked at the flower, the lower petals started to go brown and then rotted. The rot spread to the other stems and the leaves, the whole plant started falling as another shoot came up at the back of the plant from the base of the plant and grew forming another brighter flower. The whole area surrounding the plant became a garden with all different flowers growing ever upwards out of the ground. I was then given a country cottage house at the back of the garden. This house was of the sort that is white washed and was shining brightly in the sun.

From this I deduced this man started off all right in his life, he then was having or had a problem that was for him a badness that surrounded him. Something that was rotten to the core it seemed as though everything was falling around him and he was going into the depths of despair because of this badness that had happened. It was as though he was going into the mire nothing seemed to be going right at this time. Then suddenly out of the blue came a new beginning, a new growth for him, one that made him stronger in himself learning from that situation. Everything after that event began to blossom for him he was a lot brighter in himself, and so with this new found brightness everything that he looked at was much brighter for him. There were now lots of new people who were better for him in this bright new environment. This new beginning was the best thing that had happened for him in a long time, being happy within it as it progressed. The bright house was the place he was getting looked after at this present time. If needs be, the people that were around him now, were there for him at any time he was low again.

Another person could have given a totally different message from this. I will say again it is your meaning that counts not other peoples. It is your own personal link to interpret not other peoples.

By the way this interpretation for him was correct, he accepted it. He explained for me later a lot of his problem, so I know the meaning I gave was for him and correct. I will say again only use this as an exercise, please for your own sake aim for a much higher standard in your link with Spirit, ask for names fore-names and surnames, street names, house numbers, and areas that the people lived in, events that happen. Aim for the farthest star and you might reach the moon. Aim for the sky and then you might reach to the top of the highest mountain. If you only aim for the top of the mountain and you might only reach to the top of the first small hill. **Start as you mean to go on!!!!!**

# COLOURS

Colours it should be remembered are not seen as the same for every person. Remember if people are colour blind, some colours are omitted or mixed up in their spectrum range and other people have a different interpretation of certain colours of the full colour range. Remember also that colours are a vibration, a wavelength of light, one that is picked up by our seeing/hearing/feeling brain and that brain interprets all the many different colours by the individual in different ways that their mind can comprehend. Remember as well all of the colour spectrum can be measured in many different ways.

Another thing about colours that is never taken into consideration is the fact that colours are only a reflection of that part of whole spectrum of light, some colours of the spectrum are absorbed by the object you are looking at, they are colours [the vibration, the wavelength] you do not see, or should I say, are not picked up by your eyes and so interpreted by the electrical signal to your brain. The parts of the spectrum of light you do see, are reflected by the object, the parts of the spectrum that you do not see, are absorbed. Pure white light is split up into the colours of the spectrum those being red, orange, yellow, green, blue, indigo, violet, and each one of those colours having a wide range between, each colour then gradually being merged with the one next to it in the spectrum.

Each individual colour has a set wavelength or vibration of their own. Red has the longest, green in the middle, and then going to the blue side, violet has the shortest. If a circle of all the colours of the spectrum are placed on the card circle and it is spun around then the light reflected from the colours appears white. Proving all the colours that form white light does get reflected. Black objects absorb all the colours of the spectrum that is why it appears black.

This is the way some blind people can feel the colours, the vibration, the wavelength of that certain colour. You might say I don't believe that, how can they? Have you ever been into a room that has been painted blue, and felt cold? Have you ever been in a room that has been painted red and felt it being warmer or more comfortable than the blue room? Yet the room temperature is the same in both. This is you being sensitive to the conditions within that room and picking up the vibrations, the wavelength, being sensitive to the part of the spectrum that has been reflected or the part that has been absorbed by the colour from within the paint. So it is when you become attuned to objects of different colours. This is why black polythene is used to cover plants; it absorbs the heat from the light and retains it. This is why people in hot countries wear white as it reflects heat.

This is why you should not read too much into any colours that others say are the meanings of the colours. This is because we all have a different individual set of feelings that are stored in our brain, and they react differently in each and every one of us. Yes we can go by others as a guide when starting off, BUT, as we progress and learn our own patterns, we as individuals then put them into our own experiences in life, yes, believe me they might change for many of us. DO NOT try to say to any other person one way of interpreting a colour's meaning is correct and you have the knowledge. That your way is right just because another person has told you so or a particular book says "so and so" about a colour so you know for a fact.

I must stress this point strongly. Find out your own means for yourself, yes be guided in some ways by others, but be aware of your own feelings of the colours and then use your own interpretations.

I have found a great many people [Mediums] who use colours for readings change their minds as they progress in their development and their link with Spirit gets stronger, yes they change about what certain colours mean and what they mean for themselves only. So what I am saying is be flexible. People see colours in different ways not just as you see them even if you develop into a good Medium, don't push your meanings as law on to others.

What should be remembered in any colour there are/is a multitude of, a great many different shades, that some people; teachers, writers, etc. try to place set meanings into people's minds as some fixed rules that govern their thinking. You as an individual have to make up your own mind about the meanings of any colour. All right be guided at first by rules but be flexible in your outlook as you learn in life. Many a medium has changed their minds over meanings others have given them early on in their learning of their craft. Have you ever looked at the many different shades of colours? If you have not, look at nature, look in the park, look in your garden at the many shades of green for instance. They can range from a yellow/green, blue/green through to a brown/green. Where does the yellow start and the green begin? Where does the brown start and the green begin? It is only **in your mind** that these things can be worked out.

Look at the colour black some people say it is a person who is solid, can be relied on, a person to be looked up to. Yet others say it is a colour of foreboding, one that shows the person is in deep despair, if the colour black surrounds another colour it can show the person has had a worry or a black cloud hanging over them for some time in the past.

When using stones or any other object for reading, try to pick up the vibrations of the colour being reflected back out [the colour of the spectrum that you can see] off the stone. Each mineral which has definite properties of their own, as has every object, and those vibrations you can pick up from the stone itself [the colours that have been absorbed] and the vibrations that have been absorbed by the stone/object over a period of time, these should be also learned by you and the ways to feel them. Remembering that they all will be different so practice your skills. When you as a person has had your sensitivity developed you will be able to pick up either one or the other or both vibrations; absorption, and/or refection [most pick up reflection, but I do not wish to influence you, please remember you are an individual] and the ones placed there over a period of time, you will be able to then apply them to best of your ability to help others.

Another exercise you could use is to close your eyes and have a friend to place a gemstone into your hand and see whether you can tell your friend what sort of gem it is. With practice you will even surprise yourself. Try to pick up the colour of it.

Some people heal with colours and to me that makes sense, the reason being is; all colours have a different vibration that is reflected. Red can make a mentally ill patient worse. Blue calms them down. So using colours to heal makes sense. Some spiritual healers try to imagine the colour they feel is suitable for each individual disease of the body. I personally just use the all-powerful, pure, healing Divine Light. Some people while meditating visualise breathing in the colours to stimulate the power points/chakras in the body. Lilac/purple for the crown, Indigo for the third eye/brow, blue for the throat, green for the heart, yellow for the solar plexus, orange for the sacral/belly button area, red for the base. Try it for yourself; all these things are put in the book for you all to try at your leisure.

Try the exercises in the section about E.S.P. with coloured cloth and see how much feeling you have with the different colours. Practice, practice, practice.

Spirit are now telling us they use different colours to help the individual in the development. A different part of the colour spectrum is used for a different person and for their personal use. It should be remembered that the vibrations from the colour spectrum is subtly used throughout its range. Spirit tells us there are literally thousands of slightly different in between vibrations in the range of colours going from black and white and they all have their uses in different combinations.

# AURAS

An aura is a power or a vibrating energy that is given off by everything on this planet alive or dead at different levels. Some heave a strong vibrating power of the energy that could/can be measured by Kilner photographic methods or should I say be photographed by the late Dr Kilner. Through experimentation it has also been shown, that all energy giving plant food has an aura of a more or lesser degree. The human body or parts of it were one of the first things to be photographed, then the experiments went on to the food crops, these experiments are still going on today in Edinburgh University, Scotland; and sometimes at Stansted Hall with different objects by Lionel Owen, who lectures there at Stansted. I had my hands photographed there by Lionel for all to see the aura around my hands, I think on his part it was to prove that was still alive.

It has been shown that if a person is ill their aura is different to a healthy person's. Some Mediums can see the illness that another person has by just looking at their aura. Some see the colours in a person's aura and use it for a diagnosis of a patient. I will say again the colours that an individual sees can be or might not be, the same as another person sees even though they might be next to them. This is because of our own personal intake of the vibrational waves the colours give off that our eyes pick up, and from the eyes how our own brain interprets those vibrational waves in the way of electrical impulses of any colour. Also each individual might be at a different stage in their development, each person can see the aura differently the reason for this I am not fully sure. Some people can see an aura yet the person next to them cannot see anything this means it is not part of physical phenomena, the aura being see clairvoyantly. I must also add here that the aura does not stop just around the head of a person as seen in some religious pictures, the aura goes completely around the full body and around the full object no matter what it is animal, or vegetable, or mineral. Some people see the Aura subjectively, within the minds eye, others objectively, as an object in front of them, as in clairvoyance. Complicated?

For this reason I am not putting any set colour guide for the reader. It is up to you to see your own and accept it. In one book I read there was a definition for gold as a colour [now me being brought up with the jewellery trade, I know there are many shades of commercial gold going through the range from white then yellow then through to red. The same as there are many, many, many shades of yellow] and on the same page there were definitions for yellow then different definitions for gold. Where do you draw the line? Another comment was "the pure colours are the best indicators of good health". But what is a pure colour, because none are; they are all a mixture of others in varying degrees. So I will say to you all, do not go by any other person's guide for colours, read a lot of books on the subject then find the colours **BY "YOUR" EYE** that suit you alone, and make your own colour guide for the aura which is personal to you. **SEE YOUR OWN**, then judge.

I prefer to say clarity of colour rather than pure in the seeing of an aura. The clear, opaque colours are better **FOR ME** when looking at a person's health but on saying that in some books I am told that a transparent colour is the sign of purity, and half of the people I look at who have clear/transparent colours certainly are not pure. Where do we go now? Only back to ourselves, and our own experiences for our own guiding influence.

To see an aura around a person some say it is best to have them against a plain light coloured wall in subdued light. A white or black or single colour background I find is best. Then stare at them for a while not blinking until your eyes go slightly out of focus, then you can generally see a haze or a smoky white surround of that person, after a while you will be able to see the colours on the outer rim of the person's aura it will become clearer coloured with practice. It will come in time; so do not try to force it. Practice, practice, practice. Lots of people tell me they can see whether a person is good or bad, and so they then can avoid them. Well all I can say is, I would rather get to know a person first, and make my own mind up about them, otherwise I would miss out on a lot of learning of the good and bad things in life that goes along with mixing with all people of all types. Also I would like to put the point forward to all, that people's aura changes at different times so be careful what you put into a reading of an aura.

People have different auras because they are individuals. Some auras have a softer edge to them like a mist fading away [a more open person]. Some have a hard, well-defined edge [a conventional person]. Happy people have brighter auras. Sad people have dull ones.

A recent aura of a lady I saw had a smoky white inner and a hard fixed edge of red on the outside, yellow next then a type of green/yellow on the inside next to the smoky inner. The aura was about 12 inches around the person and all the outer colours were about half an inch wide. I did not know the person or what they felt.

I would advise people to make their own colour guide and keep to that, **BUT** altering it as they become better and more experienced at the art. For those of you who would like to know what I have found at this time for myself here is a personal list of colours.

**Black** can mean the person is in very lowest depths of despair, very low in their opinion of themselves, do not seem to be able to help themselves, at the lowest point in their lives can be contemplating a bid on taking their own life, in need of immediate help. Should be counselled and watched with care. Can be ill, especially in the mind.

**Black is black,** but from here on we have colours that can have many shades so it can be difficult to explain. This is why you need your own chart and where care is needed for any reading of the aura.

**Grey** is a person who will not help themselves, always looks on the dark side of life keeps on reminding themselves life is awful, there does not seem to be a light at the end of the tunnel, depression, but if talked to can be turned towards the light, but of course it depends what shade of grey it is. The lighter the grey the easier for the person to change, the darker the more work that needs to be done with this person. All this can be changed if a person puts their mind to it, with goodness; kindness and the loving help of others, it succeeds quicker. **Very light grey** can mean a person has been in the position of the darker grey but they have managed to overcome their problems even though it has been an upward struggle and they are now on a smoother upward path having gained inner strength with possible help from others but have a way to go, they can see the light at the end of the tunnel. Here it should be pointed out the colours can be a blend of others with tinges of other colours mixed in. Look at the greys around you in life. They can be a variation of blues, reds, greens, and browns.

**Brown** dark brown is a colour where the person is stuck in their ways with problems surrounding them and there does not seem to be any way out at the moment for them. They are a worrier; carry life's woes on their shoulders. Seem to look for life's troubles, a typical "woe is me" sort of a person.

**Very light brown** becomes a solid sort of a person one who has their feet on the ground especially if tinged with a touch of red to make them warm in their friendship. If the brown is like a stain in the aura it can be a person who is lacking in their emotions, very little control on them

Here we come in to another problem because of a person's interpretation of a colour of aura. In one book I read recently the writer explains about a person with a muddy aura as being ill. Now mud from what I have seen, depends on what part of the country you live in. Where I live on the Cheshire plains, mud is black. Where a friend of mine lives in Bewdley in the midlands mud is a reddish sandy colour. In other parts of the country it can be orange sandy colour, yet another it can be brown. On the chalk downs in the south the mud can be grey. See where the confusion comes in? The same comes in where a specific animal comes in with a colour. A writer describes cancer as the person having a crab attached to the spot in the aura where the cancer is affecting the body. Crabs are of multitude of colours from purple to red to brown to green. What should have been said was the cancer; the colour it was; the colour extended out and was shaped like an animal with arms or tentacles going to the effected spot, or a crab like formation of colour.

**Red** as we all are told is for passion **BUT** too much passion can cause problems; need to look out for the intensity of the red and how deep it is whether it is a fiery red, a warm red, or an unpleasant, angry red. This is a person who has an eye for the arts. Warm and heartening to be around. Look to where the mix of the colours come in and then try to marry the meanings up e.g. more darker means more black in the mix so could mean there could be problem if their passion gets out of control, might send them off the rails if they let it.

**Lighter red** are inclined to be laid back in the things they do while going about their business. In the extreme could be classed as lazy. Here you are bringing in yellows and whites.

The **light red** I class as pink is love but it can become mixed with other colours I have found, so I look to them in the reading. It also can be loving. But what kind of loving is it going to be passionate red to yellowing; is it going to be calm loving a tinge of blue; or green, being stable with their partner.

**The red** can be seen as a mixture with yellow like a fire glow sometimes with tinges of blue, a candle flame red/yellow, colour this I class as a person who has been put on a pedestal by others looked up to because of their integrity and honesty, a good person by any person's standards.

**Mauve/purple** look at the mixture in between the red and the blue, this is a person who is likely to be a helper, honest in their approach with others. Helping the most needy not making a song and dance about it. Possibly a counsellor, one who listens, has sympathy, empathy with others in a less fortunate position than they themselves have; a true friend. Bright purple shows the highest possible integrity in this person, they can be very spiritual in their approach to others and their problems.

**Blue** here is another colour that has many facets. Blue for me is truth, genuineness, honesty, a person who always wants to seek it out the true meanings of everything. Has to be accurate in the things they do in life, exacting, upright, honourable, a person of virtue. But in other blues lighter ones like ice blue; in the extreme can be a cold person, not feeling, not caring.

**Green** here is a colour that is classed as being one of an intelligent person. Showing that they are growing in their knowledge. A person who knows what to do in many circumstances where others would fail. They have the knowledge of words and education, and the ways of how to make the best use of them. Generally can be relied on to guide others along life's highway. A sharp darkness in the green is jealousy and can be underhandedness.

**Yellow** is the colour of a person who is looking for the right path to the higher life, spiritually aware if there is a purple tinge in the mix. Can be always studying the ways to get enlightenment. A great reader, of intellect and brains, a brightness in them.

Here we can come into what is termed gold. I class this as pure gold not a mixture and put it with the yellow because I cannot differentiate it from yellow in an aura.

**White** as I see in an aura it is total purity, just as I see in lots of Spirit beings, but this is a special type of white it is as though it can be slightly "see through", as though it is transparent a white fog type of white as I see it, if that makes sense. This is for me the Spirit of the person emanating from them. This white Spirit is one of such intensity you will recognise it when you see it.

Please do not take too much notice of aura drawings that are produced by computers from software written programmes. They are only a bit of fun; treat them as such they only churn out what has been put into them by the software programmer.

There are said by some (I don't agree with all of them, it is something that has to be proved to me. I have not seen them as such) to be three different outputs of a person's aura. These auras can be expanded and retracted by some people; here is some idea of them. You will have to experiment for yourself with others :-

**The mental aura.** This is the aura that is generally drawn in religious pictures. Sometimes called a halo by people. It is of different magnitude depending on the spiritual development of the person this can be detected allegedly up to 25-30 inches (64-76 cm. I do not see it this big myself) away from the inside of the head where it starts in the pituitary gland. This is where the person picks up the link with those of the higher realms for clairvoyance, clairaudience, and clairsentience. As well as I know now by my own development the link being made when linking with Spirit for transfiguration. I know this as Spirit link comes and goes out of the back of my head, or should I say the power link I feel comes and goes out of my head that way.

**The physical aura.** This particular aura surrounds the whole of the body from the outer parts of it, namely the skin. I believe people have different sizes of auras because of what I have seen emanating from them, but what should be remembered the Kirlian detection system only picks up the physical aura and shows it, only about 2 inches (5 cm) from the subject. At present this is the only one I see around people and things/objects.

**The etheric aura.** This aura is said by some to allegedly expand outwards for a distance of 50-60 inches from the power point of the body that is known as the solar plexus. When giving out power to a Medium in a cabinet or in a Closed Circle, a pull in the solar plexus can be felt. This is the reason I believe this etheric aura can be expanded out to link with the person's aura who is being developed. This is the aura that is being mainly used for the link of clairsentience BUT not only this aura, all are used in different strengths at different times when linking with Spirit. I feel it is only Spirit that has the full knowledge of what degree of each section of us and our aura they use, and really does it make any difference to know?

The aura is for us, the link we have to the outside world of the unseen. How many times have you said to another person or when you have been on your own and had a feeling, an inner feeling that something is going to happen before it does, or the person who you are with being aware of their upset? That gut feeling (the solar plexus area) is a picking up from or being sensitive to the higher realms, or another person's output of feelings. How many parents or loved ones can pick up the vibrations/feelings/sensations from their loved ones in distress or when they are placed in peril? These things are being picked up through the aura, which I believe are transmitted from those in the higher vibrational levels of Spirit.

An exercise that can be done to show how much you can expand your aura is to sit in a chair with eyes closed, your back to a group of people. Asking as always for the help of Spirit within the mind, then when the link is established, have one of the group walk slowly up to the chair behind you. Say when you feel them come into your auric field. Then with Spirit's help, you can try to say who the person is; Male of female and perhaps height and appearance of them. Then try to give a reading. Do not look around to see if you are correct. Do not have the person answer any of the yes no questions, have others there or a leader say the answers, which when given should be shown and be acknowledged by the person by the shake of the head in only YES or NO fashion. If the person in the chair gets things wrong they should be told to go back to Spirit in their mind and ask for more help. They should be always asking Spirit to be helping with the answers as they go through this exercise as a matter of course.

# MEANINGS of GEMS
# &
# PRECIOUS STONES

Now to confuse you the reader a little bit more I have included a little of the other book I have written about how to use reading tarot cards as a lifetime business. **"The Keeways "Unlock the Tarot"** book. At present it is in the form of A4 and has about 150 pages in it. But not fully completed. I started the Tarot book before I started this one, but I had such a compulsion to write and complete this Oneness book everything else was put aside.

For very general readings of the gemstones or crystals, look at the colours, and see that which is written, BUT, remember, ALL COLOURS are NOT SEEN THE SAME by everyone, also all gem colours are different hues and can be a mixture of the set colours. Again it is up to you the person who gives the reading to put your own interpretation onto a particular coloured stone, because the colour reading is for the colour you see through your eyes, and not anyone else's.

# BIRTHSTONES

Birthstones for **January** the first month, **Garnet, Amber.**
Birthstones for **February** the second month, **Amethyst, Azurite.**
Birthstones for **March** the third month, **Aquamarine, Bloodstone.**
Birthstones for **April** the fourth month, **Diamond, Rock Crystal.** [**Zircon** or **White Topaz**]
Birthstones for **May** the fifth month, **Emerald, Jet.**
Birthstones for **June** the sixth month, **Pearl, Moonstone.**
Birthstones for **July** the seventh month, **Ruby, Onyx.**
Birthstones for **August** the eighth month, **Peridot, Tiger Eye.**
Birthstones for **September** the ninth month, **Sapphire, Quartz.**
Birthstones for **October** the tenth month, **Opal, Jade.**
Birthstones for **November** the eleventh month, **Topaz, Citrine.** [**Malachite** can be use]
Birthstones for **December** the twelfth month, **Turquoise, Jasper.** [**Goldstone** can be use]
**Diamond** and **Goldstone** can be used, giving to special people at special times e.g. Xmas, Birthdays, joining together people, personal times, etc., as can all the other stones, if the person giving feels the stone is appropriate to the occasion,
**Agate, Coal, Granite, Marble,** can be used to help loved ones when given as an adornment, they can be used also to brighten up a person's life, as any gemstone gift does.
Some people use these beautiful stones to cross over the months as their star signs do, it is up to you the individual, which ever you feel comfortable with, there are no set in stone rules so it gives more choice for the wearer.

# GENERAL MEANINGS OF THE COLOURS IN GEMSTONES

**BLUES.** These stones are for a calming effect, healing qualities, cooling the troubled mind, uplifting, fortifying, can be good for pains, and headaches, ideal for mentally disturbed people, helps to calm people within. A person who wears this is said to be cool, calm collective, and can be deliberate. Blue is said to help to be so in these virtues. This person has a tendency to be the controlling influence in another person's life, a person who can be there as a stabilising influence. A pillar to be leaned on.

**REDS.** These stones are for helping where heat is needed, with blood disorders, and water circulation, blood circulation, bringing more of a stronger passion to a person's life, a surge of passion. Must not be use as a medical/mental aid to a disturbed person, can act as a red rag to a bull, raising too much passion. A passionate person associates with this colour. Can be sexual passion or angry passion. If deep red, the passion is much stronger.

**GREENS.** These stones are for healing as well as subduing, calms malice, subdues jealousy, suppresses possessiveness, calms envy, lifts people from insecurity and mistrust, can help with a person who is feeling flat, down and/or low, ideal for mentally disturbed people, helps a person reflect on their jealousy and put things in the right prospective for themselves. A person who is most of the time thinking of earthly things and nature's ways, quite often a person who thinks of others more than themselves; can be too caring sometimes, so leaving themselves to the last. Puts a person into a better frame of mind. Can help them become more level headed. A stone of growth, showing the person that has grown in their life more than they ever thought they were going to.

**BROWNS.** These stones are for giving warmth where needed, helping emotions, deepening and strengthening passions, strengthening friendships, some are said to help with certain peoples sex drive, points to a solid, sexy person who can be relied on. A lover of the earthly things and nature. Can point to a down to earth person.

**PURPLES.** These stones are for giving inner strength, strength of character, bettering self, giving a regal feeling, liberating, uplifting. This can be a person who always tries to better themselves, tries to have the best they can afford, can sometimes point to a person who thinks they are above others.

**YELLOWS.** These stones are for helping with kidneys, liver, blood and water disorders, for brightening the person's spirit. Can be a person who always looks on the bright side of life, one who looks for the best in others, tries not to have any negative thoughts.

**ORANGES.** These stones are for livening people up, uplifting a person, helps with general body health; to help with digestion and the inner workings of the body. Points to a person who can be bright in most circumstances, generally the life and soul of the party. A happy go lucky person. One who has a lot of emotions even if they do not show it towards others.

**PINKS.** These stones are used for their slow warming properties; slowly releasing deep benefits when needed, especially if sleep is being a problem, or relaxing is being a problem. Helps calm the savage beast within, slows down an over active mind, slowly and surely deepening a relationship that lasts longest. A person who, when in a relationship is very true to themselves, very loving and passionate when with the right partner.

**WHITES.** These stones are used for helping with bone problems, also helping to clean the inner most parts of the mind, body and soul. A purifying stone. Points to a person who knows what they want out of life and goes for it. They like to keep a clear conscience. Usually thinks good of most other people. Tries to look on the bright side of things in their lives.

**BLACKS.** These type of stones are for helping a person who needs extra inner strength and the outward strength to show other people they are better than they are perceived, helps a person when they are troubled with insecurity, makes them feel better. A coloured stone that gives a solid confidence to the wearer.

**GREYS.** These stones help the wearer slowly into a better way of life giving strength in every way, in a slow, methodical, deep way, can show an inner calmness. Helps a person to show they are better than others, they themselves are the best person, wards off worry, bringing a carefree attitude to the wearer.

**CLEAR.** These type of stones are said to help the wearer ward off evil, ill health, help keep away malice and anger, keeps the mind clear, reflects the nastiness away from the wearer, chases away badness, throws evil back at the perpetrator. Points to a person who cannot hide most things from others, they are open and can be transparent to their fellow man. This person sparkles at the right times and can bring happiness into the lives of others.

One small thing that I feel I should point out is :- these gemstones if charged up under a glass dome for three weeks in an active Spiritual Circle of people, the stones then have remarkable properties. A lot then gaining remarkable healing properties, (especially the clear quartz as when used in the physical circles with energy). They can gain three to four times the vibrational strength/power. I will put in more information when/if received from Spirit. Some extra information of the gemstones to what has been put down here is written in the pages of my "**Keeways Tarot Card Book**".

The fuller meanings are included in my other book that comes with the "**Keeways Tarot Book**" and the "**Keeways Tarot Cards**" in the lifetime business pack. This book and pack shows you how to run a small business and if needed, keep the wolf away from the door for the rest of your life with the reading of the Tarot.

## DIVINING/DOWSING RODS/STICKS

Please remember that the dowsing rod can give only answers of yes and no for you, just as the dowsing pendulum which swings in different directions that gives answers of YES or NO.
Most divining rods/sticks are made of hazel or willow, BUT any "L" or "Y" shaped wooden straight off the tree sticks that works with you can be used. Some are better than others; well that is what I have found, but most work. Two bent [into an L shape, 4-6 x 12-18 inches] wire coat hangers have also been used by me at times. This is the most common way to make a dowsing implement with the "L" shaped metal divining rods.

Find a bush or tree. [The hazel is the branches most preferred by dowsers, some use willow] You can have a choice of the one or two branch method to use. Any branch can be used from any tree or bush

The Single Branch Method entails finding a branching stick in a Y shape that comes off a bush at an angle of about 20 – 45 degrees. The thickness [about ¼ - ½ inch thick, any thicker it makes the job difficult] of the branches similar–ish.
Try to get the branches as near to a shape of an upright capital "Y".
The two branches of the "Y" should be of nearly equal length of about 18- 24 inches; the single length of the Y should be about 6-8 inches.
Hold the two lengths firmly in your hands, your knuckles pointing in towards each other, with the smaller part of the "Y" pointing to the ground.
Hold your arms out to the front at a level in between your shoulders and your waist.
Make the smaller part of the "Y" point to the front of you, and 90 degrees to the ground while still having tension on the two parts of the "Y". Your knuckles should now be pointing to each other and approximately parallel to each other. The two parts of the "Y" stick in your hands should be coming out of the little finger side of the hand. With bending, tension on the branches.

Now ask in your mind, a question that can be answered with yes or no, ask the higher source, Spirit for what you want to find. Then walk in the directions where you think you are likely to find it. Ask for underground water, ask for a piece of metal, ask for pipes, ask for a water course, ask for buried ruins, ask for a buried wall, etc. keep on asking Spirit the same question as you walk and looking at the stick.
When the spot is found and you have got the method correct, the stick will start to shake and a little further on, the pointed end will drop to the point in the ground where your find will be, and if you dig, then hopefully your dig will be successfully found. To find out how deep the dig is ask the yes/no questions. First ask is which way is yes, then which way is no. It will surprise you how accurate you can become. You can also use the pendulum or the wire rods. [Yes some people use YES and NO but the vast majority of dowsers only say the dip or movement of the dowsing rod only happens when the answer is "yes", nothing or should I say the "no" of the answer the dowsing implement stays still.]

Using the "Two Branch Method", start looking for a good bush select two small "L" shaped branches, if they are nearer to a right angle of 90% the better [a bit bigger than a twig] about 1/8 to ½ an inch thick, no thicker as they will be a bit heavy, the smaller length of the "L" should be about 4-8 inches long, The longer end should be of about 12-18 inches, these measurements do not have to be exact. Have both sticks about the same thickness then cut both approximately equal in length.
A pair of wire coat hangers can be use for this method. I have found the wire coat hanger or welding rods for this two-branch method better. A straight section of the wire is cut to about 18 inches long then bent

at right angles forming an "L" shape at the 12 inch mark. The ends are smoothed out so they are not sharp, there you have a set of dowsing rods that will last a lifetime and give you hours of fun.
A great many people use the wire "L" rods for answering their yes/no questions. The enquirers used them by asking a question they know the answer to first, to which the answer is, either "yes" or "no". The wires are placed pointing ahead and horizontal to the ground. A question is asked either in the mind or out loud.
Some ask "which way is yes?" Then wait for the answer to be pointed out. Then ask "which way is no?" This is to test the pointing of the wire dowsing rods (wires). One way will be crossing and the other way will have the larger lengths pointing away from each other. Some people get the opposite to others, so check for yourself.

Now you have two options in the ways you can support the rods (wires).
You can use a roll of card/paper in which the smaller length fits loosely in some people use the outer plastic holders of "Biro" pens.
Or
You hold the smaller ends loosely in each hand.

When looking for things outdoors, using either method, have the larger length of the "L" shaped sticks, or wires parallel to each other pointing forward of you as you walk, and the smaller ends in a sleeve of cardboard or paper; or you can just hold the small ends very loosely in your hands remember the larger lengths are 90 degrees to the ground pointing forward of you as you walk. Asking again from the higher side of life, Spirit, for the thing you wish to find. When you come over the chosen spot the sticks/wires will come together or part like magic. Remember to keep sincerely asking and talking to Spirit within your mind as you walk asking only questions that can be answered by yes or no.
Set into your mind to what you want to find, be it an underground stream, an old sunken well, an underground watercourse, a buried water main, an underground electric cable, a burial ground, a "Ley line" [a magnetic force field found within the earth and they are placed all over the world. For meditation this is one place to sit. When you find where two "Ley lines" meet, try and sit there, you will find the energy from them amazing], minerals, oil, radiation. In fact anything under the ground you wish to find. If you do not have anything to look for, have a friend go into a field and place something in it and then you can have a go at trying to find it. As a test exercise in the classroom situation have someone place one object in a box among many empty boxes and have the dowsers find which box the object is in.

Another method of dowsing is with the use of an elastic band held at tension hooked over the thumbs of each hand. The arms are stretched out in the front of the person at chest height, as the elastic is tight across the thumbs. The same method of sincerely talking to the higher realms for help in finding the source of the water is applied. When the position of flowing water is found underneath the ground one hand goes up and the other goes down. The other position is for depth of the water is when the both arms go down. Try it and find out which way your arms in tension react for you.
As with any dowsing to get it accurate in the beginning it is necessary to do your dowsing over an underground steam you know is there and the depth of it also. That way through your practice you will become more efficient and will definitely become far more accurate in the long run.
One place that you could start off practicing would be to try dowsing over culverts or over streams that go under the road.

# PENDULUM DOWSING

Here we have a method of using a hidden power that every person can use from the start, and with a great deal of practice can be a very rewarding pass time if used to help people. This method of dowsing can compliment the dowsing stick method so expanding your horizons.
All it entails is a weight of any kind, a piece of wood, a piece of bone, a button, a ring, a stone, one that is your favourite, perhaps your birthstone, any precious gemstone, a piece of silver, a piece of gold, these are generally pointed at the bottom of the pendulum [but need not be]; then they are suspended on a piece of string, wool, cotton, or even on a chain of silver or gold. That is how easy it is. Find yourself the pendulum of your choice. Make the dangling length that is comfortable for you to use. People I know have it about a foot long in length, some others have it a lot shorter though, down to 2-4 inches, it is a

personal thing, there are no set lengths. You are now ready to begin.

Get yourself a piece of paper, and draw on it a half circle with arrows going clockwise.
Then on the paper draw another half circle and arrows pointing counter/anti-clockwise on it.
Now draw a line going horizontal with arrows going both ways on it.
Next draw a line going vertically on the paper with arrows going both ways.
This is to set your rules for the pendulum, if one rule suits you, use it, if another one that contradicts me that you prefer, use it. It is only **you** that are linking up with your higher self and the power that is going to be used in any dowsing method, and that is personal, BUT the rules have to be set once and kept. DO NOT change the rules after you have set them for yourself from the start of your dowsing just to make the answers fit.
I personally most time use the Clockwise direction for meaning "YES". BUT the directions can change for some reason, so check beforehand.
The Anti-Clockwise direction meaning "NO".
The Horizontal marking on the paper I class as I do not know or unsure, not a definite.
The Vertical line I use as meaning possibly but again unsure. That way for these two directions I can structure the questions that I ask. With practice and **I mean practice** most situations can be found out.
The way to practice is to ask Spirit to help you each time and sit each day for about half an hour to an hour with your piece of paper in front of you asking questions that you have to find the answers of by the "Yes", "No" method, but the answers to the questions can be checked at a later date.
Have your pendulum in the hand you use most. Between your fingers [between the thumb and fore finger I find is comfortable for me] holding the string or chain dangle it over the first half circle. Keep your arm as still as possible, rest your elbow on the table and the pendulum swinging over the marking you are using at the time. **DO NOT FORCE THE DIRECTION** it will go on it's own accord. Be true to yourself AND to the people you are going to help, lies will always find you out.
Start saying to yourself out loud, positively, meaning it. "This clockwise direction means "YES", go in a clockwise direction".
Keep doing this. Each time when the pendulum starts going really well, stop the pendulum from swinging in the clockwise direction in a circular motion and start again, repeat the steps doing it again and again for another five minutes.
If it ever goes in a wrong direction start from scratch again.
After saying it out loud, say it to yourself in your mind.

Next start saying to yourself out loud, positively, meaning it. "This anti-clockwise direction means "NO", go in a anti-clockwise direction";
Keep doing this. Each time when the pendulum starts going really well, stop the pendulum from swinging in the anti-clockwise direction in a circular motion and start again, repeat the steps doing it again and again for another five minutes.
After saying it out loud, say it to yourself in your mind.

Next go to the horizontal marking on the paper say to yourself, " This horizontal direction means, "I do not know, go in a horizontal direction". (left to right) [BUT a lot of people prefer not to have this position drawn for the pendulum to swing along. Sticking to the clockwise or anticlockwise swing action of the pendulum.]
Keep doing this, each time when the pendulum starts going really well, stop the pendulum from swinging in the horizontal directional in a linear motion and start again, repeat the steps doing it again and again for another five minutes.
After saying it out loud, say it to yourself in your mind.

Next go to the vertical marking on the paper say to yourself, " This vertical direction means "possibly", go in a vertical direction". (Forward and back. Away from you, towards you). [BUT a lot of people prefer not to have this position drawn for the pendulum to swing along. Sticking to the clockwise or anticlockwise swing action of the pendulum.]

Keep doing this, each time when the pendulum starts going really well, stop the pendulum from swinging in the vertical direction in a linear motion and start again, repeat the steps doing it again and again for another five minutes.

One of the better books ["The complete guide to Dowsing"] on dowsing is written by a dowser, George Applegate, who has travelled across the globe finding underground water for all kinds of people. It is well worth a read.

Some dowsers go into the realms of map dowsing [teleradiesthesia], or finding of lost people helping the police with their searches. This can be very rewarding for the individual. Bringing self satisfaction.

The way to do this and to practice this form of dowsing is firstly to log everything in a notebook you receive from your experiments. This way you can look back at incidents you have tried to solve and help people with. You might have better ideas than the one I will be putting down here.

Follow the write up in the papers about a missing person. You should be trying to pinpoint where they are, or perhaps a person who has been found dead, then it will be your job to put down in your note book through the process of elimination, where the person who has done the murder lives. Perhaps try to say who it was.

On the process of elimination of places on a map goes. Have the pendulum in one hand and then slowly go over the map with your other hand using the finger as the pin pointer of a place. Asking the higher source through the pendulum for help for helping others find the person/persons.

Always remember you have to say words to the higher source asking for their help in your helping mission.

Now for the next steps in another exercise.

Before asking the questions I always say a few words upstairs to the higher life, Spirit, asking for help and guidance. Say your own small affirmation or prayer.

Get a map to start testing yourself. Have a friend write different questions down on a piece of paper, information that they would like you to answer. They of course, will know the answers to the question. E.g. (1) "Does the town of Liverpool have a cathedral?" Later on (2) "I would like to know the district is in ----? Is it in---?" Using the pendulum to answer the first question is a simple yes/no. Then using the finger of the other hand, the person trying to find out a position on the map would go slowly across with the finger, while asking in their head the questions. Trying to make sure that the questions put are only answerable in yes/no answers. E.g. Am I near? Is it near Wavertree? Is it within two miles of Kirkby? Is it near the Mersey? So you gradually whittle the places down. Of course Liverpool has two cathedrals but are fairly near each other, so there are two places where the pendulum would be guided to on the map. That question is only a guide for you as the references on the map have the location of churches/cathedrals.

To use the pendulum in a situation with the Dowsing rods is managed in a similar way to find the depth of your find. Asking say, the depth of the – "under water stream". When you have found the stream you get the pendulum out and start asking the depth. "Is it five feet ?" "Is it six feet?" Yes and no answers to the questions.

You can use these methods for fun in your love life, buying a car, looking for a place to eat, a holiday, anything. But be careful make sure you are well practised before you take any real notice of the things that you think are advised. Even then I would only trust your own sensible judgement.

Some people use the pendulum for diagnosis of bodily problems. I personally would not, but it can be done.

When you start to do pendulum dowsing, you will start to suspect the people who have their pendulums swinging fast in a circle. You will find the pendulum **starts** going around slowly not suddenly at speed as I saw on a T.V. programme.

The pendulum if used suspended on a tripod cuts out the possibility of the Medium or the dowser spinning the dowsing implement with their hand/arm whether it is consciously or unconsciously done. The hand of the Medium/dowser is placed on the top of the tripod and the questions are then asked ready for the yes/no answers.

Nostradamus was said to use a pendulum dowsing instrument over a bowl of water as a focus point or was it a way of asking for answers? The bowl was said to be divided into the astrological map, in a segmented way.

Nostradamus left a rhyme of himself working, remember it was written not in English, but in "**OLD**"

French, NOT MODERN FRENCH, which is different than the language today with slightly differing meanings and spellings.

Seated at night in my secret study,
Alone, reposing over the brass tripod.
A slender flame leaps out of the solitude
Making me pronounce which is not vain.

When I look at the words. I see them as telling of him sitting in a darkened room with only a candle as the source of light. The (possibly brass or pottery) bowl of water is suspended under a brass tripod, with the pendulum centre slung, swinging over the bowl just above the water as the questions were asked of it. I should imagine the person [Nostradamus] asking the questions had their hand on the top of the tripod to form the link with the pendulum. I will have to make one and try it out.

I should imagine it could have been possible for Nostradamus to have had letters of the alphabet and numbers on the sides of the bowl, and the swinging pendulum could have been directed to the letters and numbers, by the unknown power of the time [Spirit] to be written down by the enquirer [Nostradamus]. Or could it have been a flat brass segmented disk or lettered disk? OR Did he only have the water in a brass bowl for the purpose of scrying?

Some say it was a forked dowsing implement that was used, but remember many people have said many differing things about Nostradamus' verses over the centuries. Try to look at things logically and how they work, or could have worked, remembering your guess is as good as the next person's, because no one knows for certain.

One last point I would like to put is :- I have of late when using a pendulum for dowsing been getting the wrong answers to my yes/no questions. The pendulum has for some reason for me changed in its direction for the answers yes and no. I now ask at the start, which way is yes? and which way is no? before starting off on my quest for any answers. So be careful with the unseen people you work with test, test, test, and test again, and then and only then trust their answers.

Here is an exercise using the pendulum that could be done in a group or in pairs.

Use a set of closed envelopes perhaps a dozen to twenty six could be more of course, [But you could have for beginners only from nought then one to nine making it single numbers] in this exercise there are three bits of information that the person/persons have to tried to find out. First the number, the colour, then the thing written down, the drawing or single picture.

Write down on paper or put pictures into the envelopes.

Write down on each envelope "A", then the next "B", the next "C", then "D", and so on ---through to ----"Z".

In the envelope "A" place a paper (or a picture) on which is written, No 6 (or any other number but never duplicated) yellow (or any other colour), bus.

On the outside of the envelope next to the "A" put on "a person carrier".

In the envelope "B" place a piece of paper (or a picture) on which is written No 8, (or any other number) purple (or any other colour), wallpaper.

On the outside of the envelope next to the "B" write on "a covering".

In the envelope "C" place a piece of paper (or a picture) on which is written No 5, (or any other number) pink (or any other colour), slippers.

On the outside of the envelope next to the "C" write on "foot protection".

In the envelope "D" place a piece of paper (or a picture) on which is written No 2, (or any other number) black (or any other colour), paint.

On the outside of the envelope next to the "D" write on "metal protection".

In the envelope "E" place a piece of paper (or a picture) on which is written No 3, (or any other number) all colours (or any other colour), rainbow.

On the outside of the envelope next to the "E" write on "a mixture of rain and sunshine".

In the envelope "F" place a piece of paper (or a picture) on which is written No 4, (or any other number) red (or any other colour), chair.

On the outside of the envelope next to the "F" write on "a supporter of people".

In the envelope "G" place a piece of paper (or a picture) on which is written No 7, (or any other number) blue (or any other colour), the sea.

On the outside of the envelope next to the "G" write on "surrounds the earth".
In the envelope "H" place a piece of paper (or a picture) on which is written No 9, (or any other number) purple (or any other colour), wallpaper.
On the outside of the envelope next to the "H" write on "a covering".
In the envelope "I" place a piece of paper (or a picture) on which is written No 11, (or any other number) green (or any other colour), leaf.
On the outside of the envelope next to the "I" write on "part of a plant".
In the envelope "J" place a piece of paper (or a picture) on which is written No 12, (or any other number) brown (or any other colour), bark.
On the outside of the envelope next to the "J" write on "on a tree".
In the envelope "K" place a piece of paper (or a picture) on which is written No 14, (or any other number) orange (or any other colour), an orange.
On the outside of the envelope next to the "K" write on "a fruit".
In the envelope "L" place a piece of paper (or a picture) on which is written No 10 (or any other number) yellow (or any other colour), pear.
On the outside of the envelope next to the "L" write on "a fruit".
In the envelope "M" place a piece of paper (or a picture) on which is written No 15 (or any other number) yellow (or any other colour), book.
On the outside of the envelope next to the "M" write on "words and pictures".
In the envelope "N" place a piece of paper (or a picture) on which is written No 17 (or any other number) blue (or any other colour), sky.
On the outside of the envelope next to the "N" write on "surrounds the earth".
In the envelope "O" place a piece of paper (or a picture) on which is written No 16, (or any other number) green (or any other colour), curtains.
On the outside of the envelope next to the "O" write on "opens and closes".
In the envelope "P" place a piece of paper (or a picture) on which is written No 19, (or any other number) red (or any other colour), bulb.
On the outside of the envelope next to the "P" write on "off and on".
In the envelope "Q" place a piece of paper (or a picture) on which is written No 24, (or any other number) yellow (or any other colour), daffodil.
On the outside of the envelope next to the "Q" write on "a spring flower".
In the envelope "R" place a piece of paper (or a picture) on which is written No 20, (or any other number) brown (or any other colour), earth.
On the outside of the envelope next to the "R" write on "we walk on it".
In the envelope "S" place a piece of paper (or a picture) on which is written No 23, (or any other number) black (or any other colour), tarmac.
On the outside of the envelope next to the "S" write on "we walk on it".
In the envelope "T" place a piece of paper (or a picture) on which is written No 21, (or any other number) green (or any other colour), crayon.
On the outside of the envelope next to the "T" write on "small and pointed".
In the envelope "U" place a piece of paper (or a picture) on which is written No 22, (or any other number) white (or any other colour), door.
On the outside of the envelope next to the "U" write on "opens and closes".
In the envelope "V" place a piece of paper (or a picture) on which is written No 13, (or any other number) clear (or any other colour), rain.
On the outside of the envelope next to the "V" write on " in the sky".
In the envelope "W" place a piece of paper (or a picture) on which is written No 25, (or any other number) silver (or any other colour), plane.
On the outside of the envelope next to the "W" write on "in the sky".
In the envelope "X" place a piece of paper (or a picture) on which is written No 26, (or any other number) white (or any other colour), clouds.
On the outside of the envelope next to the "X" write on "in the sky".
In the envelope "Y" place a piece of paper (or a picture) on which is written No 1, (or any other number) purple (or any other colour), crocus.
On the outside of the envelope next to the "Y" write on "a spring flower bulb".

In the envelope "Z" place a piece of paper (or a picture) on which is written No 18, (or any other number) brown (or any other colour), horse.
On the outside of the envelope next to the "Z" write on "a working animal".

The envelopes are now given to the person opposite or the people in the room at random.
Each person who is going to try to find out what is inside the envelopes closes their eyes and then asks in all sincerity the higher life, Spirit for help in this task. Asking for them to come only in goodness, kindness, love and truth; to help them with the task in hand, for it to come from within the Divine Light of Spirit from within the loving harmony of the highest realms.
Each time the person who has the envelope, has to use the pendulum to find out what is in each envelope given to them, and the colour.
They have the pendulum in one hand and the envelope half under the other the pendulum hanging over the envelope. Look at the clue on the envelope, then start asking the yes/no questions to find out, what the number is, what the colour is and what the object word is.
Each person away from the others has to write down the answers to the questions against the letters of the alphabet.
Going along all the envelopes from A-Z. Put down on paper what is thought to be inside the envelope, the number/numbers, colour, and object word.
If the task is found to be too hard, then all the colours that are in the envelopes could be given out and the numbers from 1-26 and the object words. BUT the people are NOT told in which envelopes they are in.
It is only a bit of fun to practice with, it does not matter too much if people get some things wrong the exercise is to show others that it can be done with many times good accuracy.

Another way to do this if the task is going too quickly. A sequence of two tasks could be devised with the same envelopes.
First task. All there could go dowsing over the envelopes as they are given without any clues except the one on the outside of each envelop.
After all taking part in the exercise, have the participants write the answers down they think are correct.
They are now all given the set of object words that are in the envelopes, which should not be written down in the sequence that they are in, in the envelopes. The same can be done with the colours only, again not in sequence and the numbers. Then see how they all fair with these extra clues. See if any changes have to be made.
This little sequence is to get the person's awareness working.

## Prove for yourself that thoughts are a living energy

Using the two divining rod method. Get three or four people together in an enclosed space (perhaps a room or outdoors). Have one person [A] leave the room. No-one speaks except the leader, who asks another person [B] (by whispering closely in their ear) to signal, the person deliberately not speaking, (this is so nothing can be heard by the [A] person outside the room and said they heard the two points being talked about) [B] to signal/point to two points in the room preferably on opposite sides of the room, the person [B] picked out should then deliberately be thinking about placing an energy line in the ether [part of the air we breath] between the two points. The person [A] outside then comes into the room with their diving rods pointing out in front of them asking within their own thoughts for the energy line, which had just been placed, to be found; and keeps asking as they [A] walk across the space and tries to find the energy line between the two points. It will be seen that the energy line placed by their [B] thoughts, yes, **truly exists**. If done correctly it can be found by the same method, the two exact points as well as the line and the person who placed the line there for them. If needed by asking as they go to each person in turn.
Or the tutor writing down on a piece of paper where they are going to place the energy line between two points in the room or of course outside. BUT first test to see there are no other energy lines within the area where the exercise is going to be done. The students then will be asked to come into the room or area then find the connecting line between the points.

# CARD READING

Here is one subject that has had a book written by me all about card reading. The whole package is one of how to run a lifetime business reading the Tarot cards and a full business pack; so I will not go into too much detail here. As you go through the "Keeways Tarot Book" you will find out that some other tarot card writers do not explain fully the correct ways of learning the tarot, and the true ways of looking at them. Many readers only put down the "set meanings" of each card, so leading people to believe that the cards when placed down on a surface to be read within different spreads, the cards then are fixed in their portrayal of a Enquirer's destiny, this is not true. The cards are only a tool, a prompt for your inner self, your own psychic, remembering the cards are not evil, it is the people who try to use them for evil intent who are.

Each card interacts with the others in the spread placed out before the enquirer. The cards should be an extension of the inner self of the reader, which is not full explained by many writers. I believe this is because the other authors do not fully understand the ways of the cards, nor have they been taught correctly how to go about reading the cards in a proper, constructive manner. In my book the "Keeways Tarot" I have tried to lay out for my individual readers, from complete beginners, going through the best ways that I know how to expand and progress if they want to, right through to the standard of a professional reader of the tarot. I show you the rules to my mind, that can govern readings, also give you the reader, a sound grounding for the future of your craft. Each person can take as much as they need and use it; so progressing to whatever stage they want to go to. Using a dictionary and a thesaurus whenever the need arises especially in the advanced stages of learning, you will find the help from these sources invaluable. Using them regularly helps you understand more the use of your own language, they also help to expand your mind, words then come easier. What should be realised is the cards are only prompts, a trigger to get your brain working with your psyche. A help, a support, possibly a key to pull back the cover of something a person does not want to acknowledge within themselves, seeing the cards as being more acceptable to them or by the society they mix in.

The most important thing to do throughout the "Keeways Tarot book" is to "learn simply then add" to the information you take into your brain, go along the learning process at a steady pace, one that you think is suitable for you alone to do, not at any other person's pace. That book is a personal portrayal of learning the tarot, using them as prompts so leading you to a lifetime business.

Look at how the cards were first started in the beginning. The every day person could not read or write many years ago, pictures were drawn so they could understand the ways to go along in their lives when they visited seers. They were at first for the guidance of the ordinary person in their spiritual way of life then the churches in recent times saw the people were getting more from the seers than from the church so sadly, they put them down as witches.

# TEA LEAVES
## (Tasseography)
# COFFEE GROUNDS/FROTH READING

I look on this form of reading as a good practice for developing your psyche and enhancing your psychic ability. Tealeaf reading is something my sister and myself used to laugh about at home. My mother used to read the tea leaves and coffee grounds for others who used to call around for a cup of tea/coffee, and she would sometimes read the froth that was left around the empty beer glass of my dad's friends at our parties, please think on about froth. There are quite a few drinks that leave a mark around their container so many could be used.

Mum would always say it was only for a bit of fun, saying she did not believe it. When my mum did any readings, she used to say "I have to think quick and see if I had hit a right note in what I said, then work on that". BUT no matter, she was always correct in the things she used to say to the enquirers, most of them were generally neighbours and friends. No charges were ever made for her readings so people used to come back regularly to her. I remember once my mother got collared by one of the organisers at a horse jumping event, they put her in a tent with a scarf over her head like a gypsy in a fair ground and the charged 20p [in 1986 so it was not very much] towards charity for a reading of their hands, at the end of the event it was getting late, the ground was cleared except for the queue outside this tent my mother was in, still there for the reading of the hands, it was raining cats and dogs and still they waited, we still laugh about that.

Everyone I talked to over the many years said my mother was so accurate it was uncanny. I think that she must have been very psychic but did not see it as such, she said she was picking up from the person who the reading was for and using the prompts in the cups, because that is all the leaves or the grounds are; prompts or triggers for the mind. I personally think she used to see clairvoyantly in those drink containers and pick up from the people clairsentiently, but she would still have none of it. This is what happens to people who look into drink containers to give readings; they can see images others cannot. My mother used to work very quickly, not giving her mind chance to work out or analyse what she was saying. This is what should be done by anyone who is going to give any reading, trust your guide/link from higher plane. Half the time my mother did not remember what she had given in the reading, saying she had forgotten because it was only a bit of a laugh. It is only now I see what was going on for her in her mind. The rules she used to work by were.

Have a word up stairs, talk to those unseen, as she used to say, it is for a little bit of extra help, and this is from a person who did not believe in Spiritualism. She was doing the steps naturally, by asking the higher realm of Spirit for help at the start. So her natural ability must have stepped in, and her natural link with Spirit. At times she used to get frustrated at the people she was doing the readings for, showing the cup and pointing out the things she could see in it, yet they could not. This I know now was my mother's subjective clairvoyance clicking in.

Mum had the person swill the cup around with the very, very little liquid at the bottom, tip it out into the saucer then turn the cup upside down and turn it clockwise three times. Then give it to her.

Starting with the handle in her hand, pointing towards her, or a set point if it was the beer glass she was reading. But remember this is only a general guide because my mother used to be turning the cup/glass all the time.

With the handle pointing towards her, some readers start with the handle pointing to the enquirer.

To the left of the cup handle was the past.

To the right of the handle was the future.

Opposite the handle was the present. Some readers say the handle area is the present.

The bottom of the cup, was in the distance, whether it was future or past or present

Nearer to the rim was the present or near enough to that day, whether it was future or past or present

In the middle of the cup was a few months, whether it was future or past or if present, starting from that day.

Opposite the handle at the top, was outside of the home, away from it. At the bottom of the side rim/piece was someone outside the family. Not at the circular base. As within the circular base was for her classed as tears. Towards which part of the cup it was, if slightly off centre there would be the direction the tears would be for. Just outside the base circle was sadness, worry, anxiety, unease, concern, trouble over something,

Near the handle at the top was to do with family, at the bottom near the handle at the side rim/piece was to do with the where they lived, home and it's immediate surroundings.

On the left was going away from the enquirer. On the right was coming towards the enquirer.

The top of the cup is happiness, delight, high of pleasure. The centre of the cup mum classed as their contentment, well being, ease, life in general, pleasure, amusement.

Set the rules for yourself before you start and then keep to them so your link learns how you work.

Mum used to say if a tealeaf looked like something that would trigger off some story in her mind and that way she could go on. When she used to start talking about a person's past, the cup she was holding was turned in different ways clockwise [to the left]. When she was talking about the future the cup was turned anticlockwise [to the right], when she was talking about the present it was all over the place looking into it every which way.

Quite honestly half the time I wonder if she did really have any fixed rules in her readings, but that was my mum, God love her. I think she used to read from the person as much as from the cup. An idea for you would be to make a note or a list of the things you find out generally about all the human race be a sort of people watcher, write down all the little things that make one person, or a set group of people stand out from others in a categorise groups, as I have said in my other book, "UNLOCK THE TAROT" when using The KEEWAYS easy learning method. For these sort of readings read as many of the body language books as you can. **But** please do not take them as all being true of the body language of very person otherwise you will come unstuck. People are individual, always have that in your mind no matter what you read in books, or what people tell you. They will have individual feelings, individual habits, individual dress sense, and individual needs. To generalise is the best in an awkward situation in any reading, **but do not tell lies**, they will always come back to you in the most unusual ways.

# FIRE FLAME READING
## Flamography

Here is another way of improving your psychic ability try as many as you can. This will help you talk to and read for others in a great many ways.

Flames are off a burning energy source that draws air into itself to keep going, each energy source being individual. So it is when reading the flames they are all individual in the meanings for each reader/Medium. One person can be next to another reader/Medium and yet they will not see the same. It is a focus for the reader/Medium to pick up on. Mainly it is the using of your psyche.

This is a subject that is fairly easily put. All you are doing is focusing or should I say defocusing your eyes so you can see clairvoyantly. You are making yourself a point at which to aim your eyes at and help your mind to stop thinking, a sort of self-hypnosis. I remember I used to do this when we had a coal fire. You can see all sorts of wonderful things. I did not know at the time I should have been asking for help from Spirit and asked questions in my head mentally [the power of thought, a living energy] for the person who I was with, so I could have given them a reading, this was generally my sister and my mother.

What I should have done is to sit on the hearth by the fire, ask mentally for help from above in Spirit saying "I am going to give a reading for ----- [the person I was with], with your help if it is your will, I would like to help this person by giving a message". I would look into the fire at the flames, staring, blinking as little as possible. I would see in the flames pictures, which I would interpret in my own way to give a message/messages for that person. I could see a picture in the flame or a picture in my head, either/or being clairvoyantly seen objectively or subjectively. Anyway that is what happens now when I look into a fire's flames or a flame of a candle. Try it yourself it comes better and easier the more you practice.

# SAND READING (Geomancy)
# CLOUD READING (Culumlography).

Here I class these two ways of reading for others as similar, as they both use the psyche [but not always] of the person doing the reading also they take the different shadows and forms that can be seen by anyone. These two ways of looking into the shadow forms can be good easy ways of improving your ability to give messages to people, they are also cheap and cheerful as they say. They teach a person to expand on what they see, especially if done with others.

With cloud reading it is best to sit comfortably somewhere quiet with a friend out in the garden or the park. This can be done in any weather. But because of comfort, it is best done on a cloudy warm day. Ask for help from the higher source of the Spirit World asking to learn, expand and develop your ability. I quiet often look into the sky when I am travelling along as a passenger in a car, bus or train to try and see any images. I let the thoughts run through my mind as though I am giving a message to someone in particular not just the driver of the car. Often there are faces and scenes shown in the clouds before you think anything in your head. Because the clouds are always moving, and they change at different rates, which is different to the sand, which is a fixed image. In the clouds different scenes and images are produced to add to your information to be given out to the person who the message is for. Look continuously into the shadows in different parts of the sky; point the scenes and faces out the person who is there with you, (not the driver while driving the car). They might see something you have missed. You will both learn interpreting images and giving out thoughts spontaneously even if they are not at first accurate, as you relax and enjoy the movement of the clouds it will be a new experience for you. This can be a fun way of learning as you both learn to expand your psychic abilities. Each giving each other messages, or if not, information that you see in the sky then give the information you see to each other so you both can expand it and explore the possibilities of meanings. It can be very much a case of developing each other as you both look into the clouds. It can be great fun and very enlightening. You will be surprised in what truth can come out of your mind, if you first link with Spirit. This can lead to the development of many other ways of scrying.

Sand, dust, stones (reading of them is called geomancy because it is of the earth "geo"), on the other hand are static and can become a good medium to work with. Using sand for scrying has been practiced for more centuries than has been documented. What is known is; the Chinese used it centuries before the Christian calendar, as did the people of the desert and dusty regions, some used ground grain [flour], and still use these ways of scrying to this day. The way that was popular in China was to suspend a bamboo rod in a fixed position that had a dangling pointer that was placed over sand/dust. The Medium put themselves into an altered state of awareness, a Trance state, and then the bamboo rod was moved by the Medium whilst not looking at the stick or sand, looking beyond. It can be used as a focus point, a way of reading a drawing or the reading of messages in the material, the same way as automatic writing is mainly done on paper in the west.

When first starting this form of scrying it is best to get a tray or bowl of very dry sand, about 3-4 inches deep. The enquirer opposite you, blindfold yourself. Then take a stick or pencil in the hand, sit with your hand and pencil over the tray, perhaps resting on the side of the container. (Use the same implement each time). Keep asking for help in the reading in your own words over and over again in your own mind for a few minutes then give your mind a rest allowing the natural psychic force to go into your whole being and manifest itself along your arm then hand, to naturally draw in the sand. Then keep on trying for about fifteen minutes. If you **do not feel** a drive or a force to want to move the implement in the sand, DON'T force it, have a rest. Then start again. The main thing is to allow it to flow through your hand into the reading medium, the sand. Do not force any feelings that are not there. It is the build up of your psychic power that comes into play with this method that is necessary for the movement of the hand. Many a time it is a Spirit link or can be if done correctly by linking into the Spirit World.

Another way of scrying sand or fine grain powder is for you to have the sand at the similar depth 3-4 inches in the container, then have the person you are doing the reading for, the enquirer, to place their hand/hands in the sand as they feel they want to. You the Scryer, has to now put a psychic interpretation on the humps and bumps of the sand, and bring out the meaning how it looks to you and only you it is your interpretation that matters, no one else. With practice and the help of the higher force this will come eventually. Keep looking as you ask from Spirit to see.

Another way I have seen and practiced myself is to have a sieve and place some flour in it, then shake the flour evenly all over a flat surface, can be the floor [a table is ideal]. People while holding hands, sit around the flat surface, link with the Spirit World and ask for them to place a message into/onto the surface in front of them. Please remember it does not come immediately, it took my sitters and myself, about an hour for Spirit to use us to form a face in the flour. Spirit can also place messages, numbers, buildings or landscapes in the material used.

Remember the way of all readings; ask, (from those unseen from across the veil), Spirit, for help in the coming reading, ask for them to come only with goodness, kindness, love, and truth, to come in the Divine Light of Spirit within the loving harmony of Spirit of the highest realms. Then ask to keep you and your enquirer always safe from harm whether earthly, or from those unseen. Always start and finish with a prayer.

# SPIRIT PHOTOGRAPHY

These are my own thoughts again on how a person could have results produced on their films.

From my research I have found again this sort of mediumship as with others, happens differently with different individuals. When Spirit photography first started it was with big glass plates and the plates were allowed to absorb the light over a period of time 2-7 minutes perhaps more, and if needed, a flash of chemical (magnesium) perhaps being lit as a flashlight and at other times in the past with infra red lighting in a dark séance room. Now we have cameras that electrically flash bulbs, and they have quick shutter speed. A bit confusing perhaps for us and maybe Spirit to develop the chemical.

Were the chemicals on the old plates more sensitive to Spirit vibrations? Or. Were the Mediums of old doing things differently to us?

I am sure though when they have some new people **regularly** trying to succeed with their own cameras, Spirit will find a way through to the persistence of the earthly helper/camera person.

The reason photographic plate and film can pick up the vibrations/reflective light, the vibrations of our Spirit friends, and what we cannot see ourselves is because the plates/films are far more sensitive to the wavelengths/vibrations [of light] than the ordinary person in the street is. This is what Mediums are trying to do when they try to link with Spirit. They are all trying to get the tuning of their mind into a far more sensitive tuner/link state, which will pick up the unseen wavelengths that are around us everywhere. OR could it be that Spirit is using ectoplasm that is invisible to the human eye as some suggest? All these things should be taken into consideration.

The early days of the Spirit photography started by accident with many of the Mediums just taking their own photographs and thinking nothing of it. When the plates were developed there was an extra figure on the film plate. It was soon found out by trial and error if a certain person was taking the photographs, it was more likely to be an extra on the film, be it a face, full figure and sometimes an animal.

Now what have I found out?

It seems that the person has to be one of having psychic ability of some sort. BUT not always a Medium as we know one. In comes the equation of the individual and their individuality with Spirit Link.

An extra did not always appear for the people when they took their photographs of sitters to get the sitter's loved ones as well on the film, it seemed to be a bit hit and miss. BUT a large percentage of some **special people's** films came out with extras on them, so much so that certain Mediums used to earn a living by doing it. When the Medium got more developed with the practice in their art, it got better for them. BUT some lost the ability after a time.

Perhaps they abused their gift.

Perhaps they took it for granted, and not as being given by Spirit as it was meant to be put over to the general public, in comes the will of Spirit. **"If it is their will"**.

Perhaps they did not continue to link with Spirit in personal, private moments. **Forgetting to meditate** to continue being close to Spirit and develop a stronger link. After a time forgetting they were given the gift for the benefit of others and not exclusively for the benefit of themselves. **Forgetting to ask** for the photographs of Spirit, perhaps **forgetting also to thank spirit**.

Perhaps in losing their powerful gift, they forgot to keep building up their own power on a regular basis to their retain their link, forgetting to sit in the power with Spirit away from the camera, asking over and over again. In one book I read, the Medium who wrote the book seemed surprised that "thought" was a great big factor in the production of Spirit on the photographic "medium" [meaning paper or plates] how on earth did she get to be a Medium. The thought link to Spirit is the most important way of communicating. Thought is being used by the photographer and the subject being photographed; at least it should be. I think it is the thought that puts the image on the photographic plate, whether it is directly or with ectoplasm, because remember ectoplasm is produced by the thoughts of Spirit who mix the chemicals of, and from the Medium with those produced through the thought in the Spirit World.

Like in any Circle or sitting, Spirit always takes a little from everyone there that is why there always has to be peaceful loving harmony in the group. Yes the Medium is the main power link but the others there provide Spirit with what is lacking or low in the Medium's bodily and Spirit makeup at the time. Is it the same with Spirit Photography?

The most prolific people in the world to succeed in the Spirit photography were the "Crewe group". One of them was William Hope of the Crewe, Cheshire England. With the group you had to bring your own, signed photographic plates that were purchased by yourself, signed by yourself. The people were asked to examine the camera. They then were asked to place the photographic plate in the camera themselves and it was then taken out by the person themselves and then the person, took it into the dark room lit by a red light. The person had to stay with William Hope until the plates were developed then the results examined.

Another lady of the group was a Mrs Buxton. She made her results better by putting her hands over the camera, so please experiment. I suppose it was like the healer sending the power of the Spirit link through to the human body.

Sitters used to booked special photographic sessions with the Mediums of the past to be caught on camera with their loved ones who had passed onto the higher realms. Experiment yourself with different people sitting in front of the camera, asking them to send out different thoughts at different times. When sitting for different photographs try as many different ways as you can, adjust the times of the exposure of the films. Remember love and harmony at all times.

Many years ago the most famous worldwide photograph was the one of Mrs Abraham Lincoln with her "dead" husband in Spirit, the President Abraham Lincoln; he was the Spirit Extra beside her on the photograph.

A lot of the full Spirit photographs can happen by accident.

Some photographers see their photographs start changing in the early days of experimentation by having white spots, mist, and/or lines on the finished photograph. This has been found to be a starting point for that photographer in the happenings to start producing extras on film. So try it for yourself. Do not dismiss anything. Most of all do not be put off by all the sceptics. Keep asking over and over within your mind.

The unusual Spirit photographs today can also be produced by putting an **unopened film** that has come straight off a shop's shelf, still in the sealed box placed in a Circle for a good few weeks. Some unusual forms of art as well as faces and full human forms have been produced. Remember the formula; **"ASK"** Spirit for what you would like on your film, meditate to blend (altered awareness) and **"if it is their will"**, it **WILL** happen. Send your thoughts to Spirit. It is best to let Spirit have the choice themselves when first starting anything. I would just ask for a person for someone you know or someone in the Circle knows to appear on the film. Or even just something that would show that the Power of Spirit is being manifested.

Some try using 35mm film unopened, others use an unopened Polaroid type film with chemicals in it. With the Polaroid, after the time period when the film is thought to be ready and have hopefully images from Spirit on it. It is placed in the rollers of the camera to squash the chemicals together, then let the mix work, **NOT placed in the camera for the shutter to expose it the film.** Blank off the lens and shutter mechanism, make them light proof to make sure. The Polaroid film is only opened at the correct timing for the development to see if anything from Spirit is on the film.

Other ways that Spirit photography can happen is when a Circle is meeting have an automatic camera set up. One that has an automatic shutter that can be operated by the camera itself, when the time that is needed for the film to have enough light taken into the lens and an image is produced on film. [a time delaying shutter]. I have been taking some photographs on my 35 mm lens camera in red light. NO flash being use.

I have had a mist in front of one person and light being produced where there was none. **But** I have not used my camera very often.

In my Circle I have used a "Cannon A1", 35 mm SLR type of camera with ordinary film in it, using NO FLASH, the setting of the camera is set on fully automatic, placed firmly on a tripod, and I have a very, very long cable [I think it is classed as hydraulic, it has a rubber bulb on the end to squeeze] to operate the shutter from where I am seated, clicking it halfway through the sitting or towards the end of the Circle when I feel the power has built up but not late enough that the power has dropped. I experiment setting the opening of the shutter at different speeds.

A few of the older Mediums used to be in Trance, and had hold of their camera while taking the photographs, they, it has to be said produced the better results.

Some Mediums were in Trance, and another person took the photographs of the sitters in their presence and the loved ones who were extras were produced on the finished photograph.

Some photographs I have seen have had writing by Spirit on them [in the museum at the Arthur Findlay College in Stansted Hall]. In the early days in need of a name this was called **Skotography,** a word in Greek meaning allegedly "Dark Writing" from the dark writing imprinted by the World of Spirit onto the plates photographic equipment. The photographs taken by a Medium, or the method of the production of psychic photos were at one stage all being taken by a "**Skotograph**". This is photographs that were taken in the dark.

Other gifted Mediums of the time did not go into Trance, but were just holding the camera.

Some Mediums sat with two cameras on either side of them, both aiming at the person seated. The shutters of both of the cameras were opened at the same time and the resulting exposed film got different results from each camera. One photograph had an image of the person [Spirit] who was on the other vibrational level was in the finished photograph with the seated subject. And the other camera had only the seated subject on its photograph. It could be the camera has to be at a certain angle or pointing in a certain direction. Experimentation is the only way.

The placing of information from World of Spirit **on only one** recording instrument (in this instance still cameras) when there are more than one recording instrument in the exact position at the same time, we now are finding it is the same with different mechanisms, e.g. still cameras, moving/video camera, and voice recording machines. Spirit only uses **one instrument at a time** for some reason.

Experiment with different ways yourself.

Just another few confusing ideas for you to try out.

After asking Spirit for help in the usual way then waiting for a little while for the power to build up, (linking in meditation) at the same time asking and encouraging Spirit to come, try taking your own photograph in a mirror to try and get some extras on the film.

Also try experimenting aiming the camera at angled mirrors as in the psychomantium. Especially the double mirror set up. Or may be multi, I think three mirrors might be best as a minimum, BUT, experiment. This is so that the mirrors' images/reflections, the camera lens and the camera's focal image (the one you see to aim the camera at the subject through the view finder) and the other mirror image into the other mirror image are in a line that makes a complete continuous loop.

Remembering at the start of the photographic session both the Medium and the subject should say a prayer to first link with Spirit, asking for their help to put a loved one of the person there on the photographic film in the camera, bringing in Spirit closer for guidance, letting there be a loving peaceful harmony with self and the people of the highest realm, bringing goodness, kindness, truth, light, and loving harmony from the highest realms into the room. Perhaps meditate for **a while longer** to build up the power more. The photograph then being taken by the developing Camera Medium. Both the Medium and the subject should each time be asking for the help from Spirit and for them both to have sincere, positive thoughts about the outcome. Then when the photographic session is over, thanking the higher realm for coming closer. I will say again Rome was not built in a day, **it takes time to develop anything with Spirit,** so have trust in yourself and the ability of Spirit. Build the stronger link each day by meditating and asking for the things you want to happen.

As I said before, please try to place an **unopened**, roll of film, that has come straight off the photographers shelf; put it in the middle of your Circle or under the chair of the Medium in your Circle for a period of time. A lady, Janet Drewnick from Tilehurst, Reading, Kent U.K., I met at Stansted showed me a roll of 35 mm film that had holes of light on the film, it was as though the Spirit control had hit the film with spots of light and it splashed outwards in rays of light. There were about 5 spots on the roll and the lady had placed unopened the roll of film in her Circle, under the Medium's seat (herself) in the cabinet for seven weeks. Asking Spirit each week to place something on the film. Kodak had confirmed that the original unopened box of film had not been tampered with, nor had it been exposed in any way outside the box before they received it to develop.

Be disciplined in your REGULAR meditation for better contact with the higher realm for any gift development.

If you get any genuine results of Spirit photography, I am interested in them for my lectures. It is best if the results were accompanied by a letter off the reputable, Photographic Development Company who developed it to show it has not been forged, and/or a letter of explanation of the how, where and when the photograph had been done. **Even so, I would be interested in seeing anything out of the ordinary, so you can send me any results** at all that you get in this field of photography.

There have been some trials of different sorts by the "Budding Medium" experimenting, having placed the photographic light sensitive material which was open to the world in complete darkness in a red light environment, (as red light does not affect photographic film), against their foreheads and at other times at the solar plexus area and it was also done in complete darkness. Then after a period of time placed into baths of photographic developing fluid while still in the same environment, but of course if the experiment was done in the dark, the red light would be switched on so you could see what you were doing, and then the photographic paper would be placed in the solution.

Some people say the way Spirit photography is supposedly done, is by the photographic plates or film picking up Spirit produced ectoplasm. If that is so, how are the images produced by Spirit in a sealed unopened box of film? OR Are they produced purely by thought, the impression that Spirit want put on the photographic material? After all we are told time and time again that is the way Spirit communicate to us and across the veil, **by thought**.

An interesting book is "Photographs of the Unknown" by Robert Rickard and Richard Kelly ISBN 0-450-4822-5.

Battling Bertha Harris was asked by Sir Oliver Lodge to partake in experiments with Spirit Photography. The equipment used was a very simple camera that had no flash. It is said that because of her bodily chemical make up, [something was lacking] Bertha could not produce a Spirit image on the finished photograph on her own until a man was present with her, they did not need to hold on to each other or touch, only to be in their presence. The most successful partner for her was a Mr William Hope, and the most successful Circle for her was the one in Crewe, the sitters consisted of Mr Billy Hope, his assistant Mrs Buxton, Oliver Lodge, and of cause Bertha Harris. They would all join hands while Mrs Buxton and Billy Hope held the camera [plate on the camera] from either side. After saying a few prayers, they would then sing songs mostly hymns. But later on Spirit told them to sing the pub like songs and suggested "Any Old Iron", to liven up the vibrations. The Spirit extras were not in a static pose. They could be on their side, half way through the floor or at the back of the subject being photographed.

Sadly this partnership ended when the family of Oliver lodge who were not Spiritualists had him medically examined and then committed into a mental institute until his death. This was said in many circles of the time, because the family wanted control of all his money. Remember there were a lot of Christians within the establishment who were totally opposed to anything to do with Spiritualism as are many today.

# KEELIGHTS or SPIRIT LIGHTS
## MORE QUESTIONS THAN ANSWERS

I have myself since 1998 started getting what I call **"KEELIGHTS"** (some call them Spirit lights) recorded through my Infra RED cameras which is then transferred into my video tape recorder (VCR) onto VCR tape. They are of a circular shape of light. The reason I call them **KEELIGHTS"** is :- they are I believe the key to another vibrational level of existence, and it is the first three letters of my second name. In the world of the UFO hunter these lights are similar to what they call "Tesla Lights".

I started getting KEELIGHTS by accident while I was sitting on my own in meditation with a video camera pointing at me in the cabinet in my own séance room at home in Warrington while I was developing. I recorded myself because I had been told by the tutors and the other sitters whilst I was sitting for Spirit Links on the many courses at the Arthur Findlay College in Stansted Hall, Essex; that there were people in Spirit seen there with me in the cabinet each time I sat in the Circles in the rooms of Stansted Hall. I did not take any notice of the foolish people (some were tutors) who had told me it was not worth while sitting on my own to develop Physical Phenomena as Spirit would not come because they had no one to show themselves to especially as I would be in meditation and had my eyes closed. But contrary to their thoughts and advice I did just that, I even developed my transfiguration by going into a Deep Trance state on my own in front of my camera in red light and low white light. Each time I told people I was sitting on my own, some who were on the courses and others in the churches as I travelled around I got the same woolly statements. "Don't sit on your own it is dangerous". "Spirit will not come to you on your own because there is no other person to come for". How will you know if Spirit comes to you? How will you know if you are developing? These people do not have very much faith in those in Spirit, nor do they have any experience of the situation. They have only been told by others, who have been told by someone else. I say over and over again, **IF YOU CANNOT DO IT, YOU CANNOT KNOW IT !** I have developed quicker by sitting regularly on my own because good sitters are so hard to find. People who sit with you then leave, disrupt the flow of development. I always go back to the beginning of the development of Spiritualism when **ordinary people used to sit on their own and meditate to link with Spirit** and they sat far more regularly than anyone does now, especially the strong Physical Mediums of old. Not many people say they have the time, or is it perhaps they are not willing to put their spare time aside for Spirit to link regularly.

Spirit is now manipulating my bronchial tubes and altering my voice while I am sitting on my own, I am of course recording myself on video and sound, it is a funny feeling when Spirit manipulates your face and the tubes inside your body when you have no part in it. I have even thought it is not my voice recorded, and it is not coming from my voice box, the voice comes from my stomach area, it is as yet my own words coming through my own mind. I am always truthful to Spirit and myself in what comes out. I will not fool myself. I am a knowledgeable sceptic and I will stay that way, I always tell the truth where Spirit is concerned I will not embellish any part of it.

While recording myself I thought nothing of the Keelights at first, thinking they were something to do with the workings inside the camera, but they started happening more frequently on the recordings especially when I was sitting with others. I get them on the VCR recording whist sitting for Spirit in different rooms all over the country now nearly every time I set up my portable equipment. I have 26 VCR tape recordings with KEELIGHTS on them. I took them while I was in Wales at Haven-y-Coed in Abercraf, near Swansea. What a lovely setting the place is in. I have two VCR tape recordings taken in Bognor Regis at the Tudor Lodge centre. Two VCR tape recordings whilst I was attending a "Toe in the Water" weekend in Scotland at Ayr University, one VCR tape recording was of Keelights in natural white light while other Mediums were getting tested by Roy McKeag and his team, one of the team was a doctor. That doctor also tested me whilst I was there. My brain waves went into the levels of Theta while I was tested, the rest of the time my brain wave pattern was in lower alpha. My blood pressure also altered, it went from 152 systolic 98 diastolic; to, 169 systolic 154 diastolic. [my normal blood pressure is 117 over 71] I do not know what significance that this is, but, a person from a hospital who works in the operating theatre said I should have been dead! One of the twenty-five tested; their blood system actually went to 208/189.

This is the **VITAL** reason I feel for **"not touching"** or **not giving** the **"TRUE"** Trance Medium a **"shock"** while they are in a deep Trance situation.

A Medium in a Trance or very altered awareness who is put into a surprise or a shock condition **the blood vessels of that Medium could be ruptured/broken at a weak section in the already overly stretched vascular system, by the extra sudden surge of blood causing internal bleeding and endangering their life.**

This has happened in a few cases in the past, take for instance Helen Duncan; she had internal bleeding (rupture/breakage in her vascular system) after the police broke into her séance. I believe this is what happened. It was not just trauma of the ectoplasm rushing back into her body, which is dangerous as this causes psychic burning. Gordon Higginson was burned by ectoplasm many times because of foolish people not obeying the rules of the séance. Melanie Polley was bleeding out of her mouth because of a shock given to her during one of her public séances last year 2001; she took a few weeks to recover.

I have recorded the KEELIGHTS just recently in August 2001 at Reading church in a dark séance and also in red light while I was recording my transfiguration demonstration there. I had great success as well in Scotland at Ayr in white light during the testing of Mediums with Roy McKeag and on the same weekend in a private, red light, Trance séance with the Medium Melanie Polley, her guide was talking, she was sitting in my portable cabinet, also other KEELIGHTS were recorded through my camera onto VCR in séances whilst I was sitting with John (Jock) McArthur and others in the séances in the Crystal Bear Centre in Dunfermline and a private séance in Edinburgh just to mention a few over the Years which show not just one or two KEELIGHTS on each tape but many. One tape of a sitting just recently on the 23 September 2001 with Maureen Murphy and myself in my séance room I have in my own home in Warrington. I had on the recording, 82 Keelights of all different sizes over the space of ¾ of an hour. **BUT** sometimes there are none on the recording. Please remember you sometimes miss seeing some of the Keelights on a recording as they can pass across the TV screen very quickly. I now have over 300 hours of recordings to date (November 2001) 80 x 3 hour tapes a lot on long play and I am still recording and experimenting trying to get some more answers to the many of the hundred or more questions. I have written down. 99% of my recordings have Keelights on them, some more than others. Some tapes only show a couple of Keelights. On one of the five VCR tape recordings of the trance séance of Melanie Polley in Rugby Independent Spiritualist church on the 7th November 2001 I recorded many Keelights, one globe light actually comes out of her solar plexus while she is talking in Trance whilst sitting on the chair in front of the congregation. At that public séance, Melanie (Spirit spoke through her) actually spoke for two hours without a break. I asked her guide White Owl what were the globes of light I was picking up on my cameras. He said "Some are energy, some are Spirit just passing through, as they do not know they are there, others are Spirit who are deliberately there to show themselves to you on the earth plane".

Some sitters are seeing the globes in the semi darkness as Black globes; they seem to be globes of energy. A small child of ten, Joshua Cox told me that he was seeing globes, which were dark going around his room. He only told his mother after he had been to see Melanie Polley in Trance. The reason being White Owl (Melanie's speaking Guide) had told Joshua he was seeing things and had not told his mother about them.

The KEELIGHTS have a life of their own and I have shown that there is some sort of intelligence to them, attracted by some people more than others. More come when there is happiness and harmony in the area of recording and harmony in the group sitting situation. As I have said I also get the "KEELIGHTS" coming onto the recordings whilst sitting on my own in my own séance room.

The KEELIGHTS are of a circle shape on the screen that sometimes flash across the monitor screen; at other times they go slow, sometimes upwards, at others down the screen. They can go from left to right or right to left, they can be bright, or dull, or pulsating; some flashing as the progress across the recording being shown. You cannot be sure of what pathway they will take. Sometimes they can go straight and on other recordings they meander in different directions as they go in a wavy course. One or two go into the cabinet then out. Quite a few go into the cabinet and vanish in the chair I sit on, at other times they can come out of the chair area and out of the cabinet. Many come out of the cabinet structure and into the room. Some of the Keelights come straight at the camera veering off at the last minute. They can be seen on screen in all sizes, starting off as large as a person's head diminishing in size to that of a small pea looking for all the world as a form of flying insect BUT I have dismissed that because the image does not cross from one camera on screen to the other also they are circular and I have seen the moth and the fly go across the screen a few times and they look different. I now have a four cameras set up and they are recorded individually on full screen on each of the four V.C.R's then they are all recorded together through a quad machine at the same time onto two VCR recording machines with screens attached showing all four on the one screen. This is again to stop people saying it is produced by mechanical or computer enhancement. But remember there will be always those who are part of our blinkered society "there are none so blind as those who **do not want** to see"! Those people of a closed mind like my mother and sister. My mother thinks I am part of the Moonies or in a cult. She has just started going to our local Church of England church; this is after not going to any church for 80 years, now going all religious before she dies trying to catch up on lost time. How sad, but I suppose it gives her comfort. What on earth do these people like her think is going to happen when they go over across the veil? Is this sudden going to church going to help them in the after life when they have lead a not so helpful life to others?

The "KEELIGHTS" I feel could be of a disc shape, (like a throwing discus, a glass lens, or a dome shape), and of a material that can reflect or direct light in a specific direction, similar to a glass lens of a pair of glasses, or a torch, the lights showing up on the camera recording as a flat circle of light, the reason I say that design is; the circle of light only shows up in one camera, and it does not show itself onto or across in its chosen pathway into the lens vision of another camera, it being transparent/invisible in them. OR could the "KEELIGHTS" be a complete circle with a disc or dome, or a special material reflecting the light, perhaps they could be being thought controlled by a being or Spirit of another vibrational level controlling something inside by the thought to aim the light at one camera, or show itself on that single camera? (Please remember thought is a living energy). Just a complete circle could not in my opinion reflect or aim light at a single specific camera so accurately as it crosses the screen and keep the same dimensions. OR as I often wonder. Is the intelligence actually riding inside the circle of light? Pictures taken in Yorkshire in the Jean Noel centre in October 2002 by a digital camera where put onto the T.V. right after the recording of the pictures of the globes of Keelights/Spirit lights were shown to have faces in the blown up images of the Keelights/Spirit lights. The light that is recorded has to be aimed in a single direction by a reflective surface of some sort, light does not bend, as we know it, it travels in straight lines so we are taught. Is this another lesson we have to learn from Spirit?

Please think and experiment with your equipment. I have tried a few times with a camera outside to see if the lights come from outside when they appear from the window area. As yet I have had no success as I am always worried just in case someone comes along and takes the camera on the tripod from outside of the front of my home while I am in meditation in my séance room (not a very good format you will agree for attracting the lights in the first place). Another thing I should like to add is in defence of the Spirit lights only being picked up on one camera. If you read the EVP section, and Spirit photography in this book, it will be seen that the experiments with many (and cameras recording Spirit images) recorders in one room trying to record Spirit voices. Only one, at very, very, few odd time only two recorders, but mainly **"one" only** picks up the voice and very, very rarely two, and certainly NOT all of them. And it is not always the same one being used by Spirit all the time. This must be the same for some reason, only getting the recorded Spirit Lights through one camera lens. Eventually I would like to record in some physical séances where there is some ectoplasm produced, a formation of a voice box or a human or parts of one e.g. hands or torso to see if that comes through only on one camera, I am willing to travel.

Is the disc shape that is invisible to the naked eye in bright white light, concave, so it is able to direct the light from it accurately to an exact certain spot i.e. one camera?

Look at the glass lenses of the pair of glasses. If a light or sunlight is reflected into/onto another person's glasses, you can see the reflection in your own eyes but if the glass lens is turned ever so slightly or the person turns their head ever so slightly it does not reflect light into your eyes, all you see is the person's eyes behind the lens. Yet in some circumstances if you look you can still see the glass of the lens. This I feel is what is happening when the "KEELIGHTS" are recorded very transparent. Some because of their intensity of light block out the background yet at other times they can become very see through, appearing as a faint circle of light on the recording or could it be the vibrations of the area of the light from the other dimension, Spirit, are not being brought low enough or slowed down for us to be shown at their full potential? Or could it be something to do with the vibrations created by the person/persons sitting in the vicinity of the recording equipment?

I would also like to point out that the altered vibrational level of peoples' brainwaves that are around the camera, or recording equipment I personally think comes into the equation as I have had some experience with this.

In a situation at Haven-y-Coed when there were a lot of happy, harmonious people, Mediums and budding Mediums, in July 2000, in the same happy, harmonious, positive, frame of mind. I got more activity on recording of the "KEE-LIGHTS" on those weeks than others. We used to encourage the lights to come while talking to them through the closed door outside the séance room (the recording equipment was outside so we all could see the results on screen) One nice happening in that séance room which unfortunately was not recorded, (the recorder was switched off we did not know at the time, but seen on the screen outside by another group of people, was when the group were singing "twinkle, twinkle little star" and there was a lot of lights like a rainbow effect above the sitters. I was there for the four Trance and Physical weeks. Another person who recorded a year later in 2001 at Haven-y-Coed with a specialist infra red camera (mine is a cheap, infra red board camera set in a plastic wall plug housing fixed in with blue tack) got nothing, yet he and others who sat with him were I believe Mediums who can alter their brain waves to a higher level; something must be the factor. Were the people not in harmony with each other?

A person told me while I was in Scotland; it is possible that it could be me that is attracting the Spirit lights. Me being a video Medium, HA! HA! That's novel. I have never heard of one. Perhaps this is the new Mediumship of the future. BUT I think most people will be able to get these results, if they are a genuine seeker of the truth, and link in with the love and harmony of Spirit.

I believe those factors of attraction could be a combination of no bickering, no backbiting, no nastiness, no authoritarianism, no I am better than you attitude, or no seriousness, not having a blinkered attitude (not that I think anything like this had happened that time at Haven-y-Coed but one negative aspect I believe can stop any "KEELIGHT" phenomena, just as negativity stops phenomena happening in Physical Circles and this is physical because everyone can see the lights on the recordings). It must be, I feel, for a better production of the "KEELIGHTS", everyone feeling equal to each other, bringing happiness to each other, goodness, kindness within the people around the happening, looking for the truth, and being true to self and others, having an open mind, and in harmony with everything around you, last but not least having an open mind with no preconceived ideas especially in the group situation.

I now have now laid out over a hundred questions (105 to date, January 2002) and set myself a task to try and break down scientifically all of the answers, so the sceptics cannot label them as fraudulently produced. Perhaps one day I might get to the real truth of them. The only trouble seems to be the cost of the equipment, and the time it takes. I am sitting for Physical Phenomena and unfortunately my mind goes a little foggy and I seem to go around in a dozy, dreamlike state. Until you have experienced it you have no comprehension of what it is like. If I read a book nothing seems to stick in my mind, this is the same if I watch a TV programme, afterwards I wonder what it was about. It is now

February 2002 and I have not sat for four months and my mind has only just recently come back to what I class as normal. I think Spirit put things in my way to stop me sitting, this was to give me a rest and so I could finish different things in this book. I feel as though I have now put enough additions into it, so I am going to start sitting again shortly twice a day as I did before. The additions to my book have been another 161, full A4 pages of information.

Please remember you have to look at the tapes you have recorded so if you have sat for Spirit and recorded for an hour, then you will have to sit and look at the recordings for at the very least for another hour and a half to two hours, because you will have to watch the TV screen without blinking or blinking as little as possible then going back time and time again to see the quick passing of the lights on screen to make sure you of what you saw and then log the time on the video just in case people want to see where the Keelights is. I have to watch five tapes for each sitting. Think carefully before you lay out any money. It can become expensive. I am still spending out for additional equipment and boxes of VCR tapes, 50-100 at a time. After four years now I am finding still more questions that need to be answered. I go around different churches and centres as and when they want me to call to do workshops and record their séances. I always travel with my equipment to record in every different situation, as I need to find out what makes the Keelights come at different times more than others.

## BE WARNED

## THERE ARE SO MANY QUESTIONS YET TO BE ANSWERED ON THIS SUBJECT OF KEELIGHTS. IT IS ALSO <u>VERY</u> TIME CONSUMING AND DISTRACTING.

If any other people would like to try and experiment with the task of finding out some answers. Start by going through the normal routine of putting all your research data down on paper and asking the questions in each circumstance of What? Where? Why? When? Who? How? Please help me and others to understand the Keelights; by sending any data to me I would like to know your results. I will send you a sheet of data that is possibly needed.

BUT PLEASE try experimenting with different types of dust as these can foul your recordings as it will be seen if you shake a piece of cloth or a dust bag off a vacuum cleaner in front of or in the room where the camera is placed. THEN you will know how to see the difference. Your infrared light beam gets reflected back off the dust as it goes past the camera lens. Experiment with different transparent and reflective materials to see if anything matches the results you are getting on camera. I have tried aiming in different directions towards the cameras :- different kinds of dust; balls made of rock crystal, resin, and glass of different sizes. Flat glass in different shape form, as well as clear plastics. Plastic lens and glass lenses used in glasses. Try for yourself to use a fly and moths in the room you are going to record in. **It is a must to experiment in every conceivable way** to find out how and why the globes appear the way they do and what we can do to help prove to the masses the existence of another dimension. The one I believe we are all going to end up in eventually.

The Keelights can go behind the furniture in the room or people and come out the other side as if by magic, they can pulsate/flash a beam of light. Sometimes going through an object. They should be globe shape and not funny odd shaped as is the case **most** times with dust. Dust, by the way can reflect an infrared light source back into the camera looking white on the screen.

I also got some very good results from the week of experiments I did at Stansted Hall in November 2001 in the library; a lot of the lights came out of the window and wall area near the painting of Gordon Higginson. Quite a few were very bright. A lot of the lights appeared in the middle of the screen and vanished in the middle of the screen. BUT you could see the difference in the dust, it being NOT round but odd shaped objects. **BUT** I am now, through experimentation, finding out there are some kinds of dust that produce round images on the finished film I do not know if it is to do with the humidity of the surrounding and the absorbency of the dust (to that humidity) that is floating around the room. This why it is imperative to experiment in all of the things you do and go over the results so as not to fool yourself and others. Be honest and truthful even if the results hurt you and your findings when you look at them closely and do not be afraid of what others might say if your findings turn out to be something different.

And after that week at Stansted I was invited to a friends house, Montague Keen and his good lady wife Veronica, in London and set up the cameras in the bedroom I was going to sleep in. I got some good results there as well; before and as I slept. **Some are I admit, dust**.

I have been learning about the forms that flash across the screen now for about four years. I used to count the faint globe lights as significant happenings, (now counting most faint ones as dust, I might be wrong) but now it has to be a good lit up globe that interests me. On saying that, it is important for everyone to look closely at every globe that crosses the screen, then work out what it is, as you might miss something of what some people class as a normal happening in the physical phenomena sense.

When taking infrared pictures it will be found it is necessary to experiment with the modern day cloths of different kinds. The reason being, not all black cloth looks black on the T.V. screen when recording in infra red light. This is the reason a few samples should be bought before you buy black cloth by the yard/metre. Twice I foolishly bought a few yards of black material and it showed up white on the screen. And I bought 7 black shirts thinking they would be of use in my recordings when sitting. They showed up white in infrared lighting. I also tried dyeing bed sheets black without success. I then had the task of hunting down the correct cloth for the job. I tried using a few of my shirts, trousers, and the cloth I had bought as a start in front of the cameras. After a lot of hunting I have now found one type of work shirt and work trousers bought in Warrington that now look black on the TV screen.

Strangely I found that four of the 30 plus cloth off cuts from different shops on their own looked reasonably dark in the infra red light on the TV screen, BUT when put next to one of my shirts and a pair of working trousers, and recorded in the dark with infra red lighting, looking at them then on the TV screen they looked grey on the screen. So again I went hunting around all the shops in Liverpool and Manchester and found none suitable. I might have had to send away for material from Denmark where the company who makes the shirt and trousers I found suitable has their factory making them there. In the course of negotiations with the work wear company, I eventually came across a wholesale company in Manchester who had two different types of black cloth out of the eight I took off cuts from, those two where the best yet that actually showed up black on the screen.

I suppose a lot of people might think it is going to a lot of trouble for infrared images BUT it is for the sake of Spirit and to see if any ectoplasm is forming wherever I take the photographs with my infrared cameras. Ectoplasm if forming, will be showing up white on the screen like a fog and I do not want to see it on a white background, or should I say I will miss it on a white background. I want to record even a little amount if produced by the Medium, but if ectoplasm comes while using the wrong black cloth, I won't see it if there is a white produced background image in infrared on the screen instead of black. The proper black cloth when found would show up the ectoplasm.

In the olden days Mediums used to wear any black clothing in red and subdued lighting to show up the ectoplasm. This might be all right for the human eye but when you get into the realms of infrared photography things change **so take note**.

A few things I should like to point out are; the VCR tapes on which I record in Infra red lighting seem to fade to a darker state over a period of time.

And watch out for over exposing your whites on film by putting too much infrared lighting on a subject. It gives a white out effect on the TV screen recording making the images blurred and many times undistinguishable.

**If you take photographs with the modern digital cameras that have a setting for red eye this puts out first one flash then another to take the picture. Please remember most physical phenomena in a séance room setting and elsewhere, rapidly vanishes in a fraction of a second so be very wary of things you take on the camera in this setting. Also ask yourself the question; if physical phenomena vanishes in an instance what am I getting ? Is it in this case dust?**

In Stansted Hall on Judith Seaman's April 13-20th 2002 Trance week in a séance held in the main lecture hall. I was allowed to take in three infrared cameras (the other one had been short circuited at the time). I screwed them all on a drilled section of angled aluminium set on a single tripod, which I placed onto a table top, on the platform. So we all could see if anything would happen. All the recording equipment was placed outside (two combi units [a screen and recorder combined] and four VCR recorders). This being the first time anyone out of the tutors (Judith Seaman, Steven Upton, Eileen Michamson, Muriel Tennant, Brenda Laurence) had been photographed in this way did not wish the cameras to be intrusive. The other team when Judith was sitting the previously the week before had produced an apport from Spirit. In this second séance I was delighted that an apport was given to an Italian Lady who had lost her two sisters. The apport that the young Italian lady received, was a picture of a young lady above a beautiful butterfly. The young Italian lady said the picture looked very similar to the sister in Spirit and the other sister, also in Spirit liked and collected butterfly pictures, it was truly amazing. Unfortunately I did not fully get the appearing of the apport, but I did record many Spirit Lights flashing all over the room. A lot going into people and others going behind the sitters and coming out the other side the going in front the sitters and vanishing into another one of them in the group. A few stopped in mid flight then flew away at a tangent. There were forty sitters in the séance room that night. There was only one other person in the audience, besides myself who showed up on the TV screen as wearing black clothing, yet there were many there who in daylight and the white light bulb lighting, showed their clothing was black and this included nearly all tutor Mediums, (who's clothes showed bright white on screen in infra red); on the front row who wore black. This recording was shown to the student Mediums the following night in the large lounge on a big screen so all could see the phenomena if they wished too. At least Judith Seaman was confident enough to place her Mediumship on the line in the subdued red light and show there was no fraud involved and had every confidence in her Spirit Controls.

I would like to close on this subject with a short passage from the book by Podmore, **"Medium's of the 19th Century"**.

On the 19th December, 1872, the controlling Spirit, "Imperator", spoke (in darkness) in Direct Voice. There after this manifestation also was of frequent occurrence.

On December 31st yet another new manifestation was vouchsafed. Hitherto the Medium alone had been privileged to see Spirit Lights and Phantom Forms at the Circle. On this occasion both Dr. and Mrs. Speer saw a large cross of light behind the Medium's head and later "a line of light of great brilliancy, reaching several feet high and moving from side to side". This column of light was seen again on May 11th, 1873. but on May 25th Mrs Speer records that globe-shaped lights floated about the room; and from this date onwards the Spirit Lights seen, as described by both Dr. and Mrs. Speer, were mostly globular, about the size of an orange or rather larger. Mrs. Speer first describes these lights in detail in notes of a sitting held on 23rd June, 1873:-

"This evening we were told to sit for Spirit Lights. We sat in a large upstairs room communicating with a smaller one; the door between the rooms was left open, a curtain drawn across, and a large square opening made in it at the top part of the curtain. Mr. S. M. sat in the small room, Dr. S. and Mrs. S. in the larger one, at a small table just outside the curtain. Mr. S. M. was quickly entranced, and remained so for an hour. During that time many beautiful Spirit lights appeared through the aperture of the curtain; some were very large, and shaped like the egg of an ostrich and quite as large. The colour varied; so resembled pure moonlight, others had a blue tinge, while others were dazzlingly bright. They suddenly appeared at the opening, moved around, then vanished, when another kind would come, to disappear in the same mysterious manner. Musical sounds then came around us. Both rooms were often quite illuminated through the brightness of the lights. The Spirit Lights are described as hard, round, and cold to the touch."

**Another séance described by Mr. Charles Speer**.

"We were sitting one night as usual, and I had in front of me, with my hand resting upon it, a piece of notepaper with a pencil close by. Suddenly Stainton Moses, who was sitting exactly opposite to me, exclaimed, "there is a bright column of light behind you." Soon afterwards he said that the column of light had developed into a Spirit form. I asked him if the face was familiar to him, and he replied in the negative, at the same time describing the head and features. When the séance was concluded I examined my sheet of paper, which my hand had never left, and found written on it a message and signature."

**Here are a few of the questions that should be put to yourself and try to answer some of them in sequence as you go through your experiments.**

How is it that the Keelights suddenly appear out of the stonework and the woodwork, not just appearing from the outside vision of the lens of the camera [at the side of the screen] BUT suddenly appearing from the middle of the lens vision [the middle of the screen]?

How do the Keelights appear to come through or go through walls and solid objects?

Do the Keelights come through the solid walls?

If they do come through, do they show on the other side of the wall before coming through into the room?

Do they materialise and dematerialise in a room?

How do the Keelights sometimes appear to materialise and dematerialise in an instance?

How do they only show up on one single camera at a time, not crossing over as would be normal?

Why do they only show up on one single camera at a time, not crossing over as would be normal?

Is a certain type of camera specification needed?

Can the Keelights be recorded on both digital and analogue cameras in ordinary light?

Can the Keelights be recorded on both digital and analogue cameras in the dark?
Can the Keelights be recorded on both digital and analogue cameras in ordinary light with a flash?
Can the Keelights be recorded on both digital and analogue cameras in the dark with a flash?
Is one particular camera lens size required?
Is one particular size of camera lens best?
Can Keelights be recorded by ordinary cameras?
Is infra red light necessary to see the Keelights?
Why do the Keelights mainly show when using Infra red lighting with VCR recording?
Does the intensity of Infrared lighting give better results in seeing the Keelights??
Is the light of importance? Does the intensity of light give better results?
Is natural lighting best to record Keelights in?
Is the colour of artificial lighting in a room of particular importance to record Keelights?
Is white light best to see the Keelights? Is white light best for attraction of Keelights?
Is red light best to see the Keelights? Is red light best for attracting the Keelights?
Is green light best to see the Keelights? Is green light best for attracting the Keelights?
Is blue light best to see the Keelights? Is blue light best for attracting the Keelights?
Is yellow light best to see the Keelights? Is yellow light best for attracting the Keelights?
Is candlelight best to be used? Is candlelight best for attracting the Keelights?
Is it best recording in the dark with no lights for all to see Keelights?
Is best to use your voice to attract Keelights or talk through thought?
Is it best to use a recorded piece of music or song rather then the natural voice?
Is music best for attracting the Keelights?
Is a certain type of music best for attracting the Keelights?
Is singing best for attracting the Keelights?
Are the Keelights different in different lighting? Are there more? Less? Same?
Sizes; are they mainly small? Medium? Large?
Are the Keelights different when recording on camera with different music playing?
Are there more? Less? Same?
Sizes; are they mainly small? Medium? Large?
Are the Keelights being attracted different when people are singing different types of songs?
Are there more? Less? Same?
Sizes; are they mainly small? Medium? Large?
Are males only sitting, best to attract Keelights?
Are females only sitting, best to attract Keelights?
Are couples only sitting, best to attract Keelights?
Does one person in particular attract the Keelights?
Is the atmosphere a determining factor, (outside) weather wise?
Is the atmosphere a determining factor people wise?
Is it best for all in the room to be in a happy frame of mind a happy atmosphere?
Do the Keelights increase? Decrease? Same?
When the people in the room are subdued, sombre.
Do the Keelights increase? Decrease? Same?
When the people in the room are church like, a reverend mood.
Do the Keelights increase? Decrease? Same?
Does not caring play a factor in the amount of Keelights?
Does the furniture in a room make any difference for the production of Keelights?
Does temperature in the room make any difference for the production of Keelights?
Does temperature in air outside make any difference for the production of Keelights?
Does humidity in the room make any difference for the production of Keelights?
Does humidity in the outside air make any difference for the production of Keelights?
Is a certain type of room where the gathering is held best to produce Keelights?
What sort of a make up are the Keelights?
What are the Keelights made of? Why are the Keelights of different sizes?
Is there anything inside of the Keelights? Is anything controlling the Keelights?
Who is controlling the Keelights?

If there is something controlling the Keelights, by what method?
Are the Keelights controlled by thought?
If the Keelights are controlled by thought, who's is it?
Are the Keelights controlled from inside?
Are the Keelights controlled from somewhere else?
Do the Keelights only come at certain times?    Why do the Keelights come at certain times?
Why don't the Keelights come all the time?    Why do the Keelights come?
Is a set time for sitting best?
Why do the Keelights come for some certain people?
Why don't the Keelights come for some people?
Where do the Keelights go when they are not in the room?
Where do the Keelights come from?
Are the Keelights of the earth plane?
What sort of design are the Keelights?
Why do the Keelights appear global on camera?
Are the Keelights global? Are the Keelights domed? Are the Keelights flat?
Why are the Keelights the same spherical shape on camera?
Are the Keelights always spherical?
Do the Keelights act as the sun and moon effect, the sun shining onto the moon and reflecting the light?
Is the light from inside the Keelight?
Why do the Keelights sometimes pulse light?
Why are the Keelights most times transparent?
Why are the Keelights sometimes not transparent?
Why can't we see the Keelights normally with the naked eye?
Why is it some people can see the Keelights with their eyes and others don't?
Why is it some people see the Keelights with their peripheral vision?
Why are the Keelights most times only seen by the video camera?
Why can't the Keelights be captured on 35mm film regularly like on video?
Are the Keelights the portals that Spirit keeps on talking about?
Do the Keelights appear in religious buildings?
Do the Keelights appear outside religious buildings?
Is any religious building better than others at attracting the Keelights?
Is any building better than others at attracting the Keelights?
Is any place better than others at attracting the Keelights?
What colour are the Keelights?
Are they a single colour?
Are they a mixed colour?
Many of the Keelights/Spirit Lights recorded on film, we are now finding have faces in them when they are magnified.
Many people will say and have said it is dust that is being recorded.
Why is it that all the dust does not show up all the time on the screen when there is dust floating about?
If dust, why does not the dust show up on all the cameras when aimed at the same point?
All types of dust should be experimented with so it can be eliminated to your satisfaction.
Why are the Keelights/Spirit Lights now coming more to the fore with the coming of still digital cameras?
Why were there and aren't there not so many Keelights/Spirit Lights when people were filming with film on other cameras?
Why am I getting the Keelights/Spirit Lights when using cheap analogue video cameras when others do not seem to be?
Are some people more of a camera Medium than others? [that would be a new thing].
In 2003 I took 10 video cameras down to Hafan-y-Coed Spiritual development centre, Abercraf, Near Swansea in South Wales, to take a course and experiment to see what we could record with them. Only two cameras worked intermittently. When I got home and took them back to the place I had bought them from all worked properly. So if the Spirit World do not wish you to film them they can stop you. Why this time?

# OUT OF THE BODY EXPERIENCES
# O.B.E.
# ASTRAL TRAVEL

This subject is generally defined as having your body in one place, while your mind is off somewhere else, both the mind and the body existing in two separate places at once.

When a person is in the state of **O**ut of the **B**ody **E**xperience [OBE] the brainwaves have been detected at a range of 5-12Hz.

I have achieved out of the body by using the method of counting myself down into a lower level of awareness. Use the method that suits **you**, as there are many. There are also many tapes that can be bought to get you into an altered state of awareness; hopefully I will be making one as well. That is if I have the time.

O.B.E. is a state of your mind being awake yet your body being passive and asleep. That is when you start travelling out of your body.

For this method of mediumship [that is if it can be called mediumship] I have found it best to lie down on a comfortable bed, couch or reclining chair.

I concentrated on my breath then I first ask through thought for anything that is going to happen, or that is to come to me, to be brought with no harm to others, or myself; for it to come to me with only goodness, kindness, love, and truth within the Divine Light of Spirit within the loving harmony of Spirit of the highest realm, and let me return safely to my body when my journey is over. I then know the travel can happen with my mind with safety.

It is said the only link you have with your body when in this state of O.B.E. is with the etheric (some say silver) cord. Do not worry too much about that, you will not come to any harm if you trust fully in Spirit.

Here is an exercise for you to regularly practice, it is best to read it out and record it onto a tape for yourself to listen to while practicing. Go over it a few times to get it right, then when you are satisfied with it, you can use it each and every day.

I <u>see</u> myself in a warm comfortable place, (<u>see</u> and <u>feel</u> it, **fully sense it in every way).**

I <u>see</u> this place has a beautiful light that is keeping me warm. [It does not matter what colour it is, it can be blue, yellow, black, green, brown, grey, pink any colour even multi-coloured, the dark with sparkles of blue or red or yellow any colour] **I fully sense it in every way.**

I <u>see</u> and <u>feel</u> the warm comfortable light/colour, I am starting to become part of that light going deeper into it **I fully sense it in every way.**

I count one in my thoughts.

I <u>see</u> and <u>feel</u> the warm comfortable light/colour, I am starting to become part of that light going deeper into it **I fully sense it in every way.**

**(PAUSE AND SEE IT).**

I count two in my thoughts. (Or if recording this, say it ("two" and so on) on tape that way it is better as your mind is not thinking of the numbers and where you are up to in the sequence)

I <u>see</u> and <u>feel</u> the warm comfortable light/colour, I am starting to become part of that light going deeper into it **I fully sense it in every way.**

**(PAUSE AND SEE IT).**

I count three in my thoughts.

I <u>see</u> and <u>feel</u> the warm comfortable light/colour, I am starting to become part of that light going deeper into it **I fully sense it in every way.**

**(PAUSE AND SEE IT).**

I count four in my thoughts.

I <u>see</u> and <u>feel</u> the warm comfortable light/colour, I am starting to become part of that light going deeper into it **I fully sense it in every way.**

**(PAUSE AND SEE IT).**

I count five in my thoughts.

I <u>see</u> and <u>feel</u> the warm comfortable light/colour, I am starting to become part of that light going deeper into it **I fully sense it in every way.**

**(PAUSE AND SEE IT).**
I count six in my thoughts.
I <u>see</u> and <u>feel</u> the warm comfortable light/colour, I am starting to become part of that light going deeper into it **I fully sense it in every way.**
**(PAUSE AND SEE IT).**
I count seven in my thoughts.
I <u>see</u> and <u>feel</u> the warm comfortable light/colour, I am starting to become part of that light going deeper into it **I fully sense it in every way.**
**(PAUSE AND SEE IT).**
I count eight in my thoughts.
I <u>see</u> and <u>feel</u> the warm comfortable light/colour, I am starting to become part of that light going deeper into it **I fully sense it in every way.**
**(PAUSE AND SEE IT).**
I count nine in my thoughts.
I <u>see</u> and <u>feel</u> the warm comfortable light/colour, I am starting to become part of that light going deeper into it **I fully sense it in every way.**
**(PAUSE AND SEE IT).**
I count ten in my thoughts.
I <u>see</u> and <u>feel</u> the warm comfortable light/colour, I am starting to become part of that light going deeper into it **I fully sense it in every way.**
**(PAUSE AND SEE IT).**
You can use this by counting up to any number have the number on the tape, you also can say it in your mind or out loud, (**BUT** remember you are trying to still your mind and concentrate on the colour not to say the numbers), it is up to you, probably about 30-50 seems a right amount, remember we are all individuals, but please practice, practice, practice, practice.

This is a method for getting the body to fully relax while the mind is still awake.

This can be a method to use for deeper meditation or Trance. But I must say this is only a technique that is used at first, as you have to think and so use your mind. In deep Trance you have to still your mind of any thoughts what so ever [well as much as you can]. As should be seen by you the reader, this method cannot be used to go into full deep Trance.

For O.B.E. you have to have your body totally relaxed and **your mind wide awake**, this is why this method is here first

Now back to the way you can travel.

Go through the pre-meditation relaxation ritual. Some find it calming with low, soft music playing throughout. Try different ways. Here is another way.

Say your prayers and ask for what you want. **<u>Keep on asking positively and sincerely</u>** as you go deeper BUT do not let it interfere with your going deeper into the light.

Surround yourself with the power and light, **<u>see it</u>** going into your body and surrounding you.

Start to go deep into meditation, **<u>feel yourself going lighter</u>** in weight, then **<u>feel yourself</u>** having no weight at all.

In your mind **<u>feel</u>** as though you are going into a position that is alongside of yourself, as though you roll into that position, laying beside yourself, **<u>see yourself there</u>**. [Or **see yourself** above yourself, looking down at yourself]

Think and **<u>see yourself there at each stage</u>** then it becomes natural as you progress.

In your mind look at your body, **<u>see it</u>**, you are your Spirit beside your body, **<u>see it there</u>**. [or above]

Then you will start to float to where ever you want to go. Ask!

You will find you will have to practice, practice, practice. With this out of body some people find it a very hard situation to let happen, it is the letting go that is a blocking mechanism for the brain, the subconscious stopping it happening. Please remember you cannot be harmed by doing this, and it can become enlightening. Some people take only a few days; others take many weeks of practice, some many months. Some, who have a blocking mechanism of a subconscious fear, can take years.

Something that might put you off when it first happens, is the feeling when starting to be drawn out of your body, then dropped back into your body. I can only say for me it is like a feeling of having a coat on, which is touching all your body, and it being pulled once, downwards quickly on your skin, in one little jerk on the coat. Not a drag, a little jerk. Or when coming back a feeling of when you step off a small step suddenly, one that you do not know is there, and there is a little jolt to the body, or when you go to sit down on a seat, and you find it slightly lower than anticipated, about an inch or two lower, that is the similar feeling that I got when first starting Out of Body Experiences. It gives you a start but not a fright. These things can also happen, when you come back into your body after the full experience of O.B.E. travel. At least you will know that you are progressing to another stage, I didn't, I wondered what was happening at the time. There is no need to be afraid, nothing can happen to you. As I said before, I only wish while I was developing I had read some book like this one before I had started on the different stages of mediumship. The knowing of different people's experiences. It would have cut down on all the wondering and the uncertainty. When you come back into your body, the slight jolt can occur again, well with me it does. BUT remember all people can be slightly different with their reactions.

To relax you can use the method of going **up** in the lift if that suits you, perhaps you might feel more comfortable with that method. Instead of going **down** in the lift as some people teach as a way of going into a trance state. You might like to try going upwards out of your body to another level. If you feel uncomfortable in doing it alone, meet some person there first in your mind, then go with that someone who will help and guide you while you are experiencing it all.
See yourself going down in a lift into the light or warm colour, or slowly going upwards into the light upwards, going upwards, going upwards, ever upwards, at each breath. In the end you become part of the light or colour being absorbed by it, you look back at your body laying there it is you and now you are going to be free to travel. Free to go where ever you want to go.

This next method is suitable for recording in your own voice, as your subconscious mind will react earlier to the stimulus of your voice because it is used to that voice. This must be said in a voice that is slow, soft, and gentle, as though you are talking softly to a child, a small baby, calming them down in the bed/cot before they start going to sleep.

I step into a lift that is brightly lit. [Any coloured light preferably pure white] with more beautiful light streaming from above into the shaft itself. It is coming through the clear top of the lift and the clear doors it all making me feel good.
**PAUSE. See it, feel it.**
The doors close.
**PAUSE. See it, feel it.**
I see the indicator starting to move; it is showing it is taking me slowly upwards to the light that is shining.
**PAUSE. See it, feel it.**
Within the beautifully lit lift I am being taken up to the first floor I see the indicator showing ONE.
**PAUSE. See it, feel it.**
I am going up in the lift that is filled with that light shining from above, I am feeling warm within that light, I see the indicator showing TWO.
**PAUSE. See it, feel it.**
I am watching the indicator as I go further up into the light. I look out through the window of the lift and the light is looking so inviting as I go up to each floor. I see the indicator showing THREE.
**PAUSE. See it, feel it.**
I see the indicator going up further now, and I am becoming more relaxed in the bright light of the lift. I see the indicator showing FOUR.
**PAUSE. See it, feel it.**
I am starting to feel part of the light as though I belong in the light. I see the indicator showing FIVE.
**PAUSE. See it, feel it.**
As I go further into the light I am comfortable now in this position. I see the indicator showing SIX.
**PAUSE. See it, feel it.**
I look down out of the window I can see my body there where I left it ready to come back to whenever I want to, I still feel I am safe in the light. I see the indicator showing SEVEN.
**PAUSE. See it, feel it.**
I am now becoming part of the light at this level. I feel more comfortable where I am now. I am now at level EIGHT.
**PAUSE. See it, feel it..**

I look further into the light, I am nearly part of the full light, as I look upwards I can now see a person waiting there for me, they look a very gentle and kindly sort, I am at level NINE.
**PAUSE. See it, feel it.**

HERE IS A CHOICE OF TOP FLOOR ENDINGS at level nine :-
( 1    At each floor I have felt I should be here becoming part of the light, I look down at my body for the last time before looking into the light at the person waiting for me, the light is like a swirling mist which is clearing as I look at the person. The lift stops and the doors open for me and the person is there ready to greet me, I am ready to be shown the way to where I want to go, I am here at level TEN in the full light that is going to be part of me as I travel, I am completely parted from my body. I look into the clearing mist and see the person who is always going to be with me when I want them as a support)

(2    I arrive at TEN, the upper floor now and see the door open wide, on stepping out of the lift, I realise I am fully out of my body, there is a corridor full of white light ahead of me with a slight mist sort of wafting towards me. I follow the person who will be with me if I want them at any time as a support).

There is a window at the side, I am now looking down at my body laying there where I was, I am comfortable leaving my body, as I know I can return at any time I want to, just by going back into the lift.
I leave the lift behind me with its doors left open for me to return at any time I should wish it.
I walk along the corridor through the bright white mist towards the open door where the mist is coming from.
I go into the mist into the room, it is full of the nicest, pure, white, light, I have ever seen.
There I meet a person who is full of love, and compassion, that person is going to help me, it is my guide whenever I need one to call on.
This person comes to stand alongside me, putting their hand on my shoulder to help make me feel secure there. I know they are telling me they will always be there when needed; I now have two supports. It gives me more warmth and strength to carry on in my quest of knowledge.
They are giving me their strength through their hands for whatever is needed in my life.
We now go through an open space and we start to travel together. Showing each other the things we want to see.
(CAN BE PUT IN IF NEEDED) [I leave my friend at the open space knowing they will be there waiting for me]
This method can also be used to go into a trance state.

**"[This method can be used on your own, and you can travel on your own by leaving your friend at the open space, to wait for your return to guide you back to the corridor and then to the lift.]""**

**"When you have travelled all you want to".**

**""[Place this next portion on the end of the tape, so you can feel and know when the experience will end]""**

I now come back to the entrance of the open space with my friends, who now gently place me in the room that is full of the nicest, pure, white, light, I have ever seen.
I am guided out of the room, into the corridor of mist towards open door of the lift, I can see the light of the lift shining out of that open door, it has been ready for me at any time, waiting there, in that short distance along the corridor.
On reaching the lift I step into it and the doors close, I see the indicator going down each floor.
Nine, **PAUSE. See it, feel it.**    Eight,  **PAUSE. See it, feel it.**  Seven. **PAUSE. See it, feel it.**
The lift is slowly taking me downwards towards my body.
I am going down further, gently towards my body, as the brightness is slowly dulled.
Six,  **PAUSE. See it, feel it.**     Five, **PAUSE. See it, feel it.**     Four, **PAUSE. See it, feel it.**
The bright light is now fading, and I am above my body now, ready to go gently into it.
Three  **PAUSE. See it, feel it.**   Two,   **PAUSE. See it, feel it.**   One. **PAUSE. See it, feel it.**
I step out of the lift, and accept the body there, as my own.
I go gently back, into the relaxed body

I am now within my body, coming back to normality.
After this exercise you should try to do some mundane chores, house work, shopping, watch T.V. walk around the garden go for a walk anywhere to bring your awareness back to normality. Try to exercise a little, you want to bring your oxygen level back to a higher level, this is because you have been totally relaxed, in a state of altered awareness.

Another method is for you during a period of time that suits you, generally over about two months; of course it can happen at any time during the exercise, but keep continuing the whole of the routine. You can take a one or two day exercise routine. I personally recommend the two-day. All these exercises are to help make you more aware of all your senses. And make you more aware of your surroundings. You are honing your senses to another pitch or level of awareness. I recommend using a mixture of the exercises together as you go along with your development.

I am going to include here a way some people do the following exercises on different days, doing them one at a time two days at a time. It is up to you if you want to do it that way. But please go back to the beginning each time you finish one exercise, to enforce in your mind the different parts of the full exercise. This is what you should do anyway as you progress in anything you wish to learn, so you do not forget the basics, keep going back to the beginning. When doing any of these exercises please remember not to have too much of a gap in between them, as you might lose the impetuous of the exercises. Also after the week of exercises give yourself a break of one day of exercise. After each set of daily mind exercises exercise your body in some way even if it is only a walk; or shaking of hands, arms and legs if you are not mobile, something to get your heart pumping faster. You want to try and increase the blood flow that is all. Something to get your lungs moving.

Now to start.
For the first two days is for you first to get into your underwear, look at the whole of your body in the mirror, to really study it for a good half an hour to and hour, in the morning of the first day, and then again in the evening. As you are looking at your body, think of all the things it does to help you in your every day life. Go slowly through each of the actions, do not rush any parts of the exercise take at least thirty minutes or more for each exercise to do it fully, if you finish before the time suggested, go back and do it again. After each exercise have a break, and go out of your environment, go for a walk or to the shops, it is this that brings you back to normality or earth bound reality.

Here are a few more exercises to use; they can be used to bring about awareness in yourself, about yourself. Getting to know what is happening in your body, then you can put it aside ready to explore the regions of your consciousness that hitherto has been left dormant.

1. While in your underwear. You walk. Think how you walk and how it is done by your body functions. Do the actions in the mirror to show yourself; see your muscles move your legs while you think of how it is done. Feel the actions as they happen, be conscious of the happenings within your body not just the outside. See how the other muscles of the body come into the action not just your legs, see and feel them working as you walk. See and feel them first on the outside, and then on the inside, see and feel it happening on the inside, be there with that feeling at each stage. See and feel the skin over your muscles as they stretch and contract, see and feel the skin moving. Look how your tendons move the bones they are attached to, feel them as the move. Do this exercise first with your eyes open, then with your eyes closed. Feel them as they move, noting each movement as it happens.

2. While in your underwear looking into a mirror. You pick things up by using your hands try picking them off a table or the floor. Think how you pick up objects, and how it is done by your hands and arms, lift and raise the object above your head. Do the actions in the mirror to yourself, and see your muscles move your hands and arms, and what is happening to your body as you do each action, look into the mirror while you think of how it is done. Feel the actions as they happen, be conscious of the happenings within your body, not just the outside, look and feel it on the inside. See how the other muscles of the body come into the action, not just your hands and arms, see and feel them first on the outside, and then on the inside. Look how your tendons move the bones they are attached to, feel them as they move, see and feel it happening on the inside be there with that feeling at each stage. Do this exercise first with your eyes open, then with your eyes closed. Feel them as they move, know it is happening to you; note in

your mind each movement.

3. While in your underwear looking into a mirror and looking at yourself. You bend over to the side to pick things up off the floor. Think how you pick up the objects, and how it is done by your hands and arms, lift and raise the object above your head. Do the actions in the mirror to yourself, and see your muscles move your hands and arms, while you think of how it is done. Feel the actions of your torso as they happen, be conscious of the happenings within your body not just the outside, look at it on the inside. See how the other muscles of the body come into the action, not just your hands and arms, see and feel them, first on the outside, and then on the inside, feel it happening on the inside, be there with that feeling at each stage. Do this exercise first with your eyes open, then with your eyes closed. Feel them as they move, know it is happening to you; note in your mind each movement.

4. While in your underwear. Start to **feel** all the parts of your body and how the skin feels, how the skin changes on different parts of your body be aware of the subtleties of the change. **See and feel** how the hands pick up the differences, be aware of it. **Feel** the difference in the hairs of your body as you go slowly over your skin. Your head, and different parts of the body. Go to the furniture and decorations around you, and **see and feel** the difference in the hardness, softness, roughness, smooth, cold, warmth of the wood, plastics, and fabrics of different sorts. Do not rush this exploration; take your time to experience it. Make yourself more aware of it all at each feeling/touching moment. Do each of these exercises first with your eyes open, then with your eyes closed. Note each feeling you have, pause and let it sink into your mind.

5. Have a tape recorder going ready. While you are in a relaxed state. You talk to make yourself understood, think about all that you do. Talk to yourself in the mirror, be conscious of your mouth**, see and feel** what it is doing. Say to yourself on the tape what is happening. Talk when you have a smile on your face, **see and feel** the difference on the outside and the inside, be aware of that difference, be aware of any change at all. Now frown, **see and feel** the difference as you talk, **see** the difference on the outside and **feel** it, but then feel the subtle difference when you become aware of the inside of yourself as it is happening, look inside yourself, **see [in your mind] and feel** it happening on the inside, be there with that feeling at each stage on the inside and outside. Go through the different emotions. Hate, anger, happiness, sadness, being jolly/jovial, calm, brash, etc. see the difference in your face and afterwards listen to what you have said into the recorder. Do this exercise first with your eyes open, then with your eyes closed. Listen to the recording with your eyes open then closed.

6. While you are relaxed. You hear to make sense of the outside world; you hear all the different noises around you; it is not silent at all. Listen to the movement of the air; is it windy or calm? There are bees humming, flies, insects of every description making some sort of an individual, personal noise, there are birds singing. Listen to all the local/near noise that is there around you in your vicinity within fifty yards/metres. Hold onto that noise listen carefully for a while. Now listen to the noise that is far away, throw your hearing outwards to the furthest points you can hear. Listen; draw them into your mind; listen to them intently. Send your hearing into a local/near mode again, listen to the noises in your own locality, listen for a while then go back to listening to the outer fringe noises, absorb them for a short while, then go back to the local/near noises. [This exercise can be done in the park or by the sea or in a comfortable place of your liking]. Do this exercise first with your eyes open, then with your eyes closed.

7. While you are in a relaxed state. In the mirror you see with your eyes, how others see you; how your eyes and face and make expressions, when you are happy, sad, angry, thinking, etc. See how your eyes and face is different in the many moods, act out those different moods in the mirror, feel your face change on the outside and how the feeling is different on the inside, notice the difference in each mood, see the muscles change your appearance, feel that change, first on the outside then on the inside, feel it happening on the inside be there with that feeling at each stage. [This exercise can be done dressed as any of them can]. Do this exercise first with your eyes open, then with your eyes closed. Do not forget the mirror to see all that is happening.

8. While in your underwear. You breath to live, to help your body function how it should; think how you do all the actions of breathing. Look at your body's reflection in the mirror, **see and feel** how it is moving as you slowly breath in, and then slowly breath out, look at all the movement of the muscles on

the outside, **see and feel** how they manipulate each other to make room for the air, **see and feel** the moving ribs and the muscles in between the ribs at each intake of breath. **See and feel** the difference, when the breath is going out of the lungs, out of your body. See the skin expand and contract as you breath in and out, **see and feel the difference of each movement.**
Now close your eyes to start and **see and feel** the breath as a colour going into your lungs, **see [in your mind] and feel** each breath of air going into your body through your nose, then into your windpipe, then into your lungs, **feel** them expanding, **see** them expanding [in your mind], filling up with that chosen colour of air, see and feel your chest cavity filling up on the inside, see and feel the lungs pushing the chest outwards. **Feel and see** it happening on the inside, be there with that feeling at each stage. Think about the skin and what it was doing for you to help support your body frame, stretched over your organs, your muscles, your bones, and tendons. Do this exercise first with your eyes open, then with your eyes closed.

9. While in your underwear. You use your heart to keep yourself alive, think about it for a few minutes. Look into the mirror. **See** on the outside your heartbeat on your chest. At every beat **feel** how it pushes onto your chest as it is pumping, see the muscles move, think about it for a moment. Think about it being on the inside of your chest, **see and feel** your heart beating at every pulse pushing the blood around the body, all the red liquid going through your veins, **see and feel** it, all the blood going to the different parts of the body, feeding it and replenishing all goodness that is needed in those parts. Take note of the way your heart can be speeded up if you run on the spot for a minute [try it] feel the difference; watch it slow down. Go on the inside of your body to **see and feel,** then go to **see and feel** it on the outside as it is happening. Take notice of the speeding up and slowing down of your breathing. Do this exercise first with your eyes open, then with your eyes closed

10. While in your underwear, still looking in the mirror. You use your mind to control all of your body. Take a bit of time to think how your brain works, think about when it is sending out signals for the controlling of the muscles, the blood flow, breathing, movement, your eyes, your hearing, your feelings, the healing of your body when ill. When you have done that let it go and relax. Do this exercise first with your eyes open, then with your eyes closed

11. You have taste buds so you can eat the correct foods for your body to grow and sustain its equilibrium. Think about how they work inside the mouth, on the tongue, and the back of the mouth as the food goes into the mouth. Have different foods ready to taste or do these exercises while at the table to become aware of your body functions.
You also have a nose, which acts alongside the taste buds, to help with your guidance of the good, and the bad for you as a person. Get some different things out of your cupboard set out ready in containers? Salt, vinegar, sugar, jam, mustard, pepper, herbs of different sorts all separately placed. Sauces of different flavours and tastes and smells, sardine, olives, cheese, fruits of different sorts, orange, lime, lemon, grape, strawberries, drinks and juices of many kinds, cereals out of packets, rose petals if possible, marigold petals, pansy petals [yes they are edible], yoghurt perhaps different flavours, you can probably think of a great many more things. You do not have to have all of these, but try to have a wide selection. Have a small stick, which you can use for dipping into the samples.
Now go to each container one at a time first smell it then taste it. First dwell on the smell, and what it is doing to your senses. The taste a little of the container from the stick. See, and feel how it affects your taste buds, first from the smell then from the taste. [Yes if you do it properly you will be able to taste the smell]. After each sample, have a drink of water to swill away the flavour, and a few deep breaths to clear the smell in your nose. Do not eat all of them; the idea is only to taste a little of them individually, not to eat them that is the reason for the small dipstick. Do this exercise first with your eyes open, then with your eyes closed. This exercise is good fun in a group situation.

These exercises are to have you become more aware of your whole self, and what your body does for you. That way as your body becomes better known to you, it becomes easier to put it aside, also easier to come back into the body, your body, that earthly body you have more of a full knowledge of, when coming back from your OBE's.

After any of these exercises get dressed, and get back into your normal ways of going about your everyday life, perhaps go to the shops, perhaps do some housework, but as you touch an object a piece of furniture [or the things in the shop] be more aware, take an extra bit of time to look and hold it, this is to bring you back into reality/normality each time. Also at this time be aware of the difference in your body, and the normality it has returned to, notice the difference in your muscles of your body, and how much you are not now as fully aware as you were, when you were doing the exercises.

For the next two days exercises, find a comfortable chair to use or nice relaxing settee or bed. In any of the following exercises, do not worry if you fall asleep, no harm will come of you. I would personally recommend you to do this exercise as much as possible, and whenever possible as it is one of the most important.

Now is the time for you to learn how to fully relax your body but keep your mind alert.
Sit or lay down in a comfortable position.
Close your eyes and see within your mind yourself being covered in a warm comfortable colour, as you go through these relaxation points of your body, see the coloured light you see within your third eye being poured over you, imagine it going into and onto the different parts you are relaxing.

First start by relaxing your head and the hairs on your head bringing the colour onto and within them.
**Pause and think it, feel it, see yourself doing it.**
Relax your scalp, cover it in warm colour. See the colour going onto and into it.
**Pause and think it, feel it, see yourself doing it.**
Relax the skin on your face, cover it in warm colour. See the colour going onto and into it.
**Pause and think it, feel it, see yourself doing it.**
Relax the muscles on your face, cover it in warm colour. See the colour going onto and into it.
**Pause and think it, feel it, see yourself doing it.**
Relax your jaw, cover it in warm colour. See the colour going onto and into it.
**Pause and think it, feel it, see yourself doing it.**
Relax your neck, cover it in warm colour. See the colour going onto and into it.
**Pause and think it, feel it, see yourself doing it.**
See and feel the beautiful, warm, colour flowing over all and into your head and neck. See the colour going onto and into them.
**Pause and think it, feel it, see yourself doing it.**
Relax your left hand, cover it in warm colour. See the colour going onto and into it.
**Pause and think it, feel it, see yourself doing it.**
Relax your left lower arm, cover it in warm colour. See the colour going onto and into it.
**Pause and think it, feel it, see yourself doing it.**
Relax your left upper arm, cover it in warm colour. See the colour going onto and into it.
**Pause and think it, feel it, see yourself doing it.**
Relax your right hand, cover it in warm colour. See the colour going onto and into it.
**Pause and think it, feel it, see yourself doing it.**
Relax your right lower arm, cover it in warm colour. See the colour going onto and into it.
**Pause and think it, feel it, see yourself doing it.**
Relax your right upper arm, cover it in warm colour. See the colour going onto and into it.
**Pause and think it, feel it, see yourself doing it.**
Relax your left shoulder, cover it in warm colour. See the colour going onto and into it.
**Pause and think it, feel it, see yourself doing it.**
Relax your right shoulder, cover it in warm colour. See the colour going onto and into it.
**Pause and think it, feel it, see yourself doing it.**
Relax your upper body, cover it in warm colour. See the colour going onto and into it.
**Pause and think it, feel it, see yourself doing it.**
Relax your lower body, cover it in warm colour. See the colour going onto and into it.
**Pause and think it, feel it, see yourself doing it.**
See and feel the beautiful, warm, colour flowing over and into your head, neck, shoulders, your arms, your body.
**Pause and think it, feel it, see yourself doing it.**
Relax your left thigh to your knee, cover it in warm colour. See the colour going onto and into it.

**Pause and think it, feel it, see yourself doing it.**
Relax your left lower leg, cover it in warm colour. See the colour going onto and into it.
**Pause and think it, feel it, see yourself doing it.**
Relax your left foot and feel it going to your toes, cover it in warm colour. See the colour going onto and into them.
**Pause and think it, feel it, see yourself doing it.**
Relax your right thigh to your knee, cover it in warm colour. See the colour going onto and into it.
**Pause and think it, feel it, see yourself doing it.**
Relax your right lower leg, cover it in warm colour. See the colour going onto and into it.
**Pause and think it, feel it, see yourself doing it.**
Relax your right foot and feel it going to your toes, cover it in warm colour. See the colour going onto and into them.
**Pause and think it, feel it, see yourself doing it.**
See and feel the beautiful, warm, colour flowing over your legs, knees, and feet. See the colour going onto and into them.
**Pause and think it, feel it, see yourself doing it.**
See and feel the beautiful, warm, colour flowing over your head, neck, shoulders, your arms, your body, and your legs and feet. See the colour going onto and into them.

I used to have to go back and do it again in some parts, so you might also.

When you have done this, think of yourself now in a lovely warm bath of that coloured warm light, your body has no feeling at all. You are now just your mind, thinking, without your body being a part of you. Some people can feel their body has left them right away, others can feel it is heavy, some feel it is light, some take a bit longer and need to practice more just as I did. Any of these conditions are all right if they are comfortable for the person. There are no set rules. A few people might start to feel the sensation of leaving their body, do not fight it, do not analyse it, do not wonder what is happening, just let it happen, go with the flow as they say. Some here might fall asleep [I have done myself]. If you do, do not be alarmed, when you come out of the sleep, try the exercise once more now you are fully rested, do not move from where you are. Practice this exercise for about half an hour to an hour in the morning then at night. If possible have an alert mind when starting, that way you stay awake easier.

After this exercise, to regain your normality, back to your own earthly reality. Do what I generally do. I get up, swivel each of my ankles about ten to twenty times. The same with my wrists, then my arms, and then I get hold of my knees, and bring them to my chest a number of times. I then touch the furniture around me to bring myself back to earthly reality, looking at it more than I would normally do, not taking it for granted, as most of us do at times.

Now you are finding a way to have your mind alert and your body relaxed, each time you go to bed. Say in your mind "I can have an out of body experience now with safety". "I will let myself have an experience of out of the body when I want to."
Then when you wake up and your body is fully relaxed see yourself rising up out of your body. See your face and your body down below you on the bed. See yourself going off to where you are comfortable. To a park bench, to a friends house in their living room, on the beach on the sand. Anywhere in fact where you feel safe. Do this from now on while you are progressing

You can of course use the going into a lift then light method of out of the body here.

Next four days, you have to get a friend to go along with you to a place that you feel comfortable in. [you can go on your own but it is better to have someone there with you]. Have a pair of dark glasses ready, so you are not thought of as unusual whilst doing this exercise. Walking around with your eyes close can unnerve some people, they might think you strange.
When in the place of your choice, place your hand on the shoulder of your friend, and have them lead you slowly, and safely around the area, **while you have your eyes closed**.
Your friend should be now explaining to you, while they guide you, and tell you, what is around the route as you approach each point. A tape recorder is best used to talk into, so you can retrace your steps if your friend has not written the points of stopping down. You will be able to go at the same pace later

on if a recording is taken. (this part as you are recording can be done with your eyes open and going around on your own BUT it is not as efficient/effective, it does not have the same impacted on the mind BUT IT CAN WORK so try it).

Your friend guides you [you have your eyes closed] to different points telling you what is there along the way, writing down [or recording] the things done each time, so they can be done in the same sequence later.

As you go around this place your friend explains all about the route and has you touch, smell, listen, and feel different things, noting them down as each sequence is done. This is why a tape recorder is best. Note everything, with every sense that you have, within your mind, as you go through this exercise. This means using touching, smelling, feeling; remembering the feeling part of the mind is the biggest part, feel with all of your body.

E.g. :- Breath in, and take in the air, noting every smell as you do each section. Feel a tree trunk, note as much as you can in your mind, feel the bark, get you friend to pick up some leaves, you feel the ribs on them, and crunch them in your hand so you hear the sound they make. If there are a few around, best to have the leaves in a cluster on the ground or scattered in a small area so they are of significance later. If the leaves are in a cluster have your friend walk you through them, sense them, hear them, see them in your mind's eye. [eyes still closed]

If you walk along a gravel path, have your friend pick up the gravel off the path so you can feel it, smell it, hear it as you rub it in your hands, crunch it with your feet, sense what it looks like, have your friend describe it fully, see it in your mind's eye.

Go onto a piece of grass to sense the difference. Go to a wall. Go to a bench. Go up steps, down steps or levels, go to a fence, go to a car but make sure the car is one that is not likely to move off. Touch it, have your friend describe it to you. What is the smell? What are the feelings you get?

If you live near the beach go to the beach, taste even through the air [yes! you will find you can taste the air, be aware of it], **feel** with **your hands and feet**, hear, sense, the sand, the water, the seaweed, the rocks, the gravel, everything on the route. Taste the air and as much as possible so **all** your senses are aware and heightened.

If you live near a woods go there, that too can be used. Go to a shopping precinct. Try a farm, if there is one handy. Anywhere you will feel comfortable going.

When your walk is completed after about one hour or more go back to the beginning and go over the same route with your eyes uncovered, doing the exact same things in the exact same sequence. Follow the tape recorders route. See it in your mind when you were getting lead around by your friend.

Then go home and lay down in a nice comfortable place in bed or on the sofa.

Relax all your body going through the sequence of relaxation putting you body aside, but be alert in your mind and listen to your friend read out the same sequence that you have just gone through twice. This is where the tape recorder is of the greatest assistance; it can be used many times when your friend is not there. If you fall asleep doing this exercise, do not worry it will not do you any harm, when you wake up you are certain of your mind being fully awake, and your, body fully relaxed. Try the exercise then.

Practice this for about four or five times or more so you can see each location in your mind as you do it. Then repeat the exercise by going to a different location and do the same process with your kind friend.

With your long suffering friend try to go to as many different places as you feel comfortable with, I would recommend at least four or five different places. The reason being, you are now getting to a stage where you should have the images of your places of where the exercises have been done, becoming clearer in your mind. After three exercises, you will or should I say, you should be starting some free flow mind travel.

It should now be seen the difference in having your mind active in this case and having you mind stilled as much as possible for a strong link with Spirit development for mediumship, especially Trance.

# HYPNOTISM & MESMERISM

Franz, Anton, Mesmer 1733-1815 was a Swiss German Physician who was the first documented person, to be using a form of "animal magnetism", to produce an abnormal state of consciousness in his patients, in which he had control over their will. It was a hypnotic state that was induced.

Mesmer started his experiments in Vienna University, where he was a physician in the late 1760's, this was started after coming across the findings of the British physician Richard Mead, who was working on the theories of "animal gravitation" cause by the gravitational pull of the planets going around the earth. Richard Mead was working on the theory that the moods, or altered states of animals, and humans, are altered by the different pulls of the planets. Mesmer renamed his own findings to "animal magnetism," because he thought the power of the "mesmerist," was transferred to the patient. He also put his method down to all animals having an invisible fluid within their bodies that could be manipulated by other magnetic objects. Mesmer theorised that these invisible fluids could be manipulated easily by any trained person, because they followed the laws of physics that govern magnetism. He started to experiment, trying to cure people of different problems. In these experiments Mesmer was quite often brutal; if not a forceful person, when he used his techniques on his unsuspecting patients.

Quite often the patients after the treatment, in which the participant was in trance, came out of the trance in an induced fit, convulsion, or was delirious. In these experiments, a great deal of harm must have been done to the poor people. In later years Mesmer was run out of Vienna, after being accused of being a fraud by his fellow physicians in Austria. He set up a practice in Paris, France, for another six years; then he was looked at closely by a commission. They found his methods of curing people of their mental illnesses could not be proven, so his methods of mesmerism declined, but one thing he now had in his favour we can all say. The trance state experimentation of Mesmer and his followers, started off hypnotism as we know it today. Mesmer used magnets around the patients to produce a trance state. Try for yourselves by having four magnets in the four corners of the room; N-S to N-S. Experiment.

The word hypnotism was invented in the 19$^{th}$ century by James Braid from England, he and many other physicians had been using the method of Mesmer on their own patients over the many years since Mesmer's experiments stopped. Then because of the bad name of Mesmer, James Braid gave mesmerism a new name, **"hypnotism"** for the respectability the method had now found. Hypnotism is now very widely used with many patients, helping the medical profession **"experiment"** again with patients. I say **"experiment"**; because that is what they do each time you go to **any** medical practitioner/physician. No person can ever say for certain, what is going to happen when the mind is **"experimented"** on, especially when drugs of any kind are used. Remember **all drugs** have their side affects for the human body in one form or another. PLEASE for your own sake DON'T GO ALONG THAT ROUTE.

In Haven-y-Coed the year 2000 when I was there, a tutor was regressing people, (a form of hypnotism) and I saw three people upset because of the person, who in my mind was not properly taught to bring the person back to there normal state. She **thought** she had the knowledge but for me not the skill to help a traumatised person, who had had the many new dormant thoughts, brought to the fore in their mind. Those three people were left to their own devices to handle the problems brought forward by this inexperienced mind manipulator. I had to help talk through a few problems with the people afterwards, (I am a trained councillor) this is how I found out about the goings on. So if you are likely to go along the route of hypnotism have a **trusted** person NOT one who only **thinks** they can do it and are not fully qualified.

In Spiritualism, hypnotism can be used to calm a person's mind down, then a deep trance state can be reached quickly, so there is not the same length of time needed for sitting in a Circle before it is achieved, or **"so I am told"**. I might have a go sometime with a hypnotist I could trust. **"BUT WHO"** do you trust with the control of your mind?" I don't know anyone I would let control my mind except the **"good people"** from the highest realms in the World of Spirit.

To get back to the history: Quite often as things improved the swinging watch/pendulum was used, then in later years the techniques improved even more, so any patient who was wishing to be mesmerised, was softly, and gently talked into the mesmerised state. The patient was told to be concentrating on the hypnotist's voice nothing else. Different hypnotists have many different ways of practising their craft.

With hypnotism, the patient has to be willing to be hypnotised, they have to know they are able to be hypnotised. In other words the patient has to co-operate with the hypnotist; be trusting, willing, and know they will be hypnotised.

**<u>No person can be hypnotised without being co-operative with the hypnotist.</u> (It is said)**
**<u>The person being hypnotised has to have the will to do it.</u>**
**<u>No person can be hypnotised against their will</u>. (it is said)**

When doing hypnotism for Spiritualism there are many ways, here is just one. Of course it can be varied in the wording.

The hypnotist has to have the subject relaxed. Sitting (as in a group situation) or lying down in a relaxed position where there is likely to be **NO** interruptions.

The subject is asked to close their eyes, and just listen to the voice of the hypnotist. The person talking should speak in a deliberate steady, low, monotone voice; no highs or lows.

The subject has to keep on concentrating on the person's voice, nothing else.

The subject is then talked/suggested into a relaxed, slow steady breathing state.

The hypnotist talks/suggests to the subject "to go deeper into the altered state, there to link with Spirit in their goodness, kindness, and truth, Spirit is bringing into them their love within the Divine Light from the highest realms of Spirit", until they are unaware of their surrounding.

When that happens the subject is then left, and the others around in the Circle carry on in their normal manner.

All there in the group should be asking Spirit to come through to them, fill them up, and to be used as an open vessel when they feel the Power of Spirit (or if they don't feel anything, still ask for the Power of Spirit to be sent to the person developing. Each person talking all the time to Spirit through thought, asking, asking, asking) then sending the Power of Spirit to the person sitting in development, the group singing at intervals (or sitting in silence if the leader or the sitter being developed prefers) until Spirit comes through the hypnotised person, Spirit might talk through the Medium, or other things might happen.

If you record any of the other ways to get yourself relaxed as explained in the book. Remember you are used to your own voice reacting on your subconscious mind when you hear your own recording. It might sound a bit strange at first but you will get used to it. This is because your subconscious mind is far more receptive to your own voice more than any other person's voice; your own voice is trusted by your inner self. So record yourself reading the message out to yourself.

I have included in different parts of this book ways for developing clairvoyance, clairaudience, clairsentience, and clairknowing, the mental mediumships. For them try the ways of going into the lift to meet someone. Or along the beach into a hut to see them. Into the garden to meet Spirit to guide you. Into the garden then into the house or hall to see and develop with Spirit. There are many routes, so write one that suits you yourself, then record it with your own voice.

Here is another suggested method that can be used for allowing Spirit to come closer to you, BUT I personally think to use this method, you are bringing your mind into play and not allowing full access to Spirit. I am giving you all as many options as possible, so you can choose the best one for yourself. Colin Fry the Clairvoyant, Trance and Physical Medium uses this method; other people think the same as me, it is best to just to go on using the colour of light as a hypnotic aid to still the mind, which is also a self hypnosis method.

Try this next one for yourself, only you can know if it is suitable. Colin Fry's method is similar to this. I do not like it as you have to think and then you do not have a passive as possible mind.

To start with, say **a sincere prayer** or affirmation.

Visualise in your mind, two rooms, one large, the other small. In the larger room you are going to invite your Spirit friends to come into the room by asking them in your mind to come closer to you, into the room. When you feel the presence of Spirit coming close to you, thank them for coming, and you go into the smaller room to be alone in your thoughts. Then leave your Spirit friends to use your bodily form for their work. You can have a window in the small room to look out of, maybe a seat for you to sit and think. At first the room might be empty to start with, but as you progress a chair might appear, other things might be there for you. BUT I again, along with others, say you are bringing your own thoughts in to interfere with Spirit having full control. (I cannot do this method and link with Spirit anyway).

When you have finished you go into the large room and thank your Spirit friend/friends for coming and come back to reality. Say **a prayer of thanks** when finished.

# SELF HYPNOSIS

There are many self hypnosis exercises that can be used for putting yourself into a deeper altered state of awareness, a deeper Trance.

All it needs is the person to be receptive, passive, relaxed, calm, and hearing repetitive, monotonous, words, tones, music, chants or mantras.

Self-hypnotism can be achieved easily, just by looking at an object for many minutes until your eyes start to close, or you find it hard to keep them open. Keep staring at the object, and you will find you will induce in yourself a hypnotic state, it is not harmful so do not worry, and you will come out of it when you need to, it is only light hypnosis. Why should you rely on others to progress into a good Trance state to link with Spirit? Yes, you will have to sit in Circles and go to colleges like Stansted Hall to have a boost of power from Spirit. Please remember it is in yourself the link is developed with Spirit, not with anyone else.

When talking to another person or talking into a tape recorder for your self development. The voice should be in a monotone, no ups or downs. At a slow steady pace, not to be rushed.

Set in your mind the time you would like to come back to normality **IT WILL** surprise you how you always seem to come back at the required time you had set for yourself, sometimes a little before. This is why self-hypnosis is not dangerous **YOU** are the one in control. How many times have you put the alarm on to get up in the morning and have laid there waiting for the sound that was supposed to wake you go off?

The exercise I use as an aid for self-hypnosis that reinforces my belief that I am doing things correctly to slow the thoughts down in my mind. That was and still is by looking into the light, the third eye area **within my mind,** and talking to Spirit at the same time to encourage them to come near and help me in my development, in the early days at that time it was for clairvoyance, clairaudience, clairsentience, and clairknowing.

Here is a very good method of self-hypnosis, on your own or in a group. This is an exercise of looking at an **unlit** fat (about 3-2 inches across [diameter], 8 inches tall) candle, focusing on that candle or object. I just kept on staring at the candle for about five minutes maybe more, I am not certain of the time. This can be done by looking at any object on the wall, on a table, on any surface.

I kept on saying to Spirit over and over and over and over, in my own mind :-

"Divine Spirit come closer and help me in my development of clairvoyance, clairaudience, clairsentience, clairknowing, please link with me only in goodness, kindness, love and truth":

"Divine Spirit come closer and help me in my development of clairvoyance clairaudience, clairsentience, clairknowing, please link with me only in goodness, kindness, love and truth":

"Divine Spirit come closer and help me in my development of clairvoyance, clairaudience, clairsentience, clairknowing, please link with me only in goodness, kindness, love and truth":

Then "Divine Spirit come closer and help me develop". Say this over and over and over, again, again, again, and again.

After about ten minutes I started to reach a stage where the focus of my eyes went out of focus. Then the unlit candle looked as though it had a flame **inside** it, then shadows, bringing in different visions to my mind. I had learned to focus using the exterior of my eye vision, I had started self-hypnosis. Spirit came as I asked in my own mind for them to come closer and help.

If in a group situation, ask the group to let the conditions go, wait a while for each person to come back out of the Trance. When every one there comes back to normal, go around the Circle so they all can tell of what experiences they had.

This is a similar method I have been using all the time, one where I close my eyes and look into my third eye at a colour, and I found the images came from Spirit quicker into my mind, more than at any time before when using any other method. BUT remember we are all different, what works for one person, does not mean it will work for the next person.

Here is a little exercise for **self-hypnosis in a group situation** that will show people it does work **"IF"** they all go along with it in all sincerity. Not lying to the others in the group and themselves. It did it truthfully as well as two others, **BUT** the others in the Circle at the time did not put their heart into it, so the exercise for them did not work, it was a complete wash out for them. At least it showed the three of us who played our part for **"our own"** <u>**self enlightenment**</u> there in the Circle, what could be achieved, then we could at a later date put it into practice, for we then knew it would work for us. Remember there is no danger or after affect in this exercise at all. Neither is there in any of the self-hypnotic techniques. Trust in Spirit, <u>**I ALWAYS DO**</u>. Set a time to come back to reality in your mind and you will return to normal consciousness at the allotted time. Strange but true.

## The exercise:-

Have everyone seated in a circle, oval or square with a centre.

Have enough space for the person running the Circle to walk around at the back of the sitters.

Place an object, anything small [e.g. an unlit candle] in the middle of the Circle preferably on a table so everyone is comfortable looking at it for a long period of time. Not looking downwards so getting a crick in their neck.

Everyone is told to keep on looking all the time at the object until the whole exercise has finished, (as they might be asked to try again after the first time) they are to keep on looking at it without blinking (yes you will blink but try to keep the eyes open for as long as possible) for as long as possible. Keep on staring at the object and as each person does, they have to keep on asking Spirit in their minds, over and over and over and over, again and again and again and again. I started with "Divine Spirit come only with goodness, kindness, love, and truth, come near and help me with the task of talking fast and giving information to all in the Circle". Then ask within the mind, over and over and over again, "Spirit please help me with the task of giving information quickly" and "Spirit come closer and help me". Over and over and over, again and again and again.

As everyone is staring at the object and asking Spirit to help, repeatedly, over and over in their minds as in the previous section with the unlit candle. The leader of the Circle who is standing up on the outside of the Circle tells the sitters when he/she touches anyone of them on the shoulder, [the leader at intervals reminds the group in a low monotone voice, that they are going to touch each one individually]. When touched, each sitter has to say the first things that come into their minds as quick as they can, (it does not matter what comes out of the person's mouth), and keep on talking (for only half a minute or a minute not very long) until they are touched again on the shoulder, they then immediately stop talking, even in mid sentence. The leader then touches someone else. And so it goes on.

At the start of the exercise, the leader should leave the Circle alone and let the sitters stare into the object for about five to ten minutes, so that the self induced hypnotic effect can be achieved, and for each one playing their true part in the exercise, the hypnosis to work for them.

The leader of the Circle then slowly goes around the Circle touching the people in the Circle AT random, NOT in sequence on the shoulder. If any person does not do the exercise properly they can have another go at talking when again at random being touched on the shoulder after about five/ten more minutes. The leader could whisper in their ear to go back to Spirit and try again, if the time allows. IT IS a really worthwhile exercise as it shows the people who do take part in it **(if done TRULY, and GENUINELY)**, what can be achieved if they sincerely talk and encourage Spirit to come near to them for development of themselves. If anyone does not take part properly, **it is <u>only their loss</u>** not the people who learn from the experience.

A self-hypnotic tape for deeper Trance state can be easily made. It consists of yourself progressing deeper down onto a lower floor. [Yes, you can say this sequence in your mind BUT you will be using your mental ability to go into the trance state so blocking the stillness so necessary for those in Spirit to link within the mental capacity of you yourself. Please allow Spirit to use your mind, or should I say still your mental part of yourself to allow Spirit to blend with them]

The sequence is very simple, as it is very similar to those used before in the book for visualisation BUT with the one difference, it uses keywords, try recording it for yourself.

I will write out a shortened sequence for you.

You will have to write out a longer one for yourself to record depending on the length of time you wish to try it for, or how long it takes for you to go down into an altered state, a deep Trance state, where you forget to listen to the tape playing. It can be started on the 30$^{th}$ floor or the 100$^{th}$ floor depending how you feel about your Trance depth needed, of course it can be altered at any time very easily. Remembering you do not necessarily need to remember the later floors (lower floors) in the sequences. They could be blanked out by your mind because of the Trance state achieved so you might not remember going through them. Best to record longer rather than shorter.

I will start at the 100$^{th}$ step at first.

You can record this sequence saying it slow, steady, and in a low monotone voice.

Make a slight emphasis on the word **"deeper"**.

Read out all the **bold writing.**

If doing this for a group, "I" can be substituted with "you" but it is not necessary.

Say slowly or record.

Start with **a sincere prayer.**

**"Divine Spirit please help me develop. Come only with goodness, kindness, love, and truth. Come within the Divine Light of Spirit, from within the loving harmony of Spirit in the highest realms".**

**"I am going to a staircase where there are a lot of stairs going down into the wonderful Divine Light of Spirit, where I will develop for Spirit".**

"I am at the start of the stairs".

Pause slightly.

"See it, feel it, be part of it."

Pause slightly.

**"As I put my foot on the top of the first stair I can see writing on each step, I can feel everything is going to be alright for me, it is feeling comfortable, I know I should be here, I am going to be looked after and developed in goodness, kindness, love, and truth by those in Spirit in the highest realms".**

Pause slightly.

"I see it, I feel it, I am part of it".

Pause slightly. YOU SHOULD BE Seeing the light, feeling the light, being part of the light.

**"On looking down to the next step I see there are words written on it, it says "100", at each step I will go "deeper" into an altered state".**

Pause slightly. YOU SHOULD BE Seeing the light, feeling the light, being part of the light.

"I see it, I feel it, I am part of it".

Pause slightly. YOU SHOULD BE Seeing the light, feeling the light, being part of the light.

**"I step down onto the next step it says, "99" "deeper".** Pause slightly. **I am going "deeper" into the light to develop".**

Pause slightly. YOU SHOULD BE Seeing the light, feeling the light, being part of the light.

"I see it, I feel it, I am part of it".

Pause slightly. YOU SHOULD BE Seeing the light, feeling the light, being part of the light.

**"I go onto the next step looking down and reading the words written, "98" "deeper".** Pause slightly. **I am going "deeper" into light to develop with Spirit".**

Pause slightly. YOU SHOULD BE Seeing the light, feeling the light, being part of the light.

"I am relaxing, I am part of it".

Pause slightly. YOU SHOULD BE Seeing the light, feeling the light, being part of the light.

**I step onto the next step I look down and see, "97" "deeper".** Pause slightly. **I am going "deeper" into the light to develop with spirit".**

Pause slightly. YOU SHOULD BE Seeing the light, feeling the light, being part of the light.

"I see it, I feel it, I am part of it".

Pause slightly. YOU SHOULD BE Seeing the light, feeling the light, being part of the light.

**On looking down to the next step I see the words, it says "96" "deeper".** Pause slightly. **at each step I will go "deeper" into an altered state".**

Pause slightly YOU SHOULD BE Seeing the light, feeling the light, being part of the light.

"I see it, I feel it, I am part of it".
Pause slightly. YOU SHOULD BE Seeing the light, feeling the light, being part of the light.

"I step down onto the next step on it says, "**95**" "**deeper**".
Pause slightly.

I am going "**deeper**" into the light to develop with Spirit".
Pause slightly.

"I am relaxing, I am becoming part of the light".
Pause slightly.

"I go onto the next step looking down I see, "**94**" "**deeper**"
Pause slightly.

I am going "**deeper**" into light to develop with Spirit".
Pause slightly.

"See the light, feel the light, become part of the light".
Pause slightly.

"I step onto the next step I look down I see, "**93**" "**deeper**",
Pause slightly.

At each step I am going "deeper" into the light to develop with Spirit".
Pause slightly.

"See the light, feel the light, become part of the light".
Pause slightly. YOU SHOULD BE Seeing the light, feeling the light, being part of the light.

I step down onto the next step, I see, "**92**" "**deeper**", I am going "**deeper**" into the light to develop with Spirit".
Pause slightly. YOU SHOULD BE Seeing the light, feeling the light, being part of the light.

"I am relaxing, I am becoming part of the light".
Pause slightly. YOU SHOULD BE Seeing the light, feeling the light, being part of the light.

"I step down onto the next step, I see, "**91**" "**deeper**", I am going "**deeper**" into the light to develop with Spirit".
Pause slightly.

"I see the light, I feel the light, I am becoming part of the light".
Pause slightly. YOU SHOULD BE Seeing the light, feeling the light, being part of the light.

"I step down onto the next step, on it I see, "**90**" "**deeper**", I am going "**deeper**" into the light to develop with Spirit".
Pause slightly. YOU SHOULD BE Seeing the light, feeling the light, being part of the light.

"I see the light, I feel the light, I am part of the light".
Pause slightly. YOU SHOULD BE Seeing the light, feeling the light, being part of the light.

"I step down onto the next step, on it I see "**89**" "**deeper**", at each step I am going "**deeper**" into the light to develop with Spirit".
Pause slightly. "I am more relaxed, I am part of the light". Pause slightly. YOU SHOULD BE Seeing the light, feeling the light, being part of the light.

"I step down onto the next step, on it I see "**88**" "**deeper**", I am going "**deeper**" into the light to develop with Spirit".
Pause slightly, "I see the light, I feel light, I am part of the light". Pause slightly. YOU SHOULD BE Seeing the light, feeling the light, being part of the light.

"I step down onto the next step on it I see, "**88**" "**deeper**", I am going "**deeper**" into the light to develop with Spirit".
Pause slightly. "I am part of the light". Pause slightly. YOU SHOULD BE Seeing the light, feeling the light, being part of the light.

"I step down onto the keext step, on it I see, "**87**" "**deeper**", I am going "**deeper**" into the light to develop with Spirit".
Pause slightly. YOU SHOULD BE Seeing the light, feeling the light, being part of the light.

"I step down onto the next step, on it I see, "**86**" "**deeper**", I am going "**deeper**" into the light to develop with Spirit".

Pause slightly. "I am relaxing more, "**deeper**", I am part of the light".

I step down onto the next step, on it I see "85" "**deeper**", at each step I am going "**deeper**" into the light to develop with Spirit".

Pause slightly. YOU SHOULD BE Seeing the light, feeling the light, being part of the light.

I step down onto the next step, it says, "84" "**deeper**", I am going "**deeper**" into the light to develop".

Pause slightly. YOU SHOULD BE Seeing the light, feeling the light, being part of the light.

"I step down onto the next step, on it I see, "83" "**deeper**", I am going "**deeper**" into the light to develop with Spirit"

Pause slightly. "I am relaxed, I am part of the light".

"I step down onto the next step, on it I see "82" "**deeper**", I am going "**deeper**" into the light to develop with Spirit".

Pause slightly. YOU SHOULD BE Seeing the light, feeling the light, being part of the light.

"I step down onto the next step, on it I see, "81" "**deeper**", at each step I am going "**deeper**" into the light to develop with Spirit".

Pause slightly. YOU SHOULD BE Seeing the light, feeling the light, being part of the light.

"I step down onto the next step, on it I see, "80" "**deeper**", I am going "**deeper**" into the light to develop with Spirit".

Pause slightly. YOU SHOULD BE Seeing the light, feeling the light, being part of the light.

"I step down, on it I see, "79" "**deeper**", I am going "**deeper**" into light"

Pause slightly. "I am "**deeper**" relaxed",   Pause slightly,    "going "**deeper**".

YOU SHOULD BE Seeing the light, feeling the light, being part of the light.

"I step down, on it I see, "78", I am going "**deeper**" into the light"

YOU SHOULD BE Seeing the light, feeling the light, being part of the light.

Pause slightly. "I step down and see, "77" "**deeper**", at each step I am going "**deeper**" into the light to develop with Spirit".

Pause slightly,   "going "**deeper**".   Pause   "**deeper**".

Pause slightly. YOU SHOULD BE Seeing the light, feeling the light, being part of the light.

"I step down and see ,"75" "**deeper**", I am going "**deeper**" into the light to develop with Spirit".

Pause slightly. "Going "**deeper**".  Pause   "**deeper**".

Pause slightly. "I step down and see ,"74" "**deeper**", I am going "**deeper**" into the light with Spirit".

Pause slightly. "Going "**deeper**".  Pause   "**deeper**".

Pause slightly. YOU SHOULD BE Seeing the light, feeling the light, being part of the light. "I step down and see ,"73" "**deeper**", I am going "**deeper**" into the light with Spirit".

Pause slightly. Going "**deeper**".  Pause   "**deeper**".

Pause slightly. YOU SHOULD BE Seeing the light, feeling the light, being part of the light..

"I step down and see ,"72" "**deeper**", I am going "**deeper**" into the light with Spirit".

Pause slightly. Going "**deeper**". Pause  ""**deeper**" into development with spirit".

Pause slightly. YOU SHOULD BE Seeing the light, feeling the light, being part of the light.

All from here on can be repeated down in numbers

"I step down,"71" "**deeper**", I am going "**deeper**".

Pause slightly. "Going "**deeper**".  Pause   "**deeper**" into the light with Spirit".

Pause slightly. YOU SHOULD BE Seeing the light, feeling the light, being part of the light

"70" "**deeper**", I am going "**deeper**".

Pause slightly. "Going "**deeper**" Pause "**deeper**" into development with Spirit".
Pause slightly. YOU SHOULD BE Seeing the light, feeling the light, being part of the light..
"**69**" "**deeper**", "I am going "**deeper**".
Pause slightly. "Going "**deeper**" Pause "**deeper**" into the light with Spirit".
Pause slightly. YOU SHOULD BE Seeing the light, feeling the light, being part of the light.
"**68**" "**deeper**", "I am going "**deeper**" into the light".
Pause slightly. "Going "**deeper**" Pause "**deeper**".
Pause slightly. YOU SHOULD BE Seeing the light, feeling the light, being part of the light.

Etc.67,66,65, etc., 63,63,62, etc.,
Finish on **a sincere prayer of thanks** when you return to normality.

### Here is another. Using the sound of a clock ticking.

If you have a clock with a slow tick, tock, it is ideal. A clockwork one that used to be on the mantle piece many years ago is best, or perhaps a wind up grandfather clock.
Record the clock or listen to it every time it goes tick tock.
Have the tape ready then as it goes tick tock, record only the clock then at the next tick tock talk with the same rhythm along with the tick tock so your voice is louder than the tick tock. A microphone is best used here because you can take it away from the sound every other tick tock. (BUT say the words that are in **bold** in a steady low monotone voice in the same rhythm of the clock noise) :-

Say **a sincere prayer**.
**"Divine spirit please help me develop so I can prove to others there is life after our so called death. Come only with goodness, kindness, love, and truth come within the Divine Light of Spirit, from within the loving harmony of Spirit in the highest realms".**
As the clock goes tick tock say over noise and in it's rhythm **"into the light"**.
Record only the clock **"Tick Tock"**.
As the clock goes tick tock say over the noise and in it's rhythm **"going deeper"**.
Record only the clock **"Tick Tock"**.
As the clock goes tick tock say over the noise and in it's rhythm **"into the light"**.
Record only the clock **"Tick Tock"**.
As the clock goes tick tock say over the noise and in it's rhythm **"going deeper"**.
Record only the clock **"Tick Tock"**.
As the clock goes tick tock say over the noise and in it's rhythm **"into the light"**.
Record only the clock **"Tick Tock"**.
As the clock goes tick tock say over the noise and in it's rhythm **"into the light"**.
Etc, ect, etc, etc,. for as long as you want.

Finish on **a sincere prayer of thanks** when you return to normality.
Or if you like record the clock **"Tick Tock"** then say **"into the light"** record the clock **"Tick Tock"** then say **"linking with Spirit"** and so on for as long as you want the recording to last.

If there is a short rhythmic mantra you know, that could also be used in a similar way to below.

This method can also be done by using the chanting rhythm of monks. Especially the continuous OOOmmmmm. Again, say the words in **bold**. Say them to yourself or on tape.

Start with **a sincere prayer**.
**"Divine spirit please help me develop so I can prove to others there is life after our so-called death. Come only with goodness, kindness, love, and truth. Come within the Divine Light of Spirit, from within the loving harmony of Spirit in the highest realms".**
First record the **OOOmmmmm**.
Say the words in a low monotone voice in the rhythm of the chant
In the same rhythmic timing say **"into the light"**.
Record another **OOOmmmmm**.

In the same rhythmic timing say **"going deeper"**.
Record another **OOOmmmmm**.
In the same rhythmic timing say **"into the light"**.
Record another **OOOmmmmm**.
In the same rhythmic timing say **"going deeper"**.
Record another **OOOmmmmm**.
In the same rhythmic timing say **"into the light"**.
Record another **OOOmmmmm**.
In the same rhythmic timing say **"going deeper"**.
Record another **OOOmmmmm**.
Etc, etc, etc,. for as long as you want.
Finish on a **sincere prayer of thanks** when you return to normality.

Some people use their breathing as a hypnotic way to the Trance state for their development here is the exercise.
Set a time for how ever long you want to go into the Trance state, say to yourself the time to come back and you will, it is perfectly safe. Say the words in **bold** within your mind.

Start with **a sincere prayer**. Breath slow and steady
**"Divine spirit please help me develop I can to prove to others there is life after our so called death. Come only with goodness, kindness, love, and truth come within the Divine Light of Spirit, from within the loving harmony of Spirit in the highest realms"**.
As you breath slowly and steadily in, you say to yourself within your mind **"into the light"**.
As you breath slowly and steadily out, you say to yourself in your mind **"going deeper"**.
As you breath slowly and steadily in, you say to yourself within your mind **"into the light"**.
As you breath slowly and steadily out, you say to yourself in your mind **"going deeper"**.
As you breath slowly and steadily in, you say to yourself within your mind **"into the light"**.
As you breath slowly and steadily out, you say to yourself in your mind **"going deeper"**.
As you breath slowly and steadily in, you say to yourself within your mind **"into the light"**.
As you breath slowly and steadily out, you say to yourself in your mind **"going deeper"**.
Etc, etc, etc, etc,.
When you come back to normality say **a prayer of thanks**.
A lot of variations can be tried in all these small self hypnosis methods, you can say short one, two, or three words that can be fitted into your sayings e.g.
**"Into the light"**, **"linking with Spirit"**;
or **"Into the light"**, **"developing deeper"**;
or **"Into the light"**, **"deeper development"**.

A good way to help you relax, and develop is this one I use regularly.
In my mind I go into the light or colour to help Spirit to come in quicker and without any interference of my thoughts. At first asking over and over and over and over, again and again and again for Spirit to come closer to me, and help me to develop so I can prove there is life after death. Every so often I stop talking in my mind giving it a rest, so Spirit can get on with their job of developing me the way they wish. If at the start you cannot see any coloured light. Buy yourself a plain, A5, or A4 card of your favourite colour, (do not worry if the colour of light changes as it can and will. I am only putting to you all the concentration on the coloured light which will eventually become the Divine Light of Spirit) one that you think would be comfortable looking at for a while; you can always change the colour at any time. Look at the card for about a minute or two then close your eyes. You should see the colour in your minds eye. If you lose the colour open your eyes and look again at your chosen card colour for a length of time. If any images come into your mind open your eyes and bring the colour back. This is of course for the Trance state.
When advancing further along with this method for clairvoyance, and images come into your mind, do not try to break the images that Spirit is giving you in your mind, it is your clairvoyance coming to the fore. I trust you all to use common sense. But I feel this method should be used as a mind exercise for holding an image, or colour.

When using this method and holding the single colour, you are giving those in Spirit all the help you can by calming the mind of the fast thoughts that come into our minds when thinking of different things in your everyday life. This method is the best for me as I become as one with the Light of Spirit. I reach the level of Oneness with Spirit, and I must admit it has taken me many, many, many years of wandering in the dark. This is the reason for the advice being passed on to you all, so you do not have to go through all the finding out, pushing a side rubbish that is told, working out things from all the nonsense that people believe and passing on all the pitfalls I went through. I hope it will help at least one other person to help others to show there is life after our so-called death. Then I believe it all has been worthwhile.

A lot of the older Mediums used to stand in front of a wall and stare at it while asking Spirit to come near and develop them for the use of Spirit to prove there is life after death. Gordon Higginson was always made to do this by his mother Fanny, a very strict lady. Many is the time when Gordon was growing up, his mother locked him in on his own for a few hours at a time in the old church at Longton, Stoke-on-Trent, Staffordshire U.K. He was told to stay in there and link in with Spirit and talk to them.

Looking at the wall is to try and blank out all thoughts going through your mind. You are focusing on one point of the wall. It is the same as looking at a sheet of paper or into the light in your third eye and keep on talking to Spirit encouraging them to come near and help develop you. While staring you have to keep on talking to Spirit over and over and over and over again. Remember to start and finish on a prayer. Come only with goodness, kindness, love, and truth come within the Divine Light of Spirit, from Spirit in the highest realms.

Of course I have only touched on this subject of hypnotism. Mallory Stendall, Bill Nedderman, and Leonard Young from the Spiritualist National Union are the tutors to learn more of this subject with, as they are qualified hypnotists. They all teach on courses at the Arthur Findlay College at different times of the year. There are many books on this subject, but you will find they are all similar to what I have told you here in this section on hypnotism. I have tried, for all who wish to develop along with any of these methods, to adapt the known methods of hypnotism for linking with Spirit. It really works.

# MAGNETISM

Magnetic healing is when a Medium links into the patients magnetic field, or auric field, and uses their own energy to balance that of the patient [opposed to; with the help of Spirit]. Some in my opinion, who are foolish, try to take the illness into themselves, to then try to disperse it within their own magnetic field. These ways are very tiring; I would not recommend any person to go on using these methods. It actually drains the healer of their own energy and has the possibility of inducing an illness in themselves by unbalancing their own internal energy.

I will explain the reasons for this. Have you ever been next to a sick person in bed, or on a visit to a hospital, and after that visiting time you come home drained of energy? That is the person absorbing your energy out of your body through the aura. After this happening, it can take some people quite a time to regain that energy. Draining of your energy can sometimes happen on a bus, or train, when sitting next to a person who is unwell.

It is said by some, that magnets can be used to charge up the room where a Circle is held. Some people have placed place magnets in the four corners of the room, and it is said to raise the vibrations to a different level. I personally have not tried them, so I do not know. This method of using magnets in the Circle was being used in different places as an experimentation in the last century. I am putting as much as I can in this book so people can try them out. Please experiment with these different ways.

It was also said that the Trance and clairvoyant Medium was helped by the helper [earth bound] doing magnetic passes over the Medium to get them into an altered state.

This was done by passing the hands slowly within the auric field, the palms of the hand facing the body of the person about 2-3 inches away from the body not touching, slowly with the two hands at once (some use one at a time), starting the passes over the head, the shoulders and arms then the palms of the hand going outwards to each side of the Medium. Then making passes over the head and front, the head then the back, always going outwards at the end of the passing stroke. The palms of the hands should be pointing out from the person as they are swept outwards coming out and upwards in a circular movement to then start again. It was as if the helper was stroking the Medium's aura. This was done from a good few minutes up to an hour until the Medium was in the altered state. Sometimes the magnetic passes used in the last century were done by the helper to a Medium before they did any demonstration. The Medium going into the trance state for up to half an hour in an anti room **before** they went on the church platform or before the Medium did any public demonstration. This is why I believe they were such good Mediums, not just because of the magnetic passes but because they put time in to link with Spirit a good half an hour before hand. A lot of Mediums today go onto the rostrum right after arriving at the church and expect to do a good demonstration.

Some it is said might have used magnets in their hands BUT I have not read of any having held one while doing the passes, it might be worth a try, the older books unfortunately do not have clear guide lines on this. Read the books of Emma Hardinge Britten that have been reprinted by the Spiritualist National Union at Stansted Hall. They are sold at the bookshop in the Arthur Findlay College at Stansted Hall and the Psychic News bookshop in the Coach House at Stansted Hall as well.

There are a few people who have tried to sit within a magnet's, magnetic field. It is said to bring the Medium to a greater depth of a Trance state quicker. I would have thought by sitting with a few magnets laid in the same direction, negative to positive, negative to positive, negative to positive, and so on, so a larger magnetic field would be created while going into a Trance state or altering your awareness making yourself ready for a Spirit link should be tried.

Or sit in a magnetic field created by a coil of wire, which has a **direct current** of electricity might be a useful experimental way of inducing a Trance state. Try making a cabinet that has a magnetic field in it or magnets beside the cabinet.

In the 1940's a Dutch experimenter had mediumistic people hold a low voltage coil, (that created a magnetic field), in their hands and done the correct way, (positive way) it was said to induce trance BUT if done in a negative way it was harmful. (**NOT** **alternating current** or a wire wrapped around a Medium with no electric current going through it). Unfortunately he THE DUTCH EXPERIMENTER does not explain what was the positive way and what was the negative way and I have not seen any diagrams of the experiments. Remember the magnetic fields set up by our pylons (but they have VERY, VERY high amounts of electricity going through their lines, the magnetic field quickly altering in each direction, first going in one direction then in the other, this is because of the alternating current [producing an **electric field, a magnetic field, and electromagnetic radiation**]) and the alleged harmful effects they cause to the people living near by, it is said by the residents to cause leukaemia in children and cancers of different sorts. This might be because of the quick switch of the direction of the current (alternating current, A.C. current) and so the magnetic field (first in one direction then in the other). or is it the electromagnetic radiation fields that are produced. **PLEASE THINK.**

There has now in recent years been experiments reported on T.V. about a scientist ???? who has put magnets on ordinary people's eyes and at other times on the front of their forehead, by the looks of it, by their third eye. This has produced voices and images in the ordinary people (who were the guinea pigs), when they had their eyes closed and taped. So experiment yourselves with **low** [and **I mean low**] magnetic fields, perhaps using a large bar magnet. I do not know which way the magnets were placed + positive or – negative first against the head, or on an angle, at ninety degrees to the human head, or flat against the head. You will have to find that out yourselves. So good luck. BUT what has surprised me the scientist ???? had not gone back to the records of the experimenter of the ????? in Holland. Or had he, and wanted all the glory for himself? Why do not the experimenters leave detailed accounts so others can follow their findings?

**CONFUSION.**

Recently I came across a physics book that talked about magnets. In it they say the magnetic south is in the north pole area. There are two schools of thought about what is the north and the south poles of a magnet are. On a compass that sailors, scouts, and map readers use, some say it is the pole of the magnet that points (attracted to) to the **"north pole of the earth"** that is the **"N" north pole of the magnet**, and the pole of the magnet that points (attracted to) to the **"south pole of the earth"** that is the **"S" south pole of the magnet**.

BUT OTHERS say it is the **"S" pole of the magnet** that is attracted (points to) to the **"earth's north pole"** that is now opposite. And the **"N" pole of the magnet** that is attracted to (points to) the **"earth's south pole"**. In other words because the opposites attract, meaning N-S then to N-S then to N-S to N-S poles. The pole North and South on the magnet is now place the opposite ways to the others. Who is right and who is wrong I do not know. I only know that the opposite points of the compass attract each other.

**AGAIN CONFUSION.**
There is also confusion in the field of healing with the magnets while testing.
What is the best way to do it? Is it with the south pole pointing towards the patient? **or** Is it the North Pole aiming at the patient? Then what is the north and what is the south.

**Or** is it having the magnet side on to the patient, so they are sitting in the magnetic field?

**BUT** When it is parallel to the earth is the magnet placed best facing North the South? **or** Facing South to North? East to West Or West to East?

**or** Is it best to have the magnet pointing up from the ground next to the patient?

If so, is the magnet best placed with the south pointing into the earth? **or** Is it best the north pointing into the earth?

Look at the patterns produced by the magnetic fields of the magnets that are shown in the drawings; and then see and really think about the reasons how and why, the different interpretations **MUST be made clearer** by these people who are supposed to know!!!!!!

Some who are in the healing field are calling them the positive, and the negative poles. Even then it seems they have got that the wrong way round in some cases. The **positive, or "S" south pole**, getting worse results than **negative, or the "N" north pole**.

The **"N" north, negative pole** is said to help with the reduction of pain, help with the reduction of most swellings, helps a restless person at night so they with sleep more soundly, this could explain why it helps people who are of a nervous disposition. It is said to bring calmness.

The **"S" south, positive pole** is said to bring on the production of more skin and tissue acidity. Cuts down on the oxygen given to the skin and tissues of the body. Brings on anxiety and makes a person toss and turn in bed so giving them a not too pleasant nights sleep. It also can increase swelling in some people.

Scientists using a petri dish with cancer cells in them, placed the north/negative pole end of the magnet towards the dish and the cancer cells dramatically **decreased** their growth after three weeks.

Placing a magnet's south/positive pole end towards the petri dish with a similar amount of cancer cells in it. The cancer cells increased slightly, but it also showed an **increase** their volume [becoming larger], in other words they definitely multiplied.

Please experiment with these ways set out above, it is only by experimentation that things are found out. Be a pioneer. **BUT get people to sign as disclaimer** before you start doing things with them. I personally would not experiment on a cancer patient in this way there are far better ways of healing like spiritual healing as laid out in this book.

**With a <u>fixed magnet</u>, it only gives off a magnetic field.**

**BUT with an <u>electromagnetic apparatus</u>, it gives off an electric field, a magnetic field, and electromagnetic radiation.**

I have had to put in this book all the things I have found out for the sake of the ones who are genuine in their research of the truth and development. This is to help people to know there is life after our so-called death. Please forgive me if it is not what you want to hear.

One of the books on sale at this present time dealing with this subject is "Magnetism and Its Effects on the Living System" by Albert Roy Davis and Walter C Rawis jr.

# MAGNETISM

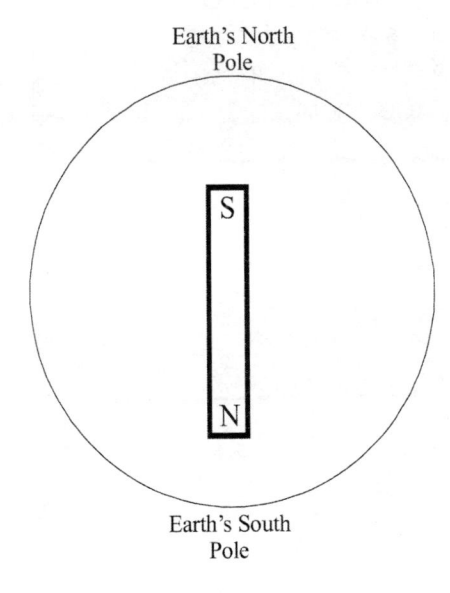

Earth's North Pole

Earth's South Pole

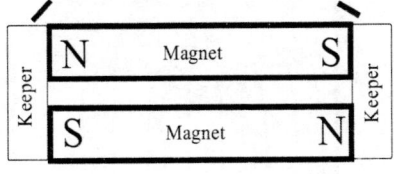

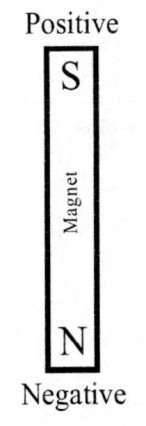

Molecular structure of
non-magnetic iron or steel
and non-magnetised iron or steel.

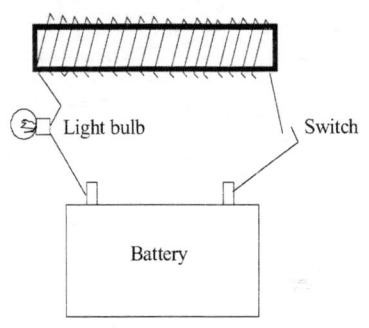

Light bulb   Switch

Battery

Insulated copper wire wrapped around a piece of steel, when connected to a battery (which everyone knows produces a direct current). When switched on produces a magnet in the steel..

Soft Iron Keepers
to stop magnets discharging
their magnetism over time

Iron or steel's
molecular structure
after being magnetised

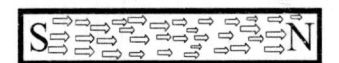

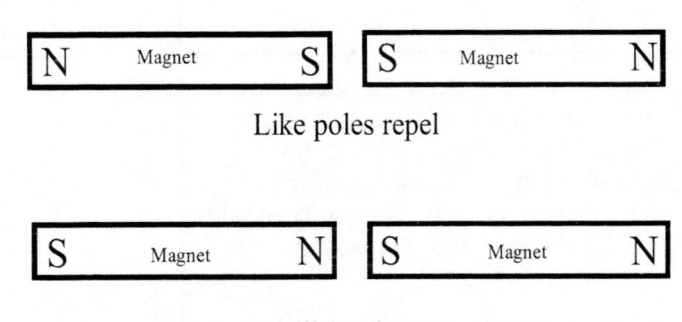

Positive

Magnet

Negative

Like poles repel

Unlike poles attract

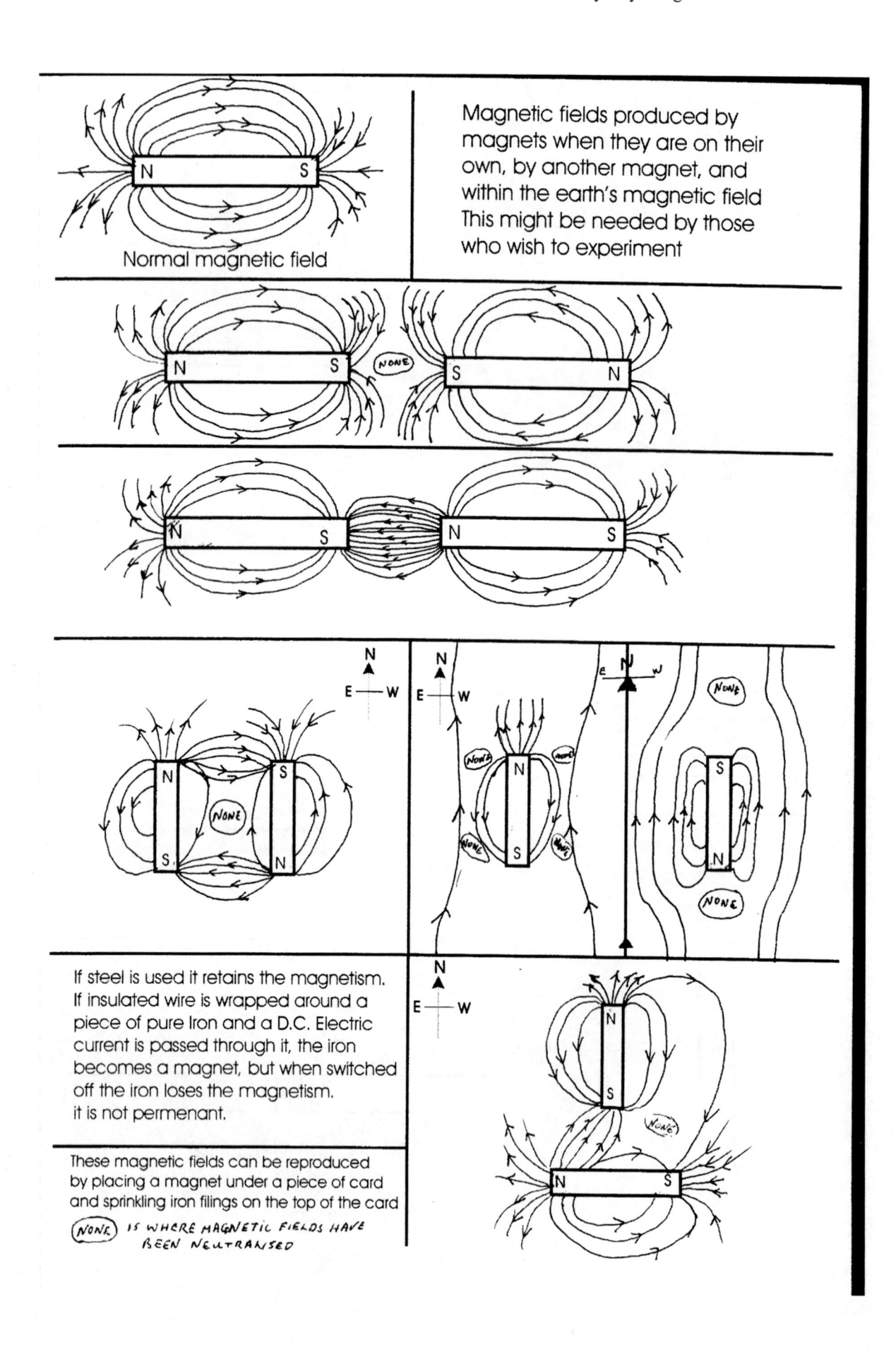

Normal magnetic field

Magnetic fields produced by magnets when they are on their own, by another magnet, and within the earth's magnetic field. This might be needed by those who wish to experiment

If steel is used it retains the magnetism. If insulated wire is wrapped around a piece of pure Iron and a D.C. Electric current is passed through it, the iron becomes a magnet, but when switched off the iron loses the magnetism. it is not permenant.

These magnetic fields can be reproduced by placing a magnet under a piece of card and sprinkling iron filings on the top of the card

(NONE) IS WHERE MAGNETIC FIELDS HAVE BEEN NEUTRALISED

## A CIRCLE WHEN SITTING FOR DEVELOPMENT OF A MEDIUM WHETHER MENTAL, TRANCE OR FOR PHYSICAL PHENOMENA

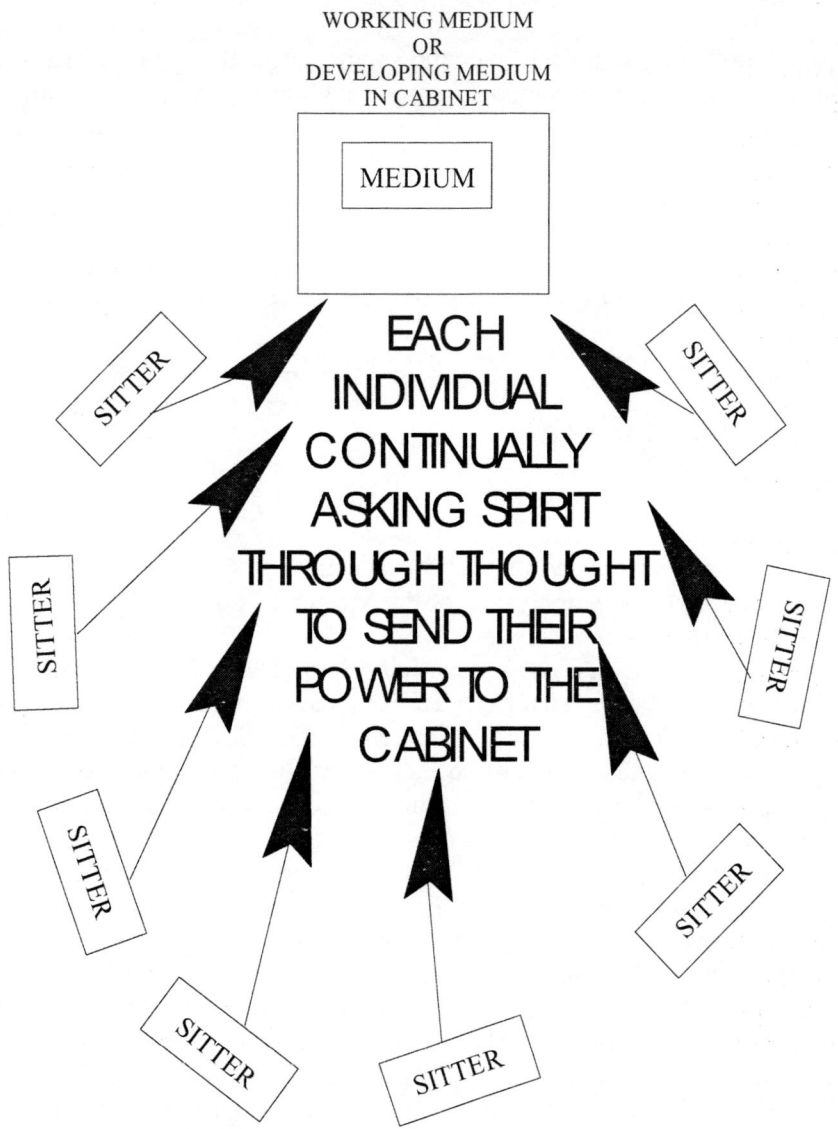

WORKING MEDIUM
OR
DEVELOPING MEDIUM
IN CABINET

[MEDIUM]

EACH INDIVIDUAL CONTINUALLY ASKING SPIRIT THROUGH THOUGHT TO SEND THEIR POWER TO THE CABINET

(SITTER × 8 arranged in a circle around the cabinet)

What you give out comes back to you ten fold.
Be generous and sincere with your power.
Keep on asking within your mind from those in Spirit,
for you to be used as an open vessel. Give Spirit permission
for you to be filled up with the power of Spirit then keep
on sending the Spirit power mentally to the person who is working
or being developed in the cabinet. If you cannot feel it, keep on asking
within your mind for Spirit to come closer and help they will eventually.
This applies in any Circle.

# PSYCHIC ART

Psychic Art and Spirit Drawing are a cross mix but I have put them in different categories. The reason I say this is because, both gifts need the Medium to be used as a link with the world across the veil and use an implement [a pen, pencil, brush, etc.] in the similar way.

Psychic art is done by the Medium linking into Spirit in a light state of altered awareness using their clairvoyant imagery. Some being in a deeper altered state [trance] than others. They then portray that image in their mind onto paper or other material, many using their own mind to control the hand, some don't only allowing Spirit to move them.

"Spirit Drawings" are done by Spirit without the awakened mind of the Medium coming into play and without their eyes to see what they are doing as the drawing are quite often done in complete darkness and if in light, the Medium is blindfolded, BUT Spirit nearly always still needing the Medium in attendance. The Medium is in a stronger sense of altered awareness (Deep Trance), many times the Medium is in an unconscious state of awareness or very deep Trance state not knowing until afterwards what went on

Spirit Drawings can also be done by Spirit alone without the need of the Medium's hand or feet being used. The implements for communication on paper, canvas or wood etc. being picked up by Spirit alone in the presence of a Physical Medium.

From the first time I saw Coral Polge the Psychic Artist, in Daulby Street church Liverpool; psychic art was something I would like to have done for people who need proof in the belief of life after death existing and also help people to come to terms with the passing of their loved ones into the higher vibrational level, showing them there is no death, life just carries on in another plane of existence. This I believe was being done through the clairvoyance of the Medium. The Medium drawing the images that were placed by Spirit in the mind of the Medium.

I started off trying this by enrolling in a part time art class at a college. Luckily at first I was left on my own to find out what I was capable of. What I wanted from that course was some hints on how to draw. I had taken a few magazines, coloured pencils, and an artists pad. When I got to the college, there were only very old age pensioners attending the class so right away I was out of the flow. The lady teacher sat us all down, and we all had to relate to the class what we individually were capable of, and what we would like to draw and achieve. I had never done any drawings of faces, so that was what I told her, and said I would like to draw faces. I did not have the remotest idea of how to draw the faces, nor how to get the faces that I was being given by Spirit in my mind, down onto paper for others to see.

I knew I had faces I could see in my head when the clairvoyance came through, all I needed to do now was to get some information on how to put the face on the paper. I did not feel confident enough to explain my Mediumship gift that I had, hence the magazines to copy from.

At the start of my drawing in the college, I closed my eyes for about a minute in front of all there as though I was thinking, looking for inspiration. In effect I was asking Spirit to guide me and give me all the help I needed for the job in hand. I said my prayer, asking for Spirit to come closer and help in the drawing task ahead, asking for Spirit to come only with goodness, kindness, love and truth, to come within the Divine Light of Spirit and to come from the loving harmony of Spirit of the highest realms and let me prove there is life after our so called death through the medium of drawing on this paper with this pencil. I got a few faces in my mind, which I should have tried to draw, instead I copied onto the pad a photo/picture of a kindly lady I had with me. I started on the hair [not, how artists who are taught do it] then worked down the face as I was drawing. I even surprised myself never mind the teacher. She said are you sure you have never done a portrait before, it was very good? **Well I DID** have the help off those upstairs in the World of Spirit. The only artwork I had ever done was at school it was silly drawing, at that time I was rubbish at it, I certainly had never done a face. At the college the next few times when I attended the art class, I copied a photograph of John Thaw the actor, again not bad. Then I copied the photograph of my girl friend. I had just split up with her at that time; again you could see the likeness. This is where the teacher stepped in with her advice. It was from that time I started going wrong with the drawings, she was trying to put her way of drawing onto me and it did not work at all. At times she would take my pencil off me and draw an oval for the start of the face and say this is the way you do it, draw another small oval for the nose, another for the ear. This way of working was a new departure from what I was seeing through my thoughts. I saw shadows, different shades of colour, lines of shading that formed a chin, darker markings that formed a hole in the ear, not an oval that had to be changed half way through to a head, an oval changed into an ear, or a nose. I was doing things all wrong according to her not going through the correct procedures. I tried her way and went down hill from there on, forgetting what I was there for, I was not asking for help from Spirit, not trusting Spirit, not trusting myself. I had started thinking of drawing whilst not linking first; so I left, not really having the confidence now to have a go again at college.

What I am saying here is, it should be trust yourself and Spirit; not some person who thinks their way is the only way. It knocked me down to such an extent that I have never done any other portraits for myself or for other people. BUT do not take my unfortunate situation in 1990 stop you going to an art class and getting some experience of other people's way of working; as with every part of any mediumship, you must practice, practice, practice. I feel if you can get this form of drawing of the images out of your head onto paper correct, it is one of the best forms of evidence for people that there is life after our so called death.

Remember to start sincerely with a positive prayer for help, and guidance with loving peaceful harmony, a special thought in your mind to Spirit. [I have my eyes closed to see them] See Spirit guiding you, being around you, helping you, being in loving peaceful harmony as one with Spirit. Ask Spirit for an image of the person who needs to be recognised. Ask Spirit for the image to be held in your head for the length of time you need it to be there. It will stay if needed, as I found out. My normal clairvoyant images generally flashed through my mind at that time. Ask Spirit for help all the time you need it **and when you think don't**. When you have finished the job/drawing in hand thank Spirit for their help and guidance, asking them to come closer each time you work with them, making arrangements with Spirit for that time you are going to sit again to draw.

I finished a course in Stansted Hall, May 1999. Not a Course that I would have chosen for myself, but all sorts of circumstances pushed me into it and I ended up going on it. Spirit works in many unusual guiding ways. I had been told there were two tutors I would like to meet on the week's course they were the psychic artist Coral Polge, [I thought she might have helped me in my psychic drawing], and Swami Dharmananda Saraswati who I would liked to have met properly and got to know her and hopefully sat with. Coral's was husband was ill and she had to stay at home. Swami was ill with an eye problem. Only for the fact of me taking someone along with me in the car to Stansted, which is something I have never done before, I would have come home and gone on another course later in the year. I stayed there and I found out how to start drawing, just by trying with the help of Spirit whilst in the power of Stansted Hall. I now know I had forgotten the one most important thing that I should have been always thinking of Spirit, also that time, that was to have **total trust in Spirit**.

I was in Janet Parker's group [a very good Medium and tutor], and I was asked to sit with my artistic equipment I had taken and have a go at drawing [a pad and a 4B pencil]. I closed my eyes, and asked within my mind for help from Spirit. I kept asking over and over within my mind for about five minutes. I was building the link stronger with Spirit as a lady who was on the platform was giving a demonstration of after life existence by giving a message to others in the group, while Janet was suggesting little helpful pointers to help with her Mediumship skills. I saw a person in my head and began to draw until the lady on the platform had finished. It was a profile drawing of a man but for me on looking back, it was a stiff drawing, just an outline with no personality. But the person recognised the man, he had passed on to the higher sphere some time earlier. I also got three names off Spirit, which I wrote down on the paper and they were accepted as correct and taken as evidence.

The next person was then up on the platform to practice their guided demonstration of Mediumship. I closed my eyes and did not get anything so I started asking over and over for help from Spirit; as I was staring at the paper, a foggy sort of a shadow came on the paper, so I started to follow the shadings with my 4B pencil; as I did this my eyes went out of focus as though I needed another pair of better glasses, my hand was working very quickly not giving me time to think of what I was doing, it turned out to be a man within a drawing of a round curly circle. The mouth was slightly wrong but it was recognised by the trainee Medium, but this person was still alive, but had been ill prior to the person leaving, [perhaps the curly ring will mean something for me in future drawings I will have to keep that in mind]. I also got another three names, which I wrote down, two were taken as evidence of after life, the single name was not recognised.

The next person up on the platform was a man who also was there for his skills as a Medium to be honed.

I started drawing from the paper as the shadows now started to form a better shape of a head on the paper, my eyes were glazed again this time. This picture took a slightly different way of working as I had more information through my mind. I got a long hairstyle and a woman's face yet I was drawing a man's ten o'clock shadow where a man shaves around the chin. The more I did the shading on the drawing the more like a man it became. When the drawing had been finished it was a cross between a lady with a ten o'clock shadow and a man with long hair. I did not feel happy with it letting my mind come into the equation. But at the end I had a "feeling" to change the hair to short so I use the rubber. The Medium came down off the rostrum and he then told me that he could accept the person who was a man, in both short and long hair. He told me that this man had a lady like face also, so I should not have doubted Spirit. I also got two names he accepted both. That week I had headaches at the back and the right hand side of the head. I do not know if that was the power of my Mediumship getting altered, my brain getting attuned to the new vibration level or what. It certainly was not the booze, as I did not drink very much at all that week. (this I now know was my link with Spirit that needed my blood pressure altering for some reason, to get a stronger link connection adjusted someway within my brain. I believe Spirit was adjusting the brain linkage to have me closer to Spirit, something like tuning a radio or TV to the correct station)

The main points that this course left me with was; I did not need an art teacher to help me with psychic art, and the other was to always fully trust Spirit and to keep on asking and encouraging Spirit over and over and over, again and again within my mind to come closer to help me with the task in hand.

Start with a prayer to those in Spirit asking them to help you and finish with a prayer of thanks arranging for those in Spirit to come again to help you when required.

I also made a lot of new friends from all over the world at Stansted that week. The power in Stansted Hall was totally different this week for me from the other weeks I have been there. It was a more of a gentle energy level but more mentally tiring. I was in bed very early 10pm that week which is unusual for me at Stansted. On the Trance and Physical weeks it has been a very high level of power energy for me. On those Physical weeks, I have been full of beans each night staying up until the very early hours of the morning (3-4am) and still getting up at 6.30am to shower.

# TEACHING CHILDREN ABOUT SPIRIT

I think something should be put here about children growing up within a spiritual family. I personally feel that the naturalness of the Linking of Spirit has started being put aside by some. It is as though talking to Spirit has become a domain of the older group in our movement. It should not be that way. Children are mostly natural Mediums, they do not think, or are not embarrassed of boldly telling the truth of their Link with Spirit. It is only the outside forces within manmade religious upbringing of people who do not understand, that quash the truth of Spirit. Let your churches or your places where you hold your meetings bring in the children and let them bring laughter and happiness into the places where you all meet. It is laughter and happiness that attracts Spirit to those places and you will all benefit from the gaiety of the surroundings. Let the children show you their gifts that they have. If they have none, teach them so they can then teach you the Power of Spirit, because they will. A solemn place is a dull place. Yes there are times when a quite place or a quite time is needed. Children know in the main how to behave. I went to a Church of England Sunday service with my mother on "Remembrance Day". I have no hang-ups because it is a house of God and I do not worry about the man made religion it represents. I will go into any church to pray BUT I believe you do not have to go into a church to be close to God. There within that Church of England church were many children, the beginnings of the mainstay of that church. All chatting away to each other it was a fun and happy place of worship.

**Where are the children in your church or meeting place?**

That church (in Roby, Merseyside, were I grew up) I went through the same things as you have, praying to God, just as the congregations do in any Spiritualist meeting: Teaching the congregation of people who have materialised (Jesus to the disciples and many others throughout the Christian bible), we have the real thing today in Physical Mediums: Teachings of people talking to the people in Spirit, Jesus talking to the prophets of old and today's congregations talking to Jesus and the saints of their churches who they could/cannot see, this is at each meeting, each and every day. NOW it is the same at the meetings held at a Spiritualist church or a meeting in a hall which has the Medium who links with Spirit: Teaching of people who heal with the power of the Holy Spirit or the God power by laying on of hands, our healers do that every day of the week: Just as Jesus and the disciples did. Levitating (Jesus walking on water), again we have proof from our Physical Mediums: Throughout the bible there are stories of people getting messages from the dead, each and every day at Spiritualist meeting we have our Mediums on the platform that link into Spirit and they give messages from the so called dead. What is the difference? Look in the bible there are lots of Mediums, especially Jesus.

**WHY LIVE ON <u>BLIND</u> FAITH of the manmade religions, when good people, many of them trained, who come from every walk of life can link with Spirit and talk to the dead. We have the truth in Spiritualist churches not fairy stories, or legends.**

The children within that Church of England building, half way through their Sunday service, went off into their little groups, one for the younger age of under six or seven-ish, the older ones into the other group, the older children take care of their younger friends and one or two older members as an observers. Each group had different ways of teaching and playing and drawing.

**Does your meeting place have any such thing for children?**

**Is there anything there in the meeting place to attract children and keep them occupied?**

**Do your meetings teach children the ways of helping others?**

**Do you explain the seven principles to children around you?**

**Do your meetings tell children it is natural to talk to God and his Angels who look after us while on earth?**

**Do you say to the children it is natural to have a two-way conversation with God and his angels?**

**Do your meetings tell your young how to link with those in Spirit because to them it is the most natural of things ?**

Unfortunately most of us older persons who are in this Spiritualism have had to **re**learn how to link, we have lost the natural way of talking to Spirit in a **TWO** way conversation we had when young for one reason or another.

## WHY Oh! WHY don't we listen to our inner self more often?

A lot of people say children should not be brought into the Spiritualist movement because it will frighten them. **Rubbish!** If taught sensibly and introduced properly to the church, their progress can be very exciting, rewarding and pleasant for the child. A lot of the really good older Mediums when they were little started sitting by the side of their parents in the Circles, a few even crawled around or sat next to the cabinet peeping in through the curtains to see what was going on with the Medium inside those cabinets, whilst they produced Physical Phenomena. It became natural to them to see it and they asked many questions of Spirit. Leonard Young a very good tutor, was one who peeked into the cabinets, and so was a wonderful person who I missed when she went, Gladys Owen of Daulby Street, Liverpool church, who herself started attending with her parents at the beginning of her life and toddling. When she was three, Gladys used to give out hymn books to the congregation as they came into the church and then after, during the service went around with the collection plate, so making her the young child part of the service. She also sat in the Home Circles, where her father who was a Physical Medium would levitate whilst sitting in a chair and four people would, with Spirit's permission, try to pull him down from the height of the ceiling [she lived in an old house with high ceilings] by holding onto the legs of the chair he was sitting on. He also produced physical phenomena in front of Gladys when she was very young. Please remember most young children naturally can see Spirit or are aware of Spirit far more than the adult who has started to come to a Spiritualist church to enquire after following blindly others in a man made religion that most of us have been brought up in.

A lot more needs to be done to help children to understand the ways of Spirit and how to keep their natural link and develop it. Children should not be forced into any religion they should be given books that will explain in simple terms the principles of the SNU if that is the pathway you would like the child to follow, if not seek out story books that will explain what happens when life in our vibrational level is ended then continued in another higher vibrational level. It is only like closing one one-way door and going into another room, you are still near the ones you love, but you cannot go back to them you have to wait on that side of the door until your love ones come to you, **and they do**. There is nothing more certain than that. We all eventually have to go through that door (across the veil) whether we are ready for the transition or not. There should be a lot more books written for the children as they grow up, so come on all you spiritual authors get on your thinking caps. Look at the other ideas from the other religions and then adapt them to the truth of Spirit, **do not tell lies or make up stories,** there is no reason to do that. Remember the different age groups and then you can figure out the best ways to help them. It is known by the man made religions if you get a child until they are seven you will have it in that belief for the rest of their lives. That is why they try to trap them in their religions, try to keep them ignorant of other religions and not let them experiment.

If the schools taught early morning meditation, then society as a whole would be calmer, as has been found by a school in the South West of England.

All that has to be done in meditation is for the schools to talk the children through a simple guided meditation. Half way through, let them meet someone of NO religious persuasion, NOT indoctrinating them the think of a person from a particular religion, then this person would be helping them with their answers to help them in the coming day. Then just to go into the God Power within their mind. Each child could have a pendant, which the string or chain could be placed on the head and the pendant itself on the third eye area to teach them where to look with their eyes closed, to look into the colour, void or light at that particular area. At the half way stage let each child go into the silence for about 15 minutes, then talk them all back along the pathway they were taken along. If the school wished the children could talk about what they experienced, BUT it is not necessary. This is only a calming down method for them. Meditation can be used to help the children [and mentally disturbed people] in so many ways.

Many years ago the Spiritualist Lyceum used to take the children under it's umbrella but that seems to be falling into something of a decline. I think it is because it has not kept up with the times and adapted. Even Spirit is trying to adapt itself within their link with a Physical Medium by trying different methods of producing Materialisation. Time does not stand still, we all have to progress, if you do not progress and adapt you will stagnate or the your ideas will die, then they become stale. Yes, we have to have a stable basis but there has to be new ideas to attract people because society changes, and in this day and age unfortunately now very rapidly.

It should be pointed out that children as young as twelve were reported to be taking their own Circles in the Spiritualist movement in the 1800's with great success, it was so natural for them to do so.

An American Medium; Miss Cora L. V. Tappan at the age of thirteen was controlled whilst in Trance by a guide "Ballou", and she was giving public addresses in Wisconsin U.S.A. at that age. Then she progressed to the capital New York; and from that time on at the age of sixteen she was known throughout the states as a Spiritual Lecturer. If you find any old books from the 1870's you will find her name. She became Cora Tappan-Richmond. She actually came to England to lecture as well. Just before the start of every lecture she undertook, the committee or the audience of the places she lectured in chose the subjects. Many of subjects she knew nothing of.

When I was little 3 or 4 until 15ish, I used to have experiences in my darkened bedroom of my mothers house. These experiences of seeing Spirit people and their faces used to frighten me because of the bad messages given out to me by my mother and my peers. I was told it was a nightmare; it is God punishing me because I had been bad, it was a ghost, it was my imagination playing tricks on me, and because I wanted the light on going to sleep, you are only a sissy being afraid of the dark. What terrible thoughts they must have given me at the time, each word destroying a child's confidence in anything. I now know it was a spiritual experience of Guardians, Helpers, Angels, the people in the Spirit World coming to make sure I was alright, keeping me safe, having a watchful eye on me. I learned to be afraid of the different things because of those adults and my peers, especially the dark. I use to hide under the bedclothes in fear away from those faces in my room. When I moved out of that bedroom, when I was about 15 years of age, into the lighter front bedroom nothing ever happened again, I now have had to relearn it all over again and it has taken a long time sitting in meditation on my own, then in a Development Circle in the low red light, in a dark room in the cabinet, and getting the afraid bit out of the way, and sitting for Physical Phenomena in the pitch blackness of no lighting at all.

Would it not have been better to put **good thoughts** into a child's head and explain that is only the higher side of life looking over you, telling the child to just talk to them in your mind, they are only being friendly, they are only your Guardian Angels friends from within the higher vibrational levels, what some call the God force, coming to make sure you are alright.

Society as a whole in their infinite wisdom suppress the natural gift of Mediumship out of our children, that which is the most natural of gifts because of the bigoted, manmade, money orientated, materialistic religions most of us are brought up in while on this earthly plane. Don't believe what I am talking about? Look at all the gold, costly buildings, idols and the places where the higher up in the churches live in luxurious surroundings, built mainly by the poor and a few rich people who gave their wealth to their religion because they wanted to raise themselves to a better heavenly place. So they thought by acting that way.

Explain to the child; "if you want them to go, just to thank your friends for coming, then ask them nicely to go, and they will, there is no reason to be afraid of the higher side of life; **it is only the people on the earth plane that you can see, that do you any harm**".

I remember being told of a little 3-4 year old girl, who when her little baby brother was born, crept into the bedroom to where the baby was sleeping in the cot next to the parents, and was heard by her parents to say "Tell me what living with God is like, I am starting to forget".

"Are you going to let the natural gift of God go; for it to be suppressed by others even perhaps by yourself?" "Will it happen to your youngsters?" "Will they have to start to relearn their gifts all over again when they get older?" That is of course if they want to, remember it is their free will.

Please believe what your young child has to say about their unseen friends. They are real to them even if you cannot see them yourself. Be thankful they still retain their gift. The child will probably start to ignore or lose their unseen, higher vibrational friends as they grow up. Just go along with them and let them live an earthly life for the present. The child **might** want in later years to go back to their gifts, it will be **up to them** when the time is right for them to do so, please do not try to force it on them, let it be a natural progression. **BUT if that gift is one that you would like to retain**, then the younger the better. It should be the most natural thing in the world for children. Nothing forced on them, make it just part of their growing up. It would be nice to see a lot more children becoming involved in the Spiritualist movement. The likes of Gladys Owen, Leonard Young and Gordon Higginson, Frank Decker; their parents kept their link going right through their childhood.

A young Frank Decker was taken to a Circle by his mother when he was ten, as she had no baby sitter. Physical Phenomena started to happen but no one knew who the Medium was, so it was decided to exclude one person at a time each week for one week to see if the phenomena continued. It was eventually found that it was the ten year old boy Frank Decker. So you can see what can be missed if we exclude children from our Circles. We need to help our youngsters understand.

I had a phone call from a 30 year old man who lived in Stoke on Trent in April 2002 asking for a book. He told me when he was young he had visions from Spirit and was given messages. He told his parents, immediately they took him to the doctors. He was examined and found to be normal. The doctor told his mother he was looking for attention and he should be taken home and given a good thrashing. Which his parents did. Months later he told his mother again about the visions and the talking in his head from Spirit. They took him to the doctors again he said he was still looking for attention, he should again be taken home and given a good hiding/thrashing again, if that did not work he could arrange with the hospital to give him electric shock treatment on his brain. From that day he did not tell his parents any more about the messages or visions. He had learned to keep his mouth shut. No more was spoken about these instances from that moment. His parting comment to me was, "his both parents were now Mediums working the platform in Spiritualist churches".

In 2001, I met a 40 year old girl friend from the North East, who I thought the world of, and still do. She told me of her Roman Catholic mother beating her with a wooden skittle because she was levitating on her bed. Her sister would shout to her mother "she is doing it again mum"! She would get locked in a dark cupboard under the stairs for hours after being shouted at and beaten for being evil. The light bulbs hanging from the ceiling would often swing when she would walk into the room. She has had wooden balls thrown at her by her parents before being thrown again into the dark cupboard. What a sad existence for a young child who should have been getting looked after. I met her in 2000 and she was still being abused by her female relation she was with (I will not give her name or her abuser to protect her). I have seen my girl friend actually shaking when this woman walked into the kitchen where she was working, as have others. Because of my previous relationships I would not give her the ring on her finger, she left to live with her daughter, to go back to the North East. I truly miss her.

# DAYS ASIDE AND PRACTICE
## for self.

What I do now just lately, is to have set days put aside for the development of my own individual Mediumship skills. I seem to have been helping others over the many years to develop and not putting any time aside for myself to develop, but on saying that, I did not feel it was right for me at the time and it was not time wasted. I did not feel it was necessary for me to develop along any set pathway. I did not have the time anyway; I had two children at the time to bring up on my own. Now I do want to develop my skills a bit better, I have the time and the inclination.

I must stress to you all that there has to be time put aside for yourself when developing, you also have to pace yourself in any Mediumship development. If you become too tired, you will not be of any use to any other person, or Spirit, never mind yourself. Then you will be blaming Spirit for not linking. A stressed or tired body or mind is in no way, in any shape or form, a good link. You must be bright, happy, and healthy in yourself. If you do not feel this way, give yourself a complete break, a good rest, then come back when you are ready. Have a holiday to recharge your batteries. I personally use my weeks at Stansted Hall to recharge, and regenerate all the ways of linking with Spirit, just in case I am getting stale on something. I go there to enjoy myself as well as to learn and develop.

At the start of the meditation I ask, in general terms, within my thoughts for the particular spiritual development I would like Spirit to develop within me, saying "IF IT IS THE DIVINE SPIRIT'S WILL I WOULD LIKE THE **what ever** GIFT DEVELOPED IN ME". Then try to still my mind as much as possible by looking into the light within my mind's eye. Becoming passive. Then let Spirit get on with what ever they need to do.

## Suggestions for
# DEDICATED DEVELOPMENT

**BEFORE EVERY CIRCLE AND EVERY TIME A PERSON SITS FOR A SPIRIT LINK. THEY SHOULD IN THEIR MIND, BE SINCERELY ASKING AND ENCOURAGING SPIRIT TO COME CLOSER TO THEM AND HELP AT ALLOTTED TIME FOR THE SITTING FOR DEVELOPMENT OR DEMONSTRATION, OVER AND OVER AND OVER, AGAIN AND AGAIN AND AGAIN, <u>AT LEAST AN HOUR</u> OR TWO BEFORE THE ALLOTTED TIME. YOU CANNOT EXPECT YOUR GOOD STRONG LINK TO COME AUTOMATICALLY AS SOON AS YOU SIT DOWN IN A CIRCLE OR DEMONSTRATE YOUR SKILL OF A LINK WITH SPIRIT.**

Once a week is the time put aside for many people, so put into place what is best for you, and you alone are the one to decide. This is the timetable for me at this time. I will explain why.

In my own home, I was sitting on my own in the dark all the time I was developing, but after going 150 miles across the country and paying £30 to see a fiasco of an alleged Physical Circle in the complete dark, and the more I thought about it, it could have been a con trick. In my own home I started sitting in the red light only after that day. Then after things started happening in Trance while I was sitting in the daylight at Stansted April 1999 I decided I was going to try midday meditating 1.00pm –2.00pm in the light and meditating 6.00pm –7.00pm in red light, but both in the room I have now put aside for Spirit. I made myself a séance room in the downstairs bedroom. I now also sit anywhere at all for my development for linking with Spirit within my meditation and I mean anywhere, and at any quiet moment if it is safe in that environment. By that I mean not likely to be suddenly disturbed. I was once nasty surprised by a loud gong being struck whilst sitting quietly meditating in a monastery just over the Scottish border near Lockerbie. So please be careful where you sit, that gong being struck finished me there and then in my meditation very suddenly and sharply. The shock upset my stomach at the time.

**Mondays** I sit for "Physical Phenomena" development.
When starting I sincerely ask Spirit to come closer around me bringing only goodness, kindness, love, and truth to blend in the Divine Light of Spirit within the peaceful loving harmony of the highest realms of Spirit with me, to bring into the room Spirit friends and the people who can help me with the production of Physical Phenomena, if it is your will. So I can prove to others here on the earth plane there is life after our so-called "death" on the earth plane. I also add. "If it is the will of Spirit for me to help by this means of physical Mediumship I would like it developed in me". When I feel Spirit near I then try to still my mind as much as possible to let Spirit do their best. I also ask from Spirit for help with the stilling of my mind. It should be said in your mind positively and in all sincerity. I go into deep meditation just looking into the light in my mind at third eye level after at first within my mind encouraging over and over for Spirit to come near. I always finish every session off by sending out the power that has been built up by the Link of Spirit and myself, in the way of healing to the others in the world, this world and the next, who are less fortunate than me. I always ask Spirit to send this residue of the power out in the way of healing. I then sincerely thank the friends from the World of Spirit for coming around me, and helping with my development, making arrangements for my next sitting with their Link.

**Tuesdays** I sit for "Automatic Writing / Automatic Drawing".
I sit with a pad and pencil beside a table in my special room that I have set aside for Spirit, my arm is resting on the table with the pencil in my hand the point of the pencil on the pad at the top. I sincerely ask Spirit to come closer around me bringing only goodness, kindness, love, and truth within the Divine Light and to blend in peaceful loving harmony of the highest Spirit realm with me, to bring into the room Spirit friends who can help me with the Automatic Writing (or/and drawing), so I can bring to the people here on the earth plain proof that there is life after our so called "death". I also add. "If it is the will of Spirit for me to help by this means of automatic writing I would like it developed in me". I go into the meditation state, and look into the light within my third eye concentrating on it. I try not to think about anything too heavy, if thoughts do come into my mind, which they often do, especially of what my hand or arm is doing. I try to dismiss it, stilling my mind as much as possible looking again into the Light within my mind. If there is any disturbance in my mind, I go back to the third eye and the light. I sometimes sit in another room in my house, I will try sitting listening to the radio with light classical music playing in the background, and/or reading a light novel. Of course I always start off, as you all should, firstly with a pray to the higher realm asking for what you want. It should be said in your mind positively and in all sincerity [or out loud, if you feel it is best for you]. I always finish every session by sending out the power that has been built up by the Link of Spirit and myself, out to the others in the world, this world and the next who are less fortunate then me. I send the residue of the power out in the way of healing. I then sincerely thank the friends from the World of Spirit for coming around me and helping with my development, making arrangements for my next sitting with their Link.

**Wednesdays** I sit for "Clairvoyance, Clairaudience, Clairsentience".
I sit in my special room, when starting I sincerely ask Spirit to come closer around me bringing only goodness, kindness, love, and truth within the Divine Light, and to blend in peaceful loving harmony of the highest realms with me, to bring into the room Spirit friends who can help me with the seeing, hearing, and sensing of Spirit, so I can help others here on the earth plane, and prove to them here on the earth plane that there is life after our so called "death" here. I also add, "If it is the will of Spirit for me to help by this means of mental mediumship I would like it developed in me". I go into the meditation state, and look within my third eye, concentrating on it while asking for the Spirit people to show me the pathway as I go through my development. I sometimes lie on the bed during the day and go into

meditation, asking Spirit to help me to see, hear, and feel Spirit. I ask Spirit to take me on a journey of learning. I also ask sometimes, for Spirit to show me the things that might help me in my learning. This is so I can gain some knowledge of what is necessary for me to do to make my learning go smoother for us both (the Spirit World and myself). This is so the pathway is not too much of an upward slope. It should be said in your mind positively and in all sincerity. I always finish every session by sending out the power that has been built up by the Link of Spirit and myself, to the others in the world, this world and the next, who are less fortunate then me. I send the power out in the way of healing. I then sincerely thank the friends from the World of Spirit for coming around me and helping with my development, making arrangements for my next sitting with their Link.

**Thursdays** I sit again for "Physical Phenomena".

**Fridays** I sit again for "Automatic Writing / Automatic drawing".

**Saturdays** I sit again for "Clairvoyance, Clairaudience, Clairsentience".

**Sundays** I just meditate without asking for anything special, and let Spirit take the initiative in my development with whatever I am lacking in my spiritual development links, but I always say to Spirit what the day is set aside for, "If it is the will of Spirit, I would like help where it is needed within my development". [I sometimes ask Spirit to take me to the halls of learning if needed]. I sincerely ask Spirit to come closer around me bringing only goodness, kindness, love, and truth within the Divine Light, and to blend in peaceful loving harmony of Spirit of the highest realms with me. All your prayers to Spirit should always be said positively and in all sincerity in your mind (some say it out loud). I then go into deep meditation. I always finish every session by sending out the power that has been built up by the link of Spirit and myself to the others in the world, this world and the next, who are less fortunate then me. I send the power out in the way of healing. I then thank the friends from the World of Spirit for coming around me and helping with my development, making arrangements for my next sitting with their Link.

I quite often have a Sunday off from meditating, and have a day in the garden or go out to socialise.

If I go on holiday I might not meditate at all, I give myself a complete break, but that is rare. I might just not meditate as long.

I have a very active mind, so the stilling of my mind has been very much an upward struggle within myself.

**Every evening** bar none, in bed I say my sincere prayers, and then give permission for Spirit to help me develop and to use me as an open vessel in the best way they can to help me progress while I am asleep bringing only goodness, kindness, love, and truth within the Divine Light of Spirit and for me to blend within peaceful loving harmony of Spirit from the highest realm, asking also for a good night's, restful sleep. Waking up in the morning fully refreshed.

We are told by Spirit the more we progress, the better we become at our helping of others whilst asleep but we do not remember it. Some more advanced people can train themselves to remember their sleeping travels of helping others. I don't.

I am waking up early lately [7 0'clock am], so I have been meditating for an hour every day before I get out of bed.

**KEEPING TO SET TIMES AND DAYS** here are another set of dedicated development for you to follow; adjust accordingly for your own development, could be:-

**MONDAY :-** Eyes closed in meditation, sincerely asking for only the gift of clairvoyance in the morning, then sincerely asking for only the gift of clairaudience in the afternoon in the evening sitting for all Mental Mediumship. Asking for all the gifts of Mental Mediumship, then meditate allowing Spirit to develop you in the direction of Mental Mediumship development they think may be a help for you.

**TUESDAY :-** Eyes closed sit in the power of the World of Spirit just talking to them at first, then meditate allowing Spirit to develop you in what ever way they see fit. Be sincere in your asking.

**WEDNESDAY :-** In the morning start by sincerely asking for only the gift of Automatic Writing, then meditate. In the afternoon asking for only the gift of Automatic Drawing, in the evening sit with a pad and paper and see what comes through giving Spirit no firm instructions for you development in what you would like, saying only that you would like the gift of helping people understand there is life after our so called death through the pen, pencil, crayon, brush or what ever medium you are using.

**THURSDAY :-** Sit in the power of the World of Spirit just talking to them out loud or through thought, bringing Spirit close to you at first, then in meditation allowing Spirit to develop you in what ever way they see fit. Be sincere in your asking.

**FRIDAY :-** Sincerely asking for only Transfiguration or any Physical Phenomena Mediumship you wish to be developed in your link on this day. As Transfiguration is a Physical Mediumship I would concentrate on it and sincerely ask and keep asking over and over again, when Spirit is felt near then try to still the mind allowing Spirit to develop your Transfiguration each sitting on the one day.

**SATURDAY :-** Sit in the power of the World of Spirit just talking to them at first, then in meditation allowing Spirit to develop you in what ever way they see fit. Be sincere in your asking.

**SUNDAY :-** Sincerely ask for Physical Mediumship and allow Spirit to work their magic on you in the direction they wish, firstly giving Spirit permission to do so. Remember you have to be subservient to the World of Spirit in all your development. For Physical Mediumship of any kind you need to be very patient as it can take a very long time in your development.

# DOORKEEPERS, CONTROLS, GUIDES, LINKS.

Before writing about guides it must be said here, that all communication on the other side of the veil is by thought. This is why in Spiritualism, Buddhism, most of the knowledgeable people around us, and within the religions of the world, it is said by them, that "thought is a powerful living thing, a living energy". It is your thoughts that help or hinder people in this world and the next. You as an individual person should be sending out good thoughts, even to the people you do not particularly like. That way you can possibly change their way in life for the better.

If you want badness you get it. If you want evil your can have it when you are here, and when you cross over to the other side of the veil. Like attracts like. All the badness and evil cannot compare with all the goodness that there is in the higher life. With your thoughts and the help of the higher life in the higher vibrational plain with those good thoughts, you/we can change things that happen here on this earth plain for the better.

When you want some person from the other side of the veil, from the higher vibrational plain to contact you. All you need is to send out your thoughts to them. If it is done with the goodness of your heart and with love, then that thought can be picked up by that person especially so in your moments of silence. This is why people who try to link with Spirit, whether they are Mediums, highly developed yoga masters, developed Buddhists, or any other developing persons, they all have a different outlook in life. They all sit in the power, the silence, in meditation, and link with the higher self and ultimately blend with the higher Spirit realm.

When you come into the link with the higher Spirit realm you are contacted by what some call doorkeepers/gatekeepers/guides; **(LETS GET IT STRAIGHT. THERE IS NO DOOR OR GATE)** these are persons who have passed to the higher realm, and have advanced to a stage where they have become part of a group, then they can be a spokesperson, or should I say a thought person [for the group]. Then they, the individual can help with the contact, making a Link with people on the earth plane. I will say here, all these labels are only names we on the earth plane have given them. Most think it is only one person that is speaking to them. I must say here, that it is the thoughts of an **individual group** that comes through to help. This is the reason a Spirit spokesperson who comes through the Trance Medium's voice box, or through an ectoplasmic voice box, always says it is a "group thought decision," meaning the answer to the question that was given to the Medium's control when a Medium is in full Trance, it is a "**group thought decision.**" These things can be found out if you ask a Medium's Spirit Control when the Medium is in **deep** TRUE **full Trance**. I must stress TRUE **DEEP Trance**, not a Medium who is fooling themselves, but a Medium that has given Spirit permission for the **full control Link**. We here on earth would probably say it is a committee decision for the ways to go about helping with the contact. The Trance Medium's Control is the chairperson [the thought person] speaking on behalf of the committee [group] in Spirit.

When the individual person like the auntie, uncle, dad, brother, sister, mother, come through into the Medium's mind. I am talking now about clairvoyance, clairsentience, and clairaudience. Those individuals in Spirit have to be brought though a system of thought, a thought process. First by a loving thought from the seeker's mind, which goes to the link group of that person who are in the Spirit realm of life, which has a spokesperson/thought person [some say this is the gatekeeper others say a Guide], to the thoughts of the mum in Spirit [or any person who comes through], the Link group making it happen through thought so helping mum, mum's thoughts to the Medium mind, the Medium's thought Link, the Medium's mouth [them speaking the message], giving the message of what has been given back to the seeker.

It is the same when a person says I have a guide who is an Indian, an Arab, a monk, a nun. These people in Spirit are only the spokesperson [the thought person] for the group, who are trying to help the Medium in their task of proving life after death. This is why I have said "do not put your Guide on a pedestal".

**I have included a lot more of this subject in the other section of the book in part two.**

# DEMONSTRATING
## Your skills

To demonstrate anything, you can read books, and be told what to do, BUT it is only by doing that you realise what is necessary for you as an individual of how to go about it. We all have our own slightly different ways of going about things.

One of the first things here must be said, is for you to be clean and tidy in the things you wear.
Be aware of your appearance in public.
Always make sure you have a good wash, bath, or shower as you would before going to meet a special friend here on the earth plain, because that is what you are doing. You are going to meet/linkup with your friends in Spirit, and meet and make new ones in the congregation [if you are working on the platform]. I am sure you would not like to meet anyone smelling of stale body odour, or one smelling of an old stale ashtray.
Make sure you clean your teeth; there is nothing worse than smelling bad breath from someone you are talking to, (but they might have a medical problem).
Try to not have a smoke before meeting people as your breath will smell, and a lot of people do not like the smell of smoke.
Pay special attention to your appearance, your hair, hands and nails. People notice and talk about your grooming, and your presentation. Be aware of the general public and the facts that some are not very nice people, always ready to put others down, and portray that person in a bad light. Lots of people unfortunately like to pick out the bad points instead of the good. Most of the public, unfortunately like to think the worst of others. I hope you are not one of them in our society, a sort of person who pulls people down.
Bad news sells. Look at the papers and on the T.V.
Make sure you are true to yourself, Spirit and the public. Do not lie to yourself or to the recipient.
When talking to many people do not have your hand or fingers over your mouth. Even if you are thinking, try to get out of the habit. The action of placing the hands or fingers over the mouth while talking is seen in body language books as the person not telling the truth. Besides the people you are trying to help will not be able to hear what you are saying. Think also of the people who are slightly deaf, they will want to lip read.
Talk clearly and with conviction. Try to work with a microphone as people at the back of the churches, halls, and theatres will want to hear clearly. Most small churches now have a public address system of some sort.
Try to have a warm, happy, smile on your face as you work, not all the time though as it will look false. Your voice sounds different when you smile; you also build yourself up when you smile. Don't believe me? Try recording your own voice first when you smile, then when you don't.

Remember your eyes and eye brows can tell a lot to people, have them bright and happy looking on the outside, even if they might be tired and heavy on the inside. Sounds stupid? Look in the mirror and make faces to yourself. Happy, sad, angry, lost, etc. see how your eyebrows change shape.

Be happy in yourself as you are working with your Angel Friends in Spirit, and then those happy feelings will show through naturally, and hopefully infect others there with you.

## YES happiness is infectious!
## GO INFECT SOMEONE ELSE!

Never be negative in your messages, finish on an uplifting thought, message, and have that bright note in your voice.

At the Daulby Street, Spiritualist Church in Liverpool. Every Monday night they have a teach-in class or development group, which is very good. The leaders of the group has people up on the platform just to talk about themselves, and what they think about different subjects. This is just to give a person confidence in talking to many, the same as they would with a church audience.

I went to a church in Stoke-on-Trent in Haywood Road, Burslem where a session of awareness was taken by a very good teacher Sally Harding, the president of the church. This is the method that we use.

A very good way of practising your skills for platform work is to have one person to run a session of learning. Best a person who has had experience of mediumship BUT not always necessary as long as they have common sense. [A leader].

Have two people on the platform, or have them at the front of everyone there.

The leader gives each person a word only when they go out to the front. The first word that immediately comes into their mind without thinking. E.g. "fear", "children" [could be any word at all e.g. stars, night, trousers, computer, bed, table, hair, garden, bus, holiday, pain, pictures, etc.].

The first person then has to go into a very light altered state, perhaps do a few deep breathing exercises, or just relax on a chair and think about the word given, this is so they are in touch with their own inner self, but not deep enough to link with Spirit.

That person then has to talk about "fear" and what it has meant to them throughout their life. The person has to **tell the "truth"** about "fear" in their life, **but not all** if they do not wish to relate details about which they are embarrassed. **The main thing is to tell the "truth".**

When this person has finished they sit down and the other person gets up and tells all there about the word "children," and how it has meant something to them in their life. **Has to tell the truth. That is the main thing "Truth".** They then sat down.

At this point, Sally gave each person a reading from the things that were said by each person on the platform. It was shown that by a person talking about themselves, an opinion of the way they looked at life, and what had gone on in their life could be seen easily, as the person truthfully opened up in front of all there; that is Sally and the training group. This was to show everyone there how to put things into context. This could be done at this point by the leader, if they were an experienced Medium that is; it could also be used as a practice point for an aspiring Medium.

The leader, Sally, then ask each of the two at the front on the platform, to go into an altered state to Link with Spirit, and ask Spirit to bring in someone in Spirit to help with their own word given ["fear" and "children"]. The two people on the platform, one at a time, then had to give a message to someone in the audience on their own word given, the word had to be included.

Spirit will give enough of a message to the person picked out to show there is significance in the word to be relevant to the person in the audience. If the trainee Medium diverted from the word, or did not bring it into the message, they were told to go back to their Spirit Link and ask for help with the message with the word.

The message should come naturally from Spirit when the Link is made and not to be a long message, the energy vibration should flow naturally and the person giving the message **should "NOT" be going back** to Spirit in their mind to prolong the message. This exercise is for the person only to continue with the single small message it will stop naturally when Spirit has given enough to the person. There is no need for many names or places, just for Spirit to mainly **use the word given** in context with the message.

This exercise is only to help the persons up at front to have more confidence, and to leave their caution/fear behind and to show there can be an easy simple link when ever needed.
It is also to show everyone discipline with the earthly link and Spirit Link, nothing more nothing less.

This was another method that was used by Sally Hardings in her teaching at the Burslam Spiritualist church in Stoke on Trent, it is another good way of practising and building up the three mediumistic skills [clairsentience, clairvoyance, clairaudience] and for the person to have practise in talking to a number of people. The person is again not told before hand what they are going to do. If they are told before, they are likely to pre-empt anything, putting thoughts into their head so contaminating the exercise with those thoughts. This is not what is required. It is a natural link that is trying to be formed.
A person is asked to go up on the rostrum, on the platform, or up in front of everyone.
For the person to meditate, to link with Spirit, for them to have total trust in Spirit. Then for the person to be told to very quickly, without any thought to it, pick a person in the audience. The person on the rostrum [I will call "Roster"] then is told to choose between a colour or a number. The person in the audience has to say the first colour that comes into their mind, or the first number that comes into their mind, which ever has been chosen by "Roster", colour or number. They should not have to have time to think of the colour/number, it has to be immediate. If any pre-thought is allowed to come into the equation by "Roster" [the picking out of the person, the choosing of the colour or the choosing of the number] then the messages can become mixed up between people in the audience amongst the people who Roster has been thinking of previously. When the chosen number [or colour] has been given to "Roster".
Roster" then has to link with Spirit for a minute or two in their own way, stand up, then give whatever comes into their head to the person in the audience in the form of a message if possible. If nothing is received then be brave enough to say so, do not be embarrassed, it comes with time. "Roster" does not go asking questions of Spirit in their head for things, the information should flow naturally after the first link, it might at first come slowly, but it does come. [This method can be used with the everyday words as well]. It does not matter what they receive it is said or described to the person in the audience, whether it is in picture, or a sequence of pictures as in a cinema, or on T.V., a name, a word of any sort is to be given out even if it means nothing to "Roster." Roster should be remembering the link; it is not to be strayed away from. If this happens then the leader has to guide Roster" back onto track, reminding them of the colour or number. At the end of the exercise the leader will ask "Roster" to go back and ask Spirit for some evidence of the link. It can come in the way of a number of a bus, a house, a flat, a train, a flower, a piece of jewellery, a clock or watch etc. If a colour was chosen, it can be a colour of a room in the house, colour of a cat, shoes some one wears, a car, the house door colour, etc. things that are relevant at the time for the person, or ones that can be checked at a later date. The idea is to let the communication just flow naturally, do not force, it lets Spirit come in at it's own pace. It is learning to have total trust in Spirit and trusting in what they are giving to you in your mind.
As "Roster" progresses, the leader can ask them to bring into their presentation their own clairsentience; how they feel about the things they are getting as they were getting it. This is a learning process for both "Roster" and the Spirit communicator link, yes Spirit has to learn as well, not all Spirit communicators are evolved to an extent they know everything, they are learning at the same rate as you are. If they did they know everything Spirit would not be at this level, they would have progressed to beyond this stage. The exercise is allowing a total trust, a Medium, a Link, to evolve between "Roster" and Spirit helpers. When practised often, the mediumistic Link with Spirit becomes a lot easier in it's flow. The main thing with this exercise and any with a Spirit Link is to have total trust in Spirit that the link will be there for you when needed. Remember the more you practice the easier it becomes just as it is with everything in life here and across the veil.

The Spirit Link learning with the group are different to the Spirit working with you individually.
A mind exercise which Sally uses, is to have the person relax and to look into their own mind, imagining they are going into a comfortable place where they are going to find people who they are comfortable with. There they are going to ask those people to help with their development and because they are people who they know and trust, they know they are going to help them. Within the person's mind anything can be asked of them. This is a very good exercise when first starting
Sadly I have just heard Sally Hardings passed away in the summer of 2001.

When people are in the presence of a Medium giving a message to others, especially in church they should be asked by the leader of the Circle or the chair person from the platform, for each person in the audience to link with Spirit, and told how to, (because the general public do not know how), talking to those in Spirit to come near and help them send the power to the Medium to help strengthen their link with their Spirit Friends. Telling the audience that the more they give unselfishly to others (the Medium) the more they will receive.

**MEDIUMS and BUDDING MEDIUMS**, please get away from asking questions of the recipient it only lowers your credibility. Don't ask the recipient e.g. Who is the person ------who wears the red hat when they go out---? Where is the place where a person--------? Where is there a church that -------? Who has a dog that is -------? What is the person who is getting a brown coat doing? When they give the answer, that person has done **your work** of the link, the lazy Medium's way of working. Then most of this type of a Medium finishes the answer with **"that is right"** I have them here. It is the Medium's job to tell the recipient, the enquirer what they are receiving and not to get fed the information. The Medium should have been going back to Spirit to gain more information of that link. Look at the platform Mediums and see how many work this way and afterwards point it out to them. Most ask questions of their enquirers, instead of giving information from their link with Spirit.

Let me put a few pointers

Don't say :- "Who is the person that has dirty boots and used to work in the building industry"?
Be certain of Spirit and trust them with the things they give you. Only say what you see.
Say "I have a person here who has mucky boots and used to work in the building industry, you know of that person don't you". [describe the person that Spirit has shown you within your mind] It is the only thing at present being shown to me by Spirit." (Go back to Spirit and talk to them.)
I am being shown a person who -----------or I have a person here who------------- . It is a person you know don't you? [describe the person that Spirit has shown you within your mind
I have a person here for you who wears a red hat it, is---------in your family. Isn't it? (or that's true isn't it?) You should have been confirming this with your Spirit link at the same time.
Or I have a person who wears a red hat who wishes to be remembered to you. [describe the person that Spirit has shown you within your mind] keep going back to your link in the Spirit World, asking them to increase the information for you.
I am being given a church on a corner of a road (describe that road, and all you can see around it) it brings in a memory of your childhood (or when ever. You should be getting information from Spirit as you ask for it). You can remember this can't you? If they cannot place it at that time ask them to hold onto the information as it came with their link.
I am getting a lady in a brown coat; she comes in a family link (or in a link of a friendship memory). The lady should be described, if you get a brown coat then you should be getting what the lady looks like what you feel about her, and the way she is looking when she came into your mind. Say what you see, or feel from Spirit, give only what you are given you might miss the vital thing Spirit wanted to portray to that person, don't make it up into a story either, as some Mediums do!!!!!.
**I see too many Mediums or "SO CALLED Mediums" giving reading, where it should be linking spiritually and giving evidence of the afterlife continuing, on the platforms of churches. Those so-called Mediums are only using their psychic powers NOT their spiritual linking with Spirit. They only give psychic reading working psychically.**

Always go back to Spirit in your own mind for more information as you should be, time and time, and time and time again. Don't allow the recipient to tell you anything more. **You are** supposed to give the enquirer the evidence, **NOT the enquirer** giving you information. **Never let the enquirer feed you.** You will have heard the saying **"Never feed the Medium"**. This is the feeding of information that you as the Medium should be getting from the Spirit link.

**The message from any church platform should be given within a link with the Spirit World then <u>at the end of the evidential message</u>, the Medium should go back to their link in Spirit and <u>ask for some evidence for the recipient that will make sure to the recipient the evidence given to them is true</u>. In other words a bit of information from the link in Spirit that WILL CONVINCE the**

recipient that the person in Spirit is who they say they are. **This practice should be done as a matter of course ALWAYS.**

E.g. I am being shown a lady with her hair in a style of the nineteen hundreds, she has a bun at the back of her head I am being shown she has a black dress which is long and of the same period. Spirit is now showing me a frame of a picture and are placing the lady in that picture frame so I know there is a picture of this lady that has some meaning for you. I am correct aren't I? (Yes) This is the evidence that the message from Spirit is for you, Spirit are giving you this as proof.

I would like the tutors of the calibre of the older Mediums who went/go straight to ONE person from the audience and give **only what they get** from the Spirit World, to teach genuine people to be our mediumistic ambassadors. If they did not get anything they were brave enough to say so. You, as they were, will be thought more of in the end because of your honesty.

If you cannot go to one person in an audience of many, **you are not developed enough for the platform**.

If you cannot give a qualified ending piece of evidence that only the single chosen recipient can take and no one else in that audience, when that piece of evidence comes genuinely from Spirit, **you are not developed enough and your link with spirit is not strong enough**

If you cannot give more than just general bits of information that any person can take, **you are not developed enough**.

If you cannot know when Spirit is linking and giving you information and distinguish it truthfully from your own imagination, **you are not developed enough**.

You must admit it and go back to your GOOD PLACES OF LEARNING AND START AGAIN. Go to back to your GOOD GENUINE TEACHERS WHO HAVE THE KNOWLEDGE AND PRACTICAL EXPERIENCE OF MEDIUMSHIP.

## SPIRITUALISM

I would suggest to all who read this book, to try and attend a Spiritualist Church at least a half a dozen times for different functions, services, awareness classes, and their specials a few times for each. Also try and visit other Spiritualist churches not just your local one and their functions. The reason for my saying this, is a Spiritualist Church is one of the places you can guarantee meeting people of the similar mind as yourself, an enquirer after truth. Here with the help of others a person can learn and expand their craft. But if you go to different churches you will have a better idea of the way things are and not just one church's perspective, and you will meet more like-minded people.

The place where most people now are going to for intensive courses is at the colleges. The most powerful one for me being The Arthur Findlay College at Stansted Hall, Stansted. Essex, England. People from all over the world travel to be amongst friends they have not as yet met. Yes each time you go there you will find a lot of good sensitive friends willing to help and share their experiences with you. I think every person who is involved with meditation, in which ever form or whichever direction they wish to travel within, should attend the Arthur Findlay College at least once. I am sure they will find once is not enough. People who go there can attend lectures and Circles if they want to or just be left alone to wander the grounds alone in the tranquil surrounding.

Spiritualism is the only religion/movement that welcomes, encourages people of all religions within it's ranks asking for nothing in return. It also does not have people who attend; follow any dogma or creed. The people in Spiritualism do not ask any person to stop going to their own churches. People who attend these Spiritualist churches are never asked to stop believing in their own way to GOD. Just to keep an open mind and a belief in life after our so-called death.

The philosophy of Spiritualism was started and it's foundations are based on the seven principles that a very great Medium in 1871, a Emma Hardinge Britten, whilst in Trance and communicating with her Spirit friend, a Robert Owen. He told her from the World of Spirit the "Seven Principles" that all who sat for Spirit and those who wished for a better life here and beyond should try to uphold and try to follow. Robert Owen, when he was living on this earth plane of ours, founded the Co-operative movement.

These words are the basis of the Spiritualist Church's "Seven Principles", the six that were given to Emma Hardinge Britten in 1871. Here are the original wordings of them:-

**The fatherhood of God.**
**The brotherhood of man.**
**The immortality of the soul and its personal characteristics.**
**Proven facts of communion between departed human spirits and mortals.**
**Personal responsibility. With compensation and retribution hereafter for all good and evil deeds done here.**
**A path of eternal progress open to every human soul that wills to tread it by the path of eternal good.**

The wording was slightly changed in 1901 by the Spiritualist's National Union on the advice of their solicitors to :-.
> **THE FATHERHOOD OF GOD.**
> **THE BROTHERHOOD OF MAN.**
> **THE COMMUNION OF SPIRITS AND THE MINISTRY OF ANGELS.**
> **THE CONTINUOUS EXISTENCE OF THE HUMAN SOUL.**
> **PERSONAL RESPONSIBILITY.**
> **COMPENSATION AND RETRIBUTION HEREAFTER FOR ALL THE GOOD AND EVIL DEEDS DONE ON EARTH.**
> **ETERNAL PROGRESS OPEN TO EVERY HUMAN SOUL.**

Modern Spiritualism as a movement was really started in The United States of America by the Fox sisters of Hydesville, who in 1848 heard "raps", and noises in their house. Now it is known by the name of "The Hydesville Rapping's". The family had only just moved into the house a few weeks previously, as on other nights, and they were kept awake again, by the noises on the night of $31^{st}$ of March 1848, so the two young children Margaretta and Kate, started clapping their hands and shouting at the noises. To their surprise the clapping of their hands was mirrored by the noises. So they experimented by clapping a number of times, then the "raps" came back the same number of times, they experimented doing different sequences. It was soon found out there was intelligence in the noises [raps]. Soon the people of the neighbourhood started to join the family with the "raps". After working out what sequence of raps were to be used for "yes" and "no" with the Spirit. One of the first questions to be asked was how many children had the mother had and their ages. The answer came back correctly but what surprised them all even more was the intelligence told the mother of the child she had who had died in its infancy. Not one of the neighbours knew of the child who had died. The people there made out a code to work with the Spirit for the alphabet. They soon found out the intelligence was a man who was murdered in 1843, his name was Charles B. Rosna, who was a peddler. He also informed the gathering, which were now all regular visitors, the previous tenant of the house, a Mr John C. Bell, had murdered him. It was not until 1904 that the remains were found in the cellar of the house as foretold by the "rapping's" and reported that year by a none Spiritualist paper. The sisters after their travelling all over the U.S.A were made to made to retract the story by the pressure of the church communities. At least the truth was found out eventually independently that it all did happen, and thank goodness it was thoroughly investigated at the time of the rapping's, just before their death the sister affirmed that the story of the rapping were true

It might seem strange to a person who has not set foot inside a Spiritualist Church that everything that goes on is like a "normal/ordinary" church service they had been brought up in.
The Spiritualist Church has the naming of children after their birth by the ministers.
The naming of adults and children by Spirit their spiritual names.
Marriages.
Before burial services, which I believe should be a celebration, because we know the person has gone to a better place and we will see them again when we go there when we die, if we live life without harming anyone or anything. Doing no evil to others.
Sunday Services and services during the weekdays on set days.
Some services are especially for Clairvoyance to prove life after our so-called death, and others as a divine service for mainly philosophy with a smaller amount of clairvoyance to prove survival after our so-called death.

The churches normally have teachers who can tell others about the "Lyceum", this is the teaching mainly of the young or new comers about the ways of Spiritualism. [which sadly is being neglected]

On other nights there are teach-ins/workshops with Mediumship training, healing training, awareness, platform work, philosophy, meditation practice, and discussions of many sorts.

On other nights most churches have an Open Circle for all to attend and on another nights generally a Closed Circle, where an invitation is the only entrance to it.

Most churches have a cup of tea ready after any meeting at nominal cost, some don't charge at all this is to get people to start talking to each other after, so if you do attend you will not be alone.

A lot of churches have or should have an appointed welcoming person to help to make new comers welcome and introduce them into a suitable group of people or stay by them talking, so they are not alone.

Many churches also try and attract the general public in through the doors by having a special night of Clairvoyance or Trance by very experienced local or visiting Mediums once a month-ish to try to boost the funds for the lighting, heating, the general repairs and running costs of the church hall.

There are no trappings like other churches i.e. NO gold and silver ornaments, statues, figurines, or icons. Only the occasional picture of past presidents, a notice board, and the seven principles for all to see in a prominent position.

Dr Cosmo Lang set up the "Report on Spiritualism", when he was Archbishop of York U.K. It had taken many years of research and investigation by the **"Commission of Churches"** but was suppressed by the then Archbishop of Canterbury. But when Dr Cosmo Lang became the Primate of England **he suppressed the findings** of **"His Own Commission"**. The findings (which were leaked) of that commission by a majority decision was that gifted Spiritualists and specially gifted people could get in touch with the dead and communicate with them. Look it up on the Internet and you will see all.

**Even the Pope in Rome is now saying it is not a sin to talk to the dead.**

Spiritualism is now since 1950 a legally recognised religion in Great Britain. But I believe, it was only put forward as such by the people in the organisations/movements, so they could take advantage of the charity status laws, which give great benefit to the money and the taxing of it.

The S.N.U. and other Spiritualist organisations were instrumental in bringing about the passing of the law which was "the Fraudulent Mediums Act" in 1951 that allowed true, genuine Mediums to practice their craft without fear of prosecution.

# R'HELP CIRCLES
## Meaning    OUR HELP CIRCLES
## Or   RESCUE CIRCLES (A name I do not like)

This form of Mediumship I feel should be used each week, **as well as healing**, for the benefit of those poor unfortunate people who have passed into the higher sphere, and cannot it seems, be able to progress towards the Divine Light. It is those Mediums who have **TRULY DEVELOPED** their Trance, Clairvoyance, Clairaudience, and other mediumistic gifts that should be giving something back as thanks to the higher realm.

This sort of work definitely needs a lot more mediumistic workers using their helpful guiding ways in **R'HELP** Circles for the ones who have gone before. Some people wrongly call this sort of a Circle a "Rescue Circle" please shy away from this label. The Spirit World is telling us there is no such thing as rescue. The young Spirits [I say young in a way they are newly in the Spirit World] who need any help are always being watched over by Spirit all the time. They are only stuck away in the grey darkness away from the Light not going towards it. Those new, ill-informed Spirits are not putting a thought out to the "White Brotherhood" who's helpers are always there ready [under the supervision of the thought guidance of the "White Brotherhood"] watching over them in the background, ready and waiting for those misguided and unfortunate people who have been stuck in limbo. They are waiting for them to send out that one thought, a single thought request for help. The White Brotherhood or any other persons in the World of Spirit cannot interfere until that thought is sent out from them individually for help. It is

Divine Law.

The reason I call it a **R'HELP CIRCLE** is, you are doing a two-way thing, something helpful for the other side of the life before you go there, and so giving you a good foundation. It can be a very rewarding part of Mediumship but you have to be dedicated to your work as it can be frustrating at times and you have to be very open minded. A lot of the souls who come through do not think they are passed over to the other side across the veil, some have the misconception they have reached their place of rest and do not like their lot at all in the lower part of the high vibrational plane. Some unfortunately cannot progress because of their indoctrination on the earth plane or do not send a thought out in the way of help to the "White Brotherhood" who are there always ready and waiting to help everyone who requires it of them.

But you should be very developed spiritually, and very experienced before attempting anything in a R'Help Circle. It can get confusing for unstable people. So choose your sitters carefully.

The person in need of help in the Spirit world has to be persuaded to send a thought out to the "White Brotherhood" for help, so they then can progress towards the Divine Light of Spirit. To go through the darkness, through the tunnel, [along the tube of darkness, the void of blackness] being guided slowly and carefully towards the light at the end. Ignoring all around.

Other stranded souls have been told different things while they were here on the earth plain that will not allow their progression into the light of the Divine Spirit, a sort of sticking point for them.

Still more of the poor unfortunate lost souls are people who have been a problem to themselves and mankind while on the earth plain, they can come through with bad language that would make a sailor blush. It can be, and is a sort of counselling session in a Circle for the lost souls/Spirits that come through.

Others who are there in the lower high vibrational plain think no one loves them, so it is not worthwhile going anywhere with anyone, and sadly they do not know what to believe.

The Circle generally starts off with prayers, and the asking for the help and guidance of the Divine Spirits of the highest level of loving harmony, ["The White Brotherhood" who will have been watching over the "lost/confuse ones"], to come with only goodness kindness love and truth, in the Divine Light of Spirit, to come within the loving harmony of Spirit of the highest realms, asking Spirit to guide the stranded souls who are there in need of help, to bring them through to the Circle. In these circumstances when a person comes through, the leader of the Circle has to ask the right questions, to find out how the person passed/"died". When they passed beyond the veil, [this can be done by finding out who was on the throne? or what sort of transport they had then? or what the housing was like? or what sort of work they, maybe one of their family member's did? What clothing did they wear? What sort of implements they used at the time when they were alive on the earth plain? You have to be a detective as well as a counsellor]. What are the circumstances of them not progressing? How old they were? About their family? Try to get the person to trust you and the Circle, to try and gain their confidence. Try to help them come to terms with their problems. Then help the poor souls progress towards the light and start upliftment from their darkness by sending out the thought to the higher levels of vibration.

Quite often it is a very good help if the Circle has a **genuine objectively seeing** clairvoyant Medium, a person who can say for certainty what the person looks like as well as a Medium who has the gifts of **Independent Direct Voice** but of course these are very few and far between, a Trance Medium has been used in the past as in the Circles in Liverpool's Daulby Street church.

The words I would like to put down here are from a person who was in a **"R'HELP CIRCLE"** for many years [she called it a Rescue Circle as this was what it was called many years ago], and is still a very respected member of the Liverpool Daulby Street Spiritualist National Union Church being president at this time 1999, I will not say her age but I can say Dorothy is very much over the national pension age and has been in Spiritualism for just a few years less than her husband Stan Tyrer.

Before he past Stan was a very good Trance Medium and an excellent speaker on the church rostrum for at least 50+ years. These are only a very few of her experiences in the **"R'HELP CIRCLE"** situation.

These words are from Dorothy Tyrer (sadly left us to go to the higher plane in 2006) [the only words I have altered are to change from **"rescue" to "R'HELP"**]:-

My husband Stan, who was a Deep Trance Medium, was in the **"R'HELP CIRCLE"** a lot longer than I was. Stan used to go to church on a regular basis and he was asked to run a Circle to help the new comers develop. So it was arranged on a Saturday evening for him to start the Development Circle. He said to the people there I am not in charge, we are all here to learn and Spirit is the one in control. He used to come home to tell me all that had gone on. Their church **"R'HELP CIRCLE"** was started by Spirit coming through an entranced Medium saying to all there in the ordinary Circle. "I think this would make a good **"R'HELP CIRCLE"** as you all have now the experience and the development necessary to go forward". From that day on we carried on with that **"R'HELP CIRCLE"** for over thirty years.

My input at that time was at home to give him different ideas on how to go about putting the questions to the stranded souls who came through each sitting of the Circle, never thinking I would get involved in it. One occasion before I sat with them, a young girl came through to the Circle by means of one of the Mediums who were in the Circle because then there were a lot of the sitters developing as Mediums. I gave him different ideas on how to approach her next time she came through. It turned out she had been murdered in a back alley in Liverpool at the time of Queen Victoria, so she was helped on our advice to go forward to the Light at the end of the tunnel. **OH YES!** There is a tunnel and there is a light that you have to go to at the end of it.

One night I went straight to the church from work and I was waiting for Stan and some person said "It is a shame you have to go home why don't you go in and sit in the Circle rather than go, you will be here with him then". After a little bit of persuasion I went in and from then on I was a regular there for more than thirty years in the Circle alongside my husband. I was not at all clairvoyant then but I could right away see all the Spirits that came into the Circle there, what was going on, and how they "died". That is how I started.

One of the White Brotherhood of Spirit came through when I started with the Circle and said to me, "We have been waiting for you to come and help". They used to show me how the person had died if the person would not tell us in the Circle. For example a young man who had committed suicide, and was too embarrassed to talk about it, he would not tell anyone why he had done it and I was shown what he had done before it had happened, what had drove him to it, so we could help him then and talk him through it.

Spirit used to open and close the Circle themselves by coming through a Medium in Deep Trance. We used to ask questions of what they wanted, it was a two-way conversation though the Medium.

One of the first people that came through, when I first started sitting (it was Armistice Day in the second world war we actually sat on), and this gentleman comes through as well as other soldiers for other people there, they said we have come through for you to help us. Then this soldier came through and I spoke to him, he came through to me. He had been killed in the first world war all the battalion had been wiped out and he had been sitting in the field all this time surrounded by barbed wire all his friends had gone forward one by one [by their asking for help through thought and then progression into the light] then one day he had thought to himself; [because nobody can progress until the first inclining of a thought comes into their mind; it is the same here if you want to progress; and so you ask questions in your mind, it is the same over there]; all his friends had been near him and watched over him, then at one point he had said "Oh God Why Am I Here" then the White Brotherhood came around him. The White Brotherhood cannot touch or come near or help you until you have that first little bit of a thought that comes into your mind, they watch over a person from a distance. He came to me then the others [the soldiers] came through to the Circle to let him know that they had been watching over him all the time he was just sitting there in that field alone. Until that thought is sent out to the White Brotherhood in the higher life, they can only stand by and watch, that one single thought has to go out from the departed soul.

We used to laugh sometimes as some of them did not know they were "dead" and when a man came through a lady medium, they used to say "These are not my clothes, I did not wear a bloody dress, what is happening", or "I did not have that bloody watch, it is not mine I never pinched it Mr". "This is not my fur coat I can't afford a fur coat". "I did not wear these clothes, these are not mine" If they came through someone else. They spoke exactly as they did when on the earth plane. One man came through very irate with himself saying, "I have just been home to the wife and that bloody neighbour was there yak, yak, yak, yak. I could not make her hear me and I have been shouting at her and she isn't taking a blind bit of notice I pushed and pushed her and it did not make a bloody difference. So I have just walked out on her". We had to persuade him that he was "dead" and his good lady could not hear him. It sometimes takes a lot of persuasion.

The funniest one was a young Irish man, he came through and he was going mad saying where the bloody hell are they I have looked everywhere for them. I said to him because he was Irish what is wrong Paddy, he said in his broad accent, "They must have told me lies, they must have told me lies there is none here, there's no bloody saints anywhere I have looked everywhere for them, they are nothing but liars the lot of them". The parish priest came through, his mother came through, and the priest said, "I did not tell lies I only told him what I had been taught, and I know different now that I am here" so did his mother; he had been looking for the saints and their lanterns. Paddy came through years later when I was on the platform. As did most of the people who we helped, yes, many came back to give us a progress report. But Paddy came back this first time, because he came back quite a few times. He said he had a new job now, he had progressed to such an extent that he was helping all the priests who came over. He helped them to come to terms with themselves after expecting so much from their personal earthly religions, sadly all the religious priests have a terrible time when they go over to the other side. What a difference in Paddy from an irate confused person swearing like a trouper who would not listen to anything we had to say for quite a while, to come back nice because of the way he had gone ahead in the higher realm but he was still his old self I felt.

Another one that sticks in my mind is the little girl who had been very ill before she "past over". Her parents had treated her like a showpiece placing her on a pedestal for everyone to see but not showing her very much love. During her illness her mother kept on saying to her when you pass over do not take any notice of anyone, do not go to anyone other than Jesus, you are very special and no one but Jesus will be waiting for you. She was very upset and confuse about where she was and where to find Jesus. We talked and talked, talked and talked. I had a very big job of trying to persuade her to go slowly towards that small light at the end of the tunnel and trying to get it over to her the light would be brighter, then there would be someone to help her there within the light. It must have taken me many weeks of heart wrenching persuasion to get her to put out a thought for herself to be helped. We eventually persuaded her to walk down the dark tunnel until it gets brighter and brighter into the light.

Another time we helped two young children who were bundled into sacks and thrown into the river and drowned, that rescue took us quite a while to persuade them that people loved them and all in Spirit were not bad. We could not find out where that happened nor where they were from as happens sometimes. But the fact that they had come, means they had sent out a little thought in their little minds that is why they were there, it was a starting point. Yes thankfully we eventually guided them to the tunnel and for them to go slowly along it towards the Divine Light.

**We did not ask for this work, we were chosen by Spirit**. One that was very satisfying was two soldiers who were apologising to each other after the war, an English soldier and a Japanese soldier.
Most of the rescue work is not normal deaths. Car accidents, train accidents, murders, suicides, religious belief problems, [the religious people have terrible problems to come to terms with when they cross over the veil], and things like that. Some people say that it is dangerous, **it isn't**, we were chosen by Spirit. It is so necessary this sort of work but I do not talk about it very often. I am only talking about it now to help others understand, and so some others people in Circles, when they come along can understand how we were able to help some poor people in Spirit, then possibly they can when they are chosen to do so.
Stan Tyrer, my husband went away to sea when he left school and two older men took him under their wing. When they came home on leave, he used to go to their house for tea one of the men's mother was a Medium and that is how Stan started. But Stan's mother was a Spiritualist. When he was little he did not know he was mediumistic. His auntie had a letter in her hand and she was crying, he went up to her saying "Don't cry auntie I know uncle is dead he got killed on the docks the other day didn't he". That was so natural for him he did not think anything of it at the time, he was about eight. Stan actually sat for Spirit the night before he died.
My husband used to say "This materialisation is not for me, the reason being if you see a materialised being, you will go home and say to yourself "did I really see that or was it a dream", but if someone gives you a message and it mentally goes into your head and there is no way a person could have known about it, that for me is best evidence you cannot doubt it. It makes them think".
This last sequence by Dorothy Tyrer was recorded by Roy Keeghan (author) in 1996 in Liverpool, Daulby St, Church.

It seems as though the Spirits that need help to progress are on a lower vibration level than when you progress into the Light.

Within this sort of a Circle it would be best if a genuine objectively seeing clairvoyant Medium was present and an Independent Direct Voice Medium would be better. But of course there are very few around these days.

Another person to help others in the lower vibrational level of the Spirit World is Ron Jordan the Mental and Trance Medium from Liverpool, he now lives in London. He told me about the time he had helped a crew of an aeroplane that was shot down over the English Channel during the Second World War; they were sadly blown out of the sky by a shell, as were many others. When they came through Ron Jordan they told of the incident. They had been flying over the English channel to drop the bombs on Germany and one minute they where in the sky and the next they where back on the ground going over into the same flight over, and over, and over, and over, and over again until they had sent a thought out for help from the higher life. When the crew came through to the Trance Circle, they gave the squadron number, all their names and addresses. And this was checked up on at a later date and all the information given to the Circle by the pilots and crew was confirmed as being correct.

So people who dismiss this type of work should sit down and think with the help of Spirit. During that time of thought they should also ask themselves; "Have I been in a R'HELP Circle and experienced it? If they have not they should say "I have not too much say in the matter until I myself experience it as reality".

This goes for all the forms of Mediumship, especially Trance if you have not had experiences in Trance yourself, do not say what should and what should not happen when in Trance. This is why it has taken me such a long time to collect the **true** findings for this book. **If you cannot do it, you cannot know it!!!!**

# EXORCISM

Here is a subject I was not going to include in my book but after looking at the word in a great many dictionaries I thought that I had better include it. I find out that the Christian church used to exorcise, expel by invocation in a low-key way. At the start of Christianity, the churches used give the task of clearing bad and evil Spirits to anyone with mediumistic gifts who belonged to the church, lay or cleric placing them just above the ordinary person. They would do a special rite and inform the evil Spirits they would have the displeasure of the Divine Spirit, God, if they did not go.

The name of an exorcist [one who exorcizes [Eccles]] is the name of one of the lowest order of cleric in a church, usually a person who belongs to the Roman Catholic Christian church or can be any Christian church. These people introduced into the religion and became part of it in approximately AD 400-ish then their status was a special lower class in the church. This is how the church brought Witches into their every day teachings, they told their congregations the person was possessed by the Devil, or a Witch had put a spell on the person who had the problems. They now had an excuse for the killing of innocent people who opposed them. Later the churches saw they had something they could keep fear in their congregation, keep control over them, so in the 6$^{th}$ century they allowed only the priests to perform exorcisms. Now in this day and age some churches only allow priests to perform exorcisms with their bishop's permission, so upgrading the status of the fear element. Most of the time the church use special rites, rituals or ceremonies. These were said to have started in Judaism and then were carried on by the Christian movement. Now the Roman Catholic Church regulates the ways of exorcism being preformed in cannon law and very elaborate rites are performed in the ritual. In the AD 200-ish the Christian churches in their wisdom "NOT", brought exorcism ceremonies into the baptism of people and it still goes on today. It is only man that pollutes another human's mind with their evil, lies, and murderous ways; sadly a lot of it comes from the leaders within a lot of orthodox religions, even today.

I think it should be pointed out here that the Christian church in the 4$^{th}$ century through the Council of Nicaea stopped Mediums practising within the Christian church. They only allowed the priest to practise the craft of linking with the Divine Spirit. Mediums up until then were held in high regard as having the gift from God, were then suddenly told they were servants of Satan and had the art of the Devil. This started the witch-hunts by the Christians, and the persecution of anyone who had psychic gifts. They killed and burned people at will and with impunity for their own ends. This was for the minds and money of the people. It should be brought to the notice of readers that there are no words for witches in the Hebrew language, the language of Christian faith and of Jesus of Nazareth, in the bible the words placed in there for the "Witches of Endor", if translated correctly should be the "Wise Ones of Endor". Yet another manipulation of the religion for their own ends.

I find it strange that most of the world religions kill people because of their religion. **Who really are the evil ones?** It is a case of if you do not believe, then die, or get put aside. **WHAT SAD SICK PEOPLE.**

If ever you feel that you are linking into the lower elemental level of Spirit tell it firmly to go into the Divine Light of Spirit. Say, you in your loving harmony within Light of Spirit, the Divine Love Light of God, are stronger, far stronger than they are.

This also applies to exorcising a person. Bring to them with your own thoughts (and/or spoken words) the Divine Light of God, which is love, and be strong in your thoughts that you send into the troubled Spirit. Send them the loving harmony and Light of God. Tell them to go into that Light, into the harmony that exists within the higher realms, which can help them. Tell them to go towards and into the love Light of God, the Divine Spirit. Comfort the person and give them healing through your thoughts and hands. Those in the true Light of Spirit will do the rest and guide them. Be a counsellor to them. Remembering that a counsellor is NOT a talker, nor an advisor, only a good listener who lets the person who has the problems decide for themselves what is right. Lets the person who is talking work the problems out for themselves through talking. A book I have found recently "The Quiet Dead" by Dr Edith Fiore ISBN No 0-345-35083-9, might be worth a read. Also Thirty years among the Dead by Carl Wickland M.D.

## UNWANTED LINKS

Sometimes when you start working with the spiritual link; Spirit will want to work with you and you might not. You must remember, it can be because the Spirit Person sometimes forget you have an earth life to lead, in those circumstances you are the one always in control. You have to tell Spirit in the way of thought or verbally out loud; [speaking to them in that thought within your head is best for most or say it through the mouth, which ever method you feel comfortable with], but say it firmly and politely you do not wish to work at that moment but thank Spirit for coming to you anyway. They might have seen their coming to you as a way of helping you in a situation. It could be in the way of Clairvoyance or Clairaudience they might make their presence known. Perhaps arrange a time to work with Spirit, tell them a time when you know you are going to be receptive to their Link. They will then break the Link for you.

**Remember you are the one who is always in control**.

If the Spirit you work with normally wants to work when you do not, mentally tell them you do not want to work and to go away until you ask for them to come. Saying " Thank you for coming to me at this time but I do not want to work, please come only when I invite you to come and work with me" "I do not want to work now but thank you for the link, let it continue when I request it as I have an earthly life to lead"

## HAUNTING AND POLTERGEISTS

Some people can have a problem with the people in lower level of the vibrational side of Spirit, the lower elementals. As I have said before there are people over the other side that are not of the kind and caring sort of nature most would expect from the higher side of life. Some can cause havoc in the earthly lives of the ordinary person. These could be Spirits that throw things around, cause havoc in the presence of a certain person, or what people call spectres/ghosts/spooks/poltergeists who frighten people, they seem to be an unwanted apparition, a presence of a Spirit on the earth plain in different unlikely, unwanted places. Most are the Spirits of people who have passed over, and do not know they have, or, sometimes can be the Spirit of a person who has no desire to go to the higher level yet, so kicks up a fuss because they are there in the nether regions, not one place or the other and lets everyone know about it.

A lot of the alleged happenings of poltergeists that have been publicised are cause by the people themselves, unhappy teenagers. But what can happen also is for an unwanted Spirit to come close to a teenager going though their upside down months/years of growing up, that is when they can attract the lower levels of Spirit. The nuisance Spirit can be of a mischievous nature around the person, violently moving things, and noise making causing a general disruption around the person. (This could be the teenager becoming a mediumistic person, so study each case separately). These can be unnerving for the person and people near to them. It should be seen in context. Spirit cannot harm you; it is only man that does any real harm to anyone. It could also be a disturbed Spirit trying to get some attention. Look at the one that started Spiritualism in America. Once people know about things and understand how they can happen, they can be controlled by the individual themselves.

To get rid of these happening and/or the unwanted presence of the a poltergeist or apparition, you have to be strong and positive in your motives, sending out a prayer of goodness, kindness and love to send/bring the truthful Light into that Spirit's being, setting up peaceful loving harmony with the higher life in the highest realms. Send out a prayer to help them progress. Tell them they have to look forward to the Divine Light and go into it, for them in Spirit to send out a thought of love and acceptance of their position as they are now. It is only by the person/spirit sending out a thought that they can be helped by the White Brotherhood. The White Brotherhood are there ready for all when the person themselves is ready to be helped, it sometimes needs the Medium or the ordinary person on the earth plain who is being troubled by the unwanted Spirit, for them to persuade the poor, troubled, unhappy Spirit it is time they went forward and not top dwell on the past. They only need to ask through that powerful living energy of thought to progress. The person/Medium talking through prayer and/or a strong thought to the lost soul and it will help them on their way. You have to be firm, positive, kind, sincere, loving, compassionate, and truly care about the lost soul, ask also for the help of the White Brotherhood to be alongside you and the unwanted Spirit. Remembering **it is only the people on the earth plain you have to be careful of; they are the only ones that can do you any harm.** Yes, it could at the time send shivers up your spine and might unnerve you, but nothing bad will happen by confronting the wayward Spirit. Try to talk to it by the means that the Fox sister did if it is a noisy Spirit. Communicate in one of the ways talked about in this book.

Have you ever wondered why the churches, their priest, vicars, ministers, and congregations of the modern religions do not try to find out about the noisy or disruptive Spirit? They never try to contact or communicate with it. Why is this so? Is it because it might be found out that there is intelligence behind the happening? Will it rock the faith they have blindly followed? It always seems strange to me that for people who say we are going to another place after we die, do not put any proof forward each and every day like the Spiritualist movement does.

I think I will tell you of the time when I came across a bad Spirit form who thought it could take me on and win.

I got involved with a beautiful lady with four children of her own I had met at a holiday camp in North Wales. This was while I was there after my divorce and on holiday with my four children. After keeping in touch by phone, I started to go down to see her and her family in Worcester, England. This one night about the third time of going down to Worcester with my children I stayed the night. My children were sent up stairs to bed, as were her children. My lady friend and myself stayed down stairs to talk and for a kiss and a cuddle. Just as she was going to bed she said to me "Would you like the light on pointing to a small tube [about two inches in height]?" I said "why" but she just laughed. I said there was no reason to have it on, as I was not afraid of the dark. With that she went to bed. Half way through the night I was woken up by something grabbing hold of me, getting on top of me and getting a vice like grip of me. I actually saw it objectively. It was like a gargoyle or a critter like thing that the pictures/films now have on them [this was before they had come out on the movies]. I did not know if the thing wanted to shake me, make love to me or squash me to death. I tried to shout but no voice would come out of my mouth, so I calmed down took a deep breath the best way I could. And said in my mind "I am more powerful than you, and you can go as I have an inner strength of love from my God and those from the higher realms of Spirit." Thank goodness it went. I was scared at the time I must admit. I stayed awake for a while then said a few words to those up top in the higher vibrational level who had helped and went to sleep surprisingly relaxed. Next day I said to my lady friend "what was that light and what is in the little cup under it". She switched it on and there was a cross inside that lit up. She said the priest had put some holy water in the cup. And that was all that was said. I said to her, "I know why you have that but it is not doing any good is it?" She just laughed again and did not say any more. She did not enquire, did not say why or anything. I left, never to return to her. The lady told me previously her husband had committed suicide by putting a pipe from the car exhaust to inside the car in their garage while in the British army and I knew that the both of them were Irish catholic. The children of the lady kept on going over to Dublin, in Southern Ireland to her relations and used to come back singing anti-British songs and IRA songs. I do not know if the evil in that house was from her, her husband or the children, but I did not see her any more after that. But there was definite evil there around them.

There are instances when the "Lower Elementals" are not in full control by the Spirit World and they can cause mischief, but it is very rarely harmful to the human race. When this occurs the person should be strong and tell the "Nature Spirits" or "Lower Elementals" to stop playing around and go back to the Spirit World and help do good and not to upset anymore people here on the earth plane. It is a forceful character that is needed, one who knows what they are doing.

# ELECTRONIC VOICE PRODUCTION E.V.P.

I was not going to put anything about this subject in my book, but there seems to be a lot of interest in it and it is very easily done if the conditions are right. Always [well, nearly always] you have to gain a link with the Spirit World first to get the true links, be very wary of other ways, investigate them thoroughly.

All that is needed is for the person who is going to investigate this subject is for them to place a tape recorder in front of themselves and talk to Spirit, requesting an answer, encouraging Spirit to speak to you.

Some try to record while playing white noise off a record. Many have got answers to their questions and information of the after life through this method. A lot of people have gained a lot of comfort from hearing their loved ones come through on the recording. It is a two-way conversation of people talking, one who is on the earth plane and the other/others who is/are across the veil. Many a time there are voices of more than one person on the recording. A lot more voices seem to come in the presence of one particular person, what you might call a recording mediumistic linking person. BUT do not run away with the idea that this is the only way that Spirit can be contacted, there are now people who are receiving messages on their word processor and computer through their word producing programmes. This by the way is without touching the keyboard of the machine.

All these different methods should be tried by each and every one of us. It is of the utmost importance that we all put as much information into the pubic domain, so we all can do our part to show there is definitely life after our so-called death.

This method of contact and every one in this book if done with sincerity, goodness, kindness, love, truth and dedication, will comfort so many people of this world of ours. Yes, you will get the ones who will not have an open mind and others who have blinkers on too, those who are set in their religious ways, but try anyway. Tell those people the Pope in Rome has actually said the church accepts this method of communication, as it does not have the interference of a Medium, so it must be so (what a laugh).

People all over the world are getting in contact with different Spirit people through this method, **BUT** I should point out there **nearly** always (BUT NOT ALWAYS) seems to be a hum or a background noise, sometimes white noise, you have to listen through. Some researchers have told of the Spirit voices saying they have to bounce their own voices against the background noises to have them recorded. The listener should look, or should I say listen for the out of the ordinary rhythm to the background noise. Many is the time during the research, the researcher has had to go over the tapes many times to listen out for a voice. Once the sound has been identified the listener will soon be able to pick out regularly other voices from the white noise or the background hum. There are some computer programmes ("Cool Edit", "Cubase" or any good music editing suite) that can clear this background noise so you can hear those from the World of Spirit better. Some researches are finding they are getting better results from having a strong Healing Medium (or a Medium who can do Physical Phenomena, Materialisation, etc.) in the same room as the recording equipment. Some of the voices come in repeating themselves and they, the voices of Spirit World, for most of the time in the early stages are hesitant and in short bursts. A lot more research should be done by all, as it is a very inexpensive method of research, all it needs is one tape recorder, and of course TIME. Try a few in the room at the same time to increase the odds of recording the voices. Cut out the obvious, always think it is not true then what cannot be explained by any normal means must be true. But then continue to pull it apart again until you are convinced. Always be a knowledgeable sceptic.

One person who did a lot to bring out the Spirit voices that were recorded, to the world at large, was an American called George W Meek from Franklin, North Carolina, who was pulled to pieces by the media (who were and still are mainly controlled by the people in the manmade religions). He realised that higher frequencies might be necessary to contact the other world. He kept recording as much as he could for a very long time. Along with his friend, he actually made a machine called the Spiricom. It should be remembered these men were levelheaded scientists. Meek spent most of his fortune on this research.

After this, there was a great deal of experimentation going on as well in Europe. A Latvian psychologist Dr Konstantin Raudive published his finding in 1968 in Germany under the name of "The Inaudible Becomes Audible" he has done a lot of work on this subject. He also had a book published by Collins called "Breakthrough", an amazing experiment in Electronic Communication with the dead.

There are another two books on this subject I have come across, try to get hold of them if you are interested in E.V.P.

One book is by John G Fuller "The Ghost of 29 Megacycles" ISBN 0-586-06869-4

The other is by Peter Bander "Carry on Talking" SBN 900675

In Peter Bander's book there is a lot said about the churches acceptance of the phenomena of E.V.P. I would like to point out the Church of Rome has now built the worlds biggest infrared telescope to look for the fingerprint of God. THIS WAS A YEAR **AFTER** an article was published in a scientific magazine on how the scientific community was looking for the "fingerprint of life" and where man originally came from. Are the man made religions getting worried? They are looking for something to keep hold of the masses purses.

Quite a lot of Circles I have been hearing about have tape recorders in the middle of them ready to pick up anything that might be said by Spirit, and getting results. It does not mean you cannot record when on your own. So try it in your own comfortable surroundings. Take one into church with you and try to record Spirit voices.

One mediumistic lady after meditating, linking with the Spirit World, talking through thought, records in the quiet of her own house (on her own and with others who want proof of after life), while asking questions a few times, sometimes out loud at other times through thought, then allowing time for the voices to come on the tape, then asks the same questions a few times, allows time for the reply, then asks different questions a few times, she then allows a good bit of time for the reply, she then plays them back, and many a time Spirit voices are there on the tape recording whereas they were not heard by anyone's ears who were there while the tape was recording. This for me is one of the better ways.

There have been scientists who have looked into these recordings and have found sometimes if the tape is played back reversed, even if the noise recorded sounded gobble-dy-gook when played correctly, in other words when playing backwards, there has been a voice being recorded when played back in reverse mode. To hear this form of recording, it is far simpler to use a computer to listen to the reverse the recording than on a cassette recorder as the tape has to be taken apart. It can be fairly easily done on a reel-to-reel tape recorder. BUT it should be warned that mistakes that can occur if using a cassette tape. They can twist in the cassette so anyone recording might think they have recorded voices in reverse mode so be extra careful.

Something that Thomas Edison said in the "Scientific American" in 1920 :-

"If our personality survives, then it is strictly logical or scientific to assume that it retains memory, intellect, other faculties, and knowledge that we acquire on this Earth.

Therefore, if personality exists after what we call death, it is reasonable to conclude that those who leave the Earth would like to communicate with those they have left here.

I am inclined to believe that our personality hereafter will be able to affect matter.

If this reasoning be correct, then, if we can evolve an instrument so delicate as to be affected by our personality as it survives in the next life, such an instrument, when made available, ought to record something".

Please do not go away with the idea the recording of Spirit voices in new. It seems to have started as early as 1855, when an American farmer was given instructions by the Spirit World to build what was called an "Electromagnetic Battery"

Then in 1909 in Brazil the Patent Office received papers to register what was called a "Vocative Telegraph"

In 1910 in Brazil it was reported that a priest, Roberto Landell de Moura was using a box to speak into and from it came voices. He used this for many years it was so well know to his flock, his congregation told other people who asked about it. The information was kept within the quiet community where he worked and lived because of the church rules, and beliefs. They would not have approved of his actions. Was this a radio or a listening device? A Dr Landell invented the radio and patented it in Washington 1904. He called it a "Wave Transmitter"

And so it goes on through this century. In 1911, an electrical machine, a "Dynamistograph", was written about in Holland in a book "Mystery of Death".

Then we come to another phenomena of voices of people who have passed over across the veil, Spirits speaking along the telephone wire to the people who they want to contact. There was a book written about this phenomena by a Brazilian Oscar D'Argonell in 1925, called "Voices from Beyond the Grave".

In 1952 there was a priest Father Gemelli in Italy, who was recording the other priests while they we chanting the Gregorian chant. As he did so, his equipment kept on breaking, he was using a "Magnetophone" a device which records on wire, and that wire kept on breaking He started to get frustrated and mentally he said, "Father help me" (his earthly father had passed away years before) when the recording of the chant was played back, on it came over and above, louder than the chant "Of course I shall help you, I am always with you"

The voice recorders of the time were also being documented being used after this period of time for recording Spirit voices, so there were many books being written about the phenomena.

1956 In the USA some results were reported in the magazine of the "American Society for Psychical Research" this person who was from California, saw the idea being possible to record Spirit voices and he got many voices on his recorder.

Then in the late1950's Friedrich Jurgenson from Sweden started to record Spirit voices on his recording device. But this was done by accident.

He was recording bird song from his window and when playing it back there was a man's voice heard above the bird song. He studied and listened to the recording time and time again. He ruled out all the possibilities of every kind and that of an accident of a recording of the radio. He came to the conclusion it was a message for him alone from someone who had passed over across the veil. This is what every person should be doing when a phenomena of any sort comes to them. That is to check, check and check again. As can be seen people all over the world have tried experimenting with recording machines and some have tried many machines recording at the same time, the same place together. In this instance many times there have been voices on one or very, very occasionally on two machines, BUT, not on them all at the same period of time, this would rule out a person in the room talking and the microphone picking their voice up. This has to be conclusive proof that the voice is not of this world. Should I say it comes out of the air, the vibration is picked up by the recording machine.

If you try to record the voices make sure you dismiss all the possibilities of you making a mistake, **BE A KNOWLEDGEABLE SKEPTIC.**

A thought I want to put into your mind and mull over.

Sound is vibration, if vibration can be recorded out of the air like radio or television. It makes sense that one-day Spirit voices will be able to be talked to, not just in a one-way conversation but a two way this form of communication will be I think when the instruments are invented that are sensitive enough to record thought waves. Remember Spirit communicates through the Medium by thought and the Medium talks to Spirit through thought. It would be nice to one day have a two way; "thought wave machine" "T.W.M." to talk to your loved ones in Spirit like you would on a telephone. I can see that day coming in the not too distant future in the coming centuries when man is ready to accept it, and Spirit is ready to give man the knowledge. As can be seen by all, technology in the field of radio and airwave vibration recording is now developing so fast.

I have found out for people who would like to use the "Scole Group Method" of talking to the Spirit World through a cat's whisker type of radio where they can find "germanium". A cat's whisker radio was a radio used at the turn of the century with no batteries, only a crystal to act on a simple form of speaker while it was vibrating, it was used as a means of picking up radio signals along the air waves. [treble check and be careful to call it Spirit sound] "The Scole Group" used a similarly built device as a means of picking up speech from the Spirit World. Germanium is used as a diode within circuitry in the electronics industry the numbers of the diodes are:- OA90 & OA91. Go down to your local electronics shop. Or buy a monthly electronics magazine from which you will be able find the addresses of suppliers to buy them from.

BUT I must warn people who use this last method, there could be a possibility of picking up outside radio frequencies so check, check and check some more. A method of this sort for recording would be to try and record in a sound proof, light proof box covered in lead, so no outside radio waves could interfere with the recording. Also every piece of electrical equipment can pick up signals of some sort or another. This is why it is imperative to treble check your experiments before saying the messages come from the World of Spirit.

## CHAPTER 1V from Mediumship of Arnold Clare by Harry Edwards pages 47-50
## SÉANCE, JULY 27, 1940 (By William E. Harrison)

PHENOMENA commenced during the playing of the first record, when four trumpets standing on the floor fell to the ground.

Two trumpets were then levitated ceiling high and were whirled about at great speed, performing circular movements, figures of eight and other evolutions. They were also used as batons to beat time to music and tapping on the floor. This continued at frequent intervals throughout the séance.

Mouth organ and small hand-bell, together with two trumpets, were levitated and used together.

Levitation of all objects was particularly good and frequently reached ceiling height some ten feet from the Medium.

VOICES. Small childish voice of child control known as Little Peter (who is the interrogator in the following conversation) greets us with; "Hello, everybody, are you all happy tonight?" Then to a young lad: "Hullo Johnny" (acknowledged by Johnny). Later: "Who bought vegetables today and left them in the shop?"

Lady says: "I did".

Peter says: "Would you like a Marrow?"

"Yes".

"I know where there is one. I'll try and get it".

After a little badinage with other sitters the marrow is brought through the trumpet and placed in the hands of W.E.H. (marrow was about 8 inches long and 3 inches wide).

Peter: "Who likes scent? There's a lot here. Have you got a bath?" all sitters then are freely splashed with perfume and we hear it splashing in the centre of the room.

Peter: "Is anyone wet through? I am sorry if you are drenched, but we couldn't help it".

Peter, later: "I want a man with glasses."

A lady answers: "Yes, he's here next to me."

Peter: "Has he been abroad?"

"Yes"

"Well, he might not recognise this." A bronze image is then passed through trumpet into sitter's hands.

Peter, to another sitter: "would you like a salt spoon?"

"Yes."

Peter: "All right, it's a big one. I'll see if I can get it." After a few moments we hear something rattling in trumpet, which is then put in lady's hand. It is a spoon about four inches long.

Peter: "Where 's the lady who plays the organ? There is someone to talk to you."

Trumpet goes to Mrs A. and a voice (not Little Peter's) says: "God bless you. Give my love to Harry and both the Boys."

This voice claimed to be the brother of Mrs A. by the name of Harold. Harold then gave a personal message, which was acknowledged by Mrs A.

Peter then gave the following messages through trumpet to sitters.

To Mrs R.: "Do you know Elizabeth Mary?"

"Yes"

"Give her, her mother's love—can't get through."

"Who is Emlyn?" "Yes. I know."

"He is here. Wasn't he very fond of cheese? He says it in a funny way." (Mrs R. says it in Welsh.) "Yes, that's it. His head is better now."

Peter, to one of the sitters: "Hello, Kirky" (acknowledged)

To Mrs Hayward: "Your mum's here, and thanks you for the flowers for her birthday" (today).
Peter: "Is there a lady here who works on the railway?"
"Yes"
"There's an old gentleman here with a big beard—says he's your granddad. He can't talk yet, he might later on."
Voice speaks to Mrs P., says he's her son Peter and gives a personal message to his family (understood). Another voice speaks, which says: "Where's Nance?"
"Here!" voice says, "It's Arthur," Gives message to his family, and speaks to his mother and brother (understood).
The Guide, speaking through Medium, asks that light be put on and the Medium given a drink, after which they would continue and endeavour to provide materialised forms. (Circle had been in progress 1 hour and 5 minutes)
On resuming, a figure builds up who is well known to regular sitters as "Peter"---the Chief Control (not the child). His features and beard were seen by all: he speaks in clear voice: "Be of good cheer, do not worry about things. All will be well."
Another figure (not very clear, but who appears to have a heavy, white beard) travels around the circle, but is not definitely recognised. Little Peter says it's the grandfather he spoke of earlier.
The next figure is the young man Arthur, who spoke a little earlier. He came straight to his mother and sister and was recognised.
The last one is a Guide of the Medium, who showed himself to all the sitters very clearly. He gave his name as Abdul and was complete with turban; appeared to be a young, olive-skinned man—an Egyptian. He gave a greeting to all sitters.
A carnation taken from a vase on the shelf is then illuminated by slate and we watch it taken across the room and put in the hand of Mrs L.
Peter now says (through the trumpet) that is all for tonight, says just a few words on need for keeping cheerful and then "Good night, everybody."
A noise of something being lifted across the room is heard, then a blessing, given through the trumpet by a voice known as "Brother Paul", brings the Circle to an end after 1 hour and 40 minutes.
Upon lights going up, it was noticed a heavy fire screen had been moved to the centre of the room and a vase of flowers placed neatly each side.

## SÉANCE, JULY 20, 1940. (By Harry Edwards)
### CHAPTER V in the Mediumship of Arnold Clare pages 50-56

*We, the undersigned, positively declare that we distinctly recognised, beyond all doubt, the materialised form of Jack Webber at a séance on July 20, 1940 (with Mr Arnold Clare as the Medium). The illumination was sufficient to permit our close examination of the features, which were clear, precise and unmistakable.*
*(Signed) W.E.Harrison, E.M.Harrison, Vera Clare, Harry Edwards, Phyllis Edwards, J.B.Webber (Mrs), Gladys Layton, Stanley Croft, M.C. Jackson, G.J.McCulloch.*

The foregoing statement, signed by ten people who knew Jack Webber well, provides yet further outstanding evidence of survival. All the signatories knew Jack Webber intimately and included Mrs Webber, Mr and Mrs Harry Edwards, six members of the late Medium's developing Circle and three other friends of the Balham Psychic Society.
The séance was held by Balham Psychic Research Society through the Mediumship of Mr Arnold Clare on Saturday, July 20, 1940.
The plaque used by Mr Clare in his Mediumship work is of large area and is so brilliantly lit it will illuminate an object four feet away; this plaque was held directly under the chins of the materialised Spirit-People; and, as may be gathered, the faces could be seen distinctly.
The first form to materialise was Peter, one of the Medium's Guides. A western face, with finely chiselled features, a slightly bent nose, and a tawny beard—totally unlike the Medium's face. Peter manifested strongly; and the plaque altered its position to show the face, such as in profile, in differing positions, proving the head was three-dimensional. Against the illumination the form of the body and

shoulders could be distinctly observed. . Jack Webber was the second form to appear. He first showed himself to the sitters on one side of
The Circle only (i.e. to Mrs Clare, Mr Harrison (present of Balham Psychic Society), Mrs Layton and Mrs Webber, in order of Seating). This first appearance was only for a few seconds' duration, and while each person recognised the Medium, not a word was said, for each felt "almost afraid to speak" –as one sitter said. The plaque fell, and a little more time was taken for Jack to build up more strongly. As the plaque rose for the second appearance, Jack showed himself to the other side of the Circle (i.e. Mrs Harrison, myself, Mrs Edwards, Mr Stanley Croft). This time the form remained for nearly two minutes; and the head came within six inches of our faces. Remember, nothing had been said as to who the visitor was. As I saw the face, I recognised Jack; I did not speak at first. I looked again, studying the features well; and only then, after I had coldly and calmly assured myself beyond all doubt that it was Jack, did I acclaim him by name. I said, "It is Jack, most definitely."

The writer noted that the illuminated surface was sufficiently bright to light up the sitters' faces as well as that of Jack; this is indicative of the strength of the light radiation, so strong that the positive statement made in the foregoing declaration can be made with absolute assurance. With this second appearance, the ectoplasmic cowling had receded back over the head, showing Jack's characteristic straight hair brushed well back. (Mr Clare's hair is shortish and rather unruly, and his eyebrows are dark and pronounced, whilst of the visitor were very light as in his physical life). Jack went from our side of the Circle to the opposite side and spoke a few words, the tonal qualities of his voice being clearly recognisable.

Again the plaque went down for a short time for a further strengthening of the form. Then for a third time Jack appeared, now with only a very slight vestige of ectoplasmic cowling, the head standing out clear and sharp.

He travelled around to all sitters within the radius of action, showing himself within a few inches of the sitter's eyes. I suggested to a near-by sitter that he should note the positive shape of forehead, nose and chin, and in response the plaque moved upright to show the whole face and head in profile against the brilliantly lit surface.

An ectoplasmic "cable" was seen connecting back from the manifestation towards the Medium.

I have seen many materialisations, but never before have I seen one so plainly. So much so, that I am prepared to swear by all that I hold sacred that it was our friend Jack who stood before us! No finer or more absolute proof of the truth of survival could be given to us than the return of Jack Webber to his own séance room, to his wife, members of his own Circle and friends.

A second control of the Medium, an Egyptian known as Abdul, next materialised, with a large squarish face the colour of sepia. This head was much larger than the Medium's.

"Little Peter", one of the boy controls of the Medium, showed himself to us, no more than three feet high; and he spoke and laughed with us.

A description of the other phenomena that occurred at this séance now follows.

At the commencement of this sitting, three large trumpets, one 30 inches high, were placed some four feet away from the Medium. As the opening hymn and prayer were proceeded with, the trumpets were in movement, their illuminated bases being easily discernible.

For the following three-quarters of an hour, two and three trumpets were in simultaneous and continuous movement. They synchronised with gramophone music or executed independent actions. They weaved intricate patterns at amazing speed; and although the Circle was fairly large, there was still insufficient room for their complete evolutions. At times, the trumpets were in movements over the heads of the sitters farthest away from the Medium, i.e. eight feet from the Medium to the nearest end of the trumpet. They turned, reversed, joined together three in a row and moved at speed far beyond that attainable by human manipulation; all this in total darkness without hitting a sitter.

During a conversation, conducted by "Little Peter" by means of direct voice through the trumpet, seven coins were apported; six of them very large ones made of copper, of the size of the old five-shilling pieces and weighing nearly one ounce each. All the coins were different, and over a century old.

One of the controls, who assists with the process of apporting, is known as "Simba". A sitter (Mrs Layton) saw him clairvoyantly, and interposed with a description of him. She asked if she had described him truly, commenting on the scar on his head. Immediately came the reply that the description was a true one, and also the information that the scar was caused in the earth life by a lion's claw. The control then said he would endeavour to show one.

Within a minute at most a lion's claw was apported followed by three more. The claws were undressed and had pieces of skin attached to them. [It is pertinent to comment here on the production within so short a time of a stated object following a casual remark. Not only was one claw apported, but four in all.]

Lastly, a solid metal idol, four inches high and weighing a quarter of a pound, was produced and given to the author. Thus nearly a pound of metal, with the coins and the idol, were apported on this occasion.

The procedure during the act of apporting was as follows: The trumpet would first be elevated with its broad end towards the ceiling as if it were searching for the apport, then it would swing and, at times, revolve very quickly; and in this movement the apport would gradually heard to take form, as judged by the strength of the taps and knocks heard within the trumpet. At times apports would follow quickly one after the other. I sat the second seat from the Medium; and I am certain that no person could have moved about to the extent that would have been necessary to manipulate the trumpets and objects in a normal manner. Further, the apporting of lion claws after only a casual remark concerning them must be accepted as evidence of a most significant nature.

We next saw a length of ectoplasmic material, some three to four yards in length, descending in front of the Medium's body, reaching to the floor and stretching out along it as far as the centre of the Circle. Its colour was a murky white, and in appearance it was like a fine quality fabric but without any weaving or pattern—not unlike fine, very thin, whitish rubber sheeting.

With the plaque held about two feet from the floor and shining downwards, we saw the above formation coming down in front of the Medium's body to the floor where it commenced to twist very tightly into rope form, the far end of which twined itself round the small end of a trumpet. Then we saw the end of the rope nearest the Medium used as a point for leverage, elevating itself rigidly on end, lifting the trumpet with it to the height of about a foot before collapsing and falling to the floor.

After a short lapse of time the plaque was on the floor about three feet away from the Medium, lighted side uppermost, when full-length materialised forms approached the area of illumination, Voluminous ectoplasmic material could be seen surrounding the forms like full skirts, the whiteness of them continuing upwards as far as the light could illumine. The heads and faces were out of vision. The forms approached the light in a gliding movement, very slowly, gradually approaching the illumination until they were within an inch or two of the plaque.

Again the plaque was placed on the floor, lighted side uppermost. First talon-like claws, about two inches long, protruded on to the lighted surface. Next, the ectoplasmic material spread over half the plaque in a single layer, almost transparent like a spider's web—no "net" or fabric marks could be seen. Then we saw an amazing thing happen. The indefinite edge of the ectoplasmic material became gently animated, and moved; and small claw-like protuberances emerged, withdrew; and emerged again. Thus we were able to see that the material possessed a degree of "life" sufficient to enable the performance of distinctive actions. The claws were dark, of full density, and their use became apparent with the next operation.

The material was cast over the whole area of the plaque; and, *immediately*, the far edge of the plaque would be grasped and pulled along the floor towards the Medium. After drawing the plaque for a distance, the ectoplasm released its hold and slid over the plaque (*the edge of the ectoplasm being indefinite*). Then the plaque was again gripped and again moved forwards, backwards, and sideways. These actions were repeated several times, and while they were taking place the remainder of the ectoplasm could be seen reaching backwards to the Medium and stretching upwards along his body. The operations took place at the writer's feet and illumination from the plaque was OF sufficient intensity to show that no other agency was responsible for the moving of the plaque. Thus we learn that ectoplasm is sensitive to intelligent control, both "nervous" and "muscular". The sure accuracy with which the fine ectoplasmic material was cast in a single layer just to reach the far edge of the plaque denotes perfect control of the material.

A more definite form of control of the plaque was seen when a small perfectly formed hand shrouded in ectoplasm held one edge of the plaque. The fingers were not talon or skeleton-like, but fully formed as human fingers. The Medium has large hands, with pointed fingers, while the hand we saw was much smaller, plumper and shorter than those of the ordinary human hand.

The séance ended with the gramophone being taken around the Circle; at times, levitated high in the air, playing all the time—the needle never slipped. It was wound up, and the sound box replaced accurately at the commencement of the record. The table on which it had stood next rose in the air and passed around the Circle gently, touching each sitter. This came to rest in the centre of the Circle with the gramophone placed on top; the mechanism was switched off; the sound box turned over to its rest and the case was closed and fastened.

When the light was switched on, the Medium in his chair was seen to have moved forward about three feet from his corner and was close to the table. During these movements not even the slightest sound was heard within the Circle that could be attributed to either the movement of the gramophone, the table or the medium in his chair.

## Séance, November 17, 1940

### CHAPTER V1 By Harry Edwards in Mediumship of Arnold Clare pages 56-70

Report of the sitting with Mr Arnold Clare on Sunday, November 17, 1940, at 30 p.m. at Balham Psychic Research Society.

Commencing from the Medium's right the sitters were: Mrs Hart, myself, Mrs Edwards, Mrs Layton, Mr Hart and Mrs Clare.

This sitting was of an experimental nature, for Mr Clare had not sat for Physical work since August, and it was a not known whether the Mediumship had suffered through in-action. Mr Clare himself was happy in mind but a little apprehensive.

In the centre of the Circle were four trumpets made of celluloid and a small one of aluminium, two large plaques liberally coated with luminous paint, a mouth organ and two small bells. Mrs Clare sat by a portable gramophone on a table between herself and the Medium. Though there were only seven persons present, the seats were spaced out widely so that the diameter of the Circle was between seven and eight feet.

The light was extinguished, and the proceedings commenced with the singing of one verse of the hymn "Nearer, My God to Thee", followed by a prayer from myself and then the Lord's Prayer.

Our fears for the Mediumship (through inactivity as previously mentioned) were soon dispelled; for immediately after the light was switched off and two lines of the hymn sung two trumpets were seen levitated high up in the room near the ceiling, gently swaying in an undulating way in time with the rhythm of the hymn; and so continued throughout the opening proceedings.

After the Lord's Prayer had ended, the trumpets explored the Circle, going from sitter to sitter and high up to the ceiling, making contact with a hanging electric pendant. It has been mentioned that the sitters were some eight feet away from the Medium at one part; yet the trumpets travelled out over their heads beyond the Circle limits; the small ends of the trumpets—that is, those ends nearest the Medium—being at least seven feet away from him.

Throughout the first half of the sitting the trumpet movements were very strong; at times two were weaving intricate patterns at amazing speed, so that the luminous bands around the trumpets appeared like blazes of continuous light (strong wind currents were created by this action); whilst at other times the trumpets would gently caress the faces and bodies of the sitters.

The small aluminium trumpet was used in the first outstanding incident of the sitting. The mouthpiece of this trumpet was barely one-third of an inch in diameter.

In between the changing of the gramophone records we sang a verse of a hymn, and while we were doing so were accompanied by a thin childish voice of the Spirit Control, Little Peter.

I was noting how clearly and distinctly the syllables of each word were being articulated, and my mind was marvelling afresh, as I had often marvelled before, that a Spirit-voice could be so perfectly produced. To my mind this conclusively demonstrated the improbability that any human voice could produce syllables so perfectly through a mouthpiece with such a small aperture.

It was as if in direct response to my thought (*it has been repeatedly observed that responsive action by the Guide or Control follows mental questioning by the sitter and similar incidents are reported by other observers*). That the Guide Peter asked Mr Hart to take hold of the trumpet and wedge something into the small end. This Mr Hart did, by screwing into it a length of handkerchief (about five inches), the remainder of the handkerchief hanging down loosely. So tightly was this screwed into the trumpet's mouth that the latter could be swung by it.

The trumpet was then passed over the illuminated surfaces of the other trumpets on the floor, so that all sitters could clearly see what had been done. The Guide Peter informed us that Little Peter would try to speak through the trumpet with its mouthpiece closed up. I was therefore intensely alert awaiting the effort.

The trumpet then rose in mid-air and Little Peter, first making an ejaculation through the trumpet, then spoke a complete sentence distinctly. To my ear the words definitely appeared to come from the open end of the trumpet—that is, the origin of the words spoken was from within the trumpet.

It is obvious from this experiment that to produce a voice speaking words from within a trumpet with one end sealed up and the other end illuminated and facing the sitters, the mechanism for producing sound waves audible to the human ear must have been situated within the interior of the trumpet itself.

A moment's reflection about this action is worthwhile. A child's voice issued from a metal cone, in mid air, with the small end, effectively sealed, facing the Medium, some four to five feet away from him. The broad end was facing the sitters and illuminated, so that any interference from that end would be immediately observed.

The first general observation is that, under the given circumstances existing at the sitting, the act so performed could not be carried out by human action without it being noticed; and therefore the fact that such an act was performed proves its super normality. And more important still, it proves that survival can be demonstrated by phenomena of this kind. Such evidence rest on the fact that, in the stated conditions, a child's voice spoke a sentence of understandable words with an intelligent meaning and one that could only have been produced by some mind-controlled, non-human, voice mechanism. The thin tonal quality of the voice was totally unlike the masculine notes of the Medium.

To continue with the narrative.

The trumpet then came to myself, suspended in the air, and the Guide Peter asked me to withdraw the handkerchief. I placed my fingers round the handkerchief, just where it entered the trumpet, and held on. The trumpet was then drawn away, pulled free from the handkerchief

I realised that a considerable part of the handkerchief had been inserted into the trumpet by Mr Hart, so, holding the handkerchief at the point where it came out of the trumpet, I tied a knot to indicate the length that had been inserted.

Peter then asked me to place the handkerchief over the trumpet so that it could be returned to Mr Hart, who sat opposite to me. As I did so it slipped off. Immediately the trumpet dipped towards the floor and in an uninterrupted movement secured the handkerchief and carried it across to Mr Hart. The time between the handkerchief leaving my possession and being received by Mr Hart was not more than a second.

As the handkerchief was returned, I said I had tied a knot in it to indicate the length inserted. While speaking, Little Peter chimed in and said he also had tied a knot in the handkerchief; and this proved to be so.

Thereby within the time-space of a second, the handkerchief being in motional the time, including its falling towards the floor and its rescue, another knot was tied. It should be remembered that the broad end of the trumpet over which the handkerchief hung was luminous and visible to our eyes all the time. Under these conditions and within a second of time, a second knot had been tied. I state categorically that it would not have been possible, under such close scrutiny and in such a fragment of time, for any pair of human hands to have tied a second knot.

At the risk of redundancy, I repeat that every sitter on this occasion had had considerable experience of Physical Circles—the novelty had worn off—had active minds trained to observe every action and to observe every gradation of light, critically and analytically, seeking the reason for each movement; and that it would have been absolutely impossible for any human hands to have taken hold of the handkerchief and to have tied the knot in it in the illumination present without it being seen.

This incident, small in itself, is typical of the ingenuity of the Spirit operators, performing new, unrehearsed acts; and so, constantly varying séances of this kind.

When the séance was over, we examined the handkerchief and the knots. I tried to screw the same length of handkerchief into the mouthpiece of the trumpet. I had difficulty in doing so, however, and Mr Hart had to complete the operation up to the knot I had tied. This, of course, shows that the mouth of the trumpet was indeed thoroughly blocked up, further, that it was not possible under given circumstances attending the incident and in the time available (the hanging end of the handkerchief being visible all the time in the luminosity present) for any human agency to have extracted the handkerchief, spoken through the trumpet and reinserted the handkerchief.

Apportation followed, a variety of coins, ten in number, in the way customary with Mr Clare's Mediumship, the same aluminium trumpet being used for this operation.

First the trumpet revolved at great speed in a circular motion high up over the centre of the circle; it then darted to a position about two feet in front of, and three feet above, the head of Mrs Clare; remained there for approximately a second of time; a tinkle was then heard as a coin fell into the trumpet, making its physical presence known. The coin was then directed into the hands of a sitter or hurled with violence to a far corner of the room. The trumpet then returned to the same place and the process was repeated, another coin received, and so on. Once the trumpet came straight to my hands and gave me two coins at the same time. By this means half the coins were apported.

Again the trumpet whirled around at great speed. This time the area for receiving the coins was quite near the floor, and it was from this position that the rest of the coins were similarly received and distributed.

Some observations are pertinent.

The manner in which the trumpet in total darkness finds unerringly and unhesitatingly the hands of the sitters, sitting spaced apart, or hurls the coins across the room without hitting any sitter. This would be an exceedingly difficult, if not impossible, task to carry out by normal action.

The ten coins came in two groups from two areas, one fairly high in the room, the second near the floor.

The coins must have been in a state of ordered suspension, while the trumpet was collecting and delivering the coins in ones and twos.

The coins in suspension were probably in a non-physical state, awaiting their re-translation into a physical state.

The coins were mainly collected singly, though once, as mentioned, I received two at the same time.

The spirit intelligences able to affect this phenomena are able to control the ordered process of re-materialisation and at the same time the distribution of a number of objects apported together in one group.

The intelligences are able to control and regulate the process of changing objects from a non-physical state to a physical state, to hold them in abeyance, and release them as and when they are required.

Owing to a metal trumpet being used, the sound of the coin could be distinctly and clearly heard as it fell (or was re-transformed back into physical shape), helping to establish the fact that from the source of arrival they were collected in a methodical, intelligent manner.

To again interpose, and revert to the argument of those who, while admitting the supernormal nature of psychic phenomena, state it does not necessarily prove survival.

Surely here is evidence of a most complicated (to us) feat of intelligently controlled chemical change. If our scientists were to try to emulate it one can well imagine the extensive laboratories and involved apparatus, which would be necessary. Yet these spirit people are able to produce the act simply, and without, as far as we are aware, the use, as we understand it, of apparatus (*these observations were written before we received Peter's explanation of the process of apporting. The points raised are relative to the subject and do not cut across Peter's statements*).

Apporting means that the form and structure of a given piece of matter, of certain shape and design, is so changed that it can be transferred instantly from place to place, no matter how far those places may be apart. That in its new formation it is superior to climatic conditions and disturbances is evidenced by the fact that if the object retained a semblance of solidity it must be affected by friction in passing through the atmosphere at tremendous speed. Also, it is able to pass through solid barriers, such as walls, with greater ease than sound penetrates, for there is no limit to the thickness or number of thicknesses an apport may pass through. It is directed to the given spot where it is to be reformed into its precise original physical condition, and held there until the moment arrives when it is to be so re-transformed.

All this, happening without any visible mechanism, is surely indicative to the active operation of discarnate minds possessing a knowledge of physics, of which man as yet is totally ignorant.

It is not a "freak" of nature. It is a planned act, carried out regularly and systematically. It can only be the result of applying definite-law-governed forces to matter by an intelligence. As man is totally ignorant of the process involved it cannot be the product of the Medium's subconscious mind, for there neither exists today, nor is there evidence that there ever has existed, any human experience from which any human mind can draw such precise knowledge.

It is futile to dismiss apporting as impossible because we do not understand the way it is done. We have an analogy in our application of radio science to sound. By means of intricate apparatus man is able to take physical sound waves in their precise form of words and syllables or musical notes; change their condition of being into a state of electrical energy; discharge that energy across the world, and at the opposite side receive it by an apparatus that changes it back from electrical energy into physical sound waves, whist retaining the clarity, precision and character of the sounds. A generation of thought has been spent upon the achievement of this modern "miracle". A wealth of experiment, of trial and error has provided the many steps along which man has progressed to accomplish the now commonly performed feat of world radio.

I hesitate again to give expression to the thought, for it is so very hackneyed, yet it is true that this very performance would have been considered absolutely impossible and a dream of the wildest imagination by many scientific minds of a hundred years ago and less. Therefore, is anyone justified in condemning as "impossible" the act of apporting, say, a lion's claw from its physical condition, lying in the African jungle thousands of miles away, transferring it immediately from the jungle to a séance room in London, and there changing it back into its original form? Is anyone justified in such condemnation, any more than the scientist of old who would have discounted the possibility of world radio?

Our difficulty is, that here we are faced with an accomplished act, without our understanding by what means it is performed. Because we, as yet, cannot see the way it is done (there not being any mechanical apparatus to dissect), it would be as short-sighted and as remote from fact to deny that it is possible to do so, as it would be to deny the fact of radio transmission.

A great wealth of thought and knowledge, slowly gained, was necessary to effect radio transmission; and is it not logical to assume that much thought and experience has been expended by discarnate minds in perfecting their knowledge of the *modus operandi* so as to apply the directive control necessary to accomplish an act of apporting? It must be the result of applied intelligence! Whose intelligence? It cannot be man's, for it is still beyond his understanding or performance, as radio transmission was beyond his understanding about 20 years ago. If it is not the mind of man, which carries out the act, whose can it be? It mist be an intelligence, which knows more of the natural laws then we do. It *must be* that of a discarnate entity.

The conclusion must be obvious, that as the act of apporting is performed, so does it prove that survival of man with enhanced opportunities for progression in all things is a reality. On this hypothesis, I suggest that a physical phenomena of this character does prove survival and that there is no other alternative.

To resume with the report of the séance.

I noted that the trumpet movements in front of my wife were characteristic. She was sitting next to me, some eight feet away from the Medium. The trumpet came to her, large end foremost, and then reversed so that the mouth-piece of the trumpet faced her, revolving, as it were, upon a swivel situated near the centre of the trumpet, an action impossible normally to perform without some mechanical appliance. It should be remembered that at this time the floor space within the Circle was occupied by luminous trumpets, and our eyes were above these, so that any form or object superimposing itself over the illuminated surfaces would have been seen.

The phenomena with Mr Clare's Mediumship are usually divided into two parts; the first part, that of the activity already described and the second half with materialisations and ectoplasmic activity. This concluded the first half.

In the second half of the sitting under review, only one materialisation of a head was seen, that of Guide Peter, whose bearded face, aquiline nose and dominant features are described elsewhere in this volume. The face was plainly illuminated by means of the plaque. The plaque then moved from the head downwards, showing the full length of his body shrouded in ectoplasmic material from his head to his feet.

The plaque was then turned over illuminated side uppermost. A white form approached it, gradually coming nearer to the plaque until it stood touching it and showing with clearness the upward stretch of the ectoplasmic material, in a rounded formation, similar to that of a gown. Although it is not possible to estimate correctly the area in square yards of the material in existence at this time, I can say, conservatively, that it was at least five feet high, and many in width (in folds). It must be remembered in the descriptions of ectoplasm, etc., in connection with Mr Clare that the plaque he uses will illuminate clearly to a distance of at least four feet.

A flow of the ectoplasmic material was next cast over the plaque in a single layer. So fine was its nature that against the brilliant luminosity of the plaque it was almost transparent; only becoming more obvious as it creased or rucked-up towards its edge.

A trumpet was next pushed outside the circle between the chairs of my wife and myself, leaving the mouthpiece halfway between our chairs; it was at least eight feet distance from the Medium. The plaque next rose on its side and moved to the trumpet's mouth where ectoplasmic material connected with it. The plaque then travelled back towards the Medium, showing the continuous length, ever broadening as it got nearer to the Medium.

Thus we could see a continuous length of ectoplasmic material stretching from the feet of the Medium to the trumpet. This material did not end at the Medium's feet but rose upwards to the source of the emergence (unknown).

Now the distance between the flow of the material and my feet was only about eighteen inches—and that is a generous estimate (it will be recalled the mouth of the trumpet was alongside my chair). Here is a most noteworthy incident. The plaque moved between the ectoplasm, myself and Mrs Hart, that is within a space of eighteen inches (*see sketch*).

A moment's reflection demonstrates that considering we could see in the illumination the ectoplasm rising upwards to the Medium, and that this same ectoplasm in front of us was clearly illuminated, it is obvious that neither the Medium nor any other person could possibly have passed the plaque between us and the illuminated structure without detection. Just another little incident in which the Mediumship is proved in a more eloquent manner than by that of ropes or other restrictions. In the clear light from the plaque we saw ectoplasm twist tightly, forming a sort of cable. It was rigid. This twisting process occurred within a space of a second, as if the material was animated by thought—as if the material was consciously organising itself into a rigid rod. Then from the fulcrum point (*see sketch*) the rigid ectoplasmic "rod" or "cable" with the trumpet attached rose upwards to an angle of about 60 degrees. The trumpet, weighing 7 ½ ozs., being held in perfect alignment with the rod. It remained so for a second or two, then the whole organisation collapsed. The trumpet fell to the floor, the ectoplasm vanished and the plaque then fell too.

A pressure of at least 3 ½ lbs. is required to lift the trumpet from a fulcrum three feet away from the trumpet mouth.

It is obviously impossible to reconstruct this feat, as described, by normal methods.

Then followed the most outstanding incident of the sitting. The plaque was placed on the floor lighted side uppermost and a stretch of a single piece of the almost transparent ectoplasmic material cast over it, reaching across two-thirds of the plaque. (*see sketch*)

Within and on the material appeared a dark mass, about two inches across and irregular in shape; indeed, its shape was never permanent as it was continuously in movement. To my very close observation—the plaque being at my feet—this opaque mass was not visibly connected to anything: it was like an island. This island effect is vouched for by my wife, but not by other sitters. At this point I would stress that I was intensely alert; and noting this effect I called attention to it, but apparently the activity of the mass so interested the other sitters that my remark was lost in the general descriptions of it being given by them. Yet I am positive that the island effect is correct. The description of what followed is vouched for by all sitters.

First there emerged from the opaque mass two pincer-like claws, quite dark and opaque, about an inch and a quarter long. The ends of the claws were sharply pointed and curved inwards; they were mobile and moved towards and away from each other in a pincer or gripping movement. These claws were visible for about ten seconds. (with faculties braced to observe every detail and action, one is apt to lose a sense of time, it may have been ten or twenty seconds—but I always endeavour to present a conservative estimate—there is no need to exaggerate). (*fig. 4*)

The claws then withdrew and were absorbed into the mass.

Next emerged two formations like finger-tips of a more evolved order, followed by two more; so that there appeared four together just like the first joints of four spatulated fingers—only they were not graded in shape like the fingers of a human hand, but were in line. They tried to grow out, but seemed to fail in the effort and withdrew into the darkness of the island mass. (*fig 6*)

The next emergence was that of two jointed formations—just like fingers, of average length, which moved away from each other at the ends, as if they were joined at the base as in the case of a human hand. These in turn withdrew. (*fig 5*)

It should be noted that while I am describing these as separate incidents, the movements were continuous; the whole mass being active and rarely still.

Lastly, we saw the re-emergence of four finger-tips, which grew outwards and absorbed the whole of the dark mass, showing as an immature hand about the size of a child of eight, except that the fingers were thick, and the ends very broad. We saw the hand, during the two or three seconds that followed, grow to the proportion of a normal hand, quite opaque but covered with web-like ectoplasm. (*fig* 7) it had four fingers and a thumb. The thumb turned to the edge of the plaque, went behind it and the hand then gripped the plaque, bending it over until it closed up, then it opened the plaque again. (This plaque was a piece of stout cardboard) the plaque was then violently folded backwards and forwards and finally was ripped into two pieces. (S*ee Chapter 12 on "Ectoplasm" for further reference to this phenomena*)

Mr Austin, of the Psychic News, and I experimented with the same plaque a few days later; and it was only with difficulty that Mr Austin succeeded in tearing the plaque in a similar manner. This indicates that the hand formed, in the way I have described, possessed considerable strength.

I cannot say at this stage that the hand was not connected to the Medium by an ectoplasmic rod or other means, as part of the hand had left the clear luminosity of the plaque, but never all of it. The fact remains that the hand itself was formed out of ectoplasm, and when finally formed had the power of gripping the plaque, bending it, and subsequently tearing it.

I reassert that all this took place at my feet, that I was bent over observing it as closely and intently as possible. My eyes were not more than thirty inches away from the plaque. My mind was intently alert and I declare that the above record is a true description of what took place. The other sitters were also observing the phenomena keenly and were audibly describing each new change and formation. I was not the only one who saw it, as the following testimonies show.

The final phase of the sitting was the draping of a single stretch of the ectoplasmic material right over the plaque. It came before the eyes of Mrs Hart and myself first. In the beginning, we could not see what we had to observe, there being what appeared to be a shadow in the top left hand corner of the plaque. The rest of the plaque looked just "light" then, by looking into the light, we could see that the whole surface of the surface of the plaque was covered by a single stretch of the ectoplasm. Readers will note that so transparent was its nature that at first we could not see it.

There were no woven or fabric marks, it was as a film or piece of cellophane.

Appreciating the difficulty we were experiencing in observing what we were given to see, the material was either thickened or rippled so that as one looked at it obliquely on could see the ripples, like "watered silk", as Mrs Layton described it. This was passed right round the circle so that each sitter could observe it. (*See further reference to this in Chapter 12 on "Ectoplasm".*)

The plaque, with its covering, returned to Mrs Hart and myself, and gently passed across our faces, touching them as it did so. Thus we were able to feel the material. To my forehead, over which the material passed, it felt quite dry and like a very soft fur. Mrs Layton described it as like chiffon. Each sitter was allowed to experience this as well.

As compared with my experiences of touching and holding ectoplasm with Jack Webber, this material was quite different. It was dry and soft, and, I should judge, of slight density, whereas with Jack Webber, ectoplasm was always wettish to the touch, and of heavy density. At this point I would rather reserve any further expression of opinion, re comparisons, for the following reasons: The material we saw this afternoon was of a very fine texture indeed, which may account for the difference in density. The material had been in existence some considerable time, which may account for the dryness, and in any event, there is a great difference between consciously feeling substance with sensitive finger-tips, in which one has ample time to receive, record and analyse impressions and a fleeting touch to the not so sensitive forehead.

With this the sitting drew to a close, the gramophone, records and table were transferred to the centre of the Circle, the record taken off, the mechanism stopped, the sound-box placed on its rest, the case closed and the clasp fastened, all by spirit agency.

We sang a verse or two of a closing hymn and the Medium returned to normal consciousness.

## Mediumship of Arnold Clare by Harry Edwards pages 71-72
### REPORT ON SÉANCE, NOVEMBER 17, 1940
(By Matthew James Hart)

Among other phenomena such as independent voice, trumpet movements and the apporting of old and foreign coins, there were two outstanding incidents which here describe.

Placed on the floor within the Circle among other things was an aluminium trumpet having a luminous band at its wider end and which was about two and a half inches in diameter. A voice had been received through the trumpet during levitation. It was placed in front of me and I was asked by the voice to block up the small end. This small end was about 3/8 ins., or slightly more in diameter, but certainly not as much as ½ in.

I did this most effectively with a handkerchief by twisting one corner up and inserting it in the small end of the trumpet, turning trumpet and handkerchief in opposite directions until I had forced a third of the latter into the aperture, leaving the other two-thirds hanging loosely.

I held out the trumpet for return and it fell to the floor; but was soon levitated again and the loose end of the handkerchief was shown to the other sitters by drawing it across and holding it in front of the luminous bands of the other trumpets lying on the floor.

The trumpet then rose directly before Mr Edwards and he received evidence of voice despite the fact that the trumpet was blocked. As if this were not sufficient, the trumpet was now given to him so that he could feel how effectively the small end was closed. He was invited to remove the handkerchief. This he did, saying at the time he had tied a knot in it to indicate the length of the part that had been inside.

The handkerchief was taken from him and passed directly back to me (no pause at all), the voice stating, "I have tied another." When the handkerchief reached me there were two knots.

.......

A luminous plaque was on the floor, luminous side up. There were two or three taps on the floor as if made by a shoe; then there appeared on the edge of the luminous surface what at first appeared to be a lady's shoe. What ever this was it is impossible to describe effectively as it was definitely not of the world we know. Not for two seconds together was it still or of a definite shape, but constantly changing. At one moment it seemed to be a small fist, from which emerged talons, short fingers or claws. At another, two claws only, resembling the nippers of a crab. Again it would change and appear as a child's hand. But never at any time was it of quite definite form.

Suddenly, as if to demonstrate the strength present, the plaque was held with one edge resting on the floor whilst pressure on the top edge caused it to bend into almost a semi-cylinder. After this pressure the board was vigorously brushed backwards and forwards on the floor and finally torn across and thrown down.

*NOTE :Mr Hart's description of the formation of the hand is not so definite as mine. The reason for this is that Mr Hart was several feet away, on the opposite side of the circle from me, and the plaque and the formation were at my feet—AUTHOR.*

## BEWARE OF
# "THE MISINFORMED"

Have you listened to people who revel in the fact there is someone there helping them who are unseen yet are described to them. What a self-egotistical set of people they are. We all must have heard something like "I have a Spirit guide who is special and does everything for me, there is no one like him/her". "No other person has one as special as me". "My Indian who is my guide with all his feathers flowing beautifully down his back". Or "My Chinese guide, he has lovely full head of flowing hair, with it plaited at the back it is so black and shiny". Or "my Arab helper with his long flowing gowns done up in a gold rope tie around his waist and a blue one around his head". Forget it!
*

Do not put Spirit on a pedestal, they are only people as they have been on this earth, but have only progressed a little bit forward. I do not mean that all Spirit are not evolved onto a very high plain. Some Spirits have progressed up to higher levels in their learning up to higher vibrational plains. When they reach the levels which are beyond the third-fourth level it is hard for them to come into contact with us here unless they have to have a good reason to return and even then only briefly. Most Spirits that come back to see us or to make contact with us are of the first, second, and a few the third plain visiting Spirits. Beyond that they find it very hard to make contact as they have far more important work to do. To learn more of this subject attend the courses at Stansted Hall with Mallory Stendall. Remember also your helpers/guides will go away from you and another will come in his/her place to help and guide you along the pathway in your Mediumship as you progress and they progress, they also have to move forward in their learning process. Yes love them, admire them, treat them with respect, but remember they are only a person [one of many] who is doing a job of work, a link who is at the forefront of the other helpers who are working in the background. **Please think**. There are another group of workers, up to sixty plus, working to strengthen and hold your link with the other dimension, especially with the specialised

Mediumship, Healing and Physical Phenomena. Spirit always work as a team, **a group thought** when they come through no matter what sort of Mediumship you work with. Do not let the others in Spirit who are there helping you be pushed out through your ignorance

*

Nothing Spirit does when using a Trance Medium in Trance they cannot do when the Medium is in an ordinary state! **WRONG.** To do some of their finer work, Spirit can only use a Medium that has a totally still mind [well as still as possible], that is when the Medium is in **a <u>True</u> Full Trance State (usually a state when the Medium cannot remember anything that has taken place)**. Spirit has to use the physical body of the Medium as a catalyst for those purposes. For example in "Trance Healing" when Psychic Surgery is performed on a patient, and some "Physical Phenomena", **most of Spirit's finest work happens when the Medium is in a state of unconsciousness**. If the Trance Medium were not in a Full Trance State with a still mind, their mind would interfere with Spirits' work and so interrupt it, in some cases stop it all together.

*

When a person is developing [you never stop developing] and then goes away from their gifts of Mediumship, they lose their gifts after a time. **RUBBISH!** (up to a point).

When Spirit works with you. You are educated with that link up to the certain development point where Spirit have reached with you, then you leave it alone for a while and do not practice the gift, you do not forget about it or where you are up to in your development nor do Spirit. Please remember where Spirit is in the higher vibrational level there is no such thing as time.

Think for a moment of yourself learning your alphabet or your maths times table, and you do not use it for a while it is just like that. Do you forget them? You might be a little slower in adding up, a bit more cautious of getting things wrong but you will never lose the adding up or the reading if you have had a good grounding, so it is with your Spirit link. You might be a little bit rusty but all the basics of the link are still retained in your subconscious, it might take you and your helpers a short while to get it together but it is all still there, what also should be remembered there is no such thing as time as we know it for Spirit, time is only a man made thing. You are going to be the only person who slows the process up and that will not be for very long, so do not worry you are only human. Start meditating again and re-establish your link it should not take long if your are positive and sincere.

BUT do not leave certain Mediumship links with Spirit alone for too long as the brain, which links with the chemical making parts of the body and the muscles through electrical impulses if not used regularly those links can die. Spirit will have to build up again the network of links in the brain for the advanced forms of Mediumship, and in some cases of Mental Mediumship can be gone for a long while before they develop again also. Look at the children who have had gifts when they were young, they have to start sitting regularly again when they become an adult if they do not keep up their link with Spirit on a regular basis.

*

Some people have been told they should not sit at home without an experienced Medium otherwise you will get some evil coming into the Circle. **RUBBISH!** The Fox sisters had no one to start them off when the rapping started. They certainly did not have anyone at all who was experienced in their phenomena. It was just Spirit who wanted to make contact. Remember always, like attracts like. If you want goodness sincerely ask Spirit for it and you will get it. I always ask for goodness, kindness, love, truth, for Spirit to come in the Divine Light and within the peaceful loving harmony from of the highest Spirit realm. And **it will come to you if you are sincere in your asking**. If Spirit is going to work with you, they are not going to do anything to frighten or harm you. To develop, sit as much as you can, linking with Spirit in meditation on your own.

*

If a Circle finishes and then after a while starts up again you have to start from scratch, the entire happening will be lost. **RUBBISH! Up to a point.**

When a Circle starts again it only has to have the human part of the equation to gel again, not Spirit. The sitters have to come together as a harmonious unit again. For all the sitters to become as one again, as they did in the Circle when it was going before, to harmonise again with each other. It is just like when a new comer to any Circle has to blend into the peaceful loving harmony of the Circle, so it is when an established Circle breaks then starts up again, the development that was there before has not changed it only has to be re-established by bring the peaceful loving harmony up to scratch, back to the good high loving standard of how it was before. Look at a Medium who goes around to different Circles to demonstrate they sit in another circle of people who perhaps have not sat together or have sat together and they have had nothing happen in the Circle. It is the link with Spirit with the one person that has attracted Spirit to help with the Phenomena.

*

## ANOTHER DAFT STATEMENT!
One blind Medium told a teaching/learning/awareness meeting at my church; "You must not meditate on your own it is dangerous". **How ridiculous,** there must be millions upon millions upon millions of people throughout the world who meditate each day on their own without any side effects what so ever. What does that person think they are doing when they focus their attention on one particular thing? That person more than most sighted people do, must focus on one thing because they are blind, because that is all meditation is, it is **"focused attention"**. They must be doing it more times a day than an average sighted person does. I had to set the record straight again on that occasion. Meditating on your own is the best way to regularly build up the power for your spiritual development. Nearly every nun, monk and eastern holy person throughout the world I have read about meditates on their own regularly. Some go into the mountains and stay isolated for many years, meditating on their own ¾ of their time there, being at one with God the Divine Spirit, in oneness, blending their own Spirit with the higher vibrational level of Spirit.

*

## ANOTHER CRAZY STATEMENT!
My friend used to go to a Circle and she started getting headaches she was told to stop otherwise she would get a brain tumour. **ABSOLUTE RUBBISH !**

Look at all of your own body and compare it as such. What happens if you exercise your legs walking or running when you have not used them for a while. The following day they are all stiff and sore. It is exactly the same with you inside your head.

When you go sitting in a Circle to develop, you are beginning to use/exercise and develop parts of your brain, which have not been used or developed for a great many years if ever. It is only another part of your body reacting the same way as your legs do.

All that needs to be done in your development is for you to have a little more rest than normal, drink more water and keep on going doing things little and often. You should do more and more exercise each time until your undeveloped parts stop hurting and are more easily able cope with those parts then tell your inner self that you can take on more work without the need to give you pain.

The reason you drink more water and should do so before and whilst sitting in any Circle as and when you feel it is necessary, is the brain is one of the parts of your body that gets starved of liquid earlier than other parts. The drink of water also puts back into your body the liquid being used by Spirit. A lot of Mediums get dehydrated when working with Spirit. If the working Medium did not drink their glass of water when they felt thirsty they would get dehydrated also possibly get a headache. Do not worry it does not last. I know many years ago I was getting headaches while I was in a Development Circle, I am alright now.

*

## YET ANOTHER
Another Medium after taking a church teaching/learning/awareness night, speaking to a lady friend of mine about meditating, who was asking for better ways of developing her gift, my friend said she meditated in bed and found it was the easiest time and the best way for her. Now was finding that she was developing very fast, the Medium was shocked at what she was doing and said to my friend, "Do not meditate in your bed because if you do and you could fall asleep you might not come back and could die", **absolutely ridiculous!** That Medium must not have any faith at all in Spirit, another stupid statement that could have put that new person off meditating all together if I had not been there to counter that damaging, dangerous statement.

I personally in my prayers each night, give permission to Spirit to develop me in the best ways possible in my learning when I am asleep, bringing only goodness, kindness, love, truth, within the Divine Light of Spirit, within the peaceful loving harmony of Spirit of the highest realms, I then ask for a good nights restful replenishing sleep, I always wake up refreshed.

While on a course at Stansted in November 2001 I was woken up early in the morning while it was still dark by someone talking in my room. I opened my eyes to see who it was, only to realise it was me being used by Spirit for voice production. It was not my voice that was coming through me, the voice was coming from my stomach area but out of my mouth as it was being manipulated I let them carry on, me being half asleep. I gave permission for them to carry on. Then I was knocked out again. Next day I was fully refreshed but did not remember what they were saying through me during the night. But at least I remembered the incident. These different things that have happened to me throughout my learning, I definitely believe they have been put in my pathways of learning, so each and everyone who reads this book can learn from them and not be afraid if any of the things that I went through come to the Budding Medium whilst learning.

\*

## ANOTHER

I was personally told by a Medium I should not meditate in a cabinet on my own as it is dangerous, I should not meditate in my room for Physical Phenomena on my own it is dangerous. At the time I was trying to build up the power, sitting ½ to 1 hour twice a day in the room I had put aside for Spirit prior to having a Physical Circle start a few months later, not trying to bring forth Spirit on my own. Yet another Medium that must not have had very much faith in the higher realms. But what I thought of later was, like attracts like; what was she afraid of?

Whilst I am sitting on my own I offer myself as an open vessel to be used as a stronger link with Spirit getting ready for the task to come and to be used in the best way possible making me a better, more able link blending with Spirit, bringing no harm to me, bringing in only goodness, kindness, truth and love within the peaceful loving harmony of Spirit from the highest realms. If Spirit is going to work with you they are not going to allow any harm come to you or put anything into your surroundings that will put fear into you.

As you progress you will possibly find as I have and many other people have also found. Those of the higher realm seem to only give you and show you things as and when you are ready for them and in ways that you can best handle what is given to you in your mind. I have heard of one Medium in the North West [I was told about him by a very respected member of the church] that used to sit for Physical Phenomena on his own, bringing Spirit into full bodily earthly view, he used to walk in the garden in Southport talking to his Spirit friends in full view of the world for everyone to see; he started getting complaints off the neighbours about all the visitors and strangers he had calling to the house and garden. Little did they know! Now **"that"** is what I call a powerful Link with Spirit.

\*

## AND ANOTHER

**Yet another misinformed Medium**. This was allegedly an experienced Medium who stayed at Dorothy Tyrer's house in the 40's. The Mediums of the day when they served the Liverpool church used to stay with Stan and Dorothy Tyrer. One of the many Mediums who stayed at her house at that time when she was very new to Spiritualism, said to her after she was talking about a Circle on the previous weekend. The Mediums said, "If you are in a Rescue Circle you will end up putting your head in the gas oven". She turned around to that Medium who incidentally had never sat in a Rescue Circle and said "You have been in Spiritualism all these years and this is your way of helping me". "You must not have very much faith in Spirit to say that to me". "It is a good job I have faith in spirit".

As Dorothy said and says to this day, "If you are going to work with Spirit, they are going to make sure that no harm ever comes to you". He went away to think about the words of that very much younger lady, he found out more about **R'HELP**/Rescue Circles, he ended up putting more of his time aside to helping others in the World of Spirit.

\*

## ANOTHER

The best way to meditate is to stare into a candle flame in the dark. **RUBBISH!** This is one way you can damage your eyes. If you want to go blind try this method, it helps. What happens to you when the light reflects from the snow into your eyes? It can give you snow blindness. This is exactly what can happen to you when you stare into any bright light. Candlelight might not put out a lot of brightness in the daylight but put it into a dark room and your eyes take in the only source of light and so it gets concentrated, so giving you pains behind the eyes [photophobia], you get the same effect from a very quick look into an arc welding light. I got the same effect when I was working on and polishing new cars under fluorescent lighting at the Ford factory for four years. So do not do it. I also saw the effect of it in a beautiful young lady at our church. Her eye surrounds were completely black and she had terrible head pains at the back of her eyes through trying this method each night. I do not know if she had weak eyes but be warned.

\*

## YET ANOTHER

Another thing that should be taken into consideration when a person tells you in a development circle you have to be upright when sitting in meditation for development, because if you are not, it blocks your energy points/chakra [meaning if you have your head relaxed on your chest] and a person is not doing the meditation the correct way if they lay down. **RUBBISH!** Look at the photographs of old, when the Mediums were in Trance, they had their heads relaxed on their chest and it was natural. If you have your head upright your neck muscles have to be taut to keep it that way. This by the way was before all the modernism and trying to find a new quick way of progressing, and all this about power points/chakras came into Spiritualism. The older Mediums at the start of Spiritualism were a lot more powerful then and there were a lot more true Mediums than there are now. So who is right? You have to be relaxed and passive if you want to have a strong link with Spirit. **THINK!** Your body does not have to be sitting or upright. If that were the case the people in Australia would not be able to link with Spirit the same as Europe or other parts of the world, yet they do. Some people are more bodily bent over that others, some of the older generation have their heads bent over yet are still fantastic Mediums. In other words it does not matter what angle your body is in, Spirit will link if they want to; if it is their will.

*

## AND ANOTHER

A Medium that came to an awareness teach-in told the people there you should not sit in more than one Circle a week. **HOW RIDICULOUS!** If you want to progress and gain as many different gifts of Mediumship you can sit in as many Circle as is comfortable for you. The days in the past, Mediums used to sit each night in their different Home Circles. At the time it was classed as party games with no TV and for Sundays it was a day of rest because they were involved with their own churches [this is before the Spiritualist movement/church was founded]. I suppose that is the reason they were far more experienced, better links, and had many more different gifts of Mediumship not just one. By the way this was a person who had been in Spiritualism since he was 17 and was now 50-ish he said to me after that, he had a Circle and he was also was sitting for Automatic Writing. He made another comment :- "It was amazing that the older Mediums of the last century had a lot more mediumistic powers than people of this century" don't these people ever stop to think. Down at Stansted where he said he had been many times, if you go down there. You will sit in a Circle a lot more than once in a Circle during the week's stay. The tutors down there sometimes sit in **different** Circles during a week, they do definitely sit in quite a few **different** Circles throughout the year, look at the time tables of the year's course. The tutors are no different than you or I. Many of the tutors after sitting in the Circle at Stansted Hall go home to sit in their own Home Circles as well. Some church Mediums sit in a church Development Circle and their own Home Circles a few times a week, that is no different. The main thing is to take into consideration is yourself and your ability to not get too tired, not to over do things. If you do over do things one week, have a rest, a break, not doing anything then continue at a slower pace, one that suits you. When sitting in most Circles you should come out refreshed, good to be alive, better in yourself, in peaceful loving harmony with all there.

When the Mediums of the last century were sitting for their development, they sat each evening for hours in each other's houses, different houses. They did not have T.V. to watch or distract them. This was their fireside fun. This was for them a worthwhile pursuit, and most of the people developed quickly. Are you going to put in that dedication they had? and put in that sort of time? Because if you want it, it is certainly there to be had. If of course it is the will of Spirit.

*

## AND ANOTHER

People who should know better have said to me "Spirit knows what you want and when you need it. Just let them do things for you, you don't have to ask it comes automatic for you". **WRONG**. If you do not ask you do not get. Remember to always sincerely ask within your mind with your thoughts. Yes ask Spirit. Until you ask Spirit for something, they cannot do anything without your request. It is the Divine Law. They cannot intervene on your behalf **until you ask** them, neither can they help you **until you ask**, nor can they know at a particular time in your development what you require until you let them know, they will then do their best. Spirit might know what is best for you, but they cannot know what you want help with nor help with development in what field of Mediumship until you ask and give them permission to help. It might be impossible for you to attain it, but they will steer you along another path some how, one that is best for you, yes, always sincerely ask for their help then you will receive it in one way or another.

\*
## AND ANOTHER
When you are developing you should be only trying to get one gift of Mediumship at a time. **AGAIN WRONG**. Think of yourself at school and if you were learning one subject at a time. You would not learn any other subject because you cannot learn everything of even one subject, neither can you become an expert of it, no matter how small a subject it is. **Think about it!** This is why the old Mediums of the past were such a diverse lot and many of them had many different skills of Mediumship, a lot had them nearly all. This was only by experimenting with all the gifts of Mediumship. Remembering you never stop learning no matter what gift of Mediumship you get blessed with. You only have to put set times aside during the week for the different Mediumship skills but try not to mix the times, that is all. You always ask Spirit through thought at the start of the session for the gift you want to develop.

\*
## YET ANOTHER ONE
I had a phone call from a friend who was on a course with a person who was going around saying "If you do not use the correct Infra Red camera you will fry the Medium". **Another ridiculous statement.** I have yet to hear of any ordinary person of the public being fried by any of the infrared camera lighting systems (unless placed very near a person as they are a heat source of lighting). Never mind the very, very low output of my four cameras. And lets face it, Mediums are only an ordinary person with no special sensitive skin that lets Infra Red waves permeate through to their inner or outer parts and cook them. **Lets please have some common sense.**

Remember the farmers use infrared lighting for rearing pigs [and pigs can suffer easily from sun or heat stroke] and poultry as it is a lighting tube with a filament that produces a wavelength of a heat source and very little light as we can see, these are of a wattage of 100-250 watts. Of course you will get burnt if you get too close to any heat source but the cameras use a very, very low output in each single light emitting diode LED each is sending out about 75 milli-watts for the camera to pick up an image, each camera generally has about six making the output of 470 milli-watts depending on the LED's. As you can see a very stupid, ill thought out statement being banded about.

The year before, I had taken my four Infrared cameras to the same place were this person had taken his camera, which was at Hafan-y-Coed in Abercraf, South Wales. In the séance room there in every Circle that I sat in and the ones I did not (I allowed the use of my Infra Red cameras) because of the good harmony within each Circle sitting there was always plenty of Spirit Lights or as I call them **"KEELIGHTS"** (because I believe they are the **key** to another vibrational dimension) on the VCR recordings while the Circle was sitting and when the room was empty. I still have the recordings.

By the way this person had his own Infra Red camera with him at the time and got very little results with it and no Spirit Lights/**"KEELIGHTS"** or any images of dust reflection in the cameras. Make your own mind up about what his angle for saying this statement was. I was told and it was said in the **Psychic News** he was supposed to be an electronics expert, but there again I am not. What do I know? I am not an expert nor do I claim to be one, I only solder my own electronic equipment together to make it work.

\*
## AND ANOTHER
You cannot sit for Transfiguration or any sort of Physical Phenomena on your own, you have you sit in Circles to have the power to do it. These people who make these statements should read all they can in the older books of the last century. The Mediums of the time used to sit on their own practising and meditating whilst linking with Spirit for all the development of phenomena no matter what it was. They would sit in the morning, afternoon and the evenings, and when the Circles were planned with others. They were mainly held in the evenings (some Circles were held during the day though, especially with the housewives and still take place today all over the country). People of that era had more time to spend away from the not yet invented technology the dreaded, all invasive, society altering, time wasting, propaganda machine called T.V.

I think people now make an excuse for not having time to sit for the linking with Spirit.

I have been told you cannot sit on your own for transfiguration as there is no one there to bring your results to, (meaning the manipulation of the face changing it from my own to the person in Spirit). There is no one for Spirit to link with. It is a waste of time for Spirit. Who on earth are they linking with when they come through me? I sit in front of a video camera on red light, go into trance, give permission for Spirit to develop me, and then I try to still my mind as much as possible. It is no use trying to sit on your own in front of a mirror as your mind is still active and you are influencing the outcome of the Transfiguration, in my opinion you are only fooling yourself that Spirit is manipulating the facial muscles. When I go into Trance my brain waves are in Theta, Alpha/Theta and lower Alpha most of the time and I know that because I have been tested by a doctor and my blood pressure was at 164 over 154 [form my normal 117 over 70] my breathing and pulse also slowed. This has been only achieved by sitting on my own regularly for the past five-six years and previously sitting in Circles since the 70's helping others to develop their link. Only take notice of people **who can to it**, what ever **"IT"** is. **If you cannot do it, you cannot know IT!**

I was taking a course in Hafan-y-Coed in 2003 most of the people were beginners and through taking my advise of getting their link first by talking to Spirit through thought for about a quarter of an hour before anything else whilst having their eyes closed, then stilling the mind as much as possible by looking into the third eye area into the void, the colour or the light, to allow Spirit to do what ever they wished. Most in that group started to have things happen to their faces. Yes most were manipulated by Spirit even though they had not had anything done to them before.

Spirit can work with the Medium in Mental Mediumship and Physical Mediumship at the same time. WRONG. At the same course at Hafan-y-Coed a developing Medium was in an altered state and Spirit was building a thin moustache on her top lip, which every person in the group saw. We even moved the red light forward to disprove that it was a shadow on her face. We also moved the light when people in the group got up and went to see the moustache from about a foot away from her face. Of course making very sure they did not touch or knock her. One of my other students ran a Home Circle in which this developing Medium was in and she said the developing Medium was going to speak. I did not want her to at that moment as the group was sitting for physical, BUT this lady thought she knew the lady best, so I let this Home Circle leader take over and she asked the developing Medium to say something. As soon as she opened her mouth to speak the words given by Spirit the moustache vanished. Remember she was still in that altered state but more aware. [perhaps in later years the strength of her link with Spirit might become so strong that both might happen without the physical phenomena disappearing but only time will tell]. That group was just one of the most harmonious groups I have taken, many are not so harmonious and they wonder why they do not get results.

Spirit still has to practise to get the links correct. This is whether you link for Mental Mediumship or Physical Mediumship. Would a person who is trying to develop their Mental Mediumship ever think of **NOT** sitting in meditation on their own? or **NOT** Linking with Spirit and asking for their development to progress whilst on their own? of course they wouldn't. Why should it be any different for Physical Mediumship? Spirit is not going to harm you if they are going to use you as an open vessel (or their instrument) to prove there is life after our so-called death. OK ! it might take a little longer to develop on your own but surely you are going to be a stronger person being used by going along that route, you can always sit in Circles as well for extra development. BUT PLEASE sit on your own developing your link with Spirit, you sometimes find out a lot of home truths whist meditating on your own when you cannot get your mind slowed down to the lower level for a deep Trance. PRACTICE, PRACTICE, PRACTICE and then PRACTICE AGAIN, **sorry there is no easy method. Only meditation, meditation, meditation, meditation, and that is** within love, harmony, dedication, sincerity, and that precious commodity **YOUR OWN TIME.**

# A FEW THOUGHTS FOR YOU TO PONDER

### HERE ARE A FEW PAGES THAT SHOULD BE READ AGAIN AT DIFFERENT TIMES OVER THE YEARS.

A saying I heard the other day was the definition of a Spiritualist, and to my mind it is very true of most Spiritualists, well me at least. **"A Spiritualist is an informed sceptic, a person who never stops enquiring, one who always has an open mind, and not wearing blinkers".** Unfortunately many of the people around that I know and those I see all around me wear blinkers. Sadly perhaps, they see but do not want to believe what they see. Many a person has a closed mind. Are you one of them?

*

Whilst living on this earth we all should realise that as you think, as you are. What you do here and now, the steps you take and the thoughts you have while you are here on this side of the veil will control and create the heaven or hell you will make for yourself when you eventually cross to the other side of the veil, when you pass over to the higher vibrational level of existence.

*

**Why, OH!, Why,** are there so many people who are in Spiritualism so jealous of other people's gifts.?

*

**Why, Oh! Why,** are there so many people in Spiritualism who back bite?

*

Why does God not heal all people who are ill rather than use a healer? Is it so we can learn from all adversity and all that goes on throughout our lives on the earth plain?

*

Why does Spirit not always give us a straight answer to all the questions we ask of them? Is it because we have to find the answers for ourselves as we progress?

*

A very profound statement that Andrew Jackson Davies made was "if you ask a question, you have the answer within yourself".

*

Mediums sit in Circles to come closer to those in Spirit and progress by being passive. Spirit uses the body of the Medium as a vessel. Mediums in this state drink a lot of water whilst working or not in a Circle. We are told by Spirit, the blood thickens because of the draining of the liquid in the human body. Is this the reason why many Mediums have high blood pressure after their Physical Circles? Is this the reason Helen Duncan naturally was drawn to whisky as her drink? (Her ectoplasm smelt of whisky). For whisky is a blood thinner; as is aspirin.

We are all made of approximately 90%-95% of water, yes mainly water with chemicals floating around in it, I do not know the exact quantity. Could it be helpful for the Physical Circles [or indeed any Circle] to help their Mediums, and possibly to help make it a safer practice for Mediums by having a bowl of water in the room with minerals, elements, vitamins, a mixture of chemical compounds in it that Spirit could use in the partial manufacture of ectoplasm, taking whatever is needed from the bowl mixture so perhaps taking the strain off the Medium's body? Could it help? It sounds logical to me. But I would change the water regularly as chemicals change their properties when mixed in water over a period of time. Perhaps a start could be made by dissolving multi-vitamin tablets in the water or get the ingredients that are on the label from the chemist/drug store not forgetting the trace elements, zinc, iron, magnesium, etc as well. Perhaps multi-vitamin tablets on their own in the raw state placed in the Circle, or would that be too strong without the water? Remember that nettle leaves [for nettle tea] have the most trace elements in them; they are very rich in vitamins and minerals. Nettle tea is used for anaemia and a blood tonic, look in the Culpeper's Colour Herbal book. This book is said by many to be the herbalist's bible. The book has colour plates to identify the plants and the old uses of the herbs according to Culpeper, and the modern uses of them as well.

*

Do you think it would make sense to have a bowl of different fresh fruits and vegetables in the room where the Physical Circle was being held as the vitamin C in our bodies does not stay in it for very long so if there was any depletion of vitamin C in the Mediums body, could Spirit use it out of the fruit and vegetables in the bowl? They use other sitters in the Circle room to build up ectoplasm, if the correct blend is not enough from the Medium, so why not? I say mixed fruit and vegetables in bowl because the fruit and vegetables grown in different areas and soils have in them different liquids, which have in them different trace elements, minerals and vitamins. Would that be best in the Circle especially a Physical Circle? The fruit and vegetables could be still eaten after any Circle as Spirit always replaces the (most) elements taken out of the Medium and the sitters, so it should be the same for the fruit. BUT it is still unwise I feel, to eat the skins of the fruit of unknown origin, as they are now sprayed with chemicals to stop them deteriorating quickly and so give them longer shelf lives in the shops. A lot of the physical Circles have flowers in their Circle room, keep up the practice and have the flowers for your household after the Circle.

*

Farmers are producing extra food for their population and it is having to be stored and sometimes destroyed. Why don't the rich nations give the food to the poor countries? Why don't we go back to producing food as we used to naturally, organically? With crop rotation. That way we would not produce too much and have to store it and waste the excess.

*

Is it possible that we are getting arthritis because we are eating chicken and other meat animals with chemicals that they feed them while growing? These chemicals are used in animal feed to put as much flesh on the carcass of the animal as possible at the expense of the building up of their bones, **yes,** the chemicals fed to the animals restricts the production of the bones. Is the residue of the chemicals still in the meats of the animals that have made the animal produce mainly meat and less bone? Especially in chicken where this sort of chemical is used a lot. Getting arthritis that way sounds about right to me, as well as osteoporosis.
*
The gillie [a man servant, a sort of gamekeeper, one who looks after the sports people who hunt and fish on large estates in Scotland] John Brown had the confidence of Queen Victoria for many years. Talking to her about the afterlife when her husband Prince Albert died. The reason being was for her to keep in touch with her husband Prince Albert who was in Spirit. Lots of people have thought it was a gamekeeper, landlady love affair, you now can hopefully see it was much more than that. Yes, John Brown put his friend Mr Slone the Medium in touch with Queen Victoria to help to bring through Prince Albert with the help of Mr Slone's Spirit Control. When placed in a situation like John Brown would you have the integrity to hold your tongue? I hope you would.
*
Does homeopathy work on the vibrational imprints of the medicine to the water given to the patient, the same as the way Spirit and the Medium does when working with psychometry?
*
There are a lot of people who hear voices in their mind naturally. If those people go to the doctors with this natural way of linking into Spirit, the doctors lock them up in a mental institute. Budding Mediums have to try and receive those voices from Spirit, with Spirit's help of tuning the mind into their wavelengths of vibration, while the trainee Medium sits in meditation. I have often wondered why the Spiritualist movement has not gone to the mental institutes and contacted the doctors, and talked to them about the people they have locked up because they think hearing voices in the head is madness, a Mental illness, all being drugged up them are turned into walking zombies. Are those people afraid of being classed as being mad, or unstable? How many natural Mediums are locked up in institutes for the insane?
*
In the 14th century the Catholic Christian church came up with another moneymaking scam. Any person could buy their way to a smoother path to heaven, by purchasing a **"letter of indulgence"** from a priest. Any person who had money could do this, even if they had killed, raped, stolen goods, committed adultery, any sin what so ever. The priest of the church guaranteed their sins to be forgiven by their church; this was supposed to be on behalf of their God. And so it goes on today in the churches, but in a slightly different way. **HOW SAD.**
*
Our trainers say we must talk to Spirit to help us get a better link with Spirit to try and draw them closer, I accept that fully. But what I do not accept is :- after you have asked Spirit for your link then try to still your mind to go deeper into Trance; is for you to talk to help Spirit to talk through your vocal cords. HOW CAN YOU TALK AND HAVE A STILL MIND? (Spirit needs a still or nearly still mind to draw closer) Your mind comes into play when using your voice. You have to think to say any words out of your vocal cords with your **own voice**.
Nor can I accept that you start talking to help Spirit to use your body functions, this for me is bringing into the equation your own mind
Nor do I accept one trainer's advice to act as though I am the Spirit person who is talking through me while in Trance. This trainer said if the Spirit passed as a hunch back; act as a hunchback, if a Spirit passed as a singer act as a singer. This is using your mind again, for me as I see it, contaminating your Spirit link. This is for me only fooling yourself and the public who will in the end find you out, then they will try to ridicule you and the movement. I cannot see how people can say they are in full Trance with a still mind that gives Spirit full control of the Medium and yet they are able to act and think what has to be done. A Medium in Trance either has a still mind or they have not. For me this person was and I think still is, an inspirational Medium. Look how a Medium works. He is inspired by Spirit.
*
No person can be psychic all the hours of the day. Do you tell the truth when you do not receive any messages from Spirit for your enquirer? Or Do you make them up to make you feel good?
*
When the pupil is ready the teacher will be there.

*

The master will mould the pupil, if they let them. The master will mould the pupil, if they are a good, kind, and caring a one. A good master keeps on teaching until they the pupil is better than the master, even then they are there for them until the end.
*

Do you look at your own failings, your own faults? Do you ever look at yourself, before you pick on others?
*

You will never know a person until you walk a mile or two in their shoes. I say ten miles or a full month but even then you will not know them fully. It is like a relationship you have to live with a person before you know them. Who can ever look into another person's mind and know only those of a high spiritual development on the other side of the veil? I know no person on this earth is able, nor will they be able to truly know what goes on inside another person's brain in the way of thought.
*

It is nearly always as children that a good foundation is laid. If they are unruly, fight and squabble all the time without a person, generally an adult, setting boundaries for them to work within as a guidance then society will be become tainted with nastiness pulling others down to their level so bringing the good in society down to a lower level.

Very rarely do people try to bring themselves up to a better standard. It far easier and less hassle for a person to lower their standard in life than make the effort to raise the standard. Don't believe me look at the estates that are around. If a person who has had a good upbringing goes onto a bad estate, the children of those parents will very rarely have success in maintaining their standard while on the estate. They are in the main brought down to a lower level. The others do not get brought up to the good people's standard. It takes a great effort to keep a set standard that is why they slip. They in the end cannot be bothered, just as the others cannot. So it is with spiritual development it is harder to maintain your development and progress. It takes effort on your part, it is easier to let it slide or not do it at all.
*

Lying, cheating, stealing, and killing will lead to disaster for people perpetrating it. These things will isolate them from their fellow man in this life and the next. That is until they learn. Then they will be able to progress.

If a cheat in this earthly life dies, they go to a place where all the cheats are and then they will not be able to trust anyone. The same goes for all the others. Murderers/killers go into a place where there are only murderers/killers. Liars go to a place where there are only liars. Again like attracts like until they learn to look into the light and be spiritually part of it.
*

One thing probably not of much interest to many people but I thought it is worth a mention, just for the child like of us, like me. The Red Indians of North America/Canada have a nice little custom, one of many. They make a "dream catcher" it is a ring with light cotton or wool across it in the form of a net; it can be decorated with tassels and small feathers tangling from each side. The parent of a child says a prayer to the higher life with the child to let all the bad dreams be caught in the dream catcher and give them a restful sleep, the child hangs up the ring with a netting to catch the bad dreams [or nightmares] of the child during the night so they do not disturb them in their restful sleep. The child then in the morning hangs it out in the sun or in a window or in the air by the door for mother nature [the good Spirits] to clear out all the badness from the dream catcher ready for the next night just in case any more strong [medicine] protection for the sleeping child is needed.
*

What I was told by a Native American (a red Indian Chief "Wananechee"). When the white man came onto the American continent if the Native American, "The Indian" did not embrace Christianity they had first had their fingers cut off then if they still did not they had their hands cut off, then if they still refused they had their feet cut off this was certainly hushed up and should be publicised.
*

The larger countries of the world are giving growth hormones to their animals that are banned in different parts of the sensible world. Look at the people in those countries and see how tall and very over weight or obese they seem to be getting. Are those chemicals still in the meats of those animals? Sounds right to me. Don't let big companies who own our governments push us all into something we do not want. Think about our future generations. Think about the unnatural things that could be happening within our bodies with these unnatural over supplied growth hormones

*

Bacon used to be salted and left to cure over a period of months. That bacon used to be able to be hung out in the air cupboards for months on end and still be safely eaten. What happens to our bacon now? It is injected with salt water which makes it swell it does not help it to keep for more than a few weeks without it being covered with maggots, yes I have seen them even in sealed packets. When you cook the modern bacon it shrinks into nothing because of all the water that has been pumped into it. They call it progress. Look at the frozen foods you buy how much has water injected into it? Have you ever left a frozen item to defrost and looked at the water that comes off? Do see what you are paying for?
*

We are now told that plants have an electrical nervous system. Are the vegetarians going to stop eating them? We are now also told the plants have feeling as they respond to stroking and touching by growing better. Also plants grow better if they are talked to in a good happy tone of voice. If you shout or scold the plants all the time they do not do at all well, yes they have feelings. Are all you vegetarians going to stop eating fruit and vegetables?

Meat eaters kill their meat humanely. Do vegetarians not understand they eat the vegetables, and salads whilst they are still alive, and vegetable are cut and harvested they must be still suffering days later? It is best not to think too much of things we eat. It is only natural for us to eat everything.
*

90% of fruit and vegetable crops throughout the world are getting sprayed with chemicals. Some crops in the poorer countries are still getting sprayed with chemicals that have been banned in the western world and by the World Health Authorities.

I think it is because the chemical companies, warehouses, and distribution companies have had very large stocks that have had to be got rid of and the companies have had to recover the costs of building the plants. OR Are they still producing those chemicals?
*

Have you looked at the salad crops and wondered how they stay on the shelf so long without wilting?
*

Have you looked at a shop bought lettuce and wondered what the pink chemical is on the stalk's base?
*

Have you looked at the fruit to see how shiny and smooth they are wondering how they get them so?
*

What has puzzled me for a great many years since I have been thinking deeply is: Why do the peoples of the world in the remote parts of the world naturally sit in circles together joining with others; as one; in "oneness" with the higher life of God they worship; yet we in the Western educated parts, supposedly knowledgeable (are not) parts of the world, sit to worship in rows pointing to an altar or a direction away from the togetherness of each and everyone who is there with us? Are we not in the West "backward" in what we do? Should we not go back to "ONENESS" with others, ourselves and GOD? Should we not start again sitting in Circles when we worship?
*

Have you tasted the coating that is on the skins of apples and wondered what chemical it is that the apple is coated with to make it last on the shelves in the shops and taste funny? They taste waxy. Is it doing us harm? It is a chemical that is not needed, except for cosmetic reasons.
*

A lot of the crops are being grown on soil that has been poisoned by chemicals over the many years. Those crops absorb those chemicals. Are you eating them?

How are the farmers who use the chemical sprays on plants going to stop the plants from absorbing the chemical, WE are going to eat that food. Plants absorb any chemicals that are in the soil by the water they drink. Plants cannot say, "I won't drink this certain chemical in this water."
*

Many farmers for the production of our food are using chemicals. In so doing over the years they are ruining the natural soil structure.

When the farmer is reliant on the chemicals and not putting any good rotting vegetable matter goodness back into the soil to build up the many, many, many diverse microbe and insect life that fight each other, live on each other and fight disease and live on plant disease, living and dying as a community in the soil making plants better as they grow using the materials that the soil community has produced and left in the soil, they are destroying the soil by using only chemical fertilisers. The farmers who use chemicals do not let the crops they grow, pick up or absorb from the soils all the very wide range of nutrients, minerals, and vitamins we should be getting from the plants we eat. "Is this the reason for all the diseases we are getting?" "Is this the reason for all the cancers we are getting?" Are we getting cancers from the crops and the foodstuff fed to the animals that are laden with man made impurities?

*

Some farmers are destroying the nourishment of what we eat, and destroying the soil it is grown in. So destroying our planet around us.

*

I know of two old Mediums who were very ill. One in Liverpool who was riddled with arthritis walked double and her hands were very bent. When she went up on the rostrum in the churches to work with Spirit all her ailment went. As soon as her link with Spirit went, she was back to her normal arthritic self. When the other old lady from Manchester who was ill, lots thought at the time she was ready to pass away, was helped upon the church rostrum she became lively and her old self as soon as her link with Spirit was broken she was her old ill self. It makes me think and I hope you also. Why could Spirit not keep them well like they were on the church rostrum all the time? What a wonderful power Spirit has when needed. Did they have no full trust in Spirit to keep them well all the time? Had they never asked for the help for themselves? These and many questions I should have asked of them when they were alive. I personally believe they could not stay like that, because the link with Spirit was gained in an altered state of awareness that could not be sustained for the everyday life that they belonged to. It would not be possible to go about life as they were doing throughout the ordinary days in a dream like state.

*

Nice simple explanatory phrase from Spirit through the Medium Arnold Clare, "As your mind demands so can the Spirit satisfy; but we cannot progress one step with our teaching until you are able to receive" see Part two

*

Don't let us be railroaded by big business into their way of thinking, which is in most cases the destruction of the natural ways of the earth for the sake of quick monetary profit. Natural might be slower but it has worked for many hundreds of millions of years and nature has had time to adjust to its way of working.

*

The ordinary person who uses the wood from the forests should plant many saplings or tree seeds to replace each one cut down so they can help preserve the woodland for future generations. Three seeds for the mammals who eat the seeds, three seeds for the insects to eat in seed form, three seeds to rot and go back into the ground as tree food, three saplings to be eaten as they grow into maturity by insects and animals, three saplings to be use by man as they grow, three saplings left to possibly grow into full grown trees.

Why don't the governments of the world pay people to plant more trees as they cut the mature ones down? Surely this would make sense for the economy of their own country and the whole world in the long run.

It should be remembered the trees and bushes are the main lifeblood of the planet as we know it, as is all plant life. They all supply the oxygen, passing it out of their leaves and themselves as a whole, we breathe that oxygen in, we all need it to survive. The trees breath in the carbon dioxide we breathe out, and produce from our factories. They are our earth's filtering system. They also hold the soil together binding it within their roots on hillsides stopping most landslides and soil erosion. All the sides of the motorways should be planted with trees for cropping and helping the planet breathe.

*

The idiotic Government of England paid the farmers to grub out the hedgerows of our countryside, which kept the wildlife at a balance that could control the pests of the farmer's crops. Now they are paying farmers to replace the hedgerows. What kind of people do we employ to look after our welfare? Again messing with the natural ways of nature.

*

An idiot of a government official in China told all the people to kill all the sparrows and finches because they were eating the seeds of the crops. The following harvest the insects killed the whole crop and there was nothing left for the local population. He was sent to prison; imagine if our officials were subjected to that sort of punishment there would be not one politician left in our parliament.

*

People are using slug pellets to kill the slugs and snails in their gardens. Slugs and snails work and live on eating vegetation, and have to produce mucus to get over and through the soil. I have always thought and I have seen that worms worked on the same principle. Worms go through the soil eating dead

vegetation and using their mucus to slide through the soil. In my opinion, if you put down slug killing pellets [made out of dead vegetation and poison] on your garden, you kill the lifeblood of the soil **the worms**, so be very careful, worms are very good at dying. They kill other insects as well, HOW or WHEN or WHERE are you going to use slug pellets?
*

I have a worry about the Genetically Modified foods that we might eat the reason being is :- Scientists are growing G. M. food crops that does not get killed by herbicides [weed killers] but they are sprayed all over the field in which they are grown by the farmers.
*

What happens to the herbicide on the leaves, does the plant absorb it like it is by the weeds? Is it drawn up from the soil into the plant like the weeds do? Plants cannot differentiate between good or bad things for us humans or the poisons they ingest.
WE EAT THOSE CROPS.
Also there are no long term tests done on them and their effects on us remembering they cannot be easily reversed if ever, when started.
Scientists are growing G.M. foods that are resistant to pests by putting the gene of snowdrops into our food crops so they are resistant to insects and bacteria. If the snowdrop gene kills the insects, WHY is it so different not to harm us? Remember we are full of bacteria keeping us going, they are only minute insects to me. They are in our stomach, in our blood, in our gut to digest our food. What is going to happen to the food there? Is it going to be resistant to our "insects" and upset them and so upset the balance of our metabolism?
*

I myself believe, a time will come when man will have to destroy the things he has made, to bring back the earth plane to a place where the humans can begin to live their proper normal lives again. The trouble will be that many of the parts of the worlds ecological system if not all, will have been lost forever to stupid mankind.
*

The farmers most certainly will have to go back to the older methods of food production in the near future. The putting back what he took out of the ground and from the land in the first place. Using the time proven way of farming a mixed farm with arable, and animal production as well as rotation of crops and grazing on the land.
I WILL ALWAYS REMEMBER paraquat many years ago when herbicides first came out. They were the modern weed killer and they were used by many a gardener and hailed by the chemical companies as the wonder answer to our problems of weeds. We all trusted the chemical companies to tell us the truth. We, us gardeners were told that when a herbicide hit the soil it was neutralised and could do no harm to anything. Now we are told that the herbicides are getting into our water after it had gone through the soil into the water table because of the over use by the council workers and farmers. What happened to the herbicide being neutralised? REMEMBER there is no known cure for herbicide poisoning [especially paraquat] it destroys the liver and kidneys as far as we are told, what else I do not know. Are we now going to eat herbicide in our sprayed Genetically Modified food? Remember, to date, the water companies **are not testing** our water **for PARAQUAT**
*

Have you ever thought of your margarine that you eat? It starts out as a flowing oil whether it is sunflower, olive, corn, rape, in fact any oil which runs freely. You know how margarine looks, are chemicals added and is it chemically changed to make it thicken?
How much of the chemical agent is left unused in the margarine ready to change your bodily oils or fats and thicken them?
"Or"
Does the chemical agent in the margarine still have the ability to change your body fat or oils that you eat into a thickened blob? Perhaps it has turned your body into a thickening blob. Do you eat a lot of margarine instead of natural butter? Ask yourselves.
My doctor told me that there are a lot more medical problems documented in the Lancet [the doctors medical paper] through people eating too much margarine than there are of people with problems through eating butter.
It makes you think doesn't it?
*

Is the reason there is so much cancer and killer diseases in us humans these days because of the many different chemicals we are subjected to in our food and water in our everyday lives?

*

Is it the food that we eat? Is it the unnatural, harmful chemicals in the foods we eat?

*

Is it that we absorb many killer chemicals out of the air through our skin and into our airways to our lungs? **WHEN WILL IT ALL STOP?????**

*

Probably only when we and our planet are dead.

*

Everyone has the God given talent to use and help everyone and everything living on this planet, BUT, each and every individual has to make it work by drawing on their own strength of their Spirit within, with the help of those helpers on the other side of life across the veil within the loving harmony of the highest realms of Spirit, and with the help of GOD the Divine Light and Power, each person can bring that talent to the fore and make it work for the benefit of other living things and themselves.

*

I would like to say here how many times have you taken a person's [say Joe] opinion of another person [say Fred], and then found out that you have been completely wrong about that person [Fred] because of the label put on them, maybe the person [Joe] did not like the other person [Fred] or they had a grievance against them. Please find out about anyone for yourself before you make a judgement.

*

Do you criticise others around you? Next time before you open your mouth to call another person for what they have done, look deeply into the mirror at yourself, look truthfully within at what you do, <u>then</u> criticise.

*

Why did God make a rainbow, it serves no purpose? Was it to lift us up when times in our life are low?

*

For those who believe no words are necessary, for those who do not believe, no words are possible.

*

People over a great many years have had their fingers tips on the planchette, also at other times the upturned glass when doing the spelling out in a Circle. I have heard of upturned glasses exploding. Is this too much energy in it having no hole for the energy to escape? I would only use an upturned glass if it was riding on a planchette with a hole in it, try it, make one for yourself to use when using the spelling out board to get the planchette moving when speaking out, requesting out loud, over and over again the questions they require answering.

*

WHY don't we say out loud our needs/requests? We are told that Spirit works on vibrations, Because of that we use singing in the Physical Circle to raise the vibration level so Spirit can come in closer? Is this a way to get a better link, a more powerful link? REMEMBER **Thoughts are vibrations of a higher level !!!!!!**

*

Also people use their fingertips on a table and the requests are said out loud, then the table with the help of Spirit Power starts to move around, make tilt and possibly dance. Why is it not the way of the newly re-discovered energy to use the dome? Why is not the way of developing a person in a Development Circle?

*

Could not each person at the start of the Energy circle put their fingers on the dome while asking the people upstairs their requests? Would that work? BUT I am told not. The Scole group tells us we should not touch the glass dome otherwise it discharges the energy to earth. STRANGE!!!!!

*

Could each person in the Development Circle not put their hands on the person to be developed, perhaps their head or body whilst asking up stairs [those in Spirit] for the person to be developed? Would that bring quicker results for that person? Would that work? Or would it be too powerful?

*

Have you ever tried lifting a seated person with only two fingers, your index fingers with help of another person; they also only use their index fingers? NO? All you have to do is place one hand on head of the person seated. The other person places their hand on your hand on the seated person's head, then you place the other hand on their hand on the head, they then place their hand on top of your hand [so you have your hand, their hand, your hand, their hand], press slightly down while saying over and over again [about seven to ten times] "we will lift this person up with our fingers, we are going to do it" and really concentrate on it believing it, asking for the help to do it, saying the words "will" and "are" more definite. Then immediately place your fingers under the chair and lift. YES it does happen.

*

I wonder whether the Egyptians lifted their big blocks of stone like that to build the pyramids. What do you think?
Is it possible?
Did they put their hands on top of each other on the blocks of stone then lift them?
Did the Egyptians have the help of Spirit to move the large blocks of stone?
If Spirit can make a person and a chair appear weightless and levitate, why not a large block of stone?
**Or**
Did they all get around the blocks of stone, put their hands on each block, ask from above for help and it came just as today people move tables or levitate them in a Physical Circle?
It is said faith will move mountains! I wonder. Did the saying come from that? The making of the pyramids. To some they are as big as mountains. Can faith move blocks of sandstone? I do not see why not.

*

Have you had a problem of insects? If you have, start linking into them within your mind, try asking within your mind with that **all powerful energy of thought** for them to move to another place because if they stay you will put poison down and they will die, BUT have a safe place for them to go to and with that thought you send out to them, direct them to that safe place, IT WILL SURPRISE YOU. When you are developing, try talking to animals through thought to find out what they are going through. If healing, ask them through thought what are their problems, it will surprise you. BUT ask with **sincerity** after linking with the Spirit World.

*

The more frequently [and longer] you sit in a Circle the earlier you will develop. The longer you sit in the power at one sitting in meditation the quicker you will progress by yourself or in any Circle, EXPERIMENT YOURSELF and know the truth

*

When Spirit comes through a Trance Medium do not believe everything that they say as though it is law. It is only their personal opinion. The opinion of the collective thoughts of their group, remembering there are other groups of thought up there in the higher vibration level also you do not know how much that Spirit or it's group has progressed in the higher level. If they do not know the answer to a question, the Spirit Communicator will generally have to go and ask their mentor for the answer. If he/she does not know they will go to the halls of learning where the knowledge is there for all and give the answer to the best of their ability to you the next time you sit in the Trance Circle with the Trance Medium.

*

The higher vibrational life of Spirit work on a thought level. [The living energy again]. What ever you want your life up in the higher level to be, so it can be up to a point you think it. If you want a nice house, bungalow it is there for you, you think it. If you want a meal of fish and chips it is there for you, you think it. Remembering you have no need for food as we know it here. This is what we are told. Get your questions ready for the DEEP Trance Medium next time you see one demonstrating.

*

Do you think when saying your prayers?
Do you say them automatic?
Do you say the words that you have said for many moons, asking for the higher life to look after the people you want them to help, saying your prayers in a parrot like fashion?
OR
Do you look into your mind, seeing the people as you ask for the help you want for them?
Try to do your best for them within your mind. BE SINCERE.
STOP, PAUSE AND **DELIBERATELY THINK** [as you say your words to the Divine Spirit] OF THAT PERSON AT EACH PRAYER FOR EACH PERSON, THINKING OF THEM!
It is a living energy of your thought that will be helping them. Sometimes I must admit, I slip and then have to pull myself back, I am only human.

*

A little something that should make you take notice. This was a message, a thought that I will always remember, one that was given to me by a very well respected older member of the church's congregation when I was at the start the upward slope of learning, thankfully it has always stuck in my mind.

Many years ago a very well known healing Medium in the U.S.A. who had done a great deal of very good healing work for people with the help of Spirit. He had a daughter who was ill for a very, very short while, then suddenly died. Distraught he asked Spirit "why after all the years of doing healing work for Spirit had my daughter died?" "Why did Spirit let her die so young?"; the Medium asked. The reply came back to him, which told him everything. "We did not know because you never asked for our help nor were we asked to heal". That person had assumed that Spirit would help and never asked for himself, **a BIG point to remember. DO NOT FORGET YOURSELF AND YOUR NEEDS TELL SPIRIT WHAT YOU WANT.** How do Spirit know what you want until you tell them? Remember to ask for your own personal needs in the way of learning, in fact anything at all that you would require from Spirit they are only a thought away [thought that living energy].

*

Keep that link open with the thoughts, your own thoughts that you give out to Spirit as I say upstairs [or to Spirit beyond the veil].

*

I believe in my heart that the two-way link to upstairs [those in the Spirit World], the other dimension will come through a machine built by man to become a regular link with them, but only when we are ready for it. I believe in the not too distant future all the man made moneymaking religions throughout the world will be found out for what they are. Those religions that are all for the wealth, the trappings, all for themselves within that religion, excluding all who do not believe in that religion, and their leaders who tend to be all power mad, getting people killed, some causing wars in the name of their religion because they do not believe in the other person's particular religion. Their leaders getting all the very best of food and material things for them alone to enjoy. Never giving back to the people who matter; the poor ordinary everyday person, they are told each person within the religion [except the higher up people] should suffer to find a higher place in their particular religion, especially when they die. **THINK ABOUT IT!** Don't believe it? **PLEASE PROVE ME WRONG.**

*

A book to read is the one that Harry Boddington wrote called "Materialisation" it has some photographs of Materialisation in it. Try and also read the book "Human Personality and Its Survival of Bodily Death" by F.W.H. Myers {1834-1901} These two are classics. Leslie Flint's book Voices in the Dark, makes a nice read also.

*

Have you ever smelt the breath of a person who has eaten garlic when you have not? You cannot mistake the smell. Now try breaking a garlic bulb and rubbing it on the foot of a person who has not eaten any garlic for a week. Smell their breath first, then a half to one hour [maybe before] after smell their breath, YES you can smell the garlic. It has been absorbed by the skin and passed through the whole of the person's system. Chemical companies try telling us their emissions from their plants/factories do not affect us from out of the air. The toxins that industry pumps out into the air we breath can also be absorbed from out of the air through our skin and kill us, never mind breathing it in. **THINK ABOUT IT LOGICALLY!**

*

When you talk to people about your experiences and the things others have experienced they cannot really and truly know what it was like. You must realise to experience reality; it is only the individual that can do **"it"**. No other person can fully show or tell others how or what **"it"** is. The individual has to experience that reality. I can explain all about **"it"**, all that I know to you. It is only when you have tried **"it"** out that you can know about **"it"**, "That then for you becomes reality". BUT is it the same reality as I had experienced? I cannot know neither can you.

**"It"**, "reality" might be totally different for me when I experience **"it"**, than from the experience that you have when you try **"it"**. The individuality of a person in this life comes into the equation again, also the mind of the individual comes into the equation as well, for no other person can see into the mind of another, nor can they sense the senses of another person, neither can they feel the feelings of another.

This is the reason no person should force any other human being to follow a religion [or something] that they have only read about and not experienced. Neither should any other person stop another human following whatever religion [or something] on this earth plain that they have not had full experience of.

*

Most of the religions of the individual regions of the world had reason for it springing up, evolving in that area, perhaps comforting the peoples when it started. As it progressed, that small isolated religion evolved their own individual rules, which protected the peoples of the area. It protected the surrounding area as well for those people. Teaching love, understanding, and caring of their fellow man, it taught the love, care, conservation, and protection of their surroundings. All was well.

What happened when others tried to force their beliefs onto another? The power trip, control of what they believed was best. The Christian religion that the intruders followed and forced onto their captors was best !!!! and their materialism (gold) came into the equation. It started wars of power and greed. Look at the North and South American Indians, they only killed for what they needed to survive on, then the white man came along and they killed for greed and wiped out the buffalo, which was the mainstay of the North American Indian. The white man killed the native Indians classing them as savages because they did not believe in Christianity and did not live as they did. Who were really the savages? The North and South American Indians of both continents had a religion, which was good for them and their country, it was a survival mechanism. This is what went on throughout the world NOT JUST AMERICA through the unsympathetic Christian missionaries thinking they knew what was best for each country. Don't believe it? **PLEASE PROVE ME WRONG.**

*

Why do almost all humans aim for higher spiritual development in ourselves?

*

Is it taught to us by our elders?
Or
Is it in us all from the start of our lives from the day we were born, natural?
Think about it! I am not going to put any answers here for you.
**ALWAYS REMEMBER** If you ask a question the answer is within yourself.

*

There are many routes to the summit, many trails up a mountain, many a track that can be trodden to your God. Please try to understand the ways of the gentle, kindly peoples of the world and do not try to change their ways. They might be on a kinder, a truer, quicker, honest, easier, more rewarding, sincere, loving pathway than the one you are treading. Forget about their colour, their background, their disability, their looks, their dress, accept each person no matter who, for what they are, as they are, and say to yourself I can learn from them.

Pick out their good points and let them grow within yourself

You are then at the start of one pathway of life to the summit.

Perhaps; if you have the eyes to see; you will then learn from both bad things and good things around. Look at bad things in someone, which you can accept and put them aside as being so in the person. Do you leave them as they are? You could look for/at the good in them and try and build up on those good things, praise the person perhaps/hopefully copy the goodness. If you can recognise things in yourself as them being a reflection of yourself, you might try to alter the badness within yourself. Perhaps point out their bad habits to the person and give reasons for it BUT do not impose your will on them. The alteration of their badness has to come from them within themselves, for themselves, and by themselves. Try to see the many good points in a person and complement them on it as much as possible after telling about the badness, only tell them once about their bad points. That way they are left with goodness in their mind not the badness you have pointed out to them at FIRST. The more you complement a person on their good points, the more the good points come to the fore. You will certainly find the person likes the complements more than the badness being pointed out to them, and then hopefully they will build on their goodness, multiplying it, making themselves a better person.

*

If you see good in others try to complement them on it, accept it as being part of that person, but most importantly, try to take part of that goodness into yourself, copy it if you can, and then try to improve on it for yourself so others can give you complements on that goodness you have started by yourself, within yourself, for yourself. So by doing that you will feel a lot, lot, lot better on the inside within yourself. Then you have your own outward appearance a lot better for all in the world around you to see. Never look for complements, do any good things for others around you for your own satisfaction you WILL feel better inside and it will show on the outside to others that way you will be always be riding on a high. You will be able to dismiss all the nastiness, jealousy, bitterness and anger that are around in the

world. So seeing it as that individual person's problem. Learn from each problem in life. Make each learning situation a positive part of your life.
*
There are many ways of looking at a situation that is correct. Try to see other people's point of view. Put yourself in another's position and try to think what you would have done in that circumstance.
*
Do not try to be two people, be true to yourself. Remember thought and power of it. "You are what you think you are", and "others will see you as the way you think you are", let it always be good, kind, happy, truthful, sincere and loving.
*
Do you love yourself? I do not mean "an I love me attitude". "Not, a being big headed about yourself attitude" Because you should love yourself, the inner self of you. What you are inside. The self that others see you as. If you do not, and you don't like what you see inwardly, how can others around you love you at all? You have to stop, think, and look inside yourself to really see what you are like. Try it and see what others see. Is it all to your liking? If you do not like what you see. Try starting today; try to change yourself for the better.
*
Complements always make a person feel better about themselves. Each day make a point of complementing someone, anyone at all you come across during the day, it will help the world to be a better place with happier people in it, all feeling better about themselves, happy to be alive. Goodness and happiness overcomes [triumphs over] badness and sadness. You try to be unhappy in the presence of happy people they always make you smile and feel better. Look at a notice, which says, "Smile and feel better NOW". All you have to do is to smile and **you do feel better**, so make one for yourself and put the notice somewhere you will see it every day. I have mine at the bottom of the stairs to remind myself. Put a notice by the telephone **"SMILE"** to remind you to smile when you use the telephone. It is amazing how much difference it makes to your voice and your own conversation to the other person when you are smiling. If you try to continue being bad or sad when there is all goodness and happiness around you, you will feel like an outcast all alone. "Do you want to stay like a sad outcast", or "do you want to belong among the goodness and happiness".
*
Put into your mind each morning "I will give out complements and be sincere to all I see today, this is to make them happy and to feel better about themselves. I will give out complements at the very least twenty times today and every day no matter who it is to and be sincere about it". It does not have to be to the same person. By doing this it will put you on a good feeling trip and the people will like you more. Everyone needs building up sometimes. Do you know what? It makes you feel good about yourself when you do give out complements.
*
Call people young lady, young man. If they say they are old [over thirty/forty], say they are younger than their age perhaps say they only look twenty three and a bit something like that. Younger people like to look older, complement them on growing up into a nice person. Complement people on the way they dress, what they have got on that day. Complement them on their hair, look for that person's good points. Complement them on their choice of plants in the garden, their garden, furniture in their home, decoration of the home, anything nice you can think of. Make your fellow man/woman feel good in themselves. Every person enjoys a complement; it always makes a person feel good about themselves.
You are showing you care, and have taken notice when others might not have done so. A little bit of kindness goes a very long way. Remember the pendulum of life, "what you give out comes back to you ten fold".
*
You are what you think you are and others will see you in that way, so let it always be happy, good, kind, sincere and full of the joys of life.
*
When you have young people who see, feel, or hear Spirit, treat them with kindness and understanding. Let them know spirit are there around them only to help and watch over them. Spirit will not do any harm to them and cannot hurt them. Teach the child to learn to love the Divine Spirit, nurture their precious gift, help it grow. Some people might try to suppress their natural gifts because of what they have been told by the bigots in the churches, whether you/they like it or not those children are the future

Mediums, the Links with Spirit for the future. Let them know it is only the people on this earth who can harm them, so don't let yourself be that sort of a person, don't become one of them.

*

Why don't we go to the true deep Trance Mediums to find out where we are going wrong with our development? That is what the older Mediums of the last century use to do; they took the advice off Spirit through the Medium and then continued along the direction that was advised by Spirit. But on thinking about it, where are they all? I mean the **true DEEP** Trance Mediums, those who have complete trust in Spirit and a link so strong that they can produce Physical while in that deep Trance.

*

A lady was looking after a very small child of a neighbour. Having been told by the child's mother of the "imaginary friend" of this child and how he/she plays with him/her all the time. The neighbour asked the child how did she/he talk to the friend. The child looked at the neighbour in a manner, which said everything [are you stupid] "I talk with my think". In other words that child thought it was normal for her/him to talk to the imaginary friend in the way of thought, in the mind, it was so natural he/she thought everyone did it, and thought the neighbour was thick/dumb for not knowing how it was done. We all had the ability to do it at one time, some stronger than others it was probably suppressed within us because of society and it's dogma. Sad isn't it?

*

I was told of a healer who kept her cut flower preserved for at least twelve years. This she did by cupping the flower in her hands each day until it was in a petrified state. The flower stayed like that with no loss of colour, and no petal loss. Why don't you try it yourself with the help of those upstairs? Those helpers in the unseen World of Spirit.

*

A person said to me the other day "I cannot alter the past". I looked at them and asked them to think a minute because that statement to me did not make sense. I had to explain to them they were making the past now here in the present. I said to them "What you have just done now less than a minute ago, less than a second ago, has now gone into the past". "You are making the past **now**".

*

So you and every person in the world should always be thinking of the things they are doing **now**! Making sure it is always good at the present so it goes into the past as good, that way you as an individual have altered the past just by altering your own way of doing things in the present, yes you have altered the past. Think about it!

*

Another thing that was said to me by a friend just recently. "I do not like the person I have just met they are nasty about others, always moaning, always angry and bitter". I said to them "personally I think you should feel sorry for that person, you can walk away from them, start doing something nice with pleasant people who you love to be with and enjoy the rest of your day not thinking of the sad unfortunate person". "That poor person who you do not like has to put up with their own company all day and all night and cannot get away from themselves". "Think about it and then if you want to, as you should". "Send some loving thoughts out to them to try and change the way they look at life". "Then next time you meet that poor unhappy person have nice words to say to them". "Perhaps they are feeling unloved". "Make them feel better and you will in yourself for doing it".

*

Don't you think it is strange that all the faiths of the world teach there is life after death, our lives continue? Yet they try to stop their followers from finding out about it and do everything in their power to try and stop their flock from proving it. Don't you think the people in those religions must be so insecure about their teachings. **OR** is it that they know their teachings won't hold water when fully examined? The set religions also will not allow other faiths to preach to their own congregations or in their churches. What are they all afraid of? Are they afraid their congregation will go over to the others that preach another way of reaching GOD?

*

Spiritualism is one of the only religions who at each of their services the chair person or the platform Medium/speaker tries to prove and most times does prove there is life after death yet the western religions of the world do their utmost to try and condemn the faith, how sad.

*

If your family told you that your granddad had said a particular statement or alleged exact wording on a day 70 years previously before his death would you believe it as a statement of fact? I know, if a friend tells me a message after a fortnight from a person that I have known for a while and they have got that message off another person which was past on to someone else, it is not going to be accurate to the exact wording. People can forget about some words of a message over a period of time even as little as one hour. That message given by another to another is either going to be exaggerated to get attention for that person or toned down to that person's belief of what should have been said. **YET! YET!** most of the religions of the world are based on the writings of people who put down as supposed fact! Alleged exact words or alleged statements of their prophets, or messiahs from which their whole religion is base on. People have written down words and statements as though their particular prophet or messiah has given that particular message as their own words to follow. In those days there were not tape recorders, neither stenographers to record the exact wording.

**WOULD YOU BELIEVE THE WORDS OF YOUR DEAD GREAT GRANDDAD BEING PAST ON BY YOUR MOTHER AS BEING EXACT, A FACT?**

**SHOULD YOU BELIEVE THE WORDS OF YOUR DEAD HOLY MAN AS FACT?**

**Or worse STILL !        DO YOU NOW?**

Let me put into context.
*
If your relations had told you your great, great, great, great, granddad had said a certain number of statements three hundred years ago?
Would you believe it as fact and then gone along with the exact wording which had been passed on by word of mouth? That is what these man made religions would have you believe. Fairy stories written hundreds of years after the death of the alleged Messiahs. **VERY** clever men over time wrote these books. I am not saying the Messiahs might not have lived **BUT** to hang on every word it seems to me ridiculous. Remembering the books of these religions have been altered many, many times over the many years by man, to suit man. Don't believe it? **PLEASE** PROVE ME WRONG.
*
Why do intelligent people fall for all the sales talk of the money grabbing religions that benefit only the higher up within those religions? Please think! It is in my opinion alright for each individual church to collect their rent money, maintenance money, money for the upkeep of their individual church **BUT** it all goes wrong when the church starts to collect for icons, statues, the layabouts who just talk, do no work, and live off the trappings of the congregation. In other words the higher up who live the life of Reilly and have the best of food, drink and material things also living with all the riches, pomp and ceremony which others don't. Golden threaded robes, gold and silver goblets used in the churches, gold covered statues etc., etc., etc. and on and on the list goes on. Don't believe it? **PLEASE** PROVE ME WRONG.
*
Please think as a rational person with a modicum of intelligence.
*
Spiritualism is a religion/movement that sets out to prove there is a life after death for each individual. It does not ask you to change your religion, or your beliefs. It only asks for an open mind that gives you the gateway to the higher life that most religions purport to teach. This is done through the links from Spirit that Mediums have made, and you yourself can do it. This is through in the most cases, the Medium's own, hard, dedicated work of self discipline over many, many years while progressing towards contacting Spirit making their link stronger whilst they are in regular deep meditation and constantly asking Spirit in their own mind as they progress. This is while they do no harm to others, they do not try to change a person's religion if they do not wish to, they do not try to indoctrinate people. They just tell the truth as they see it and let the individual make their own mind up.
Does the religion that you were brought up in prove that life after death exists as fact each time you go to church? If so, do your priests prove it to all there by demonstration each time, that fact?
Are you going along in that religion in blind faith because of what you were told when you were young and knew no difference?

**HOW SAD** if you are still amongst them!

Because, I now know the answer, one day so will you when you progress along the path with Spirit. Do not wait until the time you join them in the higher vibration level. Start NOW.

What is it said in religion? "Give me a child before/until it is seven and I will have it for the rest of its life" BRAIN WASHED INTO **"BLIND FAITH"**. Luckily the greater vast majority of us within Spiritualism have a brain that we use to lead ourselves away from indoctrination of the moneymaking religions and can think for ourselves.

### YOU DO HAVE A BRAIN. "BUT" DO YOU THINK FOR YOURSELF?
### OR
### DO YOU LET OTHERS THINK FOR YOU?

A very old saying of Al Capone, the gangster, in America in the 1920's ish said when he was alive and this saying has always stuck in my mind.

**"The only money making racket I cannot get into is, this religion".**

Think about it. From the reports coming out now, the mafia have now succeeded, laundering money through the Vatican, near Rome. Killing/poisoning Popes when they try to investigate the corruption. Three Popes in resent times. Don't believe it? Research and try, **PLEASE** PROVE ME WRONG.

\*

Look how many religions are kept going on BLIND FAITH all because their "Holy Men" [who in my opinion are not, most being far from it, quite often sending others to kill their fellow man if they do not agree with what they say or go against their religion] who are the best taught sales people in the world BAR NONE. Look at the money they bring in from the very, very poorest parts of the world with not one thought to how those people are going to survive without their meagre amounts of money that they have willingly given up. Those Holy Men must have been taught to have no conscience at all. HOW SAD! Surely no human being when born could not take off another when they the giver themselves need it for survival. How many religions of the world give money or food OUT OF THEIR OWN POCKETS, to help in any world crisis, Yes some help "BUT" the monies they use are collected from the ordinary person in the street and DOES NOT come from the coffers of any of the churches. Quite a lot of so called Holy Men and so called religious people do not even recognise other faiths as being a religion. They think they have a God given right of, we can kill or send others of the faith to kill, thinking they are all powerful and they are in the only faith that matters.

Look at the religious conflicts of **Ireland**, Christians against Christians. **Bosnia, Yugoslavia, Kosova, Serbia,** Christians against Muslims, before that it was the Muslims against the Christians. In **Germany,** Germans against the Jews. **Russia,** the state against all religions. **China,** the state against all religions. **North America,** the Christian invaders against the native populations and their religions, gods of the earth, wind, skies, mountains, and of the forests. **South America,** Christians against the native populations and their gods of the forest. **The Pacific Islands,** Christians against the native populations. **Atlantic Islands,** Christians against the native populations. **Australia, New Zealand, and the East Indies,** Christians against the native populations. **Middle East**, Muslims against the Christians and Jews, The Jews against the Muslims. **China,** the State against the Buddhists, the state against the Christians. **India,** Christians against the Hindus, Muslims against the Hindus, Hindus against the Muslims, Sikhs against the Hindus, Hindus against the Sikhs. The different fractions amongst the Muslim religion of the Middle East, see how they fight for power over their flocks of people.

**Is your religion amongst them? It does not need to be on this list.**

Can you condone these killing actions for the sake of the religion, for the sake of the God, the Messiah, Jehovah. Most acts of killing are guided by the people of upper levels within these religions? How can any sane person say it is right in anyway what so ever? Don't believe it? **PLEASE** PROVE ME WRONG.

\*

The killers go to the Holy Men of these manmade religions for forgiveness. Those Holy Men within the religions are only ordinary men in different robes. What right have they to give forgiveness to those killers it is the person themselves that will have to oness terms within, when the day comes when they pass to the higher life?

\*

The Holy Men of our time, and in the past have got and still do get money for doing nothing, perhaps a few words of comfort occasionally to some, some of them not even that. Not very many in their religions do any healing to help others as their founders did, for the body or mind.
*

The western medical establishment try to down cry spiritual healers in any way what so ever they can, and they call the healers all sorts of names for taking money to survive. What about their own religious leaders they take money for doing nothing and live in the life of luxury eating and drinking [yes and alcohol] the best of everything. While most of their staunchest supporters are living life far less a level than the people who are the ones responsible for their spiritual upbringing and lots are existing on the bread line, living in squalor, and many in extreme poverty. Don't believe it? **PLEASE** PROVE ME WRONG.
*

### All in the name of religion!
*

It has always seemed strange to me during my compulsory religious learning in school, that the so-called loving religions of the world had so many killings to force their messages onto others of the world. They always force their blind belief onto others because I believe, they, the high up in the religion wanted to control, being not secure with their religion [what are they not telling us], always letting the followers do their dirty murderous work while they sat back and enjoyed their followers' fruits; meaning money and material things. It was the forced indoctrination of their beliefs onto others throughout the world of a generally passive, kind, thinking, logical, nations of people. Wars and conflict might be disguised by politics, but it is in the main, religion at the bottom of it all. At the top is man and his greed. The need of some of the bullies in mankind to control and have power over others. There might be a kindly figurehead in that religion but you can bet your bottom dollar there are powerful people controlling and have their hands in the money pot wanting more of all that which they say is bad within that [their own] religion, their hands on the money and the material things being attracted into that religion.
"It is an all right for me to have it, but not the masses" syndrome.
And/or "Do as I say, not as I do" syndrome.
And /or "Don't question what I say or do".
And/or "Yes we are all equal, but some of us are more equal than others" syndrome.
And/or "Of course we have all the money, wealth, good food, best of drink and all the best of everything, you in our religion give it all to us to be here as we are and maintain our comfortable life style, **BUT** and **IT IS A BIG BUT** we cannot give you anything back, even if you live in poverty, are cold, are sick, and are starving, no matter what religion you are" syndrome. We now have got it and we are going to keep it. Don't believe it? **PLEASE PROVE ME WRONG.**
*

It reminds me of a saying I heard 40 years ago if when you want to keep people loyal to you. "You have to keep them well satisfied in their mind and ill shod" Just give them enough and keep some from them to keep them reliant on you that way they will be pleased enough. That way you will be in charge of them always. Another indoctrinating way of keeping people with a weak mind is to brainwash them until they grow up to be a teenager, or as other churches do, catch them when they are just a teenager when the person is unsure of anything because their body chemicals are changing. Catch people when they are vulnerable. After that it is hard for them to come to terms with any new ideas. What is it that one church [religion] says about children? Give me the child until it is seven and I will have it for the rest of its life **YES BRAIN WASHED** I say. Without any truth or substance in their religion, feeding only fiction yet people all over the world have kept it going for hundreds of years.
*

This is not fiction either: - A television a pop star "Bob Geldof" went the POPE, [the religious leader of all the Catholic Christians in Rome], with his cap in his hand, looking for money to help the starving, yes for the people of Ethiopia in Africa who were starving by the millions through a drought which had caused a famine. That religious leader could only [I am now giving him the benefit of the doubt as a person, as an individual] give to the many millions, upon millions, upon thousands upon thousands who were dying, and YES they all eventually died, he gave nothing more than the ring off his finger. That is what religion is about. That was the richest church in the world and has a separate country within a country, which also lives off the poorest of the poor in the world. Don't believe it? **PLEASE** PROVE ME WRONG.
*

It is "When we have got it off you, it is all ours and we give to nobody any time".
*
Some religions have the double standards, which we see, in the recent history as well as now in the present day. It is case of "we take any wealth from any thieves, killers, mass murderers, abusers, in fact any person here on earth no matter what they have done for we have the power to forgive" [**YES, ORDINARY PEOPLE DOING THAT**]. Think about it! Am I talking about the religion you were brought up in? Don't believe it? **PLEASE** PROVE ME WRONG.
*
The Spiritualist Church teaches that all men/women have free will to interpret the seven principles in the ways they see them.
For each individual to have free choice. Not doing any harm to others.
For every person to be the best within themselves for their own progression towards the higher vibrational plain that we all know exists. It is left to their own personal responsibility, the individual person that makes it count.
Each person is responsible for their own actions.
Is Spiritualism a religion or is it a movement? Remembering the people who are Spiritualist come from all the religions, quite often staying in their own religion. A lot of our friends in those religions agree with most of what we say in Spiritualism yet follow the path they are comfortable with because their religion has been kept up from a very young age. At least we in Spiritualism do not try to change a person's belief we only try to point out the reasons for us believing what we do. Keep it that way.
*
Do not let your Spiritualist churches get into the materialistic ways of the many religions throughout the world of putting symbols, icons, pretty ornaments, pictures of guides for others to revere, so turning them into people to be worshipped. Keep the churches simple in their decoration, just comfortable enough to attract people from all walks of life and to show them how to find their own Spirit within. Teach them as well how simple and safe it is to find a stronger link with the Spirit in the higher vibrational level of our world. Do not let our Mediums be put up on a pedestal because they have a gift that is part of the natural law that every person can have if they have a mind to.
When people, strangers, come into your church does any of your regulars go up to them and make them feel welcome? or "Is it a case of, they have not been here before, I do not know them, I will leave them alone, making some excuse for not speaking to them?" The person might look a bit untidy, they might be not very good looking, not of your colour, not of your religion, they might be a bit dishevelled, they might be down in the mouth and you cannot be bothered. This is the time that people need your churches help, your help. So look for those signs and welcome them as an opportunity to bring some enlightenment into their lives, you might find they are the best helpers your church will have or are you aware of that and do not want them to push you out of your position of power. Please ask yourself "am I falling into the trap of other religions ?" "Are you self or are you caring ?" "Are you dwelling in self glorification in your position within the church?" "I am the president so what I say goes". "I am on the committee so what I say goes". "I know better than you because I have been coming to this church longer than you have". Do you wear blinkers and do not want to see other peoples points of view?".
*

**QUESTION YOUR MOTIVES WHEN PEOPLE CRITICISE.**

**ASK YOURSELF. "IS IT BEST FOR THE CHURCH OR MEETING PLACE"?**
**Is it best for the people who come into the church or meeting place?**
**AM I ONLY THINKING OF MYSELF AND NOT HOW TO PROMOTE SPIRIT?**
**Do I do my best to help others when I am attending meetings?**
**Could I do better to help promote Spirit and the place of worship I attend?**
**Do I go to greet the new comers to my meeting place and make them welcome?**
**Could I do more to promote Spirit?**
**Do I only want people to know I am in control of the church or meeting place?**
**Do I want people to know what status I am in the church or meeting place?**
**Do I want people to know it was me who has done it all here?**
**Do I keep going quietly about my business and get things done with no fuss?**
**Do I help others and ask nothing in return?**
**Do I give credit where it is due?**

**Am I jealous of others in what they do?**
**Am I jealous of the gifts of others and their linking with Spirit?**
**If you are involved with the church or meeting place, <u>go back and read the last few sentences</u>.**
**Do I sit enough to link with Spirit?**
**Do I make excuses for myself for not sitting enough for Spirit?**

### NOW GO BACK AND ANSWER THEM TRUTHFULLY
*

Put a place aside that you can advertise as just a HEALING CENTRE allowing everyone to forget about their religion and prejudice, for them to be able to come into that place to be helped with their heads held high, not losing their own self respect and be able to keep their own religious beliefs. Because that is the thing that can stop a lot of people entering your churches or meeting places. The only guideline in any spiritual centre should be RESPECT. Respect for each other's beliefs, respect for their environment, respect for the meeting place.
*

When there are new up and coming Mediums on at your church, do you encourage them? Please advise them where they went wrong and give them to the best of your ability advice to them on how to put over their messages better to the general public, get them not to ask questions of the recipient. Remember they are the next generation of Mediums, they are serving their apprenticeship for your platform, nurture them. Give them help where needed. Don't get jealous if they have a stronger link with Spirit than you. You might be chosen for a way of helping others in a different way than them and are being guided towards it, be thankful for it.
*

Start advertising your Spiritualist Church; put **good size** notices up on your notice boards that people can read.

When a notice is completed place it in a position where it is going to attract the most readers. Stand back from it at a good distance, to a position where the vast majority of the people you want to see the notice will read it, if you cannot read it from a distance; discard it because the public will in their heads. People are in the main **lazy;** they do not go up to notice boards and read them, they have to be attracted to them by headlines as in daily newspapers and magazines. Take note of the papers and the colours they use and copy them. Notice the colours to be used on your notices from shop signs that stand out. Do not have any dark paper with dark writing on the notice; do not have any clear material covering the notice for good wearing properties. Notices have to be fresh and alive to attract. If a notice is covered with any clear material it is generally shiny and that reflects the light in certain positions so again the notice cannot be read. Yes all your notices should be new, bright and fresh looking. Look around your church and criticise any lapses of brightness in your church. Take a look at the headlines of the newspapers they generally tell all in a few words, so should your notices. Cut out as many words as you can, attract the lazy readers, which in the main the public are. Too many colours mixed confuse the eye. Use only two/three fonts [lettering type] **<u>at the most</u>** on one notice. The distant notices have to hit hard with a single large word or two, be clear and distinct. No splodges of colour to make it look nice for the person making it up. No fancy coloured pictures around the wording to make yourself look good on the computer. Black on white is the best colour mix.
*

Leave your Spiritualist papers and your church notices amongst the books in the waiting rooms of the doctors, dentists, vets, hairdressers, bus stations, the places where many people pass and rest in public places like the supermarket trolleys, on any of the public transport. Get some spare booklets and leaflets of the courses that can be taken home from the Arthur Findlay College, staple your church notices on them and leave them in all the public places, I will say again in the doctors, dentists, vets hairdressers etc. Staple your church notices on any literature and the times you are open. It does not matter if they are out of date; it is just making people aware of what is happening in the movement and in your church.

How many of your friends know that Mediumship can be learned at a college or a Spiritualist church? Whose fault is that if they don't?

OR have you got an excuse for yourself ready for not enlightening them?

Did you find out by accident about the learning of Mediumship through a centre/college course? I bet you did.
*

At Stansted Hall 1998 in the Mediums room whilst I was collecting some money for raffle tickets for the healing centre, I was once made to purposely overhear a remark as I was going out of the room from a very, very prominent short rounded male member of the S.N.U. who said I was a "Dabbler". [Yes, Leonard Young] It really hurt me very much but I did not let it show, I treated that remark with the contempt it deserved. I seem to have been put through all the aspects of this linking with the World of Spirit to write this book. I seem to have been put through nearly all the problems that can happen when developing for the benefit of others so they can have the knowledge of what can happen and not be scared.

**Think about learning at school.**
Every person as they progress in their education at school has to go through every subject in their years of learning. Some people after learning all subjects become a jack of all trades, but master of none. Some all round students become very good at all the main subjects, and other learned students specialise on one subject. So you should be able to see it is the same with the development of your mediumistic gifts. If you do not experience them all, you cannot know how you will progress in any, nor will Spirit be able to link into your natural ability if you do not give them a chance to guide you along the path chosen for you. I will let you decide for yourselves on that subject and I will forget about that thoughtless (**or was it?**), hurtful remark from a prominent alleged caring person. It took me years to stop dwelling on that hurtful remark I nearly stopped going to Stansted Hall, a place I love so much.
*

That aside, it is so sad to find in our progression in life so many uncaring and unkind people of this world we live in, many ready to bring misery and hurt to others because of ignorance, greed, power, jealousy and their own nature. Help them if you can come to terms with their own faults as you go along life's pathway, and do not get pulled into the same ways of the blinkered closed minded people who do not want to learn and progress spiritually into Oneness with God the Divine Spirit. Sadly many of them seem to belong to a **so-called** "<u>caring religion</u> !!!!!" "that are **man made**", as their cover.
*

Now you have read this book and probably pulled it to bits because it has not told you of the specific things you felt as though it should have and did not, OR perhaps you did not agree with some of the things I have said. If that is the case I am sorry, but I hope you have gained a little bit more knowledge and want to find out a great deal more. Try to read as much as you can on all of the subjects within these pages. I might write more sometime but I do not know where life is going for me as yet. I would like to thank all of you and I wish you all the very best of luck in all that you do in the years to come, **so be <u>positive</u>, <u>truthful</u> and <u>sincere</u> in all your endeavours**. Remember it as you go through life and perhaps take a course and read from a book each day. If you learn only one new thing a day and it sticks in your mind that means you will have learned 365 new bits of information each year. Now you are going to be a clever person aren't you?

## BE A KNOWLEDGEABLE SCEPTIC.
## That way you will look and find the truth.

My last message for you is to repeat to yourself out loud, at the very least three times a day.

> "Today, and each day,
> in every way.
> I am getting better, better,
> and better, and better".

This is for anything you do in your life whether it is for your business, self-confidence, or if it is to help with your health and defeating an illness. This is a very positive statement for you to give to your mind, which is the thing that truly controls all that you are.
*

If at any time you know someone who has felt uneasy about things they do not understand, or things that have entered their life, or want to know more about after life, or you/they might want to know more about Spiritualism, a person might have seen an apparition anything like that, all they have to do is to get in touch with The Spiritualist' National Union, Redwoods, Stansted Hall, Stansted Mountfitchet, Essex, CM24 8UD   England.   Phone No 01279 813636

\*
Spiritualism and life is full of conflicting statements as sometimes can be seen in this book. I have tried to put my own experiences down and the experiences of others from different sources. You will have to try everything out for yourself to know if it is true or not. That is the only way and by your own experience will you truly know. **THAT and only THAT is reality for you. Your OWN experience**.

One last thing; when doing a reading **always finish** on an **optimistic** note, and **never leave** a person **down.**

**All things if warned about or seen early enough, the outcome most times can be altered. Remember you have free will**

**I wish you all the success in the world.**

What I have tried to do in this book is to try and help you use your mind; to stimulate your own thoughts; from now on it is up to you on your own, but with the help of others from whom you ask from within your own mind, and now with my guidance and my knowledge that I have tried to put before you, you can now start to learn and grow in wisdom as you go through life at what ever rate you think is comfortable for you.

# "THIS IS NOT AN END"

# "THIS IS ONLY A BEGINNING"

### It is only now you start really learning your future craft.

---

# Part Two

A most important point that I should be put in here again is an explanation of **BEING SINCERE** as it is the basis of linking with the Spirit World:- "If you want to go through all of your development stages in linking with the Spirit World, everything should be done with **sincerity,** everyone has to be **sincere** in their linking with Spirit when talking within their thoughts and asking of the Spirit World when in any development class or development situation. This book is for the people who are coming in from the very beginning of any learning.

I will explain what being **Sincere** and **Sincerity** is. First the dictionary meanings.

**Sincere** :- free from charade, fakery, trickery, pretence or deceit; not assumed or put on; not a sham; not make-believe; being genuine, honest, frank, truthful, candid, straightforward; not assumed or merely professed. **Sincerity, Sincerely, Sincereness** :- State or quality of being sincere; honesty of mind or intention; integrity, genuineness, truthfulness, openness, reliability, faithfulness, dependability, trustworthiness.

**Being sincere** with your links with the Spirit World and the asking of it. It is the really, really, really wanting of your development, you want that link; it is the one thing in the world you want. Everything else in this world is insignificant in relation to your link. You honestly want what you are asking the Spirit World for. You are **not** wanting your gifts **for your own ego**. The gifts are for the others you wish to help along your pathways in life and to show them and prove to them there is life after our so-called death. You have to be true when going through all stages of your development. That is being true to yourself, to those you show your gifts to and most importantly true to those in the Spirit World you link with. You must not make anything up, being true all the time, as it must be realised this is a very big responsibility you are taking on. You have got to try to be there when Spirit needs you for others. They will show you where and when in their own particular ways. Yes, you have to have a life of your own; as in everything in life it is a balancing act. Keep your feet on the ground. I am not talking about the silly thing that some people say by grounding yourself what ever that might mean. Or what I was told by a silly person, go hug a tree. What are people being taught by some tutors?

# TRANCE

Every person who wishes to develop themselves in the mediumistic sense should sit for Trance at home and/or attend the Trance courses at the Arthur Findlay College at Stansted, Essex. U.K, or any other good place of learning. Trance is a technique that teaches the Budding Medium a discipline that is so vital for gaining a good link with the World of Spirit no matter what discipline of Mediumship the budding Medium wishes to train for. The Medium should aim for a situation that is second nature, one of blending with the Spirit World that becomes natural. The contact and the talking to the Spirit World should become part of their being. It is like everyone this day and age on the telephone talking to far away friends and relations. Every person uses the telephone to contact another in different parts of the world. They talk, and are now seeing the friends through the airwaves as though they are next to them it is now so natural, this is what your link with the Spirit World should be like. It can only be done by putting time aside and making an effort for meditation. This should be done before meditating, talking to Spirit through thought for at least fifteen minutes. As Battling Bertha [Harris] said "Mediums get up on the platform before they are ready. They need training, and time to prefect their Mediumship. The budding Mediums have not learned the difference between imagination and Spirit intervention. A budding Medium should not be allowed on a platform until he/she has disciplined his/her Mediumship. Some would be Mediums do not have the faculty so, if things are not going well they imagine or fabricate a few pieces of evidence. I get more help from Spirit by admitting my limitations, then they help me sort things out. With regard to deception I know there are many distinguished names who pad out their demonstrations with facts gleaned anything but spiritually. I am an old woman now, but I swear on my oath I have never cheated. Once you do that Spirit will drop you. They can't be bothered wasting their time on frauds". The frauds will have a little time then they are found out **BUT** in the mean time they have done damage to the good work being done by the true Mediumistic people.

Here we come back to the basic thing in Mediumship development **get your Spirit link strong first before all else**. Please remember your trance state and your link is always in a state of flux. Meaning it fluctuates all the time even when sitting for the physical phenomena the developing Medium can keep on coming and going in and out of the trance state until they have their link fully honed. Even then some really advanced developed Mediums can keep on coming and going out of their trance state. Remember you are never fully developed, but always be honest and true to the Spirit World and they won't let you down, please be patient, Spirit need time to develop a with a Mediumistic person, YES it is your time that they need. For the sake of your development, regularly put some time aside to sit with the harmonious group you link with in the Spirit. {I find sitting for Spirit best one my own as others do not seem to be so reliable}.

I will say again every person is an individual, what might happen to me or suit me, might not be the same for another person when linking with Spirit, especially in Trance. There are different levels of Trance, from very Light Trance, to Deep Trance, some say it starts from clairvoyance, clairaudience, clairsentience, automatic writing, inspirational speaking, healing, etc. through to the Deep Trance State where by the Medium can produce Physical Phenomena, ectoplasm, and human forms in the build up of ectoplasm, at this stage a Medium might not know what is going on around him, being in an unconscious state. Please always be truthful to yourself and then tell the truth to others about what is happening. **Most** (99 %) Trance Mediums are aware of the things at times that go on around them. Kidding [lying to] yourself holds up your development.

I personally cannot see how you can have a still mind, which is needed for a true Trance state as I know it, and then be told you are only in a light Trance, because of certain factors, i.e. your mind coming into play. For me you are in Trance, or you are not. You have a still mind or you do not. I would rather call those states of "alleged Trance", the Medium being in a state of "light altered awareness" then through to a state of "heightened altered awareness". For me a true Trance state is being totally passive to the Spirit World. Please also remember that when in an altered state of awareness, a light trance state, if you are talking you are **talking inspirational** with the guidance from the World of Spirit. Even if you talk and are in very deep trance your mind in someway CAN POSSIBLY be it only fractionally, influence the words coming from your mouth. It is only when the voice becomes totally independent of the Medium [out of the air in their presence] that it can be truly said to be from the Spirit World without the influence of the Medium. I have become very, very wary of many trance speaking Mediums of late that say "I do not know what is going on around me, and the words that I am speaking are not me, and are coming only from the Spirit World." WHY OH ! WHY can't they tell the truth????? IS IT THE EGO TRIP ????? I am better than you, I don't think so !!!! GET REAL. These are people who have only just started going into trance.

Please think about yourself as being Spirit [which you are] and the Spirit World that you do not see, both blending at different levels when you start to link, the link within your meditation and when you start speaking words placed into your mind. At the start, your own Spirit is in an altered awareness link of 90% being your own Spirit [self] and 10% that of the World of Spirit. As you progress the link becomes 80% [self] and 20%. Going along with your meditation, putting time aside to sit for Spirit, the link with the Spirit World gets stronger and becomes 50% [self] and 50%. With discipline and meditation your Link gets stronger still, your own Spirit is only 20% [self] and the Link from Spirit is 80%, and with a longer period of time in meditation and discipline over the years of regular, dedicated, **sincere meditation,** and **constantly, sincerely talking** through thought to the Spirit World in the first fifteen minutes while in the state of meditation, Spirit will take you to a level needed for the gift to be given to you, one that is personal for you. It is very, very, very rare that anyone is given any form of Mediumship over night, **YES,** it needs that most precious of things that you have at your disposal, **TIME**. It **takes time** to develop. After talking to the Spirit World for fifteen to twenty minutes, look into the light and try to still the mind as much as possible so Spirit can come closer and develop you along side your helpers/guides/doorkeepers/angels, what ever name you wish to call them.

A lot of the older generations of Spiritualists used to use hypnosis (another person hypnotising them, and self hypnosis) for the development of their Trance State, BUT what should be remembered is that hypnosis for some people could become a crutch that they could not easily throw away. It should also be remembered, that whatever another person can help you do, you can so very easily do yourself with practice, the same thing has to be said with your own will power. Never resort to the **total need** of the imposed will of others. So do not start off that way. It might take slightly longer to master by yourself in a Circle without hypnosis, but believe me; it will be worth it in the long run. I must admit I might change my mind on this, as people have been telling me to try to go deeper into my Trance and to try hypnosis to do it. But I want to have Spirit learn along side me, with a true compatible Link, not to be led into a situation that neither of us know for certain what might happen, especially me, even if they seem to be giving me some strange reactions sometimes. These reactions I have been led through by Spirit I think were given to me only so I can tell of them, explaining all that has and can happen and then others won't be surprised if it happens to them. To still my mind as much as possible I use a sort of self hypnosis technique of looking into the Light within my third eye area, a focused point and dwell in that void, light or colour because all colour is part of light, even the black void. The void is the full absorption of all the colours of the spectrum. White is the reflection of all the colours.

When a Medium is going into more of a "Trance State", normal conversation cannot be maintained. They are then going more into an "altered state of mind". Some can feel as though their mind is swimming, or the person can go light headed. As the person goes deeper, they get a better blend with Spirit. They then try to still the mind as much as possible, I look into the light, and try to become part of it, going into the light (within my mind) as much as possible I find stills my mind as much as I can, Now I am getting to a stage I use to be able to achieve easily and naturally without the fear of a shock many years ago, as happened in the early stages of my meditation, yes before my shock in my first development Circle in the late 1970's.

Some well known Mediums say they go on a journey when they go into their Trance State for Physical Phenomena or go into a room away from normal thoughts HOW ON EARTH CAN A PERSON WHO IS SUPPOSED TO HAVE A STILL MIND (or as still as possible) FOR A TRUE TRANCE SPIRIT LINK, THINK AND REMEMBER THEIR THOUGHTS WHEN THEY COME BACK TO NORMALLITY. For me this Link is only a heightened state of awareness just beyond the "Clairs". **BUT** it should be said here that awareness while in a Deep Trance State is different, being aware of what is happening to you. This is not using your own thoughts to think as you would normally.

When I first started and I was naive, of what I call being knocked out by Spirit. When I came back to the normal every day state I am usually in, I did not remember anything about what had gone on and the time went very quick, it was as though I had only just closed my eyes to meditate for five minutes, even though I had been in an hour of meditation. This depth of meditation is needed for Physical Mediumship AND to gain an uncontaminated Link with Spirit. **(which is needed in every Mediumistic "development" link with Spirit no matter what).** In later development the Medium can become slightly aware of what is happening but not always (I know a few GOOD and **GENUINE** Mediums who do not remember anything after being in Trance). How many times have you heard a **"TRUE" Trance speaking Medium** when being used by the Spirit Link, Spirit will say, "I will have to stop for a minute as the Medium's mind is interfering with the Link." BUT what should be remembered is the speaking Trance Medium with a new link with the Spirit World is **generally talking inspirational** and it is not the full Direct Voice of Spirit, or the Independent Direct Voice of Spirit. There are very, very few Direct Voice and even fewer still Independent Direct Voice Mediums, and sadly VERY, VERY few TRULY, GENUINE inspirational Mediums who have a pure link with Spirit, please do not kid yourself. {look out for Nicki Cooper from the Lake District she is very genuine} If you go to see a trance talking Medium look for the signs of hesitation, their voice coming and going away from the true Spirit link, then you will understand. No trance state stays the same; it always fluctuates when the link is not as strong as it should be. This is the reason for the Medium to always meditate, meditate, and meditate to keep that link with the Spirit World strong.

Trance is used a lot for the stronger link to the higher side of life to prove there is life after our so called "death," by allowing Spirits of the higher vibrational plane, to come through using the Medium's vocal cords or the bronchial tubes (sometimes as deep as into the Medium's stomach area) to build their voice box in e.g. Direct Voice, or the use of their body without any interference from the Medium's mind, for e.g. Trance healing, **or** building the voice box away from the Medium, [Independent Direct Voice] and other Physical Phenomena like Transfiguration and Materialisation. To have this ability, the Medium must have **total trust in themselves, total trust in their fellow sitters,** and the **total trust in the Spirit world** as well as an ability to **still the mind as much as possible** (I personally look into my third eye area into the light, and become part of it and continually talk to the Spirit World through though asking for their help to do the form of Mediumship I am sitting for until I feel them near, I then dwell in the light and become part of it).

For Trance, to take place the Medium must be **sincere**, and the Medium's mind must be **calm, harmonious,** and **submissive**. The mind temporarily becomes **passive**, as the Medium's thoughts, and their will are lowered to a level that Spirit can become as "in Oneness" with both, within the Divine Light/Power. (Spirit has to lower their vibrations, we as humans have to allow, give permission to the Spirit World to heighten ours in meditation. This is done automatically by Spirit for whatever development of Mediumship you ask for) As the Medium goes into the Trance, they become a **blend of the Medium's own Spirit and with that of the higher vibrational level, those in Spirit.** It is as though they swap/blend/become as one for a while. The Spirit from the higher vibrational level coming to use the body through the permission of mind/brain of the Medium, the Medium's Spirit going on a journey, or it is being stood aside for a brief length of time, for the mind [and/or the body] of the Medium being used as a catalyst for a time, but even then that is not wholly true. As higher-level Spirit we are told, has sometimes to manipulate some of the chemicals in the earthly body, alter the vascular system and adjust the vibration, and/or electrical impulses of the nervous system. If Spirit do not get their vibrational connection correct; shaking, twitching, tremors, and other slight abnormalities can occur at first with the Medium's body, do not be alarmed when, or if this happens, (some budding Mediums do not have any reactions at all) trust in the higher life. {BUT **"DO NOT FAKE"** ANY OF THIS MOVEMENT **IT WILL** HOLD YOU BACK IN YOUR DEVELOPMENT **AS DOES LYING to yourself, others and Spirit,** this is negativity and negativity can halt any link with Spirit}. The key here is **sincerity, to self and Spirit**.

This slight uncontrolled movement is mainly when the Medium goes into deep Trance, and going into advanced Physical Mediumship. Spirit will not, I assure you, **will not** let any harm come to you if they are going to work with you, neither will they normally have you experience anything, that is likely to frighten you before you can handle it. Sometimes though, it has happened that something has been done to make people jump because of a sudden occurrence. That generally is only the human part of you being silly, and not trusting Spirit, they (Spirit) in turn thinking you could handle it at that time. Most times it is taken away to let you experience the phenomena at a later date in your life. Always remember you are the one in control, anything you do not like, ask for it [in your mind through thought] to be taken away, and it will go, I assure you, it will go. You are always the one in control no matter what silly ignorant people say. Always ask for goodness, kindness, truth, love, within the Divine Light, and to blend within peaceful loving harmony of Spirit of the highest realms at the start of any sitting. If at any time the shaking does occur, ask for it to be taken away, as it is upsetting the vessel they are using [meaning you, the budding Medium]. But be aware that if you ask for something to go it might not return so be careful of what you ask to go. In my tutoring capacity, I always ask Spirit if they are shaking the budding Medium to treat them gentle and explain what is happening so they in Spirit can adjust whatever without harming the Medium in any way.

Lots of deeply entranced Mediums cannot remember afterwards any of the goings on that happened when in the Trance state even though they were aware of it all. It is though the short-term memory does not function properly and collate and store the information as it does in everyday life YET when reminded of the little things that happened when in the Trance state they can be brought to mind. The Medium can be talking, taking part with the helping of the link with Spirit in a Physical séance, using ectoplasm, levitating tables, bringing in apports, sending out asports, bring forth Spirit forms, Spirit using Deep Trance Mediums to form voice boxes in the air, and all this has been happening for perhaps a few hours, and still, some will not know what has happened. Others will be aware of the happening but will be in an altered state of awareness and it is as though they are at a distance from what is happening. If you do get to this level do not tell any lies to the others, do not fake, IT WILL be found out if you do. Be true to Spirit, and to yourself. It is the lies, untruths, underhandedness, insincerity, and deceit, that does block and slow people's development.

Trance, I believe is a trusted, firm, stronger than normal link with the higher life of Spirit and your own Spirit, this is where you allow the higher Spirit to be in control of your physical body/mind while your Spirit can go on a learning journey in the higher realm. But you must always know, when starting out in this quest, you are the person who has the final say in what happens to you. Some of the old writers of the 1800's classed a person in a "Deep Trance State", as being in a state of altered awareness that is next to death, as near to death as you can get. Do not worry too much about that definition, no one has died yet while in a Trance state. As long as you have good sitters, and you are looked after while in a Trance by trusted people, as well as when you are coming back out of a Trance, all will be well. I always trust in the higher life totally, it is only those here on the earth plane that you should worry about. If you are worried, go to a place where you are safe when learning and can learn more about Trance. There are many Trance courses at the Arthur Findlay College at Stansted, Essex. U.K. at different times of the year. The power is there, and it is like nowhere else on earth that I know about.

When starting to sit for Trance, you should be clean in body and soul as it is put in the older books of the last century. You should be **sincere**, spiritually good, meaning your mind, and your body healthy for Spirit to use, no badness in them either. Harmony is the word; peaceful loving harmony with yourself; peaceful loving harmony with the higher self, your own Spirit within; peaceful loving harmony with the higher vibrational life of Spirit, peaceful loving harmony with those around you, and you having total trust with the World of Spirit. Remember to have a bath, or shower, or a good wash, clean clothes on before sitting, just as you would if you were going out to meet friends, because that is what you are doing, you will be meeting your friends in Spirit.

Spirit has to have your total trust and you have total trust in Spirit to attain a good strong link.

It is recommended that a few minutes exercise are taken before any sitting, this is so the oxygen level of the body is up to scratch and the Trance state is not mistaken for sleep.

At the beginning of my development I sometimes started off by concentrating on my breath to bring and collect the ether at the root of my nose to hold the thoughts. I start looking into the light within my third eye, then I am asking within my own mind, for help in the sitting from those on the **highest** Spirit plane, and let all that come, to come only with goodness, kindness, love, truth, in the peaceful Divine Light of Spirit within the loving harmony of Spirit of the highest realms, so I can help others and to prove them there is life after our so called death.

Remember to talk in all sincerity to Spirit in your mind and continually talk to Spirit within your thoughts until they are near to you. [A lot of people can take up to a half an hour in the early stages]. Then look into the light in your third eye region and be part of it, in loving harmony with the higher force of God. [remember to ask for whatever mediumistic development you want]. I used to go through a sequence of stages to have my body relaxed. I do not have to do that now as it comes automatic after a great many years of practice. I now relax, and keep on encouraging Spirit while being sincere in every way, to come closer to me, when I feel them close; I then go fully into the light within my mind and try to still my mind by looking into that light/colour and being part of it.

BUT if Spirit comes too close I start yawning and my eyes start to stream with water I have to ask Spirit to stand a little bit away and let me blend a little better. This talking of course is going on in my mind through thought. When the adjustment is what I feel is right for me I relax in the Divine Light within my mind, in my third eye area. It is then time for you to let the Spirit World do what ever they need to do without any interference. The watering of my eyes and the yawning happens when being used as an open vessel giving energy to a person in a group who is developing. I let it happen because at that time, Spirit has to be so close and there is no interference in what they are doing, **BUT** I always tell my groups, "You are getting a true link with Spirit and it is **for your development also when it happens**, keep on asking for the energy within you as the vessel to be sent to the person developing, what you give out unselfishly to others comes back to you many fold". I have seen this time and time again.

I will go through some sequences that I have used in the past. Pick the one which is the best for you, and then stick to it, practice, practice, practice. Give one method a chance to work for you. A lot of these sequences can be used for group work. But please use this exercise to bring in harmony to the group first. I have put it in the book several times as it is important.

**Love and Harmony, Harmony, Harmony** is the most important part of any Circle to bring results.

Sit in a comfortable seat in an upright comfortable position.

Get everyone there in the Circle to look at each person individually in the group and smile at them, it does not matter if you or they feel uncomfortable and laugh, that will raise the vibrations. When that is done ask everyone to close their eyes, think about the joining together of the Circle and then smile inwardly at everyone there then smile inwardly at those in Spirit you are going to meet. Welcome them into yourself and to the Circle. Feel happy about meeting them, as they draw near to the Circle welcome them, feel the happy anticipation, the warmth of the feeling, be **sincere** about the love you are giving out to them and the Circle.

Relax, and then go through a sequence of relaxing your body. This is done by imaging [seeing it in your own mind] every sequence as you say it in your head to yourself, or record it on a tape recorder to play to yourself.

Pause at each step, so you think it, feel it, see it, so putting it aside, out of your mind, then you will be able to forget about all the parts of your body and you will be only a mind to relax ready for Spirit, ready to go into the light [that is what I do] while they work with you at each stage, see the Light flowing over and into the parts you are relaxing.

**Read out everything here :-**

Close your eyes.
First start by relaxing your head and the hairs on your head.
**Pause and think it, feel it, see yourself doing it.**
Relax your scalp.
**Pause and think it, feel it, see yourself doing it.**
Relax the skin on your face.
**Pause and think it, feel it, see yourself doing it.**
Relax the muscles on your face.
**Pause and think it, feel it, see yourself doing it.**
Relax your jaw.
**Pause and think it, feel it, see yourself doing it.**
Relax your neck.
**Pause and think it, feel it, see yourself doing it.**
See the beautiful, warm, light flowing over your head and neck.
**Pause and think it, feel it, see yourself doing it.**
Relax your left hand.
**Pause and think it, feel it, see yourself doing it.**
Relax your left lower arm.
**Pause and think it, feel it, see yourself doing it.**
Relax your left upper arm.
**Pause and think it, feel it, see yourself doing it.**

Relax your right hand.
**Pause and think it, feel it, see yourself doing it.**
Relax your right lower arm.
**Pause and think it, feel it, see yourself doing it.**
Relax your right upper arm.
**Pause and think it, feel it, see yourself doing it.**
Relax your left shoulder.
**Pause and think it, feel it, see yourself doing it.**
Relax your right shoulder.
**Pause and think it, feel it, see yourself doing it.**
Relax your upper body.
**Pause and think it, feel it, see yourself doing it.**
Relax your lower body.
**Pause and think it, feel it, see yourself doing it.**
See the beautiful, warm, light flowing over your shoulders, arm and body.
**Pause and think it, feel it, see yourself doing it.**
Relax your left thigh to your knee.
**Pause and think it, feel it, see yourself doing it.**
Relax your left lower leg.
**Pause and think it, feel it, see yourself doing it.**
Relax your left foot and feel it going to your toes.
**Pause and think it, feel it, see yourself doing it.**
Relax your right thigh to your knee.
**Pause and think it, feel it, see yourself doing it.**
Relax your right lower leg
**Pause and think it, feel it, see yourself doing it.**
Relax your right foot and feel it going to your toes.
**Pause and think it, feel it, see yourself doing it.**
See the beautiful, warm, light flowing over your legs, knees, and feet.
**Pause and think it, feel it, see yourself doing it.**

[I used to have to go back and do it again in some parts so you might.]

When relaxed.
Start to concentrate on your breath [Or use one of the other sequences] going into the nose, breathing in a warm colour, see the colour of light filling you up with the Divine Loving Power. As you breath out through the nose, you are breathing out all the badness of your body, see it as you go deeper into the warm colour you see. It does not matter if it is black with red dots, yellow with pink, grey with nothing, green, blue, as long as you are comfortable with that colour. The colours, they mean nothing, it is just to get you down deeper into a Trance state, the colours can change at different sittings so do not worry. Some people do not see colours, only a bright white light, some only darkness as I did when I first started meditating. (You are impressing onto the etheric part of the air you are breathing in, your thoughts, which are going to help you with your development of the link with Spirit. Ask for what you want developed for a few minutes, then try to still the mind within the light of the third eye, keep on concentrating on it.)
Some people at each breath, see themselves stepping down a step into a colour, or Light, then the next step down, then the next step down, going deeper and deeper, and deeper, and deeper at each step into the Light, or colour, then becoming part of the Light, or colour being absorbed in it.
Or.
Others at each breath, it is as though they see themselves going down in a lift into the light, or warm colour, slowly going down deeper, down deeper, down deeper, down deeper at each breath, in the end they become part of the Light, or colour being absorbed by it.
Here is a lift method that is suitable for recording. Only for personal use. This must be said slowly, softly, and gently.
**At each stage, Pause and think it, feel it, see yourself doing it.**

# KEEWAYS MEDITATION ONENESS written by Roy Keeghan

I step into a lift that is brightly lit. [Any coloured light]
**Pause and think it, feel it, see yourself doing it.**
The doors, which are transparent, close. The Light from below is shining up into the lift.
I see the indicator start to go down from the ground floor.
**Pause and think it, feel it, see yourself doing it.**
At each floor I can feel the light becoming part of me.
**Pause and think it, feel it, see yourself doing it.**
I am at the first floor the Light has got a little brighter for me.
**Pause and think it, feel it, see yourself doing it.**
I see the indicator is showing number two, I can see down the shaft is the Light shining upwards to me.
**Pause and think it, feel it, see yourself doing it.**
I am going deeper into the colour the Light now; I am at the third floor going deep into the light.
**Pause and think it, feel it, see yourself doing it.**
The indicator is now showing me I am passing the fourth floor. The lift is taking me deeper into the Light, I feel as though the light is becoming part of me.
**Pause and think it, feel it, see yourself doing it.**
Here I am passing the fifth floor I feel the warm feeling of the Light that I am beginning to belong to.
I am going down in a lift that is filled with that beautiful coloured Light; I am watching the indicator, as I go further down into the Light. I am looking out through the window of the lift, and through the transparent doors, the coloured Light is looking so inviting, as I go down each floor towards it.
**Pause and think it, feel it, see yourself doing it.**
I am going passed the sixth floor now it feels so right for me to be here in the Light within the lift.
I see the indicator going down further now, and I am becoming more relaxed in the bright coloured light of the lift.
I am starting to feel part of the coloured light that I am going down towards, as though I belong in the wonderful, coloured light. I am starting to feel becoming that Light.
At each floor, I have felt I am here becoming more part of the coloured Light that is getting more intense. I am nearly at the lower floor.
**Pause and think it, feel it, see yourself doing it.**
I am at the seventh floor I am arriving.
I arrive at the lower floor now and see the door open wide, on stepping out of the lift, there is a corridor full of beautiful white Light ahead of me with a slight mist sort of wafting towards me.
**Pause and think it, feel it, see yourself doing it.**
I walk along the corridor through the bright, misty, white Light, going towards the open door where it is coming from.
**Pause and think it, feel it, see yourself doing it.**
I go into the beautiful, swirling, white, mist into the room where it has been coming from, it is full of the nicest, the most beautiful, the purest, white Light I have ever seen, and now it is clear.
**Pause and think it, feel it, see yourself doing it.**
There I meet a person who is full of love and compassion, this person is going to help me, it is my guide whenever I need one to call on.
They come to stand alongside me, putting their hand on my shoulder, to help make me feel secure there. I know they are telling me they will always be there when needed.
**Pause and think it, feel it, see yourself doing it.**
This person is giving me strength through their hands for whatever is needed in my life in my development.
**Pause and think it, feel it, see yourself doing it.**

I hear them through my thoughts telling me things. I listen and take note of them.

**Pause and think it, feel it, see yourself doing it.**
I can sense someone coming up to me from behind.
I turn to face them, and they greet me with love and kindness. It is my second guiding friend.
**Pause and think it, feel it, see yourself doing it.**
This person is there to help me also. I put out my hands to hold them I can feel the loving warmth from

them; they are filling me full of their love for my fellow man. I am feeling the presence of the whole of Spirit in the Light. I am feeling the whole of the group soul and all their presence with me there. I am part of that beautiful, pure, bright, white, Light and I belong there.
**Pause and think it, feel it, see yourself doing it.**

The person who has just arrived is talking to me, advising me. I listen and take note of their advice.
**Pause and think it, feel it, see yourself doing it.**
My new friends sit either side of me, I feel I am part of them and they are part of me, we do not need to say anything because we know. It is the time for knowing, blending in the Light, and blending in each other. A time to develop together in "Harmony and Oneness". We sit in the stillness and Oneness of Spirit.

**<u>NOW LET There be a time of quietness for half an hour or so.</u>**

**At the end of the tape so you come back to reality record this sequence. Try to get hold of the longer tapes so there is a reasonable time of meditation. Or after a length of time the person says this. You go on an upward journey back to reality.**

I hug my friends individually, wishing them a fond farewell, saying I will see them again soon.
**Pause and think it, feel it, see yourself doing it.**
I turn to go into the beautiful, pure, bright, white, Light in the mist, I go to the door and walk through the mist into the brightly lit corridor.
I can see the lift door, with the coloured Light shining from it at the end; it is open ready for me, whenever I had needed it.
**Pause and think it, feel it, see yourself doing it.**
On reaching the lift I get into the bright, coloured Light; the doors close.
The lift now starts to go slowly upwards
**Pause and think it, feel it, see yourself doing it.**
I watch the indicator, as it goes from the lower seventh level, then upwards to the sixth floor.
The coloured Light's sparkle is going down from what it was.
I keep watching the indicator.
**Pause and think it, feel it, see yourself doing it.**
I have arrived at the sixth floor; the Light is not as it was before.
**Pause and think it, feel it, see yourself doing it.**
I see it is the fifth floor passing the doors. The bright Light is starting to lose its lustre.
**Pause and think it, feel it, see yourself doing it.**
I arrive at the fourth floor, looking upwards through the window of the lift, I can see daylight, it is not the same true, rich Light, as I was in a moment ago.
**Pause and think it, feel it, see yourself doing it.**
I have reached the third level; I am going ever upwards towards that daylight.
**Pause and think it, feel it, see yourself doing it.**
I arrive at the second floor and the coloured Light in the lift is diminishing, the brightness is going.
**Pause and think it, feel it, see yourself doing it.**
I see the indicator is on the first floor and the daylight is mixed with the coloured Light in the lift, the brightness of a moment ago has gone.
**Pause and think it, feel it, see yourself doing it.**
I see I am back on the ground floor and the light is normal daylight through the lift window and the doors.
The doors of the lift open and I step back into the world once more.
When I am ready I open my eyes and I am back in my normal everyday state.
  Or
Others at each breath, it is as though they see themselves on a warm, comfortable, cloud, and are sinking into it, being absorbed by it. Each breath, they see themselves sinking deeper, sinking deeper, sinking deeper, going deeper, and deeper at each breath, then become part of that warm soft cloud and are surrounded in the Divine Light.

If you listen to music while you relax, try and become part of the music, see the note, become a note, become a tone of sound of the music, get absorbed by the power of it. See your breath as a note, the sound filling you up with that certain musical tone, be part of that vibration, being absorbed by it, going deeper at each breath into it.

One tape that is very good is the continuous OOOOMMMmmmm or AUM of the monks. It is a mantra that can be used to go into an altered state if you concentrate on each omm and go into the light further/deeper at each new ooommm. I find it one of the best for me I become part of it, and it does not let you think of the tune or melody that might distract.

Another sound that you can get absorbed by is the incessant beating of a drum. This can be of any repeated rhythmic beat. Some like the ringing sharpness of the Celtic drums; others prefer the American Indian with it's duller, harder beat. These beats can become hypnotic and help certain people towards the Trance state.

At first when I started I saw myself at each breath going into a colour, a light and saw myself becoming part of that colour as I still do to this day. I have found for me this is the best way to slow down the thoughts going though my mind, many times stopping them to some extent.

At the start of going into Trance, you might feel the breathing go a little quicker, and deeper, and a strange air intake noise can be heard. The first time I heard it, I let my mind think about it, so I came straight out of the trance state, my thought interrupted the sequence of events. It often does at first I am told. The eyes will want to stay shut, do not attempt to try and open them, as it will again interrupt the flow of no thought, or should I say, interrupt the mind of still thought (or very much slowed down thought). Don't worry if it happens, we are all nosey deep down, we all want to know what is happening around us.

Some tutors say when in the Trance State in the early stages try to get the first few words out of your mouth, then Spirit will take over while you are in an altered state of none thought, well as near as possible. [When it happened to me I had a problem with this method, as there was nothing in my mind to say, I started thinking of what I should say and I came immediately out of Trance]. You will not or should not have to think of the things that are being said, the Spirit Control will do that for you, **IF you are in a true deep Trance**. Do not try to interfere with what is being said through you as this brings your own thoughts and your own mind into play, I would not try to put on an accent of a Red Indian, or a Chinese person, this will bring you down to a bad act, for which you might well get ridiculed, and so slowing up your development. Trust fully in the Spirit control that you are trying to link with. BUT it is up to you the individual. Spirit are trying with me to open my windpipe and the tube down to my stomach area, I feel them massaging and manipulate it, I do not know the reason for this at this time. It is a strange feeling that I am aware of, but at times I come out of this Trance State in a fit of coughing, my mind comes into play thinking of what is happening, try to go along with the Spirit manipulations.

Other trainers say you have to be an actor, and play the role of the person as they were in life, to take on their personality, their body language, over time I might change my opinion on this, but I am as yet just leaving my trust in Spirit alone for my development, letting them talk through me as they wish to, and I will leave the acting to those on T.V., films, and on the stage. I do not believe you should act as you will be called and actor and bring the whole of Spiritual Mediumship into disrepute. I have seen ridiculous acts of so-called Mediumship. One tutor at a well-known place of learning I helped at was talking in different accents, being asked questions and not giving answers to the questions, he evaded them like any politician. Not one bit of evidence of life after death was given and then he went into a fit of laughing for about five to ten minutes, yes just laughing, it was as though he was laughing at us for being such fools in believing he was being controlled by the Spirit World. I have seen the same laugh being played out each time I go to Blackpool pleasure funfair by the electric clown in a glass case.

When the power goes, it will be all right to come back to reality, your unseen helpers will know when the time is right for that. BUT yet again the rule of individuality comes into play.

I know of one very good world renowned Trance Medium who says you have to give all the help you can to Spirit, and if your Spirit Control comes as a hunched back person, you should become that person. If the Spirit comes as a singer be that singer in their actions. Alright if Spirit actually strongly impresses you to do that go for it; **"BUT DO NOT ACT THE PART!" I personally would ask Spirit to take away those conditions if you are aware of them.** If you are in deep Trance, and you are not fully aware of the conditions, **it is then not an act on your part. BE TRUTHFUL TO YOURSELF AND THEN YOU WILL BE TO SPIRIT.**

BUT some platform Mediums get the symptoms of the people who have gone before, e.g. a headache if they died of a head wound or brain tumour, a pain in the wrists if they suffered from rheumatism or pulled down nagging pain in their joints if they suffered with arthritis, etc., they have to ask Spirit to take away the symptom before they go onto the next message. So why is it not correct to be a bent hunchback if the Spirit World impresses the Medium to do so as long as they do it in truth? I will leave that to you. TRUTH before all else!!!

Another method I have used before going into deep meditation. Yes I have used many. This was to help me forget about my body and then to clear my mind, it was to say to myself within my mind while my eyes were closed :- (try it, and say to yourself; or better still, record it in your own voice for your own personal use, or have someone read it out to you)

I first closed my eyes. [In meditation looking into your third eye.]
I open my eyes and I am **aware of a colour**. [Any colour at all, could be a mix of colours, even blacks and greys] Close eyes seeing the colour. [If you cannot see a colour open your eyes see a colour of an object and hold that]
**Pause and think it, feel it, see yourself in your minds eye** doing it then let it go.
I can **feel my feet** placed firmly on the ground.
**Pause and think it, feel it, see yourself in your minds eye** doing it then let it go.
I can **feel my legs** pressing against the chair
**Pause and think it, feel it, see yourself in your minds eye** doing it then let it go.
I can **feel my bottom** pressing firmly into the chair.
**Pause and think it, feel it, see yourself in your minds eye** doing it then let it go.
I can **feel my back** pressing firmly into the chair.
**Pause and think it, feel it, see yourself in your minds eye** doing it then let it go.
I can **feel my hands** with the air going over them.
**Pause and think it, feel it, see yourself in your minds eye** doing it then let it go.
I **feel my arms** in the sleeves of what I am wearing.
**Pause and think it, feel it, see yourself in your minds eye** doing it then let it go.
I **feel the skin** on my head and the air around it.
**Pause and think it, feel it, see yourself in your minds eye** doing it then let it go.
I can **feel the clothes** on my skin.
**Pause and think it, feel it, see yourself in your minds eye** doing it then let it go.
I can **feel the air** going over my face.
**Pause and think it, feel it, see yourself in your minds eye** doing it then let it go.
I am **aware** of the taste in my mouth.
**Pause and think it, feel it, see yourself in your minds eye** doing it then let it go.
I am **aware of the air and the smell** that is going into my nose.
**Pause and think it, feel it, see yourself in your minds eye** doing it then let it go.
I am **hearing the sounds** close around me, I am **hearing** them **out as far as I can**, I **hear out to the furthest points.** I am coming back into my own head to the sounds close to me I then go out the furthest sounds **hearing** them, I let them go, coming back to myself. Not letting any thoughts come in, I put that hearing and listening aside.
**Pause and think it, feel it.**
**You look into your minds eye, see yourself in your minds eye doing it then let it go.**
I am **joining up with a shaft of light** to the higher side of life ready to work with them
**Pause and think it, feel it.**
**Look, see yourself in your minds eye doing it then let it go.**
The shaft of light is **filling me up with the Divine Light** and flowing over all over me, look at it as though it is expanding ever outwards, do this step for a few minutes.
**Pause and think it, feel it, see yourself in your minds eye** doing it then let it go.
Say to yourself, "I now am filled with light and ready".
Start on your breath with the eyes still closed, seeing everything in the mind.
After the relaxation of my body, **I concentrate on the breath** I am breathing into my nose.

**I visualise my breath** going into my nose, and into my lungs all the time.
I **think it**, **feel it**, **see it** myself, it is the Power of Spirit coming into my body, as I go deeper into the colour at each breath outwards through my nose. (I sometimes **think it**, **feel it**, **and see** myself as a none or any colour).
The colour is a bright light as it is going in, filling me up, (I always **think it**, **feel it**, **see** myself as in the power of love from Spirit).
I then get absorbed with that colour, [no matter what colour,] and become part of it, going deeper into it, becoming part of it.
If at any time I have thoughts of any sort, I go back to concentrate on my breathing again, **think it**, **feel it**, **see it** in myself.
I see the colour of badness going out of my body as I breath out at each breath.
The breath of the Love Light filling me up again as I breath in, and **I see** myself going deeper into the colour at each breath, so getting absorbed in the God Light of Spirit.
Always; if at any time I have thoughts coming into my head, I again go back to the breath again, and think it, feel it, see it going into myself: The more you practice these methods the more it will help. Do it on a regular basis and you **will** have success.

As with all the other meditations that start Spiritual Phenomena, a few rules should be adhered to for safety. When starting your development, it is best to be with others you have trust in, be it in a good House Circle, a Home Circle, or Church Circle. "BUT" there is no good reason not to sit on your own if you have total trust in Spirit. They will look after you. Spirit will not harm you if they are going to work with you. Trust them and only ask for the best from the best, those in the highest development level within the loving harmony they have there.

All people should be told of the rules, better still have them written down, get people to read them, then to sign them, so they know what is expected when sitting with a Medium if Trance is going to be undertaken. This is just in case anything happens whilst in with strangers.
All in the presence of an entranced Medium should be quiet at most times. (unless the Mediums tells everyone there it is all right, remember we are different).

"DEFINITELY" No **sudden** noises of any sort as the Medium is very much in a state of **very** altered awareness, and they are ultra, ultra, sensitive to any outside interference. Meaning **touch**, or **sudden noise** of any kind. Some Mediums do not believe this; all I can say is wait until they have a shock experience like I had in 1980, when I was in very deep meditation and Spirit was linking with me, I still get the reactions of a pain from that incident in the left side of the chest from that to this day, believe me it is true.
When developed, some Trance Mediums allow low talking, also questions to be asked of their Spirit control when they come through, have these rules in place "before" the Medium goes into Trance, as to what can, or cannot be said or done. Some Trance Mediums allow people to walk in, and walk out of a demonstration, **BUT** only when they are deep in the Trance **not** when they are going down into the Trance, or coming out of the Trance. That is the time when the Mediums are at their most vulnerable to the outside sounds and interference.
**This information cannot ever be stopped being told to others over, and over, and over again.**

"NO" and I mean "DEFINITELY NO TOUCHING" of the Medium, as they can be at this time be prone to psychic shock. If that occurs they can be very ill through it. (Again it is up to the individual Medium and depending on what level of altered awareness they are in), also like me they might have had their blood pressure altered ready for the work with Spirit, if the shock occurs, then the sudden increased blood pressure could rupture/break the already overly stressed veins/arteries in a weaker part of the vascular system so leading to a **very, very, serious situation of internal bleeding**. YES if a Medium is in the Trance State they can have increased blood pressure and that extra surge of blood by the heart if a shock occurs, **CAN KILL** be warned.

If doing a demonstration. A trusted person should be at the side of the Medium during the Trance, this is - to make sure the Medium is all right at every stage of the Trance, sending power to them, and to make sure no person comes to touch the Medium. In other words a minder [two is better, one at each side of the Medium, always remember the Medium's well being, also look after the Medium when the session is finished].

If doing a demonstration. When you are starting and when a Medium is coming out of Trance, all should be quiet, this is firstly to allow the Medium to go into the Trance State without interference, without them having to think about what is going on around them, then afterwards letting them come quietly back to their normal self. After they come out of Trance, the Mediums/helpers at the side of them should be talking to the demonstrating Medium in a gentle, soft, calm, soothing voice, **then and only then**, after asking the Medium themselves if it is all right, should people start to talk. DO not clap or make any sudden sounds because the Medium will be in an ultra state of awareness and their nerves will be very, very, very sensitive to sounds that are not normally a problem in ordinary circumstance, the noise of clapping can make some Mediums feel sick. The vibration of the noise can make the stomach upset. The clapping can also vibrate the nerves and that upsets the brain. It is best for the demonstrating Medium to be guided to somewhere quiet to recover. DO NOT TOUCH THEM UNTIL **THE MEDIUM SAYS** IT IS ALL RIGHT TO DO SO.

If the Trance demonstration has been done in the dark. When the Medium has finished their demonstration, the person at the side should make extra sure of the Medium's well being, and then wait a little longer to make extra sure. Quietness maintained. Water given to the Medium. Then everyone should be talking for a while before the lights are switched back on to make doubly sure, **safety of the Medium** being the watchword. People in Stansted Hall go into Trance quite happily in daylight. It is only for some Physical Phenomena Circles darkness is needed and even then it is not always necessary, a lot using low red lighting, as did Gordon Higginson in his public demonstrations with the ectoplasm flowing from him whilst walking along the isle between the chairs in the library at Stansted Hall. After dark séances be careful turning the white lights on as it can affect the eyes of everyone there. **Warn before** switching lights on.

Water should always be available for the Medium at all times, I have seen a Medium come "partly" out of a Trance because of their controlling Spirit has been worried about their throat, the throat being a problem for the Spirit Controller and the Medium, the Spirit Controller being worried for the Medium. The Medium asked for the water herself, was then handed a glass of water, the handler of the water being very, very careful not to touch the half entranced Medium at all, only gently placing the glass in their hand, then when the Medium was ready, finished drinking the water, the glass was handed back to the handler, they being very careful again not to touch the Medium, only the glass.

Never say the Medium's name when they are sitting for Trance in the early stages (I personally would not any way just in case), as it can bring them back to reality (this again is up to the individual). Saying a person's name is the recognised way of bringing gently back to normality, a Medium in any deep state of altered awareness, back to their normal state, as well as any sitter in any Circle, it makes their brain click into the normality of the ordinary earth plain life. The spoken name of the person in Trance acts within the subconscious mind as a trigger, so reacting to the request of the time to finish.

Using a battery-operated tape recorder is a good thing; this can be used for the Medium to hear anything that has been said by Spirit through them. Most times, Deep Trance Mediums cannot recall anything that has been said when in their Trance state. It gives them more confidence to carry on with their good work. A lot of Trance Mediums react as though they are normal after a Trance session but it can be a false assumption. The brain of the deep Trance Medium does not always come back to normality right away, it can be as though they are still in a fog, in a muggy feeling where nothing is taken fully into the mind. Nothing of what is talked about with them at the time is remembered afterwards.

I have started using a video camera with sound aimed at myself, while sitting in Trance alone; I sit to regularly to gradually build up the stronger link with my Spirit control; this way I can see the reaction Spirit is having on me, and if any thing is spoken by Spirit it is recorded by the camera. Later after the sitting and after watching the recording I can go back to Spirit, and ask them to alter anything they are doing with my body I think might be unnerving to the general public watching.

Now in 2005 I do not use a camera aimed at myself, as I do not want to be influenced by what I see. BUT I record others for their benefit.

If you start working in public as a Trance Medium please look after your own safety, try to **HAVE TWO** trusted people beside you if possible.

Remember not all in the churches and not all Mediums are knowledgeable about the care of a Trance Medium while they are in trance, and some can be uncaring about their care also being very ignorant of the consequences. I know quite a few so called knowledgeable church Mediums (and those on many a church committee) who have been in the Spiritualist movement a long time have very little knowledge of the care that is needed when on the platform with a working Trance Medium.

In 1999 I attended a Trance demonstration meeting, in a very large North West Church at Easter time. When the Medium was going into Trance, I told the people on the door that it should be closed, as the notice I had put up informed the public it was to be shut. I was told it was a public meeting, and a public building, and the door was to stay open for safety [politics again, I'm in charge not you syndrome]. **WHAT ON EARTH** do public buildings have fire doors on for? They are for keeping the general public out when needed, and the ones inside secure, and able to get out in an emergency, when needed. People were still coming into the hall whilst the Medium was working in Trance **[DANGEROUS FOR THE MEDIUM]**. (I know two churches also in the Northwest, who close their doors at the start of their ordinary services to avoid interruptions, which they have had in the past). Part way through the same Trance meeting, two ladies went through a door to the toilets at the back of the hall, passing near to the Medium, who was in Trance even though there was a toilet at the other end of the church. When they came back the second lady let the door bang, just as the Medium was coming out of Trance, and it shocked the Medium, the lady who let the door bang was laughing about it as she walked back to her seat. **[DANGEROUS FOR THE MEDIUM]**. I was disgusted at the lack of care shown by the church at that time. The one very, very experienced chair lady at the other side of the Medium, could not do anything about it, but she put her head in her hands upset about it [her husband Stan Tyrer, was a Trance Medium for a great many years, **BUT** he would not do any public demonstrations in Trance, because he said he was not in full control of the situation while in Trance]. All these things should be looked at before any public meeting, where a Trance Medium is concerned, any meeting what so ever. There were also no notices for the general public to follow any instructions for silence, and there was no notices giving reasons for being quiet, and for the general public to look at as reminders throughout the sitting. Notices should have been up in prominent places, **"in my opinion"**. Also the public should be asked to go to the toilet before the start of the meeting, and the chairperson explaining why. **BUT WAS THAT MEDIUM IN A "TRUE DEEP TRANCE" STATE To have allowed it?** He said after that it was all right he was not in any danger !!!!!!

When I first started with my deep Spirit control, all I can say is that I had the **"ABB DABS,"** the reason I call it this name is because it is the sound, the guttural noise that I made, when the Spirit control was trying to get my nervous system to blend with them. At my very first experience, it was the galloping **"ABB DABS;"** they were so strong but no noise from my mouth. My Spirit control had to blend in such a way, that "gender-less" [my Spirit Control I do not know who he/she is] could work my muscles in such a way as to produce a noise, we know as talking, I got shaken like anything inside the chest, throat, mouth and head, my movement looked as though I was having an epileptic fit. It really drained me, I was like a wet rag when it was finished and I had to go and lay down for an hour after the session.

Let us look at the function "verbalisation". All that talking is, is the flowing of air past our voice boxes in such a way as to make the voice box vibrate to produce a sound. The power given to me was such as to cause me to shake, and my mouth to do all sorts of strange things. I did not worry at all as I had total faith in Spirit. I allowed them to have total control, with me going along with their manipulation, I kept on looking at the light within my mind, and kept being part of it, trying to keep my mind as still as possible.

Spirit must have a lot of power to put into the human body to try and control it; they have to learn to adjust their power, and how to handle it correctly for each person. Look at it as it being similar to a power line that has 240,000 volts going through it (as in the main electric lines in Britain that criss-cross the land on pylons do) and the human body can only take the household voltage of 240volts; so Spirit has to step down their input into the human body, to make the power blend, so the static electric power can manipulate the nerves, which in turn produce the movement of the muscles in the Medium's body which control the air flow through to the voice box, which in turn vibrate while other sets of muscles adjust the vocal cords in such a way to make a noise, in us humans we class as talking, and that in turn produces our own different individual voices. Spirit have to get the functions of the nerves correct [the correct amount of electrical power into them and the correct connections for the right muscles] and that

sometimes can take quite a few sittings. Some more than others, for some a great many years.
Some teachers/tutors have the idea that you must talk when you are in this state to start, and to help Spirit. They say it is for you [the trainee Medium] to say some words to start off with, in fact any words that come into your mind. I personally do not agree with this, nothing came into my head to say at the times I have sat linking with Spirit. All I was doing was to look into the light at third eye level and being part of it, having my mind as still as I could, with no interference what so ever [or should I say as little as possible]. If you want to go along with that school of thought, it is your individual prerogative.

I personally also say you do not interfere with Spirit when they are manipulating the body of a Physical Medium when ectoplasm is being formed. Most Mediums agree with this statement. **SO Why should you interfere when Spirit is producing a voice through a Medium who is in a Trance State?** Is it the fear of going too deep? The fear of letting go. Or is it the wanting to be the person who is in control all the time.

You will find throughout all of spiritual psychic development areas there are many, many, ways to the goal we all seek, and all sorts of different ideas from all sorts of different individuals. **BUT THERE HAS TO BE A CONSTANT!!!!**

In my circumstances I go along with the way of thinking, if I interfere in the early stages bringing my mind into play, in my later development I could bring in my mind, my own thoughts into the speaking of the Spirit control, so colouring any true message from them, so I went along, and still to this day go along with the longer method of development of Spirit manipulation, of giving them a free hand, trusting fully in my Spirit helpers. Another reason I say this is for the simple fact that a lot of people are kidding themselves into the fact that it is Spirit speaking. From what I see, quite often it is only the person's imagination of Spirit and their imagination getting in the way of the truth. I would prefer the honest approach. **YES** honest with myself, and true, **YES** true and honest to Spirit with no interference on my part. I believe a lot of people cannot handle this approach because they have not the strength within their own character makeup, to handle all that Spirit throws at them in this field of Mediumship quite often wanting the quick fix method, they are the people who seem to have the biggest egos. This for me is why they fall short of the ultimate. They seem to accept a lesser level for their development. Some forget as well to keep up their meditation to keep the link built up at a strong level. For some when their Mediumship starts to go down, they resort to tricking themselves into believing the words that come out of their mouths are coming from Spirit, because they have been doing it for a while. Is this the reason that some Mediums have their gifts taken away? Is it the reason they flounder in mid-stream?

## How the system of communication with Spirit works if done correctly when linking with a Physical Medium

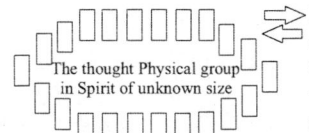

The thought Physical group in Spirit of unknown size ⇌ From the Physical group one advanced Spirit uses the Medium as a catalyst whilst the Medium is in a state of very much altered awareness [Deep Trance] ⇨ **Medium's Spirit.** ⇨ **To the recipients**
Medium's Subconscious
Most times missing the Conscious

**FULL DEEP TRANCE** Mediumship might be the hardest to master, but it encompasses all Mediumship development along the way if done correctly; all that Spirit can give to a person. Most people when they have the ability to go into very deep full Trance; gain the gifts of most of the Mediumship skills laid out in this book. That is **IF they want them and sincerely ask for them while developing** AND MOST IMPORTANTLY **if it is the will of the Divine Spirit.** This comes back again to free will. Some people might not want certain gifts, so they will not receive it, or should I say they will not allow Spirit to bring it forward, it will be still there within them in far greater strength than other people, but they will not, or should I say might not want to bring out a certain gift to the fore.

Here I would like to say something again which is personal to me. I was surprised at the way some spiritual, psychic trainers have the idea that the way Spirit energy comes through a human starting Trance, is different to any other ways. Some trainers in my opinion should not be in their position of teaching Trance. If only they would look and see, and then learn from their own experiences from what they have seen. Yes people twitch, it is a nervous reaction of the power that is being controlled by Spirit, but not sufficiently developed power going into the nervous system of the budding Medium. Some are more prone to the reaction of the power more than others. Lots seem to get a tightening around the face and mouth with the start of manipulation. BUT EQUALLY a lot of budding Mediums kid themselves that it is Spirit doing the manipulating of the body and it is only themselves. The budding Medium should ask within their mind for Spirit to come closer while going into trance state, yes, but if Spirit gives a bad averse reaction to the budding Medium's body, they [the controlling Medium by the side of the budding medium] should firmly ask Spirit for it to be taken away and to tell Spirit how to adjust and what is needed. BUT be careful, if the budding Medium asks for it to be taken away, it might not come back so soon; ask for it to be adjusted.

I found out the hard way at Stansted 1997 in the lecture room in a development Circle, whilst getting the Power of Spirit brought into the back of my body and getting bent backwards. I tried to stop Spirit bending my head backwards over the chair, and my body being straightened. I resisted and it hurt, but my head was forced further back, so I relaxed into the Spirit manipulation, then the pain stopped. The power of the energy was from the back of my head, my neck downwards to the middle of my upper back. It was as though it was a steel rod was planted into my back to keep me rigid. At the time in front of a lot of people in the development Circle, I was feeling uncomfortable and embarrassed, so as I was previously told by an old respected lady tutor Medium, if you do not like anything ask for it to be taken away, as soon as I ask for it to stop, **IT WENT immediately** then because of that and because I had let my mind interfere with the power of Spirit in which I was linked, the link went suddenly and I came immediately out of the Trance situation, and the building up of the Power with Spirit disappeared. Spirit must have been doing it for a reason. I should have gone along with the manipulation of the power in my back IT HAS NOT RETURNED TO THIS DAY five years later in 2000. I felt I was going to be placed straight across the chair and my feet lifted up with my neck only on the chair. **BUT NOW I WILL NEVER KNOW**, OR WILL I? I had forgotten to have total trust in Spirit. If they are going to work with you they are not going to do you any harm.

**THINK ABOUT IT.**
You talk to the planchette to make it move. You talk to the person in transfiguration to help the Spirit in their task to form a better ectoplasm mask over the face of the Medium or manipulate the facial muscles. You sing and laugh to bring up the strength of the vibration level in Physical Circles to bring Spirit forth. You talk to the Medium on the platform to hold the link. You talk to the table to make it move. It all needs the vibration of the human voice to make the link stronger at first. This is where the tutor who should be beside or in front of the budding Medium should be talking to Spirit, saying Spirit, (NOT THE MEDIUM) advising Spirit of the resulting and/or required manipulation or the requests of the group for the Physical Phenomena. This is done whilst the Medium has been keeping the link with Spirit and encouraging them to come closer all the time in their mind then stilling the mind by looking into the light within the mind's eye.

If in my opinion, you let the sitting developing Trance Medium think, making their mind work to try to talk, surely they are coming out of the stillness of their mind, it will in my opinion, interrupt their progress and the link. It might be all right in later stages I do not know for certain, but at first, I would not allow my mind to come out of the stillness until I was being better controlled by Spirit. I allow Spirit to be in full control, trusting in them wholeheartedly. People have said I should control the shakes and judders myself **BUT** that would not give Spirit a passive mind. Spirit themselves have to get the connection correct by trail and error; the Medium cannot know what is required of them.

Another experience whilst attending the Trance and Physical course at Stansted in November 2001, I was suddenly shot out of Trance while Spirit was still manipulating my tubes, from my throat downwards to heaven knows where in my body. I asked the tutor when I was able to speak to him in a shaking voice whether I should go back into Trance. He said "no" just to sit there in the cabinet, so I allowed the tubes to gradually come back to normal which took quite a while trying to swallow and talk to the tutor thinking I was going to choke. I sat down after recovering a bit and then about an hour after I got told off by Spirit who told me I should have gone back into trance to allow them to manipulate the tubes back to normal so as not to cause me any discomfort in the way I had experienced it. For me at the time, it was as if I was choking, I could not swallow and could not do anything about it. Later on after the class had gone to tea and I was sitting quiet on my own, Spirit told me when I give them a free clear mind (well as clear as I can) which is necessary for them, this is so they can blend with my own Spirit and the controlling of the manipulation of the body and it's functions. If the mind or something interrupts the manipulation and I get brought back too quickly, unnaturally (or any Medium gets brought back) the functions are stuck in an unnatural state for that particular human body for everyday functioning. It is necessary for myself (or the Medium) to still the mind go back into an altered state of awareness (Trance state) and allow Spirit to bring the body back ready for it's natural everyday working functioning otherwise the natural bodily functions will be out of synchronisation with brains normal pattern for that body. That night I went to bed and was woken up by someone speaking in my room I opened my eyes and realised the voice was coming out of my chest area so I thought about what Spirit had told me during the day and put myself into a trance state. I always give permission every night to Sprit to develop me. Another very good Trance Medium Melanie Polley said when she was doing a direct voice trance demonstration one time, some foolish person interrupted the flow by making a sudden noise, with the shock SHE ENDED UP AGAIN BLEEDING FROM THE MOUTH.

I watched Jean Skinner while she was in trance for transfiguration and the Spirits came through in the form of a mask on her face. Jean was being looked after by her friend, who told the people around her what to do. The best thing that I learned in that demonstration was, the people who went up to her to meet their loved ones, **had "to talk to" their formed loved one** [forming on a mask on her face], and encouraged them to build up better a mask that might have needed slight alteration and they did, becoming more strong in their developed ectoplasmic mask on the face of Jean. Surely common sense dictates it is the same for a person in Trance. If the Spirit who comes in the form of the control of the entranced person is not having the right effect, not having the right control on the person. They, the Spirit control, should be encouraged by gently talking out loud to that Controlling Spirit **by the leader of the Circle or the teacher/trainer** who should be looking after the entranced person (the budding Medium). The teacher/trainer **should be** [sadly a lot don't, not knowing what to do, they have not been taught properly] in front of the person, **never touching** the person in the Trance but **TALKING TO THE SPIRIT CONTROL** saying what needs to be done to help the person in Trance, trying to bring out the voice of Spirit, whatever, **BUT! NOT** TALKING **TO THE PERSON** being controlled by Spirit, as I believe if at that stage, they spoke to the person in Trance, it would interfere with the mind of the developing Trance Medium making them think. The person who is being controlled should have a still mind (as still as possible).
Also **DO NOT SAY THE PERSON' NAME** that will act as a trigger for them and it will bring them out of the "mind stillness" and so out of deep Trance.

I was in a Circle in the 1970's to the very early 1980's that was in a room above a butcher's shop in Liverpool. The Circle was run by a Medium, Dave Wickins from Liverpool. We, that is all the eight sitters, had no knowledge at all of happenings in a development Circle, we were all complete novices, not knowing what to expect. We were told to close our eyes and see what happens or what comes into our minds. We all just meditated in low red light looking into the colour within the third eye then at the end, we all talked about what we received in our minds. One of the ladies after a short while, [about 3-6 months] started to have an alteration of her breathing, and a strange noise started to come from her. Being nosy I had my eyes open. Dave was quickly in front of her when the breathing altered. He waited, and then started to talk with encouraging words to the Spirit Helper who had started to take control. That lady started to talk in a man's voice, one that was nothing like her own. So you can see why I do not want to let my mind be interrupted by thoughts. The trouble was at Stansted hall the power that came into me was a bit too strong, and Spirit could not control my nervous system very well, and I started shaking and twitching. This is where a good trainer/tutor would have stepped in talking, with guidance for Spirit's development with me. **NOT TALKING TO ME** TO DO SOMETHING ABOUT IT as happened at the time.

Ectoplasm for me started at Stansted in daylight lit room on the 15th of April 1999. I was in Trance and it was like breathing in and out a fluffy thing. It felt as though it was thinner, lighter more open than cotton wool. Like a thick type of air. Like thick cobwebs. Possibly like fine hair. I was aware of it coming out of my nose to my bottom lip slowly in and out as I breathed, it was seen by others in the group. It only lasted for a short while. It might have stopped because I let my mind interfere, wondering what it was, and if anyone around could see it. The next time I went into Trance, I was able to put my mind aside, and accept it, but as I went deeper I got the control of Spirit who was not used to working with me, bringing to me too much power into me at once. The Spirit Power I felt opened my wind pipe/tube, flexing it and I started to judder my inside and mouth and jaw as Spirit was trying to form words through me making the funny **"ABB DAB"** noises. I believe at that time the leader should have been talking to, and encouraging the Spirit control, and to try and help me. At least I was not scared of the happenings. I just accepted it as I had total trust in Spirit. Other people might have reacted differently.

As I said before another time, power came into my neck, back of lower head, and upper back area like a stiff rod, forcing me to straighten those parts. When it came I found it very hard to move against the power and it hurt when I did. When I asked for it to stop, as it was uncomfortable, it did. I realise now I should have let it carry on to give Spirit time to adjust my nervous system and not to resist, not worrying about feelings my the human frame. When it stopped it cause me to come out of the Trance state, again I had let my mind come into play. The next time I went along with the feelings and did not resist, I just kept on looking into the light within my mind [third eye area] keeping my mind still, not letting my mind interfere with the Spirit manipulation. I also got a tightening of the third eye area, no pain or hurt, just a gentle tightening. I also got this dreamy feeling. In the third day of sitting when the tremors came around my mouth, my bottom set of false teeth got broke by the action of the mouth and jaw manipulation not being right at that time. Again I feel the tutor should have taken control and talked to the controlling Spirit.

I can have this dreamy feeling, and tightening of the front head area about the third eye area, just before, say about a quarter of and hour before I work with Spirit, when this feeling comes in my head. I keep inviting Spirit to come closer to me (over and over and over and over again), sincerely asking Spirit from the highest realms to blend in peaceful loving harmony in the Divine Light, to work with me, letting the blending to come only with goodness, kindness, love, light, and truth, and help me in the task ahead. I have put these feelings down on paper so you will know what can happen, and when it does, it will not frighten you. Please remember this is only personal to me, many people have different experiences, some have none. Have **total trust** in Spirit, remember trance is not dangerous if you know what to expect. It is like electricity, it is dangerous if you do not have the correct training, and are not told of the ways to handle it. Electricity can do you harm, yes, but when an electrician works with it, he has been trained and no harm comes of him. What happens to electricity when the power line is cut, and it is not controlled properly? The cable keeps on arcing on the floor or on a wrong connection, the power connected cable continues to jump about, sparks fly all over the place, and the power line bounces all over the place until the power is adjusted [turned off], and when the connection is fixed into the right place, re-connected, so the flow is going along the right path, nothing happens to the cable, the electricity is still there but it is passive. The shaking, juddering, and bouncing around of the cable stops, the correct amount of flow is adjusted to the correct points. If the electrician follows the correct safety standards, and he knows what to expect, if anything does happen the electrician will not get into trouble. So it can be similar in Trance, (or any linking with Spirit) the electrical impulses to the nerves of the Medium's body, if connected wrongly by Spirit, can cause a malfunction of the body's nervous system, making the Medium do unusual things, muscle twitching, tremors, juddering, etc. It is only electrical impulses from the brain that controls the muscles of your body. Spirit has to get used to using it for their purpose of producing a voice, a change of facial features, and in advanced stages Physical Phenomena producing ectoplasm, etc.

When you see a Trance Medium, try to think of how deep they are in that Trance.

Do they keep on having to be prompted by Spirit, getting the words off them and saying them?

Is the Medium mixing their own mind in with the words that are spoken, are the words their own points of view on a subject, or are Spirit in full control?

Yes they might be in a Trance State, an altered state of awareness, **BUT HOW DEEP?**

Are they concentrating on the accents and not the words, which should be given truthfully, do you question them so their information can be checked later, where was the Spirit born? when/how did they die? Mother's name, what did they do in the way of work, etc,

I have seen a lot of Trance demonstrations, and they vary from the total control of Spirit, to the person who is kidding themselves and the others who are watching the Trance demonstration.

I often wonder why certain Trance Mediums only have the same one or two Spirit people coming through them?

Is it because the Spirit Control has had to be the only one of the few who can control the Trance Medium's body functions?

Is it because they are comfortable with them and will not allow others to come in?
Is it that they are only able to be controlled by those Spirit friends and cannot be developed any further?
Is it because the Medium does not sit enough within the Power of Spirit to progress any further?
Is it that Spirit themselves cannot bring anyone else through at that particular time? I do not know the answers, but I am always thinking and wondering, why?
Is it because they do not ask Spirit to bring others to help more people?
I have seen the same presentation from some alleged Trance Mediums, over and over again, have you? I do not mean the first few minutes of the Spirit person coming through with their introduction of recognition. I mean the same presentation that does not vary, and if it does vary, the answers to the questions being as though it is the person in alleged Trance answering, even if it is in a different accent.

Ask the **genuine** Medium about their own development. Ask about their own experiences they had when they first were starting to go into their Trance State. This is the way you learn any sort of Mediumship ask, ask, ask. Question, question, question the people who are **genuinely** doing it.

## WHAT SORT OF A TRANCE MEDIUM ARE YOU GOING TO BE?
## A **SINCERE, HONEST**, and **TRUTHFUL ONE I HOPE**.

A person in Trance is not always in the same state of awareness when they are in a Trance State, they can drift very slowly up and down in a sort of wave like sequence, for that is what they are in. They are linking into Spirit through vibrating waves of energy, and sometimes the Medium can have conditions around them that can fluctuate. The Medium themselves, Spirit Power of the Spirit Link, the sitters energy, the air, intensity of light, sounds, nothing ever stays still, they all fluctuate at different rates at times some quicker than others, and remember they all vibrate at different rates. We, and all that is around us, are all in a state of flux. The weather outside alone, can be in such a condition that is not at all as it should be for sitting for very, very deep trance. That does not mean you should not sit, far from it, it is paramount that you **do** sit for Spirit, when you feel the conditions are not quite acceptable for you, discipline yourself, do not put in excuses ready for not sitting.

Please also do not think you can be always aware of what is happening around you whilst in a Trance State. There are many and have been many Mediums, that have no knowledge of what has been happening while they have been linking with Spirit (I know as it is happening to me and has been for about four years and I know why). Being in an unconscious state of not knowing what is happening when Spirit has the use of their body for the proof of life after our so-called death. It is as though they are asleep; the Medium's brain does not function as it would normally in everyday life, in this state, the brain with the help of Spirit, blocks the memory of what is going on with their body.

Spirit and yourselves, have to learn together to cope with all the varying conditions that we have to deal with on this earth plain. This is one of the reasons that all sitters when developing should be writing down as much information, about **all** the conditions they are working in, so others can see in later times where, when, and how these Spirit Links take place. It also serves as a marker for you and your sitters, to put some extra effort to encouraging in your mind your Spirit Helpers to come closer to you, even though, you should all be doing this naturally now anyway.

All sitting in any Circle should be putting down what happens, (try to tape record each Circle session and go over it later) but for Trance more so, putting down temperature, humidity, if it is wet, dry, sunny, overcast, everything indoors and outdoors. Whether anything at all has changed from the start, during, or at the end of the session. Note also, where it has taken place, the time, the date, how many sitters, light or dark, colour of the light used if any. This is mainly when sitting for Trance for Physical though, but remember you do not know if there is going to be any progression through to Physical Phenomena, so I would personally log from the start in a diary form.

When sitting for ordinary Trance, it should be pointed out a budding Medium does not have to sit in anything other than ordinary light whether it is daylight or artificial. **BUT** I feel all Mediums should be trying to have their development of Physical Phenomena **done in the light** as well subdued lighting **AND in no light at all** as all the Mediums did in the days gone by. Perhaps put separate days aside for each method, in all honesty, I do not know for certain, but there is the new age of changing links in vibration levels that is making the Mediums of old have a rethink, experimentation is always needed by everyone, nothing ever stays still, we and Spirit need pioneers BUT again this is time consuming, if you would like to develop quicker go along in the time established method, go along with the old methods until the new methods are proven. But keep try the new methods.

If possible in the Circle, when sitting for anything, you all should be taping on a tape recorder, and if possible have the Circle recorded on a very low light (low lux) video camera. This is so that the sitters after the session can listen, and see what has gone on while they are having a cup of tea, and sweet biscuits, or cake afterwards. Perhaps sweet fruit, please remember not to leave all the expense, to the owner of the place where you sit. All who sit should put some money in the kitty or have a turn of bring the goodies.

There are many instances when unseen Spirit, and Spirit voices not heard while the Circle has been in progress, have been recorded by mechanical means, your own Circle might also be lucky if you sit in the correct conditions of truth, light, love and peaceful loving harmony, all sending the power to the person sitting for Trance. I suggest you have one night set aside, so all who sit for the Medium can have turns on a different night, sit for each person for half an hour. It will also be noted by the Medium and the sitters that the levels of Trance do fluctuate. If the Mediums voice is not true direct voice of Spirit, it will be heard on the recording that the Mediums voice [I should really put mind or thoughts] is sometimes colouring the true words of Spirit. Learn to pick out these subtleties. Budding Mediums be self critical and true to yourself and Spirit. When some Mediums come out of a deep Trance the whites of their eyes are quite often red, that is something you cannot fake, nor can you fake the sweat on the palms of the hands.

A point that was given to me by a great all round Medium Mallory Stendall [I mean that in the kindest way, as she knows (as she has been gifted with a large body) she is my little love, I call her "my little puddle duck"] was to eat a half of a Mars bar or **a banana** before, and after a sitting for Trance, because Spirit uses the sugar content in the body, and the Medium needs to make it up again. It helps ward off sugar deficiency (diabetes). REMEMBER though if you eat too much sugar the body cannot cope and that could lead to sugar diabetes as well; it is the sensible ways of eating that is most important. But if you are a person who has a problem with phlegm then do not eat the mars bar or any chocolate or **dairy product**. Only eat the banana or sweet fruit.

Try to go and have a course with Mallory, Eileen Mitchamson or any of the **experienced deep Trance** Mediums who do not try to fool themselves. Mallory set me on the correct way in my Trance work by explaining in the right way for me. Others perhaps had told me, and because of their lack of experience in what was happening to me, did not know how to explain to me how to adjust one little thing I was doing wrong, I trusted her judgement because I had seen her Trance work.

For me you have to experience Trance to teach it, because you have to **know and experience** how it can affect you. "IF YOU CANNOT DO IT, YOU CANNOT KNOW IT" Yes you can teach the basics, but as you advance in your Trance work you need in my opinion, someone who has themselves experience what can happen in Deep Trance, and the experiences that can happen when a person is going into the Trance State. Mallory Stendall got me over the hurdle of shaking too much when linking with Spirit. I was going into the light in my mind and giving Spirit the total use of me as a vessel, but I was not telling them in my mind what was going on or how it was effecting me. I now go into the light, if anything starts to react in my body upsetting my normal bodily muscle functions [shaking, heavy twitching, uncomfortable reactions] I come slightly out of the light, [void or the colour, remembering the colour you see is part of light, I personally see mainly pure white light but not always] to become a little more aware and **say in my mind** to Spirit. "Please re-adjust your power as it is upsetting my earthly body" or say what is happening to my body. Then I go back into the light encouraging in my mind, Spirit to come closer, then try to still my mind by becoming part of that light to let Spirit carry on to blend with the linking vibrations within me.

Mallory Stendall was talking to Spirit as I was in Trance and asking them to adjust what ever was happening to my body. As did Judith Seaman when I was in her course sessions, I got my first word out of my mouth in Trance whilst in her group. Both tutors encouraged those in Spirit when they were getting things correct and guiding them when they were getting things wrong also asking those in Spirit for what was require, e.g. for me to speak, to give me something to say, perhaps a message for someone there, to say something, anything, even if it was in my own voice. I at the times of going into a Trance State had nothing at all coming into my mind from Spirit, all I could see was the coloured light, then suddenly I received the word **"transition"**, and nothing more. I do not know whether it was in my mind as a voice or a written word but I know I had the word about three foot in front of me and I had to say it in my own voice. Nothing else was given to me. Since that day I have progressed like anything it is as though the floodgates were opened for me, I must have been ready at that time; Spirit must have seen the correct time and gone for it.

I think here, I will try and explain a little of what happens when Spirit begins to manipulate the vessel [the Medium] when they come nearer, when the Medium goes deeper into a Trance State.
Spirit comes close to the Medium and works mainly with the "main nervous system", "sympathetic nervous system" and the "ganglia"(where the nerves join, the junction box so to speak).
The trainee Medium when starting to sit for Trance should be submissive to the action of Spirit. Spirit has to try and get the actions within the body of the Medium, correct, for the purposes they would like to use the body of the Medium for. This is not always a smooth pathway for them, as they have many links within the nervous system to try and negotiate. This is why time; sitting in passive meditation linking with Spirit is of the utmost importance. Spirit and the Medium, have to be given time together within the power of meditation, the more time taken the better/stronger the link, each developing alongside one other. The Medium or the Medium's earth bound helper, telling Spirit where they are getting the nervous system and the ganglia wrong, by saying how they in Spirit are affecting the Medium. For the trainee Medium, it can be an uncomfortable disturbance when stimulation more than is needed is being given, or over excitement of the nerve impulses occurs. The Spirit Control has to learn alongside the Medium, how to use it's new found vessel, the Medium on how to be passive and to be used.
You might be saying, "What on earth are these parts of the body I have just been told about". So I will try to explain a little more.

The "ganglia" [ganglion, motor ganglia], are a collection of nerve points which co-ordinate the discharges of electrical impulses along the nerves (in this case, our sympathetic nervous system). The main thing to note are the "ganglia" are situated in different parts of the body, outside of the brain and the spinal cord, where most of the nerves are. I will not go into any more detail here for you; if any more information is needed look them up in a doctor's or nurse's anatomy book if you would like to know more, as it is a very complicated yet easy system indeed just like an electrician knows what he is doing when connecting the wire when he is experienced so it is with the experienced Spirit link and Medium. It is always a two-way thing.
The main parts of interest for those who would like to know about Spirit's manipulation in the Medium whilst in Trance, and the parts that Spirit uses, the main part is the system controlled by the "sympathetic nerve" branches, which are connected to the "ganglia".

There are "ganglia" controlling along the sympathetic nerve system going to the muscles that control or help with the function of. I have included what can happen when developing the altered state of awareness for the purposes of linking with those in Spirit :-
**Eye movement**, Trance subjects can have rapid eye movements (REM), watering of the eyes, tears flowing when there is no emotion, whites of the eyes turned red when trance has finished [This is something that is not easily faked].
When sending Spirit's Power to the other people in the Circle my eyes can stream with water [on the outside of the eyes, not as when you cry, the tears streaming down the face on the inside, the side nearest the nose,] when Spirit is very near me and I yawn a lot. I sometimes get this when Spirit comes too close when I am going down into a Trance State, so I have to ask Spirit not to come too close to me. I do this by thought.
**Heart beat**, Trance subjects can have rapid heartbeat, a very strong heartbeat that feels as though the heart is going to come out of the chest, (this is where the Medium can possibly have their direction of development planned out for them, making them aware or being shown if they sit with Spirit in dedication it could be for Physical Phenomena) or in others slowing down of the heartbeat as though it has stopped. Blood pressure in different Mediums is now being tested in different circumstances. Many times it increases. My blood pressure was tested before the Trance state; sitting and waiting to go into Trance for three minutes (not a normal relaxed situation) it was 152 systolic, 98 diastolic. I went into a Trance State and it changed to; 169 for the systolic pressure, 154 for the diastolic pressure; at the end I came out of Trance and was then tested again by the doctor, the blood pressure had changed again to 164 systolic, 104 diastolic. (My normal blood pressure which I had tested by my doctor in 2002 was 130 over

71; {in June 2004 117 over 71} I had not been sitting in 2002 for six months because of a split up of a relationship with a lady). Whilst I was in the state of Deep Trance and getting tested, Spirit was manipulating my face, the tubes down to my stomach, and my breathing tubes. This is the reason not to give a Medium a shock while in **"true"** Trance State. [The Trance State test had to be done for me at the end because the doctor did not do the readings at the time because she was watching the Spirit manipulation of my face, so I went into Trance and gave the thumbs up when I thought the test should be done when I was in an altered state. I was not in as deep an altered state as I was when Spirit was manipulating my face bringing others in Spirit through me]. Some 25 Mediums who were tested at the same time as me had their blood pressure up as well. These are just two of the 25 readings taken at the time, 222/102; 208/189; So it should be now noticed that something different is needed of the Medium's body by Spirit when the Medium is in a **"true"** Trance State. It is known that Spirit uses the water and chemicals from the Medium's body, which thickens the blood. So drink plenty of water while sitting for Spirit.

**The bronchi**, this is the breathing passages and the tubes that are bringing in the air to the body. Trance subjects can have a manipulation of the tubes, a heavy breathing which can sometimes produce a noise from the Medium (don't fake this as it will hold up your development), a slowing down of the breathing, shallow breathing; the Medium can yawn, take in a gasp of breath. Spirit can manipulate my tubes so I am aware of what is going on especially in the early stages. They now are manipulating them so they are wide open all the time I am in Trance, BUT **not** every time I sit.

**The alimentary system.** This is the system that brings (ingests) in the food to the body, digests it and excretes it. This more or less covers :- lips, mouth, teeth, tongue, pharynx (nasal, oral, laryngeal), oesophagus, stomach, duodenum (bile duct, pancreatic duct outer), jejunum, and ileum (plicae circulares, blood vessels, Peyer's patches), caecum, and appendix, colon (bowel), rectum, anal sphincter muscle, anus.

**Bladder.** Remember the increased blood flow/pressure in the tests.

**Uterus.** Remember the increased blood flow/pressure in the tests.

**Penis.** Remember the increased blood flow/pressure in the tests.

**Other involuntary symptoms** that can happen to a developing Trance Medium, if Spirit and the Medium are not in **full** peaceful loving harmony (**and sometimes** when they are) are :-

**The mouth waters with saliva in some developing Mediums, the mouth can become very dry, coughing.** Spirit can be using the water of the body for the person developing or others in the Circle.

**Involuntary muscle movements**, twitching, shaking, nerve endings far more sensitive than normal, many/most times becoming very extra/ultra sensitive, spasms, and convulsions through the nervous system. Spirit is starting to use and get use to the individual's body, nervous system. Sometimes the Spirit World can get the electrical connections slightly wrong hence the slight twitching.

**Face flushed. (skin colour changes)** This is when Spirit is pushing up the blood flow/pressure around the body. Using the water from the body, which consequently thickens the blood.

**Face can get manipulated**. Possible start of transfiguration Mediumship. Spirit starting to use and get use to the body's nervous system, there are forty two facial muscles that the Spirit Helpers have to manipulate if using the Medium for transfiguration when not using only ectoplasm to form the full mask.

**Facial** skin involuntarily tightens, many times uncomfortably.

**Chin area** many times involuntarily drops and tightens.

**Involuntary Lips twitching.** Spirit starting to use and get use to the body's nervous system

**Lips tingling.** Blood pressure altering.

**Lips tighten,** Spirit starting to use and get use to the body's nervous system

**Lips manipulated getting ready to talk.** Spirit starting to use the nervous system.

**Upset stomach**. Spirit using and mixing chemical of the body and getting ready to use them. Best to only have a light meal four to six hours before sitting in a trance Circle, especially if sitting for physical phenomena. Many sitters and especially Mediums have nothing at all day only water before Physical Circles.

**Fingers and hands tingling**. The blood flow increasing to the hands. Spirit starting to use and get use to the body's nervous system

**Sweating and/or sticky hands**. Can mean the start of development of Physical Mediumship. Blood flow increasing to the hands.

A lot of budding Mediums especially when sitting for Trance get **Headaches.** This again is the new blood pressure level needed in Physical Phenomena, **and possibly** Mental Mediumship, also the opening of new pathways and connections needed by Spirit for new linkage in the brain to manipulate the muscles. And those in Spirit learning to change and mix the chemicals needed within the body for the production of ectoplasm.

When I link into the Power of Spirit giving to others in the Circle, I can have my eyes watering coming out of the outer sides of the eyes, not by the nose area as would be expected, if emotions come in, and I yawn a lot.

When starting to meditate, and going into an altered state of awareness to develop, you might get different feelings in your body these should be overcome by trying to forget about the bodily feelings. This is where the looking into your third eye into the light or colour helps no end. Many budding Mediums have feelings of being pressed into the chair they are sitting on; one of their body going lighter, the body going heavier, their legs feeling as heavy as lead, or stuck to the ground, wooziness in the head, becoming light headed. Your head becoming as though it is not part of you.

Remember these are not the only parts of the body Spirit has to use when the Medium is in Trance. They quite often have to use the vocal cords, and the lungs for the air to make the vocal cords work, and so make speech. Also Spirit chemists use their own chemicals and sometimes have to use in the mixture, chemicals in the Medium's [and sitters'] body for the production of ectoplasm for the making of the voice box (etheric amplifier) inside the body cavity. Spirit might use/make things internally if they do not use the Medium's voice box. It can be for Spirit an easier start for the production of the ectoplasm internally, deeper down in the tubes and/or the cavities than the natural voice box in the body of the Medium.

I would like to point out here that a number of people have been trying to get me into the way of thinking of a quick fix method of Trance for the production of physical and a TRUE link with Spirit using the Medium's body for TRUE Direct Voice production and Independent Direct Voice production, saying it could be achieved by listening to audio tapes to send the Medium into the altered state ready for the production of Spirit talking or the production of ectoplasm. This I am finding out is not true; it might be able to send the Medium's brain waves into an altered state BUT not into the stronger altered state needed for Spirit to manipulate the metabolism of the Medium's bodily functions needed for strong TRUE evidence. Yes maybe for Mental Mediumship it **might** be used. For Physical Phenomena look at the functions that we at present can check, and have been checked on me. It is no wonder when sitting for development Mediums get headaches. Spirit has to; for some reason; alter the blood pressure that flows around the body; mine was tested in 2001 whilst in Trance at 169 over 154, as you can see my blood pressure was very, very much up. I was told I should have been dead, and this was while my brain waves were going straight into a state called Theta hardly any Alpha or Delta at all, a state where any normal patient in hospital would be expected to be in a comatose state. Imagine if you started sitting with the tapes and the body was not attuned correctly or you body was weak in certain areas imagine what harm could be done if the development was not taken gently. Look at an athlete, they have to train slowly and work up to a final push without having any damage done to their heart, muscles, bones and other vital body organs. It is exactly the same with Mediumship; you have to work slowly and steadily so when the big day comes you do not have any problems.

By starting to meditate and GRADUALLY building up your Link with Spirit, the budding Medium will have a few headaches as the pressure of the blood flow is altered, and the veins/tubes stretched in the blood's vascular system of the body. This is the main reason the **"in Trance Medium"** should not be put into a situation where shock can occur, as a shock can dramatically increase the blood flow and rupture a weaker blood vessel. So causing internal bleeding. This is when **a TRUE Trance Medium** is working, not one who is fooling themselves.

Now can you see the need for a slow steady progression in your development if you want to be **a true Trance Medium.** This is so the blood vessels can get gradually stretched to the point where it is safe for the Medium to work with Spirit in the Trance induced altered awareness ready for Physical Phenomena.

As I said before, and I feel it should be said again. At the Trance week in November 2001 run by an experienced Medium running the course "Paul Jacobs" I was thrown out of Trance very quick (I think I let my mind interfere) before Spirit had chance to bring back my tubes from my throat downwards back to **normal for my body** and I was in some distress for about five to ten minutes. Between the trying of swallowing and breathing abnormally I asked Paul Jacobs whether I should go back into Trance he said, "No just to sit there in the cabinet" where I was at the time and let my tubes come back to normal. I was told off by Spirit later for not going back into Trance so they could manipulate my tubes back to **my normality of my everyday bodily needs** from the state they were using them in for development purposes. YES Later whilst by myself, I was told off by Spirit and told by Spirit "**If in a Trance State, which is often needed to manipulate any parts of the human body to perform certain tasks needed to prove there is a continuance of life** (and in development of the Medium) **and anything like this happens again IT IS IMPERATIVE to go BACK into a Trance State so we, your helpers in the World of Spirit, can manipulate any parts of the body that were being used, back into a normality, which the body is used to, for use in your everyday life**".

I went to bed that night at Stansted and I was woken up hearing a voice talking and wondering who it was in my room, only to find the voice coming out of my own mouth. It was not my own voice but a very gruff sounding man's voice coming from my stomach area. I was being used by Spirit for practice, I was awake then, I quickly realised what was going on so I put myself back into a trance state while they were still talking and let Spirit carry on. I did not remember what was being said next morning. It was the first time that I can remember I had been used like that at night, BUT I should have expected it. I always say to Spirit during my prayers each night, "I give Spirit permission to use me as an open vessel for my development for a stronger link to prove to others there is life after our so called death as long as they come only with goodness, kindness, love, and truth, come within the Divine Light of Spirit within the loving harmony of Spirit of the highest realms, and I get a good restful nights sleep and wake up fully refreshed". I always do and I have been having the best sleep at night for years now. Even after this incident I was fully refreshed next morning. I am sleeping with a voice-activated tape recorder by my bed now.

I must say here that Spirit can talk to you, through yourself, in a Trance State as you develop and advise you. **IF and a BIG IF** you can go into very deep state of Trance, one of where you "**do not know**" what is going on while recording yourself in front of a video camera. If you "**do**" know what is going on whilst in the Trance State **it is possible** your own mind will colour the message to yourself to what you want to hear. Remember Spirit has to practice **with you and on you**, ready for the public who you and Spirit want to help. I was told by a lot of people you could not develop Transfiguration on you own **but I am**. Do not take any notice of others; go with your own instincts as to what is correct. I am developing slowly and steadily, and no serious shaking as I have told you about in the trance section.

I truly believe I have been put through all these different stages by those in the World of Spirit in the development of my Mediumship, so I can put them into book form for people to learn from and so they will not be afraid if it happens to them.

## AND YOU STILL WANT TO BE A TRANCE MEDIUM?

### BUT! PLEASE REMEMBER, IF SPIRIT IS GOING TO WORK WITH YOU, THOSE IN THE SPIRIT WORLD ARE NOT GOING TO BRING YOU ANY HARM INTENTIONALLY.

#### "IT IS ONLY THE PEOPLE ON THIS EARTH PLANE YOU SHOULD WATCH OUT FOR, THEY ARE THE DANGER"

### I HAVE TOTAL TRUST IN SPIRIT, SO SHOULD YOU. LEARN TO DO SO.

A small point that I thought might be of interest to the reader is I have tried listening to the Pan Pipes for meditating and I could not go into any sort of altered awareness. All I found I did was to listen to the tune and go along with it in my head, **for me** the Pan Pipes do not produce the sort of notes that are compatible to meditation to produce a Trance state. BUT again I must point out it is the person themselves who is the judge and the pan pipes might be OK for them to use. I have always found the lower notes seem more compatible to help make my mind alter it's state of awareness and for me to a keep in that state of silence and harmony with the Spirit, being my Spirit and Spirit of the higher vibrational level.

**All developing Mediums must learn to put their own body aside and not think about what is happening and what they are feeling. Learn to just look into the third eye area at that void, colour, or light, and become part of it, as one.**

# TRANCE DEVELOPMENT CIRCLE

**BEFORE EVERY CIRCLE AND EVERY TIME A PERSON SITS FOR A SPIRIT LINK. THEY SHOULD IN THEIR MIND, BE ASKING AND ENCOURAGING SPIRIT TO COME CLOSER TO THEM AND HELP AT ALLOTTED TIME FOR THE SITTING FOR DEVELOPMENT OR DEMONSTRATION, OVER AND OVER AND OVER. AT LEAST AN HOUR OR TWO BEFORE THE ALLOTTED TIME. YOU CANNOT EXPECT YOUR LINK TO COME AUTOMATICALLY AS SOON AS YOU SIT DOWN IN A CIRCLE OR DEMONSTRATE YOUR SKILL OF A LINK WITH SPIRIT TO PROVE TO OTHERS THERE IS LIFE AFTER OUR SO CALLED DEATH.**

**Each person should be looking forward to the Circle and linking in with Spirit in all sincerity with excited anticipation, especially in Trance and Physical circles.**

When using a light of any kind it should be set low in brightness but bright enough for every person in the Circle to be able to see the developing Medium. In most Circles people developing use a red light as it is said to be better for the seeing of any phenomena if it takes place. It is also said red light does not effect Ectoplasm the same as white light does. I would recommend the light of any sort be covered at the side facing the sitters, especially if the developing Medium is sitting in a cabinet or at the open end of the Circle. The reason for this is every person does not then become distracted by the light and can see into the cabinet or see the area of the developing Medium if any changes take place around them or on them. If the Medium is likely to walk around when fully developed producing physical phenomena and producing ectoplasm then the light should be placed in the middle of the Circle with a shade or a covering over it to cut down the glare of the light. Most circles have better results when the light is at its lowest for every person there to see things happening.

A strange thing happened to me on a week sitting in a Trance development Circle in November 2001, it suddenly hit me **NOT MANY** tutors had ever told any group I had been sitting in over the years the ways of how link with Spirit **NOR** how to send the Power of Spirit to the person developing **NOR** had they **AT THE START, TOLD THE GROUP THE RULES FOR THE CIRCLE DURING THE WEEK**.
I think I should put something down here as the leader/tutor running the Circle should have told the group at the time what was expected of them all sitting for their development as there were a few NEW comers to Circles in the group I was in. Many times they asked to go to the toilet after the Circle had started (WHICH IS A NO, NO) and were allowed to come back into the room again to sit in the Circle after going out! **HOW CRAZY CAN YOU GET ? and this was a Trance Development Circle where every person (12 in the group) was trying to develop.**
If Spirit was developing any person into a Full Trance State it could have been dangerous for that person, even life threatening. This is where rules should be set at the start of the week and at the start of the Circle. Sadly I think some tutors forget the basics over time.
AND another crazy thing was a person in the Circle moved seats to get a better view of the cabinet while the person was in a Trance situation in the cabinet without asking. This could cause an upset in the balance of the Circle conditions as does the to-ing and fro-ing, in and out of the room.
Doors should be made so no one can walk in unexpected with a lock on them or a tape right across the doorway when occupied, NOT JUST A MARKER PLACED WILLY NILLY IN A DOORWAY as a second thought.
**DISCIPLINE HAS GOT TO BE BROUGHT BACK TO CIRCLES otherwise there will be no significant development within the Circle,**

## and certainly NO Harmony built up.

## There are too many people who want a quick fix and the quick link with the Spirit World; it does not come that way.

When people come together to sit for spiritual development of their link, they should be taught how, after they have been through the different stages of relaxation.

Most of these things here are applicable to every Circle.
Every person there in the room should be told what is expected of them while sitting.
All should **go to the toilets BEFORE the start of the sitting**. If any person is allowed out of the room for an emergency, they should **NOT BE ALLOWED BACK INTO THE ROOM TO SIT UNTIL THE NEXT SESSION**. It is not fair on the rest of the group.

The sitting should begin by someone saying a simple sincere prayer. At each subsequent sitting a different person taking a turn. I always say words to the effect of :- "Divine Spirit please help each person here to develop in their own individual way to prove there is life after our so called death, only ever come with goodness, kindness, love, and truth, to come within the Divine Light of Spirit, within the loving harmony of Spirit of the highest realms, and to bring the person being developed, back after their development sitting, safely to their normal self, thank you, amen.
At the first group sitting, all the group should be told where to sit by the leader of the Circle, (male, female; masculine, feminine; strong character, weaker character; positive, negative person) they should sit placing their chairs in a horse shoe fashion, the developing person (is going to sit in the cabinet) is going to sit at the open end of the horseshoe. Leave the chair empty for the first session but in position.
The leader of the Circle should place him/herself on a chair beside the cabinet or next to the empty chair used for each person's development placed at the opening of the horseshoe shape Circle. Some leaders sit in the vacant chair left by the person who is sitting for development when they go into the development position in the cabinet, or at the open end of the horseshoe Circle (most don't, leaving the chair empty, and unselfishly staying by the developing Budding Medium as help giving their energy, talking to and encouraging **Spirit** (from within their mind, some talk very low to Spirit) **NOT the person developing**, to help that person who is developing).
Have an unselfish, giving, sensible, knowledgeable person on the other side of the cabinet/development chair.
Some leaders like to start the sequence of sitting with the people who are at the right hand side of the cabinet then go around the Circle anticlockwise, others prefer clockwise starting at the left of the cabinet
The person picked for the Circle is asked to sit in the chair at the open end of the Circle or in the cabinet.
The persons picked for development should be picked by the leader, and told previously in what sequence, **NOT in a random way,** as some might get more turns at sitting than others during the time the Circle is sitting, this way it is easier for the leader to remember who has had their turn in the cabinet (or on the development chair). It also has the added benefit of having the people who come next in the sequence prepare themselves for their next sitting. Also it **cuts out any disharmony and negativity** towards the leader that might occur so breaking a vital part of any Circle, that being the **loving harmony within that Circle**. It makes it fair for all. Some Circle leaders in development Circles I have sat in, pick out their favourites more than the others to sit for development, this way cuts it out. Be fair to all.

A drink of water should be at hand for each person that needs one, **before the circle is started**.
Each person should be told to be in their seats, settled, and eyes closed, asking within their mind over and over again and again, for Spirit to come closer and help with the development of all in the Circle, 10 minutes **before** the Circle leader comes into the room.
All in the Circle should be told to be asking Spirit to come closer and help with the coming development of the people who are going to sit and for everyone sitting to be joined as one, talking to Spirit naturally within their mind **at least an hour before the sitting** of the Circle, to prepare themselves in that way in a quiet place. It is for the benefit of the group as a whole and it brings into play **togetherness**, a greater **harmony within the Circle**, which is necessary, all thinking of each other.
Each person from that time on should be in the same seats each time they sit in the Circle. **NEVER**

moving seats and swapping seats in the Circle unless told to do so at the beginning of the Circle by the Circle leader to bring into the Circle a better balance and harmony.

When the budding Medium is placed in position, each person is asked to close their eyes and link into Spirit by asking **sincerely,** really meaning it, asking over and over and over again within their mind, for those in Spirit to come closer and fill them up with their Divine Power, asking for the group as a whole to be as one for the purpose of the individual being developed, and each person in the Circle giving permission to Spirit to use them as an open vessel for the benefit of the person sitting for their development, asking Spirit to send the power, they have received, to the person being developed. All the people in the Circle can open their eyes after about five minutes, when they feel the presence of Spirit within them, (Or when the leader asks them to come back out of meditation) and then watch the person as they sit. This is so they can report back at the end of the sitting all they have seen, felt, heard and have been aware of. The group can say what is happening during the sitting **BUT** each person should be always asking Spirit within their minds to help, (over and over and over again **sincerely** really meaning it, every so often), with the person's development and come closer and fill them up so they can sent the power to the cabinet.

It is OK, (if the person who is sitting for development says it is), for each person in the group to say at the time about the things they see, hear, feel and are aware of.

Some sitters like music or different kinds, a chant or the group singing, so have your preference or tape ready.

All this should be done for each person in the group **NOT JUST AT THE START of any sitting.**

**The leader each time another person sits for their development, asks the group to link with Spirit and ask for them all to blend and the ask Spirit to fill the Circle with the Power of Spirit, to use each individual as an open vessel and to make the Circle as one, asking for them all to blend in harmony and to send the power they all generate to the person being developed.**

**All who sit in any development Circle should be told :-
"WHAT YOU GIVE OUT TO OTHERS, COMES BACK TO YOU TEN FOLD, <u>if given unselfishly</u>, and <u>with all sincerity</u>. So do not be mean about what you give to others who are sitting in development Circles. YOUR TURN WILL COME".**

The person sitting for their own personal development, at the opening of the Circle or in the cabinet, in the Circle should have been asking Spirit to come closer and help with their development for half and hour before the Circle sitting. This is where the leader should have told the group before hand who is likely to be sitting.

When the person is sitting in the cabinet or in the chair for development they should be asking Spirit to come closer for about five minutes-ish, or until they feel Spirit near, while looking into their third eye region into the light and then stop talking within their mind and let Spirit take over and do what they have to for their development. Let Spirit use the stillest mind you can have by looking into the light. It is how we all develop, by being sincere and in a submissive state for Spirit.

One person at a time for about half an hour is asked to sit in the cabinet (this encloses the energy being generated by Spirit, the curtain can be left open or closed for a while e.g. five to ten minutes, unless it is for Physical Phenomena then the curtain is kept closed), or on the chair at the open end of the horseshoe Circle, which ever you are using.

The person who is sitting for their development should have been asking Spirit a good hour before hand in preparation, to help them while sitting in the appropriate position for their development, asking for the development they want and talking to Spirit asking them to come closer until they feel Spirit there. The person when sitting and having the power of all in the Circle aimed at them, should sit with their eyes closed looking into their third eye area into the light or a colour, while trying to still their mind as much as possible just letting their thoughts flow in and out of their mind while looking into the light or colour, and not thinking of what they want to happen. This is now up to Spirit. They will guide you if they want you to speak if doing it inspirational, or if you go into more altered awareness. Spirit might start to alter the muscles of the face so starting your Transfiguration. This at first can sometimes be seen as tubes in the face being filled with fluid. This is where the adjustable red light is so important because there might be ectoplasm started being produced so watch out for it. Ectoplasm it is said fails when there is too much white light or bright red light. BUT Spirit is trying to deal with this problem, so experiment. I know of Mediums of the past like D.D. Home, who produced Physical Phenomena in daylight. Please do not try to fool the people who are around you into thinking you have a link and you haven't, the only one you will be fooling is yourself and you will be doing a disservice to Spirit, these lies will slow your development. Remember the cause and effect, what you give out comes back to you ten fold only let it be goodness.

For the benefit of the person who had been sitting for their development. At the end of the development sitting of the person, the group who had been giving power to the person, one by one in a clockwise direction is asked to say what they have seen, felt, heard, or have been aware of as the person who was being developed is still sitting relaxing and being brought back to normality. [better to write it down for the person and go over it at a later time]. This should be done after the developing person comes out of their muggy or dreamy state or later, as some Deep Trance Mediums can take a long time to come back to normality. They can be in a dream like state where nothing sticks in the mind for about an hour or two, possibly longer. They sometimes do not realise it until later, thinking they are alright at the time, replying normally. I know, it has happened to me quite a few times at Stansted hall after sitting for my trance development.

The leader should make sure the group Circle ends the sitting with a sincere prayer of thanks, and arranges the next meeting with Spirit, saying when.

## A CIRCLE WHEN SITTING FOR THE DEVELOPMENT OF A MEDIUM WHETHER MENTAL, TRANCE OR FOR PHYSICAL PHENOMENA

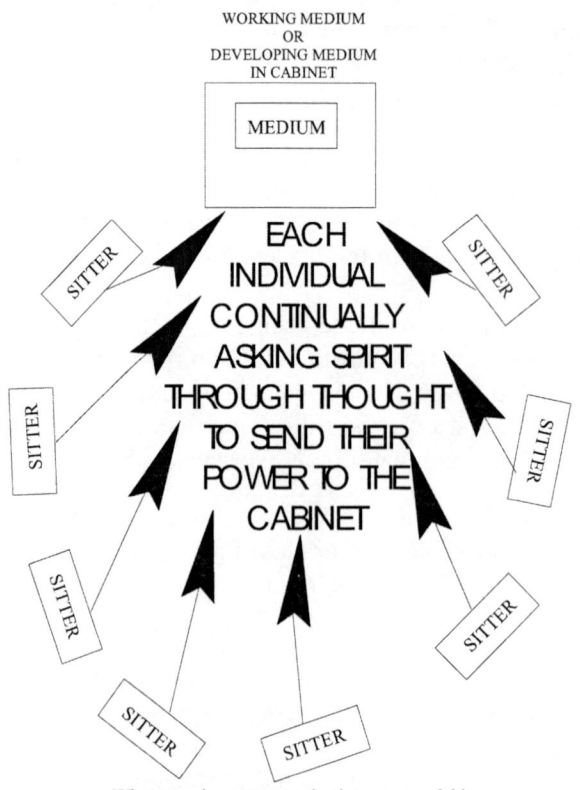

WORKING MEDIUM
OR
DEVELOPING MEDIUM
IN CABINET

MEDIUM

EACH INDIVIDUAL CONTINUALLY ASKING SPIRIT THROUGH THOUGHT TO SEND THEIR POWER TO THE CABINET

SITTER SITTER SITTER SITTER SITTER SITTER SITTER SITTER

What you give out comes back to you ten fold.
Be generous and sincere with your power.
Keep on asking within your mind from those in Spirit,
for you to be used as an open vessel. Give Spirit permission
for you to be filled up with the power of Spirit then keep
on sending the Spirit power mentally to the person who is working
or being developed in the cabinet. If you cannot feel it, keep on asking
within your mind for Spirit to come closer and help they will eventually.
This applies in any Circle and a Physical Circle

# EYE POSITIONS WHEN DEVELOPING

Please do not think these eye positions are definitely required, it is only through my own experimentation I am putting my thoughts onto paper. Other people might have different requirements. But people who I have talked to so far agree with me. I am trying to help everyone by my experiences so you do not have to grope in the dark with your development as I had done. Half the time it was like being in a secret society, not many people would tell you too much in case you knew more than them and you would displace them. I believe the pupil is ready when they know as much as you and they want to learn more. The only trouble is with your spiritual development you cannot rush it; the main thing is patience and time. It all comes when you are spiritually ready and not before. When the pupil is ready the tutor will appear. It also should be remembered that you should not be thinking of where your eyes are. These are only first and foremost exercises, yes place your eyes in the direction you wish BUT you should most of all be concentrating on stilling the mind by looking into the light within the mind so the World of Spirit has the use of your still mind, one of no thoughts or as few thoughts as possible going through it, so they can develop the budding Medium. Do not worry if your eyes do not stay in one position, this is normal. Some might dismiss the eye positions as not being relevant to Mediumship. I must say to those people it has been found out by the government and military of many countries; if a person places their eye direction towards the third eye and upwards in the head, people have what we in Spiritualism call mediumistic vision and/or experiences, so bear this in mind. This was done scientifically over a great many years, not just by experimenting on a few people, not just in any one country.

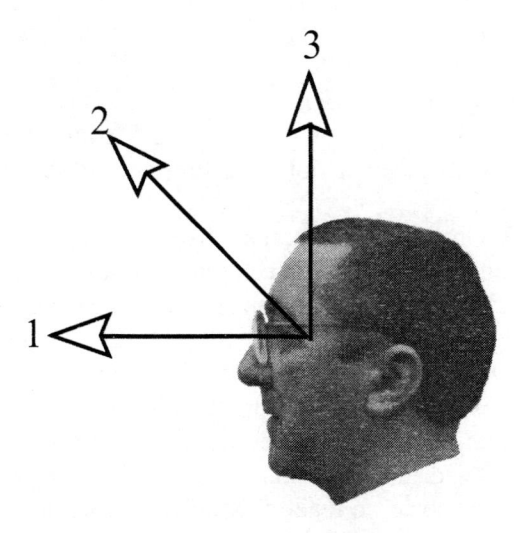

When meditating with my **eyes closed and looking into the light in my mind.**

I am finding out that the direction of my eyes for a **Light Meditation, Very Light Trance** and starting off the early stages of **Mental Mediumship** are pointing forwards as in the **No 1**.

For a development of **Mental Mediumship** and a **Light Trance** my eyes are pointing towards the third eye as in **No 2**.

For development of **Deep Trance** and the development of **Physical Mediumship** my eyes are pointing upwards as in **No 3**. This position is when Spirit can click a switch in the brain and knock you out so you can become unaware of what is happening around you.

IF YOU go too quick in these stages there is a possibility of having headaches please for your own sake go slowly and gently as you would with any exercise, you will be using muscles of your eyes in such a way you have not done before.

It should be pointed out that when advanced, some people when giving a Trance Address or doing Trance Healing can have their eyes open like in Psychic Surgery.

# TRANSFIGURATION

This is the first dictionary wording I felt that I should add to this book because of a certain lady, a Scots SNU trainer/teacher Mrs Faulkner, a person who sharply told the people who were with me in a room at the University in a test situation at Ayr, the Transfiguration that Spirit and myself were doing is not, it is moulding, because she had not seen any ectoplasm, she then stormed out of the room saying "I do not know what I am doing here". **Lets get things straight**. These books are written by individuals within the SNU, (these books are being changed all the time to suit the changing climate like at present in their healing manuals). **Who is to say ectoplasm is not being used when "moulding" is being done, for ectoplasm can be invisible.** At least she could not say it was myself trying to fool anyone, because at the time I was wired up by a doctor, my brain waves were bouncing from Beta then straight down into Theta, very little in between (Alpha or Delta), and my blood pressure was very much up (169 over 154) while the Spirit was manipulating my face (Transfiguration) as it was happening.

**Transfiguration** by dictionary definition is :- to change the figure of; a change of form or appearance; to change the outward appearance of; to change the shape of.

I think the people from the SNU should rename "moulding of the face of a Medium", as it is really transfiguration; it changes the form of the features or figure of the Medium. When ectoplasm is used, it is a covering of a thought form (and not always near to the Medium, can be as much as 20 inches away from the Medium according to Baron Von Schrenck Notzing) over the Medium's face or body to make the mask of the person in Spirit. That for me is not change of form, it is another substance, ectoplasm, which is being moulded by the Spirit World into a Spirit form. It is not transfiguration of the Medium. It is the moulding of ectoplasm.

**WHICH IS <u>TRUE TRANSFIGURATION</u>?** BOTH ARE.
**WHICH IS A <u>CHANGE OF FORM</u>?** BOTH ARE. One being the Medium form changed, and the other, the ectoplasm being change from a mist, a film, a cloth-like substance, or a gas into whatever form it is seen in.
**WHICH IS MOULDING?** BOTH ARE. One the Medium, the other the ectoplasm.

Both are change of form; one is changing the form of the ectoplasm produced from the Medium and being moulded into the form needed. Spirit also moulds or changes form of the features of the Medium's body whether it is with ectoplasm seen or unseen, it is the same. SPIRIT ARE TRYING TO PROVE TO THE PERSON LOOKING AT THE MEDIUM, THAT LIFE CONTINUES.

It can be argued that the ectoplasm changes form/shape to fit the thought form over the Medium's body parts, or the Medium him/herself changes their features/figure into the Spirit form. Why! OH! Why! Do people in SPIRITUALISM try to be so ridged in what is only a word that can have many meanings? They seem to use their little petty position of power to make themselves look important? They can be so nasty sometimes.

It is the wise man that makes things simple; it is only a fool that makes things complicated. [This is the fool trying to make themselves look clever/good].

Transfiguration is a form of Mediumship, which is another branch of Physical Mediumship. This also can **"sometimes"** require ectoplasm from the Medium and the chemicals from the Medium as well as the sitters in different quantities. The Medium can be in Trance of different levels depending on the individual. This is to form the mask or full face of the person who has passed into the higher vibrational plane onto the Medium linking with our Spirit friends. **BUT** sometimes Spirit will use the Medium's brain linkage then pass electrical impulses through the nervous system of the Medium so adjusting the muscles and the manipulation of the facial features, and Spirit can have the Medium's body pump fluids into the facial parts to swell it if the person who is across the veil had a chubby face to be recognised by. When the development of the Transfiguration is in it's early stages, tubes can be sometimes seen forming on the face of the Developing Medium. Often later on in their development, the Medium can have their bone structure stretched or shrunk where necessary. This for me is transfiguration in the true sense of the word. **BUT <u>I do not say</u> that ectoplasm is <u>not</u> being used by Spirit. Ectoplasm can be invisible in different lighting.**

When Mediums are in the process of being used for Transfiguration, they can have their hands changed into the hands of the person being shown on the transfiguration Medium (the "dead" person from across the veil, who are not dead but continuing life on another level), and sometimes it can be the hands of another person, and not the one being shown on the transfiguration Medium's face/head. The transfiguration Medium's hand/hands can shrink, become larger or smaller, be arthritic, fingers deformed the same as the person who needs his/her presence observed, and fingers becoming longer or shorter, fatter or thinner so watch out for these things.

A very famous Medium of the 1860's Daniel Dunglas Home was said by many to have changes of his full body, often being elongated, not only just his face. First it went larger, then smaller, and then normal size, the changes were extraordinary. It was said after that, the face then became gradually enlarged at all points, and then it gradually became smaller in features and deeply wrinkled and puckered" (an extract from "Shadow and the Light"). NOW **THAT IS TRANSFIGURATION** NO ectoplasm was seen in his many Transfigurations, BUT this change, and very occasionally some ectoplasm was sometimes seen if he was in the right conditions around him, even in white light and daylight conditions.

As with all Mediumship, you have to ask through thought for the gifts you would like to be given to you **before** you go into your deep meditation and so into the Trance State when your mind should be as still as possible. I do this stage of quietening the thoughts going through my mind by looking into the third eye area into the Divine Light, a colour or a void. Saying within your thoughts to those who look after you, for the things you want, say at the start of your prayers in this case for Transfiguration. You can be given the gifts even if you have not asked for them. Some Mediums just sit for Trance, and end up being given all manner of Physical Mediumship. Spirit might have guided the person along the route of their discovery to this particular field of Mediumship, or any other form of Mediumship because they have the knowledge of what would be better for the Spirit World to work with, and what would be best for the aspiring Medium.

As with all gifts, ask for the Spirit Helpers to come close to you and help, see them around you within your mind's eye, and feel them coming closer next to you, encouraging them as they come closer, by sending out your loving thoughts, being positive, sincere, asking Spirit to only bring goodness, kindness, love, truth, and asking to blend in the Divine Light of Spirit and to blend within the peaceful loving harmony of the highest and purest kind with them, so you can prove to others there is life after our so called death. Then still/quieten
the mind.

The ectoplasm that forms comes around the Medium's face to form a mask over the Medium's face. It can be seen in normal vision by all there at the séance, it is seen as real as you and I, it is not seen clairvoyantly as some people think. This is generally a face of a loved one of one of the sitters, one that has passed over to the higher sphere; it can also be a guide or helper. The Medium quite often then speaks with the voice of the loved one whilst still in Trance, and the mask still in place. Many, many times this form of Mediumship brings comfort to the sitter, knowing the person who has past over to the higher plain what is known as being dead, is still "alive" and has only progressed to another realm, a higher vibrational level of existence, YES that person **"is not dead"**!

BUT what must be remembered if Spirit starts to manipulate the face or starts putting on an ectoplasmic mask over the face and the Medium starts talking and **pretending** to be that person, the development might well stop. It is best to get one part of the development correct first before embarking on another, together with another. The one branch of Mediumship already developed might well suffer. As other students, tutors and I have seen in one Transfiguration Medium. Please remember Physical Mediumship and Mental Mediumship work on two slightly different vibrational levels. This lady was using Transfiguration and the clairvoyance/clairaudience together.

I saw this difference in vibration levels as a fact in front of about 20 students in Hafan-y-Coed in July 2003 when a moustache was physically forming on the upper lip of the student [Rosemary]. I was told by her Home Circle tutor [another student in my group] who was working with her home group that she thought Rosemary was ready to speak, I let her take over as I did not think she was at that time ready, when Rosemary and her Spirit Helper were asked by her Home Circle tutor if she had anything to say, the hairs forming on the lip vanished in an instant, then she spoke. This was a nice learning situation for all the students and tutors to see the difference in the vibration levels when the Medium is being used for physical phenomena and then mental Mediumship [but in trance or altered state].

Please remember in this situation this is NOT Spirit using the voice box of the entranced Medium direct; it is the Medium being used as an instrument for inspirational speaking. When Spirit is using the Medium direct then the manipulation of the face is still there and they are using the voice box independent of the Medium's mind [in a strong link situation], BUT even then the Medium should tell the truth as to whether they are aware of what is happening and to the amount they think they the Medium and Spirit are involved in the talking, any lies will be detrimental to the Transfiguration Medium's development.

I saw a Transfiguration Medium for the first time at the Liverpool Spiritualist Church in the late 1970's. The last one just recently was the Transfiguration Medium, Jean Skinner, (from Cleveland) at a séance at Stansted hall on a course, in 1999 (I have seen her many times since {the last in 2003}). This was done in red light. There was one light set above the blackened cabinet to shine down. And two red lights at the side of the cabinet, to stop any shadows forming on the face of Jean. Jean sat at the front of the cabinet, just inside, no curtain. There were two Mediums at the side of the cabinet sending power to Jean, one each side. Jean went into Trance very quickly. The Spirit control came through and spoke through Jean. Jean started off by a Spirit Contact coming through, and talking about the contacts they had for someone in the audience, when contact was made with the right person, the person was asked to go up to Jean, and sit in the chair that was placed in front of her about two feet away. The person was asked to send out their loving thoughts and to encourage by talking and advising the Spirit Contact to alter the mask on Jean when the Spirit coming through in the ectoplasmic form over her face was recognised. Each person who went up could see their loved ones. I personally could not see very much of the ectoplasmic mask at the front only a haze, but when I went to the side I could see the eye and nose area very slightly change, and the mask forming slightly away from her face. Towards the ending of the séance I could see a blue/white sparkling mist at the right hand side of Jean covering her right shoulder, obscuring it at times, also it covered the right hand side of the body and in the cabinet. I also saw her hands elongate at times to match the person who's mask was being formed by Spirit over Jean's face.

Jean, because of **her personal bodily make up**, has been told by Spirit to eat no red meat, and drink plenty of cabbage water, which incidentally she does not like. This she has been told from Spirit it is best for **her** body, as she said; it is personal for **her** own body needs. I personally try to eat porridge each morning. It gives me warmth when sitting in the cabinet as it can go cold when the Power of Spirit comes in strong; I also eat meat nearly every day.

Another Transfiguration Medium I saw a few times whilst attending different courses in Stansted Hall in 1999 was Dianne Elliot from Manchester, I have sat for in her cabinet in her Home Circle. Her method of Transfiguration was different to Jean Skinner's. Dianne brought her guides through as well as the guides and loved ones of some of the people in the audience; it was different to Jean's séance in as much that Dianne's face changed fully each time. It was as though it was manipulated and quite often drawn in, changing her face to someone different than her own, also it was blown up, extended, and bloated especially the lower head and neck area, the hands were seen to elongate dramatically as well at times. All and some of these things happened when different people came through with the help of Dianne's Mediumship, it was a pleasure to see both of the Mediums working with their links in their own individual ways for Spirit, to prove there is life after our so called "death". Look seriously at people's faces and see the face as a whole you will notice, the part above the eyes is nearly the same except for the wrinkles. The structure above the eye brows and the hair line are fundamentally the same this is why a lot of Transfiguration Mediums wear a black head scarf, it is to enhance the facial area itself.

Spirit is now manipulating me for use as a Transfiguration Medium, this is something I would never have thought possible as I am sitting on my own twice each day within my séance room in my open cabinet (it has curtains but not closed) for my own development and have been doing so regularly since 1998. This is Spirit manipulating/using my facial muscles through my nervous system and pumping and withdrawing fluid into and from my facial area as it happens. This can be seen in a student in the early stages on the face where tubes start to form on the face and neck, and many times after and during development the tubes can be clearly seen, remembering we are never fully developed so keep sitting for your link with Spirit.

I have been sitting on my own in very low red light in front of a video camera, which is connected to a video recording machine, going into an altered state of trance (awareness) for at least an hour a day (many times two hours one in the morning and one at night) and asking Spirit to develop me to prove to others there is life after our so called death and to prove it by Physical Phenomena, then leaving it up to

Spirit. I have of course attended as many courses in 1997, 1998, 1999, 2000, 2001, 2002, 2003, as I have been able to at the Arthur Findlay College in Stansted Hall, I think about 16 to date, so this has boosted my development no end. I am going to try and write another book and put as much as I can about my development and how I achieved it, as well as all the feelings that I had during the development of my gifts from Spirit, so others can be helped by it. I was thinking of calling it :- "Warts and All to Oneness". I also sit in meditation in the light of a morning. Even then I am also aware of the Spirit World manipulating my face. With my eyes closed, I still look into the bright light of Spirit and become part of it as they do their work in my development.

When Spirit come to my face, **at first** I am aware of the feeling it gives differently **inside** my mouth and cheeks, it is an awareness of the feeling of the muscles being moved on their own. There are no outward signs of manipulation on my face at this stage (this is noticed afterwards when I look at the VCR recordings taken by cameras, as I am aware of the feelings at the time but not part of it as it is happening). The feelings then become stronger and my facial outside muscles start to get manipulated. At the start of my development the muscles seemed to be getting stretched beyond the movement of my normal facial movement and sometimes it was **very** uncomfortable. My jaw was often dislocated and put into a longer jaw line position. Surprisingly this was not painful it just felt unusual and very strange. But at other times when Spirit stretched my jaw muscles forcing my jaw outwards, that was very uncomfortable. These different movements soon became normal and I was able to accept most of them without the discomfort I first felt when my facial muscles were stretched beyond the norm for **my** own facial features. It has taken a while for Spirit to get other people's faces (of those in Spirit) positioned onto mine in such a way that other people who sit with me can recognise them. People who have not been through this might say, "You have to tell Spirit not to do it because you are in control and they should not be hurting you". To those people I say, "You have to still your mind as much as possible and become part of the Light and Oneness of Spirit, so leaving the bodily/earthly functions at the back of your mind and try not to think about them". Yes at the time I am aware of the muscles getting stretched and manipulated bringing me some discomfort but that is not important. That discomfort goes after a while when the settings of the face are stretched or shrunk to Spirit's satisfaction, it diminishes and then goes altogether after sitting a few times. The most important thing to me is the development of my Link with Spirit to prove there is life after our so-called death, Spirit knows what needs to be done, **and "in Spirit I trust implicitly".** Remember during all the things happening to me, with my eyes closed, I am still looking into the light within my third eye region and being part of it.

Please think on about the manipulation of your facial muscles as they can be stretched beyond the normal formation of your face, so after a few years the skin of your face which in old age loses it's elasticity does not return to what it was in earlier years. If you are worried about your appearance of your face do not try to go into transfiguration, you start to look old before your years. All physical Mediumship has an effect on the body, as Spirit needs to manipulate things within the human body, which are not normal for the every day existence of living by the human form.

I often lie in my bed and meditate linking with the higher life. I do this sometimes before I go to sleep and other times before I get out of bed in the mornings. I have found whilst meditating in bed, when Spirit wish to manipulate my face rather than link for the Mental Mediumship side of things; if I have pillows propping my head up, they, Spirit, force my head back into the pillow in such a way that I have to take away the pillows to make myself comfortable, fully relaxed and in a full prone position.

I have been watching the Open University programmes on TV just recently and on one of them it was pointed out that the facial features and movement are made by 42 different groups of facial muscles. But on an American programme it said 46 facial muscles, even so, you must all surely agree it must be a monumental task for our Spirit helpers to get the faces of those gone before onto a Transfiguration Medium's face for all to recognise, that is if they use the method of manipulation through the linkage of the nervous system of the human body as they are at present using on me, and a very great and wonderful thing if they use ectoplasm, or a mixture of both, what a feat it is of the Spirit Group who do the linking of Spirit of the Medium to Spirit from across the veil.

Spirit are now we are told, are trying to make the ways easier to link with Spirit for the earthly Medium, and are experimenting with ways not to harm the Medium in the production of Physical Phenomena, as sometimes happened in the days gone before with ectoplasm which was/is dangerous for the Medium in many ways. All the ways are with experimentation with all concerned in Circles and with those who sit alone in trusting those across the veil to know what is best.

A person I met one development week when I doubted myself put this to me. "While you are demonstrating your gift to a group of people, if you help **only <u>one</u> person** by bringing their loved one forward **who <u>they</u> recognise,** it has been worth while. It does not matter what other people saw as long it was the truth and done with honesty and sincerity from you, it certainly then had been worthwhile". I thank **<u>sincerely,</u>** from the bottom of my heart, Sterling (a Physical Medium) from Ashton-U-L. near Manchester for that remark.

I saw a Transfiguration Medium who was very good go downhill over the years with her Transfiguration (at that time Spirit was building a very strong ectoplasmic masks on her), through I believe, using Mental Mediumship at the same time during her demonstration. After a while, Spirit could not build nor hold the very weakly formed mask on her face at the same strength she had years previously Now when she demonstrates you can very rarely see it. Or was it she would not let Spirit do their job of one Physical link stage and then Mental Mediumship at different times? Please remember Mental Mediumship and Physical Mediumship work on a different vibrational level to each other. The Medium, if using both in the same demonstration, has to come out of one [being adjusted by Spirit in one vibrational level] to go into the other [to another vibrational level of adjustment]. Spirit in the main [if the Medium is not fully advanced] has to link with the Medium for one then alter the vibrational linkage to try and get a slightly different level of a linkage for the other in the Medium's bodily makeup. I was very surprised in July 2003, when this Medium, what I thought was a very nice quiet subdued North Eastern lady, told me she did not say her prayers or meditate between her demonstrations. Is it any wonder that her Mediumship has gone downhill or/and was this a ploy by her to stop me developing in my constant development as many student Mediums said later. Quite honestly up until this point I had a great respect for her. I thought she was a nice quiet small person from the North East, but not any more after her being reported to the management by a lot of Students about doing her best to stab me in the back on that transfiguration week and she stupidly did it again whilst apologising in front of about twenty five-ish students. This happened after I was asked by Allan Mayze the main share holder/owner to come down to the Hafan-y-Coed spiritual centre on the transfiguration week in 2003, and support this not so nice Medium and another lady Medium [who for many years helped at Stansted hall with her husband, her husband was the odd job man then sometimes acting under-manager/manager]. Those two ladies who before that I thought were very spiritual and caring; and again on that week very much shocked me. Watch your back with these so-called spiritual people you might push them off their very high pedestal. I was very shocked also by this lady from Stansted when she was taking a joint tutorial with me the following week. When a lot of the students were in an altered state of awareness sitting around a table that we were all trying to levitate or move with the help of the Spirit World she sharply slapped the table with her hand. Everyone was very shocked by her actions. One lady had an upset stomach for a few hours after, and this was from a lady who says she has been in Spiritualism for well over 50 years.

Before any demonstrations I do, I always meditate for at least three quarters of an hour to an hour plus and I am now always asking the World of Spirit throughout the day of the demonstration to bring on my face friends and relations of people in the audience. I also talk to the Spirit World through thought over and over and over again and again for many hours before the demonstrations. Most times I start in the morning having asked in my daily prayers the night before, as I normally do. I know I am doing things correct as there are many different relations coming forward on my face for those loved ones in the audience be it two or many. My face is now being manipulated by the Spirit World, shown to the sitters or an audience in front of me in every permutation, being elongated, fat, round, and small and all the different combinations of the human face.

# THE CABINET

A cabinet is generally used in Physical Circles to concentrate the energy needed for Physical Phenomena BUT there have been many reported instances where Physical Phenomena has been produced without. The guidance for enclosing the energy to produce ectoplasm and so a human form was given by Spirit as the best way for them to use the Medium's bodily makeup and the combined energy of the Medium and the sitters.

I have made a drawing of the wooden one I have in my séance room, there are few different designs so look around for the best for yourself. Many of the books say the Mediums of old used a pole that was put across the corner of the room and a heavy dark cloth placed over it. The Medium then sat on a chair behind the curtain to concentrate the power build up and to exclude the white light that can destroy the Physical Phenomena and/or ectoplasm.

If a cabinet needs to be used in different locations one can be built out of a collapsible wooden frame covered in a cotton, woollen or as natural as possible, black (or as dark as possible) fabric. I have one made out of wooden frame six foot high, by three by three feet at the bottom of the frame; the top of it is slightly narrower because of the stability factor.

The cabinet I have at present and take around with me to different venues is frame I bought it in a camping shop and I adapted it for my own purpose covering it with black cotton. It is made out of the folding metal framing of a camping or caravan toilet tent. You have to be careful to cover the frame, as metal and ectoplasm do not mix very well. It is known that when people wear metal objects e.g. rings, necklaces, bracelets, etc., in a Physical Circle and the metal is next to the skin the person wearing the metal object they can get burned if ectoplasm is formed in that Circle. I also see in many churches, especially the ones in the North West of England are now buying chairs made of metal and throwing out their old wooden chairs. I wonder what would happen if in a Physical Circle someone got burned when ectoplasm was present. Who would foot the bill if the person sued? I bet not the person/persons who suggested the change. These things should be taken into consideration; I bet they have not by any of the church committees. OR, Is it that the people taking over on the committees do not want any Physical Circles in the churches now? It has been told by Spirit, wood acts like a battery, storing psychic energy.

## PHYSICAL PHENOMENA

The definition of physical in a dictionary is :- opposed to spiritual, of the body, of matter, pertaining to matter, something solid, something tangible, material [not moral, spiritual, or mental].

The definitions of physical for the vast majority of Spiritualist are :- As seen, heard or felt by **all** or most, there at the time [perhaps in a séance or where ever], Spirit photographs, table tilting, levitating of the Medium and objects, asports, apports, transfiguration, slate writing, Spirit breezes/winds, smells of different sorts, Spirit touches, tugs of clothing, luminous faces, luminous ectoplasm, ectoplasm, Spirit painting/art, Spirit writings, slate writings, Spirit raps, Spirit knocks, percussion in the air, direct voice, Spirit whistling, independent direct voice, Spirit music, Spirit lights, materialisation. Lights in a room being turned on and off, as well as the electric lighting being turned up and down, and the electrical equipment being altered in its operation by Spirit.

## ECTOPLASM

I think a small explanation of this most wonderful of things should be put here, as the dictionaries/encyclopaedias I have read, do not seem to know what it really is. The other names it has been called in the past in different parts of the world are **spiritplasm, teleplasm, ideoplasm, and psychoplasm**.

Ectoplasm is a substance that every living thing has to some degree or other, some more than others (as is the situation of Physical Mediums). It is a life force, a power (look at the TV programmes on DNA, it has a wispy thread like structure. Could Spirit be using that part of the Medium?). Ectoplasm is said to be developed and increased by a chemical mixture made by the Spirit chemists, taking some chemicals from the human body, [the linked-developed Physical Medium, whether they are a natural or long time meditation developed Medium] and sitters of the Circle if necessary, [sometimes building the human form with the help of the material things around in the room e.g. something from the fabric of clothing and materials also something at times from the solid things there] and some chemicals from the world of the higher vibrational level, Spirit, to produce a substance that can enable an in-between link [I was going to say visual but sometimes ectoplasm is not visible] that can be accepted by both the earth vibrational plain and the Spirit higher vibrational plane. We are told by Spirit this is not all the mixture of the ectoplasm as it is mixed with the etheric part of the air (or nature, that which is all around us) that is breathed into the Medium's nose to the hairs, where the hairs act as a filter and the ether is collected at the root of the nose of the Medium and formulated there by Spirit being connected to the Medium as a link. The Medium has to accept and give permission to Spirit within their thought to Spirit for it to happen, then be a passive vessel for the use of the World of Spirit.

Please remember the **ECTOPLASM IS PART OF THE MEDIUM.**
**ECTOPLASM IS ALWAYS CONNECTED TO THE MEDIUM.**
**ECTOPLASM IS AN EXTENSION OF THE MEDIUM'S LIFE FORCE.**
**ECTOPLASM IS manipulated by Spirit using the sympathetic nervous system of the Medium, the nerve endings (starting points of them) which are ultimately connected to the brain of the Medium. This is why the Mediums feel anything at all that is done in the way of harm to the Ectoplasm. If another person touches the ectoplasm being produced by a Medium, it is as though the person touches very, very raw flesh of the Medium and the Medium can be hurt as a consequence.**

The Medium should be breathing in and out through the nose and thinking about linking with Spirit and what they wanted to happen giving intention to the etheric part of the air being breathed in through the nose at the same time, then going passive to let those in Spirit do their job. When produced, ectoplasm is controlled by the sympathetic nervous system of the Medium, which is ultimately controlled by Spirit.

**Ectoplasm has <u>never</u> as yet been recorded as leaving a residue when it has gone back into the Medium.** So dismiss the people who say they have a stain of ectoplasm on the clothing when they come out of Trance. **It is only their saliva.**

**Ectoplasm vanishes very quickly or evaporates (it vanishes into the air/etheric and into the medium from whence it came) just like water vapour does when it comes out of a pipe in cold weather, but only seen in a reversed situation as the water vapour.**

When given permission by Spirit to be touched ectoplasm has been described as feeling wet but **<u>not wet like water is</u>**.

These forms can be solid, material like, jelly like, semi-liquid, liquid, vapour like, invisible, gas and lights [this I have included here as I feel lights "**<u>might</u>**" be formed by ectoplasm, they could be included in solids, gas, invisible in certain lighting].

To link into our earth plane, those in the World of Spirit have to lower their vibrations. Many times Spirit actually makes the ectoplasm visible in the complete dark séances, somehow by adding something similar to illuminating florescence paint to the mixture, so all in the darkened room can see the form being formed whether it is the full human form, hands, head or torso. But many other times the forms are shown/lit up in a dark séance by a plaque, (a square piece of wood or card), one side of which is coated with fluorescent paint.

Those (many needed) in Spirit who are evolved to a very high degree to form the ectoplasm are not usually the ones who speak through the ectoplasmic voice box, so it can be seen there are far more than one or two in the "group thought" that makes up any link with the Medium on the earth plane.

Ectoplasm comes out **mainly** from the orifices of the body of the Medium, and their solar plexus area but sometimes out of the areas of the joints. (Remember that the human skin is porous and can extrude fluid (sweat), just as it can give out chemicals of many kinds in normal everyday life, and the human skin can also absorb chemicals). So it could come out of the body, **anywhere** gently through the porous skin as well as the orifices. Eva C was photographed in the nude and her ectoplasm was seen coming out of her breasts.

Ectoplasm can come in differing forms.

<u>Solid</u> in the way of psychic rods that can lift heavy objects, tables, people and the trumpet. Often described as having grippers attached at the ends of the rods. It would seem the ectoplasm has different formation depending on the spiritual level of the Spirit link.

Material like, as in cloth, in the way of forming a human form over a "Thought Form" from the World of Spirit. Can be see through, or more of a crumpled up appearance, having stronger edges that seem to hold the structure more firm. Can slither across people sitting or across the floor.

Feels reptile like wet, but not wet like water. Leaving no residue when it vanishes.

The making of independent voice box (an etheric amplifier) in the séance room away from the Medium's own voice box/throat area.

Making the voice box (etheric amplifier) INSIDE the Medium away from the Medium's voice box/throat area.

The making of the Spirit mask on or near (some are said to have a mask of a person who is in Spirit formed about twenty inches away from the face) Transfiguration Mediums, manipulating and moulding the face to one of Spirit onto the moulded Transfiguration Medium.

Depending on the Medium and what they eat; ectoplasm can be brittle and it crackles; or it can be cold and damp. The best conditions for ectoplasm to be in for Physical Phenomena, is said to be when it is supple and dry to the touch.

**Semi-liquid** and **liquid** have been described by sitters as hitting them in the face as rain, and it has been seen as spots falling onto a smooth surface. Some describe it as sometimes being jelly like.

**Vapour** has been photographed when a Medium has been in a cabinet, and the vapour/mist/smoke-like substance has formed around them. There also has been a great many ordinary people having photographs where ectoplasm vapour has shown up on their film, also the vapour in some instances has formed faces of people on the processed film.

**Gas** (invisible) can be described here as the unusual smell of recognition of a loved one by their cigarette, after-shave, perfume, pipe tobacco, or bodily smell etc. Remember also there are some terrible smells that can come out of the human body's lower orifices when we use the toilet, it can be the same when the ectoplasm is being formed, so expect it.

Quite often ectoplasm is odourless. BUT often when seen in the séance room, it has also been described as dank, musty, and in many of the séances with Helen Duncan luminous. Her ectoplasm smelt of whisky as she drank it to relax.

Lastly here when explaining the **lights** I must say you will have to ask Spirit for the answer, but they are certainly produced in Physical Circles as well as some other Circles. I have recorded them in white light whilst a doctor was testing Mediums. They consist of lights the size of a pea to a half a crown/fifty pence piece going to the size of a person's head.

I have photographed them bigger than this and recorder them on a VCR with a set up of four small infrared security cameras aimed at the Mediums. I am currently getting on camera many globes or circles of lights which I call KEELIGHTS as I feel they are going to be the KEY to another dimension. I am recording on a video camera, flares of lights as well as I sit in my séance room in low red light. BUT at most times they are not seen by the naked eye, I say most times, as sometimes they are seen out of the corner of the eye in the peripheral vision. I have many hundreds recorded yet I have only seen about eight-ten through my own eyes to date. In many books especially **"Battling Bertha's Biography"** it tells of Bertha Harris and her very good friend Helen Duncan when sitting together, Helen having very many coloured lights swirling around her head, but this was only when the two of them were together.

An explanation of ectoplasm from the book "Phenomena of Materialisation" by Baron von Schrenck-Notzing puts it into context for the reader.

Before each séance Eva "C" was always strip searched, then dressed in the clothes that were kept in the séance room all the time. They seem to pick up vibrations and enhance the production of Physical Phenomena. As all of the things that are left in the séance room and not moved out of it on occasions. Stability is the watchword.

"The first stage is the appearance of a mobile substance near the body of the Medium. We may call it the stage of teleplastic evolution. The substance appears diffuse and cloudy, like a fine smoke of white or grey colour. On further condensation it becomes white, and transforms itself into amorphous coagulated masses or packets, or assumes the structure of the finest web-like filmy veils, which may develop into compact organic fabrics or conglomerates. Sometimes the veil-like forms are doubled at the margin, so that the first impression is that of a stitched hem. The veil never shows the characteristic square thread work of real veils. There is something inconstant and irregular in all these forms, and sometimes the morphological structure is different in the centre and at the rims. All observers who have touched this filmy grey/white substance with their hands agree in describing it as cool, sticky and rather heavy, as well as endowed with a motion of its own. The sensation may be compared with that produced on the skin by a live reptile."

Here is another explanation by the Baron from a séance on the 25th May 1909.

From the beginning of the sitting, about twenty minutes elapsed before the first phenomenon was seen. The curtain was drawn open from within (by Eva's feet) and remained open for the whole duration of the ensuing phenomena, so as to form a triangular opening narrowing towards the top, through which the Medium (in a Trance condition, previously being hypnotised) and the occurrences themselves could be fairly well observed in good illumination (red light).

The hands rested on the Medium's knees and remained visible during the manifestations. Eva's head was bent towards one side and almost disappeared in the darkness. The hems of the curtain touched the knees of the Medium from the outside.

Without any change in the position of the hands or the curtain, we saw first at the Medium's left side, above her left hand, an illumination of the curtain at the height of about a foot and a half. This resembled a bright phosphorescent strip, which, however, was odourless. Then out of this appeared, at about the level of Eva's head, a formless mass of a light grey colour, about a foot in vertical height, which disappeared and reappeared without a change in the position of the curtains or hands. The shape appeared at first vague and indefinite, with a fluctuating motion, then it became visibly brighter and more solid, until it changed into a white luminous material, like a heap of finest white chiffon veiling, apparently stretched out beyond the curtain by a hand and again withdrawn. Some of those present thought they saw a small female hand, which held the stuff. In spite of the most accurate observation I could not perceive anything of this. The mass dissolved before our eyes, losing first its solid shape. Finally we only saw a light strip, which ascended from the quiescent hand and gave the impression as if a column of luminous smoke were ascending from it. The total duration of this remarkable process may have been thirty to sixty seconds. After a short pause some indefinite structures of various shapes were seen, which condensed to luminous strips and balls, moved about and changed their shapes, ascended and descended, disappeared and reappeared.

The strongest impression was obtained by the observers when the luminous smoke, proceeding from the region of the upper part of the body of the Medium, changed into a long white band, about 2 inches thick and about 16 inches long, which, horizontally above the floor, at a height of 4 ½ feet, joined the two hems or the open curtain, hanging parallel to the floor. If a comparison is allowable, which perhaps does not quite apply, we might compare the optical impression of this structure with the shape of a bleached human thighbone. In this apparently solid form, which ascended and descended in the air as a broad white strip, there hung a bright white veil-like material about 16 inches square, so that the whole apparition resembled a small flag held horizontally. Without changing the position, this form ascended to a height of about 6 feet, then descended, and remained twenty seconds before it disappeared. The optical phenomena filled the whole opening of the curtains. The Medium's hands lay as before motionless and visible on her knees.

It is impossible to describe this process as it was shown to our eyes. While the white column, condensed from amorphous material, sometimes gave the impression of a solid body, it usually appeared to stream through the cabinet in strips like a white creamy substance, sometimes proceeding in a straight line, sometimes breaking into zigzags or serpentine waves, before its dissolution it became thinner, more colourless, resembling smoke, and then disappeared, usually in the direction of the body of the Medium. The reddish light in the séance room increased the attractiveness of this interesting play of colours bathing the nebulous and half-liquid or solid structures in a pale rose colour. The development of these creations took the form of an emanation of rays and streaks from the body of the Medium as from a material radiation of energy, which however, probably influenced by unconscious volition impulses, tended in its form towards definite representations, finally flowing back into the organism (like the rigid organic rays described by Professor Ochorowicz).

In the last successful sitting one could already recognise distinct attempts to produce human forms. Thus, in this sitting, the grey material repeatedly assumed a spherical shape, a more solid white nucleus formed within it, in size and shape like a human head, while the outer parts appeared to change themselves into veils and textile fabrics.

It was decided to attempt a photographic flashlight record with the consent of the Medium. For this purpose a camera had already been set up before the sitting, opposite the curtain near the stove behind the observers. Behind it a paper cylinder more than a yard long had been suspended to receive the magnesium vapour.

The curtain was opened. We again saw before us a figure clothed in a long flowing veil, which covered the face (Medium ?). The flashlight was ignited (figs 1 and 2), but, at the same moment, the paper caught fire, and it appeared as if the flames would spread. A panic took place among the audience, some of the ladies screamed with fright, and fled. But we succeeded in extinguishing the fire.

With a cry of pain the Medium (Eva C) sank back into the chair gasping convulsively. Baron Pigeard at once entered the cabinet to soothe her, but the white clothing and veiling had disappeared. The Medium had fainted, and **lay in the chair <u>bleeding from the nose</u>**, and the sitting had to be closed. I slowly wakened Eva by suggestion. A close examination of the Medium and the cabinet showed nothing suspicious. No white or veil-like materials were found.

The whole fire episode was the work of a few seconds. A fraudulent Medium would not have been able to hide the necessary masks and clothing during this unexpected interruption of her performance.

On awakening, Eva C. was obviously exhausted, and showed a trembling of the arms. Pulse 108. Subsequence control negative.

No reasonable grounds for the supposition of fraud by the Medium can be found, however strictly one may adhere to the view that these unusual occurrences require the greatest caution and scepticism.

The above record offers perhaps a contribution to the observation of a materialisation in the nascent state. The picture taken on the 25$^{th}$ November shows the head of the Medium, who had obviously risen from the chair, in the opening of the curtains. A long veil, or an obviously very transparent soft white material, whose threads reminds one of cashmere wool, falls from her head to her knees. On Eva's hair on the right hand side a soft vague and sketchy form of a miniature left hand (female), with a first finger pointing upwards, is to be seen. This starts from a sort of stalk or band quite continuous with fabric, as shown by the magnification of the photograph, and which appears to be formed of the same stuff as the veil. With the help of a artificial hand shape brought in for this purpose, consisting perhaps of cloth or paper, which then would have had to be placed on the hair under the veil, it would hardly have been impossible to obtain this indefinite shadowy form with soft fluid outline, though one has to consider a possible fault in the focusing of the apparatus.

Here is another description of ectoplasm from the book written in the 1920' by Professor Charles Richet "Thirty Years of Psychical Research". In which he talks of séances with Marthe Berand (mostly known as "Eva C").

It is a kind of liquid or pasty jelly which emerges from the mouth or the breast of Marthe which organised itself by degrees, acquiring the shape of a face or limb. Under very good conditions of visibility, I have seen this paste spread on my knee, and slowly take form so as to show the rudiment of the radius, cubitus, or metacarpal bone whose increasing pressure I could feel on my knee.

These Materialisations are usually gradual; beginning by a rudimentary shape, complete forms and human faces only appearing later on. At first these formations are often very imperfect. Sometimes they show no relief, looking more like flat images than bodies, so that in spite of oneself, one is inclined to imagine some fraud, since what appears seems to be the materialisation of a semblance, and not of a being. But in some cases the materialisation is perfect. At the Villa Carmen I saw a fully organised form rise from the floor. At first it was only a white, opaque spot like a handkerchief lying on the ground before the curtain, then this handkerchief quickly assumed the form of a human head level with the floor, and a few moments later it rose up in a straight line and became a small man enveloped in a kind of white burnous, who took two or three halting steps in front of the curtain and then sank to the floor and disappeared as if through a trapdoor. But there was no trapdoor.

Ectoplasm was tested in London in the early part of this century when a scientist described it as a material that was smelly, moist, dank, it was white, its consistency being similar to albumen that came out of the Medium's body and vanished back into it at the end of the séance. Spirit moulded the ectoplasm into whatever forms necessary by thought. It is said by Spirit that man one day will produce a machine that will produce the correct waves, Hz., and so produce ectoplasm, so the people across the veil will be seen again.

A very well known Medium, W. T. Stead in a séance he attended, had permission from Spirit to take a sample from the ectoplasm being formed. His daughter took it around all the shops of London to try and make a match of it with the cloth of the time. In a specialist drapers shop the man behind the desk said it looked like an individually handmade piece of mesh/net material. The ectoplasm only lasted for a few days before disintegrating/decomposing. This was after it being stored in an airtight container all the time. Luckily the piece was photographed. Many were the Mediums who were subjected to awful humiliating tests to show that the production of ectoplasm was not fraudulent, one being the drinking of blue dye to see if the ectoplasm (they thought at the time it was swallowed muslin cloth) or anything that came out of the Medium's body would be produced blue from the Medium. The ectoplasm came out the normal grey/white colour.

Please remember the Medium being used by Spirit for the formation of ectoplasm has to be in reasonably good health otherwise he/she will drain their own natural body immune system. To keep themselves healthy, it is so essential for the Medium to have a good varied diet. The ectoplasm produced by the Medium after the séance has finished, ends up being reduced sometimes slowly by Spirit, many times quickly, but always being replaced back into the Medium (and/or sitter/sitters from where it came from originally. In the case of full materialisation of the human form, the ectoplasmic Spirit Form shrinks downwards, many thinking it vanishes into the floor, BUT the ectoplasm is most times very quickly (in an instant) reabsorbed by Spirit back into the Medium's body the rest being etheric, is dispersed back into the air/ether from whence it came. The pure refined ectoplasm we are told by Spirit, disperses back into the etheric from where it came from. It is possible that Spirit could be using pure refined ectoplasm in the newly rediscovered energy that is being talked about at the present time. For instance look at the glass dome experiments done by the "Scole Group". Nothing is new with Spirit, it is in my opinion **NEWLY RE-DISCOVERED.**

People in our day and age have not the time, or should I say, they are not willing to put the same time aside for linking with Spirit, so the ways for Spirit contact, proof of the ability to form a materialised formation of a continuing living form who we think of a dead, and the Medium's development have had to be altered again for the sake of the safety of the Medium.

One time in a séance demonstrated by, the Medium, Gordon Higginson at the end he was found to have a safety pin beneath his skin at his stomach area this was taken in by the ectoplasm when it was withdrawing into him after the materialisation demonstration. So you can see how much care should be taken to clean the room where Physical Phenomena is to take place. Also if there is a sudden disturbance by the sitters or any external means, the non refined ectoplasm can be returned to the Medium very quickly in a matter of a fraction of a second or less and internal bleeding and/or serious psychic burns [especially if metal is worn next to the skin] can occur to the Mediums body. Eva C, Helen Duncan and Gordon Higginson are Mediums who I know were burnt many times.

Be careful of the people who say they produce ectoplasm when they only produce bubbling, frothy, spit from their mouths and then let it dribble out onto their front, also of the foolish ones who try to place muslin into their mouths, but the latter I have not seen only read about.

The reason many Physical Mediums wear black is for simple reason the ectoplasm, which is grey/white when produced, shows up best against the dark background of the cloth. Make sure you buy the correct black cloth for photography especially if using infra red in the dark séances as infra red light on some black cloth makes it show up through a camera, white on the screen, so if you use that type of black cloth you will not be able to see the ectoplasm or any energy.

The heavy black curtaining used on cabinets, is used so the Spirit World can build up the energy required in a small space, it also cuts out any light there might be in the room, which is known to have a negative effect on ectoplasm in the early stages of the it's development and the Medium's early physical phenomena development, many times destroying it completely.

Some Mediums have the strength in their link with Spirit so they can with the help of Spirit use ectoplasm in the full light of day to produce a full human form. **BUT in general, the normal day light or white light is known to destroy ectoplasm. Or should I correctly say it is not seen in its normal form, being invisible to the human eye.**

There is more about ectoplasm in the section about warnings to those who sit in Physical Circles.

A point here should be added: in one experimental test with the late Leslie Flint in a dark séance the experimenters use an infra red telescope they saw the voice box two feet in front of him. In another test the voice of spirit was very low when the infra red telescope was functioning; the telescope fused by what they think was Spirit and the volume double immediately showing infra red light has an effect on the strength of the production of ectoplasm, and the strength of Physical Mediumship as does any other light.

There are many instances recorded where investigators who were supposed to be knowledgeable scientists having no regard to the safety of the Medium. They have within their hands grabbed hold of the ectoplasm as it was being formed in the séance and it has immediately dispersed. Unfortunately it is the Medium who is harmed by such unwarranted and dangerous interference. Any investigator who commits such an action without the knowledge or permission of the Spirit World invariably causes the Medium serious harm, and does his/her cause no good at all, and is likely to be prosecuted for ENDANGERING THE LIFE OF THE MEDIUM. All who attend a physical or trance séance should in my opinion be made to sign a document agreeing to uphold the rules of the séance, and **NOT** do anything likely to hurt or endanger the life of the Medium.

I feel I should put in a little of an incident that happened in South Africa with Bertha Harris when she met a Witch Doctor. This Witch Doctor produced ectoplasm for Bertha to show he could manipulate it into any sort of form. There were fishes floating around the large hut, lions, pigs, and even a unicorn pranced around in the middle of circle of the people of the tribe, after they had gone there were foot prints in the sand to prove that the animals had been there, so do not think the Spiritualist have the monopoly for producing ectoplasm or physical phenomena.

**"The following pages are from the observations of Harry Edwards and through the mediumship of Arnold Clare on ECTOPLASM"**
**("Peter" is Arnold.Clare's Guide)**
**Chapter X11  pages 131-155**

Observation of physical phenomena, with many Mediums, at different periods and in all parts of the world, shows that a substance is produced either from or adjacent to the Medium's body, which is the "raw material" of manifestations, telekinetic action, etc.

Various terms have been used to describe this substance: teleplasm, ectoplasm, ideoplasm, etc. we use the word ectoplasm since it has been sanctioned by custom in this country.

It has been established beyond all doubt that ectoplasm is the basis for building up of materialisations, for levitation by force and for the structural mechanism in direct voice. Indeed in some form or other, visible or invisible, it is the raw material of the Spirit-folk for all their work in the séance room.

As, gradually, we are able to understand more about this "elusive" substance, so shall we be able to comprehend the manner of the performance of Spirit mechanics. But owing to its great sensitivity and its most intimate relationship to the nervous system of the Medium (if not the life force itself) it can rarely be handled or very closely studied by investigators. Indeed, apart from certain residues, which may or may not have been true ectoplasmic residue (see Peter's observation on this point), never yet has any savant been able to retain a quantity of the substance. There are records where investigators, imbued with scientific unscrupulousness, or in sheer ignorance, have attempted to take a handful of the substance with the idea of retaining it for analysis. On each occasion, although the substance was clasped within their hands, it dispersed immediately. Unfortunately it is the Medium who is harmed by such unwarrantably crude interference. Indeed, any unorthodox action by an investigator committed without the knowledge or permission of the Guide in control, invariably causes the Medium serious harm, without any advance in knowledge or credit to, the investigator.

Consideration of the descriptions of the ectoplasmic matter reported with Mr Clare's Mediumship in the first part of this book and reports that follow concerning other mediumships, lead to the conclusion that here is a substance possessing the potential of life itself; and as such, of the most delicate nature.

The substance of the living brain may be handled wisely, but no one but a fool would take liberties with it. Similarly, while at times we may be permitted to handle or observe this substance, under direction, it is only the fool who would crudely interfere with it.

He number of Mediums who have been able to produce through their Mediumship, ectoplasm that may be viewed in some degree of light, or to permit of it being photographed, is exceedingly few; though it is now hoped that photographic records may be increased by use of the infrared ray applied to psychic photography.

A close study of the major works of the past dealing with this particular phenomena discloses that our knowledge concerning it is very limited indeed; and apart from visual records and records of touch, we have not been able to approach the answer to such questions as "How is it produced? From whence does it come? To where does it disperse? What is its composition? The purpose and manner of its usage?"

For the first time, Peter has given us a detailed exposition that provides tenable answers to these leading questions, which may well provide the foundation upon which our future knowledge will be based. Naturally we seek proofs of each statement made and so perhaps at this juncture the best service that can be rendered is to take the observations of previous investigations with those of the Mediumship under review; and to see how those observations can be associated with Peter's theses.

In the author's considered opinion there is no previously recorded fact that is at variance with the explanation given.

It is not practical to include in this work summaries of all the leading investigations, so that some of the most recent investigations will have to suffice. Indeed there is a striking similarity between the records of all the published testimonies.

In the volumes published by the U.S.A., S.P.R. on the Margery Mediumship, there are many chapters devoted to the meticulous recording of ectoplasmic phenomena. They are far too extensive to reproduce here, but it will serve a general view of the Margery phenomena by reprinting the generalisations of the Research Officer of the U.S.A., S.P.R., as follows.

"………Nevertheless, from the viewpoint of sensorial experience, the word teleplasm is quite essential, and will be used without further apology. It appears that the definite physical qualities, which this substance exhibits in the performance of its many phenomena, depend on a greater or lesser density, or viewed from the other angle, a greater or a lesser tenuity. Thus when a small basket rolls on a shelf in front of the Psychic and the observer passes his clasped arms through the entire zone between the Psychic and the basket, we believe that the teleplasmic rod from the Psychic's body is either so tenuous that the arm of the observer passes through it without breaking it, or that the rod by some means comes from a four direction. When scales are made to balance a four-to-one load in red or white light we have evidence of the presence of a form of teleplasm invisible to the eye and intangible to the finger, not seen when photographed by a glass lens, but visible when photographed by a fused quartz lens. Here is apparently a psychic structure, invisible and tangible, but nevertheless emitting or reflecting an ultra-violet light. Again, when under perfect conditions of control, but in the dark, sitters receive touches by a teleplasmic terminal, we have this material in a form tangible but presumably invisible. Finally we observe teleplasm at the maximum density seen in this Mediumship, when in good red light we see, feel, handle, weigh and take the temperature of the teleplasmic mass on the table in front of us. When the substance has this density our senses not only record it, but the glass camera lens, as well as the quartz lens, confirms what we see…………

" The mass which comes from the trunk, and sometimes from the ears of the psychic, is light brownish grey colour, as seen in red light. There is a distinct variety, however, coming from the right ear, which is a dead white in colour, like wax, or slightly yellow, the colour of noodles. Both these forms are entirely opaque.

The temperature has been taken twice by having the mass laid on a chemist's thermometer. At one time it was 40 degrees Fahrenheit and the other time 42 degrees. The room temperature at the time was 70 degrees".

"The mass is cold to the observer's hand and has a clammy feeling. After the contact is broken the sitter would declare that his hands must be wet but that is sensation only. William Blake described it as "wet with the water that wets not". The mass is more or less like new rubber in consistency and resilience, but the rubber feeling is more than mere action and reaction of squeezing rubber. The mass often squirms and appears to have life itself. This liveness is further confirmed by the fact that if sitter squeezes the mass however gently, quite in the dark, the Psychic will groan as if hurt. At times the mass almost seems to be made up of individual fibres of live longitudinal cords about one-sixth of an inch in diameter. This is especially the case with the cords joining it to the Psychics organism.

"If one of the crude hands in palpated freely, we find what appear to be normal bones; in the right relationship but rarely enough of them. Thus the fingers seldom present more than two phalanges: the terminal one being missing. Fingernails may or may not be present. At one time one finger showed as if it were a fusion of two fingers with the distal phalange split and bearing two fingernails. All the metacarpals may be missing the carpals present. The forearm may contain one bone or two, as in the normal. There is generally no enlargement of the upper part of the forearm. It appears to be only skin over bone".

"The grey masses that form the crude hands are attached to the body by something closely resembling an umbilical cord. This cord is one half to one and one half inches in diameter. It appears as if twisted, as an umbilical cord frequently is. There is no pulse in it……..The white masses of teleplasm overlying the Psychic's face have cords of somewhat different character, issuing from the ear and nose…………

"………..This living mass may then extend downwards in a kind of white sheet until it reaches the table or even the floor. When it gets this size, there forms, as if for better exhibition, a long proboscis having its base on the nose, divided more or less like four legs of the Eiffel Tower. The long staff of this grows forward parallel to the floor and over this the teleplasmic sheet hands like a tent over a ridgepole. The largest one we have seen was about 24x84 inches. This sheet, which Walter calls his "shining garment", appears sometimes as a smooth uniform mass, or like coarse or fine lace. Walter declares, and close examination confirms, that the lace, however, is lace in appearance only".

The research Officer's observations dealing with the structure of the teleplasmic voice-box will be found in the chapter dealing with "Voice Mechanism"; but as the latter part of his observations relating to the dispersal of the substance are pertinent they are appended as follows:

"The disappearance of the mass may be observed. It seems to go back to the orifice from whence it comes. The last moment of disappearance we have been allowed to see twice. The mass shrinks in volume, but not continuously. The last view shows considerable mass, then all at once there is nothing. It is comparable to the cloud of white water-vapour seen coming out of a factory exhaust pipe. At first a large, white, opaque, substantial-looking cloud or mass; then all at once there is nothing……."

"The terminals have been seen and felt, most of them photographed in many forms. The mass may be amorphous, perhaps roughly like a small French loaf or like a dirigible balloon in shape. In the second period of red light it may be shown that this mass has taken on the form of a crude hand with five fingers or sometimes with two of the five fingers fused together. Sometimes the hand is observed to have a terminal with four fingers and thumb, with all extremities long, perhaps seven inches, coming to a sharp point, the region of the palm shrunken; the whole hand being a caricature of a hand, or the hand of a nightmare figure. The hand, however, may show itself in every detail of improving perfection up to what appears to be a complete hand."

The last observation is of interest when compared to the building up of a hand as reported with Mr Clare (see report) and with particular reference to Peter's comments on the subject.

A privileged and a duty of observers is to confirm the findings of others and compare results. Such comparisons over the last fifty years display a marked progression with the character of the ectoplasm formations; and generally speaking, each succeeding Mediumship provides a more refined and advanced type of phenomena. It will, of course be understood that in making comparisons, no disparagement is intended. With Margery, the ectoplasmic formations were prolific, but, from their description and photographs, appear cruder than those wince, observed, and photographed with Jack Webber and seen with Arnold Clare. It may be that the use of the infrared ray photography permitted a finer grade of ectoplasm being photographed with J.W. than with the glare of the magnesium flash permitted with Margery.

Peter tells us that no condition of ectoplasm is static; and it is interesting to observe that disappearance of the formation with Margery is the reverse of that noted with J.W. with the latter the formation of the substance commenced with seeming emission of the cloud-like vapour. Yet whether the vapour consistency is at the beginning or end of the phenomena, the similarity of description is marked; and it is quite reasonable that such a characteristic could equally well mark either the beginning or termination of the activity.

In considering all these reports, it is well to keep in mind that the ectoplasmic formations may be of various grades of refinement or development; it may be crude mass or a highly organised mechanism. The texture of the substance also varies greatly according to the opportuneness and harmony of the conditions prevailing at the time in the séance room.

It will be noted that the conclusions of the U.S.A., S.P.R. Officer quoted in the early part of his observations, refer to varying qualities of structure as probably being due to a greater or lesser degree of tenuity or density. It may well be that in view of Peter's statements a more tenable explanation lies in the varying grades of ectoplasm used and the corresponding degree of organisation within it.

Nevertheless, there are beyond any doubt characteristics in the production, formation, colour and feel of ectoplasm with each Mediumship. The foregoing descriptions of ectoplasm with Margery received before 1930, and those recorded by Baron Von Schrenk Notzing and other savants of his time, are very like those recorded with J.W. and Arnold Clare; and as we bear in mind Peter's grading of the various kinds of structures, we can obtain a truer perspective of these phenomena. While Peter has broadly graded ectoplasm formations into three categories, it is observed that there can be no ridged division; and that one grade merges into another, as all possess the potentialities of each. It is a gradual evolution from the crudest form to the most refined and highly organised kind.

Some extracts from the Mediumship of Jack Webber follow:

"In the dark séances, the process of emitting ectoplasm is often illustrated by means of luminous plaques or in red light".

"The process is as follows: The Medium's body is bent forward whilst in the ropes, so that his head is over his feet. From the mouth there commences to emerge a substance that looks to the eye like heavy vapour. As it emerges, it 'unrolls' and pours down in front of the Medium's body to the floor. At the same time, it continues to pour out from the mouth like a cascade, until there is considerable volume on the floor spreading several feet each way. The emergence is rapid and the process of emission only occupies a few seconds. There is no noise from the Medium's throat during this time.

"Rapidly, in two or three seconds only, the vapourish mass condenses or becomes concentrated, until there hangs from the mouth a length of material-like substance".

"The texture of this material varies according to the conditions prevailing at the sitting and the condition of the Medium himself. When the conditions are good the texture is fine and close. When the conditions are not so good, the material is coarser and rents may be see in the fabric".

"This material has often been handled under the Guide's instructions, by the author and other sitters".

It is moist, though not very wet and possesses a peculiar odour. On a number of occasions the author has been invited to unravel the material and open it up. To do this, however, extreme care has to be taken. The width of the material when opened out is wider than the outstretched arms of one person. Whilst unravelling the ectoplasm at one sitting, the author was unable to stretch it out to its full extent; and the assistance of the next sitter was allowed by the Guide. The full extent must have been two yards or more…………….."

"The return of the ectoplasm is instantaneous. The author has had gently hold of the material one moment; and within the second that followed, the material has been whisked away with a sound like the twang of a piece of elastic and it has disappeared……"

"Several descriptions of this material have been given by sitters as "closely woven silk of rich quality", 'like wet toy balloon rubber', 'a wide piece of thin seaweed'.

"This formation has no pattern such as 'net'. It is like a skin rather than a woven fabric…..This drapery is most gossamer-like, and is so light that its texture is as a spider's web. Yet its density is great and weight heavy to the hand".

The incident next related tells how two photographs were secured under unusual circumstances, demonstrating the rapidity with which the formations disappear.

"The author was in charge of the photographic apparatus and white light and was ready to take a photograph should the opportunity come. The sitting was proceeding and the throat noises were heard coming from the Medium, when the unusual instruction was received "*photo and light*".

"A photograph being anticipated by the character of the throat action, the infrared was immediately flashed by pressing the switch, the right hand came across and closed the shutter in front of the plate, returning to the white light switch. Both these switches were of the press kind, so no delay was caused……The three movements were therefore rapid and the only interval between the photographic exposure and the white light was the time to close the plate shutter. Two seconds is a generous time allowance.

"Plate No 11 was the first to be taken and it will be realised that the absorption back into the Medium of the ectoplasm formation was therefore instantaneous……"

"A few minutes after the plate had been changed….a similar instruction was received '*photo and light*', On this occasion Plate No 12 was secured. The author was ready for this instruction and the period between the infrared flash and the white light was not more than one second……"

There is a variation between the time taken for the disappearance of ectoplasm in Webber and Margery descriptions. Peter's explanations give the reason for this. It is in the different grades of structure present on each occasion. With Margery it appears to have been of the cruder kind and had to be returned (wholly or in part) to the body. With J.W. the formation was probably a combination, part from the body and part from the ether (it may have been that the whole came from the ether), so that its dissemination was immediate through its instantaneous return to the etheric particles from which it had been constructed.

It may be noted in my reporting of the J.W. incident I wrote "voluminous material passing back into the Medium". This illustrates how easy it is to fall into error. This illustrates how easy it is to fall into error and form the wrong conclusion by resting on observation only and forming assumptions there from; and if Peter's observations are accepted, how knowledge is slowly gained and we are forced to correct ourselves. So far, all research in the past has come to the conclusion that all grades of ectoplasm return back to the Medium's physical body. Peter says this is not so.

According to Peter, ectoplasm of *"refined"* type is not reabsorbed by the Psychic's physical organism but disintegrates back into the ether from whence it comes! This process of dissemination is both logical and practical, for when one considers the wide expanses of physically constructed ectoplasm, as shown both by description and by photographs, to assume that this volume of physical matter re-enters the throat or other orifices or sources of emergence, is far more improbable than the reasoning of Peter.

We know how materialised forms disseminate into "space" through observation of the manner of their disappearance; and therefore the dissemination of certain forms of ectoplasm follows the same process.

The two photographs referred to above demonstrate beyond question, that on the occasion they were secured the voluminous expanses of ectoplasm in a physical state disappeared within a second. This means that the intelligence in control had to negotiate the disintegration of the mass within the very limited period of time between the infra red flash that recorded the phenomena and the putting on of the white light, thereby implying instantaneous action. How well this evidence supports Peter's newly disclosed process.

Here is evidence that the scientific mind has to account for and accept. In the past scientists confronted with a phenomenon they could not account for by their previous knowledge have either discounted the act or have taken refuge in building up an argument to account for the act by fraud. Within the last two years an eminent researcher, whose name is regarded in certain national quarters as being a leading authority on physical phenomena, endeavoured to explain the process by regurgitation. That is the Medium, prior to sitting, swallowed many yards of cheesecloth, regurgitated it during the séance, displayed it for fraudulent purpose, and then swallowed it again, the process being repeated, as the Medium required. This is typical of the wilfully crass ignorance the Spiritualist movement has to encounter; and the incredible thing is, that some people prepare to accept such an absurdity rather than a simple and tenable explanation supported by abundant testimony and photographic proofs.

Here is another example of "explanation" by one who will not accept the evidence of his own eyes and senses. Dr. Dunlap, the noted American Professor of Experimental Psychology, after seeing preliminary photographic evidence of the existence and nature of psychic rods with Margery, was able to be present at sittings and to "see" for himself, yet dismissed the phenomena as being produced by the use of "the intestine of some animal, showing the stumps of some blood vessels and stuffed with some substance like cotton, through which ran several wires". So long as men of science are satisfied to discount the wonderful work of their "Spirit co-workers", so long will the true appreciation and understanding of this realm of activity be prejudiced by obstinate and brutal ignorance.

A further illustration of Peter's reference to the different grades of ectoplasm is provided by comparative photographs of ectoplasmic energy with Margery and J.W. with the former, the substance shown is of a cruder kind, Grade 1; whilst with the latter the refined character of the formation is obvious. The cruder or "fungoid" type of substance is also seen in the photographs of substances emerging from the nose and ears of J.W.

Further useful comparative study is provided by the following extracts from Geley's works and investigations, dealing with the appearance and action of ectoplasmic formations:

"The volume of substance extruded is variable, sometimes abundant, sometimes scanty, with all intermediate grades. In a few instances it covers the Medium like a mantle.

"The substance may be white, grey or black, the first being more frequent, possibly as more easily observed. Occasionally all three colours are visible at the same time. The visibility of the substance is variable; it occasionally is stringer or weaker. To the touch also it varies according to the form it takes at the moment, seeming soft and inelastic when widely spread, hard, knotty and fibrous when it forms cords. Sometimes it feels like a spiders web, but in thread-like form it seems both stiff and elastic.

"The substance is mobile. Sometimes it develops slowly, ascends and descends over the Medium's shoulders, breasts or knees with a creeping movement; sometimes its motion is very quick, appearing and disappearing in a flash. It is highly sensitive; and this sensibility is communicated to the Medium, who feels painfully any touch upon the substance. If the touch is rough or prolonged it produces a sensation in the Medium comparable to a touch on raw flesh".

"It is sensitive even to rays of light. A bright light and unexpected light perturbs the Medium, but this effect of light is also variable; in certain cases daylight is endured. The magnesium flash causes the Medium to start violently, but the substance can stand it. This allows of instantaneous photography......."

"It has a constant and immediate tendency to organise itself; and does not long remain in its primitive state. Often this organisation is so rapid that its first amorphous state is scarcely seen at all; at other times the amorphous substance and more or less complete forms embedded in the mass can be seen at the same time; for instance, a finger on the fringe, or even heads and faces wrapped in the substance".

In Baron von Schrenk Notzing's book "Materialisations", there are over three hundred pages and over two hundred photographs appertaining to the phenomena of ectoplasmic formation and materialisations, which provide additional detailed corroborative evidence supporting that already included in this book, in no case is the evidence at variance with any of the aforementioned excerpts.

The reader will have been able to observe from reports of the various mediumships quoted, that there is no outstanding departure in formation, emergence, disappearance and other characteristics including the organised creation of claws, hands, etc.

The works mentioned by no means exhaust the range of published investigations; there are many particularly continental, in which similar supporting evidence is provided. It is felt that no useful purpose would be served by reproducing here further excerpts, as the result would only be to reiterate the same symptoms, the same characteristics, the same methods of activity.

A useful purpose may be served, however, by summarising the similarities briefly before entering on Peter's explanations; and it will be seen that in no case are they at variance with the records of many mediumships, of many nationalities, in various parts of the world, that have functioned during different periods of time.

The similarities are :-
[1] The varying grades of refinement.
[2] The first appearance being of the crude type.
[3] The sensitivity of the substance and its reaction to the Medium.
[4] The ability to organise.
[5] The mobility of the substance.
[6] The feel of the substance to the touch.
[7] The characteristic of "heavy vapour" during its development.
[8] The "wetness", suppleness, elasticity, brittleness, etc.
[9] The rapidity of disintegration.
[10] The presence of cords connecting to the Medium.
[11] The unstable conditions of the substance.
[12] The formation of such members as fingers, hands, faces, from the substance. (Specially note the reports of the Clare manifestations)
[13] Similarity in colour.
[14] Similarity in source of emergence.
[15] The sheet-like structure of the formations.
[16] Its coldness.

So, bearing in mind the foregoing, we now proceed to Peter's explanations and the relating of the evidence to the thesis.

Peter introduced the subject by saying:

*Peter* :" This is a very difficult subject to tell you about. Perhaps it will clarify the general position if I tell you for the first time that ectoplasmic substance exists in three different forms. There is Grade 1, which is a crude form and which looks and feels like an inert mass of spongy substance. It is of close texture and seldom is seen in any particular form or shape. It could be best described as a fungus both in appearance and to the touch. That is the nearest description I can give".

*Question* : "What is its purpose?"

*Peter* :"It has no purpose. It comes directly from the physical body. Remember that".

*Question* : "Is it an organic tissue growth?"

*Peter* :"That is difficult to answer directly. It is organic yet not so, in that it does not reside as part of the physical organism. It is not a part of the physical body. It is produced by a method of "astral chemistry"."

*Question* : "does it contain any other elements than those of which the physical body is composed; such as salt, lime etc.?"

*Peter* :"It is very curious. It contains nothing like salt, or anything of the normal mineral world at all. It is a very primitive substance; and if we were to consider it as a fungoid growth, it would convey more clearly what it is. It is best described as a fungus as in the vegetable kingdom. It is the lowest and most primitive form of growth. Now this is important: this grade of ectoplasmic substance is withdrawn again into the Medium's physical body by its dispersal.

"It will help you understand this by considering Grade 2. This being a refinement of Grade 1 in that it is organised and can be utilised as additional members (under given conditions) comparable with those of the physical body. This substance can be transformed into rods and psychic instruments possessing great strength. In appearance it is apparently opaque. It has solidity, yet, in an instant, it can become disorganised and is inert, without life. [See plate No 10]

"Its formation is slightly different from that of Grade 1, in that from suitable centre of the Medium there is projected what can best be termed "rays" with qualities similar to that of your own wireless radio. It is of such a frequency that from particles about itself, not from the Medium but from the ether round about, so that it becomes three dimensional.

"There may be under certain conditions [that is when Circle conditions are not good] elements extracted from the Medium, but that is rather the exception than the rule".

"The mobility of the ectoplasm is controlled by the extension of the Medium's nervous system".

"Remember this always, it is difficult to give a word picture which conveys, however good the description, anything like a true picture of what it is. I will tell you this though, that one day man will be able to form this substance himself by utilisation of those rays".

*Question* : These rays. Can you tell us more about them?"

*Peter* : "Thunderbolts are formed in space by the combination, by accident of course, of certain electrical forces that fuse atoms of matter and weld them together into one whole, creating something out of an apparent void. Well, that is very similar to the process that goes on. Instead of getting metal or a combination of mineral forms you get a substance which is physical yet not physical. It has physical properties, yet to say it is flesh, or to say it is air, or to say it is composed of three parts of this and one part of that would not be correct".

Question : "The second grade is therefore a refinement of the first?"

*Peter* : "In the first grade it is not animated. It cannot be directed as in the second instance. It is a primitive substance because the Medium is not suitable, or underdeveloped".

Question : "It is recalled that on occasion, with other Mediums, sitters have been allowed to touch crude form and, seemingly, it reacted adversely on the Medium. Why is this?"

*Peter* : "It is like a jellyfish and would have a natural reaction, but not because you touch the jellyfish but because it is made from particles from the human body. The rays are not able to extract the elements of the free ether but have to do it from ether in an act of conversion through the physical body; and must therefore be like a raw spot on a tooth".

Question : "Regarding the strength of the rods, created from Grade 2, we know that this is very considerable. Can you tell us the source of the strength; from whence the power of the strength is derived?"

*Peter* : "Yes, I can tell you, but the thing is to try to convey it to you correctly. The strength of the levers or rods is not that the muscles of a physical body. It is not the same strength as brute force. The rods are rendered so rigid that if it were permissible to strike them, they would emit almost metallic-like ring through their own strength".

(The author has felt these rods, when they have contacted him by passing across his body, and they have felt of irresistible strength like "rods of iron".)

*Peter* : "Now, the application of this strength is partly by an intricate system of leverage and balance, and partly by transmitting along the course of the rod a terrific voltage, but not a voltage that can be recorded by any measuring instruments that you possess. If this power was the same as your electricity, the enormous pressure used would cause the conductor or rod to glow. I do not say that the psychic rods do not glow, but not many are able to see it. It is the indirect system of leverage plus this energy that achieves the effect of great strength".

Interjection : "I have seen terminal of such structure glow with a blue light". (See "Mediumship of Jack Webber").

*Peter* : "That is quite possible, but that is not always the present".

Let us now come to Grade 3. Here we have quite a different quality altogether. This does not proceed from or return to the Medium. It has characteristics common to the other two grades but is created by frequencies of a higher order".

*Question* : "What do you imply by the word frequencies?"

*Peter* : "Frequencies, harmony; it is all a mater of rhythm, pulsation, the frequency of the beat or harmony. It is the same instrument but a different piece of music. This allows of a greater degree of variation in that its range of operation, i.e. distance from the Medium or the central point, is limited only by the radius of the Circle; and in favourable conditions; very favourable conditions; can proceed beyond".

"This form of ectoplasm is web-like in construction and would be seen as like masses of cloud or steam, yet not spreading like that. It is used mostly in forming the outlines of the materialised figures [what you call draping]. Yet again it possesses something of the qualities of Grades 1 and 2, but in their finer forms.

"The secret of its mobility is the "ray" emanating from the Medium. It is not focused, concentrated focus, as in the case of Grade 2, but is more diffused. It can be of varied character; it has something on the nature of the rods and something of its own peculiar characteristic of fineness. Whereas you can vary the focus of this latter grade, you cannot that of Grade 2.

"You have noticed the focus of a cinematograph and the beam emitted there from. You have seen also the specks of dust playing in and out of that beam. Imagine now the beam being invested with power and the intelligence to collect those particles and to hold and mould them. If you can visualise that, you will have a pretty good idea of the formation of psychic rods and of ectoplasm in general. Switch off the beam and the whole disintegrates".

"This ray is the focal point which collects about itself by agency of the intelligence of the directive power or mind, through the Medium, those particles gathered from the free ether".

"Now I think we have covered this form very well. The whole basis of it is the understanding of radioactivity, a thing now becoming known on earth. Not only has it the power to radiate and transmit, but also to collect and coalesce atoms, from free space. We can get combinations of atoms which are unknown to you but which have the qualities of matter; and yet not be of any known matter what a job we would have to disperse them again; but I cannot pursue it any further tonight".

Two further evenings were devoted to this topic in question and answer and are follows. Many more questions rise to one's mind, but it is hoped that essentials covered give a broad view of all that Peter could tell us.

*Question* : "In a previous discussion you mentioned that ectoplasm was cell-like; and while, in your last talk, you mentioned nervous action you did not mention capillary action. Would you like to include this in the present description?"

*Peter* : "Capillary action. Well, in a way that would tend to lead to confusion if you assumed it has a similar system to yours. Have I referred to capillary action previously?"

*Questioner* : "Yes : although it is not in the records here."

*Peter* : "You see, capillary action is not always present, neither is the system it involves. It depends entirely upon the conditions and requirements at the time, and if we are going to build a form that has actual life in itself rather than a statue of the being who wishes to present itself, then this system would be present. That is where the form becomes living, having warmth and all that; but it entails a great deal of organisation and exposes the Medium to greater risks of injury. That is only natural".

"Now to give an indication of the meaning of capillary action, but yet one that is not altogether true. It is partially so yet not wholly the truth to say that it is meticulous with the capillary system of the Medium. The link between the two is atomisation. The blood is borrowed from the Medium and atomised. There is no direct action. It is extracted by a certain method of atomisation; and functions within the form, where it is kept moving by etheric beats of the heart. You must understand that apart from the physical body there must also be an etheric body. I will talk to you one day about where how the Spirit works in regard to its contact with the spiritual body. I will just give you a lead. It is directly through the blood steam". (see chapter X1X).

*Question* : "following this statement is it correct to state that ectoplasm does not carry a system of blood circulation, by means of arteries and veins, as in the physical body?"

*Peter* : "It does not carry all this as a part of its system of arteries and veins".

*Question*: "Does the transfer of blood by atomisation infer an actual quantity of blood?"

*Peter* : "That is right. But its circulation does not depend upon the heart beats of the materialised form".

*Question* : "Further, does the transfer of blood by atomisation infer that actual physical quantity of blood is taken from the Medium's blood system and transfused into the materialisation in warm physical form? If so, how is a physical fluid activated by etheric heartbeats of the Medium; or is it incorrect to state that the materialised form has a circulatory system?"

*Peter* : "It is incorrect to say the materialised form has a circulatory system. The circulation of the blood is maintained by the etheric heartbeats of the Medium. There is a sympathetic link. That is why it is often considered that the materialised form is a part of the Medium. Whilst that may be true in a sense, it is not true in actual fact. It will have to perhaps a composed respiratory action but it is always sympathetic. You must remember that the substance of which it is made is partly physical and partly etheric; and who can say where one begins and the other ends?"

*Question* : "When a materialised form speaks, does it use its own physically constructed larynx?"

*Peter* : "No. The same principle is embodied within the materialised from as that about which we have already spoken. You know the one. The etheric amplifier. (See chapter XV). Well, that is a part of the materialised form. You see, to have a larynx and everything in connection with it would make it necessary for it to have a complete system of lungs and all the rest of it. Well, ask yourself, would that be necessary?"

*Interjection* : "Yet when a materialised form speaks it speaks as though it had".

*Peter* : "Yes, and perhaps you would get a certain warmth from the mouth as of breath. Well, it is done in the same way as the circulation. I tell you that in the case of materialisation, in so far as the figure may be perfect, the rest, such as rhythmic breathing, and perhaps even warmth of temperature, may not be possible of accomplishment. The most difficult accomplishment would be the voice, which should express the personality of the figure shown. In that case it would be possible to convey the vibrations or cords of the Medium's throat and reproduce the voice by sound from the materialised form's mouth. There can be no hard and fast rule. That again depends on the completeness of the work".

*Question* : "Is the finer quality (Grade 3) linked by ectoplasmic cord or structure to the Medium?"

*Peter* : "No, it is an invisible etheric link; invisible nearly always. It depends upon where the substance begins to manifest; sometimes close at a distance, with no possible apparent contact. Where it appears to be close to the Medium, there is always that space of invisibility if it be but about half an inch. The best conditions pertaining are those where the distance between the ectoplasmic formation and the Medium is greatest".

*Question* : "Regarding the feel of the ectoplasmic substance, we have had reference to a "wetness that wets not". Can you explain this?"

*Peter* : "It is 'viscous', but I will tell you the best parallel you can get; it is comparable to the fish called the eel, but one that is not freshly caught and has lain for some days. It is wet to the touch and yet no dampness is apparent. Again, however, this does not always apply. You can have it brittle so that it will crackle like parchment, or you can have it damp and cold; and again, you can have it dry and supple. It depends upon the condition, chiefly dietetic, or the Medium. That is, the way in which the Medium lives or has lived for the few days before the sitting. Much depends upon that".

*Question* : "When you get the 'sheet' effect, is this Grade 2 ? That always feels wet".

*Peter* : "Not commonly so. The best condition for it is when it is in its supple, dry state".

*Question* : "I remember that on the occasion when you touched our faces with it, it was also dry to the touch and patternless".

*Peter* : "You will find as a rule that there is no definite pattern. You must have something definite, but to say it has a definite pattern would not be true".

*Question* : "When ectoplasm was over the plaque it was so transparent we could hardly see it until it became as if rippled. Was that rippling caused artificially?"

*Peter* : "It was a distortion of the etheric ray around which it is formed. When light of too great a density is exposed within the room, the rippling becomes so great that it disperses the ectoplasm".

*Interjection* : "At one time it appeared as almost invisible."

*Peter* : "Then we were applying unequal pressure."

*Question* : "As a preliminary to the formation of a finer grade, possibly Grade 2, there has been witnessed what appears to be an emergence of heavy whitish vapour from the Medium's mouth or other source of emergence. It has been also noted that a physical sheet of ectoplasmic substance, before disappearing, has changed into vapour. I wonder if you could tell us if this vapour comes from, and returns to the body?"

*Peter* : "To say it does not come from the body is not true, to say it has no direct contact would also be untrue. It would be very similar to water trickling out of a hose without pressure and then suddenly having pressure put behind to force it into a fixed shape; the shape of the nozzle. In the case of the vapour it is a loosely formed ectoplasm that has not yet attained physical qualities. It is in its commonest form."

*Question* : "With your Medium I observed solid claw-like growths emerge from the edge of an almost transparent ectoplasmic sheet. These gripped and moved the plaque in a controlled manner. Can you enlighten us to the thought origin that builds the claws, etc.?"

*Peter* : "You remember some time ago I told you that most formations you have witnessed within the séance room were a display of primitive life. Well, it is not far for you to go in your imagination from that stage to the forming of primitive grippers. That is what it is. Now from whence comes the motivating part? It comes from the same source as that which forms the grippers. It could not produce, in the circumstances, anything better. That force is directed by mentality of those 'entities', which are commonly termed among you as 'elementals'. Their intelligence does not go beyond that. Therefore in primitive things they use primitive methods, and that is why it is so necessary that the Guides responsible for the Medium and for the sitters should have, not only full qualifications, but also should be, with permission, invested with the authority to govern the power. The strength that is produced with lightening-like rapidity in one quick crescendo of energy is released equally like lightening. It is the culmination of a great effort wherein the innate desire of these elementals to destroy is given for a brief time free range.

"I cannot tell you in slow motion how it is achieved, but the force released for a brief period of time is tremendous, and if not controlled could slay a horse. These grippers, I tell you, could be deadly things. We utilise the different qualifications of these little people to the furtherance of our work, gradually raising them up because they have always one object and one main idea in view; that is, incarnation as a human being whom they copy so much. I could tell you of a race of them in being today; they are not related by blood ties, but they have, in this respect, a similarity of feature, height, build, and also similarities in other directions. But if you, unknowing, saw one you would see them all, and on earth today there are, at least, between 500 and 1000 of these personalities. They are what you have termed as idiots. They have no mentality and they are not violent. Their characteristics are close-set eyes, flat foreheads and altogether small head with rather thick lips that are set like a bulldog's, the under-lip protrudes and the whole shape takes a very acute upward bend. The nose is small, with two round holes for the nostrils. The face and nose lack character. You can call them freaks, but they are normal in their features; they are not unlike animals. But their character stamps them all; they are a type, which is produced from the same mould. Life is not so placid and calm; and think if you knew more you would give us more consideration as to what should be and what should not be. In their right spheres everything works for good, but man is head of all animal ambition, though some like to take short cuts.

"Man in the creative sense is the apex of the whole evolution of sub-mundane life; that is to the whole of the animal and vegetable kingdoms. And there is over all the sub-mundane life a brooding Spirit, which is not individualised. Its intelligence is colossal, in its own sphere and in its own creation; it controls its physical counterparts as a whole and not as individuals. That intelligence is striving always to keep up its creation in the scheme of evolutionary development; and if once there is a chance for these elemental to push forward and gain access to the human realm, they can never be turned out. Hence my remark and warning: perhaps you will give us greater consideration in those things that are to be and not to be. You will see now the trend of our talk."

*Question* : "At a later sitting, after having seen some more primitive-like forms, I observed a perfect hand, formed from an island opaque mass in the centre of a piece of almost-transparent ectoplasmic material draped over the illuminated plaque; and I noted its perfection as to digital phalanges."

*Peter* : "But you observed something else; you observed its gradual growth."

*Question continued* : "Yes, I did; but in your statement on materialisations you referred to materialising entity drawing unto itself particles from the ether. Am I right in assuming that there is a similarity of process between the materialisation of a whole entity and a portion of an entity? Was the hand part of a discarnate entity or was it an evolved 'thought' hand or was it from the earlier primitive growths and produced by the elementals?"

*Peter* : "It was a product of the elemental. It was a triumph for them, that progress, as you saw it, took perhaps in measure of time a 1000 years to evolve from primitive gripper to a hand with digits. It was a triumph for them and there was much rejoicing when they had done it."

*Statement* : "that demonstration is a complete answer to the opinion of those who do not agree with us that life exists beyond our present physical existence. That demonstration was most illuminating to us."

*Peter* : " Yes. We are apt to consider our life as of the moment and not to any extent of what is past and what to come. That is the whole question."

*Question* :"Ectoplasm created from etheric particles possesses physical properties of density, weight, moisture, cohesion. We can understand that matter changes its formation from solid to fluid or to gas, but in so doing it retains the elements of which it is composed. Is it possible for you to give us some idea of the constituents of ectoplasm? Are they known to man by name? For example, if water is analysed its components would be oxygen and hydrogen."

*Peter* : "Well, there again where you have not the constancy of ectoplasmic formation you cannot have constancy of formulae. There are, I believe, thirty two known atoms and from these thirty two every substance that you know upon earth is formed by various combinations. Now you understand that. Well, it is no answer to your question to say that it is two parts water. The atoms are composed of things we know. I suppose you could call it material, yet it is not material in the sense that, if it is disturbed, it is likely to be dispersed. We can vary it so rapidly that it becomes a cloud-like steam. This accelerates decomposition; and if we were able to withdraw the bound ether associated with any article such as a table, it would collapse instead of decaying. It is the bound ether, which makes it retain its character. Actually, therefore, ectoplasm is a neutral substance which is created because it best suits the purpose."

*Question* : "Is it right, then, to conclude that ectoplasm is constructed from the known atoms"

*Peter* : "From a combination of some of them but not of the whole. What decides the particular material substance is the rate of motion and combination of atoms. You see, if we slow up that process we can make it partly physical and partly non-physical: and we can finish that by saying that ectoplasm is the 'mists of borders' that link the physical to the realm non-physical. It is the meeting of the two. It is a physical substance with a non-physical existence. "

*Statement* : "Some years ago an analysis was made of some ectoplasm substance and it was said to be largely albumen. "

*Peter* : "It is true: but never forget in all these things that it may have been produced for that action; and rather than its being a true formation it may have been specially formed. If you ask these 'little people' for something they will give it, but that is not to say it is genuine."

*Question* : "You spoke of the voltage sent through psychic rods used for strength. Is there a generating source for this voltage?"

*Peter* : "You cannot generate it, but only direct it. That direction is natural. That is it comes within the same influence of control as the production of actual phenomena. It is a natural force. It is a force, which is adapted for a particular purpose in the same way as your own electricity, but of a finer kind. It is a force, which is there all the time. You simply cause it to move in a given direction along an easier path. In the first instance you will agree that magnetism is a natural phenomena; therefore it is from a combination of the magnetic forces that you get electrical energy. You magnetise and you create a field of magnetism in which you evolve another field of much electrical friction. You simply congregate it in one spot and cause it to move along the path. Electricity does not run along the conductors. They pass it on. You go round a circuit. You have in an electric generating plant a complete picture of the Medium and psychic rods. You get work done the other end according to your wisdom."

*Question* : "We come to the 'ray', which you spoke about. Can you tell me if there is any affinity between the human body and the rays and/or between the human mind and the rays?"

*Peter* : "It is always apart from the human mind, i.e. the mind of man himself. Affinity: there is a connection with the rays. It is through the Medium's soul body that the rays are directed and that is where we hold the key to switch off at the moment of any danger if conditions are not right. The Medium is the focal point, always he is the generator; but he is not fitted with 'safety fuses' so we have to stand by the switch. I tell you, in the study of anything of this nature, electricity and its laws are running closely parallel with those of the laws we are trying to propound; the only difference being that you are not yet skilled in creating etheric conductors and have therefore to use the physical ones because that is the only material with which you can work. In creating the physical part, however, there is present the etheric part by virtue of the very nature of the materials you use; hence you get the creation of the etheric field which is not within the object (or conductor) but in the ether surrounding it. You will one day be able to control these rays. Man will not be allowed to use them until he is qualified. You cannot remain in you present state of mind for always, otherwise not only are you lost but we also.

Given by Spirit through Roy [author] whilst in trance in 2006-09-06.

Ectoplasm is produced by the Spirit World using the human body as a vessel of a mixture of chemicals. But this is in your simple language. Technically we use parts of the DNA structure, parts of it that produce mainly the fluid used for secretion around the joints and from the sexual organs that produce secretion and reproductive secretion when in a state of arousal. This we mix with chemicals from our side of the veil and through thought manipulation for a short time it is fixed into various substances from clear to thick dependant on the development of the link between the two vibration levels; this is known collectively by most on the earth plane as ectoplasm. During this process we use the organs of the human body as catalysts especially the pancreas. As some people will be able to understand, catalytic actions, meaning the chemicals being used if not correct, or the catalyst is not correct, the catalyst itself can break down. This is why the human who is going into the development of the Physical Medium should be in tip top condition eating a wide range of food not sticking to a set dietary format. Every human is slightly different in the percentage of their chemical make up, BUT the constant is with Physical Mediumship, we in the Spirit World need those parts within the human frame to carry out our work, **if**, and only if the permission is given by the participating Medium, we cannot do anything without the co-operation of the human link that is the law. The ectoplasm can be manipulated through our thought into different forms as needed. When finished it is most times caringly put back into the Medium being used by us. I say most times as there are occasions when something can occur and the ectoplasm is placed back into the human frame quicker than is safe for the Medium's health, these times are a worry for the Spirit World and for the Medium as a lot of damage can be done within the human frame, a few unfortunate times the termination of the time span allotted to the human on the earth plane. We do not wish to harm a person who has placed themselves under our care nor do we want to loose a willing earthly link who has put many hours aside in our joint development to help us in our quest to bring higher knowledge to the earth plane. This is why when developing and demonstrating the gift of Physical Mediumship all safety precautions should be adhered to.

# LEVITATION [transvection]
# &
# PSYCHOKINESIS (P.K.)

This is a subject that should be placed in two distinct parts. BUT I must point out, it is only the person's Spirit, the person him/herself, and/or those in Spirit who can say if they over lap from one to another, which is which or if they are the same. One is generally mind over matter, which is called Psychokinesis or P.K., the dictionary definition is :- supposed interference with physical causation by mental influence. The other way of levitation is done by the help of Spirit **generally** through ectoplasm BUT of course, Spirit generally needs a Medium there to control the proceedings. The reason I say generally is because not all happenings can be placed there into boxes.

I cannot say that Psychokinesis is not done with the help of Spirit because we are all Spirit and all blend with Spirit to a greater and lesser degree. Most who tell about their experiences and about how they do P.K. say, "they concentrate very hard, and start willing the object to be raised off the ground." It could be this is one method how they bring in their link to help. BUT, most who try the method of P.K. generally have no belief of help from the unknown. Most end up exhausted after the demonstration.

A lady from the U.S.S.R., Ninel Kulagina concentrated so hard to levitate the objects she was mentally exhausted when she finished her task, she could hold an egg floating in the air in between her, joined at the tips, circled fingers. There are many photographs of her in books and there was a film on T.V. in 2001. The Medium from Poland, Stanislawa Tomczyk, was tested a lot by scientists. She was also exhausted when her show was over. BUT who is to say whether it was done with or not done with the help of those in Spirit?

A lot of fun can be had with experiments in your groups with this sort of thing.

Try and get a person/persons to will a ball (table tennis ball as it is light) to move across a table in a certain direction, best placed under a plastic or glass container so no wind from people blowing can influence the ball. Also try to get a pendulum to swing in a clear glass or plastic container. The best pendulum would be a piece of charcoal as it is very light or a sewing needle can be used. They are tied with cotton thread of an appropriate length, (longer the better) suspended in the middle, best supported onto the top of the inside of the container with blue tack or sticky tape.

Another experiment is to get a bit of modelling clay, "Plastercine" or "Bluetack" put it on a flat surface; place a needle in it, point upwards. Get a piece of paper or card **approx** 3 inches (70mm), by 1 inch (20mm). Fold the paper in half one way then unfold. Now fold the paper the other way in half then undo the fold so you now know the middle of the paper section. Draw something on the ends of the paper like an arrow or a dark marking. Place the paper with the markings upwards onto the needle point at its centre. Place a clear glass or plastic bowl or container over the paper, needle and holding clay. Each person has to try to get the paper to go around in a circle like an aeroplane propeller by linking into Spirit and concentrating on the paper through the power of the link. All there should be asking Spirit and concentrating that the paper for it to go around clockwise. The direction has to be set otherwise some might try to send it the opposite way to the others. The power of the thought, and the asking through that thought link with Spirit will be seen to work if concentrated on hard enough. Keep on asking, asking and asking for Spirit to help you, work together in these tasks. Ask to be used as an open vessel, give permission for Spirit to use you as an instrument

A lot more experiments were conducted in the 1940's in America with dice, with people influencing them with their thoughts. The experiments were done with two dice and a check was made to see no cheating went on. The scores were meticulously kept over a period of time of many years in a controlled environment. If you try to have a go at this experiment yourself start with one dice.

Prepare yourself for a few moments by relaxing. Ask for help from your helpers from a cross the veil to place the dice with the numbers uppermost you require and keep on asking as you do this experiment, never stop talking to them and asking, or as some do, willing the numbers to come uppermost for you over and over again. This method of "willing" can drain you of your mental strength, that is why I always ask for help from above. Never be too proud as not to ask Spirit for help. I have found they never let you down. Cup the dice in your hands and throw them against a wall, or a corner of a wall so it hits two surfaces before coming to rest, this is so the weight of the throw cannot be controlled by yourself.

The average for the numbers coming uppermost (hits) for two dice are :-

The scores for the "hits" are 15 out of a possible 36 or five in twelve throwing in a pair.

Average for throws of twelve (two dice) is 5 high scores of eight or above.

Average for throws of twelve (two dice) is 5 low scores of six or below.

Average for throws of twelve (two dice) is 2 for scores of seven.

Now you can work out if you get more than the average in your own score.

Try other experiments like tossing a coin, controlling the toss by bringing up more head or tails uppermost on the landings. I have no doubt you could think of many other experiments that could be tried have a go at them BUT keep a record for the future. The score for this would be fifty/fifty, on an average it should come down on an even score. Now you can work out your own scores.

A lot of Physical Mediums who are now in the world of the higher vibrational level had the good and trusted link with those in the World of Spirit to help with the production of the levitation of objects. But two I have not seen produce phenomena but people tell me about are Collin Fry from Brighton, and Hull's Stewart Alexander who are still alive. Gordon Higginson from Stoke-on-Trent in the 1940-80's, a Yarmouth Medium, Guy L'Estrange in the 1920's with the trumpet for Independent Direct Voice, Jack Webber levitating tables, trumpets, chairs, his coat taken of by Spirit whilst still tied up in a chair. This and many other things have been photographed and published at the time it was happening. One famous person who was regularly talked about by Battling Bertha ["Harris" from Chester] as being a small man came from Wales his name was Colin Evans. She said he often rose in his chair to the ceiling in the séances she attended whilst they were singing lustily. Then gently came to rest from where he had started from. Bertha's guide/helper was called Angelos.

The Italian Eusapia Palladino in the late 1800's were everything used to fly in her séances. Said by many to be the most documented, powerful Medium of her time (BUT was accused of cheating in later life). At that time there was an Italian man, Francesco Caracini, who whilst tied up, the furniture used to fly around the room. Remember this is with the help of their guide and the group of helpers from the World of Spirit.

If a Medium is going to be tied up and you attend the séance, **be a knowledgeable sceptic**. Check the chair they are going to be tied to. I went to a séance in Hull, where the arm of the chair (a carver chair or Windsor type) could be easily lifted off it's front dowel and easily placed back leaving [this was done accidentally in front of me when I was shown the séance room and the chair was moved forward in the cabinet] the **possibility of** slipping the wire ties holding the arms, through and off, and back again. The chair at the back that held the Medium only had the rope looped around some four or five UUUUU type metal brackets which **would be easy to** slip out of and back again, it would have been better four or five 00000 rings, the two helpers either side of him **could** easily slip off the ties and place it back at the end of the séance, remembering this séance was in **complete** darkness. Check, check and check again. BUT do not do anything until the end of the Circle sitting as it could injure the Medium and/or the sitters if the Circle is genuine. Even point it out before the Circle starts, that way things could be altered ready for a good genuine Circle. This is the reason for people to use infra red cameras to log any phenomena.

Look at the older books and you will always come across the best examples of levitation done by Daniel Dunglas Home, a Medium who had been seen by many hundreds of people and was never accused of cheating, even though many, many times all the Mediums of the time were tested and many of them tricked into performing in front of the bigots in the other religions who were trying to catch them out and put into the category of a fake. D.D. Home on the 16$^{th}$ of December 1868 went out of a window on the third floor horizontally feet first and back into another window head first at this séance.

Another occasion, he was said to have risen into the air then his body was elongated. There is a very good book written by Elizabeth Jenkins The Shadow and the Light, it is a defence of Daniel Dunglas Home the Medium, in it you will be able to read about all the different séances that he had with the royalty of Europe and others from around the world bringing forth Physical Phenomena of every kind. He was a Medium that was tested many times and was **never accused** of being a fraud **by those who tested him**.

Daniel Dunglas Home was born in Edinburgh Scotland in 1833. His rocking cradle was said by his aunt who looked after him at the time, "to be rocked by unseen hands".

He held his séances in full light and had a dislike of Mediums who held their séances in the dark.

Home levitated in a daylight séance in 1857 in front of Prince Murat and Napoleon 111.

Please remember Levitation is not a new phenomena it has been happening to people from all walks of life throughout the centuries. It is well documented in many religious books, one notable one is the Christian bible. Jesus levitated by walking on the water, this is just one I have picked out. There are many monks who have been documented in recent times that have levitated also. One monk being canonised for his sanctity and for the blessed gift he had, this was St Joseph of Copertino. YET the Christian church still killed many others outside the Christian church who had similar gifts. Joseph was documented to have levitated in front of Pope Urban V111, he saw Joseph stay in the air for many minutes. He was seen to float by the Duke of Brunswick, and the High Admiral of Castile. His levitation or as the Christian church called it, **"transvection"** was not in a controlled manner and he would take off at the most inopportune moments. One of the most memorable incidents was when he was in a garden with a fellow priest. The priest turned to him and he said, "Brother Joseph what a beautiful heaven God hath made". Joseph took off gently into the air and landed on an olive branch in a near by tree. Even though the branch was thin it did not bend under his weight. He had to be brought back to the ground by other monks who fetched a set of ladders. Joseph was said to be in a dream like state when levitating he must have been put into a trance state by Spirit. He said his head felt sort of funny and was of "giddiness". The Christian church recognise that the phenomena of levitation does happen and have from that day name it **"transvection".** Joseph died in 1663

Others in the Christian church are documented to have levitated are St Ignatious Loyola. He had the added gift of being lit up like a luminous object at different times and when he levitated. St Philip of Neri levitated during prayers as did Joseph. Another religious person in the Christian church who had this gift from Spirit was St Robert of Palentin, but he was a low flyer in their ranks only achieving the height of little over a foot to 18 inches.

In the Christian church it is said that the levitation occurs when the levitators are in deep religious prayer. The person goes into what we now call a trance like state. It should be pointed out that the people who levitated have never taken anyone else up with them when they are grabbed hold of to be brought down. The phenomena is to do with the individual and not their environment. They would it appears be made into a body that is not controlled by gravity. [this would re-enforce the theory of "bowsing" or making an etheric vacuum around only the person levitating]

Do not confuse the ways of flying that the Transcendental Meditation Natural Party had in 1962 or Yogic flying as being Levitation. I have not seen anyone through that method fly or levitate, neither has anyone else to my knowledge.

# LEVITATION

As explained from the book of the Mediumship of Arnold Clare by Harry Edwards
Chapter X111 pages 155-166
(Peter is the Guide of Arnold Clare)

The movement of objects by means other than that of human agency is termed "levitation".

This phenomena, by virtue of its definite act, has been the subject of considerable research, notably by Professor Crawford through the Mediumship of Miss Goligher.

Professor Crawford's conclusions illustrate how an advanced knowledge can be attained when there is the right combinations of understanding investigator and willing Medium and co-operative Spirit operators.

Levitation is one of the elementary and primitive forms of action with physical Mediums. It varies from wild and haphazard movement, to controlled, ordered and delicately adjusted volition. Movement of this nature is generally the first sign of the ability of operators to demonstrate through their Medium.

Professor Crawford was able to obtain photographs of the mechanism employed in lifting weighty objects; and established among other conclusions that the movement was controlled by an apparatus termed "psychic rods", constructed through the Medium's psychic faculties. He also proved by patient and exhaustive research that in accordance with the general principles of leverage these rods were used in order to move an object of greater weight than that permitted by the power of a single rod emanating from the Medium.

Further experiments with the Medium seated on the scale proved that the weight levitated was returned through the Medium's body. When leverage was employed with the rod resting on a pivot, the weight returned through the Medium corresponded with the exact pressure required to move an object of a given weight by that means.

Probably owing to the nature of the experiments and the use of white light for photography, the character of the levitation noted by Professor Crawford was restricted to the primitive or "brute force" agency described by Peter.

With Jack Webber outstanding evidence has been recorded of various grades of levitating power. Of the primitive, physical formations of great strength were observed emanating from his solar plexus. They resembled the trunks of young trees, being some six inches broad near the body and tapering off to the point of contact with the object. Heavy mahogany tables requiring two people to lift them have been moved out of a "wedged-in" position to the far side of the séance room by this same method.

Through the same Mediumship the infrared photographs of tables in levitation were secured. One of these, as shown by plate No 5, pictures a heavy table of 45 lbs. Weight in suspension; this table requires a two-handed effort to lift it, and a "husky" man to do it. The other, plate No 6 shows a lighter table in movement before Mr Bernard Gray of the *Sunday Pictorial*. No psychic apparatus is visible with either of these photographs. On other occasions the author has testified to seeing massively constructed apparatus in association with primitive levitation.

Before proceeding further with this phenomena, it is necessary to keep in mind the revelations of Peter, who divides the forces used for levitation into two main categories:

[a] Movement of objects by "ponderous and brutal" means, that is by physically constructed psychic rods.

[b] Movement by regulating weights and gravity.

These are further sub-divided, as will be shown later, but for the moment these two broad divisions will enable the reader to comprehend the different grades of phenomena and avoid confusion by associating one with the other.

The records of the movements, and the character of the action of levitated articles through Mr. Clare's mediumship, possess the same characteristics as those reported at other times and places with other Mediums. The characteristics of levitation are so similar that experienced observer at once recognises the true movement.

With trumpet levitation the movement in incredibly fast; the trumpets weaving intricate patterns, so that their illuminated bands of paint appear as fixed lines of light. When two or more trumpets are engaged in such movement they intertwine; so that if, for examples, simple figures of eight movements are in being, they cut across each other. The trumpets may be moving at great speed high up to the ceiling, with one near the ceiling and the other near the floor, in vertical action close to a wall, whilst at the same time a third may be perfectly still in the air in the centre of the activity without even a quiver of movement. The author has seen four trumpets in simultaneous levitation. To witness this elementary phenomena alone is more than sufficient to prove the presence of forces and control beyond man's knowledge.

It should be remembered that this phenomena, as just described, takes place in the dark. To the critic who laments that darkness is a subterfuge of the séance room, here is an act incredibly more difficult in the dark that in the light. At times there may be as many as twenty people seated close together in the form of a Circle, yet never is any person struck by a trumpet; nor is such a thing as an electric pendant suspended from the ceiling down to the centre of the trumpet activity ever hit. Never has a picture on the wall, or glass door or a bookcase or side board been harmed while the phenomena is normal. Only once to the author's knowledge was a suspended electric light fitting smashed in the hundreds of sittings held in strange homes through J.W.'s Mediumship, and he used long heavy metal trumpets. This mishap only occurred through the collapse of the "conditions" due to an interference.

With Arnold Clare the Circle has to be widespread in order to give room for the most expansive movement. There is no operation from the immediate neighbourhood of the Medium, but movement occurs as far a field as the extended Circle permits; and even then the trumpets travel outwards over the heads of the sitters farthest from the Medium. In this connection the most remarkable of the author's experiences was that which illustrated the prefect control of movement within a dark Circle. It used to occur frequently at Webber's developing Circle, and involved a test of nerves for the sitters. Here a metal trumpet would travel in an arc-light movement, so fast that the luminosity was just a blaze of light; and a loud swishing noise would be created by the passage of the trumpet through the air. The edge of the trumpet would come within the barest fraction of an inch of the sitter's nose. I frequently experienced this. Whilst holding myself perfectly still, the trumpet-edge would almost touch the skin but never quite—a sixteenth of an inch more and the tip of my nose must have been torn off. In a flash the trumpet would sweep over to another sitter on the opposite side of the Circle and repeat the same operation or gently caress the face, to return instantly to swish up and down just in front of my nose. (to prevent any misapprehension on the part of the reader, it may be stated that those responsible for the action described only carried it out after knowing that the sitter was able to stand it. It would not be attempted with any stranger or person unused to séance room work.)

The most delicate trumpet control, as records testify, is also witnessed with Mr. Clare.

Another form of levitation is that of the Medium himself, in his chair. This phenomena has been recorded a number of occasions with various Mediums. With J.W. there are reports in the book on his Mediumship, and all that needed to be cited here is that he has been seen in both red and white light levitating in the air; in large halls he would touch hanging pendants fifteen to twenty feet high under the roof. Mr. Clare is also levitated in his chair at close of the séance.

Thus we can arrive at the conclusion that the movement of levitated objects is sure, definite, rigidly and delicately controlled, and that such movement must be the result of thought direction with the operators positively aware of the physical features within the area of action.

We have already said that levitation is graded into different categories, and Peter's explanation of the primitive method is dealt with first, as being far less challenging than the other.

Peter said: Levitating objects by means of rods is what one, using brute force in ignorance, would call the operation. I do not say in a disparaging way, but it is clumsy and consumes great power and energy, oft-times to the detriment of the Medium. You must understand the use of rods is very awkward in the extreme and they are also subject to limitations : for as they become attenuated they lose many of their characteristics and strength.

"Therefore if we wish to lift something heavy we have to push against the pressure, or pull away from the pull ; but in pushing against the pressure a great strain is caused upon the Medium as the moisture contained in the Medium's body is absorbed at a terrific rate. That is bad, because it tends to thicken the blood." [*Peter's reference to "pushing against the pressure" will be appreciated after reading his explanation of the "refined" method that follows.*] "This method, too, lends itself to a repetition of the same phenomena through the means of subconscious and physical action by the Medium himself, which may put him in bad odour, should such movements be observed".

"For the conduct of phenomena using psychic mechanics, the conditions must be excellent. For not only are the psychic rods an integral part of the phenomena for the moment but of the Medium as well. By that I mean there is subconscious reflex action on the part of the Medium physically, because the rods contain the lower impulse that would be, in a case of normality, manipulating his limbs for the same movements. Therefore when he sits for the production of phenomena and conditions are not quite right, he is not in a state to discriminate. The impulse is passed through his nervous organism to produce reactions, and if he is not restrained the phenomena will still occur, although it is just as genuine."

"This point of Peter's is illuminating when we pass our minds back to certain supposed "exposures" of Mediums.

The findings of Professor Crawford as mentioned at the beginning of this chapter were mentioned to Peter and he was asked whether he agreed with the findings. Peter replied :

*Peter* : "That is almost so, but you must also remember that the weight of a Medium will fluctuate through the consumption of the fluid content of the body. That is a direct cause. It is a form of hydraulics. True, it is borrowed and we return it ; perhaps not quite all but most of it—but this work is not good for the Medium."

It was established several times, using the same scales before and after the séance, that J.W. lost up to 8 lbs in weight during a sitting. By taking his weight at various times following the sitting, it was found that his weight became normal about sixteen hours afterwards. Mediums whose physical powers are so used in séance work should remember this, and so give themselves adequate time for recovery before sitting again.

*Peter was asked* : "When an object of weight is lifted, where is the basis of resistance?"

*Peter* : "Well, you cannot fix that ; it would vary : but what are we going to move?"

*Questioner* : "Say a light object—such as a trumpet."

*Peter* :"The basis of resistance would then be, if it were close to the Medium, from his knee or shoulder. It would be rigid. If it were at a greater distance, the most convenient point : and from there to the Medium (acting as a "power cable") it would be relaxed, limp."

*Question* : "Would one get the cruder method for levitating objects when the control of the Medium is from 'within'?"

*Peter* : "You mean in the case of direct control of the physical organism by an invading entity?"

*Questioner* : "Yes".

*Peter* : "We have spoken of the production of phenomena and their control, that is the creation of an environment whereby the phenomena can be directed by thought (if you wish) and wherein we use a movement of brute force with rods. In this case, control from within and directive control provides almost a parallel.

"Directive control is where the instrument reaches out in thought and raises his own tonal quality to the degree where his aspirations meet and fuse with the directive thought of the Guide or Inspirer. There we have two forces seeking each other, the one lending himself to the thought domination of the other. That is in the case of directive control.

"In regard to physical control you have almost a reversal. Instead of being controlled by thought, you are entirely controlled physically, so much so that all the thought actions of the invading entity become, for the time, part of the physical organism of the instrument. The deeper the invading entity becomes immersed within the denser ether surrounding the earth, the more he loses the vision of the spheres beyond."

This answer emphasises the point made by Peter elsewhere, that it is not good for a Medium or potential Medium to encourage this form of control.

An illustration of such physical control is given in the case of Jack Webber. J.W. was about 5ft 8 in. in height, and yet on such an occasion when invested by an entity of greater stature, he would become physically much taller, bigger and stronger. Whilst under this control he would call our attention to the change, and would ask for one of the sitters, Mr. Croft a Metropolitan policeman, 6ft tall, and well built, to stand in front of him and note the expansion (this took place in red light) J.W. would then expand and grow taller until he was of equal stature with Mr. Croft. On one such occasion he took the author (5ft 8in tall and 10stone in weight) by the shoulders and swung him round as if he were a bag of straw.

We now come to Peter's explanation of more refined processes of levitation, and they contain some most challenging observations.

Before proceeding with them it may be well to recall certain definite recorded acts of levitation which, as will be seen, come within this category.

There are the Margery records, which show that sitters were not only permitted to encircle with clasped hands a levitated object, but to pass their clasped arms right over and around the object, thus proving there was no physical connection responsible for levitation. There are the photographs of the tables, previously mentioned, where no physical mechanism can be seen : and from the author's point of view, in red light, he has witnessed, with other sitters, trumpets floating or sailing around within the Circle perfectly clearly without any visible connection. This movement was described by a sceptic as like a pike swimming and darting about in a pool.

The movement of the plaque is reported in one of Mr. Clare's Circles, where at the time it passed between illuminated ectoplasm and between the legs of myself and other sitters. Had there been any physical control, however attenuated, it **must** have been observed.

It is here noted that where physical rods are employed they are always straight and rigid. (See Peter's reference to these rods in the chapter on "Ectoplasm".)

Peter commented by saying :

*Peter* : "You are already aware of the limited space wherein the directive intelligences can work, that is, within the sphere of action circumscribed by the auric field or "tent". Within that space the force of gravity is not so greatly impressed. Gravity is in a state of suspension, so that to levitate any article, no matter what the weight may be, we neutralise the already weakened pressure or gravity."

"To get a clear conception of this, one must picture the force of gravity, not as a pulling power but as a pushing power : not as a drawing towards the centre of the earth but of a push towards the centre."

"Gravity in its operation is due entirely to etheric pressure and nothing else."

"You will see that when it comes to manipulation of gross ether we are in our element, the same as you are with your wood and stone."

"Gravity operates towards the centre of the earth. This appears to you to be so because your feet are implanted on the earth and objects move towards the earth's centre.

The pressure is exerted from all directions equally, so it must get across the centre. You take the centre because you stand on a sphere and the pressure is so equal in all directions, etherically, that it tends as far as you can judge to be a pulling force directed from the centre."

"You see you are not concerned, directly, with what are the 'laws' of gravity—it is not the law you are perceiving—it is the law of force."

"The pressure of the ether penetrates all things, therefore the force of gravity operates no matter where it is."

"The magnet depends upon etheric vibrations for its manifestations. The etheric content in which you are immersed is the primitive room of all life—cosmic, solar and all forms of animated life."

*Question* : "You said that gravity is the result of etheric pressure. Can you explain this more fully?"

*Peter* : "It will help you if I tell you this. All matter is permeated by the ether!……How is this?"

"Because it is of such immense and ponderable pressure that it pushes its way through everything, so much so that whereas you consider stone and brick as solid, actually they are full of great holes due to the pressure placed upon them etherically. The spaces within and between the particles of matter are so great that in comparison and with no exaggeration the distance between each is equivalent to that existing between a football suspended in the centre of Westminster Abbey and the walls and floor and roof. It is, after all, the element within which the ordinary magnetic power operates. If you were to place a magnet within an etheric vacuum it would not operate any more than a flame in a closed jar."

*Question* : "Concerning other pressures, such as the atmospheric pressure, how is this related to either the etheric pressure or the force of gravity?"

*Peter* : "You mean the atmosphere, referring to air. Well, air ceases to exist a few miles up, and gravity ceases to operate (as far as you are concerned) because sooner or later you must reach an area where the atmosphere enters into a neutral zone. To us, atmospheric pressure is incomprehensible."

*Question* : "Referring to the answer just given—you have said that atmospheric pressure is incomprehensible to you. Why is this, for we know the atmosphere has weight and therefore exerts pressure?"

*Peter* : "Yes, of course, it has weight like everything else. That is only because it is necessary for your well-being that you should be able to assess things, and atmospheric pressure is a thing which is only concerned with yourselves. It has no existence apart from yourselves. Its depth is only a few miles of your measure, and beyond that it does not exist in any form whatsoever. It therefore has no bearing on the larger problems with which we are dealing."

*Question* : "There is also the question of attraction between matter and matter, the greater the mass the greater the attraction. How do you relate your statement to the possibility that the core of the earth, being of mineral content, may be the centre of attraction towards the centre of the earth?"

*Peter* : "It seems as if mind of man always have a core, like an apple. Why do they say it is the centre of the earth that attracts?"

Because of the great mass of the earth's mineral centre, and the consequent pulling force towards the centre."

"Well, suppose you take two large masses of matter, polarise them to the same polarity and see what happens. Actually the one would push the other away and not attract it. Well, is it not possible that the same may apply in the case of gravity? Could not the mineral contents of the earth and those in space be polarised to such a fine degree of balance that each body within the solar system maintains its position perfectly? It is the evenness of pull between the heavenly bodies and the pivot, the sun, which is responsible for keeping the earth in its place, as well as the other bodies."

"This is accomplished through that little known element, ether, a substance which can be made to bear a character according to its environs and purpose it has to serve."

"We were talking about two masses having the same polarity and making them reject each other. What actually takes place within the solar system is that the composition of each body is such that each repels or attracts the other to such fine limits that they are indissolubly bound within their particular orbit. In such a way, too, that all things relative to that body must normally remain a prisoner. Now listen to me. If you study that, you can study any mineral. You can study the large solar system that has its central pivot and round which revolve in their precise orbit electrons, so called, that determine what atom it is, it is independent, in itself, of any outside control. It shows that it has a central intelligence of its own. So far as it is concerned, nothing exists outside of itself. Now can you see? It is a world of its own. It is the cheese and not the maggot. It is the motive."

"You speak of gravity. It is not the 'law'. It is the 'effects' man studies, and they call the effects the law. Man is only concerned with effects and says it works because he knows what effect the so called law has."

"Attraction of matter to matter is something apart from etheric pressure. It has a relationship, but at the same time you have a state of unbalance because if you were to put an object between two of similar weight the centre one would remain stationary."

"You have bodies drawing out and you have certain stationary bodies, more or less on the outside fringe, pulling the other way. Well, of course that proves they could as easily be pushed as pulled. You have the core of the earth which pulls, but what is space when you are considering such forces?"

"There is no feasible evidence of the law of gravity—you just study the effects."

*Question* : "Can you tell us, when an object is levitated and is subjected to controlled directional movement, by what means this is done?"

*Peter* : "When you are sailing a boat you manipulate the sail to travel in the required direction. In the case of the directing the movement of articles, we change not the sail but the direction of the 'breeze'. We direct the 'breeze' so as to move the trumpet in the desired direction, or alternately we create an inequality of 'breezes', which is the same thing.

*Question* : "When the trumpet moves and twirls very rapidly, is this movement produced in the same way?"

*Peter* : "It is produced by the same method, but what we do, instead of directing a gentle 'breeze' is to create an etheric whirlwind which has a fixed centre and spreads out fanwise ; this carries with it the trumpet, which is caught up with the whirl. The trumpet has lost the physical qualities of weight, and therefore it is, in actual fact, non-existent physically, in so far as this characteristic is concerned."

*Question* : "Is the control of the whirl by directive thought?"

*Peter*: "The explanation of that at this point is liable to be rather confusing. You see we do not produce all this. We have to go deeper still and speak about such things as elementals."

This was the first time Peter mentioned "elementals", "the little people", "pre-humans" who have been previously described in this book. It is repeated that to comprehend them, as well as other incidental matters, one must review the thesis as a whole and not isolate one part of the explanation from another. Each aspect of the process of producing phenomena is related to the other.

It is frequently observed with trumpet phenomena that these possess individuality, indicating that a particular personality was responsible for movements. This was commented on to Peter and he further observed:

*Peter*: "Such characteristics do develop because these elementals are very primitive; and they like to be outstanding and to have characteristics of their own, but this is a subject that can be best dealt with elsewhere."

*Question*: "Can you indicate the amount of force that can be exercised? Is it considerable?"

*Peter*: "It does not matter what weight is provided we can see the content. If we can see the content, then by rarefaction there is no limit to the weight that can be used."

"The more we adjust the weight the more inert does matter become. That is the sum total of matter—inertia—the lack of desire for the thing to move. But once get it started and it would want the same power to stop it. If you could make the etheric vacuum around the Circle complete, we would have all the sitters without appreciable weight."

"Thus, movement within, as one might say, a form of 'rarefied atmosphere'. It is as if we were holding back the pressure to keep the article stationary. It requires only a little operation to make things float—these could then be directed as one can direct a feather or a light piece of paper. The weight goes when you remove the pressure of gravity. It has no weight when gravity is removed."

# DIRECT VOICE
# &
# INDEPENDENT DIRECT VOICE

Direct Voice from a Medium is the voice of Spirit coming from the Medium many times in a monotone sound that comes from the area of the Medium's body generally other than the vocal cords. This is Physical Phenomena. A lot of the time Spirit builds an ectoplasmic voice box (a word that confuses the working of the vibrations from Spirit. Spirit prefer the name of **"etheric amplifier"**) inside the tube going from the throat to the stomach many times altering the size of the tube to accommodate the **"etheric amplifier"** in it (direct voice is so called as it is direct from Spirit not through the mind of the Medium). This is achieved as the Medium gets a stronger link with Spirit or Spirit gets to know what can be achieved with their Medium who they are working with. Those in Spirit will eventually place an ectoplasmic covered/protected **"etheric amplifier"** away from the Medium's internal tubes, setting it up outside the body so it will not interfere with any problems of the Medium's earthly body. This also is to take any detrimental comments away from the Medium. This then becomes **Independent Direct Voice**, the only attachment to the Medium is the link through the ectoplasm being produced which is **sometimes** needed for the formation of the **"etheric amplifier"**. The reason I believe Spirit does this is, is to knock down the sceptics who might say it is the Medium making the voice and producing the words through their own mind. This is the reason for the need of infra red cameras in Physical Circles in the séance rooms, to record the evidence for the world at large to see. Watch out for people who say they do not want cameras in the séance room, giving all sorts of reasons for not wanting it. It might be for genuine reasons, but even then I would be wary. Infra-red lighting **does NOT** harm the Medium or ectoplasm (very rarely) nor does very, very low red light, (depending on the make up of the Medium's body) **But** ultra violet light does (i.e. as in bright daylight). It is always best to place a box which excludes all light in any room where you would like Spirit voices to be produced. A microphone can be placed inside the box if it is thought that the volume might be needed to be increased or put inside the box a small voice activated tape recorder. Try to make the box sound proof to stop any recording of outside noises.

Spirit will sometimes build the etheric amplifier at the side of the Medium's face, (independent of the Medium, Independent Direct Voice) on the shoulder or possibly in a trumpet to make the sound louder.

The **"etheric amplifier"** can be attached by an ectoplasmic cord or not. Spirit will then quite often use the trumpet to talk to an individual. Moving the trumpet by the means of ectoplasm (this can sometimes be seen, and it can be floated/moved by Spirit without any connection) from the Medium and most remarkably using the ectoplasm to form over and encase the etheric amplifier inside the trumpet as well. There are many photographs of this happening, many are on display in the museum at Stansted hall and a lot are shown in many books from the early 1900's on Physical Phenomena.

Spirit are now telling us here on the earth plane we do not have the full knowledge of the workings of the full vibration scale, especially the ones they use in the makeup of the **"etheric amplifier"**. They do not like the name voice box as it is not being used as the vocal cords of the Medium are being used in everyday life to produce sound/voice. The name voice box can confuse the way the **"etheric amplifier"** is constructed and works.

The Medium's nervous system and their etheric body are both needed to produce the vibration necessary to link with the **"etheric amplifier"**. The amplifier is enclosed within an **"etheric vacuum"**, which is often covered in ectoplasm for its protection and to hold the vacuum stable. The ectoplasm that encloses the **"etheric amplifier"** structure to protect it, is similarly being used when ectoplasm protects the structure of the materialisation of a person. They are also "within" an "etheric vacuum" to control the mechanism that can be seen. This is where the etheric is said to be '**within**' or '**without**'. **"Without"** is in the air all around us. The vibrations produced by Spirit using the Medium have to be transmitted through the etheric in the air, (which is "without"); to the structure which Spirit has constructed **"within" an "etheric vacuum"**, classed as '**within**', (it is sometimes covered/held//protected by ectoplasm, and sometimes seen) to the **"etheric amplifier"** which converts the vibrations to the sound transmitted by Spirit using the Medium. But these are not physical vibrations, they are etheric, needing also a refiner. The reason the voice often sounds like the Medium is, the Medium's etheric body which is always there part of him co-produces the sounds heard in every day life, so it becomes logical that the voice produced by Spirit is not always different from the Medium in the early stages of their development and can stay the same throughout their full development. The muscles of the Medium are used when sound is heard (BUT not always heard at the mouth area of the Medium) and often felt by the Medium being used whilst they are in an altered aware state but still slightly (different people are aware of different things at different stages) aware of happenings. The etheric sounds are produced in waves, then put out through formed ectoplasm which also protects them. Remember the **"etheric amplifier"** we are told does not act as does the physical voice box of the Medium with vocal cords being used to have the sound produced, but uses something similar to the TV and the Radio systems by plucking from the air/ether the signals necessary to produce sound through the **"etheric amplifier"**. Sometimes using the cords of ectoplasm as protection of the transmission, as in a telephone system or using the other method, by collecting, refining, then amplifying (used in both methods), the sounds straight from the air, or properly termed the etheric part of the air, to be heard.

Try to go and see genuine Direct Voice Mediums and then to Trance Speaking Mediums to see the difference. Ask questions of them, ask questions of the Medium that you think are beyond their comprehension and see how they respond.

Please do not think this is a new phenomena Spirit talking through the Medium and with the help of the Medium's body as a catalyst, it has been going on since time in memorial. Look at the text of the old books written especially the religious books if they are to be believed. The voices of Jehovah was often said to be heard by the Hebrews. Those notable ones that were written in their text were Moses and Isaiah. The basis of the Christian religion was said to be spoken by the angels or Jehovah and given through an independent voice the direction that people of a good society should follow, that was the Ten Commandments.

The most famous ones of recent history are unfortunately dead now, Leslie Flint (1911-1994) and John Campbell Sloan (1869-1951), but there is one person I would recommend to anyone is Melanie Polly, she is still very much alive. In 2001, I recorded her twice. I was recording her when I saw her go into a Trance state and link into her Spirit Friends, White Owl (who has to use ectoplasm to form the voice box internally to speak) and Marie Teresse spoke for two and a quarter hours in Rugby Church without a break or for Melanie to have a drink or to catch Melanie's breath. It was a truly remarkable demonstration and the remarkable thing is; Melanie does not remember anything of what happens during the time she is in the Trance state. Spirit knocks her out, and she says, "I feel as though I have been asleep". This is the reason for using infra red cameras and microphones to record the session for the sake of the Medium. It gives them confidence to carry on with their work for Spirit knowing afterwards things are happening to her in trance are exactly like people who attend the séance have told her afterwards. This is also the reason for the stillest possible mind of the Medium.

Most important for people who are thinking of sitting to develop Direct Voice, or Physical Phenomena is to know how to help Spirit contact as much as possible. Also if you are affected as I am with a lot of phlegm in the throat area, do not drink milk or any extract of a dairy product before any Physical Phenomena sitting. It must be water, water, water before any sitting for Spirit BUT IT DOES NOT MEAN YOU CUT OUT DAIRY PRODUCTS ALTOGETHER unless told to do so by Spirit, as they **could** be necessary for the production within your body of the things needed by Spirit in the makeup of the Physical Phenomena process. Spirit will take from you and the surrounding area chemicals needed for the production of the phenomena to prove there that life continues after we leave our physical body. The reason for no dairy products is, the throat area gets a lot of mucus and it reacts within that area which is so important for Spirit; and it clogs the airways, well in me it does. I only speak from my own experience as I have always been cloggy in the throat with milk, especially the full cream. It is most important to drink only water at least an few hours before sitting for Spirit. Every day now I only drink a very, very weak tea that is like a see through liquid of very, very light brown, I might as well drink water BUT I seem to need something that is in the tea perhaps it is the minerals and vitamins that I might be lacking. [know it cannot be caffeine as I cannot stand coffee]. But I am trying skimmed milk and no milk at all on the days I sit in the Circles. This is the reason why I am trying to tell you everything that is happening to me. I feel it is necessary because it might happen to you. It seems to me sometimes I am being used by Spirit as a person who has to experience all these things as I have the means to portray it to others. Sometimes it can be a problem for me especially in relationships. I wonder sometimes if those in Spirit realize you as a human being need a person who you can love, be there when needed, one who gives you comfort, understands and cuddles into you, at the times when you are not working for Spirit. For me a good lady is always needed. A lot of people do not understand that working with Spirit, you seem to be on a different way of thinking than the ordinary everyday person. I am sorry that might seem funny, strange, or objectionable, but it is true. Until you get into that strong level of linking you will not understand.

One book that I would recommend on this subject is one written by Rodney Davies "Disembodied Voices" ISBN 0 7090 6719 4. It goes into the past history of people who have been guided by and warned by those in the Spirit World through the direct and independent direct voices of Spirit, subjectively and objectively.

## Harry Edwards book **THE PHYSICAL MEDIUMSHIP OF ARNOLD T. CLARE**  CHAPTER V11 Pages 36-42
(By William E Harrison, President of the Balham Spiritualist Society)

On the table, as I write, lies a queer assortment of twenty different articles: an auctioneer's hammer, pieces of ivory, a lion's claw, numerous coins, an arrow, a small carved cross, a locket, three small carved images and other things difficult to describe. All of these things came into my possession in the séance room through the Mediumship of Arnold Clare; and surveying them again my mind goes back to the early days of this Circle.

We often hear how those who have developed the gift of Physical Mediumship sit patiently for many years awaiting the first movement of the trumpet; but in the case of this Medium the story is quite different and the rapidity with which the range of Physical Phenomena developed was almost startling.

My first contact with the Circle was in June 1939, at that time Mr. and Mrs. Clare with two other ladies, had been sitting for only a few months and each week I had been told of their progress, how they had had levitation of objects, strong psychic breezes and their apports.

One evening I was invited to the Circle and in a small box room at the top of the house, bare of all furniture except five chairs, I witnessed for the first time the things of which I had been told. The Medium was secured to a small armchair by tapes bound very securely around his wrists, and then over an hour there occurred the levitation of three trumpets, gramophone records being put on and taken off by invisible hands, and the appearance of two small apports (medallions) for the two ladies. But for me the most impressive event was the transportation of an object from my home about a mile away to this little room.

This is how it happened.

On the afternoon of that day my wife was sewing. She was using a thimble, which was afterwards put away in a needlework basket. Later in the day she required the thimble again but could not find it anywhere.

At the séance in the evening, Peter (the Guide who spoke through Arnold Clare), speaking through Mr Clare, mentioned the loss of the thimble and said: "we will now return it to you to take home to your wife"; and sure enough through the trumpet came the thimble right into my hands. The thimble was the one belonging to my wife, which had been lost that afternoon, and was easily identifiable by me through its special markings. Mrs Harrison was not present and was amazed and surprised to find that I was able to return it to her from the séance room. Perhaps I should add that Arnold Clare had not been in my home for more than a week previous to this sitting.

Discussing this matter later with the Guide, he said they had chosen this way of proving to me how they were able to transport objects over distance, knowing that if something from my house was removed to a distance it would give me confidence in the apport phenomena.

At a much later date a similar happening occurred to another Circle visitor. In this case a small feather was removed from a hat in a locked wardrobe at her house, and much to the lady's astonishment was presented to her in the Circle being held almost a mile away.

During the next six weeks I visited the Circle on two other occasions and witnessed the phenomena of the trumpet. The latter was always under perfect control, the movement being "clean" and rapid.

So far I had heard no voices, and although a few attempts had been made at the production of ectoplasmic structures, nothing definite or recognisable could be observed.

How ever, the apports were most prolific during this period, and frequently ten or twelve articles and coins would appear and usually were put in the sitter's hands through the trumpet.

In each case the trumpet would levitate ceiling high, and would remain stationary for perhaps a minute. The article would then be heard rattling in the trumpet. This latter would travel to a sitter and the object would be placed in his hand.

No sittings were held during August owing to holidays, and then, with the advent of war, Mr Clare was able to devote only a very limited amount of time to work. From September 1939 to January 1940 only four Circles were held. Two of these were held in my house, and it was quite obvious from the commencement of the first Circle that the rest period had produced no adverse effect upon the phenomena. In fact, the first of these Circles was one of the finest demonstrations of Physical Phenomena that I have witnessed.

There were only four of us : Mr and Mrs Clare, and Mrs Harrison and I. We sat in a semi-circle around the fireplace, almost touching one another, and in the small confines of this space all the following took place: levitation of three trumpets at once; a sewing-machine in the corner of the room moved into the circle, unlocked itself, the handle turning continuously for some minutes; oranges were taken off the sideboard and put in the writer's jacket pocket, one each side; a clock and tw3o photographs were taken from the mantelpiece and transferred noiselessly to a table the far side of the room.

A child Guide who announced himself as "Little Peter" spoke through the trumpet for the first time and amused us with his chatter. He seemed to be able to speak quite clearly and easily, and the childish intonation was particularly noticeable. This was really the first time I had heard a voice through the trumpet in this circle.

Formations of ectoplasmic substance which assumed various shapes were shown to us.

The "rushing winds" reminiscent of the Pentecostal séance recorded in the bible were much in evidence this night, and there were a number of apports.

One of these latter, a small Eastern jug-shaped object, was given to me. I held it for a few minutes and was told by the Guide to put it back in the trumpet. On doing so it disappeared. A little later it was returned to me filled with a most exquisite perfume.

Perfume had always been splashed about in small amounts in previous Circles, but this was the first time I had seen any considerable quantity.

These or similar happenings were repeated at the following three séances, at one of which the Circle was made up of fourteen people and eighteen apports were distributed to the various sitters

At this séance, January 6, 1940, the Guide said there were to be no more visitors as a further period was required for development. As a result of this, a sitting with Peter for discussion on the matter was held when only Mr and Mrs Clare and Mrs Harrison and I were present.

Peter stated they were not satisfied just to keep repeating the same manifestations, and they sought to develop the phenomena with the object of obtaining direct and independent voice. He stated they wished to build figures that could walk about, and talk with sitters, and were capable of holding sustained conversations. Mrs Harrison and I were invited to join the group, which was to remain as now constituted (four of us) and meet weekly.

We were given to understand that the apport phenomena would cease and they would only be allowed on special occasions, and in fact fore a few weeks we were not to expect any phenomena at all.

For a few weeks we sat quietly, usually for one and a half hours, and most of the time was spent in talking with Peter and John on various aspects of the work and spiritual problems. It is my one regret that these talks were not taken down by a shorthand writer, as they were deeply interesting, but many questions discussed have since been reported by Mr Edwards at special Circles.

During our talks I had referred to the subject of book tests and John promised to try this. The following week, John said I had a book called *Sunwich Port* in my library, a small brown book. I could not recall this book at all. However, he insisted that it was there and that on page 22 at the top I should find these words: "why should you think my father wanted your bed?"

On returning home I immediately looked for the book, and sure enough I found W.W. Jacobs' book, *At Sunwich Port*, a small brown book, which I had not looked at for twenty years or more. Eagerly I turned to page 22, but was disappointed at not finding the words quoted. I dismissed the matter, but two or three days later thought of it again and somehow felt impressed to look at page 122 and there found the sentence exactly as quoted.

Saying nothing of this to Mr Clare, I went to the Circle the next week and John referred to his mistake in the page and said he was glad I had looked again and found the words and that the impression which I had felt so strongly to turn to page 122 had come from them. I asked for another example of this work and he quoted a passage, which I wrote down verbatim from page 39 of Renan's *Life of Jesus*, which was in my possession and which was perfectly accurate.

Although most of the evenings during the next eight weeks were spent in taking, there were periods when attempts at independent voice occurred. Usually it was "Little Peter" whose voice was heard saying one or two words fairly clearly and from different parts of the room—sometimes over the Medium's head, sometimes directly in front of our faces, at other times at the back. Usually, towards the end of each séance, the last ten or fifteen minutes were devoted to a full operation of the phenomena, rapid levitation of trumpets and sometimes furniture, Guides speaking through trumpets, scent and slight attempts at materialisation.

The independent voice did not seem to develop very well and although several efforts were made by others to talk in this way, the only one who succeeded was "Little Peter"; and as no progress was made the guides decided to concentrate for a period on the production of ectoplasmic structure with the view to building up full size figures.

The various formations were manipulated by the operators with astonishing speed and skill, and were frequently shown to us on the illuminated side of the slate, (plaque), which clearly showed the fine structure of the substance.

At this particular period (on the Guide's suggestion) a rope was introduced into the Circle and for some weeks the medium was securely tied to the chair by the Guides. The roping was accomplished swiftly in the dark and at the end of the séance they also did the unroping.

Sometimes in the course of the séance the Medium would be unroped and Mrs. Harrison and I would be roped together by these invisible hands. Frequently they would leave the ropes tied in all kinds of fancy knots and we often found it difficult to unravel them, an illustration of the strength, which had been used in the tying process. However, this practice was discontinued as the ladies thought it might be dangerous.

By this time materialised figures were beginning to build up very clearly and "Peter" was very active in these manifestations, building up three or four times, showing himself in profile in order that we should see his pointed beard and gradually moving away farther from the medium each week and oft-times speaking a few words to each of us.

Another guide who then frequently made an appearance, but whom we had not contacted before, was "Abdul", an Egyptian, and he it was who was mainly responsible for this part of the work. It is certain that from the time "Abdul" came on the scene the materialisations became much clearer and stronger and were able to move about to a far greater extent.

About this time the guide suggested it might be advisable to hold a few public séances, inviting eight people, so that they could judge the effect of their work. Accordingly, several of these circles were held, and at each one of them the phenomena produced usually commenced without delay and carried on continuously for one and a half hours. It was quite obvious that these few weeks of development had helped the work considerably. As various records of these séances show, the voice communications were clearer and conversations prolonged. The materialised figures were able to get well away from the Medium, frequently twelve to eighteen feet away; and the control over the phenomena by Spirit operators was excellent.

After these efforts I suggested to the guide that perhaps it would be possible to produce the phenomena in a subdued light. We had a long discussion about this and finally "Peter said if we were prepared to sit for some time without results it should be possible. He stipulated that the light required should be "ice-blue"; and eventually we managed to get the require shade of light and began sittings, with a light sufficient for us to see one another clearly. *(Professor Ochorowicz employed with success a faint blue light. So did Paul Gibier, the director of the Pasteur Institute in New York. In Dr von Schrenck Notzing's : "Materialisation")*

These sittings commenced in June 1940, and for the first four weeks nothing happened, except that we could see the trumpets rocking backwards and forwards on the floor where they stood; then in two successive weeks they were knocked onto the floor and constant effort was made to lift them, but only on one occasion did they succeed in moving one trumpet to a foot off the floor.

We had now reached the middle of August and "Peter", in his weekly talks, forecast many dangers, which threatened us as a result of war conditions, saying that he thought it would be impossible to meet regularly in the weeks ahead and also that it would be wiser to abandon these sittings in the light for the time being. As we know, the September blitz on London started the following week, and from that time only a few Circles have been held at intervals.

I am sure that under normal conditions, and given a sufficient time for development, much of the phenomena now obtained in darkness could be witnessed in subdued light to the complete satisfaction of all who may be sceptical of séances held in the dark.

# THE MECHANICS OF VOICE PRODUCTION
### From Harry Edwards' book the Mediumship of Arnold Clare
### Chapter XV pages 176-191 (Peter is Arnold Clare's guide )

PERHAPS the most puzzling of all phenomena from the investigators point of view is that termed the "direct voice" This is the phenomenon of voices produced through Mediumship by other means than that of human vocal organs.

Associated with "direct voice" is that termed "independent voice". The difference between the two is that the former is manifested through a cone or a trumpet, while the latter manifests independently of any humanly constructed mechanism.

The voices purport to be from Spirit people, and there is overwhelming evidence to support this view. The words and language must be of Spirit origin, because of the very nature characterisation and information of the communications.

Two examples are sufficient to give force to this contention. The first through the Mediumship of Valiantine (see later) and secondly through Jack Webber an unlettered collier, through whom conversations were carried on between sitters and Spirit communicants in French, Portuguese Swedish and Latin, without any hesitation in the speech or a trace of an accent foreign to those tongues.

So many volumes of authenticated records of direct voice communications have been published that the reality of this manner of communication is now generally accepted. What has not so far been established is the method and means by which these voices speak. The object of this chapter is to provide a thesis for the mechanics of this phenomenon.

The following are examples of attested evidence of direct voice phenomena; and are eloquent in their proof that the mind direction for such evidence must have been from a discarnate entity.

Professor J. Hysop investigated the voice phenomena of Mrs. Eliz. Blake and his report covers over 200 pages of *U.S.A. S.P.R. Proceedings*. In it he says: "The loudness of the sound in some cases excludes the supposition that the voices are conveyed from the vocal chords to the trumpet. I have heard them 20 feet away and Mrs. Blake's lips did not move."

Mr. H. Dennis Bradley, in his book (1928) entitled *The Reality of Physical Phenomena:*

"Dr. Whynant is a great linguist speaking thirty languages and a very considerable number of dialects.

He was for many years lecturer on Chinese at Oxford University. He is not a Spiritualist. . . . At a series of sittings held in New York at the residence of Judge W. M. Cannon, a famous and wealthy lawyer of the highest credentials under the Mediumship of George Valiantine, a voice was heard speaking in Chinese, etc. In my opinion these conversations in Archaic Chinese represent perhaps one of the greatest tests ever made in psychical research and Spirit-voice communication.

"Full significance must be given to the various languages spoken and the intonation and accents of the 'voices'. I have heard 'voices' speaking in German, French, Italian, Russian, Spanish, Chinese, Japanese and idiomatic Welsh; and I have heard during the same conversation the language suddenly change into French, and the replies from the Spirit 'voices' have come through with unhesitating fluency.

"During Dr. Whynant's sittings in New York with Valiantine, Portuguese, Basque, Arabic, Sanscrit and Hindustani were spoken."

In 1927, Valiantine came to this country for a series of experiments with Lord Charles Hope and Mr. Dennis Bradley, which are fully described in the latter's books *Towards the Stars and The Wisdom of the Gods*. There are two incidents reported that are pertinent to the aspects of voice phenomena with which we are more interested here. The first is that Valiantine was quite normal while the voices were speaking, and that he would engage upon conversations himself with some sitters, while the Spirit voices were conversing with other sitters. The second was the recording of these voices on gramophone records. The recording was carried out by the Columbia Company, a telephone wire being taken from Lord Charles Hope's study, where the séance was held, to the recording studio.

Record No. 4I2-4. Confucius speaking in ancient Chinese.

Record No. 4I2-5. Chung Wei speaking and singing in Chinese.

Record No. 4I2-6. Maharajah of Manobe spoke in ancient Indian language and Sanscrit.

In the *Mediumship of Jack Webber* I have reported the speaking by Spirit communicators in Swedish, Portuguese, Latin, French and Spanish--and it must be remembered that this Medium was an unlettered collier. Reference is also made to the very loud singing of the control, Rueben, as being of full loud-speaker strength and penetrating to houses in the next street through the closed doors of the séance room. Rueben's singing was at times maintained for over an hour continuously. The words were clearly and perfectly enunciated the aperture at the small end of the trumpet used at the time being less than half an inch and generally closed up. ( At a séance held at the studios of the Mecca Record Co., Ltd., a recording of the Spirit voice of Rueben was secured, singing "Lead, kindly Light" and "There's a Land".

The ten-inch double-sided record can be supplied for 1s. 6d. from Harry Edwards, Balham Psychic Research Society, 1 1 Childebert Road, Balham London, S.W. 1 7 [this is the old address, see the new one at the end of book].

All the proceeds from the sale of records are devoted to the "Jack Webber Memorial Fund". )

These extracts do not take into account the great mass of intimate personal evidence which could only be obtained from a Spirit communicator. Notable examples of such communications can be found in Dennis Bradley's *Towards the Stars* and Gwendoline Hack's *Modern Psychics & Mysteries,* to cite but two out of a large number of records.

Throughout the history of voice mediumship there have been many references to '{voice boxes'). This term (invariably used by the Spirit operators associated with each Voice Medium) has been cloaked in further ambiguity, when questions of a pertinent nature have been asked by sitters. For example, when a Spirit operator has been asked to 'tell us how the voices are produced'^, the reply has been usually given like this: "we build a voice-box, that we can speak through", or, "we construct a cabinet with a voice-box therein, just like one of your telephone boxes", or "we fit an ectoplasmic mould over the Spirit's face", etc.

The lack of substantive data in such replies is obvious yet we should be deeply sensible of the great difficulties the Guides have had to face, when asked to explain this or that. In the chapter on the

"Development of Mediumship" reference is made to the difficulty the Guides must experience in giving reasoned explanations, through the limited mental equipment of their Mediums. Providing in advance theses which we are incapable of comprehending must present a further difficulty.

Further, not every Medium and every Guide has been willing to sit time and time again to give us instruction as Mr. Clare and Peter have done. Peter's explanations on voice phenomena alone occupied at least six evenings in order to produce a reasoned statement.

In fairness to the Guides of Physical Mediums in the past, it should be re-emphasised that we did not then possess the knowledge of acoustics, radio science, and the science of applying and relating electrical energy to sound as we do now. We can only appreciate that which we can understand. Our knowledge of law-governed forces and effects limits our comprehension. To explain any thesis beyond these limits is to embark on a dissertation that would be meaningless—even assuming our vocabulary permitted the attempt. To illustrate this point—to have used a generation ago such present every-day terms as a "moving-coil loud speaker" or "radio oscillations" would have meant precisely nothing and would have been discounted as meaningless.

It should therefore be stressed that no Guide of past days should be reproached for failure to impart information or to gently satisfy his hearers of those times by obscure references. It is obvious that until we are in a position to understand, or approach understanding intelligently, an entirely new conception, it would be a waste of time for any Guide to discourse upon it. Also we must still recognise our present limitations, and be satisfied, for the moment, if we are only dimly able to perceive a little light.

By the means of infra-red photography and other cruder methods of photography (as with Margery), pictures have been secured of an ectoplasmic mass, closely associated to and connected with the Medium by ectoplasmic connections. The Guides of those Mediums have informed us that these formations were "voice-boxes" or 'talking apparatus".

When those Guides have been questioned about these photographs (and this applies also to Guides of other Voice Mediums where photographs have not been secured) they have told us that these voice-boxes contain a "replica of the Medium's vocal organs" through the agency of which the Spirit people speak.

I refer again to U.S.A. *S.P.R. Proceedings,* Vol. II, 1926-27. The Margery Mediumship, in which Walter's speaking mechanism is described as follows:

"There is a mass which may be either grey or white, about 4 x 2 X 2 inches, resembling the size and shape of a potato. Its contour is irregular. At times, as we look at it, it seems to simulate a small face much like the dried heads of the head hunters of the South Seas, heads from which the bones have been removed. To the top of this structure from the right ear there is a white cord one-sixth to a quarter of an inch in diameter smooth. From the little mouth, as it were, of the potato-like face there comes a structure much like the human umbilical cord, one-fourth to one-half of an inch in diameter, twisted, and eight to twelve inches long. This enters the right nostril of the Psychic. The white ear cord and the twisted cord to the nose are long enough to allow the central mass to rest on the Psychic's right shoulder, or her chest or her face or her left shoulder. We have many photographs of this structure and the photographs confirm what our eyes see.... We have handled the mass and find it like the other teleplasmic masses, cold and yet vibrant with life. The fact that this structure is attached to the nose explains probably why any and every sitter is not allowed to put a hand over the Psychic's mouth whenever he chooses, as a test of the independence of the voice....

"At the end of the phenomena the mass from the ear takes two to four minutes to disappear. On exposure to red light of the masses of every origin there is immediately seen a kind of shrinking as if the light was inimical to it, or similar to that of meat suddenly exposed to a very hot fire or cautery-iron."

Peter's thesis cuts right across the view that the ectoplasmic mass contains any kind of vocal chords; and here again the suggestion is made that in the light of Peter's explanations those statements were merely the refuge of Guides from the more intricate and truer facts of the case. In my book on Jack Webber's Mediumship I adopted the safe course of avoiding theorising, except on one occasion, when I made some observations on the method of voice production; and I did this because there appeared evidential circumstances to support my contentions.

I supported the view that the voice-box must have contained a sound-producing mechanism, because I have heard on a number of occasions three voices simultaneously in being.

(1) The Guide speaking through the Medium's vocal organs;
(2) A voice in "miniature" close to the Medium; and

(3) The miniature voice being simultaneously reproduced in volume, through a trumpet levitated in the air some six to eight feet away from the Medium.

In view of the explanations of Peter I am forced to the conclusion that the ectoplasmic structure does not contain *sound-producing* mechanism, as we have been previously led to believe.

Some of the improbabilities of the original contention are worthy of consideration, if only to illustrate the human error of building up a thesis without foundations in reason or fact. In my own defence I have stated these improbabilities before, and now do so again so that the position may be better appreciated.

For a voice-box, like those we have photographed, to contain a voice-producing apparatus, it would be necessary to have not only a "replica of a human throat" but also a replica of the mouth shape, palate, tongue, lips, teeth, and air bellows (lungs), to produce the perfect syllabic sounds. Further, all of these— chords, throat, palate, tongue, lips, air pressure— would have to be controlled by some muscular action, mind controlled.

For all of these essentials to be contained within the ectoplasmic mass is not feasible; and that a Spirit communicant, whether Guide, relative or friend, in their Spirit condition could operate all these physical essentials, is not feasible either.

A further point in this connection. At times "direct' voice possesses characteristics of the Medium's speech— not always, but frequently—and this has been explained by the reasoning that, if the voice-box is a replica of the Medium's vocal organs, it is reasonable that the voice produced would bear some resemblance. This reasoning naturally enforced support for the previous contention, but here again Peter's thesis provides a stronger reason why such similarity may, at times, exist.

No tone was ever created except by means of an instrument, which means that no sound has ever been borne of space or of free ether. Further, the instrument used must correspond to the nature of the tone to be produced, i.e. the instrument must be constructed of suitable materials such as wood, wires, metals, diaphragms, to receive and transmit physical voice sound waves via a telephone, loud speaker, or other voice instrument. Therefore an etheric instrument is required for the receiving and transmitting of etheric tones.

What is more difficult to comprehend is the manner whereby the etheric sound waves are changed into physical sound waves. It is again worthy of recall that through radio science man has accomplished a similar transformation. The mind that considers it impossible for etheric sound waves to be transmitted by an etheric mechanism and then transformed into physical sounds through a delicate human receiving set— as the Medium is--is the same type of mind which deemed it impossible thirty years ago to send a voice through the ether and to hear it in millions of homes almost simultaneously.

Another good parallel is provided by the telephone, where the speaker is talking from a distance; the sound waves so created travel in a new formation along the wires to be re-translated back into physical sounds.

It has been conclusively proved beyond all possible doubt, particularly through the Margery experiments, that the voice sounds of the Spirit communicator are quite independent of the Medium. It was so proved by either filling the Medium's mouth with water or by having an inflated balloon placed in the Medium's mouth, which would whistle if air was allowed to pass out of it. Under such tests the control, Walter, would speak and whistle tunes some distance from the Medium. With Jack Webber, it was proved by hearing two, and sometimes three conversations taking place at the same time. With Valiantine, Mrs. Perryman and others, voices maintaining conversation would come from parts of the room far away from the Medium, and would continue whilst the Medium, in both normal and trance states, was also speaking. The report of the sitting on November I7, 1940, when one of Mr. Clare's controls spoke clearly through a trumpet with the mouth effectively blocked, provides further supporting evidence. The assumption has been that, as it has been proved that the actual physical sound is heard externally to the Medium, the origin of the sound waves has also been external. This has appeared as a natural and reasonable assumption—yet according to Peter it is not so.

Peter says that the production of speech has its origin within the Mediums etheric body and not in any external mechanism. Here are Peter's words:

*Peter:* "As a general rule there is no external mechanism for the creation of Physical sound. Sounds are produced through the physical and etheric bodies of the Medium. This, in itself, is a work of considerable enterprise. There is co-operative effort between the physical, sound-producing Organs and the etheric counterpart, which uses the principles of electrical force." *(Stress should be laid on the word "principles" to avoid the conclusion that it is the force of electricity alone that is the responsible agent.)* "The muscles of the throat can be felt in action when a Spirit voice is heard, but not the slightest sound is evidenced from the Medium. The sound waves are etherically created via the Medium's vocal organs and the respiratory system.

"These etheric sound waves are transmitted through an ectoplasmic and insulated tubular connection".

While this statement does not explain how two or more voices can be heard at the same time (these may well come under a varied or different process applicable to "independent" voice), it does provide a reasonable basis upon which an explanation of direct voice can be built. The Margery experiments referred to fall into line as being practical under this thesis: they also explain the essential presence of all those factors that must contribute to the creation of syllabic and dialectical words.

Following upon a number of questions relating to the above statement, Peter amplified his remarks in the statement, which follows. In this second statement is given an explanation of the term **"etheric sound waves"**. This is breaking new ground, entering into a new field of learning. One must allow here for Peter's apparent difficulty in giving a detailed explanation, which must, of necessity, command the employment of new words and meanings. I am not attempting to apologise for Peter, but to provide what is surely a reasonable explanation for Peter's difficulties.

His second statement was:

*Peter:* "The voice emanates from the ***etheric*** and physical bodies of the Medium. That cannot be disputed. I emphasise that. . . . The external fitments *(the 'voice-box'),* etc., are arrangements whereby the etheric sound vibration as opposed to physical sound vibration, passes through a system of conductors, sometimes to an external etheric amplifier which you have previously termed a 'voice-box' while that term is apt, it tends to confusion. It does not contain chords, or anything like that. It owes its peculiarity as an amplifier, to its shape. Within that amplifier, which is the 'voice-box', there are etheric whorls for the amplification or refining of etheric acoustics. This about which we are talking is no different to sound, only it is not within your ability to comprehend it just now; words do not exist in your vocabulary which would describe it, and yet be within your capacity of understanding. It is an amplifier —as is a trumpet to physical sound—but here, you see, we are dealing with inaudible sounds, that is, etheric sound. The voice-box, to use other words, is an amplifier of etheric sounds. You see, I have to use words, which you apply to your physical vocal terms in order to explain non-physical substances and action.

'After the etheric sound waves have passed through the amplifier and refiner, it is necessary to convert them into sound—audible sound. They pass down an etheric tube they have gained power or amplification, etherically, and have come to the trumpet.

"When the etheric sound waves enter the trumpet they leave the conductor tube, which has hitherto been sent into the free ether, as is general within the Circle. The change is effected by a series of explosions; actually they are little flashes of light, which you cannot see. Their transformation into audibility depends upon the vibrations, which are small explosions striking the air in the atmosphere around the diaphragm. The quality of speech or music is solely dependent on the diaphragm through which, in the case of the trumpet, the atmosphere and the ether give a cushion effect, just where the etheric wave merges and enters the trumpet. This is a series of explosions such as you get on the diaphragm of a loud speaker."

Here we have the supporting reason referred to above.

As the voice is created from the Medium's physical and etheric voice-speaking organisms, it is natural that at times the characteristics of his voice should be transmitted through this process of Spirit-voice production.

On a further occasion Peter stressed afresh, as in the next statement, that the voice-box is not a sound-producing agent, and defines its function.

*Peter:* "When you read your notes you will see that I have referred to the amplifier or voice-box. What I wished to give you was the fact that there is no sound creation in the voice-box, and no physical sound from the vocal chords or the throat. The sound-box has no characteristic of vocal chords, but its purpose is that of amplification. It is an artificial means of stimulation where a voice may be weak. Its use is not always necessary. In the case of a strong voice you would get distortion, unless it was refined within this apparatus. It does not become necessary where the voice is just right. Voice-sounds come through the vocal chords--but not in the physical sense."

*Question:* "Are respiratory sounds produced through the vocal chords of the Medium?"

*Peter:* "No, they are not. This is oft-times produced to convey something of importance. You can simulate anything by the method of which I have spoken, but in most cases it is purely the result of those explosions I have mentioned. Also note that these explosions generate heat, and heat you will feel in the air that comes from the trumpet. Though it is not always presents heat such as breath, will be evident sometimes."

*Question*: "You said, 'the voice-box owes its peculiarity to its shape' ?"

*Peter:* "Particularly true. Its substance being adaptable to shape, it can be modified. It depends on the conditions prevailing at the particular time, its shape being adapted thereto. It can be modified to produce the right volume of sound for the right occasion. There is no fixed shape for it. you can have it like a trumpet, or like a sea-shell, the whole idea being that they are, more or less, vibrations to the conditions **'without'**. The shape determines the whorls set up to give the right volume or pressure to the resultant voice."

*Question:* "You speak of a diaphragm being necessary to convert the etheric sound waves into audibility. What is this diaphragm ?"

*Peter:* "It is an extremely thin, web-like substance that is connected very delicately from the end of the tube—the etheric tube—to the mouth of the trumpet. It is of great strength and its tension is enormous; so much so that it can make loud popping sounds but it has a skin-like form of physical existence very much like the ordinary ectoplasm."

*Question:* "Is it reasonably possible to get a diaphragm left in a trumpet ?"

*Peter:* "No. It is hardly possible unless you left the whole thing."

*Question:* "Is it possible to simulate a sound not associated with the voice, the creak of a door, etc. ?"

*Peter:* "It is not impossible to make a deep sigh or anything like that, and, of course, the creak of a door is not an impossibility either; it could be even the song of a bird if the operator were skilled enough."

*Question:* Peter was asked "Whether the construction of physical sound waves bore any resemblance to etheric sound waves. '

*Peter:* 'Yes, it is very similar. There is one thing you do not appreciate, and that is that the physical sound that travels along the conductor is actually not within the conductor itself but within the surrounding ether. You see it travels along the ether owing to the etheric conditions within the conductor being not quite the same as they are **'without'**; actually because you are energising that area by the passage of an electric current. Now the same conditions appertain **'within'** our etheric tube—bound ether which enable us to create **'within'** that insulation conditions similar to your copper conductors. The insulation that we have created may vary in diameter as it is purely for the purpose of creating conditions of potentiality **'within'** the ether. When the free ether outside the insulation is too dense it would be absorbed too much: the sound travels along this conductor. If we were using a range of frequencies similar to those used by your radio, which is a form of brute force, we should have to bring it down into the denser etheric conditions nearer the earth; the principles that we utilise go far beyond your known laws of frequencies. When we use the term 'insulating' in this case, we refer to the isolation of the conditions **'within'** the etheric tubular construction from that **'without'** the tube. An explanation of that is that the etheric condition within the tube is of our making and it differs from the free ether outside in so far as it responds to our directive thought, or anyone's directive thought who is manifesting. It is nothing more or less than an etheric conductor, the same as you have your copper wire surrounded by rubber to isolate it from conducting surfaces which might be brought into its proximity." *(See Plate No. 2, which illustrates this mechanism.)*

*Question:* Peter was asked "if a communicating Spirit personality other than a Guide usually possessed the knowledge of how to use the mechanism created ?"

*Peter:* "Much depends upon the conditions that are created for him, and his ability to use it. It is very similar to your use of a telephone; you might be quite well understood at the distant end, yet someone else who is not able to use a telephone and there are many—might be, if not inaudible, at least not clear. That is the same principle. They are the only limits. Perhaps you would like it this way.... Once upon a time they found means of carrying great weights for greater distances by using circular pieces cut from tree trunks which were placed underneath the object to be moved, but look what a far cry it is from those days to now. Is it not possible that the same applies to your psychic queries ? But here, you see, we are employing purely natural forces, of which there is a close parallel between your known laws of radio activity and those we are trying to propound here. You utilise your known laws, through their manifestation, from the material at hand. That is the only difference."

*Question:* 'Do you and the other Spirit operators associated with you have to create actual 'machinery' of a definite kind for voice phenomena ?"

*Peter:* "Yes, of course, that is true, but you must not have visions of wheels. The principle is the same except that etherically we do not have to employ cumbersome things, because, you understand, we are working with a common substance ether. And that is all there is to it. free ether and employed ether--that is the secret of it. It is very similar to your damming a stream so as to make it flow another way and turn a mill-wheel."

*Question:* Can you tell us more of how the Spirit personality is able to enter into communication?"

*Peter:* "Yes, of course—you have conditions created for manifestation of voice. You have the Medium in a state of preparation for that voice. The Medium has a quality— a tonal quality—which has been built up partly by himself and partly by the assistance of the Guides. There must be harmony between the Guides and the Medium, and this is reflected within the etheric extension. This etheric extension has a peculiar quality of its own which in itself is not only a protection but is also the gateway. Any communicant attempting to approach through it must have a tonal quality almost identical to it. There you have harmony again. When one comes to communicate and he has not the necessary tonal qualifications then we help him to raise or lower it, as necessary. In the last extreme, if neither is successful we can transmit, or allow to be transmitted, all its characteristics of voice quality. In addition we are able to pass through all the things that are characteristic of the communicant which, to you, is one and the same thing."

*Question:* "Your communicant is speaking to a friend. The friend asks a question and you get the reply. Can you tell us the means by which the communicant is able to receive the thought expressed by the sitter ?"

*Peter:* "Only by thought. The expression of it helps him to do so because most people on earth cannot express thought by just thinking but only by asking aloud. Actually, it is not the voice that conveys the question but the thought accompanying it."

*Question:* "Is there any method of controlling who should so speak ? Is there a compere ?"

*Peter:* "No. I have partly answered that question. Those who wish to speak must have the qualifications necessary to make his thought (the communicant's thought) register upon the etheric extension of the Medium. Where possible we help him or her to communicate, but always with an eye to what I have told you in the last answer but one. That is the governing factor."

*Question:* "Is a Spirit communicant able to give speech by direct contact with the Medium ?"

*Peter:* "The communicant contacts part of the Medium's auric extension—any part of the etheric field—and by so doing is able to use the conditions created to communicate."

*Question:* "How is it that a childish or feminine voice is heard when using a masculine vocal etheric instrument?"

*Peter:* "The necessary physical sounds are first produced etherically via the human chords. The qualities of the etheric sounds are not limited in tone, as they are by physical chords."

*Question:* "Is there any other method of controlling who should so speak ?"

*Peter:* "That is our responsibility. We are not responsible for the phenomena, but we are responsible for the Medium and, indirectly, for everyone else. We cannot do more than provide the means—because that is our responsibility. Anything else must come as the result of patience and, unfortunately, conditions over which we have no control. There is this fact and this alone—so long as we are vested by you with the authority to control, all will be well. We hold the lever that cuts off the power, but when we are usurped from our position we cannot control."

*Question:* "For independent voice—do you have to create a similar mechanism ?"

*Peter:* "Yes. It is not 'vocal'. While the terms we are compelled to use are very elementary, the principle of amplifying is sound. The voices are created via a form of etheric trumpet within the sphere of which the conditions are controllable. The voices are produced in that way."

*Question:* "We have heard the independent voice in white light. Therefore white light does not prevent the mechanism being constructed ?"

*Peter:* "You will find that the light has allowed for dark places. It is, of course, when conditions are good. I remember we have had the voice with a light in our Circle under similar circumstances."

*Question:* "Authentic evidence has been recorded that Spirit voices have been heard in various parts of a room, with and without trumpet, through the Mediumship of Valiantine. The Medium at this time has been normal and engaged upon conversation with a sitter—consequently his physical larynx has been in use when the Spirit voices have also been audible. Does the same voice productive mechanism operate in this case as that you have described as produced via the Medium's physical and etheric larynx ?"

*Peter:* "No, that is not so. In cases like that it is a form, which is not of Physical Mediumship at all. It is a form of Mediumship wherein the conditions so combine themselves that the entities, in association with the Medium can produce directly their own voice from the rarefied ether neither directly using the Medium himself nor any part of his economy. But that is very rare."

*Question:* "Voice production ! Would it be possible to take away the side of one of these "voice-boxes" or amplifiers that is to take away the ectoplasm ?"

*Peter:* "Yes, but you would not learn anything, because its shape would be constantly altering. It would have no construction that you could understand. It would not be related to truth or permanency."

# DEVELOPMENT OF PHYSICAL PHENOMENA
By Harry Edwards in 1940's in the book the Mediumship of Arnold Clare
**Chapter X** pages 104-121 (Peter is Arnold Clare's Guide)

Any approach towards understanding the "mechanics" of psychic phenomena demands a study of Mediumship and its development.

The science of Mediumship in all its forms presents so wide a subject that no attempt is made here to deal with it generally or extensively, but rather to confine investigation to that branch of Mediumship known as "physical".

Broadly speaking, Mediumship can be divided into two sections; firstly, for want of a better word "Mental" Mediumship and, secondly, Physical Mediumship. While Mental Mediumship can be dissociated from Physical Mediumship, the latter embraces both.

Physical Mediumship presents definite acts, which must be performed through the operation of law-governed forces. Such acts are today described as supernatural because as yet man does not possess the knowledge of their manner of their performance.

Physical Mediumship may be termed that which evolves ordered movement of matter, the production of sounds and voices, the creation of ectoplasmic structure and materialisation of Spirit-people in physical form, as well as other activities.

A great deal of theory has already been advanced relative to Mediumship, but I am hesitant to add further ideas without substantiating proof to support them. In the past the difficulty has been that we have been presented with complete acts of supernormal character without our having any proven knowledge to assist us to understand the mechanics involved. It is as if a primitive man were shown a television receiving set in operation and then with his limited vocabulary and mental outlook tried to learn, in a few steps, the processes involved in producing the result. One can well imagine the difficulty a radio exponent would experience in attempting such explanation.

We are in much the same position as primitive man in our efforts to appreciate the science of psychic activity. With the passing of time and study of authenticated records, we have been able to determine provable facts by observation and comparison. The new theses advanced by "Peter" are in line with these facts, though the explanation of the manner of their production may be different from previously conceived hypotheses.

In the past, we have been too free in constructing *our* theory upon general and ambiguous statements by the operating Spirit intelligences. We must not blame the Guides because of their ambiguity, for it may well be that faced with our questionings they were in the same position as the radio exponent just referred to, who might tell his primitive man that the pictures and sound from the radio television were "pictures and sounds travelling on the winds" as being the nearest understandable formula the limited mental equipment of the questioner could appreciate. Therefore it is probable that Guides have in the past taken the line of least resistance and satisfied us, for the time being, by abstract references to "voice boxes", "psychic rods" and the like.

We are today in much the same position, but we have advanced a little; and even a lay mind can comprehend the explanations "Peter" has given.

Some of his statements affecting the mechanics of subnormal action are not as yet provable by man, but they do possess the merit of being provable and logical; other statements are definitely provable. It is suggested that when the probable but as yet unprovable statements are related to those that are provable, there is a chain of connected reasoned ideas which explain in an elementary way much that has been a complete mystery. Our ability to comprehend "Peter's" explanations has been made easier through recent advance of human knowledge affecting radio activity, which provides parallels of thought facilitating our comprehension.

The view is taken that when with different Mediums comparable results occur, and spaced apart in time and place, similar in structure or effect, then there is reason to deduce that such results are common qualities of such Mediumship. For example, with Jack Webber I was able to provide photographic evidence of a number of phases of physical phenomena. By themselves they are unique and of interest; but when similar photographic results are obtained through a number of other Mediums (if only one or two to the present time); then it is reasonable to accept that evidence as being common quality of such Mediumship; and thus what might be regarded as "freakish" becomes reasoned performances.

The proof of a statement or the probability of a statement being true may not be at once obvious from the matter immediately pertinent to the statement, as the proof, or probable proof, is only discernible by comparison with evidence relating to another aspect of the subject. For example, it would not be easy to comprehend the theory advanced for the development of Physical Mediumship without understanding the powers, functions and limitations of the Guide in control of the Medium; or why a representation made to the Guide may not be permissible without knowing the functions of the controls, i.e. the potentials of bound ether, the grades of ectoplasm, etc. therefore the reader is requested to take the whole theory advanced as a coherent structure; and not to isolate any one view from the whole text.

As a preliminary to the recordings and explanations that follow, advice from Arnold Clare's Guide for aiding development of Physical Mediumship is given, in the hope that it may benefit those seeking such development; and also as a contribution to the study of Mediumship, which after all, is the stepping-off point to the study of phenomena.

Broadly speaking, there are two conditions of trance: "partial trance" and "complete trance". To the lay mind that has not experienced any state of trance, it is difficult to define precisely in words what "partial trance" signifies. It is one of those conditions that has to be experienced to be comprehended. Suffice to say, that in partial trance the Medium is conscious of what is taking place; a degree of normality is present, though the psychic activity taking place is supernormal. Examples: A Medium speaking in partial trance may be given a free flow of oratory and of ideas relative to a subject of which the Medium knows little or nothing, and yet be conscious of the words that he or she is uttering. Physical Mediums (as with Miss Goligher, occasionally with Jack Webber, Marjorie Crandon and others) may be aware of the very act of the movement of objects. Indeed they can actually see movement taking place, and are able, too, to converse with voices produced via a trumpet suspended in the air in front of them. The condition of partial trance may be said to vary from one per cent to ninety-nine per cent.

Complete trance is far more easily explained, for then the Medium has no conscious knowledge of anything at all, not even thought; in other words, the Medium in a state of unconsciousness.

As indicated above, Physical Mediumship is possible with either complete or partial trance; voice Mediums like Valiantine and Mrs. Perriman were, to all intents and purposes, normal while their Mediumship was functioning. A developing Medium therefore should not be discouraged if he does not attain the condition of complete trance. It is on record that a photograph was obtained with ectoplasm covering the head of Jack Webber while he was fully conscious of what was taking place. Nevertheless, for physical work, a condition of complete trance is generally necessary, especially in the early stages of the development.

"Peter" (the Guide) commented on this:

"*Peter*". "It is very uncommon for voice or other forms of physical phenomena to be manifested except in a condition of absolute trance. When such occurs, the Mediumship is a freak Mediumship"

Peter gave further advice, which follows on a method he advocated for the development of Physical Mediumship. It should be observed that this information, and indeed all the information concerning the various matters on which he spoke, was obtained as the result of numerous sittings and discussions. It has therefore been collated and presented with as little interference with his words as possible. Some redundancy cannot be avoided as often a new thought has been presented in a repetition of the same subject

Preliminary to a sitting. Peter has advised.

"*Peter*". "The Medium should look forward to each sitting of the development Circle with anticipation and eagerness. It is most important that the day on which the sitting takes place should be one of complete preparation, anticipation and happy thoughts, clean line and things like that. This, will be found, is simple to learn in a very short time.

"It is better that meat should be taken sparingly. You should not sit too soon after eating. Whilst at least three hours should elapse between a meal and sitting, you should never sit hungry. Very light refreshment may be taken if it is necessary in between. **We do not impose any restrictions but we advise that less meat be eaten. The wise thing is that there should be no "Do nots" or "Dos" because if there were there would be danger of one swinging too much to one side or the other.**
" **The wise man's or woman's economy should be so trained to accept any call in reason made upon it. The meat you eat is not important, it is the method of your eating it, and why you eat it. It would be wise to deny it at first, but there is no need to feel upset because you do eat it. At least, limit it on the day of the sitting"**. (*In actual practice physical mediums do avoid meals for a time prior to sitting, except perhaps for a cup of tea. They are invariably good trenchermen and meat-eaters.*)
A summary of other suggestions by Peter is as follows:
"*Peter*". "Before sitting in the development Circle the Medium should sit quietly for a while in the séance room and engage in rhythmic breathing exercises. This exercise should be conducted with the Medium's mind and body completely relaxed."
"The air should be inhaled and exhaled through the nostrils only and not through the mouth. The breathing should be natural, excessive inhalation is a deterrent; but it is important that exhalation should be complete. Stress is laid on this point: every effort should be made to expel as much breath from the lungs as possible
"In addition to this exercise just prior to the sitting, it would be beneficial for the Medium to engage in this exercise daily whenever opportunity presents itself. He should relax his body completely and the mind should be detached from normal thought occupation".
On subsequence occasions, after the above had been read out to Peter, he added:
"*Peter*". That is right. Perhaps it would be better for me to say something more about that, because by intelligent co-operation so much more value is to be obtained. "When you breathe in always through the nostrils, you are not only inhaling the air but also the ether stream; the free ether. Now that ether is characterless, it has no character of itself; but as it passes through the sieve, as it were; the "sieve" I said; it receives its character impressed upon it by the mentality of the breather. This is important. As the nostrils are the filters for the atmosphere necessary for the well being of the body, so are they the filters for the ether rejecting all things that are inimical to the individual, whilst passing on those things that are good. But it works both ways, for it rejects also things which cannot be appreciated by the individual; that is, things spiritual.
"Therefore in this practice with inhalation and exhalation the mind should be gently focused upon the "all greatness" of the Spirit. It has the effect of creating those conditions which, individually, we have to create ourselves".
"The way of achievement by this method, intelligently applied, ensures permanency and good health, which, you will notice, many Mediums lack".
Peter was asked to give further information as to what is received and what is rejected as the ether stream is inhaled.
"*Peter*". The best way to answer is this. The ether stream, which is taken into the system through the breathing, is characterless in itself. When it has been breathed in through the normal act of inhalation, it is impressed by thought and character of the individual. That is understood. Therefore by rendering that etheric content more potent, more vital, through control of thought in breathing, you can transform that stream of ether into a veritable dynamic force. We have already spoken of the etheric body and the soul body; they both depend upon the ether inhaled with ordinary breathing for their vitality and sustenance. The more it is impressed with noble thoughts consciously directed, the more will the sub-conscious mind be brought into line with things spiritual. Therefore instead of having a part of your "household", as it were, against you, you make of the soul a strong ally; the three of you (physical, spiritual, and soul bodies) working all together, as a whole. For it must be remembered that the soul is the repository of all the experiences to do with the natural world and that world only. Therefore its desires are primitive; it is selfish. It is controlled by two strict laws, that of attraction and that of repulsion; which is oft-times the progenitor of hatred.
That is one part.
"By breathing rhythmically, the physical body profits from the air you breathe because it is taken in steadily; and therefore the heart motion is more regular with the steady supply of oxygen. The ether, which is inhaled with it does not go into the lungs, it is retained by a sieve. The sieve is contained at the

root of the nose, and it is from there it is dispersed. **There it receives the impression of the thought intention, so far as psychic work is concerned**. That is most important. Not only is it important in the way of physical health, but it gives a greater etheric vitality. I think this answers the other part of the question.

"When you breathe, it is to breathe with intention and to say, "With each breath I breathe the Spirit of Life", Each breath makes me free", "Each breath makes me stronger spiritually and physically". It is not altogether what you would term auto-suggestion, although it is true there is an element of that; but the idea is to impress the breath with your character, your idea of the moment. You can use it for weal or woe".

Peter has been speaking of the "three of you", the Physical, Spiritual, and Soul bodies. These should not be confused with the etheric or astral bodies. Peter has given the following definitions of the etheric and soul bodies; it should be observed that his concept of the soul body is at variance with the orthodox concept of the soul.

*Peter:* "Etheric body. The etheric body is only seen surrounding the physical body as an iridescent silver extension. It is a reservoir for the physical body; it's store-house.

"Soul body. The soul body is that part which belongs essentially to nature. It is primitive. By nature I mean the natural world, as associated with all the vast experiences, from mineral up to the vegetable and finally animal kingdoms, to be associated with man. It has all the experiences garnered in from those sources; therefore it has of itself no spiritual character. It is the driving force of the body in relationship to the animal realm, and "man" is the only enemy, that man has as an individual. He is the one who drives you on through desire only. He is the repository of memory".

On commenting that the above explanation differed from orthodox interpretations of the Soul, Peter added:

*Peter:* "That is where man has stumbled along. The Spirit cannot be seen except where it animates the soul body with which it has been associated for so long. The soul body is the exact replica of the physical but the Spirit is not contained in form. The Spirit is free. You cannot see the Spirit; for, if you were able to see the Spirit visually, you would see the end of all things; but when I say I can see you in a physical sense, I see your soul body.

"Astral body. The astral body proper is the soul body; that which you see clairvoyantly. It is the Spirit which animates it, as the astral animates the physical. Actually the astral body is the exact replica of the physical in ever detail whereas the etheric body is not".

*Question:* "Is ether a separate component from atmosphere? Can you give us any formula applicable to ether?"

*Peter:* "The chair in which you sit will remain a chair as long as the ether associated with the material of which it is made does not disintegrate or disseminate. The ether is associated and takes a form of individuality from that with which it is associated. You have several sorts of air do not forget. You have air in one part, which is pure; you have another which is less pure; and in other districts where there are mountains you have it rarefied. All are totally different; yet of the same substance. It is the same with ether. Ether cannot be described any better than as a huge jelly substance; if a change takes place on one side of it, that change is transferred throughout the whole. The same applies with individual ethers; i.e. those others associated with different matters and substances. With the air, you have ether in its highest form; it is finer as it bears all the potentialities of life. It does not become impressed with character, however, either for good or for evil until it reaches a certain point in man's economy: i.e. the sieve of which I spoke, situated at the base of the nose. I use the term 'sieve' because that is self-explanatory. As air is necessary for the maintenance of the physical body, so is ether necessary for the maintenance of the soul body; and as air makes it necessary for the physical body to work to contain the soul body, so does ether maintain the soul body as a fitting vehicle for the Spirit. You will understand that I am trying to explain infinite things in finite language".

A question was asked if the rapid and quick breathing, at times noticed with development, was an aid or not, Peter replied:

*Peter:* "That is wrong. That is harmful to the Medium who has to be artificially stimulated by controls. [see section dealing with the function of the Guide] but then, you see, it has to be done by them to achieve contacts for the work on which they are engaged. **It should not be a part of the development**. It is a part which is artificial and it is harmful to the Medium. It is better for him to practice rhythmic breathing, which would be a definite aid to himself.

"The method I have given to you is most valuable; and almost, I should say, essential. As you practice it, you contact sources of wisdom where we can talk; we cannot approach where breathing is speeded up. There is too much noise in that case, and we must have quiet within the Medium. Development is quick if you do it that way".

It will help the reader to understand Peter's intentions if the section dealing with the functions of the Guide and the controls are considered in relation to the above and also observations that follow.

There are two forms of control: (a) the control from **'without'** and (b) the control from **'within'**. The control from **'without'** being the control by thought "plugged in" to the Medium's etheric condition. The control from **'within'** being the possession of the Medium's body and faculties by a control. Peter instanced that "John", another of Arnold Clair's directing Spirit operators or Guides, could change with him instantly and with ease. On being asked how this was effected, he said:

*Peter:* "It is following on the present question. The idea of the system of which I have tried to tell you, is that we do not take control of the physical body of the Medium in the way that direct control can be ours. The control is not of the body. It is a control as from a distance; that is to say, we do not control the physical economy of the Medium, but do so simply by a method of 'plugging in'. The trance state is induced by the Medium. For a change over, all I have to do is remove my thought concentration and John to exert his".

Peter then gave the following analogy. His words should be borne in mind when considering it; that the trance state is induced by the Medium thereby issuing an invitation for the entry of the Guide.

*Peter:* "For example: I come into your house, I have freedom of movement, but to your private room I have no access. It is out of my range of freedom. It is, as it should be between friends, that I recognize it as your sanctuary and would not enter therein because it is a place which is private to you. But if I wish to speak to you, I knock on the door, or ring you on your house telephone".

A question was asked as to whether it is advisable to hold the breath for a short period. Peter replied, that whilst that practice was good for normal breathing exercises, it was not advisable for the exercise of psychic breathing development, and added:

*Peter:* "Suppose you were waiting here to make contact with me, you would not hold your breath then. But whilst it is good out of the developing chair in the normal practice; let me impress this upon you. For development do not over inhale for that is dangerous to you, just sufficient to fill the lungs.

*Question:* "Do you advise any number of sitters for the developing Circle"?

*Peter:* "The fewer the better".

*Question* "Is the trance state aided by our Spirit Controls or Guides?"

*Peter:* "That is true. That is why in some cases it varies. Many are rather temporary and unsatisfactory. The movements of the Medium are awkward; there is much contortion; there is much noise and there is not an easily rapid transfer of thought and movement between the Medium, now entranced, and the controller. I have said many times "We are master of originality". We can find out alternative ways to produce the same result. Well, in the case where the trance of a Medium is assisted and aided by the control, it is because the Medium knows no better and the control, ofttimes, has no patience. I tell you this in all seriousness; they should not be allowed into the sanctum of anyone persons of another world; and the wise one will not allow it. You are a kingdom unto yourself, the autocracy of which should not be shared by another, no matter how dear or close that one may be".

Following this observation, Peter was asked:

*Question* : "Most developing Mediums hope for a state of absolute trance; should he attain it, how can he distinguish who shall take possession or determine the degree or quality of possession?

*Peter:* "You must accept the control or not accept it. The fault is not with the one with the high ideals. It is a case of seeking wise leadership or not; it is often a case of getting results quickly without learning first through the wisdom of others."

This answer not being too clear, Peter was asked further.

*Question* : "Assume that I am sitting for a state of complete trance; I am willing to surrender myself for work by the control; I should welcome it ; but how am I to retain that individuality when I am sitting for complete trance? How am I to distinguish whether a control is beneficial or not if my consciousness has lapsed?"

*Peter:* "We sit here with the control that you allow. You would not be able to judge, but those with you would judge. There is no difficulty in recognising the nature of the control. You would know if the movements are awkward and there is lack of control. In the right way there is complete co-ordination; movement is natural and normal".

*Question* "Then the responsibility rests with those sitting with the developing Medium to differentiate whether the control is desirable or otherwise?

*Peter:* "Yes. For instance, you see, every method of sitting in a developing Circle is apropos to "hidden mist". Those who most desire it may miss it, although they have all the equipment; and the one you least expect to receive it, does receive it, though he may not be mentally equipped to provide a useful instrument".

*Question* : "Does not a trance state allow entry of someone else?"

*Peter:* "That is a point which is going to cause a great deal of discussion; for you must remember that development up to the present stage is built upon tradition (of development) dating from the early days when things were a little more crude. Well, the mind of the developing Medium has witnessed this before and he ofttimes goes through the same contortions, because his self-consciousness has become impressed. The point is this; in development; a Medium reaches out for someone to take control. This is not the best way to sit. There should be no endeavour to reach out for control of the body; there should be a 'sitting in silence' for the feel of a personality, which is not due to direct control, but infusing into his own mind of an impelling thought such as those which are now reaching you.

"I do not deny that the control or the system that has been used for development of psychic faculties does produce some good effects, but in one realm we are speaking of things psychic, and, in another, of things spiritual. Those that do benefit are robust people who can stand control and be quite all right: but where there is one who does profit by the association there are many more who do not; so you must judge for yourself. I am simply passing my opinion; and if they still feel prepared to take the responsibility and bring forward these controls, there is nothing against it. Someone will profit.

"I would like to clear up for you why rapid breathing throws the physical organism out of gear. Everybody has known this phenomena; and each has a form of rhythm of his own even if it is not perfect. So long as that is maintained the complete individual continues to work together in close harmony. When, however, the control begins to make his way or intrude within the individual's domain, he has gradually to speed up the breathing, which can only be done by stimulation. Thus more easily is he able to take complete control by throwing out that rhythm out. What is done, in fact, is to distort the focus between the physical, etheric and the soul body. If these three focus differently, then the control can better take command. That is the way I can explain it. The very fact of the control's gradual withdrawal means a gradual return of the Medium's full consciousness; although, of course, there is a temporary phase in which there might be an increase in the rate of breathing. I tell you this; that if you were conducting a physical Circle, through your knowing this you could teach the controls and show them the other way; you would be in a position to advise them not to be too much in a hurry; and if you were persistent in it, you would even help them do better".

*Question* : "Then does the mental equipment of the Medium limit the power of the controller to express himself?"

*Peter:* "It does in the case of the form of control we have had under discussion; the rough method (control from **'within'**). The limit is set. By the other method it is not so much limited; but the well-equipped Medium naturally is a better instrument for us; he also leaves his mind elastic, to know "why" and desires to seek further. Those with a limited mentality have set themselves a limit which they cannot pass". (*Here Peter is referring to the class of Medium who has no desire to understand the functioning of the Mediumship*)

*Question* : "Can you overcome the Medium's subconscious mind, and his own ideas, theories, etc., when you control?"

*Peter:* "The method of development I recommend is the only way by which we can do it (control from **'without'**). You see we are outside the Medium and we have not enveloped him. Therefore you will often find that were the sub-consciousness of the Medium and the desire of the control clash, it may be indicated by a pause in the speech, or a mix up of words. You may have noticed just now I wished to use the word 'method' and I said 'measure' (this incident happened, though it is not apparent in the text): that is an indication, but we correct it because we are outside the influence of the Medium. If the sub-conscious rises, then it cuts us off".

*Question* : "With reference to accelerated breathing, you said 'It is done by the controls to achieve contact'. We understand that you control the conditions that permit of phenomena; that is, control from 'without'; but do we understand the controls who work independently have to contact the Medium from 'within'?

*Peter:* "Yes in the common case. In that case the control enters entirely into the Medium's aura. Or perhaps I should put it this way; he is not in complete control but becomes the Medium and the Medium becomes the control. He takes over completely the control of the physical organism; that is by direct control, control from 'within'. It is necessary, to allow the entry of that control, that the breathing of the physical body must be speeded up so as to attain complete disruption, to throw the physical organism out of natural harmony, to create disturbance; and an intruder to break in. That is why breathing is thrown out of gear. If you were nearer to me, you would find that there is hardly any breath at all, the breathing is slow, and if you had the Medium under observation, you would find, ofttimes, that no signs of movement are observable". (This has been repeatedly noticed, the lack of the signs of breathing).

The following subsidiary questions and answers relating to the foregoing were made at a later date.

*Question* : "Are there any special attributes that a person should possess to be a suitable subject for physical Mediumship?"

*Peter:* "Well I think it will be better to stick to types of individual. At the same time it should be remembered that in speaking of types, there are always the exceptions".

"The types that lend themselves best of all for materialisation will be found among those of placid, calm mentally without the physical characteristics of being full bodied; more especially where there is an appearance of moisture in the body".

"Then you have those most suited for voice production. They are of the nervous temperament usually quick in speech and action, not over large in their proportion. I mean the little man, rather slender".

"For apports you have one who is slow of speech, not very well read and is usually fond of the open life, particularly gardens and their cultivation"

"As far as levitation is concerned, here you find the types who are usually well built, not necessarily in the sense of being tall, but in relation to their strength, and their muscular reflex: these are usually very limited intellectually. Where you get the different aspects of physical Mediumship displayed through one individual, you will find a combination of all those characteristics rolled into one. One little point I would like to add. For physical Mediumship and its development, it is the person with the moist palm to his hand that you should choose to sit as Medium; and the one with hair upon his head. There are no bald-headed Physical Mediums; for as their hair disappears, so does their power for Mediumship disappear. Loss of hair is a degeneration of the nervous part of the system and that part which we cannot do without".

*Question* :Is Mediumship more favourable to one sex?

*Peter:* "Favourable to both sexes".

*Question* : "You say the inhaled ether is received at the sieve and there dispersed. To where is it dispersed?

*Peter:* "It is definitely not material to the subject so long as the developing Medium carries out the action. I will tell you quite frankly the best type of Physical Mediumship and its extension and range depends upon the conservation of the sexual forces. The centre from which it is controlled is the base of the spine. The ethers, which you inhale when you breathe, pass alternately down either the left or right side of the spine; and according to the mental impress these ethers receive, so is the character of that carried to the spine. But it has nothing to do with researches into Mediumship for the moment. That is for private conversation".

*Question* : "When the clairvoyant 'sees', is it necessary for that part of the brain which interprets normal vision to be in action in order to receive Spirit pictures?

*Peter:* "Well, do you mean the part of the brain that registers the body's observations? This is stimulated but not used. That part is stimulated by the clairvoyant vision, so that the objective mind can construct a picture which is more or less a perfect production as observed by the clairvoyant vision. That centre must of necessity be used before a verbal description of the scene can be described. It is stimulated from another source".

*Question* :"If the reception of normal vision is dependent upon the applicable nervous system operating between the eye and the brain, is the same nervous system responsible for receiving Spirit vision?"

*Peter:* "That is a funny question. The same senses are stimulated. You understand the system of television that you use today. You are looking at a scene brought to you from as distance and reflected upon a fluorescent screen. There you have reflected precisely the same scene, though it may be many miles from the actual place of occurrence. You see that with your eyes, and to you it is almost the same as being at the actual point of observation. That is very similar to psychic vision only that you too have a screen that operates through the same Medium, ether, and stimulates the same nerve. It does not operate the same in each individual. There are some, you see, who may think they see objectively, and others by impression, but the process is the same".

*Question* : "I am quoting your words 'we borrow a little of the nearest sitters' aura and sort of blend it in'. We often notice that certain people feel conscious of being used in a physical Circle; a sense of depletion. Do you find certain persons are better subjects than others for such assistance, and not necessarily the nearest?"

*Peter:* "I do not like the word 'depletion'. What I meant by the 'nearest sitter' was where the tension was thinnest; the one nearest to the point where there is a thinness".

*Question* : "During work with your Medium, John assumes control of the Medium whilst materialisations are produced. Does this mean that John becomes the Guide? Is it correct, then, to term yourself as a control for your work in connection with materialisation?"

*Peter:* "No, I am not responsible for materialisation. There is some haziness between what is meant by Control and Guide. A Guide is essentially so because of his qualifications. I am using earth language. Those qualifications embrace a certain knowledge, which give authority to teach and instruct; the desire to be influenced by old earth conditions having been entirely lost and the role of the Guide chosen because of the attainment to the full knowledge of what that service means. That is the main difference between Control and Guide. The Control is always a Control; and refers always to those who take control of the Medium's organism by direct method. For instance, in our class of work the Controls only work within the auric field and manifest only in the direct voice or behind the scenes controlling the phenomena. Paul, John, Abdul, Peter, myself, we are what is termed the 'Band of Guides'. The controls are Simba, Little Peter and one or two lesser-known ones who may not concern us"

*Question* : "When a control is operating from **'within'**, he becomes a Medium, as it were, for the time being. How then is the Guide operating "from **'without'**" able to use the Medium's body for speech?"

*Peter:* "He cannot".

*Question* : "When phenomena is in action, you get the Guide speaking through the Medium in order to give directions. Is that so?"

*Peter:* "I cannot see how the Control could be in control of the Medium and yet the Guide speak through the lips of the Medium. That is impossible or next to impossible. You must not over look the fact that the Control may simulate the Guide, or, for instance, the Guide might prompt the Control; but the two cannot be mixed up together. If you had two incoming signals on the receiver of you wireless, what an awful noise it would be".

*Question* : "As a Guide is able to speak through a Medium in partial trance, is it possible for physical work to be manifested with the Medium's mind subconsciously present? Could such a Medium direct experimentation?"

*Peter:* "No, his sub-conscious mind could, but not consciously".

*Question*: "Is it possible for the Medium to produce phenomena in partial trance?"

*Peter:* "Yes, but it is freakish".

## INSPIRED TRANCE SPEAKING

This can be a very rewarding experience for the people who are listening to the Medium who is giving the address. The Medium generally goes into a state of altered awareness linking with Spirit, the Medium generally meditating in the stillness, **with sincerity talking** to Spirit within their own mind. The Medium giving permission to the Spirit World to be used as their instrument and always encouraging Spirit to come near and help them in the coming period of time, conversing with Spirit for about fifteen minutes or more to gain a good link. The early pioneers use to sit in a room set aside for them to Link into Spirit for half an hour to an hour before the address to bring their own Spirit in line with those on the other side, so be wary of those who suddenly go onto a platform and demonstrate this gift without sitting before hand. Of course there are always exceptions to the rules. Generally budding Mediums start off by speaking bringing most of their words from within their own mind and very little being given by the World of Spirit, (the link being 95% self and 5% from Spirit) then gradually over time when the developing Medium has been sitting in a Circle and meditating regularly each day to gain that link it becomes a better percentage. The link will get better until the link becomes 50% and 50%. This will be noticeable to others before it becomes apparent to the budding Medium even though at times they might think the percentage of the Spirit involvement has become greater than it has because of the human ego factor. **It is a must for every Mediumship gift** that the Medium must **keep on meditating in the stillness, with sincerity** talking through thought to Spirit **on a regular basis**. An aim for the Medium in this gift is a 5% of self and 95% of Spirit inspired speaking taking place, aiming for the 100% of Spirit. This can only be achieved by dedication and being truthful to yourself and Spirit.

When first starting the budding Medium will have to say their prayers and sincerely asking for the link and the gift required, to prove to others there is life after our so called death becoming more spiritual. The Medium should sit in meditation for a period of time to bring in that link closer, while talking within their mind and encouraging Spirit to come closer and help them in their task ahead, before making the address, then try a few words, sentences, just keep on talking, Spirit will then take over when they are ready. It is only by practicing that it will be achieved nothing is ever given on a plate, most things in Mediumship have to be worked for and earned. Please try to sit as often as possible in the stillness and have good spiritual thoughts going through your mind as you are doing it, whilst practicing the breathing exercises then still your mind to let Spirit get on with their job.

Many Mediums do inspirational speaking as they are being given their messages from Spirit clairaudiently, without going into the full altered awareness; so it can be seen there are many levels of awareness that can be used as long as it is the truth and no lies are used, it can be very rewarding. Remember lies are negativity, and negativity slows down and many times stops development.

This is the reason that budding Mediums should not confuse Direct Voice with Inspirational Speaking. This is not Physical Phenomena. The Medium is working on a different vibrational level, they should not be confused. If used together as I have seen done, the Physical part can be brought down to the level of the Mental Mediumship, so jeopardising the Physical producing part of the Medium's Link with Spirit, stopping it

Please remember if you are going to do some genuine Inspired or Deep Trance Speaking have your rules set out to your helpers and audience before your demonstration. Melanie Polley was given a nasty shock when a Chairlady grabbed hold of her to bring her to time at the end of the demonstration of inspired Trance Speaking during a service. Melanie was not able to work for a month afterwards; she was tasting blood in her mouth for as day or so after; so please, please treat your Trance Mediums with care. See the strong warnings section.

Do not go into an act of many different accents it sounds and looks ridiculous. It has become the fashion to talk in strange accents, instead of bringing the genuine true content from the Spirit World. I saw in 2004 the most ridiculous act I have ever seen by a novice or a very experienced person, this instance was a demonstration by a tutor at a very well known spiritual centre in South Wales. He went into his trance, then proceeded to come out with different English voices of people who were supposed to have come from different parts of the world. Irish, Chinese, American Indian, Scottish. I call them chip shop and delicatessen accents. "Wan a ba o fi a chip" Not one question that was asked by his students and fellow staff was answered in any way to prove there was life after death. Each one was put aside like a politician. The most ridiculous happening that night was he laughed out loud for five to ten minutes and that is a long time. Yes just laughing, I think he was laughing at us all in that room for sitting there and thinking it was the Spirit World. How sad to see an experienced person stoop a level so low to have students think he was in a trance and he had a link with the Spirit World and it was the Spirit World giving him the words. Most people like him put too much effort in practicing accents than they do into sitting for the Spirit World to help them as a true mediumistic link. People who have to think about the accents that they use in a demonstration rarely come out with genuinely Spirit inspired philosophy. Again there are exceptions to the rule. The idea with any sort of mediumship is to prove to others there is life after our so called death and the demonstrating Medium, with their permission is being controlled by a superior force/energy from the Spirit World, NOT put on a cabaret act.

# PHYSICAL MEDIUMSHIP

The form of Physical Mediumship is for most the crème de la crème of their training. It generally takes a great many years of regular sitting by the Medium in the same group of dedicated people, who give their power for a dedicated Medium to form a very highly developed link with Spirit. Jack Webber sat for ten years. Arnold Clare sat for twenty years, both sat regularly at the very least once a week for the development of physical Mediumship for two to three hours plus with regular sitters, and the physical Medium meditating for at least an hour, linking with the Spirit World **daily**. A lot of the old Mediums of the last century sat more than twice a week in a Circle for earlier results. Even then probably only getting raps or slight movement of the trumpet. They avoided excesses and created a code of conduct to live by, that then helped them to become more spiritual.

Physical Phenomena is the moving of objects with the help of Spirit, the bringing of gifts, even another person; out of the atmosphere [**apports**] **from another place;** other than the room it appears in, **not from the room where the séance is being held,** often appearing, being brought into the séance room when the doors are locked.

There are instances of apports being produced when the Circle has been held in candle light, coal fire lit rooms, red light and white light, especially when everyone in a Circle were holding hands.

I attended two séances in Stansted Hall when apports were produced by Judith Seaman. One in 2000 was a limpet shell produced into the hands of a lady from Warrington, Cheshire, the other in 2002 was a picture of a girl above a butterfly. The shell was said by the receiver to feel warm and like jelly, it then hardened. The picture was produced with the help of Spirit using Judith; this time while I was recording the séance with infra red cameras [BUT it was produced in red light]; The picture was placed into the hands of an Italian lady who's two sisters were in the World of Spirit across the veil. One sister looked like the girl in the photograph, the other sister collected butterflies and butterfly pictures, See plates.

Physical is the taking out of the room, objects (these are called **asports)**, sometimes Spirit even take the Medium out of the cabinet, and place them into another room or another place far away from the séance room, when the doors have been previously locked [the objects being **asported**].

Physical is also a full or partial human form being produced for all to see, and Spirit is heard through Independent Direct Voice by a voice box (an etheric amplifier) made with the help of Spirit, with or without the trumpet.

The Medium themselves, objects, or furniture being levitated by Spirit in the presence of the Physical Medium.

When a **Physical Circle** starts off with Physical Phenomena, it is best to have a lock on the door for the simple reason no accusation of fraud can be levelled at the Medium; the key should be given to an independent/impartial sitter. Spirit uses the trumpet for levitating and for the building of a voice box (an etheric amplifier) in it to talk to another sitter, so it should be in the best interest of the Medium to be tied in the chair and for the Physical Phenomena to be produced in light whether it is red, blue, green, or low white light as long as the sitters can see the Medium **after** the Physical Phenomena has started. [Spirit tell us it is harder to produce Physical Phenomena in the light. YET! It use to occur in times past in low red light, low gas light, coal burning fire light, using florescent painted illuminated plaques, and sometimes in the full daylight with strongly Spirit Linked Mediums]. Many of the older books say it is best to start off sitting in the dark to build up the energy necessary for this type of phenomena. This is the reason for the use of the cabinet enclosing the energy and the closing off of the light with the dark curtaining.

If you go to see and hear a voice Medium, a few points should be borne in mind.

On the point of the voice box (etheric amplifier). It should be pointed out the many things, Spirit coming through the mediumistic link has to remember, and put through the voice box (etheric amplifier) through their thoughts to manipulate it, and to convince the recipient it is the person they remember from the past on the earth plane. Spirit first has to produce and make the voice box, and then has to learn how to manipulate the voice box through their own thoughts. Then they have to remember how their voice sounded while on the earth plane, remembering they will be using an unnaturally moving voice box (etheric amplifier) they have not been used to, and it will be not the same voice box (etheric amplifier) as the one they had in their earthly body, (so Spirit does not always sound the same when they come back to speak quite often it can sound the same or similar to the Medium). Their [Spirit's] own mannerisms whilst speaking to prove that it is the person who they say they are, and then Spirit has to remember and give the bits and pieces of information that happened to them when on the earth plane to jog the recipient's mind, a joint complicated task for the most advanced Mediums in this world as well as those links in the World of Spirit.

The raising of trumpets is physical (a the trumpet is a megaphone shaped cone of celluloid, plastic, aluminium, wood veneer or stiff card with a strip of luminous paint about an inch wide, at the bottom and about one inch from the top [be careful of those who say you don't have a strip at the top, they the false Medium might wish to hold it themselves trying to fool the sitters]), and talking through them, the building of ectoplasmic voice boxes in the trumpet or anywhere in the séance room for Spirit to use and talk to the sitters, is Physical. The trumpet is **NOT a musical trumpet** as was being used (a scouts bugle design) by a Circle run by the local church president I was once invited to sit in at a house in Leigh Lancashire.

Please remember if Spirit makes the trumpet go around the room, then Spirit can place the trumpet back gently onto the place it came from and generally does. If it bangs walls and hits the Medium and gets flung onto the floor be suspicious, it **could** be the Medium doing it or is using Kinetic energy, **OR PERHAPS** the Medium holding the trumpet if in complete darkness, so acting out their charade. This is why it is so necessary to have infrared cameras in the séance room, if possible and if it is the wish of Spirit. I know of two physical Mediums that have been caught doing precisely this in the 1990's, so please be very aware of what can happen and what does happen. I am pointing out all these things so you can be true to yourself and to the Spirit World.

The Physical Medium after years of sitting can bring forth Spirit forms [a full or partial Spirit person, one that looks the same as they were when they were alive on this earth plane] to our own dimension so that they can be seen, touched, or have a conversation with the Spirit person to gain better knowledge of the continuance of our Spirit Form, when our body ceases to function as we know it, a so called death. This is done by Spirit using ectoplasm. This is also to prove to others that there is a life that continues, when the physical body has been left here as an empty shell, and the soul/Spirit or etheric body has parted from it and gone to a higher vibration level, in other words to prove there is life after our so called death.

Each Medium no matter what their skill, should always be trying to help others come to terms with their eventual so called death, and the eventuality of the continuance in a person's own Spirit life, and show others that there is a continuance of the lives of the Spirits of people's loved ones that have gone before from this earth plane, to a higher vibrational level. In other words life goes on after our so-called "death" here on our earth plane.

There are photographs of ectoplasmic Spirit Forms, and Physical Phenomena being produced with the help of powerful gifted Mediums. The photographs are on show in the museum, which is in the Arthur Findlay College, Stansted Hall, Stansted, Essex, U.K. There are also books with photographs in them that can be bought, or ordered at the college shop.

Be very careful about things given by others, your own illusions, and your own expectancy about things that you want to happen in any Circle.

When I was sitting in a Physical Circle with a girl friend each week for two years in the 1980's. We were travelling about 30 odd miles there and back, each week to the Circle to help this certain person to develop her Physical Mediumship, and nothing was happening. The lady who we were sitting for, turned around to me and said, "She had seen a church Medium and had a word with this Medium after the church service about nothing happening in the Circle, and this church platform Medium had said, "There was some person in the Circle taking the power out of the Circle, and it was a male" [There was another male in the Circle who lived with this person]. So my girl friend, and I were asked nicely to leave. **NEVER** think people that sit in Circles can take power **out** of a Circle, all who sit **GIVE POWER bringing it into** the Circle. BUT REMEMBER NEGATIVITY CAN HALT ANY PRODUCTION OF PHENOMENA IN ANY CIRCLE.

Looking back now I can say I was green, so was she. We were all there not knowing very much, but so was the lady we were sitting for and that church platform Medium. I can see now she never once went into Trance, never did she go to Stansted on a course to see if she had the potential, never did she ask others to test her to see her potential, never did she read the right books.

She had said at the time, that she regularly floated up to the ceiling while she was on her bed whilst meditating, **BUT** no other person had seen it, so I can only presume it was possibly out of body experience, or astral travel in the early stages, or even herself getting carried away with her own imagination. **PLEASE** for your own sake, do not get into the habit of fooling yourself, wasting your own time, and that of others. By the way, I heard that she still had not progressed any further, and that was after 20 years of living an illusion, and continually swapping the sitters. Now that is sad. Physical

Phenomena does not happen over night or in two or three years, many of the older Mediums took a great many years (ten to twenty) of sitting with **same** dedicated sitters.
She has progressed in one way now though; she has gone upstairs now to the higher life.

Read as much as you can on your subject, learn alongside people with a proven record, and take courses at the colleges. Try to attend a psychic college course at least once a year to sit in the power of that college, you will find that power is far greater than your own Circle the reason being, a college is being use every day of the year by a great many people sitting for Spirit more than once each day. Talk to all the people who attend the colleges. You learn lots from their experiences, and do not forget to ask as many questions as possible of them. Don't go there with any fixed ideas. Have an open mind for new ideas, and then try them for yourself on a separate day, but keep using your own method on your own regular days, just in case their method is not suitable for your linking.

In a Physical Circle, if you would like to try to help your Spirit link to write in the Circle, and not use a Medium's physical body, not their hand as the direct power source. It would seem to be the case of, if there is not enough power in the Circle for Spirit to hold up the pencil, use a prop to support it, one that can easily glide on the paper, e.g. a planchette type of implement on casters. Again you must experiment. Some Circles have got results from a pen/pencil and paper by just having them lying on the table in the middle of the Circle. Try a piece of charcoal, it does not take as much energy for Spirit to lift and support it to write. Charcoal is very light in weight.

A lady, Sally Hardings I met in April 1999, told me while she was reading in her bed in the early hours of the morning [during the night], She was startled by a very loud knocking on the bedroom door. So she got out of bed and opened the door to find nobody there. She closed the door and got into bed then the banging started again so she got out of bed went over to the door, opened it, there was nobody there. On closing the door again the banging started again. This time she opened the door, finding nobody there again closed it, and then she felt the door when the banging started again, slowly running her hands up the door starting at the bottom, to find the banging vibration. It was coming about head height. She opened the door it stopped again, as it had done each time the door was open. She placed her hand on the spot where the noisy vibration could be felt. Then she said aloud, "Thank you friend I can hear and feel the noise you are making". The noise immediately stopped, and it never happened again. A few months later while attending a Trance demonstration the Helper/Control/Spirit who came through the Medium on a church platform said to her amongst the other part of the message. "You are the lady who needs a hammer and chisel to get recognised."
This is one way the raps can come from Spirit but there are other ways.

In the report on Spiritualism from the Dialectical Society's Committee in 1869, they state that a series of raps were not on anything solid they seemed to be a percussion in the air.

A very well known Medium Mrs Guppy used to produce apports more or less at will. It had been known for her with the help of Spirit to apport/bring in a large block of ice from out of the etheric into the séance room.

A well-documented Medium of the last century Madame Blavatsky who helped form the Theosophical Society. When she was growing up in the Ukraine from 31.7.1831 used to tell the visitors to her grandparents home [where she was brought up] when they were going to die. She also had raps, bangs, and whispering sounds in the house whenever she was there. She wrote many books, which are now being reproduced.

One thing I should put in here is a warning to the budding Physical Phenomena Mediums who think they are going to be in a fit state, back to normality after the séance. PLEASE do not drive for many hours afterwards. The roads now are getting bad enough for the ordinary person never mind for a person who has had their brain altered into a state where they cannot function as an everyday person doing ordinary things. Allow the brain to come back to normality. I would try to have some sort of tests for the physical Medium to do before allowing them behind a wheel of a car. Take no notice of these people who say ground yourself, hug a tree, lay on the ground and be part of it, it simply does not work. **Those people have "not"** experienced what it is like to be in a true full state of Deep Trance, in a state of true deep altered awareness. When you come out of this state you are like in a fog (not your eyes), your mind is in a state of numbness, nothing really stays in the memory bank properly, nothing registers in the brain for a while afterwards. What people talk to you about does not stay in your memory, even though you are answering normally to them. Until you experience it you cannot know it.

When I was first starting to go into a stronger state of Trance, I had experiences like that at Stansted Hall while sitting in a Circle in the blue room with Lionel Owen's group. When I came out of the cabinet, Lionel had told me, and all the others in the Circle had given to me what they saw, what had happened while I was in the cabinet. An hour or two after I went over to Lionel and asked what had happened and I said "You went around every one else and told them when they sat in the cabinet, I thought you might have given me some input, could you tell me what happened to me". Looking at me strange Lionel said, "We all talked to you and gave you our input to help". I had to apologise and explain I did not remember, so please think on about the Medium when they come out of a **TRUE** DEEP ALTERED STATE OF TRANCE.

I also did a week of development for the trance/physical, and at the end of the week before going home in my car, I did not sit for the linking with the Spirit World for 32 hours, yet when driving home I did not remember going along the roads for over a distance of 130 miles. I stopped for a cup of tea and I had to ask a friend how on earth I had got to that point in my journey. NOW THAT WAS DANGEROUS so be aware of what can happen, have someone with you or have them drive you there and back.

There are not many Mediums that will risk their lives doing public demonstrations. BUT I think that should be the aim of us all so we can bring more knowledge to the world. If properly looked after by your sitters who are beside you, you should be safe.

As a Medium becomes better known their real trial begins. There becomes an enormous amount of people clamouring to see the phenomena that can be produced by him/her. Many of them being the people who had probably not wanted to sit the many hours dedicated to linking with Spirit.

As the Medium makes him/herself available, so do they become the centre of suspicion. Is it honest? Is it a fraud? The Medium might think they have to sit for a certificate of honesty, so submitting themselves to all sorts of tests. If this happens they might find themselves being put to many more test as different societies come along with tests of their own not being content to take another's word. They will be accused of being a fraud by unscrupulous societies so having to go along with that societies experimental tests. This has been known to be so in the past so be careful. Mediums also have to contend with the jealous people a very great many of whom are supposed to be spiritual Mediums.

You also have to put up with those budding Mediums and a great many established Mediums who are jealous of the gift/gifts you have been given because they cannot link properly with Spirit or those jealous ones who are not prepared to put in the time to develop, wanting it all in an instant. I have personally come across a lot who are jealously guarding their position in the spiritual circles they move in, wanting no one else to come into their spiritual circles with gifts the same as theirs, so please be careful of false, nasty people. I have been invited to other Mediums' Home Circles; afterwards finding out that I was just invited so they could see what standard I was up to, and then never invited to their home again. Not even returning phone calls in two instances.

The Medium also has to face the ever present danger that some irresponsible person will flash a light on him during the séance or interfere in some other manner while the activity taking place. Harry Edwards says he knew of one male Medium who lost his gift and his sight on such an occasion. Please be careful who you sit for, for your own sake and that of Spirit because there are too few true genuine Mediums around per head of population.

## PHYSICAL CIRCLE

**BEFORE EVERY CIRCLE AND EVERY TIME A PERSON SITS FOR A SPIRIT LINK. THEY SHOULD IN THEIR MIND, THROUGH THOUGHT BE <u>SINCERELY</u> ASKING AND ENCOURAGING SPIRIT TO COME CLOSER TO THEM AND HELP AT THE ALLOTTED TIME FOR A SITTING FOR DEVELOPMENT OR DEMONSTRATION, OVER AND OVER AND OVER. <u>AT LEAST AN HOUR</u> OR TWO BEFORE THE ALLOTTED TIME. YOU CANNOT EXPECT YOUR LINK TO COME AUTOMATICALLY AS SOON AS YOU SIT**

**DOWN IN A CIRCLE OR DEMONSTRATE YOUR SKILL OF A LINK WITH SPIRIT TO PROVE TO OTHERS THERE IS LIFE AFTER OUR SO CALLED DEATH.**

An exercise that might seem strange but it can be used to bring harmony to the Circle. YES it does work!!!
Look at each person individually in the group and smile at them, it does not matter if you feel uncomfortable and laugh, that will raise the vibrations. When that is done ask everyone to close their eyes, and smile inwardly to those in Spirit you are going to meet. Feel happy about meeting them as they draw near to the Circle, welcome them, feel the happy excited anticipation, the warmth of the feeling, be sincere about the love you are giving out to them and the Circle.

Most Physical Circles I have attended and read about, have the Medium in Trance in a cabinet to contain the power being built up, BUT there were some people who sat outside the cabinet just in front of the closed curtain. In some Physical Circles, those angelic Helpers in Spirit, can use two entranced Mediums at once, so do not dismiss this possibility in your Circle; **"BUT"** and an important **"BUT"**! Do not let any other people outside the cabinet in the Circle think themselves big and better than the other sitters, showing off to the others, and go under Trance conditions. It is up to Spirit not the sitters. All there in the Physical Circle should be sitting for Spirit and Physical Phenomena not themselves. All there should be sending their power to the **ONE PERSON** who is in the cabinet being developed. Each person who sits for the development of another should forget about themselves for a while. Each and every other person should be developing for themselves at **another** opportunity, perhaps at a different time on the same night, or in another Circle on a different night. What you unselfishly and sincerely give to that person will eventually come back to you ten fold.
The Medium should wear Black clothing so if any ectoplasm is formed it will be seen better by the sitters. With a black background even the finest, hardly visible amounts of ectoplasm can be seen, besides the black fabric increases the darkness in the cabinet. It is recommended that Medium should wear nothing white on them. The darkness behind the ectoplasm seems to be necessary for the development of the structure of ectoplasm (so says Baron von Schrenck Notzing). Please note the last part of the Infrared camera work in the Keelights section on the special black cloth itself, if it is needed for infrared photography in darkness.

Be happy and jovial when meeting anytime together for any Circle; some of the best Physical Phenomena happens in Circles that have a party like atmosphere, remember nothing is certain with a Physical Circle, only the love from Spirit. One day the Circle might be great, with all the happenings. The next time the Circle meets and every person sits, nothing happening within the Circle, some small thing might have been different to stop the phenomena. **Especially negativity**. This is the reason for constants in all Circles. Keep the same format each time you sit. OR it could be Spirit is quietly developing something in the Medium to help in later Circles.
While the Medium is sitting in the cabinet generally going into a Trance state after the prayers, which need not be religious just an affirmation of spiritual content, tell Spirit in general terms what you would like to happen, perhaps the Circle would like to sing a hymn or two but these are not essential, then the Circle should start singing "Roll out the barrel", "She'll be coming round the mountain", "Maybe it's because I'm a Londoner", "By the light of the silvery moon", "I belong to Glasgow", "Sally", "This old man", "Liverpool Lue", "Maggie May", "Underneath the Arches", " Ma she's making eyes at me", "Molly Malone", "It's a long way to Tipperary" "When Irish eyes are smiling", "John Brown's Body", "You are my sunshine", "Daisy, Daisy". Mix in old well known children songs to bring forward the Spirit children, "How much is that doggy in the window", "The Grand old Duke of York", The wheels on the bus go round and round, nursery rhymes, Jack and Jill, etc. All these should be mixed in with the typical lively pub songs, old and modern sea shanties, old music hall songs, some of the songs of the sixties, or the Beatles songs that everyone knows, in fact any of your own favourite songs as well can be sung, real lively ones so making it like a party atmosphere, if you don't know the words hum, or Lar Li Lar along it makes people laugh when you do not know the words and it heightens the happy atmosphere, try to learn the words of the songs for the following sittings. A very good vibration lifter is "Oh Great Spirit" sung over and over about twenty to thirty times :-

"Oh Great Spirit,
Earth, Sun, Sky and Sea,
You are inside and all around me".

One circle started with songs for about fifteen minutes then had three songs and had a quiet time for five minute with people having an input for that time and observations were talked about, then everyone sang for another three songs then again a quiet time to listen and observe, if the vibrations in the Circle were felt to be going flat the singing was continued for a little longer.

Try to include the continuous OoooMMMmmm in the singing.
A few Circles starting the continuous OooMmm [aum, or om] and others following at different times and everyone in the Circle continuing when their breath is exhausted, all continue when they like. The whole Circle should keep it going for about ten to fifteen minutes, it does attract Spirit World to the Circle.
Some Circles find it is best to have a tape recorder playing the tunes to keep the songs flowing, and the happy lively atmosphere going. The sitters having happy low conversation in-between songs to keeping the atmosphere, not letting it go flat, do not whisper as it can bring the Medium back from their deep meditation. Any bad/nasty, bitchy conversations or any jealousy/envy, augments, bad feelings, bad disruptions, wrong, incompatible sitters [ask them to leave], a bad illness with a sitter, if any of these are there are present, your Circle might as well be closed until the next meeting, but sort out the problem before sitting with the Circle again if you want good early results. So get some song sheets of the oldies ready for your Physical Circles, and start practising. You could record the old songs off a record to play in the Circle.
Start experimenting after the Circle has been going for a good few months, when you feel the power has been built up, get wrapped up in comfortable warm clothing, as the power from Spirit can produce cold air around the leg area, this can be felt by the hand if you place the hand palm downwards in the area. If the temperature of the room is felt to be going colder, start looking out for psychic breezes, psychic lights going around the room, and other phenomena that might start to happen. Keep **sincerely** asking in your mind often throughout the sitting for Spirit to come closer and help the Medium you are sitting for to produce the Physical Phenomena, know it can and will happen, be positive and very sincere.

One of the older Circles of the 1800's was said to have sat for 1½ hours had a break when soft drinks and a light conversation were had by all, then all there sat again for another 1½ hours. The first half they had raps, breezes, smells, Spirit lights, the second half when they all sat again the Physical Materialisation happened.

I was in the cabinet in Havan-y-Coed in July 2003 in the other cabinet opposite was another Medium Jean Blackabee, who after the séance said she was back to normality about 45 minutes before the end of the séance which was going from 9.45pm until 12.15 am. We had Spirit lights, breezes, touches, tugs, very hot then freezing cold air in the Circle. One person complaining of being hot on one side and freezing cold on the other, the sensing of Spirit being behind some sitters. All felt the cold to knee level.

Some Circles have their music playing in the Circle room throughout the day of the Circle, to build up the vibration levels, and the atmosphere in the room before the sitting of the Circle, or even a few hours before.

When the Circle has been going for a good while. Try putting a film straight off the shop's shelf and unopened each Circle sitting. Place the unopened film on the floor in the middle of the Circle [or under the chair of the medium or in the cabinet of the medium] for a few weeks/months, then send it off to Kodak [or a reputable film developing company] with a note to them, for the film to be developed, so as to see if anything comes out on the pictures. Instruct them to print it out on one continuous piece of paper so the effect can be seen. I wonder what will turn out for you? If anything! Also try using an automatic camera; I use a fully automatic "Cannon A1" at different speeds and time exposures. Try using any camera in the Circle as you progress; try, **BUT! ask permission** off Spirit through the **True and honest** deep full Trance Medium, and **make sure you get permission from Spirit to use a "flash light",** as sudden light, or sound can give a very, very bad shock reaction to the sitting entranced Medium. Some Physical Mediums have had bad internal bleeding through thoughtlessness, and some can possibly get psychic burns outside, or inside of their body if there is any ectoplasm there and it is drawn back too quickly into the Medium. Then you should try using the camera without a flash aiming at the same area of the room [the older Mediums of the last century used to use a magnesium flash for their photographs but that was **with the permission of Spirit and the Medium**]. Some photographs of the Physical Medium levitating, taken with light from a magnesium flash, have them coming downwards, the flash affecting the levitation process. It was found to be better for the Medium's safety if infra red lighting was used for photography in Physical Circles.

Try photography with, then without the red light on whilst sitting, also try black and white film, as well as colour at different times. Have each individual aim the camera to see if anyone there has a potential to be a psychic photographer, first noting down on paper the sequence of who shot what. Also the length of time the exposure of the picture took. Or talk into a tape recorder if you cannot see to write. Some unusual pictures have been produced in Circles over the years with the help of the higher life, as evidence of after life. Try to go and look at the Photographs in the Stansted Hall museum, and in the books "Mediumship of Jack Webber" by Harry Edwards, "The University of Spiritualism" by Harry Boddington, ISBN 0-85384-061-X or "Materialisation by Harry Boddington" for instance

One Circle I know of, which was going for a year, placed an unopened black and white film under the seat in the cabinet of the Circle for 7 weeks, sent it off to Kodak for development with instructions, and explanations of why it was not opened. The pictures and negative came back with what I can only describe as shooting lights on it, or a sequence of bullet holes or stones being photographed as they hit a pool of water, and the reflected light going out from the ring/the centre of light/or bullet hole, it was similar to light coming out as if it was sun rays. Kodak confirmed the film had not been tampered with nor had it been out of the unopened packet before they received it.

With my research, here are some of the "Constants" that I have found work for most, when sitting in a Circle for the purpose of spiritual, and psychic Physical Phenomena, especially from the beginnings of Spiritualism. Most things in life need constants or set formats to work. BUT there are always the exceptions to the rules. NO two Circles are the same, only similar!

Make sure the Physical Phenomena séance room is spotlessly clean. There have been instances when the Physical Medium has produced ectoplasm and when the séance had finished, it has been drawn back into the Medium, inadvertently objects being drawn back into the body of the Medium, and the objects left under the skin of the Medium, they then had to have an operation to remove it.
When Gordon Higginson used to do his demonstrations of Physical Mediumship in the library of Stansted Hall. The library used to be cleaned from top to bottom before the séance. Gordon used to produce a lot of ectoplasm for the formation of human forms. A lady, who goes to our Spiritualist church in Liverpool, attended one of Gordon Higginson's séances in the 1980's at Stansted Hall and she actually held the hands of her fully materialised mother who had passed into the World of Spirit many years previous. She has work tirelessly for Spirit ever since.

Set your rules for the sitting in the Physical Circle at the very start.
Pick a leader who can be trusted to take control of proceedings. **A must.**
Make sure the people who are going to sit in the Physical Circle can sit in TOTAL darkness. If they have not experienced it before, give them a separate viewing in the TOTAL darkness for ten minutes with just a few others of the Circle before hand. Some people cannot handle the TOTAL darkness experience or very low red light.
When sitting, keep to the light levels you start sitting in, whether it is in the dark, red light or full light. [It is known results take longer to happen in full light. This I believe should be the standard, Spirit will turn the light down if they want it so. I have been in Circles where the lights have been turned up and lowered by the unseen Spirit], my own séance room lights get tampered with by Spirit in my séance room now while I am sitting on my own.
Best to have a policy of a trial period for any new comer of about 6-8 weeks. If either party do not wish for the person to come again in that period, there will be no hard feelings and no reason need to be given for the departure. It is amazing how Spirit nearly always puts obstacles in the way of not so nice, or not needed sitters.
KEEP to the **same** people sitting for the developing Physical Medium.
New people coming into the Circle will alter the environment, [the power for a while] especially if the

Circle is only in it's infancy, just starting.

Any people who do not like each other, or who get flustered when sitting in the Dark Circle (no light in the room), stop them sitting, the conditions there will be adversely affected if you don't, it is always best to close, and ask these people quietly and nicely to leave and not to return. Best to restart at the next sitting when all bad conditions have been forgotten. (the following week) Incompatible people will stop or hinder development don't have them there. **A must.**

Do not start letting people in after the starting of the Circle. **A must.**

Stipulate a prompt time of starting; after that, no entrance to the Circle by any person what so ever. Best all to be there at least a quarter of an hour before hand. **A must.**

Any late starting of a Circle can put back the progression of that Circle.

Any person who is continually late, or a spasmodic sitter, only coming occasionally to the Circle, ask them not to attend again. It is not fair to the other sitters, neither is it fair to Spirit to think they all can put every bit of their effort into the Circle and not have a constant setting to help to make things happen for the benefit of all there. In Gordon Higginson's Home Circle, if a sitter missed once they were not allowed back into the Circle, those in the group even had to come back from holiday to sit for him on that particular weekly Circle day. Gordon used to travel hundreds of miles each week to get home to the Circle from where he was demonstrating and then travel back.

Have a comfortable room to sit in. [Some people do not alter their Circle room in any shape or form, some have no heating as well, allowing the room to find its own temperature].

Have a room preferably put aside just for purpose of sitting for any development [but is not essential].

Bowls of water placed in the room each time for the sitting. This helps to prevent the Medium and sitters getting too dehydrated. Large mixing bowls or large fruit bowls are ideal. I have three large bowls in a room of 2 metres by 3 metres.

Have a cup/glass of water for each sitter, generally placed on the floor by them [always drink plenty of water while developing it can save you suffering from headaches, remember you are developing/using parts of your brain that has had very little use, probably it has been dormant for many years]. I suffered a lot from headaches when I first starting sitting, BUT not all people do. **A must.**

All in the Circle should meditate for at least ¼ to ½ an hour in the room before the start of the Circle to build up the power within the room and all of the sitters themselves bringing in the power ready to be sent to developing Physical Medium when the Circle starts. For me a must, but some don't.

The sitters after the meditation should be ask to come back by the leader of the Circle, and for every person to link into Spirit for a moment, and ask Spirit in their heads for their power to be sent to the Medium in the cabinet for Physical Phenomena to occur. The Medium who is in the cabinet going back into, or staying in deep meditation or Trance, every other person in the Circle then quietly watching out for something that might occur. When the Medium is in Trance, all there should happily start singing to make the Circle, and the room like a party atmosphere, laughing if they go wrong, but not too loud. Quietly and happily talking in the lulls. Individual Mediums prefer different requirements. DO NOT WHISPER it can bring the Medium back as they might want to listen cocking their ears up.

A lot of Circles have three songs then listen for a while then another three, then listen and so on.

Have at least one trumpet in the circle [a trumpet is like an old fashioned megaphone or a cone] which is made of light weight things like cardboard, plastic, aluminium or thin wood veneer; if it is used in the Circle, sprinkle a little water inside it each time before the Circle starts. Other metals it is said by Spirit, effects the ectoplasmic rods that are used to hold the trumpet, but this might not be true as they have been known to lift small and large brass bells in a Circle but I think it might be the weight factor to do with the power in the Circle in the early stages. The trumpet for most Circles is about a foot to 18 inches high, one open end about 5-9 inches in diameter, the other end about ½ to 2 inches in diameter, luminous paint strip at the two ends. But Harry Edwards in his book said Arnold Clare had used three trumpets 33 inches long weighing 7 ½ ounces, made of transparent rigid celluloid kept together with insulating tape with broad strips of luminous paint all round. The trumpet should be placed on a card with a Circle drawn around it, or some use talcum powder sprinkled over it so it covers the paper it is standing on, (**BUT THINK ABOUT THE MEDIUM** and the dust this can create in the room, and the sitters in the Circle), this is to show whether the trumpet has been moved by Spirit. The trumpet is placed in the middle of the Circle on the floor, or on the table if one is used.

Some Circles have two mouth organs (Arnold Clare), a small glass pot (fish paste pot), an old fashioned musical box, and a luminous "slate" (plaque) consisting of a sheet of plywood 14 x10 ins. coated on one side with luminous paint (Arnold Clare painted his over and over again before each Circle, his plaque measured 25 inches by 14 inches) with a handle on the other side and placed in the middle on the floor. Many times placed luminous side down to the floor but a lot of the time upper most. The large one will illuminate most things to about four feet, most times the plaque is placed on the floor in front of the Medium.

A Circle of the same people each time. [Better early results within the Circle seem to work when sitters are placed man, woman, man, woman, etc. or correctly said it should be: - a manly person, a feminine person, a manly person, a feminine person. Or another interpretation :- A dominant person, a subservient person, a dominant person, a subservient person, the old school way of thinking used to say positive and negative people, meaning their energy or magnetic output].

Some Circles prefer odd numbers, the odd person being the one [Developing Physical Medium] in the cabinet, but don't take this as gospel, a great many Circles work with an even number of people.

Same placing of people in the Circle. Same seats and sitting positions for all present at each Circle **is a must**.

Chairs are best if they are upright and made of wood [wood acts as a battery type store for Physical Phenomena energy], as well as little as possible soft furnishings in the room as the Physical Phenomena energy can be absorbed into the material, there are many instances where the curtains to keep out the light, when taken down to wash fall apart. Also the clothing of the Medium can deteriorate very quickly. Metal should be avoided, as there can be flash burns when touched by the sitters. All metal jewellery removed.

Cleanliness of all sitters in mind, body and clothing.

Each person should have prepared themselves before hand, by having a shower/bath, clean clothing. Some (especially the last generation of Physical Mediums of the past) wear the same clothes for the Physical Circle but they are clean. [Most people who go out for an evening to meet a friend, or go to church to be in the presence of God get prepared with a set of clothing to fit the occasion, so should you when sitting for a link with your friends and helpers in Spirit].

ALL external daylight excluded from the room. [As this can effect the early build up of materialised Physical Phenomena] Light might be all right if the Medium is very experienced, or has developed in the light. But that would have to be experimented with after the Medium is developed.

Adjustable lighting of separate red [mainly used] and white lights, if only one can be done, use a dimmer (Rheostat) on red, and switch the white light off. [Physical Circles start off mostly in the dark, when phenomena starts, a very low covered red light is sometimes allowed by Spirit]

Some Circles start with the very low covered red light and get results, BUT a lot more get the good early regular results in the dark.

Start as you mean to go on. By that I mean if you start in very dim red light, stick by that method. It is for you to decide. In dim red light there is a better chance for your sitters to see the Physical Phenomena, and there is less chance of others thinking it is fraud. [Try sitting alternately in a closed Physical Circle, first in the light and then the following week in the dark, **and** on other days at separate set times so no one can be accused of fraud when Physical Phenomena has started, or begins to happen, or use an infra red camera at set times again alternating, use very low light cameras for in the red light and in the day light sittings].

Comfortable seats for all. All sitting comfortably upright, hands resting on the laps. If sitting around a table all to have their hands on the table, the little fingers touching to form the Circle and build up the strength of the Power of Spirit. Some hold hand to wrist, or hand to hand to form the complete Circle.

Legs of sitters not crossed, feet on the floor a comfortable distance apart [Spirit uses all the sitters if the Medium has not got the chemicals needed at the time, the ectoplasm comes mostly out of all the human orifices of the body :- the mouth, nose, ears, eye sockets, anus, vagina, penis, solar plexus and elsewhere. Ectoplasm can also come out of the skin pores. Areas of the body can be restricted if the legs are crossed, the sitters have to be comfortable, also crossed legs can cause cramp in many people].

In the entranced Physical Medium, their body and brain has to be completely relaxed, so Spirit has full access to the inner workings of the brain and so to link better with the individual's most inner workings [in other words the least possible thoughts and nerve impulses from the brain and no electrical activity to the muscles, which tenses them].

Nothing moved if possible. [Meaning changed around].

Nothing being taken out or brought into the established Circle.

New things brought into the room or Circle very gradually over a period of time.

Meditation to bring in the link from Spirit before the Circle's start, BUT punctual starting times **is a must**.

A good, happy, loving, sincere, positive, anticipating the best, almost party like atmosphere should be strived for.

Sitters should be sincere and in "peaceful loving harmony" with each other "that is essential". All there having dedication and being submissive to Spirit's needs. **A must**.

Lively, happy singing of songs old and new. [A lot of Circles now in the modern times use a **battery** operated tape recorder to play their tunes and songs to sing along with, get used to turning the tape low or off in the dark, but do not let the conditions go flat] when the phenomena happens in the subdued light, tell each other what you see, hear, feel so it can be confirmed by others in the Circle, talk in a low voice, lots talk normally, but not loudly, laughter enhances the vibration. Lots of Circles sing two or three songs then listen for a short while to see and listen for anything occurring, set the rules at the start. If the Circle sings constantly the sitters can miss out on the taps, knocks, ringing of bells, Spirit voices, etc. If anything occurs the person should say there and then, especially if it is being recorded on tape or film.

DO NOT WHISPER as it can bring back the Medium from their deep meditation or Trance. DO NOT USE THE MEDIUMS NAME as this also can bring them back to reality, it acts as a trigger to the subconscious mind of the Medium. **A must**.

No very long silences, or low periods when the power is allowed to go flat, except when the leader would like everyone to meditate, asking all to bring in/up the Power of Spirit to make a Link with the higher side of life, generally when the Circle first starts. But there might be a feeling by the leader it is necessary to build up the power again part way through either by singing or a short meditation.

No negativity allowed at all in the building or room. No bad or evil thoughts or deeds. No bitchiness, or gossip. No criticism. **A must**.

Try to exclude any heavy metals from the room.

Do not wear any metal jewellery rings, necklaces, watches, etc., in a Circle where there is likely to be ectoplasm, as psychic burns can happen to the wearer. If the wearer cannot get their rings off then cover them with a plaster or tape of some sort [masking tape is good for this]. **A must.**

Do not wear anything restricting, undo belts, scarves, collars etc. especially the developing Medium.

All to go to the toilet before sitting in any Circle so no interruptions later during the Circle. **A must**. Once all are in the séance room there **must not be any going out**, and certainly **no one** is allowed to come in during the Circle sitting.

No person is to have any preconceived ideas about what might happen, in the Circle, trust in Spirit, and send out sincere love to the higher side of life. **A must.**

Trust totally in the personal higher self and the higher life. If Spirit is going to work with you they are going to make sure everything is in your best interest. **A must**

I have total trust in Spirit but make sure I am ready for the unexpected from others who are not in Spirit. Make sure there is no chance of interruptions, no doorbells, no visitors, no telephones to ring, no sudden noise, etc. This is a **must for the safety of the developing Medium and the sitters.**

A cabinet for a person to sit in to concentrate the psychic energy power from Spirit used all the time at the start of development for Physical Phenomena. [Mine is 3 feet wide by 3 feet deep by 6.6 feet high with a curtain from the top to the floor in the front, which can be drawn shut to enclose the power for development, and a cushioned dining chair with arms, [I sit in it now to meditate each day] The cabinet is an option in every Circle except the Physical Circle, but on saying that, Physical Phenomena has been produced without, but very rarely in the early development stages. A cabinet can be made in a corner of a room with just a curtain on a pole, or a corner shower rail. But as the people became more fully developed many years ago, they had no need for a cabinet or darkness, some even sat in front of the curtain/cabinet. As did Gordon Higginson, as he was claustrophobic, Spirit took him inside the cabinet when they were ready for him so they could manipulate what ever they had to in the body, and to build up the power needed for the ectoplasm production for the full materialisations he did.

Sincere prayers to start and finish the sitting of the Circle, with the asking for what you want from the Circle at the beginning. [Most ask for **"Physical Phenomena to prove there is life after our so called death"**, and leave the rest to Spirit]. Also asking for Spirit **"to come only with goodness, kindness, love and truth, to blend in the Divine Light of Spirit within the loving harmony of Spirit from the**

**highest realms, and protection of all there, when finished to return all to the normality needed to continue their lives on the earth plane".** For me a must.

At the end just before the close, everyone is asked to send any power left to those in need of healing and a quiet moment of at least a minute. Then close the conditions of the Circle down in the form of a prayer thanking Spirit, make arrangements for the next sitting of the Circle, and asking Spirit to take conditions away, returning everyone there to their normal self, telling your angelic Spirit helpers you will be back and when, it is a commitment from all. **BUT** there are some Physical Mediums who say the Physical Circle is the only Circle you do not send out the power left in the way of healing, as it is needed there in the room to build up for the next sitting of Physical Phenomena. Others say you just send out the residue of the power and ask for some to be left for the next time. I have always been of the belief that what you give out comes back to you ten fold. I always send out any power left at the end of the Circle to those in need of healing.

No person to move out of their seats during the Circle sitting without permission of the leader of the Circle or Spirit. **A must.**

**At the start all there present being told if anything happens, not to touch, or grab out at any phenomena, or ectoplasm as it could lead to the Medium being severely injured.** <u>A must.</u>

**At the start all there present being told not to touch the Medium, as the Medium could be severely injured. No sudden or loud noises. The Medium will generally be in a deep state of meditation or Trance; bad shock could also occur. If the ectoplasm returns into the Medium too quickly, psychic burns can occur and the sudden surge of blood through a shock can many times cause internal bleeding. <u>AN IMPORTANT MUST.</u>**

Bring back any person in deep meditation by talking to the person in a low gentle voice, use their name, asking the person to let the conditions to go and to come back to normality, do not touch them. Spirit can sometimes use more than one person in a Circle but this is unusual. [Read the really old books of the last century and about their Circles, quite often you have to read in between the lines to gain any real information].

Have a person to be the guardian of the Medium, and of the Circle [a leader of the Circle], making sure that the Medium is protected from the silly person, who might not obey the rules of the Circle.

Sit the guardian and/or a trusted person at each side of the Medium to make sure at the end of the sitting they are fully returned to normality, talking to them in a soft low voice, do not touch the Medium until they are fully recovered, and the Medium themselves say they are OK. **A VERY IMPORTANT MUST**

When sitting for Physical, only eat a very light meal at least four hours before and no nuts especially peanuts as they are hard for Spirit to deal with [this has been told to us by Spirit]. I was sitting in the enclosed cabinet in a Physical Circle that went on for 3 ½ hours, by the side of me in the Circle, sitting on a chair by the outside of the cabinet was a lady who had only eaten a light meal four hours before the start of that Circle and she brought up that meal and the séance had to be closed. [Please remember that the first signs of any ectoplasm is for the person the be as though they are going to be sick, I will leave you up to your own devices for the length of time you have a meal before any physical séance]. I do not have any food for that day, only drinking water.

Many in a Physical Circle have no red meat, or fish before the Physical Circle, [this can build up too much activity in the body, heightening the person's bodily activity]. Spirit has to adjust the chemicals in the sitters bodies to help them with the correct vibrations necessary, some try to eat the same type of meal before the Circle to help Spirit. Eat your fish and meat after sitting. Lots I have spoken to only eat four hours before the Circle then nothing until after. They then have their main meal. Some don't.

No alcohol before Circle, save it until after the Circle.

Some Circles have a small bell, a little toy tambourine, and a rattle for Spirit to play with. Some have wind chimes hung up to see/hear if there is any psychic breeze happening in the room. Others have a ping-pong ball, which has florescent tape attach [there are new florescent balls now on sale] these are placed in the middle of the Circle.

Do not attempt anything other than aiming for Physical Phenomena in this Circle at this time, on this day. [No clairvoyance, messages, by the sitters, etc. as these are on a different level of vibration than Physical. Only use Physical from the working Medium unless guided by Spirit].

When any lights are switched on or off all there including Spirit should be warned [to let any ectoplasm to be absorbed back into the Medium], then it should be done only after asking if all there are OK with the light going on and then only gradually. A must.

Have a "sweet" drink and/or "sweet" cakes/biscuits after sitting to revitalise the sitters and especially the Medium that has been used by Spirit for the Link.

Salt, calcium tablets, (or crushed limestone) and crushed vitamin tablets are placed in the room by many Mediums in their Physical séances. I say what about sugar being included, because that is needed by the Physical Medium when they come out of the séance room, it might help. Try it in your Circles.

A point I would like to make here is that the human body is made up of 90% plus of water. Does it not make sense that to save the people's bodily fluids being use too much and those of the Medium in Physical Circles, by Spirit, because they have told us they in Spirit have to use some chemical salts and minerals at times that they cannot put back into the sitters' and the Medium's body. It makes sense to me to place multivitamins in water and perhaps vegetables and fruits in bowls and flowers in the room. Also some sugar, salt, minerals, calcium (which bones are made of) and vitamins in dishes. These could be eaten and displayed afterwards in the house after the Circle, or covered up for next time, so not wasted. Of course it would be up to the individual Circle. Each dish should be replaced with a new stock at intervals.

A cabinet can also be made of four poles, a type of box on top made of stiff cardboard to make it ridged, possibly stapled to the poles. This then is all covered with material at back, and sides stapled, then the front as a parting curtain to allow the Medium gain access to sit in it. That is how easy it can be.

There are few things that every person there should be watching out for when sitting in a Circle, especially a Physical Circle. These happenings have been a prelude to the starting of the phenomena in the past in many a Circle as the power builds up. Please do not dismiss them, as a lot are classed as being Physical in themselves, even if they are only a small snippet of the phenomena.

A lot of people class Physical as only being the physical presence of the human like Spirit Form this is not so. So put that idea out of your head.

The feeling of cotton being drawn over the face or exposed skin, some say cobwebs. This sometimes has a ticklish feeling around the mouth, ears and/or the nose also on the hands. This is the feeling of the power being built up and you are becoming sensitive to it. Do not scratch or itch it. Possibly ectoplasm building up there, generally it is the energy felt.

A drawing out of energy from the body, a slight suction from the area of the body, chest to the lower half, generally from the solar plexus, and it is generally going out towards the person who needs the power. This is generally the Medium in the cabinet. Every person there should be sending that energy to the Medium being developed.

Some sitters yawn a lot and their eyes water, this is the power being used from that sitter.

Some sitters feel the sensation of water or a perfume being sprinkled on them. DO NOT LET ANY PERSON FOOL AROUND AND DO THIS AS A JOKE, IT WILL BACKFIRE. Every person there should be positive and sincere in their attitude, looking for the peaceful loving harmony within the group.

Parts, or the whole body feeling light, or feels heavy.

The body feels as though it is being pressed into the chair.

Gentle touches on the body, the hair, the clothing, also slight tugs of the clothing.

Feeling your legs heavy or your legs very light and weightless.

Changes of your feelings in your hands, tingling as it sometimes happens when healing.

Smells of different kinds are produced, cigarette smoke, pipe tobacco, perfume, coal fire, fire ash smell, smell of sulphur, matches, These smells are generally indications of presence by Spirit to remind someone there of a situation and/or a memory.

The smell of ectoplasm has a smell of a dank, musty, mould sometimes a pungent sulphurous smell. These are the reasons sitters should not be wearing any perfume of any kind or after shave, nor smoking before the Circle and to only wash with none perfumed soap before any sitting in any Circle not just a physical Circle.

Tutting or lip smacking, or guttural noises in the room of the Circle or from the Medium, can mean that Spirit are trying to build up the power of voices for the Circle to hear.

A breathing of the Medium generally changes when Spirit is going to speak through them, especially when the Medium is in Deep Trance. Then it is generally a guttural monotone sound [but not always] when the Spirit talks through an ectoplasmic voice box [etheric amplifier].

Do not worry too much about people's stomach rumbling and gurgling. This often happens in any Circle it can be only Spirit adjusting the bodily chemicals of the sitter for easier use. Sometimes it is Spirit using the chemicals from the sitters to build up ectoplasm from the sitters. BUT sometimes though, it can be the sitter just being hungry. Look at all the options.

Whistling coming from out of the air; do not let any of the sitters whistle or it might confuse all there.

Watch out for psychic breezes, some Circles have wind chimes hanging in different parts of the room to detect the breeze.

Cold breezes that can be felt on the face, and hands, showing the group that the power is being built up by Spirit, and there is a presence of Spirit.

Circles I have sat in, each person could feel the coldness of the psychic power build up from the floor to about knee, or waist height. People in your Circle, I hope will be able to place their hands palm downwards and feel the height of it when your Circle gets the power there. I wear two jumpers and two pairs of trousers when sitting sometimes in the cabinet at home; it can be like sitting in the icebox when the power is built up, even with the heating on.

Tapping and raps happening anywhere in the room where the Circle is being held.

If a tape recorder is being used, battery powered is best to use in any Circle not mains electric, but at a pinch they can be used. This is because the surge of power from Spirit can sometimes blow the fuse of the mains tape recorder. It is also for the safety of the Medium as I have also heard of the volume on some recording equipment really blasting out very, very loud when the surge of power has been brought into the room by Spirit through the Medium, some equipment I have heard of being damaged by the power.

A lot of people use a microphone only in the Circle/séance room. The microphone is connected to a long lead; the recorder is placed outside the séance room. Many are the times I have the microphone in a séance room and there is a lot of crackling or interference coming through it. This static interference generally stops when the Circle goes through a low energy period and at the end off the séance.

Some Circles have a sound proof box with a microphone placed in it, on which is placed the trumpet, the leads of the microphone are then fed through the wall into another room and connected to the recorder.

Power surges of the electric by Spirit can alter the lights so they go brighter and/or dimmer.

Sometimes the lights will be switched off or on by Spirit.

A flash of light can be made by Spirit to occur in a darkened room, as has happened in my séance room many times and recorded on infra camera.

Crackling or an interference might be detected through the microphone onto the tape, this could be the start of the power being built up and things will begin to happen pretty soon.

Some voices might be able to be heard on the tape recorder when there was none heard whilst the Circle was in progress. Quite often the voices come mixed in with a sort of white noise (as though a radio is not on station) so have to be listened to carefully and heard over and over again to make any sense of them or they can be enhanced on a computer by taking away the white noise with special software and leaving only the voices on the recording.

When people have their eyes open, as all should most of the time, except when building up the power in meditation, to see if anything happens. In pitch blackness the darkness can change, some say it is a thicker blackness, then it can change to thinner, others say it is becoming blue with speckles, then can be seen to turn reddish. There might be some patches of this difference in the form of mist that is seen by all/some of the sitters. This mist can be of different colours and can have a sparkle, a sheen or be fluorescent; watch out for these and the many changes you will experience, note them down for future reference, This can be the energy changes in the Circle. [BUT do not kid yourselves; try as an experiment closing your eyes very, very tightly and then open them in a darkened room and you can then see lights, so do not be fooled].

Some of the more sensitive of you will detect a presence of a Spirit Form standing in the room, and be able to describe them, yet not see them. You can feel, and yet know everything about them, as though they are there in a physical form.

In the Dark Circles (where there is no light at all in the room), Spirit will when necessary light up the forms they appear in, whether it is the whole body form, or just part of the person.

Try to remember; to write down in a diary all happenings as they happen on that day, time can play tricks on the memory, even after one day with most people. This is why it is best to record the Circles in some way.

Every person who sees, or feels any of these bits of phenomena, should speak out about it at the time in a

low voice, so that the others who are there and do see or feel the same also should speak out, so they can confirm that they also can see or feel any happenings. That way it can be proof for the person [and the Circle] and not put down to imagination, or seeing the phenomena clairvoyantly.
Do not whisper as it can bring back the Medium out of deep meditation or Trance, if there is one being use in the Circle.

It is said, the sitters in Physical Circles should not sit in Open Circles as they might bring into the Physical Circle an unwanted presence. On this point I cannot fully comment on, but it stands to reason in my book. For one you do not know the people who are sitting and for what reasons they are sitting nor can you know what sort of a person they are. Two, you cannot know if they are selfish, nasty, evil, unkind, not caring, unstable, mentally ill, so care should be taken. I would only recommend each and everyone of you if developing Physical Side of Mediumship to sit only in Circles with people who you know, and who are giving, kind, loving, sincere and generous with their time and efforts when linking with Spirit especially when going for the Physical development links it is not so important with clairvoyance, clairaudience, clairsentience. Read the warnings.

There is a society called the Noah's Ark Society; a group that has been set up for the promotion of Physical Mediumship, at 7, Sheen Close, Grange Park, Swindon, Wiltshire, SN5 6JF in the U.K. 01793 874169 It is worthwhile sending off for their literature.

Something that should be pointed out is, some Mediums of the late 1800's who were studied by scientists, sat outside the cabinet in front of the curtain, to bring about their Physical Mediumship Phenomena. The ectoplasm then as usual being built up in the enclosed cabinet. So try doing it that way as well. Experiment for your own sake of development. **BUT give one method a chance over the years to work.** Read the books written by the scientist, the late Sir Arthur Conan Doyle.

Do not think that Physical Phenomena is a new thing of the present day; it has been going on since time began, in the tepees and sweat lodges of the North American Indians, in the mud huts of Africa, the huts of Haiti, and in the jungle huts throughout the world where they still happen, and have been documented for many centuries. People have only to look at the Christian bible for evidence. In the "Old Testament" There is one Materialisation that is documented when King Saul visited a Medium of Endor. The Prophet Samuel Materialised to him in that séance [1 Sam. 28.7 to19]. Then there is the Materialisation of Jesus after he was killed, that is documented in the New Testament. In the middle ages the churches were losing their power, or should I say their income, because of people going to Mediums/wise ones/Shaman/witches (call them what you like they were all the same to the churches) for advice, and to hear them speaking in different languages they did not understand, the Mediums then were doing Physical Phenomena and giving advice to the spiritual needy through their gifts of clairvoyance, clairsentience, and clairaudience from Spirit. So for this the church classed the Mediums as Witches, and had them killed. The churches want to forget about these things and keep everyone in the dark about their past and sadly still in this present day. Unbelievable, terrible cruelties done in the name of their religion and are still being done today, look at the wars that are going on "RELIGION". Remember there is no such word in the Jewish language for Witch, It was said the "Wise One of Endor" in early bibles. Yet again the church changing the words of the bible to suit themselves. Please think and look into the religions of the world and you will see all the religions have at their start "**MEDIUMS**" who were then put onto pedestals.

In (1909) recent investigations by W. J. Crawford have shown that white light acts destructively on the seedpods (constructed by Spirit using the ectoplasm from the Medium's body for the lifting of objects as in levitations) or psychic projections from the Medium's body necessary for the production of telekinetic phenomena. It appears to produce a molecular softening of the invisible "rod", while red light acts much more feebly. It is, therefore, necessary to consider reflection, refraction and absorption of light used in the séance room.
Professor Ochorowicz employed with success a faint blue light. So did Paul Gibier, the Director of the Pasteur Institute in New York. But, in any case, the long wave red rays are preferable, since they allow us to leave the shutter of the photographic apparatus open. On the whole it is better to renounce the show pieces of the Medium in the dark, and use a faint illumination with a feebler manifestation. It is true that

in a feeble light, and, therefore, also in as red light, we only see (with our eyes) indirectly with the retina, which are more sensitive to light, and less to colour, whereas in fixation in a feeble red light, we use the "cones", on account of there central position. But these, on account of their greater sensitiveness to colour than to light, in general give a feeble general effect. Objects on which the glance is fixed, or concentrated in a red light appear, therefore, feebler than they do subsequently on the photograph. The eye is very easily fatigued and subject to error. Hence it is advisable often to close the eye and to rest it, instead of fixing it with and effort for a length of time.

# "<u>STRONG WARNINGS</u> TO ALL WHO SIT FOR DEEP TRANCE, PHYSICAL MEDIUMSHIP AND WITHIN A PHYSICAL CIRCLE"

I would like to point out here again for all who would like to progress towards Physical Mediumship and for those who would like to sit in a Circle for Physical Phenomena, that there are dangers for all if the proper rules are not adhered to.

For the safety of the Physical Medium. All attending the Circles should be told **before** the start of the Circle, and those who do not agree to the terms of the Circle sitting, OR demonstration, **should be asked to leave**.

No person there is to make any sudden, loud, or sharp noises.

If any person/persons fool around or grab hold of any ectoplasm, or any of the phenomena, that person/persons should be restrained and the Circle should be stopped immediately for the safety of the Medium especially, but also the sitters, and the person/persons should be taken to task. In this day and age they should be prosecute if necessary, for putting the Medium's life and possibly the sitters' lives in danger.

**I think all who attend Physical or Deep Trance Séances should have to sign a piece of paper that tells the sitters what might happen if anything is done to harm the Medium, that way the offending person can be taken to task and if necessary prosecuted for endangering the Medium's life**.

I would like to write about some of the things that have happened in the past so it will reinforce what sort of a danger can befall the unwary.

Just recently a great friend, Melanie Polley of Rugby U.K. the Physical Medium, was doing a demonstration of Direct Voice sitting in a vulnerable place, someone outside of the building made a sudden noise causing a disruption during the talk by her guide White Owl. The shock was immediate for her; poor Melanie had bleeding from her mouth. The person did not realise the danger that he had put Melanie into. Spirit had built an ectoplasmic voice box in her chest/stomach area and that manipulation was/is alien to her normal bodily function. Also Spirit had increased her blood circulation to a higher pressure (as Spirit does with Physical Mediums) to quickly bring the chemicals necessary for the ectoplasmic voice box and surrounding area. The shock of the noise suddenly increased the flow of blood and it burst an already over pressurised blood vessel. Also it should be remembered the ectoplasm needed for the voice box was withdrawn into Melanie's body very quickly and it was very painful for her causing possible internal burns, so causing a life threatening situation for Melanie. Luckily the damage to her physical body was this time only small, BUT she was ill after the séance and bad for a month after.

Guy P.J. L'Estrange was injured and did not work for Spirit or sit for a very long time after this incident. An idiot of a sitter put his foot out to stop a trumpet flying around and he broke the ectoplasmic rod that was supporting the trumpet as it was flying around the room. The ectoplasm shot back into the solar plexus area of Guy's body and he ended up writhing on the floor in agony. Guy was left with a very big bruise (remember a bruise is a rupture/breakage of the blood vessels) in the stomach area and not being able to move without discomfort for very many weeks after.

A very well known Physical Medium was put in very great danger by a son of the sitter who through his action consequently killed his mother, **one of the sitters**, through the foolish action of his.

Here is an extract of the published article at the turn of the century from a séance, when the ectoplasm was starting to build up in the Circle.

"At first I did not understand it, but as the sensations of being drawn downwards continued, it flashed across me that a Spirit had materialised behind me, and someone had grasped it and was drawing it from the cabinet. In horror I cried to my friend (the hostess), who was sitting beside me, that someone had grasped the form, but she only moaned and leaned heavily against me. In an instant all was confusion. I angrily ordered the delinquent to loose his hold of the white drapery, (ectoplasm) but it was not until the order was repeated with a threat from the others that he obeyed. Order was restored and the meeting brought to a close. My friend was taken to her room, which she was scarcely ever able to leave again, until the welcome end came and she was relieved from her sufferings, not least of which lay in the knowledge that they had been caused by the act of her own son".

Another extract from the British Journal of Psychical Research.

"It took about thirty minutes to produce a large mass of teleplasm and pile it up on Hardwicke's head. Dr Tillyard obtained leave to handle it in red light, and this was granted by Walter, the Spirit Control. Just as Dr Tillyard was stepping forward to examine it, he heard Dr Crandon say to Mrs Tillyard that the Medium would groan when the teleplasm was touched, and, sure enough, as soon as it was touched, Hardwicke emitted a deep groan, although he was sound asleep. He thought at first this might have resulted from suggestion, but found later on that this is the usual result of handling the material, even though the Medium is unconscious is aware of pain in that state.

Gordon Higginson was burnt many times by the foolish people who tried to grab the ectoplasm or by people making sudden noises while in the Physical Circle or demonstration. Also he was burnt in the stomach area from a metal buckle off his belt. Once, because of people not cleaning the séance room before a Physical Circle, Gordon had a safety pin drawn under his skin with the withdrawing ectoplasm into his stomach/solar plexus area at the end of the séance.

In 1956 Helen Duncan the Physical Medium, was severely injured and consequently died by the deliberate, forced intervention by the police into her Physical Materialisation séance.
That séance was being held in a private room upstairs in a Nottingham chiropodist's home, that forced entry gave a massive shock to Helen who was in the cabinet, in an unconscious Trance State, and producing ectoplasm (so "Albert" her guide, who would come through, could [he was talking through Helen at the time of the break in] talk to the audience through Independent Direct Voice box before the Materialisation started). Helen was deathly grey, unconscious and bleeding from the mouth when the police carried her out of the cabinet into the bedroom and laid her flat out on a bed. The doctor was called, the police at first wanted to take Helen down to the police station, he refused to let them, so the police wanted him to strip her and examine her for masks and muslin cloth in **ALL** her orifices even in the state she was in. She was also in great pain the police again asked the doctor to come down to the station with her, the doctor again refused. They again tried to insist on taking her down to the police station, the doctor said "I will have no part of it, she is in deep shock," "Can't you see she is dying." "She is a diabetic and has a heart problem." "If you move her she will die." She died thirty-six days later, I now believe as a direct result of that massive shock to her human body system. Knowing what I do now.

Helen Duncan because of using her gift/powers from God the Divine Spirit to comfort people, and it conflicted with the establishment (most of whom belonged [and still do] to the Christian Church) was the last person to be prosecuted in Great Britain under the witchcraft act of 1735 at the Central Criminal Court on 3rd of March 1944. She was convicted and sentenced, then gaoled/jailed for nine months.
There are many books that have been written about her and the trial, one being the "Two Worlds of Helen Duncan" by Gena Brealey with Kay Hunter.

In the late 1970's when I first sat in a Circle with Dave Wickins, as I have already said earlier in the book. A warning to all from my own first hand experience.
One day Dave Wickins, the Circle leader, told us he was going on holiday and did we wish to carry on with the Circles as he could get another experienced, church platform Medium to look after the Circle the following week. We were all excited with the progress we were making so agreed to sit with this **k**nowledgeable **c**hurch **p**latform Medium, as we thought. He came across the Mersey from Birkenhead to

where we were in Kensington in Liverpool above the butcher's shop. Two buses and a boat for him to get there. That night we sat in the dark with a very low red light and as usual after prayers, we had all gone into an altered state then the lady in Trance was speaking in a guttural monotone man's voice. New to us all, and her knowing nothing about being taken over by Spirit. Unknown to me I was also deep in an altered state of awareness. The time was up for the Circle, and the **Knowledgeable (not) Church Platform Medium** asked us all to let the conditions to go. We were not coming back quick enough for this **k**nowledgeable **c**hurch **p**latform Medium and he went over to the lady who was talking in Trance and shook her, she screamed got up and walked out of the room never to be seen again in the Circle, and at the same time I had something immediately shoot up from both my hands, up out of both of my arms and out of my chest on the left just below my peck muscle. I still have niggledly pains in that area [2006 and have them now, as I am finishing editing this book]. I never sat for Spirit for two years after that for fear of what might happen again. I only then sat in Circles for others, sending the power to them, but I have started sitting for myself again for the past nine or ten years ish, especially on my own. Since approx 1990 ish

I will again repeat the fact that a doctor tested me while I was in a trance state, as I know it is so important for all not to forget what happens. I did not know my blood pressure rose an extra 56 points while I was in the trance state. Imagine if I was suddenly touched whilst in that state. The extra surge of blood, as happens in a shock situation, in an already over pressurised vascular system **COULD BE FATAL**.

Even the great, late Harry Edwards in his book "the Mediumship of Arnold Clare" in chapter two says, "**I know two Physical Mediums, still with us, who suffer from <u>continual internal haemorrhage</u>, the result of undue strain**".

**Please think!** You can, hurt, ruin, severely injure, or kill any Deep Trance Medium through lack of thought or deliberate mischief. So take note. You could end up a killer of an instrument of the Divine Spirit, GOD.

Go to your reference libraries and read the older books they have there. One that I would recommend is **"Shadow lands"** by Madame E D'Esperance ISBN 185 2287 098. It has just been reprinted being first written in the 1800's.

Harry Price was a self-taught conjurer, so he more or less knew the tricks of the trade, who died in 1948. He investigated with vigour the fraudulent Mediums of the day and praised the genuine ones as well, going against the established churches many times. There are many books on him and good ones written by him.

One séance he went to in 1937, in London U.K., Harry Price remark "It was the most remarkable case of Materialisation I have ever seen".
After sitting in the dark for about half an hour in the séance, a presence was felt. A lady, who was sitting in the Circle, said her daughter's name, "Rosalie" "Rosalie" "Rosalie" a few times and became upset. She then talked to her calling as she had when alive by her pet name of "My darling" Price felt a hand on his leg, so he asked whether he could feel the presence with his hands so he could be sure, and was given permission by the Circle leader, who had asked Spirit before the request was carried out. On feeling the form in the dark, which had no clothes on, Price found it was a girl of about 5-7 years of age and was about three feet tall. He actually put his ear to the child's chest and heard her heart beat, and felt her pulse on her wrist. Price was given permission by Spirit for the luminous plaque to be turned over so everyone there could see the girl standing in the Circle, they all saw it was the sitter's daughter who had died when she was six, sixteen years before. Price and the group through the leader, asked many questions trying to get a response from the Materialised Spirit Girl, but the only one she replied to was from Price who asked; "Rosalie, do you love your mummy?" in her own voice which was in a lisp she replied "Yes." It was a very emotional séance as can be imagined.
Price afterwards examined the seals on the doors and windows, and the starch powder outside and just inside the door, making sure that no one had come in or gone out of the room. No extra people were in the room at the end of the séance. Price himself had removed the excess furniture and all unnecessary

bits and pieces, before the séance was started.

The interesting point here for the people who want to try things out in Circles. The luminous plaque (some call it a slate) they had in the séance had the illuminating part facing down to start with, then with Spirit's permission, it was used to illuminate the Materialised Form. The luminous plaque (about 1 x 2 feet or smaller) is generally made of thin plywood or stiff card and painted with luminous paint, which is charged up by placing it up to a light before going into the darkened room. This is a pointer for you to look out for with frauds. After your eyes get used to the dark most people can see with the very small amount of light given off. Be it the strip on a trumpet, it can act as a small low powered torch. TRY IT AND SEE. I did after a séance in HULL U.K. in which the trumpet was hitting the walls and the Medium, it was then thrown on the floor in front of a sitter opposite the Medium in the cabinet, which I had never heard of before or since so be very wary. If Spirit can pick a trumpet up they can place it down gently after they have finished. When I tried in the séance room at home using my trumpet, I could see my camera in a completely darkened room when I pointed my trumpet at it, I could get it up to a fraction of an inch with accuracy, without touching the camera. I could see this and I was not fooling myself, because of my infrared video cameras. This is why I think infra red cameras should be used **in every Physical séance** that is of course with Spirits permission and I cannot see that being denied because I am sure they want **every one to be sure of the TRUTH**.

Another séance in Sir William Cookes' small room in 7, Kensington Park Gardens, at the turn of the century should serve as another warning. This was written by Miss F. R. Scratcherd and was published in "Survival" by Putnam, 1924.
There were present Mrs Z, the Medium, Sir William (who had an injured leg after a fall) and myself.
Once Sir William had arranged himself in his long chair, in the dark room, there was just space for two other persons to be seated, and no room for moving about without detection. One afternoon, after the lights were out and the phenomena had started, someone opened the door. A shaft of light fell full on the Medium, who gave a gasp of agony, while I called out: "Shut the door. You are spoiling our experiment".
But the door was not properly re-closed. By means of the crack of light I saw a bulky mass pass between Sir William and myself, partially obscuring the light, in places shutting it out completely. For a moment I thought the medium had left her chair, and stretching out my left hand, struck the knee of the entranced sensitive rigid in her place. At the same time a voice said, "You have hurt my Medium. You have been told you should never touch her when we are working. She was already suffering on account of the light. No, do not close the séance. We will shield her from the light, and do our best to carry on".
Sir William was literally enveloped in the ectoplasmic mist, which was apparently weightless, as he felt nothing, though it seemed to be resting on his injured leg. But the substance was so arranged as to cut off the light where it struck the Medium, while leaving enough for me to see, to some extent, what was occurring.
Meanwhile a lively conversation was in progress between Sir William and the Spirit of his late wife, who seemed to be most dexterous in managing the ectoplasmic column and manipulating it according to the slightest expressed wish of the sitters.
I did not see the formation of the hand that caressed her husband's forehead and greeted myself with a touch, but I heard Lady Crookes say in answer to Sir William's regret that he could not see her (he had his back to the door), " I am here beside you, Willy dear, listen while I carry the musical box round the room".
But I did perceive the upper end of the ectoplasmic column form itself into a rough gripping apparatus and heard it groping for the musical box at our feet.
By means of the bar of light I saw the musical box as it was whirled past the door and round and round Sir William's head.
The box had been purchased for the purpose, a day or two earlier, at Gamage's, and was wound up and stopped at our request, or at that of the unseen intelligence in a way impossible to ourselves, on account of the nature of its mechanism. It was passed gently up and down his injured leg and most of the time two or more voices were speaking with Sir William and myself. But I concentrated on observing as far as possible the behaviour of the ectoplasm, and did not make my usual record of the conversations.
I had known Lady Crookes during her lifetime, and was now witness of her attempts to make use of

ectoplasm as a means of demonstrating her survival, by actions and effects that seemed only the register of the normal five senses for their perception.

The Medium was ill for some time as a result of the shock caused by the sudden letting in of the light. Also where I had placed my hand on her knee in order to ascertain whether she had left her chair, was a huge dark bruise which only gradually disappeared during the next few days, and at first painful to the touch.

A small passage of a book now out of print, by Harry Edwards in the 1940's, "The Mediumship of Arnold Clare".

As Mediumship becomes known, the Medium's real trials commence. He is importuned by people who desire to sit with him and observe phenomena, or receive help and comfort from the " return" of their relatives and friends. As the Medium makes himself available, so does he immediately become the centre of suspicion. "Is he honest?" "Is he a fraud?" etc. The Medium may feel he would like to obtain a "certificate of honesty" and submits to "tests" in the manner described already. If he succeeds, he finds many more societies seeking further tests; and the author has known an established research society impugn a Mediumship in order to force the Medium's hands and introduce him to agree to a series of sittings for experimental purposes.

The Medium also has to face the ever present danger that some irresponsible person will flash a light on him during the séance or interfere in some other manner with the activity taking place. At the time of writing (1940's) one Medium known to the author lost both his gift and his sight on such an occasion; another well known Physical Medium recently passed over after an interference of this nature; and numbers of others have been seriously ill, many suffering internal haemorrhaging from ignorance and ill-conceived interference.

I think I will leave the last word in this section for **Melanie Polley** the Physical Medium. This is what she wrote in March 2002 for this section of the book.

I guess that all of the problems I have had with this part of my work are due to a lack of understanding. Initially, this was not just a lack of comprehension on behalf of my audience but also of myself. I had always slipped off into a "funny state", ever since I was a child but didn't realise that this was Trance until a Medium, now in the Spirit World, Sid Fitzsimmons, told me that I was going to be a Physical Medium working with Direct Voice and Transfiguration. He didn't tell me anything else and sat me in a Physical Circle straight away. I hadn't read anything about Physical Mediumship and I honestly thought until about 10 years ago, that when people talked about Trance and Physical Mediumship, that they meant what I do, and I realise that a lot of people actually don't mean that at all. Let me explain.

White Owl started to speak through me many years ago, and he did so in my voice, using my throat and mouth. He proved a real character, filled with great love and sense of humour. He talked about things I did not know and uplifted people. He would inspire me on the rostrum and seemed always to be within earshot of me. It was only when our Circle sat in our conservatory, with no curtains and in the autumn and winter months, therefore, in the dark, that things changed. Suddenly, I was not fully present when he spoke and one day, this deep man's voice came out of my mouth. Circle members said they could feel him coming way before he spoke. I went to sleep for the tail end of the Circle. As soon as the night of each Circle came, off I went and in he came. Still I still didn't know that this was Physical Mediumship awakening in me, as it had done in my childhood but I knew that we had Trance.

I was invited to attend a group that a friend of mine ran and to demonstrate Trance. During this session, which I attended alone and unescorted, White Owl apparently completely covered me and everyone could see him, complete with feathers and clothes. The stereo came on by itself and crystals flew off a table onto the floor. I was the only one who didn't take off from their chair because I didn't hear anything. When I came round, I was shocked to see everyone in the group was crying, including the men! Apparently, White Owl had spoken to everyone individually and had touched on deeply personal problems with everyone, giving advice and guidance but in a way that did not divulge private matters. This is the man I have come to know, a man of deep concern for his fellows. He talks of people being "Dear Ones".

I did another demonstration again without a minder, in a massive hall. Afterwards, I was ill for several days. I felt absolutely shattered and shaky. It was only about a fortnight later that I found out that several people had left the hall and returned banging the doors behind them. On another occasion, I went into Trance to give philosophy and the chair lady touched my arm and called me to time. I could barely stand and felt sick. I was unable to work at all for a month.

These things happen because I was poorly educated in Trance Mediumship. However, I can't put all the blame onto myself for this because the people I approached for advice either gave me incorrect information or really didn't know anything at all. I learned several things through these early experiences.

**Firstly**, a Trance Medium should **NEVER** work alone outside their own Circle environment, especially in public.

**Secondly**, **Don't assume** that long term Spiritualists know about Trance and Physical Mediumship.

**Thirdly**, **NEVER touch** a Trance medium when they are in a "Trance State".

**Fourthly**, Trance and Physical Mediumship is a very emotive subject. I have sat in four Physical Circles and in each case; nothing was happening until I joined BUT as soon as it became obvious that I could be an instrument for the Spirit World in a Physical way, I was quite literally "turfed out". I have even been accused of "having an evil presence with me" and "working with the wrong kind of energy" because the tables run around the room when I touched them and don't just wobble a bit. It is very important to sit for development of any kind of Mediumship in a harmonious group.

The Physical Circle that I now sit in is wonderful. Everyone is sitting for "the gift". We all know that we are equally "important" to the development of "the gift". All the Circle members bring their own individual energy and together we create the right power for the work to carry on. The power in a Physical Circle vibrates totally differently to that in a Mental Mediumship Circle but there is a definite kinship to the power vibration in a Trance Circle. I think of Trance Mediumship as a stepping stone to Physical Mediumship.

What would I say to a member of a Circle who is sitting to develop a Trance or Physical Medium? Forget yourself and what you might gain from the experience. Remember that you are sitting there giving love and energy to the Spirit World to use with the developing Medium in order that someone who does not have the abilities to perceive Spirit, as you do, or who is desperately unhappy because they have just lost someone and they don't know where they have gone, will find comfort and support in the knowledge that only our material body dies, "we" do not. Imagine the joy of joining a mother and child together once again. THAT is what you're there for.

What would I say to an attendee at a Trance or Physical Mediumship Demonstration? NEVER, EVER, EVER, make loud noises, get up, never move around too much, never leave or touch the Medium, even if you think the Medium is a fake. You may be wrong. If you have a problem with the demonstration, then tell the organisers afterwards. NEVER endanger the health of the Medium. I have bled, been bruised and felt like I've gone twelve rounds with a heavyweight boxer when people have been inconsiderate.

However, now that I understand my Mediumship more, now that I realise that I go into deep altered states and even what many would erroneously call, a Trance Demonstration, I am working with Physical Mediumship, I am very picky as to where I work. My Circle members are even pickier! It astonishes me how even when I explain in detail what my needs are to demonstrate, people just don't get it. They tell me that they are Trance Mediums too and cannot understand why I need red light and hush. I have my own beliefs about this.

It appears that many Spiritualists believe that to be in Trance, the Medium has to be unconscious for the whole of the time. This is not the case. As soon as the Medium in linking with the Spirit World, they are in an altered state, i.e., in a Trance. A Medium can pick up inspiration from Spirit on a surprisingly low level of altered awareness. By calling "Inspirational Speaking Trance, people have become confused. Of course it is a form of Trance, but people don't realise that there are loads of levels of this, from slight overshadowing through to Deep Trance, where the Medium in unaware for long periods of time. I feel that many Mediums fool themselves into believing that they are not fully present when they deliver an inspirational address, when really they are aware but just not as they usually are in their normal day to day living. The Medium knows that he is receiving inspiration and that "it's not him speaking" but due to his lack of education and that same lacking in his audience, he believes that he cannot be in Trance unless he is oblivious all of the time. So, some people say they are oblivious when they are not. He is likely to be oblivious "some of the time". We need to be made aware, as a whole Movement that Trance covers a whole range of "Brain Patterns" and "States of Awareness".

People are not stupid and when they see a Medium who is in a state of overshadowing, or light Trance, saying that they are completely "gone out", the audience know it's untrue. This means that when someone really does go into these deep altered states, they are not believed and the needs they have are not met. It also means that those who are able to deliver the most wonderful Philosophical Addresses from the Spirit World in not so deep states of Trance don't feel supported and actually stop working. This is a sad state of affairs. There is nothing better or worse about the depth of Trance. A Deep Trance Medium is not better than an Inspirational Speaker, they are just different and they can both be used for great works, and indeed dependent on their level of spirituality, they can both be used for not so great works.

I think perhaps with any form of Mediumship, truth of the pudding is in the eating and if someone is interested in a particular form of Mediumship, then they should go and experience it themselves. There are some interesting Physical Mediums about as many people are being inspired to develop this kind of communication at this time. There are all sorts of Trance Mediums about, all working in many levels of awareness, personally, I find the closeness of the Spirit World with this kind of work stimulating and encouraging. I have never felt so loved by God and the Spirit World, as I do when being taken into Trance and carried back again.

I have never bled in my own Home Circle, as it is obviously totally controlled and safe. However, I have had two experiences when I have been demonstrating outside where I have been injured and bled through the shock.

I am not happy about stating where these demonstrations were held nor for which organisations as I have informed the relevant people of the problems I experienced, and I feel sure that these conditions will not be repeated. There is no doubt in my mind that both of these unfortunate incidents occurred because the organisers just did not understand that there is a different set of needs for Deep Trance Mediumship to lighter states. Also, there is a lack of education in Physical and Trance Mediumship at this time.

The first time I was injured and bled was when I was demonstrating Deep Trance, Non Independent Direct Voice and Transfiguration. I had been seated in a curved window area. It was in the evening, so it was dark outside and I did not know the area, nor did my colleagues who had accompanied me to the centre. No one thought to say that the window opened out into a car park. Right in the middle of the demonstration, someone got into their car and slammed the door; the car was right in front of the window in the bay of which I was seated. I did not stir at all, in fact White Owl told everyone that there was going to be a loud bang and there was nothing the Spirit World could do about it. He chose to keep me in Trance, as it was safer than returning me to consciousness quickly. He had also said to a colleague when we started and I was in Trance, that the conditions were by no means perfect but that they did not wish to disappoint the audience or me. It was after this demonstration that he said that they would try one more outside demonstration and if they had any more problems, then they would restrict the work to only two locations and then only with the attendance of at least one Circle member or two selected people who the Spirit World refer to as "family". If there were requests to work elsewhere, we would need to ask for direction in the Circle before accepting or rejecting. I had blood in my mouth and could taste blood for several days afterwards.

The second episode happened in a private demonstration, with a Circle member present at one of the two outside locations the Spirit World operators consider to be safe. Everything should have been all right. The room was secure and people had a reasonable understanding of the needs of the session. However, someone actually forced their way in, going past signs refusing admittance. They let in white light, banged the door on a large, snail shaped, concrete door stop and banged the door shut as they left. Again, White Owl saw it coming stating that he would withdraw as quickly as he could, hoping I would be better with him out rather than in when a disturbance happened. He handed over to Marie-Therese who works without the need for ectoplasm. Unfortunately, I had a nose bleed that lasted off and on for five days.

The Circle Guides are endeavouring to work in all kinds of light, from pitch dark as they develop new areas, to red light and subdued white light. White Owl has successfully spoken maintaining his voice box within my body when the white light has been on. He does this to keep me safe and so that we can work in public. The voice box has been clearly seen, recorded in infrared lighting on my shoulder when conditions are good.

### Appendix 1 - BREATHING RATE

| MEDIUM | 1 | 2 | 3 | 4 | 5 | 6 | 7 | ** 8 | 9 | 10 |
|---|---|---|---|---|---|---|---|---|---|---|
| Per min before Trance | 18.66 | 11.33 | 19.33 | 15.3 | 14.3 | 15 | 13 | 21.3 | 13.6 | 23.6 |
| Per min during Trance | 12.33 | 9.33 | 16.66 | 11.3 | 9.6 | | 13.3 | 23.3 | 12.6 | 17.3 |
| Per min after Trance | 14.33 | 11 | 18 | 16.3 | 16.6 | 16.3 | 14 | 14.3 | 14 | 20.1 |
| *before & during difference* | -6.33 | -2 | -2.67 | -4 | -4.7 | | 0.3 | 2 | -1 | -6.3 |

| MEDIUM | 11 | 12 | 13 | 14 | 15 | 16 | 17 | 18 | 19 | 20 |
|---|---|---|---|---|---|---|---|---|---|---|
| Per min before Trance | 15.3 | 24.3 | 19.3 | 17.3 | 17 | 15.3 | 11.6 | 22 | 16.6 | 18.6 |
| Per min during Trance | 13 | 17.6 | 17.3 | 12.6 | 14.6 | 15.6 | 13.6 | 17.6 | 16.3 | 16.3 |
| Per min after Trance | 16.6 | 21 | 18.6 | 19 | 17 | 15.6 | 12.6 | 21.3 | 19.3 | 18.3 |
| *before & during difference* | -2.3 | -6.7 | -2 | -4.7 | -2.4 | 0.3 | 2 | -4.4 | -0.3 | -2.3 |

*** did not go into a trance state.*

| MEDIUM | 21 | 22 | 23 | 24 | 25 |
|---|---|---|---|---|---|
| Per min before Trance | 18 | 20 | 15.3 | 24.3 | 16.3 |
| Per min during Trance | 18.6 | 17.3 | 10.6 | 15.6 | 19.3 |
| Per min after Trance | 17.6 | 21.3 | 15.6 | 21 | 17.6 |
| *before & during difference* | 0.6 | -2.7 | -4.7 | -8.7 | 3 |

| | | |
|---|---|---|
| **Breathing decreasing during trance** | 18 | 78% |
| **Breathing increasing during trance** | 5 | 22% |
| | 23 | 100% |
| **Error** | 1 | |

> 18/23 mediums, 78%, showed a decrease in Breathing during mediumistic trance.

### Appendix 2 – PULSE

| MEDIUM | 1 | 2 | 3 | 4 | 5 | 6 | 7 | ** 8 | 9 | 10 |
|---|---|---|---|---|---|---|---|---|---|---|
| Before Trance | 71 | 51 | 71 | 92 | 100 | 59 | 101 | 62 | 75 | 84 |
| During Trance | 89 | 60 | 100 | 88 | 142 | | 111 | 71 | 74 | 82 |
| After Trance | 78 | 54 | 75 | 72 | 110 | 60 | 100 | 53 | 70 | 80 |
| *before & during difference* | 18 | 9 | 29 | -4 | 42 | | 10 | 9 | -1 | -2 |

| MEDIUM | 11 | 12 | 13 | 14 | 15 | 16 | 17 | 18 | 19 | 20 |
|---|---|---|---|---|---|---|---|---|---|---|
| Before Trance | 69 | 82 | 86 | 80 | 87 | 100 | 105 | 78 | 101 | 100 |
| During Trance | 71 | 83 | 88 | 85 | 89 | 93 | 84 | 83 | | 84 |
| After Trance | 68 | 72 | 68 | 76 | 85 | 92 | 87 | 77 | 84 | 88 |
| before & during difference | 2 | 1 | 2 | 5 | 2 | -7 | -21 | 5 | -101 | -16 |

** did not go into a trance state.

| MEDIUM | 21 | 22 | 23 | 24 | 25 |
|---|---|---|---|---|---|
| Before Trance | 84 | 127 | 65 | 76 | 104 |
| During Trance | 81 | 121 | 60 | 77 | 114 |
| After Trance | 84 | 108 | 57 | 72 | 65 |
| before & during difference | -3 | -6 | -5 | 1 | 10 |

| | | |
|---|---|---|
| Pulse decreasing during trance | 10 | 43% |
| Pulse increasing during trance | 13 | 57% |
| | 23 | 100% |
| Error | 1 | |

13/23 mediums, 57%, showed an increase in Pulse during mediumistic trance.

## Appendix 3 - TEMPERATURE

| MEDIUM | 1 | 2 | 3 | 4 | 5 | 6 | 7 | **8 | 9 | 10 |
|---|---|---|---|---|---|---|---|---|---|---|
| Before Trance | 35.5 | 35 | 36 | 36 | 37 | 36.5 | 36.5 | 37 | 36 | 38 |
| During Trance | 37 | 36.75 | 38 | 37 | 38 | | 36.75 | 38 | 36.5 | 38 |
| After Trance | 36.25 | 35.75 | 37 | 37.3 | 38.5 | 39.5 | 36.5 | 38 | 36.25 | 37.5 |
| before & during difference | 1.5 | 1.75 | 2 | 1 | 1 | | 0.25 | 1 | 0.5 | 0 |

| MEDIUM | 11 | 12 | 13 | 14 | 15 | 16 | 17 | 18 | 19 | 20 |
|---|---|---|---|---|---|---|---|---|---|---|
| Before Trance | 36.5 | 36 | 36 | 35.5 | 36.5 | 36 | 35.5 | 36 | 36.5 | 36.5 |
| During Trance | 36.75 | 37.5 | 36.5 | 38.5 | 38 | 35.5 | 37 | 35 | | 37.5 |
| After Trance | 36 | 37.5 | 37 | 36 | 37 | 35 | 37 | 35.5 | 36 | 36.5 |
| before & during difference | 0.25 | 1.5 | 0.5 | 3 | 1.5 | -0.5 | 1.5 | -1 | | 1 |

** did not go into a trance state.

| MEDIUM | 21 | 22 | 23 | 24 | 25 |
|---|---|---|---|---|---|
| Before Trance | 37 | 37.5 | 36 | 35.5 | 35 |
| During Trance | 38.5 | 38 | 36 | 37 | 34.5 |
| After Trance | 36.5 | 37 | 35.5 | 35 | 36 |
| before & during difference | 1.5 | 0.5 | 0 | 1.5 | -0.5 |

| | | |
|---|---|---|
| Temperature decreasing during trance | 3 | 14% |
| Temperature increasing during trance | 17 | 77% |
| Remaining the same | 2 | 9% |
| | 22 | 100% |

Error 2

> 17/22 mediums, 77%, showed an increase in Temperature during mediumistic trance.

Here it should be pointed out that the blood pressure of some of the Mediums being tested are at the start abnormally high. This is I feel because the weekend we were being tested, the Mediums were already in a heightened state of altered awareness. My normal blood pressure as tested at home by my own doctor is 130 over 71, yet in the test it started at 152 over 98.

I would like to thank the people who together monitored the Mediums and collected all these bits of data and are continuing to do so. They are Roy McKeag who watched over much of the sessions and wrote it all up, as did Jim Brown, and Duncan Muir and his good lady Linda one of the organisers. Evelyn Armstrong, the doctor who was at the side of the Mediums all the time, two other hard workers were Trish Robertson, Mary Armour.

### Appendix 4 - BLOOD PRESSURE - SYSTOLIC / DIASTOLIC

| MEDIUM | 1 | 2 | 3 | 4 | 5 | 6 | 7 | **8 | 9 | 10 |
|---|---|---|---|---|---|---|---|---|---|---|
| Before Trance | 141/82 | 143/71 | 146/88 | 154/85 | 176/100 | 137/97 | 152/67<br>170/75 | 113/80 | 150/70 | 148/89 |
| During Trance | 153/88 | 165/75 |  | 156/92 | 222/102 |  | 171/76 | 172/96 | 156/67 | 140/85 |
| After Trance | 131/85 | 159/70 | 154/92 | 147/91 | 173/96 | 163/110 |  | 140/86 | 152/68 | 132/87 |

| MEDIUM | 11 | 12 | 13 | 14 | 15 | 16 | 17 | 18 | 19 | 20 |
|---|---|---|---|---|---|---|---|---|---|---|
| Before Trance | 188/92 | 165/95 | 150/72 | 119/76 | 148/56 | 192/116 | 180/100<br>178/91 | 189/86 | 208/96 | 190/85 |
| During Trance | 193/88 | 154/87 | 167/72 | 154/87 | 142/73 | 208/189 | 157/97 | 203/98 |  | 207/94 |
| After Trance | 129/86 | 129/86 | 145/60 | 137/79 | 155/69 | 181/115 |  | 172/92 | 204/100 | 175/89 |

*** did not go into a trance state.*

| MEDIUM | 21 | 22 | 23 | 24 | 25 |
|---|---|---|---|---|---|
| Before Trance | 159/93 | 160/96 | 152/98 | 182/101 | 171/109 |
| During Trance | 121/98 | 166/106 | 169/154 | 176/111 | 185/107 |
| After Trance | 166/100 | 114/94 | 164/104 | 172/101 | 160/96 |

### PLEASE NOTE THESE FIGURES FOR TRANCE MEDIUMS

ALL TESTED AT AYR IN November 2001    **no 23 is my readings**
Normally 130 over 71 As taken August 02

This is the reason I feel why **NO** Trance Medium should be touched OR given a shock whilst in a trance situation. A sudden increase of blood pressure as brought about in a shock could cause the already over stretched vascular system of the entranced Medium to break/rupture causing <u>internal bleeding</u> leading to <u>possible fatal consequences</u> for the Medium.

**SIT WITH PEOPLE WHO UNDERSTAND**

## IF YOU CANNOT DO IT  YOU CANNOT KNOW IT

## Appendix 5 - BLOOD PRESSURE - DIASTOLIC

| MEDIUM | 1 | 2 | 3 | 4 | 5 | 6 | 7 | **8 | 9 | 10 |
|---|---|---|---|---|---|---|---|---|---|---|
| Before Trance | 82 | 71 | 88 | 85 | 100 | 97 | 67 | 80 | 70 | 89 |
| During Trance | 88 | 75 |  | 92 | 102 |  | 75 | 96 | 67 | 85 |
| After Trance | 85 | 70 | 92 | 91 | 96 | 110 | 76 | 86 | 68 | 87 |
| before & during difference | 6 | 4 |  | 7 | 2 |  | 8 | 16 | -3 | -4 |

| MEDIUM | 11 | 12 | 13 | 14 | 15 | 16 | 17 | 18 | 19 | 20 |
|---|---|---|---|---|---|---|---|---|---|---|
| Before Trance | 92 | 95 | 72 | 76 | 56 | 116 | 100 | 86 | 96 | 85 |
| During Trance | 88 | 87 | 72 | 87 | 73 | 189 | 91 | 98 |  | 94 |
| After Trance | 83 | 86 | 60 | 79 | 69 | 115 | 97 | 92 | 100 | 89 |
| before & during difference | -4 | -8 | 0 | 11 | 17 | 73 | -9 | 12 |  | 9 |

*** did not go into a trance state.*

| MEDIUM | 21 | 22 | 23 | 24 | 25 |
|---|---|---|---|---|---|
| Before Trance | 93 | 96 | 98 | 101 | 109 |
| During Trance | 98 | 106 | 154 | 111 | 107 |
| After Trance | 100 | 94 | 104 | 101 | 96 |
| Appendix 5 - before & during difference | 5 | 10 | 56 | 10 | -2 |

| | | |
|---|---|---|
| Blood Pressure decreasing during trance | 6 | 29% |
| Blood Pressure increasing during trance | 14 | 67% |
| Remaining the same | 1 | 5% |
| | 21 | 100% |
| Error | 3 | |

> **14/21 mediums, 67%, showed an increase in Blood Pressure during mediumistic trance.**

## Appendix 6 - EEG - BETA

| MEDIUM | 1 | 2 | 3 | 4 | 5 | 6 | 7 | **8 | 9 | 10 |
|---|---|---|---|---|---|---|---|---|---|---|
| Before Trance | 96 | 100 | 24 | 50 | 68 | 33 | 57 | 34 | 90 | 32 |
| During Trance | 39 | 59 | 23 | 17 | 21 | 21 | 7 | 54 | 78 | 47 |
| before & during difference | -57 | -41 | -1 | -33 | -47 | -12 | -50 | 20 | -12 | 15 |

| MEDIUM | 11 | 12 | 13 | 14 | 15 | 16 | 17 | 18 | 19 | 20 |
|---|---|---|---|---|---|---|---|---|---|---|
| Before Trance | 32 | 94 | 96 | 96 | 72 |  | 30 | 24 | 43 | 73 |
| During Trance | 25 | 34 | 64 | 36 | 64 |  | 60 | 12 | 17 | 32 |
| before & during difference | -7 | -60 | -32 | -60 | -8 | 0 | 30 | -12 | -26 | -41 |

*** did not go into a trance state.*

| MEDIUM | 21 | 22 | 23 | 24 | 25 |
|---|---|---|---|---|---|
| Before Trance | 63 | 19 | 98 | 27 | 99 |
| During Trance | 8 | 99 | 83 | 26 | 65 |
| *before & during difference* | -55 | 80 | -15 | -1 | -34 |

| | | |
|---|---|---|
| **EEG Beta decreasing during trance** | 20 | 87% |
| **EEG Beta increasing during trance** | 3 | 13% |
| | 23 | 100% |
| **Error** | 1 | |

> 20/23 mediums, 87%, showed an decrease in Beta activity during mediumistic trance.

### Appendix 7 - EEG - ALPHA

| MEDIUM | 1 | 2 | 3 | 4 | 5 | 6 | 7 | **8 | 9 | 10 |
|---|---|---|---|---|---|---|---|---|---|---|
| Before Trance | 1 | 1 | 64 | 25 | 15 | 8 | 4 | 46 | 2 | 22 |
| During Trance | 16 | 9 | 50 | 14 | 6 | 23 | 6 | 24 | 8 | 39 |
| *before & during difference* | 15 | 8 | -14 | -11 | -9 | 15 | 2 | -22 | 6 | 17 |

| MEDIUM | 11 | 12 | 13 | 14 | 15 | 16 | 17 | 18 | 19 | 20 |
|---|---|---|---|---|---|---|---|---|---|---|
| Before Trance | 40 | 3 | 0 | 4 | 26 | | 10 | 24 | 1 | 2 |
| During Trance | 19 | 1 | 2 | 57 | 31 | | 34 | 12 | 3 | 5 |
| *before & during difference* | -21 | -2 | 2 | 53 | 5 | 0 | 24 | -12 | 2 | 3 |

** *did not go into a trance state.*

| MEDIUM | 21 | 22 | 23 | 24 | 25 |
|---|---|---|---|---|---|
| Before Trance | 21 | 1 | 0 | 66 | 0 |
| During Trance | 6 | 0 | 3 | 51 | 1 |
| *before & during difference* | -15 | -1 | 3 | -15 | 1 |

| | | |
|---|---|---|
| **EEG Alpha decreasing during trance** | 10 | 43% |
| **EEG Alpha increasing during trance** | 14 | 61% |
| | 23 | 100% |
| **Error** | 1 | |

> 14/23 mediums, 61%, showed an increase in Alpha activity during mediumistic trance.

### Appendix 8 - EEG - THETA

| MEDIUM | 1 | 2 | 3 | 4 | 5 | 6 | 7 | 8* | 9 | 10 |
|---|---|---|---|---|---|---|---|---|---|---|
| Before Trance | 3 | 0 | 11 | 19 | 7 | 41 | 14 | 16 | 4 | 27 |
| During Trance | 28 | 12 | 22 | 30 | 12 | 31 | 10 | 12 | 11 | 12 |
| *before & during difference* | 25 | 12 | 11 | 11 | 5 | -10 | -4 | -4 | 7 | -15 |

| MEDIUM | 11 | 12 | 13 | 14 | 15 | 16 | 17 | 18 | 19 | 20 |
|---|---|---|---|---|---|---|---|---|---|---|
| Before Trance | 17 | 2 | 1 | 0 | 2 |  | 10 | 10 | 14 | 6 |
| During Trance | 7 | 4 | 11 | 1 | 4 |  | 4 | 3 | 15 | 20 |
| *before & during difference* | -10 | 2 | 10 | 1 | 2 | 0 | -6 | -7 | 1 | 14 |

** did not go into a trance state.

| MEDIUM | 21 | 22 | 23 | 24 | 25 |
|---|---|---|---|---|---|
| Before Trance | 17 | 3 | 1 | 3 | 0 |
| During Trance | 12 | 1 | 7 | 8 | 2 |
| *before & during difference* | -5 | -2 | 6 | 5 | 2 |

| | | |
|---|---|---|
| EEG Theta decreasing during trance | 8 | 35% |
| EEG Theta increasing during trance | 15 | 65% |
| | 23 | 100% |
| Error | 1 | |

**15/23 mediums, 65%, showed an increase in Theta activity during mediumistic trance.**

# PHYSICAL PHENOMENA WITH ENERGY

There is a "new," or should I say a form that has been "newly **re**-discovered," that is being used to bring into the séance room, Spiritual Psychic Physical Phenomena by using "enclosed energy". This method has been re-introduced, and is being re-experimented with by the people who started the Spiritual Scientist, and now run their own group, that being The SCOLE GROUP, in the Street Farmhouse, Scole, Diss Norfolk, IP21 4DR in the U.K. phone No. 01379 741 945. It is said to be safe for the Medium, as ectoplasm is not used. It is worth sending away for the leaflet, and the back copies of their experiments over the years, and their results.

This method is done by people sitting in a Circle around a table. On the table is a domed glass [clear], like the ones over a large carriage clock, mine is the minimum size to be recommended to be used. It is 12 inches tall by 8 inches wide [or a bell jar can be use] with an open bottom. The glass dome has to be a completely enclosed, domed, top inside, no opening at the top, only the base is open, but the wooden base on which the dome sits, has a ½ inch hole in the centre of it to allow the energy through, to expand and contract, the dome and wooden base are placed on a small open stand, the four legs are about 2 inches tall, the stand has to have a larger hole in it, to let the energy out of the base of the jar to go down to the table freely [I have a 2 inch hole in the centre of my stand], the whole structure is placed in the middle of the table. Then there is a clear quartz, crystal cluster with at the very least two points in it, placed on the table to bring up the power, these have to be held, and dedicated to the psychic phenomena required [e.g. physical phenomena; I have two crystal clusters, a large one 3 x 3 inches, dedicated to the development of Physical Phenomena, and the other of a medium size 2 x 2 inches crystal cluster, which is dedicated to the psychic development of all sitting in the Circle within the room] by the person who is running the Circle, at the start of the Circle when placing of the crystals on the table. **Do not change** the things you have dedicated the crystals for, so think for a while before dedicating the crystal cluster.

Four other single (about 1 ½ to 2 inches long) quartz crystals points are also on the table, placed at the 4 points of the compass [so get yourself a compass] to send out healing with, these are also dedicated; they are dedicated for the purpose of healing. The points of which are pointing inwards to the dome. Do not touch the glass dome between Circle sittings, as the person touching it discharges it [earthing it]. The power then has to be built up again over a period of time within the sitting Circle, always lift by the wooden stand.

A person I met at Stansted from Wales, who has used the dome and crystals, got Spirit Lights darting around in the room the first time her Circle use it, but this was in an established Circle and they had a full Trance Medium sitting in the cabinet. Also there was second dome, placed in another part of the room, that was charging up other crystals inside it, I do not know if this had anything to do with the Spirit Lights' immediate start.

Another lady from Egypt I met at Stansted said she had pictures on her T.V. screen [it was not even connected to the mains electric] whilst she was sitting alone with the glass dome and crystals, and wished she had, had a camera set up at the time to collect the evidence. I would not expect a miracle like that from mine as some people sit for years just to get Physical Phenomena, others in the other extreme get it after a few sittings if everything is right for Spirit.

The lady from Wales said, that music was use throughout the sitting after their affirmation/prayers, then meditation of quarter of an hour-ish, to build up the power in the room and Circle. The Circle went on for about two hours but no set finishing time was laid down at the start. The Circle was not closed until the power had gone down, [this can generally be felt by the sitters].

The Welsh Circle was held on set days, twice a week. Their Medium who sat in the cabinet had the gift of Trance Mediumship. When in Trance she then produced Direct Voice, so any advice was taken from Spirit that way. I have been told, it is not necessary to have a cabinet, or a Medium to have Physical Phenomena happen in this type of Circle. As it is new to me I cannot comment on this. It is now 1999. Best to let Spirit do what is necessary for the Spiritual Psychic Physical Phenomena With Energy, and just go through the motions of a normal Physical Circle only asking for Physical, saying prayers, meditate, then sing, let Spirit pick out the person to be the Medium who is used, if any. The one chosen by Spirit is not always the person who is chosen by the Circle, and can sometimes be two people picked out by Spirit, to be used as an instrument not just the one. When you buy crystals for your own Circle, they have to be charged up under the domed glass for about three to four weeks within the Circle while everyone is sitting before they become effective, and left under the dome for the full period of time, not touching the glass of the dome, apparently then having four times the strength of energy of normal uncharged crystals.

In the Scole group they had physical phenomena of different kinds happening most weeks. They have had Spirit forms, being shown, Spirit touches, Spirit lights, and Spirit voices on a crystal wireless, made from germanium (note the spelling) explained more in the EVP section.

The Scole Group have now disbanded but there is a book out called "The Scole Experiment" by Grant & Jane Solomon. ISBN 1-7499-2032-7 hbk Published by Piatkus.

# SLATE WRITING
## Psychography

This form of phenomena is classed as Physical. It seems to have fallen out of favour with Mediums at this time. It used to consist of a piece of slate, which had a border of wood around it, like a frame on a picture. The children used to use them at school to write on; the wooden border was for safety as the slate could be sharp. A small piece of slate, or pencil, [now we use chalk], was at the time given to each child with the classroom slate to write with. So it was with the Mediums, they had the slate with the small piece of slate [I will call it chalk from now on] to write with.

The slate was generally placed under the table facing upwards, flat against the top underside of the table, with the chalk (slate) placed in between the slate, and the tabletop underside. The Medium held the slate firmly against the table underside with their fingers; the thumb was on top gripping the tabletop topside, and was on show. [At this point the lights were generally turned low but all able to see the Medium's thumbs on the top of the table, or sometimes the lights off, using slate sandwich ]. Quite often the noise of the chip of slate (chalk) against slate was heard. When the session was over there was writing on the slate. Another way was to lay it out on the séance table; there were two slates with wooden edges tied together, with the chalk (sliver of slate) in the middle of the sandwich of slate. The slates nearly always when untied had writing on them, a message for the sitters. The sitters in the early days used to sit around a table in the different séances; some held hands, others had just their fingers touching. Try slate writing, experiment with a pair of small black boards or make your own slate drawing boards. About the size of an A4 or A5 sheet of paper, or 8 inches x 10 inches.

Other documented slate writing séances had the table covered with a heavy tablecloth so it formed a cabinet type of environment [encapsulated, enclosed psychic power and in a darkened space]. The Medium held the slate under the table with one hand; the other hand of the Medium was on the tabletop. Sometimes a sitter had their single hand on the slate as well, so they could feel the writing by Spirit taking place.

There are some hinged slate boards [wooden edged] and a slate board with Spirit writing on it owned by the tutor/Medium Lionel Owen, and many more séance things in the museum at Stansted Hall college.

Most Mediums have to develop themselves over a period of time in the power of the Circle, while meditating for their own spiritual awareness, some of the better Mediums regularly meditate alone at set times every day as well, to gain a lot more within their own link development. It is up to you yourself to ask for the gifts that you want to be developed while meditating. As far as I can see, nothing is guaranteed with Spirit only their love light as we do not seem able as yet to have a reliable system, that is a two way link to guide each one of us individually. Spirit it seems, have to try and do their best with each individual Circle and each individual Medium, some being a better link than others. The vast majority of us mortals have to work hard at our development. The natural Mediums are few and far between. Remember we all have the ability of Mediumship but most have let it lapse over the period of time throughout our lives before it was ever recognised.

Remember to ask for development while you sleep as well each night.

Each night after my prayers sincerely thanking the Divine Spirit for all that has gone on in that day, I personally give Spirit permission to use me as an open vessel to help make me a better link with Spirit, to continue to develop my psychic and spiritual ability in every way within me as I sleep, asking sincerely for it to come with only goodness, kindness, love, truth, within the true Divine Light of Spirit and to blend in peaceful loving harmony of Spirit of the highest realms, letting me have a good nights sleep as well. I ask to see, hear and feel Spirit better in every way, so letting me prove, and show to others, there is a life after our so called death on this lower vibration plain.

# AUTOMATIC WRITING
# INSPIRATIONAL WRITING
# SPIRIT WRITING

A lot of people mistake inspirational writing with automatic writing. Inspirational is when something within you inspires you to put pen to paper and a flow of words come out on a page. This could be an inspiration from the World of Spirit or it could be from your higher self. A lot of people in this world get inspired to write books of glowing quality. This should not be confused with definite Automatic Writing from the World of Spirit where the link between the vessel/Medium being used is constant and irrefutably not the work of the earthly vessel/Medium. The confusion comes in when anyone starts off in trying to gain the gift, "is it me, is it them (Spirit)?" being asked all the time, this is how it should be until that definite proof comes in the way of a different hand writing, different words being used that are not in the vessel/Medium's repertoire, or words of a language that the Medium does not know. Also the Medium should in time as others have done in the past, be able to just balance the writing implement [pen, pencil, crayon, etc.] on part of the hand to take the weight of the pen/implement to make it slightly easier for those in Spirit to put the words down on paper.

For Automatic Writing you have to have patience as you have to have with all psychic phenomena, sitting with no thoughts in your head [well trying not to, stilling the mind as much as is possible, the best way I have found is to look into your third eye into the colour, the void or the divine white light of Spirit] with a piece of paper and a pencil in your hand for hours on end. A lot of people say that you have to have the pencil in between fingers of the hand, that you do not hold the pencil/pen within your own normal circumstances, rubbish! Try writing with your own hand and try with all different combinations that you can and your handwriting comes out similar to your own normal handwriting. Yes you can fake it but try to keep it up for hours.

When you are Automatic Writing, the handwriting comes out totally different to your own handwriting **BUT**, and it is an important **BUT!** the hand writing style is **not** like your own, importantly <u>**it is constant, consistent,**</u> and <u>**it is sustained**</u>.

Some people write with their eyes closed, some blindfold themselves (which is best so you cannot look at the work being done and it does not detract from your Spirit link), others go into what can only be called a dreamy state or an alter state of consciousness/awareness, some in different deeper levels of Trance. Some use the ectoplasmic power of Spirit to write with a Spirit formed hand, but this is going into the realms of strong Physical Phenomena. Some sitters need others in the room they are working in, this is to help with the power build up for their work, try at first developing with a partner if you want to. Some writers get the impression of the words just before they are written [this is classed as inspirational writing], others don't. Some feel a sensation down their arm and hand, others don't. As I keep saying we are all individuals in every section of Mediumship. No two people it seems are totally alike in their contacts with Spirit. Some write slowly while others write at an unbelievable speed, where the pen/pencil does not leave the paper and the letters are all joined together. Some write right to left; others write left to right. Others are known to have written in languages that they do not understand. Some do what is called mirror writing, the type of writing you have to read in a mirror after it is complete. You never know what to expect with Spirit Contact, at least done the correct way it is always of a good nature. Quite often very educational in the way it happens.

Try putting down the sensations you felt; when it happened; all the things that were around you and the conditions of the weather and the room in a diary, that way you will know how to react if it happens again.

The best way to develop is in a Circle situation where there is more than enough power there within that Circle so a person can develop quicker, and the Automatic Writing Mediums who are working are not drained by having to use only their own power, but on saying that most automatic writers develop on their own in the quiet of their own home.

One of the most famous automatic writers the Rev W. Stainton Moses, the automatist, got his automatic writing to such a level that he could read a book or do others things while the Spirit Control who was doing the writing through him just kept going and going. That is how much his own mind was detached from the script being written. That is what is to be strived for by all. He made all sorts of tests for himself to make sure it was genuinely from Spirit, and not himself coming in with his own ideas from the subconscious, in other words he had a still mind, or a mind detached from the functions of Spirit. Even he said his writing was slow to start with and he had to look at it as he was writing at first, but as time went on the speed went up, and the unseen power controlling it, got more efficient. That is what all who try Automatic Writing should do; they should not try to kid themselves and others that they have this God given gift.

Rev. W. Stainton Moses was an English Protestant Priest/Minister born on the 5th November 1839 in Lincolnshire, England. He became one of the of the last centuries greatest automatic writers. His books were published in the name of M. A. Oxon.

He tested himself many a time by putting a pen in each hand and one fixed in the toes of each foot so he had four pens going at once, all four writing something different in totally different languages and in a different hand writing. Yes quite often he used to write in languages he did not understand, it might happen to you. Lets face it there are a great many more people that speak a foreign language to us that have died and gone to the higher realm than people of our own language, no matter where you live in this world.

Let Spirit take control fully, it is only trust that is needed. A graphologist would be able to say without a shadow of doubt that the handwriting was not of the person's with the pen/pencil in their hand. But do not take on board or should I say do not believe everything that comes through from Spirit as there are many unhappy souls [lets put it that way kindly]; who have passed on before and they can come through trying to guide you along the wrong path, this is why being sincere is so important. I always ask for Spirit to come with only goodness, kindness, love and truth, and me to work in the peaceful Divine Light within the loving harmony of Spirit of the highest realm and that and only that to come around me when working with Spirit, always sincerely asking to blend in peaceful loving harmony with them, and even then I double check. Never go along with people who come through to tell you or others to change completely your way of life, unless of course it is sensible for you to do so.

Please think and be sensible if you have a go at it, the inspirational thoughts of your own can come into the equation. Look at the musicians of many years ago who wrote musical scores, painters, writers, play writers, artists who also lived years ago. They probably had help from above and a link with their higher self, and not a direct link to Spirit for their output on to canvass or paper. But what is Spirit? You are and you can link with Spirit on different levels make sure it is with the highest.

What I have been told by others, you should first write your passage out fully [that which is written by your Spirit Control] then look at it, do not examine the writing as you are doing it as this puts a block in the way of your progress (you will be thinking of what you are doing, not automatically doing the writing). Go over the writings at a later time, say ten-twenty minutes after you have finished and are back to normal mentally.

Some Mediums who use this method of communication with the Spirit World can do written readings for sitters. They started giving readings after they had become proficient, and it was proven to them beyond a shadow of doubt that the communicator was not part of themselves.

Remember if you do have a go at automatic writing for sitters, that the writing for the sitter and all that is contained in the writing belongs to the hand that wrote it. In a few cases contested through the courts in Great Britain and Europe, it is the Medium who wrote the words down that own the copyright of the message. Yes! It is worth your time and effort as it can mean such a lot to others getting a letter, a word off their loved ones, those who have past into the higher realms. It can bring a great deal of comfort to them.

The ancient and present day Japanese, Chinese and Eastern Asian people used/use a suspended stick not held by anyone to write in the sand, others balanced the stick on their hand, the Medium is not controlling it, they are just the instrument of Spirit, that is their way of automatic writing. This way of working is generally done in Trance, after a prayer and/or ceremony. So as you can see there are many ways of trying this form of Mediumship.

Here a few pointers for you to try if you would like to develop automatic writing.

At a set time of the day, each day for half an hour, to an hour (at the **very, very least** three times a week) sit with a marker in your hand, a pen or pencil or crayon, holding it very gently, a piece of paper or preferably an **A4 pad** or larger. This is because you do not know how much is going to come through in the way of writing at one sitting, a drawing, a message, or could become a small book, anything.

Be passive; do not try to do anything with your hand, that is Spirit's job.

Start by saying a prayer.

Sincerely ask for goodness, kindness, light, love and truth, to be with you all the time, ask to blend in the Divine Light within the peaceful loving harmony of Spirit from the highest realm.

Ask for what you are looking for, a message for someone, poetry, whatever, a contact to help you help others, or just let Spirit decide, just ask to be used as their instrument in the form of automatic writing. Keep asking over and over and over in your head through thought to bring Spirit near and then wait.

Sit in the quiet with your pencil in your hand placed on the paper. Some people have developed whilst reading a not too heavy reading book to pass the time. I do not know whether listening to a low radio programme, or light music would work as I have not heard of it being used when developing but I should imagine it might be all right. I would say T.V. is a no, no. The reason being, it puts out a lot of radiation into the room and it would in my opinion interrupt or interfere the link, but again it is up to you. Others just sit with their eyes closed **asking sincerely constantly** through thought for the link with Spirit. I would suggest at intervals, keep on asking Spirit to come closer to you and help. Keep encouraging them in their efforts. Also for lengths of time try to have a passive, a still as possible mind, letting Spirit take control of your hand. It can start with little swirls and lines that you have not controlled. Do not pretend or lie to yourself as this is negativity and this can stop any development.

Do not analyse, criticise or think about the writing as you are doing it, just accept it.

When you finish thank the higher vibration level [Spirit] for coming around you and helping you to develop.

DO NOT BELIEVE EVERYTHING THAT COMES THROUGH. If any persons who have been bad on the earth plane, ones who have been blatant liars, or ones who try to make out if you do certain things against your fellow man which is evil will be to your advantage; if that sort of a person comes through, ask them to leave with a kind, sincere prayer, that will help them on their way to a higher level where they will progress upwards into the Divine Light, thanking them for coming but saying firmly in your own mind you do not want them to ever come again, this is why **it is so important** to sincerely ask for goodness, kindness, truth, love, light, and peaceful loving harmony from Spirit of the highest realms. Remembering at all times, you are the one in control. If you get warnings, suggestions, prophecies for the future. Keep them but do not believe them until you find out who and what sort of a person you are getting the writings from and whether you can trust them, and even after that you should always test, test, check, check and double check. Post them to yourself after taking a copy of the writing. That way people will believe what is written is truly from those in Spirit.

When you as a Medium become attuned to the higher vibration level with your writing. It is possible to write in a foreign language to that of your own language, the language being of the person controlling the hand of the Medium, and the Medium's hand writing mimics the handwriting of the control as well. There are many people in America and Europe who have had this ability in times gone by. Read about them in the older Spiritualist books in your libraries. I have met some people who do automatic writing now. They were on the courses I attended at the Arthur Findlay College at Stansted Hall Essex U.K.

There are many different types of people doing this sort of thing so do not think they are special to start doing this automatic writing. Quite often Spirit start with what I would call doodling, it might be dots, squiggles, a few words, and drawings, in fact anything might start it off. One person I was speaking to at Stansted Hall only got a name for weeks on end, that stopped then came bits of sentences, and she has or should I say her contact through her has started now writing all sorts of philosophy from the Spirit World. If you start to get scrolls or pictures that does mean something, and for you it means you are starting along the right road. Do not think it is always going to be the family or close friends that come back to talk to you, remember there have been millions of very kind and NOT SO KIND people who have passed before your family and friends, so weed out the worst; and stick to the best. It is always best to start off in the correct way by loving prayer. Leave those not so nice people up there in the nether-land ready to be helped and perhaps rescued by Sprit and taken into the Light. When finished thank the Spirit Helpers for coming and arrange the time of your next meeting.

Automatic writing is where Trance comes into the way a Medium can gain a stronger link for Spirit to prove there is life after our so-called death. Trance can for some Mediums encompass a great many of the fields of Mediumship with the help of those guiding influences in the world of the "unseen" helpers. Over and over, and over again and again and again, Ask, ask, ask, ask, those in the World of Spirit for what you want of them.

There are a few books from the Automatic Writing Mediums of the past, two most recent that I have read are :- **Beyond the Horizon By Grace Rosher. 1961.** [published for the churches' Fellowship for Psychical Study by James Clarke & Co. Ltd. 33, Store Street London, WC1. Grace must have been a remarkable Medium, one I certainly admire. She did not go to the people who would have taken her gift as normal into the realms of Spiritualism. Because she was brought up a Christian she went to the Churches' Fellowship for Psychical Study because she was a sceptic, she did not believe in her gift, she was very cautious and because of her upbringing. At the time she did not like the thought of being called a Spiritist.

Her friend Gordon Burdick died and she had communication off him as she says, by telepathic communication. This book was written four years after the communications first came to her in a mixture of stumbling, urgency, and with excitement as she puts it.

Her first automatic writings were faltering and not clear to whose hand writing it was, but as time went by the proof within the wording was over whelming and the handwriting then definitely not hers, (Spirit moved her hand along the page, as the words were told to her) the fountain pen at first was held ordinarily as she would do in her every day life, then she was told by Spirit to hold the pen in between her finger and thumb very lightly, then after an argumentative **thought with Spirit** (if your so clever lets see if you can do it on your own), she just placed the pen **"balanced"** on her closed fist between her first finger and thumb, and Spirit, a Mr Gordon Burdick who did the writing with Grace Rosher as the instrument, used to lift the pen at each words ending. There are photographs in the book of Grace being used as the instrument with this method of the fountain pen balanced on her closed fist as it was normally happening. See photograph.

KEEWAYS    MEDITATION ONENESS  written by Roy Keeghan

GRACE ROSHER

The other book written in 1965, I have just picked up from a second hand bookshop is called **Swan on a Black Sea by Geraldine Cummins** who lived in Glanmire, County Cork, Ireland. Over 40 different communicators came through this lady. Her writings were tested by "The Society for Psychical Research" in the period of 1957-1961. In this book are writings through Geraldine Cummins from another Automatic Writing Medium who is in the World of Spirit having gone to the higher realms, "died", in 1956, she used the nom deplume of Mrs Willett. When living, this Medium a Mrs Charles Coombe Tennant, was also tested by the S.P.R. Mrs Coombe Tennant (Willett) when on this earth plane of ours was also a very good Trance Speaking Medium.

Battling Bertha [Harris] was told of her house being flooded while she was two hundred miles away from it. The pen she was holding wrote what it wanted not what she had intended to write. She had to ring the water board from where she was and they confirmed it. Bertha and her husband Robert quickly returned home.

Emanuel Swedenboug was a scientist who lived in Sweden in the $18^{th}$ century who also did Automatic Writing. In his diaries he says his hand when doing Automatic Writing had a mind of it's own, and quite often wrote about things he disagreed with.
All of these automatists sat for Spirit at a set time, started off with a sincere prayer and finished with one, thanking those in Spirit for their time and effort in developing the gift given to them.

A way of trying to have a go at Automatic Writing in a one to one situation with a friend is to get yourselves seated comfortably sitting opposite each other. One person says a prayer to Spirit, then both linking into Spirit by meditating, both encouraging Spirit within the mind to come closer and help. Do this for about five minutes, then one person picks up the pen/writing implement (with eyes open or closed) both go into and altered state of awareness. The one with the pen/pencil asks Spirit to be allowed to be used as an open vessel for the work of Spirit to communicate through the pen/pencil or writing implement they are holding. The pen holder then tries to still their mind by looking into the light in the third eye area and become part of it and then leaves the rest to Spirit. The other person opposite asks of the Spirit World for them to be filled up like an open vessel to bring in the Power of Spirit into themselves and when full to overflowing for it to be sent out to the person sitting opposite to help them in their quest to automatically write with the help of their link in Spirit. They keep on asking for the help for the person over and over again until they finish.
This can be done in a group situation, where again one person holds the pen, who then goes into a state of altered awareness asking Spirit for help and giving permission to be used as a vessel for communication through the pen. The others link with Spirit asking within their minds to be filled up as an open vessel with the Power of Spirit, when after a set time about five to ten minutes. They unselfishly ask Spirit within their minds to send that power to the person holding the writing implement, and all sincerely ask Spirit to help the person in their quest. This they keep on doing until the session has

KEEWAYS    MEDITATION ONENESS  written by Roy Keeghan

...ot try using the planchette. In the 1870's there was a book written and advertised as being written by the planchette, it was called "Destiny of Man" by Fred Griffin.

### **SPIRIT WRITING** within a séance situation is best describe by Harry Edwards in his book "The Mediumship of Arnold Clare" from page 42-47.

During the sittings of the Home Circle in March and April 1940 the Guide was asked whether he thought it possible that if a pencil and paper were provided in the Circle written messages could be given. "Peter" agreed that it could probably be achieved, and was worth trying.

Accordingly a small writing pad was laid on the floor of the Circle together with a pencil; and at the first sitting we heard the pencil scratching over the paper, which was then torn off the pad. Eagerly we awaited the end of the Circle to see what had been written, and found that two pieces had been detached from the pad; on one was written, "John greets you" and the other "God bless you all, Peter". One was heavily written (John's), whilst Peter's was much more lightly scrawled.

This seemed a good start, and for some weeks we never failed to put pencil and paper in the Circle, and each week we received two or three different messages. Some were messages of affection from our loved ones; two were sentences foretelling developments in the war both of which turned out to be correct with regard to developments in the East. "Little Peter" seemed to be delighted with this method of communication and never failed to write some simple message, which he sometimes accompanied by a drawing. One of these drawings is particularly good, having regard to all the difficulties under which it was accomplished.

The drawing is of a flower (intended for a carnation) with a 3 inch stem and leaves, against which leans a small ladder. At the foot of the ladder is drawn a small elfin figure. The remarkable part of the drawing lies in the fact that it was drawn in the dark and yet not one line overruns another; it is perfectly spaced in every way and is right in the centre of the page. Had it been drawn in full light it could not have been spaced more perfectly. Anyone who has tried to write in the dark will appreciate the remarkable result achieved by "Little Peter" under these conditions. The drawing took little more than five minutes and was the only one received that night; and during the time it was being done we could hear the pencil working at what seemed incredible speed. To hear the pencil moving over the paper naturally gave rise to the thought, "If we could only see it working" and the wish was expressed to "Peter". At the next sitting he promised to try and show us this phenomena illuminated by the slate (plaque).

The following week he kept his promise. The illuminated slate was lifted sufficiently to allow the light to spread over the floor immediately in front of it for about a foot. In this lighted space the Spirit operators placed the pencil and pad so we could see them quite easily. Slowly the pencil was raised by what appeared to be two small prongs or pincers, which slowly moved the pencil point to the blank paper. The pencil then began to move rapidly until a sentence was written and then the sheet of paper was detached from the pad. It was most fascinating to watch the movement of the pencil over the paper. After this we were given the opportunity of watching the experiment several times and in all cases the procedure was exactly the same.

We thought this method of message giving very helpful and in the later séances, where visitors were invited, a number of people received messages from their Spirit friends, which can be truly called "Letters from Heaven".

# PSYCHIC ART

Psychic Art and Spirit Drawing are a cross mix but I have put them in different categories. The reason I say this is because, both gifts need the Medium to be used as a link with the world across the veil and use an implement [a pen, pencil, brush, etc.] in the similar way.

Psychic Art is done by the Medium linking into Spirit in a light state of altered awareness using their clairvoyant imagery, some in a deeper state of trance than others. They then portray that image in their mind onto paper or other material, many using their own mind to control the hand, some don't only allowing Spirit to move them.

"Spirit Drawings" are done by Spirit without the awakened mind of the Medium coming into play and their eyes to see what they are doing as the drawing are quite often done in complete darkness and if in light, the Medium is blindfolded, BUT Spirit nearly always still needing the Medium in attendance. The

Medium is in a stronger sense of altered awareness (Deep Trance), many times the Medium is in an unconscious state of awareness or very deep Trance state not knowing until afterwards what went on
Spirit Drawings can also be done by Spirit alone without the need of the Medium's hand or feet being used, the implements for communication on paper, canvas or wood etc. being picked up by Spirit alone in the presence of a Physical Medium.
From the first time I saw Coral Polge the Psychic Artist, in Daulby Street church Liverpool; psychic art was something I would like to have done for people who need proof in the belief of life after death existing and also help people to come to terms with the passing of their loved ones into the higher vibrational level, showing them there is no death, life just carries on in another plane of existence. This I believe was being done through the clairvoyance of the Medium. The Medium drawing the images that were placed by Spirit in the mind of the Medium.
I started off trying this by enrolling in a part time art class at a college. Luckily at first I was left on my own to find out what I was capable of. What I wanted from that course was some hints on how to draw. I had taken a few magazines, coloured pencils, and an artists pad. When I got to the college, there were only very old age pensioners attending the class so right away I was out of the flow. The lady teacher sat us all down, and we all had to relate to the class what we individually were capable of, and what we would like to draw and achieve. I had never done any drawings of faces, so that was what I told her, and said I would like to draw faces. I did not have the remotest idea of how to draw the faces, nor how to get the faces that I was being given by Spirit in my mind, down onto paper for others to see.
I knew I had faces I could see in my head when the clairvoyance came through, all I needed to do now was to get some information on how to put the face on the paper. I did not feel confident enough to explain my Mediumship gift that I had, hence the magazines to copy from.
At the start of my drawing in the college, I closed my eyes for about a minute in front of all there as though I was thinking, looking for inspiration. In effect I was asking Spirit to guide me and give me all the help I needed for the job in hand. I said my prayer, asking for Spirit to come closer and help in the drawing task ahead, asking for Spirit to come only with goodness, kindness, love and truth, to come within the Divine Light of Spirit and to come from the loving harmony of Spirit of the highest realms and let me prove there is life after our so called death through the medium of drawing on this paper with this pencil. I got a few faces in my mind, which I should have tried to draw, instead I copied onto the pad a photo/picture of a kindly lady I had with me. I started on the hair [not, how artists who are taught do it] then worked down the face as I was drawing. I even surprised myself never mind the teacher. She said are you sure you have never done a portrait before, it was very good? **Well I DID** have the help off those upstairs in the World of Spirit. The only artwork I had ever done was at school it was silly drawing, at that time I was rubbish at it, I certainly had never done a face. At the college the next few times when I attended the art class, I copied a photograph of John Thaw the actor, again not bad. Then I copied the photograph of my girl friend. I had just split up with her at that time; again you could see the likeness. This is where the teacher stepped in with her advice. It was from that time I started going wrong with the drawings, she was trying to put her way of drawing onto me and it did not work at all. At times she would take my pencil off me and draw an oval for the start of the face and say this is the way you do it, draw another small oval for the nose, another for the ear. This way of working was a new departure from what I was seeing through my thoughts. At the start I saw shadows, different shades of colour, lines of shading that formed a chin, darker markings that formed a hole in the ear, not an oval that had to be changed half way through to a head, an oval changed into an ear, or a nose. I was doing things all wrong according to her not going through the correct procedures. I tried her way and went down hill from there on, forgetting what I was there for. I realised later that I was not asking for help from Spirit, not trusting Spirit, not trusting myself. I then because of her, started thinking of drawing not linking first, so I left, not really having the confidence now to have a go again at college.
What I am saying here is; it should be trust yourself and Spirit; not some person who thinks their way is the only way. It knocked me down to such an extent that I have never done any other portraits for myself or for other people. BUT do not take my unfortunate situation in 1990 stop you going to an art class and getting some experience of other people's way of working; you must and practice, practice, practice. I feel if you can get this form of drawing of the images out of your head correct, it is one of the best forms of evidence for people that there is life after our so called death.
Remember to start sincerely with a positive prayer for help, and guidance with loving peaceful harmony, a special thought in your mind to Spirit. [I have my eyes closed to see them] See Spirit guiding you,

being around you, helping you, being in loving peaceful harmony as one with Spirit. Ask Spirit for an image of the person who needs to be recognised. Ask Spirit for the image to be held in your head for the length of time you need it to be there. It will stay if needed, as I found out. My normal clairvoyant images generally flashed through my mind at that time. Ask Spirit for help all the time you need it **and when you think don't**. When you have finished the job/drawing in hand thank Spirit for their help and guidance, asking them to come closer each time you work with them, making arrangements with Spirit for that time you are going to sit again to draw.

I finished a course in Stansted Hall, May 1999. Not a Course that I would have chosen for myself, but all sorts of circumstances pushed me into it and I ended up going on it. Spirit works in many unusual guiding ways. I had been told there were two tutors I would like to meet on the week's course they were the psychic artist Coral Polge, [I thought she might have helped me in my psychic drawing], and Swami Dharmananda Saraswati who I would liked to have met properly and got to know her and hopefully sat with. Coral Polge's husband was ill and she had to stay at home. Swami was ill with an eye problem. Only for the fact of me taking someone along with me in the car to Stansted, which is something I have never done before, I would have come home and gone on another course later in the year. I stayed there and I found out how to start drawing, just by trying with the help of Spirit whilst in the power of Stansted Hall. Just before that time I now know I had forgotten the one most important thing that I should have been doing and that was to always be thinking of and talking to Spirit within my thoughts, also that time I had forgotten to have **total trust in Spirit**.

I was in Janet Parker's group [a very good Medium and tutor], and I was asked to sit with my artistic equipment I had taken and have a go at drawing [a pad and a 4B pencil]. I closed my eyes, and asked within my mind for help from Spirit. I kept asking over and over within my mind for about five minutes. I was building the link stronger with Spirit as a lady who was on the platform was giving a demonstration of after life existence by giving a message to others in the group, while Janet was suggesting little helpful pointers to help with her Mediumship skills. I saw a person in my head and began to draw until the lady on the platform had finished. It was a profile drawing of a man but for me on looking back, it was a stiff drawing, just an outline with no personality. But the person recognised the man, he had passed on to the higher sphere some time earlier. I also got three names off Spirit, which I wrote down on the paper and they were accepted as correct and taken as evidence.

The next person was then up on the platform to practice their guided demonstration of Mediumship. I closed my eyes and did not get anything so I started asking over and over for help from Spirit; as I was staring at the paper, a foggy sort of a shadow came on the paper, so I started to follow the shadings with my 4B pencil; as I did this my eyes went out of focus as though I needed another pair of better glasses, my hand was working very quickly not giving me time to think of what I was doing, it turned out to be a man within a drawing of a round curly circle. The mouth was slightly wrong but it was recognised by the trainee Medium, but this person was still alive, but had been ill prior to the person leaving, [perhaps the curly ring will mean something for me in future drawings I will have to keep that in mind]. I also got another three names, which I wrote down, two were taken as evidence of after life, the single name was not recognised.

The next person up on the platform was a man who also was there for his skills as a Medium to be honed. I started drawing from the paper as the shadows now started to form a better shape of a head on the paper, my eyes were glazed again this time. This picture took a slightly different way of working as I had more information through my mind. I got a long hairstyle and a woman's face yet I was drawing a man's ten o'clock shadow where a man shaves around the chin. The more I did the shading on the drawing the more like a man it became. When the drawing had been finished it was a cross between a lady with a ten o'clock shadow and a man with long hair. I did not feel happy with it letting my mind come into the equation. But at the end I had a "feeling" to change the hair to short so I use the rubber. The Medium came down off the rostrum and he then told me that he could accept the person who was a man, in both short and long hair. He told me that this man had a lady like face also, so I should not have doubted Spirit. I also got two names he accepted both. That week I had headaches at the back and the right hand side of the head. I do not know if that was the power of my Mediumship getting altered, my brain getting attuned to the new vibration level or what. It certainly was not the booze, as I did not drink very much at all that week. (this I now know was my link with Spirit that needed my blood pressure altering for some reason, to get a stronger link connection adjusted someway within my brain. I believe Spirit was adjusting the brain linkage to have me closer to Spirit, something like tuning a radio or TV to the correct station)

The main points that this course left me with was; I did not need an art teacher to help me with psychic art, and the other was to always fully trust Spirit and to keep on asking with sincerity and encouraging Spirit over and over and over, again and again within my mind to come closer to help me with the task in hand.

Start with a prayer to those in Spirit asking them to help you and finish with a prayer of thanks arranging for those in Spirit to come again to help you when required.

I also made a lot of new friends from all over the world at Stansted that week. The power in Stansted Hall was totally different this week for me from the other weeks I have been there. It was a more of a gentle energy level but more mentally tiring. I was in bed very early 10pm that week which is unusual for me at Stansted. On the Trance and Physical weeks it has been a very high level of power energy for me. On those Physical weeks, I have been full of beans each night staying up until the very early hours of the morning (3-4am) and still getting up at 6.30am to shower.

# SPIRIT DRAWING and SPIRIT ART

This is something I have not as yet experienced, but there are a great many Spirit drawing in the museum at the Arthur Findlay College at Stansted Hall. One that stands out for me was done by Spirit through the Mediumship of "Mr Robson". He painted the picture called Psalms of Life. "Mr Robson" was blindfolded and in the completely darkened room he completed the oil picture in three, ninety-minute séances in 1890. The séances were in the home of another person who laid out the oil paints, brushes, linseed oil and turpentine that is what they use as thinners. On the finished oil painting appeared gilt this was not supplied by the homeowner "William Smallin". "Mr Robson" was an ordinary post office worker, who had never had artistic training. In his normal everyday state he had no skills what so ever of an artist.

There **were** (they have disappeared, I went to try and see them) some pictures in the church at Southport, Merseyside, England, done by Spirit through the Trance Mediumship of Lizzie and May, the "Bangs sisters." Who lived in Chicago U.S.A. in the late 1800 and early 1900,s. The sisters used to have séances with people who brought along the photographs of their loved ones, BUT NOT SHOWING the photographs to the sisters. They would proceed during the séance with the help of Spirit and by Spirit the sisters only being the instruments of the Spirit helpers produced a portrait of the person's loved one. I have heard there are no brush marks on the pictures. People do not know how it was done by Spirit. Many of these pictures were done in the light, in front of people, with just the hand of the sisters over the card. The way this was done and this has never been produced in this way since as far as I know. The ladies placed a blank sheet of paper in between two wooden framed canvasses that were placed together, then placed in front of the window whilst being held each side by Lizzie and May. With the daylight coming through the window the canvas allowed the light to pass through it so when the phenomena produced by the World of Spirit started, the drawing/portrait could be seen to build up before the sitters' eyes many being done in a very fast time of five minutes. The paintings when examined immediately after the séance were wet and done with what looked like a stippling effect as though it was blown on with some sort of an airbrush type of thing. What is surprising is that when the séance finished and sometimes over the following days, some of the paintings still changed, jewellery being added, details of the clothing being altered, the eyes of the person in the portrait being also altered some opened when they were closed and others closed when they were originally open. There was never any sort of trickery employed and as far as everyone who attended was concerned, nor could it have been in the circumstances. This particular phenomenon is a one off so it seems. Their pictures are on display at the Spiritualist Centre in Chesterfield, Indiana. U.S.A.

Another famous person who used to do drawings in a darkened séance room was David Duguid. His drawing was done in 30 seconds by Spirit while the light had been switched off. When the light was put back on, the drawing was there on the card, which had been placed under his hand. More of this subject and Spirit photography can be obtained from Mr Lionel Owen who lectures at Stansted Hall. Send your letters there for him or me, they will be passed on to him or me, if you include a stamped envelop, the college will put his address on it, mine is at the front of the book.

Another tutor I met, and had the good fortune to sit in her experimental group at Stansted Hall was Eileen Taylor. She showed the group there how to use a graphite stick or graphite pencil to draw with the help of Spirit. The only trouble was the extractor fan was on and I got a nasty shock from a sudden bang from the closing flaps when I was in Trance, so be careful if you try and link whilst in a Trance State **anywhere there might be sudden noises,** especially if you go into a **(true)** deep Trance state. I have been trying in my own way so I will now pass the method I now use, to you the reader.

Get yourself some large wide pointed graphite pencils, or graphite sticks (wrap these in masking tape half way to help reduce the mess that is generally put onto you fingers), preferably soft to medium in the sticks and 4b and lower in the pencils or perhaps the pastel pencils. Have a piece of paper on a fixed hard surface. (I use a sheet of A4 on a clipboard) Sitting comfortable with your eyes closed. Go into a link state with Spirit to the level of Trance or deep altered awareness, ask Spirit to help you in your quest of helping others, to prove there is life after death, to bring forward those in Spirit who would like to be remembered, and Spirit to help you become the link to be used with the drawing of those loved one who are across the veil so they can be shown to their nearest and dearest as proof that life continues. You give permission to Spirit to use you as an open vessel to be used by Spirit for the time necessary to draw what ever is put into your mind in that trance state. **STILL with eyes closed** better still, **blind folded.** You now start rubbing the graphite across the paper in the direction you are inspire to, varying the pressure as you and your Spirit Link feel it is necessary. (you should be looking into you third eye area into the light to let Spirit have the best use of the uncluttered mind. many times I get images there) As your own link gets stronger there becomes faces, sometimes figures, for others, perhaps a scene on the paper that will bring back a memory to a person who you are doing the drawings for. It is surprising how much comes through. Do not forget to say to Spirit you need help whist practicing, and remember to keep the drawing for a later date as Spirit might have given you images for someone you are going to meet in the future. Keep them tidy in a sleeved folder; **Spirit knows**.

If you do get images in your mind try drawing them with your eyes closed trusting in Spirit to place the pencil on the paper at the correct place. At first the results might be worse than you think they should be, but with practice, **Spirit will help you**. As you go deeper into a true Trance state, Spirit will take over from you and they will then have the knowledge (if you have been practicing regularly while linking) of how to manipulate your muscles necessary to put drawings onto paper. Please practice both ways, it is necessary to help Spirit to help you as much as possible; as long as you are truthful and sincere with yourself and Spirit, anything can be made possible.

Another method to try is with a mixture of either different coloured felt tips, colour pens, coloured pencils, coloured crayons, pastels, oil paints, water colours (with the paints I would suggest the use of a lot of different brushes at the ready) etc. there can be many coloured mediums/implements you could use and experiment with.

Place the coloured (I will call them **all** crayons for now) crayons on a table, bench or in a container near you. Blindfold yourself, then within your mind **sincerely** ask Spirit :- "Divine Spirit please help with the task of drawing to prove that life continues after our so called death, please only come with goodness, kindness, love, and truth, come within the Divine Light of Spirit and from the loving harmony of Spirit of the highest realms. Go into an altered state of awareness linking within the Light of Spirit within your third eye area. Let Spirit start at the beginning inspiring you to pick up a certain crayon then put it onto the paper and make a drawing of some sort, when you feel it is necessary, change the crayon and continue. Another way is to let Spirit completely take over you and then they can do the drawing totally on their own using you as their instrument. (with the blank mind that is always looking into the light in your third eye) BUT remember it is practice that makes it all happen. Always thank Spirit at the end with a prayer making arrangements for the next session.

If you would like to try experiments with your groups. Try Spirit/psychic art with three to six people in a group or Circle, one person to try the linking with Spirit to do art, by the graphite stick or pencil method. For that matter any form of drawing for Spirit, because it is the sitting in a spiritual power situation of Spirit when everyone there within the group links into Spirit that gives the extra bit needed for a kick into starting the flow for some people at the start. But I will just talk of the one method for now.

First every person in the group has to be sitting comfortable facing into the centre of the group or facing towards the one who is seated at the open end of a horseshoe shaped Circle, this is the person who is going to be the artist. All close their eyes. All in the group should link with Spirit, all of them asking Spirit to help with the task in hand, which is giving the power to the artist (who has the graphite in their hand and the paper on the firm surface), to help them link with Spirit and draw someone's loved one in the World of Spirit. After say about five minutes all except the artist, asks Spirit, to be filled up with the power of Spirit and to be used as an open vessel, sending the Power of Spirit they have within themselves to the artist, they should keep on asking throughout the sitting.

Keeping their eyes closed, the artist should try and go into a deep state of altered awareness (Trance State) linking with Spirit asking for the help in their task then leave the rest to Spirit using their (the artist's) arm to scratch the graphite across the paper in a way that it comes into their head with their link (eyes still closed). I cannot tell anyone nor will I be able to, which is the correct way as everyone is different in the way that they do everything in this life of ours, please experiment in everything. Children are very good at this, help them, use it as play thing as it comes very naturally to them. All children should be encouraged to develop at an early stage.

In the days gone by, 1860's, the painting Medium David Duguid, from Glasgow with his eyes closed and many times, blindfolded and he did his drawings in a Trance State. He did not charge for his séances and even at the early stages allowed strangers to sit with him. One séance he was painting on canvas, at an easel, in subdued gas light and the people there put a screen in between him and the subdued light to block out more of the light so it went down to a glimmer on his canvas, and even then placed a hand held screen in between his eyes and the canvas, yet he kept on drawing very fast and effectively. He drew a landscape with hills, lakes, mountains, steams, and waterfalls all with the help of Spirit. Notice it is generally in subdued or very little light that Spirit generally needs to work in when dealing with Physical Phenomena as in Direct Spirit Drawing in complete darkness. I must admit I do not fully know the reasons why.

## SPELLING OUT BOARDS

If you ever try the spelling out board, treat it with caution, it can bring in lies as a lot of people have found out to their mental cost, remember like attracts like. So let your Spirit Link be good and do not believe all that is given, always double check. The troubles start with fools and the unstable who try to mess around with the board. THIS IS MAINLY by those who treat it as a joke and do not go through the correct procedure. There has been very good proof given through the board of the after life existing, but on the other hand there have been mischievous messages given.

If you do use one, **always start and finish** with the asking out loud and **most importantly through thought to the world of the unseen** in the form of a prayer and ask for only goodness, kindness, love, truth, and blend in the true Divine Light of Spirit, within the peaceful loving harmony of Spirit of the highest realms; surround the Circle (or the table where the numbers and letters are) with light and love asking for help, protection, and understanding from those unseen helpers from the world of Spirit. Lots of people use letters of the alphabet, then YES, the numbers 1-9 and (some use a 0 some don't as the O in the alphabet suffices) then NO. All are written out on pieces of paper then they are placed in a circle or oval in that sequence on a flat shiny surface. A manufacturer made one and called it a "Ouija" board. Meaning "Oui", yes in French and "Ja", yes in German.

I personally do not recommend using the spelling out boards with a small upturned glass as a lot of people use. This is because the small upturned glass holds the energy enclosed inside it, so then the energy has no place to expand to when the power is very good and extra powerful, it can in some cases, make the glass explode and frighten people. Look at the newly **re-discovered** method of using a glass domed container in the Physical Circle using energy, the base is wooden BUT it has a round 1/2 inch hole in middle of it for somewhere the expanding energy to go to, when it gets too much for the glass dome to hold. So please use a planchette, when using the spelling out board, anyone can see one and how it was designed many years ago, they have two in the Arthur Findlay College, museum at Stansted Hall.

A planchette is a triangular or heart shaped (most widely used) piece of wood with three casters and a pointer to pick out the letters. The one at the college has a brass pointer attached to it at the pointed end. The pointer is used for spelling out words on a spelling out board, when all the participants place their fingertips very lightly and gently on it.

Another type of planchette has two/three casters attached, and a holder at the pointed end for the pencil or fine, fibre tipped, pen for Spirit to write out messages, or Spirit can use it to draw many different sorts of pictures, when one (a Medium or budding Medium) or all the participants place their finger tips very lightly and gently on it, after saying their prayers to Spirit.

I have heard about a planchette being used that had only small posts with a piece of felt glued on the base of them instead of casters, but this sort could only be used on a very shiny, polished surface.

These two designs of planchette can be used safely on your own to communicate with Spirit [But they are hard to get moving with one person if not developed, remember you have to start somewhere]. Use the spelling out board with a positive, caring and sincere attitude. Start and finish with prayer, also give thanks to the people in Spirit when they come to the Circle, and then all should be well for all concerned. Start by sitting around in a Circle with the sitters' finger/fingers gently on the planchette, after the prayer, start asking questions one at a time out loud, asking for your unseen friends to come to the Circle and communicate, sometimes a question has to be repeated a great many times to start the planchette moving. Remember one question at a time; do not go on saying different questions because one does not get the planchette moving. Have a pen and paper ready to write down what the pointer is showing you all. Do not push or pretend the planchette will move if you are positive and sincere. Most start off with "is there any one there to communicate with us". Then asking the name. Be wary of people who have the whole of the hand on the planchette [they can turn and manipulate the direction of the planchette] or ones who press and push, [you can sometimes see the pressure of the fingers that turn white] use one or two **fingertips only.**

It is the same with the planchette with the pen in it, instead of having around the board on a table, on which are pieces of paper with the alphabet "A-Z, numbers "Zero, 1-9", and "yes, no" at either side of the board, you just have the "pen holding planchette" marking out letters, drawings or messages on a piece of paper. Do not run away with the idea that the spelling out board is a new invention, it has been used for many thousands of years, there is documented evidence that the ancient Egyptians used to use one and that they also used a pointer that was dangled over a ring of letters and numbers, something like a dowser is doing when they channel their energy into their personal pendant.

# MECHANICAL SPELLING OUT MACHINES

In the early 19$^{TH}$ century, a machine called a "**Reflectograph**" was being used for communication with those on the other side of the "Veil" (in Spirit). This machine was bulky, and not suitable for carrying around from house to house. So a group of three people came together in 1930 and formed the "Ashkir-Jobson Trianion". For the soul purpose of researching, and experimenting with different mechanical ways of the contacting of Spirit, to prove there was indeed life after our so-called death. This group used different ways, a wide array of instruments, some home made vibratory tests, photography, thermometers, and anemometer, etc. The group consisted of Mr George Jobson, Mr B. K. Kirkby, and A. J. Ashdown. The lighter machine was eventually made, and they called it the "**Communigraph**," using the patented drawings of the "Reflectograph" machine and adapting them.

Sitting with the "Reflectograph" the long wait of three years, praying and meditating, eventually paid off using the "Reflectograph" and the Physical Mediumship of a Mrs L. E. Singleton, who was in deep Trance at the time, and her feet and hands were securely bound onto a chair in a cabinet, the "Reflectograph's keyboard was placed outside. Mrs Singleton had a guardian and communicator who was an African Zulu Chieftain "Karahnuta"; he guided the sitters along in their quest. Mrs Singleton after the long wait brought forth an ectoplasmic hand, which pressed the keys, and lit up the lights of the letters on a board, to advise the group in their quest.

The "Reflectograph" looks like a very large typewriter keyboard, or organ keyboard and it was the size of an organ; fifteen keys on the top level and fifteen keys on the bottom level; with a backboard of squares, which light up individually for all to see as the individual lettered, or numbered keys, were pressed by the operator in Spirit.

At the séance Mrs Singleton went into Trance some hymns were played on the gramophone, time was given for those in Spirit to build up the power, then the materialised hand of "Ethel" the Spirit Operator was slowly formed. The hand played on the keyboard so as to get used to it, then rang a bell, which was attached to one of the keys to tell all, "Ethel" was ready to start, then the start of the communication began. The bell rang [by Spirit] in between each word. When the message was finished for a particular person, there was a blue light in the shape of a star that came on when Spirit pressed a certain key. And so it continued along those lines, until the sitters with the help of those in Spirit put together all the information needed to build another machine that was reasonably lightweight. The group named this new machine a "Communigraph".

Each one of the newly made "Communigraphs", as they were completed, went to the "Beacon Sanctum" to be consecrated. There, they had special sittings conducted by the wardens, and helpers, to find out the Spirit Operators who would be using the individual machine. They were chosen by Spirit, who usually pick out relatives, or special friends of the group who were going to use it (these operators of course, were in Spirit themselves). The warders and helpers also helped with the training of the operators over periods of weeks, doing trails. The reasons being, each group when they took delivery of the "Communigraph," had an operator in Spirit, who had a slight knowledge of the machine; they had been trained in the use of it. This way the "Communigraph" could be used in a normal home Circle, by ordinary people/sitters, none of whom needed any special psychic, or mediumistic powers. This machine it has been found can be used by ordinary Circle even now, there is one in the museum at Stansted Hall, and this has been used a few times there in Circles.

The "Communigraph" looks like a round table, with a square hinged glass opening at the top, to gain access to the wiring of the bulbs inside. The glass screen is covered in red plastic so the lettering and the bulbs are invisible to the sitter's eyes. The lettering shines out in red, when the bulbs are lit by the contact being made by the counter weighted pendulum ball in the partially enclosed chamber when it connects to the brass "studs"; on which are the lettering; on the lower circular platform, which is called the "dais". There is a large chamber underneath the table top to house the components, and the mechanical working parts of the unit, the lower half being open, but it is low enough to hide under the wooden skirt the pivoted rotating arm of the counter balanced brass arm. The contact, and the ball can be seen, as can the "stud" lettering. The pivoted arm is extremely free working, but limited in movement, so that when the ball is rotated round the "dais" by Spirit until the ball is directly over the desired letter "stud", it is then lowered by Spirit, to make a contact, which lights up on the top of the "Communigraph". Each leg has adjusting screws on their bases to make the "Communigraph" level on any surface. The pivoted arm is adjusted so it is approximately a millimetre above the "studs" and able to rotate freely without touching the "studs".

A panel in the centre of the hinged top can also be lit by a switch under the surface of the table.

There are thirty-one contacts ["studs"], which are embedded in the lower round "dais" about an inch away from the edge. These are the full alphabet, yes, no, interrogation, star [which indicates the word has finished being spelt by Spirit], and the bell, which tells the sitters, the communication with Spirit has started and finished.

The most important part of the equipment is the vibrator or "soul".

The vibrator also acts as a timer, giving signals every 40 seconds when the central panel is on, and every 37 ½ minutes during the sitting, which is two in the hour and a quarter [then considered the length of the sitting]. The setting or the buzzer can be altered at the discretion of the leader of the Circle sitting.

In order not to startle the sitters when the buzzer sounds, the central panel is designed to light up just before it activated, and then the panel light is immediately switched off.

When used in the Circle of sitters; this machine is only as good as the sitters, the Spirit Helpers, Spirit Guides, Spirit Controls, (harmony and sincerity) and the instrument itself, as is any machine like a computer, typewriter, etc. All there sitting in the séance, should be in loving peaceful harmony with each other. Not just then in the Circle, but in their every day lives, this applies to every sitter, in every séance Circle.

The sittings were done at first in the dark then after the link was made with Spirit and it was felt the power was strong enough, the dimmed, deep red light was used.

The Ashkir-Jobson Vibrator.

It is said that vibration is the key or link that binds the World of Spirit and that of the earth plain. So it has been for centuries. As said before the "Trianion Group" did many experiments with vibrations amongst other things.

They came to many feasible conclusions :-

That all sitting in the Circle, MUST be sincere in peaceful, loving harmony.

The group looked at the music in churches, and the gatherings of people in most religions of the world. The singing in séances, home Circles, physical Circles. Playing of gramophone music, old hymns, old songs, and some modern. Through experimentation they concluded that; some we like and enjoy immensely, but they can sometimes only bring to those in the Spirit realm, vibratory disturbance. This means that only parts of music are stimulating to Spirit. Only certain parts of the tune are potent as he puts it.

Harmony so sweet to us sometimes causes disagreeable reaction to those in the higher spheres of life.

That of a long sustained note is much better. Look at the Eastern religions, where the Holy Men chant in a deep, droning, monotonous manner.

The sound of the tuning fork is the most powerful influence [the one of the frequency of lower "A" gave the note most appreciated by Spirit], with the exception of the double-diapason note from a large organ pipe.

The vibration of the "vibrator", was the single most effective source of development that helped the link with Spirit.

The tuning fork in the "vibrator", is set into oscillation by winding up a clockwork mechanism, and tuning in by a controlling handle. The "vibrator" then sends out sonorous sustained vibration of great power, but with very little sound, thus causing strong waves to be generated into the surrounding atmosphere for about 2 or 3 hours. {I think personally a tape recorder or CD player of superior quality **might** succeed in making, and holding the sound for a length of time, perhaps a good computer programme of quality, and a good quality set of speakers **might succeed**.] It might be worthwhile trying these methods out, to help Spirit come closer earlier in an ordinary Development Circle, Trance Circles, and Physical Circles. I might try and make a tape or CD (which I think would be better because of the longer length of time CD's or now DVD's have just come in this last year; time for me is the factor) for that purpose.

**Using the "Communicator"**

Every sitter should be a person that lives their lives by being good, sincere, clean, and harmonious. To be in peaceful loving harmony with all there sitting. Be well balanced, be positive and **sincere** at the séance, no others should be invited. Only those who will maintain sympathy, restraint, and implicit obedience to the Circle leader to be invited. Any highly sceptical, supercilious, exacting persons, or those under those under the influence of excessive emotion, should not be invited to take part in these sittings.

The "Communicator" should be set on a firm surface, and levelled by the screws on the four legs.

The long brass beam set so it freely turns about the axis. The ball contact pointer should be riding about 1 to 2 millimetres above the contact "studs" on the "dais".

The leader takes their seat at the side opposite the opening end of the top glass door flap, the hinged end.

The leader switches the red light on in the centre of the "Communicator". This light is switched on at the beginning, at the end, and if needed at any time there is a disturbance in the Circle.

The Vibrator is started and might need adjusting during the séance.

There is a dimmer on the lights, if needed during the séance.

There is an electric chime for Spirit to use at the end of each word spelt.

Do not ever place anything on the "Communicator".

Place the people sitting, positive and negative as in any Circle, or at the discretion of Spirit.

It is recommended that a piece of paper is placed over the red light in the middle of the table so each light comes through the appropriate letter and not confuse the sitters.

A person should be given the task of writing all the words given as the sitting progresses.

All should sit with their hands on the knees, palms turned upwards.

It greatly assists in the building up of suitable conditions if there is a special room set apart for this purpose.

Start always in the same way, with the same opening hymn, or record. Music can be used, but if the vibrator is used it is not necessary, as some might prefer to sit quietly.

Light conversation can be carried out, BUT arguments, controversy, back biting, nastiness, all should be ruled out. The development of the Circle is very greatly impeded by not being punctual, and the leader of the Circle should make sure every person is there to begin at the appropriate prearranged time.

Any member of the Circle, who is consistently a bad time keeper, being late, irregular in their attendance, and shows the least signs of declining interest, zeal, and begrudges coming to the Circle should be ordered by the leader, not come again to the Circle.

All should then be standing and holding hands around the "Communigraph". The light put out. Then the light of the central panel of the "Communigraph", switched on.

Any interruptions by a sitter should not be encouraged, as they can curtail the previous question's answer.

Questions should only be put when the starlight is on signifying that previous message has been completed by Spirit.

It is the usual practice for the Spirit Operator to pass the ball around the "dais" a few times and over the "studs" making a few practice letters.

When the friends in Spirit are ready for the first communication, they ring the chime and light the star in the top panel. All this should be explained out loud to the sitters, guides, and helpers on both sides after the invocation referred to below.

The following notes were dictated by a Guide from the higher plain to members of "The Ashkir-Jobson Trianion", on the occasion of the dedication of the instrument, and the latter part explains the procedure, which should be carried out faithfully at each Circle as directed :-

"You have in your new instrument, an exact plan of the great scheme of all life. All is perpetual motion.

"The sound given by the vibrator is the pulsating breath of life working in perfect harmony in the divine scheme of all being. That is why those who are tuned up to these high vibrations will have perfect success, while to others it will be worthless.

"You have somewhat of a replica in this Communigraph of the way in which the higher scale of beings sends down its wave lengths to the lower scale of beings; the wave length of Love, Duty, and Service.

"Each lettered spot indicated on your instrument represents various planets, all working and revolving the same yesterday, today, and forever; the sphere or ball then working round the Grand Centre of all. The power descends to ascend, to reflect and connect all minds from the highest to the lowest, and the lowest to the highest.

"Rest assured all this has been planned by a great architect and master mind, to work in perfect loving harmony with the power called Life Force.

"Before using the instrument, the sitters must stand round holding their hands with points of fingers of all in contact for three minutes, at a distance of five inches above the table. Then repeat these words all together :-

**"I AND MY FATHER ARE ONE. MAY THE BREATH OF GOD BREATHE ON THIS WORK, AND SO SET UP THE NECESSARY VIBRATION FORMING THE LINK BETWEEN THOSE WE WISH TO LOVE AND SERVE; TO THE GLORY OF GOD, AND THE ADVANCEMENT OF SPIRITUAL TRUTH, FOR LOVES SAKE.   AMEN."**

At the end of the sitting, the Guides and Helpers should be thanked for their co-operation. The centre panel light can be switched on again, and a closing prayer given by the leader. After about a minute, the main light can then be switched on, after warning all that are in the room to shade their eyes.

I have heard of people in séances that have excellent results with the help of Spirit using older typewriters, electric typewriters, and computers with and without the keyboards (I would try with the keyboards first). So please experiment in your Circles.

Read as much as you can about any of these subjects I have glossed over. Write for the book list from Stansted Hall. One book I would certainly recommend is the "University of Spiritualism" by Harry Boddington. As well as some of the books that have been written by Arthur Findlay.

# TABLE TILTING
## Typtology

A table with three/four legs or more is fine to use, to start with, make it light enough to move, but heavy enough for people to know it is not a con. [But on saying that, very, very, heavy Victorian solid oak tables have been used]. One finger each can be enough to place on the table, but a lot of people use all their fingers to start it off with, the fingers placed on the table touching the person next to you. Some have all their fingertips on the table all the session to keep all the power concentrated in the table. The first time I had a go at this was fun, as I had thought it could not be done. We had an old fashion, small, centre pillared, four legged, coffee/corner table dancing around the room. Different people kept on coming off the table to allow others a go; they were also swapping their fingers on the table to let others on, so we all knew that it was not a trick. BUT it can be seen that it is not a trick when a table climbs up the wall as has been done many a time at Arthur Findlay College in Stansted hall and at the Spiritualist Association of Great Britain [S.A.G.B.] in London.

After a prayer and a meditation to build up the power in the room. (remember to ask for only goodness, kindness, love, and truth to come from within the loving harmony of Spirits in the highest realms). The table was started by asking out loud to those above [Spirit], "are there any friends there to give us a message"? Asking our friends above for the table to move, and give us a message, the same question being repeated over and over. "Come on friend contact us", "we are waiting for a message off you friend" [like the spelling out board] "Is there any friend who would like to contact us?" Repeating the question over and over, each time waiting for the answer by table movement. All there sincerely within their minds encouraging Spirit to come closer. Some saying it out loud and others say it in their mind. All who were there concentrating on the table, every person had their fingertips very lightly on the table. We all started to feel the slight vibration from the table, it was as if the table was alive, and the table felt as though it was wanting to move. We kept repeating the questions and kept encouraging the friend in Spirit to come through. The table rocked slightly then started to go around in a circular motion on the legs. As we encouraged it, the top was sliding through all our fingers, so I could say not one person was able to keep it going as it was moving. As we encouraged it out loud, "come on you are doing fine", it started to go faster some let go, as they could not keep up with it. We then thanked our friend, and asked it to calm down, swapping the fingers and the people on the table, some people dropping out for a while. The table then was rocking from one leg to the two legs in a slow rhythm. The leader asked for the person's name. The unknown Spirit friend spelt it out on each rocking motion, from one set of legs to the others, by going through the alphabet as it rocked, so we spelt out the alphabet out loud to help A, B, C, etc. It stopped the rocking motion at the correct letters.

We asked many questions and we always received an answer. So have a piece of paper and a pencil handy. I would now say it is better to go A, and, B, and, C, and, D, and, E, and, rather than A, B, C, D, E, on each table leg rocking movement, as some confusion was found that first time and we had to re-ask the questions over again because a few of the unsure words to get the message correct. Get the format of the code being used correct, so the force/Spirit driving the table knows what format you are using.

I have been told of tables rocking around the room, and climbing a vertical wall with the participants only having **their fingers <u>on the top</u> of the table**. **REMEMBER ON THE "<u>TOP</u> ONLY"**. Some actually levitating. It can be an eye opener, and a different thing to try to break the monotony of people just sitting meditating.

A small, round/square, four legged, wooden pub type table can be used, or a plant stand type. One that can stand the buffeting of the rocking motion. A Medium who I have the greatest respect for, Ron Jordan told me he has had a very large heavy oak table levitating at about 5 foot when he and six others had their fingers on the table. This was done by asking out loud over and over for Spirit's help to lift the table, and when it started the internal vibration began [yes you can feel it], encouraging Spirit out loud when it begins. WAS THIS THE WAY THE EGYPTIANS BUILT THE PYRAMIDS?

In the 1800's the moving of tables was it seems commonplace with Physical Mediums. The happenings sometimes used to occur unexpectedly when a certain Medium was present in the room especially Andrew Jackson Davis. The movement of tables by Spirit were documented many times; they were very, very heavy in construction [read the History of Spiritualism by Sir Arthur Conan Doyle, you can buy it from Stansted Hall]. I have included some of the happenings of the 1860's at the end of the book.

Please to not be silly and fake it as I have seen it done, the movement will come with time if you are sincere and patient.

One foolish happening during a demonstration of table tipping that I attended in Liverpool's very large North West of England Spiritualist church, the group who took the particular séance thought they had movement and levitation of the table because they, the leaders of the demonstration, (all the group of about twenty plus and a lot of new comers who have not been seen since, attending a Monday night's gathering were told it was Spirit levitating a table), were having Physical Phenomena in their Home Circle. The Home Circle group gathered around the table and placed their full hands on it, some placing their thumbs **under (a definite no-no)** the table to get it moving. After that fiasco was another, three people started to lift the table placing their fingers UNDERNEATH (**should NEVER be done**) the table and one let go then two of the Home Circle started to go up and down with it. It was the best circus juggling act of a table I had ever seen. When I remarked at what they had done, they insisted that it was Spirit moving the table through them. This was a vice president/secretary/Northwest area president [Coral Matthews] and the healing leader [Mike Dempsey] of the church who were leading this demonstration, so be very careful who you take notice of when you attend these things. Read as much as you can about the subjects about Spirit contacts.

The people who attended this Circle, who had not attended very often must have gone away laughing their heads off thinking how stupid the people in that church were. I certainly did, I had been attending the church since the 1970's. Luckily they have learned a bit more since.

I have been in a Circle of a well known Medium [Jean Noel] and she does table tipping all over Europe. I have seen her support the table with her knee when it was at an angle, saying "it is standing in it's own", BE CARFUL who you trust. I have seen in a teaching centre in South Wales, a tutor/manageress [Jean Duncan] on the table rocking it with their knees. If you do have a go yourself be truthful to all who you sit and try these things with, and especially yourself; you will be found out at the worst possible time.

BUT there are genuine Circles and Mediums around to learn from. One Circle in Blackpool run by Helen Taylor at the present moment are getting the table to move without anyone touching it. The table is being lifted by Spirit, going upside down, and placing itself on top of the sitters' heads and touching them very gently.

In Gordon Higginson's home Circle the cane table used in the middle of Circle each week would walk back to the corner of the room at the end of the séance without anyone touching it, there it stayed until the next séance

In one séance in the 1800's it was said by Crawford: "during levitation, the table would immediately sink to the ground if the Medium touched it with her bare hands, but if she wore gloves, or touched it with her shoe, it did not fall so abruptly or remained unaffected.

It is now known if a completed Circle is formed by sitters holding hands, or touching fingers on the table, or hand to wrist, the Phenomena happens earlier/quicker.

In an experiment done by Crawford in the 1800's it was found after sitting for less than a half an hour the table rose into the air and was held suspended by an invisible force where strong men tried to push it down to the floor and failed. Other times the table appeared glued to the floor and would not move until permission was given by Spirit. Then it would become unlocked and free to move about.

Another good physical and all round Medium of this century Battling Bertha Harris. She was at a party with her very ill husband, in which the sceptics were goading her about the abilities of her and the Spirit World. One person in particular who she called the jester challenged her to prove the existence of Spirit. She pointed out a very large table across the other side of the room and said to him "if that table rose off the floor would that convince you of the existence of Spirit". He replied, "it would". Bertha went to one end of the table, her husband Robert went to the other end. They both placed their fingers on the top of the table and after well over a quarter of an hour the table was still on the ground as the party crowd around them were laughing at them while making wise cracks, and hilarious comments so pleasing the jester, but making them look foolish. Then slowly as the table began to rise the two kept their fingertips on the table until it spun and threw their hands away. The unnerved hostess ran to get the dishes off the table and dropped a bowl with trifle in it on the floor to add to the confusion. The table on its own, while in mid air, went to the jester and pinned him to the wall. It slowly gained height until he was taken off his feet and pinned by his throat as he was shouting hysterically. And Bertha shouting at him "For god's sake say you believe or it'll kill you". The jester spluttered, "I believe, I believe", he shouted the table immediately left him and he fell to the floor. The table had not finished it rose to the ceiling and it took the chandelier upwards shattering it, the table then slowly came back to the floor in the original position it had started from even to the extent into the sockets that protected the carpet from the legs. That man became a convert to Spiritualism for the rest of his life.

# APPORTATION

Pages 167-176 in the Mediumship of Arnold Clare

"APPORTATION" is the producing at a given place of an object [an apport] from a distance. The object may be composed of any material and be of any size. The distance from which it is brought may vary from a few yards to thousands of miles.

While it is contended that the phenomena and teachings reported in this book proves the case for survival, apporting lends weighty support to this conclusion.

Apport Mediumship is one of the rarest forms of Mediumship. The number of authenticated reports of apporting is very limited, some of the most notable being those associated with Charles Bailey of Australia, Count Rossi, Maria Silbert, Estelle Roberts, Jack Webber, Arnold Clare and I have witnessed an apport in a séance at Stansted Hall with Judith Seaman as the working Medium. It is noteworthy that all these mediumships are of comparatively recent times; and this may indicate that either earlier apporting may not have been recorded, or that it denotes an advance in the knowledge and adaptability of the Spirit Operators in the use of their human instruments. Yet we are told by Peter (Arnold Clare's Guide/Helper) that where such Mediumship can function, apporting is a relatively simple performance.

While the act of apporting, or its opposite "asporting" (that is, when an object [an asport] is taken away from a séance room by the Spirit World), may be a simple one to the Spirit Operators, yet these acts appear incomprehensible to the human mind. It means that an object, say a stone, a piece of glass, metal or a vegetable product, is taken from a distant place and produced in an instant of time within the four walls of the séance room. To achieve this the physical state of the object is transformed into another state, so permitting its instantaneous transportation and passage through solid objects such as walls, doors, etc., with greater ease than sound or electrical energy can penetrate such obstacles.

No wonder that "scientists" have so far frowned upon this form of phenomena, for it appears so demonstrably impossible. It is this apparent "impossibility" that must argue the presence and action of discarnate minds to accomplish it; the fact of its performance strengthens the case for survival, otherwise how can one explain the presence of the operators ?

As a rule, a condition of darkness is necessary for apporting, though cases are reported of the act being performed in light. I have witnessed the arrival of two apports (with Jack Webber) in a red light sufficiently strong to show clearly the bound Medium and all sitters; and, more noteworthy, a recent apport was received through Mr. Clare in bright white light. On this occasion the four people present (including the Medium, in trance) stood upright with all hands linked. The apport which fell into their midst was a large and heavy copper coin. The light on this occasion was an I00-watt white electric lamp.

While other forms of phenomena have been tentatively accepted by some scientific faculties, apporting has not yet been accepted. In the realm of Spirit activity the scientific mind has always lagged behind knowledge gained in the séance room, but doubtless the time will arrive when the seeming 'miracle' of apporting will be accepted.

It may be said that there is no form of physical Mediumship that is so open to fraudulent deception as that of apportation. Short of the most intimate search of the Medium— and indeed all sitters—probably by X-rays, it is difficult to conceive precautions that would satisfy an investigating commission. Incidentally, it is not easy to obtain the services of an investigating commission composed of persons whose authority is unquestioned. Even if it were, it might well be that the unusually severe conditions imposed would be so restrictive and artificial that, coupled with the strained mental attitude of the sitters focused upon a set result, the sitting would be rendered abortive. True, we have succeeded in obtaining an infra-red photograph of the act of an apport being re-materialised in ectoplasm (through Jack Webber), but even this might be said to have been "framed", despite the twenty independent sitters present on that occasion. Similarly, to have an object passed into a locked and sealed box in the darkness of a séance room would have to meet the charge of its being a conjuring trick. The time will doubtless come when the Spirit Operators will be able to devise a test that will be indisputable; and until this occurs we shall have to be content with the reports of sitters and investigators. It need only be added, once more, that in recent years our scientists have been able to produce results that would have been totally rejected a decade ago.

There is a further aspect of this question that may command some weight, and that is the process of apporting is but a part of the general phenomena associated with physical Mediumship. It is illogical to believe that a Medium in the trance condition necessary for phenomena would be able to return to normality consciously to commit a fraudulent action. Yet for apporting to be fraudulent this absurd contention would need to be maintained.

No medium of repute would jeopardise his or her Mediumship by such artificial means. He or she would know it would be to invite exposure, and to destroy the confidence of friends and others in their Mediumship. Finally, it is exceedingly doubtful whether the Guides would continue to work with such a Medium. Therefore, apporting should be considered with the rest of accepted activity.

The detailed happenings respecting apporting through Mr. Clare's Mediumship reported in the first part are eloquent of the act; and the reports independently subscribed by a number of writers testify to the similarity of procedure and result. By report of the séance on July 20, 1940 tells not only of the apporting of nearly a pound of metal in varied forms, but also of the apporting of four lion claws which arose from an unrehearsed conversation. For the conversation to have been anticipated is beyond credulity; whilst for the Medium or his friends to have secreted the objects and produced them by the methods reported, movement and actions would have been necessary, and these must have been discerned by myself and the other experienced sitters present.

In passing, it may be stressed that those accustomed to the work of dark Physical Circles develop an extra-perceptive sense. This results from their being so familiar with activity in the dark that eyes, ears and mind become tensely alert. Even the most insignificant rustle of clothing in movement is noted, and it would be most difficult, if not impossible, for anyone to rise up from a chair without being observed.

Peter, in his quiet way, has given us in the explanation that follows the procedure adopted, within the measure of our understanding. He leads us further to the contemplation of a form of life that has its nearest parallel in the fairies of our childhood. This form of life (which he calls the "little people") is as a link in the chain of life's evolution and progression. Failing more definite evidence of their existence, we can only accept the 'little people" as one of the "wonders" of Peter's revelations. Some of these revelations are provable, many more when related to authenticated evidence are most probable, and it may serve, for the time being, to receive his story of the "little people" as knowledge "in reserve" in our pursuit of truth and wisdom.

Peter commenced by saying:

*Peter:* "No better start could be made than to consider an article that is intended for use as an apport. In normal apporting simple articles, such as stone, metal, dried grasses, wood and soil, are most easily apported, and the range proper would be things composed of these materials. New articles such as jewellery, handkerchiefs and animal life should be considered as freak apports, and can only be produced under very special conditions. You see, I am not quite satisfied with the procedure we are adopting—we are not going right down to the facts, to the nature of intelligentsia who deal with this activity. Now, an article, which is to be apported, must normally have rested in its hiding place (I do not mean it is hidden) for a considerable period before it can be used. This is not a normal qualification but one of becoming steeped in its local environment. The reason is that it must not of itself set up individual radiation otherwise there would be a disturbance within the ether at that point. This would prevent the successful construction of the etheric vacuum around the object to be transported. To explain this etheric vacuum, one might say that it compares, which is as near as one can get, to an egg, with all the possibilities it contains of life, and even to its 'shape'. Perhaps now you can see how we get back to the beginning of life, and how the life first reached the earth through an etheric vacuum."

*Question:* "What is an etheric vacuum ? Are we right in assuming an etheric vacuum describes a condition in which there is no ether ?"

*Peter:* "In your vacuum ether still exists. In our vacuum ether also exists when the air has been excluded there-from. With your vacuum you change the character of the ether because you have removed the bound ether associated with that air. An etheric vacuum is precisely the same. The ether **'within'** is different from that **'without'**. The character has been taken out of the ether within the vacuum."

*Question:* "Did life originate in this vacuum ?"

*Peter.* "You see, we are carrying out the reverse action by placing the object into an etheric state, and what is to prevent us carrying it further into a spiritual state, by the same means of working in reverse ? Now you can see how fish can be in a pool that has never had any spawn in it. I warned you that in dealing with this matter we were dealing with primal powers that were responsible for the beginning of life."

*Question:* "Could I call it, or would you consider it as a sealed birth ?"

*Peter:* "We will talk about that question later, comparing it with the birth and growth of things. Remember, we have spoken of these things as being primitive.

"Here is a passing thought. Our globule or egg. Is it not remarkable how nature manifests itself ? — always forming new life and possibilities within spheres and ovals; I mean in shape.

"Now studying the etheric vacuum in relation to an egg simplifies the process of explanation. Within the egg you have all the potentialities of life awaiting only the opportunity which will transform it from potential energy into pulsating active life The same takes place within the etheric vacuum, only in the reverse way. You have something which has life, in so far as shape and quality goes which is just awaiting the opportunity for the change to be brought about. Now we come to the roads where we start to lose you again. Like the egg, the conditions **'within'** the etheric shell of the vacuum are not the same as those **'without'** and through the directive play of attractive etheric forces (corresponding to heat, as in the case of the egg) life (in the case of the object to be apported) is speeded up, so that the atomic structures change. When this occurs the speed becomes so great that all physical semblance disappears. This is just the reverse of that of the egg, where the fluids become solidified and take on its form according to the germ implanted therein."

*Question:* "Is the action of change automatic as soon as the necessary condition is created around the object?"

*Peter:* "It is automatic. Now this is a point which will interest you. The sympathy between that object at a remote distance and the Medium does not pertain, as is generally supposed, but where the sympathy or harmony does exist is between the operators and the Medium. It is there and not with the distant object. It is a natural sympathetic understanding between the soul in human form and, for want of a better name, the 'Nature Spirits' which serve."

*Question:* "You state it is the sympathy between the soul and the 'Nature Spirits'. How does this operate?'"

*Peter:* "They, the 'Nature Spirits', are unconscious of the directive mind of the Medium. They are directly associated only with the soul of an incarnate human being. Any direction that is passed on to these little people is via the Medium himself or through his aura. I am speaking chiefly of apports now. Look—you have a pretty fable, *Gulliver's Travels,* where you have one giant amongst a crowd of diminutive people. It is very similar to that, but they cluster around the human being who has a physical body. That is absolute."

*Question:* "Does that apply to any human being?"

*Peter:* "Yes. The harmony may be not so complete but I cannot go into that now. Have you ever heard of the expression 'Green Fingers' ? They can resuscitate plants. Well, it is the same sympathy or harmony which exists between these little people."

*Question:* "The point which is puzzling is the direction that the little people get in a séance in order to obtain apports."

*Peter:* "The fact of the Medium sitting shows that he is giving his consent for others—that is the controls to give the direction. Now it is necessary for this work that there must be a Control who is as near to them in sympathy as it is possible to get. Hence, in this case, the employment of our friend Simba. You see, the Control works within the aura of the Medium and is, for the moment, using the Medium's authority for that direction. If the Medium were to employ the same powers consciously, then he could 'receive food from the ravens in the wilderness', but as that is not possible, he must have an assistant which is the same thing."

*Question:* "Do the little people create the etheric vacuum ?"

*Peter:* 'Yes; but mark you, it is confined always to simple things. They cannot rise above that."

*Question:* 'Does not that require a great amount of knowledge on the part of the little people?"

*Peter:* "No, that is the hod in which they carry their stones. They are using their everyday means for the production of what you would consider the miracle, but to them it is simpler than the eating of your meal. The difficulty arises not in the construction of the etheric egg and the dematerialisation of the object within it, but in returning it to its normal physical state within the Circle. That is the real difficulty. Observe, in the first instance, I have stated the ideal conditions are those wherein the object must have rested in its position so long as to absorb its environment. In bringing it to the Circle, they have created deliberately just those conditions which they would normally avoid. That is the difficulty. That is why oft-times an object will come to you with condensation upon it, or extremes of temperature."

*Question.:* "Can you tell us the method of transportation ?"

*Peter:* "Transportation is very simple once the article is rendered into its etheric components (you appreciate that)— it is no more than moving it in its material shape one small fraction of an inch, because, you see, space does not exist. It is hard for you to imagine, I know."

*Question:* "I can imagine its passage through obstacles, but I cannot conceive the method by which it is directed from one place to another."

*Peter:* "Well, there is no need. For instance, to you Africa is a long way, and the lion's claw which your lady wears was brought from there to your own residence in less than an instant of time. Well, space is only a sign of your limitation. Africa is no farther away to us, in fact is not so far, as is your hand from your face, otherwise if that were not so radio impulse would take time to travel the earth. It is of the same realm, only quicker. There is an appreciable time lag so far as radio is concerned, but not in the finer ethers in which they and we would work."

*Question:* "Are you able to hold up the reforming of the object ?"

*Peter:* "Very simple. Once we have achieved the initial dematerialisation and, of course, conditions being equal within the Circle itself, it does not matter how long it is before it is reformed. We could almost bring a large supply, although depending always upon circumstances relative to your physical state. It depends upon that."

*Question:* "Do the natural elements make any difference—thunder, etc. ?"

*Peter:* "Not directly--only in so far as they affect the Medium. If he is affected by it, then, of course, that is passed throughout the whole system, physical, etheric and mental as well."

*Question:* "Is apporting possible while the Medium is not sitting ?"

*Peter:* "Yes. You will laugh at this perhaps. It is not necessary for the soul to be occupying the same seat, or any position as the body at any time during the day when you are working, much less when you are sleeping, because distance is no object. That is why you have often heard of cases where one has been thinking deeply of another and that other has been seen at a distance from his or her body. So you can appreciate that when you become etherically unconscious you can think without the limitations of distance, time and space. The man who keeps an open mind all the time is likely to meet more wonders than he who keeps the door shut."

*Question:* "Apporting a lance, for example. Would that give any particular difficulty ?"

*Peter:* "No. We could bring you a couple of elephants if you wished. That is quite 'on the cards'. Size is no difficulty."

Reference was made to the photograph received of the materialisation of an apport with J. Webber in the following question.

*Question:* "Is it possible, according to your line of reasoning, for an apport to be produced via the Medium's body ?"

*Peter:* "It is not impossible, but it is not normal. Can you see any reason why it should be ?"

*Comment:* "It was said that it was produced via the body?"

*Peter:* "Well, it might have been the place where it was rebuilt. I should hardly say it was brought via the body. It is not normal and I would not say impossible; but it is unnecessary. It may have been necessary to re-materialise close to the Medium, more especially if it was not a branch with which this Medium was associated. The Guide knows nothing about it. He is powerless to produce one little thing. He is responsible for the well-being of the Medium and, to a lesser extent, the sitters within the environment. Like many others, however, the Guides must qualify for the work--to know how it is done. It is like a man who has control of a vast concern. He may not be able to carry out each operation necessary for the production of an article, but he knows how it is done and he owes his position to his organising ability and his power of vision for the future. That, in regard to the work of development, is very necessary. A man might be able to design aircraft but never be able to fly one himself.'

*Question:* "In view of what has been said concerning the construction of matter, can you give us any idea of the condition into which an article is changed for the purpose of apporting ? Does it still retain its atomic form ?"

*Peter:* "Yes, only it has become speeded up, or, in other words, has had its frequency increased it ceases to be matter temporarily, although it is not exactly disintegrated; for it retains its form in an invisible state. In your science I think you will find that some materials readily give off under condensation, electronic forces or streams. What happens then is what would be termed 'ionisation'. You employ it in your radio valve. You encourage this electronic flow by introducing within the construction of the valve's filament a coating of material or a substance (I believe you call it thorium) which under heat from a local battery of some sort creates a cascade; this rises out of the filament and falls back again like balls on a water fountain But as soon as you introduce a positive potential, the flow ceases to be a disorganised cascade, and becomes a direct path from the filament to the positively charged conductor A similar kind of process is employed in regard to the article. That is the best analogy I can give. Moreover, and this is important, before you can obtain these conditions in regard to this radio valve, you must create for it its own vacuum similar to the etheric vacuumed."

# MATERIALISATION

I was not going to put a special section in the book about Materialisation as it has been covered in previous pages. I got told off by some of the people who had bought the earlier book. A lot of information can be seen in the sections dealing with Trance, Physical Circles and others.

To gain this special gift requires a lot and I mean a lot of dedication in linking with those in the World of Spirit and getting the harmonious blending with them to the $N^{th}$ degree through dedicated meditation in a Deep Trance State (mainly an unconscious state, [Gordon Higginson used to say he was aware of some of the things that were happening with him] after asking through prayer for the development of Physical Materialisation) and letting Spirit manipulate over a period of time the things inside your body necessary to produce ectoplasm. When that has been achieved over the many, many, many years of sitting in a dedicated Physical Circle, by the earth bound Medium; it is then up to those in the World of Spirit to say if you are suitable, some might never be. It is now accepted that not all Mediums' bodies are suited to the necessary makeup for the production of the ectoplasm or the amounts needed to produce a part or the full human form with this sort of amazing phenomena. Please remember it is not only the bodily make up of the Medium, but their mental ability to cope with the strains put on the body and the mental strains put on them over the days, weeks and years after the development has started, this comes from the hypocrites and bigots in all the religions (including Spiritualism) in the outside world at large. It is not an easy everyday life to lead.

One of the most famous Materialisation Mediums of recent times that I met was Gordon Higginson from Stoke on Trent. He used to have his public séances in library in the Arthur Findlay College at Stansted UK. He used to sit outside the cabinet as he suffered from claustrophobia, then when he was knocked out (put into a Deep Trance State), Spirit would take him into the cabinet and work on him. He many times would walk down the safe passage laid out in between the chairs in the library while there was ectoplasm coming from him like a mist of linen folds, they were then built up from the floor into a part or full human form. Sadly towards the end of his life the strength of his human body was such that only parts of the human form appeared.

Here within this book I have had the kind permission to put all the sections of the book by Harry Edwards about a very good Physical Medium Arnold Clare, who produced the human form through ectoplasm, he was also a Transfiguration Medium, he passed on many years ago. Arnold was many times tied up to a chair by the group, and the coat he was wearing was passed through the ropes and thrown on the floor by Spirit. He was photographed as he levitated tables, and trumpets.

A person most people know of is Helen Duncan, there have been many books written of her and her life as a Materialisation Medium. Also of the fact that she was the last person to be prosecuted under the Witchcraft act in Britain. The prosecutions were brought by the establishment who were, and still are mainly Christian, who in my opinion were and still are fearing the upsurge of genuine Mediumship, which is bringing the truth to the masses, and the gaining of support of the gifts she had, BUT all the publicity served to help the spiritual movement as a whole. Helen Duncan sat inside the cabinet or enclosed places that formed a cabinet, e.g. the corner of a room covered by a curtain. Both Gordon Higginson and Helen Duncan as Mediums in their own right were both stripped and searched before each of their own individual séances, this was done so none could accuse them of fraud. You often find the Physical Mediums have the other mediumistic gifts of one or all of the "Clairs".

Physical Mediums nearly always have the gifts of Mental Mediumship, BUT purely Mental Mediums never have the gifts of Physical Mediumship.

Experiments were done to prove the materialised form was there in the darkened room if Spirit had not illuminated the ectoplasm to show itself. This was done by the group who held the séance, asking Spirit to put their hand in molten wax a good few times so a strong cast could be made from the hardened wax. When the ectoplasm was withdrawn, the wax model shell ended up looking like a glove of sorts. This was then was filled with plaster and the wax melted leaving a hard formation of what ever Spirit had placed into the wax bath, which was generally contained in a large heated bowl. In the early séances, Circles produced masks of face, the feet and also the hands of those experimenters in the World of Spirit. Some can be seen in the museum in Stansted Hall. We should be getting back to things like this now, BUT, where are the **Genuine** Materialisation Physical Mediums of today?

# MATERIALISATION
### As told by Harry Edwards in his Book of the Mediumship of Arnold Clare
Chapter XV1 pages 191-202

ONE of the highest developments of Spirit activity through human Mediumship is the materialisation of a person, who was known to the sitters during his earthly life, whereby this person is able, for a brief period, to rehabilitate himself in physical form, to be clearly recognised and to converse with his friends and relatives. There can be no weightier evidence to demonstrate the truth of survival.

The history of Physical Mediumship presents an accumulated mass of evidence relative to this phenomenon; and the primary conclusion from the study of the evidence is that this phenomenon is only produced in association with physical Mediumship. It cannot be produced in a laboratory or by chemical or instrumental means. This conclusion not only applies to the full-length materialisations but also to its associated phenomena.

Materialisations are not hallucinations or the result of mass hypnotism; for not only do all the sitters present witness the phenomena, but also from time to time the camera has recorded the phenomena.

As ectoplasmic structures and their development into living formations possess similar characteristics, so are there similarities governing the building-up of Materialisations, their functions and dissolution.

Study of the records associated with the names of investigators such as Sir William Crookes, Baron Son Schrenk Notzing, Professor Charles Richet, *S.P.R. Proceedings of Great Britain,* the U.S.A., and the Institut General Psychologique of France, as well as the many other published accredited records, gives complete confirmation that the principles governing this phenomenon are the same. In no record has there been shown any fundamental departure from the general method of its creation, movement, activity and dissolution.

In studying the records it is noteworthy to recall, that when a Medium has been found to possess the faculty for this phenomenon and has been reported on by an accredited observer, further investigations have invariably followed by other competent investigators or national psychic research societies.

In most cases the phenomenon with its characteristics has been confirmed by the various commissions, no matter is what country it has taken place. The importance of this is obvious, when critics assume that a person may fraudulently produce effects in his own home by artificial means. It is beyond credulity that any deception would be possible in the séance rooms chosen by the investigators. Also the Medium is under continual close scrutiny during his stay with the investigating commission and his body is subject to particular search immediately prior to any sitting.

One of the conditions necessary for this phenomenon is that the process of building-up of the materialisation must take place in darkness. When built up it may be viewed in a degree of light and has at times been photographed by electric and magnesium light.

A further characteristic is that the built-up form is generally shrouded in ectoplasm, which appears to the eye as a voluminous white or shining drapery.

These two characteristics have lead sceptics to assert that there must be trickery. They instance the darkness, and suggest that some fabric must be hidden in the darkened portion of the room where the Medium sits. They suppose collusion on the part of a confederate, or that the Medium secretes material in or about his person.

The stringent restrictions and searchings that always accompany reports of investigations refute the sceptics' assertions. It should be obvious that the keen minds of the investigators, who are aware of the methods of fraudulent practice, would take every precaution against such crude attempts to deceive. Indeed, the history of the evidence shows that the precautions taken have been extreme.

Mediums after external search of their bodies, and being kept under the close scrutiny of an attendant for some hours prior to the sitting, are then draped in a single garment provided by the commission, or have sat nude. In Schrenk Notzing's work there are hundreds of photographs of structures and materialised forms and it is further reported how, on occasion, the Medium would be hypnotised, taken into another room, undressed, and whilst in a nude state the emanation of ectoplasm and its evolvement would be observed—the emanation coming from various parts of the body.

Happily such drastic conditions imposed upon Mediums fifty years ago (at the turn of the century) are now being replaced by more enlightened and understanding methods of control. It is asserted here, that if investigators will abandon their crude methods of restriction and search and will co-operate with the controlling intelligence in a friendly way, the operators will produce phenomena in such a way that the most critical mind will be convinced of the supernormality.

Sir William Crookes succeeded in obtaining photographs of the materialised Katie King, showing the entranced Medium in the same picture. His testimony goes to prove the above assertion; for he obtained not only the confidence of the Medium but also that of the operators and Katie herself: also he was permitted to walk arm in arm with her, take her pulse and temperature; and to be with her at her building up and dissolution.

Schrenk Notzing secured a number of photographs of full-length materialised forms standing by the side of the nude Medium.

With Jack Webber, the narrator "with witnesses" saw in a reasonable degree of red light—which was gradually increased by a rheostat, until there was sufficient brilliance to see clearly each sitter and the roped Medium—the materialisation of his Control, Rueben. From an ectoplasmic mist associated with the Medium, by a process of contraction or solidification, Rueben emerged; and the records state how he took hold of the author's hand with his and passed the former over his face so that the texture, smooth and clean feeling, could be felt; how he repeated this with other sitters, and spoke for a number of minutes in a deep resonant voice. It is further related how he elevated his entire form to the red electric globe some nine feet high to illumine his face all the more clearly, then descended, shrinking downwards towards the floor, just as a snow man would disintegrate in a strong heat, and finally disappeared—the process of disappearance taking but two seconds.

Quite often the materialisations of heads are appreciably smaller than normal, yet are perfect three dimensional heads subject to muscular control, with movement of eyes and lips through which comes articulated speech.

One can watch at times the building up of these heads. At first there appears, over the illuminated plaques a mist of indeterminate shape but oval in general appearance, which, when seen sideways, looks like a disc of bluish dim light. As second follows second the shape of the head appears within the mist, forming first the outline, then the features, gradually becoming stronger until perfect and often recognisable. A fairly good simile is that of focusing a camera or a picture on a screen. From a haze of light there first appears the blurred indefinite image, which leads to the precise features as the picture is brought into correct focus.

On occasion, the author has noted that if the visiting entity possessed a moustache or beard, these would be the last to form and has noticed at times that they were white, as if there was an absence of colouring pigment. On other occasions the hair would be of full colour, brown, black or red.

That the heads are three-dimensional is proved by the showing of the head in profile; and if plaques are used to illumine the manifestation, the Guide will have the plaque moved to illustrate this.

Heads are more commonly formed, as they take less power and preparation than full forms.

The records of materialisations with Mr. Clare's Mediumship in the first section of this book are eloquent of this type of phenomena, particularly of the occasion when Jack Webber was able to return for a short time. He materialised at two other sittings (not reported) about that time.

The appearance of the smaller forms of children three or four feet high, or of forms larger and taller than normal, certainly smaller or larger than the Medium, are often seen. Sometimes one sees two or three forms simultaneously. Peter explained the reason why some forms appear so large.

Peter tells us that the creation of hands, claws or similar formations may be produced by a different process from that of materialising a discarnate entity; and such phenomena should not always be associated with materialisations.

As already stated, the building up of materialisations invariably takes place in total darkness. When the Medium sits in the Circle—that is, not within a cabinet--as does Mr. Clare, complete darkness is an essential. The more general practice is for the Medium to be seated either in a cabinet with curtains in front of the opening or in a curtained recess to a room that permits of the shutting out of all light. In either case the room may be illumined by a subdued light, though the usual practice is to illumine the materialisations by means of a plaque.

No strict laws govern physical work of a psychic nature; and there have been occasions when witnesses have been able to see the building up of the form, as with Jack Webber or the presence of a form, as described by Colin Evans, in the light of an electric fire.

Due to this necessary condition of darkness, records of materialisations generally commence with the appearance of the built-up form emerging through the curtains or by the pulling apart of the curtains.

The French physiologist, Professor Charles Richet, described the building up of a materialised form as follows:

"I see something like a white luminous ball of undetermined outline suspended above the floor. Then suddenly there appears emerging from this white orb of light, as from a trap door, the phantom 'Bien Boa'. It is of moderate height. He is halting and lame in his walk. One cannot say whether he walks or glides.... Without opening the curtain he suddenly collapses and vanishes on the floor.... Three or four minutes afterwards the same white orb appears in the opening of the curtain, above the floor, then a body is seen quickly rising straight up and attaining the height of an adult, and then it collapses on the floor."

Richet adds:

"Before my eyes outside the curtain, a living body has been formed, which emerged from the floor and - vanished into the floor."

Similar phenomena were witnessed through the Mediumship of Eusapia Paladins as with a number of other Mediums of her time, like Home, Slade and Eglington.

In more recent times we have had the records of materialisations with Estelle Roberts, Jack Webber and Arnold Clare. In no case where observations have been possible has there been any variance in the general principles of the method of building up, the creation of ectoplasmic drapery, the gliding or floating movements and the dissolution.

It was recorded by Sir William Crookes how on one occasion the materialisation of Katie King cut off portions of her ectoplasmic "garment" and gave portions to those present. She then passed another part of the drapery over the gaps and they were immediately made whole. Despite the very closest investigation Crookes was unable to find the place from whence the pieces had been cut (there was no seam).

For the first time it is believed, Peter explains, the source from whence the special quality of ectoplasm for materialisations comes, and the purpose of the "ectoplasmic drapery". It will be seen that the thesis he presents is in harmony with the experiences recorded.

The gliding or floating movement of the forms is another general characteristic. As they move across a room, the motion is invariably described as floating or gliding along. This may signify that the legs and feet have not been physically formed and it is believed that the extremities are the last to be built up. It is fairly positive that the forms do not touch the floor.

The Guide of Jack Webber once asked that the floor space within the Circle should be covered with white powder. This was done, and a number of forms were seen to build up and cross the space in red light—the white floor space showing up very plainly. There were no marks of footprints nor was there any disturbance of the powder.

This does not signify that not on any occasion are the legs and feet materialised: it should be as easy for them to be solidified as a hand or a head. Indeed, if evidence of a personality can be given this way it is done. An example of this is . . . when Pedro, one of the controls associated with Mr. Clare's group of Spirit people, makes his presence known. He manifests with a wooden "peg leg", and one hears the sounds of one foot and the stump, as he walks around the Circle.

In order to save the Medium from strain and to conserve energy, only sufficient of a Spirit body is materialised to satisfy the immediate purpose. If the visitor is a foreigner who comes back to his relatives and speaks to them in his own voice, dialect, and tongue then the respiratory and vocal organs would be built up. Another example might be one whose identity would be absolute by showing a scar upon the face or a deformed hand. Then the effort would be concentrated to this purpose and it may be, as Peter says, the voice may be produced by other means. The author has witnessed the movements of the lips of materialised Spirit people consonant with the words being spoken and which do come from the mouth of the visitor (this has been confirmed by a number of independent witnesses, including critical journalists). Geley says:

"To build up in a few seconds an organ or an organism biologically complete—to create life—is a metaphysical feat which can rarely produce a perfect result. That is why the great majority of materialisations are incomplete, fragmentary, defective, and show lacunae in their structure." A warning about this work is also given by Peter, who says the Guide has to exercise care, in regard to the extent to which the visitor is permitted to reassume physical life.

Peter opened his observations upon this phenomenon by Saying:

*Peter:* "The first condition essential for materialisation is complete darkness within the immediate vicinity of its formation.

"After the materialisation is formed according to the conditions prevailing, it may, in given circumstances, be exposed to indirect light rays. This condition is the exception rather than the general rule. That provides a summary with which to begin.

'This is a condition which cannot be broken away from."

"Now what is a materialisation ?"

"It may be the birth of a thought or it may be a complete birth of an entity, except that its birth has not been carried to its material or physical completeness.

"For a complete materialisation, under normal conditions it takes about nine minutes in your time.

"First of all, there is formed for it an ovoid, matrix or moulded. This is very similar to the etheric envelope of which we have spoken in our talk on apportation. Within this ether-tight matrix the manifesting entity commences to draw about himself particles from the ether, the special ether, that is, within the mould. They can only form to his personality and not to any other. As he gains greater proficiency so does his density become more pronounced.

"Within the limits of the ovoid the form is dressed about with a material of different character and is what you call ectoplasm. That is the part which you have referred to as Spirit robes' but it is not primarily for the purpose of dressing the entity but of protecting it from the etheric bombardment **'without'**. It is, I agree, quite often draped around the form as a sort of robe, but that is more to complete the picture which is oft-times, in itself, very imperfect.

"Now what is the relationship between the now materialised form and the Medium ? It is this. Take, for example, the complete materialisation—by complete I mean one that has all the members associated with the body: heart, lungs, hands and feet, which have been constructed by the same means. To give forms of this nature complete action there is a corresponding link-up with the Medium's physical organism; all the functions of his body are projected into that of the materialised form.

"This transfer is carried out over a network of etheric nerve cords which passes from the Medium's solar plexus to that of the manifesting entity. I will carry this perfect case a step further and say that if this entity were so empowered as to be able to extract from the ether atomic particles to build up his form, it could become a three-dimensional being as solid as you are yourself; the only difficulty in this instance being that it and the Medium could not both live at the same time. That shows how vital it is for the existence of a perfect control between the Spirit Operators associated with the Medium and this particular phenomenon.

"It is, in effect, an accelerated process of bringing to birth an entity which is only one stage removed from the physical, actually it is closely allied to the earlier stages of the natural period of conception but is very much speeded up. In the normal birth of a child the incoming soul must pass through the several forms of birth, entering, as it were, one lock at a time before passing down into the next stratum, each deeper and denser than the previous one."

*Question:* "That is from strata to strata or plane to plane, but from whence ?"

*Peter:* "That does not matter, because if it did we should have to go into very deep things. Let the question remain and perhaps it will form a basis for something else. It is all very well to say 'from whence' but you would still have to justify that by explaining 'why' and I am afraid that would be beyond me for the present.

"Now at the beginning I said the materialisation could be of a thought or the person of an entity.

"In the case of the materialisation of a thought this is not a true materialisation. For instance a person who has passed over to the other side of life may not be able, for various reasons, to accomplish a complete materialisation but only able to build around the thought something that would express sufficient of his character and personality to make it recognisable. In such a case it would be just a head and a feature; and you can always recognise this phenomenon by the fact that it has no life or animation. It would be like a sculptured head, oft-times dimensional, at other times cloudy with just a faint suggestion of the eyes and nose and mouth. Now these may or may not be true expressions and do not constitute the proof of survival that you see, but it is interesting in so far as it is not of your world. Now where can I proceed from there ?"

*Question:* "Has the thought formation a similar linking up to the Medium's solar plexus ?"
*Peter:* "Not necessarily."
*Question:* "It may be built up from ectoplasm emerging from another part of the body ?"
*Peter:* "Yes."
*Question:* "Can you tell us how the thought formation is able to build ? You spoke of the visiting entity gathering unto himself qualities to enable him to materialise. Is the thought materialisation created by a different process ?"
*Peter:* "Yes, slightly different, in that the formation does not have lifelike qualities. It is moulded from the ordinary ectoplasmic substances of a slightly different quality. It is formed from that; and, of course) may vary considerably in Size, being smaller or larger according to the governing factors at the time."
*Question;* "Do the controls have any work to do in regard to materialisations ?"
*Peter:* "Yes, but not upon the forming of the figure. They maintain the right etheric conditions and help with the processes associated with the Medium—always directly with the Medium—which enable him to withstand etheric shocks. You might term the latter, voltages. These would, without our assistance, nearly reduce him to a wreck. We direct the forces and currents through him to provide the conditions necessary for the building-up of the materialised form. That is where our operation commences and ceases. We have our hands upon the taps that control the flow."
*Question:* "We have been told from other sources, that materialisations are created by the controls moulding ectoplasm around the astral body of the entity. From your explanation that is incorrect?"
*Peter:* "No. You see, I cannot say that that is impossible, but it is not the way it is normally done."
*Question:* "You stated that the visiting entity gathers to himself particles from the ether. That presumes sufficient willpower on the part of the entity to permit him to materialise. Is that all he has to have, or does he have to possess technical knowledge as well ?"
*Peter:* "He has to have knowledge . . . he must have knowledge. I would rather not take up that subject because it has to do with a qualifying form of development of the entities.

"This I will tell you, as it may stimulate your interest. People who have lived on earth and were born with a physical defect are often provided with the opportunity, when conditions are right, to materialise. You are thinking 'why'—of course the eternal 'why'. For this reason, they are born oft-times—not always—imperfect in their body, indicating an imperfection within the soul. That imperfection is a lack of wisdom and so they are given opportunities to build perfectly, down to the stage where the next step would be the physical. We cannot escape it, we are going to come to it sooner or later because they will have to come again."

**NOTE:** The foregoing statement implies reincarnation.

*Question:* "You have said the materialisation was three dimensional. We have felt their hands. . . they must possess weight. Could one be weighed ?"
*Peter:* ('Yes, but you must remember that they are not solid right through. It is often an incrustation, a veneer."
*Question:* "Yet the lungs must work ?')
*Peter:* "Yes, but they can get to work in the same way as the lips move when 'a man pulls the strings'."
*Question:* "Can you give us the relationship of the materialised form to the Spirit Entity himself ?"
*Peter:* "The Spirit Entity is always, and for ever, seeking knowledge, and he can gain it that way; but it is the soul of the one who is manifesting which is responsible for the work. The Spirit is the observer, as it were, for the soul. The purpose is served by the experiences gained in the handling of the various potentials of the realm in which he finds himself. He desires to build a body if only of an etheric nature. In that way there is a gaining of wisdom, because it is the most difficult work there is to do."
*Question:* "Is the materialised form the soul body of the person or an astral shell ?"

*Peter:* "It is he who has returned in reality. You have spoken of an astral shell but this is a term we do not like and you should find a better one to supplant it. But there are such things, just the same as when you have no further use for the physical shells they are laid in the ground. So the astral shell, when the soul has no further use for it, just remains a shell with no animation. They are oft-times perceived by the undeveloped clairvoyant, but it is a graveyard of {astral bones' and they always appear to your mental vision grey and lifeless. It is a place unattractive and desolate."

*Question:* "You spoke of the transference of functions from the Medium to the materialised form. Does that imply that for a materialised form to walk or give speech that the directing thought emanates from the Medium and not from the Entity ? "

*Peter:* "The moving and speech is that of the Entity, but the means whereby it is achieved is taken from the Medium and travels via his nerve trunk."

*Question: "So* the nerve trunk provides the power for animation ?"

*Peter:* 'Yes, and though the organs are complete within the materialisation they have not quite the same character as that of the normal physical body, but are more or less copies. They carry out the functions, though mark you, they are not entirely necessary to the form that is materialising; but to give it a vitality of its own it must be more or less complete."

*Question:* "If that entity had the power could it draw from the Medium sufficient life as to become physical again? Might it be possible, if the control was not on guard, for the form to take on renewed physical life again ?"

*Peter:* "Yes, but the organs are not complete. The Guides have their hands on the taps and there are therefore limits to which the form can be permitted to build. That is why you seldom find a complete materialisation."

*Question:* "You have spoken of the etheric qualities which are used for materialisations. Is there any special characteristic denoting these ? Are they different from other atomic structures known to us ? Is there anything particular about them which permits their use for the special purpose ?"

*Peter:* "No difference that I can mention worthy Of note It is only the looseness, the polarising agency that makes the difference—the agency of nature which materialises concrete things. The largest star in your system is still half formed. It owes its size to them, yet it exists materially. It is measured; therefore it is three dimensional, yet it is not as solid as your earth. As it solidifies so it becomes smaller. That is a parallel to the answer to your materialisation, and that is why most materialised forms seem so tall. They even have to bend for you to see them. That is why you are often asked to stand."

## SPIRIT CHILDREN'S CIRCLES

This is generally done for the children who are in Spirit in the form of a Physical Circle, when there is a well-developed Trance Physical Medium present. It is good to make the Circle a celebration of the children's birthdays on the earth plain, also any of the celebration times on earth that they are likely to remember, but if living in a Christian culture mostly at Christmas time. Or make it any other religious festival. This is when all the toys, and the Christmas tree, all things of celebration are placed out for the children still here on the earth plain, or any festival time. Quite often the children in Spirit like to remember those times, but remember the children in Spirit can come through to any Circle, at any time, just to get themselves noticed. This is why the singing of children's songs and nursery rhymes should be sung in all Physical Circles.

When the Spirit children come through to the Circle, they can ask through the entranced Medium [using his/her voice box] or through Independent Direct Voice using the power from the Medium, by using the ectoplasmic voice box somewhere in the room where the Circle is being held, sometimes asking for their own little toys. Toys that they like to play with in the house where the Circle is being held. Sometimes it has been known for the Spirit children to go to one of the sitter's houses, to play with the toys, which are there under the Christmas tree. Some Circles place toys all the year round in their Circle for the Spirit children to come and play with them. This is best begun when a Circle starts getting some children coming through on a regular basis. Requests from the children in Spirit through the deep trance Medium are then quite often given to the sitters for special toys. The Spirit children can ring the bells; play with the small musical instruments, use drumsticks or a small xylophone and things like that.

I have spoken to a number of people who have had Spirit children's celebration Circles. Here are two.

A lady and gentleman who I met at the Arthur Findlay College were talking to me in the long gallery one day about the Physical Circles they had sat in over the years. The conversation came up about all the older Mediums who are now sadly passing away and not many memories of the children's Circles were left for others to try to help the children in Spirit, so making the children happy by bringing back their own earthly memories of playing with earthly toys and I thought the ways should written down to be preserved and to try and get people who sit in Physical Circles to revive them.

The Daulby Street Liverpool church used to have Circles for children at the Christmas time in the early days when Gladys Owen was a young person and throughout her whole life within Spiritualism which was 80 plus years, and in later years within the church when Stan Tyrer the Trance Medium was alive. A lot of the regulars used to attend. They were happy times for the members and the children who came through. A tree was always set up for the Circle and presents placed around for the people who attended, and the same toys each year placed for the Spirit children to play with and to make a noise with. Please try to revive the practice in your own Circles and in your own church Circles, think about the children who have passed on to the higher vibrational level and who have memories of the earth plane.

I was talking to one older Medium who wishes to remain anonymous. She was saying in her "Home Physical Circle" they always had a Christmas séance for the children when everyone brought presents. The children who came from Spirit used to take the presents (apport them) to the deprived children of the earth plain throughout the world. What a wonderful thing/Circle that must have been, and what an experience it would have been to be a part of.

# THE GUIDES AND CONTROLS
Written by Harry Edwards, Mediumship of Arnold Clare, Page 45-47

The chief spiritual leader of this Circle is Brother Paul, a monk who one evening gave an account of the many years he had spent when on the earth at Beaulieu Abbey. Many details we afterwards verified on a visit to Beaulieu in 1939. Paul finds much difficulty in coming into the earth conditions and it is only when conditions are exceptionally good that he speaks for any length of time. He has on occasion materialised and sometimes given a blessing at the close of a Circle in direct voice (through the trumpet). Most of the talking is left to Peter who. As he has often said, finds it easy to work through the Medium and so becomes the second-in-command and the mouthpiece of Paul, as he never fails to remind us when giving some lengthy discourse on spiritual things.

Peter is a most interesting personality and I have never known him avoid a question; his replies are usually given without the least hesitation and always to the point. {That is the true nature of a Spirit link. DRTK.]

He has materialised once in a Physical Circle and always makes a point of showing his short pointed beard. I have never heard him speak much of his earth life, but he has stated he passed over a hundred years ago. When Peter is occupied in the physical work, he leaves the Medium in control of John.

I have always liked the personality of John, it has a certain similarity to that of Peter and yet there is a subtle difference. He has a keen sense of humour and is quick at repartee; and whilst he will talk on general thing, can seldom be drawn into a deep discussion.

These three Guides are the only ones I have ever known to control the Medium, and each one seems to give the impression of acting as a Medium for the other. Indeed, this is the idea which Peter has frequently mentioned when we have discussed the work that takes place on their side. Each one is a link in that ever-ascending chain of the angel ministry.

Farther down the ladder we have the invisible helpers; and in this Circle we have Simba, the African. When Simba first manifested in the Circle things were moved with great power and speed. He it is who is mainly responsible for the rapid swirling of the trumpets and other objects and levitation. Peter has often said Simba has a heart of gold but simple child-like mind and takes great delight in displaying strength and power in the movement of these things. He, too, has a great deal to do with the production of the apports which, Peter states, he does in conjunction with the 'little people' (Peter's favourite expression for 'Nature-Spirits' and those lower down in the scale of evolution).

Another helper who used to be more in evidence in the early days but who does not come forward so much now is Pedro, a one-legged sailor. There is never any mistake when he appears, because he pads around the room exactly as a man with a stump would do. He is usually accompanied by "sea breezes"; and sometimes the rushing cold wind has been so violent that is has billowed the curtains. We heard little of Pedro after Abdul came on the scene, and apparently he receded into the background when the work of materialisation was pushed forward. Certainly Abdul made a tremendous difference in this aspect of the work. He (Abdul) was able to show himself very clearly, and frequently the jewel in his headgear was easily visible and the swarthiness of his skin most apparent.

The perfume which is always a feature of the phenomena, we were told, was produced by the power of an Indian Girl and though most often reminiscent of Parma violet, other distinct perfumes have been given. On one occasion a small potted-meat jar was filled for us and the contents kept for months without losing strength.

The other personality is one whom all sitters very quickly come to know: "Little Peter", who passed over in early life. Sometimes he used to bring with him a little girl who, he said, was his sister. Little Peter was always full of fun and mischief and fond of pranks. One night he took a packet of cigarettes out of my pocket and told me I should find them in my overcoat which was outside the room in the hall; and after the Circle that's where I found them. On another occasion he told me to hold my wife's handbag very tightly over the clasp, as he wanted to get some of the things out. Within a minute or so, although I held the bag tightly and I know it was not opened, a comb, and a small pair of scissors were taken from the bag and put into my wife's hand. Many instances similar to this could be quoted and we had only to suggest to him that something was beyond his power and he would constantly try, until he succeeded.

He often attempted to materialise, and although we could always see his small figure the face was never sufficiently clear, but he certainly was the most proficient speaker through the trumpet, and would often sustain quite a long conversation. His main work seemed to lie in keeping the Circle atmosphere bright and cheery; and after perhaps a tense moment of communication, he would interpose some remark which immediately lightened the atmosphere. He seemed also to be the one to encourage the Spirit people to use the trumpet; and we have often heard him talking to them and telling them just what to do. If a Spirit could not give the message, Little Peter would invariably do so; and he took great pains to make things clear and give the evidence in a satisfactory way.

This completes the "family" of helpers to whom we owe so much. Their untiring efforts, their patience, their loyalty, and the sincerity of their desire to maintain a clear channel of communication by which the vital message of man's spiritual destiny may be given to this stricken world, leaves us with happy memories and a debt of gratitude for their companionship. It is a debt which we can endeavour to repay only by passing on to those who have not had this privilege, the knowledge and experiences which we have gained; and by devoting ourselves to this cause of truth for the benefit of mankind.

# THE FUNCTION OF THE GUIDES AND CONTROLS

Written by Harry Edwards, Mediumship of Arnold Clare, Chapter X1 pages 121-130

In dealing with the functions of the Guides and of the Controls, it is well to recall that any act of organisation demands the presence of an organised mind. The purposeful movement of a finger, or the lifting of an object from one place to another, requires mind direction to accomplish the act. Therefore when deliberate or planned act is performed and carried out by non-human agency, it is obvious that the agency of a non-human or Spirit mind is employed.

The reports of phenomena through Mr Clare's Mediumship are sufficiently decisive for certain declaration to be made, that they were supernormal in character and performance.

A theory has been advanced that, admitting the Medium is in a state of unconscious trance, the acts may still be performed through the knowledge contained in his subconscious mind. Not one shred of evidence exists to support this theory. The subconscious mind of a man can only retain knowledge that is gained from past experience; and no evidence exists that man, in any age, either through knowledge, or through other mediumships, has been able to perform such acts as have been authentically reported here.

The levitation of a solid object into the air, without any from of humanly constructed apparatus, requires the application of a force to counteract the force of gravity. When the object is of a material that is non-receptive to any of our known forces such as magnetism or electricity, it appears that some forces other than these two is employed. Further, after the act of lifting the orderly controlled movement of that object denotes a control that is not automatic but intelligent. When the object moves at once as desired at the audible request of a sitter in any direction, up or down, to the left or right, fast or slow, further evidence is obtained that the directing intelligence is responsive to the sitter's directions.

This intelligence must possess not only an intimate knowledge of the natural laws as known to man, but also law-governed forces unknown to man. In addition, this intelligence must possess further knowledge of how to combine and co-ordinate these forces with those we know.

Still further evidence is provided of the greater power possessed by Spirit intelligence, by the knowledge it must have of human anatomy and understanding of the human mind. This must be obvious to the reader who stops to consider what is implied by the creation and the potentialities of ectoplasmic activity. Thus one conclusion is immediately apparent, and that is, that when through human Mediumship phenomena are manifested, there must be present a directing intelligence of great wisdom.

With all Mediums there is another common factor; and that is the "personality" who makes himself known through speech, via the Medium or by means of the "independent voice". This personality is in command of the Medium and the proceedings at the séance. We have Walter with Margery, Black Cloud with Jack Webber, Peter and John with Arnold Clare; and so on with every Medium.

It is noticed that two personalities have been cited with Mr Clare. This is not unusual; with Jack Webber, Black Cloud would on occasion leave the Medium for one of the other Guides to take charge. (for the purpose of clearness, the term Guide is used in this book to denote the personality in charge of the Medium and the proceedings at the time; the other Spirit Operators present being termed Controls).

The Guide during a sitting is an autocrat, governing the proceedings with a "rod of iron". He is the sole arbiter of what may be allowed to proceed or not. As a rule, such Guides are most anxious and will to co-operate with the sitters when their requests are reasonable.

These Guides are not vague abstract personalities, they are known by names, tell you of themselves, their nationality, the work they were engaged upon when on the earth; and at times have provided evidence to prove their earthly existences.

It is not of great importance, however, whether the controlling genius possesses a white or red skin during his earth life. The salient fact is that these personalities must be in a condition of active existence. To prove that, they carry out their work amongst us.

There is another aspect that may well be recorded. When one has been privileged to work consistently with a Medium, and has come into frequent touch with the Guide, he becomes much more than a "personality" or the "voice" through the Medium. One learns to know him, and he becomes a close personal friend, almost as "one of the family"; and very human. He enters into the family lives of the sitters, is solicitous and loving and is revered as counsellor, guide, and loved friend.

Peter has told us that the Guide has responsibility of creating the "conditions" in which the Controls can present the phenomena. The Guide in control does not produce an act of levitation, apportation, or any other of the acts performed. It is as if he were in charge of the power and the power switch. When the Guide has built up the necessary conditions at the séance, it is the individual Controls who carry out the jobs of work.

Before dealing with the *modus operandi* described by Peter, of how the right "conditions" are created, some evidence is given to support the statement above.

On the hundred and more occasions when I sat with Jack Webber, I was able to observe the variation of the quality of the phenomena, the facility of difficulty of their production according to the nature or disposition of the Medium. When the general conditions at the séance were co-operative and easy, the phenomena would flow freely from act to act without a pause. The movements would be strong and sustained and, at times, so strong that the Guide would express himself through the Medium asking for caution. The closing act of the sitting was often the levitation of the Medium into the air, bound to his chair, where he travelled around and above the heads of the sitters, finally alighting on the far side of the Circle or, at times, on the outside of the Circle. The Controls responsible for this act were often impatient, and did not want to wait, so that on occasion one heard the Guide admonishing the Control, especially when the Medium had been slightly levitated in the middle of the séance. At times, when after admonition the Control persisted in levitating the Medium, the Guide would ask imperatively for the light to be put on; thus breaking down the conditions in which the Control could act. On other occasions, when sitters were non-co-operative, or some new restriction had been imposed on the Medium, or the Medium himself been upset, there appeared difficulty in producing phenomena; movement or activity would be short, snappy and with long time-pauses between each movement. Then would be heard the voice of the Guide speaking through the Medium saying "Do your best now", "Do this", "Do that", clearly indicating that it was outside his own province to perform the act.

Peter describes the way in which he creates the right condition for action as "extending the auric field of the Medium", his words on this point are of interest.

*Peter* : "The phenomena take place within the extension of the Medium's aura. This is done by means of **bowsing-bending-reflecting**". (here Peter seems to have given us a new word **"bowsing"** to convey a meaning, for which our vocabulary has no word). "It is not the sort of bending as is pictured when you bend a piece of metal, but a bending under strain like the cover of an umbrella. Can you imagine a flame being bent over for no apparent cause, as if deflected by a steady directive wind? It is most important to get the idea. It is, as it were, bent over by an invisible power.

"If, in the circumstances, the Circle is not properly arranged, the aura of the Medium cannot be **'bowsed'** or extended sufficiently to include all the people. If the edge becomes thin, due to certain conditions associated with the sitters, we borrow a little of the nearest sitters' aura and blend it in

"There you have the tent or umbrella, under stress enveloping the whole Circle. This tent or umbrella covers a certain area inside which are sitters.

"Etheric conditions **'within'** are not exactly the same as the conditions **'without'**".

"**Within** that area the Controls can work their will, to a certain extent, that is".

"If there are any leaks in the umbrella **'within'**, the conditions are not so good for the production of phenomena".

"We have an atmosphere of freedom in which we can operate without limit; that is without limitation that would be imposed outside the tent. It is **'within'** the pressure existing inside the tent where the Controls are able to perform their will".

A drawn impression of this gives the author's idea of what is intended. The Medium has seen this and, through him, the Guide has said it certainly does give an impression of what takes place.

A summary of a previous talk with Peter was then read to him as follows:

"The Guide in control creates the conditions necessary for phenomena to be manifested".

"These conditions are an extension of the auric field of the Medium. Help may be obtained from sitters for this purpose".

"The auric field is composed of [a] the aura pertinent to the physical body, which extends to about three inches around the physical form, misty silver in colour; and [b] the auric atmosphere that is limitless in extent: a storehouse of electric energy which belongs to the soul body and is subject to pull from each condition".

"To create séance conditions, the auric field is controlled and concentrated into the area **'within'** which phenomena are to be created, like and umbrella or tent".

"Psychic breezes are caused when the auric properties of the sitters are employed".

Peter replied:

*Peter* : "Not quite right. I do not like the phrase, 'Aura which extends three inches'. Let me tell you once again".

"Around the normal human being there is an extension. You said pertinent; that is a good word. It means 'close to'. This etheric extension is the reservoir of strength. It has no character of its own, but is simply a storehouse of etheric energy used for the complete and successful working of the physical body".

"It is not wise for me to give measurements in regard to this, it varies so widely in extent".

"Close to the physical body it has the property of scintillating colours. This is due to the mental changes of flux of the individual. The aura proper has its own basic colour. All other colours are added by mental stimulants. I mean, of course, anger, sorrow, and things like that. It has for basic colours, orange, purple, and slate grey. These are always impressed first. That is the aura or atmosphere; and that is the part which is capable of extension".

Peter was asked if he could say whether the forces used could be compared with any of the forces of which we are aware, he replied:

*Peter* : "The nearest force we know comparable to that used in producing action is a magnetic force, but this force is of a different quality and stronger in character. A compass point can be diverted from its position by directive power. This magnetic force is superior to your known force. It is allied to electrical energy. This power force has potency different from that of the forces known to you: for example wood is a good conductor of the superior force, whereas it is impervious to your known electrical and magnetic forces. Tin is a good conductor, aluminium is not so good; but the difference is slight and would not impede action".

"You will notice that while I am talking, the respiration of the Medium is almost non-existent.

You will find this is only during speech, and that it is not because he can hold his breath but because of the relaxation of the body. Hence no ill-effects are felt by the Medium".

*Question* : "With regard to the work of the Controls and the reference you made to the "little people", would you like to speak to us on that and tell us something more of the 'people' who work in the séance room?"

*Peter* : "With pleasure, I can deal with that. I have told you about the Guides I think; (yes).

"Controls are called by that name because they do not qualify for the standard of Guides and their work is completely different".

"They are called Controls chiefly because of their method of control, which is, to enter into complete possession of the physical organism of the Medium, i.e. they impart directly through that organism their entire personality. This is a fault, because there is not the perfect development of the Medium spiritually. Now that does not sound very happy. The reason brings us back to those very vexful questions; spiritual development and psychic development".

"In the case of controlled Mediumship [I use that term for want of a better] you have a display of purely psychic phenomena with very little of the spiritual. The Controls themselves are quite good but they are little removed from the limits imposed upon man in the flesh. Their range of vision is very much restricted; and can act only within the realms adjacent to earth. It is the natural phenomena of man since the dawn of history; and you might call it quite simply primitive religion; very primitive. They can perform what would be termed miracles, but it stops at that. It goes no further; and in this scale of operation you have at once all the elements that comprise ancient magic, both black and white, the difference being intention and the will of the Medium and those who comprise the group".

"Now that is Control and its function".

"I have referred on several occasions to the 'little people' (for want of a better term). These people are know by the name 'Nature Spirits' or, collectively, as 'Elementals'. They are very similar to the human race, but possess certain features which are accentuated, that is to say their bodies, if you could see them, are slightly out of proportion with features which are characteristically the same no matter what particular force they represent. Temperamentally they are light-hearted. They lack completely moral character, as you know. They are neither essentially bad nor good. They are every ready to obey the direction of the human mind where there is close kinship between the mind of the man or woman and themselves".

"They are able to manipulate the natural laws of ethers with the utmost ease, producing natural things such as stone, flowers and all things like that".

"In the scale of evolution, they stand between the animal realm and man himself. The one goal they desire to attain is the physical form complete. In the séance room as far as physical phenomena are concerned, their services are very necessary; in fact no work could be achieved without their aid in producing solid objects brought from a distance. In many other forms of phenomena, their services are utilized; but always under direction of the Control, who is very closely allied to themselves yet superior in mentality. [In the case of this Medium (Arnold Clare), the one called Simba] they love to disport themselves by simple antics such as causing things to move; and invariably their presence is betrayed by aimless moving of objects within the vicinity of the Medium, that is, more or less, movements without a definite purpose.

"They, too, are responsible for the maintenance of séance conditions; and their services are quickly withdrawn if any offence is given by anyone present unless the Control has instituted some form of discipline. They are subject to discipline, but that is only in relation to their normal work, which ranges from the geological realm up to all activities of nature, including flowers and insects; they are even associated with the air that you breathe, and the water that you drink".

"That is why I have said séance room work is a natural religion, a primitive religion of mankind. That is why we are anxious to lift it more from the realm of the soul and the natural side of man, so that it may be directed purely by the spiritual, of which man, more and more is becoming aware. That is our mission and our work to do".

"You will remember, too, that I have said on one occasion that phenomena would go on in the presence of the Medium without intervention from a discarnate entity, but it will lack purpose and be entirely sporadic because of the familiarity and link between the Medium and these little people".

*Question* : "That explains the movements we sometimes see in the presence of a Medium, when he is normal."

*Peter* : "That is right".

"The same 'little people' can be pressed into service even for certain types of healing; but their services are not often used; only for psychic healing; and then for the ailments affecting chiefly the bony structure and deformities".

"To sum it all up, you might say they are the soul of nature. As man himself has many complex parts working together to accomplish something far too immense for the ordinary mind to grasp. They are not left to wander aimlessly in space but are directed by superior intelligences who press them into service according to their capabilities, with only one purpose in view, development and progress along the road of the whole realm of nature, to keep it in step and in tune with the whole life and scheme of creation whilst working ever towards the perfect plan ordained by God".

*Question* : "We have often been told that there are other workers such as Spirit Chemists in the séance room. Are they there in addition?"

*Peter* : "Not through any direct interest in the production of the work or of the séance, but witnesses learning the laws. They are there in order that they may impart their experiences to man if he is sufficiently attuned to their own minds to be receptive".

*Question* :"We are also told that healers associated with a Medium are there to protect him or look after him".

*Peter* : "No, not essentially there to protect him any more than they would function in that capacity in any other form of work. No, they are there because of their knowledge of cosmic rays which are so essential to the healing mind and body of the sufferer. The benefit of these rays is very similar to that gained from your radiotherapy. You see they make use of certain wavelengths or frequencies, which are coarser form of finer cosmic rays. You see the association.

*Interrogation* :"We have pictured a number of personalities each doing his different job!"

*Peter* : "If you demand an answer from a Control you get it, but they may not have sufficient understanding to answer it correctly although they think it is the truth as they see it. I would not deny that such personalities are present, but they are there only as observers".

*Question* : "You said the method of control depended upon the fact that the Medium had not attained spiritual perfection to any extent. Is it possible for the Medium to attain it?"

*Peter* : "How do the Controls work in the case of one who has not attained spiritual perfection? In this case, the Controls are still associated with the Medium but work without his spiritual aura. They are similar to the 'little people' in that they follow the direction of the Guides. They are happier working thus; they are freer. In the case of one who works spiritually, he must have always the ideal in front of him; for once he loses faith in himself the contact is snapped".

*Question* : "With the Medium who is psychic only, the phenomena is still produced?"

*Peter* : "That is quite correct, and usually more robust too. There is nothing to learn from it".

## WHITE BROTHERHOOD

The White Brotherhood are different groups of very advanced people in the Spirit World. Ones who have aspired to the level of teachers, healers, and ones who have the knowledge of how it is best to help others on the earth plain in specific situations. Quite often Mediums see them as people in white, I have seen them subjectively in the halls of learning, and objectively within the Circle between the chairs of the sitters at Stansted Hall in the blue room in a Circle run by Lionel Owen.

The names given to those within the groups are called by other peoples of the earthly world, Masters, Mahatmas, Great Teachers, Maharishi, or Enlightened Ones.

One group it is known, help to watch over the people when they pass over to the other dimension. Helping when they first pass across the veil, those who have had their troubles here on earth. Those poor souls of fixed, unshakeable beliefs, and those who are not ready for their sudden transition into the higher vibrational level. Those sad people who think no one loves them, and they are all alone.

The "White Brotherhood" are there always waiting by the unfortunate, waiting for them to send out a thought, so they can step in to help. It is the divine law that they cannot help, or do anything without first being asked, by word of mouth [if still on earth] or a sent out thought of a need for help through the mind of the person in need, here on earth and in Spirit.

Within the "White Brotherhood" there are also groups of teachers of the higher levels of philosophy. But it must be remembered here it is only their individual group thoughts' on the subject, yes it is to the best of their knowledge, so do not take their words as being the whole truth. Those in Spirit also have to advance along the many more pathways of learning, just as we do here on the earth plain.

There are also groups of the "White Brotherhood" who are dedicated to helping Circles develop, especially in the ways they think best for each individual, in each individual group here on the earth plain. Some of those people of the "White Brotherhood" I have Clairvoyantly (this was objectively) seen sitting within the Circle with us. This was in 1996 whilst sitting with Lionel Owen's group in the Blue Room at Stansted Hall.

Some other groups of the "White Brotherhood" watch over the sick and the infirm, giving the healing to the patients sent out by others on the earth plain and magnifying it with their own power. Other groups help the Healing Mediums on the earth plain.

Some help the Physical Mediums in their work of Linking with those in Spirit and producing phenomena.

Some watch over what we would call tricky situations. When at times we humans get into difficulty, and we are helped when we think no other person is around. Sometimes in those situations suddenly we are out of that tricky situation, and out of danger not fully understanding how it happened.

We might have been heading towards a crash and the next thing we know, we have had something turn the tables, and we are out of that predicament. We are left wondering after the situation how it happened. Often we have in that split second sent out a quick thought of help. This is where the "White Brotherhood" have stepped in quickly, and most times very briefly into your life to help in your hour of need, or should I say the fraction of a second of need.

That is how quick and wonderful the power of Spirit can be.

Be thankful for it, and be thankful for those who have developed into the realms of "White Brotherhood" group.

**YES; all it needs is a simple thought, for that help at that crucial time**.

# OUR LIFE CONTINUED ACROSS THE VEIL.
# Or LIFE AFTER LIFE.
# Or LIFE AFTER DEATH.

Many people if not all the people in the world when getting on in years, or laying in a hospital bed or ill at home, start to think "what is going to happen to me when I pass from this body into the unknown which is called **"death"**?" Please let me reassure them that **there is no "DEATH"** only a progression into the wonderful spiritual world that is full of love and Light of God, if that is what you have worked towards on this earth plane of ours. Those who have not, will have stay in gloom and grey darkness until they start thinking about working towards the higher vibrational plane into the loving harmonious Spiritual Light asking to be helped along the way when they are ready to do so. It is only the individual that knows when that is. It will be when they have found out their problems and addressed them, put them aside, and then let the loving harmonious Spiritual Light come into their being, **then and only then** by the **asking to be helped** will they then progress.

Countless books written by **TRUE** Deep Trance Mediums, **TRUE** Automatic Writing Trance Mediums, and people from the pages of different religious books have been given messages from the world we are all going to progress into one day. That is the one certain thing for all who are living here on this earth, we all will progress to our level in the World of Spirit according to our level of loving spiritual lifestyle on this earth plane of ours. There will be many an alleged religious person who will not progress very far because of the bigotry, evil, and nastiness they have in their hearts for their fellow man and the many living things for whatever reason. **Remember all religions of every kind on this earth plane of ours are man made**.

Also in the Spirit World, after earthly life, many a non-religious person will progress far because of their kindly loving lifestyle they have continued with throughout their lives. Many will progress a lot further than the many two faced religious people who kill, destroy, and mess up people's mind with their blinkered ways of living **within their insular man made religions.**

When we leave our earthly bodily shell to go into the grey darkness and progress to the level of spiritual light we have earned through our progression on this earth plane because of the sort of life we have led.

After a transition period, we are met by those we love, to be shown by them to a place of rest where we can adjust to our new surroundings. The people who think they have no one to greet them are met by compassionate people who will show them love and will care for them in the confusing transitional period. Those new surrounds are placed in our thoughts by the supreme power we call God, for when we are in Spirit we all communicate by thought, **thought the all powerful living energy**, the energy which is supposed to be a medium of life on earth, but it is in reality **THE living power** of life here and life ever after in the higher levels of existence.

The new place we will be taken to will be the same as we have been used to whilst on the earth plane, so it is not too much of a shock to/for the person who has gone to the other side of the veil.

Some people who have been taken by a sudden passing as in an accident, or an earthly disaster, do not even know they have crossed the veil, they have to be treated with care and compassion. Many find it hard to adapt because of leaving loved ones suddenly. It is the helpers at this time who have been trained for this purpose that come around them. It might be people of a different nation speaking in a language that would have been foreign to them on earth plane that might help, but because of the transfer of thought to communicate and not words, everything is understood.

The people who communicate from the higher spheres, the higher vibrational plane, tell of the things that are seen in the World of Spirit are more beautiful; stronger, more vibrant colours of everything there that are pleasing to the eye. Flowers that do not die but fade away into the air when finished, only to be replaced by new ones. There is no need for food to eat, as it is not necessary for people to survive. People do not grow old but stay at their prime. The children who pass very early grow up to stay at their prime. The ability to learn at your own rate, to progress as an individual person to the different levels of spirituality.

Most communicators have other work to do in the World of Spirit, many tell of helping others to progress and teaching them to learn of the progression possible into the other levels. Seven levels are spoken about, whether that is seven in each one of the seven of seven or just seven seems a bit of confusion. I go along with seven of seven and possibly of seven until seven levels. BUT it is said development is infinite. How that is achieved beyond a certain level is left as a mystery by the communicators because those in Spirit can only go up to a higher level into the brighter light for a very short time with a person of a higher dimension but finds it hard to stay there and adjust to the conditions because of their own spiritual development, the higher vibrational level is said to be not compatible to the soul who has not developed and the light there is said to be too intense for a lesser developed soul.

There at this higher level we are told the Light is much brighter and the colours are much more vibrant. Those who are not developed enough cannot stand the higher quality of the environment.

It is so natural for us as human beings to wonder what is going to happen to us when we die. Of that I have first hand experience in so much as I have partly gone to the place where I eventually will end up when this earthly body has had its time for me. Nothing is more certain than that one thing that we call "DEATH". That act of dying is going to happen to us all, no matter what.

There are a lot of books written by people who have had near death experiences and they all say the same, you go along a dark tunnel towards the Light and the ones you love are waiting to greet you at the end within that Light.

I was very ill in the 1970's after buying four parrots, which I was going to breed off. They died within a week and I was taken VERY ill. I was confined to bed and given the highest dosage of antibiotics you can be given. I did not remember four days of my illness after that, and I lost two stone in the week. I had I believe, double pneumonia, an infection on each lung. Before the illness had taken its course I was taken by Spirit up towards a window and through that window was the most beautiful valley, hills with grass, trees and water of the most vibrant, alive colours I have ever seen. I am not a person who says look at that beautiful view if I look across any hills and valleys, I have always took them with a pinch of salt because they are just there, this was something totally different. If at the time I would have gone through that window, I know I would have been there with my dad, he was waiting around the side I could not see, ready for me. But I was taken back down to the bed to where I was a sick person. After that incident I got better. This all happened when I was happily married with four children, and had no thoughts of going into a Spiritualist church. I started in Spiritualism in the late 1970's.

Another incident I had was in meditation just before going into the Light within my third eye I was taken to the halls of learning to gain knowledge, of what sort I do not know, because after seeing the "White Brotherhood" I was knocked out and I do not remember anything else for half an hour, until I came back into my normal state for my getting on with my life.

We are told time and time again there is a dark tunnel, a black tube, a cold bleak cylinder, an empty murky passage, a dim gloomy void we go into. If stuck there because of the life style we have lived, we have to ask for the help needed to progress. We have to go along through that bleak darkness, blackness, and gloom, through the empty murkiness, along the dark tunnel towards that Divine Light of Spirit that we all should be aiming for. That is **IF WE WANT TO for remember we all have free will.**

If for some reason we have had the life of a murderer, a liar, cheat, bully, thief, a nasty person. We end up in that darkness until we see the error of our ways; yes, we get the justice we deserve in the next life mixing with like souls, until we are ready to progress into the Light.

Some souls feel as though they are still alive and so they stay close to the earth plane vibrations, this is where ghosts and poltergeists come in. BUT the advanced souls who make contact with the Mediums of this earth plane have been developed to such an extent they can lower their own vibrations to such an exact level, with the help of highly developed people in the realms of Spirit, that they can communicate and act as a constant contact through thought for those who have passed on to the Spirit world. It takes a group thought to do this, **NOT just one person's thought**. Please remember **THOUGHT IS A LIVING ENERGY**.

We are told by the Deep Trance Mediums, when we pass over to the other side we are greeted by our loved ones, after that we are taken to what only can be described as reception centres like a caring hospital where the etheric body (what the person who has passed is now in) is rested and acclimatised to the higher vibrational levels, and different vibrating colours, which it is in. The colours there are of a brighter hue. Nothing dies it just goes on, there is no decay.

We are also told that a disorientated person should ask for help if they are lost and go towards the Divine Light of Spirit so they can be helped BUT until that thought is put out by that person of the need for help, nothing is done. Yes there will be others there near by for their protection; that single thought has to go out from the individual, as Spirit cannot interfere until asked to do so by the individual. It is the act of asking for help that triggers the help that is there in an instant.

Communication is by thought, but if you want to use speech it is alright to do so.

You can go to lectures, concerts, walks, work, learn, and are helped with your development in Spirit.

One of the most simple and easily read books on this subject is "More Truth" communicated by Arthur Findlay through the Mediumship of Eileen Winkworth.

There are many more in the psychic book shops but I have not read them.

# RUNNING A COURSE

There are many examples in this book of things to do in your courses but here are a few more.

A few suggested points to think about for running a course for the help of others to learn how to gain a stronger link with Spirit. The most important thing is to GET A LINK FIRST in any form of development. Get your students to close their eyes, and to talk to the Spirit World within their minds 10 to 15 minutes BEFORE the students try to develop any kind of Mediumship. I would say longer if they are only just beginning. Keep on reminding them to talk to the World of Spirit in their thoughts every five minutes just in case someone is not thinking about it fully, their mind is wandering, or they are falling asleep. The tutor MUST stress the importance of truth, honesty and sincerity in all things when dealing with the World of Spirit. If lies are told it is negativity, and negativity slows down, and many times stops development in the mediumistic person. It is in the students' own interest to be positive in all things.

A most important point that must be said here is training of Mediumship is not like any other teaching as it entails more compassion than normal. Most people when they are learning Mediumship become what can only be described as over sensitive with their emotions and this should always be borne in mind. The ordinary person becomes ultra sensitive, so be careful how things are said in the way of criticism, and how you go about guidance as everything said if wrongly put; can be taken to heart and destroy a person.

Don't be like me and go all around the houses to explain, I do this sometimes. I hope you do not say things as I sometimes do, back to front. Or, Saying one thing and mean another. **YES folks, I am**

**dyslectic.** I even don't see some words on a line sometimes when I am singing hymns I miss them out. I cover it up well though and get through life you have to learn to adapt to get through life. I had a haulage business for about 9-10 years. I have been a trainer [then took a course for a trainer's trainer] of people with learning difficulties, social problems, abuse, and drug problems. Yes, educating them all up to the standard of the "Royal Society of Arts, and "City & Guilds" for the government Vocational Certificates. I am also a trained counsellor; my course was taken in a Manchester Business College. I use to feel very proud of my position when the trainees used to come to me and say, "I wish you were my dad". I would often go home thinking about the day with my eyes watering, as I cycled the approximate 15 miles home, to cook the tea for my two children, and myself; Julie was then 13, and Tom 8.

Tell the truth to your trainees do not flannel them with false build ups of what they are doing. Tell them straight. Stop them if they do things in your opinion are wrong. It is better for someone to be told in their early stages than to go on in the false assumption they are getting things right. BUT always think about everyone being an individual and doing things slightly different to you.

Give praise and encouragement whenever you can to bolster the students confidence to help them go forward. Yes point out their failings but put it in such a way that they do not feel hurt. One way could be to say, "if I were doing this I would be doing it this way **because-------**". Or "don't you think it would be better doing it this way **because-------**". "I use to do it this way **because** then I found other ways did this-------**and this what happened for the better when I changed----**". Give credibility for your ways of doing the job in hand. Always give a reason for the change of direction you want a person to go along.

Point out the failings first then let them go, do not dwell on them, always finish any lesson on a positive note for anyone, pick out their good points and build on them. Make sure you have more good points than bad. People will respond better and quicker this way. Give plenty of praise to all who learn because they have put in an effort.

Give plenty of advice and mix with them whenever you can.

**DO NOT** go into the tutors room and hide away thinking you are special, because **YOU ARE NOT** far above the trainees, and they are not beneath you.

Quite often you learn far more of life from those you are teaching than from those in the staff room. Some in that staff room could have, as I have found out, insular and blinkered thoughts on their subjects. It also keeps you in touch with the real world, instead of keeping in your own cocoon of a teaching/learning environment. Are you keeping your head in the sky, thinking you are head and shoulders above everyone else?

Try to learn as much as you can of the subject that you are going to try and help people with. If you don't you will be found out early on.

**If you don't know how to do it, how can you realistically teach it?** OR as a true specialist in the same work he did from boy to man, a 90 year old friend said to me :-
    **"If you cannot do it, you cannot know it".**

**If you get someone who thinks they know it or how to do it,
ask them to demonstrate it.
Say "Now you show me how"!!!!**

Ted, my 90 year old friend always used to quote a friend of his serving his apprenticeship, who was saying to another workmate who was trying to tell this person he was going about a job he was doing the wrong way. He stood back and said right **"you show me how"** and that person could not. He only had the theory, not the practical experience. Saying "see you do not know it, so do not teach me to suck eggs". Learn and practice your craft, then teach it. He also quoted an incident with a very experienced surveyor he had a brush with while on a very big site. This surveyor came along while he was in the middle of a very intricate job of replacing some fancy plaster coving in Liverpool town hall and the surveyor told Ted he was going about it all wrong. Ted who had been doing his master plaster's job for more than fifty years, did no more than come down the ladder and gave the Surveyor his tools and said you do the job and walked out of the building to get his dinner and stayed off the job for four hours. That surveyor thought Ted was walking off the job and he did not know what to do. But he had learned a valuable lesson from that incident. That was NOT to tell people who have been doing the job correctly for many years how you are supposed to do it when you have had no **hands on experience** of the particular job.

If I can help people to learn, anyone can. Yes I believe every person can help others if they want to. YES I am dyslectic, I know what I want to say but **sometimes** the words do not come out the correct way for people to **sometimes** understand me. When I write things down I have to go over the written word about ten times before I am satisfied that my meanings will be understood. Even then I have to get others to check.

Tutors should **not try to separate themselves** from the pupils/trainees, by sitting separately from them while eating on a separate table. Each tutor should be on a different table with the pupils. Mixing with other pupils when ever possible. Perhaps each day swap tables so everyone has a chance to mix and talk to each tutor.

Over the years I have taken courses with trainers who have had very bad knowledge of the subject they were teaching and the way training should be done to develop a person's abilities in meditation, trance, [especially] spiritual, psychic. In my opinion the tutors should have not been taking those courses.
One lady tutor in Stansted taking a Trance course I was on, after she told us to go into deep meditation and link with Spirit was asked by a student in our group Circle :- "When we in the Circle are in an entranced state, then Spirit comes through us. If one person starts talking in Trance, when the person has finished speaking how will we know who is to talk next" the lady tutor in question said "When the person who has been talking has finished they should touch the person next to them, so they can then say something". **SO MUCH FOR KNOWLEDGE** of her subject. **You must never touch a person** in meditation never mind a person who is in a very much-altered state of awareness, one of Trance or Deep Trance, which is generally necessary for **"TRUE"** Trance speaking. I say again, **especially** not **one who is in a TRUE DEEP Trance State.** When in a trance state the Medium is not in full control of self.

I found this Medium's statement absolutely **RIDICULOUS**. Generally Spirit will know who is to talk. It would not have mattered if three people were talking at once. The idea of the course was to gain a better link with Spirit in the power of a strong Circle in the powerful atmosphere in that place. Spirit in that situation would have known who was ready to talk and when to talk. BUT there again, it could have been the person going to talk knew what was going on around her (not being in deep Trance) and wanted to have a clear field for her **"act"** of Trance or Linking with Spirit!! **So many people DO fool themselves that it is Spirit linking and Spirit is talking through them when it is only them and their imagination.** People in a light trance state can be inspired by Spirit to use words they would not normally use. This is inspirational speaking which is a wonderful thing in its self more people should try it. But please do not confuse it as speaking in a deep trance state. When the world of Spirit is using the Medium in a very deep trance state.

One time in a development Circle, a tutor kept on saying my name [and also he kept on using other people's names while they were trying to go deeper into a Trance State], this was when I was learning to try to go deeper into Trance State and hold a contact with Spirit with a stiller mind. He kept on breaking my mind stillness, bringing me back to reality by saying my name when explaining to the others in the group what was going on in the cabinet; this was by the way a very experienced man who regularly did Trance demonstrations. He is a really decent man, but for myself all the other people who have sat with him and I have spoken to, say he is not a trainer. Perhaps if both of them got the correct training off others with greater knowledge, and then **take notice** of their advice, they will then because of their experiences become excellent tutors. The trouble is some people think they know **all** that happens in the Linking with Spirit if they are an alleged Medium of one speciality. Teaching and training is totally different to telling people about a subject. It is an art, so get some training before teaching or training anyone.

**Lecturing on a subject is NOT teaching or training someone to do something practical. Lecturing in many circumstances is generally only a person's theory, a speech.**

If you go in for teaching people in a college, you will probably have to be assessed at one of the colleges "MAKE SURE" that the person or persons **"who are assessing you" <u>can do the subject itself,</u>** the one you are taking the assessment for. I mean DO they do it practically, and are they practicing it regularly? Especially deep Trance work. Unfortunately a lot of the so-called tutors in these teaching centres and colleges do not do it genuinely. They are not True Trance Mediums.

It is just like some man saying to a woman who is having a baby **"I KNOW WHAT YOU ARE GOING THROUGH?" Just as if** !!!!! Even a **woman** who has <u>**NOT had children** cannot know</u> what having a baby is like.

I had to have the qualifications myself <u>**AND practical experience**</u> to teach for industry. I taught 16 to 25 year olds in Warehousing, Storage and Distribution, Computer Studies, Cooking, and Life Skills. I gained those skills over the many years I had been doing them. I had been a heavy goods Wagon driver, I had had a Haulage business, I cooked most Sundays when I was married, I brought up two children on my own and cooked for them from their ages of 8 [son] and 13 [daughter] until they left home, both now cook very well themselves. I went to day and night school to take different courses of computing so I had the knowledge, and I bought a computer so I could go beyond the things taught at school. *I Had the were with all* to tell and show those students how to go about those skills they needed for their life outside **BUT MOST IMPORTANTLY**, I had the experience and knowledge to teach and assess those Students ready for their assessment by the Royal Society of Arts and City and Guilds examiners who came around to see what level of competence each student was at. **YES I knew how to do all the things I was teaching.**

**I HAD TO BE AT A STAGE OF COMPETENCE <u>ABOVE</u> THE STUDENTS.**

**HOW MANY ASSESSERS CAN SAY THAT THEY ARE ABOVE THE STAGE OF COMPETENCE OF THE STUDENT THEY ARE ASSESSING AT THE PSYCHIC COLLEGES? Especially in trance work. Have you as a tutor been sitting for many years for trance????**

I have been sitting for the Spirit World since the 1970's and I have been through most stages of development as can be seen in my book, and I see so many people who think they know what they are doing in the way of assessing and muddling through teaching in their not so good ways of linking with Spirit, it is so sad to see. There is only one way to know how to link with the World of Spirit for assessment purposes and that is through experience. Nothing more, Nothing less.

Would you let any none competent person assess you for a job in industry if they had not done it themselves. Would you pay out your own money to an incompetent person to serve any of your customers you might have and give advice to them, so they would come back to you again. **OF COURSE YOU WOULD NOT!!!! We need the TRUE, ABLE, dedicated workers who can do the job and NOT the ones who pretend to be able to.**

I go back again to

# IF YOU CANNOT DO IT, YOU CANNOT TRULY KNOW IT.

Talk to as many people as possible at the colleges who practice all types of Mediumship. Ask them about their experiences, and all about when they were learning their craft, what they went through. I learned much more from the pupils at the colleges than I did from the tutors when I was attending on different courses. I must admit some pupils were as old as 70+ many with more than 50 years experience of sitting for Spirit. Some of the tutors I have spoken to have only been practicing sitting for Spirit for under five years some less than that. Sit in the other classes when you have time, take notes, ask questions of the other tutors when they are on their own. Have those questions written down ready so you can remember them.

A tutor should get used to the method of Mediumship they are going to teach and practice it in Circles, practice it on their own, sit in other practical, knowledgeable people's teaching Circles at the colleges to see how they go about their craft.

Try sitting for the type of Mediumship you are going to teach in, in as many different circumstances, tutorials, and courses. Go to as many as you can, so you can experience good and bad points of other tutors and their ways of teaching others, sit with as many other people as you can.

Go to see as many Mediums as possible who practice the form of Mediumship you are going to be teaching. This is so you can give examples of the good and bad points of the ones you saw [leave personalities out of the equation]. If you cannot get around to see as many as you would like, read as much as possible on the Mediums who have experienced in/of that form of Mediumship.

When asked to run a course, plan each day, and have a few extra subjects at hand just in case things do not turn out correctly on say, two days. Get ready some things you have written out, planned already, ones that you can do immediately, at the drop of a hat if one thing goes wrong.

**At the start get your rules for the Circle, or the teaching within the room set at the start of the session.**
**Have your rules and restrictions of the Circle, your practical sessions or your lectures for the week written down so you do not forget any.**
**Discipline has to be brought back into the teaching and the sitting in the Circles.**
**Start on time with a prayer and finish with a prayer.**
**Be firm and fair with all, no favourites.**

**Tutors should tell each individual student to be bringing Spirit near, asking Spirit for help in the coming Circle and to come closer them at least an hour before the sitting and keep on doing it during the Circle sittings.**
**Tell them what they give out sincerely to the person developing (others) comes back to them ten fold.**

**You cannot expect any Link with Spirit to suddenly come in moments in a newly formed Circle. It needs as much help as possible from the newly brought together sitters and those in Spirit to get that harmony built up in the Circle as soon as possible for the sake of everyone's development.**

How many tutors think of trying to get the **harmony** into the Circle before the start of any sitting because they are tired, busy or have not thought about it, and yet **it is the most important part** of the sitting in any Circle.

An exercise that might seem strange but it can be used to bring harmony to the Circle. YES it does work!!!
First the leader then each person in turn has to look at each person individually in the group and smile at them and say with **feeling, and sincerity** out loud "hello and welcome to our group", it does not matter if you feel uncomfortable, silly and laugh, that will raise the vibrations. When that is done ask everyone to close their eyes, think about the joining together of the Circle and then smile inwardly at everyone there, then smile inwardly at those in Spirit you are going to meet. Welcome the Spirit World Helpers into yourself and to the Circle. Feel happy about meeting Spirit as they draw near to the Circle, welcome them, feel the happy anticipation, the warmth of the feeling. **Be sincere** about the love you are giving out to those in Spirit and the Circle.

Say a prayer that everyone can relate to before any start.
Use the one that I always use in its slightly different wording. "Divine Spirit please help us all to develop in our own individual way but only come with goodness, kindness, love and truth, come within the peaceful loving Divine Light of Spirit within the loving harmony of Spirit of the highest realms lead us towards gaining oneness with God".

**The most important lesson BAR NONE at the beginning of any development class for the students, whether beginners or experienced, [this is the basic thing that most tutors I have sat with have forgotten to say to the students at the start of the development Circles] is for the tutor to tell their pupils how to bring Spirit to the environment around them, how to get Spirit World to come**

**...ose to the individual so Spirit can develop the individual. For experienced people/students, this gets the whole group in harmony and it shows you are in control of the situation and know what you are doing.**

Have the student/students sit comfortably, at a suitable distance from each other so they do not touch. There should be no possibility of a sudden shock being given to anyone there. No mobile phones left on, all phones off the hook. No chance of any person walking into the room where the development sitting is taking place. No flash cameras.

The student should always be encouraging within their mind Spirit to come closer and to ask within the mind for Spirit to help them with the task that is needed in the Circle situation or where ever. The older experienced Mediums of the last century sat down in meditation for at least half an hour to an hour before any demonstration, talking to Spirit within their mind encouraging their helpers to come closer and to help them on the platform, in a group situation, with physical demonstrations, and also whilst sitting on their own for development. I personally can be sitting or slowly walking around in the quiet, talking to Spirit within my mind asking for help and encouraging them to come near, just as I do while sitting in meditation to bring in a stronger link with my Spirit Helpers before I sit in a Circle. Each student should be encourage to do so before each Development Circle sitting outside somewhere quiet, or inside the room where it is going to take place, and the reasons why explained to them.

The time for enjoying yourselves and messing around are after the sittings are over, or at the nighttime get together in the lounges or bar, not during the learning periods. BUT the learning situations do not have to be stuffy and stiff, remember most phenomena and happenings with Spirit come when the people are enjoying the atmosphere, happy, and in harmony with each other, development comes quicker in that atmosphere. It is up to you to make it so.

The best atmosphere to learn in is a happy, lively one. Never serious, Spirit always comes closer when the atmosphere is lifted. It is the serious, inflexible Medium tutors that can ruin a course for the students, then they, the pupils will not come back to any more courses, remember they are adults NOT children and they will have paid for their courses. **BUT** rules in Circle **NEED** to be adhered to. They are there to learn during the day. **"REMEMBER" THE EVENINGS AND THE NIGHT IS THEIRS (the pupils)**. It is their free time of winding down relaxing, **IF** they, the pupils want to go to bed and be quiet let them, if they wish to be boisterous and jolly let them, if it does not interfere with the quiet ones.

A lot of people who go to the colleges to learn for the week, it is their one and only holiday of the year, please make it a memorable one for them, it will encourage them to come back next year.
If people are happy learning, they learn more and find it far easier to learn in a happy, relaxed atmosphere. Happy and satisfied people always look forward to coming back to the next course meeting. Why on earth do the parties happen on the last night of the courses when everyone on the course has got to know each other over the week? The get together and/or party should be on the first night or day of the course. That way people get to know each other from the start and the atmosphere is happy from the start. This will relax all there and lower their barriers by mixing earlier with most there on any course, so bringing in the "harmony" quicker, which is so necessary, with all there.

The trainees/pupils should be told the more you meditate in a Circle with people of like minds, the stronger the Link becomes with those in Spirit who are going to help. It is like you are meeting friends each time, because that is what Spirit is, a group of friends. Imagine if you have a friend here on the earth plain. You have grown up with them. This person starts to drift away from you, because you do not see them so often, you are not keeping in regular contact with them, the loving link gets weaker, the Spirit link can sometimes die. Look at Spirit, they are only ordinary people who have progressed to a higher vibrational level, one we as yet cannot fully see or fully understand. But we can become close to and we can link better and stronger with those there in Spirit by keeping regular, happy, loving contact with Spirit, this fact must be stressed to all. There is no quick fix; it is only in meditation that the link gets stronger!
The longer you meditate the faster you progress. Quite often an hour to two at a time is long enough for most, but if you have the time and inclination meditate longer during the day.

When taking a Circle, you, the tutor should not meditate. EXCEPT at the start [about five minutes] to help build up the power of the Circle (while talking to Spirit through thought, asking for their help. This should have been taking place by the tutor automatically before hand anyway). Then the tutor should be watching out for anything that is happening with the students. Especially in a Trance and Physical Circle. It should be remembered that **in any Development Circle** a lot of wonderful things **can and do happen**.

The tutor at the start of the meditation should have told the students to keep talking **sincerely** to Spirit in their mind **with their sincerest thoughts**, over and over and over again and again and again, encourage Spirit to come near and help them develop within the student whatever they are sitting for. This should be done for at least about a quarter of an hour or so to start with [This should be done at the very start of any teach in]. This is the one most important things that the tutors all seem to forget. You have to **ask Spirit sincerely** for development and encourage the Spirit World to come near to you, to come closer and help. Then the students should be told after a period of time to try and still the mind by looking into the Light within the third eye area for at least a quarter of an hour, then again **ask sincerely** and encourage Spirit within the thoughts in their mind, then try to still the mind looking into the third eye area looking into the colour void, or the Divine Light [which will come to all in time], to give Spirit a chance to do their work of development.

This should be repeated for the hour or an hour and a half. As this is needed for the first part of the course as it should be used as a basis for the week. This should be reminded of at each session, at the start of each Mediumship development sitting.

The tutor **should not say the students name** if anything starts to happen with them in deep meditation. As by saying the name of the student can act as a trigger to the subconscious mind and bring the student back to reality out of that altered state of awareness when their development is starting to happen, by saying the name of the student it brings their mind into the equation and subsequently makes them think, so can break the link with the World of Spirit.

Tutor should stand in front (or be sitting at the side) of the student if Spirit tries to come through when the student is going deeper into Trance. When in front of the student the tutor should be **talking to Spirit**, **NOT the student**, encouraging Spirit to come through. Helping by telling Spirit how the manipulation (if developing transfiguration or trance) of the person is going, and which way Spirit should do things better for the student. Sometimes if a person is starting off in Trance the student can be shaken, have twitches, mouthing of words with no sound. I think the trainer should NOT ask the student to say something [they will have to think of what to say, so bringing themselves out of a still mind (or slowed down thoughts going through the mind) breaking the clear link with Spirit]. All they should do is trust in Spirit, help and advise Spirit with the development of the vessel [the budding Medium] they are working with.

Students should be made aware of the possible happening when a person goes into deep meditation BUT do not make them fearful of any happenings, if Spirit is going to use them, the Spirit World are not going to bring any harm to them.

Keep reminding the other students to ask Spirit **sincerely** to come with only goodness kindness love and truth to be filled with the Divine Light of Spirit from the highest realms of Spirit and then give their own power from Spirit unselfishly and **with all sincerity** to the person being developed. Reminding them what is given out sincerely and unselfishly, comes back to you ten fold, this should be done until it is their turn to sit in front of the group in a cabinet or at the open point in the horseshoe shaped Circle.

Make sure you have a list of the very basics of how to go through the procedures of the course you are training people for. Lets face it you might have forgotten little pointers over the years, so have them written down so you can look them up from time to time. This is to remind you and they act as a prompts when rushed or tired. Even some so-called experts forget their basic training; perhaps this is why they fail in their Links. Yes, we all can take things for granted, and carry on in that way until we are pulled up and reminded. Remind yourself before others do it for you. Perhaps others you are training might not come back for any more training off you.

Have mixed activities ready to be tried in the groups. This will break the monotony of sitting in meditation all the time.

Have table tilting. This, it should be remembered was the way the last generation was guided by Spirit, as were the spelling out boards (Ouija boards) I would recommend trying to get a good, truthful link and then ask for advice; Or are you one of the people who rely on the words of Mental Mediums. I personally don't; and looking at some mental Mediums on the platform, I would not in a million years be guided by most of them. Some Mediums [alleged Mediums] seem to get a Link and then interpret it in the strangest ways imaginable. This unfortunately is when they think they can do the job of Spirit, bringing their own mind into the equation. The message is not pure, direct from Spirit, it is being coloured by the [alleged] Medium's mind.

Try mind games sending colours of cards [which are facing away from the other person] to each other; get the students to try to improve on the scores they get. Remember each time to have the students get their Link with Spirit first, to ask for their help.

Have Psychometry exercises by the owners placing their objects on a tray so no other person touches the goods except the owner and the trainee Medium who is doing the reading off the object.

Have the student Mediums give a reading off one object each.

Have colour readings for each other off a drawing each student has done for the other, but with the student Mediums first linking with Spirit. Using Spirit's help.

Put pictures in sealed envelopes, and have the student Mediums ask Spirit for help to find out what is in the envelopes. Have the students individually write the information down.

Have two student Mediums sitting in a chair each, back to back, [at different times have the students front to front] have them first meditate for five to ten minutes, asking for Spirit's help bringing in the power through thought. Then before they come out of meditation have the students imagine their auric field expanding, try to get them to see it in their mind going outwards, as it expands it goes around the person at the back [or front] of them enveloping each other. They hold it there. Each person with Spirit's help [asking through thought] has to try and pick up any complaint the other has. Also they have to try and pick up any other feelings, thoughts, hunches, anything they can about the other person while still in meditation. Each person in turn gives to the other [or to the group] what they received and what it meant for them. A reading of sorts. This is another mind exercise for any Medium.

Meditate using different methods as described in the book. I am sure many of you can think of different ways to keep your students happy in various ways. So do not get bogged down in the same old routine that will put off the regulars.

Here is one form of meditation exercise that might be of use as an icebreaker on different subjects of your own choosing.

Using this form of meditation activity is to involve a group of people. It might be in a church hall or in a work place depending on what outcome is needed.

A "leader" has to pick a subject, a statement or an idea for each group of three to six people.

Let us first start as an example with a Spiritualist church hall situation.

The people in each group sit in their own individual Circle, slightly away from the other groups if possible.

The "overall leader" of the get together, asks for complete silence off all that are there from that moment on, and no person has to talk until asked to do so. **This is important.**

The "overall leader" gives the leader (**spokesperson**), of each individual group, a piece of paper on which is one of the seven principles of Spiritualism, (or any other subject).

The **spokesperson** shows each person in the group what has been written. NO TALKING.

Then all are asked by the overall "leader" to go into meditation to link with Spirit for about a quarter of an hour. Each person there are told to be talking to the Spirit World over and over and over again through thought so that it is certain the Spirit World is close to each individual, and continually reminded at intervals of every few minutes.

The "leader" talks through the group into the meditation, if needed by some. With or without music. So the options are many.

I will give an example of a talking meditation [contemplation] so if needed the "whole room group leader" can read out from this book. Talk your listeners through it in a gentle voice, and very slowly. Never rush a meditation talk. Pause longer than normal at each full stop. Let all in meditation see and feel the place they are in within their mind's eye. [This form of meditation can be used for mental Mediumship development as it can for some people put relevant pictures of the scene into the budding Medium's mind and so Spirit can see how their mind mechanism works].

See yourself at the start of a pathway going through a large garden, which is leading to a large building. You open the gate and walk along the path.
As you go along this path you see flowers of all the seasons blooming all at once. It is a fantastic sight.
There are beds of spring flowering bulbs, crocus, daffodils, bluebells, tulips and snowdrops, all mixed with all the summer and autumn flowers. It looks amazing, what a wonder to behold.
As you walk through the garden you hear the birds singing in the beautiful pink, red and yellow flowering shrubs. You stop for a minute and listen.
Your eyes then are drawn to a white buddleia the butterfly bush, there is a purple one beside it; they are attracting the butterflies by the hundred. There are butterflies of every shade and colour. This sight fills you with wonder.
You walk further along the pathway towards the building, while breathing in the fragrance of the flowers around you.
On coming to the building you see the door is open ready for you. You enter and go into a large hall where there are people ready to help you with what ever you wish to know.
Ask the people in your own mind for what ever you want answered by them. If needed, you are shown towards a large screen where the answers to your questions are being shown for you to go into your mind.
You sit in front of this screen with your helpers by your side. Anything you do not understand you only have to ask of them within your mind with your thoughts.
If the helpers do not know any of the answers to your questions, some of them will go to the vast array of books on every subject and find out, another few helpers will go and look for the answer on computers, others will put out a thought to a higher level of consciousness to find out some answers for you. No stone will be left unturned for the answers. There are many helpers there ready to help you, put your thoughts out to them. Nothing is impossible in this atmosphere of love and light.

**Each individual is to keep asking Spirit to come near in the normal way, (in their own mind with thought), and help with the task, to give them something that is relevant to the meaning of that single principle for themselves. What that single principle means to them individually.**
**The "leader" of the whole room group when the time is up will start to talk the whole room back through the meditation, back to reality.**

The time is now coming to an end for your questions.
Thank your helpers for being there with you, start towards the door of the building.
You go into the warm daylight in the garden.
Going through the garden you remember and turn to the butterflies flying around their own, special, flowering bush. You stand and watch them for short while.
But now time is pressing.
Going further down the path you pass the birds still singing out their own special songs of joy, it is good to be here in this garden again. Stop and listen for the short moment. [pause]. Listening and looking at all the beautiful flowers.
You carry on along to the end of the path, leaving the multi seasonal flowering garden behind you.
You close the gate behind you, leaning on the gate and having one last look into the garden. You thank those in the Spirit World who made it all possible. You sincerely ask for it to be possible for you to be privileged to return at a later date when you need the answers to some other questions.

**The "overall leader" then after a few moments asks all there to let the conditions go and open their eyes to come back to reality.**
**The "overall leader" then asks all the groups to go through the following sequences.**

The **spokesperson** in each group asks each person what they received whilst in meditation; also what they were given that was relevant to the principle or subject. The **spokesperson** writes down what is said by each person, on a spare piece of paper.

After each person in the group has had their say, each person in each of the groups has then the opportunity to comment on the comments of the others.

The "overall leader" has been going around and only listening to the conversations, not joining in with them.

This is then stopped by the "overall leader" after a set time that is felt appropriate by them.

The **spokesperson** of the first group has then in order, the opportunity to say to all the other groups there in the room, what each person in "group one", said about the principle or subject that was given to the group and what it meant to each person. They then say what each person in "group one" has received whilst in their personal meditation.

At the end of that each person in "group one" then has the opportunity to comment about their own experience, and what they received while in meditation describing it more fully.

When each person has had their say, the floor is then open for all in the room to comment, or ask questions of the first group. A time limit should be placed on each session here; otherwise it could go on too long in some cases.

The "overall leader" then stops the conversation and the next group has their turn, and then the next.

After all in the groups in the room have had their turn the leader then closes down the get together.

The session is then closed down in the usual manner, the "leader" asks for a short silence, asking Spirit for the power that has been built up in each individual Circle of friends and in the room, to go out in the way of healing to those who need it, and the thanking for the help and the link with our Spirit friends.

This form of get together can be used as a brain storming method of working to get the church committee members together to find methods of raising funds for the church, ways to attract more people through the doors of the church, how to advertise, where to advertise in the best places to attract. What words to put up on the notices. In fact anything in your church that is a sticking point or needs sorting out can be done in this way. By putting down the correct sentence or statement for each group it will get sorted out easily.

This method can be used to sort out problems in business, when the business has problems that are a sticking point. When a business needs to progress along in a different direction, so finding the best way for all to go in the working environment. How to advertise, where to advertise, the best ways of getting more money, better profits, new lines to sell, new ideas, better conditions, better safety, etc., in fact anything.

If you have problems with getting all the ideas for a new course to run, use this method; it works in different ways for all sorts of people. It also can be a very good way of problem solving in every day life, bringing answers to many sticky problems. If you have no partner to read out the meditation in this sequence, record it for yourself and leave a time lapse of about twenty to thirty minutes before recording the bringing yourself back to the gate and out of the garden. I will try and make recordings of these meditation sequences if people would like them just drop me a line. Just say which one you would like.

One way to try and get people to trust each other in the séance room situation is for them to practice what is called "**trusted closed eye flying**". With gliding meditation music playing.

This method is done by people being placed in pairs. Have them standing up and facing each other. One person is to be the guide and the other the person is going to be the flier. The guide stands feet slightly apart, comfortable and balanced, with their hands palms facing the flier, in front of the flier. The flier then places their hands onto the palms of the guide's left to right, right to the left one. The flier stays in their position standing with their feet slightly apart putting their weight **slightly** onto the guide's hands **leaning** onto the hands as the guide moves slightly away [less than one step, ½ to a ¼ ] from the flier. The guide should feel the slight pressure of the flier's body through their hands. The leaning position of the flier can be adjusted by the guide as the sequence is gone though. {*It should be noted it is only **slightly away** from the guide and the flier, as any more is too much pressure on the hands of the guide and it becomes tiring as the flier becomes heavier*). The flier should feel as though they are **slightly** leaning onto the guide. The flier closes their eyes as a piece of soothing music is played. The guide now talks to the now blind (*eyes closed*) flier, as they both go through the imaginary sequence of flying as a bird would. The flier should remember they should be always having their weight on the guide's hands. This is where the trust is, and knowing they, the flier will not fall.

The guide or the person at the front who is take the class (one to one interaction is best, as the story can be made up along the way with the appropriate actions at the correct times by the guide) talks as they are thinking how the bird would move and react with their wings.

E.g. See yourself as a bird flying as you are going over the hedges, trees, mountains and the clouds. To start off, you take off from a high cliff top (*slowly flaps the arms up and down to start off, the guide opens up the arms wide as they glide across*), you glide down over the trees on the mountainside. As you pass the trees, you hear the birds that are singing in the trees as you fly by, listen to them, don't they sound lovely? They make you feel wonderful to be alive. (*the guide moves the flier's left arm down to one side the right going slightly up so it is as though the flier is turning in a circle to listen to the bird song*) you are now turning and soaring around the high trees listening to the bird song. (*be silent as the guide moves the arms first one way slowly up then the other way slowly as the bird song tape is listened to*) you feel the wind rushing under the wings as you fly around. You are feeling warm, comfortable and secure as you glide across the sky at this height. (*the guide slowly takes the flier's arms slightly lower to have them feel as though they are going downwards towards the hedges which are below the tree height*) Going slightly down towards the hedgerows you can see the flowers in the fields along side the hedges as you go across them. Here is a larger hedge to go over (*as they both sway ever so slightly slowly and gently, first to one side then swaying to the other side [the guide still taking the weight of the flier on their hands], the guide gently lifts ever so slightly the arms of the flier as a bird does with their wings the flier feeling the sensation of going over the larger hedge*). You are starting to go higher into the sky up towards the clouds seeing the ground below you (*as the guide raises and opens the fliers arms gliding ever upwards*), it is looking beautiful. You are feeling the air rushing under your wings as you fly towards the clouds (*the guide is slightly swaying the flier as though they are going first one way then the other. The arms of the flier are still apart as though they are the bird gliding, the wings are never flapped*). Here you are gliding across the countryside in the higher parts of the air way above the trees, and hedges, which you can now see as small bushes on the ground way below you. In the distance you can see a mountain ahead of you. You want to go and see what is on the other side. Heading towards the mountain, you can see the purple heather covering the sides of the mountain as you get closer to it. You go down to see what is at the base of the mountain. (*the guide lowers the arms of the flier ever so slightly*) you are reaching the bottom of the mountain it is necessary to fly now upwards to avoid crashing into it. (*the guide lifts the flier's arms slightly higher*) it gives you a wonderful feeling going ever upwards so quickly over the purple heather. (*the guide keeps the flier's arms higher until the top of the mountain is reached*) as you reach the top of the mountain you can see over the other side a wonderful richly coloured green valley where the plants are growing so lush over you go across the mountain top going down to the valley below (*the guide taking the flier's arms slightly lower and swaying slightly one way and the other slowly*) as you go down the other side of the mountain you are avoiding trees that are on the mountain side. Etc. etc. etc Make up your own route as you talk the people through the sequence. The guide has to take the flier's arms higher or lower depending on where they are said to be flying or from side to side if drifting or one arm slightly up and the other down depending on the turning the guide is taking the flier. Never moving from the spot, the feet must stay on the same spot, especially so the flier. Some fliers as they are flying upwards have a tendency to go up on their toes do not worry about this as it is a common reaction. **A leaning pressure** has to be maintained onto the guide's hands **at all times** by the flier

Here is a good way of showing people how Mediums work with their link.

Without at first giving the questions to be asked of Spirit or how to go about it properly. Use a role-play action of the mechanism of the Spirit World and the recipient of the messages from/through the Medium. This can be shown by having two people who know each other fairly well (or pretend they know each other fairly well) stand each one at the side of the Medium (a person acting as the Medium). The person on the left is acting as the person who is the Spirit World [Spirit contact]. They have to tell/explain to the acting Medium all about themselves so those on the earth plane would recognise the person in the Spirit

World, any little bits of information that can be relevant to the person (who is acting as the recipient of the message from the Spirit World) on the right of the Medium. The Medium then has to relay what is being said and they keep on going back to the Spirit (the person who is on the left) just as a Medium does while linking with Spirit asking the relevant questions to glean the right answers. They are to try and convince the person (the recipient, the audience) they are who they say they are in the World of Spirit. The audience can participate after by having an input of the questions they would have asked if they were in that situation. How they would have gone about it. It is a helping situation for all. Most forget about asking for the person's name, only giving information of happenings.

Examples would be :- **Who** do you wish to give a message to? Are you a man? Are you a woman? Are you a child? **How** old are you? **What** work did you do? **Where** did you work? Explain **how** you dressed? **What** did you wear? **How** many children did you have? **When** did you live on the earth plane? **When** did you pass across the veil? How did you die? What did you die of? Etc., etc., etc. **THE Where, What, Why, When, Who, How**. At the end of the message the acting Spirit is asked by the acting Medium to give some form of evidential proof. This is something which should be done by all Mediums every time when giving messages to the public. This should be put into the minds of the students. By telling them it is no use just giving the people messages if they cannot be backed up by some **strong last message the is true evidence for the person.**

After the trainees are settled, a prayer said, all there should meditate bringing Spirit into their being and encouraging Spirit to come closer to them and help them in their exercise. This should always be done before any session. And close the session with a prayer of thanks.

Have a large piece of card, or paper on which is placed pictures of various sizes, perhaps faces of different kinds, objects, small different scenes. Randomly write (or cut out of a newspaper and glue them on) words on the paper that stand out, and some that do not stand out too much  Write out or cut out short sharp words, something that could be made to fit an incident for someone in a Spirit linked message situation. E.g. Car crash, motorbike, red house, yellow brick surrounded garden. The Oak Tree, Camping, Boat, Red hair, Bald head, Cancer, Zimmer frame, (names of people, etc.) place only a few of each, not too many as the information has to be picked up fairly quickly as you yourself as a Medium does when linking with Spirit. Sometimes the picture and/or words from Spirit can be given in the mind for a split second and then they are gone.

What you are doing is to trigger responses from your trainees and show how the World of Spirit can show you images and words for the Medium to give evidence of survival after our so called death.

Get them to show how they would individually tell of the things they were receiving from Spirit. During this session, a lot of the trainees will try to make up stories from the words and images. This is where a selection of words on cards should be brought out to be shown to the students, the words can be got found in any dictionary. Choose words with the same meanings or sounding the same but ones having different meanings, e.g. KEY, HORSE, TANK, WOOD, SET, SERVICE, etc. On the back of your selection of words have the different meanings ready to be read out to the trainees. This is to show the trainees that what they say or think that should be said is not always correct meaning that Spirit wants to put forward.

After this has been done it should be firmly told to the trainees **"that the evidence only shown by the Spirit World or heard from Spirit should be given; NOT anything they think might have been meant by a word, picture or image.** If this is not done as suggested you are going along the road of a psychic and not a Medium, and the trainee Mediums will be letting their own mind interfere. This is where many Mediums go wrong with their messages and get them totally wrong. It is the subtle single image or word properly and truthfully explained/described that has the most impact for the recipient. A lot of Mediums can go off the message or block the message's meaning by enlarging on the words or images into things that were not given by the World of Spirit, leading to the recipient not recognising that the message was for them. The single subtle image or word from Spirit could be the one thing that will be the evidence for the recipient of the message to convince them that it is their mother or uncle Bert that has come and is giving them the evidence, and the Medium by trying to be clever and bringing their own mind into the equation could hide the true message in their interpretation of the image or word given by the World of Spirit.

Each card or collage that you have made, in turn should be held up at first to the students for a few seconds. Then as you go through your pictures, the time should be whittled down to a fraction of a second, just giving the student a quick glimpse.

After each showing of a picture, each person should be asked what they saw, and asked to give it out what they got as though they were giving a message from the World of Spirit to someone in the audience making sure they are **NOT asking questions** of the recipient, and the trainee Medium should be told to tell the recipient they are to only answer YES or NO.

I was given a picture of ........????, which was .....(**trainee Medium is to describe it**) near it was given the words .......????? [Trainee Medium says what words were give by Spirit] etc., etc., etc.

These sort of pictures that you have made for the exercise, and being describe by your group should be used for a while to let the students get the hang of things. To let them explain properly without questioning the recipient to glean information off them.

A good simple grounding makes a good Medium in the long run. Clairsentience (feelings about the pictures and words) should come later otherwise there could be a conflict of a person's imagination. But on saying this, go along with your own gut feeling. Most people seem to be going along the route of psychic rather than spiritual and this is where we are going wrong. In this instance the cards can be used again and the trainees explaining them as though they are receiving information from Spirit.

## One way to teach Trance or Transfiguration

in a group situation is to have [this can be two to many] four or five developing people [these are the sitters] on chairs in the front of the group there. Place the 4 seats facing the others [the observers], You must have a good number of observers so they can see what is happening, split the group sensibly. Have a space in between the sitters so they do not touch each other while in their altered state of awareness. This is done in low red light, or low white light, BUT no shadows are to be cast on the faces of the budding Mediums. If any shadows are suspected then the lights should be mobile so they can be lifted up during the sitting to see if there is a shadow or not, or if the alterations to the face of the budding Mediums are tubes supplying the facial skin area ready to eventually manipulate it into a different facial formation, may be a moustache or beard forming [with true hair], etc. or perhaps a full facial change to Spirit on the face of the budding developing Medium.

After the prayer or affirmation it should be pointed out to the students that linking with the Spirit World is always done in **sincerity and truth** and to be **in harmony** with all sitting in that room with them. If anyone lies about what is happening they are only fooling themselves no one else and Spirit will not give them the gifts asked for, they will be destroying the harmony so slowing down/blocking the development of self and the others. They will certainly be found out in the long run.

## Tutoring of Trance [plus transfiguration]

Have the four developing sitters close their eyes and talk to the Spirit World through **sincere thought**.

In their mind, each sitter is to keep encouraging the Spirit World **with all sincerity** to come near and help in their development of Mediumistic physical development e.g. Transfiguration or Trance Speaking. Tell the students, both the sitters and the observers, they have to keep on talking to the Spirit World through **sincere** thought for about ten minutes or so. The tutor in a low voice has to keep on reminding the students throughout every few minutes to keep **sincerely** talking to the Spirit World within their minds.

The observers at the start are also told by the tutor to close their eyes and continually talk to the Spirit World through their **sincere thought** asking to be filled up with the spiritual power as if they are an open vessel [the tutor in a low voice has also to keep on reminding them to do so] or continually asking the Spirit World to come near and fill them with the Spiritual energy ready to be sent to the developing sitters.

After about ten minutes or so, the sitters [budding Mediums] are told to stop talking to the Spirit World and just to look into their third eye area and get lost within the void, colour, or light that they might see in their third eye, they are to do nothing else {BUT if an individual feels that the Spirit World are not close enough, for a short while after, they should go back to the encouraging of the Spirit World through **sincere** thought to come closer and help in their development].

The observers are asked to keep sending what spiritual power they get from Spirit to the people sitting opposite them who are developing, pointing out at this point whatever power from the World of Spirit that is given out to others unselfishly by them, comes back to them ten fold, this is done at the tutor's say so. <u>The observers</u> after that ten minutes or so, then open their eyes and observe what is taking place, and over different intervals of about five to ten minutes right through the exercise, the observers are reminded by the tutor to be still sending their Spirit [they should be still asking the Spirit World for their help within their minds for the help with the spiritual energy and power for the sitters] given energy and power [through **<u>sincere</u>** thought] to the four developing Mediums. If and when it happens, the tutor can point out the swelling of the tubes on the face [at the side of the nose, along from the jaw to the outer eye socket area, across the top of the eye brows] and again the neck at the side slightly to the front [around the artery area] as well as sometimes forming a hole-like indentation of the neck at the front centre [where the collar bones join and dip, this can be the Spirit World working on the voice box area], and looking out for energy, the distortion of the visible (or the altering of the vibrational which is normally invisible) waves going through the air to the sitter's head generally at the back. This is like a heat haze on the road in summer. All this phenomena can be produced by the Spirit World during a budding Medium's development. This is the energy being given to the Medium being observed, this many times is seen at the back of the neck area, and **in rare cases** watch out for some ectoplasm [generally out of the orifices, e.g. nose, eyes, ears, mouth; sometimes the skin]. Each person, who is observing; as they see these things, should be pointing it or them out to the group and saying out loud, NOT SHOUTING just <u>in a normal voice slightly subdued</u>, **importantly NOT whispering** about what is happening with each developing Medium. Like the swelling and shrinking of the face of the particular budding Medium [this is if the budding Mediums are sitting for transfiguration; BUT it can happen in Trance Speaking sometimes as well so watch out for the signs]. There should be no pulling of faces and falsehoods by the budding Mediums otherwise it will hinder their progress. Everything should be done in truth, and honesty. All that is needed is the help of the Spirit World through **<u>sincere</u> thought**, allowing the Spirit World to do any manipulations **<u>NOT</u>** the Medium themselves through their own thoughts.

It should be pointed out to the students that physical phenomena is when all there in the room see the changes and faces placed on the Medium. Many are the times that a lot will see clairvoyantly so please know the difference.

**But <u>think</u> on;** when a Medium is developed and sitting for the people in the demonstration room, if their relation from the other side comes, does it matter if it is shown physically or clairvoyantly if it gives comfort to them.

## Tutoring of Trance Speaking and Inspired Speaking

When tutoring/developing students for "Trance induced Speaking" whether it is in a lighter state of trance for "Inspirational Speaking", or a deeper state of trance for "Deep Trance Speaking" both must be practiced with a **<u>clear link with Spirit</u>** [deep trance speaking can become direct voice, this is when Spirit take over the voice box of the Budding Medium or builds an etheric amplifier below the voice box]. It is imperative that the tutor knows the difference and the budding Medium also, so they do not fool themselves. It is also important to tell all the students to tell the truth in what they are doing and getting. The Students should explain to everyone there all about their feelings as things were happening to them; all the experiences have to be asked about and talked about. This is so important for all to learn from other people's experiences **as long as it is the <u>truth</u>**. Many will lie to build themselves up better than they are, others will fool themselves because inexperienced people have told them what they think was the truth in the person's development and they unfortunately, generally want to believe it, so be careful of the people who you believe. There are some not so truthful people in this spiritual movement, and many who come into tutorials try to become a Medium build up themselves into a person they think others will take notice of, becoming a puffed up ego balloon.

It should be pointed out to all the sitters, that when sitting for Spirit Voice manipulated vocal cords, this type of physical phenomena does not happen overnight. It takes the Budding Medium a long period of time sitting and linking with the Spirit World in a meditative state to get the Spirit controlled manipulations of the Medium's body correct [especially the vocal cord section if they are going to use it that way] if done in truth. So it will be seen it is the inspirational speaking development that will come first. This is why it is so important for students to know and realise this, please do not let anyone fool you or themselves.

In a group situation, have the four [more or less depending on numbers] developing sitters sitting at the front, close their eyes and talk to the Spirit World through **sincere thought**. To keep encouraging the Spirit World to come near and help in their development of Mediumistic Trance Speaking. Tell the students they have to talk to the World of Spirit for about ten minutes. Many times it should be done a lot longer especially in the early stages of development. [It also should be pointed out to students that their development never stops, no one is ever fully developed, so it is logical that their linking with the Spirit World should not suddenly stop even if the Medium themselves thinks they are developed]. The tutor in a low voice has to keep on reminding the students throughout, that is to say every few minutes reminded to keep on talking to the Spirit World helpers through **sincere** thought asking for help [the sitters who are getting developed should have given permission to the Spirit World to be used to prove there is life after our so called death, they are going to be subservient for Spirit's use]. The observers opposite are also told by the tutor to close their eyes and talk to the Spirit World through their **sincere thought** asking to be filled up with the spiritual power as if they are an open vessel and send it to the developing sitters. The tutor in a low voice has to keep on reminding the observers to keep talk to the World of Spirit through **sincere** thought, this is most important. After about ten minutes or so, the observers are asked by the tutor to keep sending what spiritual power they get from Spirit to the people sitting opposite them who are developing, the tutor pointing out what ever is given out unselfishly comes back to them ten fold, the bringing back of the observers is done at the tutor's say so [meaning, telling them to open their eyes and observe]. They then open their eyes and observe what is taking place, and over different intervals of about ten minutes are reminded by the tutor each student is to be **sincerely** talking to the Spirit World within their minds and sending their Spirit given energy and power [through thought] to the four developing Mediums. There should be no deliberate falsehoods; everything, when developing with the Spirit World, should be done in truth. All that is needed is the help of the Spirit World through **sincere thought**. If anything [words, comments, speeches, thoughts, etc.] comes into the mind of the budding Mediums after the truly linking with Spirit World, the words are given off through their **ordinary normal everyday speech** whilst in a trance/altered state, NOT IN MICKEY MOUSE ACCENTS, not in Homer Simpson, or any cartoon character accents, not in alleged American Indian accents, not in Chinese chip shop language, not in Italian delicatessen owner accents nor Asian kebab house accents, Irish, Scottish, Cockney, Scouse, Brummy, etc. If the foreign accent route is taken, then the accent becomes more important than the message from the Spirit World for the Medium and to the observers. Often it will be shown by the honest students, if the link with Spirit is a true one, the speech can and should become very quick and **without hesitation** or interruptions or the err's, ahh's, without the Medium's **own thought process** coming into the equation, this is where the use of a tape recorder can be brought into the session. Many are the times that can be pointed out the different levels of the Medium's trance state. The state of trance is never constant. The trance state in even the most advanced Medium often shifts quite a lot. That does not matter and should not be dwelt on. All that matters is for people to tell the truth in what they are doing. The use of a tape recorder can also show the students how foolish they sound to the public when not done in truth. It should be the aim of every tutor and student to be the best and the most honest Medium there is. Every developing person no matter who; should endeavour to sit for the highest standards possible, even if it takes a little bit longer, it will be worth while for them and for the sake of the Spirit World, the God Force they will be serving. I will say again lies are negativity and negativity slows down and many times stops the Sprit link. Spirit inspired speaking can become such a wonderful thing to listen to when it comes from the soul which is true.

The tutor should be observing the linking Mediums and over time will become accustomed to the energy from Spirit surrounding them, and when the start of a Spirit Linking Developing Medium is ready to speak. When the Medium is ready to speak they are approached very carefully by the tutor so they do not touch or knock the altered state developing Medium, and in a very low voice and very near them [this is so the others do not think they are being allowed to speak, who will be aware of the tutor speaking as will the budding Medium] some tutors give each Medium a number, **BUT in transfiguration** only give numbers to the developing Mediums at the front after they have closed their eyes, so only the observers know which Medium is what number. This is to stop the developing Mediums from influencing the manipulation on their faces. The tutor talking to the Spirit World, who should be now linking with the budding Medium, and not talking to the budding Medium directly, the tutor goes to the budding Medium [who will be aware of what is being said; **make no mistake about that**] and says if you wish to speak and give some words of wisdom which will help us all, slowly lift one finger [tutor looking carefully at the fingers]. If there is no sign of any fingers being moved, after a short period of time, the tutor should say "if you do not wish to speak and wish to stay developing together with Spirit in the power, please lift one finger slowly". If that happens then the tutor goes to the next budding Medium sitting, or the budding Medium who they think is ready to speak. This is where discipline comes into the equation; the Budding Medium is to speak only when asked to do so. Many a new Medium will rather sit in the power and develop, a lot will not have anything to say, especially if the Spirit World have not placed anything in their mind. That budding Medium, and only that individual Medium can know when they are ready to speak. This is when developing inspirational speaking from Spirit is done in truth. It should be pointed out to everyone there, that at the start of the development of the budding Medium, the link with the Spirit World will only be about 10% of Spirit and 90% of the Medium. It is only by sitting and meditating, **sincerely asking** and **sincerely talking** through thought to the World of Spirit and then stilling the mind [by looking into the colour, the light or the void] to allow Spirit to develop your passive mind, that the link gets stronger, nothing more nothing less.

Tutoring of Altered state Development for Mental Mediumship.
**People often ask me how do I get the Spirit World to give me names, full addresses, house numbers, telephone numbers, jobs people do, how they travel, etc. Everyone in this world is an individual and as such is slightly different in their learning BUT there must be a constant.**

That constant is :-
"**TALKING** to the Spirit World and **ASKING** through **SINCERE** thought".

# TUTORING MENTAL MEDIUMSHIP

## GETTING NAMES, ADDRESSES, TELPHONE NUMBERS, SMELLS, TASTES, FEELINGS.

Here is a form of contemplation, [or guided meditation as some call it], that can put your clairvoyance into a better format. Bringing in a better understanding between Spirit and the student. A way the Spirit World can see the way your or your student's linkage [within the brain area] within the mind puts images into your student's or your own third eye region.
Have your students sit comfortably. Get the group to close their eyes and with **sincerity** start talking to the Spirit World within the mind, in thought, asking those helpers across the veil to come and help with the fixing of images in the third eye region, and to learn together.
The tutor should keep on reminding the students at a few minute intervals to keep asking **sincerely** for the Spirit World bring themselves closer to the individual, and each person in their own minds to be doing this for about ten minutes to a quarter of an hour over and over, and over again. At the end of the quarter of an hour the tutor stops the students from talking through their **sincere** thought to the Spirit World and asks the students to keep looking into the third eye region [still with the eyes closed not opening them at any time] if they have not already been doing [this which they should have been doing all the time], the tutor now can go through the sequence. For a few more minutes the students asking the Spirit World to heighten all their senses as they go through the exercise. They should ask Spirit to see, hear, feel, sense, smell and taste everything that happens. They should be doing this exercise with their whole being. Each student being **very, very sincere** in their asking, and keep on asking if they don't get what they request.
The tutor should now ask the group or individual to relax and look into the third eye region.
The tutor talking to the group in a steady, calm, and relaxed voice.
A suggested format would go like this:-
You are staying in a yellow, sandstone, three bedroom, Victorian terraced single fronted house for a short break while you learn different things that will help you in your life. It is a nice warm sunny day, you come out of your yellow sandstone three bedroom Victorian terraced single fronted house door out onto the pathway, you turn around get hold of the 'cold brass knocker' and close the 'purple door' locking it with your 'brass coloured key' in the mortise lock, notice how cold the 'brass knocker' and the 'brass coloured key' are in your hand. You see the number of your house just above the 'brass knocker', it is '2' and the 'number 2' is also made of brass. You turn around and walk to the 'brown wooden gate' at the

bottom of the 'gravel path'. You open the 'brown gate' by holding the top of it, notice the different feelings you have between the 'brass' and the 'wood' of the 'brown gate', you go through. Closing the 'brown gate' behind you stroke the 'wood' then look back at your 'purple door' with the 'cold brass knocker' and the 'brass number 2' on it. **Look at it, see it, sincerely ask the Spirit World to show it to you clearly, sincerely ask Spirit to place the feelings of the brass and the wood into your senses.** You turn right and start walking down the paved area of this new street you have just moved to. Along the street you see a street sign set on 'two small concrete posts on the opposite side of the road. The sign says Jervis Street it is positioned next to the gate of the only double fronted semi detached house in the street and against the green hedge of number 3. The silver number 3 is on the plain wooden gate, look at the street sign Jervis Street and the plain wooden gate with the number 3 on it just for a minute; see how Jervis Street is implanted in your mind's eye. Register it. See Jervis Street on the sign and the bold lettering it is in; see the number 3 on the plain wooden gate. See the position they are in within your mind's eye when you see it clearly. Through a single thought, **sincerely** ask the Spirit World to always place your street names in this format within your mind's eye or perhaps in a better, clearer format as the case may be. Then let that thought go.

You start walking further along Jervis Street. Now start looking at the Victorian terrace three storey type houses on both sides of the road as you pass them. Look at them and study them so the images become clear in your mind's eye. **[Say this passage from the start at least twice to imprint them into the minds of the students].**

Walking along the pavement you stand outside the next Victorian terrace, three storey type house, the house that is next to yours. You look over the small green hedge, across the well kept lawn surrounded by its neat borders full of tulips, you look along the paved path and see the wooden four panelled pink door of number 4, the number 4 is in chrome metal. Look at the number 4 on that wooden four panelled, pink door and see how the number 4 is formed in your mind's eye. Recognise it. **[Pause a moment]**. If you see the chrome metal number 4 in your head clearly, **sincerely** ask the Spirit World to place the door numbers in your mind in this format for you in the future into your mind's eye when you require it in your mental Mediumship. Let that thought go.

**[Say this passage from the start at least twice].**

Walking further along the pavement you stand outside the next Victorian terrace three storey type house, you look over the short wooden fence, across the light brown gravel where there was once a lawn in that part of the front garden. There are small evergreen conifers in pots, on the edge by the black tarmac path are a lot crocus of different colours coming through the light brown gravel, you look along the black tarmac path and see a flat plain red door. The flat plain red door has a laid out surround square of white beading on the outer edge of the flat plain red door to make it look a bit more personal. It has a number 6 in silver on it, look at the silver number 6 on the red door for a short while. See the colour of the flat plain red door with a square of white beading on the outer edge of the door also see the silver number 6. Implant the colour red onto the door with a square of white beading on the outer edge of the flat plain door that has a silver number 6 on it. See the colour red of silver number 6's door. Still see the shining silver number 6 on that red door. [Pause a moment while the students sincerely ask the Spirit World to place the images in their third eye region. Tell them to do so].

**[Say this passage from the start at least twice].**

**[It is important for each person to see through thought what is being told to the group** as a person's **own** images in their mind are a distraction of exercise and should not be classed as a good thing. It is no use the Spirit World giving everyone in the group an image and one person changing it to suit him/her self. **That is not the correct way to do this exercise.** These images given often do not appear in the budding Medium's mind immediately so do not have the students worrying. It is only through a great deal of practice that things happen].

Moving further along the road to another yellow sandstone Victorian terrace three storey type house you see the number 20 in white on a pale green wooden six panelled door. Count the panels on the pale green wooden door see the white number 20 at the top of that door. You stay for a while and look at the white number 20 on that pale green six panelled door as it is being shown to you by the thought, that thought is placed at first now by you, but those in the World of Spirit have to learn as well as you so the Spirit World know to how your placement of all images works best for the individual within their mind. Look and see the number 20 in white on the pale green, wooden six panelled door. Stand back a little and look at the Victorian terrace three storey type houses. Look again at the number 20 in white on the pale green, wooden six panelled door, again count the panels and look at the white number 20 at the top of the pale green wooden door, see it. If you don't see it all, SINCERELY ask the Spirit World to place the images into your mind's eye for you.

**[Spirit has also to learn how the mechanisms of your own individual thought process works. How they can place meanings and images in the individual's mind that the individual and the Spirit World will understand how to work together within oneness within their harmony together in the future].**

As you walk steadily further along Jervis Street, you look across the road at another street sign Jervis Street on the opposite side of the road. This sign is attached to two small concrete posts, which are positioned next an old dirty brown wooden gate of house 27 you can see the number 27 on the top of the old wooden gate and the street sign is against the green hedge of number 27. The hedge is growing over the sign nearly covering the letters you can just see it has the name of Jervis Street on it to remind you, see it and remember it. Then you see a small brown, long haired, Yorkshire terrier dog at your feet, look at the dog. Looking at the dark brown leather collar it has around its neck. You can see the large chrome nametag on the small brown long haired Yorkshire terrier dog's collar, the name on the large chrome tag is the name of the dog, his name is Rex. Look at the small brown long haired Yorkshire terrier dog and the chrome name tag that has Rex on it, look at them for a short while, see how real the image is, you can see all the markings of that small brown long haired Yorkshire terrier dog and the brown leather collar with the large chrome name tag that has the name Rex on it.

**[Pause to let everyone see the dog and the collar in their mind's eye. Remind the students they should be sincerely asking the Spirit World for help].**

As you watch the small brown long haired Yorkshire terrier dog Rex go on his way, he stops at the edge of the road still on the pavement and waits for the noisy red single decker, number 346 bus to go passed him. The bus has the number on the front. Listen carefully. Can you hear it? Can you smell the horrible diesel fumes it is putting out into the atmosphere? When the road is clear of this traffic he goes across the road. You see Rex walking along the pavement on the other side of the road. Rex has now stopped outside number 37 Jervis Street. Rex crouches down and springs over and through a space in the dark brown wooden gate that has 37 in black on the top bar that goes across the gate. This yellow sandstone Victorian terrace three storey type houses is where the small brown long haired Yorkshire terrier called Rex lives. You notice the number 37 in brass is on a six panelled, wooden, varnished pine door. Pause a moment. Count the panels as you look at the six panelled, wooden, varnished pine door. Look at the six panelled, all wooden door, look at the varnish and how it shines on the pine door, it is glistening in the sunlight even the brass number 37 on it is shining. This is a very well looked after house. See Rex the small brown long haired Yorkshire terrier dog now as it sits on the red painted step. Listen as Rex barks for the owner.

Did you hear that bark? If you didn't, keep asking the Spirit World to put into your mind all the sounds, smells, and all of the actions in the picture formed as you go along the streets and roads.

**[Perhaps go over this section once or twice to reinforce the images and sounds]**

Listen as the owner comes to the door along the wooden floored hallway in the house you can hear shoes clip clopping. Listen to the noise as the owner undoes the door's deadlock with a key, and then you hear the clunk of a bolt, which is also locking the door. It is a lady of the age of 25 that comes out to let Rex into the house; she is dressed in a light brown sweater and denim jeans. The lady is wearing her slippers, which are red slip-ons with a piece of red fluffy feathery material across the top. As the door opens you get the smell of her cooking it of kippers being grilled. Smell those kippers. As you breath in the smell of the grilling kippers, the lady speaks to you and you hear her say; My name is Julie Peters it is my birthday today I am 25, you can keep in touch to hear how my dog Rex is getting on, phone me on 01975 822 199.

As you hear her name and phone number, be conscious of the way you hear them. You also see the name Julie Peters, the lady's age of 25 and all her phone number 01975 822 199. They are all being placed by the Spirit World above her head as you listen to her name of Julie Peters, see her name, see her phone number 01975 822 199. Remember you are being given them all into your thoughts by the Spirit World. See and hear that name, the age of the lady and phone number. See Julie Peters and how she is dressed in a light brown sweater and denim jeans. See Julie Peters is wearing her red, slip-on, slippers; see they have a piece of red fluffy feathery material across the top. Julie Peters waves you goodbye and you listen as Julie Peters shouts to you. Please do not forget my name Julie Peters and my phone number 01975 822 199. You bid her goodbye and thank her for showing herself to you.

You continue along Jervis Street see Jervis Street on that street sign at the side of the road on the small concrete posts. As you pass the next house you notice the number 39 in black which is on a fancy flowery, square pottery plate that has a white background with green leaves, and stems, as well as pink and blue flowers on the outside area. On the plain white centre there is a black number 39. This fancy, flowery, square, pottery plate with the number 39 is positioned on an area at the side of a light brown door, the door looks as if it is made of a light brown solid fibre glass substance.

[Each student should now as a matter of course, be **sincerely asking the Spirit World** to place the numbers of doors, telephone numbers, and numbers of every description, colours of every kind in life, the different designs of the house and doors, names of the streets, roads, places, people and animals, ask Spirit to hear the lady speaking her name, and the bark of the dog, and all different smells of every day life; yes **sincerely ask the Spirit World helpers** to place them all clearly into each individuals mind ready to be used for the help of others proving to them there is life after our so called death].

[PAUSE a few moments after each section; these short intervals are to consolidate the images in the mind, so the budding Medium and the Spirit World can learn the process together]

Pause again for a moment.

**[Go back and read this section over again].**

Along the road again you come to a corner, looking upwards on the wall of the yellow sandstone house you see the sign again for Jervis Street, look at it, see how clear it is, look at the sign and plant it in your mind's eye, it has just been erected by the council, that is how new and clear it is.

Pause a moment.

On the other corner fixed onto a small red brick wall is the name of the Street you are going into, it is Park Road. This also is a newly painted black and white sign, it is very clear to you. The houses in Park Road are different to the others in Jervis Street. The houses in Park Road have their design of rooms, two up and two down, they are rows of red brick terrace houses, you turn around to see the both road signs, one high up on the house wall, the other on the small red brick wall, note how they are implanted in your mind ready for the next time that the Spirit World shows you the images. You also see the difference in the houses in both roads, Jervis Street and along Park Road.

Pause a moment.

In Park Road, there is a blue door which has painted glass in leaded mosaic set in it's 6 panels on this one terrace house that stands out for you. The door of this small red-bricked terrace house has the white number 6 on the top of it. You can see the blue door and the painted glass in leaded mosaic set in it's 6 panels with the white painted number 6 on it at the top, **mentally note how it is all placed in your mind.**

[**Pause a moment**, each time even go over the previous paragraph a few times to implant the images in the minds of your students especially if they are new or not very well developed in Mental Mediumship].

Along Park Road there in the middle of very tall green leafed trees is a dark dirty old blacken reddish brown bricked church, which is surrounded by a three foot high wall of dirty red brick, on top of which is a rusting four foot high metal railing. Walking about fifty yards along this three foot high wall of dirty red brick you look inside the grounds and see you have come to the black wooden notice board of the church, it is of a round topped structure with a plain grey cast metal cross at the top of it, on the notice board are the times of the services written in faded gold lettering, mass at 8.00 am, service at 10.00am, another service at 12.00 noon, then an afternoon service at 3.00pm. The name of the church is :- The church of The Virgin Mary; the name is at the top of the black notice board, which has the plain grey cross in cast metal about a foot high at the very top of the round-topped notice board. See it all in your mind's eye.

**Pause a moment**.

[Those who cannot see it should each time be **sincerely asking** the Spirit World through thought over and over and over again to be helping them in this exercise].

Walking further along, alongside the dirty red brick wall and looking through the four foot high rusting metal railings, you see there are graves in the churchyard with many types of gravestones on them. Some have large crosses, some small crosses, others just of the plain white or black marble slab type with writing on them. On one grave near the wall that has a white marble angel on top of a flat white marble headstone, you can see the carved black writing on it, it says "In loving memory of Jim husband of Ethel, loving father of Grace and Barbara". Next to that grave you see a 'large headstone in black shiny marble with gold inscription' on it. The inscription says, "Gone but not forgotten, "Gladys Taylor", underneath that there are more words "Wife of Tom", and underneath them, "Loving mother Gladys, mother to Jimmy, Joan, and Kim". There is also picture of an old lady in an oval frame on the gravestone, at the top of the right hand corner. It must be Gladys. See those words and the picture on that gravestone see the large headstone in black shiny marble with gold inscriptions and the white marble angel on top of the flat white marble headstone with the carved black writing on it. See those two graves. Ask Spirit to show you those words and those headstones. **[Pause a moment], Go over the paragraph again and remind the students to still be SINCERELY asking for help from Spirit in their minds through thought over and over and over, then let the request go].**

Walking further along Park Road, you see leaning on the dirty red bricked wall of the churchyard there is an old priest, he is dressed in a in long heavy black overcoat to keep the chills out, he is wearing his black shirt, a white dog collar, black shoes and trousers. He is next to the open part of the fancy, double, heavy metal gate both of which have crosses on them. The priest is part leaning on the dirty red bricked wall and bent over with his two hands on a light brown wooden walking stick that has a black ferrule on the bottom of it to protect the wood on the floor, as you come to him you can smell the 'pipe tobacco' off his clothes. He introduces himself to you. You hear him say "My name is father Michael O'Grady, I am 70 years old and I have arthritis in my knees and I live in the old House over there beside the church", he points to it. It is an old blacken reddish brown-bricked double fronted house with a dark brown door. You can see the large black knocker and a lever and chain pull bell. Beside the door on a black plaque, it has the words in a dirty white on the black plaque at the side of the door, "Please knock and wait". The church and the house have been blackened by the soot from the coal fires of many, many years gone by, breathe in and smell the coal fires in the area. You can feel the twinge of pain in your knees just as father Michael O'Grady is feeling the twinge of pain as he stands there by the gate. You also see the name father Michael O'Grady above his head. You bid him goodbye and thank him for showing himself to you.

**[Pause a moment].**
**Go over the paragraph as the students sincerely ask for help from Spirit in their minds through thought.**

As you pass by the old priest father Michael O'Grady, further along Park Road there are two children playing on the pavement by the side of parked cars one is a silver estate car the other is a florist's small pink flowery painted van. There is a 7 year old, blonde haired girl in a smart pink dress that has clean white cuffs and collar, she is wearing white socks, black shoes and is skipping with a rope, and the 9 year old, dirty faced boy in a pair of short grey trousers, grubby white shirt and a blue V necked jumper and dirty scuffed trainer shoes. The boy is splashing in a puddle and playing in the gutter with a frog. They both look up as you reach them and they greet you with their names as they say their names, you see the names above each child's head. Listen as they tell you their names, you can hear them speak. "My name is 'Pauline Hopkins' and I am '7' and I live over across the road there in 'number 16 Park Road', the one with the 'yellow door'", says the girl pointing. You look over and see the red bricked terraced house with the yellow door that has the number 16 made out of brass on it. Listen as the boy says, "My name is 'Derek Pinter', I am '9' and I live on this side of the road in number 21 Park Road. That house with the black door that has a shiny number 21 on it". With that they carry on with what they were doing before you reached them, the girl skipping, the boy playing with his frog in pool of water in the gutter. You look over and see young, Derek Pinter's red-bricked terraced house with the black door that has the number 21 made in chrome metal on it.

**[Pause a moment]. Go over the paragraph as the students ask for help in their minds from the Spirit World through <u>SINCERE</u> thought.**

Along Park Road you see a happily married couple who are holding hands coming towards you. The lady is around five foot six inches tall, aged about fifty with salt and pepper hair colour [she had been dark, but the grey is coming through], she has a uniform on and the name Asda on her uniform. The man is around six foot tall, sixty and is very bald in the middle of his head with grey hair around the edge of his head to an inch above his ears. He is dressed in a dark grey suit and is wearing a dark blue tie with a motif on it. They introduce themselves to you. "My name is Mike Butchard and this is my Good Lady, Joan. We live in that house over there on the other side of Park Road in number 33. Our house is the one with the mushroom coloured door, you can see our number 33 better at night as it is lit up in an orange light behind the plastic plate". Mike Butchard says to you "I work in the 'Barclays Bank on the corner of Park Road and Hillside Avenue, that is why I am dressed in a 'dark grey suit and I am wearing my dark blue Barclays' tie with the Barclays' emblem on it. My wife Joan works in the local Asda supermarket, that is why she still has her uniform on and the Asda name on her uniform". Joan says to you "Why not call us on our phone tonight, the number is '0987 654 321'. It is just so we can have a talk, remember our phone number is '0987 654 321'". As they leave you, you are left with the perfume of the lady around you; it is a heady fragrance channel No 5.

**[Pause a moment].**

**Go over the paragraph a few times as the students SINCERELY ask for help in their minds through thought.**

Going a hundred yards along Park Road you come to a 'T junction' there is a bank on the corner it is Barclays Bank, look at it and the sign above. As you look upwards you can see the sign Hillside Avenue just under the first floor window on the grey brickwork. Next to the Bank is a Newsagent's shop with papers in a rack outside hanging up at the side of the glass door you can see it is called Nelson's Newsagents. Next to the Newsagent's is a vegetable shop called Waterworth's Fruit and Veg, it has lots of boxes of different fruits, and vegetables outside on the pavement. Going along you see there are three grey bricked terrace houses next to the shops, then there is a ladies hairdresser's shop with pictures of models with different hair styles in the large plate glass window of the hairdresser's. You can see three ladies of different nationalities sitting in chairs all covered with white protective gowns. The nearest lady to you under the drier is a young 18 year old Asian lady, she is sitting with her eyes closed and has ear phones on listening to her music, the lady in the middle, who is reading, is a heavy well made, middle age, Afro-Caribbean lady. The other furthest away from you is a middle aged Oriental lady just sitting there and staring into the mirror. One large black haired white European lady dressed in a black dress also covered with white protective gown is having her hair washed. Look and see the actions in the shop.

There is a Chinese takeaway next to the hairdressers you can smell the cooking coming from the door as you pass. There are two black haired Chinese ladies one with a long plat and the other who has a short-cropped hair; both are wearing small white hats on their heads. The lady with the black platted hair is serving a young black haired bearded man about 25 who is wearing grey trainers [shoes], blue jeans and a white shirt, he is with a blonde haired girl of the same age, she is wearing a short blue skirt with a white top. Take in all that is happening in the shop before you move on. You look up above the shop at the notice board; the shop is called "Ho Chin Take Away". There is a phone number on the board for people to ring in their orders, it is 01925 845 876, look at it and say it to yourself to place it in your mind, 01925 845 876 ask for help from Spirit to place it in your mind's eye for you. See it

**[PAUSE and remind the students they should be always SINCERELY asking and talking to the Spirit World for the help they need at any time]**

After the Chinese take away food shop, there is a space before the next building. It is an entry with rubbish bins in it ready to be collected. This is before you come to the red-bricked modern flat, single fronted, semi-detached houses, which are set back from the road. The first house you come to has a large front garden with a border full of flowers on either side of the full length of the path. The path is straight and it is leading to the frosted patterned glass front door that has a grey curtain behind it. You can hear a large dog barking at the back of the house. As you go to pass the gate, a very light brown and black German Shepherd dog comes bounding up to the gate barking and wagging its tail at you. Can you hear her? The very light brown and black German Shepherd dog puts her paws on the top of the brown, wooden gate as she gives a woof. There is no anger in the dog so you go over to it and see the very light brown and black German Shepherd dog has a brown collar with a large shiny metal name tag attached to it, you can see in large lettering the name of Kitty engraved on it. Kitty is very friendly and you stroke her calling her by name. As you stroke Kitty, you look over her and see the name on the white plate on the door of the house, it is Keeways written in black lettering, and the number of the red bricked, modern, flat single fronted, semi-detached house, it is 34 also in black. Yes you can see the number 34 is on the white nameplate, it is written in black underneath the "Keeways" in black on the white nameplate. The white nameplate with the black lettering of "Keeways" and number 34 stands out for you, you immediately notice it is positioned on the red bricked wall at waist height on the right hand side of the door.

You turn around hearing someone shouting to you. You see it is a van driver who has lost his way. The man pulls up beside you in the large white van; you notice the smell of the petrol coming from the van as he leans out of the cab's window asking you the way to Coventry town centre. You see the van has the name of Phoenix Transport in bright red on the side of the white van with the phone number 0191 354 963 in bold black writing and underneath also in black the Email address of phoenix@bird.com. You point out the directions and he thanks you then indicates, after first letting a dark blue estate car go past. The driver of the white van pulls out into the traffic and then continues along Hillside Avenue. As you watch the man drive the white van down the road, you see in the distance there is a green bus with the number 54 on the front coming towards the bus stop on the opposite side of the road where there are four people waiting to board the bus. Waiting for the bus, is a man who is in his dark brown overalls and a black duffle jacket, in his hand he has his lunch in a clear plastic box with a blue lid. The man is talking to a lady who has a bright green scarf on, she is dressed in a long green winter coat, she has two small boys beside her who are very smartly dressed in their maroon school uniforms, maroon caps, shiny, black shoes and grey trousers. It looks as though their mother is taking the children to school. The bus stops at its stop, and the driver lets the people onto the number 54 bus. Look, listen and breathe in; see, hear and smell the bus as it goes on its journey.

Now looking at another house along the road you see it has a very nicely built natural coloured wooden porch that has pot plants growing in it, all the window frames in the house match the natural coloured wood of the porch, this is house number 46. The number is in brass and the name of the road, Hillside Avenue is also on the door in brass lettering. Looking up you can see on the windowsill in the front upstairs window, there is a large grey and black tabby cat sitting looking out of the window.

As you pass the nicely trimmed four-foot high conifer hedge that was growing in-between 46 and 48 you see in the next-door house's driveway there is a young 30 year old man washing a silver sports car. You hear him talking to another person who is stretched out underneath a bright metallic green, four-door, saloon car. This bright metallic green, four-door, saloon car is jacked up and has the near side front alloy wheel off, you can see this wheel is lying beside the car. The younger man is calling to him "Dad do you want a hand while I am here", and the father is saying Jim to his son "Jim just pass me the ring spanner out of my tool box next to the alloy wheel. Listen to the names and the words spoken place them in your mind see them. The man under the car is in a pair of blue overalls that is all you can see of him.

Going past the father and son you look up and see an aeroplane overhead, it is leaving a vapour trail in the sky as it is flying high above you then another aeroplane noisily comes over a lot lower going into the local airport. You can see and hear there is a helicopter hovering over the house in the distance there must be a problem over there you think.

Going along Hillside Avenue you can see a black London taxi has drawn up outside of house number 56. The taxi has the phone number 0161 700 700 on the side door, the number 56 of the house in Hillside Avenue the taxi is outside of, is in bright red on the fancy black metal gate. All along the front of the house there is a two-foot high red brick wall above which is a small foot high fancy metal railing topped with gold painted acorns instead of the spikes.

Next door in garden of house 58 there is a window cleaner up his ladder. He is whistling a happy tune as he cleans the muck off the glass. In the downstairs front window a movement attracts your eye, it is a bird in a cage, which is hanging on a hook inside the house, you can see it is a brightly coloured, yellow songbird, it looks like a yellow canary. Looking down in front of you, there is a lady dressed in a green smock, wearing a white hat and green gloves, weeding the border of garden in number 58. See this number 58 is in black on the front green painted wooden gate. The lady takes a break from the weeding and looks up at you and says her name. "My name is Hilda Spencer, this is 58 Hillside Avenue", then goes back to the weeding. The flowers in the border are blooming in their glorious multi-coloured splendour. Looking away from the flowers, up the road you see in front of you is a bridge over which is a train drawing into the station at the right hand side of it. You can see there is another train already at the other platform. You can see all the people coming and going, off and on the train, some leaving others arriving. You stand and watch for a while before continuing along to the corner of Hillside Avenue where there is a seven-foot tall set of black metal railings with the name of Hillside Avenue on a sign attached to them.

There is a park on this corner of Hillside Avenue; you look at the road sign on the high black metal railings nearly hidden by the hedge. You turn the corner there is another road sign, it has Cinnamon Lane on it. Along Cinnamon Lane you have come to a gate to the park, and you go in. Turning into the park there are two joggers running along the path together, One is a blonde long haired man is dressed in tight blue shorts and white T shirt, he has blue and white running shoes on. Running alongside him is a dark brown haired woman with a ponytail tied with a yellow ribbon. She is dressed in a bright yellow running outfit. The joggers shout over to you. "My name is John Smythe" calls the man, the lady shouts over to you in a puffed voice, "my name is Mary Tottenham", they keep on jogging along the path. As those joggers go into the distance, you see coming towards you an elderly lady with bright red dyed hair, long grey coat and brown shoes pushing a double dark blue pram with baby twins in it, you look and see there is one baby dressed in a blue bonnet, the other dressed in a pink bonnet. She introduces herself to you "My name is Winifred Farier and these two lovely children are granddaughters, my daughter's twins John and Sophie"; she bids you farewells and continues along the path.

You walk towards the lake where there are a family of mother, father in their 20's, and very young before school age, son and daughter feeding the many different ducks. They introduce themselves to you, "My Name is Vicky and this is my husband Mike Holden" as they both hold out their hands to shake yours. "These are our children Samantha Holden and Kayleigh Holden they love animals", continues Vicky Holden. Wanting to go further into the park you wish them a pleasant day and continue along through the park. As you go into the quietness of the park your ears pick up the melodic sounds of an unusual harmony in music. You hear the pleasurable music in the distance, it is a very pleasant sound to the ears, it is the blending of the guitar and a flute. As you round a bend in the path just beyond some bushes on a seat are a teenage couple playing in this harmony. The boy playing the guitar is in jeans, a plaid shirt and brown walking boots, his lady partner playing the flute is also in jeans, and brown walking boots but is wearing a most beautiful flowery loose top. They put down their instruments and say their names. "My name is Susanna Filton" says the girl. "My name is Isaac Cohen", says the boy, they kiss each other, then go back to playing their melodic music. Listening to it as you walk along among the flowering shrubs and trees at the side of the pathway there is a different type of music coming to your ears, you stand for moment and listen. It is a brass band playing in the middle of the park.

**[Pause here to allow the students to engage in the hearing and seeing of the events, Remind them again (and keep on doing so) to keep sincerely asking for the help from Spirit World helpers].**

As you walk towards the bandstand which is surrounded by a well maintained border, filled wall boxes and overflowing hanging baskets in which are flowers of every description, you can see all the players are men, women, boys and girls of all ages who are dressed in a military type uniform of red white piping and gold. The white piping is so vivid, the brass buttons and the gold braid are all glittering and shining in the sunlight as all of the band move with the rhythm of the music. It is as though the whole world is smiling at you through that exciting rhythmic big band sound of the music. What a wonderful place to learn with those in Spirit World. As you look at them playing you see the notice board at the front, it has the name of the band "All Ages, Musical Big Band". You stay there for a few moments listening to the music. **[Pause a few moments, remind the students they should be always SINCERELY asking and talking to the Spirit World for the help they need at any time].**

To go back to the house where you came from, you are going to go along a different route. You turn along another path among the trees and flowering bushes going out of the park, out of another gate into Cinnamon Lane. You turn left and come to a corner of the railing that signifies the parkland has finished, you see the name of Cinnamon Lane on the railings. At the turning the corner left, you start to see hidden by the tall trees of the park there is a large ugly dirty red bricked factory, on the wall of which is the name of the road you are now in. The sign says "Cobble Stone Road". There is a name on the wall, which you did not see at first, it is the name of the factory in very large blue neon lighting; it says "FITTERS" "THE MAKERS OF THE FAMOUS FITTERS SHOES". There are a lot of cars parked in the front of the building; it looks as if it is the office at the front as there are a lot of people sitting down at their desks in front of computers conscientiously typing away. A motorbike goes slowly passed and you can see there are two people riding it. They are dressed in black and blue leathers to match the colours of their motorbike and its electric blue luggage panniers and the both riders' electric blue helmets. Next to come down the road as you are passing the famous Fitters shoe factory is a white police car with the siren blaring and the blue light flashing. The police car has fluorescing stripes along the bodywork of the car that light up in the sunlight. Fast on its heels is an ambulance with its lights and siren going just like the police car. The noises of the sirens are going out into the distance now, listen until you can hear them no more. As you walk further passed the factory you can hear the noise of the machinery as it makes the shoes for the people to sell in the shops and markets. Just beyond the factory building there is a busy open-air market that is selling everything you can imagine. Red meat joints fresh chickens ands turkeys, which are hanging up on one stall so you can see them, vegetables and eggs all neatly placed in racks on another, ladies and gents clothing on the next stall, underwear on another stall across from it, bedding and linen for the house are displayed to its best on another stall. The smells, the noises and atmosphere are truly wonderful.

As you walk through the market looking at each individual stall you look at the things more closely. You look at the fresh meat stall. **[pause]**.

Going along you look at the fruit and vegetable stall with its eggs of different sizes in trays **[pause]**.

The next stall is selling ladies and gents clothing of every size; all are placed on hangers and are under a large covered area just in case the weather changes to rain. **[pause]**.

The one next to that is an underwear stall. Some are plain and white, others in many colours are for the younger ladies, and they are very fancy and sexy. This stall also sells underwear, socks and Tee shirts for men and silk stockings for the ladies. **[pause]**.

There is a jewellery stall that sells a lot of watches, gold and silver trinkets, bangles, chains and pendants. **[pause]**.

On the deli stall there are hot freshly cooked chickens, hams, and black puddings, many cold cooked meats and spicy sausages hanging up and the stallholder displays many under glass. They are all shapes and sizes and come from all over the world; you can smell the wonderful garlic and spices. There are pieces of cheese on the counter so you try a few different types Danish Blue, mild Cheddar and a small piece of mature Canadian Cheddar and buy half a pound of the mature red Canadian cheddar.

**[pause, remind the students to keep sincerely asking Spirit to place the taste and the feel of the taste of each cheese and smell it. Smell the different aromas of the different products that are on the stall at this time, try also to conjure up the flavours into your mouth as well.** Say each different product then pause for a little while so the students do not break their concentration and their link with the Spirit World].

Further along the isle past the hardware stall, the car accessory stall some distance away from the food stall, there is a pet stall selling birds, rabbits, and guinea pigs in cages, goldfish in tanks and food for all sorts of pets. **[pause** and remind the students to notice the different smell and different noises].

You pass the electrical stall and the fancy goods stall. The last stall on the end of this row is a sweet stall so you buy some mint imperials. And pop one into your mouth.**[pause and** remind the students to feel and get the taste of the mint sweet, there are different sweets to try here you can go through different sweets in the range on the stall chocolate, toffee, nuts, etc.].

You miss the rest of the stalls as you have come to the end of an isle in this market, so you carry on along into Cobble Stone Road and come to a Public House. Needing to go to the toilet you go in through the smoky atmosphere to the back of the room in which there are men and women drinking and having a laugh. You see two youths playing pool and another playing the fruit machine **[reach with your inner self and Spirit the smell of the smoke and the beer]**. You go into the toilet it smells like a stale old person. Not wanting to be in the pub longer than necessary, you go back out into the street and turn left along Cobble Stone Road towards the health centre where you see the young looking 30 year old doctor in a white coat with his stethoscope around his neck and a nurse in her blue uniform with her watch on her chest of her blue uniform rushing towards the black car with a green light on the roof. They start the car, switch on the flashing green light and go off into the distance very fast. You come to a T-junction at the end of Cobble Stone Road. In front of you is a row of shops, a brightly lit jewellers with a window full of watches and clocks, in its other brightly lit window are bracelets, lockets, and chains of differing weights and styles. Above the window is the name of the shop it is called "LOGIC" there is an advert across the bottom of the window saying "Be logical buy from LOGIC" above the Jeweller shop sign LOGIC is the name of the road you have just come into, it is "Bents Road". Along to the right next to the Jewellery Shop is a Motorbike shop; there are large and small motorbikes and scooters of every colour outside. Next to that is a general store selling pots, pans, knives, forks, garden implements, seeds and fertilizers in fact everything for the home, a good shop to have near you. Suddenly out of the fire station at the end of the block of shops next to the greengrocer comes a fire engine with the firemen getting dressed in the large cab as the fire engine goes quickly away from you towards the docks. **[pause]**. As you walk along the main street in the area called "Bents Road", you are looking at the people walking aimlessly along a lady bumps into you, you see it is a friend you have not see for a while. Greet her and remember her name. After a little talk you excuse yourself and carry on along your way. You have reached the dock area and walk into a Cobble Stone Road. The name of the road is "Hard Stone Way";

you can see a cruise liner at the landing stage in the dock. It is a very large ship; take a note of it and how big it really is, look at the people taking their baggage up the gangplank ready for the trip they are going on. Turning around as you are walking along the side of the docks in "Hard Stone Way" you can smell smoke, it smells like burning rubber. You turn a bend in "Hard Stone Way" and you see a lot of activity with blue lights flashing on a lot of vehicles. As you get near the activity a lady about 50 years of age wearing a brown coat speaks to you explaining what is going on. An ambulance quickly goes passed you in the opposite direction.

**[Now each student should be looking at the scene as it is described, and placing it in their mind's eye. SINCERELY ask for help if needed from the Spirit World through thought]** The lady tells you there was a crash between a green car and a large brown articulated lorry with people trapped in the green car. The police, the doctor and the nurse came first, they are standing talking over there across the road, look at them talking. Then the fire engine came to cut the people out of their vehicles, the car caught fire just after the people were cut out of their vehicles. A second fire engine was called to stand by because the lorry is carrying something that can catch fire very easily, it is rolls of paper, and if it did catch fire it could make the situation a lot worse. Can you see the smoking crumpled green car and the damaged large brown articulated lorry over there by the spare ambulance with its blue flashing light and the doctor's black saloon car, the one with a flashing green light on top. The doctor's black car is next to the police car with its blue light flashing. I think the danger is now all over though. The injured have been taken to hospital in that ambulance you saw go passed you a minute ago, none of the people are really badly hurt just cuts and bruises. **[pause]**.

After this excitement you walk along Hard Stone Way into Bents Road passed all the shops in the busy road right along to the end of Bents Road towards the corner; it is a T junction. Opposite you on the other side of the road you come to another sign on the pavement, it says Enfield Park Road. Turning right into Enfield Park Road you see you are on the other side of the park you were in just before. You can hear the big band playing very clearly. Walking along a little further you can see the bandstand inside the park. The band of men, women, boys and girls are still playing in their splendid colours of red and gold. The white piping on the uniforms is very bright in the sunlight. You pause a minute in the sunlight to listen to the wonderful music and watch the activity of the joggers John Smythe and Mary Tottenham still going around the park trying to keep their weight down and keep fit. You see Winifred, the old lady pushing the twins in a pram is still there, the lovers in the distance sitting and cuddling, who are not at this time playing their own musical instruments, they are just listening to the sounds around them. You watch a small bent over gentleman in a drab brown over coat with a stick slowly walking passed the bandstand with his plump black Labrador dog on lead. It makes you think about the slowness of the pace of life within the park, it is so soothing to the eyes and relaxing to the mind, become part of it. **[pause]**.

You leave the scene before you and continue along the road as a young dark brown haired boy with a yellow baseball hat with a red motif on the front of it, wearing a light grey coat with a hood folded on his back, he has short black trousers and shoes. As he comes towards you riding his red bike nearly bumps into you. The young dark brown haired boy is about 4. The young boy is closely followed by his blonde haired sister who is slightly older, but not by much, she is riding a pink bike with white handle bar grips with different coloured streamers coming from them. She is wearing a pink flowery dress, white socks and white shoes. They shout to each other "You will have to go slower for me James", shouts the young girl. "I will race you to the shop Pricilla", shouts James. As you see the two youngsters go around the bend on the pavement you walk on and come to a café, feeling like a drink you go in, as you walk through the door the coffee aroma hits you and you can now see it is an internet-café with a lot of computers at the tables. After paying for the cup of tea and a digestive biscuit [ask Spirit to place the taste of the tea and the biscuit in your mouth] and getting them from the counter off a large homely grey haired lady about 50 years of age who has her name of "Jean" on her white uniform, you sit down and look at the screen of the computer on the table in front of you, there are messages for you coming on the screen. They are telling you the names, addresses, telephone numbers and details of people you have not met before but instinctively you know you must tell other people about all this information. This is so people can understand the people whose details are there on the screen; that those people have not gone away. You instinctively understand from this computer screen, this is one way you can get information placed into your mind's eye in the future to help others. Ask the Spirit world to place it there for you in the future as you see it.

You see the message with the full address, post code, and telephone number in front of you on the

computer screen :-
Spell the words out. Each time the students see the name and address, they say it quietly out loud.

>Mr David Smith,
>17, Alder Lane,
>Princess Park,
>Liverpool 8,
>Merseyside,
>L8 9AH
>Phone No   0151 709 421

Another message comes up on the screen in full detail :-
**[Each student should be looking at the screen as it is described, and placing it in their mind's eye. SINCERELY ask for help if needed from the Spirit World through thought]**
Spell the words out. Each time the students see the name and address, they say it quietly out loud.

>Mrs Annie Hastings,
>35, Crosswood Crescent,
>Huyton with Roby,
>Liverpool 36,
>Lancashire,
>WA2 4QM
>Phone No   0151 480 241

I worked in Owen Owens in Liverpool city centre behind a counter for 40 years. I lived in this house for 30 years with my mother Mrs Wilson and my son Norman. My husband died during the war in France in 1941. I had a granddaughter Valerie who was killed by the milkman's horse and cart in the road outside the house when she was only 3. I left the earth plain in 1961 6 years after my mother Lillian.

Another message comes up on the screen in full detail :-
Spell the words out. Each time the students see the name and address, they say it quietly out loud.

>Malcolm Tennison,
>Llwyn Farm,
>Heol Tawe,
>Abercraf,
>Swansea,
>SA9 1TJ

I worked on the farm for 70 years until I was put to bed because of an illness and I went to sleep, for my body was all used up. On my farm I had the occasional pig, but mostly I had hens, sheep and cattle on my farm all my days. Our farmhouse is made of blue grey slate with a slate roof to match; there are three barns for the cattle, sheep and the large open one for the animals' fodder. Many is the time that we have owls nesting in the barn and the surrounding trees. There are many trees on our farm a collection of which is towards the end of the lane. Locals call it Bluebell Woods. I have three sons Glynn who is 34, Gwylam 32, and Taff 30. They looked after the farm after I fell asleep in 1890. My wife, Gladys fell asleep in 1874, 16 years before me when she was 54. We all attended the local chapel in the village each Sunday, as did all my family members for as long as I can remember.
Spell the words out. Each time the students see the name and address, they say it quietly out loud.

>Dennis King,
>84 Simpson Street,
>Hobson's Creek,
>Hobart,
>Australia,

I was born in England in 1942. I did not know my parents. I was placed in a Catholic orphanage from the age of 6 by a lady, I and was shipped across to Australia when I was 8 this was all taken care of by the church orphanage. I was placed in a hostel with the brothers of charity. I was there until I was 12. I ran away one night to get away from the cruelty and abuse. I ended up with a very nice family who owned a sheep farm in the outback. It was hard work but I was happy and well fed, not as it was back in the hostel. I ended up as the foreman of the farm and when the owners died, they left it all to me as they had no children of their own. I ended up a very wealthy man with a good wife and four children two girls

Julie born in 1965 and Pauline born in 1966 and two boys. Derek born in 1969, and Tom born in 1970. They run the farm and the other businesses now. They all get on together and are all doing very well for themselves. My wife Caroline is still working around the farm cooking for the workers who tend to the sheep and now cattle. She was a good caring wife. I passed away to the higher life after a bad accident on a horse in 1980. I fell off after the horse's leg went into a rabbit burrow and the horse rolled over on top of me, this happened while I was on a round up in the bush.

You see the last message with the full address, post code, and telephone number in front of you on the computer screen :-
Spell the words out. Each time the students see the name and address, they say it quietly out loud.

      Mr Jon Noble,
      167, Berry Lane,
      Old Kent Road,
      Oxford,
      Oxfordshire,
      WA2 8OX
      Phone No  0770 896 654

After seeing this last message on the computer screen you **<u>sincerely</u> thank** the Spirit World for showing you all this information in this format within your mind [or if the information is not how you would like it to be seen in your mind, you **<u>sincerely</u> ask** for help and make arrangements to sit again and go over a similar situation or the same, to place clear images in your mind by the Spirit World helpers].

[If need be, the tutor can have notices on paper for the Students to look at and laid out in the format above as on the computer screen to place the format into the third eye of the students (just as in the colours in previous exercises in the book). The addresses are printed out as they are on the computer screen but in heavy bold print, one at a time on a one sheet of paper. The sheet of paper on which a single address and information is written on is placed in front of the eyes of the student in focus so they can read it, the student reads it quite a few times focusing on the address and information and nothing else, then closes their eyes and all that is written on the page in front of them should be seen in the third eye. It might be preferable at the start to have just the addresses on the paper first, then later on the full information. If the information does not stay in the third eye area at first for very long, do it over and over and over again. It is only with practice and the **sincere talking and asking** for help from the Spirit World that things happen, as they should].

After this last message on the computer screen you get up off your chair, thank the homely grey haired "Jean", who is still behind the counter with her white uniform on. You go out of the door into the street and see the street sign Enfield Park Road next to the bollards on the pavement in front of the supermarket across the road. The car park is full of cars and people to-ing and fro-ing through the doors with their trolleys. Walking on along the road you come to another junction. You see there is a crossing just further up so you go to it. Waiting to cross the road you see a large white van delivering electrical goods to the shop the company name on the van is Philips Electrical you can see it comes from Barking, London, you can see it all in black lettering against the white of the van with the phone black number 0181 945 258 and the black Email address Philips@hotmail.com.
The lights on the pedestrian crossing now have changed to green with the little man flashing. Going across the road on a pedestrian crossing you see a small frail old man fall on the pavement in front of you. He had a black walking stick with badges all over it; this is beside him on the floor. You see he is alright, this old man has only had a bit of a shock, and you bend down to help him up off the floor, hand him his decorated black walking stick and dust the dirt off his trousers and jacket of his brown tweed suit. He says "my name is Freddy Giddings and I live in number 12 Jervis Street, just around the corner" so as you are going to Jervis Street you walk with him. He tells you all about his family as you walk around the corner into Jervis Street. Looking away from Freddy, you see the name of Jervis Street on the road sign, which is fastened on two concrete posts in the ground on the pavement, which are next to a telegraph pole against the small red-bricked wall. This is my house says Freddy as you pass a well kept garden hedge looking into the pathway you are standing in front of you can see the white number 12 on the brown front door, you bid Freddy farewell. As you carry on to your own front door it is starting to

rain heavy, you open your front gate and scurry up the path to the door of the house you are staying in, open it with your key and go inside the front door of the house you have been staying in for this short time. When you are ready, thank your helpers in the higher vibrational level who have been learning how to place the images in your mind's eye. Make arrangements to meet them again when you are going to sit in meditation for them to link with you, open your eyes

For some of these exercises especially if you are tutoring in a small group or in a one to one situation. When the students/student has the image placed into their mind's eye with the help of Spirit they should say it [give it off] as though they are giving a message to a recipient in the audience or another person in a reading. I can see this person [describing them], or I hear the name of ****, [the student should/could say it out loud and say how they are being given it], or explain about the scene they are being shown in their mind's eye, or say how they are seeing the telephone number or say if they are being told it by Spirit. It is so important to do it this way for the simple reason, people who will eventually receive the messages will know you the student are not fooling them. The students should be told all these exercises have to be done with sincerity, in truth and honesty so no negativity holds you back. LIES ARE NEGATIVITY. Negativity, very much slows down development and **many times stops it.**

Tutor now after a short period of time a break a cup of tea or something like that, go back to the beginning and read the whole section out loud in full again so it can become clearer in the mind of the students.

[What should be said after the full exercise, is to ask the students to say truthfully what sort of a street sign, notice board, what sort of a cross, what sort of a dog, what sort of a woman, what sort of a priest, what sort of numbers and house doors, what friend they met, etc. What each student individually saw the first time of reading then after each sequence was read over and then after the whole passage was all fully read out to them in one full sequence. Go around them all first asking them individually what they saw in their guided meditation. It is a must to tell them to tell the truth. Ask if they saw the cross as a crucifix (with Jesus on it) or a different dog or a dog of a different colour or a door of a different colour than the one said to them, if they have they have **NOT** done the exercise correctly; if they have placed into their own minds anything extra to what has been said. They have **NOT** done the exercise correctly at all. All that was told to them was a cross, a small brown Yorkshire terrier dog, and a certain colour or number of a door. This **HAS** to be corrected from the beginning; because each person has to learn to place into their minds **only what has be told to them** by the tutor and with the help of the Spirit World which they should have been asking for from the beginning, and concentrating on **THAT ALONE. Also only to give off what has been seen, NOT to add anything in any reading**].

[**If doing this exercise in your own words**, It is so important to write on paper **as much detail as you can** for your guided contemplation so you can go over the same sequence and so you can place into each person's mind **as much detail as possible** in each described development meditation [developmental contemplation]. This is so each person can gain something from each guided meditation [developmental contemplation] even if it is only a little at each reading. Most developmental meditation should be said more than a half a dozen times to any group to get the images with the help of the Spirit World fixed onto the set pattern of mind's eye of the budding Mediums so they, the Mediums, can eventually recognise the difference between their imagination and the messages given to them by the Spirit World].

When your students get a bit more advanced have one individual [or yourself] each week in turn stand up [after linking with Spirit for a quarter of an hour] and give their interpretation of a walk, so students can have their own individual images placed into their minds by Spirit. The student or tutor should only give there is a street sign, what does it say? Look at the door, what type of door? What number? Meet two [or how ever many] people? What are their names? What are they wearing? See a van looking at what is on it? What telephone numbers? Address? Email? The number of the bus, how many people at the stop? Name of shops, look at every day things and have a few general walks ready for the following weeks. Afterwards in turn, the students tell of the images that were placed into their minds as they went along their walk in their third eye region.

When you see these images and hear the voices, [or the impressions of the images and impressions of the voices], talk to the World of Spirit and tell your helpers this is how you want [or not, as the case may be] the images and informative voices to be, please make sure it is what you want though. If you want clearer images tell the Spirit World. If you want the images to be for the past on the left in your mind's eye, the front the present and the images on the right of the mind's eye for the future being on the right, **say so** through **sincere** thought. Tell the Spirit World what you want and the ways you would like them to work with you, they are going to be working with you for the rest of your life, make sure you have good solid foundation for your learning. NOT RUSHED. Let it be slow, steady, **sincere**, **honest** and **true in that Divine Light of Spirit of the HIGHEST REALMS** that is where learning should be done. NOT RUSHED. I assure you that you will not be disappointed if done correctly in this correct manner. Remember this is only one method BUT it is the best one I have found as yet.

Having guided meditation going down through the woods and by the seaside might be OK for your fantasy or relaxation, it is not much use for placing everyday images in your mind to help with your development alongside the Spirit World helpers. Those mundane everyday images are the images that have to be planted in your mind for Spirit to understand how to work within your thought pattern then expand on them. Write down and record [so you can listen in your own quiet time] as many things as you can to place the everyday images in your thought pattern.

I repeat, and so should you to your students; tell them the most import thing in any development group is to get the students talking to the Spirit World as they would do to their friends, for that is what the Spirit World should become to each individual, **good genuine friends**. It is so necessary for each student to understand that this is what the Spirit World is, and will become to them throughout their lives, yes **good genuine friends in the World of Spirit who listen, who can/will do things with the student's permission, together with the student, prove there is life after our so called death.**

**One last thing for me to say to every tutor, you should be helping every one of your students and to be teaching them as though you are the receiving party, then they will be taught, as you would want to be taught yourself. Tell them** everything as **you would want to receive it,** NOT as much as you want them to know up to that stage you want to leave them so the students can come back to you again to learn more, just as some tutors do. Teach in all honesty, **so every person can go out into the wider world to help others understand there is life after our so called death, hide nothing,** then, and only then you will be respected, be open to all no matter what!!!! **Do not** and I mean **do not** tell others what they want to know if it is not the truth or what you think they want to know, **NEVER** try to build them up by saying they are doing well when they are not, **tell the students the whole truth, always tell the truth to everyone as you see it.** Sometimes the truth can hurt but please try to be compassionate when you do so, it is best in the long run to tell a person the truth about what they are doing especially if they are going about the learning of their Mediumship in the wrong way. There are a great many tutors who are so ignorant about the true ways of linking with the Spirit World who are still teaching others. THERE ARE MANY WHO SHOULD NOT be in that position, please weed them out and educate them. Make suggestions to make them better tutors.

It is so important to have the Mental Medium to go to the correct person who a message is for and NOT throw out information to a wider audience. [This sort of thing is called fishing] This should be taught from the early stages of Mediumship. This can be brought to the attention of budding Mediums through a tutorial.
Have a Medium [a Mental Medium of experience] at the front of the class. Better with a lot of participants.
Have a large flip chart or large marker board ready.
Have the Medium link into the Spirit World ready to give a message to the audience [the class].
Have all the class stand up.
Have the Medium give one piece of information from Spirit, then it is written down on the flip chart. All those who cannot take **any** of that information should sit down.
The Medium gives the class another piece of information from Spirit. It is written down on the flip chart. All those who cannot take **any** of that information should sit down.
Medium gives the class another piece of information from Spirit. It is written down on the flip chart. All those who cannot take **any** of that information should sit down

So it goes on. Until there is only one person left standing who can with certainty, take **ALL** the information from the Spirit World via the Medium.

It will soon become apparent that there is a lot of general information that comes from the Spirit World via **some** Mediums to their audience that can be taken by a lot of people. Generally about ten to fifteen bits from Spirit, sometimes more. This is why I always say it is so vital to have a good link with the Spirit World before any sort of Mediumship is taken to the public domain and then **only go directly** to the person in any audience who the message is for.

At the end of the demonstration the experienced Medium should give a piece of evidence to the remaining recipient that they cannot dispute. This is only done by going back to the Spirit World and asking them. If you do not keep talking to the Spirit World through thought it is using your psychic and generally not being evidential in Spiritual Mediumship.

## HOW TO INVESTIGATE SPIRITUAL PHENOMENA
## By J. Burns. 1871

Written in the year of 1871. It is common but very significant saying that to cook a hare you must first catch it; and the suggestion thus conveyed indicates the prime necessity in attempting a study of Spiritualism. Reading is all very well, for the experience of others is a valuable aid to progress, but it can never stand in place of experimental knowledge. Hence the cry, when a man is assailed by some irrepressible Spiritualist, how or when can I see anything of it? The public have a vague impression that some one called a Medium is necessary to elicit the phenomena, and that his assistance can only be obtained by those who have the money to pay for it. This notion is only partly true. There are but few professional Mediums in England, and these are able to obtain some of the more remarkable and special phases of phenomena. Once they were sceptics, and quite unconscious of the wonderful power, which is daily being exercised in their presence. Circumstances introduced them to a Circle or enabled the manifestations to occur spontaneously. Their friends begged of them to sit for investigation; gradually the circle of enquirers widened till the Mediums' time became so much occupied that no other avocation could be followed, and a charge had to be made to provide means of substance and afford protection from the importunities of sitters. In this way all public Mediums have been produced. The function of Mediumship is not an art, which can be acquired by tuition or dexterity, but it is a natural endowment dependent upon bodily temperament, and it may be developed by exercise and propitious circumstances. Mediumship thus being a natural faculty, it ought to be of frequent occurrence; and so it is. It is probable that there is a latent Medium of one sort or another for every family in the country. Not that there is a Medium in every home, for several families may be found in which there are no Mediums, while the members of another family may be all of them Mediums. Like literary talent, mechanical skill, and other qualities of mind, Mediumship is not by any means found equally represented in each individual.

---

Such being the case, and Mediumship being a principle inherent in man, the question of spiritualism is capable of universal solution. Do not, then, take any man's word as finality, whether he declares in favour of Spiritualism or against it. Do as the sub-committees of the London Dialectical Society did (see their separate reports) sit down, observe the conditions, and produce results for yourselves. Spiritualism is simply a branch of science, treating of an unexplored region of human nature. It discusses not only man's relations to the Spirit World, but demonstrates what man is, what his powers are, whither he is bound. If man is immortal, he must be so in accordance with natural law; and if immortality be a fact, it must be capable of discovery. There is therefore no superstition or credulity in spiritualism, but each investigator speaks as he finds, and reasons according to the facts presented to his intellect. To remain in ignorance of any department of man's being is to leave the field to the occupation of that grim giant, Superstition, whose two heads, Negation and Credulity, by their withering scowl, reduce to tyranny, slavery, misdirection, and misery, the ignorant denizens of an otherwise fair world. That all may by experiment satisfy themselves of the existence and nature of spiritual phenomena, there is herewith placed freely at their disposal—

## RULES AND CONDITIONS FOR THE SPIRIT CIRCLE in 1869

**Atmospheric Conditions**—The Phenomena cannot be successfully elicited in very warm, sultry weather, in extreme cold, when thunder and lightening and magnetic disturbances prevail, when the atmosphere is very moist, or when there is much rain, or storms of wind. A warm, dry atmosphere is best, as it presents the mean between all extremes, and agrees with the harmonious state of man's organism which is proper for the manifestation of spiritual phenomena. A subdued light or darkness increases the power and facilitates control.

**Local Conditions** –The room in which a Circle is held for development or investigation should be set apart for that purpose. It should be comfortably warmed and ventilated, but draughts and currents of air should be avoided. Those persons composing the Circle should meet in the room about half an hour before experiments commence; the same sitters should attend each time, and occupy the same places. This maintains the peculiar magnetic conditions necessary for the production of the phenomena. A developing Circle exhausts power, or uses it up.

**Physiological Conditions**—The phenomena are produced by a vital force emanating from the sitters, which the Spirits use as a connecting link between themselves and objects. Certain temperaments give off this power; others emit an opposite influence. If the Circle is composed of persons with suitable temperaments, manifestations will take place readily; if the contrary be the case; much perseverance will be necessary to produce results. If both kinds of temperaments are present, they require to be arranged so as to produce harmony in psychical atmosphere evolved from them. The physical manifestations especially depend upon temperament. If a Circle does not succeed, changes should be made in the sitters till proper conditions are supplied.

**Mental Conditions**—All forms of mental excitement are detrimental to success. Those with strong and opposite opinions should not sit together; opinionated, dogmatic, and positive people are better out of the Circle and room. Parties between whom there are feelings of envy, hate, contempt, or other inharmonious sentiment should be excluded from all such experiments. The minds of the sitters should be in a passive rather than an active state, possessed by love of truth and of mankind. One harmonious and fully developed individual is invaluable in the formation of a circle.

The Circle should consist of from three to ten persons of both sexes, and sit round an oval, oblong, or square table. Cane-bottomed chairs or those with wooden seats are preferable to stuffed chairs. Mediums and Sensitives should never sit on stuffed chairs, cushions, or sofas use by other persons, as the influences which accumulate in the cushions often affect the Mediums unpleasantly. The active and quiet, the fair and dark, the ruddy and pale, male and female, should be seated alternately. If there is a Medium present, he or she should occupy the end of the table with the back to the north. A mellow mediumistic person should be placed on each side of the Medium, and those most positive should be at the opposite corners. No person should be placed behind the Medium. A Circle may represent a horseshoe magnet, with the Medium placed between the poles. Sometimes a single individual possesses all the conditions necessary for Spirit-communion in his or her person. When this is the case the phenomena may be obtained by such a person sitting alone.

---

**Conduct at the Circle**—The sitters should place their hands on the table, and endeavour to make each other feel easy and comfortable. Agreeable conversation, singing, reading, or invocation may be engaged in—anything that will tend to harmonise the minds of those present, and unite them in one purpose, is in order. By engaging in such exercises the Circle may be made very profitable apart from the manifestations. Sitters should not desire anything in particular, but unite in being pleased to receive that which is best for all. The director of the Circle should sit opposite the Medium, and put all questions to the Spirit, and keep order. A recorder should take notes of the conditions and proceedings. Manifestations may take place in a few minutes, or the Circle may sit many times before any result occurs. Under these circumstances it is well to change the positions of the sitters. Or introduce new elements, till success is achieved. When the table begins to tilt, or when raps occur, do not be too impatient to get answers to questions. When the table can answer questions by giving three tips or raps for "Yes" and one for "No," it may assist in placing the sitters properly. The Spirits or intelligences which produce the phenomena should be treated with the same courtesy and consideration as you would desire for yourselves if you were introduced into a company of strangers for their personal benefit. At the same time, the sitters should not on any account allow their judgement to be warped or their good sense imposed upon by Spirits, what ever their professions may be. Reason with them kindly, firmly, and considerately.

**Intercourse with Spirits** is carried on by various means. The simplest is three tips of the table or raps for "Yes and one for "No." By this means the Spirits can answer in the affirmative or negative. By calling over the alphabet the Spirits will rap at the proper letters to constitute a message. Sometimes the hand of a sitter is shaken, then a pencil should be placed in the hand, when the Spirits may write by it automatically. Other sitters may become entranced, and the Spirits use the vocal organs of such mediums to speak. The Spirits sometimes impress Mediums with messages, while others are clairvoyant, and see Spirits, and messages from them written in luminous letters in the atmosphere. Sometimes the table and other objects are lifted, and moved from place to place, even through closed doors. Patiently and kindly seek for tests of identity from loved ones in the Spirit World, and exercise caution respecting Spirits who make extravagant pretensions of any kind.

## From the Book by Harry Edwards
## "The Mediumship of Arnold Clare" I think might be of interest for some.
### CHAPTER ONE pages started at 21-27
## The Medium, Arnold Clare

Arnold Clare was born of Suffolk parents at Felixstowe, in 1901, where his father owned a hand-made basket business.

Arnold went to school until he reached the age of 12, when he took up employment in a grocery establishment. At the age of 15 he went to sea under sail; and shortly afterwards, during the World War and at the age of 15 ½, joined the Royal Navy

His first war service was spent in destroyers and light cruisers on ocean convoy work; and with the Dover patrol.

In 1917 his duties took him through the Mediterranean to Mount Athos, where he was engaged for a time on shore duties in the wireless station.

It was here at Mount Athos that Mr. Clare, not yet 17 years of age, met a personality who influenced his life from that time onwards.

At one of the monasteries he met a Greek Father, named John, who could speak English fairly well. He was an old man, and a strange friendship grew up between them. Arnold spent much of his free time at the monastery, listening to the wisdom from the lips of the old monk. One can perhaps picture the venerable white-haired and bearded monk and young sailor discussing mysticism and philosophy amid the background of the stone ruggedness of the monastery. Mr. Clare does not remember much in particular of the old man's teachings, but does remember that he was greatly impressed at the time by their profundity. Before leaving Mount Athos John said, "I won't say good-bye, my son; we will meet again."

Mr Clare's service in the Middle East did not end there. He went overland to Baku on the Caspian Sea, where his duties took him on board a Russian ship, the Emile Nobel. His naval service on this ship lasted for nine months.

The ship was navigated by a Russian captain between whom and Mr. Clare grew up a close friendship. One day the captain took him home to tea, and this visit was to prove the forerunner of many more. One evening, after tea, the family drew round the fire, the captain on one side, his wife on the other, and his two daughters and Arnold completing the fireside Circle.

The wife would play a mandolin and then commenced to talk in a strange tone in Russian. Though he did not know it then, Mr. Clare was at his first séance, for at that time he had no idea of Spirit intercourse and did not recognise the trance state of the lady.

Mr. Clare often joined the Circles they held—for, as he says, there was nothing else to do—but he was not greatly interested in any of them since the language used was unintelligible to him. One night, however, the lady ceased speaking Russian and spoke English in John's voice. Here was a peasant type of lady, who knew only the local patois, speaking English in a voice and with an intonation unmistakably

John's and reproducing his natural inflexions. Still Mr. Clare did not appreciate the significance of the phenomena, which he was witnessing.

"I told you, my son, we should meet again." Said the voice, and each evening, while the Circle was held, John would speak and continue his teaching from the point at which he had left off in Mount Athos. John told his listener that he had work to do and that he was being prepared for it. Mr. Clare says today, that not knowing of the meaning of survival, he did not realise the meaning of John's words or even that he had passed on since he had left Mount Athos. So natural was the conversation that he did not think he could be "dead".

The time came for Mr. Clear to leave, though neither he nor the captain had any knowledge of this yet. On what turned out to be the eve of departure John said: "I must now say farewell for a little while." Mr. Clare thought this meant that John would not be speaking again for some time, but the next morning surprise orders started him on his homeward journey. This was 1919.

Mr. Clare tells how in the excitement of coming home, and during the post-war activity, he lost sight of the intimate meaning of John's teaching. He was engaged on wireless work at a Government station; and about this time met Miss Vera Lawson, who later became Mrs. Clare.

They have three sons: Stanley, aged, 18, now serving in the Army: Tony, aged 17: and Pat, aged 11 years.

One day Mr Clare picked up an old magazine, and read an article by Conan Doyle. This described an Egyptian bronze vase with inscribed figures around the edges. Conan Doyle speculated as to its use and thought it might have been used of old for divination with a pendulum. This article so impressed Mr. Clare that he wondered, "Why have a bronze vase, why not do without?" So taking a sheet of paper he wrote the letters of the alphabet around the edges; and tying his collar stud on to a short length of thread, held it over his letter chart. The stud moved as if propelled by a persistent force and spelt out the word "John".

Mr. Clare tried automatic writing for a time and found that information was given to him on topics he knew nothing about. He did not attach any great importance to them; and they have not been kept. At the same time he had many other interests and the automatic writing was only engaged in spasmodically as a means to pass an idle hour.

At the age of 28 Mr. Clare sought an extension of Government service and went to the medical officer for an examination. The doctor told him he could not be passes as fit as he was suffering from tuberculosis. This was a great shock; and the doctor was asked if he would agree to consider the examination as "off the record", and to study Mr. Clare's condition at a future date. This the doctor agreed to do.

Mr. Clare went home and gave Mrs. Clare the doctor's report. He says he then commenced to pray as he had never prayed before and continued doing so nightly. As the nights passed so he became conscious of the presence and personality of John. He received the impression that he was not to be unduly alarmed, that he would be made well, and that he had to work to do.

Two months later Mr. Clare again went to the medical officer and he was given a clean bill of health.

From this time onwards Mr. Clare sat in solitude every night whenever possible, from half an hour to an hour, mainly around midnight. It was in this way he primarily developed those powers of which this book speaks.

It will be seen that the pattern of "John" is interwoven through Mr. Clare's life, that the development of his spiritual gifts took place in spite of himself, and the Spirit people associated with him gradually directed his life for the work they had to do.

Mr. Clare's association with Spiritualist Churches began with the church at Scarborough where he was a Vice-President; he followed this by commencing a healing circle at a Winchester church, of which he later became hon. secretary. Coming to London in 1933 Mr. Clare continued his solitary development. It should be noted he was averse to trance work; and when he undertook services for churches would not allow himself to be a trance subject. During the latter part of his solitary development he again felt the presence of John. One particular physical reaction he noted was that he felt incapable of movement for the time being.

At this time Astrology became his hobby and he lectured on this topic a number of times in London.

In 1937 Mrs Clare and he joined the Balham Spiritualist Church; and he became hon. secretary in 1939. During these two years he conducted Healing Circles in the church and was intimately connected with all its branches of activity, giving addresses, clairvoyance, psychometry as well as healing.

At this time a small home circle of church members was sitting privately for development of a Mr. Edwin Twitchett, who showed signs of Physical Mediumship. The guide of this Circle directed that Mr. and Mrs. Clare should be invited to join. Knowing of Mr. Clare's aversion to trance work they said they did not think he would join. The guide replied, "You ask him, and he will come". Mr and Mrs Clare were thereupon approached and they consented. This Circle had been sitting weekly for eighteen months and signs of movements were being observed. Mr Twitchett, however, left the Circle, which carried on in the hope that he would return. Subsequently, on New Year's Eve, 1938, Mr Twitchett agreed to return, and a sitting was arranged for that night.

At this time the sitters were a Mrs Sheppard, Mrs Shelston, Mr and Mrs Clare and two others.

On that New Year's Eve, Mr and Mrs Harrison were at tea with Mr and Mrs Clare when the telephone bell rang, and a message given that Mr Twitchett could not attend. Mr Clare felt that no matter what happened, the sitting should take place. It did, and that night Mr Clare's physical Mediumship functioned for the first time. There were apports and Mr Clare's Guides made themselves known.

The story is continued by Mr Harrison, but this chapter must not end without recording Mr Clare's gratitude and thanks to his wife for her unfailing help and courage through all the days of trial, for her unbounded patience in the Circles, and her energy for the work. This culminated in February of 1941, when Mr and Mrs Clare opened their own church, "The Trinity of Spiritual Fellowship".

To inaugurate a new centre of devotional activity during the topsy-turvy conditions of this war year denotes both courage and confidence; and, to date, the new church has shown every sign of making progress.

Finally, the author desires to express his personal thanks to Mr Clare for his ever-ready willingness to give up so many hours of his all too limited home time for the purpose of this book. Never on any occasion was this co-operation refused, nor has any effort on his part appeared too great to render whatever service he could.

One afternoon, when Mr Clare's son, Tony, was thirteen years old he was in his room, and commenced to draw upon a sheet of paper. The drawing of Brother Paul was the result.

Tony says that while the he appeared to take over the drawing appeared very short, he was surprised to find, when he had finished, that evening had set in. he did not attach any importance to the drawing and put it away, without saying anything to his parents.

It was some time later, when Brother Paul first made himself known through his Medium to the development Circle. On his first appearance he startled Mr and Mrs Clare with the statement that they had a picture of him in their house. They said they had no knowledge of it, but Paul said there was such a picture and they were to ask their son for it.

Returning home, they asked Tony if he had any picture, and he went to his room and returned with the drawing.

A peculiar characteristic is the squared nature of the drawing; and a decided technique is shown by the effect of light and shadow imperceptibly produced by the shading of the squares. Paul said that he had impressed Tony to draw it and it could be regarded as a reasonable likeness.

The author has seen other drawings made by Tony, and their undeveloped technique bears no comparison to the drawing of Paul. He has never produced a similar picture either before or since.

It appears from Tony's uncertainty as to the way or manner in which he drew the picture—he says he does not remember having a rubber—that he was inspired in his effort, being in a state of natural semi-trance, unknown to him at the time. It is definitely stated that the technique employed is far beyond his normal accomplishment and indeed when he tried to copy this drawing he could not do so with success.

## HEALING OF Mrs CLARE

As Peter's discussions were drawing to a close, Mrs Clare was taken ill and entered hospital, where she underwent a surgical operation. An unexpected complication set in, and the medical authorities decided that it would be necessary to set Mrs Clare's body in plaster of Paris for nine months. She was moved to a country hospital for this purpose.

The matter was discussed with Peter on the Sunday evening of the day Mrs Clare was moved to the country hospital. It appeared that Mr Clare and his sons' minds were a little upset that the Spirit Healers had not been able to avert the trouble and restore Mrs Clare to health. On the evening in question, Mr Clare being in trance, his sons raised the issue.

Peter replied that so far no effort had been made to ask for Spirit assistance. The matter had been regarded casually; and it had been taken as a matter of course that Spirit healing would be given. Peter seemed to resent this, but a request by the sons being made for help, Peter agreed they would see what could be done in the matter.

That very night Mrs Clare, in her new hospital, felt the change taking place within her; and when on the following morning a specialist arrived from London to undertake the plaster of Paris casing, Mrs Clare surprised him by asking if she could sit up. The specialist knew this should have been impossible. Mrs Clare, however, not only sat up, but stood up and walked about the ward. In a short while she was home and able to walk fairly normally. Without doubt, there is definite evidence of another "miracle" healing, the direct result of Spirit intervention. [*A further work dealing with the science of healing, spiritual and magnetic, has already been commenced by the author with collaboration of and explanation by Peter*].

## CHAPTER TWO in Mediumship of Arnold Clare pages 28-36
## OBSERVATIONS ON THE RESTRICTION OF MEDIUMS

In recording the psychic manifestations received through the Mediumship [of Mr Arnold Clare, criticism is anticipated from those who deem that the most rigorous control of the Medium's body is essential before super-normality is proved. There would be justification for such criticism if the events reported were limited to the immediate proximity of the Medium's body; also were there no other factors such as light, time and other evidential data to determine beyond all doubt that supernormal energy and activity were present.

With modern physical Mediumship, the technique of the Spirit operators (who are masters of ingenuity) provides far more intelligent "tests" proving super-normality than the most inquisitorial fettering of the Medium's body by means of ropes, wires, cottons, sticking-plaster, electrical gadgets, adhesive tapes, cages, etc., so dear to certain types of minds associated with psychic research.

Obviously the way to obtain the greatest proof of Spirit activity is to give the Medium and the Spirit operators' comfortable and amenable conditions in which to work. If conditions under which the sitting is held are hard, un-natural, and foreign to the Spirit people, no one should blame the Medium or the operators if phenomena are scanty or absent. One of the most important factors contributing to success is that the Medium's mind should be confident, and sure of successful issue, happy and without any mental strain or anxiety. Mediums, as a rule, are more sensitive than ordinary people and therefore the preliminaries before a sitting should take into account the psychological reactions of the Medium to the conditions, if any, to be imposed.

A professional Medium who demonstrates his/her gifts in order to secure a living is more or less bound to submit to being restrictively controlled. Most professional Mediums welcome and invite some sort of "reasonable" control, though at times there will be differences of opinion as to the interpretation of reasonable control. There is also the professional Medium whose outlook is selfishly limited to financial advantage and is not concerned with any scientific approach, no matter in how friendly a manner this may be introduced. A reason for this is that the Medium is aware of the harm that has been caused to other Mediums by research groups imposing conditions involving strain to the physical body. He/she therefore regards investigators as enemies rather than "understanding friends". There is some justification for this attitude of mind since a number of Physical Mediums have had their gifts impaired whilst others have suffered physically from the strain imposed—**I know two Physical Mediums, still with us, who suffer from <u>continual internal haemorrhage</u>, the result of undue strain.**

Another important contributory factor to success or non-success is in the nature of the sitters themselves. There is a vast difference between a Circle of alert-minded yet co-operative sitters and a Circle of people mentally obstructive and non-co-operative. When Jack Webber sat for "test" séances where extra-restrictive control was employed, or at séances where the hard non-co-operative mind predominated, it invariably followed that the operators found it much harder to manifest phenomena. When they did appear they were spasmodic, jerky, with time-gaps in between each action—so different from the continual free flowing activity at a normal séance.

Few words are more ambiguous or less understood than the word "conditions" as applied to psychic matters; yet it is of paramount importance for successful results for all present to attain to harmonious mental co-operation. The scientific mind that regards the universe as matter only has to learn the importance of the reality of the dimension of thought before it will make progress in comprehending the realm of Spirit activity.

There is the type of Medium of which Margery (Mrs Crandon) is perhaps the finest example, who had no need to demonstrate for financial profit, yet was willing to undergo every kind of restrictive and humiliating control—short of crucifixion—such as may at times be devised by the investigators. So mush thought has been devoted to the various ways in which the human body can be deprived of independent muscular action that it seems that the science of the control of the Mediums has become more important to the investigators than the phenomena itself.

((*According to the proceedings of the American Society for Psychical Research volumes dealing with "the Margery Mediumship", Margery {with the consent of her husband, the Late Dr. Crandon} permitted herself to be used without any restraint.*

*Baron Von Schrenk Notzing visualised a special kind "of psychic laboratory, furnished for all kinds of experimental psychology and psychophysics. Registration should of course be made independent of the sense organs, which are subject to deception, and should, as far as possible, be transferred to physical apparatus. A self-registering balance, the full use of photographic and electrical aids {such as photographs with ultra-violet light}, the use of various degrees of brightness of light and spectrum colours, thermometers, and other specially constructed instruments may find their place in such an institute. Other apparatus of a more physiological kind would be necessary for investigations of the Medium's organism".*

*One can well imagine the reactions of a sensitive Medium to such an environment, and his or her shrinking from placing either himself or herself in a hypnotic or trance state at the mercy of psychic "vivisectors". It would be hard to imagine conditions more prejudicial to satisfactory issue than these*))

Margery knew the potency of the forces used through her Mediumship, and knew also when she surrendered herself to those exacting conditions she was in constant danger of injury to health, if not to life, as the following may indicate.

From U.S.A. S.P.R. Proceedings, page 357:

"I, Grace V Reuter, certify that I assisted at the disrobing of Margery, and thoroughly examined the dressing–gown in which we wrapped her, after which I controlled her hands until she was led into the glass cabinet on a floor two stages higher. There she was wired in the glass cabinet, hands and feet, so that any movement of the extremities was impossible. Her head was bound to the ceiling of the cabinet with a thick rope which fastened around her neck so that she could not move her head without danger of suffocation." (Page 372) "The psychic is clad in a single garment, (kimono) stockings and shoes. She and her garments are examined by a woman at the request of the commission before and after the sitting. In bright light now, there are tied around the Psychic's wrists and ankles long pieces of No 3 picture wire. The part going round the limb is protected against cutting the skin by rubber tubing. All knots are either made, observed in the making, or tested by the Commission. A leather collar is padlocked around the Psychic's neck by the Commissioner and the key kept in his possession. The Psychic is now conducted by a Commissioner into the red-lighted séance room and there seats herself in a Windsor chair in the Richardson plate glass cabinet. The ends of the wrists and ankle ties are threaded through and round fused closed–ring eyebolts on the floor and through the sides of the cabinet respectively. They are securely tied, observed in the tying, or inspected by the Commission and the ends threaded through American Railway Express lead seals and sealed by a member of the commission. Heavy twine is tied by a commissioner to the leather collar in knots peculiar to himself and the other end is similarly tied to a fused eyebolt in the roof of the cabinet. The excursion for the feet is not over six inches. The excursion for the hands is not over two inches; for the head not over six inches forwards, nine inches sideways."

It has been truly said that Mediums who so voluntarily place themselves at the discretion of investigators enter upon a martyrdom as great as that of any other of our fellows who have sacrificed themselves for the sake of posterity.

There remains yet another class of Medium, in which Arnold Clare may well be placed, that self-sacrificing body who do not profit materially from their Mediumship. They regard their gift as of a spiritual or divine nature to be used for the comfort of the distressed and for the enlightenment, by teaching, of man's present materialist conduct of life. Such Mediums do not demonstrate purely for the scientific mind, they are not concerned with it; and are quite indifferent to the approval of any Society or group. (My first request to Mr Clare to agree to sitting for infra-red photography was refused, mainly for the above reason; and that he only wished to serve those who sought his help in a spiritual sense.)

The position should therefore be clear, that one cannot expect every Physical Medium to suffer the indignities freely for the glory of a halo from any particular society. The number of such societies and groups who seek to investigate phenomena thus far exceeds the number of Mediums available, and few societies will accept the evidence of another society, insisting upon their own research. The demands upon a Medium, for "a series of test sittings" becomes more and more numerous as his Mediumship is established. Thus the attitude of Physical Mediums is better understood when at times they refuse to agree to submit themselves to "tests"; and are content to put up with the opprobrium they receive when they also refuse to be "tested" by any society wishing to investigate their powers.

It would, however, be most unreasonable to reject *authenticated* reports of phenomena, simply because Mediums have not been willing to sit in almost strapped nudity. When they state that they are not willing to be treated with so much suspicion, they are quite within their rights.

Each case of Mediumship should be treated individually, and proof that supernormal action takes place should be considered according to the nature of the evidence the operators are able to provide. I do not hesitate to emphasise that these remarks should be taken as expressing, on behalf of Mediumship, a plea for a more discriminating and intelligent outlook than that of the rope and straitjacket.

Before evidence is submitted to illustrate how supernormal action is provable without restriction, a few general remarks concerning Physical Mediumship will not be out of place.

Before any person is able to demonstrate in public as a Physical Medium, a wealth of labour and sacrifice has been necessary. As a rule a number of years (in Jack Webber's case ten years, in Mr Clare's twenty years) are devoted to developing the psychic faculties. This means that for at least one, probably two nights every week, the potential Medium and a number of friends sit for an hour or so with utmost regularity. It may be that for years no movement is observed, and so far as the persons themselves are concerned, both potential Medium and sitters, they may be just wasting their time.

There are in Great Britain thousands of such Circles sitting week after week and year after year, but it is only very rarely that the Circle produces a Medium able to demonstrate publicly. In addition to the weekly sittings, the Medium devotes a part of each day preparing himself for future use. He lives an abstemious life, avoids excesses, and creates for himself a code of rules as spiritual as he can. After the passing of years of endeavour, phenomena may at last become noticeable, perhaps only raps, or the slight movement of the trumpet. When these signs are obtained the development settles down in earnest, and as a rule, several more years of continual sitting week by week follow before the Medium is able to demonstrate outside his home Circle.

Actually, the development is never complete, and continues even after the Mediumship has been acclaimed.

As the Mediumship becomes known, the Medium's real trials commence. He is importuned on all sides by people who desire to sit with him and observe the phenomena, or receive help and comfort from the Return" of their relatives and friends. As the medium makes himself available, so does he immediately become the centre of suspicion. "Is he honest?" "is he a fraud?" etc. The Medium may feel he would like to obtain a "certificate of honesty" and submits to "tests" in the manner described already. If he succeeds, he finds many more societies seeking further tests; and the author has known an established research society impugn a Mediumship in order to force the Medium's hands and induce him to agree to a series of sittings for experimental purposes.

The Medium also has to face the ever-present danger that some irresponsible person will flash a light on him during a séance or interfere in some other manner with the activity taking place. At the time of writing one Medium known to the author lost both his gift and his sight on such an occasion; another well-known Physical Medium recently passed over after interference of this nature; and a number of others have been seriously ill from ignorant and ill-conceived interference.

Reverting to the mediumships under review, the following are examples of what is intended by Mediumship being able to prove itself, without fettering restraint.

Mr Arnold Clare uses a fairly large plaque, measuring 25 ins x 14 ins. This plaque is, as a rule, freshly painted before each sitting with luminous paint, to give maximum luminosity. The degree of light from this plaque will illuminate an object four feet away, and ordinary 10-point type (slightly smaller than used for this book) can be read at a distance up to three feet, so that it will be noted that any article lying on top of the illuminated surface would be seen very clearly indeed. At times, with Mr Clare's sittings, this plaque lies on the floor, illuminated side uppermost. Over the bright surface ectoplasmic material is cast. In appearance it looks like a spider's web, very fragile and almost transparent. This substance is lying perfectly flat, without a crease, on the plaque.

Sitters can thus observe the web-like substance become animated at the *edges only*. There is no question of the whole piece being shaken or moved, the edges only assume life, and move and form prehensile projections, like small fingers. They come and go. As they build up, it is noticeable that they cease to be transparent and appear dark and opaque. These protuberances grip the edges of the plaque and draw it towards the Medium. The plaque stops, the protuberances loosen their hold and take a fresh grip on the sides of the plaque, which is then moved in a controlled manner sideways, forwards, backwards. The whole material is withdrawn, whisked back; and a second later again cast over the plaque, lying on it perfectly smoothly. As it rests on the plaque, so immediately is the plaque gripped and moved about the floor. Clearly here is observable supernormal activity, judging by the rapidity of movement, the sureness of the cast, the animation of a transparent web-like substance into solid fingers or claws, the controlled and ordered movement of the plaque. The word supernormal is used to denote the action that cannot be imitated under the same given condition by human means. In the incident just described, it is asserted that man cannot produce the same effect under any conditions, even given the use of mechanical means or by the employment of electricity, magnetism, or any other force we know.

A further supernormal performance is demonstrated when the plaque is held about two to three feet from the floor, illuminated surface shining downwards upon a length of ectoplasmic material stretching from the Medium towards the trumpet about four feet away. The material being of a whitish colour, is very clearly seen in the illumination from the plaque against the dark colour of the linoleum. The substance becomes animated, its farthest extremity extends towards the small end of the trumpet, and grips hold of it firmly. Whilst this is taking place the flaccid diaphanous-looking material twists together tightly, but only from the trumpet to where it reaches the floor in front of the Medium. Then, using the end of the twisted material near the Medium as a point for leverage, the twisted material, now rigid, raises itself up on end (nearest the Medium) with the trumpet held in perfect alignment. All this in clear light. This position is maintained for a second or two before the trumpet falls to the floor. These and other still more remarkable incidents are described in the records that follow.

It should be noted that Mr Clare's trumpets are not of the light aluminium kind, but are made of celluloid and insulation tape. They are 33 inches long and weigh 7 ½ ounces and to lift up this weight the tension on the small end of the trumpet is equivalent to 3 ½ pounds, from the point of the fulcrum, about three feet away.

Jack Webber's Mediumship was also proved by visible and audible demonstrations, as for instance the removal of his stitched up coat while his hands were held; the instantaneous putting on of white light immediately before and after the phenomena. Details of all these will be found in the volume The Mediumship of Jack Webber, as well as such other examples as: the time factor in a number of varied acts of phenomena; the act of switching on white light immediately after such activity as the photographing of expanses of ectoplasmic materials, the movement of trumpets and objects in distinguishable red light and a number of other acts of phenomena reported and verified.

Jack Webber was controlled by various methods: ropes, cottons, seals, etc., but not so restrictively as by those imposed upon Rudi Schnider or Margery, yet no one, on the evidence, would dismiss the reports as being valueless because the Medium was not so controlled. Neither should any reasonable mind, taking into account the testimony accompanying the reports of Mr Clare's Mediumship, refuse to accept the fact of the phenomena simply because Mr Clare was unfettered.

In this presentation of further evidence of Spirit activity, the sceptic should remember that if a certain incident appears to partake of the "miraculous" as being contrary to, or outside of the range of, ordinary human experience, such incident may well be only the extension of experiences already noted and recorded by responsible and reputable observers. It is suggested that to reject such an incident on the ground that it is of novel or supernormal character would indicate a negation of the scientific outlook on the critic's part.

It would seem only reasonable to accept fearlessly all problems presented fairly and not to reject the implications arising there-from without careful investigation of the evidence, past and present. In this world, governed by the Cosmic law of evolution, will be found problems untold in scope and number for probing investigation and analysis: they will only be solved satisfactorily if implications arising are faced without fear of consequences.

## REPORT BY Mrs GLADYS LAYTON
### Mediumship of Arnold Clare pages 72-73

At the request of Mr Harry Edwards, I am reporting my witnessing of two remarkable incidents at the sitting.

During the course of the séance, varied phenomena have taken place, during which a trumpet went to Mr Hart. Child Peter, one of the controls, asked him to block up the small end of the trumpet, which he did with a handkerchief, twisting it into the small aperture. This being done, about half the handkerchief was left hanging down from the small aperture, which could be seen over the lit-up surfaces present. The trumpet was then levitated and Little Peter spoke to us in a remarkably clear voice. The trumpet then went to Mr Edwards who, on Peter's direction, took hold of the handkerchief and the trumpet was pulled away from it. He was then asked to lay the handkerchief on the trumpet, which slipped of towards the floor as he did so. The trumpet, in a continuous sweeping movement, rescued the handkerchief and in the same movement gave it to Mr hart. As this was being done, Mr Edwards said he had tied a knot in the handkerchief to mark the length of its insertion into the trumpet, and then Little Peter immediately interrupted by saying he had tied a knot as well. On inspection, this was found to be so, though only a second had passed between Mr Edwards placing the handkerchief on the trumpet and its delivery to Mr Hart. The Handkerchief was within my view during the whole process.

Later on occurred the second incident. On the brilliantly illuminated plaque, which was lying on the floor, lighted side uppermost, there appeared in a film of ectoplasm, that had been cast on to the plaque, a dark mass about the size of an egg that was in continuous movement, and constantly changing its shape. There protruded from it a number of distinct formations, claws and fingers, and finally it resolved itself into a perfectly formed hand which moved to the edge of the plaque, gripped it and bent it double several times quickly, and finally ripped the plaque into two pieces. This feat required considerable strength.

## SÉANCE, NOVEMBER 30, 1940 (Report by Colin Evans, B.A.)
### CHAPTER V11 in the Mediumship of Arnold Clare pages 73-81

I was invited to sit on Saturday, November 30, 1940, in a large group séance with A.T.Clare as the Medium. He is secretary of the Balham Spiritualist Society, on whose platform he sometimes gives the address and clairvoyance at the Sunday services, but I was told that he does not sit professionally. I did not count the other sitters, but am under the impression that they numbered about eighteen. I did not inquire nor learn whether any of the other sitters either paid any person or organisation or donated or subscribed to any Society or other fund; the manner of my own invitation prevented the question from arising in my case.

The séance lasted about two hours. It was held for the most part in darkness, but dull red light and firelight were at numerous intervals switched on for fairly long periods, during which similar phenomena occurred as in the dark (details below). No test conditions of any sort were imposed, though one test tentatively suggested by me during the séance was readily most successfully complied with. The Medium was not subjected to any restraint or check or control by sitters. The general effect produced on my own mind was one of complete genuineness in respect to all the phenomena; but only in respect to some of the phenomena was there such proof of genuineness as would have ruled out any possibility of doubt if a sitter had any predisposition to suspicion. The fact, however, that some of the phenomena concerning which there was fool-proof evidence, making doubt impossible, were among the rarest and most important of the phenomena, than the ones otherwise liable to be most doubted, lends a presumption of genuineness to the rest.

After the extinction of lights, the séance was opened with a brief invocation and the Lord's Prayer. Three "trumpets" all made of transparent rigid celluloid with broad strips of luminous paint all round, two of them about twenty-four inches long and one about eighteen inches; two "mouth-organs" (not luminous) and a small glass pot, such as is used for some brands of fish paste, etc., examined and empty; an old fashioned musical box, and a luminous "slate" consisting of a sheet of plywood (larger than the "slates" commonly used—I guess its size as 14 x 10 ins., perhaps) coated on one side with luminous paint with a handle fixed to the other side, were placed in the middle of the floor. The Medium sat in one corner of the room and I was seated in the diagonally opposite corner, with other sitters all round the walls. The distance between my seat and the Medium's was perhaps 20 ft., with the accessories mentioned placed halfway between us, or about 10 ft. from the Medium.

During the short invocation there were loud sounds of a sort of fumbling kind, with rappings and knocks against the trumpets in the middle of the floor, two of the three trumpets were seen to be jerking slightly; they fell over; one of them was righted, rose a few inches wobbling in the air, and fell and rolled in a direction away from the Medium towards my right. At this time, a small electric fire, giving a red glow and a little dim visibility, was still alight. There was no sign of movement by the Medium, either visible or audible.

One of the Medium's Guides then spoke, giving a brief address. This Guide was named "Peter", and spoke perfect English with a slight but noticeable accent of a cultured foreigner. This control's accent is noteworthy for this reason; I have some knowledge of phonetics, and am convinced that the control's pronunciation—with its characteristic vowel qualities, and certain consonants, were such as would be beyond the mimicry of anybody who was not either a trained phonetician, an accomplished linguist or a very exceptional able actor with special dialect training—in fact, I do not believe the last-named could do it unless he were also one of the two former; I noted particularly the non-diphthongal character of the long vowels, the particular nuance of broad e's and o's, long and short, and narrow short o's; the difference between the English so-called dentals, and the genuine dentals of the control (point-tooth, not point-gum, plosives), and absence of aspiration in the phonetics sense in the phonetic sense with voiceless plosives; also the nuances of syllabic stress and of phrase-intonation. The timbre of the voice itself also was, while quite unforced, natural and very resonant, entirely different from that of the Medium's own voice. The latter's speech is that of the average middle-class Londoner of secondary education. Peter's speech was not in direct voice but by means of trance control of the Medium—Peter himself drawing attention to the fact "for our information". After the electric fire had been extinguished, first one then both of the larger trumpets were levitated almost to the ceiling—to a height of some seven feet—and floated all round the room, with perfect controlled and unhesitating steady movement, pointing first to one sitter then to another, with motions of the two trumpets quite mutually independent, the broader ends being often 12 or 15 ft. from the Medium, but always pointing away from him, so that the narrow ends, nearer him, must have been not nearer to him than 10 or 13 ft.

As Peter finished speaking, these two trumpets lowered their broad ends to the floor and, with a little fumbling, picked up the third (smaller) trumpet between them; after which all three remained suspended in the air and moved about independently of one another for a few moments.

During most of the séance, records were played softly on an electrical gramophone and amplifier in a corner of the room away from the Medium's corner, the lady in charge of the gramophone tried to change a needle and reported that she had dropped the needle on the floor and could not find it in the dark. The Medium's child control (also named Peter, but called "Little Peter") spoke in direct voice coming from close to the gramophone and well away from the Medium's chair; and apparently found the lost needle, without the intervention of the lady in charge; then a box of gramophone needles was levitated and floated around the room, rattling. No needle was on the floor when looked for in full light after the séance.

From this point on "Little Peter" seemed to take charge of the séance, and was speaking most of the time, in direct voice, usually coming, beyond doubt, through one of the trumpets; sometimes when broad end of the trumpet was right against my face; sometimes in mid-air or near ceiling in middle of room; sometimes close to other sitters; at other times apparently from high up near middle of room away from all trumpets. The voice and intonation suggested a cockney child, but (possibly through imperfection of ectoplasmic voice-box or distortion by trumpets) sounded always a little unnatural in timbre (which I have noticed to be the case with many child Guides using adult Mediums).

Disconnected notes were rather unmusically played at intervals through the mouth organs or one of them, apparently about breast-high in middle of the room while trumpets were whirling; and in a not very successful attempt (musically) to "accompany" the singing of a song.

I was frequently tapped or touched or stroked by trumpets, with what seemed a perfect control of their movement, suggesting that the responsible agency could see me clearly despite the complete darkness then existing. The movements by which I was touched were too rapid and assured and direct to be consistent with a groping or tentative feeling way; and never either just missed or hit with violence; but were such as a person seeing what he was doing would have made.

Strong and very cold winds blew at intervals for about a minute at a time, about six times during the séance. This phenomena was much more pronounced than the wind that could have been made by movements of the trumpets which were in motion at the times.

About three-quarters of an hour after the commencement of the séance there was a very strong smell of a floral perfume, suggestive to me of an ordinary commercial toilet scent, as used by women; and a considerable quantity of liquid perfume was sprinkled in drops over my head and face, feeling like heavy rain, while other sitters all round the room reported the same thing at the same time.

Four different sitters, all at some distance from me, but also at some considerable distance from the Medium's chair, were personally addressed by "direct voice" through one of the levitated trumpets, in voices not loud enough to be very distinct from were I sat, but all of which were apparently readily accepted by sitters addressed as the distinct and recognisable voices of friends and relatives ("dead") well known to them. The conversations which ensued were apparently fully evidential and satisfying to the sitters concerned. One of these sitters was a young lady who, I learned later, in conversation with her and others after the séance, was attending her first séance; and was a complete stranger to the Medium.

Two of the trumpets having fallen to the floor, the third continued to float around the room; and I saw it approach a sitter and apparently tip itself up, when that sitter announced that a coin had fallen into her lap. A moment later the same trumpet, clearly visible by its bands of luminous paint, came to me, without for an instant having ceased its steady movement round the room with its wide end pointing away from the Medium, and touched my hand; then tilted up and from its wide end fell something which alighted by my foot, which I stooped and picked up, finding it to be a very large heavy coin, about the size of an English five-shilling piece. On examination in the light after the séance it proved to be a Russian coin. A similar thing then happened to five other sitters, and then the trumpet floated towards the ceiling, remaining poised about the middle of the room; and at slow intervals further coins; to the number of another sixteen, were dropped to the floor one by one, "Little Peter" counting aloud as they dropped. A few of the larger ones I was able to see as they passed the luminous band on the transparent trumpet, thus seeing that it was from within the wide end of the trumpet they dropped; but at no time was there any sound of more than one coin rattling in the trumpet; and I satisfied myself after the séance that the larger coins could not be passed into the very narrow small end of the trumpet. One of these additional coins, a German 10-pfennig piece, was dropped into my own hand. Others proved afterwards to be English coins of bygone reigns (George 3, etc.) and foreign coins of various countries, including India. A lady present mentioned that at a previous séance with the same Medium she had by a similar process received a spade guinea.

Brother Peter then asked for full lights to be turned on for a few minutes prior to an attempt to produce a different "phase" of phenomena. This proved to be materialisation, as a number of materialisations followed, taking up most of the remaining time of the séance, after the lights had been again extinguished.

While the lights were up, the Medium was seen to be in an apparently unbroken deep trance in his chair, exactly as before the commencement of the séance and its conclusion.

After the break, when the room was again darkened, the luminous slate was seen to be raised very slowly from the floor, reaching a height of about eight inches, still with its luminous surface floorward and moving upward with a purely vertical movement impossible if normally lifted by human agency unless the person lifting it had been standing in the middle of the room and leaning directly over it—and this movement commenced instantly the light was extinguished, without allowing time for the Medium or any sitter to leave his chair with sufficient stealth to be unheard; while the use of an outstretched arm or foot or any kind of rod or tongs or other accessory for lifting it from a distance would have lifted it with a slant or tilted to one side or the other. It was much more brightly illuminated than most luminous paint-covered "slates" which I have seen used at séances, and gave a light which appeared equal in visibility—conferring power to that of a pocket electric torch shaded with two thicknesses of tissue paper or one of newspaper. The brightly illuminated patch of floor beneath the slate when it reached a height of about eight inches, or perhaps rather more, was then gradually veiled by what looked like a fine semi-transparent textile fabric of very subtle texture gradually materialising "from nothing" until fully formed, draped over the slate. There was no rustle or sound of any material.

The slate then descended slowly to lie on the floor again, then rose suddenly and swiftly to about six feet from the floor, and took up a horizontal position, luminous surface upward, and then slightly tilted upward, till it was seen to be held immediately below the chin of a fully materialise head, whose features and head-dress were as clearly and distinctly visible as if lit by a pocket-torch held close up to it. The head-dress appeared to be some kind of white or whitish thick-textured woollen hood, rather suggesting a monk's cowl widely opened to give a clear view of the face. A curled moustache and small but distinct "imperial" goatee beard were seen, being that of a living entity and not of a mask or inanimate structure. The features of undisguisably different from the Medium's; the nose fuller and more fleshy; the mouth thinner lipped and of more sensitive shape; the eyes quite different, more deep-sunk, and the eyebrows fuller; the forehead larger, broader and higher, and with fuller curves at the temples; and the chin and jaw larger. The remainder of the figure (apart from head and head-dress) was not visible at all. The materialisation made the circuit of the room close to the sitters, pausing opposite each sitter and (in my case, certainly—and I think in the case of the other sitters) bringing its face to within twelve inches of the sitter's eyes for careful scrutiny, with the luminous slate held immediately under chin.

By the Guide's request during the first materialisation, all sitters linked their hands. To do this, I had to put away the note-book in which I had been making notes of the phenomena as they occurred, and my report of the séance from this point on is therefore from memory immediately after the séance and not from notes made while it was in progress, as in the case of the earlier part of the séance.

Sitters were allowed to release their linked hands during later materialisations, the Medium, I was told, was not linking hands with sitters.

A second materialisation was produced and shown in similar manner, and was that of another Guide with quite different features. He was wearing a large turban, with a sparkling jewel of some kind set in it. While this entity was showing his features I, without speaking aloud, formulated a clear-cut mental request to be allowed to see more of the figure than the head. As soon as I formulated this mental request, the slate was lowered so that at first it showed nothing, then, starting near the floor, it was made to shine on and show the clear outlines of legs from the ankle upward, and body up to waist, clothed in close-clinging but heavy textured whitish material of some sort, and then showed what looked like a misty unoccupied gap above the waist. Brother Peter's voice obviously coming from the direction of the Medium's chair at some distance from the materialised form; while the materialised form was still visible about eight feet from the Medium's chair. I then made another mental request, which was apparently ignored or not sensed by any human or discarnate intelligence operating; and I therefore repeated it aloud. It was that we should be shown the Medium while we were shown a materialisation, so that I could repeat to sceptics the fact that a materialised form and the Medium's own body had been simultaneously rendered visible in different places.

At first there was no reply. The materialised form disappeared, but the slate remained levitated. Then there followed the heavy noise of the portable electric fire being lifted from the hearth and placed on the floor nearer the middle of the room. Suddenly it came alight, having apparently been supernormally switched on without the action of any sitter. In the reddish but clear light of the electric heater and in front of the electric fire there was seen slowly materialising what appeared to me a baby's form in white clothes, moving slightly, and seated on the floor silhouetted darkly against the electric fire on its further side (to me) while his clothes, partially transparent, allowed the fire to be seen through them where they were draped loosely away from the body. Luminous slate was shone on the face and body for a moment on the side unlit by the electric fire. The then floated across the room and was carried up and down clearly showing the Medium's face and figure in his chair in the corner of the room. While the Medium was being shown by the luminous slate, the child was seen slowly de-materialising until there was only a small amount of transparent drapery or textile of some sort fluttering in front of the electric fire; this drapery then vanished completely, appearing not to move away but to thin into non-existence. Immediately after, the plug of the electric fire was abruptly pulled out of the wall socket without human intervention. Trumpet levitation, complete with rod-like structure, was shown in the light of the fire.

A final materialisation seen clearly by me was that of Jack Webber, the Medium who passed on recently. Brother Peter had asked if any sitters knew Jack Webber; and I replied that I did; so did some other sitters. His characteristic features, full face and profile, were clearly shown and were unmistakable, the slightly receding chin and low forehead being such as would have required amputation of solid masses from the Medium's face and head in the event of impersonation by him. I knew Jack Webber very well by sight, and was under no possibility of doubt as to the features I saw in the materialisation being the same as those with which I became familiar during Webber's earth life.

Little Peter then materialised, showing only his face, at a height of some three feet from the floor. The face was obviously too small to be that of any adult. It was obviously a complete face and not a middle portion of a larger face partially surrounded by any black covering; and it was obviously alive. However, its features were not clearly visible to me in detail, though I gather that they were to other sitters.

I did not get any clear view of materialisations of personal friends or relatives that I think, I gathered, were recognised by two other sitters.

At the end of the séance, the small glass pot, slightly damp inside, was found on the floor near the farthest wall from the Medium. It smelt of the perfume with which we had all been sprinkled.

## PART TWO CHAPTER V111
## INTRODUCTION TO PART TWO
### In Mediumship Of Arnold Clare pages 82-88

When the discussions with Peter commenced and the idea of publishing them was first formed, I had in view a series of talks that would be confined to explaining the simple mechanics of each phase of phenomena. I soon realised that to present a cogent chair of reasoning, the explanations travelled far beyond the mild comprehension of myself and those present.

It is obvious that the limited knowledge of the sitters handicaps the Guide in his explanations; for unless we were able to comprehend his observations we could not proceed intelligently.

Had our sitters been composed of members who were authorities on physics, philosophy, radio-activity, biology, chemistry and so on, Peter would have been able to give more advanced wisdom, again up to the point of their ability to understand. Further, the questions put by such authorities would have elicited more detailed answers to the points at issue.

This position is frankly realised by the author and his friends, but to obtain such a well-versed commission was, for a number of reasons, out of the question, especially in wartime.

Firstly, the scope of the work in this section is the product of sitting on an average once a week for nine months; and it is extremely doubtful if any expert would have been willing to devote so much time to the matter. The difficulty did not end there; for owing to Mr Clare's war service and his uncertain free hours the meetings could not be held regularly, so that no advance dates could be determined. It must also be kept in mind that Peter's explanations cannot be divided into water-tight compartments, for the whole story is a related structure; and the reader will not be able to obtain a true picture until he has read every chapter, for each part dovetails into the rest.

This presentation will, however, serve a useful purpose, firstly because it will be understood by the majority of those interested in survival; and secondly it will serve as a foundation for the extension of the knowledge by more technical minds at a later date. I am permitted to say, that should any commission of experts be formed in the future, Mr Arnold Clare would be most willing to collaborate.

I am mindful of an attempt to arrange through the good offices of Miss Mercy Phillimore, Secretary of the London Spiritualist Alliance, a representative commission to observe the Webber phenomena. It had to be abandoned as it was not possible to obtain the services of suitable commissioners under the conditions extant in these days.

In spite of the obvious great importance of this work and the benefit that would accrue to humanity from a fuller understanding of the spirit realm, science, as represented by its leaders, is generally reluctant to devote any appreciable time to its study.

Seventy years ago Sir William Crookes cited:

"I have both seen and heard, in a manner which would make unbelief impossible, things called spiritual, which cannot be taken by a rational being to be capable of explanation by imposture, coincidence or mistake. So far I feel the ground firm under me; but when it comes to what is the cause of these phenomena, I find I cannot adopt any explanation which has yet been suggested".

Since that time a number of noteworthy mediumships have functioned, and in some cases well-authenticated reports have been published. As a rule, these recordings have been restricted to a recital of the bare facts—and rightly so—with no attempt to provide explanation of causes and *modus operandi*.

It would be natural to conclude, following the published weight of evidence of unexplained acts and forces, that scientific faculties would have been very keen to conduct research on the issues; but experience has shown that this is not the case. Again I refer to Sir William Crookes who lamented;

"I confess I am surprised and pained at the timidity or apathy shown by scientific men in reference to this subject……..I invited the co-operation of some scientific friends in a systematic investigation. But I soon found that to obtain a scientific committee for the investigation of this class of facts was out of the question".

That attitude of seventy years ago has unfortunately mainly continued unto the present day. True, we have had the support of a number of individual scientists of repute, such as Sir Oliver Lodge; but we have not had any investigation by scientific associations, who invariably have ignored the findings of individual investigators. These remarks do not apply to Societies for Psychic Research, whose careful and meticulous investigations have proved to be so valuable, but to scientists in general, who have formed the opinion, without investigation, that all séance-room phenomena are fraudulent. It is a position based on the premise that as spirit activity seems so opposed to the factors governing matter and known natural laws, the Spiritualist case must be wrong. They have ignored the view that if a new fact seems to oppose what is termed a law of nature, it does not prove the asserted fact to be false, but only that we have not yet ascertained all the laws of nature and forces that are so employed, or that we have not learned them correctly.

The recordings in the first part will have been seen to be outstanding in character; and having assured ourselves of the truth of the facts, and also that they are confirmed by similar occurrences at different times, in different countries through different mediumships, it would be cowardice to suppress the truth. It would also be cowardly to ignore the facts and the teachings of Peter simply because they may cause to be altered, readjusted or re-written some of the presumed established conclusions of psychic science.

It is with no apology therefore that in the second part of this book a challenging contribution is made towards the fuller understanding of the laws and forces involved.

... ... ... ... ...

Throughout the whole history of investigation one essential has been found absolutely necessary for the production of phenomena. Whether the Medium be primitive, lettered or unlettered, the presence of a guide has always been required to direct through the medium's voice or by other means the conduct of the work.

This presence has proved to be one of the major obstacles the scientific mind has to face and accept. The weight of evidence and communication has made the acceptance of the reality of the Spirit Guide more easy in these days; but it presented a difficult problem in the early days; for a while they found it difficult to countenance the presence, they had to endure it, with scepticism. The savants of those days took the naïve and sublime view that the Spiritualist theory should be discarded *during the experiments*, but when the manifestations were accompanied by intelligence they needed the Spiritualist hypothesis but only as a *working* hypothesis. In other words, the investigator must, in order to get results at all, adapt himself to the presence of the Spirit operator under whom all Mediums in trance state work.

One of Arnold Clare's Guides, Peter, is mainly responsible for the phenomena and teachings here described, and it is noteworthy that he has been able to deal fluently with a vast range of subjects. He would speak so fast that it became difficult for the experienced stenographer to take the words down, and he had to slow up his delivery. It has been an achievement that would give pause to any exponent of the art of oratory.

His observations disclose a realm of vast activity, containing potentials the magnitude of which cannot yet be even dimly comprehended. They disclose not only the methods whereby the so-called dead can for a brief time rehabilitate themselves in physical garb, but also deal with elementary and primitive forms of life and their functions.

The references dealing with the "little people" throw some light upon a comparatively new conception of a state of being; and the detail with which this is narrated provides abundant food for speculation. If one admits the reality of life at all in the Spirit World and that life is thereby progressive, it can only be one of degree; and as we in this life have witnessed the evolution of living things from the jelly-fish upwards to man, so it is not unreasonable to assume that there are also gradations of life in Spirit

It is easy for a critic to dismiss the matter as absurd; that course has been the refuge of foolish sceptics in the past who denied with equal vehemence that the earth was spherical or that a heavier than air machine would ever fly.

More pertinent is this challenge. Here we give you the recorded fact and explanation of its accomplishment given by the chief operator. One cannot deny the former for it is the truth, no matter how strange it may appear; and if the fact of its performance is strange, why refuse categorically the explanations because they too must of necessity seem strange.

What alternative reasoned hypothesis can the disclaimer put forward to account for phenomena?

It would have been far easier for Peter to have contented himself with repeating theories we had formed previously, or to cloak the performance of Apportation in ambiguity. Why need he have introduced such a revolutionary explanation of the force of gravity or cut across our preconceived theories of the functions of "voice-boxes"?

Every inquirer should be bound by a law of honour to face fearlessly every problem and every hypothesis presented to him, and it is with this object that the explanations are submitted.

We are, as Peter says, "paddling on the foreshore" of a realm of infinite activity; and as such, the explanations are in their early stages. We have first to grasp an idea—its development being a heritage of the days to come.

... ... ... ... ...

An effort has been made to summarise previous knowledge and experience so they may be related to the explanations. In presenting such summaries, difficulty has been experienced in choosing from the accumulated mass of evidence the most relevant and important items. I have stressed the fact that there has been close similarity between all the various reports of each phase of phenomena, and therefore the summaries and quotations given have been chosen as being generally representative of the whole. They include extracts from incidents in the mediumships of Margery Crandon, Rudi Schnieder, Miss Goligher, Valiantine, Count Rossi, Donald Dunglas Home, Slade, Eusapia Paladino, Jack Webber and others. I have had to rely upon printed records, but with Jack Webber I write from an intimate association; therefore if the references to this Medium are frequent it is because I prefer to speak of what I know rather than what I have reward.

As one studies the history of physical Mediumship, it becomes clear that with each succeeding Mediumship progress is made in the character and quality of the phenomena; this progress is illustrated in the photographic records. So it with Arnold Clare, who today is able to have manifested through his Mediumship phenomena of the highest order.

In the past many phrases have been used by Guides (Peter uses new ones) to name a certain structure or processes. We have such phrases as Walter's "talking apparatus"; D'Angello's "magnetic fluid" and "vital power"; Professor Castellani's "X force", radio-active potencies" and "the psychic force that holds the molecules of the astral body together"; Muldoon's "positive and magnetic principle" and so on. Sir William Barrett, in summing up some of these references, "attributes the phenomena to some extension in space of the nervous force of the Medium, just as the power of a magnet or of an electric current extends beyond itself and influences and moves certain distant bodies which lie within the field of the magnetic or electric force".

By themselves these phrases and inferences mean little, and indeed, may be misleading, causing theories to be built up upon abstract references by the Guides, who, when asked for an explanation, simply provided the best phrases likely to be within the comprehension of the receiver sitter. But now, in view of Peter's explanations, these seemingly ambiguous terms take on a new significance; they come to life and we can begin to perceive intelligently and more accurately the intention behind the references. They build up a composite picture providing a related tenable hypothesis covering the whole field of manifestation.

Peter's statements may create some controversy among those who subscribe to certain theories elaborated from man's interpretation of the circumstantial evidence of the séance room. Further, the nature and the work of "nature spirits" may not be to the taste of those who have regarded all physical phenomena as of a purely spiritual character; and they may be shocked to read that certain works they may have witnessed were the result of labours of sub-human entities.

It is felt essential, however, no matter how adversely the explanations may affect some readers, to publish faithfully the explanations as given. By doing so, expression may be given to one new proven thought, or probable line of reasoning capable of being proven subsequently. If one part can be shown to be wrong, then it may be all wrong; but if one part is proven and it stands up to reason as a coherent whole, then the entire structure is worthy of our most earnest consideration.

## THE ETHERIC REALM
### CHAPTER 1X Mediumship of Arnold Clare pages 88-104

It has been somewhat puzzling to determine the exact order in which Peter's revelations should be given so that the sequence of chapters will build up a constructive story step by step.

What has made it even more difficult is that no part is complete in itself, each chapter having a direct bearing upon others.

It would have been preferred for this opening chapter to have been last owing to its complex nature. Yet it must come first for it deals with a subject that is the basis of all Spirit activity and it is essential for the reader to have in his mind the foundation upon which each explanation depends.

It is therefore necessary to provide first of all a general statement as to what is known by science to be the meaning of the realm etheric and the constitution of matter.

Peter's statements in this chapter were last to be received. It will be found that they contain references to some of his previous statements (appearing in subsequent chapters). This may render the reader's appreciation of this chapter a little difficult to grasp its meaning and implications on the first reading. It is suggested that this chapter be read through to obtain a general idea of the subject, continuing with the rest of the book returning to re-read this chapter again afterwards.

Until recently matter was known to be composed of molecules and atoms, just little lumps of matter, coalesced together into large or small lumps. The invention of the X-rays disclosed subsequently that atoms are made up of electrons and protons whirling round within an etheric content. Perhaps the best description is that given in the words of Sir Oliver Lodge in his book Ether and Reality as follows:

"We can now summarise briefly what we know. The two opposite charged particles, the negative and the positive, are called respectively an electron and a proton. They are both exceedingly minute. They are far smaller than atoms, incomparably smaller, the smallest things known; even if there were a hundred or a thousand of them in an atom, they would not be in the least crowded, there would be plenty of empty space. Different atoms are now known to be composed of a different number of electrons; and by their different number and grouping they constitute the different chemical elements. The atoms of all the chemical elements are built of electrons and protons and of nothing else.

"On this view the existence of an electron can be fairly understood. Can the existence of a proton be understood too? No; there we are in a difficulty.

The proton is more massive than can be easily accounted for: and why it is more massive we can only guess, or at least the guesses are not very satisfactory. That remains at present an outstanding puzzle: the question is one that has hardly yet been faced. One guess is that the electron is hollow like a bubble that it has an electric field, which by itself would cause the bubble to expand, but that it is kept in equilibrium and of a certain size by etheric pressure. On this view there is no substance in its interior: in itself such an electron is not massive at all, its apparent mass is due to its electric field and nothing else. Whereas the interior of a proton, instead of being hollow, may be full-filled with an extra ether. : all that which was removed from the electron being crammed into the proton, so as to account for its great massiveness or what we may call its weight. A proton is more than a thousand times as heavy as electron, about 1,840 times by direct measurements; and what is called "the atomic weight", for the weight of an atom depends almost entirely on the weight of the protons it contains. The hydrogen atom contains one only, the helium atom contains four, the lithium atom seven, the oxygen atom sixteen and so on—in accordance with the list of atomic weights long empirically known in chemistry, the heaviest being uranium, which contains 238. the atomic weights are certain enough; the number of protons in a specified atom is fairly certain also. But what is not known is why the proton has such weight, and why the weight of an electron is so much less. In every other respect the two charges seem equal and opposite; electrically they are equal and opposite.....

"we are safe in saying that the weight of matter depends on protons, that is the positive units, which go to form the nucleus of the atom, while the chemical properties of the atom depend on the electrons which circulate around the nucleus. These planetary electrons are active and energetic and produce conspicuous results; they characterise the atom by its spectrum; they confer on its chemical properties; but they add to its weight hardly at all...."

So we see that matter is not solid at all, it is a vast number of revolving electrons around a nucleus. Thus we are able to perceive clearly that all matter is in a state of vibration; and the manipulation of vibrations or frequencies is the method the Spirit Operators employ for certain phenomena in the séance room.

The electrons and protons move at great speed within the framework of the atom, and are so small that they may be compared in Peter's words to footballs whirling around inside Westminster Abbey; the space within the atom in which the electrons and protons move being occupied by ether. This ether thus takes on the characteristic of the particular atom, so becoming, in Peter's words, "bound ether".

Certain conclusions carry us further. As electricity is a vibration of ether, and the atom and its components are electrical energy, so is all matter ether in a particularised condition.

Matter, therefore is a combination of positive and negative electrical charges moving in an ordered manner associated one with the other by the ether which is thereby the basic substance of the whole universe.

We know that ether fills all space and is the medium by which light and heat reaches us. It has been computed that etheric waves move at nearly 200,000 miles a second. Although we have been unable to measure or weigh ether, we know that it must occupy what we call space because heat, light, and sound waves travel trough it at ascertained rates, particularly does this apply to radio waves, proving there must be a medium through which the waves can regularly travel.

Its pressure, as Peter says, is immense, ponderable, and penetrates all things. Its pressure may be so great that no adequate concept can be given in finite understandable terms; it may be millions of tons to the square foot.

It is difficult for the mind of man to conceive ether as it is, as we are in it, like deep-water fish in the depths of the ocean; we are part of it, as it is the all-pervading interpenetrating power. Without it we could not se, as there would be no medium to carry light to our eyes; we should be utterly cold, as there would be no means of conveying warmth throughout the world.

Peter tells us that the manipulation of gross ether is the raw material of the Spirit people as wood, iron and clay are ours, so that ether must be a connecting link between the realm physical, the realm of energy and the realm of Spirit.

In our world our senses only permit us to perceive a very limited range of etheric vibration. That extra vibrations exists we know by the limited range of light waves that our eyes permit us to see, or the limited range of sounds that are audible to our ears.

We know of the presence of the ultra-violet, infra red, unknown and X-rays, which our eyes cannot receive. We know there are extensions of sound vibrations at both ends of the scale which our ears cannot record. Thus human reception is extremely limited as compared with the known range of experiences that might be ours were we to possess extra perceptory senses.

The fuller life open to Spirit people can be more clearly visualised if we use the argument that, as our soul body and mind leave the prison cell of the physical body, an extended etheric sensory perception naturally follows. This argument is supported by our knowledge of the spectrum which tells us that outside our very limited perception there is a vast field of ordered frequencies with potentialities permitting another from of tune-in existence to receive and use those potentialities.

This modern knowledge presents a picture that would have been an inconceivable fantasy to the scientist of a century ago. May it not be that this glimpse we are seeing of the realm etheric provides a definite postulate for much that the Spirit-guides could only hint at obscurely in the past.

Peter refers many times to bound ether, that is, ether associated with a given condition. When it loses that boundness or character, decay sets in. Here again is a firm argument. Compare a piece of tough oak with another piece that is in the process of decay. Some change has taken place, in which the piece of live tough substance has been transformed into a condition of crumbling dust. Some quality has left the original oak. Its character, its personality has gone; and there is no organisation within it. This change is consistent with Peter's explanation. For if we bear in mind our knowledge of the construction of matter and the importance of the vehicle of ether for its being and motivation, we arrive at the thesis that, as the forces within the atom disseminate, the ether loses its character or boundness; and so the vibrant organised mass comprising the piece of oak loses its character and its organisation. The individualised ether in the fullness of time changes from the condition of bound ether to free ether; and so this piece of oak loses its character and decays.

Another simile may assist towards visualising the realm etheric. We are told that all matter (including our dense bodies) is subject to the ponderable inter-penetration of ether. The living sponge at the bottom of the sea provides a good illustration. There is the pressure of the water, equal intensity all around it; and penetrating throughout its whole being. Thus we have to view our bricks and mortar, our chairs and tables, our dense bodies, as sponges in the etheric sea. This may be hard for many to conceive or accept, and yet it is in perfect line with our knowledge and Peter's observations.

As all matter is a state of vibration formed from etheric potentials, and each matter component possesses its own individual vibration, yet still allowing co-operation and association with other components, so there can be no rigid dividing line separating one piece of matter from another, solid from fluid, fluid from gas, or physical substance from substances built by Spirit action, such as ectoplasm.

We are continually discovering both slower and quicker vibrations or frequencies than those previously known. We are learning how by different amalgamations of electrons, protons and their associated forms, we are able to obtain substances with new potentials. What is there then to debar the probability that there is no borderline between that of matter as we know it, and dense or gross ether. If we admit this probability we draw a step nearer to realising how for various kinds of manifestations, i.e. ectoplasm, materialisations, voice instruments, rods of strength, and so on.

Just as man is able, through his knowledge of atomic structures, to form new agencies, so are the Spirit-people, with their greater wisdom and their closer affinity to the realm etheric, able to build up, for a period, a materialised form or an etheric structure to carry out the purpose of the moment.

As energy is the foundation of matter, and as man is able by directing that energy to accomplish his set purpose, so does it become tenable that Spirit-people can direct similar energy or other qualities of that energy to the etheric potential; and so create substances or instruments to accomplish their purpose. When they withdraw the energy, in a similar manner to man cutting off an electric current, it is understandable that the created substance or instrument will disintegrate back into the ether from whence it came. This readily explains Peter's references to the dissolution of ectoplasmic material.

Worlds are still being formed in the solar system; and as we know, they are also immersed in an etheric surround—otherwise we should not be able to see them—the assumption is tenable that they are subject to similar etheric activity and influence.

It is perhaps permissible to remark here that as we know each solar system to be the ordered revolution of bodies around the nucleus (the sun in our case) we thereby have a vastly enlarged example of atomic movement. Since the same principle of ordered movement applies to components of an atom as to the components of a solar system, it is surely pertinent that ether and its potentials are "father and mother" of both.

As the reader keeps the sense of this in mind, so will he be able to understand more readily Peter's explanations, which permit the curtain to be lifted a little and allow a glimpse into that which has been for so long an impenetrable mystery, cloaked in obscurity by the vague term 'astral" or "cosmic" chemistry.

Peter's observations followed this question:

*Question* *:( Unless otherwise stated, all the questions to the Guide were from the author) "You have spoken a great deal about ether and it would be most helpful if you can
tell us more about it. (The discussions on this topic were some of the last to be held.) We recognise the vast scope of the subject, but perhaps it would clear the air if you could give some definition of the classifications of what is bound ether and gross ether."

*Peter:* "Except for one or two points, it is a mighty big task In referring to 'bound either' and 'dense ether' I think those terms are synonymous—they can be interchanged.

"If we were referring to Bound Ether in relation to the medium's form we should be referring to that part which is the etheric body. It is what one might term differentiated ether. It has character because it is in a different state of motion or vibration from that of the free ether. Bound ether can be considered as like the air you put into a bottle, it is confined there whilst the free ether would be comparable with the atmosphere outside. It has no character of its own apart from its essential make-up except in such cases as where it is related to certain areas, such as hilly districts, heavily tenanted quarters and the places which are beautiful or foul, in which case the air and ether would become affected.

"Bound ether maintains the life of its material counterpart so long as that life serves a useful purpose; and decay sets in when the ether becomes loosened It reduces its vibration and as it slackens it gradually becomes absorbed into the free ether) very much like the slow removal of the stopper from our bottle of air. As this bound ether disintegrates so does the physical counterpart crumble. Now can you see the purpose of it ?

"That is bound ether—it is ether which has character— the character of the object with which it is associated. It is the egg to the pudding—the binding, do you see ?

"Ether, as a whole, fills the whole of space. If it were possible to fill it, that is in the sense that you would use the term. Space is limitless, as you know, but I must use terms which are readily understandable by you. It is not quite the same ether as you know on earth, because the earth itself bears an ether with character. To you, as to all other **things upon earth, it is without character, in the same way** as the negative polarity of your electricity is of the same polarity as that of the earth.

"Ether being characterless can be impressed by the minds of man. It will take on, almost permanently, conditions of its environment; because remember ether is ponderable in that it does not shift or move. You can compare it with a jelly. If you tap it on one side, the vibration is felt at the other—the whole wobbles. You cannot measure ether at the moment. Scientists have tried to measure ether drift the drift of the sea of ether past the earth; they were on the right road, in a way, when they sought the highest points, but they did not go high enough. They would have to ascend to at least a height of eighty miles above the earth's surface, and then it would perhaps be impossible to measure with their present-day instruments. The earth carries its own ether, but it soon becomes isolated from the sea of ether. That is a good term—lithe sea of ether". It fills all space. It interpenetrates everything. It is denser than material for it has no holes or spaces in it. It has no chemical composition. It is more solid than the earth--in reference to its own environment and not yours. You know how you walk through water. As you walk through it up to your waist you push it aside. Well, you do almost the same in ether; but you do not create a space behind you. Water and you cannot occupy the same space at the **same time but ether** can and does. But you see what I **mean.** It is equally as solid and real as are your bricks and stones."

*Question:* "A glass of water is permeated by ether. We conclude the ether content within the glass of Crater differs from that without ?"

*Peter:* "Yes, of course. That is why I have referred to it as bound ether."

*Question:* "It has weight ?"

*Peter:* "Its weight is so great that you cannot measure it, because all your standards and measurements are taken within the etheric mass. You see, it is so vast and it so fills all space that you do not and cannot comprehend it. We cannot get outside of it to weigh item Ether has a frequency, and when a change is made within the ether, material bodies are formed. What takes place is a change of frequency in the immediate environment of the material body in such a way that it is different from its apparent source.

"It is operated on by the intelligent mind in a case of usage of the natural processes by the higher developed mind. A man operates upon it by his thoughts; and the level of those thoughts is determined by the quality in which they are radiated. And so you have, as it were, etheric thought strata—the strata or layers of different combinations or rates of vibrations. If you cut through the surface of the earth, you would see a sort of graining, marking the different periods during the earth's formation. It would be precisely the same if you could take a large knife and slice through the lower stratas of ether, that is those strata associated and bound by the earth's area of influence.

"You can tune in to these strata according to your own mental processes. They are, as it were, mental records wherein are stored the thoughts of the ages. They are the very source of knowledge—memory, experience, to which the whole of man's and nature's evolutionary processes have subscribed.

"If you think of water and its natural characteristics, you have something of the idea of ethers You see ! **But** not quite the same thing. It fills **everywhere it flows, although,** of course, there are wider differences. Consider it as being constantly in a state of motion without the whole of itself moving; the movement within the whole being aided, fluctuating, as it were, according to the pulls it receives from the thought-force finding its level or strata according to its intention. The thought gravitates to that stratum most in harmony with it for good or for ill."

*Question:* "With regard to ether and health ! I believe that we can do a great deal for ourselves by consciously tapping etheric vitality. Can you give us any idea of that ?"

*Peter:* "Yes, of course you can. That is right: but first of all you have to convince yourself that such a thing is possible. You must remember always the trinity of man's make-up, the triune constituted by his physical body, his soul body and his spirit. I have already told you of the soul body which carries on certain processes of mind control, and operates in relation to all things concerning the natural realm, within which realm comes the realm of ether.

"If there is complete understanding between the mind— which is of the soul, in this instance—and the brain, one is able (referring to the soul) to demand the necessary health and power, which is in effect a sympathetic vibration; and so incorporate it into oneself and ultimately into the body For remember this, that before a mould manifests physically it exists etherically, i.e. within the soul. God loves the mar} who, when fortune goes against him, keeps his own fortress unharmed, i.e. he retains all his physical potentialities. God has not forsaken that man. A human physical {ailing is a disharmony within the soul or a lack of its wisdom. It seems a far cry from ether, but it is not. It is not even next door—it shares the same room."

*Question:* "You have said that health and illness are first built in the soul body. Can you explain to us how it is that, say, a healthy physical body obtains a complaint such as headache or nerve trouble ?"

*Peter:* "It is so simple yet I cannot say yes or no. you will probably think I am, what you might term, 'going a **long way** round'. If you can fix in your mind the idea that the soul existed before the body (you will not dispute that) there you have the answer to your question. The soul is by no means perfect, in so far as its desire for life is concerned; and it likes to enjoy the lusts of the flesh whatever they may be. If you get headaches, they may be due to several things. One might be due to over-indulgence, which is a form of unwisdom or, if it is more deep-seated it is a deficiency within the constructive powers of the soul to complete the building into the physical of a durable nervous sensorium in regard to that particular part. Now you want to know what this relationship has to healing.

"First of all, you have to have faith in the healing power. You have to be conscious of the existence of that power. You see, all of that which contributes to life is linked so closely together, that when you start to talk of one thing, you are not far distant before you have crossed the bar into the next realm. It is difficult unless you can envisage the whole thing completely."

*Question*: "That implies that harmonies and disharmonies, health and illness, are built up first in the soul body, therefore the soul dominates the physical body ?"

*Peter:* "There you have it perfectly."

*Question:* "I am puzzling how those conditions can be built within the soul body in the first place ?"

*Peter:* "We go back to our first words, to what I have told you about breathing—rhythmic breathing—not only in relation to the balance of air but primarily to the supply of bound ether associated with that air for the maintenance of the etheric body through which the soul works. You can by thought-control direct the temperature of the body; but, in the main, because of your form of living, the body is more susceptible to temperature changes than it would be if you lived more naturally. I told you, you were paddling on the foreshore that separates your known from the unknown~ You say the earth is real and concrete. It is concrete but not real. Only **those things** that are permanent are real. It is we who stand upon the shore of reality facing you; and you are facing reality, but the distances are so vast that you cannot take it in, in one glance. But we are talking about ether—the common denominator that separates the visible from the invisible (invisible to you), separating the perceptible from the imperceptible."

*Question:* "Is ether the vehicle of the spirit world and essential for the existence of spirit people ?"

*Peter:* "No, not in the sense in which we have been speaking of it. It is the realm or the material of the soul. It is what I have called the material with which the soul works. It is its clay and stone."

*Question:* 'You say that in the manipulation of gross ether you are in your element. If gross ether is your clay or stone, are you not akin to it, or related to it ?"

*Peter:* "Would you relate yourself to a clay building ? Would you consider yourself a part of the bricks of this house or the coal that you burn in your fire ? The same applies; and, do not forget, the word 'gross' is used, which gives a different significance. Many beautiful paintings that you see upon walls are of similar material to the clay within your bricks. It is the application that makes all the difference. I have used the word 'ether' generally for all things when referring to the various substances through which we work and which we use, although there are perhaps other names you would give it; but my answers would then have become too involved. Where I have specified, I have said the 'gross' ether or the 'bound' ether, whereas perhaps other people would use other names. Dense ether is a gradation of the gross but similar."

*Question:* "Referring to psychic rods and their etheric conductors ! Can you tell us how the voltage you spoke of is applied to them ?"

*Peter:* "Well, it is the same principle as those employed by you, with this difference: that it has the same qualities but it is of such a frequency that you cannot record it. You have upon earth what is known as low-frequency and high-frequency current. Low-frequency travels through the mass of the conductor but the high-frequencies travel only upon the surface. As the frequency increases, it is taken further from the centre of the material towards the surface—which I believe is termed the 'skin effect'. If you were to link yourself with high-frequency (not a high voltage) you would find it would burn but seldom kill because of its 'skin' effect, showing a tendency to travel rather more within the etheric part of the conductor than in the material. It is an easier passage for it, so therefore if you could increase the range of its frequency intentionally it would become further removed from the conductor. You almost have it in the case of what you term 'radiated frequency'.

Through the coils they use for its inductive qualities, the frequencies travel almost clear of the physical conductor. And so you go on; in the case of radio telegraphy you have its radiation across distances via the ether. The disturbance at the terminal, or what you have termed the antennae— aerial--agitates the ether throughout. We carry it beyond the stage that you have reached by bringing it within the scope of those voltages spoken of in connection with the psychic conductors, or what you have termed Prods'. Do you see, and cannot you see that with the advance of your knowledge of radio activity you are coming to closer contact with understanding the principle of etheric energy ?"

*Question:* "May I refer to the talk on ether which we had last time ? There are one or two points which perhaps you would elucidate a little more. You spoke about the zones of ether that carry thought and experience. The first question is: Do the spirit-people draw from and contribute to those same zones ?"

*Peter:* "On the one hand, they draw from, and, on the other hand, they influence those zones which are available to the mind of man. Their own intelligence, however, is drawn from zones or strata far higher and beyond the receptivity of their minds. For instance, in the case of making revelations to the earth you call it new inventions--they are placed within handy reach of the mind so attuned to receive them. What use man makes of them thereafter is man's responsibility."

*Question:* "The wisdom that you have. Is there a sort of stratum or zone of wisdom for record purposes that you can draw from ? Is it the same as that you have just mentioned ?"

*Peter:* "It is the same but, of course, there is a residuary intelligence--that which we can draw upon from our own strength, but anything beyond that we must have recourse to those zones of supply. remember they are limited. We cannot reach out for everything any more than you can, but only according to our illumination. You must consider the realm which we are discussing as being ever present, there is no past and no future—just experience."

*Question:* "Do the zones only contain the experiences of the immediate present and of the past ?"

*Peter:* "They contain in the records everything from the commencement of evolution insofar as the material and physical realms are concerned. Simply, before there was matter, life existed within the ether; and those records are the same now as then, and always will be. The other zones are Progressive— they are constantly being added to Prom the experiences of the past, so that when the mould is full and the physical pattern complete, you have the end of that evolutionary cycle. Can you see ?"

*Question*: "Could you ever reach the end of a cycle of that nature ?"

*Peter:* "Yes, of course. You do not think so because that is not within the ken of the children of today. Your geologists, however, will tell you that during certain periods of the earth's history, there has been some unexplainable catastrophe which has occurred with great suddenness. 52,000 years is approximately the period of one of these cycles."

*Question:* "And these catastrophes--are they arranged or do they evolve ?"

*Peter:* "They are arranged by nature. There is intelligence behind nature. I have been instructing you in that. I have spoken of an over-soul which is not individualised. That is the difference between man and animals in its wider and larger aspect. With man you have an individualised or polarised spirit intelligence. The use of these two words no doubt will help all your readers to understand my meaning. The egotist will understand 'individualised' and the scientist will understand 'polarised'.

"Man being an individualised or polarised spirit, each is different from his neighbour, but in all nature and especially in the case of animals, you have not that difference. If you study one only of a particular type, say a lion or a tiger, you study the species. They have no individuality. They have what is known as the over-soul which copies them as a species, but not as individuals. You say, (I have a cat or a dog which definitely has an individuality !' My answer to that is 'yes' because of their close association with the human being. Who can say that at some time in the future that cat or dog you fondle so much will not earn the right to become your brother and that it will stand on two legs rather than four ? It is not beyond the realms of possibility, but r am not going to express any opinion now."

*Question:* "With reference to bound ether. Can you associate that with the physical construction of atoms, or can you explain the relationship of ether to the atom and its component parts ? Does that association create the boundness of ether ?"

*Peter:* "It is easy to ask the question but difficult to discuss something which for you does not exist. It is the nearest approach to the real thing that I can see, but there may be others more qualified than I to give an analysis of what an atom looks like. Imagine a dewy morning with many gossamer threads: hanging at the end of each thread there is a little scintillating globule of water, and if you examine one closely you will find that it is constantly moving. Can you picture that ? That is what atoms look like reaching out into infinity ! Have you seen a waterspout ? Well, that is like the atom in action within ether. It is a whirl of energy; and it is its speed or its vibration or its frequency of motion that gives it its peculiarity. It has a positively charged centre, 'proton' (that is your word for it). Now you have a positively charged body. Very well—that is not happy by itself, it is unbalanced; so it attracts to itself negative charges or what you call electrons. Very apt names, I would agree. As soon as it has collected about it sufficient to neutralise and to render it satisfied, it has no further concern, no interest in anything without itself. Do you See ? During this process it is still whirling round, and according to the nature of its centre so are governed the numbers of electrons necessary to render it static. Almost immediately following that, there is set up within itself a state of stress within its ether. This is due to torque which characterises the ether or etheric medium through which these natural forces can operate. That ether becomes individualised because of the strain. It has a zone or sphere or influence around it which makes it similar to our globule of water.

"In a few words you have seen the creation of the atom as directed by some superior mind in the beginning, and it was not until that action took place that you had anything living physically. That was the work of God in the first day of creation. The first 'day' was of a length or period of 52,000 years; and the six days it took to create the earth was actually six times that time. A truer story was never written if only we had the right mind to read it."

*Question:* "What was the implication of the gossamer thread ?"

*Peter:* "They stretch into infinity. Now you take in imagination a bunch of those threads with globules I mentioned attached; and whirl them around your head in such a way that, in a manner of speaking, they are equally spaced. You would have them revolving, with you as the pivot at the centre. The invisible connection between that power and the atom is intelligence, which is concentrated at the centre. It is, if you likes a polarised radiation similar to that radiated by man--individual man."

*Question:* "Regarding decay, you told us that ether loses its characteristics. Is the initial movement towards decay from the ether or from the forces within the atom ?"

*Peter:* "It is due to your being within the sphere of influence of the larger atom which is the earth and of the forces pushing towards its centre. There is definitely a pressure. And this pressure is great. All the same there is bound to be a reaction otherwise you would have a destruction of time, in fact the earth would not exist. You must remember that a given action always calls forth an opposite, or reaction; but although the opposite reaction is oft-times observed in other things, there is reaction."

*Question* (Mr. Hart): "Do material and ether occupy the same space at the same time ? An article develops, or has with it, its own characteristic ether which remains bound to the object and keeps it intact According to our science, no two materials can occupy the same space at the same time but r now- find that material and energy or force can occupy the same space all the same time. Therefore do ether and material occupy the same space at the same time ?"

*Peter:* "Yes, definitely."

*Question* (Mr. Hart): "Science, I think, is beginning to realise that the true life is spirit. You are living the true life ? . . ."

*Peter:* "No, I am not. I am still living a life just as speculative as yours; but we are one jump ahead of you. We have gathered, too, facts which are a part of reality and which show you, as a Comparison the enormity of the findings of the great journey that yet lies before us. We have a greater awareness of the reality; and we have a better understanding of the unity of life. That is why we are here to bring it home to you."

*Question* (Mr. Hart): "Life is spirit; and life on earth is merely the existence of spirit in material. You, as spirit, exist without material. That is the difficult part for us to understand. Is our existence in material merely for experience, to improve our life, to progress upon our path-way ?"

*Peter:* "As blinkers are to a horse, so with a physical body is your understanding upon earth. It can only see a little bit ahead. It has to be blinded to all else otherwise it becomes fearful. But the horse wishes to shed its blinkers; and because you would know, you feel that also. It is the feeling that any normal being has the craving to know what is outside those 'blinkers': the trouble is the finding of the key, which will open the way. Yet the finding of the key is so simple that it is profound. You have the right idea, and we will pursue it further."

## DISCUSSION ON PLATES NOS. 3 , 4, 5 AND FIG. 3
### CHAPTER XV11  Mediumship of Arnold Clare pages 202-207

THESE three photographs are typical of "light formations" received through psychic photography. Hitherto no explanation has been given to account for, or explain, their meaning. Certain conclusions can, however, be stated with confidence, as follows:

(I) Photographs of this nature, while not abundant, are not rare.

(2) They possess Similar characteristics, of formation, convolution and construction.

(3) On two appear a central well-defined and perfect sphere of activity.

(4) They are only obtained when Spirit forces are present, in the presence of a Medium.

(5) They cannot be obtained by normal photographic process.

Professional photographers cannot explain them yet they are definite results obtained under certain given conditions. The "given conditions' being; a plate exposed in a camera in the presence of a person (or persons) possessing mediumistic powers. Therefore such photographs can only be the result of psychic forces expressed through Mediumship

The cameras and plates used were of the normal kind. Time exposures of varying periods were made in each case therefore no set exposure time governs the result. The probability is that the formations were only momentarily in being (photographically).

A short description as to the manner in which they were received by the persons concerned follows.

**Plate No. 2** was secured by Mr. R. F. Bounsall, of Worthing Mr. Bounsall, senior, states that the photograph was secured by his sixteen-year-old son, at a home circle consisting of his wife, son and himself. The plate was *partially exposed* in normal light *before the sitting commenced,* so that the image of the room-was first recorded. The trumpet on the table appears transparent; this was due to the trumpet being placed on the table during this first exposure The lens was closed. The sitters took their seats, the light was extinguished and the lens opened again. The medium Mrs. Bounsall} sat in the chair on the right-hand side, where the formation commences. There is a distinct "cable" running from where the medium sat, throughout the whole length of the formation through an "insulation" to where it reaches the trumpet. The trumpet appears to have other effects (light or ectoplasm) oil it.

By means of the double exposure we are able to see the directive action of the phenomenon. One other point should be mentioned: behind the screen is a bowl of water; though whether this has any significance is not known.

Peter tells us what this formation is; and it is pertinent that Mrs. Bounsall was sitting for the development of voice Mediumship.

**Plate No. 3** was secured by Mr. S. J. Spiller, of the Ewell (Surrey3 Spiritualist Society. It was taken at a sitting of a home developing circle. The exposure was approximately ten minutes in white electric light—a shaded 100-watt electric bulb.

**Plate No. 4** was taken by Mr. O. MacKinnon Charles, B.Sc., leader of the Merton Park Spiritualist Church. Exposure approximately eight minutes in darkness.

Peter's observations on these three photographs followed the question:

*Question:* "Regarding the photographs I have shown your medium tonight, can you tell us whether there is any connection between them and what you have told us concerning voice production, or whether they give a picture of any etheric energy about which you have spoken?"

*Peter:* (**Plate No. 2**.) "The structure proceeds to what appears to be a trumpet. Now that is a pretty good example of the etheric sound conductor, though it is not completely organised, of course. You see, there is a knot in it. If you could straighten that out you would have the voice right away. This does not of courses illustrate the power of levitation. It has regard to voice alone, and would only be responsible for the production of voice. It has no power to levitate."

*Question:* "We understand that there are two distinct processes ?"

*Peter:* "Yes there must be, but for perfect working the formation shown on that picture would have to be much more concentrated. That is to say, not so wide. It may be that for the purpose of demonstration they have widened it to give a clearer idea of its formation."

*Question:* "Is the shaded part what you have called the insulation ?"

*Peter:* "Yes, and the centre line is the conductor or the conveyor."

*Question:* "The insulation appears to commence where it would leave the Medium's body ?"

*Peter:* "That is right. Whilst that is not a true picture it is useful as an example or illustration. It had to start from somewhere and the commencement, in this instance, is on the right of the photograph: then it is gradually built up and developed as it proceeds towards the trumpet. There you have as complete a plan of the principle of voice production as you can be shown. But mark you this somewhere along the length of the conveyor, according to conditions) there would develop a bulge, a mixing chamber you might say, or your beloved 'voice-box'* This may be near to the medium, or to the source of emergence, or it may be further along towards the trumpet. In the case of independent voice, when no trumpet would be used, the 'voice-box' would be almost solid—that is dense ectoplasm."

*Question:* 'Now can you give me any reason why the plate would receive that formation in the dark ?"

*Peter:* "There is no evidence that they exposed the plate in the dark. You are relying upon people's good faith."

*Question:* "Their story is, that they exposed the plate in the darkness ?"

*Peter:* "If that is so, I cannot tell you. There is no reason why they should not so expose it, but I cannot say yes in this instance, because I do not know."

*Question:* "The photograph [**Plate 3**] was received in ordinary electric light ?"

*Peter:* ('*Why* not ? There you have a picture of etheric energy, but completely disorganised. It may be due to several reasons. There were people present who were about to sit for a circle, that is, conditions were being built up preparatory to the sitting; and it is, more or less, a radiation from the sitters. If you could get a good photograph of a circle complete you would not have that ribbon formation wandering aimlessly around like a wisp of silk in a breeze you would have it linking up perfectly with each sitter."

*Question:* "*That* lacy appearance within the ribbon of light [**Plate No. 33,** does that indicate any particular characteristic? "

*Peter:* "That just happens to be etheric ripples in the substance; yet it is not substance (it is difficult to find words with true meaning). It is a slight luminosity beyond the range of human vision. It could be made tangible by a little more organisation. Do you follow ?"

*Reply:* "Yes, except that I do not know the purpose for which it is used."

*Peter:* "*It is* not used for any purpose. In the photograph it is disorganised: it should be linked with each sitter."

*Question:* "That implies that it would be the work of the Guides or Controls to control the formation ?"

*Peter:* "That is right. It is the rim of the bowl that links each sitter; and from that upwards would rise the ribs or the points of contact. I cannot quite explain it in your language. "

*Question:* "In two photographs we have what looks like a ball or a sphere of light. Has this any special significance ?" **(Plates Nos. 3 and 4.)**

*Peter*: "It is the ball or sphere so common in nature and science which contains the possibility of any form of phenomena."

*Question:* 'Do you mean, like the etheric egg that would bring an apport ?"

*Peter:* "Yes, of course; but it is exaggerated in comparison to the size of the exposure. It looks very large but there again, it is because of its lack of organisation."

*Question:* "Then the actual size of such a formation would be very small ?"

*Peter:* "Quite; in fact the more perfect it is, the smaller it would appear."

*Question:* "That drawing I made~[**Plate No. 26**]. Does this give any indication of the appearance of the dowsing' of the auric field ?

*Peter:* "It is very good, but you cannot impart to it the tenseness. I do not think it is possible for you to do that. Still, I should use it, as it gives an impression. The rim of the pull would be at the base of the line linking each sitter. The sitters would not be subscribing necessarily to it, but it would be the point of contact."

*Question*: "You are referring to the ribbon of light ?" **(Plates 3 and 4.)**

*Peter:* "Yes. When it becomes organised, it links each sitter. It is a protective ring which brings them within the influence of the tent. It is the rim of the umbrella."

*Question:* "Can you give us any technical reason which permits these formations, which are invisible to our eyes, to be picked up by the lens of the camera ?"

*Peter:* "The receiving of such pictures does not depend on any particular plate, but rather on the peculiar properties of the lens; and the conditions governing the objective which enable it to be received by the lens at that moment. It is purely a matter of . . ." (here Peter hesitated). "There is no word which I can use that will describe the peculiar property in the lens that permits it to receive this activity in the formation about which we are speaking. It collects, under some peculiar conditions, light. Light is an etheric radiation; and light exists even where it is dark to you. It is discernible to an extra sensory perception which has a degree of recording ability. The lens, by chances might be so set at such an angle and at such a focus from the activity, that it combines a set of circumstances permitting it to record itself with the sufficiency of light existing at the time. Actually it is a combination of circumstances, a combination of lens and plate. So that really you cannot lay down any fixed rule except this: that where persons have been successful in obtaining such photographic results, they should always set their camera at the same angle as in the first instance and then their success is more sure."

*Question:* "Do you know whether the luminosity of the activity comes within the field of the unknown light ray as distinct from the ultra-violet ray or the infra-red ?"

*Peter:* "Not necessarily so. you do not know of the light characteristics then employed because they have not yet any purpose that would be of service to you."

*Question:* "Even though a room may appear dark to us it does retain some light ?"

*Peter:* "Yes, though it is darkness to you, it is probably not dark at all. The whole thing hinges upon the ability to receive the existing properties within the lens."

## PART III Mediumship of Arnold Clare
## CHAPTER XVIII pages 207-212   INTRODUCTION:

THE phenomena recorded in Part I and the explanations in Part II would be purposeless were it not for the motive behind it all. In this section an effort is made to show the purpose behind Spirit activity.

Spiritualists are often asked: What is the purpose of phenomena ? Why should it be necessary to lift a table or play a tambourine? What is there spiritual in such elementary activity ? How do these actions imply survival ?

While a distinction can be drawn, as Peter points out, between the psychic activity of brute force carried out by primitive spirit agencies and the purposeful phenomena of far more enlightened intelligences, both "brute-psychic" and "spiritually-psychic" activities imply operation by discarnate minds.

We are here concerned with the point of view advanced by Peter. We can surely recognise that the simple act of levitating an object is but a method of communication, a way of attracting our attention by unusual means. It is a planned act, deliberately performed in such a manner that it intrigues man by its supernormal character. The act of lifting an object is in itself of no importance: but the manner of its performance must impel man to think and, in thinking, draw the only possible conclusion, that it is the result of forces applied by a living discarnate intelligence. This intelligence is capable of effecting an organised result by methods unknown to man. Therefore the intelligence operating must belong to a different state of being to that of man in the mould of matter. Direct voice communications and materialisations force this conclusion home, for here there is the evidence of individuality.

One of the main fundamental reasons that distinguishes man from the animal realm is that he is conscious of unrest and discontent. He possesses an irresistible urge to over-come difficulties, to give pleasure to his senses and to see progression towards a more perfect state—both physically and ethically.

Man is a spiritual being animated by Spirit. From the earliest times when he became a conscious personality he has ever striven towards an ideal-- towards perfection—as he is doing today. As consciousness quickened and perception developed, so did his ideology likewise evolve.

It is shown that as we enter into the new sphere of activity after transition, we carry with us the experiences of our earth life . . . vice and virtue . . . character, good and bad, developed or undeveloped.

With this purposeful progression of life from phase to phase, we see how the interest and activity of the spirit realm is intimately woven into a fabric of which our earth life forms an important part.

It follows, that as both earthly and Spirit progression are bound up in each other, spirit intelligences who are able to communicate in any way through a human medium will do so for the purpose of influencing us for good. So we have Guides, like Peter, serving as missionaries for the progression of spirit through the enlightenment of mankind. Their activity will, in the end, bring all mankind together and give each individual truer appreciation of his place and function in the purpose of life, quickening his evolution from grossness to spirituality.

To convince man of survival is to assure him of his own spirituality. Convince him of the purpose of life, of which he is a part; and also of the part he has yet to play in ageless time to be; and, beyond all doubt, he will so order his life here on earth and influence that of his fellows. It will become an existence of preparation for the greater life and thereby the, negation of his animalistic existence today, which is motivated by greed and selfish profit.

In these days of war, when millions of men are engaged in destroying one another and the might of nations is organised for mass destruction, the one great hope of all mankind is that out of Armageddon a new order will evolve in which peace and brotherhood will endure.

Upon what does that depend ? Not treaties, conventions, partitions or armaments, but upon the building up of a great impelling moral and spiritual force within the very heart of man.

We can take courage from lessons of the past. In those days man suffered for ideals which then seemed so remote but which are now part of our accepted life. They came not by legislation, but through the enlightenment of man's consciousness and a change in the heart of humankind.

It is the age-old story of human progression, and if we, in our generation, are to make a worthy contribution to the future, we must turn our thoughts to the method whereby it may be attained. We must ask ourselves by what means can an enduring peace be secured and upon what foundation can we establish a code of enlightened conduct.

Can the churches of today provide the urge and enthusiasm for a great and permanent spiritual uplift ? Their ritual has lost its appeal. Their doctrinarian philosophies have fallen far behind the times. Their legendary sophistries I10 longer are accepted as truths. Virile youth, so rudely jerked out of complacency by war demands and education, no longer accepts teaching simply because it is preached to them by pseudo-authority or because their parents subscribed to it. The decline in churchgoers indicates there is but little confidence in the church as it stands today.

On the other hand, we can no longer rely upon the efforts of Statesmen After the experiences of these times we cannot pin our faith on treaties, conventions and protocols: neither have we any reason for believing that peace can be secured by legislation, national or international, so generally based upon sectional and vested interests.

What else is there ?

Before this question is answered, let us see what has happened within a lifetime. We have seen the birth and growth of modern Spiritualism succeed against the greatest of odds. Founded in the humblest of circumstances in poverty and without leadership, it has had to face the opposition of the Church, the law, and the ridicule of the press. Every man's hand was turned against it. Public opinion was prejudiced by charges of the fraudulence of mediums, and that Spiritualist practices were unclean and the works of the devil. Yet, in spite of all this it has grown until today its churches are numbered by the thousand and its Home Circles by the scores of thousands. It has received the support of some of our greatest scientists and thinkers.

The investigation carried out officially for the Church of England by a commission of the Archbishop of Canterbury's choosing has not led to a published report. The Archbishop has banned its publication. Why? Because the majority of the commissions after two years' investigation, found that the case for survival as expressed by Spiritualism was proved.

The literature of Spiritualism is prolific. Impartial psychical research societies, backed by men of the highest integrity, have been established in all great countries. They have investigated phenomena most meticulously; and their proceedings have added weighty testimonies to the ever accumulating mass of evidence.

Spiritualism has penetrated most countries, particularly this country, America, Sweden, France and Germany (where it is now forbidden by the German Government). The national life of Britain and America, in particular, reflects its teachings; and its implications are found in general literature, the stage, films, sermons) the radio, etc.

One of our national Sunday newspapers computed the number of Spiritualists in Great Britain as 3,000,000, and just prior to the outbreak of war the finest tonic for a newspaper's circulation was an investigation into Spiritualism. These investigations were carried out fairly and frankly by experienced hard-headed journalists who invariably added their testimonies to the truth of survival.

In peacetime, every large meeting-place in central London was booked for Sunday services.

All this has been achieved in eighty years, and most of it since I920.

What, then, of the future ?

Is it beyond reason to assume that in these days of war, and particularly in the days to come, when peace is with us again, the peoples of all nations will be demanding a new concept of enlightened philosophy ?

The progress of awakening the peoples to the implications of survival will be so great that the spiritualisation of mankind will come within the bounds of probability.

The truth of survival with individual responsibility is not an ephemeral thing; it is capable of being proven over and over again. The great majority of Spiritualists today are Spiritualists only because they have received personal proof of the continued existence of their loved ones.

Here then is the foundation of the future. Here is a movement that will be ever new, and cannot grow old. Here is a field for science, the possibilities of which transcend every other avenue of research. Here is a dynamic living truth that can influence the whole conduct of human affairs.

This is the answer to those who ask "What is the purpose of Spirit activity ?"

In this section, Peter goes further than these generalisations: he tells us of the relationship of the Spirit to ourselves; and gives us a new thesis of life.

In this year, 1942, the author's fervent hope is that the Spiritualist movement in general will be able to cope with the demands the future will make upon it. That mankind will learn from the bitter experiences of these days to provide for the children of tomorrow a better heritage than that through which we are now passing.

# THE BIRTH OF THE SOUL
## CHAPTER X1X Mediumship of Arnold Clare pages 212- 217

MAN possesses his physical body, his soul body and his spirit. At the physical transition he dispenses with his physical body, the soul body motivated by the spirit continuing on.

The soul body is most closely allied to our present state of being. Peter has explained several times its functions and its relation to the physical body.

In the past there has been much confusion between the meaning of the soul and the spirit and if we accept Peter's definition it certainly puts the relationship of one to the other in order Religious denominations of all kinds have failed to provide any reasonable explanation of what the soul body really is. They refer to it in the most ambiguous of terms and have never been able to define it.

According to Spiritualist reasoning in general, and Peter's in particular, the soul body is a functioning organism, the repository of experience, the propellant to the physical.

That each person possesses a soul body is proved through the act of Spirit communication—there can be no other there is no other, alternative.

We know how all things in the universe are subject to determined laws; and of course this applies equally to the soul body. It cannot be either an intangible, incomprehensible, abstract force, form or thing, it is definitely positive. Every lesson we have learnt from nature speaks of an evolving process; and the soul body is likewise subject to ordered law-governed change.

This view is not a conception, it is cold, hard, materialistic reason. The infinite wondrousness of the evolution of the individual soul provides a far more spiritual vista than the blind, unreasoned, superstitious views of the past.

As we so regard our own soul body, so should we give it its rightful place in our individual scheme. Its culture and development should become our main incentive. It is immeasurably more important than acquiring possessions, wealth or power.

An enduring philosophy for the right government of human conduct, individually and communally, must rest upon established and demonstrable truths. The implications that follow the proven fact of survival provide this. In the following chapters Peter not only satisfies the reasoning mind of the functions of the soul body but engages in an effort to give us more understanding of the laws that govern it.

We know the soul body leaves the physical at transition---Peter tells us how. He also describes its relationship to the Spirit and the way it first contacts its human counterpart.

Peter's explanations arose out of our question as to the way the Spirit contacts the physical body. He said:
*Peter:* "I think we will start by calling it the birth of the soul because we cannot deal with soul and omit the spirit, nor can we omit the spirit and deal wholly with the soul.

"I do not intend to go into the initial stages where conditions are created for the formation of the physical part It may be little understood that the order of birth into the physical realm of an individuals spirit is strictly controlled. Further, it may not be generally realised that whilst the spirit has a choice of parentage, it has not the choice of the time of birth. That is fixed and irrevocable.

"You will asks why does the Spirit have choice of parentage ? The answer is that in such manner it is enabled to choose the correct environment in which to function and to provide the necessary experience for its own development.

"We are not now considering the earthward travel of the Spirit through its many planes of earlier existence but only its last phase, that of physical birth.

"The spirit itself stands apart from the actual development of the form it will subsequently activate

"The soul has complete control in the formation and the development of the child within its mother's womb . . . the building from the materials provided by the first act…moulding and forming according to its own wisdom, begotten by long experience.

"When it has attained a certain degree of development) a more positive association between the soul and body commences. That is the period termed the 'quickening'. A further period of development from close association with the body takes place before the child is born

"During the time of the first period, the soul of the child is closely linked to that of the mother. That is why changes in her outlook, tastes and, oft-times, temperament are so noticeable; for it is through the soul body of the mother that the soul works until a period of four and a half months has elapsed. It then has a little soul. It is full of wisdom, as it is today. The soul is closely associated with the child's development and growth in its post-natal days until approximately seven years of age.

"During that period there is little or no close association with its Spirit. That is why a child up to this age is nothing more than a healthy animal, driven only by its primitive desires.

"Having reached the approximate age of seven, a change takes place. The Spirit, instead of brooding, one might say, over the young form, now becomes definitely and positively linked through the soul to the body.

"That is when the child changes from the 'me want' stage to the 'I want' stage. It has then realised intuitively its own individuality as expressed in the word 'I'. It is not the result of education, it comes naturally and as a matter of course. This period is sometimes accelerated--it might be five years— or it might be retarded according to the individual condition.

"Now I feel that this brief description will be sufficient to create some measure of controversy; but viewed reasonably there can be no young spirits, for spirit cannot be created; and the universal anvil from which the sparks were struck originally can only be struck but once.

"The spirit, by the way, holds dominating control over the body through its contact direct with the blood stream. It requires wisdom to control the rhythmic beating of the heart so that the Spirit which animates it may become attuned to it. Now you see the processes whereby knowledge of spiritual worth and value passes down almost without let or hindrance. Now you can appreciate why we have stressed the importance of the rhythmic system of breathing, to bring the heart of the individual into the rhythm and pulsation of its universe.

"All spirit is the same whether it is polarised, as it is with a human being, or contained in the vastness that fills eternity—if you can appreciate that expression.

"The spirit of man is a part of that universe, flawless filled with beauty, with power unlimited; but it is the soul that stands between man as the spirit and man as the physical counterpart.

"The soul carries with it the characteristics portrayed by the young life in its first four to seven years of earth life. That period is activated by three things—to eat, to live and to possess all the things that he sees, at the expense of anything that would oppose him.

"I cannot say any more in your all too few words, but that is briefly how it is. The soul is the screen that passes on the deep rays of the eternal sun of the Spirit."

*Question:* "Then the Spirit attached to one person is not individualised ?"

*Peter:* "Yes, it is. Through its association with the soul and the body it naturally has an individuality, the totality of which is from the reactions between the three.

'¢It is the same with the ether, the free ether, and that which is bound or individualised. Its nature is essentially the same. It is its performance which makes the difference. It has the same potentials plus its individuality.

"You can appreciate that if all things are perfect there can be no attainment of greater perfection; and perfection in one direction may not be perfection in another. We are speaking in the one sense of the universal spirit; you must remember that you who are part of the universe proper, are still confined to a spiritual orbit within a solar system which too has its own individuality."

*Question:* "If the soul that comes to a new being is full of wisdom, are we to understand that it has been in existence a long time ?"

*Peter:* "That is right. I said that the soul was full of wisdom, taking it for granted that the one who read those words would also remember that I had said the soul belongs to the natural worlds having, thereby, only primitive instincts. Its wisdom therefore can only be in relation to its experiences through its own development from the mineral kingdom, the plant kingdom and the animal realm.

"All the forms and processes of growth and development have fitted it out for its development and evolution to the status of man.

"You might say to me when you come to ponder that point--that pertains to the birth of a soul, *but* what hap pens when it ceases to animate the body at its physical separation, called death ? Without the body, can that soul remain individualised ?

"The answer is 'yes'. so long as the spirit animates the soul for the collection of the experiences received during its sojourn on earth; and for the further working out of the many problems that it could not complete during the school hours of the earthly life.

"You are thinking, what happens when the problems are solved ?

"Death—so called takes place again . . . there is a severance, or a rupture, of the points of contact between that which is called the soul body and that which is spirit. Like the physical body, the soul body, too, gradually breaks up. It is re-absorbed into the stream of the substance of which it is made, in the same way that your physical body breaks up in your earthly conditions.

'A questioner would say: 'How is it that the soul of a man who has passed on a long number of years ago still manifests ?'

"The spirit, if it wishes to make its presence known to a man still on earth, can, with ease, gather about itself particles of the several realms through which it may have to pass to get back to earth conditions, until finally it clothes itself temporarily, with an ether. It materialises down as far as the ether realm, and dissolves when the thought that gave it birth, or the Spirit which animates it, has no further use for it.

"Remember, all the consciousness of the spirit is focused and contained in its inferior member (the soul body). One must dies either permanently or temporarily, just as man dies now before the known superior (again the soul body). Neither can have full sway.

"It is like your own body, the whole of your consciousness is concentrated within an aching member be it tooth or foot; because it is where the greatest action is taking place.

"The physical body is but a *limb* of the spirit. It is no more perhaps than a little finger or toe, but how infinitely important

"You might say that you are part of the universal one you call God.

"The difficulty is that, what you now consider as reality is but the shadow. What you consider as the cause is but the effect. That is the difficulty. It is a reversal It explains itself in what I have said. The inferior plane is always the seat of consciousness and activity, and that is why the realm you live in is apparently the only one.

"There is no past, no present and no future. Life is a slow unfolding of the plan.

"Is the setting out of the details, growing and expanding all the time, just for you to return to spirit, do you think ? No. For a time yes, while there is work to do; but not work to fill you with dread because of the humdrum existence of earth life. One Man gave you the answer once: 'I must be about my Father's business', and that is about as good an answer as anyone can give."

## TRANSITION
### CHAPTER XX from Mediumship of Arnold Clare pages 217-219

Over the next occasion we met we asked Peter if he would carry on, from "The Birth of a Soul' to the next stage. Peter commenced by saying:

*Peter:* "One of your playwrights said 'All the world's a stage', and it is across the stage that you act your part and then pass out and are clapped or booed as pleases the audience. Life is very similar to that.

"My opening words on this phase of the relationship are these: Life does not commence where you of the earth apprehend it, nor can it cease when it passes from your ken".

"Life is as a mysterious stream ever flowing onward bearing all creation with it. Life as manifested in man is the advance of evolution. It is, broadly speaking, the cosmic experiment wherein the spirit is polarised and allowed to function, having, in certain measures the quality of free will.

"It is only in man that you find spirit segregated and individualised from the rest of life which is Spirit. When man begins his earth life, it is as if man, meaning spirit (that is the meaning of the term), begins the descent of a ladder each rung of which represents a different phase of existence until finally he emerges in the physical realm in this case your earth.

"After having completed this life, the spirit of man leaves by the same ladder to which has been added another rung.

"That is a crude illustration that will appeal to any ordinary reader.

"At the death of the physical the first to leave the association of the body is the Spirit. It is like the extinguishing of a flame. The SOUND however, has much to do and is not really dissociate from the body completely until after a lapse of two to three days, seldom more.

"The Spirit has direct control in the matter of life and death only. Mark that, it is important. In no other bodily function has the spirit any authority, but the way of the birth and the precise second of physical death are factors directly controlled by the Spirit.

"Now you would say to me, 'But how is this accomplished ?'

'You have been taught that the spirit, through the soul, is linked to the physical body by a silver cord. That is true. We have been trying to separate (though wrongly so in the sense of the word 'separation') the spirit from the soul. There is a distinct difference; but then, you cannot understand the difference without presuming a separation, so remember I am discussing at the moment the spirit.

"The Spirit's control over the manner of life and death is in connection with the heart. The association of the blood with spirit can be easily seen as having something in common; for as the blood stream is to the body, so is spirit (the life stream) to the universal body. To permit the Spirit to escape easily, it is only necessary to raise the bodily temperature, through heart action, to find an easy means of exit. A man is termed 'hot blooded' when he is not controlled by the Spirit of reason. That is why a child is so unreasonable, for a child lives on the borrowed blood until he is between five and seven years old. The Spirit enters the blood stream of the child when he realises his own individuality and uses the word 'I' instead of 'me'.

"I have spoken already about the spirit and soul of the child. Now we have to take it in the reverse order because we are talking of the exit. Ashen the spirit withdraws its control from the blood stream, the soul cannot for long maintain its hold upon the physical body. It is like an engine with the governor gone, it races and slows up, finally tearing itself to bits. Right. The soul body is above all things instinctive; the desire to manifest in the world of fact—the physical world—is so overpoweringly strong, that it will cling to the body for two or three days. It is this power, or lack of power in controlling the blood action, the heart action, that subsequently defeats him.

"Then you have the severance of the silver cord which is the point of contact between the physical and the soul body.

"Now a word about the etheric body ! I will remind you that the etheric body has no characteristics that is, personality or temperament. It has no reactions similar to that of the soul. It is purely bound ether that might be likened unto an expanding bag (Little Peter says 'rubber balloon') taking the outline of the physical body. It appears to be the same viewed from whatever angle, never reaching more than about three inches from the body, when the person is normal in health and is well fed and rested. It varies according to the vitality of the individual; the aura is beyond that. The etheric body has no colour change. It is ever the same—more or less, a misty silvery colour. We will talk about the aura by and by.

"The etheric body gradually loses its shape, which is the only characteristic it does have (the outline of the physical), as decomposition sets in, and is always associated with the body until decay is complete. That is why the modern idea of destruction by fire is excellent, provided always that three days have elapsed. If you could witness the place where you bury these bodies, you would find there is present an etheric mist made up from the etheric odours from decaying bodies. It is equally as dangerous as if you left the bodies where they died. I will speak one day about destruction by fire. Now that is briefly the procedure of the exit."

# THE PURPOSE

## CHAPTER XX1 from The Mediumship of Arnold Clare pages 219-224 to the end of book

*Question:* "As many people say to us, 'What is the purpose of phenomena?' would you give us a lead on the reasons for your work ?"

*Peter:* "That is the only logical point to which we can influence anything. Cast your mind back to the early days of Christianity, or perhaps I should say pre-Christian days.
Christ showed marvels and wonders through the working of so-called miracles. In that, you saw every phase of the phenomena that have been witnessed in the séance rooms of today
"You have seen also the miracle of healing and the materialised form in comparison with that of Christ.
"If you will ask yourself this question, Which has lived longest in man's mind and what has been responsible for influencing thoughts along spiritual lines since His day ? Was it the record of His miracles or was it the beautiful philosophy that He taught ?
"We today are in almost the same position. We have to produce something out of the ordinary to indicate in an objective way operations beyond the normal range of man's understanding.
"Perhaps it is a forlorn hope that man, of his own initiative, will strive to follow the lead given him in all these manifestations until it guides him further and further away from the realm material. But unfortunately in the great majority of cases he has gone just the opposite way by bringing it down to purely physiological limits. We intend that man should follow the other way, to find the link between himself and the realm of spirit.
"It was not intended that the phenomena of the séance room should be given such a place of importance within our scheme; but we are helpless, as Christ was. We cannot go beyond man's understanding or give a greater illumination than that which can be received by the minds of the people who gather within the range of our voice and operations. In itself the work of the séance room is unimportant, in so far as that those who witness it fail to understand or to realise the immense possibilities that it has.
"It is, in fact, the harnessing of natural forces under the guidance of a directive mind or intelligence. Those same forces could be utilised by the minds of carnate man in the setting-up of conditions of great value to the human family; and, of course, in the reverse sense also.
Today, it is the mission and the plan of the superior spiritual intelligences to create again opportunities upon earth, much the same as they did years ago when man first attained to spiritual freedom. I will tell you for the first time that there will be given another John the Baptist—I mean, in the same sense. Indeed, there is in the world today one such as he; and he is calling in the wilderness
"This movement of spiritual forces found in manifestations is a counter to the forces of evil now rampant throughout the earth and the spheres adjacent thereto.
"It is only through the power of the spirit, weak as it may appear to be, that an antidote can be provided to save the rapid dissolution of the moral fabric of humanity.
"We have to find many ways in which to manifest to you; and we oft-times do not have to be too particular what channels we users
"The day is soon to come, I mean *soon,* when our voice shall be heard in no uncertain volume- and at the right moment when spiritual leadership is needed.
"All this has had and will have its inception within the séance room. It has already succeeded in focusing man's mind beyond the realm of the purely physical and has made him more aware of some force without himself, that is all we can expect to achieve at the moment.
"In that upper room 2,000 years ago, the man Jesus did manifest behind the locked doors. It required His almost physical presence to convince the founder members of Christianity of the reality of life beyond death: but having once had that proved to them, they were more than ready to carry out the instructions they had received from their risen Leader. Instructions, mark you, that no man today knows about. He had so increased their spiritual consciousness that they were minor reflections of their Master and Leader. Can you see ?"
*Question:* "They have not given us any such communication ?"
*Peter:* "No, they could not do that any more than I can give you instructions how to achieve certain things. But if I could gather about me men of the same calibre and with the same readiness to appreciate spiritual unfoldment as Christ did, then I could confer (through contact) the same powers of Spiritual awareness that we have through years of patient toil been able to confer upon the medium; but, of course, to a far lesser degree than that enjoyed or borne by the Master Jesus. You understand that.
"You employ the same methods today. The Medium gathers friends about himself and, through patience, develops similar gifts. It is by using the medium as a focal point, that these powers are quickened. It is similar to the magnetisation of a piece of steel by bringing it into contact with a magnet of greater permanency. It is the same law. By signs and wonders we try to attract and retain the interest of those witnessing such things; so that a few, who are thus impressed to pursue it further, may gradually be led

into the understanding of our way; and so that we may send them out into the highways and byways, doing and living the way of life that we always try to inculcate.

"It is very important: because consciously, or unconsciously, they are all linked together today; and they spread the seeds of spirituality within the souls and the minds of those they contact, both subjectively and objectively. So the way is prepared; and one day you will see the small growth of the tender plant. Then almost before you realise it that plant will flower and be of great strength and of wondrous beauty.

"We do not come to tear down the ancient fabrics of your Christianity but we come to fill the gap whilst the present Church lies gasping because of its antiquity in the spiritual sense. We have come to imbue it with new life and with a fresh power; a power which is dictated by the common standards of spiritual valuation, which is directed towards the lives of all and not to the lives of the few. To replace outworn dogmas and creeds. To give the power of spiritual interpretation to those suited to dispense it. To remove the Church from the rut worn so deeply and to give it a place again within the lives and the homes of all children: to make it a constitution, and not an institution. A place where all may come to derive spiritual sustenance, rather than to receive the cold comfort of the literal interpretation of the life of one man; a man who can only live in the spirit and who can only be interpreted within the soul. By no other means can his power to influence be felt within your life, except it be through service in a like manner. That is the next step from the séance room. That is our place of commencement '

*Question:* "You agree with the view that today we have great need of spiritualising humanity, by knowledge and understanding of the things about which you have been speaking to us ?"

*Peter:* "Yes, that is true: but knowledge and understanding cannot come except that it be with the realisation of all that it implies. You have to regard it as a leavening power, rather than as a science of angles and views, and it is only by stimulating that, that the purpose can be achieved. If it shall be by the path of knowledge, then by that path it must be accomplished. But a slow and painful job it will be where the minds of certain individuals are so blinded by the tradition of Scientific knowledge that spiritually they are deaf. Whereas a more humble individual, knowing nothing of the law and the mathematics of science, can achieve in one stride the secret of the knowledge we try to teach. That is our difficulty"

*Question:* "The view is held that spiritual development will arise from the demonstration of survival after death?"

*Peter:* "That is the difficulty. The demonstration of survival is the least part of our difficulty. It is its implications that are important. What a difference it can make, knowing as a fact that life proceeds unbroken; what an effect, too, the accumulation of experience here and hereafter will have upon your own life and the lives for whom you are responsible. There is a purpose behind all things if you could but see it. For instance the production of this book . . . It will be produced. You have found the channel for its launching, and you may think you have done it yourself; but have you ever considered whether it was your own idea or how much you are being made the instrument of forces without yourself ? And the same illustration can be used for most things in the ordinary individual's life. Why should anyone take a step forward or a step backward at a precise time for apparently no reason at all ? Yet in the next instant his or her life has been saved or destroyed physically by taking such action. These are little problems little pointers worthy of consideration

Mr. Hart here interposed with a question: "It is difficult to distinguish between natural laws mental laws, and spiritual laws ?"

*Peter:* "You have got a little mixed. The question is now: 'What is the spiritual and what is the mental ?' I do not want to launch out upon a discussion tonight upon the mental processes of man, because it would bring us again into that realm of strata; and the mind itself has layers and certain frequencies that can respond only to certain stimuli

The mental processes are played upon by other forces, the spiritual on the one hand and the etheric on the other; both radiate from other minds and from the very house of the soul itself. And you must understand, too, that spiritual pain and suffering mean nothing. Pain and suffering are only things experienced by the soul. you cannot quite appreciate that. It is a very important factor because that is a part of the natural life, not of the spiritual; and it is where you will become confused by saying that natural law is spiritual law. It is not. one is a reflection of the other. Both operate in harmony, although to you oft-times they appear in apparent disharmony. And that is why man today is such a puzzle to himself; because whilst the evolutionary process is proceeding there is a grafting process going on the spirit of man is trying to graft himself upon the flesh of the beast. Do you remember a picture of that figure 'Centaur', where you have part man and part animal ? There is more in that figure, interpreted spiritually, than at first sight may be apparent to you. There is another symbol pictured by the ancient painting of two children called 'The Twins'. I believe it is marked in the Heavens as Gemini. You might consider that as a superstition, but that too has its story. Those pictures are symbols containing within their stories the history and evolution of man; and illustrate his emergence from the animalistic stage and his entry into the spiritual stage Everything has a meaning and a purposes and the desire within you is to come into harmony with the spirit. As your mind demands so can the spirit satisfy; but we cannot progress one step with our teaching until you are able to receive."

*Peter went on:* . . . "Why do we bother to speak to you ? Why do we make it our concern, aching and burning to help ? Because we understand the true meaning of 'Brotherhood'. You have often heard me say that 'All life is one unity', therefore I am of your life. Your life is my life; and so long as there is one member of the whole body that aches or suffers, the whole body suffers with it."

"Now for a preliminary, I think we have covered some good ground."

# Investigations by the
# THE LONDON DIALECTIC SOCIETY   1870
## REPORTS

These few "Reports" are from one book of many pages, and the society has investigated many more incidents, which are written in many more books beside. They are true extracts from a book printed after the report from the London Dialectic Society [England] on Spiritualism which was made public on the 20th July 1870. I have picked out pieces of the report I think might help others in their quest for development, also might help people setting up Circles and some with general interest value. If asked for in later years I will write all the report out.

## Table tilting and moving

**Page 41:** If the muscles of the back and shoulders are kept in a certain degree of tension, and the arms drawn backwards until the wrists and hands only rest freely on the table, the pressure then becomes about 2 lbs. This is the attitude most commonly assumed, so that the pressure of 2lbs may be taken as the usual amount of force exerted by an attentive sitter, though, when some of the more active "manifestations" are in progress, the pressure which each person exerts generally ranges downwards from this to less than an ounce, or to the lightest touch possible.

**Page 42:** By careful experiments with the smaller of the tables, we have found that the force necessary to tilt it when applied at the most favourable angle, viz., 90 degrees to the legs, is nearly twenty and a-half pounds. But in applying the force in this direction, some obstruction must be placed on the floor against the legs, otherwise it will slide and not tilt at all at this angle.

## Levitations

**Page 117:** (part of the paper by **Mr Jencken**)
---------------These levitations you will find recorded as having occurred as far back as 1347:- (see Spiritual magazine, November, 1868)--and another instance is cited as having taken place, in the year 1697. On the latter occasion, a certain Margaret Rule is described as having been raised to the ceiling of her room: and Goethe refers to the wonderful fact of levitation in his life of Phillipinari. The levitations of Mr Home are so well known, that I need not more then allude to them—upwards of one hundred levitations have taken place during his lifetime, of which perhaps the most remarkable was the carrying of his body out of the third floor, at Ashley House, into an adjoining window; and the lifting of his body raised 3 or four feet off the ground at Adare Manor for twenty or thirty yards. As regards the lifting of heavy objects, these I can testify to myself; I have seen the semi-grand (a piano) at my house raise horizontally 18 inches off the ground, and kept suspended in space two or three minutes. I have also witnessed a square table being lifted one foot off the ground, no one touching or near to it, at the time, a friend present seated on the carpet and watching the phenomena all the time. I have also seen a table lift clear over head, 6 feet off the ground; but what may appear more remarkable, I have witnessed an accordion suspend in space for 10 to 20 minutes, and played by an invisible agency.----------------------

**Page 119:**

I have seen Lord Adare hold in the palm of his hand a burning live coal, which Mr Home had placed there, so hot, that the mere momentary contact with my finger caused a burn. At Mr S.C. Hall's a large lump of burning coal was placed on his head by Mr Home; and only within these last few days, a metal bell, heated to redness in the fire, was placed on a lady's hand without causing injury. At Mrs Henning's house I have seen Mr Home place his face into the flames of the grate, the flame points penetrating through his hair without causing injury. -----------------------The next class of phenomena are those extraordinary elongations of the medium's body, (I have been fortunate to see a demonstration of this phenomena at Stansted Hall on Manchester week by the transfiguration Medium Dianne Elliot) of which we read in the "History of the Mystics," but until witnessed could be credited. It has been my good fortune to witness the elongation and shortening of Mr Home's person many times, and at Mr S.C. Hall's, about three months ago, Mr Home and Miss Bertolacci were simultaneously elongated. The elongation usually takes place from the hip, a span wide, and on one occasion I measured an extreme elongation of the body of fully EIGHT inches. The shortening of the body is equally marvellous. I have witnessed Mr Home shrinking down to about five feet; again, as described in "Human Nature" March 1869, I have measured the expansion and contraction of the hand, arm, and leg. Fortunately these expansions and contractions have been witnessed by fifty people at the very least, and now placed beyond doubt.

"I will pass over the numerous phenomena of holding of fluids in space, without vessels to contain them; extracting liquids from bottles---which I have witnessed; nor will I burden you with a description of the perfuming of water, or extracting the scent from flowers; or the alcohol from spirits of wine; but will pass to the appearance of **_hands, arms,_** and **_spirit forms_**, wholly or in part developed. Fortunately within the last few months instances have repeated themselves, so that I could name a score of witnesses, within the Circle of my own friends, who have seen spirit forms or appearances. As these facts go far towards establishing the truth of Spiritualistic phenomena, I will with your permission dwell more upon these manifestations.

"**Spirit Hands** are usually luminous, and appear and re-appear all but instantaneously. I have once been able to submit a spirit hand to pressure. The temperature was, as far as I could judge, the same as that of the room, and the Spirit hand felt soft, velvety; dissolving slowly under the greatest amount of pressure to which I could submit it. I have, however, been informed by friends that they have seen spirit hands break a stout piece of plank in two, and that the temperature of the hands, tested by a delicate thermometer, was usually equal to that of the room.

" **Spirit Forms**---They usually appear with head and bust developed and very luminous, the outline rarely well defined, and generally the form seems to float, rather than walk. These appearances however, present very different aspects at different times. I have often urged upon my friends to get some facts to guide in ascertaining the physical property or character of these forms. At a friend's house, some short time ago, the Spirit form cast a shadow and slightly obscured the light of the gas-burner:---------------( page 121) This phenomena repeated itself over and over again, the figure disappearing whenever those present became too positive; of this Mr Home, who was in a trance the whole time, warned us. When I say too positive, I mean "too intent." A figure also developed itself next to and above Mr Home, as he stood half covered by the curtains against the light of the window; but the outline was so indistinct I could not well discern its form.-----

**Page 127:** **Mrs Honywood**, in answer to a request from the chair, stated that she had witnessed some remarkable phenomena at the residence of Dr Gully, "While sitting in a Circle recently, the table rose, and the room vibrated to such a degree that an engineer who was present declared that nothing but the strongest machinery would have been sufficient to account for it. An accordion was played in the air, Mr home holding it with one strap, and not touching it in any other way. The room was fully lighted. Three or four persons, unknown to Mr Home, mentally wished for particular tunes and they were played."
**Page 128:**
The **Hon. Mrs**---gave evidence in the following words:-
"the most remarkable manifestations I have seen, were those of last Sunday at my house. We were seated in a partially darkened room. We first heard raps and then saw a human figure at the window. It entered and several other figures came trooping in after it. One of them waived its hands. The atmosphere became fearfully cold. A figure which I recognised as that of a deceased relative, became behind my chair, leaned over me, and brushed my hair lightly with its hand. It seemed about eight feet high. Then approaching the Master of Lindsay it passed right through him, causing him to shiver with cold. But the

most extraordinary thing of all was the laughter. One of us said something and all the Spirits laughed with joy. The sound was indescribably strange, and it appeared to us as if it can from the ground. It was the first time we heard Spirit voices."---------------------------------------- Mr Home was present on this occasion, but I have seen things when Mr Home was not present. We sat in a Circle at first, and were seven in number. Five of the seven saw just what I have described, and the others saw something, but not so distinctly.------------------------------ It was stated that Mr Home had no previous access to the room beyond having dined there.

**Page 129:**

**Mr T.M. Simkiss** evidence-------------I have been a spiritualist for nearly sixteen years , and have examined the various phases of Mediumship, with all the critical research of which I am capable.

" I am not myself a medium in the common acceptation of the term, though I have tried hard to become one. I have tried in a variety of ways to see, hear, or feel Spirits myself: by sitting frequently in circles as passively as possible, by submitting myself to repeated mesmeric manipulations, and by sitting alone in the dead of night for many hours in a room that was used for some years exclusively for the purposes of Spirits and mediums, and might be considered to be thoroughly permeated with spiritual magnetism; but all with no apparent effect.--------------------"For the past three years my wife has been a Medium.------------one Spirit who at this time very frequently possessed her was that of a Scotchman, who invariably spoke broad Scotch through her, which she is quite unable to do in her normal condition.

"This trance state, unsurpassed as it may be for test purposes, is detrimental to the nervous system if much persisted in. In the case of my wife it appears to have been a transition stage that she passed through as means of developing her interior senses, so as to enable her to see and converse with Spirits, without put closing of any of her external senses. She is now as wide-a-wake and fully conscious when seeing Spirits as any person with whom she is in company. She not only sees them, but occasionally gives the full names, both Christian and surnames, of total strangers, and by this means has convinced many persons of the truth of spiritualism and immortality, about which they were previously doubtful.-----------

**Page 133:** (evidence of **Mr Blanchard**).
-----------"Beyond solving the important question "if a man shall he live again?"—by the very fact of spirits communicating and proving their identity, there is to me little that is consistent or reliable in what is revealed through different Mediums. And perhaps this is very wise. For if man were led to rely much upon Spirits for advice, his own judgement and energy would be in danger of being weakened thereby."-- ----------**Page 134**:----------"That between the years 1858 and1863 the despondent was frequently present at "circles" formed for the purpose of investigating "Spiritualism," and that he has always subjected the evidence adduced to the most rigid scrutiny, and tested in every instance the truthfulness of the so called "Medium" by every expedient that common sense could suggest.

"That Amongst other places, hr pursued his enquiries at the rooms of Mrs Marshall, and on these occasions he has seen tables rise from the ground without the slightest possibility of human agency; that he has heard guitars played and bells rung without the least chance of feet, fingers, machinery or electricity being employed to produce the effect. That he has repeatedly seen "The Spirit Hand" under circumstances which rendered deception impossible, and that he has frequently received at those "circles" written communications which could not have been given by any person present in the flesh. Some of these communications bear the signature of a departed friend, and these signatures, when compared with the autograph of that individual written before his departure from earth, have been by competent witnesses declared to be singularly identical. On one occasion the deponent has found himself raised in a chair at least six inches from the ground without such levitation being due to mechanical forces. Handkerchiefs knotted in a minute, heavy slates raised by the "Spirit Hand" and placed on the table, and instantaneous writing on whitened glass, slates, and note paper are among his familiar experiences.-----------------------**page 135**-----------"
On January 11th 1862, The deponent in the company with Mr Cornelius Pearson the artist, and Mr Thomas Spencer the well-known analytical chemist, visited a "medium" named Foster, at 14, Bryanstone Street. Names previously written on slips of paper and rolled up into pellets were brought by each person, and these names were quickly and correctly given by "Raps," without the possibility of "the medium" acquiring a knowledge of the contents of the paper beforehand. On the arm of the "medium" appeared in red letters "William Blanchard" the name of the deponent's father, and immediately afterwards appeared on the palm of the medium's hand, the numbers "27" indicating in answer to a

question put, the exact number of years which had elapsed since the said William Blanchard had ceased to exist on earth. All this was done very rapidly, the deponent and his friends being utterly unknown to the "Medium," and the letters and numbers disappearing in sight of those present, without the arm of the medium being withdrawn.----------------

**Page 139:** (**Mr Coleman's** evidence)-----------I was walking round my neighbour's garden one fine summer evening, when the full moon was above the horizon and Mr Home, who was present, suggested we should have a "sitting"-------------------------- The drawing room to which we retired was level with the garden; the centre table (a circular one) was cleared of books and cover, and seven persons, myself included, sat around three parts of it, leaving the forth part blank opposite the window. There was light enough from the moon to enable us to see each other, as well as every object between us and the window. I asked Mr Home to place both hands in mine, which he did, and I continued to hold them thus throughout the séance which followed.---------------The table then gradually rose from the ground, and it became necessary for us all to stand up; to continue ascent until it touched the ceiling, quite out of reach of all of all excepting myself, the tallest of the party. It then as gradually descended and resumed its original position, with no more sound than if it had been a snow flake. A hand-bell was then placed upon the table, and a hand and arm of feminine proportions were observed to rise from beneath the blank side of the table—and, which, reaching towards the bell, took it up, rang it, and carried it from our sight. In an instance afterwards, I felt a hand patting my knee; I put my hand down, received the bell and placed it upon the table.

" I then asked to be allowed to feel the hand, and putting my own hand open beneath the table, I felt a soft feminine hand placed in my own, which was again slowly withdrawn. It was of a velvety softness, neither warm nor cold. The arm was draped, as we all of us saw and remarked upon, in a gauze-like sleeve, through which the full form of the arm was distinctly visible.

"Three or four of the party had rings on their fingers, and one of them said, "My ring has been taken off my finger by someone" Another said, So has mine;" and four rings in all were thus taken away. Presently, a hand presented itself, exhibiting the four rings upon its fingers, and then, inverting itself, the rings were scattered upon the table.

"On another occasion, in the same house, I witnessed the following when *Mr Home was absent*. I saw a long dinner table rise up, supported only by its two legs, and remain steadily poised at an angle of forty or fifty degrees. The gentleman of the house then said to me, I will show you my confidence in the spirit's intelligence and power." He then placed his hand flat upon the floor and said, "Now spirits, I know you will not hurt me. Bring the table gently down upon my hand." This was done, and his hand, though pinned fast by the weight of the table, was not in the least hurt. The table was then slightly eased, and he removed his hand.--

----------I and my family spent the day out, and returned home between ten and eleven o'clock at night; when my wife and daughter retired to bed and left me in our sitting-room. Shortly afterwards, Willmore, in great excitement came to me, and begged that I would come down stairs immediately for he did not know what to do; he said, his wife, his daughter, and Miss Lee were all in hysterics. I followed him at once, and upon entering the room, a small three-legged table met me at the door, *no one touching it,* and made a graceful bow as if to say, "how do you do?" On of the females was on the sofa screaming, and the others in different parts of the room throwing themselves about in a state of great distress. I went up to the other end of the room to Miss Lee, the table following me standing by my side whilst I endeavoured to calm her. I had nearly succeeded in doing so, when the table made a jump at her and threw her again into violent hysterics; her screams were responded to by the other females. Matters looked so serious that I felt it necessary to take part with the table, and seizing it with both hands, I lifted it into the centre of the room, and said, Now spirits, you have done quite enough, I command you to leave this place in God's name. They appeared to obey my injunction, for nothing further took place. When the party had calmed down, they told me that they had a very interesting séance in the afternoon, at which it was said, through the table, that Willmore and his daughters were Mediums, which induced them after supper, and long after the Marshalls had left, to try whether they had any power of Mediumship; when to theirr great surprise the table responded, gave truthful answers to many questions on family matters, and at length became so active as to frighten them all, and they assured me that this had been going on about half an hour, chasing them into different corners of the room, creating great confusion, and causing Mr Willmore to rush to me for assistance.----------------.

**Page 143:** --------"I have in my possession several coloured drawings, done through the hands of ladies, who, I have every reason to believe, have no knowledge whatever of the art. Two of these were drawn through Mrs Mapes, the wife of Professor Mapes, the well known chemist of New York. One is an Iris, and the other, a collection of autumn leaves.

"Good artists in water colours declare they are both very perfect drawings, and could not be copied in the ordinary way in less than two days. They were presented to me by Professor Mapes, who assured me that both of these pictures were commenced and finished in little more than and hour. I have also a number of drawings in pencil and colours, of birds and flowers, which were done in my presence in New York, without any human agency whatever, and the time occupied in their production varied from ten to fifteen *seconds*.

Judge Edmonds, Professor Lyman, Dr Gervais, and others were present with me when these drawings were made,----------------------------

**Page 145** (Witness **Mr Jones** ) the night was dark, as the moon had not risen, but as there was a conservatory at the side of the drawing room, in which some eight persons sat around the loo table, and a window in front, he could see all in the room distinctly. As it was unusual for Mr Home to sit in a dark room for physical phenomena, he (Mr Jones) mentally determined to play sceptic. A sofa behind him moved away from the wall and passed in the rear of his and Mr Home's chairs, no one being near them. By sounds and raps it was said, "Mrs------, rest on the sofa." She got up and did so. He (Mr Jones) then saw the vacant chair rise in the air, float over the lady, pass in front of Mr Home (whose hands were on the table) and ascend till vertically over his (Mr Jones's) head; then the chair descended, and the under portion of the seat rested on his head. On mentally declaring himself satisfied, the chair arose again, floated in the air, and descended on to the loo table. Mr Jones also stated that at his house, Enamour Park, in a well-lighted, large room, at a circle of only his own family and the Medium (all hands on the loo table), he and all his family saw his aged mother and the chair she sat on, rise in the air, till her knees were on a level with the rim of the table. He had, at previous sitting, seen Mr Home rise in the air, and held his hands while he was rising.

**Page 145:** Tuesday, 11<sup>th</sup> May 1869.
Chairman, Dr. Edmonds.

------------ "We have done all we can to convince you that we live, and that god is love" Such was the message collected from the telegraphic knocks, between eight and nine o'clock last evening, at my house, on a breakfast table, in a large room, sixteen feet by thirty four; the blinds being drawn down and the gas full lighted.-------

**Page 150:** **Mr Borthwick**, now Lord Borthwick, in reply to a question put from the Chair regarding some spirit drawings that had been produced in his presence, said:-

"I was present when these drawings were produced. I did not hear any explanation of them. There were about twelve or thirteen people present. A table was placed in the middle of the room, and we sat around it—a shawl was drawn around it and tied—the paper was put into form by Professor L— and handed to me, I marked it. I was then asked to place the paper under the table; on this being done, we heard sounds like the scribbling of a pencil or brush upon paper; a stop watch, in the possession of some one present, indicated that about seven or nine seconds elapsed from the time when it was placed under the table until it was brought out, wet with paint upon it, and handed to me. Mr Coleman retained some of the papers. I have no opinion my self as to how they were done."

The Chairman then remarked to Mr Jones that he believed his daughter was present, who could give them an account of what she saw at Stockton when Mr Home was there.

**Miss Alice Jones** then said:-

"I was at Stockton at a séance which took place about eight o'clock in the evening, when Mr Home was present with others. He seemed very ill, and said the spirits were in him and did not understand him, and he must go out and get rid of them. He went out and walked up and down the verandah, and we saw a bright light issue from him, upwards, of a conical shape; it reached about half his own length; it looked very much like phosphorous. All the time he was away there were perfumes in the room---each had a different perfume—one eau-de-cologne, etc. He went out again, and was carried across the lawn, a distance of over 100 feet, to a rhododendron bed; and, when he returned, all said there was a light down by the bed; and he said, "Yes, it is a Spirit I have left there," Although it was raining there was no rain on his coat, neither were his feet wet. He floated over the verandah, which was about ten feet from the lawn, in an up right position, and his body seemed elongated. He observed, as he went out, that we should all have perfumes, and we did. We heard him walking on the gravel path, and yet his feet were perfectly dry.

During this séance I felt and pressed the hand of the spirit who was producing the phenomena. -------------------**Page 151**:----------He further observed that if Mrs Burns and her sister were in a dark room with others, they would see light issuing from the various heads, they would see flashes passing from the brain of one to another, and could tell those who were congenial to one another. His wife's sister sometimes went into a trance, and described accurately things at a great distance which she had never seen. They developed automatic writing too; these writings came from the Spirits, and were in different styles of handwriting, sometimes when Mrs Burns was observing what was going on around, she would sketch out a little flower; she had done a great many of these, although she had never even heard of the names of the materials usually employed to produce drawings. Her sister wrote out the names of the materials, where she could get them, and what they would cost, and they were obtained. Mrs Burns drew flowers of various kinds in crayon, water colours, and oil. Sometimes she wished to alter the sketch, but found herself unable to do so, and the message came to her sister that the Spirits knew best, and she must only allow herself to be used as an instrument in the matter. Mrs burns was ill upstairs, and it crossed her mine as to whether the spirits could help her. The sister, in another room, was influenced to write a prescription which gave instant relief. Since that first instance the Medium has written a number of medical prescriptions. Thus on two occasions, when my wife has been ill, the Spirits have prescribed remedies which cured her as soon as they were applied.

One night we were at Mrs Marshall's; I have been there twice, with Mrs Burns; we sat next to Mr Jencken; Mrs Burns, in the dark, saw a hand approaching her, but she could see nothing in the hand, when a voice called her by name and told her to put out her hand, she did so, and in it was placed a peach, which she gave to me. Mr Jencken held out a small tambourine, but the spirits could not take it away. Mrs Burns saw them throwing their influence over a part where the tambourine was, but there was something coming from Mr Jencken which neutralized their influence.

The Chairman then asked Mr Burns whether he had any theory as to whether the Spirits were matter or not? To which Mr Burns replied that he did not know what matter was.

Mr Thomas Sherratt Then produced some Spirit writings, and remarked, concerning them, that they were done in his presence at a séance at Mrs Marshall's at Bayswater, in a fully lighted room; the paper was place under the table, with a pencil and during the time the writing was going on, they could hear the pencil moving over the paper; it was a peculiar kind of paper, brought by himself, viz., lithographing paper.

Miss Houghton then produced some very interesting drawings, done by spiritualistic agency, and made the following statement:-

On the 20$^{th}$ of April, 1867, we held a séance for my birthday; Mrs General Ramsay, Mrs Gregory, Mrs Cromwell Varley, Mrs Flinders Pearson, Miss Nockolds, Miss Wallace, and Miss Nicholl (now Mrs Guppy) being present in addition to Mamma and myself. The doors and the windows were all closed, and we were in complete darkness, which is indispensable for some kinds of manifestations; and at the séance at our house, we are always particularly quiet, and as still as possible. We had at first some few messages, but after a time, I (who had been seated between Mrs Ramsay and Mrs Gregory) was impressed to rise from my chair, and place my hand on Mrs Ramsay's shoulder, so that I was quite out of reach of any one in the circle. Suddenly I felt something on my head, but said nothing about it, and Miss Nicholl exclaimed, "Oh! There is something so bright on Miss Houghton's head; do you see how it glitters?" Well, some could see it, and some could not; so we asked and obtained permission to have a light, when we found that the spirits had brought me as a birthday present a lovely wreath of everlasting flowers, with which they crowned me. I have since had a case made for the wreath, which remains in my possession.

"On The 3$^{rd}$ of October, 1867, I went to a dark séance at Miss Nicholl's (Now Mrs Guppy) own house, on which occasion there were eighteen ladies and gentlemen present, with all of whom I am acquainted. The table was small, therefore only six sat at it, the others being seated round the room. I sat on one side of Miss Nicholl at the table, with her father on the other, and Mrs. Cromwell Varley beyond him. By raps the spirits desired me to wish for fruit, and I chose a banana, which they promised me, and then said, "Now all may wish," which they did, for various fruits, sometimes having their wishes negatived, but in most instances, agreed to. The fruits were then brought in the order which they had been wished for. One lady said, "Why do you not ask for vegetables; an onion, for instance?" and even as she said it, the onion came into her lap. I will give you the list of the various things brought: a banana, two oranges, a bunch of white grapes, a bunch of black grapes, a cluster of filberts, three walnuts, about a dozen damsons, a slice of candied pine apple, three figs, two apples, an onion, a peach, some almonds, four very large grapes, three dates, a potato, two large pears, a pomegranate, two crystallised greengages, a pile of dried currants, a lemon, and a large bunch of beautiful raisins, which, as well as figs and dates, were quite plump, as if they had never been packed, but had been brought straight from the drying ground.

"I will Now give some account of how the drawings were done, of which I have brought the tracings. They are what is termed *direct* drawings, i.e., done by the Spirits themselves, without the agency of the human hand.

"Miss Nicholl held a séance at her own house, on the 5th of December, 1867, at which about two dozen persons were present. There were on the table two sheets of drawing paper, a lead pencil, a sable-hair pencil, some water, and a tube of water-colour, madder brown, some of which Miss Nicholl squeezed into a saucer. After the gas had been extinguished, we heard the sheets of paper (which from and accident had been drenched with water), being fluttered about the room. Presently, one was brought to me, and laid between my hands, and we heard it being patted for some time, as if to dry it. The Spirits then made me hold it length wise before me, with finger and thumb of each hand. We then heard the brush dipped into the saucer of colour, and then applied to the paper, the movements being very rapid. The paper was laid, for a while, flat on the table, and I feared the moist colour would be smeared; however, it was lifted up and again worked upon. A light was then demanded, and we saw the sketch of "the Guardian Angel," which was still moist. To my surprise, I found that the drawing had been done on the side of the paper next to me, as if the Spirit executing it had occupied my place, or been, as it were, within me; so that when laid upon the table , it must have had the wet colours upwards, instead of running the risk of being spoiled, as I had feared. There was but one colour on the table, but a second was employed in the drawing, so that our Spirit friends must have themselves supplied it.

"At Mrs Guppy's *séance*, March 4th, 1868, the first message that was given (by the alphabet) was, "You must undergo a process of purification before I can draw. I will draw the emblem of spiritualism." Mrs Guppy and I were lavishly sprinkle with perfume, after which we were all desired to sing. Pens and ink were then demanded, and on a sheet of letter paper, the corner of which was placed under my hand, a drawing was executed of a dove, hovering over the world, and holding in its claws a palm branch, and an olive branch, while rays flow down from it, as if to enlighten the world. A message was then given; "This séance is the first of a series of illustrations of passing through death into life. I will try to solve and explain by drawing the poetry of spirit life."-------------------

**Page 184:** --------**Mr Hockley**, the next witness, spoke as follows:-

"I have been a Spiritualist for 45 years, and have had considerable experience. This is a crystal encircled with a silver ring, as a proper crystal should be. It was formerly the custom to engrave the four names of God in Hebrew on this ring. I knew a lady who was an admirable Seeress, and obtained some splendid answers by means of crystals. The person who has the power of seeing, notices first a kind of mist in the centre of the crystal and then the message or answer appears in a kind of printed character. There was no hesitation, and she spoke it all off as though she was reading a book, and as soon as she had uttered the words she saw, they melted away and fresh ones took their place. I have 30 volumes, containing upwards of 12,000 answers received in this way, which I keep carefully under lock and key. A crystal, if properly used, should be dedicated to Spirit. Some time ago I was introduced to Lieutenant Burton by Earl Stanhope, and he wished me get him a crystal, with a Spirit attached. I also gave him a black mirror as well, and he used that in the same manner as you would a crystal. You invoke the person whom you wish to appear, and the seer looks in and describes all, and puts questions and receives answers. Lieutenant Burton was greatly pleased and went away. One day my Seeress called him into the mirror. She plainly recognised him, although dressed as an Arab and sunburnt, and described what he was doing. He was quarrelling with a party of Bedouins in Arabia, and speaking energetically to them in Arabic. An old man at last pulled out his dagger and Lieutenant his revolver, when up rode a horseman and separated them. A long time afterwards Lieutenant Burton came to me, and I told him what she had seen, and read the particulars. He assured me it was correct in every particular and attached his name to the account I had written down at the time, to certify that it was true. These books are locked up and nobody can see them; and sometimes, if I repeat some previous question which has escaped my memory, I am referred to the book in which it has been previously answered. The seers are generally of the female sex, and it is impossible to tell by their personal appearance whether they have the gift or not. I once knew a Seeress that weighed 19 stone. The only way to tell whether a person is a Seeress is by trying. Two persons occasionally see the same thing at the same time. On one occasion a lady was looking into the crystal, and when the mist divided she saw her husband in conversation with a lady, a friend of hers, and then a boy made his appearance. A friend looked over her shoulder as she had put it down to rest her eyes and saw precisely the same thing. Although I have had a crystal since 1824, I have never seen anything myself. My Seeress was perfectly in a normal condition, and in full exercise of all her faculties, and used to give answers to metaphysical and other difficult questions, which she could not possibly understand. I have nearly 1000 volumes on occult sciences. I do not think it has anything to do with mesmerism. I put a crystal in the hand of a Spiritualist, and she became quite rigid, and I had to make a pass before she could see. Some ladies would look five minutes, others ten minutes, and others fifteen, before they saw anything, but if it appeared to them foggy it has merely to be developed. The words would appear on the mirror the same as a crystal. The girl sits in front and you ask the question. The answer appears on the glass in printing than writing, and as she repeats the words they disappear. Only the girl sees the writing on the mirror. Gentlemen come to me and say, "" want to see my Guardian Spirit." The girl sees and describes the appearance. It appears in the same form as in life.--

**Page 188**: -----(witness Mr Home)-----The Chairman: "can you state the conditions under which manifestations take place?"

**Mr Home:** "You never can tell. I have frequently sat with persons and no phenomena have occurred; but when not expecting it, when in another room, or even sleeping in the house, the manifestations took place. I am, I may say, Extremely nervous, and suffer ill-health. I am scotch, and second sight was early developed in me. I am not imaginative; I am sceptical, and doubt things that take place in my own presence. I try to forget all about these things, for the mind would become partly diseased if it were suffered to dwell on them. I therefore go to theatres and to concerts for change of attention."

**The Chairman:** "Will you give us some information relative to external physical manifestations, such as the lifting of tables or persons? Do you go into trance?"

**Mr Home:** "Certain things only occur when I am in trance. But the trance is not necessary for all the phenomena, the only thing necessary is that the people about should be harmonious. At times I have been awoke at night by a presence in the room, and then the Spirits would dictate what was being done in another room. I wrote it down, and found it always correct."

**Mr Bennett:** "What are your sensations when in a trance?"

**Mr Home:** "I feel for two or three minutes in a dreamy state, then I become quite dizzy, and then I lose all consciousness. When I awake I find my feet and limbs cold, and it is difficult to restore the circulation. When told of what has taken place during the trance it is quite unpleasant to me, and I ask those present not to tell me at once when I awake. I myself doubt what they tell me. I have no knowledge on my own part of what occurs during the trance. The "harmonious" feeling is simply that which you get on going into a room and finding all the people present such that you feel at home at once. Manifestations occur at all times—during a thunderstorm, when I am feverish or ill, or even suffering from haemorrhage of the lung. Scepticism is not a hindrance, but an unsympathetic person is. Sex has not any influence. As for Mediums they are generally very nervous. Since I was born I was not expected to live, but I found the manifestations beneficial if not overdone. It is calming. At the age of six I was not able to walk. I have been given over by Dr. Louis, of Paris. The Spirits told me I should get better. At the time of the law suit with Mrs Lyon I had congestion of the brain. I was paralysed; my memory left me. They told me I would get well again, and I have done so."

Mr Atkinson asked the witness the difference between manifestations in and out of trance.

**Mr Home:** "In trance I see spirits connected with persons present. Those spirits take possession of me; my voice is like theirs. I have a particularly mobile face, as you may see, and sometimes take a sort of identity with the Spirits who are in communication through me. I attribute the mobility of my face , which is not natural, to the Spirits. I am most frequently in the air when I am awake. When I am in a trance I frequently take a live coal in my hand. I was sceptical on that point, and on taking one in my hand when awake I raised a blister. I have never been mesmerised, and cannot mesmerise. I have an exceedingly soothing power, an exceedingly gentle way of approaching any one, whether well or ill, and they like to have me near them. I may say I am exceedingly sick after elongations. While in Paris I saw the figure of my brother, then in the North Sea. I saw his fingers and toes fall off. Six months afterwards tidings came of his having been found dead on the ice, his fingers and toes having fallen off through the effects of scurvy."---------------------**page 190:** ----Mr Coleman-----------He also remembered seeing Mr Home, while at his house, lifted from his seat, carried into an adjoining room, brought back again, and laid on the table. Mr Home knew he was so, because he asked for a pencil and wrote on the ceiling.

Mr Home; "Yes I recollect that perfectly. In the houses of several people I remember constantly being lifted. On one occasion. I was staying at the chateau of M. Docosse, the Minister of Marine. I was then lifted half a foot in the air. The movement was so gentle that I had not observed it in the least. I moved back from the table to see if it would occur when I was standing. It did occur. The Count de Bourmont, one of the senators, was staying there. I had evening dress shoes on. He took hold of the shoes when I was in the air; they remained in his hand, and I was carried up. One Sunday Evening Lord Adare was told to put flowers outside a window; we saw the flowers brought into the room where we were. The Master of Lindsay was present as well as Lord Adare. Instead of my body being lifted, the flowers were taken from one window to another. I do not remember being taken out at one window and in another, for I was unconscious, but numbers witnessed it. Once I was elongated eight inches. A man was standing holding my feet. In one case I was laid on the floor, and Lord Adare had hold of my head, and the Master of Lindsay of my feet. The elongations were not confined to my legs, for I seemed to grow very much from the waist. I have seen a table lift into the air with eight men standing on it, when there were only two or three other persons in the room. I have seen the window open and shut at a distance of seven or eight feet, and curtains drawn aside, and, in some cases, objects carried over our heads. In the house of Mr and Mrs S. C. Hall, a table went up so high in the air that we could not touch it. I have seen a pencil lifted by a hand to a paper and write, in the presence of the Emperor Napoleon. We were in a large room—the Salon Louis Quinze. The Empress sat here, the Emperor there. The hand was seen to come. It was a very beautifully formed hand. There were pencils on the table. It lifted, not the one next it, but one on the far side. We heard the sound of writing, and saw it writing on note paper. The hand passed before me, and went to the Emperor, and he kissed the hand. It went to the Empress; she withdrew from its touch, and the hand followed her. The Emperor said, "Do not be frightened, kiss it;" and then kissed it. It was disappearing. I said I would like to kiss it. The hand seemed to be like that of a person thinking, and as if it were saying "Shall I?" It came back to me, and I kissed it. The sensation of touch and pressure was that of a natural hand. It was as much a material hand seemingly as my hand is now. The writing was an autograph of the Emperor Napoleon 1. The hand was his hand, small and beautiful as it known to have been. In the house of Mr Bergheim a smelling bottle on the table began to tremble, as if some one with a very shaky hand had taken hold of it, and then it began to spin round the table; it span a minute at least. There were three witnesses who saw that. I went into a trance immediately afterwards, and told them that a Spirit named James was present. I learnt afterwards that James had a very shaky hand. The Emperor of Russia, as well as the Emperor Napoleon, have seen hands, and have taken hold of them, when they seemed to float away into thin air. I have never seen material substances brought into a room when doors and windows were closed. Flowers have been brought in from a parterre, but the Spirits always asked for the window to be open. When other witnesses were present they have seen heads. One witness will testify to having see heads in her lap at night. They were luminous; there was quite a glow from them."

**Page 197:** (witness Signor Damiani) I have been present at séances when a sheet of blank paper and a pencil have been placed under the table, and a few seconds afterwards, these things being picked up, sentences have been found written on the paper. How do I know that it was not the Mediums toes did this? You may ask. Well, I can only reply that in such case the Medium must indeed have possessed most extraordinary toes.

"Whilst in Sicily, quite recently, a most telling poem, two hundred lines long, in the Sicilian dialect, besides communications in German, French, Latin, and English, have been received in my presence, the medium in this case being singularly illiterate person of the artisan class.

I have met in Clifton with a boy Medium, between ten and eleven years of age, who would write long essays on spiritual philosophy the matter and manner of these essays being such as would have been accepted from any accomplished writer of mature age who was conversant with the subject.----------------
------I have frequently held Spirit hands (at all events, hands not attached to any corresponding body) in my grasp. The touch of these hands differed so much from that of human hands, that I can bring nothing like analogy or comparison to bear upon it. They were not so warm as human hands, and ordinary (though not invariably) were softer in texture. Their contact has generally sent a thrill through my frame, somewhat resembling a slight electric shock. These hands would melt away and dissolve in mine. I have often *seen* hands. They are generally beautiful in form, with tapering fingers, such as those Canova gives

to his ideal nymphs and goddesses. Sometimes they present a whitish and opaque appearance, at other times I have seen them pink and transparent.

## Tuesday, 6th July 1869.
### (witness Master of Lindsay)

"Another time, at Mr Jencken's house, I saw a crystal ball placed on Mr Home's head, emit flashes of coloured light, following the order of the spectrum. The crystal was spherical, so that it could not have given prismatic colours. After this it changed, and we all saw a view of the sea, as if we were looking down at it from the top of a cliff. It seemed to be the evening as the sun was setting like a globe of fire, lighting up a broad path over the little waves. The moon was faintly visible in the south, and as the sun set, her power increased. We saw also a few stars; and suddenly the whole thing vanished, like shutting the slide of a magic lantern; and the crystal was dead. This whole appearance lasted about ten minutes and pleased us very much, both on account of the curious nature of the vision, if it may be called such, and from the really beautiful effects of light, etc., that we had seen.

" there were two candles and a bright fire burning in the room. We noticed that the flame of the candles was depressed occasionally as if some gas had been poured over them, and again at other times they would gain in brilliancy.

"I saw a grand pianoforte raise in the air about four inches, without any noise; and subsequently the note were struck, although it was locked and the key taken away.---------------**page 203:** I have frequently seen Home, when in a trance go to a fire and take out large red-hot coals, and carry them about in his hands, put them inside his shirt, etc.. Eight times, I myself have held a red-hot coal in my hands without injury, when it scorched my face on raising my hand. Once, I wished to see if they really would burn, and I said so, and I got a blister as large as a sixpence; I instantly asked him to give me the coal, and I held the part that burnt me, in the middle of my hand, for three or four minutes without the least inconvenience.

"A few week ago, I was at a *séance* with eight others. Of these, seven held a red-hot coal without pain, and the two others could not bear the approach of it; of the seven, four were ladies.-----------------Mrs Honywood said she had never seen Home give a live coal to anyone. He had in her presence carried one in a hand bell, and had placed the coal upon his hand on a piece of paper. He afterwards handed it to Mrs Hall and another lady; the paper was not injured in any way.-----------Miss Douglass continued: "Mr Home held the hot coals a long time in his hand, till they were nearly black. He then place them between his shirt and coat, and they did not singe either. I then touched them, at first they scorched me, but immediately after they felt cold like marble."

**Page 210:** In answer to Mr Wallace, Miss Douglass said she had no preparation on her hands when she touched the coals.

**Mr Rowcroft** next gave evidence; he said he had seen a hand playing upon an accordion and apparently suspended in space. This was at Mr Jones's house, where he met Mr Home, Mr Jones, with himself, a friend and Mr Home sat at a table, and in ten minutes raps came. The raps were to the effect that witness was a medium, and that if he remained that night "they" would develop his power for him. The initials A. E. R., were then given, and on further questioning the spirits, the name Albert Edward Rowcroft was given in full. Mr Home then held the accordion, and it played most beautiful music. When the music ceased, the accordion left Mr Home's hand and came under the table. I said "I see a hand;" the instrument then went round the table and came back to Mr Home. Witness considers the agency on this occasion was spiritual, since no one present could have produced the phenomena. He continued; "That was the first *séance* I had ever witnessed, but I have since had some further experience, and with regard to messages conveying information, I may say I have a sister who was coming from America; I did not know when she would come, but I asked the table and the answer was, the first week in July; at the time I asked the table, she had not then started; The prediction was quite true."

In answer to Mr Gannon, witness said he knew July was a favourable month for crossing the Atlantic.

**Mr Wallace:** " With reference to the accordion, was there sufficient light to enable you to see clearly?"

**Mr Rowcroft:** " There was plenty of light; six gas burners were lighted. I saw the hand for about a minute; it accompanied the instrument round the chairs. I was the only person who saw the phenomena, and there were *nine* persons present. When Mr Home held the accordion, I saw it open and shut, and he frequently exclaimed, "they are pulling," and he was obliged to exert considerable force against the unseen player. Mr Home's disengaged hand was resting on the table; all present saw the accordion float in space. At Mr Jones's suggestion we sang a hymn, the accordion gave the key note, and after a pause it accompanied us. On the same evening I saw something like a hand creep between the cloth and the table; I felt the fingers distinctly; my friend saw the shape also; and every one present touched it."------------I have frequently seen forms like hands under the table-cloth; I have felt them and, when pressed, they always seemed to dissolve. I have frequently been touched; the touch is peculiar, like that of a glove filled with air. On one occasion I laid my handkerchief over my hand, it was then pulled, and on looking I found a minute knot had been tied in the corner. When I have such phenomena as these, coupled with intelligent and trustworthy answers, I Cannot but believe them to be spiritual.

" I have seen Mr Home's levitations. I saw him rise and float horizontally across the window. We all saw him clearly. He passed right across just as a person might float upon the water. At my request he was floated back again. The window blinds were then moved up and down without any one touching them; this seemed to be done to tone the light. I may add that all this took place at the house of Mr Milner Gibson."

**Mr Jones** then produced a handkerchief which had been tied in a knot by the "spirits." He said, "The handkerchief was folded when I took it from my wife's draw; at the séance that evening I laid it down at my feet. Shortly after I looked down and found the handkerchief gone. It was under the centre of the table. I took it up and found that it was tied in a "country girl's knot."

In continuation witness said; "I heard music Mr Rowcroft referred to, and I know no human hand touched the accordion. I did not see the spirit hand. I don't remember seeing the accordion, but heard the music. I understand Mr Rowcroft saw it, but I did not."

**Dr Edmunds** (to Mr Rowcroft): "Was the accordion in such a position that others could see it?"

**Mr Rowcroft** then described the position of the instrument, from which it appeared that it was on a level with the table. Witness said, in continuation of his evidence; "My friend, Mr Milne, did not see the hand though he sat next to me. It was above the accordion and therefore higher than the table."

**Mr Holyoake:** "If the instrument travelled round the table all must have seen it?"

**Witness:** "Certainly."

**Mr Holyoake:** "But not the hand?"

**Witness:** "No."

**Mr Jones** was then recalled. He said: "After exquisite music had been played, someone suggested "God save the Queen." It (that is the spirit) said "yes," But added, "you sing," referring to me. I then sang, and it accompanied me exquisitely. The instrument, on this occasion, was in Mr Home's hand close to the ground, and I and others saw it swaying up and down.

"Home was obliged to keep hold on account of the power exercised by the spirits; his disengaged hand was on the table. The accordion belonged to Mr Milner Gibson."

**Mr Volckman**: "did any person see Mr Home's feet?"

**Mr Jones**: "I cannot say."

**Dr Ellis**: "Does Mr Home believe all this is done under spiritual influence."

**Witness**: "Yes."

**Mr Jones** then said: "I have paid five guineas to obtain a special sitting with the Davenports. I thought they were impostors and did my best to discover the trick. We had a dark sitting. I helped to tie the young men and I placed paper under their feet and marked the shape of the feet with a pencil. On the table was a pile of musical instruments. I had provided myself with some phosphorised oil which I poured over them; My party then held hands. The oil flared, and the instruments flew up and round the room; the light from the oil was sufficient for us to see all persons present. I asked mentally, to be struck on the head and was struck by a guitar very powerfully. So far as my experience went I did not discover any imposture. The young men's feet had not stirred a hairs breadth."

Mr Swepstone addressing the Master of Lindsay, asked whether the elongations referred to in his paper were in the trunk or the legs of the subject?

**The Master of Lindsay**: "The top of the hip bone and short ribs separate. In home, they are usually close together. There was no separation of the vertebrae of the spine; nor were there the elongations at all like those resulting from expanding the chest with air; the shoulders did not move. Home looked as if he was pulled up by the neck; the muscles seemed in a state of tension. He stood firmly upright in the middle of the room, and before the elongation commenced, I placed my foot on his instep. I will swear he never moved his heels from the ground. When Home was elongated against the wall, Lord Adare placed his foot on home's instep, and I marked the place on the wall. I once saw him elongated along the ground. Lord Adare was present. Home seemed to grow at both ends, and pushed myself and Adare away.

" I have seen the levitations, But not in a brilliant light. Home on occasion was sitting with me; in a few minutes he said, "keep quiet, I am going up;" his foot then came and touched my shoulder; I then felt something like velvet touch my cheek, and on looking up, was surprised to find that he had carried with him an arm chair, which he held out in his hand and then floated round the room, pushing picture out of their places as he passed along the walls. They were far beyond the reach of a person standing on the ground. The light was sufficient to enable me to see clearly. I saw the levitations in Victoria Street, when Home floated out of the window; he first went into trance and walked about uneasily; he then went into the hall; while he was away, I heard a voice whisper in my ear, "He will go out of one window and in another." I was alarmed and shocked at the idea of such an experiment. I told the company what I heard, and then we waited for Home's return. Shortly after he entered the room, I heard the window go up, but I could not see it, for I sat with me back to it. I, however, saw his shadow on the opposite wall; he went out of the window in the horizontal position, and I saw him outside the other window (that in the next room) floating in the air. It was eighty-five feet from the ground. There was no balcony along the windows, merely a strong course an inch and a-half wide; each window had a small plant stand, but there was no connection between them. I have no theory to explain these things. I have tried to find out how they are done, but the more I studied them, the more satisfied was I that they could not be explained by mere mechanical trick. I have had the fullest opportunity for investigation. I once saw Home in *full light* standing in the air seventeen inches from the ground."

**Dr Edmunds**: " have you ever obtained any information which could not have been known to the medium or any one present? I may say I have received score of letters from people who are utter strangers to me, asking the Committee if our spiritual friends can assist them in finding lost wills, and registers of birth and baptism; do you know of any of that kind?"

**The Master of Lindsay**: "I know of one such fact, which I can relate to you. A friend of mine was very anxious to find the will of his grandmother, who had been dead forty years, but could not even find the certificate of death. I went with him to the Marshall's, and we had a *séance*; we sat at the table, and soon the raps came; my friend then asked his questions *mentally*; he went over the alphabet himself, or sometimes I did so, not knowing the question. We were told the will had been drawn by a man named William Walker, who lived in Whitechapel; the name of the street and the number of the house were given. We went to Whitechapel , found the man, and subsequently, through his aid, obtained a copy of the draft; he was quite unknown to us, and had not always lived in that locality; for he had once seen better days. The medium could not possibly have known anything about the matter, and even if she had, her knowledge would have been no avail, as the questions were mental ones.

**Dr Edmunds**: "Have you seen any apparitions of deceased persons?"

**The Master of Lindsay**: "When I first saw Home, we had a *séance*. I was late for the train, and stayed the night with him, he gave me a shake-down on the sofa in his room. There were no curtains to the windows, and the ground was covered with snow, the reflection from which made objects in the room distinctly visible. After I had been in bed twenty minutes, I head raps, and my pillow went up and down in a curious manner. That might have been the result of imagination; a few minutes after, I saw an apparition which seemed like a column of vapour or an indistinct shadow, which grew eventually into a definite shape, and I then saw the form of a woman standing *en profile* to me. She stood between me and Home, I saw the features plainly, and should have recognised them again anywhere. She seemed to be attired in a long flowing gown which hung without a belt from the shoulders. The figure seemed quite solid, I could see not through it. I spoke to Home, he said he saw her distinctly, and that it was the apparition of his late wife; she often came to him. She moved and stood by his side. She then walked to the right of the bed and rather behind it, but not out of my sight, and then slowly faded away like a column of vapour. The next morning I found an album, and on looking over the picture carelessly, I saw a photograph exactly like the figure I had seen . Mrs Jencken said it was the likeness of the late Mrs Home."

**Dr Edmunds**: " Have you ever seen the apparitions of the lower animals or of trees?"

**The Master of Lindsay**: "Never. I was once subject to a singular optical illusion. I used to see the spectre of a black dog. It seemed to glide along; I never saw it walking. I often went up to it, and sometimes passed a stick through it. It was the result of over-work; I was at the time studying for the

army, and reading sixteen hours a day."
**Dr King Chambers**: "Are your family subject to "second sight?"
**The Master of Lindsay**: " Yes, such things have been in our family."
**Dr Edmunds**: " What do you define "second sight" to be?"
**The Master of Lindsay**: "Second sight in an intuitive knowledge of an event which is going on at the same moment in another place; and also of events which will happen. I will give you an illustration, for the authenticity of which I can vouch. A lady of my acquaintance married an officer in the army, who went out to India before the mutiny. One night in the drawing room she screamed and fainted; on recovering, she said she saw her husband shot. The time was noted, and intelligence arrived that he had been shot at the precise moment when she saw the vision.

It has just occurred to me that some people might think as I did many years ago WHAT IS THE VEIL that you go across? The older Mediums that I spoke to and the books that I read, they always talked and wrote about "across the veil". I only found out after about 15 years of sitting for the Spirit World even though I had been linking with them for many years previously. To this day 23.6.03 I still occasionally get the veil in my mind's eye. It is a wonderful experience when it happens. I get a sort of film of light in a red-ish, orange-ish, yellow-ish colour, no strong colour of any kind, which turns into a lacework, netting, type pattern. That then turns into visions of many kinds from the World of Spirit, it took me many years to go beyond that veil though. I also get a fantastic pure white light within my mind the likes of something I have never experienced before it envelopes me wholly, it is truly wonderful. I believe it came when I was ready, as all things in my development with the Spirit World did, and not before.
I am starting to get deeper into my trance state, I only say deeper as it is how I feel. This is only a figure of speech, not going down into anything physically. The World of Spirit is knocking me out of the equation more. In reality, I am being taken away from my normal self a lot more and being zonked out completely for an hour or more [after giving Spirit permission to develop me in which ever way they wish]; this is after about 30 years of sitting. The past few days [now 23.6.03] and I mean days I have been having a bit of trouble in getting the effects of my trance and linking into the Spirit World away from my body or better put, away from my mind. It is a strange feeling that has me feeling very, very woozy and my eyes do not want to open, they try to keep closed, even when I open my eyes or try to open them they are so heavy they want to stay shut and close again. When my eyes eventually open through me forcing them with my best will that I can muster [this is not as I would sometimes wish, as I love to be in the state of linking with the Spirit World, I would stay there all day but I need to come out of it as I have an earthly life to lead, and I might be in a demonstration situation] they close again. BUT when that is happening, what I am finding is the focus of my vision is not right. I have to force open a little at a time and close my eyes many times now before they focus for my every day life. It is very strange. This is another one of those things that you have to experience yourself to know it. I have put it down on paper so you will not be scared if it happens to you. Please do not be stupid and fake it, if you do it is only yourself who will be loser. All I can say is, it must be needed in my development for my body/mind to be used in this way by the Spirit World, otherwise Spirit would not put me into this state. Be aware of this, don't worry it is not scary, for me another thing that is just unusual.

### "To the Committee Of the Dialectical Society Investigating Spiritualism."
### Page 354:

Ladies and gentle men—I have been desired by the Committee of London Dialectical Society now investigating spiritual manifestations to furnish them with some account of my experience therein. I do so with pleasure but I omit details as much as possible, as no doubt you have been overwhelmed with accounts of phenomena of common occurrence. I may state that I have got no power peculiar to mediums, nor am I conscious of spiritual existence, except through the most palpable physical manifestations; I am, therefore, constitutional an unbeliever in such things; and in all matters a rationalist. My personal presence at the spirit circle is even an impediment to the success of the phenomena; and this and other facts have led me to the discovery that Mediumship does not depend on belief or scepticism, but upon organic conditions or temperamental peculiarities. I am of that physiological type which is the opposite of Mediumship, but Mrs Burns and her sisters are of purely mediumistic temperament; on account of which I have had very special opportunities of becoming acquainted with the subject, and I now report on behalf of these ladies rather than myself.

"Mediumship, then, is a natural faculty peculiar to certain individuals, which the spirit circles does not create, but merely calls to exercise. From childhood Mrs Burns has been a Medium, and in the darkness of the evening could perceive the odie emanations from graveyards while yet a child, and many years before spiritualism was heard of. About eight years ago, during my prolonged absence from home, Mrs Burns and her sister Mary sat at the table, after the manner of spiritualists, and readily produced all the phenomena. Their sister Caroline was also found to be a powerful medium, and the table would walk about the room if she simply placed her finger on top of it. It would also lie down on its side, or turn its legs up in the air with its face downwards if desired. We never took the least trouble to cultivate these manifestations, as much more interesting phenomena occurred.

"Spontaneously, Miss Mary was found to be a very superior Writing Medium. By taking a pencil in her hand she would write automatically in response to mental questions. I have seen her write on different subjects with a pencil in each hand, without giving any attention to what she was doing. In desperate case of illness we have repeatedly received medical prescriptions in this way, the application of which was of immediate benefit. This young lady also has the faculty of conversing with Spirits, face to face. A brother of mine, whom she never saw and knew nothing about, thus appeared to her and conversed with her a long time; and the description she gave of him, and the information he communicated, was ample evidence of the identity of the spirit, and of the fact that there was a spirit in the matter.

We have also cultivated the trance. Mrs Burns has been in a state simultaneously with Mrs Everitt and Mr Cogman, while sitting together in *séance*. They met in the spiritual state, and conversed and walked together. When they returned to physical consciousness, they each gave the same testimony as to their spiritual experiences.

Mrs Burns and Miss Mary see spirits quite readily while in trance. By this means the Spirits have been seen scattering perfumes in the form of flowers. Mrs burns will exclaim "There they are, throwing the flowers!" and instantly a puff of cool air and the most delicious perfumes are experienced. These experiments have been repeatedly verified at Mrs Everitt's and other Circles. The spirits are also seen producing the direct writing, but the details of the process are not very minutely observed. I was at Mrs Everitt's house when Spirit "John Watt" wrote his name on the ceiling with a pencil. Mrs Burns and two other clairvoyants were present, and they all described the event at the moment of its occurrence, and before the light was struck. The Spirits are also seen to move physical objects and touch persons in the Circle. Miss Mary saw the Spirit take the coat off Mr Fay's back while his hands were tied, at the public *séance* given by the Davenport brothers. She was also astonished at the light which came out of the cabinet while the manifestations were going on inside. Mrs Burns saw the spirits at Mr Alsop's circle carry a bible, upwards of eleven pounds in weight, from the sideboard on to the table. This process of carrying has been observed many times. The spirits do not put their hands under objects when they carry them; they place their fingers on top and seem to move the objects by magnetic attraction, in the same manner as spiritualists move a table by placing their fingers on top of it. When spirit voice is heard, Mrs Burns sees the spirit holding the tube and carrying it about the room. She has thus observed "John Watt" at Mrs Everitt's, and "John King" at the séances held by Messrs. Herne and Williams. She also saw spirits untie John Blackburn, a Medium from Halifax, who had been previously tied in a most extraordinary manner by the spirits while he was in a trance. The rope was manipulated by the spirits by a kind of magnetic attraction proceeding from their hands, and not by the ordinary form of leverage with the finger points.

"We make use of this seeing faculty as a means of communication with the Spirits. To practice it, we retire to a darkened room, and, in a short time, if conditions are favourable, the spirits appear in groups in the vicinity of the persons to whom they are attached. By this means, persons now deceased have been accurately described by clairvoyants. The spirits communicate their information by writing it in luminous scrolls, which are promptly read. These spirits are of various historical periods and counties, and their appearance is very peculiar. Sometimes they write through Miss Mary's hand automatically, and in different styles and languages. On one occasion a gentleman translated one of these communications; it was in Spanish, and the spirit had described himself as a Spaniard. In the trance she has also spoken in various languages. I have had a test of the genuineness of these clairvoyant observations, which I shall here detail.

"Mrs Burns and myself were present at a séance at Mr Mylne's house, in Islington. A female figure was minutely described by Mrs Burns as standing near me, who said she was related to me. My family connections are very few, so I had no difficulty in recalling them all, and I was obliged to deny that I had ever had such a relative. A few months afterwards I visited my parents in Ayrshire, accompanied by my sister-in-law, Miss Mary, who had not been at the séance at Islington. We had a sitting, and she described the same spirit as standing between my mother and myself, and said that she was a near relation of mine, who was attracted to me on account of my literary pursuits. I replied that I was certain there was some mistake, as I could recall no such person as having been a member of our family. As soon as my mother heard the full description of the spirit she said it applied to an only sister of hers who died upwards of seventy years ago, and of whose existence I had never heard. She had been a precocious child, passionately fond of books, and died when quite young. As soon as my mother recognised this fact, the spirit was seen to give manifestations of assent and pleasure.

"Mrs Burns sees spirits in attendance on public speakers, and has also observed them in the theatre, inspiring the leading characters. She perceives that they touch the head, or send down a shaft of light upon it when striking a thought or original idea is to be uttered.

"I have not mentioned many cases of physical phenomena that have occurred in our experience, as you will doubtlessly have been liberally supplied with such accounts.

"The result of my experience has been to establish to my mind that there are two kinds of matter—one peculiar to the physical world, and one peculiar to the spirit world;

"That every object has a spiritual, as well a physical condition;

"That certain individuals give off this spiritual matter in such a way as to relate them peculiarly to the spirit world; which constitutes such persons mediums;

"That this spiritualised form of matter is that of the objective personality of spirits is composed; that it is the link which enables them to control physical objects; and also that it is the bond which connects mind with matter in the physical state.

"J. Burns
15, Southampton Row,
London, W.C. 21 April, 1871.

**Page 369 No 5—The Hon. Mrs-----**
"From among the many remarkable instances of spiritual phenomena which I have witnessed, I will cite the following :- It was on the evening of the 17$^{th}$ of March, and there were five persons present. Mr Home, in the trance state, walked to a table on which stood a moderator lamp burning brightly, removed the glass globe, and then the lamp chimney, and brought it to me, holding it firmly in his hands. I declined to touch it, knowing it was burning hot. Mr Home then said, 'have you no faith? It is quite cool.' I consented to take hold of it, and found to my astonishment that it was hardly warm; another lady present likewise felt it, and made the same remark. Mr Home then passed the chimney, he said, in a sad, low tone of voice, as if deprecating anger, 'It is necessary to confirm the faith of others, that this should be made hot for you.' The gentleman then lightly touched the glass with one finger, and found that it was so burning hot that even in those few seconds of time it had raised a blister on his finger, which remained for three days afterwards. Mr Home then proceeded to the fire, and thrust the lamp glass into the middle of the burning coals, and after waiting and watching it for five minutes he took it out, and held it tightly clasped with both hands. Fetching a Lucifer match from the writing table, he brought it to me, and desired me to touch the glass with it. Of course it instantly ignited, owing to the great heat; and having pointed this out carefully to all present. Mr Home thrust the burning chimney into his mouth and held it there, observing at the time the tongue was the most sensitive part of the human body. Not apparently satisfied with this, or thinking that he had failed to show us that it was done by supernatural agency, he again proceeded to the fireplace, took out a red hot coal and placed it inside the chimney, then brought it to me and dropped it on to my white muslin dress, where it remained for some seconds, as it was so hot we all feared to touch it. My dress, though made of finest muslin, was not ignited, and we even failed to detect the slightest trace or mark of any kind after the closest examination. Mr Home remarked that we need not be afraid as they (The Spirits) would never hurt us. He then took a flower, and after breathing gently over it, passed it several times through the flame of the moderator lamp; after showing us that its leaves and blossom were untouched, he took it to the fire, and held it in the smoke and moved it gently about amongst the coals; then bringing it back again to us, he made us observe that there was no smell of smoke or burning about it, and that it was precisely in the same state as when he first plucked it. "On other occasions I have seen chairs moved and brought by invisible hands from the other side of the room, three or four musical instruments played in harmony together at one time, and have likewise heard voices, sometimes speaking together at an apparent great distance, and at other times close to me. But

perhaps the most remarkable spiritual manifestation is what is called 'direct drawing.' Pencils and paper are placed either on the table or under it, and in a few minutes, there will be found something drawn or written upon it. I have seen drawn most beautiful faces, sometimes touched with a little colour, only a pencil sketch. On one occasion I placed a pencil and paper *on* the table, and looking at it ten minutes later I found a complete programme of a concert written out, which the spirits told us they would play in the course of the evening; and this promise was faithfully carried out, and all the pieces of music played in a most masterly manner on different instruments, a violin, flute, piccolo and concertina, all lying on the table. I must add that these spiritual drawings, etc., are best obtained when the lights are extinguished."

---

### Page 371:     No 6.--Mr Guppy
*Séance with spiritual Society of Florence.*

"The *séance* opened with a message; 'It has been asked in this Society if spirits can distinguish colours; we will show you.'

"A noise was heard on the table, and the light showed a heap of sugar plums of all colours mixed together—about a handful. Light put out again; we heard a rattling; lighted the candle and found the sugar plums all assorted in little heaps of separate colours.

"Saml. Guppy."

### No 7. –Mr Guppy.
*Another séance with the same Society.*

The room, at my request, had been made very warm, as at the previous *séance* we were shivering. Some of the most eminent Florentine literati were present. First came a shower of fresh flowers, which fell all about the table while Mrs Guppy's hands were held. The light was put out again, and ten minutes an awful crash was heard on the table, as if the chandelier had fallen down. On lighting the candle, we found a large lump of beautiful ice, about a foot long and one and a half inches thick which had fallen on the table with such a force that it was broken. It began to melt immediately, and was put into a dish. This was more than an hour after the beginning of the séance, in which time the ice would have melted had it been in the room.

"Saml. Guppy"

### Page 372:     No 8. –Mr Guppy.
Test séance with Mr Adolphus Trollope, Mrs Trollope, Miss Blayden and Col. Harvey.

"First, the room was searched by the gentlemen while Mrs Guppy was being undressed and re-dressed in the presence of Mrs Trollope, every article of her dress being closely examined.

"We sat at the table, Mrs Guppy firmly held, both hands, by Mr Trollope and his wife, while Colonel Harvey and Miss Blayden held my hands and touched Mrs Guppy's. In about ten minutes all exclaimed, "I smell flowers," and a shower of flowers came. On lighting the candle the whole of Mrs Guppy's and Mr Trollope's hands and arms were found covered with jonquil flowers. The smell was quite overpowering. The doors had been locked, the windows fastened. Had a bunch of jonquils been in the room before the séance it would have been detected by the smell.

"Saml. Guppy."

### No 9. –Mr Guppy.
Mrs Guppy went to a séance at the Ambassadors, Sir Augustus Paget; present, Lady Paget, Count and Countess Moltki, and a daughter of Sir Digby Murray. They held Mrs Guppy firmly, and asked for a noise; and there was a loud concussion on the wall, like a gun. Flowers were afterwards brought.

"Saml. Guppy"

**SOME OF THE EXPERIMENTS ARE THE SAME, GETTING THE SAME RESULTS, SO I HAVE NOT INCLUDED THESE. But I have included some the same because of slight differences that might help some circles of the present day. (ROY: The Author)**

## Minutes of the sub-committees.
### Experiment 1

**Feby.24th, 1869. Six members present. Circle formed. Private house. Medium non-professional.**
All hands resting on a square heavy dining-table on four legs with casters. For one hour and a quarter no motion or sound. Two members left; the four remaining sat for a hour. Phenomena at intervals. 1st. Motions of the table, sometimes very gentle, then rapid, and such as would require, to produce them voluntarily, a great and visible exertion of muscular force. A slight rising of the table from the floor. This was easily seen by all present by reason of the corner of the table being close to the writing table, one inch and two thirds higher, up to the level of which it was raised twice. 2nd. Sounds. These consisted of creakings and taps. The former were such as would result from efforts to move the table by the legs or from unequal strains applied to various parts of it; the latter were such as could only be produced by distinct blows with a pencil, finger tip, or light hammer. On questions being asked, they were followed by one, two or three sounds. During the whole time the hands of those present were laid flat on the table; the room was well lighted with gas, and everything could be distinctly seen. At the termination of the sitting there was quite a volley of raps, according to request preferred that "Good night!" might thus be signified. *Note*: all present were members of the Committee, and declared upon their honour that none of these motions or sounds were produced voluntarily or consciously by themselves. Moreover they have found, by repeated experiment, that they are not able to produce similar sounds or motions when endeavouring to do so.

### Experiment 1V.

**March 9th. Nine members present. Conditions as before.** The following phenomena were produced; 1st. The members of the circle standing, rested the tips of their fingers only on the table. It made a considerable movement. 2nd. Holding their hands a few inches above the table, and no one in any way touching it, it moved a distance of more than a foot. 3rd. To render the experiment absolutely conclusive, all present stood clear away from the table, and stretching out their hands over it without touching it, it again moved as before, and about the same distance. During this time, one of the committee was placed upon the floor to look carefully beneath the table, while the others were placed outside to see that no person went near to the table. In this position it was frequently moved, without possibility of contact by any person present. 4th. Whilst thus standing clear of the table, but tips of their fingers resting upon it, all at the same moment raised their hands at a given signal; and on several occasions the table jumped from the floor to an elevation varying from half an inch to an inch. 5th All held their hands close above the table, but not touching it, and then on a word of command raised them suddenly, and the table jumped as before. The member lying on the floor, and those placed outside the circle, were keenly watching as before, and all observed the phenomena as described.

It may be observed that the motion of the table, whether upwards or horizontal, was not produced by any *sensible* attractive force of the hands of those present. The persons forming the circle were quite unconscious of any expenditure of attractive force, but the force, whatever it was, seemed to obey, to some extent, the will of those present.

### Experiment V111.

**March 30th. Conditions as before. Six members present, and one visitor. Sitting at 8p.m., lasting about two hours**. A member of the Committee having objected to the assumption of one and three sounds meaning no and yes, it was asked, "If one sound means 'No,' give three raps;" which were immediately given. Again it was asked, "If three sounds are to mean 'Yes,' let three more raps be heard. It was thereupon agreed that, in future reports, it will only be necessary to speak of answers being in the negative or affirmative, without specifying the number of raps or sounds indicating such answers. That one rap shall be taken and expressed as negative three as an affirmative, and two as uncertain; the sounds hitherto, by this interpretation, having conveyed intelligible answers.

A round tripod table, smaller and lighter than the square table hitherto used, was employed for the first experiments. All hands were placed on it, and every member of the circle placed each of his feet in contact with that of his neighbours on the right and left. The Unusual tapping sounds were speedily produced, and when questions were put the table tilted once or thrice on one side, the elevation varied from one to about three inches. It also moved along the floor, but with the hands resting on it. These manifestations becoming weaker, the circle was formed at the square table. This, in the course of the evening, moved along the floor, but not without contact with hands, although the experiment was tried more than once. But sounds which came from the table, sometimes during conversation, as if in approval or dissent of remarks made, and those following the questions put consisted, not only of gentle tappings and distinct raps, but sometimes of heavy blows; and occasionally, when a physical manifestation was asked for, as that the table might be raised, of creaking, cracking, scratching, and other sounds quite indescribable, coupled with trembling or vibratory movement of the table.

Five distinct raps followed a repeatedly expressed wish for physical manifestations, the alphabet, as on a former occasion, was used as a means of communication, and the following sentence was formed, "Do keep your mouths shut;" another was as follows, "This is a great work; it demands your life, your soul, your all; go on friends, God prosper your work."

Occasionally, to save time, when a word was partly spelled out, a guess was made at the remainder and the question asked, "Is it such a word?" The answer being in the affirmative the word was written down accordingly. But in more than one instance the answer was in the negative, and the supposed word only formed part of another word. It is to be remarked that the sounds in correction of the letters and formation of the words of communications were very sharp, distinct, and regular. During the whole of the time the communications were being spelled out every member of the circle placed each of his feet in contact with that of his neighbour, and his hands on the table.

**Experiment 1X**

**April 6th. Conditions as before. Five members present.** Raps were heard proceeding from the table. The alphabet was proposed, and on enquiry it was found, that a certain number present was to call the alphabet. On his doing so, the table rapped at certain letters which were written down and a sentence was thus spelt, and the communication caused considerable amusement. Other questions were put and answered by the usual signals. The raps, however, at times seemed to manifest the most lively disposition and occurred continually during conversation; they also distinctively kept time to music with perfect accuracy.

**Experiment X**

**April 11th. Conditions as before. Six members present. The sitting lasted about one hour and a half.** In less than five minutes tapping sounds heard, proceeding from the leaf of the table; at first faint, but soon they became louder, and so continued during nearly the entire sitting. During conversation, they were of sharp, decided, and lively character, often occurring in volleys, and came from different parts of the table according to request. There were also motions of the table. These consisted: (1.) Of a rapid to-and-fro movement along the floor, in one instance while only the tips of the fingers were in contact with the table. (2.) A peculiar tremor of the whole table followed by a sudden jerk, somewhat similar to the jolting of a cart. (3.) Tilting of the table three times on a question being put, the elevation being about half an inch.

**Experiment X1.**

**April 15th. Conditions as before. Eight members present. Sitting at 8pm.** Within five minutes tapping sounds were heard on the leaf of the table. Various questions, as to order of sitting, etc., were put, and answered by rappings. The alphabet was called for, and the word "laugh" was spelled out. It was asked if it was intended that we should laugh. An affirmative answer being given, the members laughed; upon which the table made a most vigorous sound and motion imitative of and responsive to the laughter, and so ludicrous as to cause a general peal of real laughter to which the table shook, and the rapping kept time as the accompaniment. The following questions were then put and answered by the number of raps given;--"How many children has Mrs M--?" "Four;" "Mrs W--?" "Three;" "Mrs D?" No rap; "Mrs E--?" "Five" "Mrs S--?" "two" It was ascertained, upon inquiry, that these replies were perfectly correct, except in the case of Mrs E--, who has only four children living, but has lost one. Neither the medium nor any person present, was aware of all the above numbers, but each number was known to some of them. The enquiry for a written communication being responded to by three raps, some sheets of paper with a pencil were laid under the table, and at the end of the sitting examined, but no letter or mark was found on the paper. In order to test whether these sounds would continue under different conditions, all sat at some distance from the table, holding hands in the circle round it. But instead of upon the table as before, loud rappings were heard to proceed from various parts of the floor, and from the chair on which the medium sat; while some came from the other side of the room, a distance of about fifteen feet from the nearest person. A desire of having been expressed for a shower of raps, loud rappings came from every part of the table at once, producing an effect similar to that of a shower of hail falling upon it. The sounds throughout the evening were very sharp and distinct. It was observed that, although during conversation the rappings are sometimes of a singularly lively character, yet when a question is put they ceased instantly, and not one is heard until the response is given.

### Experiment X11.

**April 20th. Eight persons present. Conditions as before. Sitting a little before 8, lasting about two hours.** Sounds from the table were heard within ten minute. On a song being sung rapping commenced immediately. A lively air was always accompanied by a spirited beating to time, the sounds, in harmony with the song sung, being loud or soft, and following the measure note by note, conveying as much musical expression as such an accompaniment was capable of. The sounds were frequently accompanied by slight vibratory or trembling of the table. It was asked—"Will you answer a question by the alphabet?" to this the usual token of assent was given. A member of the committee wrote on a slip of paper;" What is the name of my sister?" but what was written was not disclosed to any person present. The word "MaryAnn" was spelt. The answer was not quite correct, it should have been Marian. In order to place beyond doubt that these sounds could in no way be produced by any person present, the back of every chair was turned to the table, and at some distance from it, each person kneeling upon the chair and resting his arms on the back, with the tips of his fingers only upon the table.

### Experiment X111.

April 29th. Nine members present. Medium and conditions as before. In about a quarter of an hour the table made sundry movements along the floor with rapping. The sounds at first were very softly given but subsequently became much stronger. They beat time to airs played by musical box, and came from any part of the table requested by the members. Some questions were put and followed by raps, but more frequently by tilting of the table at its sides, ends, or corners, the elevation being from one to four inched. An endeavour was made by those sitting near, to prevent the table from rising, but it resisted all their efforts. The chair on which the medium was seated was drawn several times over the floor. First it moved backwards several feet; then it gave several twists and turns, and finally returned with the medium appearing perfectly still and holding her feet above the carpet; so that during the entire phenomena no part of her person or of her dress touched the floor. There was bright gaslight, and the members had a clear opportunity to observe all that occurred; and all agreed that imposture was impossible. While this was going on, a rapping sound came continually from the floor beneath and round the chair. It was suggested that trails should be made if the table would move without contact. All present, including the medium, stood quite clear of the table, holding their hands from three to six inches above it, and without any way touching it. Observers were placed under it to see that it was not touched there. The following were the observations.

1. The table repeatedly moved along the floor in different directions, often taking that requested. Thus in accordance with a desire expressed that it should move from the front to the back of the room, it took that direction, and on approaching the folding doors and meeting with an obstruction, turned as if to avoid it.
2. On a given signal all raised their hands suddenly, and the table immediately sprang or jerked up from the floor about one inch.
3. Without any movement of the hands the table jerked off the floor, sometimes at one side or corner, sometimes at another, according to request, the elevation varying from one to four inches.

The distance of the Circle from the table was now considerably increased, all standing about two feet from it, and without extending the hands towards it. The same phenomena were frequently repeated. Once the table jerked up on one side, making a considerable forward movement, and again it moved along the floor about two feet, rising at one end and causing some noise in its fall. After a time, the power appeared to fail, all approached the table, placing their hands in contact with it. Then on withdrawing all hands suddenly, the same movements were renewed.

During many of these phenomena, various members of the Committee volunteered took turns to keep watch below the table, whilst others standing round them carefully noted everything that took place; but no one could discover any visible agency in their production.

---

**THE END at long last, this book is hopefully finished, February 2007.**

## "THIS IS NOT THE END <u>FOR YOU</u>"
## "THIS IS ONLY THE BEGINNING"

It is only now <u>YOU</u> really start learning <u>YOUR</u> future craft of
## "MEDIUMSHIP"

**LOVE TO YOU ALL. TAKE CARE.**

**MAY YOUR UNSEEN HELPERS, AND YOUR GOD, THE DIVINE SPIRIT, BE WITH YOU ALWAYS** in the love and light of all that IS.

**MAY YOU LOVE, BE LOVED, AND BE LOOKED AFTER ALL THE REST OF YOUR DAYS, BRINGING HAPPINESS AND COMFORT TO OTHERS, AS YOU TRAVEL FORWARD ALONG THE PATHWAYS OF LIFE, LEAVING A HAPPY TRAIL BEHIND YOU.**

Remember **LOVE AND LAUGHTER CONQUER ALL**.

I send you Love and Light to pass on to everyone and everything throughout the world to make it a better place for the future.

## I will always think of you all learning from this book, and helping others with your new found wisdom.

I send to you all that you wish for me ten times over, I hope it comes with goodness kindness love and truth.

### Good night and God bless you all.

## There is only one truth.

### We do not die, life is everlasting.

**When we pass from this realm, we go to a higher vibration level of existence to join loved ones.**

## The genuine Mediums
### with their special gifts developed with the help of Spirit can prove it is so.

# THERE IS NOTHING HIGHER ANYWHERE ON THIS EARTH AND BEYOND, THAN;

## LOVE, TRUTH,
### and the
## DIVINE LIGHT OF SPIRIT, GOD

### Your job now begins to prove to others there is life after our so called death

With kind permission from the Harry Edwards Healing Trust I have put details and photographs from Harry Edwards Book now unfortunately out of print.
"The Mediumship of Arnold Clare"
I felt so strongly about the book's content, I felt that it would help others understand and all must be included here for you all in my hopefully informative book. I hope you understand the reasons why after reading Harry's Edwards book in its entirety.
The trust still sell all of other Harry Edwards books down at :-
**"The Harry Edwards Spiritual Healing Sanctuary"** and in **The Stansted Hall**, **Psychic News bookshop** and **Arthur Findlay College bookshop**, Essex, UK., and all good bookshops. Also on the internet sites in :-   ebay.co.uk and amazon.com   the World Wide bookshops

A lot of other books are available in the two above shops. Ones that I recommend are as follows :-

| | | |
|---|---|---|
| All the Books written | by | **Arthur Findlay**. |
| All the books written | by | **Harry Boddington** |
| All the Books written | by | **H. H. Dalai Lama** |
| All the Books written | by | **Emma Hardinge Britten** |
| All the Books written | by | **Harry Edwards** |
| **The Boy Who Saw True** through | by | **Cyril Scott**  A story about a young boy and the traumas he went because of seeing Spirit |
| **History of Spiritualism** | by | **Sir Arthur Conan Doyle**   (vol one & two) |
| **Modern American Spiritualism** | by | **Emma Hardinge Britten**   (vol one & two} |

**The Scole Experiment** by **Grant & Jane Solomon**
**Stephen Turoff Psychic Surgeon** by **Grant Solomon**
**Two Worlds of Helen Duncan** by **Gena Brealey with Kay Hunter** Autobiography of Helen Duncan
**My Living Has Not Been In Vain** by **Mary Armour** Autobiography of Helen Duncan.
**Unlock the Tarot** by **D.Roy.T. Keeghan** Teaches you how to use the tarot cards and explains how to run a lucrative business for life using any tarot card set, as well as the full 165 <u>very</u> <u>special</u> set of tarot cards with the book..
**Unlock your Healing Potential** by **D.Roy.T.Keeghan**
**Battling Bertha [Harris]** by **M Leonard**

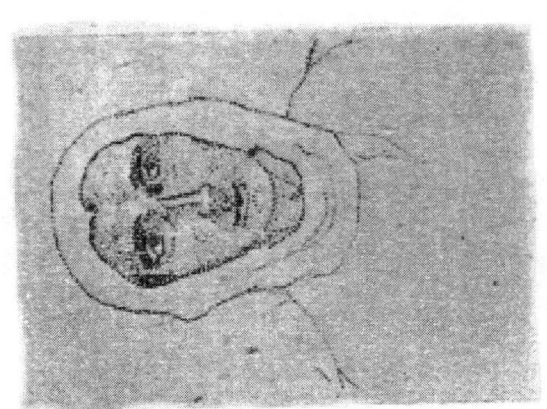

**Fig 1.**
Brother Paul, chief Guide to the medium, as drawn under unusual conditions described, by Tony Clare.

**Fig 2.**
A drawing in the dark by a spirit child control (Little Peter) during séance

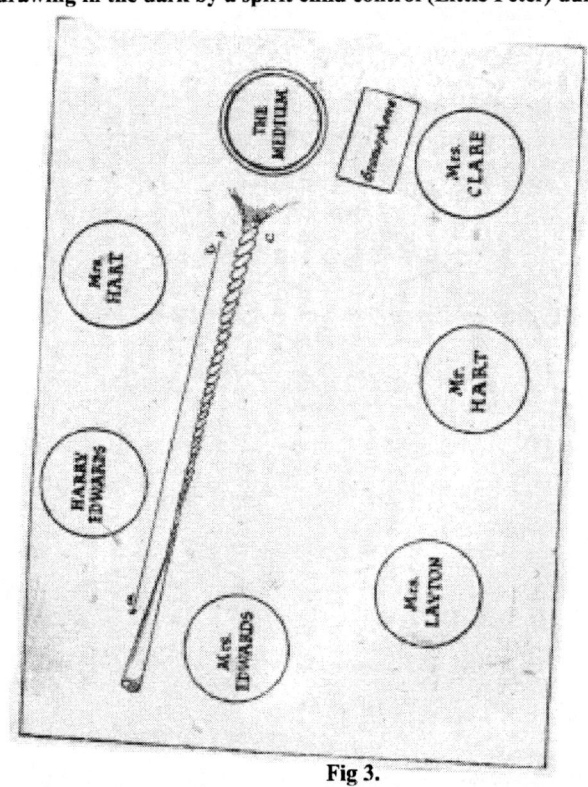

**Fig 3.**
Diagram showing the movement of the plaque between the phenomena and the sitters.
The Line a-b indicates the position of the moving plaque. The fulcrum is denoted at c.

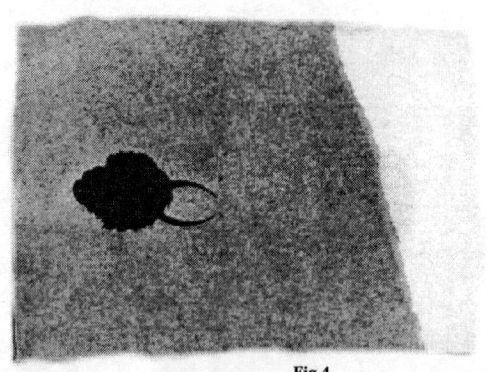

**Fig 4.**
An impression of the emergence of two claws from the island opaque mass in the centre of the almost transparent ectoplasmic material spread over the illuminated plaque.

**Fig 5.**
The two finger-like formations emerge.

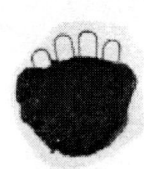

**Fig 6.**
Followed by the tips of four fingers.

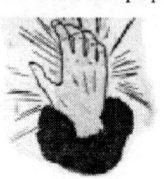

**Fig 7.**
Impression of the fully formed hand that moved to the edge of the plaque and tore it into two pieces.

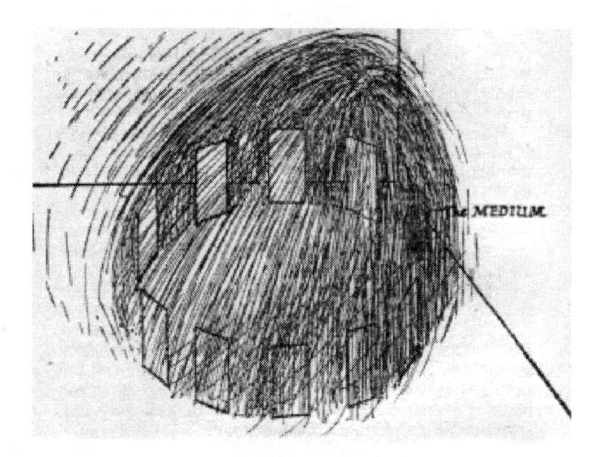

**Fig 8.**
An impression of the bowsing of the auric field; creation of conditions to permit phenomena action. The rectangles represents sitters.

Harry Edwards
the famous healer

PLATE 1
THE MEDIUM—ARNOLD CLARE

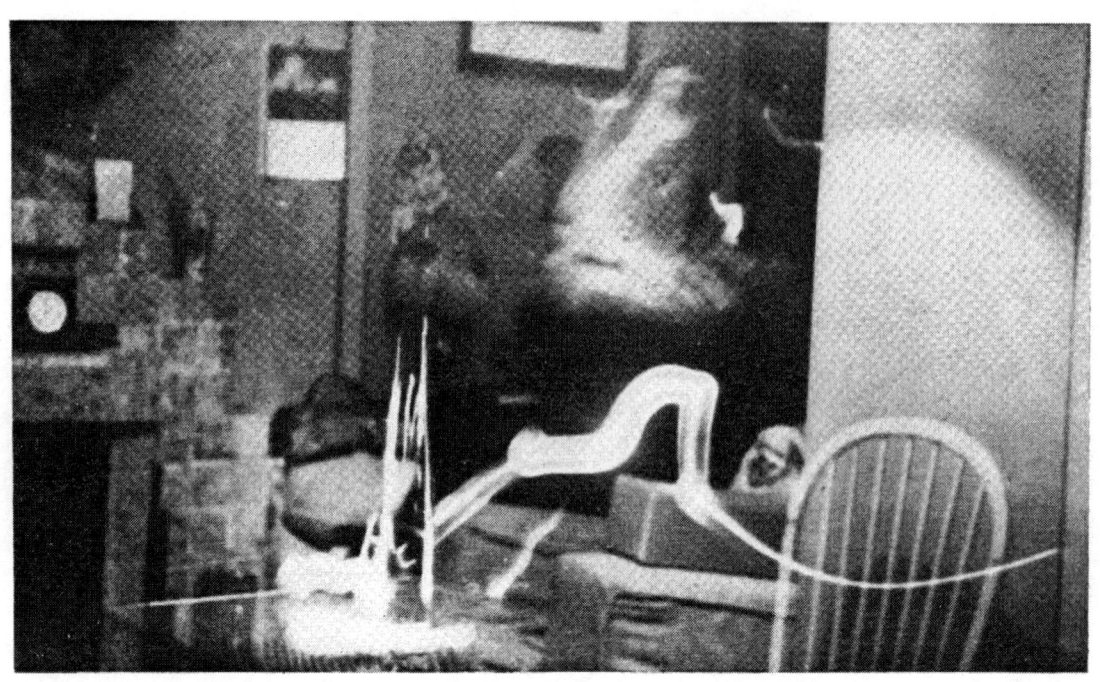

PLATE 2

The mechanism used for conducting "direct voice" to the trumpet. The conductor which conveys the etheric sound waves is housed in an insulation, which protects it from external etheric bombardment. (See Chaps. XV and XVII.)
*Photograph by Mr. R. F. Bounsall.*

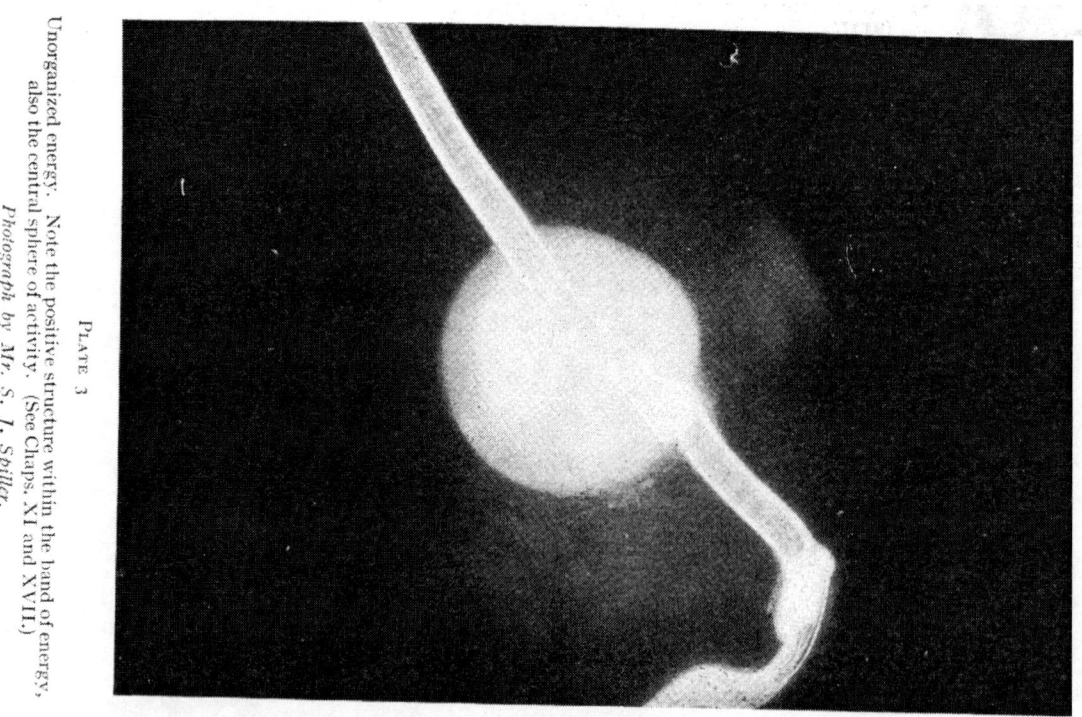

PLATE 3

Unorganized energy. Note the positive structure within the band of energy, also the central sphere of activity. (See Chaps. XI and XVII.)
*Photograph by Mr. S. J. Spiller.*

Please remember that some of these photographs are time lapsed, is it possible that the energy that is shown in some of the photographs is the Keelights or energy balls we are still getting on our photographs today

**Plate 4.**
**Unorganised energy similar to Plate 3. See chapters X1 and XV11)**
**Photography by Mr O MacKinnon Charles B.Sc.**

**Plate 5.**
**A 45 lb table levitated by manipulation of gravity and etheric forces. Note the absence of physically constructed ectoplasmic rods. (see Chapter X111)**
**Infra red photography by Leon Isaacs.**

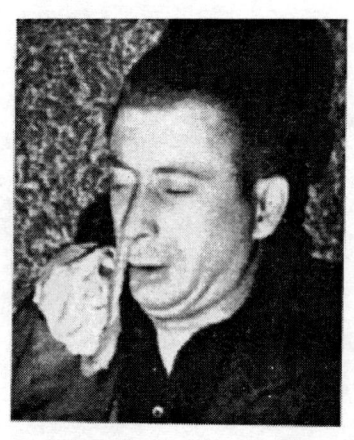

**Plate 7.**
Grade 1 crude ectoplasm emerging from nostril.
(See Chapter X11)
Infra red photography by Harry Edwards.

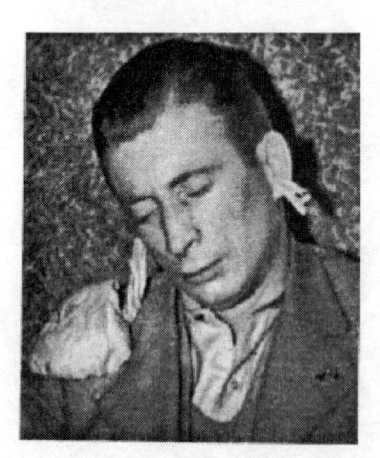

**Plate 8.**
Grade 1 Crude Ectoplasm emerging from both ears.
(See Chapter X11)
Infra red photography by Leon Isaacs.

**Plate 6.**
Lighter table levitated by similar process to table in plate 5. (See Chapter X111)
Infra red photograph by Leon Isaacs.

**Plate 9.**
**Grade 2. Ectoplasmic formation showing tendency of extremity
to organise. (See Chapter X11)
Infra red photograph by "Daily Mirror" staff photographer.**

Two, Grade 2, ectoplasmic formations, organised for voice and forceful levitation purposes.
The formations have considerably depreciated from their actual working condition to
withstand the stress of impure infra red rays used for the photographic exposure.
(See Chapters X11 and X111 .
Infra red photograph by Leon Isaacs.

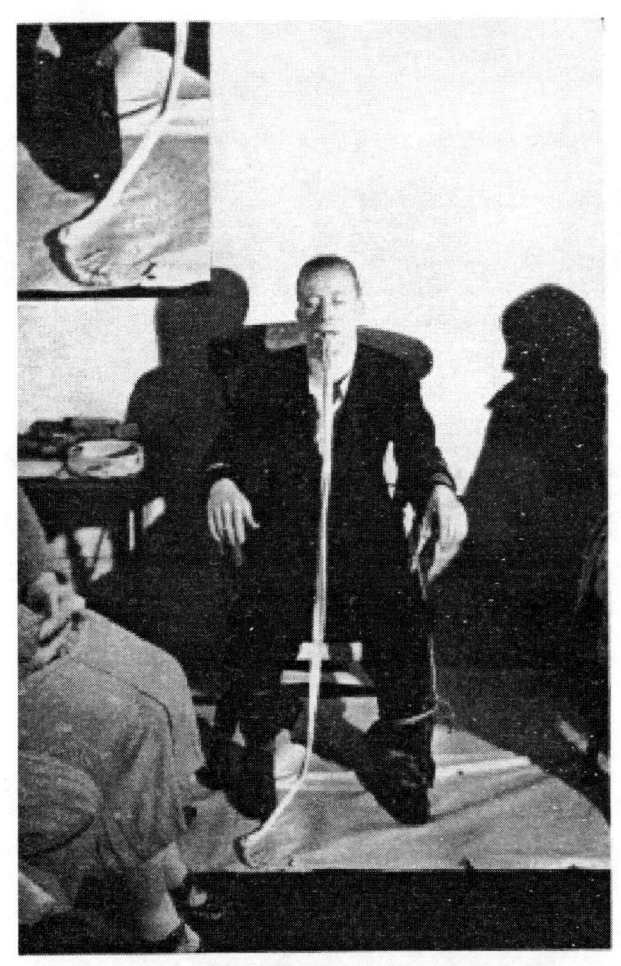

**Plate 11.**
Ectoplasmic formation of Grades 1 and 2.
This formation disperses within a fraction of time
following photographic exposure. (see Chapter X11)
Infra red Photograph by Harry Edwards.

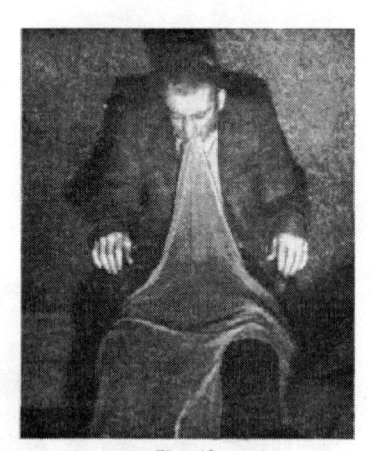

**Plate 12.**
Ectoplasm formation of Grades 1 and 2,
which also dispersed within a fraction of a second.
(See Chapter X11)
Infra red Photograph by Harry Edwards.

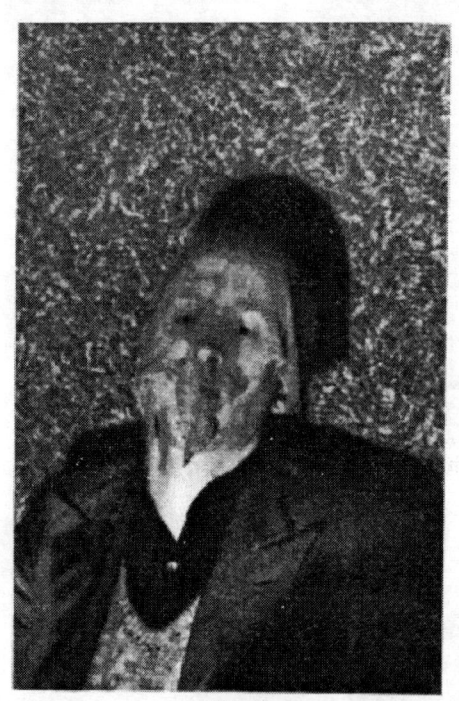

**Plate 13.**
Ectoplasm formation of Grades 1 and 2.
Photographed over the face of the entranced medium in red light.
Infra red Photograph by Harry Edwards.

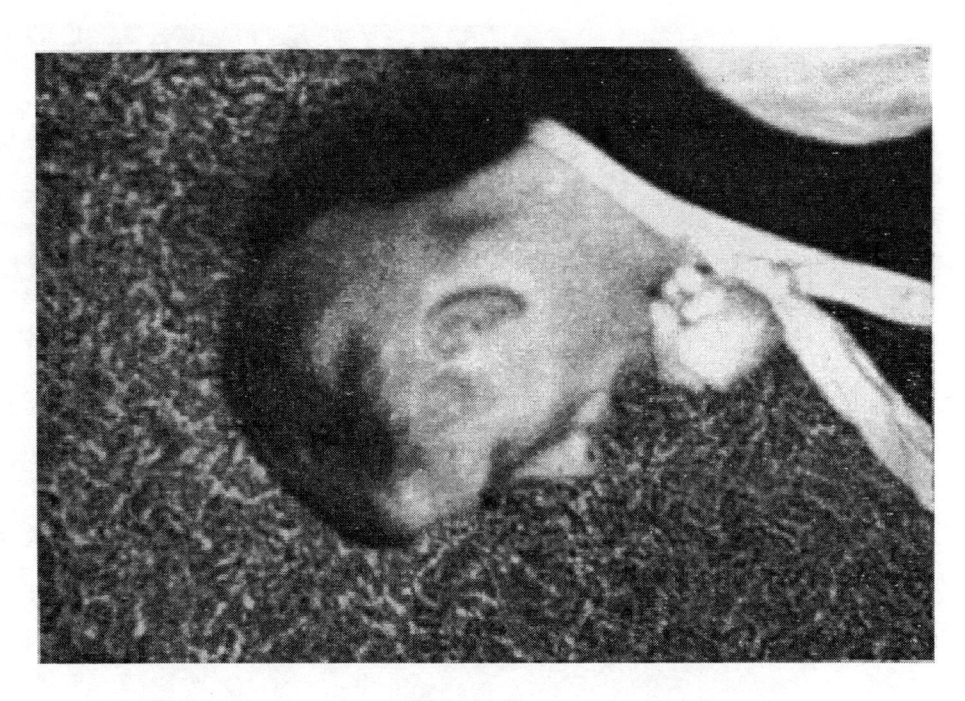

**Plate 14.**
**Ectoplasm formation of Grades 2, Previously described as a "voice box"
with cable leading to trumpet. (see Chapter XV)
Infra red Photograph by J McCullock.**

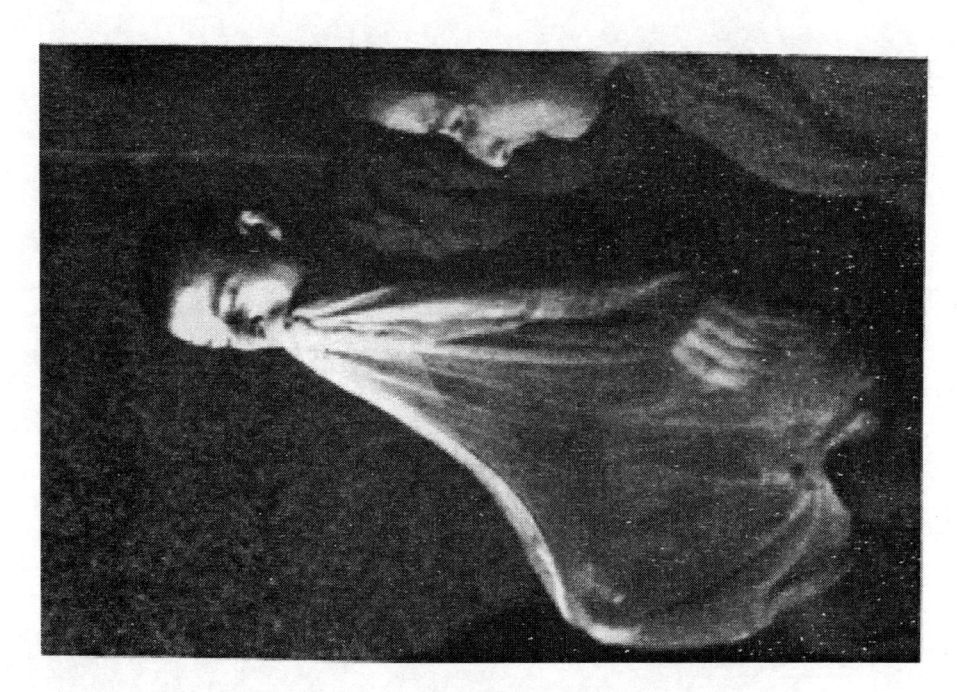

**Plate 15.
Ectoplasmic material Grade 2. (see Chapter X11)
Infra red Photograph by J McCullock.**

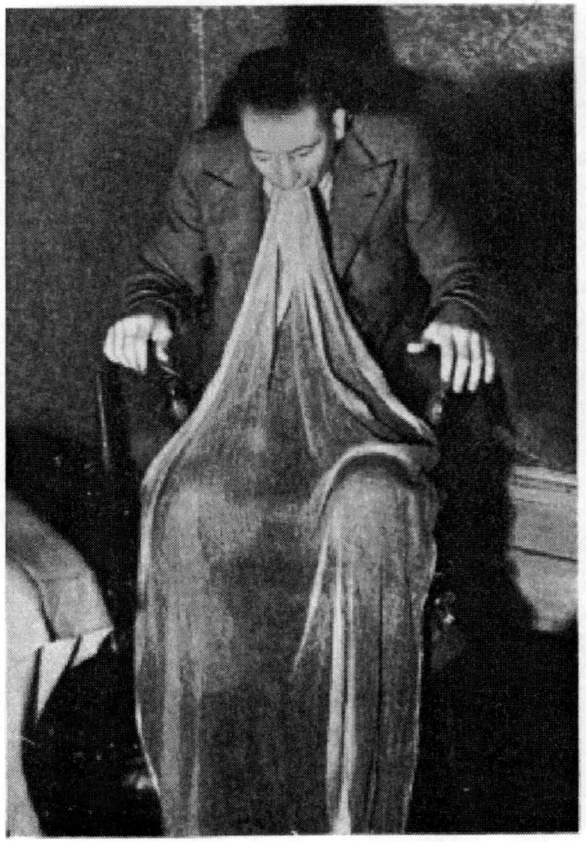

**Plate 16.**
Considerable volume of grade 2 ectoplasmic material. This disperses in a fraction of time. (See Chapter XII) Infra red photography by JmcCullock.

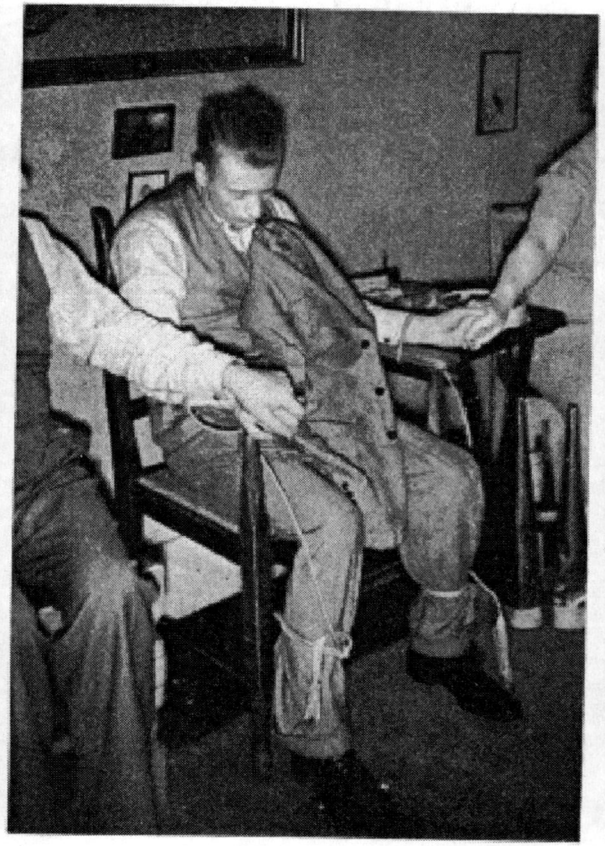

**Plate 17.**
The medium is roped to the chair. His hands are held by two sitters. His coat, previously stitched up from lapel to skirt is drawn through the medium's body, illustration the process of dematerialisation and the passage of matter through matter. (See Chapter XIV) infra red photography by Harry Edwards.

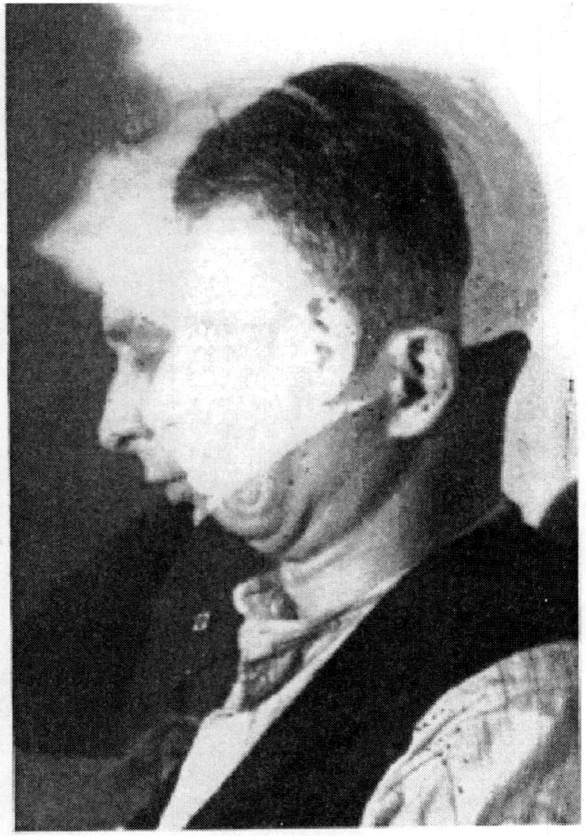

**Plate 18.**
This photograph shows the manner of dematrialisation. The coat is shown in semi-density. The face of the medium's soul body has been recorded with the inner face strongly transfigured by the Guide. Note the harmony in the partial densities of both heads and coat. Full density is where two heads merge. The different alignment between the eyes, nose, mouth and the ear and read of the head indicates that rotary movement is necessary to bring both heads into alignment; indicating that both heads are three dimensional.
Infra red photography by W Clayton.

SEPTEMBER 1998

**BOOKS OBTAINABLE FROM**
**THE HARRY EDWARDS SPIRITUAL HEALING SANCTUARY TRUST**
**BURROWS LEA : SHERE : GUILDFORD : SURREY GU5 9QG**

---

### THE POWER OF SPIRITUAL HEALING — by HARRY EDWARDS

This commanding book has been widely acclaimed as one of the finest works on spiritual healing ever published. Harry Edwards presents his subject in plain speaking terms, emphasizing his points with case histories drawn from his unparalleled healing experience.

Illustrated £12 post paid.

### SPIRIT HEALING — by HARRY EDWARDS

The whole panorama of spiritual healing from its theory to its practice, answering all those inevitable questions which arise in the lay mind. Should convince the most sceptical enquirers.

Illustrated £12 post paid.

### THE HEALING INTELLIGENCE — by HARRY EDWARDS

Spiritual healing is not mysterious, but it is often thought to be so. It is, in fact, a spiritual 'science' and this book explains how the healing processes operate and how one can more closely co-operate with the healing purpose by employing the various bodily systems we possess.

Illustrated £9.50 post paid

### A GUIDE TO THE UNDERSTANDING AND PRACTICE OF SPIRITUAL HEALING — by HARRY EDWARDS

A guide in every sense of the word, every page being of inestimable value to the healer who is just beginning to develop his or her healing gift; and as it embraces concepts of advanced healing knowledge acquired from Spirit, so the experienced healer will also find it a book of tremendous scope which he or she will want to refer to again and again.

Illustrated £12 post paid

### LIFE IN SPIRIT — by HARRY EDWARDS

Just what is life like in the Beyond? A unique and absorbing adventure into the realm of Spirit, sensitively envisaged by Harry Edwards. Truly wonderful reading.

Illustrated £12 post paid

### THE MEDIUMSHIP OF JACK WEBBER — by HARRY EDWARDS

An eye witness account of one of the most remarkable mediumships of our time, presenting unshakable evidence of the reality of the Spirit world. Contains 36 full page photographs unique in psychic history, testifying to the thoroughness of Harry Edwards' investigations.

Illustrated £8.50 post paid

### HARRY EDWARDS — by RAMUS BRANCH

The lively fascinating story of the greatest healer of our time, told by his close associate in the healing work at Shere. From his family background and rumbustious childhood, the story is traced through his working life as a printer into which he blended a stormy political career which, in itself, was to prove the forerunner of the glorious life of healing service he was to render humanity.

Illustrated £12 post paid

| | |
|---|---|
| Absent Healing | 95 |
| A Few Thoughts to Ponder | 208 |
| Apportation, Asporting | 351 |
| Astral Travel, | 141 |
| Auras | 112 |
| Automatic Writing | 335 |
| Awareness | 109 |
| Birth of the Soul | 427 |
| Birthstones | 116 |
| Cabinet | 260 |
| Card Reading | 125 |
| Chakra, Power Points | 52 |
| Circles | 55, 60, 164, 258, 262, 320, 414 |
| Clairaudience, Clear Hearing | 27, 31, 398 |
| Clairdelusion Clear Delusion | 27, 34 |
| Clairgouterience, Clear Tasting | 27, 33, 398 |
| Clairsensatience, Clear Feeling | 27, 32, 398 |
| Clairsavoirience, Clear Knowing | 27, 32, 398 |
| Clairsentience, Clear Sensing | 27, 32, 398 |
| Clairsentirience, Clear Smelling | 27, 32, 398 |
| Clairvoyance, Clear Seeing | 27, 30, 398 |
| Cloud Reading, Culumlography | 127 |
| Coffee Grounds [reading of] | 125 |
| Colours | 110, 115 |
| Communigraph | 357 |
| Conclusion | 226 |
| Crystal Ball Gazing, Crystallomancy | 108 |
| Days Aside and Practice for Self | 172 |
| Dedicated Development | 172 |
| Demonstrating your skills | 176 |
| Development Circle | 61, 165 |
| Development of Physical Phenomena | 298 |
| Direct & Independent Direct Voice | 286 |
| Discussion on plates and fig | 423 |
| Divining, Dowsing Rod/Sticks | 118 |
| Ectoplasm | 261, 267 |
| Exorcism | 186 |
| Extra Sensory Perception, ESP | 77 |
| Electronic Voice Production, EVP | 189 |
| Etheric Realm (the) | 415 |
| Eye Positions when Meditating | 255 |
| Fire Flame Reading, Flamography | 127 |
| Froth [reading of] | 125 |
| Functions of Guides & Controls (the) | 364 |
| Gemstones (colours of) | 116 |
| Guides, Controls, Doorkeepers | 175, 363 |
| Healing | 91 |
| Healing Circle | 96 |
| Healing exercises with sound | 101 |
| Haunting | 187 |
| How do I meditate? | 39 |
| Hypnotism | 150 |
| Imagery Clairvoyance | 110 |
| Inspired Trance Speaking | 305, 384 |
| Inspirational Writing | 335 |
| Investigate Spiritual Phenomena 1871, | 400 |
| Keelights | 132 |
| Levitations, Transvections, | 278, 281, 433 |
| Life after Life | 369, 415 |
| Links [of spirit] | 29, 94, 175, 235 |
| London Dialectic Society 1870 | 433 |
| Magnetism | 160, 163, 164 |
| Materialisation | 356, 357 |
| Mechanics of Voice Production | 291 |
| Mechanical Spelling Out Machines | 346 |
| Meanings of Gems & Precious Stones | 116 |
| Meditation | 10, 23, 26, 34, 39, 46, 152, 432. |
| Mediumistic Inspiration, | 69 |
| Mediums, Mediumship | 41, 152 |
| Mesmerism | 150 |
| Mindfulness, | 38 |
| Mirror Scrying, Psychomantium | 107 |
| Misinformed (beware of) | 202 |
| Music, Sounds and Brainwaves | 49 |
| Observations, Restrictions of Mediums | 405, |
| Ouija Board, Spelling Out Board | 345 |
| Our Help Circles, R'help Circles | 182 |
| Out of Body Experiences, OBE | 141 |
| Overshadowing | 73 |
| Part Two | 227 |
| Pendulum Dowsing | 119 |
| Physical Circle | 164, 310 |
| Physical Mediumship | 208, 306, 402 |
| Physical Phenomena | 261, 297 |
| Physical Phenomena with Energy | 333 |
| Poltergeists | 186 |
| Precognition | 74 |
| Psychic Art | 166, 340 |
| Psychic Awareness | 79 |
| Psychic Surgery | 105 |
| Psychokinesis, PK | 278 |
| Psychometry | 78 |
| Reflectograph | 357 |
| Rescue Circles | 182 |
| Rules & Conditions for Spirit Circle 1869 | 400 |
| Running a Course | 371 |
| Sand Reading, Geomancy | 127 |
| Séances | 193, 196, 201, 288, 291, 409, |
| Seers | 75 |
| Self Healing | 97 |
| Self Hypnosis | 153 |
| Sensitivity | 109 |
| Shamanic Trance | 20 |
| Slate Writing, Psychography | 334 |
| Spirit Children Circles | 362 |
| Spirit Drawing and Spirit Art | 343 |
| Spirit Lights | 132 |
| Spirit Photography | 128, 233 |
| Spiritualism | 180 |
| Spirit Writing | 335, 340 |
| Stress Reduction | 14 |
| Strong Warning to all | 321 |
| Suggestions for a Safe Circle | 56 |
| Symbolism | 71 |
| Table Tilting, Typtology | 350, 433 |
| Tarot | 479 |
| Tea Leaves [reading of] Tasseography | 125 |
| Teaching Children about Spirit | 168 |
| Telepathy | 78 |
| Test data on Mediums | 328 |
| Trance | 228, 239, 241, 351 |
| Trance Development Circle | 251, 254 |
| Trance Healing | 102 |
| Trances Speaking | 384 |
| Transfiguration | 256, 383 |
| Transition | 449 |
| Tutoring Mental Mediumship | 386 |
| Unwanted links | 187 |
| White Brotherhood (the) | 368 |

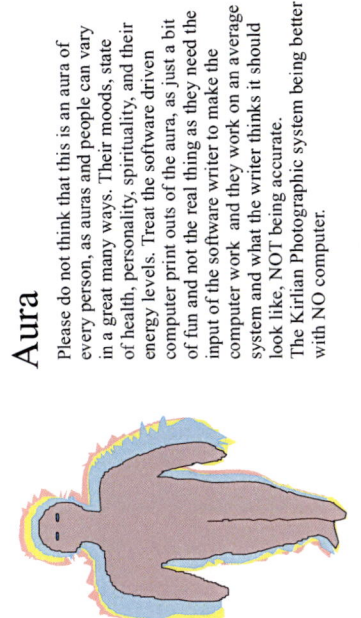

# KEEWAYS MEDITATION ONENESS written by Roy Keeghan

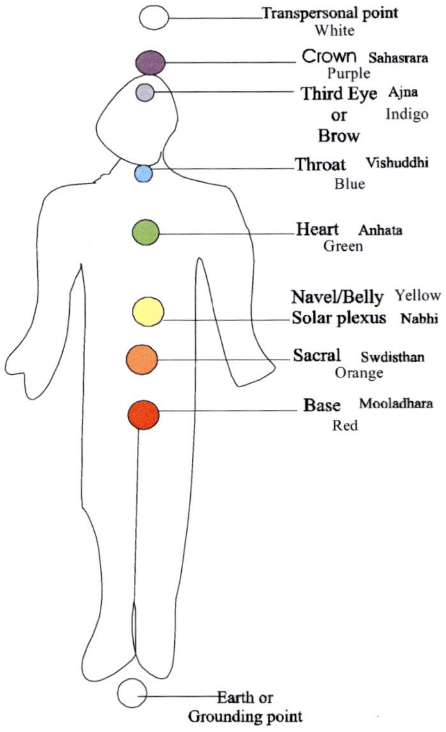

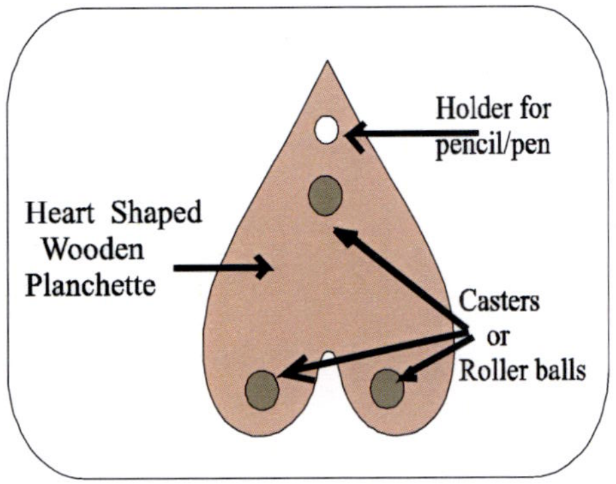

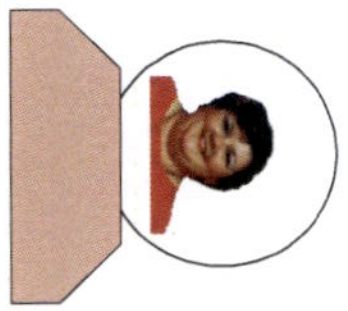

## Crystal ball made from rock crystal glass or resin

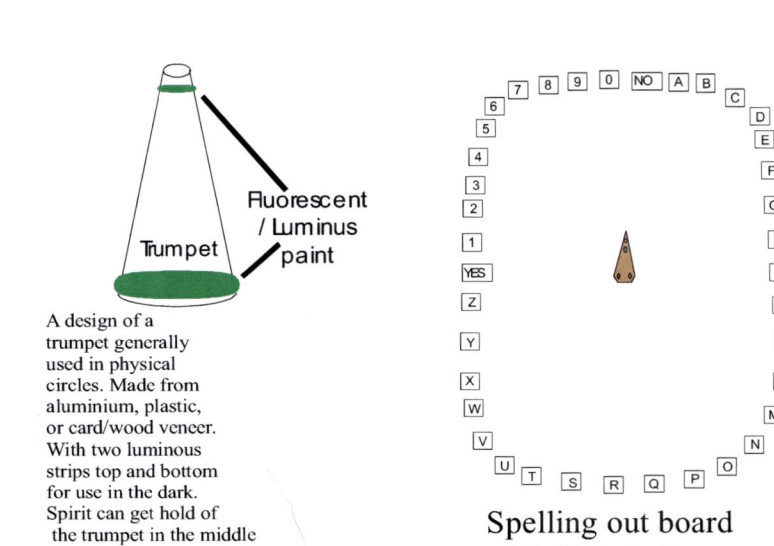

## Spelling out board with Planchette
Can use pieces of paper on a shiny surface (table)

## Heart Shaped Wooden Planchette
- Holder for pencil/pen
- Casters or Roller balls

## Trumpet
- Fluorescent / Luminus paint

A design of a trumpet generally used in physical circles. Made from aluminium, plastic, or card/wood veneer. With two luminous strips top and bottom for use in the dark. Spirit can get hold of the trumpet in the middle.

## Aura

Please do not think that this is an aura of every person, as auras and people can vary in a great many ways. Their moods, state of health, personality, spirituality, and their energy levels. Treat the software driven computer print outs of the aura, as just a bit of fun and not the real thing as they need the input of the software writer to make the computer work and they work on an average system and what the writer thinks it should look like, NOT being accurate.
The Kirlian Photographic system being better with NO computer.

## Chakra power points

- Transpersonal point — White
- Crown Sahasrara — Purple
- Third Eye Ajna or Brow — Indigo
- Throat Vishuddhi — Blue
- Heart Anhata — Green
- Navel/Belly Solar plexus Nabhi — Yellow
- Sacral Swdisthan — Orange
- Base Mooladhara — Red
- Earth or Grounding point

## CHAKRA Or power points

Chakra comes from a word in Sanskrit, it mean wheel. There are said to be over 88,000 different points on the human body. But the main ones are shown in the drawing. The vibrational colours of the main power points/chakra are generally represented by the ones as shown. Lots of other names are given to them as well. In some books they are given slightly differently, BUT they are in these approximate positions and these main colours. Please remember these points are of interest to some. But it should be pointed out these are only a recent addition to the world of spiritualist from the eastern practices. Chakras were not even heard of in the 1950's by most of the population of spiritualist. They only became fashionable with the event of the Hippy travellers going to the far east and exploring the different cultures of the large Asian continent.

With the help of spirit when I linked and asked. Some of the drawings I did using a 4b lead pencil. Drawings were all originally on an A4 size page. Colour photographs are nearly the same size.

John Thaw an actor, who I copied from a Magazine

A drawing from a magazine

Jean, who was once my beautiful lady friend.

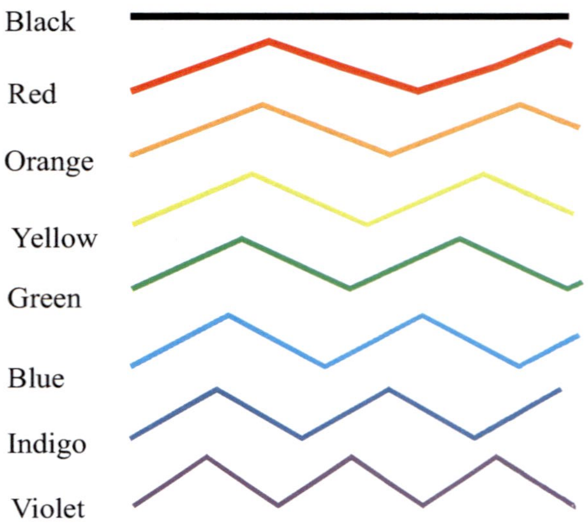

Another design of a dowsing implement made of a coat hanger wire I saw being used by a dowser. The tension is put on the outer points and the wire twists one way for Yes the other way for No.

The Dowsing implements. The two wires with sleeves. The forked stick and some of the many the pendulums. Here also is the diagram drawn for your use when you start practicing

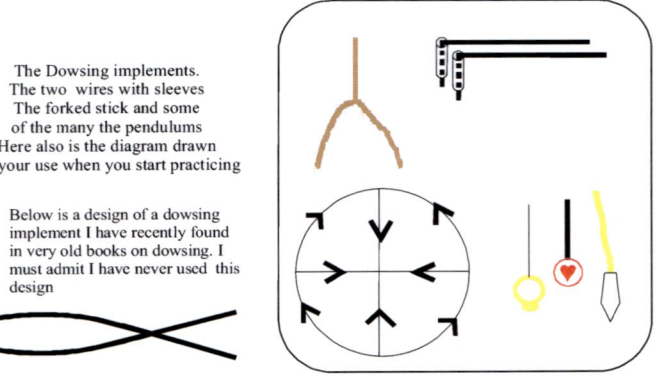

Below is a design of a dowsing implement I have recently found in very old books on dowsing. I must admit I have never used this design

## Vibrational Wavelengths of Colour  NOT EXACT

Black
Red
Orange
Yellow
Green
Blue
Indigo
Violet

As a guide the wavelength of red is approximately twice that of violet.

Red, green and blue are classed as primary colours because if these three colours are mixed together in equal portions they make white light

Examples of drawings to explore a persons psyche to use in a practice reading

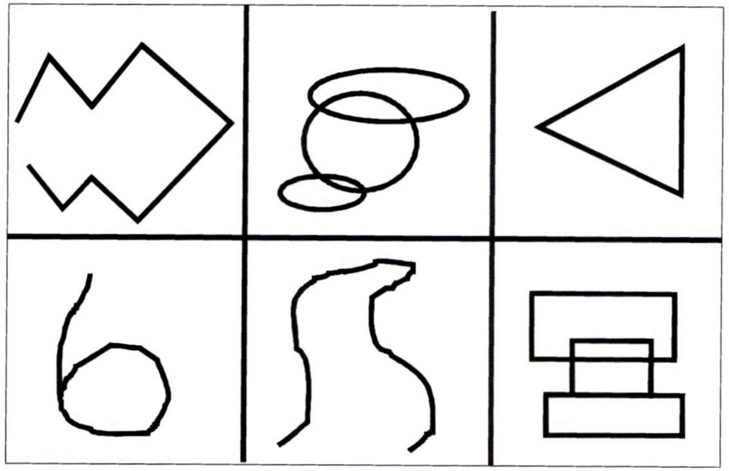

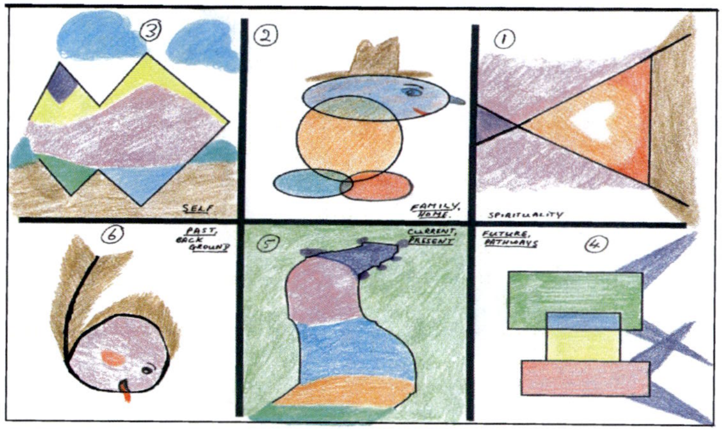

| Top row | Self | Family/Home | Spirituality |
|---|---|---|---|
| Bottom row | Past/Background | Current/Present | Future/Pathways |

See explanations in text on subject

## PSYCHOMANTIUM

Single Mirror

Two Mirrors

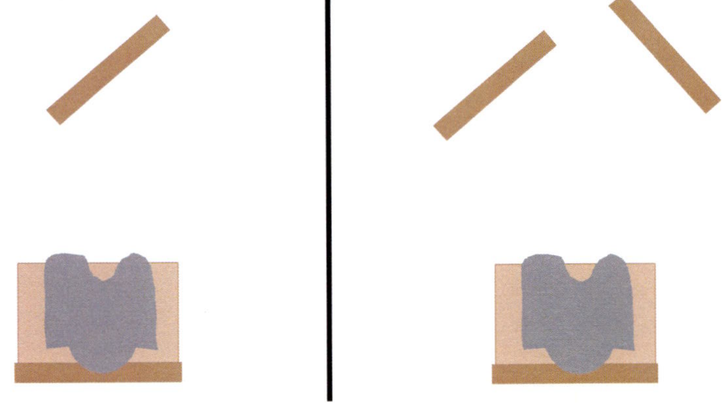

Best Seating Positions are where you cannot see your own reflection
The size of the mirror is not important

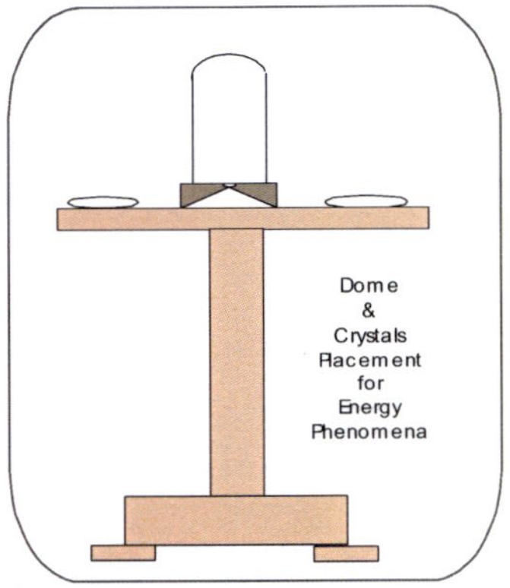

## COMMUNIGRAPH

Dome & Crystals Placement for Energy Phenomena

Clear Quartz crystal points for healing placed at four compass points N, S, E, W, pointing inward the clear quartz clusters for dedication are placed anywhere on the table.

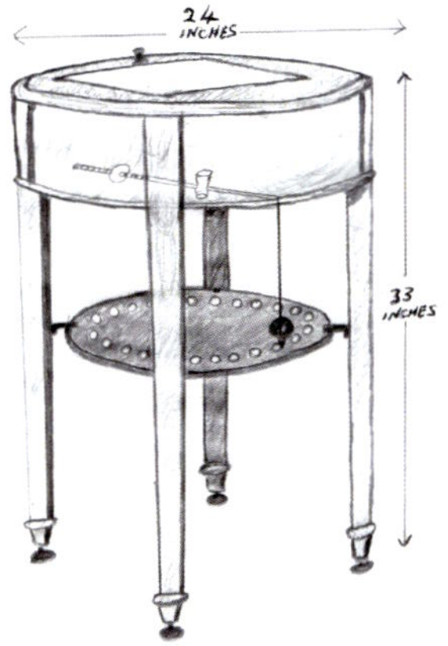

# Some Portable Cabinet Designs

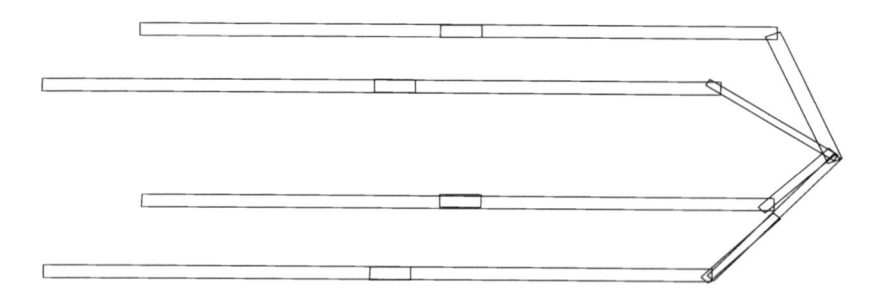

Here are two metal structures, when covered in black cloth, could be used as cabinets. Both are used in the camping and caravan industries as toilet or storage tents. The most important thing is to cover the metal in fabric as there could be a possibility of ectoplasm being produced. Ectoplasm and metal do not mix around humans. As it is could be possible that psychic burns of the Medium could occur. Both of these designs fold neatly into bags for carrying and storage. Could be made from wood which would be far better.

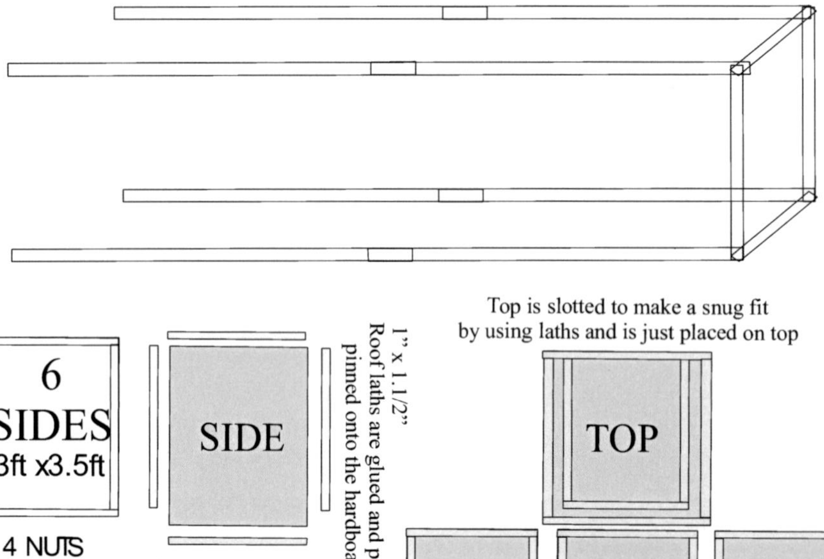

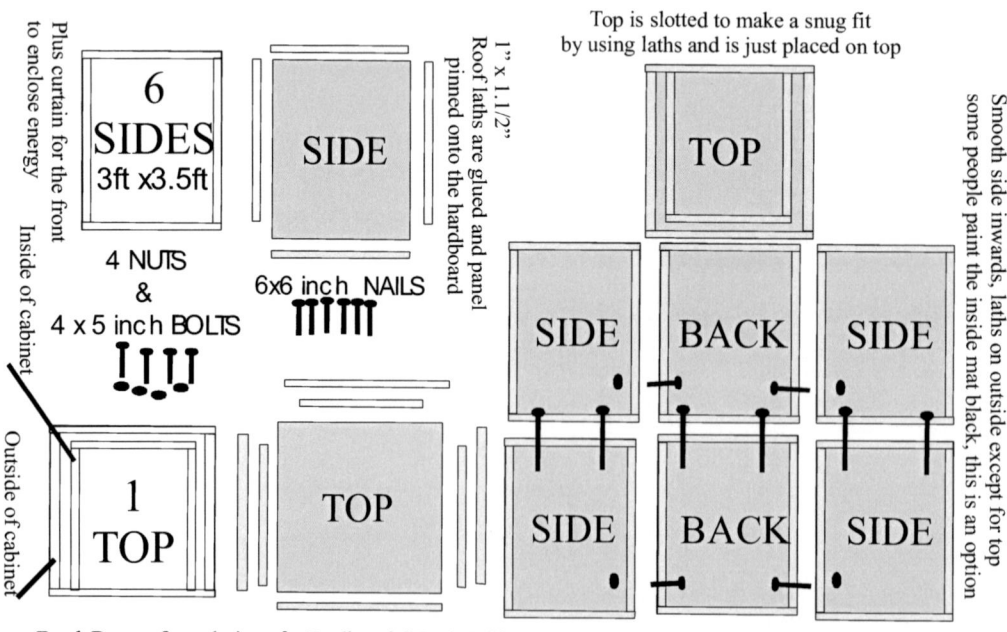

Break Down of one design of a Hardboard & Lath Cabinet, another could be three sides and a top with the curtain in front. Mediums in the early days used to sit in the corner of the room behind a curtain that was pinned to the wall and supported by a pole placed across the corner. The reason for a small enclosed space is to enable the Spirit World to concentrated their energy and build up in harmony with the Medium's physical and psychic energy in a small confined area which is so necessary in the early build up of the combined energy to form ectoplasm through the Medium for physical phenomena to occur. Many times forming a Spirit human form to prove there is life after our so called death. YES, life exist across the veil.

## TAROT

After a lot of people asking for the information of the Tarot and how it relates to the linking with the higher vibration level I have now included a small snippet. The reason it is only a little, as you can see I have written a full book about the subject.

The Tarot in picture form was used in the first instance because people could not read the written word, so the pictures and symbols on the cards/tablets were used as an interpretation of the person's destiny. Over the years readers found that they were becoming more accurate in their reading if time was put aside to quietly relax beforehand; then later on they must have with the eyes closed talk within their mind to their inner self before any reading given, and then as they progressed, they talked to the higher levels, then as things became more accurate still they must have thought I will ask for help from my Gods.

To this day, most professional Tarot card readers who are accurate put time aside to talk to the Spirit World and ask for help before any reading and then meditate for a short while; 15 minutes to half an hour.

Please remember that the reading of the Tarot itself is not evil it is the people who have evil intent within their hearts that are. The giving of any information should be to help and uplift any person and not to bring them down lower in their moments of despair.

The using of the Tarot is only another tool in any person's development. It should be reminded that the cards are only **prompts** for the beginnings of Mental Mediumship. BUT on saying that, there are many good and accurate Mediums who like to use the Tarot cards to help their enquirers They feel comfortable as do their enquirers, when the spread of Tarot cards is laid out in front of them, and many go on using the cards throughout their lives, as it gives them extra income to survive.

## CONCLUSION

I have given you all in this book, and the other parts in other sections [part two etc] the best ways I have found to link with Spirit, those in a nut shell are as follows :-
Within meditation, and time put aside, you develop with those in the Spirit World.
When starting with the exercises for your awareness or guided meditation (it should be called guided contemplation) where the mind is used (and you are thinking about the story) to put images away from the outside unseeing imagery (eyes closed), into the third eye region of the brain. These images are at the start mainly you, the developing Medium. Yourself producing the images from your own brain out of your imagination, the equation being, 90% plus, and 10% coming from the linking with Spirit. This is why it is vital, so imperative, after asking Spirit to come near and help over and over again and again, at separate set times put aside to try and look into the light, the colour, or void within the mind at the third eye area. As the link gets stronger the Medium learns to slow down the thoughts going in and out of the brain, by becoming part of that colour, void, or light, being as one with it, the link becomes better, 40% self and 60% from Spirit help. As you progress the link gets far stronger **if,** the discipline of focused attention (meditation) has been applied. The aim is for at the most 10% of self or lower, and 90% plus information from the Spirit World. The aim by all should be 100% information from the Spirit World.
In your mind with the power of thought, (or if you prefer, out loud), you have to **ask** Spirit **then encourage**; **ask** Spirit **then encourage**, then try to **still your mind for a time** to give full access to Spirit; **ask** Spirit **then encourage**; **ask** Spirit **then encourage,** then try to **still your mind for a time** to give full access to Spirit. So you as a Medium can prove to others there is life after our so-called death. That should be your aim, your only aim, so you can help others who are finding it hard to come to terms with the loss of a loved one, to help the bereaved.
Every discipline written about in this book has to have the developing Medium **SINCERELY encouraging** through thought the Spirit World to come closer and link with them. Then for the Budding Medium to try and still the mind so those in the Spirit World can have an uncluttered access to the

complex workings of the brain connections. This for me is the only way to gain a stronger link with those angelic helper in the World of Spirit.

It is the easiest thing in the world to link with Spirit, the hardest thing is trying to quieten, to slow down incoming and out going thoughts. Find your own way to still the mind so Sprit can develop you the Budding Medium. The only way I have found that is suitable for me is to look into the Divine Light [or a colour or the void, which of course is all part of light] within the third eye region and become part of it, as one with the Divine Light of Spirit.

The Medium talks to the participant in the church when they make contact with their loved one they are said to work on the vibration of the reply and the voice of the person perhaps the thought. People talk to Spirit when they talk to the planchette encouraging Spirit, people talk to Spirit and encourage them to come and make contact with them when using the Reflectograph, and the Communigraph, people trying to make contact with Spirit on a spelling out board talk and encourage Spirit to spell out their message People for centuries have been talking to Spirit when using the table, to make it move with the help of Spirit.

**WHY should any other link with Spirit be any different?**

**WE ALL SHOULD USE OUR VOICE OR YOUR THOUGHTS to attract Spirit.**
**Thoughts are living energy !!!!! Look in the dowsing section and prove it to yourself and others.**

People in a Physical Circle sing to bring up the happy joyful vibrations to attract Spirit. So try it yourself. Each person has to be open to Spirit and **trust fully** in those Guardian Angels in Spirit, entrusting them with each individual's development.

Each person, if in a group development, has to be <u>**sincere in their thoughts**</u> **that are sent out to Spirit**, and to blend in loving harmony with all of those there within that group, and most of all aiming to be in peaceful loving harmony as well with those in Spirit, after asking for their development of a gift from Spirit, then enter into meditation with a quietest mind possible letting those in Spirit have full access, to use your mind for the purpose they know will help you prove to others there is life after death, each person individually giving permission to Spirit to be used as an open vessel. The Medium has to be subservient to Spirit especially in Trance and Physical work with the World of Spirit.

Each person should try all the mediumistic developments in this book so Spirit can guide the Budding Medium towards the mediumistic discipline they have been chosen to use by Spirit.

Each person **who genuinely and unselfishly sits <u>for another</u>** person to develop in a Trance Circle, blends faster with Spirit in their own development no matter what, but has to sit for themselves as well (at a different time). This is because **it is the act of unselfish <u>GIVING</u>** of each individual's own power to the Trance Medium, whilst **not asking** for development of themselves. What you give out **without asking for anything in return**, comes back to you ten fold.

**When you sit in a Trance or Physical Circle, the phenomena happens earlier if everyone holds the hands of the person next to them, touches their skin (finger to finger as on a table), holding hand to wrist, in other words "completes a complete linked Circle".**

**It is best to start in red light, having the cabinet to be use as a darkened room/space/area.**

Each person has to be happy in themselves, about themselves; **NO <u>negativity.</u> NONE** <u>what so ever</u>.
Each person has to know how to love themselves, so they can know how to love others.
**If you do not love or like yourself, how can anyone else? Cut out any negativity or nastiness within.**

Each person has to put their time and effort aside for the Angels, with sincerity to ask within their own thoughts to blend with Spirit bringing, <u>**happiness**</u>, <u>**goodness**</u>, <u>**kindness**</u>, <u>**love**</u>, and <u>**truth**</u> in the <u>**peaceful loving Divine Light**</u> within the <u>**peaceful loving harmony of Spirit from the highest realms.**</u>

Know in <u>**all sincerity**</u> the link with Spirit can and will happen. <u>**Be positive**</u> **with yourself.**

To gain the link with Spirit above all else it must be to help others, before yourself. To prove there is life after our so-called death, this is for the benefit of others on each side of the veil. Man on the earth plane and those in Spirit on the higher vibrational plane.

It is imperative that time is put aside, each day if possible, to sit in the "Power of Meditation Oneness" to become as one with those in the Light of Spirit. Even if it is only half an hour or less. It is the only way to draw close to those Guardian Angels in Spirit. Meditate, meditate, meditate, meditate. Practice, practice, practice, practice, **Practice makes perfect.** Then you will gain that special link with Spirit. This should never be forgotten even when you think you are developed. **You are never ever fully developed so KEEP ON MEDITATING.**

To gain a stronger and earlier link with those Angels in the Spirit World, it is necessary to sit in Circles with others, **BUT it is not essential**. I still sit on my own and have got on very quickly, but remember I have attended a lot of courses in the Arthur Findlay College [Stansted] where there is a lot of power within it's walls. This is so Spirit could hone within me any bits needed with that extra power. I am now having sitters wanting to sit with me so Spirit seems to have guided them to me when necessary for their work with me.

Music, singing and happiness raise the vibrations to help those Angels in Spirit to come closer with their link for us.

The reason time is needed for the development of mediumship is; Spirit needs that time to help the physical body change. Changes the same way that a radio and TV engineer needs time to connect different wire connections to bring into the receiver more channels for the person who is listening or watching the broadcast on the extra channels from the new linkage. So it is with the Medium and the Spirit channels. The Medium's brain linkage needs new extra connections making (or helped to develop in the Medium's brain) by the specialists in the World of Spirit, so the Medium can receive the thought messages sent by those in the Spirit World in word (hearing) or picture (seeing) form. If the person when little had the gift of Mediumship, and it was not kept up on a regular basis; the linkage, the connections die within the brain of the youngster. If that gift was needed in later life then the person has to put time in with spiritual meditation to regain and again grow those new precious linkages within their brain needed to receive those thought links for clairvoyance, clairaudience, clairsentience, clairknowing, etc., from the World of Spirit. Then after their development, it is imperative for the Medium with those gifts to regularly sit so Spirit can maintain those links in good working order and to see that they do not get broken, like any linkage in a radio or TV set might break when they are being misused or if not used for a period of time, rot or disintegrate. Please remember all the cells in the human body and our brain cells die and renew themselves when used regularly this is done with help of the inbuilt natural function of the human body on a regular basis, so it makes sense that the meditation needed for the work of Spirit is needed regularly for Spirit to maintain a good standard of our Mediumship thought linkage, if this is not done, then the body will revert back to the natural, normal brain linkage that it was programmed to do at the start of life, so losing the linkage that was so necessary to link with those in Spirit.

If the person wishes to progress further along in the field of Mediumship and sits for physical Mediumship then it gets a little bit more complicated for the World of Spirit as specialists in the field of chemicals as well as specialists for making special connections to produce those functions necessary to change the chemicals in the body come into play.

The human body has been programmed at conception, it grows within the womb for nine months to birth, and then as the human body grows to only function for just ordinary every day life on this earth plane. When the ordinary person wishes to become a Medium, it is then by meditation, Spirit can help alter and adjust the functions of the human body to produce the chemicals when needed for Physical Phenomena. This adjustment for the safety of the Medium and their physical bodily makeup, might take many, many years.

When sitting in a séance for Physical Phenomena when the Medium has been developed, it will also be noticed that the functions necessary to take place take a little while to be brought into play and do not immediately happen. The functions necessary if they were there all the time in the Medium's body in the everyday life could do untold damage to the human body as a different mixture of chemicals are needed in this case. Some chemicals are brought from the chemists in the World of Spirit and others are from the Medium and the sitters. So it should now be obvious that this would not be correct for the everyday working functioning of the Medium's body.

Also it now has been found through experimentation with Mediums, testing of them in a Trance State, that the World of Spirit needs to alter the flow of blood for some reason to produce Physical Phenomena, which is not fitted normally in the everyday use within the Medium's body. Spirit increases the blood flow, a high pressure, so the vascular system has to be made safe by Spirit for the Medium if they are going to produce Physical Phenomena for the world to see, making the blood flow correctly for their purpose, and afterwards return it quickly and safely to normal so as not to damage the human body must be a feat in itself. It must be realised that all of the brain is very sensitive and the blood vessels are very small and there are very many which need to be adjusted and strengthened to accommodate the altered blood pressure that is needed in this form of mediumship. This is the reason for headaches in some budding Mediums when they start from scratch; it is nothing to worry about. It is like the muscles of the body when they have not been used for a while and when you use them, the day after they hurt or ache. If Spirit are going to work with you they are not going to bring any intentional harm to you. It is total trust in Spirit, trust that is needed when developing. I hope you can now see why every person here on this earth plane of ours cannot become a Physical Medium producing Physical Phenomena, not everyone's body could take the alterations needed.

One point I must put in here is the experiments also showed that the Medium's pulse and breathing slowed as well as the brain wave pattern altering at the same time and this does not go along with medical thinking. BUT it must be pointed out this was only in a **"True Trance State"**.

Also there is a lot of water loss from the trance state Medium, it can be proven by weighing the Medium before the séance and then after before they have a drink of water. The human body needs at least 16 hours to fully recover after a TRUE deep trance demonstration. That is true deep state trance speaking, true transfiguration, or a true physical séance. If you do not believe that, look at the people who sit to link with the World of Spirit in development Circles with their glasses of water beside them. They get thirsty. Look at the people who do demonstrations when linking with Spirit on the platform they have a drink of water when they are finished. They get more thirsty. Go to a demonstration of a TRUE trance Medium and see how much water they drink. They get thirstier still. Look at the Physical Medium when they come round after being used by Spirit, they are the most thirstiest Medium of them all. Does it not make sense that that the water is being used in some way by the World of Spirit when linking? Does it not also make sense that the water comes from all of the body? That being so, Spirit must use the liquid from the blood system and so thickening it. This must be the reason for the heightening of the blood pressure of the TRUE deep trance state Medium, which includes the Physical Medium. Imagine if the Medium does not carry a lot of bulk that is storing a lot of water in their body, surely that Medium must have a higher than normal blood pressure when linking. BUT all that being said as a theory, WHY is it that as soon as the Medium comes back to a near normal state their blood pressure drops. This is before they have had a drink of water to give the medium's body back the water taken from it by Spirit. DO Spirit give back some of the water to the Medium as they return from their deep state of altered awareness? Not as much as is needed if they do. Are Spirit using the heightened state of the blood pressure for some reason, which we do not as yet know about?

**Remember IF YOU DO NOT USE IT, YOU WILL LOSE IT. It is the same with your mediumistic gifts from Spirit; meditate, meditate, meditate and keep on meditating even when you think you are developed. You never are fully developed. So keep on using that tuning mechanism which is the brain.**

I feel we all need to help with these mediumistic gifts in our workers and trainee workers, who on this earth plane work for Spirit and God, and for the truth to go out to all mankind. I feel we must have our mediumistic people attending colleges of learning on a regular basis and help them to do so, BUT better still, have them supported in residential colleges and taught **properly** within the correct environment and within the discipline needed of how to Link with Spirit on a regular basis. Look at the man made religions of this planet as an example and the way they are taught and what they do with their ministers, vicars, priests, mullahs and Holy Men of the east. They are taught in their monasteries, convents, colleges, holy places, or retreats. The Mediums should be protected from the idiots who can harm them and eventually those trained Mediums should be brought out from their places of learning for the public meetings at appropriate times **"protected"** to prove through their gifts there is a continuance in our existence when we pass into the higher side of life across the veil, **BUT,** and a **BIG BUT NOT** to be put onto a pedestal and to be treated as a God figure or someone special, **NOT to be revered**. When certain people are good enough from that environment, for them to go onto other places that should be set up across the world for the progression of the teaching of linking with Spirit for the benefit of mankind in a proper manner, **importantly** and I mean this sincerely, **IMPORTANTLY** not to make money for all the pomp and splendour that the man made religions thrive on, keeping the hangers on in a good life of luxury.

When we link with the Spirit World no matter how well we know our Link, the Helper, the Angel looking after us, we do not know for certain what is going to happen. Keep that in mind. This is the reason to ask for the highest of guidance.

When teaching others I want them to be better than me, otherwise I have not done my job properly. I want those students to come back to me and say to me "you taught me properly," and I am going to show you I am now higher in my development than you are. I am then feeling as though I am on the top of the world. I thank the unseen Power of God, for my gift of teaching of my gifts; and because of the guidance of Spirit, those people I taught can now go forward and tell others as I couldn't when learning with bad tutors, and because I am dyslectic. YES I get tangled up with words. I know I should have said something that was in my head, yet it comes out differently as I wanted it to be put, but that is my problem not yours. I know Spirit is working through me with my difficulties to help the world as a whole to progress and understand there is life continuing after our so-called or man made label called "DEATH", this is the reason for the large teaching book I have written called "Meditation Oneness" This is the way EVERY TUTOR should look at their teaching otherwise is it NOT TRUE, this is what I believe. Many tutors are only teaching for their own ego. Sadly a lot do not go along my way of thought. I will continue along that pathway until I pass into another level of consciousness, NOT death, just the continuing my life. I feel sorry for people who are not TRUE to themselves, and not true to the higher force of God we call Spirit.

Mediumship in my opinion is going downhill, only relying on Mental Mediums of **not so high levels** of development, many of the so called Mediums kidding themselves they have a gift to use before they are ready. A lot of bad Mediums and charlatans do not sit regularly in meditation, they should be looking into the light to develop their link with Spirit and make it stronger. A lot only want to be in the **star status and be a fortune teller, most of them asking questions of the recipients to gain insight of them**, instead of giving information from Spirit, and evidence of the person in Spirit is who they say it is. It is no use giving out names and the areas, which could apply to nearly all sitting in the room. It needs the Medium to go back to the Spirit contact and ask for evidence applicable to **that person only,** so they can identify with the person, the area, and the names given. Many an alleged Medium wants a quick fix and do not see the need for sitting in the Power of Spirit. The only reason people should be giving readings, clairvoyance, clairaudience, etc. or sitting for Physical Phenomena, is to prove there is life after our so called death.

Physical Mediumship takes years of dedication and regular sitting for Spirit. Leslie Flint took seven years sitting in a regular dedicated Circle for his gift of independent voice and even then never stopped sitting and developing. As did Gordon Higginson the materialisation, independent direct voice, clairvoyant, clairaudient, healer, the good all round Medium, who because of his strongly disciplined mother's guidance was sitting and developing all of his life. Fanny Higginson had been told of a child of her's was going to be a Medium when Fanny was only still fifteen years of age. As with Gordon Higginson's, and Gladys Owen's Mediumship, Mediumship should be taught early and developed in all people who have the desire to dedicate themselves to help others, for the sake of mankind. Not for the benefit of those in high places with their comfortable lives and riches, which are gain on the backs of the dedicated ones who put their time and effort into linking with Spirit and proving there is life after our so called death, as every religion has done over the ages.

Come on you churches and meeting places, start saving and get a fund going to send your brightest and the most dedicated, **NOT YOUR FAVOURITES**, send them to **good** places of learning for a good few, **good** development courses each year, or allow them to stay as a resident for the year, maybe two, the dedicated hopefully more.

I have notice there are many more places where everyone can go to, to learn the art of mediumship. BUT be careful of the people who are buying big places/buildings and calling it places for Spirit when in all honesty they are only buying the place or building for the benefit of themselves and their family. You will see they are earning as much money as they can from the spiritual needs of others as the religious leaders of times gone by did.

I know I will not earn much money from my writing. The shop, the printers, the paper, advertiser, photographers, distribution costs; they all need a cut from **my years research and my years of writing**, (many are the times while working on this book up until the wee small hours [4-5 am) and YES most of all **MY TIME, all of my hard work of years of learning all since the 1970's**. Yes I had the phenomena from very young 3 ish-16, but I had put it aside, then had to work long and hard to bring it back.

When writing a book yourself, it is like the petrol in England. The petrol companies receive about 2-5 pence profit out of each gallon sold for £4.50 at the garage pumps, most is taken by the government in tax something like 95%, then there is production costs, distribution cost, etc. and the petrol companies have done all the hard work. So it is with book writing, most goes to the publishing houses, and all the vultures waiting in the wings for their cut. If you want to write a book buy the Writers' & Artists' Yearbook and it will give you all the relevant information.

BUT PLEASE PASS ON YOUR <u>TRUE FINDINGS</u>, SO IT BECOMES YOUR KNOWLEDGE. WHEN GIVEN TO OTHERS IT BECOMES YOUR WISDOM. **Please be WISE** and <u>most of all</u> <u>**TRUTHFUL**</u> in what you give to others, so others can **learn from the truth**.

 

**We are conceived in joy, <u>love</u> and <u>harmony</u> of our <u>Spirit</u>.**
**We are made in the body within joy, <u>love</u> and <u>harmony</u> of our <u>Spirit</u>.**
**We are brought forward into the world in joy, <u>love</u> and <u>harmony</u> of our <u>Spirit</u>.**
**We continue to grow in joy and <u>love</u> within our earthly lives of <u>harmony</u> of our <u>Spirit</u>.**
**When we pass over we are received in joy and <u>love</u> by loved ones into the**
<u>**Loving Harmony of the Spirit World.**</u>

 

**IT IS THAT <u>JOY/HAPPINESS</u>, <u>LOVE</u> AND <u>HARMONY</u> THAT MAKES THINGS WORK.**

 

**It is up to you to bring love, and make it joyous within your own Spirit, in harmony with Spirit, becoming part of the whole so you are at one with Spirit,**
**you <u>will feel</u> that "ONENESS".**

 

## IT IS WITHIN THE GARDEN OF PATIENCE
## THAT INCREASES THE STRENGTH

 

**With your sincerity, truth, love, and trusting fully the help of your angelic helpers in the Divine Light of Spirit of the highest realms there within their loving harmony,**
<u>**you will achieve your goal.**</u>

### Remember :-

**"There are none so <u>blind</u> as those <u>who do not want to see</u>"**
**"There are none so <u>deaf</u> as those <u>who do not want to hear/listen</u>"**
There are none so <u>insensitive</u> as those <u>who do not want</u> to be aware.

### and again
## most importantly

## "<u>IF YOU CANNOT DO IT, YOU CANNOT KNOW IT</u>"

With kind permission from the Harry Edwards Healing Trust I have put the details
and photographs from Harry Edwards Book now unfortunately out of print.
"The Mediumship of Arnold Clare"
The Trust still sell all of the other Harry Edwards books in the
"The Harry Edwards Spiritual Healing Sanctuary" and at Stansted Hall
in the Psychic News bookshop, and the Arthur Findlay College bookshop.
and the internet from the book sellers :- ebay.co.uk and amazon.com

In the Harry Edwards' Book "The Mediumship of Arnold Clare" If you would like to read this book in the order as Harry wrote it. The pages in my book are set out in his book in the following printed order. 406, 409, 294, 345, 368, 188, 190, 192, 413, 413, 417, 420, 303, 369, 273, 287, 357, 297, 362, 427, 429, 431, 434, 435.

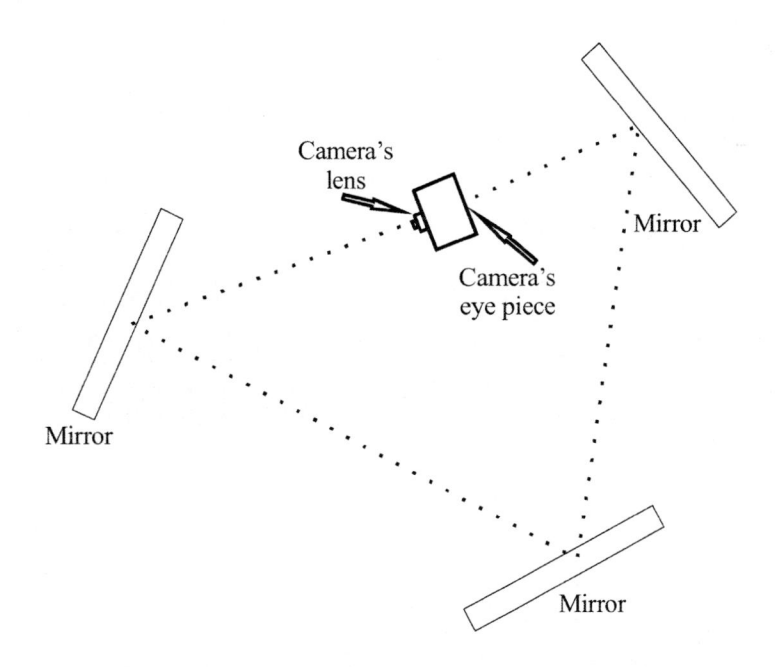

This is a three mirror and camera set-up. The layout is in a continuous loop, the mirrors and then through the eyepiece then out through the camera lens and around again

The camera can be a still camera or video camera being used. It is said to produce a certain image of Spirit given the correct environment of spiritual harmony around the given area where the experiment is to take place. Before starting, remember to talk to the Spirit World and bring into yourself the link with Spirit.

I believe with all my heart that all children are naturally talented in the ways of linking with the Spirit World; they should be educated by spiritual people and spiritual example, and not by religion or religious people. It is only the religions and the religious people that destroy the truth in what youngsters say naturally about the Spirit World and what they see.

It is the children we should look at to see the ways of truth through their simplicity. It is so natural for them to talk to God, the Spirits they see. That is how every Medium should gain a greater link with Spirit doing it naturally as a child. Simple EH?

Evil comes from within. Anger comes from within.
Hatred comes from within. Deceit comes from within.
Badness comes from within. Sadness comes from within.
Dishonesty comes from within. Illness comes from within.
**To find self, go within.**
Goodness comes from within. Loving comes from within.
Silence comes from within. Calmness comes from within.
Stillness comes from within. Strength comes from within.
Honesty comes from within. Healing comes from within.
Through knowledge, wisdom comes from within.
The God Force comes from within.
**YES, to find self, go within.**
**BUT to LIVE totally within, is to go without.**
By D Roy. T Keeghan

## LOVE TO YOU ALL. TAKE CARE.

**MAY YOUR UNSEEN HELPERS, AND YOUR GOD, THE DIVINE SPIRIT, BE WITH YOU ALWAYS IN LOVE AND THE LIGHT HERE ON THIS EARTH PLANE OF OURS AND IN THE SPIRIT WORLD.**

**It is only now YOU really start learning YOUR future craft of "MEDIUMSHIP" within Meditation when you become as one with the GOD force.**

© This book is covered by copyright 1980-2007  Keegan Family Quayle Family Carolan Family 34, WA2 OBS  England

**BEGINNERS and PROFESSIONALS**

# UNLOCK
### PLAY SOCIALLY
### USING

**KEEWAYS** EASY LEARNING METHOD

## THE
# TAROT
### Enhance Your
### PSYCHIC ABILITY

### INCLUDED
## LIFETIME BUSINESS PLAN

**IS YOUR JOB TRULY SAFE ?**

**SHOWN HOW up to £100 plus a day is possible**

**ISBN No 978-0-9554590-1-6**

The detailed, simple to learn method in this TAROT Book shows how <u>it is easily possible,</u> to earn in your first few readings, the money you paid out for the book and cards, then continue <u>at your own rate</u> to earn <u>extra money</u> <u>throughout your lifetime</u>. At today's rate [2007] earn from £15 to **£100 PLUS A DAY. Easy to learn, Easy to use.**

The Tarot is explained in expanded detail, going through the basic rules that govern the readings. The cards have been so designed to help the reader BUT keep the air of mystery for the recipient. Each suit set has an extra 5 cards, the Tarot cards have been expanded also brought up to date and added to near what it was many, many years ago. In this full set with the book there have been 22 planet cards added totalling 165 cards in all, they are in linked packs of 41, 44, and 80. All this book has been put together after a great many years of cajoling my mother and my relations for their handed down knowledge, much research, plus too many months to count, writing, drawing and designing the cards' also setting out all the book's layout.

After reading this book and thinking I also have a book inside me, why not give it a go. The people who have printed this for me have been very helpful and have been in business for many years so are not likely to fly by night.

All you have to do is to get hold of a computer and write the book in Microsoft Word. Space it and format it how you want it to look. By going to and working in the print layout [typing in the **print layout** under **view**] you can see how it will look on the page. Write you own life story, a children's book, about your hobby, something in nature you like, the history of your own area, in fact anything.

The printers address is :-

Dale Burgess. M.D.
**code DRTK**
Print on demand,
1 First Drove,
Fengate,
Peterborough
PE1 5BJ

Pop a letter in the post and get a quote for your book, give the **code DRTK** and you will get a very good price and the best thing about it, **you can order as many as you wish**. The more you order at once, better the price you get.